THE

DEBATES

OF THE

CONSTITUTIONAL CONVENTION

OF THE

STATE OF MARYLAND,

Assembled at the City of Annapolis, Wednesday, April 27, 1864:

BEING A FULL AND COMPLETE REPORT OF THE DEBATES AND PROCEEDINGS OF THE CONVENTION, TOGETHER WITH THE OLD CONSTITUTION, THE LAW UNDER WHICH THE CONVENTION ASSEMBLED, AND THE NEW CONSTITUTION.

OFFICIAL:
WM. BLAIR LORD, REPORTER—HENRY M. PARKHURST, ASSISTANT.

VOLUME III.

ANNAPOLIS:
PRINTED BY RICHARD P. BAYLY.
MDCCCLXIV.

Mr. Abbott. It does not accomplish the object which I have in view, which is to test the question at once.

Mr. Thruston. I will withdraw the amendment for the present.

Mr. Morgan demanded the yeas and nays upon Mr. Abbott's amendment, and they were ordered.

Mr. Stockbridge. I do not know that there is any object to be attained by taking up the time of the convention by any discussion of these two great systems. They have been before the country a great many years; and probably every member of the convention has his judgment fully matured upon the subject. I shall therefore not take up the time of the convention by any discussion. I have my own opinion upon the subject, very clearly defined, what is best for the people, and what is best for the State. That opinion is embodied in the report. I am satisfied that the plan here presented for the consideration of the convention is the one which in the end will give most satisfaction to the people of Maryland. I am satisfied of it upon general principles, and as the result of observation during the last fifteen years in the State, under both systems, first the one and then the other. But there are other gentlemen present who have perhaps had the same opportunities for observation that I have. I am satisfied that all the essential qualities of a judge, as set forth by us in two of the sections of the declaration of rights, can better be attained under the system reported here than by the adoption of the proposition of my colleague (Mr. Abbott.) We have said:

"Art. 18. That every man, for any injury done to him in his person or property, ought to have remedy by the course of the law of the land, and ought to have justice and right freely without sale, fully without any denial, and speedily without delay, according to the law of the land."

We have said also:

"Art. 32. That the independency and uprightness of judges are essential to the impartial administration of justice, and a great security to the rights and liberties of the people."

In the adoption of these two cardinal principles, I believe we are all agreed. The only question which divides us is, which of these systems will best conduce to the great objects there specified and aimed at. I have no doubt upon that subject.

It should be borne in mind that the judicial office is in no sense a representative office. Wherever the people are to be represented through their agents, it is undoubtedly best that the people should freely and intelligently exercise their choice. But this is one of the offices which calls into requisition higher qualities than what are supposed to constitute the popular man in the community. A fluent tongue, and a knack of getting elected to office by a constituency, are not the highest recommendations for a judge. I think the experience throughout the country, wherever it has been tried, is that the independency of the judiciary is better promoted by a system such as is here recommended. I shall therefore vote against the motion which has been made by my colleague.

Mr. Thomas. I am as much indisposed as my colleague (Mr. Stockbridge,) to make any extended remarks in relation to the proposition submitted by the gentleman from Baltimore city (Mr. Abbott) to strike out the word "appointment." And I am as fixed in my opinion as to the expediency and justice of the election of judges as of all other officers of the people, as he is in relation to the appointment. I will say here in relation to those opinions that they are not newly born. I have held them from the time I was a boy; from the time I first commenced to mix and mingle among the people of the State. While the gentleman says that he believes that a great portion of the people of the State are in favor of the appointment system.

Mr. Stockbridge. I did not say that.

Mr. Thomas. Then I beg pardon; but I assert that in so far as my immediate constituency is concerned, that portion of the State which I represent, being the working men of the State, they are unwilling to give up this right of the election of judges by the people.

The gentleman has read from the bill of rights in relation to the uprightness and integrity of judges. I suppose that he wants to argue from that that the people cannot elect good and upright judges. We have had an experience of fourteen years in the State of Maryland under the elective system; and I assert without any fear of contradiction from any quarter, that as a general thing the judiciary of Maryland this day is as good as could be selected for the price you pay to the men put in office. There is another principle in the bill of rights which is as much to be regarded by this convention, in the provisions which they will put into this new constitution, as the section which the gentleman has read. The first article of the bill of rights says that all government of right originates in the people; and the second section says that the people of the State have the sole and exclusive right of regulating the internal government and police thereof.

The gentleman says that the judicial power of the State is not a representative power. I will admit it; but still it is a power of the State. It is the most important power of the State. Your legislature, which is to be the immediate representative of the people, might go to work and pass its laws; and if those laws are unconstitutional they are to go before the court of appeals, and their constitutionality is to be decided by that court of appeals. So far as that is concerned, your court of appeals does represent the people, because the judiciary is the check upon that branch of the government, to prevent their passing illegal and unconstitutional enactments.

The judicial power of the State acts more closely upon the people than any other department of the government. I assert that the poor man, the man of bone and sinew, the real working man of the State, looks and feels as strongly towards this principle of the election of judges and sheriffs and clerks, as to the election of the man who is to represent him in the legislative halls. I deny that if the people are competent, as they are, to elect the governor, and members of the general assembly, that they are not as fully competent to elect their judges. There may have been abuses in the elective system; and under what system have there not been abuses? You cannot change human nature by the system of appointment. The governor of the State is a mere man; and when he exercises the right which the constitution gives him, in appointing men to office, in nine cases out of ten he will appoint his own political friends. It is not the same way with the people of your State. The people of your State, as a general thing, when they can get hold of an honest man for judge, will elect him in preference to a dishonest one; and they can more easily discriminate among the men who live in their own neighborhoods, as to who is honest and who is dishonest; who is learned in the law, and who is unlearned in the law, than the governor of your State. There have been evidences of partisanship under an appointed judiciary that we have not seen under an elective judiciary. It is but the other day that I heard it asserted by a gentleman in my city that the supreme court of the United States in making its decision in the Dred Scott case, had acted as a partisan court; and he made a good argument to prove it. That is one of the illustrations of the appointive system; and it is one of the evidences to show that the appointive system cannot change human nature. Wherever you find human nature you will find it subject to sympathies and bias. The mere appointment or election of a man to an office cannot take away from him that sympathy or that bias.

Believing therefore as I do that the people of the State will not consent to give up this power they have exercised for fourteen years, a power which the convention of Maryland in 1851 gave them in good faith, and which they of right ought not to be deprived of, because it is a right which they have exercised fourteen years and should have exercised ever since 1776, and in my opinion would have done it if it had not been that the old convention of 1776 were acting under the old prejudices derived from the colonial government, and derived this idea of the appointive system from England and incorporated it into the constitution, where it stood until the days of reform swept it away—believing this, it is my candid opinion that if any other system were to be incorporated into the constitution than an elective system of the judiciary, it would injure the constitution before the people and it is this which induces me to support the amendment of my friend from Baltimore city (Mr. Abbott.)

Mr. Thruston. I think this is a question upon which we are all bound to give our testimony so far as we can with regard to which is the preferable system. The people whom I in part represent are made up mostly of mechanics and laboring men. I have taken great pains to converse with them whenever an opportunity occurred, and I have found them almost universally in favor of an appointive system. They have lived under both systems. We find that the elective system does not secure judges as unbiased and free from prejudice as the appointive system, of which my constituents, I am sure a large number of them, are in favor. I am sure that if we incorporate that system into the constitution it will secure in that neighborhood additional support to it.

Men are not fitted from mere personal popularity to fill the judicial offices. So far as my experience goes, we rather find men who are sometimes unpopular even more fitted for such offices than those who have attained great personal popularity—those who seek popularity for their own purposes. We know further that seeking for popularity and electioneering for office creates a state of mind wholly inconsistent with the proper exercise of the judicial functions. I am sure that the appointive system will gain strength to the constitution in the county which I represent, and so far as my own experience goes, having practiced under both systems, I have not a shadow of doubt that the appointive system gives the greatest satisfaction.

Besides, the people do in fact elect the judges even under that system, for they elect the man who has the appointing power. They control the party who appoints the judges, and it throws such a guard around the appointment that it may be said that the people do practically elect. I am confident that the appointive system is most popular in my section of the State.

Mr. Stirling. It seems to me that this amendment is rather premature. I do not think it will settle anything; for the next section says that the judges shall be appointed by the governor.

The President. That can be stricken out.

Mr. Stirling. It seems to me that the motion of the gentleman from Allegany (Mr. Thruston) ought not to have been withdrawn, because whether you adopt the appointive system or the elective system, there will certainly be judges appointed to fill vacancies. I cannot therefore vote to strike out the word "appointment," whatever my views may be with regard to the best system to adopt.

The PRESIDENT. It is to test the sense of the convention.

Mr. STIRLING. It will test it wrongly then, if it leads us to strike out what ought to be in there.

Mr. THRUSTON. I only withdrew my amendment temporarily. I shall renew it afterwards.

Mr. RIDGELY. I do not see the slightest necessity for the amendment suggested by the gentleman from Baltimore city (Mr. Stirling.) There is a special section which provides for the case of death, resignation and removal from office, which meets that difficulty. Here the word first occurs, and this, is the appropriate place, it strikes me, in which the sense of the house ought to be tested.

Mr. CHAMBERS. I have but a word to say. I have heretofore expressed at large my views upon the subject. I have not altered any opinion I entertained since the convention of 1851. But I may be permitted to say that what I considered then as probable, all the mischiefs I foresaw have not only been realized but have been experienced to an extent far beyond my anticipation at that time. I hold, as I always have held, since I have had any intelligence upon the subject, that the tenure for life or for good behavior, and the system of appointment are both important, and the former I deem still more important than the latter.

I merely mean now to have my opinion recorded as not only unchanged, but confirmed. All the experience I have had is that you have lessened the character of the judiciary; and I was going to say, you have abolished the respect to the organs of the law, which those organs have in former times universally experienced at the hands of the people. But upon my opinion I do not deem it necesssary now to enlarge, or the reasons for it. I understand that opinions have been formed.

But I rise now for the purpose of suggesting the fact that this proposal is out of time. There are persons upon this floor who will advocate the appointment of a portion of the judiciary, and the election of another portion of it. I shall vote that way. I now believe that a majority of this body will certainly adopt a system of appointment, so far as the judges of the court of appeals are concerned. The idea of giving to the men in a distant part of the State the appointment of a judge of the court of appeals, whose sole authority is to decide questions of law; the idea of giving to the man who lives at the remotest distance in the State, whose habits have never claimed the exercise of one moment's reflection upon the qualifications necessary for a judge of the court of appeals, who perhaps may not know how many judges sit there, or whether there is such a court at all; the idea of calling upon such a man to elect a judge to the highest judicial tribunal of the State, is one which I hope will not be considered proper.

If you undertake to decide the question of the election of the judiciary as an abstract question, and preferable to their appointment, you embarrass those who intend to make this distinction. I suggest, therefore, that this is a merely verbal alteration. Undoubtedly if the house shall at a future time decide that the court of appeals shall be appointed, and that the circuit judges shall be elected, nobody will hesitate to turn back to this section and add the necessary words to meet that state of the case. The gentleman from Baltimore will therefore perceive that he has been in great haste to make this change, because there is not now the slightest necessity for it. There is not a man here, certainly, be his opinions upon this question what they may, who would for a moment hesitate, if the house should decide that the court of appeals shall be appointed and the circuit judges elected, to say it is right to make the change in this section necessary to conform to that decision

Mr. SANDS. I do not purpose now to argue the comparative merits of the two systems, appointive and elective. I should not have risen at all had I not some days ago intimated that I might perhaps as a member of the judiciary committee, submit a minority report. Circumstances induced me to alter my mind with regard to that matter, believing that I could attain any ends I might have in view as well by amendments of section after section, as the judiciary report shall be read, as by a minority report.

There have of course to my mind, as well as to the minds of other gentlemen, been reasons suggested for and against both systems. I know that the judiciary power of our system of government is perhaps the most important branch of the government; because it does not matter what laws you have upon your statue book, if your judiciary misinterprets or misconstrues them. We are all satisfied of the necessity of wise, learned and impartial judges. The question of course with us all is how best to obtain them. How shall we best obtain the man for the place?

Although the remark of my friend from Baltimore city who has addressed the convention might at first strike the ear as not containing the truth of the matter, that the people of the judicial district or circuit were better qualified to judge of the man as to his moral character, and as to his legal learning, than the governor of the State, although it may have seemed to have little weight or truth in it; yet reflect: you are to have a man to occupy the bench of one of your circuits. He is either to be chosen by the people or by the governor. The chances, I presume, of the selection of a good, and learned, and impartial judge, would depend very much upon the knowledge which the parties making the selection have of the character and legal abilities of the party proposed, whether he is to be appointed or elected. I venture to say that there is not a judicial circuit in the State that has within its limits a man really learned in the law, passionate in the practice of his profession, but what that fact is as notorious to the people of that circuit as any other thing which is a fact.

The qualifications of a lawyer are something that cannot be hidden, or his disqualifications at the bar. If he is successful, if he is learned, if he is able, if he is eloquent, the men who are called upon to select him are constant witnesses of his professional career; and I do not know one fact more certain than this, that the popular appreciation of a judge's character and ability, is its very best test. It is that teaching which is attained by experience. He has practiced for years in the courts of his circuit, and the people having causes there have intrusted them to him. They witness his management of their causes, and of the causes of other parties, and there is nothing more certain than this, that when a party has a suit to be brought in any court of the State, he knows exactly the man best qualified to try it, and he will go to him.

On the other hand, the governor of the State appoints a man whose face perhaps he has not seen a dozen times, or half a dozen times; and appoints him how? It would hardly be dignified for the gentleman to go and solicit the appointment. He would better solicit it at the hands of the people than at the hands of the executive. How does the governor hear of him, or what does the governor know of him, except through the recommendations of his personal and perhaps of his political friends? That is the amount of the governor's knowledge of the man; while the knowledge the people possess concerning him is that which has grown up perhaps from an experience of twenty or thirty years' active professional service in the community.

This being the case, who is the best qualified to judge what man can best occupy the bench, the governor who knows him only from the recommendations of his personal and political friends, or the people who have been the witnesses of his course of conduct for twenty or thirty years? I say the people are the best judges And the people have a very just appreciation of the importance of the judicial office. They know that their property, perhaps their lives, their interests of every character, are under his especial guardianship. They know that not only upon his impartiality but upon his legal wisdom perhaps depend the positions they hold. They may be brought into court any day; and they know the man who is to decide there ought to have sound legal learning, ought to be impartial, fair and just. I verily believe that in ninety-nine cases out of one hundred they will choose such a man.

Practically to the people of the circuit or district in which I live, it has been one and the same thing, whether elected or appointed. The present incumbent there has occupied the bench for thirty years. Certainly he has not been re-elected time and again because he was the sort of man to pander to the populace, and to deal with a light hand with crime, rowdyism, profligacy of any sort that came under his judicial notice. It has got to be a saying among the people who are in the habit of coming into our courts—don't fall into Judge Pryor's hands; if you do he will give you the extent of the law. Why do the people re-elect him? Why have the masses voted for him? Because he was tolerant of popular abuses, rowdyism, drunkenness, rioting, and everything of the sort. No, sir; that is not the secret of the matter; it is because the people who have elected him once and again, have observed for many years his conduct as a judge, and they have faith in his legal learning, faith in his integrity, and know he is just the man to whom they can safely intrust their interests; and the consequence has been that he is now filling by appointment and by election, his third term in that service.

I did not propose to say as much as this. These thoughts suggested themselves to me. I do believe that the people are the best judges of the character and qualifications of their judges, and they have such intimate knowledge of the men at all times and under all circumstances, personally, morally, and professionally, that they know into whose hands to intrust themselves and their welfare.

Mr. Negley. I do not intend to say much upon this matter, but I am inclined to favor the amendment of the gentleman from Baltimore city (Mr. Abbott.) I do not believe that the operation of the elective system of the judiciary of Maryland for the last fourteen years has been found to depreciate the character of the judges, in the circuits at least. In our own district we have on the bench a man who was on the bench under the appointive system, and I think altogether as competent and as good a judge as it would be possible for the legislature or for the governor to give us; because I believe that the people of the district are the best judges of the integrity and legal capacity of the man to be selected for the office. The constitution provides that the citizens shall not go out and select A, B and C, without any reference to their integrity or legal capacity. The constitution restricts the selection to men learned in the law. With that restriction, I think that the people of the several districts are abundantly capable of making the selection for themselves.

Is it not a notorious fact that a man can go into any judicial district in the State of Maryland, into any county of the State of Maryland, and inquire of the most ignorant man he can find there, who is their best lawyer, and he will immediately be told. In our own county the little boys, the children in the streets, can point out the best lawyer in the county. So that the parties who are to make the selection in our county are better qualified to do so than the governor or the legislature, of whom not five men, three men, and perhaps not one man out of the county will know anything about the party to be appointed. The governor and the legislature must rely upon information obtained from others, from the delegates or senator from the county, or they must rely upon personal representations made to them as to the fitness of the party who asks for the office.

I am one of those who are willing to trust the honesty of the people in the selection of their officers at all times. There is just as much corruption, just as much wire-pulling, just as much personal preference in the selection of judicial officers by the governor and the legislature, as there is among the people; and more so. They are appointed through the representations of personal friends; and there is just as much liability to get incompetent men as there is by allowing the selection to be made by the people. After all, these things are to be judged by their results. The elective feature has been adopted, I believe, in most of the States; and I have yet to learn that the bench in the States is now more corrupt or less competent than it was under the appointive system.

Therefore I am in favor of the election of the judges by the people, not only in the circuits, but in the court of appeals also. It has been argued that the man in a distant county of the State has no interest in the selection of a judge for the court of appeals.—He is as much an integral portion of the State of Maryland and of the population of Maryland, living in the county of Allegany, as if he lived in the heart of Baltimore city; and he has just as much right, and perhaps just as much interest to the extent of his finances, in the selection of a judge of the court of appeals as the man who lives in the heart of Baltimore city. The man whose jurisdiction extends all over the State, over every part of it, is as much the officer of the individual who lives on the top of the Alleganies, as of the man who lives on the shores of the bay; and the one citizen is just as much interested in the selection of that officer as the other; and it is just as right and proper that he should vote for him. Hence the propriety of electing judges of the court of appeals by general ticket. This system of selecting judges of the court of appeals by districts is not proper, because every man in every portion of the State has an equal interest in the selection of the judges of the court of appeals, because they preside over his cases and determine them. The judge of the court of appeals does not decide the cases that arise particularly in the district in which he is chosen, but he sits in judgment upon cases that come to him from districts that have no voice in his selection. There is injustice in that; and as a State officer he ought to be elected by a State ticket.

A State officer is the servant of the entire people of the State, and the entire people of the State have an equal interest in his selection. So I am really on principle inclined to favor the election, both of judges of the court of appeals, and of judges of the district courts. I believe it would be most hazardous to attempt to take away this right of selection from the people.

Gentleman in this convention have been speaking much about the apprehension that they might do something to jeopardize the adoption of this constitution. In my humble judgment you cannot more effectually jeopardize the adoption of this constitution than by attempting to take away a right which the people know that they possess. The people are jealous of being deprived of power they once possessed. You would a thousand times better never have given it to them at all; there would then not be so much difficulty in withholding it. But having possessed it, having exercised without any dissatisfaction to themselves or any detriment to justice throughout the State, they will be very loth to give it up. If gentleman are sincere in their disposition to insert nothing in this constitution that may jeopardize its passage, I think they would better be very careful about attempting to take away from the people this privilege.

There are a few of the lower officers of the State, such as constables, road supervisors, and perhaps magistrates, whom there may be some ground for appointment; at least the constables and road supervisors. But as to the higher officers, the judiciary, I am not inclined to touch them, or to change the principle concerning them which now exists in our constitution. The people have not suffered. The complaint in our county is not about the circuit judge, or not about the court of appeals particularly, except that they think they ought to have a chance to assist in the election of officers who preside over their cases if they are elected at all; but it is with regard to these little petty offices where they have suffered. But there is no complaint; there is no wish or desire, I believe, among the people to have a change in regard to the mode of selecting circuit judges or judges of the orphans' court. There may be some difference of opinion with regard to these lower offices; and I am not so very particular about them, whether you elect the magistrate, or give to the circuit judge the power to appoint him. But I am decidedly opposed to appointing the court of appeals or the circuit judges; and I shall therefore vote for the amendment.

Mr. RIDGELY. I shall follow the example of my friend from Baltimore city who opened this debate (Mr. Stockbridge.) He occupied a very short time. The experience which I have had in the last fourteen years has confirmed in my mind the fitness and propriety of my vote in the convention of 1850, to make this system an elective system. In that respect my experience differs from that of the gentleman from Kent (Mr. Chambers.) My experience has not assured me that we have lost anything from the change; but on the contrary in the judicial district in which I reside my experience has been that we have gained by the change.

It may be that we have not in general obtained judges so profound in judicial learning as we had under the former system; but we have obtained judges who have in the opinion of our people met the wants of the people.—It is not *per se* judicial learning, learning in the law, that makes up all the elements of character necessary to constitute a good judge. There are other elements of character besides that of profound legal learning; and they have been eminently displayed in my judicial district. We have had two judges under this system; the one the lamented Alfred Constable; and the other the present judge, John H. Price. The business habits of those gentlemen, their accessibility, their irreproachable private character, superadded to a reasonable amount of judicial learning, has eminently fitted those gentlemen for the positions which they held.

Nor have I observed that in other quarters of the State there has been any lessening of the amount of judicial learning or fitness for the position upon the bench, among the various incumbents of the bench. If you will look around through the various circuits, beginning at Allegany, who is upon the bench there under the elective system? Look again at Frederick and Carroll; who are upon the bench there under the elective system? Passing by the district in which I live, and of which I have just spoken, to the Eastern Shore, we come to Judge Carmichael, who was succeeded by judge Ricaud; and in the lower district, judge Spence. I put it to the convention whether the bench has fallen very far below what it was under their predecessors? In my opinion they level up fully to the standard of their predecessors as a whole.

It is true they have been unfortunate in Baltimore city; but it was in the inception of the system when Baltimore city had the misfortune to make a selection which probably they would not have made under a larger experience. At present the bench of Baltimore city, generally speaking, is highly respectable. Indeed I know of no judge who has conferred higher honor upon his office, either in the court of appeals or on the lower bench, than the justice of the superior court of Baltimore city, Judge Martin.

With this experience and this observation, I am unwilling to turn back to the point where we stood in 1850. I find the opinion I entertained in 1850 confirmed and sustained by the past.

There is another reason for my vote. This is a very important movement. Neither my people nor the people at large have ever been consulted upon this subject When we were sent here as members of this convention, this question was not raised before our constituency. I hold that I have as much a duty to perform to represent my constituency here, as if I were in a legislative body. It is my duty to reflect what I believe to be the wants and the will of that constituency. Never having specially discussed this question, it never having been particularly brought before the people, we are asked, without any sort of information upon this subject, boldly, at once to cut loose from the system which in general has worked well, and to fall back upon the old system which we know in the experience of the past, did not work well.

Just turn to our experience anterior to 1850, and see what was the condition of the judiciary under the appointing system. I happen to be cotemporaneous with that system, and know something about it, and I here challenge, with the exception of the court of appeals, a comparison between the associates upon the bench under the old system with the bench of the circuit courts now under the new system.

For these reasons I am unwilling to vote to change the mode of selection, and to return to the old system of appointment anterior to the adoption of the present constitution.

Mr. BOND. I have no doubt that it is the wish of every member of this convention to adopt that mode, whether appointment or election, which is most conducive to the public good. The only difference between us seems to be, that some think that the public good would be better promoted by the elective system; and some on the contrary think it would be better promoted by the appointive system.

In the early part of the session I had the honor to submit to the consideration of the judiciary committee the outline of a system in which I proposed an elective judiciary. I am free to say it was not because I regarded it as the best system; but I really supposed it would probably be the only tenable system. Since I find some of our friends upon the other side in favor of an appointive system, being very glad to find that it is so, I now say that I am an advocate of the appointive system, and will vote for it.

These gentleman who have occupied the floor in favor of the elective system, seem to me to lose sight of a very important consideration; that in the election of an officer by the large mass of the people, there is no means of fixing the responsibility of the incumbent upon anybody. It is divided among the whole mass of voters; whereas in the appointive system the governor himself is held responsible. The court will, therefore, always be more carefully selected from men suited to the place.

Besides, our government is not a pure democracy. It is not even so far a democracy that the people have a right to elect. It is a representative democracy, it is true; but it has conservative elements in it as well. One of these conservative elements is and should be, that the judiciary should be as far removed from the people as compatible. What I mean is this; that there should be no judge placed in such a position or condition that his supporters or friends can claim that he should yield to them a favor which he would not grant to a stranger.

It is absolutely certain, since judges are but men like all the rest of us, that if there be a highly influential individual in the county or the district, who has zealously supported the individual as a judge, it is natural that that judge should have a leaning towards him and his interests, whereas a judge ought not to know anybody. It would often happen in the election of judges by the people that the most popular man was by far the least qualified for the place. In fact, it is well known that some of the very best men, the men best suited for such a place as judge of the court, would perhaps obtain the fewest possible votes. Instead of pushing himself, and endeavoring to secure votes, probably the most suitable man would be a man who would shrink from being dragged before the public and made a candidate for their suffrages.

It is for these reasons, briefly stated, that I shall advocate the appointive system. I have no objection in the world to exercising every right in voting which I think would conduce to the public good. But as it has well been suggested the office of judge is not a representative office. He ought to stand aloof, far above any communication or political affinity with anybody in his district. These are my reasons for supporting the appointive system, and I shall do so with a great deal of pleasure.

The question being taken, the result was—yeas 51, nays 19—as follows:

Yeas—Messrs. Goldsborough, President; Abbott, Annan, Audoun, Billingsley, Blackiston, Carter, Crawford, Cunningham, Dail, Davis, of Charles, Davis, of Washington, Dellinger, Dent, Duvall, Ecker, Edelen. Galloway, Harwood, Hodson, Hopkins, Jones, of Somerset, Keefer, Kennard, King, Lee, Marbury, Markey, Mayhugh, McComas, Mitchell, Morgan, Murray, Negley, Nyman, Parran, Peter, Purnell, Ridgely, Robinette, Sands, Schley, Schlosser, Smith, of Carroll, Smith, of Dorchester, Smith, of Worcester, Swope, Thomas, Turner, Wickard, Wooden—51.

Nays—Messrs. Berry, of Baltimore county, Bond, Brown, Chambers, Daniel, Earle, Hopper, Jones, of Cecil, Lansdale, Miller, Mullikin, Parker, Pugh, Russell, Stirling, Stockbridge, Sykes, Thruston, Todd—19.

When the names were called,

Mr. Davis, of Washington said: My vote on this question indicates my individual preference. At the proper time I shall with a great deal of pleasure vote to allow Baltimore city such a system as will suit them best. But with reference to the system for the whole State, I vote "aye."

Mr. Stirling said: I do not vote upon this question with any reference whatever to the question of the elective or appointive judiciary; but I think this word ought not to be stricken out, no matter what the convention intends to do; and I therefore vote "no."

The amendment was accordingly agreed to.

Mr. Thruston. I move to amend this section by inserting after the word "election," the words "or appointment."

Mr. Thomas. What is the object of that amendment, I would ask the gentleman?

Mr. Thruston. I think the object is very apparent. If we adopt an elective system of judiciary, then in case of vacancies there must be appointments made by the governor for the rest of the term so vacated, or until an election can be held. And the obj ct of my amendment is to provide that the same qualifications shall be possessed by the persons who are appointed to these offices, that are possessed by those who are elected to these offices.

Mr. Thomas. If that be the object of the amendment, there is a section in the present constitution, which I will submit at the proper time, and which will provide for the very same thing which the gentleman desires to provide for. It is the section in relation to vacancies occurring in consequence of death, resignation, or disqualification of judges. I do not think this is the proper place for this provision, and therefore I shall vote against the amendment now offered.

Mr. Stirling. The convention has emphatically determined in favor of an elective judiciary, and we may as well make all necessary provisions as we go along. And unless you make some such amendment as that proposed by the gentleman from Allegany (Mr. Thruston,) the governor can appoint to fill a vacancy a man who has not resided in the State one day.

Mr. Thomas. I submit that the better way would be to provide by a separate and distinct section, in relation to vacancies caused by death, resignation, or otherwise, and not mix it up with a section which provides for the election of these officers.

Mr. Stirling. You are fixing the qualification about residence now.

Mr. THOMAS. That can be done in a separate independent section.

Mr. THRUSTON. That is taking a whole section to do the work which two words will do in this section.

Mr. THOMAS. It looks to me as if it were providing for both appointment and election.

Mr. THRUSTON. It is.

Mr. THOMAS. That is what I object to. It looks like submitting both an elective and appointed judiciary to the people.

Mr. THRUSTON. I have no such object.

Mr. JONES, of Somerset. The gentleman from Baltimore city (Mr. Thomas) is mistaken. It merely prescribes that when there is a vacancy, which the governor will be authorized to fill by appointment, the one so appointed shall have these qualifications herein prescribed.

Mr. THRUSTON. I will modify my amendment so as to insert after the word "election," the words "or appointment by the executive, in case of a vacancy by death, disqualification, or otherwise."

Mr. SANDS. I would just like to suggest that the proper place for this amendment would be in the third section. If the members of the convention will look at the report, they will see that it being based upon an appointive system, there is no section in it in regard to vacancies. And we will have to incorporate in it a section providing for the filling of vacancies occasioned by death, resignation, or disqualification. And in that section would be the proper place to include the idea of my friend from Allegany (Mr. Thruston;) that in case of the death, resignation, or disqualification of any of the judges, the governor should appoint for the unexpired term a person learned in the law, as judge of said circuit; and said person shall have all the qualifications heretofore prescribed for the judges of this State.

Mr. STIRLING. That is what the present constitution says, but it says what is a technical absurdity. It says that a man shall possess "the same qualifications." And when we look back to the section prescribing the qualifications, we find that he must have resided in the State for five years preceding "his election." Now a man not elected but appointed cannot have resided in the State for five years before his "election." I know that the proper construction would be that he must have resided in the State five years preceding his appointment. But why not make this section read properly while we have it under consideration?

Mr. SANDS. We must have a section in this report providing for the filling of vacancies. And when we do that, we can prescribe the same qualifications for the judges appointed that we prescribe for those elected. What are those qualifications?

Mr. STIRLING. It requires a residence of five years before election.

Mr. SANDS. Certainly; you fix the age, and the number of years that he must have been a citizen of the State. You will want an additional section in regard to filling vacancies. And this amendment certainly does impair, it seems to me, very much the phraseology of this section.

Mr. THRUSTON. This is the only and the proper place for it.

Mr. JONES, of Somerset. I would suggest to the gentleman to add the words "as hereinafter provided."

Mr. THRUSTON. I desire to read for the information of the convention, this section as I propose to have it amended:

"The judges of the several courts, except the associated judges of the orphans' courts, shall be citizens of the United States, and of this State, not less than five years next preceding their election or appointment by the executive, in case of a vacancy by death, disqualification, or otherwise," &c.

We are here prescribing the general qualifications for any one to be a judge; and here is the proper place to prescribe the qualifications for appointment or election to the office of judge, whether you have another section for filling vacancies or not, the judges must all possess these qualifications, and this is the proper place to prescribe these qualifications for all judges, whether appointed or elected.

Mr. STIRLING. I will also add that this very question has already been raised under the present constitution. And while it was not decided, because it was finally determined that the judge had the proper qualification as to residence, the question was actually raised that because the present constitution said that the judge shall have resided one year next preceding his election in the judicial district for which he was elected, that was not binding upon the governor in case of appointment. And I know that in the case of the appointment of the present judge of the criminal court, the governor took the ground that he had a right to appoint a man to fill the vacancy without any reference to the fact of his residence, because the constitution said one year before he was elected, and that if a man was not elected but appointed, that did not apply to him.

The question then being taken upon the amendment of Mr. THRUSTON, upon a division—ayes 32, nays 18—it was adopted.

Mr. ABBOTT. I move to strike out the words "appointed" and "appointment," wherever they occur in this section, and insert the words "elected" and "election."

The question being then taken, the motion to so amend was agreed to.

Mr. STIRLING. I move to strike out the words "and not less than one year next preceding their election resident in the judicial district or circuit, as the case may be, for which they may be elected." If the people have the right to elect the judges, they should have the right to go outside of the judicial districts if they desire. It may be a matter of practical convenience in some districts to do so.

Mr. SANDS. Will that enable the people to go outside of their own judicial district for a judge?

Mr. STIRLING. Yes, sir.

Mr. SANDS. I am opposed to that.

Mr. RIDGELY. The amendment of the gentleman from Baltimore city (Mr. Stirling) refers also to the circuits, and allows a judge from one county to be elected to serve in another county.

Mr. STIRLING. If you are going to give the election of judges to the people, let them have that power to the fullest extent. In the present condition of affairs in this State it may be very necessary to take a man from one county to be judge in another.

The question being taken upon the amendment of Mr. STIRLING, it was rejected.

Mr. THRUSTON. I now move to strike out the words "or district," so as to allow the judges of the court of appeals, who are to be elected on general ticket to be selected from any part of the State, and not to be confined to their special districts.

Upon this question Mr. MARBURY called the yeas and nays, and they were ordered.

The question being then taken, by yeas and nays, it resulted—yeas 18, nays 43—as follows:

Yeas—Messrs. Annan, Chambers, Cunningham, Daniel, Davis, of Washington, Hopper, Keefer, McComas, Mullikin, Negley, Russell, Schley, Schlosser, Stirling, Stockbridge, Todd, Thruston, Wooden—18.

Nays—Messrs. Goldsborough, President; Abbott, Berry, of Baltimore county, Billingsley, Blackiston, Bond, Brown, Crawford, Dail, Davis, of Charles, Dent, Duvall, Earle, Ecker, Edelen, Galloway, Harwood, Hodson, Hopkins, Jones, of Cecil, Jones, of Somerset, Kennard, King, Lansdale, Lee, Marbury, Mayhugh, Mitchell, Miller, Morgan, Parker, Parran, Peter, Pugh, Purnell, Ridgely, Sands, Smith, of Carroll, Smith, of Dorchester, Smith, of Worcester, Swope, Thomas, Turner—43.

The amendment was accordingly rejected.

Mr. NEGLEY, when his name was called, said: As these officers are to serve for the whole State, I think the people of the whole State ought to be permitted to take them from any portion of the State. I therefore vote "aye."

Mr. ABBOTT. The section now reads—

"They shall be not less than thirty years of age," &c. I move to strike out the word "thirty" and insert the word "forty."

The question being taken, the motion was not agreed to.

Mr. STIRLING moved to strike out "thirty" and insert "twenty-five."

The amendment was rejected.

Mr. DAVIS, of Charles, moved to insert the word "five" after the word "thirty."

Not agreed to.

Mr. MILLER. I move to strike out the word "circuit" and insert the word "county," in the clause of the section which now reads, "resident in the judicial district or circuit." The convention had determined by a very large vote to adopt the elective instead of the appointive system. They have refused to allow any judge of the court of appeals to be taken outside of the judicial district. Now, if there is to be one judge for each county in the State, who shall be one of the judges of the circuit court of the three counties of the circuit, and also to be placed upon the bench of the orphans' court, then properly to carry out that provision each county should elect its own judge. It will be found that by the nineteenth section of this report the State is to be divided into eight judicial circuits, providing that each circuit shall consist of three counties. In each of those circuits are to be elected three judges; that is, one judge for each county. He is required by the provisions of this report to reside in the county for which he is to be the judge, and if the elective system is to be carried out, it is but proper that the people of the county should be the proper constituency to elect that officer, and not permit the counties of St. Mary's, Charles and Prince George's, for instance, to elect three judges, all three of whom may be elected from one of those counties, and require two of them to remove to the other counties to reside. You should let the local bar of each county furnish a man to be the judge in that county.

Mr. CHAMBERS. They may not be able to do it.

Mr. MILLER. I think they can.

Mr. SANDS. I would suggest to the gentleman from Anne Arundel (Mr. Miller) that his amendment is premature. The subsequent action of the convention upon other subjects may require us to come back to this section and reconsider it. If the convention determine against the three-judge system, we would have to go back and strike this out.

Mr. MILLER. I will withdraw the amendment now, but shall probably introduce it at some other time.

No further amendment was offered to this section.

The next section was then read as follows:

"SEC. 3. The judges shall be appointed, commissioned and designated as chief or associated justices, by the governor, with the advice and consent of the senate. Each judge shall hold his office during good behavior, or until he shall attain the age of sixty years, when, in the discretion of the governor, by and with the advice and consent of the senate, he may be re-appointed for a term not exceeding ten years, after which he shall not be re-appointed."

Mr. THOMAS. I move to amend this section as follows:

Strike out all after the word "judges," in the first line, and insert the following:

"Of the several counties of this State, shall be elected by the qualified voters of the counties and the city of Baltimore, in the manner hereinafter prescribed."

Mr. CHAMBERS. I would suggest to the gentleman who has offered this proposition, that it is not at all cognate to the subject under consideration. If I recollect aright, there is no other provision in this report for this purpose.

Mr. THOMAS. I propose to offer another section for that purpose.

Mr. CHAMBERS. If the idea of the gentleman is to have the tenure of office changed, then let us understand it.

Mr. THOMAS. I do not know what the convention may want to do about that.

Mr. CHAMBERS. The tenure of office is another subject. This section applies to the tenure of office. Strike it out here, and then it is not in the report. The matter of his amendment is entirely different from the matter of this amendment.

Mr. THOMAS. I understand the gentleman to make the point of order that my amendment is not in order. If the president decides that question, I will be satisfied.

On motion of Mr. STIRLING,

Section three with the pending amendment was informally passed over.

Mr. SANDS. I would suggest——

The PRESIDENT. The president has heard so many suggestions, that hereafter he will require all matters to be reduced to writing.

Mr. SANDS. I merely wish to save time. We have settled the elective feature of this report. We better decide now whether we shall have three judges for the bench or not.

The PRESIDENT. Does the gentleman from Howard (Mr. Sands) submit a motion?

Mr. SANDS. No, sir.

The following sections were then read, and no amendment was offered thereto:

"Section 4. Any judge shall be removed from office by the governor, on conviction in a court of law of incompetency, of wilful neglect of duty, misbehavior in office, or any other crime, on impeachment according to this constitution, or the laws of the State, or on the address of the general assembly, two-thirds of each house concurring in such address, and the accused having been notified of the charges against him, and had opportunity of making his defence.

"Sec. 5. All judges shall, by virtue of their offices, be conservators of the peace throughout the State, and no fees or perquisites, commission or reward of any kind shall be allowed to any judge in this State, besides his annual salary or fixed per diem for the discharge of any judicial duty.

"Sec. 6. No judge shall sit in any case wherein he may be interested, or where either of the parties may be connected with him by affinity or consanguinity within such degrees as now are or may hereafter be prescribed by law, or where he shall have been of counsel in the case."

Section seven was then read as follows:

"Sec. 7. The judge or judges of any court may appoint such subordinate officers for the respective courts as may be found necessary, but none other; and no crier shall be appointed in any court, but clerks or assistant clerks, sheriffs, or their deputies, or bailiffs, as the court directs, shall, without additional compensation, perform the duties heretofore performed by criers."

Mr. STIRLING. I desire further time to consider this section, and therefore I move that it be informally passed over.

The motion was agreed to.

Section eight was then read as follows:

"Sec. 8. The clerks of the several courts created or continued by this constitution, shall have charge and custody of the records and other papers, shall perform all the duties and be allowed the fees which appertain to their several offices, as the same now are or may hereafter be regulated by law."

No amendment was offered thereto.

Section nine was then read as follows:

"Sec. 9. The legislature shall provide for the trial of causes in case of the disqualification of all of the judges of the circuit, but the parties to any cause may, by consent, appoint a proper person to try said cause, and may try any cause before the court without the intervention of a jury."

Mr. MILLER. This section embraces a new feature in the judicial system of this State, and I would like to hear some reasons assigned why it should be adopted. It provides that parties by consent may appoint a proper person to try any cause, ignoring entirely the judge, if I understand the section aright, even if he is not disqualified. And if the section is not susceptible of that construction, then it is liable to another objection. "And may try any cause before the court without the intervention of a jury." That applies as well to civil as criminal cases. It seems to be a sort of invasion of the right of trial by jury, by allowing parties by consent to take a case before the judge and try it upon the facts as well as upon the law, without a jury. It seems to me that is imposing upon the judge a duty which has not hitherto been devolved upon him. It may devolve upon him the trial of a long case in which, besides the construction of the law, the facts may be complicated. I think the trial of facts in all civil cases should be left to a jury, under such instructions as the court may give them in reference to matters of law. I can see no good reasons for the change here proposed.

Mr. CHAMBERS. Persons familiar with the practice of courts, will readily recollect a great many cases where the facts are perfectly simple, dependent upon the testimony of one witness, or two at the best. Hours might be occupied before a jury, while the matter would be disposed of before the court in a few minutes. The putting labor upon the judge is a consideration, I think, hardly to be regarded as worth estimating in such cases. It is only where both the parties desire it, that they are to have this privilege And if it was an onerous case to the judge, I think the principle of common delicacy would lead them to forbear exercising this privilege. I know that has been the practice. I know that the judge of the court has repeatedly urged counsel not to submit cases of a very serious criminal character, to his decision, when they expressed a desire to do so. And as gentlemen would always do, they have courteously acceded to the judge's request, and have gone before a jury. Now, where there is a very simple case, where much time may be saved, and where both parties desire it, why forbid parties from exercising their option? I confess, that I can see no objection to the section.

Mr. THRUSTON. I think the section will be made less ambiguous by changing the word "and," to the word "or," so that it will read: "but the parties to any cause may, by consent, appoint a proper person to try said case, or may try any cause before the court without the intervention of a jury."

Mr. STOCKBRIDGE. That changes the meaning of the sentence somewhat, as I understand it.

Mr. THRUSTON. I do not so understand it. The change I propose would carry the idea of consent into the latter clause more clearly than it now does; and that I suppose is the intention. If it is left as it now stands, the words "by consent," ought to be inserted into this latter clause also.

The question was upon striking out the word "and," and inserting the word "or;" and being taken, it was agreed to.

Mr. NEGLEY. I think this section should not be passed in its present form. This section contemplates a three-judge system. It say, "The legislature shall provide for the trial of causes in case of the disqualification of all the judges of the circuit, &c." Suppose we adopt a one-judge system, then we will have to go back and change this.

Mr. SMITH, of Worcester, moved that the convention take a recess; but withdrew the motion at the request of

Mr. BERRY, of Baltimore county, who asked and obtained leave to submit the following report, which was read the first time, and ordered to its second reading:

The committee on militia and military affairs respectfully submit the following report:

MILITIA AND MILITARY AFFAIRS.

Section 1. The militia shall be composed of all able-bodied male citizens, residents of this State, being eighteen years of age, and under the age of forty-five years, who shall be enrolled in the militia, and perform military duty in such manner not incompatible with the constitution and laws of the United States, as may be prescribed by the general assembly of Maryland.

Sec. 2. It shall be the duty of the general assembly to provide for and perfect from time to time the enrolment of the militia, and also for its effectual organization, and to make for this purpose such a division of the State into military districts as may secure these results, and in so doing to especially pass such laws as shall promote the formation of volunteer militia associations in the city of Baltimore, and every county, and to secure to them such privileges or assistance as may afford them effectual encouragement.

Sec. 3. The adjutant general shall be appointed by the governor, by and with the advice and consent of the senate. He shall hold his office for the term of ——— years, and receive for his services an annual salary of ——— dollars.

JOHN S. BERRY, Chairman,
JOSEPH B. PUGH,
H. W. DELLINGER,
D. C. BLACKISTON,
GEORGE PETER.

Mr. WICKARD, from the same committee, asked and obtained leave to submit the following report which was read:

The minority of the committee on militia and military affairs, respectfully submit the following report:

Section 1. The militia of this State shall consist of all able-bodied male citizens, between the ages of eighteen and forty-five years, except such persons as now are, or may hereafter be exempted by the laws of the United States or this State.

Sec. 2. Persons whose religious opinions or conscientious scruples forbid them to bear arms, shall not be compelled to do so in time of peace, but shall pay an equivalent for such personal service.

Sec. 3. The general assembly shall provide for organizing, equipping and disciplining the militia, in such manner as shall be most effective to repel invasion and suppress insurrection, not incompatible with the laws of the United States.

Sec. 4. The militia officers shall be chosen or appointed as follows: Captains, subalterns and non-commissioned officers shall be chosen by the written votes of the members of their respective companies; field officers of regiments and separate battalions, by the written votes of the commissioned officers of their respective regiments and separate battalions to which they belong; brigadier generals and brigade inspectors, by the field officers of their respective brigades; major generals, brigadier generals, and commanding officers of regiments or separate battalions, shall appoint the staff officers of their respective divisions, brigades, regiments or separate battalions.

Sec. 5. The governor shall nominate and, with the consent of the Senate, appoint major generals, an adjutant general, and other members of his staff, and their commissions shall expire with the time for which the governor shall have been elected.

Sec. 6. The general assembly shall, by law, fix the time and manner of electing militia officers, and of certifying their election to the governor, who shall grant their commissions and determine their rank, when not fixed by law.

Sec. 7. In case subalterns, captains or field officers shall refuse or neglect to make such elections, the governor shall have power to appoint such officers, and to fill all vacancies caused by such refusal or neglect.

Sec. 8. No commissioned officer shall be removed from office but by the sentence of a court-martial, or by the senate, on the recommendation of the governor, stating the grounds on which such removal is recommended.

Sec. 9. In case the mode of election and appointment of militia officers hereby directed, shall not be found conducive to the improvement of the militia, the general assembly may abolish the same, and provide by law for their appointment and removal.

J. WICKARD.

Mr. SMITH, of Worcester, renewed the motion that the convention take a recess.

Mr. DANIEL called for the yeas and nays on the motion, and they were ordered.

The question being then taken, by yeas and nays, it resulted—ayes 26, nays 37—as follows:

Yeas—Messrs. Berry, of Baltimore county, Billingsley, Blackiston, Chambers, Crawford, Dail, Davis, of Charles, Davis, of Washington, Dent, Duvall, Harwood, Lansdale, Lee, Marbury, Mayhugh, Mitchell, Miller, Morgan, Murray, Parran, Peter, Purnell, Smith, of Worcester, Thomas, Thruston, Wickard—26.

Nays—Messrs. Goldsborough, President; Abbott, Annan, Brown, Carter, Cunningham, Daniel, Earle, Ecker, Edelen, Galloway, Hopkins, Hopper, Jones, of Cecil, Jones, of Somerset, Keefer, Kennard, King, Markey, McComas, Mullikin, Negley, Parker, Ridgely, Robinette, Russell, Sands, Schley, Schlosser, Smith, of Carroll, Smith, of Dorchester, Stirling, Stockbridge, Swope, Sykes, Todd, Wooden—37.

The motion to take a recess was not agreed to.

JUDICIARY DEPARTMENT.

The convention then resumed the consideration of the report of the committee on the judiciary department, which was on its second reading.

The ninth section as follows, was under consideration:

"Sec. 9. The legislature shall provide for the trial of causes in case of the disqualification of all of the judges of the circuit, but the parties to any cause may, by consent, appoint a proper person to try said cause, and may try any cause before the court without the intervention of a jury."

Mr. NEGLEY. I move to strike out the words "all of the judges," and insert the words "any judge," so that it shall read "in case of the disqualification of any judge of the circuit,"&c.

Mr. SANDS. I think that amendment is entirely out of place as to time. We have not determined the main features in this report upon which will depend all these details. I think the convention will save a great deal of time by first acting upon the controlling features of this report and afterwards it will be easy to provide for the minutiæ. We have decided to have an elective system. Now let us determine the number of the judges; then the tenure of the office, and we can then very soon fill up the details. If this amendment is adopted we may have to go back and strike it out.

Mr. STIRLING. I hope this question will not be pressed, unless the house is going to investigate this subject. If we go on making amendment after amendment without due consideration we may abolish the half of this report right off by incidental motions. This report provides for three judges in the circuit court. If we are going to decide that we are to have a one-judge system we ought to have our eyes open. I confess that I am now in favor of the one-judge system.

On motion of Mr NEGLEY,

The ninth section with the pending amendment was informally passed over.

TAKING OF TESTIMONY.

Mr. DANIEL. I move to insert after the ninth section, the following as an additional section:

"Sec. 10. The testimony in equity cases shall be taken in like manner as in cases at law."

I think this is the proper place for this section. I have copied it in exact terms from the New York system. I have done it because I believe it will save a great deal of time in the taking testimony by commission as is now practiced. Cases are frequently delayed day after day under the present system in this State. One party may be placed almost in the entire control of another party, who wishes to delay a case and put it off by the taking of testimony day after day before a commissioner. I call to mind now a case, an important case of injunction, where the party who wished to delay it was allowed to take testimony before a commissioner. The case has been delayed in this way day after day, a great number of witnesses having been examined, until now that injunction has been lying for months and may lie for months longer before it can be tried. I think, therefore, it is better to have all witnesses come before the judge of the court of equity as they do at common law and give in their testimony there, so that the judge can observe the manner of the witness, hear his cross-examination and keep out all improper questions and answers. I think that will not only promote justice, but will tend very much to save time. A case may be tried before the judge of a court of equity in one or two days, when the same case before a commissioner would occupy, in the taking of testimony, several weeks, if not months.

Lawyers who are constantly employed in business will not find it possible, perhaps, to appoint more than one day in a week, sometimes not more than one day in two weeks to take testimony before the commissioner. And you must suit the convenience of both lawyers, and the witnesses have to be examined in this tedious way. Every word must be written down; every answer must be propounded in writing; every question must be reduced to writing. One or two witnesses are examined in a day, or one but partially examined, and then comes an adjournment over for a week, perhaps two weeks. A long case may in this way occupy months where one of the parties is disposed to delay, or where it may not suit the convenience of parties to examine the witnesses right straight through, and the very same case in a court of equity might not occupy more than a day or two. And I think the advantage of seeing the witnesses while under examination, and the having the examination properly conducted, and rapidly conducted as in other cases, will lead to a saving of time and promote justice, besides being a saving of expense. In a suit at common law, say involving $500, a man brings his witnesses before the court and has them examined at once before a jury. In equity a case involving the same amount requires you to go before a commissioner with all this delay, yet in the one case as in the other it may be important to have the witnesses before the tribunal that is to determine the case. I think it will lessen the expense, be a saving of time, and promote justice, to adopt this provision. I find it in the constitution of New York, and I understand it has been found to be very beneficial in its effects there.

Mr. Sands. I would like to call the earnest attention of the members of this body to the proposed amendment and the objects which it will really attain. I think there is no question but that our present system is deficient in this; that it causes great delay and vast expense. For instance, generally the person appointed a commissioner to take testimony is not a professional man, and even if he is, he cannot decide, for he has not the power, upon the competency of a witness or the admissibility of his testimony, and no matter what irrelevant questions may be put to a witness all you can do is to except to them. And I have known many cases where parties who were irresponsible for the costs, in order to compel the opposing parties to compromise, have gone on increasing the record until the testimony in the case was almost as much as the Bible, and the ends of justice have been entirely defeated. You might go there day after day, have A, B, C, brought in as witnesses, of whom the most irrelevant questions will be asked, spun out to interminable length, all written down and put upon record, you objecting to them on account of their utter irrelevancy, and the commissioner replying, "I am no judge of that matter; put it down, and the answer to it," and then you enter your exception.

I say I have known many such instances. I call to mind now one case where the purposes of justice were entirely defeated, because the party defendant was advised by his counsel that he better settle and pay the demand than have more eaten up in the costs of the suit; and he did so. And I say that it ought to be taken out of the power of parties thus to defeat the ends of justice. I had a case: A wife had petitioned for separation and alimony. The husband in that case is bound to pay the costs, no matter whether the petition is granted or not. I, myself, sate taking testimony in that case for weeks, and the record would make such a one as I do not suppose one man in a hundred gets to see. Then I had to advise the party, because he would have to make payment of the costs in the end, to make the best settlement he could. She did not care, her counsel did not care, which way the suit went as far as the costs were concerned, and it was evidently their purpose to force him to a settlement in this way. And our system at present tolerates this abuse.

If we adopt this amendment then the testimony is taken before the court, and all these evils are met. The judge would at once exclude irrelevant testimony, and would confine it to proper issues, and within proper bounds. This is certainly a great abuse, and I think if we can by such a change in our system as would be made by the adoption of this proposed amendment cure these abuses, we will have done the State of Maryland great service.

Mr. Miller. The legislature has full control over this matter; if there is any abuse existing, the legislature can correct it at any time it sees fit. There is no necessity for putting this in the constitution, for if that is done, and it is found to work badly, it cannot be changed or repealed, as it could be if it were a legislative enactment and not a constitutional provision. The gentleman from Baltimore city (Mr. Daniel,) and the gentleman from Howard (Mr. Sands,) have spoken about the trial of these cases before the court below. Now a commission is issued, testimony is taken, and written and submitted to the judge; the parties having a right to except to any question they may consider irrelevant. The court below decides upon that case, and then it goes to the court of appeals on appeal, and they decide whether the court below decided correctly or not upon those exceptions.

Now, under this amendment, how are cases in equity to be tried in the court below? Are we going to call witnesses up, and every instant have disputes about the admissibility of testimony, have exceptions taken, and then have the record go up to the court of appeals, just as if it were a common law case? Is that the mode of proceeding that the gentleman desires?

Mr. Sands. The testimony is to be taken under this provision, before a court competent to decide the competency of witnesses. Does it not operate to the good of the party by saving to him the cost of the immense record that is made up before commissioners?

Mr. Stirling. The record must go up any way.

Mr. Sands. It must be made up, I know. But if the testimony is taken before a judge, three-fourths of what is now upon the record would never get there.

Mr. Thomas. Suppose in an injunction case, you go before a court and take testimony, and the party against whom the injunction is issued conceives that the injunction is not rightfully issued, and you have to send up in the record of the court of appeals the facts upon which the court below acted, in order to obtain a reversal of his judgment. You lose all the time of the court below in taking down the testimony in the injunction case, and putting it in the record to go up to the court of appeals.

Mr. Sands. My idea is to provide that testimony shall be taken before a court competent to judge of the relevancy of the testimony.

The President. The court would have to sit all the year.

Mr. Sands. That may be an objection; but certainly the other objections which have been made here are not objections.

Mr. Jones, of Somerset. The purpose which the gentleman (Mr. Sands) has in view of abridging the testimony, in saving the consumption of time by this mode, cannot be effected, where a party is disposed to prolong it factiously. A lawyer upon the one side or the other will object to every question, and will take exceptions if overruled; will argue before the judge the question of the admissibility of each question, and the judge would be bound to hear him, or if he did not it would be discourteous. And then when the judge decided against him, he would take a bill of exceptions. Therefore so far from abridging the record, I think it would lead to an almost interminable consumption of time, where the disposition is to prolong; and as the President has well suggested, it would require the judge to sit the whole year, and if the judge hears the testimony, you would have to have a clerk to take down all the testimony. If irrelevant testimony is taken down before the commissioner, the lawyer knows it would be ruled out by the court?

Mr. Sands. I admit that there is something in the objection in regard to occupying the time of the judge in taking testimony.—But I ask my friend this: Does he believe that any man who had a decent regard for his own standing in court, would before any judge put such questions as you find put by the hundred before a commissioner.

Mr. Jones, of Somerset. If he is paid for it, I reckon he would put all the questions his client desires.

Mr. Sands. I would not.

Mr. Thruston. Any radical change of this kind is a very dangerous thing. If there are any defects in our present system, it is perfectly competent for the legislature to change it. It is a dangerous experiment, I think, to change almost the whole equity records of the State.

Mr. Stockbridge. I am greatly in favor of every proposition which can expedite business in courts of law or equity. For these delays have existed ever since the time of Shakespeare, who considered the law's delays one of the things which would justify suicide; and I do not think it has improved since. But I do not think that this amendment will accomplish the object sought.—There are suits in equity and suits at law, begun in the time of our grandfathers, which are not decided yet. I think the law as it now stands affords greater facilities for suits in equity than for cases at law; provided the attorneys are disposed to press their cause. Our code now says, in reference to chancery matters:

"With a view to the speedy execution and return of commissions to take testimony, the court, or any judge thereof, shall prescribe such rules as the nature of the case may require."

The courts have acted upon that, and have prescribed rules wherever there is a disposition to delay trivially. It is the easiest thing in the world for a solicitor in a cause to obtain a special rule from the judge requiring the commission to return in so many days. It is an every day practice with solicitors who press their causes.

Suppose you adopt the system proposed by this amendment, and I am disposed to fight for time. Is it not easy enough for me to want John Smith, whose testimony I cannot get; he is in New York, and you can only take his testimony before the court, or send a commission. You send a commissioner there and he finds it difficult to find John Smith. There will be commissions taken out under this system as under the other, for you will always have the right to send abroad. And under the rules already prescribed in the code, which can be modified at any time by the legislature, when they work hardship, you can have all the expedition that the occasion requires.

I know it has always happened, where a lawyer has lost a cause, he is sure the jury was corrupt, or stupid, or the judge was wrong, or something of the kind, and he will go to the legislature and get a law passed to apply to his particular case. My colleague (Mr. Daniel) has met with some hardships, and he offers this amendment. My friend from Howard (Mr. Sands) has met with some hardships, and he thinks this may remedy it in that divorce case of which he speaks. Possibly it might; and then it might operate injustice in a hundred other cases.

Mr. Stirling. I agree with my colleague (Mr. Daniel) as to some of the evils of which he speaks. But I would like to know what this constitutional convention has to do with this subject? This is a matter regulating the practice of the courts. And we might as well go to work to fill up the constitution with the whole practice of the courts. And if all the lawyers would get up here and jaw about the details we might sit here until kingdom come.

Mr. Daniel. The gentleman voted to go into all the details in regard to the public schools. I find that whenever it suits members to go into details they always do so; when it does not suit them to do so, then they say it is a matter for the legislature. I say that we have the example of New York, one of the largest States of this Union; and I suppose they had as good lawyers in their convention as ever were in any convention. The lawyers there put this in their constitution in very short phrase; and I think it is a very good precedent.

In reference to what has been suggested by gentlemen in reference to delay, that this amendment I have offered will cause more delay than the present practice. Now my experience has been different in reference to the trial of causes at law in comparison with the trial of causes in equity. You generally get through your case sooner at law than in equity, for you have a jury there and are assigned your time. And I do not see why you cannot take your testimony, every point that is to go up before the court of appeals, before the judge of the court below, or at the time of your trial in equity, just as you do at law. I know that sometimes in the trial of equity cases weeks and months are occupied in the trial of equity cases; whereas at law a great number of witnesses are examined in one day. I do not see any more reason for a long record in equity than at law. There are a great many questions and points that lawyers would waive when they come before the court of equity. They would certainly presume that the court knew something, whereas they presume that the commissioner knows nothing. And when these points are submitted to the court of equity and argued, they would waive them, and thus they would not go up to the court of appeals and increase the record. There is a section in this report that you may waive a jury at common law as well as in equity. And why should we reverse and alter the whole practice of the State heretofore, which has always required all matters of fact to go before a jury? And yet you think this is an anomaly and not to be put into the constitution, because it is properly a matter of legislation.

Mr. Stirling. If we do not put in the constitution a provision permitting a question to be tried without a jury, you cannot do it at all; fifty thousand legislatures could not authorize it to be done, because the constitution guarantees the right of trial by jury; and you must put such a provision in your constitution or not have it at all.

Mr. Daniel. Be that as it may, I think this will save expense and save delay, and will give the judge what has always been considered the very great advantage of seeing the witnesses and cross-examining them in his own presence. And I have no doubt that very frequently a case would be decided upon the justice and equity of the case in a different way if the court could see the witnesses upon the stand, hear them testify, see their manner, see them under the fire of cross-examination, by which you test not only his recollection, but his honesty and motives.

LEAVE OF ABSENCE.

Mr. Dellinger asked and obtained leave of absence until Tuesday of next week.

Mr. Ridgely asked and obtained leave of absence for his colleague (Mr. Berry, of Baltimore county,) on account of indisposition.

Mr. Davis, of Washington, moved that the convention take a recess.

The question being taken, upon a division —ayes 30, noes 25—it was agreed to.

And the convention accordingly took a recess.

EVENING SESSION.

The convention reassembled at 8 o'clock, P. M.

The roll was called, and the following members answered to their names:

Messrs. Goldsborough, President; Abbott, Annan, Audoun, Belt, Billingsley, Blackiston, Brown, Carter, Crawford, Cunningham,

Daniel, Davis, of Washington, Dent, Duvall, Earle, Ecker, Edelen, Galloway, Harwood, Hodson, Hopkins, Hopper, Jones, of Somerset, Keefer, Kennard, King, Lansdale, Lee, Marbury, Markey, Mayhugh, McComas, Mitchell, Miller, Morgan, Mullikin, Murray, Negley, Nyman, Parker, Parran, Pugh, Purnell, Robinette, Russell, Sands, Schley, Schlosser, Smith, of Carroll, Smith, of Worcester, Stirling, Stockbridge, Swope, Thruston, Todd, Turner, Wickard, Wooden—59.

On motion of Mr. STIRLING, it was

Ordered to be entered upon the journal that Mr. Cushing was detained from his seat on account of indisposition.

INTEREST AND USURY LAWS.

Mr. BELT. I move that the rules be suspended in order to enable me to make a report from a committee, so that the house may be put in possession of it, and that it may be printed.

The motion was agreed to, and the rules suspended accordingly.

The report was received, read the first time, and ordered to be printed, as follows:

The committee heretofore appointed to consider and report upon section 49, of article 3, of the present constitution, having reference to interest and the usury laws, beg leave to report their unanimous recommendation, that the following section be added to the article on the legislative department.

Sec. —. The legal rate of interest in this State shall be six per centum per annum, except in cases where a different rate may be agreed upon between contracting parties; and in all cases of private contract, the rate of interest agreed on, or contracted for, shall be recoverable; and the general assembly shall pass all laws that may be necessary to carry this section into effect.

EDWARD W. BELT,
Chairman of the Committee.

JUDICIARY DEPARTMENT.

The convention then resumed the consideration of the report of the committee on the judiciary department, which was on its second reading.

The pending question was on the amendment submitted by Mr. DANIEL, to wit:

Insert as an additional section, the following:

"Sec. 10. The testimony in equity cases shall be taken in like manner as in cases at law."

Mr. DANIEL. I wish to say a few words so as to place myself right upon this subject. Since I had the honor to introduce this amendment, I have been examining the debates of the New York constitutional convention upon this subject. That convention was composed of some of the ablest lawyers of New York, of whom Charles O'Conor was one, Mr. Tallmadge another—Charles O'Conor standing pretty much at the head, if not at the head of the bar in this country, I think. And I find that this very proposition I have submitted here was introduced by Mr. Charles O'Conor, and was incorporated unanimously into the constitution of New York. I beg leave to read a few remarks of some of the able lawyers who advocated this proposition.

I will first read some of the names of the lawyers to show some of the lawyers in that New York convention: Messrs. Tallmadge, Shepherd, Harrison, Shaw, Witbech, O'Conor, Taggart, Bouch, Worden, Marvin and St. John. All of these gentlemen reported systems of judiciary; and in a great many of those reports was reported some section of this sort making proceedings in equity similar to those at law. A very full discussion was had. I will show that the very proposition I have submitted here was introduced into that convention by Mr. Charles O'Conor, and unanimously incorporated into the constitution of New York.

I read now some of the remarks of Mr. Stetson on this proposition. He said:

"But first he would here express his heartfelt thanks to the honorable gentleman from New York, (Mr. O'Conor,) who has so ably, eloquently and triumphantly vindicated the principle of the union not only of the equity and law jurisdiction in one, but of the uniformity of practice and proceedings upon the two remedies. There should be a similarity of proceedings in all cases, and whether proceedings should assume the form of equity proceedings, or the simple and well known proceedings of an action on the case, was of comparatively little importance. His impression had been that the better method would be to assimilate all actions and proceedings to the simple form of an action on the case as now used. That the multitude of civil actions now in use, should be abolished, and one plain, simple remedy provided in all cases. On this subject he did not know but he stood alone in his profession, and it was highly gratifying to him to find in the honorable gentleman from New York so able a champion of that principle. The gentleman and myself desire to arrive at the same result, and it matters but little by which course of proceeding we shall so arrive at it, whether by the simple action on the case, or by a plain, concise, and simple bill in equity."

Mr. Jordan, another very able gentleman, a lawyer from New York, makes use of these remarks, upon the discussion of this question:

"Although the senior of the honorable gentleman from New York (Mr. O'Conor) in years, he would not pretend to the same amount of practical experience and accuracy of observation; yet he had seen enough to convince him that if the one or the other must fall, he would cling to the common law; its remedies were bounded by right lines, it did not and could not follow the zig-zag, crooked and searching tracks of the court of chancery, but so far as its remedies extended they were direct and perfect. He who sued for justice there could march forward to her altar and receive from the hands of her priest that measure to which he was entitled. The systems of equity were adopted from necessity; and nothing but necessity would drive any sensible man into that forum—a suit at law was no mystery—everybody could understand it sufficiently, and calculate with proximate certainty its expenses and its delays, but the purlieus of the court of chancery were shrouded in darkness and mystery, and his client generally when informed that no adequate remedy existed elsewhere, would shrug his shoulders and shrink back as from the horrors of annihilation. Much of this it was true, arose from the manner in which justice had been administered in that forum; much simplification, much reform, in that department might doubtless be attained, and he trusted would be, in whatever court its powers might be vested, though in its best estate if the one system or the other must go by the board, he would take leave of it forever and take the hazard of moulding the remedies of the courts of law so as to attain the end of justice."

And not only was the proposition discussed to make the proceedings similar, but they discussed the proposition to blend both law and equity together. Previous to that time there was a sort of entire court of chancery. Now I say the argument holds strongly in this State; for with the exception of Baltimore city, our courts of law are courts of equity, and the same judges administer equity that administer common law. And as one gentleman from whom I have quoted says in his very able argument, the distinction was so nice, especially where one of the judges administers both, that his mind was constantly running from the common law channel into that of the other.

Mr. SMITH, of Carroll. As the gentleman seems so familiar with the judicial system of New York, will he tell me whether or not there are masters of chancery in that State?

Mr. DANIEL. They abolished them by this constitution. I copied the provision I have offered here, from the present constitution of the State of New York, as published in the book of constitutions with which members have been furnished. The ground taken there was the same ground I have taken here to-day, that it does save time, and in my judgment it saves expense to suitors. We have the same thing in the United States court in Baltimore city every day, sitting as a court of admiralty. Judge Giles in all cases of admiralty hears testimony and decides upon it without the intervention of a jury. The proceedings are similar to those in equity. You commence with something like a bill of equity; and then the answer is put in, and you take testimony before the court, and the court prepares a decision in the case. I would not destroy the commissioners, for where the witnesses cannot be present at the trial, and the lawyers agree, you can take the testimony of witnesses before a commissioner.

Mr. STIRLING. You cannot do that if this is put in the constitution.

Mr. DANIEL. Mr. O'Conor said distinctly it could be done.

Mr. STIRLING. It cannot be done under our practice, if this proposed section is adopted, except out of the city or county.

Mr. DANIEL. It can be provided for. And I think in all cases like these it would afford greater facility. I was very much surprised to hear my colleague (Mr. Stockbridge) say to-day that the experience was that cases at common law were as tedious or more so than cases in equity. And he illustrated it by saying that some have been in court since the time of our grandfathers. It may be that some have hung on like that, but I think experience is to the contrary. In a case at law you try the case before a jury, you have the witnesses before the court and can see their manner and all about them, and get through more rapidly than in cases of equity. It is a common tale about the great delays in suits in equity; novels have been written about it.

Mr. STIRLING. Is that applicable to this State? It may be applicable to such cases as Jaundice *vs.* Jaundice, but not to cases in our courts. The docket of the superior court has cases on the docket longer than those in our equity courts. It takes two years longer to try some cases there than in the equity court.

Mr. DANIEL. That does not at all meet the objection I am making. It is said that proceedings are necessarily longer at common law than in equity, that is because that court is crowded with cases, and you cannot get at the case.

Any man who has been in courts of justice, and seen witnesses come in and be examined orally, one come in, be examined and then go out, and another come in, etc., must know that it is a shorter process than to take testimony before commissioners, by filling up the record with exception after exception, to go up to the other court. Some of the lawyers from which I have read speak of the interminable delay of cases in equity. One of them said that when his client was told that he must go into chancery, he would shrink from it as from annihilation.

Mr. MILLER. I should regret very much that gentlemen should go to the State of New York and bring here all the new-fangled notions of law that prevail in that State. In reference to the matter of expense, about which so much has been said by the gentleman from Baltimore city (Mr. Daniel,) the experience of New York lawyers will show,

I think, that instead of the expense being diminished, it has been vastly increased by their attempts at reforming law proceedings. The cost even of collecting a promissory note of $120 or $130 there, would amount to about double the sum recovered.

It seems to me that the difficulty in adopting this provision is this: In our State equity and common law jurisdictions have always been kept separate and distinct, and gentlemen forget that it is at last the court of appeals which in equity cases is to decide upon facts; and these facts must appear before that court upon the record. There may be some difficulty, and there is, in the court below in having testimony taken down before the witnesses; and the witnesses have to appear before the judge; and that testimony must in some way or other be embodied in the record and submitted to the appellate tribunal, because the court of appeals under our system of procedure, when acting upon equity causes, is both judge and jury. That court must have the facts before them, in order to review the decision of the judge below in reference to the facts. Now, how is that to be brought about? Are we to go into the trial of a cause in equity, and raise exception after exception before the judge as to the competency of a witness, and have the testimony written down word for word, as it was delivered, and then have it embodied in the record, and sent up in the shape of exceptions as we do in a case at common law? It seems to me much simpler to have the testimony taken first before the commissioner, and then submitted to the judge, and then the same testimony, in the same form, submitted to the appellate court.

Now in reference to delays, that has been a charge against equity proceedings from time immemorial. That is not, however, it seems to me, an objection that should prevail. It is an objection which is not true in point of fact. I have had some experience in reference to equity causes, and have had some knowledge of equity causes coming into the appellate court, and so far as the records go of cases that come up to that appellate court and are decided there, I think I can safely say they have not been of so long standing as cases at common law.

Mr. THRUSTON. I know there are some evils in connection with our present system. But my objection to this amendment is that I think it would be extremely dangerous for us to attempt to make this change without seeing what the effect will be. The legislature has power to change it if necessary, and they can look into it and see how far it is necessary to change the equity system. Now it is very common, in applying for an injunction affecting great public interests, interests of large bodies of people, for the judges to grant this injunction upon terms; that is to say, with leave to move for a dissolution of the injunction upon five days' notice, and commission the parties in interest to take testimony. Here is an injunction upon stocks in certain manufactures: the judge says—I will grant the injunction upon the case stated upon the bill, but with leave to the other party to move for a dissolution upon five or ten days' notice, with leave to parties to take testimony. Suppose a case arises when the judge is absent. Is it for him to leave the county he may be in, and go there to take evidence? Or when there is a vacation of the court, when the judge is entirely occupied in determining how to decide certain questions? This is but one difficulty.

There are many difficulties that occur to my mind, showing that it is not proper to introduce such a change as this into the law, without providing in other ways for its effects. Judges will not sit upon the bench all day, and then sit up all night to take evidence in a case; and unless you can provide some mode for evidence to be taken at the time, injunctions of this character would be carried over until the county court sits for the testimony to be taken in court. I think it would be exceedingly dangerous to make any such change as this in this way, without seeing its effects, without providing for those effects, as they may affect our system of equity jurisdiction. I am therefore opposed to this amendment as a dangerous amendment.

The question being taken upon the amendment of Mr. DANIEL, it was rejected.

TRIAL OF CAUSES, ETC.

Mr. THRUSTON. I suppose it is the wish of this body to perfect this report as we go along, if it can be done. The ninth section was passed over this morning, because no amendment was proposed that covered the whole case. Since that period I have prepared an amendment, which I think will not be objected to. I would, therefore, ask the convention to take up section nine, for the purpose of enabling me to offer what is in effect a substitute for the whole section, which I think will suit the views of all parties.

The question being taken, the motion was agreed to.

Section nine was then read as follows:

"Sec. 9. The legislature shall provide for the trial of causes in case of the disqualification of all of the judges of the circuit, but the parties to any cause may, by consent, appoint a proper person to try said cause, and may try any cause before the court without the intervention of a jury."

The pending question was upon the motion of Mr. NEGLEY, to strike out the words "all of the judges" and insert "any judge."

Mr. NEGLEY withdrew his amendment.

Mr. THRUSTON. I now move to strike out all after the word "the," in the first line, and insert:

"General assembly shall provide for the trial of causes in case of the disqualification of all the judges of the circuit to hear and determine the same, but in case of such disqualification, the parties thereto may by consent appoint a person to try the same; and the parties to any cause may submit the same to the court for determination without the aid of a jury."

That permits parties to submit their causes to the court without the intervention of a jury, and also provides for the case of the disqualification of the judge, and it does not mix up the two subjects which were intended to be included in this section.

Mr. SANDS. I would just remark that the proposition submitted by the gentleman from Allegany (Mr. Thruston) proceeds upon the supposition that we have already determined to have a plurality of judges in the several circuits. Now I do not think from what I know of the temper of the house, that that is likely to be the prevailing sentiment here.—The language of the amendment as read certainly implies that we have decided in favor of a plurality of judges in the circuit. This says "in case of the disqualification of all the judges of the circuit," &c. Now from what I have learned by conversation with other members, I think it is pretty well determined that we are to have but a single judge in the circuit, and perhaps a new districting of the State.

Mr. THRUSTON. The language I have used will cover the case whether there are one, two, or three judges. If there is but one judge he will be "all of the judges of the circuit."

Mr. STIRLING. The committee on revision can alter it if necessary.

Mr. THRUSTON. It will be construed to mean but one judge, if there is but one.

The question being taken upon the amendment of Mr. THRUSTON, it was adopted.

No further amendment was offered to the section.

REMOVAL OF CAUSES.

Section ten was then read as follows:

Sec. 10. The judge or judges of any court of this State, except the court of appeals, may order and direct the record of proceedings in any suit or action, issue or petition, presentment or indictment pending in such court, to be transmitted to some other court in the same or an adjoining circuit having jurisdiction in such causes, whenever any party to such cause, or the counsel of any party, shall make it satisfactorily appear to the court that such party has a substantial ground of action or defence, and cannot have a fair and impartial trial in the court in which such suit or action, issue or petition, presentment or indictment is pending; and the general assembly shall make such modifications of existing law as may be necessary to regulate and give force to this provision.

Mr. STIRLING. I move to strike out the words "has a substantial ground of action or defence, and." It will then read—"make it satisfactorily appear to the court that such party cannot have a fair and impartial trial in the court," etc. I am not prepared to say whether I like this section or not. It restricts the right of removal which now exists, and requires a party to satisfy the court that he cannot have a fair and impartial trial there, before he can remove his cause. He can now remove it upon his own affidavit, and I also cannot see how you should require a criminal to disclose his defence, in order to satisfy the court that he has a good ground of action.

Mr. STOCKBRIDGE. I greatly prefer the section as it stands, to the section as it will stand if the amendment be made which my colleague (Mr. Stirling) has proposed. No person who is at all familiar with the course of proceedings in this State for the last fifteen years, but knows that one of the greatest abuses which has grown up in our courts, has been the constant removal of causes without any reason, and for the purpose of promoting delay, and the promoting the ends of justice from being accomplished. Civil causes and criminal causes alike have been removed upon the affidavits of parties, and the records of the State, I am sorry to say, will show more utterly reckless and unconscionable swearing in that respect, I think, than in any other. It is an every-day practice for persons to go into court professing a readiness for trial, in criminal cases and in civil cases. But if they find the adverse party there with their witnesses ready to proceed, then they make affidavit that they cannot have a fair trial, and ask that it be removed, in the hope that, being sent to some county at some distance, ten, twenty, forty or fifty miles away, the witnesses would not follow; that the adverse party will be worried out. It has often happened in criminal cases, when the State was represented in one county by an able district attorney, and indifferently represented in the adjoining county, that they have sought to avoid an able prosecution against them, by putting it into the hands of a different State's attorney, who being separated from the witnesses, probably never seeing them until the cause is ready for trial; and then perhaps being compelled to go into court with but a part of the witnesses in the cause. I know that the court in many counties have used great efforts to procure the attendance of witnesses, and required them to follow parties where the causes have been removed. The removal of the cause often operates, in the first instance, a long postponement of the cause. Then after the postponement has continued, witnesses must make a long and expensive journey. And sometimes witnesses to a small matter of theft have found it much cheaper for themselves to refund the loss to the parties who have lost by the theft, than to follow the causes to the places to which they have been removed, and consequently cases have been informally dropped and thus the ends of justice have been defeated.

This section is an exception to the general power of removal on the naked affidavit of the parties. It was thought wise also to provide that parties should in some way satisfy the court in making the application that it was not done to delay the cause and run away from the witnesses, or the person in whose hands the cause was placed; so that the court might see that there was some ground of action or defence, as the case might be. I do not see that it can operate any hardship to any one. It is true the objection may be to the court that is to try the case. I suppose an objection of that nature, stated in any court, would insure instantly the removal of the case. If any man who had a cause on trial felt that the personal relations between himself and the judge were such that he could not have a fair trial before him, and that was stated to the court, then I suppose that no judge within the State, or whom we are likely to have in the State, would retain jurisdiction of the cause and proceed to the trial. In a case of that sort an order for removal would follow of course, and in other cases I am satisfied that the ends of justice would be attained by this section.

Mr. Stirling. This section undoubtedly involves a matter of very grave importance, and whatever is done in regard to this matter ought to done very deliberately. There is no doubt that, as my colleague (Mr. Stockbridge) has said, there have been gross abuses growing out of this system. But at the same time it is a system which has been in force in this State for a very long period of time, and like most things that have some value they are the very things that are abused. I have seen men in court, just as their causes were being called for trial, move for an order of removal with no other object than to get rid of justice. It was not because they were allowed to do it on simple affidavit, so much as because the disposition to extend this right of removal has been carried so far as to lead to the abuses which have grown up under it. The laws of the State gives the party the right to move for a removal at the first term of the court; and the legislature has given the right still further to do so at any subsequent session of the court. The difficulty is that there is no time fixed, no limit. If the judges of the court were authorized to prescribe rules in regard to this matter, so that they could compel a man to decide within a certain time after his pleading, the great evil would be remedied. The legislature of 1862 was importuned principally through the instrumentality of the judge of the criminal court and myself to pass a law to alter this thing, and they did intend to do it; but the law was so botched up before it got through the legislature that the matter really stood as it was before. The difficulty arises from allowing a party to remove his cause at a second term of the court. This section would abolish the right altogether hereafter. A criminal cannot show why it is that he cannot have a fair trial, for to do so he must make known his ground of defence; and in a civil case it cannot be done. It rests upon matters which a man cannot see, but very often cannot prove. Take a man who is to be tried in some county for a criminal offence. His counsel knows, and he himself knows that he cannot have a fair trial.—His offence has prejudiced every man in the county, and each one of those men, unless he is an extraordinary man will carry those prejudices into the jury-box. The judge sympathizes with his fellow citizens in the county. Innocent men have been acquitted in this State solely because they had the power to have their causes removed. Now I do not see how a man is to show that he has a good defence. This does not say that he is to swear to any affidavit, but that he must make it satisfactorily appear to the court.

Mr. Thruston. Suppose you insert the words "by the affidavit of the party," after the word "shall," so that it shall read "whenever any party, &c., shall by the affidavit of the party make it satisfactorily appear to the court," &c. In that way it would be necessary for the party to set out what his case was, and his ground of action upon oath; and the court could judge whether they were such grounds of defence as were reasonable and proper. Suppose the section were to read in this way, "shall make it satisfactorily appear by his affidavit to the court that such a party has a substantial ground of action or defence," &c. Then the affidavit of the party would be all that the court would require. In regard to the defence, it would be necessary for me to set out in the affidavit only so far as to show that he had a substantial defence. I think that would meet the objection of the gentleman, and would avoid some of the abuses to which the system is liable.

Mr. Stirling. I think this amendment is absolutely indispensable. unless you are to change the whole right of removal. I would rather leave this section out entirely. If you put it in here the legislature cannot restrict it. But leave the law to stand as it is, you will leave it subject to such revision as the legislature may deem necessary. I think the legislature will be disposed to restrict this right. But if you put it in as it stands in this section you shut the door to fraud, and to everything else also.

Some time ago I had a civil case against a corporation. The president of the corporation made oath that he could not have a fair trial; I knew he could not have it. But if I had been called upon to satisfy the judge with proof, I could not have done it. There were circumstances which satisfied us that there were certain general reasons why the jury would not render an impartial verdict. That was just as apparent to us as a thing could be; yet it was not susceptible of proof.

Mr. THRUSTON. It was a matter of belief.

Mr. STIRLING. The difficulty at present is that men put all sorts of interpretation upon it. But that can be cured by legislation, and it might just as well be left to the legislature. If men are not ready to proceed to trial, they will swear that they cannot have a fair and impartial trial, if you do not give them time. That is where the abuse is; and that abuse can be remedied without taking away the right. I would not want to deprive a man of the right of removing his case; because the very court to which he appeals may be the very thing which he desires to get rid of. If he goes up to the judge and tells him that he thinks he is something he ought not to be, I think the judge most likely would get mad and remove the case. But you do not like to tell the court that you cannot trust them; it is a delicate matter. I do not wish to amplify the question. But it seems to me it is dangerous to go to the extent this section does.

Mr. STOCKBRIDGE. The considerations urged by my colleague (Mr. Stirling) and the suggestions of the gentleman from Allegany (Mr. Thruston) were all thoroughly canvassed by the committee. The precise phraseology which the gentleman from Allegany has suggested should be modified was framed of deliberate intent. He shall make it satisfactorily appear, without any limitation whatever, by his own affidavit, by the affidavits of other parties, in any other way or form—giving him the largest latitude possible. He may satisfy the judge by a simple statement without any affidavit; if the judge becomes satisfied, that is sufficient.

So far as the other objection is concerned, that you may be compelled by that prematurely to develop the whole line of defence in your case, which it is important to keep secret. That is an objection which lies to other things just as well as this. For instance, my friend is in court ready to try the case, with the exception that one witness is absent, a vital witness He makes application for a continuation, because that witness is not there. How is he to obtain it? He must develop the facts which he expects to prove by that witness if he were in court. This may compel him to unfold his whole ground of defence, just as much as on an application for removal. This notion of diplomacy, in cases at law, is getting a great deal out of vogue any how. If gentlemen go into courts to obtain their rights and justice, it is right that justice should be done. And in those cases, and they are rare, where a fair trial cannot be had, where there is so much prejudice, excitement, in those few cases I think this section makes a sufficiently broad provision. I see no way at all by which justice can be more thoroughly obtained than under this section. Ordinarily a case is to be tried where it is to be brought; in those extraordinary cases they can be removed. We have laid it down in the declaration that the trial of cases where the controversy arises, is one of the great means of promoting justice. By our laws, we do not allow any suit to be brought against a man, save in the county where he resides. But that avails nothing, if the plaintiff having brought such a suit, can forthwith compel it to be removed elsewhere. And he cannot do it under the law, except with this provision in the constitution.

Mr. NEGLEY. I think the limitation upon this power of removal contemplated in this tenth section, is a very salutary one. I know that this unlimited right of removal has been most outrageously abused in my own county. Parties on trial for some petty larceny, have absolutely made affidavit and had their causes removed to Frederick county, and subjected the county to heavy expense. Not that they could not have justice done in our county, but in order that they might not have justice done in the county to which they removed their cases, because their character was so well known in the community where the offence was committed that they had not much chance to escape justice. And their cases were removed for the sole purpose of being enabled to go free and unwhipped of justice. This does not shut the door of removal at all.

Under the old constitution, it was in the discretion of the party himself. Whenever he chose to make an affidavit that he could not have justice done, the case was removed. Under this section, the discretion of removal is in the breast of the judge upon sufficient cause shown. If there is sufficient ground, can it not be shown by the affidavit either of the party himself, or some of his friends, or of his attorney? And is it to be presumed that the judge in such a case will deny the application? The presumption, if it is worth anything at all, goes against the competency of the judge, for if the judge will not do justice in this case, he will not do it in any case. You cannot go upon such a presumption as that against the bench; it will not do. If a party goes into court, and asks for a removal upon a proper foundation, either upon his own affidavit, or of some friend, or his counsel, and that is fairly presented to the court, then I guarantee that there is not one case where it ought to be removed that it will not be removed. And especially if it be intimated that it is not proper that the judge on the bench should try the case, if he had the slightest self-respect, he would at once grant an application if there was no offence in it.

I would like to see this section passed as it is. I know the section in the present constition has been scandalously abused in our county. Parties have gone unwhipped of justice just because the cause was removed. I think there is that disposition in the breast of all the men of a community, that there is a sufficient guarantee that they will not convict a man when he ought not to be convicted in any case. And in case where there is an overwhelming prejudice against a man, any excitement against him, cannot that fact be brought before the court? There is no trouble in the case; this leaves the door open wide enough.

Mr. Stirling. My amendment only strikes out that which requires him to show to the satisfaction of the court, that he has some substantial ground of defence.

Mr. Sands. If the argument of the gentleman from Washington county (Mr. Negley) amounts to anything, it is simply this: that for fear a rogue would take advantage of a removal, all honest men are to be deprived of it. That is just the sum and substance of his argument.

Mr. Negley. Is not the power of removal still open under this section? Or is it closed?

Mr. Sands. Very nearly; so nearly that it does not suit me at all. I say, if the argument of the gentleman from Washington county amounts to anything, it is simply this; because a rogue would take advantage of the right of removal, all honest men in Washington county ought to be deprived of it. This section as it stands is a virtual deprivation of the right of removal. Examine it; you first require the party to make oath, and then you leave it to the discretion of the judge, after that oath is made to say, "prove that you cannot have a fair trial." What are the elements that enter into this matter? There may be prejudice against the party in the community, if there is a criminal case.

Mr. Thruston. Not on the part of the judge.

Mr. Sands. On the part of the judge.

Mr. Thruston. The judge is the one to decide upon the removal.

Mr. Sands. I know all about that; I am talking about the whole matter. There may be a prejudice against the party; and he knows he cannot remove that prejudice from the jury. He may believe that there are upon that panel a number of men from whom he could not have justice. Can he prove that fact? Suppose my judgment was convinced that A, B, C and D, upon the jury were my enemies, and that I could not have at their hands a fair and impartial verdict, and I called you up as a citizen of the community to prove that. Would you swear to that effect? Certainly not; assuredly not.

We have abundance of law upon this subject already, it is said. Well, the gentlemen are on the two sides of the fence, just as it suits occasion, upon this matter of putting things into this constitution, or allowing legislature to control it. A few moments ago an amendment was offered here looking to the correction of great abuses in our present judicial system. The answer on all sides was: "You need not put it in the constitution; leave it for the legislature," although the amendment was but a single line. Now, when we have in our present code law covering three or four printed pages, regulating this matter of removal in all its details; when we have the whole subject in the power of the legislature, to be modified by it at its will and according to its best judgment from time to time to suit peculiar views, then we are told that we must put it in the constitution in the form of this tenth section. Now, under the provision in section twenty-eight of the present constitution, and under the sections of the code touching this right of removal, the oath of the party compels removal.

Now in regard to the objection urged here, that the party may put off the cause from time to time until he is about to be forced to trial, and then have the cause removed. Certainly gentlemen have not looked at the provisions of the code upon this subject.—The law is now that if a party does not remove his cause as soon as the issues are made up, he cannot have it removed at all, without further showing to the court that, since the making up of those issues, matters have occurred which have created in him the belief that he cannot have a fair and impartial trial, then what is the practical result? A and B are parties to a suit in Baltimore city, and A wishes to remove it; he must do it just as soon the issues are made up or he cannot do it at all.

Mr. Stirling. That is not the law in the code.

Mr. Sands. Let us see.

"Such suggestions shall be made before or during the term in which the issue or issues may be joined in said suit or action, issues or petition, presentment or indictment."

Mr. Stirling. "Unless"—go on.

Mr. Sands. There is nothing in that clause which will do your side of the question one bit of good; for I stated a moment since that a party had further to make oath to show to the satisfaction of the court that circumstances have occurred since the making up the issues.

Mr. Stirling. They will always swear to that.

Mr. Sands. I will read, just for the information of my friend, from the code:

"In all suits or actions at law, issues from the orphans' court, or any court sitting in equity in petitions for freedom, and in all presentments and indictments instituted in any of the courts of law in this State, the judge thereof, upon suggestion in writing if made by the State's attorney or the prosecutor for the State, or upon suggestion in writing, supported by affidavit made by any of the parties thereto, or other proper evidence that a fair and impartial trial cannot be had in the court where such suit or action at law, issues, petition or presentment and indictment is pending, shall order and direct the record of proceedings therein to be transmitted to the court of the adjoining county, whether such adjoining county be within the judicial circuit or not, for trial, which court shall hear and determine the same in like manner as if it had been originally instituted therein."

And then this comes in:

"Such suggestion shall be made before or during the term in which the issue or issues may be joined in said suit or action, issue or issues, presentment or indictment, unless the party applying for such removal shall, in addition to such affidavit, further state he had come to such belief, or had been convinced of that fact since the issues had been made up—"

That is the law upon this subject in this State to-day.

——"on which additional statement being made and filed, the cause shall be removed, notwithstanding the issues had been made up."

What is clearer than this fact: that the law, as I stated it before reference to the authorities, is just exactly the law of the book?—How does it practically operate? In Baltimore city, for instance, a party must demand his removal at the term in which the issues are made up; or if he neglects to do it then, he cannot do so afterwards, unless he assures the court that since the issues were made up he has been convinced that he cannot have a fair and impartial trial, and he therefore asks the removal that he did not ask before.

Now, I say we have in the code here several pages upon the subject of removal. And I suggest that it would be right to leave it as it is, as gentlemen are so fond of leaving things to the discretion of the legislature, to be modified at their will. When in urging the other amendment, which I thought would have a very salutary influence, I suggested that we better put it in the constitution, it was said—"No, do not put it in there, because it cannot be changed." Yet you propose to make provision to have your constitution amendable by the people. I do think this right of removal is a right which honest men very often desire to have, which it is very vital to them in many cases to have, and of which we have no right at all to deprive them. Now, the section as it stands here; the action of the committee has been referred to. There was never a vote taken upon this section.

Mr. STOCKBRIDGE [interrupting.] The gentleman utterly mistakes. If he had attended half the meetings of the committee, he would know more about it than that.

Mr. SANDS. Well, all I have to say——

Mr. STOCKBRIDGE. I wish once for all, as a matter of personal right and privilege, to state that I did not bring in any report from that committee that was not the report of the committee. And I will not submit here or elsewhere to any imputation of that sort thrown upon me as the chairman of the committee which made this report.

Mr. SANDS. I make no imputation.

Mr. STOCKBRIDGE. Is it no imputation to say there was no vote taken upon this subject?

Mr. JONES, of Somerset. I know there was a vote taken, after full discussion.

Mr. SANDS. It was not taken in my presence. I know if I had ever been called upon to give a vote, it would not have been in favor of taking away from a man the right of removal, which right might be vital to him in relation to his property or his life. And believing that we have plenty of legislation upon this subject already, and believing that this right is one of which the citizens of this State ought not to be deprived, I hope the section will be stricken out.

Mr. THRUSTON. I think it is right to explain to the convention the object of this law, which the gentleman (Mr. Sands) has not done. In the first place, it is well known to the profession that in nine cases out of ten the issues are never joined until the parties are ready for trial. And the object of putting the law in this way is this; if a party joins issue and gives no notice to the other party, that he is going to move in the case, until the other party is just going into the trial, it takes the party by surprise. That is the reason why the law is put in this way; that before a party joins issue he must give notice that he wishes to remove the cause to another court for trial; otherwise the other party goes to all the expense of getting ready for the trial in the court at which the issues are joined. Nine times out of ten, the term at which the issues are joined, is the trial term. And when that is not the case, it is but right that the party should notify the other of his intention to remove his cause, and not make him go to all the expense of getting ready for trial, and then remove to another court.

Mr. MILLER. I merely wish to say in reference to this subject of removals, that the difficulty, if there has been any difficulty, is not attributable solely to the present constitution of this State. It has been the law of the State since 1804, that in all criminal proceedings a removal might be made upon a bare suggestion made by the party. And in 1838 the privilege of removal was given in civil cases. In 1849 a case came before the court of appeals where that privilege was exercised by a person indicted in Baltimore city. After ten jurors had been sworn to try him, he filed his suggestion for a removal, and the case was removed to Anne Arundel county, and tried there. The case was taken before the court of appeals, and they held that the removal was properly made, upon the construction of the old law of 1804, which gave the right of removal in its broadest terms; upon the mere suggestion made in writing by the party, it was obligatory upon the court to make order for the removal. In the trial of that case by the court of appeals a suggestion was thrown out by the court that a further provision in regard to the removal of criminal cases would be a proper one, but that it must originate with the legislature, and if adopted it would doubtless be guarded by limitations which might prevent this abuse. It was argued in that case that the party had really submitted his case to the jury on the day the jury had been summoned, and ten of them had been sworn to try the case. In the estimation of the court it was an abuse of that privilege for the removal to take place after the case had got thus far towards a trial.

That case was decided in 1849. Immediately after that decision the constitutional convention of 1850 met. It was composed of the most eminent men in the State; there were many lawyers in the body. And they adopted the provisions of the present constitution, which have been cited by the gentleman from Howard (Mr. Sands,) the code merely codifying the provisions in the constitution. They restricted the right of removal in accordance, I suppose, with the suggestions of the court of appeals in the case in 1849. They allowed the suggestion to be made by the party; they did not leave it discretionary with the court to remove; but required the court to remove it upon such suggestion, provided, however, "that such suggestion shall be made before or during the term on which the issue or issues may be joined in said suit or action, issues or petition, presentment or indictment." That got rid of the difficulty; and I suppose that was the only difficulty the convention of 1850 saw in this subject of removal. The old law that had existed since 1804 and '05, was a constitutional provision, allowing the removal to be made at any time, even after eleven jurors had been sworn, as the court of appeals had decided in 1849. The convention restricted the right of removal to the term at which the issues were joined.

If abuses have crept in under this system, since the adoption of the constitution of 1850, it would seem that we get rid of the abuses by providing that the removal should be made within a certain specified time after the indictment is found or the action commenced. It should not be left, as this section now leaves it, entirely discretionary with the judge to allow the removal or not. It has grown up in this State to be considered almost as a matter of right that a cause should be removed to an adjoining county for trial upon the suggestion of the party. The old common law required the jury to come from the vicinage where the act was committed, or where the party lived. But in very early times, both in England and in this country that was departed from, and this right of removal allowed.

It seems to me this section will in effect shut out the right of removal in many cases; it is shutting it up a little too close to leave it entirely discretionary with the judge, to require the party to disclose his ground of defence to the judge.

Mr. Sands. The legislation subsequent to the adoption of the present constitution, shows that it was the sentiment of the legislature thus acting, that the right given by the constitution should be enlarged instead of restricted. I will read the two sections, and that will be seen at a glance. The first, from the present constitution, is as follows:

"And provided also, that such suggestion shall be made as aforesaid, before or during the term in which the issue or issues may be joined in said suit or action, issues or petition, presentment or indictment, and that such further remedy in the premises may be provided by law, as the legislature shall from time to time direct and enact."

The provisions of the present code show that when they were adopted the legislature deemed the provisions of the present constitution too strict in thus binding the parties down to the time of the joining of issue; that it was impeding his right of removal, therefore the legislature went on to say in section seventy-two of article seventy five of the code, that even after the issues were made up, if the party became satisfied after they were so made up that he had not the chance for a fair trial in the court in which the issues had been made up, even then he should be entitled to the right of removal. The action of the legislature, as it stands embodied in the code, shows that they thought the provision upon this subject in the constitution needed enlarging rather than restricting.

Mr. Kennard. I do not rise for the purpose of engaging in this discussion. But from my intimate relations with one of the courts of adjudicature in Baltimore, some matters of this sort have come under my personal observation. During the present term of our court there have been twenty-three cases removed from our city to the adjoining county; and I believe it has been done in every case for the purpose of avoiding justice. At a previous session of the court a party was on trial for bigamy. The main witness was living at a distance, and the court ordered him to be brought to Baltimore city at an expense of over one hundred dollars. The very day the witness arrived there the party had his cause removed to an adjoining county.

Mr. MILLER. The case was removed to Anne Arundel county; the witness followed, the man was tried and convicted, and is now serving out his time in the penitentiary.

Mr. KENNARD. The removal, however, was to avoid justice.

Mr. STIRLING. It seems to me this section would be sufficiently stringent if the alteration I propose be made in it. It will then require that the party shall make it satisfactorily appear to the court that he cannot have a fair and impartial trial, and that is enough to require. I do not see how any one charged with being a criminal can swear that he has a defence. The State is bound to prove a case against him. He may have no defence at all, and yet be perfectly innocent. A defence means that you have something to show against what is on the other side. Now, a man may be perfectly innocent, and yet have nothing to show at all; yet the other side may break down for want of proof. A man in that case must either commit perjury, or else merely swear that he is innocent. It is making a man swear against himself. The section goes still further; even if it is made substantially to appear to the court that there is a good ground for defence, or action, or that a fair trial cannot be had, the judge is not compelled to remove the case. The section only says he "may order and direct the record of proceedings * * * * * to be transmitted to some other court," &c. I submit that even if this part is stricken out about showing the ground of defence, the section is strong enough to cure all the evils which I admit do exist.

Mr. BELT. It seems to me that the explanation which has been given by the gentleman from Baltimore city, the chairman of the committee on the judiciary (Mr. Stockbridge,) cuts away all the foundation upon which this proposed change in the law rests. As I understand it, his explanation of the motives which guided the committee is that they proposed to give to the courts the utmost latitude upon this subject. That is, causes shall not be removed hereafter upon the suggestion and affidavit of the party as now; but the court must be satisfied that there is a proper defence, in the first place; and in the second place a proper cause for removal. And as an argument in favor of the proposed change in the constitution the gentleman says that nobody knows what view the court may take of the subject, what they may propose and insist upon. They may take any point in the wide range, from the simple statement in the ear of the judge if the party wishes to remove his cause, up to the most stringent regulations upon the subject that it is possible to conceive of. Now this which is advanced as the strength of the proposed change, is in my judgment the very weakness of it. How can we determine upon what principles the court may act? The explanation shows that the proposed change is liable to abuses in both ways.

If the court adopt such regulations and rules in this matter as that a man charged with a criminal offence shall be obliged to disclose his whole defence, or that a man in a civil proceeding shall have to open before the court his whole case—and gentlemen will bear in mind that it is not to the judge that this is to be made, but to the court in its public capacity; the court is to be satisfied, and this exhibition to whatever extent it is to be made, is to be made openly before the court—if the regulation and rule is such that a man must expose his defence, nobody can doubt that it would be an almost inconceivable and intolerable hardship, and in this particular against the whole practice of courts of law in this State.

On the other hand, if you leave the court full of latitude upon this subject, the abuse will be equally intolerable. The court may not require sufficient ground for removal; it may not even require the personal guarantee of the affidavit of the party. It may take the statement of some parties and refuse that of others. They may adopt the most arbitrary, or the most lax and most unsatisfactory rules for their government in this particular. And there may be a great many men on the bench who will avail themselves of this extreme official latitude given them, to divest themselves of the responsibility of trying cases between their neighbors. They not only may make it easy, but they may make suggestions to parties, may facilitate, and urge, and take an active part in having cases removed from before them.

Now I will propose an amendment to test this matter, to find out whether or not this convention will embark in this latitudinarian sea, which the committee on the judiciary through its chairman proposes; or whether we shall stand by the old landmarks of the State. I propose to guard the affidavit in this particular; to have the party to swear not only that he cannot have a fair and impartial trial in the county where the venue rests, but that the cause is not removed by him for any purpose of delay, or to evade justice. I propose to insert before the words "and the general assembly shall make such modifications," &c., the following:

"And sufficient proof to entitle the applicant to such removal shall be the affidavit of the party to the effect that he cannot have a fair and impartial trial of the said issue, petition, presentment or indictment, and also that the said removal is not applied for with any view of delaying such trial, or of evading justice."

The PRESIDENT. The question will be first

taken upon the amendment of the gentleman from Baltimore city (Mr. Stirling.)

The amendment of Mr. STIRLING was to strike out the words, "has a substantial ground of action or defence, and"—so that it will read—"shall make it satisfactorily appear to the court that such party cannot have a fair and impartial trial," &c.

The question being taken, upon a division—ayes 27, noes 20—the amendment was adopted.

The question was then taken upon the amendment of Mr. BELT, and upon a division—ayes 22, noes 28—it was rejected.

Mr. STIRLING. There is one other amendment which perhaps should be made. I do not know but that the same construction would be put upon it by the court, whether the amendment be made or not. It now reads: "The judge or judges of any court of this State, except the court of appeals, *may* order and direct the record of proceedings * * * * * * * * * to be transmitted to some other court," &c. I suppose that if it shall satisfactorily appear to the court that a party cannot have a fair and impartial trial there, it must order a removal. It seems to me that to rid the matter of all doubt the word "shall" should be substituted for the word "may." However, I will not move the amendment.

Mr. SANDS. Well, I will make the motion to strike out "may," and insert "shall." I would just say that if you leave the word "may" here, then even after proof has been made to the satisfaction of the judge that the party cannot have a fair and impartial trial there, the removal is left entirely to the discretion of the judge. If the party has made satisfactory proof is it not his right to have his case removed? And shall we leave it in the discretion of the judge to say, "even though you have made your case you shall not have your right?" It seems to me that it is monstrous to make such a provision as that. For whom are we legislating? For the citizens of the State. Are we trying to protect them in their property and their lives, or are we simply trying to lodge arbitrary power in the hands of the judges?

The question was upon striking out the word "may" and inserting the word "shall."

The question being taken, upon a division—ayes 25, noes 19—no quorum voted.

Mr. TODD called for the yeas and nays on the question, and they were ordered.

The question being then taken, by yeas and nays, upon striking out "may" and inserting "shall," it resulted—yeas 30, nays 24—as follows:

Yeas—Messrs. Billingsley, Blackiston, Brown, Carter, Crawford, Davis, of Washington, Dent, Edelen, Galloway, Hodson, Hopkins, Jones, of Somerset, King, Lansdale, Lee, Markey, Mayhugh, McComas, Mitchell, Mullikin, Nyman, Parran, Pugh, Robinette, Sands, Smith, of Carroll, Smith, of Worcester, Stirling, Wickard, Wooden—30.

Nays—Messrs. Goldsborough, President; Abbott, Annan, Audoun, Cunningham, Daniel, Earle, Ecker, Hopper, Keefer, Kennard, Marbury, Miller, Murray, Negley, Parker, Purnell, Russell, Schley, Schlosser, Stockbridge, Swope, Thruston, Todd—24.

The amendment was accordingly adopted.

Mr. MILLER, when his name was called, said: I shall vote against this proposition, because I conceive that the word "may" in this connection implies an obligation on the part of the judge to order the removal, if the satisfactory proof is made out before him It means the same as it would if the word "shall" were put in. I vote "no."

Mr. SANDS. In the clause which reads: "shall make it satisfactorily appear," &c., I move to insert after the word "shall" the words "by affidavit or otherwise."

Mr. PUGH. It does not seem to me that this is necessary. According to my understanding of the section as it now reads, the party, by affidavit or otherwise, can make it appear to the satisfaction of the court that he has a substantial ground of action, etc., and he can do no more if the words proposed are inserted.

Mr. SANDS. No, he cannot. If the gentleman will read the section in the old constitution, and the proposed section here, he can see the difference at once. I wish to have it definitely fixed that if the party makes affidavit he shall have the removal.

Mr. PUGH. This will not do it. The gentleman proposes to insert the words "by affidavit or otherwise."

Mr. SANDS. As it is now the court may allow him to make affidavit or not, as it pleases.

Mr. STOCKBRIDGE. With that explanation of the meaning of this amendment, is it not the same as the one proposed by the gentleman from Prince George's (Mr. Belt,) and voted down by the convention?

The PRESIDENT. The chair is of opinion that it is not the same proposition.

The question was upon inserting the words "by affidavit or otherwise" before the words "make it satisfactorily appear," etc.

Upon this question Mr. EDELEN asked for the yeas and nays, which were ordered.

The question was then taken, by yeas and nays, and resulted—yeas 20, nays 23—as follows:

Yeas—Messrs. Billingsley, Blackiston, Crawford, Dent, Edelen, Galloway, Hopkins, Jones, of Somerset, King, Lansdale, Lee, Marbury, Markey, Mayhugh, Mitchell, Miller, Parran, Sands, Schlosser, Stirling—20.

Nays—Messrs. Goldsborough, President; Abbott, Annan, Audoun, Brown, Carter, Cunningham, Daniel, Davis, of Washington, Earle, Ecker, Hodson, Hopper, Keefer, Kennard, Mullikin, Murray, Negley, Nyman,

Parker, Pugh, Purnell, Robinette, Russell, Schley, Smith, of Carroll, Smith, of Worcester, Stockbridge, Swope, Thruston, Todd, Wickard, Wooden—33.

The amendment was accordingly rejected.

No further amendment was offered to the tenth section.

PERSONS ALLOWED TO PRACTICE.

The next section was then read as follows:

"Sec. 11. Every person of good moral character, being a voter, shall be admitted to practice law in all the courts of this State, in his own case."

Mr. Stirling. I move to stricken out the words "of good moral character, being a voter." I do not see why a thief should not be allowed to defend himself, if he does not choose to employ a lawyer. People of good moral character do not want to defend themselves. At common law every man has a right to defend his own case. This was originally put in the constitution for the purpose of allowing everybody "of good moral character, being a voter," to practice law, and then on the motion of some one the words "in his own case," were added, which cut the thing right down at the roots. It is a restriction of the common law right to say that a man shall not defend himself unless he has a good moral character. Who is to decide that question? The very people who want to defend themselves have no good moral character. If a man is fool enough to try his own case and not employ a lawyer, I want him to show his folly, if he wishes.

Mr. Stockbridge. And there is another reason for it. That much of the practice of law may ruin what little moral character he had to begin with.

The question being then taken upon striking out the words, "of good moral character, being a voter," upon a division—ayes 30, noes 23—it was agreed to.

Mr. Stockbridge. I would call the attention of the convention to the condition in which this section is now left.

"Every person shall be admitted to practice law in all the courts of this State, in his own case."

That leaves it ambiguous as to whether a woman would not be admitted to practice.

Mr. Stirling. I move to stricken out the section, as it is wholly unnecessary. Every person has that right at common law.

The question being taken upon the motion to strike out the section, it was agreed to.

On motion of Mr. Todd,

The convention then adjourned.

SEVENTY-SIXTH DAY.

Thursday, August 18, 1864.

The convention met at 10 o'clock, A. M.

Prayer by Rev. Mr. Owen.

The roll was called, and the following members answered to their names:

Messrs. Goldsborough, President; Abbott, Annan, Audoun, Barron, Berry, of Prince George's, Billingsley, Blackiston, Brooks, Brown, Carter, Chambers, Clarke, Crawford, Cunningham, Cushing, Dail, Daniel, Davis, of Charles, Davis, of Washington, Dennis, Dent, Duvall, Earle, Ecker, Edelen, Gale, Galloway, Hatch, Hebb, Hodson, Hopkins, Hopper, Horsey, Jones, of Cecil, Jones, of Somerset, Keefer, Kennard, King, Lansdale, Lee, Mace, Marbury, Markey, Mayhugh, McComas, Mitchell, Miller, Morgan, Mullikin, Murray, Negley, Nyman, Parker, Parran, Peter, Pugh, Purnell, Robinette, Russell, Sands, Schley, Schlosser, Smith, of Carroll, Smith, of Dorchester, Smith, of Worcester, Stirling, Stockbridge, Swope, Sykes, Thomas, Thruston, Todd, Turner, Wickard, Wooden—76.

The journal of yesterday was read and approved.

ABSENT MEMBERS.

On motion of Mr. Hebb,

It was ordered to be entered on the journal that Mr. Greene, of Allegany, is detained from his seat in the convention on account of sickness.

On motion of Mr. Smith, of Dorchester,

It was ordered to be entered on the journal that Thomas J. Dail, is kept from his seat in the convention by indisposition.

On motion of Mr. Barron,

It was ordered to be entered on the journal that if John Barron had been present he would have voted for the test oath offered by Mr. Stirling, and would have voted for the amendment to the report of the committee on the judiciary offered by Mr. Abbott.

LEAVE OF ABSENCE.

Mr. Thomas asked and obtained leave of absence for a few days on account of illness.

Mr. Thruston asked and obtained leave of absence until Monday next.

Mr. Wickard asked and obtained leave of absence from the session of this evening, being slightly indisposed.

Mr. Brooks. I desire to be excused from attending night sessions, and I will assign my reason for the request. I believe that it is generally known to this convention that I am commissioner of enrolment for the third district. It is necessary for me to be in Baltimore some time each day to sign certain papers. When I return to Baltimore at night, my clerk brings the papers to my house and I sign them. It is therefore imperative that I should be in Baltimore some time each day. I hope the convention will indulge me by granting this request.

Leave of absence was accordingly granted.

Mr. Barron. I would like very much to have the convention excuse me from attendance at night sessions, for this one reason. I have a very severe affliction in my family. My wife attends in the day time, and I have to attend a portion of the night at least to relieve her. I would like, therefore, to be excused for some time at least, from attendance at the night sessions of this convention.

Leave of absence was accordingly granted.

THE DRAFT IN MARYLAND.

The convention then took up for consideration the following preamble and resolution, submitted by Mr. MARBURY on the 16th instant.

"*Whereas*, The citizens of the State of Maryland have been drafted until the draft has reached the home of nearly every able-bodied man in the State; and whereas the slave counties of the State have almost been depopulated of their whole laboring force; and whereas the slaves who have been enticed or voluntarily gone off from this State, and entered the service of the United States, have nearly all of them been accredited to other States, contrary to the laws of the land, and in violation of every principle of justice and right; and whereas, the upper counties of this State have been so entirely laid waste and so depleted of their population that they have scarcely men enough left to protect and support the helpless women and children who are entitled to their care; therefore,

"*Resolved*, That the members of this convention deem it a duty they owe their constituents, to appoint and do hereby authorize the president of this convention to appoint a committee of five, of whom he (the president) shall be one, to wait on the proper authorities at Washington, explain the condition of our people, request and urge that they be relieved of all further draft during the war."

Mr. MARBURY. I think that the propositions contained in this resolution are so eminently just and proper that it is hardly necessary to say anything in advocacy of them. If I am correctly informed, the State of Maryland has furnished far more troops in proportion to her population than any other State in the Union. It is a well-known fact that in the lower counties of the State, in all the slaveholding counties, there have been recruiting officers for months at a time. Independent of that there have been a great many slaves forced off. A great many have been put into the service without any authority from the federal government. A great many have gone off voluntarily and joined the regiments of other States. We want to find out if possible how many have been taken from the State of Maryland, and by what authority they were taken. I think if we can ascertain these facts, and have the proper credits for the slaves which have voluntarily gone off, the government will see the justice and propriety of our being relieved in the future. In my own county, in Upper Marlboro', there was an officer there for months at a time recruiting. We supposed he was acting under authority from the government. But afterwards a gentleman from the county who was formerly in the military service himself, went to Washington and made investigations, and found that the recruiting officer had been acting without any authority whatever, and that all the slaves he had taken from the county had been taken without any knowledge of it on the part of the government.

There was General Birney down on the Patuxent river; he certainly acted under authority of the government. He carried off a great many slaves who were mustered into the service, but they were credited to other States. I think we should have some justice done us in this matter. It is necessary that our people should have this thing investigated. If I am correctly informed, our county, that has furnished hundreds, I may say thousands of able-bodied slaves for soldiers, has only been credited for three slaves. Where is the justice of that?

And I think the other branch of the proposition equally demands investigation and remedy, if possible. Certain portions of the State, if I have been correctly informed, have been laid waste, devastated, and the people have been crippled in their means in every possible way. It is impossible for them to support their families, unless they can retain among them the laboring force they now have. Unless the laboring men, the men who have families to take care of can be left at home, the greater portion of the population must be great sufferers. I think that in consideration of all these facts, the proposition that I have made is eminently just and necessary, and one which our constituents demand of us. I confess that it is not exactly within the scope and objects for which this convention was assembled. But certainly it is equally as much within the sphere of our duties as many other propositions which have been presented for our consideration.

Believing as I do that this is a matter in which the people of the whole State from one end to the other take a deep and abiding interest, I feel no hesitation in bringing it before the body as I have done.

Mr. JONES, of Cecil. I offer the following amendment; add to the resolution the words:

"And we will in all other respects sustain the administration to our utmost ability in suppressing this most unholy and wicked rebellion."

The PRESIDENT. The chair must rule that amendment out of order, as not germain to the proposition under consideration.

Mr BERRY, of Prince George's. There is more in the resolution offered by my colleague (Mr. Marbury) for the consideration of the convention than upon a cursory view of it would appear. I can state without fear of contradiction that Prince George's county has furnished for the service of the United States, able-bodied men enough to fill the quota of our congressional district under all the drafts that have taken place. And why is it that we are not credited with these men who have been mustered into the service of the United States? It is because there is no person to take an interest in it with a view of seeing where they have been received into the service, and to what State, or to what district of this State, they have been credited.

Now General Birney, in his camp on the Patuxent had upwards of 10,000 able-bodied negro men recruited for the service of the United States. He was acting under the authority of the government of the United States. And I am not here to say that he was not authorized, or that the government was not authorized to take them for military purposes. A large number of those negroes, or the majority of those negroes then mustered into the service were from Charles, St. Mary's and Prince George's counties, and many were taken from the eastern shore. But the majority of the whole command were taken from those three counties. And I understand that the whole number credited to Prince George's county although there were upwards of two thousand taken from it, were seventeen. And there were other cases cited by my colleague.

In November of last year, there was a whole New York company came to our town and took up their station there and remained until April. They had wagons going constantly from our town to Bladensburg, and they were constantly taking off our servants. The officer who was in command stated that he was there recruiting under the authority of the United States. He got about one hundred and fifty men in our neighborhood; all whom he could induce to enlist, by any inducement he could offer, he prevailed upon to enlist. We took it for granted he was acting under the authority of the United States government, and no hindrance was offered by the people to his recruiting. He went about the neighborhood, saw the negroes, talked with them, and offered them inducements to enlist, and many of them did enlist. About the time he left in April, not having up to that time furnished certificates to parties whose servants,he had enlisted, he was called upon to give them certificates. His excuse was that he had not the necessary forms, but would procure them and hand them over to the various owners. He left there, and Major Lee, of my neighborhood, three of whose servants had been enlisted by him, went to Washington to see about the certificates. He was there informed by the proper authorities that this New York officer had been there without the authority of the government. These men were placed to the credit of New York.

And I have heard of other instances where men were thus enlisted and placed to the credit of Massachusetts and other northern States. They come in our midst and take our servants, pretending they were acting under the authority of the United States government, and we take it for granted that those men will be placed to the credit of Maryland. And when it is too late for us to notify the government and have it stopped, we find that they are credited to other States of the union.

Now, is it not right, is it not just, that an inquiry should be made into the matter? And an inquiry made under a resolution passed by this body would have a force greater than any inquiry of any set of men from any one of the counties of the State would have with the authorities at Washington.

Our servants have not only been taken away in this manner, but they have been drafted in our county in the last two drafts. And I do not think that there are fifty able-bodied men in our county now, either white or black, who have not been drafted; and I suppose the September draft will take the balance of them. That state of facts exist; we have furnished more able-bodied men for the service of the United States than has been the quota of our whole congressional district, had they been properly credited to our county. Let gentlemen reflect upon this, not come to a hasty conclusion that this is an effort on the part of the minority of this convention to accomplish some end that they do not understand at this time; let them reflect upon this state of facts. And then I ask them if there is not a great deal of justice in appointing the committee contemplated by this resolution.

I would not advocate such a resolution in this body, if I had not precedent for it in the action of this body upon other subjects. But we have precedent after precedent in resolutions offered upon the other side through the whole session of our body. And therefore the majority will not oppose it on that ground. If they want to accord justice to us, if they are willing that we should have right accorded to us, I think there is not a sensible man in the convention who will hesitate to vote for this resolution. There is nothing secret, nothing hidden in it. It is a simple inquiry with a view of arriving at some means by which this wrong can be remedied, and justice be done to every part of the State.

I find that in the draft that is to take place in September our congressional district is put down for upwards of three thousand, a larger number than any other congressional district in the State. And I will venture to assert that our district now has a smaller population than any other district in the State. I ask gentleman in fairness to look at this question, to give us this inquiry, and let us have the advantage of the inquiry emanating from this body; because in doing that we may accomplish some good to the State much more readily than if a number of gentlemen were to meet in the several counties of the State, and pass resolutions and appoint committees to wait upon the authorities at Washington with a view of having this matter investigated.

Mr. SCHLEY. Like the gentleman from Prince George's (Mr. Berry,) I have felt a great deal of interest in the matter of the impending draft, and like him, too, I thought that perhaps much injustice had been done to various sections of Maryland by a failure to credit on their quotas the number to which they were entitled by reason of negroes enlisted and credited to other States.

But upon speaking of the subject on my recent visit home, I was credibly informed that on the previous drafts, to cover and more than cover all such complaints, we have been credited with upwards of eight thousand men. I deeply regret that I have not the exact figures of the table which a friend showed me, so that I could present them to the convention here. But I did not anticipate any necessity for it. That number, however, has been struck off the amount which Maryland was called upon to furnish. Now I think it would be more advisable to institute an inquiry into the facts, for the information of the convention instead of our sending forth the statements contained in this preamble and resolution, with the authentication of our adoption of them. The facts can be very easily ascertained by any gentleman who will inquire of the provost marshal of the State, at Baltimore.

Mr. MILLER. I understand the gentleman from Frederick (Mr. Schley) to say that there had been a credit given to the State of eight thousand men?

Mr. SCHLEY. Eight thousand of the deficiency has been stricken off.

Mr. MILLER. Was that credited to the State at large, or was it credited to the several counties from which they were supposed to have been taken?

Mr. SCHLEY. I would not undertake to answer that question without knowing more of the facts than I now do. But that that much of the deficiency of the State has been stricken off I have no doubt is the fact. And I know it as well as I can know anything that I do not know of my own knowledge. I shall, therefore, urge upon the convention to pause before it adopts this resolution, that it may not commit itself to any erroneous statement.

Mr. PETER. I will not pretend that we have a legal right to demand this at the hands of the government. But if justice entitles us to it, it is certainly not going too far to have this matter investigated. If our several counties have furnished more than their quotas, and if by the acts of parties representing other States they have been unjustly deprived of that to which they are entitled, is it fair, is it right, is it honest, that we representing the people of Maryland should sit idly here and see our constituents imposed upon? I do not say that we should send a committee to Washington and demand this thing, as a matter of legal right, from the President and the Secretary of War. But I do say that it is but fair, it is but right, it is but doing our duty to our constituents to send a committee there to fully investigate this matter, and to ascertain what has become of the number of slaves that have been taken from the State of Maryland.

I know that an immense number have gone from the counties, the most of whom are in Washington, employed in some way or other in the several military departments. If they are not in the army as soldiers, they are acting as teamsters, or in some way engaged in the service. And if they are thus representing our counties as able-bodied men, for it takes able-bodied men to perform the duties that they perform, is it not right that we should have credit for them?

Another important point which suggests itself to my mind is this: In the late draft that was made in this State, many negroes were drafted who are now lounging about the streets of Washington, the officers not having thought proper to go and arrest them and force them into the service as they would other drafted men. Is it not right that we should appoint a committee to investigate this matter? And if we can show the government that numbers of drafted men from this State are now hanging about the streets of Washington, is it not right that the government officers should take those men, or else give us credit for the deficiency occasioned by their failure to report.

I cannot see this thing in any party light at all. If we represent our constituents here, and can rightly be of any service to them in relation to this matter, why not do it? Why should we not aid them, so far as we can justly do so, by having this matter investigated? If these slaves are now hanging about the streets of Washington doing nothing, though their names have been drawn in the late draft, why should we not ask the government to place them in the service and give us credit for them, or strike that much from our deficiency? I believe that if our county could have this matter fairly and fully investigated, it would be found that more able-bodied negro men have left that county (Montgomery,) than would fill its quota, and I further believe that a great majority of those who have thus left, are now in the employment of the government of the United States.

I do not ask gentleman to take my mere assertion here that such is the fact. But I ask them to appoint a committee to investigate the subject, and to ascertain if what I say be true. And if it be true, are we not fairly entitled to credit for them? Again, what harm can result from an investigation by a committee of this character? Suppose upon a full and fair investigation of the facts as they really exist, what we believe to be true is found to be without foundation. Certainly it could do no harm to the interests of the government, and could in no way damage any portion of our State. But on the contrary, if the facts were found to be as we believe them to be, would it not, in this hour of distress, result in great amelioration to our people?

I can say for our county that famine almost stalks abroad in our land. A draft is impending over us, and we are continually, day after day, subject to bodies of military passing to and fro. I do not say it with any view to disparage our forces, but it is well known that there is no army, however well disciplined it may be, but what has its attendants, camp followers and stragglers. And I do say most unhesitatingly that it is necessary in many instances, especially after the officers have left that some male person should be about the premises to protect the females. I will say that in our town, in most if not in all instances where officers have been present, they have readily granted relief when we have been imposed upon by stragglers and camp followers. But when officers are not present it is necessary for some man to be there to assert his rights; and not only to assert his rights, but to throw around those who are endeared to him by every tie of affection that protection which they need and which they ought to receive.

Another difficulty under which we labor in our county results in consequence of the late raid. Many of us who were able but a few months ago to have placed substitutes in the service, and thus been enabled to remain with our families, are now left in a manner destitute. Is it anything more than fair and right, after we have been subjected to these heavy losses, not occasioned by ourselves, not the result of any acts of which we have been guilty—is it not fair that the government should at least be inclined to show us some little favor? Because the distinction between the portion of Maryland which I represent, and New York, Maine, New Hampshire, etc., is that they hardly realize that there is war in the land. They do not feel its desolating effects; they do not feel the terrible scourge which has so lately visited us.

Now if we have suffered in this respect, as every person must admit who will visit our county, is it but fair, if we can show this to the government, that it should at least show us some little favor, although we cannot ask it as a legal right? Again, are we not entitled to the slaves which have left our State, if they be in the government employ?

Our slaves up to this time do not stand in the position which the free white men of other States stand in. I will admit that as a free white man of the State of Maryland, if I had chosen to go to the city of New York and accept the larger bounty which that city offers, it would have been fairly entitled to the credit on my acceptance. But was that the position occupied by our slaves? They had no right to leave our employment. No man from the State of New York, or from Massachusetts, or from any other State in the north, had the right to get one of our slaves by giving him the bounty from one of those States, and thereby get credit for him for that State. These slaves were our property, and they have no right of their own to leave this State, or to represent any other State in the service, without first obtaining the consent of their masters. Then if we have been deprived of the credit these slaves would have given us, by the large bounties offered in other States and cities, it is a wrong unjustly perpetrated upon us. And unless such State or city, obtaining a credit for our negroes, could show that it was by the express permission or license of their masters, then I contend that the government is in all honor and all justice bound to give the people of our State a fair credit for them. And not to the State at large, but to the county from which those negroes were obtained.

I do not think any gentleman of this convention can discover anything sinister in a motion of this kind. I do not think any gentleman in this body, as the representative of his county or of his district, can under any circumstances refuse to vote for a resolution of this character. It can of itself do no harm. It can throw no obstacle in the way of the general government, in carrying out the draft as soon as it may think it right and proper to do so. It will be a mere matter of investigation. If we are fairly entitled to it, let us have it. If not, then the government can refuse to grant us the favor. They have the right to refuse, whether we are rightfully entitled to this credit or not. But the question with me is this; if we present to them a fair, honest, and just case, will they turn a deaf ear to the petition of the people of Maryland through this convention?

I would like to see every man in this convention vote for a matter of this kind. It would then have force in it; it would carry weight with it; it would present this State as a body to the government, and the government merely as a favor might perhaps grant it—for we can only ask it as a favor, not as a legal right.

Now as regards the State being credited with eight thousand men. Perchance she may be so credited; perchance she may have that many regularly enlisted. But is that a fair proportion of the able-bodied negro men that have left our State? It is a matter, I will admit, that I have not fully investigated, that I have not examined into. But if other counties have furnished able-bodied negro men in proportion to our county, then the State is certainly entitled to a much larger credit than eight thousand.

Mr. SCHLEY. I do not say that only Maryland has been credited with only eight thousand men. But I say that eight thousand and more of her deficiency has been stricken off, been obliterated from the requisition made upon her.

Mr. Berry, of Prince George's. There may be a great deal of force in what fell from the gentleman from Frederick (Mr. Schley,) that this convention would not be in a condition to vote upon this subject properly, until we had the statistical information. And if it meets the views of my friend (Mr. Marbury,) as we seem to be at a loss for this information, I will submit a motion that the further consideration of this resolution be postponed, to be called up at any time when we have obtained the necessary information, and then I will submit a motion that a committee be appointed to correspond with the proper authorities and obtain the information desired.

Mr. Peter. Permit me to add a few remarks before I close. Suffering as I have been for some time with an affection of the throat, I may not be able to attend the sittings of the convention; or if I do, I may not be able to speak. I have arisen here to-day to discuss this subject as a matter of justice to my people. And I would ask any man in this convention to go to my county and view the situation of our people there as it is at present. And I think if he will honestly take a view of that portion of our county bordering on the Potomac river, and extending out from nine to twenty miles from the river, he will say—"in all conscience do not oppress this people any more; the scourge of war has already devastated them sufficiently; do not put any more burdens upon them; let them at least be spared any further oppression of any kind from this war." As to this postponement, I think myself that we better first investigate and ascertain all statistical information as to what numbers have gone, and how they are credited.

Mr. Thomas. I move to amend the preamble by inserting after the word "population" the following:

"By the incursions and raids of those in arms against the United States, and by the wholesale desertion of men of said counties to the confederate armies."

That portion of the preamble will then read:

"And whereas, the upper counties of this State have been so entirely laid waste and so depleted of their population, by the incursions and raids of those in arms against the United States, and by the wholesale desertion of men of said counties to the confederate armies, that they have scarcely men enough left," etc.

Mr. Berry, of Prince George's. I now move that the further consideration of this preamble and resolution be informally postponed.

Mr. Stirling. That was the motion I was about to make. But I thought the gentleman was to accompany that motion with a motion to appoint a committee.

Mr. Berry, of Prince George's. I will do that afterwards.

Mr. Stirling. I am opposed to the appointment of a committee. I am perfectly willing to have this matter laid over until we get the necessary information. But I think we can get it without a committee. I think there is great liability that we may be taking a leap in the dark about this matter. I know that the State has suffered a great deal, and that it has never received full credit. But I am very much inclined to think that the State has never been called upon for the full number of troops the government had a right to demand of it. And if we call for justice, we may be told that we shall have it, and be called upon for more men than we may be ready to furnish.

Mr. Billingsley. We want only justice in our section. I understand that a difficulty has occurred between the national and the State governments, in relation to this matter. All we want is to be credited with such a number of our population as have been enlisted in the army, and been mustered into the service of the United States. That return has not been made by the proper officer. I understand there is a difficulty between the State government and Colonel Bowman, in relation to this matter. And I think it would be but an act of mere justice to the people of the lower counties of Maryland, if this draft is to go on, that they should receive full credit for those who have gone into the army from those counties. That cannot be done until the proper returns are made by Colonel Bowman. I understand there is a negotiation going on between the State government and the government of the United States, to have this correction made. And if there is shown a disposition on the part of the convention to do us justice, I do think the government of the United States will afford us some remedy.

Mr. Cushing. I merely wish to say that while I have no objection in the world to justice being done to all the counties of this State, yet, as the coming draft will probably take place on the 5th of September, and as it would be impossible for the United States government to revise the quotas for the different States before the fifth of next month, so as to make good any allowance for Maryland, this will practically result merely in an obstruction in the way of raising the troops now absolutely needed. I think it would be much better for those counties that have been "oppressed," to do as other counties in the State have done, raise their quotas by offering bounties for volunteers, and then get the credits that may be due them allowed on the next draft.

I agree fully with my colleague that if all the troops raised in Maryland, be put down to her credit, it will be found that she has not furnished to the armies of the United States, the number of able-bodied men which her population would require. Nor do I think there would be any practical justice in crediting these men to the counties from which they came; for, had the counties desired to have them so credited at the time, there was not a particle of impediment in the way of their enlisting them. There was no motion on the part of any one in those counties so to aid the government. On the contrary, the right of the government to take those negroes was in all cases declaimed or inveighed against. The representatives of Maryland, in Congress, denied the right of the government to take them. Those counties, so far as I know, have never admitted the right of the government to take those negroes. And if they are to be credited to the State, I think they should be creditied to the general quota of the State.

But I think the practical question for us to consider, is that before the 5th of September, it would be impossible for the government to do anything in this matter. There is but about two weeks now to the time fixed for the draft. And if it should be decided that we are not to furnish the number we have been called upon to furnish, then the quotas of a l the States of the Union must be revised to make up the number for which Maryland would be deficient.

Mr. JONES, of Somerset. The gentleman from Baltimore (Mr. Cushing) has most extraordinary ideas of logic and of justice. Because the people in the counties do not admit the right of the government to take their slaves and put them in the army, when they are so taken and put in the army, the counties are not entitled to any credit for them. Why, sir, every man who is drafted goes unwillingly, and the same objection might there arise. He does not go willingly, does not admit the justice of being taken from home and put in the army; therefore, the county from which he is taken should receive no credit for him.

I think it seems to be generally conceded that there has been great injustice done many portions of the State, in not giving the proper credit for persons who have been taken and put into the army of the United States. I saw in the newspapers some time ago, the statement that representations had been made by the governor, authorities, and some of the leading men of Kentucky, to the administration at Washington, that a very large portion of their population had actually left the State, and gone into the service of the Confederates, and therefore a draft upon the residue, based upon the entire population as if these men were still there, would be most unjust to those remaining. For those men who had left the State and had gone into the Confederate service had expatriated themselves, and were no longer to be considered a part of the population of Kentucky, supporting the government of the United States, and from which a draft should be made. And the authorities at Washington, upon these representations, allowed a credit of twenty-five thousand to Kentucky upon the draft.

It has been stated that a great many have left this State and gone away. Who is responsible for that? They have taken their lives in their hands; they have left the State; they are no longer citizens of this State. We admit the right of expatriation; we admit that a man may leave the State and go elsewhere, to Great Britain, to France, to any European country, and if their laws allow, he may become a citizen of those countries. If they are gone, is it proper and just that they should be considered as still here and liable to the draft, and their absence made up by the heavier draft upon those who remain.

And besides, the gentleman from Frederick (Mr. Schley) states that he has been informed that a lumping credit of eight thousand men has been made upon the deficiency of Maryland, by the authorities at Washington. Now, if that credit is on the score of the slaves that have been taken away from the several counties, then I submit most respectfully that such a credit operates most unjustly to the counties that have furnished these eight thousand men. The people of Frederick, and Washington, and Allegany, and Baltimore city, and all those populous portions of the State that have furnished very few colored recruits to the army of the United States, would get the benefit of this credit, in precisely the same manner and in a greater ratio than the counties that have furnished them.

Mr. SCHLEY. We have furnished white men.

Mr. JONES, of Somerset. I apprehend that all the counties have made efforts to raise their men. And I know that more than a thousand negroes have been taken from Somerset county, and very few have been credited to that county. My friend from Dorchester informs me that of two regiments enlisted in the city of Baltimore there were a great many men from his county, and from my county, who had gone to the city of Baltimore and enlisted there, and that city has the credit for them. Now that is not just.

There ought to be an inquiry into this matter. We have suffered injustice enough already, in a variety of ways. I have no doubt that the governor and the adjutant general have been doing and will do all they can to put this matter right. I trust they will push this investigation, which more properly belongs to them, and endeavor to ascertain how many have been taken from the several counties, in order that the proper credit may be given to those counties which have furnished the troops. I trust that the difficulty which has existed with Col. Bowman will be disposed of in some way, and that the government will see the justice of having the authorities of the State furnished with correct lists of those who have been mustered in the service of the United States, who have been in the recent battles, some of whom have been killed, and many of whom have been wounded. The counties that have furnished these men, should receive credit for them. There should be some way of ascertaining this matter.—And if this subject is postponed, I trust that before it again comes up for consideration, we will be enabled to have some definite information from the proper authorities as to how this matter stands.

Mr. ABBOTT. Has the county of Somerset offered any bounty for troops?

Mr JONES, of Somerset. No, sir; the county has offered no bounty, but she has filled her quota, either in person or by substitute.

Mr. BERRY, of Prince George's. I will give one reason why I think it would be wise to postpone the further consideration of this subject. It is admitted on all sides that great injustice has been done to the State of Maryland. But we want the data before we come to a just conclusion. The object of postponing is to have that data before us. I propose to follow up the postponement with the motion that a committee of three or five be appointed to make the necessary inquiry in order to obtain from the proper authority the requisite information. The gentleman from Baltimore city proposes to hurry this thing through without that information.

Mr. CUSHING. I propose to vote it down in this convention.

Mr. BERRY, of Prince George's. He proposes to vote it down. He says it is all just and proper that whatever number Prince George's county has furnished should be credited to the whole State. Now is that proper? Does he forget that the quota of every county and district in the State is fixed by the provost marshal? Does he forget that each county and each district in each county has to furnish the number allotted to it? I should say there was not the slightest justice in crediting the number to the whole State; that it was contrary to the spirit of the law. The law enacts that each county should be credited with whatever recruits it may furnish to the army. I say it would be not only unjust, but contrary to the law. Before I conclude I propose for a moment to refer to the negro population of our county.

Mr. STIRLING. What is the use of postponing this subject, if we are going to take up all the morning in discussing it?

Mr. BERRY, of Prince George's. I do not propose to discuss it all the morning.

Mr. STIRLING. I do not refer to the gentleman from Prince George's (Mr. Berry) in particular. I refer to all.

Mr. BERRY, of Prince George's. I do not mean to discuss the question now. I only desire to say that the negro population of our county was 12,479; and I am satisfied that of that number 5,000 able-bodied negro men have been taken for the army. We have, therefore, furnished enough able-bodied negro men to fill the quota for our entire congressional district.

The question was then taken upon postponing informally the preamble and resolution submitted by Mr. MARBURY, and it was agreed to.

Mr. BERRY, of Prince George's, then submitted the following:

"*Ordered*, That a committee of three be appointed by the president to correspond with the proper authorities, and furnish this convention with the number of recruits, both white and black, which have been received into the service of the United States, from the several counties of the State, and the city of Baltimore, and also the number credited to the said counties and city respectively."

Mr. CHAMBERS. I would suggest to my friend to have one committee man from each congressional district.

Mr. STIRLING. I am opposed to sending a committee to Washington. It is the governor's business to look after this matter. I do not understand that he has made any publication of wrong having been done. I offer the following amendment: strike out all after the word "ordered," and insert—

"That the governor is hereby requested to furnish this convention with any information he may have as to the quota of the State, and the credits that have been given for inhabitants of the State, white or black, who have been enlisted in the service of the United States."

Mr. BERRY, of Prince George's. The governor could not possibly give us information of the number received into the service of the United States. That we can only get from the provost marshals and the authorities at Washington. My order does not contemplate the sending a committee to Washington; only to correspond with the proper authorities.

Mr. ABBOTT called for the previous question.

The call was sustained, and the main question was ordered.

The question was upon the substitute submitted by Mr. STIRLING.

The question being taken, upon a division —ayes 34, noes 27—the substitute was adopted.

The question then recurred upon the order of Mr. BERRY, of Prince George's as amended.

Upon this question Mr. GALE called for the yeas and nays, and they were ordered.

The question being then taken by yeas and nays, it resulted—yeas 38, nays 33—as follows:

Yeas—Messrs. Goldsborough, President; Berry, of Prince George's, Billingsley, Blackiston, Brown, Chambers, Clarke, Crawford, Davis, of Charles, Dennis, Dent, Duvall, Edelen, Gale, Hodson, Horsey, Jones, of Cecil, Jones, of Somerset, Lansdale, Lee, Mace,

Marbury, Mayhugh, Mitchell, Miller, Morgan, Negley, Nyman, Parker, Parran, Peter, Sands, Smith, of Carroll, Smith, of Dorchester, Swope, Sykes, Todd, Turner—38.

Nays—Messrs. Abbott, Annan, Audoun, Barron, Brooks, Carter, Cunningham, Cushing, Daniel, Davis, of Washington, Earle, Ecker, Galloway, Hatch, Hebb, Hopkins, Hopper, Keefer, Kennard, Markey, McComas, Mullikin, Murray, Pugh, Purnell, Robinette, Russell, Schley, Schlosser, Stirling, Stockbridge, Thomas, Wickard—33.

The order as amended was accordingly adopted.

Pending the call of the yeas and nays, the following explanations were made by members as their names were called:

Mr. ABBOTT. Believing this to be a matter with which this convention has nothing in the world to do, I vote "no."

Mr. BERRY, of Prince George's. Believing this to be in keeping with precedents established by this convention, I vote "aye."

Mr. KENNARD. Believing that the information desired can be had, and ought to be had, without recourse to the means proposed, I vote "no."

Mr. NEGLEY. Believing it is the duty of each citizen of the State to see that justice is done to every citizen of the State; believing that it is right that this information should be had, and that Marylanders should look after Maryland interests, I vote "aye."

Mr. STIRLING. I am perfectly willing to make proper inquiry of the government in regard to this matter. But as I conceive it is an utter usurpation of power on the part of this convention to undertake, over the heads of State authorities, to correspond with the authorities at Washington in regard to this matter; and as I think the gentlemen interested in this proposition refused a fair compromise, I take great pleasure in voting "no."

Mr. SANDS. I should like to understand from the gentleman (Mr. Berry, of Prince George's,) who offered the order, whether this committee is to correspond with the governor of Maryland or with the President of the United States? I have voted "aye," because my impression was that the committee was to correspond with the governor. If that is so, then my vote shall remain as it is. If it is to correspond with the President, then I shall change my vote, as I believe the matter to be peculiarly appropriate to the governor of the State.

Mr. BERRY, of Prince George's. My object was to ascertain the proper authorities, and then correspond with those in authority.

Mr. STIRLING. It says "authorities in Washington."

Mr BERRY, of Prince George's. No, sir; it says "proper authorities."

Mr. SANDS. I merely wish to say that if the committee is to correspond with the governor, I shall vote for the order very cheerfully. But if it is with the President or with any federal authority, then I shall vote "no." If the gentleman who offered the order will assure me that the committee is to correspond with the governor, my vote shall remain as it is.

Mr. BERRY, of Prince George's. It says "to correspond with the proper authorities."

The PRESIDENT announced the vote to be, yeas 38, nays 33.

Mr. STIRLING. Has the vote been read over by the secretary?

The PRESIDENT. The assistant secretary informs me that the roll has been read over by him.

Mr. STIRLING. I think the secretary is mistaken. I do not think the roll has been read over since the vote was taken.

The PRESIDENT. The chair will direct the roll to be read over again.

Mr. CHAMBERS. By what authority is that order made?

The PRESIDENT. There seems to be some misunderstanding as to whether the roll has been called off properly. And the chair has directed the secretary——

Mr. CHAMBERS. I ask under what rule that is done?

The PRESIDENT. The gentleman from Kent (Mr. Chambers) is out of order.

Mr. CHAMBERS. I say the chair is out of order.

The PRESIDENT. The chair was announcing what had been done, and before he had concluded, the gentleman from Kent interposed, in which he was out of order.

Mr. CHAMBERS. The president has authority, I know, but it is authority to enforce the rules.

The PRESIDENT. And the president will see that the rules are enforced; he will compel the enforcement of them, if he has any power in this body. The president called upon the clerk for the purpose of ascertaining whether the roll had been read over, being under the impression that the roll had not been read. The clerk informed the president that it had been read over, and thereupon the president announced the vote. There seems, however, to be some misunderstanding on the part of several members of the convention in regard to the subject, and the president will therefore direct the roll to be read over again. There can be no harm done. The trouble has occurred only from the interposition of the gentleman from Howard (Mr. Sands,) who asked several questions of the gentleman from Prince George's (Mr. Berry,) after the vote had been taken but before it had been announced. If gentlemen will just be quiet, and interpose at the proper time, there will be no difficulty about the matter. The president will take care hereafter that the rules are strictly enforced. While gentlemen are walking all about the hall, and indulging in conversation, it is utterly impossible to keep the convention in proper order. Hereafter, should this again occur, the president will suspend all business until order is restored.

Mr. CHAMBERS. I had understood from the use of the term "calling the roll" that the idea was to take the vote over again, and to that I had a positive objection. I have not the least objection to the vote being read over again. I misunderstood the announcement, and supposed the president had assumed the power to have the vote retaken.

The names of those in the affirmative and in the negative were again read over.

Mr. TODD. Would it be in order to change my vote now?

The PRESIDENT. No sir; the vote has been announced. The president has permitted the vote to be again read over, for the purpose merely of correcting an erroneous impression.

Mr. TODD. Then I move to reconsider the vote just taken.

The motion to reconsider was seconded by Messrs. NYMAN and SANDS.

Mr. JONES, of Somerset, called for the yeas and nays on the motion to reconsider, and they were accordingly ordered.

The question being then taken, by yeas and nays, it resulted—yeas 42, nays 30—as follows:

Yeas—Messrs. Goldsborough, President; Abbott, Annan, Audoun, Barron, Brooks, Cunningham, Cushing, Daniel, Davis, of Washington, Earle, Ecker, Galloway, Hatch, Hebb, Hopkins, Hopper, Keefer, Kennard, King, Markey, Mayhugh, McComas, Mullikin, Murray, Negley, Nyman, Pugh, Purnell, Robinette, Russell, Sands, Schley, Schlosser, Smith, of Worcester, Stirling, Stockbridge, Sykes, Thomas, Todd, Wickard, Wooden—42.

Nays—Messrs. Berry, of Prince George's, Billingsley, Blackiston, Brown, Chambers, Clarke, Crawford, Davis, of Charles, Dennis, Dent, Duvall, Edelen, Gale, Hodson, Horsey, Jones, of Cecil, Jones, of Somerset, Lansdale, Lee, Mace, Marbury, Mitchell, Miller, Morgan, Parker, Parran, Smith, of Carroll, Smith, of Dorchester, Swope, Turner—30.

The motion to reconsider was accordingly agreed to.

The question recurred upon the adoption of the order as amended.

Upon this question Mr. JONES, of Somerset, called for the yeas and nays, and they were ordered.

Mr. BERRY, of Prince George's. Before the vote is taken, I propose now to make the motion to postpone this subject until to-morrow morning. In the meantime I will ascertain who are the proper authorities from whom this information can be obtained.

The question being then taken upon postponing the further consideration of the order until to-morrow morning, upon a division—ayes 44, noes not counted—it was agreed to.

JUDICIARY DEPARTMENT.

The convention then resumed the consideration of the report of the committee on the judiciary department, which was on its second reading.

Mr. KING gave notice that at the proper time he would submit the following amendment:

"That the judicial districts in the several counties of the State be as reported by the judiciary committee, except Frederick and Baltimore counties, each to be separate judicial districts."

PERSONS ADMITTED TO PRACTICE LAW.

Mr. MULLIKIN moved to reconsider the vote by which section eleven of the report of the committee on the judiciary department had been stricken out.

The section as reported by the committee was as follows:

"Section 11. Every person of good moral character, being a voter, shall be admitted to practice law in all the courts of this State, in his own case."

Previous to its being stricken out, it had been amended, on motion of Mr. STIRLING, by striking out the words "of good moral character, being a voter."

The question was upon the motion to reconsider, and being taken, *viva voce*, before the result was announced—

Mr. ABBOTT called for the yeas and nays, which were ordered.

Mr. NEGLEY. I hope the convention will reconsider the vote by which this section was stricken out. It is the provision in the last constitution by which every man is allowed to go into court and appear in his own case, and thereby save to himself an appearance fee at least. It was adopted by the last convention, and is a concession, not to the bar, I know, but to the people generally, and I should like to see it retained.

The PRESIDENT. Is it not a common-law right?

Mr. NEGLEY. Then why was it put in the constitution at all? The practice in all the courts, previous to the adoption of the present constitution, was that no man could appear except by attorney.

The PRESIDENT. I venture to say that before the adoption of the present constitution there were more of such appearances than now.

Mr. JONES, of Somerset. The party need not appear in his own case now. But this gives him the right to appear in person and confess the judgment, as has been done from time immemorial; or he may try his own case. He has a common-law right to do so. A lawyer is but the agent of the party. The party may appear in person and try his own case, if he chooses, notwithstanding the old adage that "the lawyer who tries his own case has a fool for a client"

The PRESIDENT. There is no use in putting this in here; you cannot deprive a man of that right, for he has it at common law.

The question was upon the motion of Mr. MULLIKIN to reconsider the vote by which the eleventh section was stricken out.

Mr. ABBOTT called for the yeas and nays upon this question, and they were ordered.

The question was then taken, by yeas and nays, and resulted—yeas 44, nays 26—as follows:

Yeas—Messrs. Abbott, Annan, Billingsley, Blackiston, Brown, Cunningham, Cushing, Davis, of Charles, Davis, of Washington, Dennis, Dent, Ecker, Hebb, Hodson, Hopkins, Horsey, Jones, of Cecil, Keefer, Kennard, King, Lansdale, Mace, Marbury, Markey, Mayhugh, McComas, Morgan, Mullikin, Negley, Nyman, Parran, Robinette, Russell, Sands, Schlosser, Smith of Carroll, Smith, of Dorchester, Swope, Sykes, Thomas, Todd, Turner, Wickard, Wooden—44.

Nays—Messrs. Goldsborough, President; Audoun, Barron, Brooks, Carter, Chambers, Clarke, Crawford, Daniel, Earle, Edelen, Galloway, Hatch, Hopper, Jones, of Somerset, Lee, Mitchell, Murray, Parker, Peter, Pugh, Purnell, Schley, Smith, of Worcester, Stirling, Stockbridge—26.

The motion to reconsider was accordingly agreed to.

The question was stated to be upon agreeing to the section, as amended, which was read as follows:

"Every person shall be permitted to practice law in all the courts of this State, in his own case."

Mr. MULLIKIN moved the following as a substitute for the section:

"Every person, being a voter, shall be admitted to practice law in all the courts of this State, in his own case."

Mr. CLARKE. It might be considered that, being an attorney, the vote in favor of striking out this section was one in which I was interested, as being one who, to a certain extent, probably might be benefited thereby, by the exclusion of parties from acting in their own cases. But a very limited experience on this subject has convinced me that not only is the profession not interested in having this left out, but I think the public would be benefited, individually, by not having this right extended to them. I understand that at common law any party who is sued in court has the right to come in and have his personal appearance entered. I once brought suit against a person, and he undertook to conduct his own case. We had a rich scene there, I can assure gentlemen, such as I never saw before. During the pendency of the trial almost a fight took place in the courthouse. The party seemed to be entirely ignorant of every form connected with his case. He filed a plea covering from ten to twenty pages, and going into everything except the real merits of the case. There was a demurrer to that, and he filed another plea; to that there was a demurrer, to which he again filed a plea. And finally he had to get a lawyer to take part in the case, while it was before the court. Of course the lawyer who came into the case then, had no knowledge of it. The result of that case was that costs accumulated to such an extent that the party was really damnified. The case went up to the court of appeals, and we agreed to leave out a great many issues, it was so complicated and involved. If this provision had never been in the constitution, I think a great deal now on the records of the courts would never have got there.

Mr. MULLIKIN. I only want that in a plain case, involving a hundred dollars for instance, a man shall not be compelled to employ a lawyer, but shall be allowed to try his own case.

Mr. PARRAN. I move to insert the words "in this State," after the words "being a voter."

Mr. JONES, of Somerset. I move to strike out the words "being a voter," so as to leave the matter where the common law leaves it. For fear that legal gentlemen here might be under the implication of striking out what may be considered by some, who do not know what the common law is, their constitutional right, it would be as well to incorporate the broad provisions of the common law. It can do no harm; it is but an affirmance of the common law; and having been put in the present constitution, if it is stricken out of this the ignorant might suppose the lawyers struck it out for their own benefit. It takes very little experience to convince a man to the contrary. A man never tries that thing but once. He may go up and confess judgment, that is done every day. But as to a man's trying his own case, I never knew an instance of a man doing that the second time. I knew a case once of a shrewd man, who tried his own case, examined his own witnesses, etc. His case was just as plain a case as possible, and if he had employed some one who understood the matter to ask the proper questions he would have been cleared. There happened to be two cases against him. In the first one which he undertook to manage himself, he failed to make out his case, and the judge decided against him. He then asked me how it was he had lost that case, and I told him. He then asked me if I could get the case opened again, I told him it was doubtful. He told me he would give me ten dollars if I would try. I went to see the judge, who said the case was closed. Then said the man to me—"I will get you to try the next case any way." Now if a man trusts himself to draw up a declaration on a note for one hundred dollars, or something of that kind, he may perhaps be able to do it from the code. I, however, once knew a justice of the peace, who accepted the office, when appointed to it, for fear the governor might consider it discourteous in him to refuse. He was called upon to draw a deed, which he did, following the old forms of 1805; but when he came to the description, he copied so literally that it read —"beginning at a stone and going to the end of the description," and that is so recorded to this day in Somerset county.

Mr. SCHLEY. This section was amended yesterday before it was struck out, by striking out the words "of good moral character, being a voter." The action of the convention therefore has been had upon the words "being a voter." Is it competent now for the gentleman from Talbot (Mr. Mullikin) to offer an amendment to the section including those words?

Mr. PUGH. The action of the convention of last night has been reconsidered.

The PRESIDENT. If a proposition is reconsidered, everything in connection with the proposition is also reconsidered, and the whole subject is opened up again.

Mr. STOCKBRIDGE. The words "of good moral character, being a voter," were stricken out of the section last night. What was left then was the following:

"Every person shall be admitted to practice law in all the courts of this State, in his own case."

Now, having voted to reconsider the vote by which the entire section as amended was stricken out, is not the question again upon the motion to strike out the section?

The PRESIDENT. The gentleman from Talbot (Mr. Mullikin) has moved an amendment to the section, in the nature of a substitute.

Mr. NEGLEY. Which substitute is the same as the section stands amended, with the exception of the words "being a voter."

Mr. DENT. According to my understanding the last vote upon the section yesterday was upon the motion to strike out the section. That vote is the one which has been reconsidered this morning. And after that reconsideration, the motion to strike out the section is again before the convention.

The PRESIDENT. The gentleman from Talbot in lieu of the section that had been stricken out proposes another section, to which the gentleman from Calvert (Mr. Parran) moves an amendment, to insert the words "in this State," after the words "being a voter."—The first question is upon the amendment of the gentleman from Calvert

Mr. MULLIKIN. I will accept that amendment.

The question was upon the substitute as modified.

Mr. JONES, of Somerset. I move to strike out the words "being a voter."

Mr. MULLIKIN. That will admit colored people to practice.

Mr. JONES, of Somerset. Well, if a colored man chooses to try his own case, let him do so; I see no objection to that.

Mr. BERRY, of Prince George's. So far as the members of our profession are concerned, if we looked alone to our interests, we would greatly prefer to have incorporated into the constitution a provision allowing every person to practice law in all the courts of the State in his own case. It has been my experience in the practice of law, that those who have no practical knowledge of the law have been the means of making more law-suits than there would have been without their assistance. I know various cases arising in our county: I call to mind now one in particular, a criminal case, where the party attempted to defend himself. The jury found him guilty without leaving the jury-box, though it was the opinion of every member there that if he had had a professional man to defend him he would have been acquitted. There was another case of assault and battery, with which there was no aggravating circumstances connected. The party undertook to defend himself, and was found guilty and fined three hundred dollars.

It has been my experience that it is a great deal better for our profession, if we look at it in that light, to let every man practice law, for they make more law-suits. We have found the old adage true, "that he who tries his own case, has a fool for a client."

Now I came here to try and make an organic law that would meet the wants of the people of the State for all time to come. I did not want them to have another constitutional convention called within my lifetime.—But my opinion has now very much changed —I want to see another constitutional convention in this hall in less than three months. And if it could be done, I would have every one of the majority here turned out and what I consider better men politically, put in their places. I am here to do my duty to my constituents, and that I intend to try to do in my own way. I am here to try if I can to get a perfect organic law for the people of this State, and therefore I am prompted by no desire to put in any provision which will assist my profession, or any other profession.

Now, individually, I have no objection to this section. But let me ask if it is better to allow every citizen to practice in his own case, however inexperienced in the practice of law he may be, and however little knowledge he may have of it? I say that the citizen is much better off when he gets a professional adviser and gives him a fee to try his case. If the majority of this convention desire to have this section incorporated into the constitution, I want them to understand that I vote against it only because I think our citizens generally would be benefited by not having it in the constitution. Under the laws of Maryland, any man in the State can practice medicine and charge for it. But would any man not a physician, among those members of this convention who favor the adoption of this section, attempt to treat a bad case of disease, or to give a diagnosis of it? While I have seen a man try his own cases in the courts, I have never in my life seen a man, not a physician, employed by his neighbors to treat diseases. Now any man in the community is as capable of forming a diagnosis of the most obscure case known to medicine, as he is, uninformed and unpracticed in the law, to go to your court-house and try a legal case before the court and jury.

I shall vote, therefore, against retaining this provision in the constitution, because I think to do so would be doing our citizens an injustice. Not that I think that keeping this section out would benefit my profession at all; for I believe it would be a greater benefit to the profession to permit every man to practice.

The question was upon the motion of Mr. JONES, of Somerset, to strike out the words "being a voter."

Upon this question, Mr. JONES, of Somerset, called for the yeas and nays, and they were ordered.

The question being then taken, by yeas and nays, it resulted—yeas 14, nays 58—as follows:

Yeas—Messrs. Chambers, Crawford, Daniel, Dennis, Edelen, Hatch, Horsey, Jones, of Somerset, Lansdale, McComas, Mitchell, Murray, Schley, Stockbridge—14.

Nays—Messrs. Goldsborough, President; Abbott, Annan, Audoun, Barron, Berry, of Prince George's, Billingsley, Blackiston, Brooks, Brown, Carter, Clarke, Cunningham, Davis, of Charles, Davis, of Washington, Dent, Duvall, Earle, Ecker, Gale, Galloway, Hebb, Hodson, Hopkins, Hopper, Jones, of Cecil, Keefer, Kennard, King, Lee, Mace, Marbury, Markey, Mayhugh, Morgan, Mullikin, Negley, Nyman, Parker, Parran, Peter, Pugh, Purnell, Robinette, Russell, Sands, Schlosser, Smith, of Carroll, Smith, of Dorchester, Smith, of Worcester, Stirling, Swope, Sykes, Thomas, Thruston, Todd, Turner, Wickard, Wooden—58.

The amendment was accordingly rejected.

Mr. DANIEL, when his name was called, said: I shall vote for this, for I can see no reason why a man twenty-one years old should be allowed to defend his own case, and not a man who is twenty years and eleven months old.

Mr. THRUSTON, when his name was called, said: Inasmuch as this amendment if adopted would permit citizens of other States to practice law in this State in their own cases, I must vote against it.

Mr. CHAMBERS submitted the following amendment:

Strike out the words "admitted to practice law," and insert the words "permitted to appear and try his own case," and strike out the words, in the last line, "in his own case."

Mr. CHAMBERS said: I have made a business of the practice of the law in my State from the year 1805 up to the 18th of August, 1864; and I think it is entitled to some respect at the hands of this convention when I say that a man who knows nothing of the law cannot be admitted to practice it. You may pass an ordinance or a constitutional provision, but you cannot enable a man who is fool enough to go into court to try his own case, not being a lawyer, to practice law. It would be a libel upon the profession, were we to assert such a thing.

The amendment was agreed to—ayes 44, nays 14.

The question was stated upon the motion to strike out the section.

Mr. CHAMBERS. I rise to excuse myself from voting to accomplish an object I have no desire to accomplish. By common law every man has a right to appear and try his own case. Gentlemen seem to think that they are conferring a privilege upon a particular class of persons. That is altogether a mistake. This is restricting a right which they already have. I vote against it because it restricts the right of the voter coming into the State, and having all the qualifications except residence. A man coming here from Massachusetts, although he may be a lawyer, cannot be admitted to try his own case unless he comes to the bar and qualifies. But another man alongside of him, with no pretensions of law, because he is a voter can try his own case. I do not see the necessity of restricting the privilege. Any man has a right to spend his own time and money foolishly; to employ his time, talents, money, reputation, as he pleases, provided he does not injure his neighbor by it. Why then restrain him? The inference would be from inserting such a clause that this class of persons is to be prohibited. I do not want them prohibited. I think it is an invidious distinction between persons who stand in this respect in the same category. When a man has just come into the State or into the county, I do not see why he should not be as much as any other man in the State, permitted to try his own case. I shall vote against the insertion of such a clause.

Mr. NEGLEY. What will be the effect of striking out the entire section?

The PRESIDENT. The gentleman from Talbot moved to reconsider the vote by which this section was stricken out. After that vote had been reconsidered, the gentleman from Talbot moved a proposition which the house has been perfecting. After they have perfected it the convention must go back to the motion to strike out.

Mr. NEGLEY. And in order to get this proposition in the house must strike out the original?

The PRESIDENT. Yes, sir.

The motion to strike out prevailed.

The PRESIDENT. The question recurs upon the substitute submitted by the gentleman from Talbot (Mr. Mullikin) as amended.

Mr. THRUSTON. I move to strike out "voter in this State" and insert "citizen of the United States;" because the constitution of the United States requires that "the citizens of each State shall be entitled to all the privileges and immunities of citizens in the several States" [art. 4, sec. 2,] and I do not want to have our constitution at variance with the constitution of the United States in any way.

Mr. NEGLEY. I think that is an edge tool that will cut two ways. It is competent to allow a man who has not been naturalized to vote for State officers; yet he could not vote for United States officers.

Mr. THRUSTON. It is not competent to give a privilege to citizens of Maryland in a suit at law, that citizens of other States have not a right to. I do not want to have a useless conflict between our own constitution and the constitution of the United States, because our constitution must give way to the constitution of the United States. That is the reason for my motion.

The amendment was agreed to.

Mr. NEGLEY. I move the following amendment, being section 31 of the article in our present constitution:

"Every person of good moral character, being a voter, shall be admitted to practice law in all the courts of law in this State, in his own case."

The PRESIDENT ruled the amendment out of order, having already been acted upon.

Mr. CHAMBERS demanded the yeas and nays upon the adoption of the section as amended, and they were ordered.

The question being taken, the result was—yeas 40, nays 32—as follows:

Yeas—Messrs. Abbott, Annan, Audoun, Barron, Brown, Crawford, Cunningham, Daniel, Davis, of Charles, Davis, of Washington, Dennis, Duvall, Ecker, Galloway, Hebb, Hopkins, Hopper, Horsey, Jones, of Somerset, Keefer, Kennard, King, Lansdale, Markey, Mayhugh, McComas, Mullikin, Negley, Nyman, Robinette, Sands, Schlosser, Smith, of Carroll, Smith, of Dorchester, Smith, of Worcester, Sykes, Thomas, Thruston, Wickard—40.

Nays—Messrs. Goldsborough, President; Berry, of Prince George's, Billingsley, Blackiston, Brooks, Carter, Chambers, Clarke, Dent, Earle, Edelen, Hatch, Jones, of Cecil, Lee, Mace, Marbury, Mitchell, Morgan, Murray, Parker, Parran, Peter, Pugh, Purnell, Russell, Schley, Stirling, Stockbridge, Swope, Todd, Turner, Wooden—32.

When their names were called,

Mr SCHLEY said: For the same reason I voted for striking out yesterday, I vote "no."

Mr. STIRLING said: I do not know that this section can practically give any rights a man cannot exercise now; and I think it is only calculated to produce confusion, and perhaps restrict some rights. I therefore vote "no."

Mr BROOKS said: Under the explanation of the gentleman from Baltimore city (Mr. Stirling,) I will change my vote and vote "no."

The section was accordingly adopted as follows:

"Sec. 11. Every person, being a citizen of the United States, shall be permitted to appear and try his own case."

The next section was read as follows:

PART II.

Court of Appeals.

"Sec. 12. The court of appeals shall consist of a chief justice and four associate justices, and for their selection the State shall be divided into five judicial districts as follows, viz: Worcester, Somerset, Dorchester, Talbot, Caroline, Queen Anne, Kent and Cecil counties, shall compose the first district; Harford and Baltimore counties, and the first seven wards of Baltimore city, shall compose the second district; Baltimore city, except the first seven wards, shall compose the third district; Allegany, Washington, Frederick, Howard and Carroll counties, shall compose the fourth district; St. Mary's, Charles, Anne Arundel, Calvert, Prince George's and Montgomery counties, shall compose the fifth district; and one of the judges of the court of appeals shall be appointed from each of said districts."

Mr ABBOTT. I move to strike out "appointed" and insert "elected" in the last line.

Mr. JONES, of Somerset. I would suggest to the gentleman to insert "by the qualified voters in each of the said judicial districts."

Mr. STIRLING. It would be better to take the vote first upon the amendment as offered, and afterwards upon the mode of election.

Mr. SANDS. That can be provided for by inserting in line two, after the words "associate justices" the words "to be elected on general ticket by the qualified voters of the State."

Mr. SCHLEY. I give notice that I will move to amend by inserting "to be elected by the qualified voters of the State" in the second line, and to strike out the last clause, and let the justices be elected from the State at large.

Mr. DENT. I will move to amend by adding at the end of the section, "by the qualified voters thereof."

Mr. THOMAS. I give notice that at the proper time I shall offer a substitute for the whole section.

Mr. CHAMBERS demanded the yeas and nays upon Mr. ABBOTT'S amendment, and they were ordered.

The question being taken, the result was—yeas 42, nays 19—as follows:

Yeas—Messrs. Abbott, Annan, Audoun, Berry, of Prince George's, Billingsley, Blackiston, Crawford, Davis, of Washington, Dennis, Dent, Duvall, Ecker, Edelen, Gale, Galloway, Hatch, Hopkins, Horsey, Jones, of Somerset, Keefer, Kennard, King, Lee, Marbury, Mayhugh, McComas, Mitchell, Morgan, Murray, Negley, Parran, Purnell, Robinette, Sands, Schley, Schlosser, Smith, of Carroll, Smith, of Dorchester, Thomas, Turner, Wickard, Wooden—42.

Nays—Messrs. Goldsborough, President; Brown, Chambers, Clarke, Daniel, Earle, Hebb, Hopper, Jones, of Cecil, Lansdale, Mullikin, Parker, Peter, Russell, Stirling, Stockbridge, Swope, Sykes, Thruston—19.

When their names were called

Mr. CLARKE said: I was not here when the former vote was taken. I am in favor of the court of appeals being appointed, and the circuit judges being elected. I therefore vote "no."

Mr. JONES, of Somerset, said: In committee I voted for the appointive system for the court of appeals; but the house yesterday manifested its disposition determinedly, by a large majority, to have an elective system. I do not consider the mode of appointment so important as the character of the men to be appointed. I am not afraid to trust the people. Therefore I shall vote "aye."

Mr. STOCKBRIDGE said: I was willing to accept the decision of the house yesterday as the settlement of this question, and I had hoped that the time of the convention would not be taken up with calling the yeas and nays upon a settled question, but as they are called I shall vote in accordance with my real opinion. I vote "no."

The amendment was accordingly adopted.

Mr. DENT submitted the following amendment:

Add at the end of the section "by the qualified voters thereof."

Mr. THRUSTON submitted the following amendment to the amendment:

Strike out the word "thereof," in the last line, and insert the words "of the whole State."

Mr. THOMAS submitted the following amendment:

Strike out all after the word "The," in the first line and insert the following:

"The court of appeals shall consist of a chief justice and four associate justices, and for their selection the State shall be divided into four judicial districts. Allegany, Washington, Frederick, Carroll, Baltimore and Harford counties, shall compose the first; Montgomery, Howard, Anne Arundel, Calvert, St. Mary's, Charles and Prince George's, the second; Baltimore city the third; and Cecil, Kent, Queen Anne's, Talbot, Caroline, Dorchester, Somerset and Worcester, shall compose the fourth district; and the chief justice shall be elected by the qualified voters of the counties and the city of Baltimore on a general ticket.

"And one person from among those learned in the law, having been admitted to practice law in this State, and who shall have been a citizen of this State at least five years, and above the age of thirty years at the time of his election, and a resident of the judicial district, or if chief justice a resident of the State as herein provided, shall be elected from each of said districts and the State, by the legal and qualified voters therein as a judge of said court of appeals, who shall hold his office for the term of fifteen years from the time of his election or until he shall have attained the age of seventy years, whichever may first happen, and be re-eligible thereto until he shall have attained the age of seventy years, and not after, subject to removal for incompetency, wilful neglect of duty or misbehavior in office, on conviction in a court of law, or by the governor upon the address of the general assembly, two-thirds of the members of each house concurring in such address, and the salary of each of the judges of the court of appeals, shall be four thousand dollars ($4,000) annually, and shall not be increased or diminished during their continuance in office, and no fees or perquisites of any kind shall be allowed by law to any of the said judges."

The question was stated upon Mr. THRUSTON'S amendment to the amendment.

Mr. THRUSTON. The effect of my amendment is that the judges of the court of appeals will be elected by general ticket.

Mr. DENT. The object of the amendment I proposed was this: Since it had been determined by the convention that the judges of the court of appeals should be elected, I wished to provide that it should be by the voters of the district from which they should be elected. It seems to me much more proper that they should be elected by the voters of the district from which they are to be elected, than that they should be elected by general ticket, as proposed by the amendment of the gentleman from Allegany (Mr. Thruston.) The question is simple and plain between the two, and it is unnecessary to make any extended remarks upon it.

Mr. BERRY, of Prince George's. I object both to the amendment offered by the gentleman from Allegany (Mr. Thruston,) and to that offered by the gentleman from Baltimore city (Mr. Thomas.) My objection to the amendment offered by the gentleman from Allegany is this; that it proposes that the judges of the court of appeals shall all be elected by general ticket. Under the present constitution the members of the court of appeals are elected by the qualified voters of the several districts from which they come. There are many reasons why I think that under that system we can get a better man for the court of appeals than by a general vote of the whole State.

I must confess, although a member of the bar, that if I were called upon to vote for the most competent man in the particular district represented in part by the gentleman from Allegany, I should not be half as competent to judge who was the most fit person to sit upon the bench of the court of appeals, as the gentlemen who reside there. The same principle would apply to being called upon to vote for a member of the court of appeals from our section of the State. I am familiar with all the members of the bar in our section of the State. I know their standing at the bar, and their legal attainments, and therefore I should be better able to judge who would be most competent in my section of the State to sit upon the bench of the court of appeals than the gentleman from Allegany.

I therefore prefer the provision of the present constitution. Let gentlemen think of it for a moment, and ask themselves how we can obtain the services of the best men to sit upon the bench of the court of appeals. As a matter of course we must know the men from whom we make the selection; and, although a member of the bar, I must say that I do not know personally who would be best suited for that place in the section of the State represented by the gentleman; and I take it for granted that the same remark will apply to him. Therefore there is manifest wisdom in adhering to the present system.

Let each district elect a judge of the court of appeals by the qualified voters of the district. We then have the assurance that we shall get good men upon the bench, and I am sure it is the desire of every one present that that should be accomplished. I think that this is reason enough why every member of the convention should vote to allow them to be elected by the qualified voters of the district from which they come, according to the provision of the old constitution.

Mr. Stirling. I hope very sincerely that the amendment of the gentleman from Allegany will prevail. It strikes me that there is a manifest propriety in this mode of electing the judges. I was very much struck yesterday with the remarks made incidentally by my friend from Washington (Mr. Negley) with regard to this subject. It is a fact that the judges of the court of appeals represent the justice of the whole State. Under the old system they were appointed by the governor who represented the whole people. The judge of each judicial distrcit represents the people of that district, but the judges of the court of appeals are obliged to decide cases which come up from every portion of the State.

Mr. Berry, of Prince George's. Will the gentleman allow me to ask him a question? The appointment having been made under the old system by the governor of the State, was it not the uniform practice for the governor in the appointment thus made to require recommendations from the members of the bar from the section of the State from which the judge was appointed?

Mr. Stirling. I suppose it was. That was the mere ascertainment of his fitness for the office. Every citizen of the State has an interest in every judge of the court of appeals, and he has just as much right to vote for him as to vote for the governor of the State. They equally exercise a general authority over the whole State.

So far as regards the selection of a proper man, I believe that the State convention of any political party will in every instance nominate a better man upon the State ticket than would be nominated upon a district ticket. In the first place, candidates are selected with more care by the members of nominating conventions. They come together from all parts of the State, and there are more men among them acquainted with the qualifications of members of the bar.—Not only that, but they have an interest in putting on their ticket their strongest man because it has an effect upon the strength of the rest of their ticket.

It is a positive fact, so far as I have had an opportunity of hearing about it, that the judges of the supreme court in New York State have been less influenced by politics and have been more able men than those of any other courts of the State; and I believe this is largely attributable to the fact, that while the district judges are elected by the vote of the districts, the judges of the court of appeals are elected by a general vote of the State, and both political parties have taken pains to keep their ablest men for the court of appeals. We all know that when the question of the constitutionality of the legal-tender law came before that court, Judge Denis gave a dissenting opinion against the law, and yet his character was such that when his party came to nominate a justice of the court of appeals for the next term they unanimously gave him a renomination. I rather think that if he had been required to be nominated by a district convention political prejudice would have absolutely turned him off the bench, because he decided contrary to the political feeling of the party. There is less liability of political feeling being excited against a judge for deciding contrary to the prejudices of a particular district than when the election is by general ticket. The individual citizen is very often brought before the court in antagonism with the people, and the judges under the elective system are sometimes inclined to represent the people against the individual. I think that by enlarging the sphere of selection you cure some of the acknowledged evils of the elective system. There is certainly a manifest propriety in it upon principle, because they do represent the whole justice of the whole State.

With regard to the State convention, we know that practically judges will be nominated. It is all nonsense to shut our eyes to it. It necessitates the nomination of judges of political views. I do not care whether they are politicians or not. They will be nominated as they always have been nominated, more or less directly. When the State convention meets, the gentlemen coming to that convention from the different districts will know whom they want, and they will try to get their best man, and a much better man will be nominated than could be selected by the governor, or by a county or district convention, and there would be less chance for undue influence to be exerted.

Mr. Miller. One word in reply to the gentleman from Baltimore city (Mr. Stirling.) This system of electing judges is all wrong, and I am happy to have voted against it. But if it is the opinion of the convention, as it has been expressed, that judges shall be elected, I think it is manifestly proper that the election of the judges of the court of appeals should come from the district as they have heretofore done. The gentleman has put the case of New York where it may have worked well, but taken as a general thing it works badly. In the upper district of this State the two parties nominate a judge. Each party makes its nomination and has a candidate for judge of the court of appeals. There may be no comparison between the two men selected as to fitness to fill this position; and yet if the man least qualified for the position is the nominee of the party which happens to be the strongest in Baltimore city and other parts of the State, his election will be secured. Whereas by letting the majority of the district select their best man, we should get the best man for the bench of the court of appeals. It may be so in all the other districts of the State. I do not want the controlling political majority in the State to ride down at any time, or to vote down a good judge, or a good candidate that may be nominated from any particular district in the State.

Mr. Sands. I think that the concluding remarks of my friend from Baltimore city were really conclusive upon this point. I have been a member of some State conventions, and I have never known them to undertake to dictate to the people of any district whom they should have. On the contrary the practice has been to say, "You must have a man from your district; whom do you want?" They generally have their committees, and the different delegations consult among themselves. They say, "Mr. A. is our best man." "Well, we will vote for Mr. A. then." They do this mutually, one district for another, each selecting the best man in the district as their candidate. I have never seen this rule contravened. Suppose the delegation from the first judicial district say, "We want Mr. A." Those from other districts never say, "No, you shall not have Mr. A, whom you do want, but Mr. C., whom you do not want." Practically, as you district the State, requiring one member from each district, the whole matter of the choice rests upon the people of the district.

This is a court in which every citizen of the State is equally interested, from one end of the State to the other. It is a court that sits in final judgment upon cases, and every man who has occasion to go into court has an interest in the question, who shall sit in the courts. Therefore the plan of election by general ticket has my concurrence. I repeat that from my experience in nominating conventions the nomination is invariably left to the people of the district from which the man is to be taken.

Mr. Dennis. If we are to have an elective system at all, it seems to me certainly desirable that each district, in every part of the State should be represented. It may very well happen that if you elect by general ticket the man in Allegany and the man in Baltimore city may select a man from St. Mary's or a man from Somerset whom the people of that district may be opposed to. It is desirable to have every part of the State represented. It is not the mere location of a man which is necessary to make him the exponent and the representative of a district. If you take from Somerset a man with the views and wishes and sentiments of the people of Allegany, and make him a candidate, no man can say he is a representative of the Somerset district. Where is the propriety, and where is the necessity of dividing the State into districts—the convention has already determined to divide the State into districts, taking a judge for the court of appeals from each district in the State—and where is the propriety of this if you are to elect by general ticket?

Mr. Stockbridge. That has not been acted upon.

Mr. Dennis. True; that is a part of the report not acted upon; but everybody seems to think it proper to divide the State into these districts; and yet it is proposed that the election shall be by general ticket. It seems to me that you might as well take them all from Allegany and Baltimore city at once, as to have them elected by general ticket.

Mr. Schley. In reply to the remark of the gentleman from Somerset (Mr. Dennis,) that you might as well take the judges directly from Baltimore city, I say, not at all. We know that practically, as has been stated, each division of the State puts its own man into nomination, to be placed upon the general ticket.

In reply to a remark which fell from the gentleman from Prince George's (Mr. Berry,) I merely wish to say that there is no such superfluity of good legal and distinguished men in the State, that the election should not be coextensive with the limits of the State. I do not see any force in the objection that a man who happens to be a resident of one district is not known in other districts of the State. The remarks of the gentleman from Baltimore city (Mr. Stirling,) and of the gentleman from Howard county (Mr. Sands,) appear to me to cover the whole ground. Every man has an interest in the court of appeals, and ought to have a voice in their election. I hope the motion will prevail.

Mr. Negley. If the arguments of the gentlemen who oppose this amendment be worth anything, they would apply with equal force to the election of governor. Under the present constitution, and I suppose under the one that we intend to make, the State is divided into three gubernatorial districts, and the candidate comes alternately from each one of these. But because he comes from one of these, is that a reason why he should not be elected by any but the legal voters of the district from which he may happen to come during that gubernatorial term?

Mr. Berry, of Prince George's. If the gentleman from Washington will allow me, I will give him the keynote of our whole action here; and perhaps he will be better able to answer the arguments offered. It is this, that we do not propose to make the judgeship a political matter at all. We do not propose that they shall be nominated by convention. The very strong reason which the gentleman seems to think he offers in support of his position is the very greatest objection to my mind to adopting the principle. If they are to be nominated, as the gentleman from Baltimore city says, by a political convention——

Mr. Stirling. I only said that they always have been.

Mr. Berry, of Prince George's. I have never known them to be in my district.

Mr. Stirling. There may have been an exception in that one district, but I know that in every other district of the State from the eastern shore to Allegany, they have been nominated by political conventions.

Mr. Berry, of Prince George's. I have not known such a state of things to exist.

Mr. Stockbridge. At the last election of judge of the court of appeals, were not both candidates nominated in convention?

Mr. Berry, of Prince George's. No, sir; they were recommended without any nomination. It is our desire that they should not become connected with politics, one way or the other, but should be kept separate and distinct from every political movement of the State. We want the judgeship of the State to be held as a high and exalted position, above the politics of the present day, so high that they can look down upon and scan the action of political men of the day, and I have no doubt that in many instances, it will be with great contempt. I want them to be separate and apart from politics; and in our district I have never known them, since they have been elected under the revised constitution, in the slightest degree connected with politics. I do not think I could vote for a judge who would go to political meetings and electioneer for such a position. I think it would be a sufficient objection in my mind to any man, no matter how well qualified in other respects, if I knew him to enter into the general politics of the day and to attend political meetings, or if he were to solicit votes as a party candidate for such a position. The man who would do that, I should conceive to be incapable of holding such a position, and unfit to hold it.

I say that it ought to be kept clear of politics. If not, they may carry their political prejudices upon the bench with them. They will not administer the law in the spirit of the law, but they will carry their political prejudices upon the bench and degrade the profession and the high position of judge. I say, therefore, that the very reason the gentleman assigns as the strongest reason why they should be elected by general ticket, is the reason why I shall oppose their being elected by general ticket; if it is to result in their being nominated by a party convention.

Mr. Negley resumed: I understand the gentleman from Prince George's (Mr. Berry) to shift his ground of objection.

Mr. Berry, of Prince George's. No, sir; I do not shift; I add that as another reason.

Mr. Negley. Then that is another count. Now as to this last reason, he says he desires to keep the election of judges of the court of appeals away from politics. What is your government? What are the executive, legislative, and judicial departments of your government? Do they not all pertain to politics? The very name of politics embraces the executive, legislative, and judicial departments of any government. It is a part of the business of the public, as the derivation of the word signifies You cannot separate the judicial department of the government from politics You cannot make it something outside and disconnected with it. There is a common principle connecting the judicial, executive, and legislative forms of all governments, and you cannot separate the judicial department. It is a manifestation of the same general principle in one direction; a manifestation of the national mind. What is government? The national mind. The form of government is the form in which the national mind shows itself to the world It shows itself to the world in three distinct forms; but the underlying, the life-giving principle is the same. The idea of separating the judicial department of the government from politics, from the government, is absurd.

I think if we do elect the court of appeals in Maryland by districts, it is the only State in which it is done. In Pennsylvania, in New York, and in all the States, they are elected by general ticket; and why? Because they are the representatives not of a particular district or division of the State, but of the entire State; just as much so as the governor is the representative of the entire State, in the executive department. The court of appeals represents the entire State in the judicial department, just as much as the governor represents the entire State in the executive department. Therefore strictly, and on principle, it is altogether right to elect by general ticket; and it would be wrong, and violate a principle to elect the judges of the court of appeals upon any other system than general ticket; because they are the representatives of the entire people of the State, and as I said the other day, in the beginning of the debate, the man on the top of the Alleganies has just as much interest in the selection of a competent man for the position of judge of the court of appeals, as the man who lives in the extremest corner of Worcester. They are upon a common platform and a common basis, in that these men administer the entire judicial forms of the entire State.

It is different in regard to the district courts; because when you cut up the State into judicial districts, for district purposes, then I, in Washington county, have no right to have anything to say in the selection of the judge in Prince George's county, because I have no interest in the decisions which he may make. Neither has the gentleman from Prince George's any interest, or any right to claim any interest in the selection of the judge who is to preside within the district of Washington or Allegany county. It is therefore altogether right that the people of the several districts should select the district judges, on principle, because they are their representatives in the judicial department of their section of the State, and their jurisdiction extends only to the limits of the district. In the districts the voting power extends just as far as the jurisdiction of the court extends. Why not apply the same principle to the State? Why should not the voting power, in the selection of judges of the court of appeals, be coextensive with the judicial power of the men selected?

I say therefore, strictly on principle, that if you select the judges of the court of appeals in any other way than by general ticket, you violate a principle; and there is no question about it. We do the same thing in electing a governor from the separate gubernatorial districts. The State is divided into three districts, in order to let men from each portion of the State have a chance to fill the gubernatorial chair; and it is done only with that view. It is only that the honors may be distributed to the eminent and fit men in each portion of the State. It is exactly upon that principle that I would be in favor of taking these judges of the court of appeals from the five different districts, one from each, that the judicial honors of the State may be distributed among the people generally, so far as it can be done. The men being equally fit, I think it is the only correct way; and that is the only reason why we require any selection from different districts. The particular reason is that the judicial honors of the State may be distributed among the five different judicial districts of the State. It is for the purpose of letting all have a fair chance to attain this judicial position.

As regards their nomination, you cannot help it. I know we have had two elections of members of the court of appeals under the present constitution in our district, and they were both nominated; and there was quite a fight over the second nomination, I know; and there was quite a quarrel over the first. They must be nominated either by the district or by the State; and I think it is better that they should be nominated by a State convention. All the quarrels of the parties of the district from which they are to be selected will be adjusted by the balance of the State not implicated in them; and they will therefore be more likely to take a proper man. I am decidedly in favor of the amendment.

Mr. PETER. I suppose as to the object to be attained in the selection of the court of appeals, there can be no difference in this convention. Our object is to secure an unbiased court, which will render to every man the law as it stands; a court which shall try causes, not according to political bias, but which shall mete out justice according to the law and the evidence. This is the object to be attained.

I think none of us can doubt that the court of appeals, differing politically, as they would more probably differ, elected by districts, would be more likely to mete out justice, than a court selected by the whole and entire State, which would be of one political opinion. If we could attribute any bias to the mind of the court, from politics, that bias would certainly be more likely to arise in a court entirely of one political complexion, than in one differing in political views.

Therefore we might presume it to be a natural consequence, if the State be divided into judicial districts, and if a judge be elected from each judicial district, that there would be some difference of politics upon the bench; but if the election be by the entire State, as gentlemen here would have it, we may say with almost entire certainty that if one of the judges upon a ticket shall be elected, that entire ticket will be elected. Therefore if our object be to attain that purity upon the bench, that circumspection and examination which should dwell with these keepers of the law, and of the rights of the people, we should use the means likely to produce this effect.

If there be different political parties in the State, why not intermingle them upon this bench, that they may watch one over the other? Suppose a case arises upon the political subjects of the day; for under the law now we very often have political subjects before the court. The court being elected by the entire State is, as I argued before, of one political party; and there is no person in that court to represent the other political party.—Whatever the rights of the person of the other political party may be, there would be no person to represent him; and the decision of one would undoubtedly be the decision of the entire court.

The gentleman from Washington county (Mr. Negley) argued that as the State was divided into three gubernatorial districts, why not let each district elect a governor?—For the simple reason that there is but one governor for the State. If we were to have three governors, I certainly should insist that the governors should be selected by the people of each gubernatorial district separately, and not from the entire State. The gentleman's argument as to that point, I may say is an impossibility; because during the term of any one governor, the other two-thirds of the State would be unrepresented. The idea in having one governor is that the entire State may be represented.

The gentleman from Washington argues further that separating the court of appeals from politics is absurd. Has the day arrived in the State of Maryland when it has become an absurdity to separate a court from political bias? I think the universal wish of the people of Maryland should be that the court should be placed as far as possible above all political bias; that it should not cringe or bow to person or party; that it should hold its balance equal in its hands unmoved by any personal or political influences which may be brought to bear upon it, and look only to the law and the evidence as it exists in the case. I have always believed, and I have always thought that the opinion of the people of Maryland was, that courts should be governed and ruled by the law and by the testimony, and not by political bias.

The gentleman tells me that politics reflects the feelings and opinions of the nation. Do we not find politics one day running in this direction, and the next day in that? If the court is unbiased, let it hold that intermediate position, that it may not be swayed either this way or that by its influence.

The gentleman from Washington says again that the court of appeals represents the entire State, and therefore should be elected as an entirety. As the gentleman from Somerset, I think argued, let us suppose a case, of a nomination in the district in which Allegany county is. We will suppose that two candidates are nominated in that district, there being two political parties. Might it not be possible—aye, is it not probable, that one of the existing political parties will have some jurist whose attainments and whose integrity, whose fitness for the office towers above that of the candidate of the other party? I do not say, nor will I pretend to say, that the party to which I claim to belong, have men in it who are superior to those of the other party; but is it not probable that such a case would arise? Then I ask the gentleman what I would know about their integrity or capacity? Although in his judicial district the vote might be overwhelming in favor of the man whose judicial attainments and integrity towered above those of the other, perchance the political majority of Baltimore city or of the rest of the State would more than counterbalance that majority which his legal attainments and his integrity known at home would give him there. The consequence would be that the man representing the strongest political party in the State would be elected, although less qualified, over the man well known at home to be far better qualified.

The gentleman argues that the circuit courts are right in themselves; that it is right that those judges should be elected in the circuits, for the reason that they merely represent the interests of these circuits. I do not know how it may be with the rest of the circuits of this State; but I unhesitatingly say that the docket of our court may be examined at any time, and during my practice there, not of very long duration, six or seven years, it will be found that in the majority of cases upon that docket the parties have been strangers in that circuit. His argument therefore is not good. There are many cases upon our docket from the city of Baltimore, many from Washington county, many from Allegany county, and many from other counties in the State.—Therefore, according to his idea, if you were to carry it out, if all the parties who have the right to come there and institute suits in our circuit court ought to have a voice in the election, our circuit judges ought to be elected by the people of the entire State; for the cases that come up there represent the different parts of the State almost as much as the cases before the court of appeals. His argument then will not hold good in that respect.

Therefore, Mr. President, I think it would be doing great injustice to the people of the judicial district to take from them the selection of a man known to them, a man whose integrity and legal attainments would fit him for an office so high, because we almost always look to the court of appeals as the highest officers of the State. I, for one, although it has been carried in this convention, shall ever be opposed to a court which shall occupy so high a position, being selected by political conventions. My opinion is that that court, should not only be above political bias and political influences, but be above all influences whatever, save and except the law; that the law alone should govern and rule the mind of the court. As this convention has decided otherwise, let us use the means which will give to us as pure and as honest a court as we can get.

Mr. MILLER. One word with reference to an assertion made here to the convention respecting the election by general ticket of these supreme judicial officers in other States. It has been asserted that that is the universal doctrine practiced by all the other States of the Union. That is not the fact. In the great States of Illinois and Indiana, two of the great northwestern States, the supreme court is divided into districts, and the electors of the several districts vote for them in these several districts only. So it is in Kentucky; and so it is in Oregon. How it may be in other States I do not know; having only examined a few. It is not therefore the prevailing opinion of the people who are most experienced in an elective judiciary, that they should be elected by general ticket.

I think it is best to keep out of politics the election of these judicial officers. Under our present constitution, when the election of judges was first thrown before the people in our judicial district, two gentlemen of high standing, both belonging to the same political party, came out as independent candidates for that office, recommended by their friends. I hope it may continue to be so in other districts of the State. Chanceller Johnson was one of the candidates, and the gentleman who was elected, Judge Tuck, was the other. They both belonged to the same political party, and both received votes from each of the two parties. I trust that the nomination of judges never will be made a political matter. If it is, I have great fears that the judicial department of the government, the most important of all, will degenerate into the same state that some of the other departments of the government have degenerated into.

Mr. NEGLEY. Will the gentleman allow me to ask him one question? Did any President of the United States ever appoint a judge of the supreme court from any political party but his own?

Mr. MILLER. No sir; I do not know that he did.

Mr. NEGLEY. Did you ever know a State governor to recommend to the legislature when he had the power to appoint, any judge except of his own party?

Mr. MILLER. I am not upon the question of appointment or election. Yes; in our own State, Governor Hicks appointed a gentleman of the opposite political party from his own; and Governor Thomas did the same thing.

Mr. JONES, of Somerset. I will state that not only did Governor Hicks appoint him, but when the time came for a new election, both parties concurred and elected Judge Carmichael without opposition. Judge Barton also was appointed by a political opponent.

The question being on the adoption of the amendment of Mr. THRUSTON to the amendment of Mr. DENT;

Mr. STIRLING demanded the yeas and nays, and they were ordered.

The question being taken, the result was—yeas 39; nays 30—as follows:

Yeas—Messrs. Annan, Audoun, Barron, Brooks, Cunningham, Cushing, Daniel, Davis, of Washington, Ecker, Galloway, Hatch, Hebb, Hopkins, Hopper, Jones, of Cecil, Keefer, Kennard, Markey, Mayhugh, McComas, Mullikin, Murray, Negley, Parker, Pugh, Purnell, Robinette, Russell, Sands, Schley, Schlosser, Smith, of Carroll, Smith, of Worcester, Stirling, Stockbridge, Sykes, Thruston, Wickard, Wooden—39.

Nays—Messrs. Abbott, Berry, of Prince George's, Billingsley, Blackiston, Brown, Chambers, Crawford, Davis, of Charles, Dennis, Dent, Duvall, Earle, Edelen, Gale, Horsey, Jones, of Somerset, King, Lansdale, Lee, Marbury, Mitchell, Miller, Morgan, Parran, Peter, Smith, of Dorchester, Swope, Thomas, Todd, Turner—30.

When their names were called,

Mr. ABBOTT said: Much preferring the system proposed by my colleague (Mr. Thomas,) to divide the State into four judicial districts, and to elect the chief justice by general ticket, I vote "no."

Mr. KING said: For the reason assigned by the gentleman from Baltimore city, preferring Mr. Thomas's amendment, I vote "no."

The amendment to the amendment was accordingly agreed to.

On motion of Mr. GALE, on division—ayes 35, noes 26—

The convention took a recess until 8 o'clock, P. M.

EVENING SESSION.

The convention met at 8 o'clock, P. M.

The roll was called, and the following members answered to their names:

Messrs. Goldsborough, President; Abbott, Annan, Audoun, Berry, of Prince George's, Billingsley, Blackiston, Brown, Carter, Chambers, Clarke, Crawford, Cunninghan, Cushing, Daniel, Davis, of Washington, Dent, Duvall, Earle, Ecker, Edelen, Gale, Galloway, Harwood, Hebb, Hodson, Hoffman, Hopkins, Hopper, Horsey, Jones, of Somerset, Keefer, Kennard, King, Lansdale, Lee, Marbury, Markey, Mayhugh, McComas, Mitchell, Miller, Morgan, Mullikin, Murray, Negley, Nyman Parker, Parran, Pugh, Purnell, Robinette, Russell, Sands, Schley, Schlosser, Smith, of

Carroll, Smith, of Worcester, Stirling, Stockbridge, Swope, Sykes, Todd, Turner—64.

On motion of Mr. ECKER,

It was ordered to be entered upon the journal, that Mr. Wooden is detained from his seat, having been unexpectedly called away on important business.

Mr. DAVIS, of Washington, asked and obtained leave to absent himself from the sessions of the convention for a few days.

ELECTION OF COURT OF APPEALS.

The convention resumed the consideration of the report of the committee on the judiciary department; the twelfth section being upon its second reading as amended as follows:

Sec. 12. The court of appeals shall consist of a chief justice and four associate justices, and for their selection the State shall be divided into five judicial dirtricts as follows, viz: Worcester, Somerset, Dorchester, Talbot, Caroline, Queen Anne, Kent and Cecil counties, shall compose the first district; Harford and Baltimore counties, and the first seven wards of Baltimore city, shall compose the second district; Baltimore city, except the first seven wards, shall compose the third district; Allegany, Washington, Frederick, Howard and Carroll counties, shall compose the fourth district; St. Mary's, Charles, Anne Arundel, Calvert, Prince George's and Montgomery counties, shall compose the fifth district; and one of the judges of the court of appeals shall be elected from each of said districts.

The pending question was upon the adoption of the amendment of Mr. DENT, as amended, as follows: to add at the end of the section, "by the qualified voters of the whole State."

Mr. BERRY, of Prince George's. I move to postpone the section informally, as the house is not full, and we may have a full house to-morrow.

The motion was not agreed to.

The question recurred upon the adoption of the amendment as amended.

Mr. BERRY, of Prince George's, demanded the yeas and nays, and they were ordered.

The question being taken, the result was—yeas 34, nays 27—as follows:

Yeas—Messrs. Annan, Carter, Cunningham, Cushing, Daniel, Davis, of Washington, Ecker, Galloway, Hebb, Hopkins, Hopper, Keefer, Kennard, King, Markey, Mayhugh, McComas, Mullikin, Murray, Negley, Nyman, Pugh, Purnell, Robinette, Russell, Sands, Schley, Schlosser, Smith, of Worcester, Stirling, Stockbridge, Swope, Sykes, Todd—34.

Nays—Messrs. Goldsborough, President; Abbott, Audoun, Berry, of Prince George's, Billingsley, Blackiston, Brown, Chambers, Clarke, Crawford, Dent, Duvall, Earle, Edelen, Gale, Hodson, Horsey, Jones, of Somerset, Lansdale, Lee, Marbury, Mitchell, Miller, Morgan, Parran, Smith, of Carroll, Turner—27.

The amendment was accordingly agreed to.

The question recurred upon the adoption of the substitute moved by Mr. THOMAS as follows:

Strike out all after the word "the," in the first line and insert the following:

"The court of appeals shall consist of a chief justice and four associate justices and for their selection the State shall be divided into four judicial districts. Allegany, Washington, ton, Frederick, Carroll, Baltimore and Harford counties, shall compose the first; Montgomery, Howard, Anne Arundel, Calvert, St. Mary's, Charles and Prince George's, the second; Baltimore city, the third; and Cecil, Kent, Queen Anne's, Talbot, Caroline, Dorchester, Somerset and Worcester, shall compose the fourth district; and the chief justice shall be elected by the qualified voters of the counties and the city of Baltimore on a general ticket.

"And one person from among those learned in the law, having been admitted to practice law in this State and who shall have been a citizen of this State at least five years, and above the age of thirty years at the time of his election, and a resident of the judicial district, or if chief justice a resident of the State as herein provided, shall be elected from each of said districts and the State, by the legal and qualified voters therein as a judge of said court of appeals, who shall hold his office for the term of fifteen years from the time of his election or until he shall have attained the age of seventy years, whichever may first happen, and be re-eligible thereto until he shall have attained the age of seventy years, and not after, subject to removal for incompetency, wilful neglect of duty or misbehavior in office, on conviction in a court of law, or by the governor upon the address of the general assembly two thirds of the members of each house concurring in such address, and the salary of each of the judges of the court of appeals, shall be four thousand dollars ($4,000) annually, and shall not to be increased or diminished during their continuance in office, and no fees or perquisites of any kind shall be allowed by law to any of the said judges."

Mr. STOCKBRIDGE. My colleague is not here to-night in his place. I should like to know whether his amendment has any indorser here.

Mr. CLARKE. I have been absent; and I understand that the convention have already adopted a number of general qualifications and rules with reference to the judges of the court of appeals as well as the other courts. Now if in the sections relating to the court of appeals and the circuit judges we are to go again into the questions of qualification, age, removal from office, &c., we shall have first a series of general provisions, and then a series of particular provisions for each court which will take the place of the general provisions.

Mr. SMITH, of Carroll. It strikes me that

this suggestion is entitled to very serious consideration; and I will therefore move that the section be passed over informally until to-morrow. The gentleman who moved this amendment is obliged on account of illness to absent himself, and I think it is just to him as well as to ourselves to postpone it until we can give him an opportunity to be heard upon it. This report will undoubtedly occupy the attention of the convention a long while, so that we can wait without damage to the interests of the State for the gentleman's return.

Mr. DANIEL. I think the proposition has been printed.

The PRESIDENT. No, sir; it is in manuscript.

Mr. DANIEL. Whether it has or not, I see no necessity for passing over it. The main feature of the proposition submitted by the gentleman from Baltimore city (Mr. Thomas,) if I understand it, has twice been before the convention; and that is whether they will elect by districts or by general ticket The proposition of the gentleman brings us right back to the district system with the exception of one judge; and this question was so fully discussed this morning, when we voted upon it twice, that I see no reason for postponing. After the vote was taken I mentioned to my colleague that I supposed the vote taken to-day would destroy his proposition effectually, or pretty much so; and he said he cared very little about it; that he had to go home; that he was sick and should not be back for several days.

Mr SMITH, of Carroll. Whether he cares about it much or little is not the question before us. He has submitted a proposition to the convention, and we are as much interested in that proposition as the gentleman himself. The election of these judges is not to take place, some of them for three years, and others for six or seven years; and there can certainly be no political object in the proposition to elect by general ticket. I take it that the sense of the convention has not yet been taken upon the proposition. It is not to be supposed that judges elected in any manner would be controlled by personal or political feelings. It appears to me that the people in electing their judges decide some of the most momentous questions before them. They have an opportunity to judge of the qualifications and fitness of those for whom they are called to vote. Can a convention assembled from every part of Maryland be as well qualified to determine in regard to the qualifications of men for this office as the delegates from the immediate vicinity in which they live? I think that the gentleman from Allegany ought not to be asked to vote for the candidate coming from Worcester. We can only know their qualifications by making the districts so small that any lawyer of any prominence will be known to all the people, so that they may know who is fit, and whom they are willing to trust. Considering the vital importance of the question, and the fact that the gentleman who proposed the amendment is absent, I think it is but just that we should postpone the section. The system which he proposes is a mixed system; and the sense of the convention has not been taken upon it; nor has the attention of the convention been invited to it. It is a system providing for the election of the chief justice by general ticket, and of the four associate justices from their several districts.

Mr. JONES, of Somerset. I concur most heartily in what has been said by the gentleman from Carroll (Mr. Smith.) This proposition has not been printed upon our journals, and I should like to have an opportunity of considering it very deliberately. It seems to be a sort of compromise proposition, between those who go for election by general ticket, and those who go for election by districts. I concur in all the gentleman from Carroll has said with reference to the importance, if we are to have an elective court of appeals, of electing them from the several districts of the people, where they live, and where the people are best qualified to judge of their qualifications.

I voted with the majority in relation to the elective system, upon what I supposed to be the determination as manifested by the vote of yesterday, to adhere to the system which we now have, which is the system of election of the judges of the court of appeals by districts. But the vote to-day has entirely disappointed me; and I am frank to say that if this is persisted in I shall return and vote for the appointment by the governor. I have conversed with several friends, and found the same view; and we shall go for the appointive system, if the judges are not to be elected by districts. I concur with the gentleman from Carroll in the desire that the section may be postponed informally, that it may be printed, and that we may have an opportunity of seeing the proposition and consulting about it.

Mr. CHAMBERS. I rise simply to do an act of justice to an absent member. I think the gentleman from Baltimore (Mr. Daniel) has mistaken the feelings of his colleague (Mr. Thomas) with regard to this amendment. That gentleman is absent to-night, not from any unwillingness to be in his place, but from sickness. I saw Mr. Thomas after the house adjourned, and I remarked to him that I regretted the vote of the house; and he had high confidence, or seemed to have, that his proposition would be carried. I rose to correct that error, in order to do justice to an absent member.

Mr. ABBOTT. In behalf of my colleague who is now absent (Mr. Thomas,) I will say that I had some conversation with him with regard to this amendment after the adjournment, and he regretted exceedingly that his health was such that he was obliged to go home; and he expressed a strong desire that this proposition should receive the attention of the house, and be carefully considered. I for one hope it will be postponed. It is worthy of consideration by the house; and I think it is a proposition, that when it is examined will be found to be a proper one. It combines both the ideas that have been proposed for the present section, providing for the election of a chief justice by a general ticket, and of the associate justices by the different sections of the State. I am sure that no gentleman here desires to alienate the feelings of one part of the State against another by selecting all the officers from one section of the State, as might be the case.

Mr. CLARKE. I was not here during the debate upon the general question of the appointment of judges by the executive or their election by the people. It is evident that there is a very great diversity of opinion upon this question when we come to reach the details of it. By the vote taken yesterday it appeared that there was a large majority of the house in favor of an elective judiciary, provided that elective judiciary would be so organized that the State would be districted, and the people of the districts might have an opportunity of choosing their own judges; the result of which would be that the political complexion of the court would not be determined by a vote upon general ticket; but there might be in one district a judge elected of one political party, and in another district a judge elected of a different political party; the result of which would be to deprive the court of appeals of anything like a political bearing.

We have voted to adopt the elective system. We have followed that up by a vote which determines that the court of appeals shall be elected by general ticket. What will be the result? Simply this: that the nominating State convention will determine who are to be the candidates of their political party. That will determine the entire court; and the result will be that the entire court of appeals will become a mere political machine or political body. If you district the State, and have one judge of one class of political sentiments, and another judge of a different class of political sentiments, there will be no such political agreement on the part of the court of appeals.

Mr. HEBB (interposing.) I rise to a question of order; whether it is in order to discuss the merits of a question, upon a motion to postpone.

Mr. CLARKE. I am not discussing the merits of the question, but the operation of the different propositions to combat the view taken that this question has been already settled. The propositions have been presented in various forms and various phases; and the proposition is now presented in such a form before this body, as to convert, in my judgment the court of appeals into a mere expression of the political sentiments of a party.

Mr. STIRLING. The gentleman is not in order. He is arguing against what the house has done.

The PRESIDENT. The question is upon the propriety of postponement.

Mr. CLARKE. I am just coming to that. I say that is the result. Now there is another proposition, to change the character of the organization of the court of appeals, providing that the chief justice shall be elected by the whole State; to a certain extent changing the character of the court, by having one elected by general ticket instead of by the bench, and coming back to the district system to a certain extent. Inasmuch as the desire of the house seemed yesterday to be in favor of an elective system, and now the character of this organization is such that it will convert it into a political machine, the gentleman from Somerset (Mr. Jones) and probably other gentlemen may desire either to adopt the proposition of the gentleman from Baltimore city (Mr. Thomas) or to reconsider the proposition by which the house determined to have an elective judiciary instead of having them appointed. I believe the views of gentlemen have changed upon the question of appointment, and I should like to see the question raised again.

Mr. SANDS. I think nothing will be lost in passing this section for the present. As to gentlemen changing their views from the appointive system to the elective, and from the elective back to the appointive, from political motives and considerations, I suppose that is a game that may be played at by both sides of the house.

Mr. CLARKE. I hope the gentleman did not understand me as saying that gentlemen proposed to change their views from political considerations.

Mr. SANDS. What I understood from the remarks of the gentleman from Prince George's was this: that many who started for the appointive system became converts to the elective, and would modify their opinions under some new state of affairs, and become willing to turn back to the appointive system. I am satisfied, myself, that they shall have either one or the other; because if they are going to turn it into a political machine, that matter cuts both ways. I concur very heartily in the suggestion to postpone this.

Mr. DANIEL. I wish simply to say in explanation of what has been stated with reference to my colleague from Baltimore city (Mr. Thomas,) that the casual remark which fell from me will not operate at all upon my vote upon this subject, nor do I wish the convention to be influenced by it. I would just as cheerfully vote for postponing it, had the remark not been made. But the remarks that have been made by every gentleman who has advocated the postponement, show that that it is the very same ground which was discussed over and over, and over again this morning, which was the propriety of electing by districts, and not by general ticket. That seems to be the main proposition embraced here; and I think we are just as well prepared to settle it to-night as at any other time.

The question being taken upon the motion to postpone the 12th section informally, it was agreed to—ayes 40, noes not counted.

Mr. BERRY, of Prince George's, gave notice that when the section was again considered, he would submit the following amendment:

Strike out the words in the amendment "for the period of fifteen years," and insert "for life, or until they shall arrive at the age of sixty years."

The next section was read as follows:

"Sec. 13. The court of appeals shall hold its sessions in the city of Annapolis, on the first Monday in April, and the first Monday in October, in each and every year, or at such other times as the general assembly may by law direct, and it shall be competent for the judges of said court, sufficient cause appearing to them, temporarily to transfer their sittings elsewhere."

No amendment was offered.

JURISDICTION OF COURT OF APPEALS.

The next section was read as follows:

"Sec. 14. The jurisdiction of the court of appeals shall be coextensive with the limits of the State, and such as now is or may hereafter be prescribed for it by law, and its sessions shall continue for not less than ten months in the year, if the business before it shall so require."

Mr. MILLER. I wish to ask the chairman of the committee what is meant by the provision "such as now is or may hereafter be prescribed for it by law?" The court of appeals under the present constitution has appellate jurisdiction only; and it is impossible for the legislature to confer upon it anything except appellant jurisdiction. But if this constitution is adopted it does away with the old constitution entirely, under which the court of appeals now has its entire jurisdiction. What jurisdiction then would be referred to by the words "such as now is or may hereafter be prescribed for it by law?"

Mr. STOCKBRIDGE. As the gentleman is well aware, we have several acts of assembly in our code, referring to the jurisdiction of the court of appeals. It was designed to sum the whole up in one expression, to avoid a very long definition It is true it is entirely appellant; but at the same time the jurisdiction has some limitations or definitions; as on the 23d, 25th, 27th, and various other pages of the first volume of the code.

Mr. MILLER. These are provisions regulating the mode of appeals simply.

Mr. STOCKBRIDGE. Saying who may appeal, and in what cases the court shall have jurisdiction.

Mr. MILLER. But by virtue of the provisions of the present code, it is appellate jurisdiction only. The provision is: "The court of appeals shall have appellate jurisdiction only, which shall be coextensive with the limits of the State." But by adopting the present constitution we repeal that; and it seems to me that it would be proper to say in this constitution that the court of appeals shall have appellate jurisdiction only, and then it may be subject to all laws applicable to the new court of appeals as well as to the old.

Mr. STOCKBRIDGE. It makes very little difference what the committee or anybody else, understands by this section. It should be so plain as to be understood by anybody of ordinary capacity; and if it is not so plain, I hope the gentleman will make it so by an amendment. There may be one or two instances, as in cases of *habeas corpus*, where the court of appeals have entertained jurisdiction not appellate.

Mr. MILLER. That was by virtue of their being judges, and not as a court.

Mr. STOCKBRIDGE. Precisely; and if there be any jurisdiction of that sort, they will still have it under this provision; but not otherwise. Still I should like to hear the gentleman's amendment.

Mr. MILLER submitted the following amendment:

Strike out down to the word "and," in the third line, and insert "the court of appeals shall have appellate jurisdiction only, which shall be coextensive with the limits of the State."

The amendment was rejected.

No further amendment was offered.

The next section was read as follows:

"Sec. 15. Any three of the judges of the court of appeals may constitute a quorum, but no cause shall be decided without the concurrence of at least three judges in the decision, and in every case decided, an opinion in writing shall be filed within six months after the argument or submission of the cause, and the judgment of the court shall be final and conclusive."

No amendment was offered.

SALARY OF JUSTICES.

The next section was read as follows:

"Sec. 16. The salary of the justices of the court of appeals shall be four thousand dollars each per annum, payable quarterly."

Mr. MARBURY moved to strike out "four" and insert "five."

Mr. DAVIS, of Washington, moved to strike out "four" and insert "three."

The amendment submitted by Mr. MARBURY was rejected.

Mr. GALLOWAY demanded the yeas and nays on the amendment to reduce the salary to $3,000; and they were ordered.

The question being taken, the result was—yeas 36, nays 25—as follows:

Yeas—Messrs. Goldsborough, President; Annan, Audoun, Billingsley, Brown, Carter, Cunningham, Davis, of Washington, Duvall, Ecker, Edelen, Galloway, Hopper, Horsey, Keefer, King, Lee, Markey, Mayhugh, McComas, Mitchell, Mullikin, Murray, Negley, Nyman, Parran, Purnell, Robinette, Russell, Sands, Schlosser, Smith, of Worcester, Swope, Sykes, Todd, Turner—36.

Nays—Messrs. Abbott, Berry, of Prince George's, Blackiston, Chambers, Clarke, Crawford, Daniel, Dent, Earle, Harwood, Hebb, Hodson, Hopkins, Jones, of Somerset Kennard, Lansdale, Marbury, Miller, Morgan, Parker, Pugh, Schley, Smith, of Carroll, Stirling, Stockbridge—25.

The amendment was accordingly adopted.

No further amendment was offered.

PUBLICATION OF REPORTS.

The next section was read as follows:

"Sec. 17. Provision shall be made by law for publishing reports of all causes argued and determined in the court of appeals."

Mr. MILLER submitted the following amendment:

Add to the end of the section the words "which the judges shall designate as proper for publication."

Mr. MILLER said: The language of this section departs from that of the old constitution in requiring the reports of *all* causes argued and determined in the court of appeals to be published. It is well known that the object of the publication is for the information of members of the bar and the profession generally. If all causes are to be published, the volumes of reports will accumulate so that in a few years we shall have a library of our own reports. The publication of reports of all causes argued, it seems to me, would be very absurd, because frequently cases come up in the court of appeals, generally equity cases, where the judges decide simply upon questions of fact, deciding no matter of law which would be of any interest to the profession, which could not be cited as a precedent in any other case, unless another case should arise with facts precisely similar. Under the amendment I offer, the judges can designate such cases as are proper for publication. They ought to be the best judges of that. The volumes of reports will then contain only the leading cases, principles of law, and new doctrines or new decisions made upon important points. In reporting every case we should have two or three volumes where we have perhaps one now, reporting every case, and spreading the facts upon the record.

Mr. SANDS. I really think the amendment is one that ought to meet the approbation of the convention. Of course there is something to be regarded in the mere matter of cost to the State, in the printing and publishing of these reports. I think the gentleman is entirely correct in his view that the reports should not be cumbered with unnecessary matter.

Mr. STIRLING. It seems to me that the suggestion is a very proper one; but I do not know how it will affect the State reporter. I suppose he would get more money for reporting all the cases than for reporting a part; and you might so cut down the duties of his office that it would not pay a competent man to take it. But I do not exactly see the necessity of saying anything about it in the constitution. There is nothing in the old constitution about it.

Mr. MILLER. Yes, sir; in the second section.

The amendment was adopted.

No further amendment was offered.

The next section was read as follows:

"Sec. 18. The court of appeals shall appoint its own clerk, who shall hold his office for six years, and may be reappointed at the end thereof; he shall be subject to removal by the said court for incompetency, neglect of duty, misdemeanor in office, or such other cause or causes as may be prescribed by law."

No amendment was offered.

The next section was read as follows:

PART III.

Circuit Court.

"Sec. 19. The State shall be divided into eight judicial circuits, in manner following: The counties of St. Mary's, Charles and Prince George's shall constitute the first circuit. The counties of Calvert, Anne Arundel and Montgomery, the second. The counties of Allegany, Washington and Frederick, the third. The counties of Baltimore, Howard and Carroll, the fourth. The counties of Harford, Cecil and Kent, the fifth. The counties of Queen Anne's, Talbot and Caroline, the sixth. The counties of Dorchester, Somerset and Worcester, the seventh. And the city of Baltimore, the eighth."

Mr. HEBB submitted the following amendment:

Sec. 19. Strike out all after the word "the," in the first line, and insert:

"State shall be divided into twelve judicial circuits, in manner following: The counties of St. Mary's, Charles and Prince George's shall constitute the first circuit; the counties of Anne Arundel Calvert and Montgomery, the second; the county of Frederick, the third; the county of Washington, the fourth; the county of Allegany, the fifth; the counties of Carroll and Howard, the sixth; the county of Baltimore, the seventh; the counties of Harford and Cecil, the eighth; the counties of Kent, Queen Anne's and Talbot, the ninth; the counties of Caroline and Dorchester, the tenth; the counties of Somerset and Worcester the eleventh; and the city of Baltimore, the twelfth."

Mr. HEBB said: I will state that if this amendment should be adopted, dividing the State into twelve judicial districts, instead of eight, I shall offer another providing one judge for each circuit, making twelve judges. The system reported requires twenty-two judges—three for each of the seven circuits—and one for the eighth circuit. My object is to have one judge in each circuit instead of three.

Mr. KING. Would it not be better to pass over this section informally until we come to the 21st, to know whether we shall have one judge in each circuit, or three? I make that motion.

The motion to pass over the section informally was agreed to.

Mr. CLARKE. I will offer a proposition when it shall be in order, to test the sense of the convention upon the question whether there shall be a judge for each county in the State.

The next section was read as follows:

"Sec. 20. In each of the above named circuits, except the eighth, there shall be three courts, one to be held in each county; they shall be called circuit courts for the county in which they may be held, and shall have and exercise all the power, authority, and jurisdiction, original and appellate, which the present circuit courts of this State now have and exercise, or which may hereafter be prescribed by law."

Mr. AUDOUN moved to strike out "three" in the second line, and insert "one."

Mr. HEBB submitted the following amendment:

Strike out the section and insert:

"Sec 20. One court shall be held in each county of the State; the said courts shall be called circuit courts for the county in which they may be held, and shall have and exercise all the power, authority and jurisdiction, original and appellate, which the present circuit courts of this State now have and exercise, or which may hereafter be prescribed by law."

Mr. SANDS. I do not see how we can properly act upon this until we have decided whether we shall have three judges to a circuit, or whether we shall have three counties to a circuit, or one county in some cases, two counties in others, and three in others, as proposed by the substitute of the gentleman from Allegany (Mr. Hebb.) I move to pass over the twentieth and twenty-first sections informally.

Mr. STIRLING. It seems to me if we are going to do that, we might as well pass over all of it; we shall have to meet the question somewhere.

Mr. SANDS. I will withdraw the motion, if we can have the question at once.

Mr. STIRLING. The whole report will have to be recast; and if the house come to some conclusion upon this point, the committee can more readily revise it. This whole part was very carefully drawn for a three judge system, and it is now proposed to have a one-judge system.

Mr. AUDOUN withdrew his amendment.

The question recurred upon Mr. HEBB'S amendment.

Mr. BERRY, of Prince George's. Does that mean that only one term of the court shall be held in each county of the State?

Mr. SANDS. Certainly not.

Mr. STOCKBRIDGE. The twenty-first section provides for that.

This amendment, I think, brings before the convention fairly the question of the system of circuit courts they may choose to adopt. As such I am very glad it has been offered. This is perhaps as good a time to decide that question as any As there have been several indications on different sides that this report has not been read or considered in its entirety, but only in its separate parts, I wish to say a word with reference to the system, as a system, that is reported.

There have been a variety of amendments offered, not systematized at all, not fitting the one into the others, and several of them adopted, sufficient to make it clear that we are not to have a judicial system at all, but a thing of shreds and patches, a little of this and a little of that.

The effort of the committee at which they worked a long time, was to digest and prepare a system; and they settled two or three cardinal principles, and fitted every detail to these principles.

There is a necessity for four different kinds of jurisdiction in the State, aside from the court of appeals; that is, the ordinary common law, civil jurisdiction, criminal jurisdiction, equity jurisdiction, and the jurisdiction of the estate of deceased persons.

The effect and design of this system was to cover the whole ground, to form a system which should give sufficient force to meet the wants of the people in all these departments, which should give no more than was necessary, which should be at all times accessible, and which should be able to render justice promptly to all suitors.

The system which has prevailed for the last fifteen years in the State has been a circuit court system, with but one judge upon the bench in any place. That system has some advantages; the chief one being its very great economy, there being but one judge over sometimes one county, and sometimes two or more. But there has been this practical difficulty, that the judges have been overworked in almost every instance, and in many instances they have not been at all times accessible for the discharge of what are called the chamber duties of the court in the discharge of equity business. When engaged in business in a different part of the circuit, if an injunction were needed, or any equity business, it was an impossibility to procure a judge. Men have ridden fifty, sixty or one hundred miles, in an inclement season, over roads which were almost impassable, then to find that the judge had gone to another part of his circuit. It has been a denial of justice in many of the counties of the State. I appeal to the experience of gentlemen on all sides of the convention, if this has not been the case, to a greater or less extent, in all the counties. In most of them the ordinary civil business has greatly accumulated. I hardly think I should exaggerate if I should say that in all of them the equity business has greatly accumulated, and is undone.

Another difficulty which has been experienced has been that under the system which has prevailed, worthy, and excellent, and well-meaning men have been elected to fill the judgeship in the various orphans' courts, in utter ignorance of the testamentary law of the State and of the general princples of common law as applicable to them. What has been the result? They have administered the law, as they have said, upon the plain principles of common sense; but although the unwritten law and the statute law are of course consonant with common sense, yet in the imperfection of human reason, it has sometimes unfortunately happened, that the common sense of the judges has not accorded with the common sense of the law.

Again, as under that system the real estate of deceased persons could not be interfered with by orphans' courts, estates have remained unsettled. When there was a small amount of real estate; from the trouble of bringing an action in equity, the judge being off in a distant part of his circuit, and coming then but once or twice a year, it has been almost impossible to procure a settlement.

I need not speak of the delays in the discharge of persons arrested for crime. In some instances it has occurred that persons have been confined awaiting trial, longer than would have been the punishment if they had been convicted of the crime for which they were arrested and charged with having committed.

In digesting and preparing a system, the committee strove to remedy, so far as possible, all these defects. For this purpose they decided upon a system of circuits, three counties in each circuit, and three judges to compose a bench. This enabled them to obviate another difficulty which has been at times very serious. When a judge has been disqualified from sitting in a pending case, or unable to sit on account of his health or for any other reason, it was provided that one of the judges should be resident in each county, so that while the judges should sit in the discharge of ordinary *nisi prius* duties as a bench in all the counties, yet during the greater part of the year, one judge would always be at or near the county seat of every county, accessible for the discharge of equity business; and there would be no unnecessary delay on that account.

Then yielding to what seemed to be the desire on all sides, that the entire real estate as well as the personal property might be administered in the orphans' court, this report purposes to add to the jurisdiction of that court concurrent jurisdiction so far as the real estate of deceased persons is concerned with the equity courts; providing that the circuit judge resident in the county should sit as chief judge in the orphans' court, thus securing at all times one judge upon that bench who from education and habits may be presumed to know something of the law of the State. Some of them perhaps would not know as much as they should; but they would be more likely to know something about it than those who had never paid any attention to it at all.

As to the system proposed by the amendment of the gentleman from Allegany, I do not know that I should call it a system, but the plan proposed—it is of course a sufficient deviation to render it an impossibility that the county judge can act as chief judge of the orphans' court; because in some instances he has to sit as judge, and alone at all times, in three or four different counties. With that plan it will be impossible to secure the other end at which the committee aimed, to provide that there shall be a judge for the transaction of equity business accessible in each county; because he can at all times be accessible only in his own county for the discharge of important business.

It is of course for the convention to select between these plans. So far as the compensation of the judges is concerned, the amount which the State will pay for salaries upon the plan or project of the gentleman from Allegany has an advantage over that of the committee. I think if this State is not already surfeited with cheap justice, they have but to adopt this plan, and in a little while they will become so. I thought they had become satisfied that cheap justice like cheap law, and cheap medicine, was in the end a very dear article. I know that by dispensing cheap justice, suitors have lost more in a single suit, than the entire difference of expense between these two plans for a single year. That is for gentlemen to consider. I am satisfied that under the system as proposed by the committee, justice can be administered with a promptness, a certainty, and an accuracy, such as it never can do under the other system. Of course the convention will decide whether the expense is too much to pay for it. I do not think it is.

Mr. STIRLING. My colleague has very well explained the principles of this report. There is no doubt that it is a general principle which the convention are as competent to decide now as at any other time. I agree with him in nearly everything he has said; although I do not agree with him precisely, for this reason. I had made up my mind to accept the report of the committee. I thought that the committee having investigated and digested a plan, it would be much easier to take the system substantially as they had adopted it, so far as its general principles are concerned. I would not have bound myself to all its details. But the convention has absolutely modified that principle. The system proposed in this report is a system of three judges, going back to the plan before the present constitution, when the judges were appointed by the governor during good behavior. The convention has determined that its judges shall be elected, while I was perfectly willing, so far as my individual opinions were concerned, to vote for the three-judge system as proposed in this report, I cannot agree to vote for three judges according to this plan, to be elected by the people. It will run the elective system into the ground, to cause such a large number of judges that it will positively bring the judicial office directly into politics. It will offer so many offices to the competition of members of the bar, that there will be constant elections of judges from among them. I do not believe it is worth while to incur the expense of a three-judge system, to be chosen in the mode in which the convention have determined to choose them. I am not willing to incur the expense of this system, the judges being elected under the present system. I think the result will be that we shall not be able to come to any conclusion if we attempt to perfect such a system. It seems to me that all the convention can do now is to adopt and modify the system of the present constitution.

It requires some modification because it works some injustice. There are some circuits in this State in which it is absolutely impossible to transact their business. I think if my friend from Baltimore county were present at this time, he could give some practical experience how the matter works there. In the circuit composed of Baltimore, Howard and Cecil counties, there is an absolute denial of justice. It is impossible for suitors to get their suits tried; for no mortal man can discharge the duties of these three counties. Baltimore county alone has business enough before its court to test the capacity of any single man. I am satisfied from what I know of the practice in some of the other counties of the State that there are one or two other counties which have business enough for a single judge.

I should prefer, as the matter now stands, that we should have a one-judge system, and so reduce the larger districts that business may be transacted by one judge. I do not see that we can do anything else. There is no doubt that there will be great difficulty about the expense of the other system. I do not consider it too much to pay, but other members of the convention will consider it too much to pay. I shall be disposed to vote for the proposition of the gentleman from Allegany substantially, because it does remedy the practical difficulties by diminishing the size of the circuits, while it keeps the one-judge system in operation.

Mr. Jones, of Somerset. I do not know whether the chairman of the committee (Mr. Stockbridge) adverted to the fact that the one-judge system necessitates the employment of special judges to a very great extent; and I question whether, if the account were strictly kept of all the employment of special judges, the expense would not be found sufficient to employ at least one additional judge; and whether it is not worthy of consideration that in the three-judge system you have a far greater certainty of having a judge whose regular business it is to hold courts, who has been regularly appointed or elected and commissioned to that office, to hold a court, and need not resort to special judges in so many cases. I think one of the principal reasons for resorting to the three-judge system is the frequent necessity for resorting to special judges and the expense attending it.

The other consideration is important also, that in many of the districts the distance of the judge from some portions of the district is such that it is impracticable to reach him, which amounts to a practical denial of justice, especially in cases of injunction. I have had myself in urgent cases to ride fifty miles in the winter season by a private conveyance to find a judge to get an injunction, and if he had happened to be away from home I should have had my whole trip for naught. I have ridden fifty miles and back, making one hundred miles, and in other parts of the district they would have to ride seventy or eighty miles. This is an inconvenience.

I do not think the additional expense at all is to be compared to the additional convenience afforded to the people. Where there are two or three judges it would certainly avoid the delay. In Baltimore county they could divide the business between the three judges, one hearing appeals, another criminal matters, and the third equity matters, for instance; and they could all be together to hear cases tried at common law before juries. I submit that I think it will be very great economy ultimately, as well as a very great convenience to the people, to adopt the three-judge system.

Mr. Audoun. My friend opposed the amendment offered by the gentleman from Allegany county, because it does not provide for one learned in the law, for the orphans' court. If he will turn to page 446 of the journal, he will find a section offered by

Mr. Thomas, which does provide for one learned in the law upon the bench of the orphans' court. I think that will obviate the difficulty named by my friend. The provision is this:

"Section 24. The qualified voters of the city of Baltimore and of the several counties of the State shall on Tuesday next after the first Monday in the month of November, 1867, and on the same day in the same month in every fourth year thereafter elect three men to be judges of the orphans' court of said city and counties respectively, one of whom shall have been admitted to practice law in this State for at least five years before his election, and who shall be the chief justice of the orphans' court, and who shall be citizens of the State of Maryland and citizens of the city or county for which they may be severally elected at the time of their election, and each of said judges shall be paid an annual salary of fifteen hundred dollars, except the chief justice, who shall receive an annual salary of two thousand dollars, and which shall be paid by the said counties and city respectively."

Mr. STOCKBRIDGE. I do not think it will by any means insure its having one learned in the law, if he is simply to have been admitted to practice law for five years, and if he is to hold the office for a salary of $2,000.

Mr. CLARKE. I do not see how I can well raise the question before the convention without offering an amendment to that offered by the gentleman from Allegany county (Mr. Hebb,) which I will read to the convention, carrying out the idea I suggested when I was up before. If it shall be adopted it will be necessary to vary several other sections, and I have sketched a plan for this. But really it is impossible, as said by the gentleman from Baltimore city (Mr. Stockbridge,) with the report cut up in the manner in which the convention seems determined to do it, for any gentleman to submit an amendment which contains any idea of any plan or judicial system whatever. A gentleman offers a proposition which is an amendment of a section, and is part of a system, but it is so cut up, and the whole thing is so mixed up that nobody can tell what system we are considering.

There can be no doubt that the present judicial system is imperfect. The people are involved in heavy costs by reason of the impossibility of conducting the business with despatch. Especially is it so with regard to equity business, and so in many cases with regard to getting injunctions. It is a notorious fact that all the equity business is despatched at the end of the common law term. What is the result? Members of the bar are crowded with business; the judge is crowded with business on the common law side of the court, and many orders are drawn and signed by the judge just as he is about to get into his carriage to drive off. I do not mention this as the fault of the judges, but of the system.

The proposition which I have to offer differs very little from that which is here reported by the committee, but it is varied a little, as I thought it would tend more speedily to despatch the equity business of the various counties. Upon this question I really think the convention ought to take some other than a mere dollar and cent view of it. It is the great question of dispensing justice to the people of the State. It is the great question whether or not your courts are to be a mere place for parties to become involved in, where but few shall have a speedy decision of the merits of their cases, driving the people of the State out of your courts to settle their cases by arbitration, or to settle them in modes which give up all their rights rather than to be involved in this direction.

We have here attempted to frame a system, believing it would carry out the views of the convention, yet when we come down to this system of dispensing the justice of the State to the people, questions of expense are raised, whether we shall pay $50.000 for one system, or what will be the saving to the people of the State by a different system. But I will not take up the time now with discussion. I will offer the following amendment to the amendment:

"Sec. 20. There shall be a judge for each county in the State, who shall be elected by the legal and qualified voters thereof, from among those learned in the law."

I will simply read the section I have drawn up to show the system with which I propose to follow this up:

"Sec. — There shall be a court in each county in the State; they shall be called equity courts for the county in which they are held. The judge elected for each county shall be the judge of the said court, and shall have and exercise in the county for which he is elected the full and exclusive power, authority and jurisdiction of a court of equity in their said county, with all the chancery powers which the present circuit courts have as courts of equity in the several counties, or which may be hereafter prescribed by laws made pursuant to this constitution, with the right of appeal to the court of appeals, as is now or may be hereafter provided for by law."

The result of this is to have a judge in each county, elected in the county, with chancery powers to despatch the equity business. Instead of having the appeals from magistrates heard only twice a year, they will be disposed of four times a year or oftener by the county judge, disposing of them rapidly, and saving costs in small cases. These small cases have heretofore often consumed in costs more than the amount involved. We have then a judge in each county—that is a chancellor—and hears the appeals from magistrates where the parties desire to appeal to the circuit court of the county.

Then put three adjoining counties into a circuit, and let the three judges constitute the circuit court, with full common law powers and criminal jurisdiction, and thus you bring home to the people a more speedy and rapid settlement of the business, not only of the equity court, but in hearing appeals from magistrates, and all questions of common law or of criminal jurisdiction. Yet it does not increase the number of judges.

Mr. JONES, of Somerset. I merely wish to add to what I have said that it is a maxim of law that it is for the interest of the republic that there should be an end to litigation. I think that the experience of the one-judge system in this State has shown that it tends to multiplicity of appeals, and especially in those districts where the judge is overworked and has to decide without due reflection. In our district the judge has not been overworked. He is an excellent judge, learned in the law and the decisions, remarkably accurate, and in the few appeals which have been taken he has generally been sustained. But in other districts, where the judges have been overworked, where they have done more than could be done accurately, exceptions have been taken and often sustained. The bar would not have that confidence in the decision of one man that they would in the decision of three lawyers of good standing, agreeing upon a point of law; and in the latter case there would be fewer appeals. I think this is worthy of consideration. These appeals cost money to the litigant, and it is for the public interest that they should be as few as possible. I think that consideration is worthy to be taken into view in deciding whether to adopt the three-judge system or the one-judge system.

Mr. HEBB. The reason why I did not put in the section that they should be elected by the people, was that the general provisions pass upon the mode of election, and all the clauses there are applicable to all the judges.

Mr. MILLER. This is one of the gravest subjects we have had under consideration since we have met in convention. The administration of justice in the counties of the State especially is a matter of deep interest to the people of those counties. The system that is proposed by the gentleman from Allegany may work very well for the counties in the western portion of the State. He has there by his system all the benefit of the one judge for the single county. He makes Frederick, Washington and Allegany counties, each to compose a judicial circuit, where one judge is there to administer the law. He is easy of access to every part of the county and can be approached on business matters readily.

But in the other portions of the State, as I caught from the reading of the amendment, a large number of the counties would still be left without a judge—that is, the judge would have to go from one county to another.

I hope that the amendment of the gentleman from Prince George's (Mr. Clarke,) or the report of the committee will be adhered to. The gentleman from Baltimore city, the chairman of the committee (Mr. Stockbridge,) has very ably set forth in his remarks to-night the advantages of the system which he has proposed. So far as our own judicial circuit is concerned we have had a very able and excellent judge upon the bench. But it is true that business has accumulated on his hands, and there are instances of delay, and complaints made by the judge himself, that he is overtasked and overworked. If upon a proper consideration of the expense to the State we should adopt a system by which one judge should be appointed in each county, having equity jurisdiction, and presiding over the orphans' court, we should bring home the administration of justice to the doors of the people of the State generally.

We have declared in our bill of rights that it is a fundamental principle of all government that every man for every injury done to his person or his property ought to have justice, speedily without delay. The complaint that has been universally heard in the State under the present system is the delay in the hearing of cases which are brought before the courts. It has been in many instances almost intolerable. It is conceded on all hands that there must be some modification of the present system to meet the wants of the people. I can conceive of no better plan than to have the judges appointed in each county, and then to throw three adjoining counties into a circuit for the purpose of having civil and criminal cases tried before three judges.

Now, although we have had no complaint of that kind in our judicial circuit, yet I have heard lawyers from other parts of the State complain, and the people generally complain of this one-man business, this one-man power, in judging and determining every case that comes before them. The concurring opinion of three eminent and distinguished men upon the bench would carry with it a weight which no one man could possibly have.

Under the old system appeals were less numerous to the court of appeals. Now, in almost every case where one man decides it, under the present system, an appeal is taken. Litigants would oftener be satisfied with the decision of three men upon the bench in important cases, than with that of one, and would save themselves the trouble and expense of appealing; and I have no doubt that the time and labor of the court of appeals would be saved in hundreds of cases by having three judges upon the bench instead of one.

With reference to the orphans' court system, which is necessarily connected with this question now before the convention, it is a matter of importance that there should be upon the bench of the orphans' court some judge who knows something of the law. It must of necessity be so, if we adopt the provision recommended by the committee, to give the orphans' court jurisdiction over the administration and distribution of real estate, concurrent with that of the court of equity.

The expense to the State may be a little more. I cannot state whether, if we adopt a system of having a judge for each county, it might not be so modified that where the counties are small, and their business would be less onerous than in the larger counties, there might be such a modification of the salaries in those cases as to save some expense to the State. Let the administration of justice, however, come home to the people of every county. Let every man have free and easy access to the judicial tribunal of the county. By the one-judge system, the judge living in one of two or three counties, that is an impossibility in the lower sections of the western shore, and in the lower sections of the eastern shore. In Allegany county, according to the gentleman's scheme, they will have a judge there; in Washington county they will have a judge there; in Frederick county they will have a judge there; but gentlemen from Calvert, Prince George's, or Anne Arundel, will have to go entirely out of their counties before they can reach their judge for the purpose of transacting important and pressing business.

Then in reference to the appeals from magistrates, important matters of litigation are constantly going on before the justices of the peace of the several counties; and if those appeals could be taken at once, as they can be under a provision for having in each county a judge, and decided at once, a great deal of expense, a great deal of annoyance, and a great deal of difficulty would be saved to the citizens of the several counties in that particular.

From all these considerations, I trust that this mere matter of additional expense to the State will not be taken into consideration. I wish the convention to consider that we are now framing and organizing the most important branch of our State government, in comparison with which all other departments in my opinion, sink almost into insignificance. What does the governor of our State do, or the legislature even, in comparison with the administration of justice, in contact with which the people daily and hourly come? The administration of the executive branch of our government is now but a mere nominal affair. Our legislature is to meet but once in two years, and then sit only for a short time. But the judges are constantly at their labor, administering the law, protecting the weak, redressing wrong, disposing of the estates and property of individuals. We are daily and hourly brought in contact with the judicial department of the government. Why should gentlemen stop, when we are organizing such a branch of the government as this, to weigh dollars and cents, in comparison with the great object to be attained, a judiciary which will administer equal and exact justice to all, placing upon the bench men of learning, of integrity, of high character, who will hold the scales of justice evenly between man and man, free from political bias, free from party prejudice?

There is no function that a man can perform on earth, it seems to me, equal to that of judge. A community can be cursed with no greater evil than having over it an unjust, a partial, or a corrupt judge. If gentlemen would reflect upon the great importance of this branch of our government, it seems to me that these considerations of expense would be lightly weighed. I believe the people of the State would willingly bear the expense for the purpose of obtaining a judiciary such as I have indicated.

The gentleman from Baltimore city who last spoke (Mr. Stirling) said that in the election of so many judges we were running the doctrine of election into the ground. I was opposed to the elective system altogether; but there is this about it. Elections will not be very frequent under this system, if we provide that the tenure of office shall be during good behavior or until a specified period of age. The independency and uprightness of judges will be secured I think vastly more by giving them an independent and long tenure of office than by the mode in which they may be selected. Elections will not occur frequently. It will only be in case of death or the resignation of one of the judges, which may not occur for twenty or thirty years. Taking any one of the counties, electing a man thirty years of age, or thirty-five years of age, a man at the bar and in good practice, a man of integrity, giving him a sufficient salary, so that his time may be devoted to the discharge of his official duties, electing him once for this long tenure of office, during good behavior, and elections will not occur frequently in that county for a judge; and the election of judges will not be brought into politics; which is the strongest argument that the gentleman from Baltimore city has urged against this section. I hope that the amendment of my friend from Prince George's (Mr. Clarke) will prevail.

Mr. STOCKBRIDGE. I desire before the convention adjourns to-night to add a single word, lest any one should suppose that the accumulation of equity business is the result of the inattention or negligence of the judges. It is incumbent upon them by law, in all equity cases, to file an opinion in writing when they pass a decree or decretal order. A judge cannot decide a case in equity and pass an order at random. He must do it with deliberation, writing and filing his opinion—that involves time, investigation, examination—in order that if the case should go up to the court of appeals, it may go up properly represented. This renders it impossible for judges having three, four, and in one instance five counties on his hands, with all their business, to attend to this business and prepare and file his opinions. Some remedy must be devised for this. The system proposed by the committee I suppose will remedy it.

As this is an important measure, and as the amendments proposed have not been printed, and cannot therefore receive the consideration to-night which I am sure we are all disposed to give them, I now move that the convention adjourn.

Mr. HEBB. Will the gentleman withdraw that motion for a moment, that I may give notice of an amendment?

Mr. STOCKBRIDGE. Certainly.

Mr. HEBB gave notice that he would submit the following amendment:

Strike out section 21, and insert:

"Sec. 21. For each circuit (the twelfth excepted) there shall be one judge; the said judges shall be styled circuit judges, and shall hold a term of their courts in each of the counties composing their respective circuits at such times as now are or may hereafter be fixed by law, such terms to be never less than two in each year in each county; special terms may be held by said judges, in their discretion, whenever the business of their several counties renders such terms necessary.

On motion of Mr. STOCKBRIDGE,

The convention adjourned.

SEVENTY-SEVENTH DAY.

FRIDAY, August 19, 1864.

The convention met at 10 o'clock, A. M.

Prayer by the Rev. Mr. McNemar.

The roll was called, and the following members answered to their names:

Messrs. Goldsborough, President; Abbott, Annan, Audoun, Berry, of Prince George's, Billingsley, Blackiston, Bond, Briscoe, Brooks, Brown, Carter, Clarke, Crawford, Cunningham, Cushing, Daniel, Davis, of Charles, Duvall, Earle, Ecker, Edelen, Gale, Galloway, Harwood, Hatch, Hebb, Hodson, Hopkins, Hopper, Horsey, Jones, of Somerset, Keefer, Kennard, King, Lansdale, Larsh, Lee, Markey, Mayhugh, McComas, Mitchell, Miller, Morgan, Mullikin, Murray, Negley, Nyman, Parker, Parran, Pugh, Purnell, Ridgely, Robinette, Russell, Sands, Schley, Schlosser, Smith, of Carroll, Smith, of Dorchester, Smith, of Worcester, Sneary, Stirling, Stockbridge, Swope, Sykes, Todd, Turner, Wickard, Wooden—70.

The proceedings of yesterday were read and approved.

On motion of Mr. AUDOUN,

Ordered, That the minority report on militia and military affairs be printed in bill form, and furnished to members of the convention.

ADJOURNMENT TO MONDAY.

Mr. MORGAN submitted the following order.

Ordered, That when this convention adjourns to-day it stand adjourned to meet on Monday next, at 12 o'clock, M.

Mr STIRLING. I shall vote against this because I think we ought to stay here to-morrow, although it would be a great convenience to me to go home. But I hope that gentlemen who vote against it will let the convention know whether they mean to stay here; for although there is now a full house there may be to-morrow no quorum. I stayed here in Annapolis a week ago and that was just the result. I hope no gentleman will vote to stay here to-morrow unless he intends to stay himself. I call for the yeas and nays.

The yeas and nays were ordered.

Mr. DANIEL. I hope gentlemen will be excused from attendance by leave of the convention and not by their votes.

Mr. CLARKE asked to be excused for a few days.

The request was granted.

Mr. DUVALL asked to be excused until Monday.

The request was granted.

Mr. TODD asked to be excused for a few days.

The request was granted.

Mr. SYKES asked to be excused from this night's session.

Mr. DANIEL. Gentlemen seem to be asking to be excused without assigning any particular reason for it. It seems to me if no reason is to be assigned we might as well repeal the rule at once.

Mr. JONES, of Somerset. I think members of this house ought certainly to be trusted as honorable men, not to ask to be excused unless for some reason. I think that for the house to require gentlemen to assign their reasons is to ask more than should be asked of honorable men.

Mr. DANIEL. Then what is the use of the rule?

Mr. JONES, of Somerset. So that members

may not absent themselves without notifying the convention.

Mr. SYKES was excused.

Mr. KEEFER asked to be excused for to-morrow.

The request was granted.

Mr. McCOMAS asked to be excused until Monday noon.

The request was granted.

Mr. DAVIS, of Charles, asked to be excused until Tuesday morning on account of indisposition from recent illness.

The request was granted.

Mr. ABBOTT. I move that those who have been excused, be also excused from voting upon the question of adjournment.

Mr. KENNARD asked to be excused until Monday morning.

The request was granted.

Mr. RIDGELY. I ask leave to be excused from attendance on Monday next, as I cannot make a connection to get here on that day. I mean to be here to-day and to-morrow.

The request was granted.

The question was then taken on the order to adjourn until Monday, and the result was—yeas 44, nays 29—as follows:

Yeas—Messrs. Goldsborough, President; Audoun, Belt, Billingsley, Blackiston, Bond, Briscoe, Brooks, Chambers, Clarke, Crawford, Davis, of Charles, Duvall, Edelen, Gale, Harwood, Hatch, Henkle, Hodson, Hopkins, Hopper, Horsey, Jones, of Somerset, Keefer, Kennard, Lansdale, Larsh, Lee, Marbury, Mitchell, Morgan, Mullikin, Parran, Ridgely, Schley, Schlosser, Smith, of Dorchester, Smith of Worcester, Sneary, Stirling, Sykes, Todd, Turner, Wickard—44.

Nays—Abbott, Annan, Brown, Carter, Cunningham, Cushing, Daniel, Earle, Ecker, Galloway, Hebb, King, Markey, Mayhugh, McComas, Miller, Murray, Negley, Nyman, Parker, Pugh, Purnell, Robinette, Russell, Sands, Smith, of Carroll, Stockbridge, Swope, Wooden—29.

When their names were called,

Mr. CLARKE said: Having been excused from attendance, I think it is proper that I should be excused from voting; but as that is not to be expected, I will vote "aye."

Mr. McCOMAS said: I ask to be excused from voting, having been excused from attendance.

Not being excuse, he voted "no."

Mr. MULLIKIN said: I see very clearly that we shall not have a quorum to-morrow; and I vote "aye."

Mr. STIRLING said: I am satisfied we shall not have a quorum. I am not willing to run the risk of being left here; and vote "aye."

Mr. TODD. I should prefer to be excused from voting; but as there appears to be an indisposition to excuse members from voting who were excused from attendance, and in view of the fact that it is rather doubtful whether there will be a quorum here to-morrow, and being unwilling to afflict unnecessarily those who remain, I vote "aye."

Mr. WICKARD. I am quite confident that there will be no quorum here to-night or to-morrow. The result will be as it was last Friday night and Saturday. I therefore vote "aye."

The order was accordingly adopted.

On motion of Mr. RIDGELY,

It was ordered to be entered upon the journal that Mr. Hoffman, of Baltimore county, is detained from his seat in this convention by reason of the dangerous illness of a member of his family.

On motion of Mr. DUVALL,

It was ordered to be entered on the journal that Mr. Peter is detained from his seat in this convention on account of indisposition.

ORDER OF BUSINESS.

Mr. STIRLING. I move to postpone all prior business in order that we may proceed to standing orders upon their third reading.—We have several reports standing upon their third reading; and unless we take them up soon we shall have all the argument at the tail end of the session.

Mr. STOCKBRIDGE. I hope that motion will not prevail. There are several of these reports which have been printed as ordered to be engrossed, upon their second reading, and laid upon our tables. So far as I am concerned, not supposing the regular order of business would be interrupted, I have not examined these reports, going over them carefully as I designed to do upon their third reading; and I presume that is the case with other members of the convention. As this is to be the final form of them, I think it is proper that every member should go over them carefully and examine every word before they are put upon their third reading. They cannot be amended after that. That finally disposes of them. It would suit me much better to have this made the special order of the day for a time certain, when we shall have completed the present report, or at some hour on Monday, to allow some little interval to enable every member to make this critical examination of them which it is important should be made by every member. Until that is done I hope the reports will not be taken up. I think we should lose time by it.

Mr. HEBB. I would suggest that the convention take up the report of the committee on State's attorneys.

Mr. STIRLING. I am not in favor of taking up any other report on its second reading.—I do not desire to press my motion.

Mr. STOCKBRIDGE. There are at least three reports unacted upon.

The PRESIDENT. The report on State's Attorneys, on the Militia and on Usury, are on their second reading.

THE JUDICIARY.

Mr. CLARKE. I now offer the following sections to the report of the judiciary committee, in order that they may go upon the journal as amendments to the different sections. If we should immediately go on with the judiciary report, I suppose they would come up at once.

PART III.

County and Circuit Courts.

"Section 19. There shall be a judge for each county in the State, who shall be elected by the legal and qualified voters of the several counties. He shall be a resident for one year in the county for which he may be elected next before the time of his election, and shall reside in the county for which he is elected while he continues to act as judge."

"Section 20. There shall be a court in each county in the State; they shall be called equity courts for the county in which they are held. The judge elected for each county, shall be the judge of the said court, and shall have and exercise in the county for which he is elected, the full and exclusive power, authority and jurisdiction of a court of equity, in their said county, with all the chancery powers which the present circuit courts have as courts of equity in the several counties, or which may be hereafter prescribed by laws made pursuant to this constitution, with the right of appeal to the court of appeals, as is now or may be hereafter provided for by law. He shall hold at least four terms of the equity court for the county, or oftener if required by law, and shall be ex-officio chief judge of the orphans' court of the county for which he is elected.

"Section 21. Same as section 19 in the report of the committee.

"Section 22. In each of the above named circuits, except the eighth, there shall be three courts, one to be held in each county; they shall be called circuit courts for the county in which they may be held, and shall have and exercise in the several counties of the respective circuits all the common law power and authority, original and appellate, and criminal jurisdiction which the circuit courts for the several counties now have, hold and exercise, or which may hereafter be prescribed by laws made pursuant to this constitution.

"Section 23. The judges of the several counties comprising the said judicial circuits shall be the judges of the circuit courts for the respective counties embraced within the said judicial circuits. The governor, by and with the advice and consent of the senate, shall designate the chief justice of the several circuits. The said judges shall hold a term of their courts in each of the counties composing their respective circuits at such times as now are, or may hereafter be fixed by law, such terms to be never less than two in each year in each county. Special terms may be held by said judges, in their discretion, whenever the business of the several counties renders such terms necessary; a single judge may hold sessions of the circuit court for the disposal of all business merely formal and uncontested, such causes civil or criminal as the parties litigant shall consent in writing to try before a single judge, and appeals from justices of the peace where the parties agree in writing to waive a trial by jury, and to try the appeal before a single judge.

"Section 24. The chief justice when so appointed as herein prescribed, shall when attending, preside in said courts, and in case of his absence or his withdrawing from the bench, the judge next in seniority, to be determined from the date of the commission, who shall be present shall preside therein; and in case of the death, disqualification or refusal to act, of the person appointed chief justice as aforesaid, the judge next in seniority as aforesaid, shall be the chief justice of the said court until a new appointment of chief justice shall be made as aforesaid."

The convention resumed the consideration of the article on the judiciary department on its second reading. The pending section was the following:

"Sec. 20. In each of the above named circuits, except the eighth, there shall be three courts, one to be held in each county; they shall be called circuit courts for the county in which they may be held, and shall have and exercise all the power, authority, and jurisdiction, original and appellate, which the present circuit courts of this State now have and exercise, or which may hereafter be prescribed by law."

Mr. HEBB had submitted the following amendment:

"Sec. 20. One court shall be held in each county of the State; the said courts shall be called circuit courts for the county in which they may be held, and shall have and exercise all the power, authority and jurisdiction, original and appellate, which the present circuit courts of this State now have and exercise, or which may hereafter be prescribed by law."

Mr. CLARKE had submitted the following amendment to the amendment:

"Sec. 20. There shall be a judge for each county in the State, who shall be elected by the legal and qualified voters thereof, from among those learned in the law."

Mr. HEBB. I think the gentleman's amendment more properly belongs to the next section. It refers to the judges, whereas the section refers to the courts.

Mr. CLARKE. I withdraw it.

The question recurred upon Mr. HEBB's amendment.

Mr. NEGLEY. In some respects I like the amendment offered by the gentleman from Allegany (Mr. Hebb) better than the original article. But I think it increases the number of judges beyond the necessities of the case. It provides that we shall have twelve districts.

Mr. HEBB. That is the nineteenth section, which was informally passed over.

Mr. NEGLEY. I thought the nineteenth section was the amendment pending.

Mr. CLARKE. I withdraw my amendment with this view, that we cannot vote understandingly upon section twenty without understanding the system which I propose to offer, and of which the amendment last night was only one branch. I think if I read the amendments I propose to offer, the convention will be in a better frame of mind to understand the different sections as they may be offered, section by section as the several sections are taken up.

[Mr. CLARKE again read sections nineteen to twenty-four, inclusive, of which he had given notice immediately before taking up the report this morning.]

This will bring up the question of the two systems at once. If in order, I will now offer section nineteen, as an amendment to the present amendment, so that it shall read as follows:

"Sec. 20. There shall be a judge for each county in the State, who shall be elected by the legal and qualified voters of the several counties. He shall be a resident for one year in the county for which he may be elected next before the time of his election, and shall reside in the county for which he is elected while he continues to act as judge.

The PRESIDENT. That does not seem to be strictly germain to the amendment of the gentleman from Allegany, which is a section relating to the courts, that one shall be held in each county.

Mr. RIDGELY. I understand the proposition of the gentleman from Prince George's (Mr. Clarke) to be a part of an entire system, which contemplates a circuit and equity judge in each county. I would ask him what compensation he has in view for these judges?

Mr. CLARKE. I will state that the plan which I propose embraces no more judges than the report of the committee. Instead of having three counties brought into a circuit, you have one judge for each county all through; and the resident judge in the county shall discharge the chancery powers. The expense is the same as that contemplated by the report of the majority of the committee. There are no more judges; and the expense is identical.

Mr. HEBB. I offered the proposition in this form in order to conform to the general features of the report of the judiciary committee. The difference between the proposition I offered and that contained in the report is this: The report proposes twenty-two judges, one for each county, three judges in the circuit. My proposition is to have one judge to each judicial circuit, and to have a circuit court in each county over which that judge is to preside. There can be no difficulty about it. Any one in favor of having one judge in each circuit, whether there are eight, ten, twelve, or fifteen circuits, will be in favor of my proposition.

Mr. NEGLEY. I conceive that there is no earthly difference between the section offered by the gentleman from Allegany and the one reported by the committee, except that the section offered by the gentleman from Allegany looks to a one-judge system, and the other looks to a three judge system; so that when we vote, those who are in favor of a one-judge system will vote for the proposition of the gentleman from Allegany; and those who are in favor of a three-judge system will vote against it.

Mr. HEBB. That's it.

Mr. NEGLEY. We can alter it hereafter to make twelve, nine, or fifteen circuits, as we please.

Mr. SANDS. I was very much interested last evening in the remarks of gentlemen to whom I listened. The more that has been said upon this subject—that is, the question of three judges upon the bench or one—the more I have become interested in it. I should like to hear the views of all gentlemen, professional and non-professional, upon the subject. I do not think that the one consideration with us should be the consideration of expense. By calculation, we will find that the expense of the system as proposed by the committee, will be about 4 cents on the $100. The assessable property of the State is about $300,000,000. The estimated cost of this system is about $100,000. After all, the expense of this system would scarcely be felt in the taxation of the St. te.

The convention has already by its action appropriated $400 000 annually to the public school system of the State. We have provided that $300,000 shall be raised to defray the immediate expenses of the system, and a sinking fund created, by a tax of 5 cents on the $100 on the assessable property of the State, making in all a levy of about $450,000 annually.

Now I humbly submit that a matter so important to the people of the State, their welfare and their safety, their convenience and their happiness, as the judiciary system of the State, should not be controlled by the bare consideration of expense. I for one would be willing not to take the expense of the two systems into consideration; because, as I said, the taxation to which the State will be subjected for its judiciary will be not over 4 cents on the $100. It seems to me then that the sole consideration with this convention should be, which is the better system, as proposed to this body.

To the system as reported by the committee there are some objections. Some of the circuits are very small. Some of them are so large that the judges could scarcely discharge the duties of their circuits within the year.—For instance, the report puts Carroll county and Baltimore county and Howard county in one district. I think that the business of Baltimore county alone will occupy at least six months of the year. The business of the Howard county court will occupy six weeks or two months more, making eight months. I am not familiar with the Carroll county court. I do not know what amount of time is occupied in the discharge of the business of the court there; but in that circuit, according to my best information, ten months in the year would absolutely be required to discharge the business of the circuit. That is one objection to the system as reported by the committee.

The substitute offered by the gentleman from Allegany, that the State be divided into twelve circuits; that the larger counties be erected into circuits themselves; and that circuits composed of smaller counties shall go to make up the number presided over by a single judge, has many things to recommend it. Baltimore county would be erected into a circuit by that system. Frederick, Washington and Allegany counties, all large and populous counties, and each affording sufficient business for a court, would each be a circuit.

I am, I confess, at a loss to select between the systems proposed; and I do not think we could spend an hour more profitably than in listening to the views of gentlemen, professional and non-professional, upon this subject. I think our sole object ought to be to decide upon the merits of the systems proposed without any regard to the question of expense. If it is so important to the State at large that the children of the State should be educated, that intelligence should be diffused, that we are willing to spend almost half a million annually for this purpose, are not these tribunals which have the custody in fact of the lives and the properties of the citizens of the State, of equally great importance, and equally deserving of our fostering care and consideration? I scarcely know of any subject which has interested me so much as that now before this body. I hope we will take time. We are going to adjourn to-day at half-past one o'clock; and I do not think the time to elapse between the present moment and that hour could be more profitably spent than in carefully considering this subject.

Mr. Ecker. How does the gentleman know that we are going to adjourn at half-past one o'clock?

Mr. Sands. Well, I feel it, sir; and I think we could scarcely spend the time more profitably than in listening to the views of gentlemen of all sides of the house in regard to this matter. For one I would urge upon the convention the propriety of settling upon the merits of the systems without any regard whatever to the cost. If you can go out from this convention and say to the citizens of this State that the education of the children and youth of the State is so important a matter as to justify you in expending half a million annually upon it, can you not go out and say to the people that the judicial system of the State is so important that you may be justified in devoting to it at least one-fifth of that sum? I want to listen, instead of talking about this matter. I really desire to be instructed as to the merits of the two systems.

Mr. Stockbridge. I would like to inquire of the gentleman from Allegany, whether under the system as he proposes it, he designs that the circuit judge should be the chief judge of the orphans' court of the circuit?

Mr. Hebb. It would be impossible for the judge of a circuit of two or three counties to be judge of the orphans' court.

Mr. Stockbridge. Then there would be a difference in expense, for that reason, of twenty or twenty-five thousand dollars annually.

Mr. Smith, of Carroll. There is very great force and propriety in the remarks made by the gentleman from Howard county (Mr. Sands,) and I hope they will receive the attention they deserve. We have waited a very long while for the report of the committee on the judiciary, and supposed they would be able to submit a report which would be acceptable to the majority of the convention. We have not individually, many of us, provided anything as a substitute in its place. A number of independent propositions have been forced upon us, very hastily; and we have not had the opportunity of giving to them the attention which their vital importance and the interests of the State imperatively demand.—We are determined to adjourn to-day, and are very much like school boys, anxious to get away as soon as vacation comes. I believe the temper of the convention is not such as to be competent to investigate this matter properly. I think we would better fulfil our trust by postponing the consideration of this report until we assemble again on Monday.—To-morrow we shall have an opportunity, many of us, of conversing with our constituents and ascertaining their opinions. They will read the papers very carefully, and make suggestions to us, and enable us to come back on Monday more fully prepared to unite on some system which will command general approbation. I move that the further consideration of the report be postponed until Monday. We can take up the report on the State's attorneys, which will require very little discussion, and finish it to-day.

The President. It is not likely that we shall have a full convention on Monday.

Mr. Belt. I would suggest to the gentleman from Carroll that the amendment of the gentleman from Allegany, and of my colleague, be printed.

Mr. CHAMBERS. Let them all be printed.

Mr. BELT. It is a matter of special importance, and these amendments all go to the very root of the system; and I should prefer that they should be printed in bill form.

Mr. JONES, of Somerset. Before the vote is taken, in response to the desire of the gentleman from Howard (Mr. Sands,) that those who have reflected upon this question of the judiciary should give their views to the convention, there is one point upon which I desire to throw out a view suggested this morning, in order that gentlemen may give it such weight as they deem it worth; and it will operate against the amendment of the gentleman from Allegany. He says that under this system it will be impossible that the judge of the circuit should be the judge of the orphans' court.

The PRESIDENT. The motion to postpone is now pending. If debate is allowed upon the question itself, it may be interminable, one gentleman speaking and then another.

Mr. JONES, of Somerset. I hope the gentleman will withdraw the motion.

Mr. SMITH withdrew the motion.

The question recurred upon Mr. HEBB's amendment.

Mr. JONES, of Somerset. I merely wish to address my remarks to one single point. I think there cannot be much difference of opinion, with those who are well acquainted with the matter, that our past and present orphans' court system is very defective. When you come to consider that about once in a generation the entire personal property of the State passes through the administration of that court, and when you consider the innumerable questions which arise there about the distribution of that property, where infants are concerned most frequently, I think it will be seen that a different system ought to be adopted, and that there ought to be at least one, the chief judge, a lawyer, well acquainted and informed, and learned in his profession, as well as of the strictest integrity and business habits, to supervise the administration of this personal estate.

The PRESIDENT. That is not the question before the convention.

Mr. JONES, of Somerset. I suggest it in this view. It is an argument against the amendment of the gentleman from Allegany, because it does not provide for a judge for the orphans' court with legal qualifications.

The PRESIDENT. The gentleman has not made any proposition of that kind; only that one judge shall be established in each circuit.

Mr. STIRLING. It seems to me that this question is inevitably concerned in it. Gentlemen may vote against the proposition of the gentleman from Allegany on the ground that it renders the presiding of the circuit judge over the orphans' court impossible.—Any proposition which provides one judge for a circuit, of course prevents any such change in the orphans' court as is proposed by the committee.

The PRESIDENT. He might propose for the equity judge to sit.

Mr. STIRLING. He could not do that. It is impossible.

The PRESIDENT. If the gentleman from Allegany, in proposing one judge for each circuit, also proposes an equity judge to take charge of equity business, he might preside over the orphans' court.

Mr. STIRLING. He does not do that.

The PRESIDENT. The chair does not know what the plan of the gentleman from Allegany contemplates.

Mr. HEBB. It only contemplates these three amendments, to the 19th, 20th, and 21st sections.

Mr. JONES, of Somerset. I will not occupy the time of the convention; I am willing that the subject should go over on the motion of the gentleman from Carroll (Mr. Smith.)

The PRESIDENT. The gentleman has withdrawn that proposition. The question is upon the amendment of the gentleman from Allegany (Mr. Hebb.)

Mr. JONES, of Somerset. I will say that the chairman of the committee, and many of its members, have been indefatigable in their endeavors to digest a system, and they have reported a system. If the convention upset it in detail, as has been commenced, we shall be very much at sea. I think it is well worthy of consideration whether it would not be better to recommit with all the amendments for the committee to reconstruct their report. If the convention go on and amend by detail, they render the whole system incongruous.

Mr. STIRLING. It strikes me that there are some things this convention must settle before we can emerge at all from the confusion in which we are placed. If these things are settled, the confusion can very easily be remedied. We have decided that the judiciary shall be elected. That guides us in some respects in casting our votes for the details of the system. There is another proposition which must be settled before any of us can vote understandingly; and that is the tenure. There is no use in recommitting the report for the committee to consider and put into shape, if the committee does not know the sense of the convention upon the tenure.—The committee has reported an appointive system. The convention have substituted an elective system. If the committee report it back with the tenure unchanged, and we do not accept the tenure, we are at sea again.—Men may be willing to vote for a system with a certain tenure, and not be willing to vote for it with a different tenure.

Another thing to be settled is the orphans' court. All these systems depend more or less upon the construction of the orphans' court. I suppose nobody will vote for a system of three judges in each circuit, unless one of the judges is to be judge of the orphans' court in each county. I suppose in any system of one judge to each county, that judge will have jurisdiction over the orphans' court, either entirely or to a great extent. So far as I am concerned I am opposed to any change whatever in the orphans' court. I am opposed to substituting any system of judges of probate in the place of the present orphans' court system. I shall cast my vote with reference to this thing. I shall not cast my vote for any system which vests in the judge of the county jurisdiction over the orphans' court.

I am not going to argue that. I say that the orphans' court system has stood longer than any other system in the State. There is no popular movement against it. It is a system eminently popular in its character.—Gentlemen talk about being unwilling to take the election of judges away from the people. There is no system in the State which more nearly concerns the people, or in which they feel more interest; and I really believe the orphans' court system is more popular than any other system in the State.

I know that a great many lawyers look down upon it as a lay court; but for that very reason the great mass of the people prize it. It is a system involving the personal property of the State, and which has been in existence from the establishment of the testamentary act down to the present day; and there has never been a dollar stolen or wasted. I do not believe any other system has worked better. They have a probate system in New York; and it is neither as honest nor as well managed as the system in Maryland. If I am not mistaken some of the most eminent lawyers in other States have expressed their approbation of the testamentary act of Maryland as the most complete testamentary system that exists in the United States.

It seems to me that we ought to take some action upon this report, to establish these general principles. Let us know whether the convention intends to alter the orphans' court system; let us know what tenure the judges are going to have; and after we have done that, we can more easily come to some conclusion with regard to the circuits. For manifestly, if there is to be one judge, as my friend from Allegany proposes, in three counties, or in two counties, that judge cannot preside over the orphans' court. It is perfectly impossible. If you have one judge in each county, he can administer the orphans' court; but I should like to have it explained how a judge of three counties can attend to or administer the functions of judge of the orphans' court.

Mr. Daniel. I agree in part with my colleague as I understood him, as to the propriety of voting upon these questions at once. I should be sorry to have it postponed until Tuesday.

The President. The motion o postpone was withdrawn.

Mr. Smith, of Carroll. I renew it; I move to postpone it until Tuesday next, at 12 o'clock.

Mr. Daniel. I was going to say that we have a very full house to-day, some seventy members here, and as my colleague suggests, there are certain principal features about this report which pretty much all the members I think have thought more or less about; and I think, as suggested by the gentleman from Howard, we might have a sort of experience meeting, to hear what members think about it, just as well now as at any other time; because this thing will all have to be gone over again. I am for a short session, and I presume every member wants to get away from here and hasten home as soon as possible. But there are matters before us that members have thought of, and we can as well discuss now, while here in a full house, as at any other time. If we put it off three or four days, I think we shall be losing valuable time. We have just determined to adjourn over the night session to-night as well as tomorrow. There are seventy or more members present to-day, and I look upon this proposition to postpone until Tuesday, as about effectually losing this day. Therefore I think we would better go into the discussion of this question. If we do anything wrong or hastily, we have a right to re-consider; and if we do it right we shall not have to go over it again. I think it would be better to save all the time we can, by going on with this discussion at once.

Mr. Stockbridge. I would suggest that half past ten o'clock would be better than twelve; for there would be as many members present at that hour as at 12 o'clock.

Mr. Smith, of Carroll, modified his motion accordingly.

The motion to postpone the further consideration of the report until Tuesday next at half past ten o'clock, was agreed to—ayes 48, noes not counted.

On motion of Mr. Belt,

All the proposed amendments to the report were ordered to be printed in bill form.

THE DRAFT.

On motion of Mr. Berry, of Pr. George's,

The following order submitted by him on yesterday, was taken up:

"*Ordered*, That a committee of three be appointed by the President to correspond with the proper authorities, and furnish this convention with the number of recruits, both white and black, which have been received into the service of the United States, from the several counties of the State, and the city of Baltimore, and also the number credited to the said counties and city respectively."

Mr. BERRY, of Prince George's, submitted the following as a modification of the order:

"*Ordered*, That a committee to consist of nine members of the convention, be appointed by the president to wait upon his excellency, Governor Bradford, and respectfully request him to ascertain from the proper authorities and report to this convention at his earliest convenience, the number of recruits, both white and black, that have been received into the service of the United States from the city of Baltimore and several counties in the State respectively, since the beginning of this war, also the number that have been credited to the said city and counties respectively, and if possible to have the enrolment so revised and corrected, as to give the said city and several counties a credit for all the recruits furnished by them as aforesaid, also take such steps as may be necessary, to have credited to said city and counties all persons who may have been enlisted by military officers in the employ of the United States, under the pretended authority of the government, and transferred by them and credited to any of the States of the Union."

Mr. BERRY, of Prince George's, said: The object is first of all to furnish data to the convention before they act upon the resolutions offered by my colleague, as to how many have been received into the service of the United States in the various counties and the city of Baltimore, and to see whether they are correctly credited to the several counties from which they came or have been enlisted. The other inquiry is to ascertain how many have been taken and enlisted in the State of Maryland for other States in the Union, and to try to have the draft credited, or the enrolment list so revised and corrected as only to require of Maryland her proper quota. At the time the enrolment was made in my county, there were at least 4,000 or 5,000 capable of bearing arms more than there are at the present time. The quota to be furnished by my county, and I take it for granted that the same principle applies to nearly all the other counties of the State, is predicated upon the old draft of 1862. Since that time more than one-half the able bodied persons of our county—I speak particularly of the colored persons of our county—have been either taken away and enlisted by officers of the United States service, or have gone away, and their masters have not been able to reclaim them. They therefore do not form a part of our population. To do justice to our county, or to any other county of the State, the quota ought to be fixed upon the present inhabitants capable of bearing arms. It is with that view that I add that portion of the order which differs from the order which I submitted yesterday.

I have made the committee to consist of nine members to be appointed by the chair, with the view that we may to-morrow go and see the governor and converse with him freely; and I am sure he will give us all the information now in his possession; and if necessary he will go to Washington and claim the right there to procure such information as may be necessary to place before the convention before it acts upon the resolution of my colleague. This was admitted on all hands yesterday to be necessary before we could act intelligently upon the subject. I cannot imagine how any gentleman can oppose the passage of this order, because it is a mere inquiry which I am sure the governor of the State will be very happy to answer; and I am sure it will facilitate in every way the proposed apportionment of the draft among the several counties of the State and the States. But it is no more than an inquiry for information I am sure he will willingly give us.

Mr. BELT. I wish to state in connection with the proposition of my colleague, what action has been taken by the authorities in our section of the State in reference to the draft. I will mention one instance, as an illustration how the matter was arranged with us. About last November there came into our county, whence I have not been able to understand, or by whose authority, a detachment of forty soldiers, under the command of an officer, to the county seat, Upper Marlboro'. They located themselves in a house that did not happen to be occupied, where they remained until near the time for the meeting of this convention. They succeeded by various inducements, in getting away to Baltimore and other districts, almost every able-bodied man. Great efforts were made by our leading citizens, by approaching the military authorities of Baltimore and Washington, to throw some light upon the question by whose order these men came there; but no military man was able to inform us. They did not know they were there, who sent them, or for what purpose.

They stayed, and succeeded in robbing the whole county of its able-bodied labor. Where did they go? It was not credited to the county or the State. We were willing, if we could get the credit of these two or three thousand able-bodied men, after the county was free, to let the rest go to the credit of the whole State, to relieve the white population. Not so. The truth finally leaked out, not in the way of absolute, demonstrative, legal proof, but with sufficient moral evidence to satisfy us about the fact, that these men were sent there by the colonels of their regiments, and came there to recruit negroes, and were paid for doing it, in order to relieve certain parts of the States of New York and New Jersey. And one of the moral evidences of the fact, was that fifty and one hundred dollar New Jersey bills were just as common as leaves on the trees, in the hands of these soldiers. That is one of the abuses and outrages that I want to see corrected by the proper authorities; and I want it to have all the moral weight this convention can bring to bear upon it. If the Southern counties of the State had the credit they are entitled to, for the class of men surreptitiously carried off in this way, the whole State would be nearly relieved of the burden of an excessive draft.

Mr. HEBB. I hardly think it is necessary to have a committee of nine; and I move the following amendment to the amendment:

Strike out all after the word "that," in the first line, to the word "to," in the seventh line, and insert the words "the governor be respectfully requested to communicate."

Mr. BERRY, of Prince George's Really I cannot see what objection any gentleman can offer to this order. The object is to get the information; and in case the governor is not possessed of the information, to desire him to write and procure the information; and he will do it with a great deal of pleasure, with more than the gentleman from Allegany (Mr. Hebb) will vote for this proposition, I am sure. This is a mere subject of inquiry, admitted on all hands on yesterday to be necessary. It is merely with a view that we may have a consultation, that gentlemen of this body may have a consultation with the governor upon the subject, and devise some plan to meet this want, that the order is offered. I did not really expect any opposition to the order. I think it is drawn up in respectful terms, that he be respectfully requested to furnish us with the information; and I cannot imagine why gentlemen should arise in their seats and offer objections and amendments with a view of killing off a subject which they admitted yesterday was of so much importance.

I think the information desired by the convention can be more readily had in the mode pointed out by the order which I have had the honor of presenting. I said some days ago, and I shall follow out the rule, I meant this only as a suggestion to the convention; not that I expect it to pass anything coming from me or my colleagues, but I merely made the suggestion, predicated on reason and founded on justice, which I did not suppose any man through prejudice or any political bias would oppose in this convention.

Mr. HEBB. I believe I did not violate any rule of the convention by offering an amendment to the gentleman's order. If the gentleman supposes I have any prejudice upon this subject, he is very much mistaken. If there is any prejudice, it is on the other side of the house. So far as the information is concerned, if the gentleman desires information, and the governor has the information and is ready and willing to furnish it, he can as well furnish the information to the convention by a communication as to nine gentleman sitting there and conversing with him. That is my view of the subject.

Mr. MILLER. I think it would be entirely respectful for a committee to wait upon him, rather than for the convention to pass a mere order requesting him to communicate the information to us. That is certainly in accordance with precedents, to communicate with the governor by means of committees; and I can see no objection to the appointment of a committee to bring the matter more respectfully and formally to the attention of the governor, than it would be by the mere passage of an order. This is a subject of grave importance to the people of the State, and especially to the people of my congressional district Now I have been credibly informed this morning by those connected with the department, that in this congressional district, with two of the counties nearly exempt, Calvert and St. Mary's, the people in this district have under the present draft paid a quarter of a million dollars in the way of commutation money for the procurement of substitutes; and notwithstanding that, it is a well known fact, not legally known perhaps, that a large number of slaves of this district, and able-bodied free negroes have been taken from the district and enlisted, and credited either to the other portions of the State, or to the city of Baltimore, or to the other States in the Union. Yet in the coming September draft, the quota of this congressional district is three or four hundred more men than in any other congressional district in the State. I say that is a matter of injustice. It ought to be remedied if possible. This matter ought to be inquired into and the facts made known, and the enrolment lists corrected, and the quotas properly assigned to the several subdivisions of the State. There cannot be anything but justice in this proposition, and if the information is possibly to be obtained, let us have it.

Mr. ABBOTT called for the previous question.

The call for the previous question was not sustained.

Mr. STOCKBRIDGE. I desire to say a few words upon this question. I have always been averse to sending committees to the executive of the State for information. I think the more usual custom is to communicate in writing, sending him a respectful communication, and asking for a reply in the same form. That is better for many reasons. A committee waits upon the executive, and makes a statement of the thing that has brought them there, and asks certain questions; and they obtain replies.—Then in their own manner they communicate what they said or designed to say, and what they understood the executive to reply. If the communication is made in writing and a written answer is returned, we know precisely what was represented, what was inquired, what was said to the executive, and precisely what he said in reply We have all the information to act upon which the committee would have in the other case, without any misunderstanding or possible misrepresentation. I therefore greatly prefer that form of communicating, at all times, with any other department of the government.

There is another thing to be said with reference to this. If it is impossible to remedy the injustice on writing, however great it may be; it is useless and worse than useless for us to squander the time of this convention upon the subject. Now what can be done? Take the facts as stated by the gentleman from Prince George's yesterday, as stated by his colleague this morning, precisely as stated, what is it possible to do under the circumstances? As I understand the statement, an irresponsible body of men, sent by no officer of the government, and it is not known who——

Mr. BERRY, of Prince George's. Let me correct my friend. He was sent by the colonel of his regiment stationed at Bladensburg, and the negroes taken from our county were taken to Bladensburg and not to Washington, and were never reported to the department.

Mr. STOCKBRIDGE. So I said; they were not sent by an officer of the government, they were not acting officially. Whether the order came from a sergeant, a captain, or a colonel, still it was not from any proper official source. It was something outside. They took certain men. These men, as I understand it, have been credited by the government to the place where their names were entered, and where perhaps bounties were paid. How is it possible to trace these men upon the muster-roll? Or beginning at the other end, taking the muster-rolls, how is it possible to trace these men back as Maryland men? That class of people change their names whenever they please, without waiting for acts of assembly. They may have gone under one name or another name. So far as I can conceive, it is altogether a matter disconnected with the government, and one in which it is impossible to trace the men so as to rectify any injustice that has been done.

Mr. BERRY, of Prince George's. If the gentleman will allow me, I will say that if the inquiry is set on foot by the proper authorities, I will undertake to prove every individual so enlisted, and can trace them to one particular regiment in which they were placed by this officer. I will have them all identified

Mr. STOCKBRIDGE resumed: I will only say that it will come very near the power of omniscience if that can be done.

Mr. BERRY, of Prince George's. Not at all.

Mr. STOCKBRIDGE. It will not fall much short of it. I was going on to add one other remark, that if it could be done, supposing for a moment that it could be done as the gentleman seems to suppose, they have been credited to a certain part of the State, or if they have gone out of the State they have been credited to another State. Does it not necessarily follow that if it could be done, the whole apportionment within the State, or as between the States, has got to be remade, and a readjustment and new apportionment to be made? Does there not necessarily follow an entire suspension of the draft for 500,000 men, indefinitely, blocking the operations of the government for months, to rectify it? It seems to me perfectly plain that it is so; and that the government will not be disposed to submit that its operations shall be so embarrassed and impeded, for the very reason that they will say, if this injustice was committed, it should have been noticed in a proper form, and at the proper time. It certainly would not have been half as hard to follow and identify these men, to tell where they were then, as it would be now after the lapse of time. If you have the power now to trace them, much more had you the power then, and you should have attended to it at that time. In the exigency upon us now, in the necessity for men, in our requirement of an army, the United States shall not be delayed until this investigation can be made, and this readjustment. It seems to me therefore, in the first place, useless. At the same time, I have no objection to vote to send a communication of inquiry to the governor.

Mr. BERRY, of Prince George's, demanded the yeas and nays upon the amendment moved by Mr. HEBB, and they were ordered.

The question being taken, the result was—yeas 40, nays 32—as follows:

Yeas—Messrs. Goldsborough, President; Annan, Bond, Brooks, Carter, Cunningham, Cushing, Daniel, Ecker, Galloway, Harwood, Hebb, Hopkins, Hopper, Keefer, Kennard, Larsh, Marbury, Markey, Mayhugh, McComas, Mullikin, Murray, Negley, Nyman, Parker, Purnell, Robinette, Russell, Sands, Schlosser, Smith, of Carroll, Smith, of Worcester, Sneary, Stirling, Stockbridge, Swope, Sykes, Todd, Wooden—40.

Nays—Messrs. Abbott, Belt, Berry, of Prince George's, Billingsley, Blackiston, Briscoe, Brown, Chambers, Clarke, Crawford, Davis, of Charles, Dent, Duvall, Earle, Edelen, Gale, Hatch, Henkle, Hodson, Horsey, Jones, of Somerset, King, Lansdale, Lee, Mitchell, Miller, Morgan, Parran, Pugh, Ridgely, Smith, of Dorchester, Turner—32.

When their names were called,

Mr. ABBOTT said: Believing this to be a matter entirely out of the province of the convention, I shall vote against every proposition of the kind. I vote "no."

Mr. SANDS said: Believing this a matter of sufficient importance to be acted upon by the convention, and believing that we shall all be convinced on reflection that we would better address the governor a communication than to send a committee, I shall vote for the order as amended by the gentleman from Allegany. I vote "aye."

The amendment to the order was accordingly agreed to.

The question recurred upon the order as amended.

Mr. BRISCOE submitted the following amendment:

Strike out all after the word "that" in first line, to the word "the" in the ninth line, and insert the words "the governor and adjutant general of this State be requested, in conjunction with a committee of the members of this convention, to be appointed by the chair, to proceed to the war department, and after conference with the proper authorities to obtain."

Mr. BRISCOE said: My own view is that even if the order is adopted by the convention and sent to the governor, it will result in no practical good, at least to us in that section of the State in which I live. It would merely indicate a disposition on the part of our friends to protect the citizens of that part of the State in which I reside. But I am fearful, and really think from what has taken place in the past with reference to this whole system of drafting, that it will acccomplish very little good. My own idea is this: that all the evils and the injustice that have been heaped upon our section of the State have resulted from that system which has been inaugurated by the government of the United States, and recommended by the President of the United States, in calling out directly by authority emanating from the central government, all the forces of this country, to carry on this war. The view we take of it is that these requisitions should have been made by the States. The States alone should have controlled that; and if that mode of proceeding had been adopted by the government at first, it would have tended more to accomplish the purposes for which the administration were conducting this war.

It is not necessary for me to go on and give in detail the manner and character of the operations of the government in that section of the State which the gentleman from Prince George's and myself represent with regard to this whole matter. We know very well that the governor of Maryland is as helpless as a new-born infant; that this convention is helpless; that there is no authority within the State of Maryland, unless it be by the concession of the authority at Washington, that can bring any relief to us, so long as this system operates as it has in the past. We know very well that we have been compelled to characterize that proceeding as a usurpation of power upon the part of Congress and the government, and on the part of the President. We denounce it now, and we will continue to do it as long as this oppression is upon us. As to the details, as to the manner in which these things have been carried on, I have only to say that there are now hovering around the limits of my own county nefarious bands of ruffians who have mounted their gunboats, and armed themselves, and are passing through our section of country, stealing, breaking our jails, and stealing from us our property, under the pressure of this draft, for the relief of the city of Baltimore and other parts of the State. We know that to be a fact. It has occurred within our own midst within the last week.

Not expecting myself that it will lead to any great practical good, I have offered this amendment simply with the desire and the hope that if this is adopted, some step will be taken by the executive of Maryland, weak as it may be, insignificant as the State of Maryland may be in this condition of affairs, that if anything can properly be done, it may be accomplished by the proposition I have offered. With this communication the information can be got from the governor of Maryland and after having it, it seems to me that this committee, composed of three gentlemen of the convention in conjunction with the governor and the adjutant general, will convey to the department in Washington all the information they require on the subject, if there is any mode of conveying to them the extent and the actual condition of outrages heaped upon us. That will be the most efficient mode of doing it, if it is done at all; and I hope the amendment will be adopted.

Mr. HENKLE. I sincerely hope something will be done by the convention in this matter. It will come with more force and authority, if it comes from the convention. There is a great defect in one particular with regard to the draft of the State, and I want to call the attention of the convention to it particularly, as my attention has been called to it; and that is in regard to the enrolment of the State as it now exists. I see that a meeting has been recently called in Baltimore county in the vicinity of Towsontown, where they have appointed a committee to wait upon those in authority to revise their enrolment and perfect it. There are many names on the enrolment list which should not be there; some men who are away, others already in the service, and others over age; and in our section of the State particularly great numbers have absconded, because the enrolment embraced all the slaves of Maryland who were here in the beginning of the war; whereas in my section of the State nearly all the slaves of the military age have left. So the enrolment, as it stands in my county, and I believe in every county of the State, contains a number of names vastly greater than it should be, containing those in the federal army, many over age, and others whose names for other reasons should not be there.

For that reason there is a great necessity that the enrolment list should be revised, and that the attention of the authorities should be called to this matter before the coming draft is put into effect. Not that it will derange it at all. I cannot see that it will derange the operations of the general government with reference to this matter. I suppose the quota of Maryland at large will be the same, but that the relative proportion furnished by the different counties and the city of Baltimore will be changed by correcting the enrolment. I have just received a letter from a provost marshal that the quota of the 5th district of Anne Arundel county, including the deficiency of the present draft, will be sixty-one. The number liable to draft after making all deductions is three hundred and three. Now I am prepared to prove in any court of justice that there are not two hundred and fifty persons in that district liable to draft. The same thing prevails all over our county, and not only in our county but in all the counties of the State. We poll from two hundred to two hundred and twenty votes in our district. That includes the old men, and it includes a great many persons physically unfit for military duty; and the negroes are gone. I know personally that upon revising that list nothing like that number will be found subject to draft. Go over the whole county, and it is the same. You will find in the enrolment of Anne Arundel county an enrolment of at least one-third more names than she should have; and as the quota is based upon the enrolment the quota for Anne Arundel county would be at least one-third more than it should be. The quota would be vastly larger, because the basis for it is larger. When they made the draft here in June, one-half that they drafted were runaway negroes that were not there. They were there at the beginning of the war; but now they have gone into the federal army, the majority of them, but we have had no credit for them.

I am not so sanguine as my friend from Prince George's that I could trace these negroes to their regiments and find them, so as to have them set down to our credit. It is impossible for us, I believe, even to get credit for them. There have been harpies hovering over the country, and they have carried off our negroes, the Lord only knows where. We know they are gone. Still we are charged with them, and the draft is made as if they were still in our midst. We ought to have a just and accurate enrolment.

Mr. Stirling. I would like to ask the gentleman a question. If the government has upon its enrolment lists two or three thousand people who have actually gone away, are not those names liable to draft, and if they are drawn, does not the government lose just so many, not being able to find them?

Mr. Henkle. In June they drew twenty-five names in my district, and got thirteen of the twenty-five. For the other twelve they drew twenty-four more names, and out of the two dozen they only got six; not because they were exempt for physical disability, for our surgeon does not exempt any, but because they were not there—not to be found. It is not only of my own district that I speak; for I am familiar with others, and what is true of my district is true of every district in the county, and the slaveholding section of the State.

This is a mere matter of justice, and I earnestly hope the convention will do something in the matter. I hope they will ask for a correction of the lists, and that the apportionment of the State may be made in accordance with the corrected list. The government can make it up with a very little trouble, by the aid of the provost marshals, who can give them the information in two days, or even in twenty-four hours, all that is necessary with regard to my district, and so of every district in the whole State.

Mr. Pugh. My objection to the intervention of this convention in this matter is simply this. The first reason why I object to it is on account of its impracticability In the first place, I understand that the governor, who is requested to be one of a party to investigate this matter, according to the amendment of the gentleman from Calvert (Mr. Briscoe,) and to be requested to give us the information according to the amendment of the gentleman from Allegany (Mr. Hebb,) is not in Annapolis at this time. Even if he were here, I have not heard anybody that has been able to show that there can be any practical result reached in time to meet the difficulty suggested before the coming draft of the 5th of September. Now I respectfully suggest to the gentlemen from these counties that they have deferred the matter entirely too long. In our county, and in every district in the county, I believe the quota has been filled up or very nearly so. I know that if it were not the case there would be very little hope then of having anything done about the quota for the present draft, between now and the 5th of September. In my judgment it can amount to nothing. The arrangements cannot be made to arrive at a proper result before the present draft takes place. I fear that the only result that can happen at all will be interfering with the draft. If the counties have not prepared to meet it, and if they have any grievances, they should certainly have taken some measures themselves. If they have not, it is very unfortunate for them that they did not urge this matter upon the convention some time since. I shall oppose this for the reason I have stated, and for no other, that it interferes with the draft.

Mr. Henkle. I am astonished that it should be said to produce delay. I can see no difficulty at all. It is not a matter which would require a week to readjust entirely.

Mr. Pugh. I do not acknowledge the justice or propriety of this; but I acknowledge that the counties should have looked out for this matter. I believe that was their duty.

Mr. HENKLE. And because our county has not sent emissaries down to buy up their quota, instead of filling it up in a proper manner, gentlemen are to vote against a resolution which they must acknowledge is a matter of justice, to give us simply a corrected enrolment.

Mr. AUDOUN. Allusion has been made to Baltimore city receiving more men than she was justly entitled to. Baltimore city through its mayor and city council, has offered large bounties for the purpose of assisting the government. The difficulty I ascribe to the counties is just this, that there is no disposition on the part of persons in the counties to fulfil their responsibility, and to assist the government. Hence, this difficulty that they call upon us to relieve them from.

Mr. BERRY, of Prince George's. I will ask the gentleman whether every county of the State did not pay ten cents on the one hundred dollars, to pay the bounties appropriated at the last session of the legislature? I know that every man in my county did. We offered no objection to paying it.

Mr. MAYHUGH. I am in favor of the resolution as perfected by the adoption of the amendment of the gentleman from Allegany (Mr. Hebb.) I should have voted for the amendment of the gentleman from Calvert (Mr. Briscoe,) but as he has denounced the very authorities from which he seeks favor, I must vote against it. I think it is proper that Maryland men should take care of the rights of Marylanders. If there is no power in the State of Maryland to take care of ourselves, then the whole resolution is out of order. But I know in my experience in my own county, that dead men have been drafted; that men who went into the confederate army have been drafted; that men who enlisted for the sake of the bounties in other States have been drafted. These things have been enacted in our midst, and we have been negligent about it. It has occurred a thousand times in our county; and yet our quota stands. But I have no objection to receive the information. It is but just and right that we should receive it. I shall therefore vote for the resolution as amended; but I must oppose the amendment of the gentleman from Calvert.

Mr. BRISCOE. I enunciated my opinions about the mode in which the draft should be made. I recognized the doctrine that it should be left to the States themselves to provide the number of men required, upon a requisition made upon the governor in the constitutional mode. I say that the President of the United States should have made a requisition upon the States for their quotas, and the quota would have been provided from the States by the State authorities. If that proceeding had been adopted, instead of the mode that has been adopted, I believe that it would have more successfully operated to bring forth the men of the country to fight its battles.

As to the political question, I simply state now that I do regard it as an unconstitutional proceeding upon the part of the government to call directly upon the people of the States without the interposition of the State governments for the men to go into this war. That is offered as an individual opinion. That is my opinion of the constitutional powers of the State and of the general government. As to the actual mode in which this draft has been made and carried practically out, I have simply to say that I believe the President of the United States has already declared to the governor of Maryland that these acts have been done without his authority. I know very well that officers and men in the uniform of the army of the United States come there, with assumed authority from some quarter, and perpetrated these outrages upon us. We denounce them coming from any quarter.

It is a matter of great astonishment to me that although a gentleman upon the other side recognizes the wrong perpetrated, and thinks there is injustice being done to some portions of the State, and even to his own section, he is unwilling, because I have undertaken to express my opinion as to the constitutional question, to vote for that which he conceives to be right. If the gentleman is prepared to take that position, he may have the benefit of it. I know very well that the practical operation of this thing, so far as it affects my section of the State, has been an unmitigated outrage upon it. I did not charge the government of Maryland with it. I did not denounce the governor of Maryland for it. But I said that helpless and insignificant as we were in this conjuncture of circumstances, I did not see that any practical good could result from the whole thing; but if any good was to result I thought the amendment I proposed was the most efficient mode of reaching it.

I care very little whether this convention adopts it or not. I care very little whether they vote it down or not. I simply desire so far as I am concerned, by my vote to do what I can to protect our rights. I think we should not undertake to ask through the State. My mode of doing it, if I stood in the majority here, would be to go and demand it, and to tell them when they put their hands on us, that they are violating their oath, that they are perjurers. That is my mode of doing it. I would have no half way mode of doing it. I would demand it as the representative of the majority of the people of Maryland.

I simply propose that amendment because I think it would be the most efficient mode of reaching the object of the gentleman from Prince George's (Mr. Berry.)

Mr. STIRLING. I move that this subject be indefinitely postponed.

Mr. BERRY, of Prince George's, demanded the yeas and nays, and they were ordered.

The question being taken, the result was—yeas 44, nays 28—as follows:

Yeas—Messrs. Goldsborough, President; Abbott, Annan, Audoun, Brooks, Carter, Cunningham, Cushing, Daniel, Earle, Ecker, Galloway, Hatch, Hebb, Hopkins, Hopper, Keefer, Kennard, King, Larsh Markey, Mayhugh, McComas, Mullikin, Murray, Negley, Nyman, Parker, Pugh, Purnell, Ridgely, Robinette, Russell, Schlosser, Smith, of Carroll, Smith, of Worcester, Sneary, Stirling, Stockbridge, Swope, Sykes, Todd, Wickard, Wooden—44.

Nays—Messrs. Belt, Berry, of Prince George's, Billingsley, Blackiston, Bond, Briscoe, Brown, Chambers, Clarke, Crawford, Davis, of Charles, Dent, Duvall, Edelen, Gale, Harwood, Henkle, Hodson, Horsey, Jones, of Somerset, Landsdale, Lee, Marbury, Mitchell, Miller, Morgan, Parran, Smith, of Dorchester, Turner—28.

As their names were severally called, the following members explained their votes:

The PRESIDENT said: I have some difficulty in voting upon this question. I have always evinced every disposition to give gentlemen all the information upon any particular subject that they may desire; but from the tenor of the debate it seems that gentlemen of the opposition do not ask this as a matter of favor upon the part of the convention, but demand it as a matter of right. It might be to some extent a matter of right, were this a properly constituted body authorized to make the demand; but I do not conceive that the convention, having been assembled for a specific purpose, has strictly anything to do with this question. I would have been perfectly willing to vote for the proposition of the gentleman from Allegany, considering it a concession upon the part of the majority toward the minority. That concession I conceive has not been met in a proper spirit; and conceiving that this discussion may have some ulterior object not directly indicated by the proposition, I am constrained to vote for the motion of the gentleman from Baltimore city. There is such a thing as killing a proposition by talking it to death, and I think this has been effectually killed. I vote "aye."

Mr. BERRY, of Prince George's, said: I did not offer this proposition with a view of creating any ill-feeling in this convention. If I had supposed that any ill-feeling would have been created, I would not have offered the proposition. I thought it was a fair one. It was acknowledged yesterday to be a fair and just one. But I did not regard it as a favor of the majority, but as a right which I took it for granted, that the majority of this convention as sensible and honest men, desiring to render to every one justice, would accord to the minority. I shall vote against the motion of the gentleman from Baltimore city to postpone indefinitely. I think the minority of this convention have a right to complain of the action of the majority. I vote "no."

Mr. BILLINGSLEY said: I believe that St. Mary's county has not received the credit she is entitled to receive. Believing that this order is calculated to accomplish that object, I am in favor of it; and any disposition to postpone indefinitely an act of that character, I deem gross injustice to the people whom I represent. If we have slaves in the service of the United States, for which we have not received a credit; and we can by any possibility through the action of this convention obtain that information, it is your duty as honest and as honorable men, to accord it to us. So far as I am concerned, I seek not to accomplish any other object than justice to the people of Maryland. I have no other principle in this, or in any other vote which I have ever cast in this convention. I vote "no."

Mr. BRISCOE said: So far as my vote is concerned, gentlemen upon the other side may take the responsibility of their position, and I take mine. I do not care whether the proposition be killed by talking it down, or in any other way. I know what I consider right. I know that the governor of the State of Maryland has been treated in the past with ignominious contempt by the President of the United States, even on the matter before the convention. He went and saw the President personally, and he says:

"I complained of these proceedings to the President of the United States, and was informed that no orders upon the subject had then been given, and that it was under consideration. After the lapse of a month, the practice still continuing, no order relating to it yet appearing, and continued complaints from loyal owners still reaching me, I addressed a written communication to the President, remonstrating against the practice, and invoking his interposition.

"This led to another conference with him and the secretary of war, the result of which, as I thought, was the suspension of the practice until an opportunity could be offered to the owners to voluntarily offer their slaves to the government at a certain rate of compensation, and to meet by that means its supposed necessities. But the suspension did not take place, and the practice still continued with as little system as ever on the part of the recruiting officers."

The governor has already been there and complained of this injustice, and no practical good resulted from it in any way. I should be willing to put it into such a shape that I could hope it might accomplish the object, and I shall vote against the postponement. I vote "no."

Mr. CHAMBERS. I repudiate all untold,

latent, backstair purpose, in giving this vote. I disclaim now and forever any such purpose. I repudiate the suggestion of any motive other than that these gentlemen think they can obtain justice by this process. I desire to say that I have taken no interest in it because I was hopeless of justice, so far as any particular part of the State was concerned. I desired to give them an opportunity, because they supposed it would be of some advantage. And I therefore vote against the postponement, "no."

Mr. DENT said: I am not in the habit of explaining any vote which I am about to give at any time; but as it has been intimated, I supported the proposition for the purpose of ascertaining facts which we considered important for our section of the State to relieve us from what might be considered an oppressive drain upon our population. As it has been said that it would be a concession upon the part of the majority towards the minority, to afford them the opportunity asked for, I must say that I repudiate it entirely as a concession. It never is a concession to accord justice and right—never. It is one of the matters which minorities have a right to demand. Majorities can enforce them; minorities have to ask for them, and we have asked for it. The opportunity will be denied us, I suppose, by the prevalence of the motion which has been made to dispose of this matter; but I shall vote "no."

Mr. HEBB said: I offered the amendment in good faith, intending to vote for the proposition as amended; but for the reasons so well set forth by the president, I vote "aye."

Mr. JONES, of Somerset, said: The gentleman from Kent (Mr. Chambers) has expressed my sentiments very well on this subject. I knew nothing in the world of the proposition until it was submitted, nor have I heard anything outside of the house with reference to it. All that I know of it has been said upon this floor. In fact I saw very little difference between sending a committee, and sending a letter, and should have preferred the amendment of the gentleman from Allegany, except that I did not think it was of sufficient importance to interfere with the proposition as made by the gentleman from Prince George's (Mr. Berry,) not varying the language, but being only another mode to effect the same purpose. I should have been very much gratified to adopt either mode, personally, although sending written communications has been most usual. The governor has certainly been in correspondence with the federal government upon this question. What has transpired we do not know. The governor is under no obligation, and it would not perhaps be proper for him, to communicate to us the information without being asked. The idea of there being a majority and a minoriy of the convention upon such a subject as this, is one which I am sorry to hear. This is a question which concerns the quota of Maryland; and is there any portion of Maryland, any county of Maryland, that has so fallen under the ban as to be unworthy of putting an inquiry, and that the remainder of the State, and the majority of this house shall be perfectly careless whether the whole population is swept away unjustly by the federal army, and the women and children left to perish with cold and hunger through the coming winter, or not? I wish the information to be given. I am not particular about the mode. I trust our friends will agree together upon the mode, and will permit a respectful note to be addressed to the governor, and that the governor will give us the information he may have from the authorities. I vote "no."

Mr MARBURY. I repudiate the idea that in supporting this order I am influenced by any unfair motive whatever; either at first in introducing this subject, or now in voting upon it. I considered it a subject in which the whole State of Maryland, and more particularly my portion of the State, were deeply interested. I have been frequently talked to upon this subject. I have heard it talked over and over again for the last five or six months, and have understood that private individuals had sought for the information time and time again, without any success. I thought the State convention of Maryland, men coming from all portions of the State, would carry a great deal more weight in anything they might present to the consideration of the government; and that the adoption of this course would prove much more successful.

But I have derived the consolation from the defeat of this, that perhaps there will be another exhibition to the people of Maryland of the temper of this convention called by the people to frame a new constitution. There are some most extraordinary and most offensive provisions in this constitution, and they will see in this a manifestation of the same disposition that incorporated them.

I beg gentlemen if they have any regard whatever for fairness, that they will consider this subject and see if there is anything latent. Let some gentleman here suggest an idea of anything latent in a proposition of this sort, and he can at once arouse a prejudice against it. I merely desire to get this information upon which men in this State can bring their influence to bear. It was with that object that the subject was first introduced into this convention by myself. I vote "no."

Mr. MAYHUGH. As I have expressed my willingness to vote for the proposition as it stood amended on the motion of the gentleman from Allegany, it is necessary for me to say why it is that I change my vote. I believe the order before the convention entirely out of place, so far as the duty of this convention is concerned; that as a duty incumbent upon any member of this convention, they are not compelled to vote upon such orders as that. Desiring the information, as I observed before, I would have voted for that order, and against the amendment proposed by the member from Calvert (Mr. Briscoe,) but it is not too late yet for the people of my county to get the information, provided they attend to their duty. I was willing to vote to favor the counties which could not have the same privilege or benefit, upon the ground that I believed it was a favor to those counties.

But when gentlemen get up in this convention, and declare in their conversation and in their speech that it is the duty of members of this convention, and they demand it as a matter of right, then I get up and say it is outside the duties of this convention, and there can be no such proper demand made by any gentleman upon this floor. I was willing to give them all the influence of this convention to favor these counties that complain so much, knowing at the same time that the information could be obtained in my own county as yet, and that we could have the matter adjusted there properly. But as they take it as no favor, as they regard it as no concession whatever upon the part of the majority of this convention, I do not wish to throw the moral weight of the convention in their favor. I vote "aye."

Mr. Negley said: For the reasons so forcibly expressed by my colleague (Mr. Mayhugh,) I vote "aye."

Mr. Stirling said: I had intended and made up my mind to vote for the proposition of my friend from Allegany, although I did it with a great deal of reluctance. I thought from the statements made that there might have been some injustice done in the enrolment, and although I did not like to give the expression of the sense of the convention in favor of a positive revision of the enrolment, yet I was willing to meet the matter fairly, and to give the moral weight of the convention in favor of inquiring into the matter. But I do not recognize the right of anybody to offer a proposition here and insist upon its being adopted. We offered an amendment and they voted against it on the other side. Then another member rises and makes another proposition, and makes an assault upon the government. When a proposition of this sort is urged upon us, and made the basis of denouncing the government, and abusing it, I wash my hands of the whole transaction, and vote against sustaining any such proposition. I vote "aye."

Mr. Belt said: I merely wish to say, to explain my vote in part, that it strikes me as exceedingly rich that the gentleman from Washington, and more particularly the gentleman from the city of Baltimore, should object to the passage of a resolution of this kind; because not germain to the proper functions of this convention. No such objection was urged by those gentlemen at the time a resolution was offered calling upon the military authorities to banish half the people of this State from its limits, or to assess the damage inflicted upon the property of certain classes of our own people upon them. That was just as far from the business of this convention as this order is. I vote "no."

Mr. Mayhugh. I was not here at the time, and did not vote upon the resolutions.

The motion to postpone indefinitely accordingly prevailed.

ATTORNEY GENERAL AND STATE'S ATTORNEYS.

On motion of Mr. Stockbridge,

The convention proceeded to consider the report of the committee on State's attorneys, which was on its second reading.

Mr. Belt moved that the convention adjourn.

The question being then taken, upon the motion to adjourn, upon a division—ayes 29, noes 38—it was not agreed to.

Section one of the report was then read, as follows:

"Section 1. There shall be an attorney general elected by the people of the State on general ticket on the ——— day of ——— next, and on the same day ——— every ——— year thereafter, who shall hold his office for ——— years from the first Monday of January next ensuing his election, and until his successor shall be elected and qualified, and shall be re-eligible thereto, and shall be subject to removal therefrom for incompetency, wilful neglect of duty, or misdemeanor in office on conviction in a court of law."

Mr. Daniel. I move to amend this section by striking out the words, "elected by the people of the State, on general ticket, on the ——— day of ——— next, and on the same day ——— every ——— year thereafter," and insert the words "appointed by the governor, by and with the advice and consent of the Senate."

I have but a word or two to say upon this question. My reason for moving this amendment is this: this officer, judging from his duties as prescribed in this report, seems to be a sort of confidential adviser of the governor, as well as an officer to defend the interests of the State. It seems therefore peculiarly proper that the governor should have the selection of an officer who is to be consulted by the governor, in all matters where his advice and counsel are desired.

Mr. Thruston. I am disposed to favor the proposition of the gentleman from Baltimore city (Mr. Daniel.) But if this officer is to be appointed by the governor, I would suggest that his term of office should be made to correspond with that of the governor.

Mr. DANIEL. This question will test the question in regard to the mode of appointment. The other question can be decided afterwards.

Mr. SMITH, of Carroll. I desire to say a word, to show that there is no inconsistency between the vote I shall give upon the proposition of the gentleman from Baltimore city (Mr. Daniel,) and my action in having reported this section from the committee. I am generally in favor of giving the people the right to elect their officers, and not to deprive them of any privilege in that regard which they have heretofore exercised. And one strong argument introduced here in favor of an elective judiciary, is that the people having once exercised that privilege are not disposed to abandon it. That argument, however, does not apply to this case.

I think that the confidential and intimate relations that must necessarily exist between the governor and the attorney general are such as make it very advisable that he should be appointed rather than elected. The governor of the State will be forced to appoint a person learned in the law, and of honor and integrity. And the governor would be held responsible for the faithful discharge of the duties of the officer thus appointed. If this constitution be adopted by the people, I have no doubt that a great many important questions will be submitted to the attorney general, for the many changes we propose will bring up many questions to be decided. I think, therefore, under the circumstances, considering the relations which will exist between these two officers, that the governor ought to have the privilege of making the appointment. In my estimation it will better subserve the public interests.

The question was upon the amendment of Mr. DANIEL.

Upon this question Mr. DANIEL called the yeas and nays, and they were ordered.

The question being then taken, by yeas and nays, it resulted—yeas 24, nays 33—as follows:

Yeas—Messrs. Goldsborough, President; Bond, Briscoe, Chambers, Clarke, Daniel, Davis, of Charles, Dent, Earle, Edelen, Hopkins, Lee, Mitchell, Miller, Mullikin, Parker, Parran, Purnell, Ridgely, Russell, Smith, of Carroll, Stockbridge, Sykes, Todd—24.

Nays—Messrs. Abbott, Annan, Audoun, Blackiston, Brooks, Brown, Cunningham, Duvall, Ecker, Gale, Galloway, Hatch, Hebb, Horsey, Jones, of Somerset, Keefer, Kennard, King, Larsh, Marbury, Markey, Mayhugh, McComas, Murray, Negley, Nyman, Robinette, Sands, Schlosser, Stirling, Swope, Wickard, Wooden—33.

The amendment was accordingly rejected.

Mr. HEBB moved to fill up the first two blanks in the section, so that it should read—

"There shall be an attorney general elected by the people of the State, on general ticket, on the Tuesday next after the first Monday in November, in the year eighteen hundred and sixty-four."

The question being taken, the motion was agreed to.

Mr. SMITH, of Carroll, moved to fill the other blanks, so that it would read—

"And on the same day in every fourth year thereafter, who shall hold his office for four years from the first Monday of January next ensuing his election," &c.

Mr. HEBB. I move to make the term of office two years, so that it may conform to the terms of the comptroller and treasurer.

The question was stated to be upon the longest time, being that proposed by Mr. SMITH, of Carroll, which was agreed to.

No further amendment was offered to the first section.

Section two was then read as follows:

"SEC. 2. All elections for attorney general shall be certified to, and returns made thereof by the clerks of the circuit courts for the several counties, and the clerk of the superior court of Baltimore city, to the governor of the State, whose duty it shall be to decide upon the election and qualifications of the person returned, and in case of a tie between two or more persons, to designate which of said persons shall qualify as attorney general and to administer the oath of office to the person elected."

No amendment was offered to this section.

Section three was then read as follows:

"SEC. 3. It shall be the duty of the attorney general to prosecute and defend, on the part of the State, all cases which at the time of his election and qualification, and thereafter may be depending in the court of appeals, or in the supreme court of the United States, by or against the State, or wherein the State may be interested; and he shall give his opinion in writing whenever required by the general assembly, or either branch thereof, the governor, the comptroller, the treasurer or any State's attorney on any matter or subject depending before them; and when required by the governor or the general assembly, he shall aid any State's attorney in prosecuting any suit, or action brought by the State, in any court of this State; and he shall commence and prosecute or defend any suit, or action in any of said courts, on the part of the State, as the general assembly or the governor, acting according to law, shall direct to be commenced, prosecuted, or defended, and he shall receive for his services an annual salary of ——— thousand dollars; but he shall not be entitled to receive any fees, perquisites, or rewards whatever, in addition to the salary aforesaid, for the performance of any official duty, nor have power to appoint any agent, representative, or deputy, under any circumstances whatever."

Mr. AUDOUN moved to fill the blank so as to

make the salary three thousand dollars per annum.

Mr. STIRLING moved to make the annual salary twenty-five hundred dollars.

Mr. EDELEN moved to make it two thousand dollars.

The question was first upon "three thousand dollars."

Mr. MILLER. I would state before the vote is taken upon this question, that by a report made by the comptroller or the treasurer in the early part of our session, it appears that there has been expended by the general assembly of the State for special counsel fees, under the provision in the constitution, allowing the governor to appoint special counsel for particular cases, the sum of $24,475, or nearly $2,000 a year since this present constitution went into operation. And that expense has been in consequence of the want of such an officer as an attorney general. I think that according to the rate of payment hitherto made for special counsel fees, taking into consideration also the present state of the currency, three thousand dollars a year is little enough compensation for such an officer as this.

Mr. BRISCOE. The amount expended for special counsel since the adoption of the present constitution, has been much more than $24,000. I have ascertained that special counsel have received fees and commissions to the amount of $12,000 or $15,000. If the commissions were taken into calculation the amount paid to special counsel for the last thirteen or fourteen years, would be found to be at least $40,000.

Mr. MILLER. That would make it about $3,000 a year.

Mr. KING. A portion of that, some $3,000 or $4,000 was paid for counsel to go out of the State.

Mr. MILLER. The attorney general is to perform that duty under the proposed article.

Mr. JONES, of Somerset. Under the provisions of the constitution as proposed in this respect, the attorney general will be subject to be directed by the governor to assist in the trial of criminal cases of every kind. He may be ordered to go to Allegany county, or Washington county, or Somerset county; all over the State. And his time will be very nearly exhausted in giving opinions to the governor, comptroller, treasurer, State's attorneys, and other officers, on all subjects, and I think he will have very little time for other practice.

Mr. NEGLEY. I am as much in favor of keeping down salaries as anybody. But you better strike out this provision altogether than to put in an inadequate salary. Because if you put in an insufficient salary, you cannot get the services of a man whose services will be worth anything. And rather than have a second or third rate man in the office, you better strike out the provision entirely. Three thousand dollars a year is little enough for such an officer. They are the younger members of the bar who are elected State's attorneys, and they will be continually calling upon the attorney general for his opinion, and perhaps require his personal assistance at the trial. He is to be besides the legal adviser of the governor, comptroller, treasurer, and even of the legislature; he will have his hands full. Three thousand dollars a year is not too large. Let us have salary enough to secure a good officer, or let us have none at all.

Mr. BOND. In my judgment, a salary of three thousand dollars a year is little enough for a good lawyer. The attorney general, by this report, is forbidden to receive any other fee or compensation whatever, except his salary. As has been well remarked by the gentleman from Washington county (Mr. Negley,) you better strike out this provision entirely, than not get a good man in this office; and you cannot get a good one, unless you give him a good compensation.

Mr. MAYHUGH. I very much regret to see the disposition on the part of members of this convention to make new offices, and to increase the salaries of old ones. This is not increasing salaries, it is true; but is creating a new office. For the last fourteen years, the expenses for special counsel fees has been about $1.800 a year.

A MEMBER. It has been a great deal more than that.

Mr MAYHUGH. If gentlemen desire to defeat this constitution they can accomplish that purpose by weighing it down with such things as these. I am opposed to the creation of new offices, especially when they are unnecessary; and I am decidedly opposed to any increase of salaries. Whenever I have voted I have voted against them, and I intend to continue so to vote. I have a constituency who will hold me responsible for my action here. In this time of heavy taxation, especially when the people of western Maryland have been plundered and robbed, and almost deprived of the means of carrying on their necessary business, when they are taxed by the county, and by the State, and by the federal government, it is decidedly out of place to be creating new offices, and increasing the salaries of old ones. I must oppose all these measures, and shall do it at all hazards. And I shall at least vote to make this salary two thousand instead of three thousand dollars.

Mr. STIRLING. I think the views of my friend from Washington (Mr. Mayhugh) are correct so far as the general principle is concerned. I have myself on several occasions voted here not to put these salaries too high. I have no objection to putting the salary of the attorney general at $2,500, though I think that is full low. But I suggested that sum, because I know there is an indisposition to pay large salaries.

This is not really creating a new office. It is merely re-distributing duties that are now performed under another name, and so far from increasing expenses to the State, it is saving expenses. It is true that so far as this report of the comptroller shows, the expense for the last fourteen years for these duties have not averaged much over $1,800 a year. But last year it was considerably in excess of $3,000. But the report does not include those cases in which gentleman have been employed by the treasury department and have received commissions out of moneys collected for the State. I know that one gentleman under the late comptroller received a very considerable commission; not too much, for it was a very valuable service which he performed. In regard to matters of that sort, whenever that kind of compensation is made it is not contained in the report of the comptroller or treasurer. Now if you take into account the commissions which have been paid for these services, it will amount to much more than $1,800 a year.

Now you must have for attorney general a man who is accustomed to trying cases, or he will not be fit for the office. And any man who has a good practice trying cases makes a considerable sum of money every year by trying cases against the State. But if such a man accepts this office, he must give up entirely that portion of his practice. Taking all these things into consideration, I believe a competent attorney general at three thousand dollars a year will be a saving to the State of at least a thousand dollars a year.

Mr. EDELEN. I would ask the gentleman from Baltimore city (Mr. Stirling) if in his opinion, the duties which this attorney general will be required to perform will be sufficient to occupy all his time? In other words, would he not have time to transact and attend to considerable private practice?

Mr. STIRLING. I suppose he would have some time. But no man will be willing to engage himself as the permanent counsel of the State, unless he gets a competent salary, for it will greatly affect his practice. There are many lawyers who receive from five hundred to a thousand dollars a year from criminal practice alone. If a man takes the position of attorney general he must resign all that portion of his practice, because he cannot take a case against the State. Then the attorney general would necessarily be required to reside in Annapolis a great deal of the time during the session of the legislature, and would have to pay board while here, and he must also go about the State a great deal.

In regard to the necessity of such an office as this, I think every one who has paid any attention to the subject has been convinced of the vices of the present system. The governor has absolute discretion to employ any counsel, and any number of counsel he pleases; and so with other officers of the State. And it has become a sort of favoritism to reward certain lawyers. And it has got to be the practice that no man comes down here to perform such services for the legislature but what he expects his five hundred or his thousand dollars. And every man considers it a sort of grab at the treasury, as the only kind or instance of that service that he will get from the State, and he therefore considers himself entitled to a good fee. And besides the opinion of a man who has no official responsibility is not such an opinion as the State is entitled to. The opinion of such a man is not matter of record to the extent that the opinions of the attorney general would be. Besides that, you now have half a dozen men, one of whom may give one opinion and another give another opinion, which will control the action of the State authorities upon the same subject in the course of two or three years. But by having this officer, you at least secure uniformity of opinion during the term of his office.

Besides that there is a supervision exercised over the State's attorneys. This does not go back to the old system, but secures advice and co-operation in such a manner as to give us a uniformity in the criminal administration of the State. As it is now, with the different views that may be taken by different State's attorneys in regard to criminal law, one man may be acquitted by one State's attorney in one county, and another convicted by another in the next county, on the same charge. It is an anomaly that the criminal administration of the State of Maryland should be represented by twenty-one different officers. This office unites the judicial system of the State so far as responsibility is concerned. And I am of the opinion that if you give this officer three thousand dollars a year you will save at least a thousand dollars a year to the State, if not more.

Mr. BOND. There is one thing to be said; it is made the duty of the attorney general to try all cases in which the State is interested, in the supreme court of the United States, as well as elsewhere, and I suppose his travelling expenses, and expenses at Washington, will amount to at least five hundred dollars a year.

Mr. STOCKBRIDGE. I suppose that any one at all familiar with the legal business of the State, must feel the absolute necessity of the office proposed in this report. Without any disrespect to those officers, it is a notorious fact that the State's attorneys in some of the counties are far from being qualified to discharge the duties which devolve upon them, even in the local trials there. And when the cases which they have tried there come up here to the court of appeals, they are utterly incompetent to follow them up here and try them. The consequence is that it has been a necessity forced upon our governors almost if not quite without exception, since the present constitution has been in operation, to employ additional counsel. I do not know to what extent; I have not looked over the list of counsel employed, very carefully; but I know there is at least one mistake in it. I am aware of the employment of at least one attorney who has received fees from the State who is not included there.

The PRESIDENT. Some of them have been employed under acts of the general assembly.

Mr. STOCKBRIDGE. If we compare the salary proposed here with that paid to any great corporation, municipal or otherwise, for similar services, we will find that the largest sum which has been named here is a moderate one. The Baltimore and Ohio railroad company pays very considerably more than that every year for its counsel fees.

Mr. ABBOTT. Allow me to correct the gentleman. Mr. Latrobe manages the business of that company for a thousand dollars a year.

Mr. STOCKBRIDGE. He transacts a part of it; he is only one of three or four employed.

Mr. ABBOTT. He transacts the attorney general part of it.

Mr. STOCKBRIDGE. Not at all. I happen to know that there are several counsel who do business for that company who receive that sum. The amount Mr. Latrobe receives is the same he began with years ago; and as far as I am aware it has never been raised. But they have a great many special counsel. It is notorious here; I know any number of counsel employed by them.

Mr. CHAMBERS. The late Mr. Scott did more business for that company than did Mr. Latrobe.

Mr. STOCKBRIDGE. The corporation attorney of the city of New York receives, I believe, five thousand dollars a year. And certainly the business of the State of Maryland is of quite as much importance as the business of that corporation. The cost to the city of Baltimore for legal services, year by year, is more than the largest sum named here. And whether we look to the services required to be performed, or the importance and the delicate nature of them, or the great interests involved in comparison with the duties of other attorneys, we shall find that the largest sum named here is moderate.

Mr. EDELEN. I wish to make but one remark. I dissent altogether from the views taken by the two gentlemen from Baltimore city (Messrs. Stirling and Stockbridge,) in instituting any comparison between what has been paid to special counsel in times past, through the medium of the legislature and other authorities, and the salary now proposed to be given to the attorney general. We all know that sometimes for very slight services very liberal fees are paid by the general assembly of Maryland.

The view upon which I act in regard to this matter is this; we have already determined that the judges of our court of appeals shall not receive more than three thousand dollars per annum. When they go upon the bench they are debarred from all practice. They have to devote their time, their abilities, their labor, to that one thing. They are employed constantly nearly ten months in every year. When not actually engaged in court they are required to devote their time to preparing opinions. And after a careful examination of the duties of the attorney general, as enumerated in section three of this report, I have come to the conclusion that he will have ample and abundant time for the prosecution and transaction of a large private practice.

I wish to correct the impression which was made upon my mind—I do not know how it was with others here—by the remark of the gentleman from Anne Arundel (Mr. Miller,) in relation to the attorney general being cut off from any other fees and perquisites.

The section reads—

"But he shall not be entitled to receive any fees, perquisites, or rewards whatever, in addition to the salary aforesaid, for the performance of any official duty," &c.

That only means that he shall not charge any fees to the State, but does not debar him from private practice. That I submit is the true construction.

And I differ altogether from the construction of this section as given by my friend from Somerset (Mr. Jones.) It does not require the attorney general to go to the several counties of the State and take part in the prosecution of any criminal upon any indictment at the suit of the State of Maryland.

Without wishing further to transgress upon the time of the convention, I will say that I think all of us recognize the truth of the remarks of the gentleman from Washington (Mr. Mayhugh,) that we ought to reduce the expenses of this State as much as possible, in consideration of the fact that the people of this State have now, and will have for many years to come, to bear heavy taxation. I think, under all the circumstances that two thousand dollars a year is an ample salary, one abundantly sufficient for the attorney general.

Mr. CHAMBERS. I desire to say a word or two in regard to this matter, and the illustration offered by the gentleman from Baltimore city (Mr. Stockbridge.) I happen to know something about the conducting of the business of the Baltimore and Ohio railroad company. The late distinguished and intelligent gentleman, Mr. Scott, who resided for a long time in Harford, was perhaps the most active lawyer in trying the causes of the Baltimore and Ohio railroad company: if you go by per centage, he tried ten to one of any other counsel. He had half a dozen associates. The late Hon. Mr. Pearce was one;

Mr. Thomas was another, and there were others. However, we are not to be governed by the action of the Baltimore and Ohio railroad company in this respect.

The idea which has been suggested that this is increasing the expense of the State, is altogether a mistaken idea, as much so as any idea that ever was presented. It is just the reverse. The State, since this office of attorney general has been abolished, has not only actually paid more than it did before, but it has committed—I will not say fraud—but great injustice in many cases. You know, Mr. President, as well as I do, a case in which I was concerned for one month. The president of this convention was the special judge. That was eight years ago, and to-day I have not received one dollar for my services in that case.

Some gentlemen in the house, when they hear of a lawyer receiving one or two hundred dollars for his services, think it a very great affair, and go to talking about what a day laborer receives. But notwithstanding all this injustice, which I suppose has been perpetrated upon others as well as myself, the actual cost to the State has been greater than when we had an attorney general. Let gentlemen take up the statutes and turn to the comptroller's account and they will find that the State has paid more for these legal services than it would cost to have an attorney general at three thousand dollars a year. We have suffered nothing but evil, inconvenience and mischief, since the destruction of this office. We all know that at the last convention this office was discontinued, not from any belief that the office was unnecessary, but purely from personal considerations, having relation to the individual who it was supposed was going to have the office. It was abolished not in consequence of any judgment formed in regard to the expediency of the matter, but solely from personal considerations.

Now let gentlemen listen a moment to the duties to be performed by this officer, and they will find that it is perfectly impracticable for him to do anything else, if indeed he can discharge all the duties required of him by this section three of the report.

"It shall be the duty of the attorney general to prosecute and defend, on the part of the State, all cases which at the time of his election and qualification, and thereafter, may be depending in the court of appeals, or in the supreme court of the United States, by or against the State, or wherein the State may be interested; and he shall give his opinion in writing whenever required by the general assembly or either branch thereof, the governor, the comptroller, the treasurer, or any State's attorney, on any matter depending before them," &c.

Every county in the State is to have its State's attorney, and every attorney of every county is to ask the attorney general, just as often as his own ignorance may require, for information which the attorney general is obliged to give. But that is not all.

"And when required by the governor or the general assembly, he shall aid any State's attorney in prosecuting any suit, or action brought by the State, in any court of this State; and he shall commence and prosecute or defend any suit, or action, in any of said courts, on the part of the State, as the general assembly, or the governor, acting according to law may direct."

Now, how can any individual occupying this position, and liable to be sent off to any part of the State at any moment, attend to any private business? Talk about three thousand dollars being a large sum! It is payable in the present currency, and in point of fact it amounts in good money to less than fifteen hundred dollars. What an enormous sum! for the whole time of a man, who, unless he is one of the first lawyers in the State, is not fit for the place. You expect to obtain a man possessing the first legal abilities of the State, and you propose to pay him fifteen hundred dollars for the performance of duties which will separate him entirely from his own private concerns. I do hope this house will give this officer the highest salary which has been named, for it is not one cent too large.

The question was on the motion of Mr. Audoun to make the salary of the attorney general three thousand dollars a year.

Upon this question Mr. Mayhugh called the yeas and nays, and they were ordered.

The question being then taken, by yeas and nays, it resulted—yeas 30, nays 31—as follows:

Yeas—Messrs. Goldsborough, President; Audoun, Blackiston, Bond, Briscoe, Brooks, Carter, Chambers, Clarke, Dent, Duvall, Earle, Galloway, Hopkins, Kennard, Lansdale, Larsh, McComas, Miller, Negley, Nyman, Parker, Ridgely, Russell, Smith, of Carroll, Sneary, Stirling, Stockbridge, Sykes, Wooden—30.

Nays—Messrs. Abbott, Annan, Billingsley, Brown, Crawford, Cunningham, Daniel, Davis, of Charles, Ecker, Edelen, Gale, Hatch, Hebb, Hopper, Horsey, Keefer, King, Lee, Markey, Mayhugh, Mitchell, Mullikin, Murray, Parran, Purnell, Robinette, Schlosser, Smith, of Dorchester, Swope, Todd, Wickard—31.

The motion was accordingly not agreed to.

Mr. Abbott, when his name was called, said: As compared with the salaries paid for other services, I do not believe that there is a lawyer in the State whose services are worth more than two thousand dollars a year.

Mr. Ecker, when his name was called, said: I am in favor of making the salary of the attorney general twenty-five hundred dollars, and therefore cannot vote for this proposition, though I never did like to see anything mean. I do not want a man to work for me for nothing. But there is another thing which

I hate a great deal worse; and that is being bored almost to death by candidates for such offices. Therefore, with all due respect for the opinions of my legal friends in this case, I must vote "no"

The question then recurred upon the motion of Mr. STIRLING to fix the salary at twenty-five hundred dollars.

Upon this question Mr. WICKARD called for the yeas and nays, which were ordered.

The question being then taken, by yeas and nays, it resulted—yeas 42, nays 20—as follows:

Yeas—Messrs. Goldsborough, President; Annan, Bond, Briscoe Chambers, Cunningham, Daniel, Dent, Earle, Ecker, Galloway, Hatch, Hebb, Hopkins, Hopper, Horsey, Jones, of Somerset, Kennard, King, Lansdale, Larsh, Markey, McComas, Miller, Mullikin, Murray, Negley, Nyman, Parker, Parran, Ridgely, Russell, Schley, Smith, of Carroll, Smith, of Worcester, Sneary, Stirling, Stockbridge, Swope, Sykes, Todd, Wooden—42.

Nays—Messrs. Abbott, Audoun, Billingsley, Blackiston, Brooks, Brown, Carter, Crawford, Davis, of Charles, Edelen, Gale, Keefer, Lee, Mayhugh, Mitchell, Purnell, Robinette, Schlosser, Smith, of Dorchester, Wickard -20.

The motion of Mr. STIRLING was accordingly agreed to.

Mr. MILLER moved to strike out the words "or any State's attorney," in the clause enumerating the parties authorized to call upon the attorney general for a written opinion on any subject depending before them.

Mr. SMITH, of Carroll. I hope that amendment will not be adopted.

Mr. MILLER. I was going to say one word in explanation of my motion. By this provision, as it now stands, it is made the constitutional obligation of the attorney general to "give his opinion in writing whenever required by the general assembly, or either branch thereof, the governor, the comptroller, the treasurer, or any State's attorney, on any matter or subject depending before them."—It further provides that "when required by the governor or the general assembly, he shall aid any State's attorney in prosecuting any suit or action brought by the State in any court of this State." Now there are twenty-one State's attorneys in the State, and, under this provision as it stands, they are at liberty to require an opinion in writing from the attorney general upon any subject matter before them, and the attorney general is subject to be required to go and help them try their cases.

Mr SMITH, of Carroll. It means all official matters before them, not any private matter.

Mr. MILLER. Of course it refers to State matters. Suppose my learned friend, the chairman of this committee, (Mr. Smith, of Carroll,) is elected attorney general by the people of this State, as I hope he may be. He would sit down in his office, or wherever he might be, and I venture to say there would not be a day pass through the whole year in which he would not be required to give his opinion in writing to some State's attorney. I think it is enough for the attorney general to do to give his opinion in writing to the general assembly, the governor, the comptroller and the treasurer, when required, and also be sent to assist any State's attorney whenever the governor sees that the business of the State is not well conducted.

Now, according to this section as it now stands, it is not discretionary with the attorney general, but it is made a constitutional obligation upon him to answer all the letters of these twenty-one State's attorneys in the State upon official business pending before them. Now that is imposing upon him an amount of duty that I would not be willing that the gentleman from Carroll (Mr. Smith,) if in that position, should be made to perform.

Mr. KING. It appears to me that this is a very wrong time to bring this matter up, as we have fixed his salary. One of the arguments in favor of a high salary was that the attorney general had to aid the State's attorneys throughout the State. That was one reason why I voted for twenty-five hundred dollars.

Mr. BILLINGSLEY moved that the convention adjourn.

The question being taken, upon a division—ayes 25, noes 28—the motion to adjourn was not agreed to.

The question recurred upon the motion of Mr. MILLER to amend section three of the report by striking out the words "or any State's attorney."

Mr. SMITH, of Carroll. I hope this amendment will not be adopted. This provision was inserted here for the express purpose of making it obligatory upon the attorney general to give his opinion to the State's attorneys, who in all conscience need it greatly in some of the counties. Still I do not think it would be fair to impute so great ignorance to them as to suppose it would be necessary for the attorney general to be giving them opinions all the time. I know there are many intelligent gentlemen who occupy that position. But there are some who are not so learned in the law, for the simple reason that the fees of the office are totally inadequate to secure the services of good men. We have made provision for them to receive a certain salary, which will compensate gentlemen of ability, and enable the people to obtain their services.

I think we will be destroying the efficiency of this section, if we strike out these words. The State's attorneys throughout the counties have the right to require the opinions and the services of the attorney general upon all matters in which the State is interested, and unless there is a provision making it obligatory upon him, some gentleman occupying that position may not think it necessary to respond to all the appeals made to him by those who really need the information for the benefit of the State.

The question being then taken upon the amendment of Mr. MILLER, it was not agreed to.

No further amendment was offered to the third section.

Section four was then read, as follows:

"Sec. 4. No person shall be eligible to the office of attorney general, who has not been admitted to practice the law in the State, and who has not practiced the law for ——— years, and who has not resided for at least ——— years in the State."

Mr. SMITH, of Carroll, moved to fill the first blank with the word "ten."

Mr. SCHLEY moved to fill it with the word "five."

The question was upon filling the blank with the word "ten," involving the longest time.

Mr. SMITH, of Carroll. I think a man who is called upon to fill this responsible position, ought to have practiced law for ten years at least. It is one of the most important and responsible positions in the State. And from the circumstances that now surround us, from the changes proposed to be made by this constitution, it is evident that we require in this position the services of one who has occupied a leading position in the profession for ten years at least.

Mr. STIRLING. I partially agree with the views of my friend from Carroll (Mr. Smith.) This is a question which does not affect me one way or the other. I do not expect to fill this office, and I have practiced law for ten years. But it is possible that there is some one who has practiced law but nine years, or eight years, who is well qualified to fill this position. I do not think the people are likely to be careless in reference to this matter. I know that gentlemen have occupied places heretofore in this State probably as prominent as this, who had not practiced law for ten years. Certainly some gentlemen have been upon the bench in this State who had not practiced law for ten years. The last chief j stice of this State had not practiced near ten years, when he was called to that position. And he certainly made one of the best judges the State has had. Though I did not agree with him in politics, and he had some few failings which his friends might very well regret, still all that had nothing to do with his age, or his practice at the bar. He was abundantly able to fill the position of judge, and fully competent to fill the position of attorney general. I refer to the late chief justice LeGrand, who had not practiced law five years when called to that position. Take such a man as Judge Constable; I have no doubt everybody would have thought him fit for the place of attorney general even before he had practiced law for five years. I think you may safely trust the people to exercise a proper discretion in regard to the matter. I do not deem it a matter of very serious importance, but I shall support the proposition to fill the blank with the word "five" instead of the word "ten."

Mr. SCHLEY. I am somewhat concerned in this matter, as a citizen of this State. I am sure no one is more desirous than myself to secure ability and learning in this high office. But it occurs to me that if after a practice of five years an attorney at law does not show a fitness for this office, he will not do so after fifty years of practice. He may not have acquired as much legal acumen and learning in five years as he would in a longer time; but his legal acumen and learning will show themselves in that time.

Mr. STIRLING. I will state another instance. Governor Hicks offered the most important judgeship in Baltimore, before Judge Martin accepted the position, to a gentleman who certainly had not practiced law for five years. He offered the place to him with the entire approbation of a large portion of the bar; but he declined.

Mr. SMITH, of Carroll. I know there are instances of rather extraordinary men. But a gentleman may be learned in the law, and yet not knowing about the duties of attorney general. I think ten years is short enough time to require of one who will be called upon to apply himself to the practice of law in all its branches.

The question was upon the motion of Mr. SMITH, of Carroll, to fill the first blank with the word "ten."

The question being taken, upon a division —ayes 24, noes 26—the motion was not agreed to.

The question recurred upon the motion of Mr. SCHLEY, to fill the blank with the word "five."

Mr. CHAMBERS. I propose to fill the blank with the word "seven," as I believe seven years is as short a time as can enable a man to fit himself for this office.

The question was upon the motion of Mr. CHAMBERS, embracing the longest time.

The question being taken, upon a division —ayes 42, noes not counted—the motion was agreed to.

The question was next upon filling the blank in the last clause of the section, which read as follows:

"And who has not resided for at least ——— years in the State."

On motion of Mr. STOCKBRIDGE,

The blank was filled with the word "five."

On motion of Mr. ABBOTT,

The words "next preceding his election" were added to the clause.

On motion of Mr. CHAMBERS,

The word "therein" was inserted after the words "practiced law."

Mr. CHAMBERS. I did not notice the question at the time the last blank was filled with the word "five." In order to make the term of residence correspond with the time for which the party to be eligible to this office must have practiced law, I move to reconsider the vote by which the term of residence in the State was fixed at five years. I think the practice required should be in this State. A gentleman may come from another State in which he has practiced twenty years, and yet be quite uninformed in regard to the mode of practice, and the peculiar statute law of our State, which is the great subject of criminal jurisdiction.

The motion to reconsider the vote by which the word "five" was inserted, was agreed to.

The question recurred upon inserting the word "five."

Mr. CHAMBERS moved to insert the word "seven."

The question was upon inserting the word "seven," being the longest time.

Mr. STOCKBRIDGE. Instead of that, I will move to strike out the words, "and who has not resided for at least ——— years in the State." If that is adopted the section will then read—

"No person shall be eligible to the office of attorney general who has not been admitted to practice the law in the State, and who has not practiced the law therein for seven years next preceding his election."

Mr. STIRLING. That does not exactly fix the term of residence in this State at seven years. It is possible that a man may have practiced law in this State for seven years and not have resided here for that length of time. In New York it often happens that a man practices law there for years, and does not live in the State at all. I know gentlemen who reside in this State and go to Washington day after day and practice law. I think the section is better as it is.

Mr. STOCKBRIDGE. I will not press my motion.

The question recurred upon the motion of Mr. CHAMBERS, to fill the blank with the word "seven."

Mr. SCHLEY. I move to strike out the word "seven" where it first occurs, and insert "five."

The CHAIRMAN (Mr. Daniel.) It is not in order to move to strike out what the house has voted to put in.

The question being then taken upon the motion of Mr. CHAMBERS to insert the word "seven," it was agreed to.

Mr. STOCKBRIDGE. I move to transpose the words "in the State" from after the word years to after the word "resided." The clause will then read—

"And who has not resided in the State for at least seven years next preceding his election"

The question being taken, the motion was agreed to.

No further amendment was offered to the fourth section.

Section five was then read as follows:

"Sec. 5. In case of vacancy in the office of attorney general, or of his removal from the State, or on his conviction as herein before specified, the said vacancy shall be filled by the governor until the election and qualification of his successor, at which election said vacancy shall be filled by the voters of the State for the residue of the term thus made vacant."

Mr. MILLER. I would suggest to the chairman of the committee (Mr. Smith, of Carroll,) that there seems to be some inconsistency in this section. The section provides that in case of a vacancy it "shall be filled by the governor until the election and qualification of his successor." That covers the case of a vacancy during the time for which he was elected. And yet the section goes on to provide—"at which election said vacancy shall be filled by the voters of the State for the residue of the term thus made vacant."

Mr. CHAMBERS moved to adjourn—not agreed to.

Mr. STOCKBRIDGE. I move to amend this fifth section by striking out the words "until the election and qualification of his successor, at which election said vacancy shall be filled by the voters of the State"—so that that portion of the section will read—"the said vacancy shall be filled by the governor for the residue of the term thus made vacant."

The question being taken, the amendment was agreed to.

Mr. MILLER. I move to amend the first part of the section so that it shall read "in case of vacancy in the office of attorney general, occasioned by his death, resignation or removal from the State, or his conviction as hereinbefore specified," &c.

The question being taken, the amendment was agreed to.

LEAVE OF ABSENCE.

Mr. MARKEY asked and obtained leave of absence for a few days.

Mr. HOPPER asked and obtained leave of absence until Monday next.

Mr. HATCH moved that the convention adjourn.

Upon this question Mr. HEBB called the yeas and nays, which were ordered.

The question being then taken, by yeas and nays, upon the motion to adjourn, it was agreed to—yeas 33, nays 24—as follows:

Yeas—Messrs. Audoun, Billingsley, Blackiston, Briscoe, Brooks, Brown, Chambers, Clarke, Davis, of Charles, Dent, Edelen, Gale, Hatch, Horsey, Jones, of Somerset, Keefer, Kennard, Lansdale, Lee, Markey, Mitchell, Miller, Mullikin, Murray, Nyman, Parker, Parran, Pugh, Smith, of Dorchester, Smith, of Worcester, Sneary, Stirling, Wickard—33.

Nays—Messrs. Abbott, Annan, Cunningham, Daniel, Earle, Ecker, Galloway, Hebb, Hopkins, Hopper, King, Larsh, Mayhugh, McComas, Negley, Purnell, Ridgely, Robinette, Schley, Schlosser, Smith, of Carroll, Stockbridge, Swope, Wooden—24.

The convention accordingly adjourned until Monday next at 12 o'clock.

SEVENTY-EIGHTH DAY.

MONDAY, August 22, 1864.

The convention met at 12 o'clock, M. Mr. PUGH in the chair.

Prayer by Rev. Mr. Owen.

The roll was called, and the following members answered to their names:

Messrs. Abbott, Audoun, Berry, of Prince George's, Billingsley, Brooks, Brown, Carter, Chambers, Clarke, Crawford, Cunningham, Cushing, Daniel, Dent, Duvall, Earle, Ecker, Gale, Galloway, Harwood, Hebb, Hodson, Hollyday, Hopkins, Horsey, Jones, of Somerset, Keefer, King, Larsh, Lee, Mayhugh, Miller, Murray, Nyman, Parker, Parran, Pugh, Purnell, Robinette, Russell, Sands, Schley, Schlosser, Smith, of Carroll, Smith, of Worcester, Sneary, Stirling, Stockbridge, Swope, Thomas, Thruston, Valliant, Wickard, Wooden—54.

The journal of Friday last was read and approved.

ATTORNEY GENERAL.

The convention resumed the consideration of the unfinished business of Friday last, being the report of the committee on State's attorneys, which was on its second reading.

The fifth section, in relation to the attorney general, was under consideration, having been amended to read as follows:

"In case of vacancy in the office of attorney general, occasioned by death, resignation, or his removal from the State, or his conviction as hereinbefore specified, the said vacancy shall be filled by the governor for the residue of the term thus made vacant."

Mr. CHAMBERS. I move to amend this section by striking out the words "for the residue of the term thus made vacant." I hope to see a provision incorporated in this constitution that wherever an election takes place to fill an office, the whole term of which has not been occupied by the party first elected, that election shall be for the full term provided for the office. A man who is elected to an office for a number of years, may quit it just a short time before the election. He may have served within a short period of the whole term. As the provision now stands an officer is to be elected for the balance of the term, and then at the next election the office is to be again filled by a new election. Now, I hold that we are just as competent to elect an officer for the full term at one time as the other. I suppose nobody wishes to have a repetition of elections for the same office, short of the time for which the office was originally intended to extend. I therefore move to strike out the words "for the residue of the term thus made vacant." That will leave the general provision requiring an election to fill the office for the full term.

Mr. SMITH, of Carroll. One objection to the amendment of the gentleman from Kent (Mr. Chambers) is that it destroys the uniformity established in regard to other officers. A similar provision to the one inserted here has been adopted in regard to other officers, and I do not see any reason why it should not be retained here.

Another objection to the amendment is that it prevents the term of office of the attorney general corresponding with that of the governor. As they are in confidential relations to each other, I think they should hold office for the same time, and go out together.

Mr. CHAMBERS. It is undoubtedly true that by having the elections at one time, the terms would be the same, so far as depends upon the officers immediately elected. But I would be pleased to hear what advantange there is in that. One may die at the expiration of the first year, and his successor will be appointed for the balance of the term. The other officer may die at the expiration of the second year. Now, according to my amendment, whether his successor is appointed or elected, he will hold for a full term. I see no advantage in their holding for the same terms. What advantage or benefit can accrue to a man in Carroll county because he may be elected to an office on the same day, on which a citizen of Kent county may be elected to another office? It does not affect his office at all. The attorney general is a man by himself. I admit the fact that if my admendment prevails the terms of the attorney general and of the governor may be different. But I see no good consequences to result from a different state of things. Will the gentleman enlighten us upon that subject? I see no advantage to result to a person holding the office of State's attorney, or judge, or anything else you please, in one part of the State, whether or not he holds his office at the same time, for the same term, and goes out on the same day with some other officer in some other part of the State.

Mr. STOCKBRIDGE. The section has been already amended by providing that the governor shall fill the vacancy for the residue of the term; thus requiring but one election for each term.

Mr. CHAMBERS. I was not aware of that. I only desire that when an election takes place, it shall be for the full term. I will withdraw my amendment.

No further amendment was offered to this section.

The next section of the report was then read as follows:

STATE'S ATTORNEYS.

"Section 1. There shall be an attorney for the State in each county and the city of Baltimore, to be styled "the State's attorney," who shall be elected by the voters thereof, respectively, on the ———, and on the same day every fourth year thereafter, and hold his office for four years from the ——— next ensuing his election, and until his successor shall be elected and qualified, and shall be re-eligible thereto, and be subject to removal therefrom for incompetency, wilful neglect of duty or misdemeanor in office, on conviction in a court of law "

On motion of Mr. SMITH, of Carroll, the first blank was filled with the words, "Tuesday next after the first Monday in November, 1867."

On motion of Mr. SMITH, of Carroll,

The second blank was filled with the words, "first Monday of January."

No further amendment was offered to this section.

The next section was then read, as follows:

"Sec. 2. All elections for the State's attorney shall be certified to, and returns made thereof, by the clerks of the said counties and city to the judges thereof having criminal jurisdiction, respectively, whose duty it shall be to decide upon the elections and qualifications of the persons returned, and in case of a tie between two or more persons, to designate which of said persons shall qualify as State's attorney, and to administer the oaths of office to the persons elected."

Mr. MILLER. I know this section follows the phraseology of the old constitution, but it will depend upon the new organization of the courts, whether these words "having criminal jurisdiction respectively" ought to be inserted in this section.

Mr. THOMAS. There will always be some court in the counties, and in the city of Baltimore which must necessarily have criminal jurisdiction. I can see no difficulty in this section.

Mr. MILLER. These returns are to be reported "to the judges."

Mr. THOMAS. The gentleman can secure his object my making it read "to the judge or judges."

Mr. SMITH, of Carroll. The committee on revision can determine that after we shall have completed the report of the committee on the judiciary.

No amendment was offered to this section.

SALARY OF STATE'S ATTORNEYS.

The next section was read as follows:

Sec. 3. The State's attorney shall perform such duties, and receive such fees and commissions as are now prescribed by law, and such other duties, fees and commissions as may hereafter be prescribed by law, and if any State's attorney shall receive any other fee or reward than such as is, or may be allowed by law, he shall on conviction thereof, be removed from office; provided, the State's attorneys of the several counties shall receive not less than —— dollars per annum; and provided the State's attorney for Baltimore city shall have the power to appoint one deputy, at a salary of not more than —— dollars per annum, to be paid by the mayor and city council of Baltimore, as city officers are paid.

Mr. THOMAS submitted the following amendment:

Insert after the word "than," in the seventh line, the words "eight hundred."

Mr. THOMAS said: It very often happens in some counties of the State that the office of State's attorney pays so badly that we cannot get a member of the bar to take the position with the trouble it gives him, unless he is guaranteed a certain salary. The idea of the committee, or at least a portion of them—for I do not know whether the committee was unanimous upon the subject, or not—was that $800 should be fixed, so as to insure the State's attorney at least $800 as a salary, which I think is very small, to be paid by the county commissioners.

Mr. DANIEL. I move to fill the blank by inserting "five hundred." In some of the counties the State's attorney has very little to do. Besides that, it is frequently a very excellent school for practitioners, and I have known it to be one of the best ways of introducing young practitioners in their professions. It does not interfere with their practice; and I think that $500 would be ample, especially as I know that in many counties the fees do not amount to more than $200 or $300.

Mr. BERRY, of Prince George's. I should think, if it could be accomplished, that it would be better to leave it to the commissioners of the several counties to fix the salary to be paid to the State's attorney. With us, we have a good deal of commercial business, and the State's attorneyship is worth $1400 or $1500. In some counties it is worth very little. If you fix a uniform salary for all of them, you give those who have a good deal of work no more than those who have little to do.

Mr. SMITH, of Carroll. That is not the construction we have given to the language. It is to give them this amount, at least.

Mr. MAYHUGH. I should prefer to substitute the compensation now allowed by law.

Mr. CLARKE. Is it proposed to pay the deficiency, if there should be any, from the county or the State treasury?

Mr. SMITH, of Carroll. It is to be paid by the county commissioners. I have an amendment to meet that.

Mr. DANIEL demanded the yeas and nays, and they were ordered.

Mr. MILLER. I do not see what objection there can be to filling the blank with $800, especially as the committee proposes to provide that the county shall pay it. If the gentlemen from the counties that would have to pay it object to it, we might vote against it ; but I cannot for my life see why the delegation from Baltimore city should oppose it.

Mr. DANIEL. We are legislating for the whole State.

Mr. MILLER. We think in the counties that $800 is little enough to pay any man. By a previous provision in this section we give them the fees now prescribed by law, so that they may get a much larger sum than $800; and if so the counties will not be asked to add anything to the fees of the office. But if in any county it should happen that the fees of the office should run short of $800, he will be entitled to receive from the county commissioners enough to make up that sum. It is not a tax to come upon anybody except the people of the counties where they happen to be.

Mr. PURNELL. While I am entirely willing that the city of Baltimore should compensate the State's attorney in proportion to the amount of business, in the county of Worcester I am very well satisfied that the salary proposed is too much for the services required. At the last session of the legislature there was a special law passed with regard to Worcester county, by which the fees were regulated, at the suggestion of the State's attorney himself; and as it was entirely satisfactory to him. I think that so far as Worcester county is concerned, $400 would compensate the State's attorney for the amount of service required of him. There is very little business in that county of that character. Not that we are a more law-abiding or moral people than other counties; but it has so happened that we have very little of that business requiring the services of a State's attorney. The practice has been to elect a man who would accept the office as an introductory matter, and for the sake of giving a little more character to his profession, and after serving a term or two, the office passes into other hands under like circumstances. I think that $500 would very liberally compensate him in Worcester county ; and I suppose there are other counties where $500 would be a very liberal and fair salary for the amount of labor imposed upon the State's attorney. I suppose that $800 would be too much for the labor required for that office in the county which I have the honor in part to represent.

Mr. SANDS. I must say to the convention before I make any further remark, that I am not at all interested personally in the sum with which this blank is to be filled, as the fees of the office which I hold amount to twice that sum and frequently to more; but I want to suggest to my friend from Worcester (Mr. Purnell) some facts in connection with this provision which may induce him to change his mind. There are many counties in the State where a large amount of criminal business is done. Now I am prepared to say that no very young gentleman is qualified to discharge that business I think any one whose experience in courts of justice is such as to enable him to determine about this fact, will agree with me, that where there is any quantity of criminal business to be done, a very young and inexperienced man is by no means the individual who ought to have charge of it.

What is of more importance to the people of the State at large, than the administration of the criminal justice of the State? I can say that in my observation, on account of the inefficiency of the prosecuting officer, I have seen criminals turned out of court unwhipped of justice, who, had they been properly prosecuted would have got it to its full extent. I would suggest to my friend that there are other considerations besides the mere amount of actual service done, which will always operate upon competent men. I have myself individually had to refuse a fee of $500 to defend, when as prosecutor I could receive but a fifth part of that sum. Gentlemen of experience, ability and capacity are not going to accept positions which necessitate such things, unless those positions pay him otherwise, not only for his services, but remunerate him for his losses.

The convention will understand me that I am not personally interested at all in filling this blank, because my own salary for nearly ten years past has been largely beyond it, nearly double the amount proposed. But I know from observation that there is no more important post than that of prosecuting attorney, scarcely excepting that of judge.

Mr. STIRLING. I should like to learn from the convention what counties there are in which the fees of the State's attorneys are below $800. I know there are some, but my impression is that there are very few, and that in those few the services rendered are so small that anybody can be got to do the work.

Mr. SANDS. I do not know. I cannot inform my friend as to the number of counties where the fees are below this sum. But I know this, that whereas the lives and property of citizens are measurably in the protection of this officer, and in a large measure, he ought to be a man at all times well qualified for his post. I repeat that I have frequently seen criminals dismissed unwhipped of justice, merely from the inefficiency or want of experience and knowledge of the prosecuting officer.

We have been fixing the salaries of judicial officers liberally. I declare it as my conviction that in every county, next to the judge presiding over the circuit in which the county is included, the prosecuting officer is the next man not only in responsibility but in utility to the community to which he belongs I throw out these ideas for the consideration of the convention; and I say again to my friend from Worcester (Mr. Purnell,) that it is not so much the services that the State's attorney is called upon to render as the fact that his acceptance of that position cuts him off from other practice, which, if he be a man of ability, will pay him frequently more in a single case than you propose to give him for a year's salary. The consequence is that no competent person can accept. I should like to have these offices always filled by a competent person, skilful, and not an inexperienced individual who for $500 and as his first step in life is willing to take the position. There is scarcely any individual officer in he community in whose ability the safety of the citizens of the community is so much involved.

Mr. Purnell. My friend from Howard (Mr. Sands) doubtless misapprehends me when he supposes that I wish for one moment to depreciate the office of State's attorney. That is not my purpose. I only spoke with reference to my particular county, and with reference to the extent of the business which was required of that officer. If the office is so important and so necessary to be filled by an able man, it seems to me that a salary of $800 would be wholly inadequate to command the services of such a man. The truth of the matter is, as I observed, that this office is generally taken by some young practitioner of the bar for the purpose of introducing himself into practice, acquiring a notoriety and celebrity which he could not otherwise acquire in the same length of time. — Having served one term his aspirations are generally gratified, and he resumes or goes on with his practice; for this forms a very unimportant part of the practice of his profession, and he pursues his profession as though he did not hold the office, except that he cannot take a fee against the State; but in civil practice he has the opportunity of taking all that offers. He only holds this office as giving him to some little extent an importance in his profession, being the representative of the State in that community. I presume you could not get in the county of Worcester a man who is engaged actively in his profession for the sum of $800 a year; for in a single isolated case $500 might be offered which would more than cover the amount of salary he would receive as district attorney. You cannot get a lawyer in such a position to accept the office for a salary of $800, limiting him to prosecution for the State.

I am aware of the necessity of bringing in all infractors of the law, to justice; and perhaps the gentleman's estimate is no higher than mine of an efficient State's attorney. The young men we have had in Worcester as State's attorneys have been energetic and talented; and I do not know that any offenders have escaped unwhipped; I do not know that any who have violated the law have escaped without being punished for it, under the efficient district attorneys it has been our good fortune to have.

The question being taken upon filling the blank with "800," the largest sum, the result was—yeas 30, nays 21—as follows:

Yeas—Messrs. Audoun, Berry, of Prince George's, Billingsley, Brooks, Carter, Chambers, Clarke, Crawford, Cunningham, Dent, Earle, Galloway, Harwood, Hodson, Hollyday, Horsey, Jones, of Somerset, Keefer, King, Lee, Miller, Russell, Sands, Schley, Schlosser, Smith, of Carroll, Stirling, Swope, Thomas, Wickard—30.

Nays—Messrs. Abbott, Brown, Cushing, Daniel, Ecker, Hebb, Hopkins, Larsh, Mayhugh, Murray, Nyman, Parker, Parran, Pugh, Purnell, Robinette, Smith, of Worcester, Sneary, Stockbridge, Valliant, Wooden—21.

When his name was called,

Mr. Sands said: I ask to be excused from voting, being one of the unfortunate class of State's attorneys.

Not being excused, he voted "aye."

The blank was accordingly filled with "800."

Mr. Audoun moved to fill the blank in the ninth line with 1500.

Mr. Stirling. I have an amendment to offer, not with regard to filling the blank, but the clause as it at present stands is not exactly correct, and would have the effect of absolutely increasing the salary of the State's attorney by $1500, which I know was not in contemplation. After consultation with my colleague who now holds that office (Mr. Thomas,) I have prepared and now offer the following amendment:

Strike out all after the word "the," in the tenth line, and insert the words "said State's attorney, out of the fees of his office, as has heretofore been practiced."

It is important to tell where the money is to come from before filling the blank. Nobody is interested in it but the State's attorney who will have to pay it.

Mr. Audoun withdrew his amendment temporarily.

Mr. Miller. Under the present constitution of this State there is a provision that all officers must account to the treasurer for the amount of all fees received at any time over and above the sum of $3,000 per year. The State's attorneyship of Baltimore city has been always a paying office; for the amount of fees there has always exceeded $3,000 a year, and the surplus has been paid over into the State treasury. This amendment offered by the gentleman from Baltimore city (Mr. Stirling,) takes from the treasury, from what has been hitherto paid into it of this surplus, $1500 a year.

Mr. STIRLING. The gentleman is entirely mistaken in his facts. I do not see the absolute necessity of having this clause at all, except that it is well to have the whole law on the face of it. The law fixed here by the amendment is precisely what has always been allowed ever since the constitution has been in force. It does not change the law or the fact.

Mr. MILLER. I see no use in putting it into the constitution.

Mr. THOMAS. The only object of putting it into the constitution, is that no comptroller may hereafter deny the right of the State's attorney of Baltimore city to pay his deputy.—It might happen that the comptroller might refuse this amount of money in the account of the State's attorney of Baltimore city. It is utterly impossible, as is known to almost every one connected with the bar, for the State's attorney there to get along without a deputy; and in order to get a good deputy, he must pay him a good salary, something to live on; because it takes the whole of his time to attend to the grand jury. It does not take a dollar from the State, for the reason that ever since the adoption of the present constitution, for fourteen years, the comptrollers have been allowing to the State's attorneys of Baltimore city this amount of money out of the fees which came into their hands.

Mr. MILLER. I would suggest that the present provision of the constitution appoints an attorney general, who will no doubt have his residence in Baltimore city, and who will attend to a good deal of the important criminal practice in the city of Baltimore.

Mr. THOMAS. Will the attorney general go before the grand jury and write out indictments?

Mr. MILLER. No; but the important business will be attended to by the attorney general, capital cases, &c. I know a former attorney general, Mr. Richardson, used to say that he did most of the work himself.

Mr. STIRLING. Mr. Richardson acted as his own deputy; and he himself tried all the cases, and got the fees of the State's attorney

Mr. MILLER. If this deputy is made a constitutional officer, as provided here, it would not be possible for him to keep any fees beyond the $3,000.

Mr. THOMAS. He cannot do it now.

Mr. MILLER. I understand that now the State's attorney has the power to employ Mr. A, Mr. B, or Mr. C to attend to cases.

Mr. STIRLING. The gentleman does not understand the facts of the case. The facts of the case are these. Under the old constitution the attorney general always prosecuted the cases in the Baltimore city court; and he did that for the obvious reason that there was all the important business, and all the profits of the attorney general came out of the Baltimore city courts. He employed no deputy there except to attend to the grand jury and draw indictments. Mr. Pinkney was deputy attorney there during many years. He attended the grand jury and drew the indictments, and Mr. Richardson himself received the fees of the attorney's office and tried the cases.

Since the present constitution the same state of facts has existed all the time. The State's attorney has had a regular appointed deputy, one single person and no more, who always attended on the grand jury and drew the indictments; and the only effect of this provision is to cover still more under the direct provisions of law, what has been covered heretofore by the entire practice both of the treasury department and of the court. The deputy attorney of Baltimore city goes to the grand jury room, goes as State's attorney to the grand jury room; and he does it for the simple reason that it is impossible for any State's attorney of Baltimore city to try cases and attend the grand jury, because the grand jury is in session when the petit jury is in session, and no case can ever be in two places at the same time. It is not to render temporary assistance that a deputy is temporarily called in.—He is a regulur officer, and as such is required to take the oath of office under the constitution; but he will be to no further extent a responsible officer than he is now. He does not now take any fees. It is an incident of his place that he is never to take any fee as counsel against the State. If he does he must resign his position. He has no right to receive any; so that this does not at all prejudice him in his personal rights. This is exactly the same thing that has been done all the time; and this is only an additional sanction to the responsibilities of the place. I did not know that there would be any provision of this sort placed in the report. I do not agree with my colleague (Mr. Thomas) that any comptroller could make any difficulty about it, because the thing has been settled by the uniform practice of the departments. But it can do no harm to put this in, and there can certainly be no objection to it.

The amendment was agreed to.

Mr. DANIEL. I will renew the motion to fil the blank with "1500."

Mr. THOMAS. Fifteen hundred dollars has always been the usual allowance.

The amendment was agreed to.

Mr. PARRAN. I move to insert after the word "counties," in the seventh line, the words "except the county of Calvert." We have very little use for this officer in my county, and I can hardly believe that his salary ever exceeds four hundred dollars; and, considering the rate of taxation in our county, I propose this amendment.

Mr. HEBB. I think it is very hard to make any county pay a larger salary than the county desires to pay to its own officer; and I will therefore move to strike out this clause, to leave it exactly as it is in the present constitution, to let the county commissioners fix the salaries they will pay. I move to strike out the words "provided the State's attorneys of the several counties shall receive not less than eight hundred dollars per annum."

Mr. PARRAN withdrew his amendment temporarily.

Mr. HERB's amendment was agreed to.

No further amendment was offered.

The next section was read as follows:

"Sec. 4. No person shall be eligible to the office of State's attorney, who has not been admitted to practice law in this State, and who has not resided for at least one year in the county or city in which he may be elected."

No amendment was offered.

FILLING VACANCIES.

The next section was read as follows:

"Sec. 5. In case of a vacancy in the office of State's attorney, or of his removal from the county or city in which he shall have been elected, or on his conviction as herein specified, the said vacancy shall be filled by the judge of the county or city respectively, having criminal jurisdiction in which said vacancy shall occur, until the election and qualification of his successor, at which election said vacancy shall be filled by the voters of the county or city, for the residue of the term thus made vacant.

Mr. STIRLING. I move to strike out the word "election and qualification of his successor," and to insert the words "until the next election thereafter held for members of the general assembly." There is an ambiguity in the section, which was copied from the old constitution. I do not think the meaning is different; and I know the language of the old constitution is very ambiguous on the subject. It is a matter of serious doubt whether the provision does not mean that he shall hold over for the four years. The first section says that he shall hold his office for four years; and whether a successor could be elected before the four years should expire is a matter of very grave doubt. The officer usually holds his office until the next general election of members of the general assembly thereafter.

Mr. CHAMBERS. I would suggest to the gentleman that he should strike out "at which election said vacancy shall be filled by the voters of the county or city, for the residue of the term thus made vacant," to make the election for four years instead of two.

Mr. STIRLING. I have no objection to that. I think it is perfectly proper as a general provision, applicable to other officers also. As the section now stands, as copied from the old constitution, it is very difficult to make any meaning out of it at all. It says "until the qualification of his successor," and nobody knows what successor is meant. If it means the successor of the original State's attorney, then the appointee would hold until the next regular election of State's attorney. But that has not been the interpretation placed upon it, although it seems to be the interpretation that ought to be placed upon it. A man may resign just two years before the election of members of the general assembly; and if at the end of the term a man was elected to fill the vacancy, he might only stay in office from November to January. I accept the amendment.

Mr. SMITH, of Carroll. It seems to me that the language of the constitution can have no other than the plain and simple construction. If a vacancy occurs the judge is to fill it until the election and qualification of his successor. The election, it seems to me, would necessarily take place by a simple, fair construction, at the next general election of members of the general assembly.

Mr. STIRLING. There is no provision except that for election for four years.

Mr. SMITH, of Carroll. There is no direct provision; yet it is until the election and qualification of his successor. If the amendment prevails there might be a hiatus, and there might be no State's attorney at all; because the person appointed might not be qualified until the first Monday in January.

Mr. STIRLING. That can be remedied by retaining the words "and qualification of his successor." I will modify my amendment so as to retain these words.

Mr. SMITH, of Carroll. I think that will accomplish the whole object. I think that will do away with any difficulty, and leave this section to correspond with all the other sections in reference to tenure of office, so that the vacancy shall be filled for the residue of the term, and not for four years, as the gentleman from Kent (Mr. Chambers) proposes.

Mr. STIRLING. I think I would better not accept the amendment of the gentleman from Kent. I agree with it, but there may be a difference of opinion about it, and I think it would better be left as it is. I think myself that is the proper way to put it.

Mr. CLARKE. As I understand the amendment, it adopts a principle of electing to fill offices simply for the residue of the term. We have not acted upon the case of clerks or registers. I think it was determined in committee, in relation to the report on the judiciary department, that when an election should take place it should be for the full term of six years, or whatever term might be assigned for these various officers. I would suggest while upon this branch of the question that this is a proper veiw to be taken of this matter. What is the necessity, when the people themselves elect, the office being vacant, of having an election for two years, and then another election for six years? The one elected to fill the vacancy is as much a party selected by the people as the one elected at the expiration of that term. But you elect a man for the short term, and when he is just becoming experienced in the office you turn him out and put in a new man. For that reason also I think the election should be for the full term, and not simply for the unexpired term left vacant.

There is another reason for this. I think it is highly important that these offices should not all expire at one time. If we have the election always take place for the unexpired term, we shall have all the offices expire at one time; and at a certain period throughout the State we shall have our elections of registers, clerks, State's attorneys, &c., leaving the State with entirely new and inexperienced officers coming in. I think it is better that the offices should expire at different periods. In consequence of deaths and resignations it will so happen; and in one county the office will expire at one time and in another county it will expire at another time. We shall not therefore every four or six years have throughout the State an entire new set of officers. But every two or four years there will be some of the counties electing new officers; and you will have partly old experienced officers, instead of entirely new and inexperienced ones. For this reason I hope the amendment of the gentleman from Kent will prevail.

Mr. STIRLING. So far as my amendment is concerned, it is a mere verbal criticism. The interpretation which it puts upon the words of the constitution has been the interpretation always put upon it in fact. I say that the section was doubtfully drawn. It is perfectly susceptible of the other construction. It is proper to put it in such a form that a man shall hold office until his successor shall be qualified. Then the section goes on to say that when a man is elected he shall hold for the residue of the term. The gentleman from Kent proposes that it shall say that when he is elected it shall be for a new term of four years. That has nothing to do whatever with my amendment. There is no inconsistency with it.

You do not hold any election for members of the general assembly except every two years; but you hold elections under the constitution for county officers, the next year. You should fix the election day upon one or the other of the two, either to say it shall be at the next election thereafter or at the next election of members of the general assembly.

Mr. DANIEL. My colleague will see that this only fixes the day at which the man shall be elected, and says nothing about how long he shall hold. The law is that the judge can only appoint until the next general election, and then somebody must be elected.

The question was stated on the amendment of Mr. CHAMBERS, to strike out the latter clause of the section.

Mr. SMITH, of Carroll. Then we shall have to go back and strike out the provision with regard to other officers. In every single instance heretofore the provision has been retained to fill the vacancy for the residue of the term made vacant.

Mr. CLARKE. With reference to the clerk, the provision in the present constitution was construed in this way. The clerk elected to fill the vacancy in the office, held for six years.

Mr. SMITH, of Carroll. I am speaking of the constitution we are framing now, and not of the constitution under which we are living.

Mr. CLARKE. I understood that the judiciary decided that he should hold for six years.

Mr. CHAMBERS. That was our understanding in the committee room.

Mr. CLARKE. And that report embraces the most numerous class of officers in the State.

Mr. THOMAS. I will state that the court of appeals put the construction upon this, as stated by the gentleman from Prince George's (Mr. Clarke.) The phraseology with reference to judges in the old constitution, is peculiar:

"Section 25. In case of the death, resignation, removal, or other disqualification of a judge of any of the courts of law, the governor, by and with the advice and consent of the senate, shall thereupon appoint a person duly qualified to fill said office until the next general election for delegates thereafter; at which time an election shall be held, as hereinbefore prescribed, for a judge, who shall hold the said office for ten years, according to the provisions of this constitution."

But when it comes to the State's attorney, instead of specifying the term for which the party is elected to fill the vacancy, it says: "at which election, said vacancy shall be filled by the voters of the county or city, for the residue of the term thus made vacant;" clearly showing a distinction made in the present constitution between the two tenures of office as to the judge and clerk, and the State's attorney; the one to be filled by the qualified voters of the county or city for the full term of his predecessor, and the other for the residue of the term thus made vacant.

Mr. DANIEL. I cannot see why the same provision should not apply to the State's attorney that applies to the judges and others, as a matter of principle. I do not see the use of having two elections of State's attorney, when there is only a year or a year and a half remaining to be filled. The judge appoints first, and when the next election of members of the general assembly arrives, you elect for the vacancy, and the year after must elect again. Let the judge appoint until the next election, if you please; or I would be perfectly willing to let him appoint until the term expired; but at any rate when you do elect, elect for four years, as you elect the judge for ten years. It is of no use to have two elections following, one this year, and another it may be the next.

There is another reason for it. You may elect a man for a year or a year and a half, and break up his business in other respects. This does not apply so strongly to the State's attorney as to some other officers; but if you elect a man for a portion of the time his business will suffer greatly, and then in a short time you elect somebody else. I think therefore that when he is elected it should be for the full term of four years. The people are just as competent to elect at one time for a term of four years, as at another time for a term of four years. I see no use in electing a man to an office, and just as he becomes acquainted with it turning him out and putting another one in. I think that on principle it ought to be just as it is in the case of the judges.

The amendment submitted by Mr. STIRLING was agreed to.

The question was stated upon the amendment submitted by Mr. CHAMBERS, to strike out the latter clause of the section.

Mr. STOCKBRIDGE. What will then be the construction?

Mr. THOMAS. That the State's attorney elected to fill the vacancy, will serve for the full term of fours years, as I understand it.

Mr. STOCKBRIDGE. If that is the operation of it I am ready to vote for it. That makes it accord with what has been recommended by the committee on the judiciary department, although not acted upon by the convention as yet. It is precisely the provision reported by the committee on the judiciary department with reference to registers of wills, almost in the very terms. But to make it clear, I will propose an amendment.

Mr. SMITH, of Carroll. I desire as far as possible to preserve a uniformity of tenure of office with that prescribed by the report on appointment, tenure of office, &c., and that was the reason for making the election for the residue of the term made vacant. But I do not care whether he is elected for four years or two years.

Mr. STOCKBRIDGE. In all the cases so far as I have observed, in the report referred to by the gentleman from Carroll (Mr. Smith,) the persons were appointed, and not elected for the residue of the term.

Mr. STIRLING. It seems to me that the convention ought to adopt one of two courses. Either the appointing power, when it fills a vacancy, should fill it to the end of the term; or if the convention is not disposed to authorize that, but is disposed to require an election by the people, when the people elect they should elect for a full term. If you require the people to elect only for the balance of the term, this state of things can arise under our present constitution. If a man resigns the office of State's attorney in October, the judge appoints until the first Wednesday in November, and at the first Wednesday in November the people may actually have to elect two State's attorneys, one for four years and the other for two months. That is the law as it is under the present constitution. When a vacancy occurs towards the end of a term, the people have to elect two men, one to fill the vacancy, and one for the full term. It is an absurdity. I agree with the gentleman from Carroll that the convention should make up its mind to adopt one thing or the other.

Mr. STOCKBRIDGE moved to strike out after "occur" in line five, to the word "for" in line seven, so as to read:

"Section 5. In case of a vacancy in the office of State's attorney, or of his removal from the county or city in which he shall have been elected, or on his conviction as herein specified, the said vacancy shall be filled by the judge of the county or city respectively, having criminal jurisdiction in which said vacancy shall occur, for the residue of the term thus made vacant."

Mr. THOMAS. That does away with the amendment of the gentleman from Baltimore city (Mr. Stirling,) already adopted.

Mr. STIRLING. Yes, sir; and I think it is a very sensible amendment.

Mr. THOMAS. The only objection I have to that amendment is this; that in the case of a vacancy in the office of State's attorney, the judge and the State's attorney being so intimately connected, as they are in the transaction of business, it gives the judge the power to appoint a person as State's attorney who might perhaps be too much under the power of the judge. I think the amendment just adopted a better one, to let the judge appoint to fill the vacancy until the next general election, and then to let the people elect for four years.

The question was stated on Mr. CHAMBERS's amendment.

Mr. CHAMBERS. My object was to avoid too frequent elections. I did not care about the form of it, and I will withdraw it.

The amendment submitted by Mr. STOCKBRIDGE was agreed to.

No further amendment was offered.

ATTORNEY GENERAL.

The next section was read as follows:

"Section 6. It shall be the duty of the clerk of the court of appeals, and the commissioner of the land office respectively, whenever a case shall be brought into said court or office, in which the State is a party, or has an interest, immediately to notify the attorney general thereof."

Mr. STOCKBRIDGE. This section relates to the office of attorney general, and not at all to State's attorneys, and seems to be misplaced. I move to strike it out here, and to insert it after section five, under the head of "attorney general."

The amendment was agreed to.

The first section upon the attorney general was again taken up and read as amended as follows:

"Section 1. There shall be an attorney general elected by the people of the State, on general ticket, on Tuesday next after the first Monday in November, in the year eighteen hundred and sixty-four, and on the same day in every fourth year thereafter, who shall hold his office for four years from the first Monday in January next ensuing his election, and until his successor shall be elected and qualified, and shall be re-eligible thereto, and shall be subject to removal therefrom for incompetency, wilful neglect of duty, or misdemeanor in office, on conviction in a court of law."

Mr. GALLOWAY moved to strike out the word "people" in line second, and to insert "qualified voters."

The amendment was agreed to.

QUESTION OF ORDER.

Mr. AUDOUN moved to increase the salary from two thousand five hundred dollars to three thousand dollars, and to add "he shall not, during the time he shall so hold office, engage in the practice of the law, except in behalf of the State."

Mr. HEBB. I rise to a point of order. That is in section three; and we have got through with that section. It is not in order to go back to it now.

Mr. CLARKE. Unless the previous question has been called, we can recur to the section by a mere motion.

Mr. SANDS. If that is the construction of the rules, what binders a recurrence to everything we have done, even including the adoption of the fourth and twenty-third articles of the bill of rights, during the four or five months we have been sitting heie? What hinders it if we can go back and recur to a section that has been passed to a third reading?

The CHAIRMAN (Mr. Pugh.) This section has not been passed to its third reading.

Mr. SANDS. It has been acted upon.

Mr. DANIEL. The section was not passed over until the president had asked if there were other amendments to be offered to it; and then passing it over had the effect of voting that it should be the section. It superseded the necessity of voting, and took the place of the previous question. If the previous question is not moved, we pass on to another section, and that has the effect of a vote.

The CHAIRMAN. The chair does not so understand it. The section was not voted upon, the previous question not having been called upon it.

Mr. SANDS. Then under the ruling of the chair, we can go back to any section in any report, where the previous question was not called.

Mr. CLARKE. All the other reports have passed to a third reading. This is still on its second reading; and that is the distinction. We simply recur to a section that was passed over, in order to amend it and put it in perfect shape.

Mr. HEBB. I have never seen such a course adopted before. The president announced the next section, which was equivalent to the unanimous consent of the convention to pass that section. The only way to get back to it is by reconsideration. Any one can move to reconsider, the vote being unanimous. The proper time to offer an amendment to an article is when it is under consideration. We have passed through all the sections reported by the committee, and of course they have all been acted upon. If we wish to recur to any we must vote to reconsider.

Mr. CLARKE. It is a mere point of parliamentary law; but it is better to be correct. If the house desires not to act upon the amendment, the house will vote not to recur to the third section; so that the matter is fully under the control of the house. But if we were to reconsider, what vote have we got to reconsider, no vote being taken? The journal does not show that any vote was taken, and unless a vote was taken, there is no vote to reconsider.

Mr. DANIEL. It was taken by unanimous consent, and hence anybody can move to reconsider.

Mr. CLARKE. The journal does not show any such unanimous consent.

Mr. SANDS. I think the views expressed by the gentleman from Allegany (Mr. Hebb) are conclusive. The question is put to the house, are there any more amendments? If there are none, unanimous consent is given to pass to the next section.

The CHAIRMAN. The chair decides that it has been the course heretofore to recur to a section for the purpose of amendment, and that it is in order to recur to this section by a motion to recur. The question therefore is, will the convention recur to section three for the purpose of amendment?

The question being taken, the motion to recur was rejected.

The report was then ordered to be engrossed for a third reading.

MILITARY DEPARTMENT.

Mr. STOCKBRIDGE moved that the convention proceed to the consideration of the report of the committee on the militia.

Mr. WICKARD. Inasmuch as the minority report has not yet been printed in bill form, I suggest that we pass over that for the present, and I move that we take up the report of the committee on usury.

Mr. STOCKBRIDGE withdrew his motion.

The motion of Mr. WICKARD was agreed to.

RATE OF INTEREST.

The convention accordingly proceeded to the consideration of the section reported by the committee on usury, which was read the second time as follows:

'Sec. —. The legal rate of interest in this State shall be six per centum per annum, except in cases where a different rate may be agreed upon between contracting parties; and in all cases of private contract, the rate of interest agreed on, or contracted for, shall be recoverable; and the general assembly shall pass all laws that may be necessary to carry this section into effect."

Mr. DANIEL. I move to amend by striking out "six" in the first line, and inserting "seven." I make this motion simply because I think it will be greatly to the interest of the State of Maryland to adopt the rate of interest which is allowed in New York. It is still higher in some other States; and business men, large financial operators tell me that the effect has been to drive a good deal of capital out of the State of Maryland, simply because by the provision in our constitution the rate of interest has been confined to six per cent. I know that at the principal banks in the city of Baltimore they are discounting more New York paper at the New York rate than of Baltimore paper. They prefer it because they get a larger rate of interest; and thus our money is going out into other States, and the State of Maryland is drained of its capital.

I very heartily agree in the subsequent provision, that money ought to be like any other commodity in the market, open to contracting parties. Whether you prescribe it in the constitution or not, money will range according to its value; and the effect of attempting to control it is to prevent honest men from bringing their money into the market, and to enable another class of men who are sharpers, to take advantage of the high rates, and to charge a higher rate than would be charged if money was free. If the market is left open, as soon as the rate of interest gets a little higher than usual, money would be thrown into the market to such an extent that the rate of interest would immediately go down again; and thus it would regulate itself like any other commodity in the market, according to its value.

'According to the law now upon the subject, that is nearly the proposition upon the statute book, that the rate shall be as agreed upon by the contracting parties, the law being that if a party is sued for an excess of interest, and the party does not come in and plead usury, and tender the amount with simple interest, you can recover the whole amount, no matter what rate of interest is agreed upon. That is the law as decided in the courts. It amounts therefore simply to this, that a party must plead usury, to avoid the payment, and there is scarcely a man willing so to injure his character, for he could never go into the market again. As the law now stands therefore it amounts to this, that in nearly every case where the interest agreed upon is above the legal rate, the party can recover it.'

I tried a case in the superior court of Baltimore city in which this question came directly in issue. The rate of interest agreed upon was some eight or nine per cent. The party pled that we could not recover that rate of interest; but he did not plead usury and tender the amount with the legal rate of interest; and we recovered the whole amount of interest.

I think the legal rate of interest should be seven per cent. and that contracting parties should be allowed to fix the rate higher or lower in particular cases as they think proper, according to the condition of the money market. I think it will work greatly to the advantage of our State to adopt seven per cent., the rule in New York, instead of six per cent.

Mr. CLARKE. I move to add to the section the following: "provided that the said rate of interest shall only apply to contracts for the loan of money made after the adoption of this constitution." I do not know that it is necessary to say anything except a mere statement of the case. A number of contracting parties have made large loans of money five or ten years ago, and a great deal of money is now seeking investment, and the parties are making their arrangements in reference to the present rate of interest. These contracts are existing contracts; and I think it may be fairly contended that any contract made when the law limited the rate of interest to six per cent. could not be subjected to a higher rate It is no more than just that the change of rate should apply only to future contracts.

Mr. SANDS. I must say I have listened with surprise to the amendment offered by the gentleman from Baltimore city (Mr Daniel,) and with still greater surprise to the remarks made in support of it. What should be the object of all just legislation? Should it be to protect those who need protection, or should it be to confer upon those already in power? So far as this question is concerned, it affects two classes of people. I do hope the members of this convention will give this matter their careful and serious consideration. This question affects, I say, two classes of people; and who are they? Money-kings, who have at present power enough in their hands. Money is power everywhere. And it affects, secondly, the honest, enterprising, industrious, working classes of the people. It was said by a man who was a very close observer of men and things that the most powerful sovereign on earth was the head of the house of Rothschilds.

Mr. STIRLING. Will the gentleman allow

me to ask him the question whether he thinks he is protecting the honest working classes of the people of the State of Maryland in allowing the Rothschilds of New York to take away the money of the State of Maryland to help build up their colossal fortunes?

Mr. SANDS. The gentlemen will have plenty of time to argue their view of the case after I get through with what I have to say. I say that it was said of that house, the great moneyed house of the world, that it was the most powerful sovereign on earth, and that every loan was not merely a speculation, but, might be made to fix a sovereign or upset a throne. That was so. Money is the great social lever; and it is the great political lever too. It is a power that needs no legislative protection. It is, so far as society is concerned, the Archimedean lever.

Now what is it proposed here to do? It is proposed to add to the power of the money seller the right of an additional one per cent. of interest. Against whom do we discriminate? Against the laboring poor. A poor man who is perhaps trying to set up a little store in some corner, or along one of your streets, wants a bill of goods, or he wants to get into this or that vocation, and he wants money. He is the man you want to pay your money-king one per cent. additional on his money. So you will make the laboring man, the working man, the enterprising man, the man who wants money above all others, and is least able to pay for it, pay one per cent. more into the funds of the money king.

I say in my view of the case that is iniquitous. It is a discrimination in favor of money, when money has power enough. Then the question reduces itself to this. Is six per cent. a fair remunerative rate of interest to the moneyed man. I suppose the answer to that question has been given practically in this State for a long time, and is to be found in the fact that at that rate of interest it does not take a great many years for capital to double itself. That is an answer to the question whether this is a sufficient rate of interest or not?

Again, sir, looking about at other money markets across the water, where is there a nation of people that pays the same rate of interest we now pay to-day? In the great commercial centre of the world—in England and France—what have been the rates as compared with the rates of American interest? Much less.

As to this idea that a six per cent. rate of interest is going to keep capital out of Maryland, it is utterly fallacious. If capital is coming to Maryland, what does it come here for? To be invested at a mere six per cent. or seven per cent.? Not a whit of it. If New York capitalists, according to the argument of the gentleman from Baltimore city (Mr. Daniel,) draw away capital because they pay one per cent. higher interest, will they be induced to bring their capital into Maryland for seven per cent. when they can get seven per cent. for it in New York? What is the object to be attained in coming down here and investing money at seven per cent., when everything is unstable and shaken to the centre, if he can get seven per cent. to-day at the great commercial centre of the continent? It would be foolish? No, sir; seven per cent. is not the inducement which is going to bring New York capital or Boston capital into Maryland.

Mr. DANIEL. It is to keep our capital from going there.

Mr. SANDS. Well, it is one and the same thing. It is to keep our capital from going there. What is going to bring capital into your State? We hope that under the new order of things your lands, your mines, your manufacturing facilities, everything you have at stake, are going to be doubled in value. When a New Yorker invests a hundred dollars, or a thousand dollars, or a million dollars, it is not simply with the hope of getting the same interest that he can get in New York city. If he invests money here in your mines, or lands, or in putting up manufactories along your excellent and beautiful streams, it is because that land for which he pays you fifty dollars an acre is going to be worth one hundred dollars an acre. It is because he sees and knows that you have commercial, manufacturing, mining resources, which, if properly developed, must make an empire out of your State. It is this which is going to bring capital into Maryland.

It is waiting now, not for a sufficient interest, but waiting and knocking at your doors. A member of this convention, not now in his seat, said to me a few days ago, that to his knowledge there were now ten million of dollars of capital waiting to be invested in Maryland. Was it waiting for this amendment to raise the rate of interest, so as to get seven per cent.? Not at all.

How is this section to operate? "In all cases of private contract the rate of interest agreed on or contracted for shall be recoverable." How will that operate? Here is a poor fellow in the city of Baltimore, who in some mercantile crisis gets involved, his credit is at stake, and he must pay his note at the bank. There is the man struggling to meet his payments on the one side. Here is a money-king sitting in his broker's office, with plenty of money on hand, just waiting for his victim, as the spider watches for the fly, who knows that the other man wants money and must have it. He says, "Yes, you may have it, but you must pay me for it." And how? At the legal rate of interest recoverable in the court? No, sir. "You must pay me just according to your necessities. You are to break to-morrow. Pay me twenty or twenty-five per cent. and I will give you the means to keep your head above water to-day." And the poor fellow is entirely at his mercy.

The law as you want to fix it is a beautiful protection to the class who need protection in the State. I trust that the men who want protection, the poor, the up-struggling, will find it, and not those who, when they are struggling to keep above the water, are pressing them down under the flood to engulph them.

Six per cent. is enough interest. In twelve years it doubles the capital at that rate. And if six per cent. be enough for the lender, why put it in his power to demand ten? This report puts it in his power to demand ten, fifteen, twenty, or one hundred per cent. if he pleases, just according to the necessities of the poor fellow who goes into the market to buy.

The gentleman has attempted a parallel with other commodities, but it does not hold good at all. A man goes into the market to buy flour. It has a fixed price. Suppose the holder of that flour had it in his power, by legislation in his behalf, to say to the buyer, "You shall starve, or pay me thirty, forty, or fifty dollars per barrel for my flour. Because you are starving I will sell it to you at a starvation price. Starvation looks you in the face, and you shall give me what I demand." And the poor fellow might have to do it. Just so with the poor man seeking relief. He can give the capitalist the honest six per cent. But he may be sinking, and need the money to save him; and yet we come forward here in this usury report, and say, because it is a fact notorious that the money dealers—I do not mean by that gentlemen who invest their means in stocks and securities at the legal rate—but it is a notorious fact that the professional money lender, the real Shylock, the fellow who must have what is nominated in the bond, takes and receives in the streets of Baltimore city from poor necessitous men five per cent. a month, yet you say that shall be a valid contract, and the terms shall be enforced by the courts of your State.

Away with it! It does not deserve to be seriously entertained by the men of this convention or any one else. Is there any reason in it?

Again, I would urge upon certain gentlemen of this house another view of the case. If you are going to declare as a rule that the poor borrower must pay seven per cent., I want to know whether you do not in that by just so much embarrass the operations of your government? If you put the legal rate of interest up to seven, eight or ten per cent., when the government goes into the market do you not demand that it shall pay the same? Of course you do. I do not know of a single proposition which has been offered upon this floor which strikes me as more unfair, more unjust, more reprehensible than this, that goes to aid the power of money, itself the great power in the community, that goes to add to the power of money at the expense of the poor men of the State—the borrowers, for they are the poor men. The rich men who want to make some great speculative hit, and turn their hundred thousand or two hundred thousand, do not borrow money at six per cent. It is the poor man, the man of enterprise who is the borrower; and it is him that you tax the additional one per cent. by this report as it is proposed to amend it.

I hope there will be found upon this floor, irrespective of party or anything else, gentlemen enough to stand by the interests of the people, and to say that they are heavily enough taxed now. It is the poor people who feel the tax. I should like to pay Stewart's tax and the tax of some other gentlemen. I should like to be in that category. I hope there will be gentlemen enough irrespective of party upon this floor to set the seal of condemnation upon this, and to retain the old order of things.

Mr. Chambers. I rise to express my concurrence in the views just expressed by the gentleman from Howard (Mr. Sands.) It has been a very long period since I first entertained the idea that it was necessary to arrest by some legal provision the enormous appetite of the money-lender. It is a difficult matter to date the period at which the system of usury laws commenced. It seems that it is not now deemed altogether proper to abandon restrictions upon that class of people. The proposition is to increase the amount of interest. It is not to abolish the usury law, but to increase the amount of interest. It is not to abolish the usury law, *eo nomine*, but effectually and really to do it. So far as my experience goes, there is a class of persons who own money, and there is a class of persons who being without immediate funds desire to obtain money for the purpose of improving their condition, and who can expend it profitably. The money lenders need no protection. They are sagacious, discreet, and perfectly capable of taking care of themselves. It is not for the benefit of that class that usury laws are provided.

But there is another class, different altogether. Young men coming of age, who have been educated in the enjoyment of means larger than at the death of their parents they have found themselves possessed of. They are unwilling to retrench, but go heedlessly into the market, and unfortunately there they find sharks prepared to meet them and to devour them. It is notorious that the man whose business has been habitually that of a money lender is as utterly destitute of conscience as an animal who never was designed to have one. It is from these people that these young men need and should have protection.

I agree that it is impossible under any system of legislation heretofore adopted to afford them perfect protection. Means of evasion have been found, and they have been victims to the inordinate demands which have resulted in grasping as high as twenty-five or thirty-three and a third per cent for debts perfectly well secured. I do think that this is a great and dangerous innovation. We have got along very well without being obliged to go to New York. If they insist upon going to New York for seven per cent., and if it is necessary to make the rate seven per cent., make it so; but I utterly protest against throwing down every sort of protection to the thoughtless young men who come into life, weakly confident, calculating upon profits which they will never realize, and becoming victims to the first sharper with whom they come in contact. Make your interest what it should be. Let it be seven per cent. if you will make it so. There is a difference of opinion upon that subject in spite of the alarm lest New York should take away all our capital. I hold in my hand a letter from an intelligent gentleman in the city of Baltimore, who says in so many words that six per cent. should be the legal rate of interest, and that most alarming, dangerous and mischievous results will follow if that ceases to be the rate. He says:

"As this question is of very great and vital interest to the citizens of our State, pardon me for saying that the means, thrift and industry of the State at large should be carefully guarded," &c. "The statute rate of interest should be six per cent. If it be thought proper agreements might be made for sixty or ninety days with a larger interest—seven per cent."

Mr. DANIEL. Who is that?

Mr. CHAMBERS. James W. Allnut, a very highly respectable president of the Bank of Commerce. I maintain that the policy of this report has been found through all time to prejudice the pecuniary interests of a State. I do not think that moneyed institutions have gone on better in New York than in Baltimore, or better in the State of New York than in the State of Maryland.

There is another argument. Our people are paying seven per cent. in fact. I suppose now it may be said to be the universal practice everywhere, and I am prepared for such a proposition here, to charge to the borrower the taxes due to the government of the United States, and the State and the county, making up just about one per cent. This makes the interest just about seven per cent., which the borrower pays. You may assume money to be any standard you please, except that which merchants engaged in large speculations, and making in anticipation enormous profits, place upon it, and this is about as much as money is worth in the ordinary pursuits of life. Farmers do not make six per cent. on their capital. I venture to assert it as a fact, having been in that department myself for some forty odd years. I say that farming throughout the State of Maryland does not produce six per cent. on the capital employed. I say that human employments, except those which are carried on at a great risk and therefore produce great profits, do not pay that amount, a business which pays six per cent. in Baltimore being regarded a fair business.

But I say again, I do not care so much what rate you fix, if you will restrain the money lender, and protect those who are borrowing money from his high rates. My own opinion is that six per cent. is enough, and I shall vote against increasing it; that is, six per cent. with the addition of the taxes and dues, making it about seven per cent., is as much as I think persons out of the city can possibly derive a profit from by the loan of money. In the city there are thousands of ways by which mercantile men manage to get more. They put their funds into a bank, and get their discounts, and make their arrangements by which they can get one, two, or three per cent. a month. I am willing to let them manage their business as they like. But there is a class of people, chiefly those residing in the country, young men coming into the possession of real estate, who have all the confidence and ambitious expectations of youth, who hope to realize the largest crops from which they are to obtain almost fabulous sums; and it will lead to nothing but damage to let them go heedless and thoughtless into the market, even under the very shadow of your constitutional provisions, to find themselves victims, ruined and penniless. I ask for protection for these. At the proper time I shall offer the following amendment, which I hope the chairman of the committee will adopt:

"It shall always be lawful for parties having money on bond or mortgage judgments or other security to contract for the payment of taxes, and dues to the United States, the State of Maryland, the county and other public dues by the borrower, so as to retain to the lender the clear amount of legal interest."

Mr. SANDS gave notice of the following substitute for the report of the committee:

"The rate of interest in this State shall not exceed six per cent. per annum, and no higher rate shall be taken or demanded, and the legislature shall provide by law all necessary forfeitures, fines and penalties against receiving or demanding any higher rate of interest."

Mr. MILLER. The subject-matter now under consideration, is certainly one of great importance. We cannot touch this question of money very well in this convention, without its being felt by the people of the State, very generally, in one way or another, for good or for evil. The provision in the old constitution required that "the rate of interest in this State shall not exceed six per cent. per annum; and no higher rate shall be taken or demanded and the legislature shall provide by law all necessary forfeitures, fines and penalties against usury." That has received judicial construction and interpretation by the court of appeals, to the effect that it is a valid defence only in case a plea of usury is set up, in which case the surplus will be forfeited. Our old usury laws of the State of Maryland dating back, I think, as far as 1715, provided that the rate of interest should be six per cent., and the contract should be forfeited if any higher rate was taken or demanded, and it imposed a severe penalty upon parties for contracting to pay a higher rate. The present constitution changed that to the extent of saying that six per cent. should be the rate of interest and nothing more should be taken or demanded, and imposing upon the legislature the right to fix the penalty for usury; which was considered to mean taking more than six per cent. The legislature provided that in that case, the lender could recover his principal and the legal rate of interest. And the courts have decided that you can go into a court of law and enforce a contract, unless usury be pleaded against the contract, in which case you can only recover six per cent. and the principal. That has been the policy of the State of Maryland for a long number of years.

Some of the States of the Union have adopted a different rate of interest from six per cent. About one-third of the States have adopted a rate exceeding six per cent. I have been furnished by my friend from Baltimore county with a list of the States, by which it will be found that New York, South Carolina, Georgia, Michigan, Wisconsin and Minnesota allow seven per cent. as the legal rate of interest; Alabama, Florida, and Texas eight per cent.; California, Kansas, and Oregon ten per cent.; Louisiana five per cent.; and all the other States in the Union six per cent.

There should be some good reason urged upon the convention, I submit, why we should change the rate of interest as proposed by this report. I do not care so much, as the gent eman from Kent (Mr. Chambers) says, about the change of the rate of interest, from six to seven per cent., to make it conform to New York and other States, allowing, as the gentleman from Prince George's (Mr. Clarke) proposes, existing contracts to stand at six per cent., although I think that six per cent. with the taxes and dues paid by the borrower, is enough for the borrower to pay.

They have tried in some of the States the provision that is contained in this report, of allowing parties to make such contracts as they please with regard to the rate of interest on money. It has worked a great injury upon the interests of the State, and they have repealed it. I think it was so in the State of Georgia. I remember reading in my Georgia reports a case that occurred there, in which the law allowed them to make such a contract as they pleased; and two parties came together and made a contract for a loan of $4,000, upon such a rate of interest demanded by the lender and agreed by the borrower to be paid, that in the course of ten years a decree was passed by the court setting off from the man's estate the amount of $40,000 to pay the loan of $4,000.

It is to that provision of this bill that I especially object. It must be remembered that money is not like any other commodity which men can deal with as they please. It is the measure or standard of value, by which the intrinsic worth of all other commodities is measured. The divine law prohibited the Jews from taking usury from each other, although it allowed them to take as much as they pleased from the heathen or the gentiles. It is against this provision of the report that I protest. The gentleman from Kent has well stated the objection.

A contract in law is an agreement of two minds to one particular thing. It is a consent. When men come to contract for the loaning of money, the man who goes to borrow and the man who has the money to lend, do not meet on equal terms. Hence the borrower requires the protection of usury laws. In many cases he is under necessity. His pressing wants require that he should have this money. Or he thinks that he can make money enough to pay almost any rate of sacrifice which the lender may choose to demand. He flatters himself with the idea that in a short time he will be able to pay this money back and save his credit. But he is under the pressure of circumstances; and his mind is not in that clear and calm mood which is required for him to make such a contract as that. His creditors may be pressing upon him. He may think that he will in a few weeks be able to pay off the money at an enormous rate of interest. But in nine cases out of ten it is far better that that man should just take his property and put it into liquidation and pay his creditors off and start the world anew than to go into the hands of sharpers, and finally let them get all his property while his honest creditors are cheated out of it. It is far better that that man should be protected by law against making such a contract as that, than that he should have the privilege of going on, and borrowing money, and that the courts should enforce such contracts as he may make under such necessitous circumstances.

It is for that that I object especially to the provision put into the latter part of this section; that in all cases of private contract the rate of interest agreed upon in the contract should be recoverable. We must remember that we have a law of this State allowing parties to go into a court of justice, and swear to their own case. The money lender would go before the jury, and his word would be as good before the jury and the judge as that of the money borrower. Men meet in private and agree, without any writing, upon certain terms for the loan of money. The borrower may understand it one way, and the lender in another way; and when they go before the court, the shrewd, sharp, cunning money lender will convince the jury in nine cases out of ten that the contract was as he understood it, rather than as understood by the honest, and poor, and needy borrower. I am opposed to all such provisions as that. It is wrong for the law to protect parties who come together to make contracts in regard to such loans of money, which is the measure of the value, the standard of the value of all commodities in the market. It is right and proper that the usury law should interpose between the poor borrower and the grasping money lender. If he makes his contract under the law as it now exists, and should by inadvertence or from necessitous circumstances agree to pay ten, fifteen, or twenty per cent., and it should turn out that his expectations were not realized with regard to his ability to pay that money, honesty and justice to his other creditors requires that he should go into court, as against the man who had loaned him money at this exorbitant rate of interest, and plead usury, and get rid, not of the fair amount that the man is entitled to, with the legal rate of interest, but of the excess of interest beyond the rate established by law He should do that, and no injustice would be done to any one. The money lender would get his due, and the *bona fide* creditor would get his share of the estate. I think the money lender is sufficiently helped by allowing this. If it turns out that the man's circumstances are favorable, and he can pay this large interest, that is a matter for him then to decide whether he considers it honorable to have borrowed the money at that rate and having the means to pay it, to decline to pay it simply because there is no penalty fixed by the law under such a contract as that. I am willing for parties to fulfil such contracts when they choose; but I am opposed to any such extension of the right to contract as to give the lender the right that this section proposes.

Mr. Cushing. Mr. President——

Mr. Audoun. If my colleague will give way, I will move that the convention take a recess.

Mr. Cushing gave way, and on motion of Mr. Audoun,

The convention took a recess until 8 o'clock, P. M.

EVENING SESSION.

The convention met at 8 o'clock, P. M., Mr Pugh in the chair.

The roll was called, and the following members answered to their names:

Messrs. Abbott, Audoun, Billingsley, Clarke, Crawford, Cunningham, Cushing, Daniel, Dent, Earle, Ecker, Gale, Galloway, Hebb, Hollyday, Horsey, Jones, of Somerset, Keefer, King, Lee, Mayhugh, McComas, Miller, Murray, Nyman, Parker, Parran, Pugh, Purnell, Ridgely, Robinette, Russell, Sands, Schley, Schlosser, Smith, of Carroll, Smith, of Worcester, Stirling, Stockbridge, Swope, Thruston, Wooden—42.

There being no quorum present,

Mr. Audoun moved that the convention adjourn.

Mr. Swope demanded the yeas and nays, which were ordered.

The question being taken, the result was—yeas 19, nays 22—as follows:

Yeas—Messrs. Audoun, Crawford, Dent, Galloway, Harwood, Hollyday, Horsey, Jones, of Somerset, Keefer, King, Lee, Murray, Nyman, Parran, Ridgely, Russell, Sands, Schlosser, Smith, of Worcester—19.

Nays—Messrs. Abbott, Billingsley, Cunningham, Cushing, Daniel, Earle, Ecker, Gale, Hebb, Mayhugh, McComas, Miller, Parker, Pugh, Purnell, Robinette, Schley, Smith, of Carroll, Stirling, Stockbridge, Swope, Wooden—22.

So the convention refused to adjourn.

On motion of Mr. Sands,

The convention adjourned.

SEVENTY-NINTH DAY.

Tuesday, August 23, 1864.

The convention met at 10 o'clock, A. M., Mr. Pugh in the chair.

Prayer by Rev. Mr. Owen.

The roll was called, and the following members answered to their names:

Messrs. Abbott, Audoun, Berry, of Prince George's, Billingsley, Blackiston, Bond, Carter, Clarke, Crawford, Cunningham, Cushing, Daniel, Dellinger, Dennis, Dent, Duvall, Earle, Ecker, Edelen, Galloway, Harwood, Hatch, Hebb, Hodson, Hollyday, Hopkins, Hopper, Horsey, Johnson, Jones, of Cecil, Jones, of Somerset, Keefer, Kennard, King, Larsh, Lee, Mayhugh, McComas, Mitchell, Morgan, Mullikin, Murray, Negley, Nyman, Parker, Parran, Peter, Pugh, Purnell, Ridgely, Robinette, Russell, Sands, Schley, Schlosser, Smith, of Carroll, Smith, of Dorchester, Smith, of Worcester, Sneary, Stirling, Swope, Sykes, Thomas, Thruston, Turner, Valliant, Wickard, Wilmer, Wooden—69.

The proceedings of yesterday were read and approved.

LEGAL RATE OF INTEREST.

The convention proceeded to the consideration of the report of the committee on interest and the usury laws, as follows:

Section —. The legal rate of interest in this State shall be six per centum per annum, except in cases where a different rate may be agreed upon between contracting parties; and in all cases of private contract, the rate of interest agreed on, or contracted for, shall be recoverable; and the general assembly shall pass all laws that may be necessary to carry this section into effect.

The pending question was on the adoption of the amendment submitted by Mr. DANIEL, as follows:

Strike out the word "six," in the first line, and insert the word "seven."

Mr. PURNELL gave notice that at the proper time, he would submit the following amendment:

Section —. The rate of interest in this State shall not exceed six per centum per annum, and no higher rate shall be taken or demanded; and the general assembly shall provide by law all necessary forfeitures and penalties against usury.

Mr. CUSHING. The question before the convention is one of finance alone; not to be argued upon the old ground of Jewish enactments, or old prejudices against usury and money lenders; not to be declaimed against by representing all men of means, and all individuals connected with banking institutions as Shylocks; not to be rejected for the benefit of a few borrowers in the rural localities, nor upon the ground that an increased rate of interest or an unrestricted ability to make contracts to any amount may be the cause of financial ruin to a few spendthrifts anxious to procure the means to indulge in their extravagance, and foolish enough to pay any amount of interest necessary to secure the gratification of their present desires.

It is a question affecting the future welfare of our State; a question whether our mercantile classes and laboring men shall receive at your hands due protection, or whether you will, on the other hand, go again to the old superstitious and old world fables, and come here and raise the cry so popular among demagogues, of the antagonism between the rich and the poor. It is a question whether you desire to protect in your State, men of means, or whether, when means have been brought here, you will allow capital to be employed in the State of Maryland on an equality with the neighboring States, so as to give the lender a fair compensation for the use the borrower makes of his money.

It is to-day a notorious fact that but a small part of your banking capital remains in the city of Baltimore. More of it is used to-day in discounting New York paper by telegraph, than is used in discounting Maryland paper. Your banks, for instance, having $500,000 to loan this morning, do notoriously loan by telegraph some $400,000 of that in New York; and when their boards meet at 10 o'clock in the morning, there is but $100,000 left to divide among the customers of the bank, with applications possibly for the loan of the whole amount of $500,000. Why is that? It is because New York banks can discount paper at seven per cent., and in Maryland, they are restricted to six.

Who borrow from your banks? The commercial classes in your State; the very class referred to by the gentleman from Howard (Mr. Sands,) the men of small means, but of good reputation, who desire money which they can use profitably at a fair rate of interest. They come to your banks; and the money which under the provision of the amendment would be loaned to them at seven per cent. by the banks of the city of Baltimore, has been transferred to New York, to be used at the rate of seven per cent., and these poor men have no chance left them. The men who stand high in your banks, and whose necessities are imperative, get all the money that is left in the banks to be used for purposes of discount at home; and the men of moderate means, whatever their necessities, are thrown out.

The national banks in the State of Maryland, that are now or may hereafter be created, are by law, and in fact not on an equality with those in New York, because by the terms of the law under which they exist, they are allowed only to charge the rate of interest that is the legal rate in the State in which they are located. So that while in Maryland they can only use their money at six per cent., they have not the means of transferring it to New York, and using it at seven. It is notorious to gentlemen of the convention acquainted with mercantile usages—among whom I do not count the gentleman from Howard—that the merchants from your State are now putting nearly the whole of their surplus means on deposit in New York city. The extra rate of one per cent. interest is a sufficient inducement to them to pay one-half of one per cent. exchange and transfer their money to New York, and keep it there on deposit.

That the question of the increased rate of per centage of interest allowed to be asked, is against your poor men and in favor of the rich, is, with all due deference to the gentlemen who advocated it, merely an absurdity. The rich men who want to use their money at seven per cent., can use it to-day in New York city; and they will not lend it to your poor men in the State of Maryland, at six. The question resolves itself into this, whether your poor men shall have any money at all, and not whether rich men shall receive more or less, because they can make their extra one per cent. interest by transferring their capital to New York.

Then there comes in another grave question. Your savings banks in the State of Maryland have deposits from poor people, and in the city of Baltimore, one of them has deposits solely from poor people, ranging from five dollars up to a thousand; and in the aggregate, it amounts to millions of dollars. That money must be employed by the bank, and by law at six per cent. interest. Out of that has to come the hire of the clerks of the bank, much increased beyond what it was at the time when living was less expensive than now. The tax of the United States, and the tax of the State of Maryland, must be paid out of that six per cent. So that when the time comes for the bank to declare its extra dividend, the poor people must be told that out of this six per cent. the bank has not been able to make enough to declare the dividend. All of the money goes to the poor; not one cent to the men who conduct the bank, not one cent to any stock, because there is no stock. All the money they make goes to the poor who deposit in the bank; and at six per cent. interest, they cannot make enough to declare the extra dividend to the frugal poor who there deposit their savings.

So far then, from the operation of the amendment being, as the gentleman from Howard described it, against the poor people, it is a benefit to the poor people; because the bank at seven per cent. would make one per cent. more, and it would distribute the money among the poor.

Mr. SANDS. I suppose the poor people are the stockholders of our banks.

Mr. CUSHING. There are no stockholders to the savings banks. I am glad the gentleman asked the question, because it shows that he argued the question before the house without the mere fundamental elementary knowledge of it. He comes before the house and treats a question of finance as a question of stump oratory, or question of antagonism between the rich and poor, altogether ignoring the fact that by a just use of money the poor are benefited, ignoring the fact that by the proper use of money in your State the majority of the people in your State must be benefited. He treats it as a question of oratory, forgetting that the judicious use of money for the interest of the moneyed class, is also for the interest of the laboring class; that as soon as you depress the use of money, and drive money out of the State, your poorer classes go down; making no distinction between the question of the appointment of an attorney general, and the question of dealing with the finances of your State; as if to the people of your State the questions were synonymous at all, to be treated in the same way, or to be argued on the same grounds. It is to be expected that in the formation of a constitution, gentlemen shall give a consideration to questions in some direct ratio to the importance and character of the questions themselves, and not take everything as a case of declamation before the body, and to be treated under political prejudices.

The gentleman from Kent (Mr. Chambers) introduced, or gave notice of an amendment which, after an argument against the injurious effects of an unlimited rate of interest, gives up the whole principle, and allows an indefinite rate of interest always to be charged. Examine it, and see if that is not the effect of it. The gentleman declares that it is utterly indifferent to him whether six or seven per cent. is charged.

Mr. CHAMBERS. Not indifferent. I said I preferred six to seven; but objected particularly to the additional authority legalizing any rate agreed upon.

Mr. CUSHING. The provision which the gentleman introduced to take the place of that second clause, is a provision that in all cases the borrower shall pay all the United States, all the State, and all the county taxes. That is to say, every man in your community that loans money shall forever be free from all share in your taxes; that he shall always be released by law——

Mr. CHAMBERS. It is not an obligation but an authority.

Mr. CUSHING. Because the amendment proposed here gives only authority to make such contracts, and not an obligation, do you suppose that the lender would not always force the borrower to pay the tax? They will always do it. Is it not human nature, that when you give authority to enforce the payment of the taxes by the needy man, he will always pay them? The provision of the gentleman from Kent is eminently wise, for the interest of bank stockholders, and eminently unwise with regard to any other class of people.

The amendment as proposed, to raise the interest to seven per cent., protects the interest of the stockholder of the banks; yet it does not throw upon the borrower from the bank the *onus* of paying all those taxes. In any bank the money used is not the capital of the bank, but the deposits in the bank. You would then have the deposits in the bank used by the bank, not paying one cent of taxes from the bank, but rolling up dividends to the stockholders in property amounting in some cases to five or six times their capital. For instance, a bank has a capital of one million, and deposits amounting to five millions of dollars; and uses the whole deposits to loan, on which it receives interest at six per cent. Under the provision of the gentleman from Kent, it would receive on the capital loaned, in addition to the six per cent., the United States tax upon the bank, the State tax upon the bank, the county tax upon the bank, and the city tax upon the bank, if there were any. What is the result? The stockholders owning one million of dollars and employing six millions, receive upon their one million of dollars the interest upon six millions, secured from all share in the city, county, State and United States tax. You have the result that one class in the community is always exempted from every particle of your tax. That is the policy of the amendment of the gentleman from Kent.

The proposition of the report is fair both to the lender and to the borrower. It gives a chance to the stockholders of the banks, after paying their taxes, city, county, State and United States, upon the capital of the banks, if their deposits shall have been used at the rate of seven per cent., to pay probably a dividend clear of all taxes, of six per cent. upon the amount of their capital; because they will have used, to loan, five or six times the capital of their banks. That is fair and just. But the instant you transfer the whole burden from the money lender's back to the shoulders of the men who have to borrow, you are exempting the wealthy class of men in the community from paying taxes, and forcing all the taxes to be paid by the poor.

Mr. Sands. Will the gentleman allow me to ask him a question?

Mr. Cushing. Yes; if the gentleman will confine himself to a question, and not make an argument.

Mr. Sands. I would like to know if the gentleman has been accustomed to prepare mortgages for money lenders?

Mr. Cushing. I presume that is nearer the business of the gentleman himself, than to mine; and if in drawing them he was instructed to put it twelve per cent., I think he would do it. I do not think he would be found arguing with the man who asked him to draw up the mortgage that it was immoral to require twelve per cent., but I think he would simply inscribe upon the paper what he was told.

We have heard a great deal said on the floor of the house about money lenders being Shylocks. It is patent to every sensible man that all the men of means are not Shylocks, with a most ferocious and villainous countenance, peering about the highways and alleys of the towns, to see if they cannot destroy some poor man. It is a fact well known that all the impetus through the length and breadth of our land has come from moneyed men; that every great enterprise is carried on only by moneyed men. It is a great fact that from the beginning of the war, it was the moneyed men, and the banks, which supplied the money needed by the government. The Rothschilds are not in the habit of going around lanes and alleys for poor victims to devour; but their's is such an institution that I doubt whether without it many of the governments of Europe would have to-day been in existence.

If the gentleman means to represent all the great banking institutions, the Barings, the Bank of England, as many kings, combining together to destroy and take away the poor man's earnings, the thing is so absurd that except to a congregation of men assembled to hear a stump speaker, it would hardly meet with an attentive audience. Let wealth have its true place. Recognize it for what it is, a great lever and necessary instrument in working out the advancement and progress of the people. Let it be understood that with increase in wealth comes increase in refinement, increase in comfort; that just in proportion to the increasing wealth of the State, the laboring classes, and the poorer classes are better provided for.

We had an appeal from the gentleman with regard to the agricultural classes; that by imposing seven per cent. interest, the agricultural classes would be depressed. If the agricultural classes want money, it is certainly desirable that they should be able to get it. As it is now, they do not get it at six per cent., because it is gone to New York at seven. They cannot get it through the regular channels, the banks, and they are forced to go to men whom they oblige by the inducement of gain to break the laws of your State and demoralize both the lender and the borrower, the one by inducing to break and the other by breaking the law. You have the gentleman from Anne Arundel (Mr. Miller) arguing here that when a man has gone to a money lender and has obtained from him money at a given per cent., it is the borrower's bounden duty to the rest of his creditors to go into a court of law and to claim the benefit of the law, and to say that this interest has been usurious; to confess that under a false confidence in him he has induced a man to lend him his money; to break away all reliance between man and man in regard to money contracts, and to reduce the whole business of borrowing money throughout the State to the mere question of diamond cut diamond, and let the man who is the sharpest, and can lie the best have the benefit of it. Thus he raises the interest to ten per cent. or more on account of the danger of going into the courts of law and pleading usury. He would actually break down all confidence between man and man, and take advantage of having broken the law. It is truly a novel way of improving the character of the money lender. It is a comical way of making the money lender a less disgraceful person than he has been represented to be upon the floor of this house.

The gentleman from Howard (Mr. Sands) seemed to think that every money lender was a pawn-broker, sitting on the front steps of some house in a little alley with three gilt balls over his door, decoying in the poor to their destruction. That is a way of dealing with questions of finance to which I must confess I have not been accustomed. The gentleman may say that they get along in Pennsylvania with six per cent.; but it is a notorious fact that in every community where six per cent. is the rate of interest, there is more money loaned to-day at twelve per cent., more money at twenty, more money at thirty, than there is at six. The law may be evaded by selling your note for any amount, whatever may be its face. The law can be evaded at every step and turn you choose to take; and the man that must have money will have it at any price. There are times that come to every man that needs money when money may be worth twenty, thirty, or forty per cent. In the crisis of 1837, when the largest merchants of the whole United States went down, there were times when they offered cent per cent., offered all they were worth in the world if they could but raise money enough to pay their mercantile debts; brought down the accumulations of years of business, and offered them all for money enough to be advanced to save their mercantile credit.

An act to restrict the rate of money? It flows like water. If money is plenty and is not worth six per cent., men of undoubted security can get it for less. But the man whose security is not good will not get it for six per cent. because the lender runs a risk of losing the whole. It is not to be expected that a man who may break to-morrow can obtain a loan of money to-day at six per cent., which to-morrow may be gone. Is it according to the ordinary operations of trade, and ordinary common sense, that a man will lend money to-day at six per cent., taking the risk that to-morrow the man may break and he may lose the whole? No; they ask enough in addition to pay for the risk, whether that risk be twenty, thirty, forty, or fifty per cent.

The gentleman from Anne Arundel (Mr. Miller) brought up the case of the man in Georgia who borrowed four thousand dollars at such a rate that estate to the value of forty thousand dollars had to be sold to pay principal and interest. If the money was not worth an amount sufficient to swamp his whole estate, he need not have borrowed it. Nobody forced him to borrow it. The lender did not force his money upon him at such a rate. It was because the security he had to offer was such that he could not command the money at a lower rate. If the security had been undoubted, there were men enough who would have been ready to lend him their money at the market rate of money at the time.

The gentleman brought forward an argument that money was different from any other commodity because money is the representative of value. Why is it the representative of value? It is because the precious metals have in themselves the most labor in the least quantity, that they serve as a circulating medium, for large representative values, for purposes of commerce. They have always been used for this purpose; but they have not always had the same value in themselves. It is within the memory of every gentleman upon this floor, that but a few years ago the Congress of the United States found it necessary to debase the whole silver circulation of the country, because silver had become proportionately higher than gold in its value. And if the discoveries in gold continue, the time may come when the world may be driven to employ some metal still more rare and valuable than gold or silver, as its circulating medium. Gold is to-day used as an article of commerce; it is shipped from your mines unstamped as an article of commerce. The only thing which gives the least shadow of weight to such an idea, is that the government puts its stamps upon it to attest that it has been assayed and weighed; and it has the seal of the government to show that the coin contains a definite value. It is shipped every day in the form of dust and bars, as a simple article of commerce.

(The twenty minutes allowed by the order having expired, the hammer fell.)

Mr. CHAMBERS Mr. President——

The CHAIRMAN (Mr. Pugh.) The gentleman has already spoken upon this question.

Mr. CHAMBERS. If there is any other gentleman who wishes to speak, I will give way with cheerfulness. I have not a word to say that I cannot say two hours hence as well as now.

Mr. THOMAS. I give notice that I will at the proper time move an amendment that the rate of interest shall be six per cent. per annum; but that parties may contract for any higher rate of interest not exceeding seven per cent.

Mr. THRUSTON. I give notice that I will move to amend the report by inserting after "recoverable" the words "not exceeding seven and three-tenths per cent." My object in fixing this sum is that seven and three-tenths is a very convenient rate for computing interest; and that it is a little above the New York rate of interest, and therefore will have the effect of bringing home that capital which has been sent there at seven per cent. I am opposed to allowing contracts at any rate of interest.

Mr. ABBOTT. I have an amendment of which I wish to give notice, that the legal rate of interest shall not exceed seven per cent., leaving to the legislature the power to fix a lower rate if they think proper.

Mr. CHAMBERS. I have been exceedingly surprised at the argument which has been urged by the gentleman from Baltimore (Mr. Cushing,) with regard to stump-speaking, &c. I understand that that is passed over to another gentleman; for I do not suppose the gentleman alluded to any remarks of mine.

Mr. CUSHING. I had no allusion to the gentleman.

Mr. CHAMBERS. The argument of the gentleman is that if we limit the rate of interest on money loaned to six per cent., the available funds of our State will be transferred to the use of the people of New York. The next argument, to enforce it, is that the banks in our State are making such an inordinate profit that if you allow them to charge to the borrower from their banks, the taxes due upon the amount, they will make an enormous and most outrageous profit. How these things can be dovetailed together, I do not know.

Mr. CUSHING. I said under the operation of your proposition.

Mr. CHAMBERS. The gentleman seems to have forgotten altogether that at present your lenders of money can charge the taxation.—The code says that the proposition to increase the rate of interest seems to overlook this provision. The simple purpose I have is to have it noticed, that it may be decided by the provisions of this constitution. The additional clause I propose is no new law; it is the law now. I say further, that it is not only the law, but that it is the practice. Money lenders now exact from those that borrow a stipulation to pay the taxes. I have acted as agent for several individuals in the city of Baltimore, and they have forwarded printed mortgages; and I have not seen the first one yet that did not contain this provision.

Mr. SANDS. It is universal.

Mr. CUSHING. That refers to a small part of the money loaned in the State—the money loaned on mortgages.

Mr. CHAMBERS. I care not whether it is large or small. I say it is the law and the practice, whether large or small, that privilege is now reserved to the lender of the money. I do not use such harsh terms as the gentleman—"nonsense," &c; but I say that any prudent man, no matter what the rate of interest may be, will take care to secure himself a certain sum; and the only mode is to guard against his being made to pay taxes out of his six per cent. Six per cent. is the value of money. We can go to the bank, and deposit it, and can receive there six per cent., and they pay the taxes. The taxes, as I said yesterday, amount to about one per cent.

I will not dwell upon the remarks of the gentleman about money lenders. I have been selling out my stock, and have found it necessary to take care of what I have. I have not denounced money lenders, all of them, as sharpers, sharks, Shylocks, and all that sort of thing. Those remarks of the gentleman cannot apply to me. They belong, as I say, further on. But I do say this, that where persons adopt that profession or occupation of shaving paper and loaning money as a business or trade, those men become presently, by habitual indulgence in large extensions of their conscience, if I may so term it, a very elastic material sometimes, beginning with seven, eight, and nine per cent., and finding the receipts very pleasant, unable to be satisfied with less than twenty-five or thirty-three and one-third per cent. I defy the gentleman to name a man who has been ten or fifteen years in the business, habitually lending money, who is satisfied with less than twenty-five per cent. on good bond and mortgage.

It is that class of people that we are to guard against. It is to that class of people that young men go, when they come into their estates, to get money in advance, speculating upon future imaginary profits. It is to that class of people that these young men go, to persons extortionate in their demands.

The argument that the gentleman urges upon us strongly is that if you make the borrower pay the taxes, the banks will make inordinate profits. If that is the case, six per cent. is enough, and we ought not to give seven. The law now authorizes that, and I presume there is no intention to change the law. Why then increase by one per cent. the enormous profits of the banks? I have been a director in some one or another of the banks in Baltimore for the last five and twenty years, and though I have as little knowledge of their actual operations as anybody else, I believe they never have adopted the practice of exacting more than the legal rate of interest. It is not to the banks that this particularly refers. It is to gentlemen who have some surplus money, and in the present condition of the country being utterly at a loss where to place it, have loaned it out to agricultural men at a legal rate of interest, requiring the payment by the borrower of the taxes that may become due on it, so that they may know exactly what their income is—a clear six per cent.

With regard to the agricultural matter, the gentleman has misunderstood me. I do not mean to say that agriculturists were those who took advantage of the wants of others and victimized them. I mean to say that they cannot afford to pay more than six per cent. That is the idea I have of the agricultural interest. When a farmer borrows money and pays six per cent. interest, and pays the taxes on the loan, I say that is about as much as he can expect to realize out of the amount he borrows. The agricultural interest of the country is not receiving as much as six or seven per cent. profit out of the capital which they have invested.

My proposition is first that six per cent. is the value of money. There are some facts known to us by which it can be estimated.—Take the bonds of the Baltimore and Ohio railroad, the Northern Central railroad, or any other perfectly well secured bond in the State. A Baltimore and Ohio railroad bond, for one hundred dollars, will yield its owner six per cent. From that six per cent. he has to pay the State twenty-five cents on one hundred dollars capital. He has to pay the county forty-five to sixty-five cents on the one hundred dollars of the capital. He has to pay the United States, at present, three to five per cent. upon the interest. All this is to come out of the six dollars which he is to receive for the one hundred dollar bond. It reduces it to about five per cent. A Baltimore and Ohio railroad bond, which does not yield above five per cent., is selling to-day at one hundred and fifteen or one hundred and sixteen dollars. What does this prove?

Mr. CUSHING. How much did the same bond sell for three years ago, when money paid the same amount of interest? Less than forty dollars.

Mr. CHAMBERS. That has about as much to do with this question as what it will sell for three years hence. Three years ago a very different state of things existed. They were in debt, had all sorts of obligations imposed upon them, and they had been struggling to make a dividend. I say as a fact within my own personal knowledge—and I appeal to gentlemen everywhere about me to confirm it—that money has been abundant.—Your newspapers have been advertising it. Every lawyer in the country I suppose has had offers from gentlemen of funds in Baltimore to loan out money at six per cent. interest. There are now outstanding offers ready for the acceptance of anybody who will give ample security in real estate, to loan money at six per cent.

Mr. SANDS. Will the gentleman allow me to read some quotations from this morning's paper? "Baltimore city 6 per cents., due in 1870, 116; United States 6 per cent. bonds, coupons, 106¾; 5-20s, 111." These are all six per cent. securities.

Mr. CHAMBERS. These are six per cent. securities; and in these cases the parties who own the stock have to pay the taxes. I say further that money may now be had at five per cent., I believe in abundance, by persons who can give real estate security, the only security that is now thought to be perfectly safe. I have lent to gentlemen myself a few dollars, and my contract is that it shall not be paid; I will not allow it to be paid until the circulation becomes more settled, and money has a more definite character than at present. I have been applied to within a very short time afterwards to receive the money, because the gentleman could go and borrow it at five per cent.

Mr. SANDS. If the gentleman will excuse the interruption, I will say that here is an offer in to-day's paper of $40,000 at five per cent.

Mr. DANIEL. On what sort of security?

Mr. CHAMBERS. Another argument of the gentleman was that gold was only the representative of value because stamped by the government.

Mr. CUSHING. I said that that made its circulating value; but that did not give it its actual value.

Mr. CHAMBERS. The government stamp cannot make a circulating medium. You may indorse a man of ample means, and your indorsement does not have much effect. Does the government stamping ingots make them a circulating medium? It is a mistake. Gold has an intrinsic value. Silver has an intrinsic value. That value is derived from the fact that there is a limited amount. Greenbacks have not that value; because the authorities in Washington can manufacture them as fast as they can get them printed. I do not believe anybody participates in the apprehension of the gentleman from Baltimore city that gold is to be so plenty that we shall look for some more precious metal. It has been the standard of value for all time, and I think it will continue so for all time to come.

I therefore say that the evidence is all around us that six per cent. is enough. We have always been limited to that. The country is habituated to it. There has been, so far as I know, no complaint about it. Money is abundant at that price. The very moment you advance it to seven per cent. interest it will be all the other way. There is no mistake about that. But I say that is not a just rate. I say that six per cent. is enough. And I say, above all, do not legalize the extravagant amounts which young men, indiscreet persons, of unripe judgment, and choleric or any other habits, of strong anticipations about future profits will agree to pay, and thus enable that class of people thoroughly to ruin themselves for the benefit of others who are certainly not particularly entitled to claim our protection. The additional section which I propose, I take it for granted would have been adopted by the committee if it had been before them—the provision for the payment of taxes. I intend to move it as a separate section if not adopted as an amendment to this.

Mr. NEGLEY. The gentleman from Kent (Mr. Chambers) seems to argue that in order to prevent the prodigal and reckless young man from spending his patrimony, it is necessary to prevent him from borrowing money at a higher rate than six per cent. That I understand to be his proposition, and that is the reason he gives why there ought to be a prohibition upon the lending of money throughout the State of Maryland, to confine it to six per cent., because if that be not done some extravagant and reckless young man may go to a money lender and agree, in order to get money, to mortgage his property, or pledge it in some way, so that he may have the means by which to squander his estate. Does the gentleman forget that we ought to prevent that same young man from going into the market and buying at an extravagant price a pair of fine horses or a magnificent carriage?

Mr. CHAMBERS. Tell me how to do it, and I will accomplish that.

Mr. NEGLEY. You cannot do it; and it is utterly useless to attempt to curb him in one direction when he squanders his money like water in every other imaginable way. That very thing shows the utter folly, the utter absurdity of trying by legislation to make a man keep money when he has a disposition to spend it. If you do not allow him to borrow money at a greater rate than six per cent. is there no way of whipping the devil around the stump? Is it not done every day?

JUDICIARY REPORT.

The hour having arrived for taking up the order of the day, being the report of the committee on the judiciary department,

On motion of Mr. STIRLING,

The order of the day was postponed until after the consideration of the matter pending.

LEGAL RATE OF INTEREST.

Mr. NEGLEY resumed: Why are there such men in the world as have been described by the gentleman from Kent? Why are there money lenders that have secret places with by-ways by which men can get to their offices to get money? Why has it been so for centuries? It is because the government has not placed money upon the proper level with other things. Allow a man to borrow money as he is allowed to buy a horse, and you destroy these obnoxious characters. You take up the evil by the root. At one fell swoop you destroy the entire class of money lenders, if you allow a man to go into the market and borrow money, as you allow him to go into the market and buy a peck of apples, a ham, or anything else.

What is money? It has a commercial value like anything else. A man who goes to the mines of California and digs out the precious metal, by the time that metal goes through all the processes and receives the stamp of the United States upon it, finds that it costs him one hundred cents to the dollar, just as much as it costs one hundred cents for the man to go into the field and plough his land and raise a bushel of wheat. At the same time that it is a commercial medium for the disposition of things between man and man, it has another character. It has a value in itself. It has a double character. It has an intrinsic value at the same time that it is used as a means of exchange. Hence it is that money is governed by the same laws which govern other things, the perpetual and unchanging laws of supply and demand.

If money in the community is abundant, if the supply is increased, the demand being the same, what is the result? The interest goes down. We are way behind England. We are way behind France. We are way behind the German States. Has not the Bank of England a sliding scale? When money is abundant it goes down; just like the scale that operates of itself in the community. When any commodity is abundant, and the supply remains the same, the value of the article goes down. It is so every day in the streets of New York and Philadelphia and Baltimore. Why is it that you see money quoted at seven per cent. one day and seven and a half per cent. another? Not all the legislation in creation would affect these rates. You cannot trample the eternal laws of political economy under foot. It is utterly absurd and preposterous to attempt to hedge in and prevent the obtaining of more than six per cent. or seven per. cent., or eight per cent., by any legal enactments.

What do you do in the present constitution? You license a set of men—this very class that the gentleman from Kent talks about—to take the paper which you will not allow me to negotiate myself, and hawk it about the streets, and sell it at six, eight and ten per cent.; whereas if you would allow me to do it myself, without any interference by statutory enactments, or constitutional prohibitions, I would go to my neighbor who has money, and I would make a contract with him to suit my own convenience. If he asks me more than I choose to give, it is no bargain. It is just upon the same principle as if I wanted to buy a horse, and you should make me apply to a licensed broker to buy that horse, under a constitutional provision that a man who sells horses shall not be allowed to ask more than so much for them. You might as well fix a maximum value upon every horse that is sold, and every carriage, and every bushel of wheat, and everything else that you get money for. You might as well say that a livery man shall not have more than a dollar and a half a day for his horse, or his buggy, as to say to me that I shall not have more than six dollars a year for the use of a hundred dollars. Is there any difference in principle? I hire my money to a man who gives me a certain reward for it. I hire my horse and buggy to a man who gives me a certain reward for it. What is the difference in the principle? There is none. It is governed by the same law. If there are many livery stables, and an abundance of horses and vehicles, I can hire at a low rate. If there is an abundance of money in the market, I can hire money at a low rate. If horses and carriages are scarce, and there is a great desire to ride, the rate increases. The demand being increased, and the supply remaining the same, they will command a higher price. Just so it is with money.

Our sister States are getting awake to this fact. Shall we go trudging along in this old beaten path, and force away the capital from our own State? I tell you that capital, like water, will seek its level. Wherever capital can receive the most profitable investment, it is going just as surely, just as certainly as that water will run down hill. If in the State of Pennsylvania a higher rate of interest were allowed than in the State of Maryland, as a consequence capital would be lent where the owner could make the most out of it. I know that in my own county $6,000 have absolutely gone to Ogle county, Illinois, to seek investment there at ten per cent. Seven per cent. is the legal interest and they are allowed by private contract to run it up to ten. This capital never would have gone there if the parties had been allowed to make such a bargain here. It would have remained in the county. So in Baltimore city, I have no doubt that thousands upon thousands of dollars go out of the city to seek investment, where the money receives a higher rate of interest.

You do not avoid the very thing which you aim to avoid. It is utterly useless by any legislative means to attempt to prevent the obtaining of more than six per cent. I know hundreds of cases; I know cases in my own county. What do the parties do? A wants money, and B has got it. Here is a constitutional provision that A shall not pay more than six per cent. But they go into a room and make a contract. A gives B his note for $1,000 at the legal rate of interest payable six months after date, and B hands him $950. If you would allow A to go out in the street and contract for himself; if you would allow him to go openly and above board, and make inquiry, and make an open, fair, legal contract, he would not have been asked, and would not have been compelled to pay those $50. This is done continually. I know one of the wealthiest men in the county of Washington, who loans out the most of his property, and he never loans it at six per cent. He always gets more; but he gets it in advance, and he manages in this way. There is the note. The parties are by themselves. How can you get at it?

Why not leave this open? Why impose a restriction? It has a bad effect. It demoralizes the public. It holds out inducements to men to do that clandestinely and illegally which the law does not permit them to do. It has a bad effect upon the public morals.

I am in favor of this section as reported by the committee to let the legal rate of interest be six per cent.; but then, in God's name, allow a man the liberty of making a bargain for himself. Why do you insert six per cent.? Why is there a necessity for the insertion of any amount at all? Simply because if there were no stipulation in the contract, and a question were to go before the jury, it would be necessary to adduce testimony to show how much money was worth at the time; and it would lead to interminable litigation, and a great deal of cost in adjusting the rate of interest. Hence it is always better that a legal rate of interest should be fixed to apply to all cases where the parties leave it a blank. Then when they come into court and introduce testimony, the rate will be according to the instrument itself, or if no rate is mentioned, the legal rate. Beyond that, let this question be open as you let everything else be open. Let me, if I want money go and contract for it, just as you allow me to go and contract for a horse. I know something of my county, and if these rebel invasions continue much longer they will want horses infinitely more than they want money, and they will be more likely to be imposed upon in the purchase of horses than in borrowing money; and therefore I respectfully recommend to this convention, if they will restrain my ability to borrow money, that they should put the same limitation upon the men who come to Washington county to sell our people horses, that they shall not charge more than such a price for them. They have an equal right to do it, and can do it with just as much propriety.

The history of the world, and the history of the age, shows that this species of legislation is the very worst kind. The curse of over-legislation is infinitely worse than the curse of under-legislation. Too much legislation is infinitely worse than too little.—This is one of those delicate questions of political economy, that the price of money is governed by the same law that governs everything else. If this convention acts wisely it will do as our sister States have done; it will leave this question open. It will fix a legal rate of interest; and after fixing that, it will allow parties privately to contract at least up to a certain amount, say 10 per cent.—You may put on that limit if you think proper; but there is no harm in leaving it open to any extent, I conceive. If a man chooses to squander his property he will do it. A young man who has a disposition to waste his estate will do it, not by borrowing money at larger rates than 6 per cent, but will do it in every possible way in which men do spend money, going to restaurants and having magnificent dinners, calling for wines of extravagant price, and inviting his friends in.

It will not do to pass laws to hedge in men in their rights in this way. You must leave men free. You must provide in your schools to make moral men. Teach them their duty, that when they grow up they may be a law unto themselves. That is the way to rule these things, and not by legislation; not by cutting off one branch and leaving the others to flourish in undisturbed luxuriance.

Therefore, sir, I am opposed to this amendment for 7 per cent. Yet I do not conceive that we should lose by it. New York allows 7 per cent, and I think Pennsylvania allows 6.

Mr. Daniel. Many of the States allow more than 7.

Mr. Negley. I know they do; but money being abundant I think the rate of interest is likely to go down rather than to go up. It is probable, from the very fact that it is governed by the same law. The amount of money in the country is vastly increased. Hence the price of everything has gone up. Money being cheap, everything is dear. The worth of money, therefore, instead of increasing, is rather depreciating. The fact is that 6 per cent. now is a depreciation. If the interest had kept up, it would be 9 per cent., and ought to be 15 per cent., if the interest had kept up with the increase in the amount of circulation, for everything has advanced that much in price; everything but money; and it has been kept down by the simple fact that the supply has been so abundant that money could be borrowed on accommodating terms. I do not know that I would be in favor of disturbing the rate of 6 per cent. as it is now. I certainly am in favor of the section as reported by the committee.

If it shall be passed, the convention will have made a very considerable stride towards bettering the condition of the people, in taking away the restriction of these usury laws that have come down to us from Bible history.—Why is it that so much odium was attached to usury among the Jews? It was to prevent the Jews from borrowing money, because when they got into debt they were sold into slavery, and because the Jewish law put its face against slavery. It liberated all Jewish slaves at the end of every seven years. This was one means of producing slavery. Borrowing money and not being able to pay when pay-day came, the Jew had to go into slavery; and hence the odium which has come down to us. But that does not apply at all to a commercial age of the world. You might as well say that bigamy being recommended once, or rather permitted once, it is advisable to be recommended and lived up to now. The fact is that it was there in the Bible, and that the circumstances out of which it grew have entirely changed; but it has come down to us with the odium of the Jew; and to this day the money lender and the Jew are connected together, and we associate them together.—Whenever you talk about a Shylock, it is synonymous with a money lender or a Jew.

Mr. Thruston. I do not think there is anything more apparent now than that money is not worth more than 6 per cent. when we see 6 per cent. securities selling above par in the market. The difficulty is that gentlemen call money that which is not money. Money—gold and silver—is very scarce, and very hard to be got. But when you offer the right kind of security you can get it at 6 per cent.; and the proof of that is that good, undoubted securities are selling for less than 6 per cent. So that money now is not worth 6 per cent. Currency is a very different thing from money. Currency refers to money for its value; but it is not money itself. We know that the experience of civilized nations has been that it is necessary to have some moderate rate of interest fixed by law. That has been the experience of the civilized world for the last fifteen centuries. I think that this idea that the money lenders, the people whose only trade and business it is to lend money, are themselves best fitted to take statesman-like views upon the subject of usury is an anomalous argument. Persons can generally look at things in which they are not interested under circumstances more favorable to coming to a right conclusion, than those whose interest it is to make them work in one direction, and one direction alone. A man whose trade it is to loan money, finds it to be for his interest to get as much for the use of money as he can; and therefore it is his interest to go to the persons most needy and necessitous to obtain money, to lend his money to them because he can get a higher rate of interest for it

There is one argument which, to my mind, is unanswerable against giving no rate at all, but allowing any rate to be agreed upon by contract; and it is this. Men who are in debt upon contracts at a small interest, unable to pay it at the stipulated time, feeling themselves in depressed circumstances, will go and borrow money at any rate, 50, 60, or 100 per cent.; and when their creditors come to be paid from their estates, the honest debt contracted by them when they borrowed money at 6 per cent. or bought goods to be paid for on time, will be placed upon an equality with debts to the man who has loaned them money at 50 or 100 per cent. A man in failing circumstances wants $1,000, and perhaps he never expects to pay it. The creditor runs a great risk and demands a double payment. He rather thinks it is good, but he asks 6 per cent. interest and 10 per cent. for the risk. People who loan money will always loan it so as to make the greatest profit out of it.

In the amendment which I propose, and which goes as far as I am disposed to go, allows parties to contract at seven and three-tenths per cent.; and gentlemen must reflect that that is equivalent to 9 per cent. if you stipulate, as you may stipulate, as the gentleman from Kent (Mr. Chambers) argued, that the borrower shall pay the taxes; for with the taxes, seven and three-tenths per cent. will amount to 9 per cent. which you may receive for your money. That is a sufficient interest, especially in times when, as I say, undoubted security does not command 6 per cent. In other words you must pay such a price for the bond that it really brings but 5 per cent. I think that seven and three-tenths is sufficient. It is a higher rate than is allowed in any of the States around us, and therefore it will keep our capital at home, instead of going to adjoining States, or neighboring States, where a higher rate of interest than our own now prevails. I have drawn up my amendment in the form of a substitute for the section which I will read, remarking that I require the contract to be in writing so as to avoid frauds or disputes, which might occur if the rate of interest were to be left to verbal agreements:

"The legal rate of interest in this State shall be six per centum per annum, except in cases where a different rate may be agreed upon in writing between contracting parties, not exceeding, however, seven and three-tenths per cent. interest in any case; and the general assembly shall pass all laws necessary to carry this section into effect."

I will merely say in conclusion that six per cent. legal interest with the taxes now amounts to seven and one-half per cent., and that seven and three-tenths per cent. with the taxes added amounts to nine per cent. I think that is interest enough if the borrower has any reasonable security to offer. If he has not good security, the lender exacts exorbitant interest which is in fact paid by the party's creditors and not by the party himself. I think the substitute goes as far as it is proper to go, and is a reasonable proposition.

Mr. Daniel. I confess that I do not see the force of a good many remarks that have been made. The gentleman who has just taken his seat, it seems to me, in his remark that every civilized nation has thought it proper to fix some moderate rate of interest, does not invalidate this proposition at all, nor any proposition that is upon the table, because it certainly seems to me that while some States are charging ten per cent. interest it cannot be said that seven per cent. is an immoderate rate of interest.

Two gentlemen, one from Howard and the other from Kent, have arisen to address the house, and two subjects seem to have been the burden of their remarks, two great grievances which they wished to remedy. The gentleman from Kent (Mr. Chambers) wants to provide against the lavish expenditure of their fortunes by improvident young men; and the gentleman from Howard (Mr. Sands) wants to keep the poor out of the hands of the Shylocks. The one is the especial friend of the poor, and the other is the especial friend of improvident young men. As has been very well said by the gentleman from Washington county (Mr. Negley.) the idea of our trying to prevent improvident young men from spending their fortunes is an utter absurdity. The experience of every man is to the contrary. It has been in our constitution from time immemorial that six per cent. only shall be charged. Is it not the experience of every man in this convention that notwithstanding this, young men have spent their fortunes, and have paid a great deal more than six per cent. for money in order to get it to spend? I have young men in my eye who inherited a fortune, and yet in a few years spent their fortune, and spent it in part by borrowing money at fifteen, twenty, twenty-five or thirty-three and a third per cent., of which the gentleman from Kent has spoken.

The gentleman from Kent is contradictory with himself; because he states here in one proposition plainly upon this floor that money is worth six per cent. and only six per cent., and that men derive the value of it when they let it for that rate; and yet he tells us almost in the proposition immediately preceding that every man's experience is that every money lender does charge twenty-five to thirty-three and a third per cent. and gets it.

Mr. Chambers. The gentleman from Kent said no such thing, "every money lender!" I said that men habitually received that. I tried to explain it before, and it is hardly worth while now.

Mr. Daniel. So I understood the gentleman. The gentleman certainly stated that twenty-five to thirty-three and a third per cent. were obtained for money. I do not care how it was obtained; for if it were paid the money must have been worth that in the market.

Mr. Chambers. That is the language of every money lender.

Mr. Daniel. The language of every money lender? I know some men who would not have it if you would give it to them; who would not take more than six per cent. although money might be worth ten or twenty per cent. Some men will not have it. But the very fact that the gentleman stated, that money has commanded such rates, and the gentleman says that is the experience of everybody that money is lent in the community at such rates, shows that those who pay these rates cannot get it cheaper. If money was worth only six per cent., they would have gone to somebody else and got it at six per cent.

Now I ask if the rate does not depend in a great measure on the character of the investment. The gentleman from Howard (Mr. Sands) has flourished here advertisements in the newspapers. He is the especial friend of the poor man; and he has told us that $40,000 are advertised in this morning's paper to be loaned at five per cent. Now let us see how this money is to be loaned. "For five or ten years; the security must be ample; located either in the city of Baltimore or in Baltimore county; in one sum of $40,000, or four sums of $10,000." I think the poor man would be badly off if he had to take $40,000, or even $10,000. And then where is he to get the security? It must be good city security, ground rents, or something of the kind. When the poor man comes from Howard county wanting $1,000, applies for it, the answer is, "No sir; I cannot take your security; I want security in Baltimore city or county." Or if he says he only wants $1,000, the answer is, "No sir; I will not loan that amount; I want to loan it in large sums. The lowest sum I will let is $10,000. Then I get my interest easily, and do not have to go around and collect it, $1,000 from A., $1,000 from B, and $1,000 from C. I collect my interest easily, and therefore I can afford to charge less."

It is plain, as the friends of this measure have argued, and as was argued especially by the gentleman from Washington (Mr. Negley,) that if you allow money to go into the market, like any other commodity, to be regulated by the law of supply and demand, you will have interest at less than seven per cent., and even at less than six per cent. oftener than you will have it above. That is the experience in New York. The experience there is that more money is loaned in New York city to-day at five per cent. on good investments than at seven per cent., although seven per cent. is the legal rate. When you allow money to go into the market, as soon as the market is supplied the rate of interest goes down; but if you keep money out of the market by a forced rate of interest, you force it into other States, and it becomes scarce, and the rate of interest goes up; and you force the poor friend of my friend from Howard right into the hands of the Shylock by the very provision intended to keep him out.

The gentleman from Kent stated another proposition which is not good upon its face at all. He spoke of the value of the bonds of the Baltimore and Ohio railroad company as being an argument to show that money is only worth six per cent. Does not everybody know that a while ago, before the crisis, they could be bought for sixty or seventy per cent., so that the interest was seven or eight per cent.? It was because the credit of the Baltimore and Ohio railroad company was involved, although they paid their interest of six per cent. annually. Look at our city sixes, with the city property pledged to the payment of it. Persons can invest there and have ample security. But suppose a poor man comes up, and wants a small amount upon security in Howard county, to pay the interest semi-annually, or even if he is to be trusted and has property, will he not be charged for contingencies? Certainly he will; and money will range higher on that account.

I say therefore that instead of aiding the poor man, as the gentleman from Howard supposes, by refusing to allow seven per cent. to be taken, we are legislating against the poor man. And if we allow seven per cent., it will be legislating in his favor. Our experience under the law confining it to six per cent. in this constitution, has shown that it has worked against the poor man ever since it has been in the constitution. So long as you make it a prohibitory law upon the statute book, you will find that honest men owning property will not go into the market and lend to A, B and C, because they can invest their money in stocks or otherwise, and derive a more certain or a larger amount of interest than the rate of interest fixed by law. The poor man who wants money must go to the men who are willing to evade the law if you will pay them for it; and they fall into the hands of the Shylocks. But if you change the law, honest men can go into the market with their funds as money lenders, and you will find money more plenty, and poor men can get it at a less rate of interest.

Again, I deny that all the favor is toward the money lender, even at the highest rate of interest. A poor man has the sheriff ready to come into his house to levy an execution upon his property, and sacrifice all the little means he has, and unless he can get money his property will be sacrificed, and he will be turned loose upon the world. He goes out and tries to borrow money at six per cent. Money is worth more and he cannot get it. Honest men with money to lend can do better by it; and he is thrown into the hands of other men. And even if they do charge him ten or twelve per cent., I say that it is to that man's advantage to save his little property at ten or twelve per cent. rather than to allow it to be sacrificed.

Again, there are men that want money to invest. They are engaged in a great enterprise. Money is worth twelve or fifteen per cent. on the street to-day. But they know that by engaging in this enterprise, and obtaining the loan of money, they can make fifty per cent. Is there any hardship in taking twelve or fifteen per cent. from that man? You are doing him an actual favor by loaning him the money at that price, from which he can realize double or treble the amount of interest you charge him.

I have had a little experience in lending money on mortgage. I know from my own experience, and I think it is the experience of every gentleman who has lived in a commercial community and engaged in money transactions, or who has been in a condition to observe them, that money will range according to its value, whatever laws you make to prevent it. Money will bring its value. I know in my own experience, with my own clients and others, that when money is worth twelve or fifteen per cent. on mortgage, it will bring twelve or fifteen per cent.

Mr. Sands. How do they get it?

Mr. Daniel. I will tell you. A comes up and wants to borrow $1000, on mortgage. B has the money to loan. But B says, "I cannot lend you that money unless you will give me twelve per cent." "Very well," says A. Then B takes out a year's interest, $60, and hands over to A $940, and takes his note for $1000 with interest at six per cent.

Mr. Miller. Would it not invalidate the contract, if these facts are proven in a court of justice?

Mr. Daniel. No sir; it would only invalidate it in case the party should come into court and plead usury and tender the amount.

Mr. MILLER. Certainly; but that would invalidate it.

Mr. DANIEL. I will come to that directly. I say that this is done every day. In my own experience I know it. It is customary for every money lender and broker in Baltimore city to do that same thing. Money will have its value. But the gentleman says it will invalidate it in a court of justice if the party comes into court and pleads usury and tenders the amount of the principal and six per cent. interest.

Mr. PETER. Would not a court of equity say that that is a debt, like any other debt, and compel the creditors to pay it back?

Mr. DANIEL. I do not think it would; but the question has never been tried. At any rate the only way to avoid it is for the party defendant to go into court and plead usury and tender the principal sum and interest; and I say that no man who has any respect for his character in the commercial community will ever do that; and I think the history of Baltimore will bear me out in that. There has been perhaps but one case known where a man has ever done it under the present constitution. A man goes upon the street, and goes to Mr. A. who has money to loan; and Mr. A. says, "I cannot lend it to you unless you give me twelve per cent. He says, "I know it is worth that, and I am willing to give it to you;" and he contracts positively on his honor as a gentleman to pay that amount. Then when he fails to pay it, and you sue him in court, he comes in and says, "true, money was worth it; and true, I promised to pay it; but the law says I need not pay it, and I will plead the statute of limitations and avoid it;" because it is in effect a statute of limitations; and no man that places any value upon his character would ever plead usury upon a contract; just as no man of honor will plead the statute of limitations upon an honest debt. A man who has agreed to pay twelve per cent. deems it beneath his dignity and honor to come into court and plead usury. And I say it would be doing injustice, although the gentleman from Anne Arundel (Mr. Miller) called it justice to plead it. I say it would be injustice after going to a man and privately contracting with him to give him twelve or fifteen per cent. and knowing that he relies upon your honor to pay it, then to go into court and plead usury to avoid, because the law allows him to do it,—plead that he has made a dishonest contract which is void in law.

I wish further to say in reference to the plea made here that money lenders and money borrowers are not upon equal terms, that I think that money borrowers are a great many of them about as sharp as money lenders; and I have seen some quite as sharp. The man whose interest it is to borrow generally studies his interest, where he can do best, as much as those who lend. Human nature everywhere is the same. It merely depends upon the peculiar acuteness of the man who borrows and of the man who lends, as to who gets the advantage in the bargain.

I will say, moreover, in conclusion, that the court of appeals and the legislature of Maryland have tried to avoid these onerous laws by construing them liberally; and the legislature have passed laws so as to avoid this very thing which gentlemen would have us confined to, that money should be loaned at six per cent. Chief Justice Taney said that under this very constitution of Maryland, if any man loaned at a higher rate than six per cent. it was absolutely void, and the man forfeited the contract, principal and interest. Yet in the very face of that decision, our court of appeals was so earnest to construe this law liberally, that commerce might be promoted, that contracts between men might be observed, and that money might have its own value without being restricted by a construction that was not the law, settled the principle that a man could only void the contract by pleading usury, and if he did plead usury he must tender both the principal and legal interest.

I saw this very matter tried in the superior court of Baltimore. A party had agreed to give more than six per cent. He did not plead usury, but he tried to avoid it as being illegal; and the court gave the instruction that the plaintiff should recover the full amount, the interest which was contracted for, being, I think, eight per cent. That is the law now. Courts and legislatures have so construed it as to break down this provision of the constitution, with regard to usury, so far as its original intention is concerned, in order to promote progress. As sure as you adopt such laws, while your neighboring States, New York and others, allow a charge of seven, eight, or ten per cent., you cause money to flow out of Maryland into those States, and make it harder for the poor men, the particular friends of my friend from Howard, to get the little sums of money which he may need. He cannot borrow because the money will not be here to loan.

I know of my own knowledge that banks in Baltimore city find at their desks when they come there in the morning as many letters from New York as they can answer, for money in large sums to be loaned upon good security at seven per cent. And some of the largest banks of Baltimore city tell me that they do not care to loan money in the city of Baltimore, they can do it to so much better advantage in the city of New York. The result is to cripple us and put us into the hands of Shylocks, to whom we must pay exorbitant interest, because you do not make it worth while for honest and honorable men to loan money, for you do not allow them to charge a proper rate of interest, to supply the poor men and to keep the improvident young men from spending all their means.

Mr. CLARKE. In my humble judgment this is not a question in the determination of which we are called upon necessarily either to protect the poor man or to protect the improvident young man, although those two classes may more or less be affected; but the question is what provision shall be inserted in this constitution which is best for the general interests of the State, which best protects the wants of the community. It is the question whether or not we should fix a certain rate of interest, whether we shall leave it entirely open to the private contract of parties. It is a question the right determination of which will decide what is the real value of money when loaned out, looking to the general wants of the community and looking to the general value of money.

It cannot be denied that however currency may fluctuate, there is such a thing as a real value of gold and silver. Money, as represented by gold and silver, has a real value. The present experience of this land shows it. You have legalized paper. You have made it a tender, so that a dollar of paper money extinguishes a dollar of debt. But what is the result? Do you buy the commodities of life at the same price at which you bought them before? Not at all. You can go, if you pay the gold, and buy at the same rates. Hence the result of it is that paper money is all brought down to one standard, that of gold and silver, which is real money, having a permanent and fixed value.

Money having a fixed value, in the sense in which I have referred to it as being represented by gold and silver, the value of the use of money should be fixed and permanent. Why is this? Could men engage in permanent legitimate operations without any knowledge of what they are to pay for the use of money except for the passing moment? How can a farmer, for instance, purchase real estate, and make improvements upon it, to be paid for five or ten years hence, if it is uncertain what value he is to pay? Who will loan money unless there is some fixed value for the use of that money? If you leave this matter to the determination of private parties alone, you will have the rate of interest dependent not upon the real value of money for the legitimate purposes of trade, but governed by the spasmodic speculations of the commercial cities. What will be the result then? It will be that men cannot pursue, as they now do, upon a legitimate and fixed basis, schemes of operations based upon fixed rates of interest. The farmer or mechanic, or any man in the community who prefers to plan out a scheme of life based on fixed principles, will no longer be able to pursue it; but he must adapt his schemes to the fluctuations of the money market produced by speculations in trade.

It being desirable then that we should have a fixed basis, I would ask whether the rate of six per cent. is not near the true value of the use of money. At one particular period, in any particular crisis, money may be worth more than six per cent. to some men. In the crisis which occur in the trade of all large cities, brought about not by pursuing the legitimate benefits of trade, but by speculative operations, money may to some men be worth more than that. But we should be governed in fixing the rate of interest by what is the legitimate value of the use of money. I take the case of farmers. I take the case of any man who enters upon legitimate trade, or legitimate business based on prudential and wise principles. I take even the man engaged in commercial business, who pursues not a wild scheme of business, but carries on his business on sound and just principles. And I say it is very rarely that men can make on sound principles of trade and of business more than six per cent.

Take the case of the farmer. I know that in our own county, I know that in the history of the State many men do by work, hard toil and labor, realize six per cent. on the capital invested. A man who has his property safely invested, who toils hard and works hard, is very glad at the end of the year if he has realized a clear gain of six per cent. Yet the money lender can sit down quietly at his desk and draw his note and throw it upon the market, and sell it for that; and you propose to raise the rate of interest to protect him in taking advantage in any way he can of trade at a particular period, and making more in that way than men can make upon safe and sound investments, where they can bring their own labor and skill and toil to bear upon their own capital. The high price of money at certain periods in our large cities is based upon the demoralizing feature of American trade, a character or feature which never existed more prominently than at the present time, when instead of the whole attention of the country being turned to schemes of speculation, we should turn to the more legitimate duties of the hour.

How does it operate any better that at certain periods money brings seven or eight per cent. and at other periods three or four per cent.? How can men who desire to operate upon fixed principles make loans, and make any calculations upon such a fluctuating basis?

Hence I prefer the present provision in the constitution to fix it at a permanent rate, and that rate six per cent.

The reason why some men are willing to pay twelve, twenty, and even thirty per cent. interest, is found in the character of the trade in the large cities, where the great mass of men operate not upon a fixed capital, but are engaged in schemes of speculation. A man goes and buys $100,000 worth of stock, and it goes down and he is unable to pay for it. If you demand the payment, he has no real basis upon which to meet it. Money becomes tight; and the result is that if he is compelled to pay, he loses everything. Of course he will prefer to take the chance of paying thirty-three or even fifty per cent. interest, and running the chance of a rise in the market by which he can save something, rather than to sell out entirely, fulfil his engagements, and lose all. But if the money lenders will advance him the money, it will be with a full knowledge of his condition. They take advantage of it. The result is that these men are the only men who are able to pay these high rates of interest—the men engaged in these schemes. They are able to pay it, because if they do not get the money they lose everything; and if they pay it they are no worse off than if they do not, and they may be so energetic as to succeed in the operation. Losing everything unless they get the money they can very easily afford to divide one-half with the man who comes forward and prevents the loss of everything.

It is this kind of trade, these operations, which reduce to such a spasmodic condition the money market; and it is to control to a certain extent, and so far as we can, such spasmodic conditions of the money market in the State of Maryland, which never has existed here to the same extent as in the city of New York; it is to prevent these operations in our large cities from coming in and controlling the agricultural interests and the mechanical interests of the State, and all classes of men who prefer the pursuit of trade upon sound principles of business; it is to protect the men who base their business upon accurate calculations instead of being governed by these spasmodic conditions of the market; it is for this that I prefer, and shall vote to maintain in this constitution the provision which forbids a higher rate of interest than six per cent., as it is contained in our present constitution.

Mr. Dennis. Of all the articles that I have heard read, I decidedly prefer the report of the committee. I go further, and say that I prefer the section in the present constitution even to that; and I hope to see that adopted by the convention. I concede that there is very great force in many of the arguments that have been used. It is desirable that all the capital of the State shall be kept here so far as possible, and that as much shall be brought here as can be brought. I presume it is true that when a higher rate of interest is offered in a neighboring city than is offered in our own State, our own capital seeking investment, will, as a matter of course, go where it gets the greatest return. As to all the argument about taking care of those that cannot take care of themselves, the oppression of the poor, the exorbitant operations of the money lenders, and all that, I leave it out of the question. I do not think it properly enters into the discussion of the question at all. Practically the six per cent. rule is not observed now. Practically, I understand—for I really have no knowledge of it, for I never went into a bank to borrow a dollar in my life—when they lend a thousand dollars they take the interest in advance, which amounts to more than six per cent. Instead of lending one thousand dollars, they take out the sixty dollars in advance, leaving nine hundred and forty dollars, with the interest on one thousand dollars; so that practically the bank gets more than six per cent. And this question should decide the real point in issue. The question is whether or not the interest on money ought to be regulated by law, and how it ought to be regulated. This is a question that has been settled by universal experience. It is true that seven and eight per cent. are paid in New York; but I do not think we ought to make our action conform to the state of things existing in New York; because while that regulates our markets, you may say that Europe regulates New York. One is the mere adjunct to the other: and the circle flows throughout the world.

We must determine for ourselves whether money is to be regulated by law, and if so how far, and what regulations. Looking at the experience of all time past since we have regulated this thing by law, and looking at the present condition of things, looking at the investment of other forms of human industry, farming, mechanical, and other interests, pervading our various relations, I cannot but think that six per cent. is a fair, and just, and reasonable compensation. Thinking so, I hope the provision in the old constitution will be adopted, and that all this matter about private contracts will be stricken out, and that it will stand where it has been established, where the decisions of the courts have placed it, that six per cent. and no more is to be taken.

Mr. Thomas. The proposition which I suggested by way of substitute, I offered simply as a kind of peace-maker between the two divisions, one demanding seven per cent. and the other demanding six per cent. I am myself in favor of the proposition submitted by the gentleman from Howard (Mr. Sands.) I am in favor of six per cent. I do not think the legal interest ought to be more than that. I will even go further than that. I am in favor of putting a proposition into the constitution that all contracts or agreements for any higher rate of interest than six per cent., shall be absolutely void, in order to meet the suggestion which was thrown out by my colleague, in the remarks which he made some time ago, as to the decision of Judge Taney. I will offer my proposition at the proper time, in case that which I like better, offered by the gentleman from Howard, does not pass.

Mr. CUSHING. The gentleman from Kent (Mr. Chambers) spoke of the stock of the Baltimore and Ohio railroad company being at one hundred and fifteen. My colleague (Mr. Daniel) met that conclusively by showing that when it paid six per cent. in gold the price only ranged about eighty, and has been as low as sixty, and the gentleman from Kent does not claim that because it was then nearly a twelve per cent. stock, that twelve per cent. was a fair price for money. While the prices were so reduced, possessing some four and a half million of dollars, they declared no extra dividend. They had one million dollars of United States stocks, one million in bank, one million in Northern Central stocks and one million in Central Ohio, which would make it about a twelve per cent. stock, while it is now at one hundred and sixteen, and may be had in the market at one hundred and fifteen. Parties have forced it up to one hundred and fifteen, buying it at that rate to control the stock.

Mr. CHAMBERS. It was the bonds I spoke of, not the stock.

Mr. CUSHING. The bonds have been as low as eighty, as mentioned by my colleague.

The gentleman from Prince George's (Mr. Clarke) spoke of the legitimate value of money. That is a question which the world has been debating from the time there was any circulating medium until now, and I venture to assert that never on two days has the value of money been the same. It has fluctuated from three per cent. to forty. It fluctuates from day to day in every civilized country in the world. There never has been any barometer found delicate enough to measure the fluctuations of the money market.

Mr. CLARKE. The use of money, I admit, fluctuates, and I desire that some fixed rate should prevail in the State of Maryland. I said that gold and silver have a real fixed value. Their use fluctuates from time to time, but I desire that in the State of Maryland it shall be made a fixed rate.

Mr. CUSHING. That is to say, for the good of the State of Maryland we are to take the winds from every quarter of the world and fix them stationary by some human law in the State of Maryland. We can no more fix the fluctuating value of money in the State of Maryland, while it rises and falls in every other State and in every other country of the civilized world, than we can stop the wind from blowing or the rain from descending. It is beyond the reach of human law. You may make penalties, but you dare not enforce them, and cannot. The instant you attempt to enforce them you destroy the whole commercial progress of the State. You might as well attempt to regulate the price men shall pay for flour as to regulate the price they shall pay for the use of money. You might as well pass sumptuary laws with regard to every single thing you use, to fix the price, as to fix the price of money by your law.

The gentleman has told us that mercantile men in sound business do not require money at more than six per cent.; that they cannot afford to borrow money at more than six per cent. I have no doubt the gentleman thought that that was so. Yet, if he will inquire into the commercial history of the mercantile men of the United States, he will find that the soundest men of business, with the largest capital, not only do but can afford to borrow money at ten and twelve per cent., or whatever it is worth, provided they can use it to make it worth more. If the gentleman had been acquainted with our commercial history he would have known that for years throughout the commercial community of the United States the rule of six per cent. has been replaced by a rule of five per cent. for six months credit, which amounts to ten per cent. per annum interest which the purchaser pays for the use of the money.

Mr. CLARKE. That is the difference between cash and credit.

Mr. CUSHING. And as to the farmers who cannot make six per cent.—if you take a farm where there is a capital invested of one thousand dollars, and if including the labor which he puts upon it, out of the whole proceeds he cannot make sixty dollars a year, I ask you how he can live? The gentleman must not forget in estimating what he produces to take account of what he consumes. A man in business takes what he makes and pays his expenses out of it, and the farmer must do the same. And if it were true that the farmers throughout the United States do not make, labor and all, six per cent. upon the capital invested in the farms of the United States, it would amount to starving every man who ever went upon a farm. A man upon a farm of one hundred acres at one hundred dollars an acre has a capital of ten thousand dollars. Will not that produce six hundred dollars a year? Will not the man with a thousand acres realize six thousand dollars a year? We know that sometimes they make sixty thousand dollars. It depends entirely upon the culture of the land, the kind of product, the state of the market, and a thousand fluctuating things.

The same thing that makes corn worth a dollar a bushel here and in the State of Illinois ten cents, the difference of circumstances, causes money to have a high price in large cities. The gentleman says it is due to speculation and extravagance. That is new to me, that speculation, unfounded upon any sound business, has been the cause from the beginning of our commercial history until now, for the fluctuating interest on money in the larger cities. If that be so has not speculation controlled the money market from the beginning of the civilized world until now? There never has been a time in any com mercial community from the earliest days until now when money has had any fixed value.

What is speculation? What does the gentleman call sound business? What has made the commerce of the United States but speculation and the reaching out of the arms of merchants to the trade of foreign countries, and finding a sale for the products of other lands? Speculation! Without speculation the commerce of the United States could not exist one day. It is speculation going solely upon judgment in many cases, failing and failing and failing again, but out of this failing they come to final success. The first new thing in a country has hardly ever been successful; but they have gone into the hands of men who have made them successful by repeated trials and repeated efforts time and again, and thus the commerce of the country has been made what it is. The rate of interest has depended upon the wants of men who have properly employed money in carrying out these enterprises, and in supplying the commercial requirements of the country.

How can a man who desires to operate with money, the gentleman asks, do it when money fluctuates? How can a man who desires to farm, do it when oats are fluctuating? How can a man who desires to go into business of any kind, do it when the prices of merchandise are fluctuating? Does the man who goes into business require to know what will be the prices of merchandise? Does he require that the prices shall be fixed by law? He takes the risk of the market. So the man who wants money does not require to know whether it will fall or not. He makes up his mind according to the best of his judgment, and comes to a determination whether he can employ it profitably at the rate he borrows it, knowing that the price of money as well as the price of anything else is constantly fluctuating. In every business, in every calling, is the element of fluctuation. But the fluctuation of money has nothing to do with this question, because the man knows what he is to pay by his contract, and that is what he must calculate upon.

But how allowing the right of making private contracts makes money fluctuate I do not see. If I see that I can employ money at an advantage for six months at twenty per cent., I make the contract, and it does not fluctuate during that time. During that time it is fixed and immutable. If I borrow more money three years hence, at a different rate, that has no reference to what I borrow to-day.

How is it in England? The Bank of England fluctuates, changing its rate every day. To-day, perhaps it is eight per cent. and to-morrow five or six. They fix the rate as they think proper. They ask no consent from anybody. It is a power given to them in their charter. The security is that they state the rate of interest publicly in the market on the day on which they intend to sell at that price. To-day they say it is eight per cent., and ask who wants it at that price. If it is not worth eight per cent. to-day no man will be willing to take it, and to-morrow they may publish that the rate of interest is five per cent., and ask who wants money to-day at five per cent. The thing is open, fair and above board. There is no chance for men to grind the face of the poor that gentlemen have talked about so much. If a man has good security to offer he goes into the market and takes the money he requires at eight per cent., or five per cent., or whatever may be the published rate.

When a man goes into the market to make a contract for money he goes exactly as he would go to-day to buy gold. The first broker charges him 2 60 and the next one perhaps 2.58, and he buys it where he can get it at the lowest rate. So in borrowing money, he goes round to find where he may get the money at the least rate upon his security. The man is safe. It is a fair open transaction. The lender estimates the risk which he runs in taking that security, and fixes the rate at which he will lend the money, and the borrower takes it or not as he pleases.

It is notorious that in New York city, where the rate is seven per cent., money is loaned at five, when the security is undoubted. If the security is not undoubted the price runs up, until the security gets so bad that no man will touch it at any price.

The money borrowed on real estate, to which the gentleman from Kent referred, is not one tithe of the money used. The money borrowed upon real estate is generally used to make improvements upon that estate; but the bulk of the money used is used for commercial purposes in the country and goes from one end of it to the other. It is constantly circulating. The amount of money borrowed in the State of Maryland for a whole year on real estate I do not believe equals the amount borrowed on the streets of Baltimore in a period of commercial activity in a single day. They go and borrow it upon the security of commercial paper, or bonds, city bonds, or Maryland bonds, or others, which are held until the note is paid. There is very little money borrowed for commercial purposes on real estate.

The gentleman says that in Baltimore and in Maryland we are not subject to the spasmodic contractions of the New York market. I tell the gentleman that if this morning, at 8 o'clock, it had been telegraphed to Baltimore that money was tight in New York, at ten o'clock you could hardly squeeze out a dollar in Baltimore. As fast as the telegraph could bring them there would be calls for money from New York, and in any part of the State of Maryland the money would be instantly withdrawn from the market.

Mr. CLARKE. I think the gentleman misunderstood me. I spoke of trade. That our merchants had not been subject to such spasmodic changes of trade; and not of the value of money.

Mr. CUSHING. If I recollect right the gentleman said that the object of these restrictions was to control the spasmodic contractions of the money market to which fortunately we had not been so much subject in the State of Maryland as in the city of New York. The money market of Maryland is acted upon instantaneously by the money market of New York.

It was said by the gentleman from Somerset (Mr. Dennis) that the banks take their six per cent. in the beginning, which is true, and that this makes it more than six per cent. They do another thing. They very often discount paper and give the man uncurrent money. I have known cases in Baltimore city where money which was five per cent. discount was taken for its face. That made the interest nine or ten per cent. paid at the banks, though nominally the law was observed. The necessities of a man may be such that he will be willing to take uncurrent money, and pay the bank in current funds when the note is due.

The gentleman well said that the question turns upon the point whether money ought or ought not to be regulated by law. Believing as I do that money is a marketable commodity in the whole present range of commercial business in the civilized world—believing as I do, and as the whole history of the mercantile world teaches, that the use of money fluctuates in value from day to day—that the money itself changes, and that its value to the people desiring its use varies from day to day—that the opening of a new market makes the value of the use of money borrowed to-day totally different from what it was yesterday—that the opening of a new market to me for my produce, which I knew not of yesterday, makes it worth while for me to pay largely for money to invest in sending that produce to the new market, beyond what I could have afforded to pay yesterday—all this coming from the fact that money is unequally distributed—I believe that it is against all sound political economy, and against all sound political liberty, to force a man to give to another that which he himself owns, unless he pleases, except for purposes required by the State or national government, or unless at a rate which shall represent its value to him.

When men desire to use money for purposes of speculation, or business, or enterprise, of necessity they must have regard to what is paid for the use of money in the community, to the willingness of those who hold it to lend, and to the value at which they hold it. If therefore, Maryland money can be sent to New York and used more profitably than it can be in Maryland, I am under the disadvantage in Maryland when I apply to the people who own the money to lend it to me, that I cannot by law pay an equal rate, and if the man to whom I apply is of such a character that he will not evade the law, he can only say, "I am sorry; I had the money and would have preferred to lend it to you at a given rate than to any one else, but the law says that I shall not lend it in Maryland above a given rate, and I have therefore sent it to New York where the law allows me one per cent. more." It is a matter of regret to me, but the man looks after his own interest. If I could have had that money at seven per cent. it would have been a benefit to me, and possibly to the community, and possibly a benefit to the State, as all enterprise is a benefit. But my enterprise must be given up because by law we have prohibited the use of money from seeking its level according to the law of supply and demand. So the money has been transferred from the place where it was needed and sent to be used by a more liberal people.

I think with the gentleman from Somerset that the whole question comes back to one simple matter, whether money ought to be regulated or not? I think it ought not. But as it has been the custom of this State to regulate it, and as it seems to be the intention of this convention to regulate it, I desire to have it regulated in a manner which will give the State of Maryland the use of money where there is no contract upon a par with the State of New York, and not so that New York shall have power by paying one per cent. more to draw the capital of Maryland away from the State. Then by allowing private contract at a rate agreed upon by the parties, you put the matter upon the fairest possible basis.

If money is not worth the price which is demanded, I will not contract to pay it. If it is worth that price, what right has the State by law, to prevent me from purchasing it? It does not prevent me from purchasing flour at sixteen dollars a barrel, which I could have purchased at one time for eight dollars. It does not interfere with my paying sixteen dollars for coal to-day, which a year ago was five dollars and fifty cents, because coal to-day is worth sixteen dollars.

My colleague (Mr. Daniel) brought up the instance of a man who may owe fifty dollars for rent. His goods are distrained and to be sold at auction; and he cannot obtain the money at six per cent. But he might have gone to a man at eight per cent., and obtained the money, and could afford to pay eight per cent. for years, until he could repay the principal, rather than to have his goods sold.

There seems to be a feeling in the minds of the people, especially in the State of Maryland, beyond that of any State I ever saw, that money is some sacred thing, which to own is a sin, and which owning it is a greater sin to lend to any other man at a price beyond that which the law may choose to fix. The legislators of Maryland have assumed to decide that money under any circumstances, can never be fairly worth more than a certain amount, and have made it a crime to ask more than that amount for it. Here we have my colleague (Mr. Thomas,) not only fixing the rate, but wanting to invalidate all contracts whatever by which money is loaned at a higher rate than six per cent. He is not even content with the present condition of the law; but actually wants to put into the constitution of Maryland, an enactment which would forever cripple all enterprise in Maryland, which would drive all money out of Maryland, put a stop to any man ever entering into business in Maryland, who was not already rich when he began the business, and prevent any poor man in Maryland from ever undertaking any business whatever.

I think one of the gentlemen from one of the counties argued that the people in the country were extremely indisposed to allow this thing. Yet, I have been very credibly informed, that one of the constituents of that gentleman has been known to loan parties money at three per cent. a month. That is just the way this matter always operates. If a man has money, he always wants to get all he can for it.

I think the question is a very simple one to be looked at. If six or seven per cent. interest is not unfair in New York, if the State has thriven under it, if more people do not break in New York than in Baltimore, if the commercial community in New York is as sound as in Baltimore, if capital is driven from Maryland more than from New York, then I ask gentleman to consider this matter.

Mr. SANDS obtained the floor, but having spoken once upon this question, the floor was awarded to

Mr. STIRLING, who yielded to

Mr. SANDS, who said: I will not speak more than five minutes. I should not have risen now if I had not felt myself necessitated to do so from the criminations indulged in by the gentleman from Baltimore city (Mr. Cushing) this morning. As I listened to him, this question first of all came up in my mind. Which of the two positions, that of superintendent of public instruction, or the rostrum of the sanctum of the Rothschilds, ought the gentleman to occupy? He certainly seemed to know all about finance, intricate as the subject is, and delivered his views as if they ought to be accepted here without question. Now, I do not accept them. And I must say, that while he expressed them with his usual eloquence, he certainly manifested a disregard of fact and of law, that in these times is really refreshing. And he manifested a sublime indifference to the facts and an amount of indifference to the law which he knew must be familiar to gentlemen upon this floor, which was equally refreshing; for he told you that in the great and prosperous State of Pennsylvania, at a regular rate of six per cent. interest, this matter of fixing the rate of interest was got around by a man giving his note for a hundred dollars, and taking seventy-five dollars for it.

Mr. CUSHING. Does the gentleman allege that I made any such statement?

Mr. SANDS. I think that was your argument.

Mr. CUSHING. You think wrongly, then.

Mr. SANDS. I appeal to the house if the argument the gentleman used was not that the legal rate of interest was got around in that way.

Mr. DANIEL. I stated that it was done in that way in the case of a mortgage.

Mr. SANDS. That was the ground taken by gentlemen who argue the pro side of this question. Now, it is known to every gentleman that in that case the maker of the note could plead want of consideration, and have so much of the claim deducted as was usury. Another gentleman goes so far as to say that the court of appeals has decided either that the constitution is unconstitutional, or that they in their capacity of the court of appeals of Maryland, can set the constitution aside.

Mr. DANIEL. They construed it to mean differently from what the circuit court did.

Mr. SANDS. And the legislature did the same thing, said the gentleman. Now, here is the constitution as it stands:

"That the rate of interest in this State shall not exceed six per cent. per annum, and no higher rate shall be taken or demanded; and the legislature shall provide by law, all necessary forfeitures and penalties against usury."

That is, the constitution says plainly that if six and one-tenth, or six and one-hundredth per cent. is demanded and taken, then that one-tenth or one-hundredth per cent. is usury, and the legislature shall see that usury is not practiced in this State. And yet, the gentleman says, with this section standing here in the constitution unrepealed, that the court of appeals, the creature of that constitution, has decided that this section is a thing to be evaded by reason of commercial necessity.

Mr. DANIEL. I did not say any such thing.

Mr. SANDS. My friend from Baltimore city (Mr. Daniel,) drew a parallel between the Bank of England and the money sharpers of the great commercial city of this country, as if he did not know that the Bank of England was regulated by and under the control of the government. I suppose then that an institution which is controlled by the government which has at heart all the interests of the nation stands upon a par with those people "who do hang out their three balls at the door and wait for their victims." It did suggest itself to my mind that some other emblems would be very appropriate in some cases ; the cap and bells, for instance.

I have nothing further to say, except as to its being a sin. We have got the good old Book for that, in which it is especially denounced as a sin and a crime to take more than the money's value as interest. It is a sin to take more than money's value, unless things have changed. What is money's value? Look at the advertising columns of to-day's American, the chief journal of Baltimore city, which city the gentleman represents. They show this fact that people who have large sums of money to loan are willing to go into the market and loan it for five or ten years at five per cent. ; and they will lend as small a sum as fifteen hundred dollars at six per cent. In no case do they demand more than six per cent. Baltimore city securities bearing six per cent. interest are selling at 116; and United States six per cent. securities are selling at a premium. What do those facts all go to show, if not the worth of money to-day in the market? Gentleman have argued that we might have a condition of things which would put down the value of money, that what we have passing as money now is currency, and it is to meet that view of the case I presume that they urge propping up the currency by a constitutional provision increasing the rate of interest.

I am satisfied, however, not to consume any more of the time of the house. I think I have consumed not more than five minutes now. I think the house has decided not to pass this section.

Mr. STIRLING. It strikes me that this debate is very interesting, but it has gone to an extent that I do not think practically tends to bring us to any conclusion on this question. We have here the whole question, and it is a very complicated question, in regard to the propriety of fixing the rate of interest for money. The report before us assumes the absolute doctrine that under all circumstances, any amount of interest contracted for shall be recoverable in courts of law. Now I am very free to say that I cannot support that proposition, even if I believed it to be good sense and good law, still I should be opposed at this time to putting into the constitution of this State any such broad proposition, one so contrary to the habitual practice of the community.

But it seems to me that a great deal of the debate upon the other side has been just as radical, and just as radically wrong, as the proposition of the committee. I believe there may be a practical question as to what the rate of interest ought to be. But so far as the law itself stands on the subject, I do not know that there is any great complaint at the existing condition of the law. On the contrary, the gentleman from Howard (Mr. Sands) seems to wish to go to the extent of forfeiting absolutely the whole claim.

Mr. SANDS. That is not my idea.

Mr. STIRLING. That is the tendency of the gentleman's argument. I think one of the propositions before this body absolutely goes to that extent. I prefer greatly that the convention should not interfere with the existing law on that subject. As the law now stands in the code, it has been decided by the court of appeals not to conflict with the constitution. It amounts to this; if a man is forced to bring suit on his contract, he cannot recover more than six per cent., if the other party sets up the defence of usury ; but the party who borrows the money must pay the principal and six per cent. interest.

There is only one practical difficulty that exists now, and that will be remedied by the proposition of the gentleman from Kent (Mr. Chambers,) which proposition I sincerely hope will be adopted. It has been a question whether if a man lends money, and stipulates in the contract that the borrower shall pay the taxes on that money, such a stipulation is legal. There is no reason why it should be considered more than six per cent interest. There is a difference of opinion about it. But the practical facts exists that there is a doubt; and those persons most scrupulous, most honest, are afraid to put in their mortgage or contract a stipulation that the borrower shall pay the taxes. There is no reason why a man should not have the right in a contract to require for himself, with the consent of the other contracting party, a clear interest of six per cent. That is especially important at this time when the tax upon money may decrease the rate of interest to three per cent. I think the convention ought to clear up that doubt and provide that the stipulation with the borrower to pay the taxes shall not be considered usurious.

I should be perfectly willing to support the proposition of the gentleman from Allegany (Mr. Thruston,) which I think is better than that of my colleague (Mr. Daniel,) in that it does not change the legal rate of interest. The government of the United States has offered to borrow money at seven and three-tenths per cent. interest. That has become a very favorite rate of interest, by reason of its being so easily calculated. It is a great deal easier to calculate than six per cent., and much simpler, being two cents per day on each hundred dollars. That was the reason, doubtless, why that rate was determined or rather than the rate of seven per cent. The national banks under the first law were authorized to charge seven per cent., but are now restricted to the legal rate of interest of the States in which they are located. The banks of this

State are therefore placed at a disadvantage compared with the banks of New York. I would be willing on that account to support a proposition to allow a rate of interest not greater than seven and three-tenths per cent. That does not raise the rate of interest absolutely to seven per cent.

The difficulty in regard to the proposition of my colleague (Mr. Daniel,) raising the rate of interest to seven per cent. is that it will have the effect of raising the rate of discount to seven per cent. everywhere throughout the State—unless the state of affairs should be such that money should fall to five or six per cent. Everybody would put the rate of seven per cent. in their contracts, and it would actually raise the rate of interest from six to seven per cent. But if you merely provide that not more than seven and three-tenths per cent. may be taken, it will not have that effect.

I do not wish to enter into a full discussion of this question. I will merely say that the reason why I do not believe that the report of this committee is founded upon a true basis is this: it absolutely destroys the permanent fixed value of money for a long period of time. Contracts for a long period of time will be made by people at the existing rate of interest. Now money is not worth more than six per cent. as a general thing, though for a short period of time it is sometimes worth more than that. But men will not lend for six per cent. for one or two years, if they can get seven or more, because that rate is not worth the trouble of turning over their money. Nor will they lend at six per cent. if the borrower is in such circumstances as to make it any risk to lend him money. There is no usury under the law in buying a promissory note in the market at ten cents on the dollar, if the note is not worth more than that. There is no usury law or anything else which prevents a man from selling his paper at what he can get.

Mr. Daniel. Accommodation notes, just made for the purpose of being sold for what they will bring?

Mr. Stirling. Certainly; he can put his own notes on the market. But as I said before, there is a practical difficulty, in consequence of this offer of the government to pay seven and three-tenths per cent. for money, which I think justifies the proposition of the gentleman from Allegany (Mr. Thruston,) to allow persons under private contract to ask and receive that rate, if the parties to the contract agree to it. There is no reason why the people should not be allowed to borrow or lend at the same rate which the government is willing to pay.

Mr. Daniel. I will ask the gentleman a question for information. Does he consider that, under the proposition of the gentleman from Allegany (Mr. Thruston,) if a man charges more than that rate, it absolutely vitiates the contract?

Mr. Stirling. No, sir; I do not understand that that is the effect of the proposition. I understand that that matter is left precisely as the code leaves it now. The truth is that, except so far as I should like to see the proposition of the gentleman from Kent (Mr. Chambers) carried, settling this doubt about the question of taxes, I do not see what is the use of putting this in the constitution at all, if the convention is not disposed to make any change in the rate of interest. The act of assembly fixes the rate of interest at six per cent. By virtue of an act of the assembly banks are authorized to take interest in advance; and the court of appeals has decided that the code is not in conflict with this provision of the constitution, and having decided that, I do not see the necessity of having anything in the constitution except for the purpose of settling the question met by the proposition of the gentleman from Kent. I think it is utterly useless to adopt this report. In fact I may say that I know it is not going to be adopted, and therefore I think we better come to some practical conclusion upon the subject, and vote upon it. I do not think this report will get a corporal's guard in its support in this house, and there is no use in going into the general subject of finance, when we have every reason to believe that the report will not be adopted.

Mr. Ecker moved to lay the whole subject on the table; but at the request of several members withdrew the motion.

Mr. Abbott. When the question is taken, I hope the subject will be divided. Let us first decide whether we will have six or seven per cent.

Mr. Miller. I know that the convention is weary of this debate, and I propose to detain them but a few moments in reply to some remarks of gentlemen upon the other side. I allude more particularly to the remarks of the gentleman from Washington county (Mr Negley.)

The question involved in this part of the report allowing persons to contract for whatever rate of interest they please, is simply a question as to whether or not we will any longer have any usury laws in Maryland. It is said that the State of Maryland is in that respect behind the civilized and commercial world; that England, France, and all those countries have got rid of these usury laws long since. That is an argument which if established, would be of great force in this convention; for if we are in that position we should step forward into the broad sunlight of progress.

But what is the fact in regard to this question? Civilized, commercial and enlightened England this day has upon her statute book a law forfeiting absolutely the entire contract, all the money loaned, besides imposing a penalty of treble the amount of money loaned, if more than five per cent. interest is charged. And this privilege of the Bank of England, about which the great financiers of this body have talked so much, is simply a provision passed in the time of George I, allowing the Bank of England to borrow money at what rate it pleases. France has the same usury laws. Every enlightened commercial State of this Union has them. New York has them; Pennsylvania has them.

What are the provisions in New York down to this day? They forbid the recovery of more than a fixed rate of interest. And the courts of that State have put it upon the ground of protecting the weak against the oppressor. Chief Justice Savage, in speaking for the supreme court of New York, declares in one case:

"In making this remark, I mean not any reflection on the justice or policy of the laws prohibiting usury. On the contrary, I believe such laws perfectly just and proper.—They are necessary to protect the necessitous against their own acts of indiscretion. Nor would I impute moral guilt to those who receive more than the legal rate of interest, provided their exactions do not become oppressive. Usury is *malum prohibitum*—not *malum in se*."

And that is the ground upon which these usury laws are based. It is to protect the necessitous against the exactions of the oppressor. And here is a law as late as the year of grace 1860, of our neighboring State of Pennsylvania, where the rate of interest is six per cent. By that law all the excessive interest is forfeited, and a man who has paid it is allowed to go into a court of law and recover the amount of excessive interest he has paid, upon an action of assumpsit. What does the learned court of that State say upon this same subject? It was an action brought after a man had paid more than six per cent. interest.

Mr. CUSHING. Cannot seven per cent. interest be recovered in New York to-day?

Mr. MILLER. I say that if more than seven per cent. is taken in New York you can recover it back. And in Pennsylvania, where the rate of interest is six per cent., the court has taken this ground:

"The early disposition of the English courts was to deny the right of a party paying such interest to recover back any portion of the money paid, for the reasons that both parties to such a transaction were deemed to be "*in pari delicto*," and the excess of interest was regarded as paid voluntarily, so that the maxim "*volunti not fit injuria*" would apply.—[1 Salk., 22] The authority of this decision, however, was soon questioned, Lord Mansfield declared that the case had been decided a thousand times. [Cowper, 199.] At a later day a distinction was taken between transactions under statutes enacted on grounds of general policy, where each party violating the law is held to be in equal fault, and transactions under the usury laws, enacted to protect the weak and needy from being defrauded and oppressed. To the latter the law does afford relief. It regards the lender or usurer as an oppressor, and the borrower as the injured and oppressed."

The supreme court of Pennsylvania sanctioned that doctrine as late as 1860. Every one of the commercial States of the Union has the same provision. All the New England States, New York, New Jersey and Pennsylvania have it. And it is only in some of the western and southwestern "wild-cat" States where they have allowed parties to contract for what rate they please, in order to induce capital to go into those States. And in some instances capital has been induced to go there by the opportunity of investing at fifteen and twenty per cent. And capitalists have made a permanent investment, never having got one cent back.

Mr. CUSHING. How is it in Ohio?

Mr. MILLER. I have not looked at the provisions of Ohio. Gentlemen say that the plea of usury is a rogue's plea. Why, gentlemen who are lawyers know that in every court in this country, and in England, too, there is no head of the law under which so many cases are decided, as the head of "usury." The books are full of cases in which the usury laws have been enforced. Time and time again in England penalties have been recovered of treble the value of the amount loaned. The courts have said that the plea of usury was a just plea, and Lord Mansfield declared that it was beyond the device of man, by any contrivance whatever, to avoid the usury laws. If the contract was a contract for the loan of money, and more than five per cent. was taken, it was usury. You might cover it up as you pleased; yet a court of equity would ferret out the transaction, and if it could find the usury, it would strike down the contract, principal and all, and impose the penalty. These laws have been always the favorite of the courts; they have always enforced them.

With these views, I submit that the question is directly up before this convention, upon this report, whether we are any longer to have usury laws in Maryland. If you allow men to contract for whatever rate of interest they please, and make that contract valid, you are in effect breaking down your usury laws.

Mr. NEGLEY. The gentleman from Anne Arundel (Mr. Miller) says that the Bank of England is allowed to borrow money at any rate it pleases; and he also says that there is a law in England fixing the rate of interest at five per cent., and that any individual who takes more than that is liable to a forfeiture of the whole contract and a penalty of treble the amount. Now I suppose that corporations would not be allowed any privileges that are not allowed to individuals. I have yet to know the State that grants privileges to corporations in their corporate capacity, that would not be allowed to individuals with an equal amount of money. If it is usury for an individual to loan money for more than five per cent., of course corporations cannot. Was the Bank of England organized to borrow money?

Mr. MILLER. Certainly.

Mr. NEGLEY. What does it do to-day? Every steamer brings to us the rate of discount at the Bank of England, not the rate of borrowing. At different times we find the rate of discount stated to be three, four, four-and-a-half, five, six and seven per cent.

Mr. DANIEL. It is up to eight and nine per cent. now.

Mr. NEGLEY. Yes, sir. Then the gentleman is in this predicament, if his law is correct; the government of England grants privileges to corporations that she denies to her citizens.

Mr. MILLER. Will the gentleman allow me to read the statute?

Mr. NEGLEY. There are other banks in England, and I suppose they are put upon the same footing with the Bank of England. They are chartered by the government, and I suppose are allowed to charge this sliding-scale of interest. Why is it permitted to the Bank of England? Because the fluctuations of trade require it. It is so in France; if money is abundant it goes down; if it is scarce it goes up. Is the Bank of England organized by the British government for a public benefit or a public nuisance? If it is organized and created for the public benefit, and I take it for granted that it is, then this privilege is given for what purpose? So that the wants of the public might be subserved; so that in a time of abundance of money they might get the benefit of it, by obtaining it at a low rate of interest. That is it. Suppose you fix a rate of interest that a bank may demand; sometimes it may be too high, sometimes it may be too low. A party can never obtain it for less than that rate; he is bound up to that sum; and the bank can and absolutely will not loan at a less rate.

I would like to see the law of Maryland conform to the law of Missouri on this subject. By that law the rate of interest is fixed at six per cent., but parties may agree in writing for the payment of interest not exceeding ten per cent. per annum, on money due or to become due on contract. Something of that kind should be adopted here; there ought to be a limit. Let the rate of interest be six per cent.; then give some liberty of choice, some freedom to persons who want money, but say that the rate shall in no case exceed ten per cent. The gentleman from Allegany (Mr. Thruston) proposes that it shall not exceed seven per cent. Look at what has been done by the government of the United States. Did it not go into the market at the beginning of the war and offer seven and three-tenths per cent.; next its five-twenties at six per cent.; then its ten-forties at five per cent.; then back to six per cent., and now up to seven and three-tenths per cent. again? Why is this? Because of its need of money; that renders it necessary that it should change its rate of interest. Would it be right or wrong that the government should be tied down to offering a particular rate of interest? It is free to choose, and the rate is regulated by its necessities and its wants. If you were to tie the government down to six or five per cent., it might not be possible for it to borrow a dollar. It may have to pay more than seven per cent. bye-and-bye, we don't know.

And it is the same with an individual. His necessities may require him to have money, and it may be his salvation to get it at seven, eight, nine, or even ten per cent. I know a case in the city of Philadelphia, of a man owning immense quantities of coal lands; who, if he had not succeeded in getting money two or three years ago at more than ten per cent., would have been a broken and ruined man to-day. He got the money on those conditions, and to-day is worth a million of dollars. If a man thinks his financial affairs will justify him in giving six, seven, or eight per cent. interest, he will do it. And in God's name is not he, rather than this convention, the best judge as to his ability to give six, seven, eight, nine, or ten per cent.? Why not leave it discretionary with him? If you legislate upon the hypothesis that a man is not intellectually or morally competent to make a contract as to the value of money, you strike at the foundation of all competency for individual self-government. To that extent you strike even at the personal liberty of the individual; you interfere with his right to pursue his own happiness, and look after his own interest in the way he may choose.

These usury laws come down to us from antiquity, from the middle ages. We know that in the period of the middle ages, the money lenders, the Jews, were looked upon as outcasts; were not allowed to live in the heart of any city, but were kept outside, in their own peculiar quarter. So far did that prejudice go during the middle ages, that the Jews were denied the privileges of citizens on account of money lending. But we have outlived those prejudices, and in this country Jews are allowed the privileges of citizens.

But our constitution, as it now stands, makes this the paradise of money lenders, of Shylocks, because you guard their privileges; you make them a privileged and a prerogatived class. You say to the citizen that he shall not borrow money, unless he does it through the instrumentality of the money changer. I say, let us go into their temples and overturn their tables. Let the people contract for themselves: let them go into the public markets, and bid for money on their own personal responsibility. Do not let us force them to go into the highways and byways, and secret places of these money lenders, and in the dark places where there is no eye but that of the money lender and the money borrower. You may strike this from your constitution or not; you are not going to change the eternal laws that govern commerce, the laws of supply and demand. These same outrages upon the oppressed will go on.

Strike this out of your constitution, and you will confer upon the poor and oppressed a benefit. They are now at the mercy of the money lender. A man cannot now go to A, B or C, and get money upon his own note, with his neighbor as security. If the man chooses to take the note at six per cent. he can do it; but if not, then the needy man must hunt up the office of the licensed broker. The poor borrower, the distressed and money-needing man must pay the licensed broker his license, interest and brokerage. But if you allow him to go into the market in open broad daylight, he would save the percentage and brokerage, and the license of the broker. But instead of favoring the oppressed, you do them an injury by your constitution. Strike out this provision, or at least do partial justice. Fix the rate of interest; I have no objection to that, because it is absolutely necessary to fix some rate of interest, otherwise how are you to ascertain what money is worth, in the absence of any agreement? If the State fixed no rate of interest, and there was none named in the contract, then you would have to go into a particular investigation as to how much the loan of that particular sum of money was worth to that particular individual, and that would lead to interminable litigation. Hence the necessity of fixing some rate of interest. Let the rate be six per cent. where the parties do not agree upon any particular rate. And then give them some choice. And to guard against extortion, let the rate be limited in the other direction to ten per cent. Let us make some progress in matters relating to the commercial world.

It has been gravely argued here that if you prohibit excessive interest, you absolutely prevent financial crises. Was there ever anything so wildly absurd? Was not there a financial crisis in 1857? Did not money command exorbitant and enormous prices at that time in New York? And upon the same day that the banks were closed in New York, were they not closed in Pennsylvania, Maryland and Virginia? What was the result of that crisis? It not only affected every little town and hamlet in this entire country, but England and France felt it. It was supposed by financiers that Amsterdam, having a purely metallic currency, would not be affected at all. Yet, strange to say, that crisis affected the commerce of Amsterdam just as much as the commerce of London and Paris. These things are independent of the prices you pay for money, and are governed by different laws: the law of supply and demand. You might as well try to iron and hedge in the waves of the ocean as to iron these waves of commercial crises. They will come in times of great commercial agitation; they will roll up and break upon the wharves of every country. You cannot control them; they are a part of human society. You cannot make any provision against these things.

I am for the largest liberty compatible with the public good. It is the true doctrine not to tie down and hem in by law on every side.

As to the proposition of the gentleman from Kent (Mr. Chambers,) I am utterly opposed to it, and will vote against it, because it is giving a privilege to the man who owns money which you deny to the man who owns lands and houses. The owner of lands and houses is taxed by the federal government and the State government, as well as the owner of bonds and securities. If you make an exemption in favor of the one, do it in favor of the other.

With these views I shall vote against the proposition of the gentleman from Baltimore city (Mr. Daniel,) to make the legal rate of interest seven per cent. instead of six per cent. And I shall advocate the adoption of a provision allowing private contracts to be made as high as ten per cent., and require them to be made in writing.

Mr. Jones, of Somerset. I do not propose to trouble the convention except for a short time. All this discussion has not removed the result to which the wisdom of ages has come, that this matter of interest in all well regulated communities ought to be regulated by law. The theory of perfect free trade without any sort of restriction, including free trade in the lending and borrowing of money, is a very beautiful one, and very plausible and taking. But it has not very generally been found to be very acceptable to the great body of the people, or one applicable in practice.

A great many years ago, as a part of my education, I studied very thoroughly Say's political economy. He advocated this theory of free trade, and especially makes an assault upon usury laws, and all rules regulating interest upon money. Although that work has been published a great many years, I do not find that, even with all the power of the money lenders of France, they have been able to break down the laws of France regulating the loan of money. During all the revolutions they have had in France, those laws have stood unimpaired. So whatever may be said of the theory that demand and supply will regulate the value of money, precisely as it does the value of corn, wheat, flour and all such things that enter into consumption, in practice there is in fact a difference. The value of daily food and clothing depend upon a great many more contingencies than does the value of money. The contingencies of season, climate, rain, drought, war and peace, affect the value of those things. Those circumstances occasionally somewhat affect the value of money, but not to so great an extent. Money is affected more by seasons of speculation, demands for speculative purposes. Notwithstanding all the experience of the past, those seasons of speculation will start, money goes up, the fever rages, and it goes on until one of those periodical collapses occurs, with which we have become so familiar. And then men begin to get cautious for a time. But soon experience is forgotten, and the whole thing is gone over again. When one of those collapses take place, as in 1857, it necessarily affects the monetary affairs of the whole civilized world, because to a greater or less extent the system of credit prevails everywhere, and there are debtors and creditors in all civilized countries. And where one of these collapses takes place debtors are found to be in a very bad condition; and those who depend upon them for the means to pay their debts are also in a bad condition, and so on.

And the result of all this is that it has been found necessary in practical experience that this matter of interest should be regulated by law. And I think that such is the experience of the country; such is the demand of the country. And why do I think so? Because it is certain that money is power, as much so as knowledge or anything else. As it is regulated in this country now, it is very much in the hands of the few. How many men are there in our counties who have surplus funds on hand and undertake themselves to loan them out? They take their money to the cities, and place it in the hands of their commercial agents, the brokers and bankers, whoever they may be; and the money is left there for investment under the direction of those who make finance their study. The man does not trouble himself about it, provided he gets his interest. There are many persons who do that; and that is one reason why money is so hard to be obtained in the country. That would not be altered by the repeal of your usury laws. On the contrary, I think the trouble would be increased. The matter is now in the hands of the financiers of all your cities, who are all more or less connected together. They all have their correspondents, and their houses of connection, throughout the entire country, from one end to the other. If they do not have in every office a telegraph connection with their correspondents in other cities, they certainly have telegraphic communication with every city, and not only daily but hourly reports of the condition of the money market in those cities. With all this power of concentration in the hands of the few, and with all the numerous conventions and legislatures everywhere, yet they never have been able, notwithstanding the terrible onslaught that has been made, to break up these usury laws.—It is true that in the western States, where there is a great demand for money to make improvements, they have necessarily to make a higher rate of interest in order to attract capital. But capital that far from home is somewhat in danger. A man has to intrust his money to the management of others. If he has a mortgage on land in Missouri or Illinois, the interest on it must be collected by others; so that the farther from home money goes, the more danger there is of losing it. And hence there are very few who are induced by the higher rates of interest to venture their funds so far.

I have been very much surprised to hear that in consequence of money bearing seven per cent. interest in New York, capitalists in this State are sending all their money there to be invested, and that too in face of the advertisements read by the gentleman from Howard (Mr. Sands,) that money is offered for five and six per cent. in Baltimore city today. I was told by a gentleman in Baltimore within the last six months that he could borrow all the money he wanted for five per cent. for one, three, five and ten years.

Mr. Stirling. The longer the time the easier it is to get it on good security.

Mr. Jones, of Somerset. I do not see that there is any necessity for sending money out of the State, when it can find investment here, such as it is. Old Ben Hardin, of Kentucky, used to make a great many speeches on every financial bill in Congress, and uniformly wound up with the declaration—"Finally, Mr. Speaker, I am in favor of good money, and plenty of it."

This legislating upon money, except to the very limited extent to which it has gone in regulating the rate of interest, has no very good effect. And I think it has been found by the experience of all ages, and by our own experience, that the removal of the restrictions by the last convention of this State, is going quite as far as public opinion would justify or require. I think the matter is now in a very safe condition. I think there were many onerous and harsh conditions imposed before those restrictions were removed. The forfeiture of three times the amount loaned, because a greater than the legal rate of interest was taken, in many instances might operate exceedingly unjustly. I do not think it at all immoral for a man to loan his money for whatever he can get on good security. But assuming that it ought to be regulated, there are many instances of oppression, as in other articles necessary for life. But it is more easy to give protection in this case; there are more persons affected by it.

I think the law as it stands now is very good, as it has been construed by the court of appeals, and is well settled with the exception of the point in relation to the contract for the payment of the taxes by the borrower. I am myself doubtful whether such a contract would be justified under the law. It is certainly an indirect mode of taking more than six per cent. For, if the taxes amount to one per cent., the making a contract at six per cent. with a stipulation that the borrower should pay the taxes, would be the same as if the lender took seven per cent. and paid the taxes himself. It is usual for the borrower to pay all the expenses for executing the contract. And if he makes a contract to pay the taxes also, and the money is worth that to him, I do not see any great objection to it. As it is now, the contract may be entirely confidential between the parties. And out of a million of contracts I do not suppose that more than one or two out of a hundred become subject to the laws about usury. Among commercial men it is understood that no contract of that sort should be set aside by the plea of usury. Still the law in some cases may avail for purposes of justice and to prevent oppression. And it may be some restraint upon those who would be grasping, who would take every advantage of a man's necessities. It is true you cannot prevent that altogether. A man who has his corn house full while his poor neighbor has not credit to get it ten or fifteen miles off for a less sum, may charge him more than the market price for it. That is a practice which is wrong; it is not doing as he would be done by; it is against the moral law, and is immoral in that aspect of the case. But those cases are few, and public opinion will regulate that matter to a great exent.

While I disclaim any idea that there is any immorality in a contract for the loan of money, yet I know there are times when six per cent. would not be an adequate compensation. And in those cases the party may contract for and receive more than six per cent., (it is done in thousands of instances,) if there is no litigation about it. But if it does come into litigation and there has been oppression practiced, the party is relieved to the extent of the interest above six per cent. This is to be said in favor of that; that whereas those who engage in any other business, in farming, merchandise, in speculations of various kinds, have to run the risk of the loss of all they have invested, it is not so with the money lender. A man invests his money in manure, puts it upon his land, sows his seed, bestows upon it all his labor, and then a blight comes, upon his wheat crop especially, a week or two before it matures, and his prospects are blasted, and he loses all his money and labor. But for those who lend money on interest, the interest goes on whether it be cold or hot, whether it rains or shines, day or night, whether he sleeps or wakes; his interest is all the time accumulating, if his loan is well secured. In that respect he has a great advantage over those engaged in other kinds of business, which are attended with great hazards.

With all due respect, therefore, to those who have submitted propositions here, I think that the present system which has now been in operation for some twelve or fourteen years, is about the best. The system relieves the subject from the idea of attaching immorality to such contracts, and I think we better leave it as it is. Let a man make his contract; let him take his chances; let him be sure of the man he deals with. He can tell if he is a fair and honorable man, and can contract with him according to the money market. In the city those who lend understand very well the character and standing of those who borrow. And in the counties a man is very apt to know to whom he lends, and takes care of the security. I think we cannot better the present system. As to what New York does, all I can say is that Pennsylvania and Philadelphia, being between us and New York, get along very well at six per cent. And I cannot understand why capital should pass through Philadelphia and go to New York, especially when after it gets there it is beyond the personal supervision of those who own it, and is in the hands of the money brokers and capitalists of New York, who will have their percentage on all the investments they make. I do not think capital is sent there to any great extent. I am, therefore, in favor of retaining the present system, leaving contracts between parties to the operations of the law as it now stands.

The question recurred upon the motion of Mr. DANIEL to strike out "six" and insert "seven" as the legal rate of interest.

Mr. THOMAS called the yeas and nays upon this question, and they were ordered.

The question was then taken, by yeas and nays, and resulted—yeas 8, nays 63—as follows:

Yeas—Messrs. Abbott, Cushing, Daniel, Gale, Hatch, Hopper, Parker, Ridgely—8.

Nays—Messrs. Audoun, Berry, of Prince George's, Billingsley, Blackiston, Bond, Briscoe, Carter, Chambers, Clarke, Crawford, Cunningham, Dellinger, Dennis, Dent, Duvall, Earle, Ecker, Edelen, Galloway, Hebb, Hollyday, Hopkins, Horsey, Johnson, Jones, of Cecil, Jones, of Somerset, Keefer, Kennard, King, Larsh, Lee, Mayhugh, McComas, Mitchell, Miller, Morgan, Mullikin, Murray, Negley, Nyman, Parran, Peter, Pugh, Purnell, Robinette, Russell, Sands, Schley, Schlosser, Smith, of Carroll, Smith, of Dorchester, Smith, of Worcester, Sneary, Stirling, Swope, Sykes, Thomas, Thruston, Turner, Valliant, Wickard, Wilmer, Wooden—63.

The motion was accordingly rejected.

Mr. CHAMBERS moved to strike out all after the words "six per cent. per annum," and insert the following:

"And no higher rate shall be taken or demanded; provided, it shall be lawful for parties loaning money on bond, mortgage, judgment or other security, to contract for the payment of taxes and dues to the United States, the State or county, and all other public dues, by the borrower, so as to retain to the lender the clear amount of the legal interest."

Mr. THRUSTON asked for a division of the question.

Mr. RIDGELY. I hope the house will be able to reach some conclusion upon this question. The proposition now before the house brings us to the privilege of adopting the constitutional provision as it now exists. It is perfectly competent, as suggested by the gentleman from Allegany (Mr. Thruston) for the house to divide this question, and take a vote upon so much of the proposition as corresponds with the existing provision of the constitution. In doing so, we shall adopt what we now understand, because all the decisions and interpretations which have been made by the courts in relation to the existing provision of the constitution are perfectly intelligible to us, and is known as constitutional law. I hope therefore that the house will take the question upon this proposition in its divided form. I shall vote for the first part of the proposition which corresponds with the provision of the existing constitution; but I cannot vote for the second branch of it.

The question was stated to be upon adopting the first branch of the proposition submitted by Mr. CHAMBERS, being as follows:

Strike out all after the words "six per cent. per annum" and insert "and no higher rate of interest shall be taken or demanded."

Mr. THOMAS demanded the yeas and nays upon this question, and they were ordered.

The question was then taken, by yeas and nays, and resulted—yeas 59, nays 10—as follows:

Yeas—Messrs. Abbott, Audoun, Berry, of Prince George's, Blackiston, Bond, Briscoe, Carter, Chambers, Clarke, Crawford, Cunningham, Dellinger, Dennis, Dent, Duvall, Earle, Ecker, Edelen, Gale, Galloway, Hebb, Hollyday, Horsey, Johnson, Jones, of Cecil, Jones, of Somerset, Keefer, Kennard, King, Lee, Mayhugh, McComas, Mitchell, Miller, Morgan, Mullikin, Murray, Nyman, Parran, Peter, Pugh, Purnell, Ridgely, Robinette, Russell, Sands, Schley, Schlosser, Smith, of Carroll, Smith, of Dorchester, Smith, of Worcester, Stirling, Swope, Sykes, Thomas, Thruston, Turner, Wickard, Wilmer, Wooden—59.

Nays—Messrs. Billingsley, Cushing, Daniel, Hatch, Hopper, Larsh, Negley, Parker, Sneary, Valliant—10.

The first branch of the amendment was accordingly adopted.

Mr. NEGLEY, when his name was called, said: I am in favor of fixing the rate of interest at six per cent. in cases where there is no contract. And I would be glad to vote for that. But as the question is now presented, it does not meet my approbation, because it forbids the making of a private contract. I therefore vote "no."

The question recurred upon the second branch of the amendment, as follows:

"Provided, it shall be lawful for parties loaning money on bond, mortgage, judgment or other security, to contract for the payment of taxes and dues to the United States, the State or county, and all other public dues, by the borrower, so as to retain to the lender the clear amount of the legal interest."

Upon this question Mr. WICKARD called for the yeas and nays, and they were ordered.

The question was then taken, by yeas and nays, and resulted—yeas 27, nays 43, as follows:

Yeas—Messrs. Berry, of Prince George's, Billingsley, Blackiston, Bond, Chambers, Clarke, Duvall, Earle, Edelen, Gale, Galloway, Hebb, Hollyday, Hopper, Jones, of Cecil, Kennard, King, McComas, Mitchell, Miller, Peter, Pugh, Sneary, Stirling, Thruston, Valliant, Wilmer—27.

Nays—Messrs. Abbott, Briscoe, Carter, Crawford, Cunningham, Cushing, Daniel. Dellinger, Dennis, Dent, Ecker, Hatch, Hopkins, Horsey, Johnson, Jones, of Somerset, Keefer, Larsh, Lee, Mayhugh, Morgan, Mullikin, Murray, Negley, Nyman, Parker, Parran, Purnell, Ridgely, Robinette, Russell, Sands, Schley, Schlosser, Smith, of Carroll, Smith, of Dorchester, Smith, of Worcester, Swope, Sykes, Thomas, Turner, Wickard, Wooden—43.

The second branch of the amendment was accordingly rejected.

The following explanations were made by members, as their names were called:

Mr. MILLER. I consider this proposition as merely allowing what the law of the State now permits to be done. But the question has arisen, and there is a doubt in the minds of some professional gentlemen in the State whether that provision of the code is constitutional or not. I think that question ought to be settled, and that the borrower ought to have the privilege of stipulating in his contract that he will pay the taxes. I vote "aye."

Mr. MULLIKIN. I wish to say that no selfish motives will control me in my vote upon this question. I have never been a money borrower; I do not know that I ever shall be. I have had the fortune to loan a little sometimes. And I think the man who has money to loan is better able to pay the taxes, than the man who has to borrow. For that reason I vote "aye."

Mr. PETER. I understand this proposition merely leaves it optional with the borrower whether he will pay the taxes or not.

Mr. CUSHING. No, sir; optional with the lender whether he will charge the taxes or not.

Mr. PETER. I vote "aye."

Mr. RIDGELY. I vote "no," for the reason that I think it very unwise for us to encumber our constitution with details of this kind, which belong more properly to the legislature.

Mr. SANDS. I shall vote against this proposition because it relieves the lender from the payment of any taxes either State or federal, and throws it upon the borrower. I vote "no."

Mr. STIRLING. This is law now. The code provides expressly that this can be done. And legal consistency will lead me to vote "aye."

Mr. RIDGELY. In order to make this section conform exactly to the provision in the present constitution, I move to add the words that were omitted in the amendment just adopted, viz:

"The legislature shall provide by law all necessary forfeitures and penalties against usury."

Mr. SCHLEY. I have not taken any part as yet in this debate; but at the proper time I will offer an amendment which I will now read for information. Perhaps the gentleman from Baltimore county (Mr. Ridgely) will accept it, to precede the amendment he has just offered. I propose to add the following to this section, as amended:

"Except in cases where a different rate, not exceeding seven and three-tenths per centum per annum, may be agreed upon or contracted for in writing."

Mr. RIDGELY. I cannot accept that amendment; but I will withdraw mine in order to let that take precedence.

The amendment of Mr. RIDGELY was accordingly withdrawn.

Mr. CHAMBERS. It may be necessary perhaps that I should explain why I omitted the words which the gentleman from Baltimore county (Mr. Ridgely) has indicated. I did so because they are perfectly useless. The legislature has that power already, and there it is not necessary to give it to them. They have all the necessary powers to inflict penalties for the violation of any law.

Mr. RIDGELY. I propose to make it mandatory that they shall pass such laws.

Mr. SCHLEY. I move the following as an addition to the section as amended:

"Except in cases where a different rate, not exceeding seven and three-tenths per centum per annum, may be agreed upon or contracted for in writing."

Mr. CHAMBERS. I did not offer the words indicated by the gentleman from Baltimore county (Mr. Ridgely,) because it was perfectly idle, the legislature already having power to provide penalties for anything prohibited by the constitution.

Mr. RIDGELY. Allow me to say one word in reply to the gentleman from Kent (Mr. Chambers.) It may be true that the legislature has the power. But in the absence of any mandatory provision in the constitution, it is entirely discretionary with the legislature whether they will exercise that power or not. I propose to make it obligatory upon them to pass such laws.

The question recurred upon the amendment proposed by Mr. SCHLEY.

Mr. THRUSTON. I merely wish to suggest to the convention that the substitute which I have offered accomplishes the same purpose in fewer words.

The CHAIRMAN (Mr. Pugh.) The first business before the convention is to perfect the proposition under consideration. A substitute therefore is not in order until the proposition is perfected.

Mr. THRUSTON. I know it is not now in order. I merely wish to suggest that the substitute accomplishes the same thing in simpler language.

The question was then taken upon the amendment of Mr. SCHLEY, and, upon a division—ayes 21, noes not counted—it was rejected.

Mr. RIDGELY. I now renew the amendment which I offered a short time since, viz:

Add to the section as amended the following:

"And the legislature shall provide by law all necessary forfeitures and penalties against usury."

Mr. MILLER. I think that amendment is necessary, because if you leave the section to stand as it now is, prohibiting the taking or demanding any higher rate of interest than six per cent., then any contract by which more might be taken or demanded would be void *in toto*, and the whole amount, principal and interest, would be forfeited.

Mr. RIDGELY. Under existing acts of the general assembly?

Mr. MILLER. That provision of the constitution, providing for penalties and forfeitures has never been carried out. It is therefore important that this amendment should be adopted. If not, then we should have to go back to the old common-law doctrine, that any contract which is contrary to the provisions of the constitution is null and void, and you cannot recover even the principal.

The question being then taken upon the amendment submitted by Mr. RIDGELY, it was adopted.

Mr. CLARKE. I have one amendment to offer, in order to make this section conform exactly to the one in the present constitution. The section as reported by the select committee reads: "The legal rate of interest shall be six per cent. per annum," &c. The section in the present constitution reads: "The rate of interest shall not exceed six per cent. per annum," &c. I move to strike out the word "be," and insert the words "not exceed."

The amendment was agreed to.

Mr. MILLER. I move to strike out the word "legal;" that will leave the section exactly as it is in the present constitution.

The amendment was agreed to.

On motion of Mr. HEBB,

The words "general assembly" were substituted for the word "legislature."

The question then recurred upon the following amendment submitted by Mr. THRUSTON:

Strike out all after the word "the" in the first line, and insert, "legal rate of interest in this State shall be six per centum per annum, except in cases where a different rate may be agreed upon in writing between contracting parties, not exceeding, however, seven and three-tenths per cent. interest in any case; and the general assembly shall pass all laws necessary to carry this section into effect."

Mr. CUSHING. I ask for a division of the question. I can vote for the first part of the amendment, but I cannot vote for the second part.

Mr. HEBB. Have we not already voted upon the first branch of this proposition?

The CHAIRMAN (Mr. Pugh.) The chair sees no other course to pursue except to put the question, although the house has voted upon it once. The substitute being in order, and a division having been called for, the vote must be taken.

Mr. CLARKE. I think the best way to get rid of this matter will be to vote down both branches of the proposition. That will leave the section to stand exactly in the form in which it has been adopted by the house.

The question was then taken upon the first branch of the proposition fixing the legal rate of interest at six per cent., and it was rejected.

The second branch of the proposition was also rejected.

The report of the select committee as amended was then ordered to be engroseed for a third reading.

ADJOURNMENT SINE DIE.

Mr. STIRLING. I move to reconsider the vote of the house a few days since, adopting the resolution fixing the day for the final adjournment of this convention. I do so for this reason: while I still hope that we may be able to adjourn finally by the thirty-first of this month, I merely propose, therefore, to have the resolution laid over informally. There are some circumstances which render it somewhat doubtful, and therefore I think we better keep ourselves free. It is not unlikely, judging from the critical state of military affairs, as announced in the papers this morning, that we may have more trouble in this State.

The question being taken upon the motion to reconsider, it was agreed to.

The question then recurred upon agreeing to the resolution.

On motion of Mr. STIRLING,

The further consideration of the resolution was informally postponed.

LEAVE OF ABSENCE.

Mr. STIRLING. I am requested by my colleague, Mr. Stockbridge, to ask leave of absence from this convention for a short time. He left suddenly last night for Baltimore in consequence of the death of Colonel Dushane, being one of his legal advisers, and required to take care of his interests and those of his family. He will have to be absent a few days. As I understood from him in conversation last night, he desires the convention to proceed with the consideration of the judiciary report in his absence.

The leave of absence was accordingly granted.

Mr. CLARKE. I desire to obtain leave of absence for a few days. Leave of absence was granted me on Friday last, but I did not avail myself of it.

Leave of absence was accordingly granted.

Mr. HOPKINS asked and obtained leave of absence from the evening session, on account of indisposition.

Mr. EARLE asked and obtained leave of absence for a few days.

Mr. KING asked and obtained leave of absence until to-morrow.

Mr. SANDS asked and obtained leave of absence for to-morrow.

Mr. JONES, of Somerset, asked and obtained leave of absence for a few days.

Mr. THOMAS moved that the convention adjourn.

Mr. SANDS moved that the convention take a recess.

The question was first taken upon the motion for a recess, and upon a division—ayes 37, noes not counted—it was agreed to.

The convention accordingly took a recess until 8 o'clock, P. M.

EVENING SESSION.

The convention reassembled at 8 o'clock, P. M. (Mr. PUGH in the chair.)

The roll was called, and the following members answered to their names:

Messrs. Abbott, Annan, Audoun, Billingsley, Blackiston, Bond, Briscoe, Brown, Carter, Chambers, Cunningham, Cushing, Daniel, Dellinger, Dent, Duvall, Earle, Ecker, Edelen, Gale, Galloway, Hebb, Hodson, Hollyday, Hopper, Horsey, Keefer, Kennard, King, Lee, Mayhugh, McComas, Mitchell, Miller, Morgan, Mullikin, Murray, Negley, Nyman, Parker, Parran, Pugh, Purnell, Ridgely, Robinette, Russell, Sands, Schley, Smith, of Carroll, Smith, of Worcester, Stirling, Swope, Sykes, Thomas, Thruston, Turner, Wickard, Wooden—58.

JUDICIARY REPORT.

Mr. AUDOUN asked and obtained leave of the convention to offer the following :

Ordered, That the report of the committee on the judiciary, with all pending amendments, be recommitted to the committee, with instructions to prepare and report an article embodying the present judicial system of the State, with the following modifications :

1st. To provide for the formation of a fifth judicial district of the State, composed of Baltimore city, and the election of a judge therefrom, so that the court of appeals shall consist of five judges, with a compensation of ——— each.

2d. To provide for the formation of two additional circuits; the first to be composed of Baltimore county, and the second of Frederick county, and for the election of circuit judges therein—and fixing the compensations of each of the circuit judges of the State at ——— per annum.

3d. And empowering the general assembly to re-arrange and increase the circuits from time to time, as the public interest may require, and to provide for the election of such judges as may become necessary in the event of the increase of circuits.

4th. That all elections for judges under this constitution shall be held in the month of May instead of on the day for the election of members of the general assembly, except in the case of the first judges in the new circuits hereby provided for.

Mr. AUDOUN said: My object in offering this order is to bring the session to an early close, an object I believe desired by every member of this body. And I believe this order if adopted, will accomplish that result.

Mr. SCHLEY. I hope that order will be amended as far as Frederick county is concerned. We do not wish to have Frederick county erected into a separate judicial circuit; we prefer the circuit as it is now established. We have no objection at all—indeed we can see that there is a manifest propriety in Baltimore county being erected into a separate judicial circuit. But we do not care to have Frederick county alone made into a circuit, because we do not think there is work enough there to occupy the time of a judge.

Mr. AUDOUN. I had understood from some of the members from Frederick county, that they desired to have it made a separate circuit; hence I inserted the name of Frederick. I have no objection to withdrawing the name from the order.

Mr. SCHLEY. If you will do that we will not object to it.

Mr. AUDOUN. My object is to accommodate the wants of the counties as nearly as possible. Some of the smaller counties do not at this time require to be made into separate circuits. But I have inserted a provision for the general assembly to provide for them at such times as they may require.

The order was accordingly modified by striking out the words "and Frederick county."

The question was on the order as modified.

Mr. DANIEL. My only objection to this order is that I think it will delay our proceedings instead of saving time. If the house determine that they prefer the old system, then it is much easier, with the report already before us, to substitute section for section, than it will be to recommit the report to the judiciary committee, with the necessary delays which are frequent in getting meetings of the committee, and all the discussions which will come up in the committee, a great deal of which discussions will come up again before the house. The report is now before the house, and I think we better determine upon the various propositions which are proposed to be sent to the committee, when the report comes up for action. If the spirit of them is adopted, it will shorten our labors very much. We are better prepared to do it right now, and we will save time by having one discussion here in place of the whole. I think therefore this order better be laid upon the table for the present, and let us go on with the report. Gentlemen can submit section for section, and amend it in that way, which is the easiest, and I think we will get through in half the time. I move to lay the order on the table.

Mr. SANDS obtained the floor.

The CHAIRMAN (Mr. Pugh.) The motion to lay on the table is not debatable.

Mr. DANIEL. I will withdraw the motion if the gentleman will renew it.

The motion to lay on the table was accordingly withdrawn.

Mr. SANDS. I think the speediest way to dispose of this judiciary question would be to substitute for the report of the committee, the present judiciary system as embodied in our constitution. That would enable us to take up section after section as we proceed, making simply the changes suggested by the proposition of the gentleman from Allegany (Mr. Hebb,) or any other change which might occur to members as necessary. We have the present judiciary system all printed here, in article four of the present constitution, and we might take it up as a substitute and amend it as necessity requires. We would find that a large portion of this article would be left to stand as it does in the present constitution. Alterations would be necessary only in those sections which provide for the division of the State into judicial circuits. I think it would simplify the whole matter and tend greatly to facilitate the action of this convention, if some such course as that was adopted.

Mr. RIDGELY. The difficulty about the course suggested by the gentleman from Howard (Mr. Sands) appears to be this: the gentleman knows very well, that according to fixed parliamentary law, the friends of a measure are entitled to the privilege of perfecting their measure before the house, and no vote upon a substitute for the entire proposition could be taken before the friends of the pending proposition had had an opportunity of perfecting. Hence the course he has suggested could not be adopted.

Mr. SANDS. I suppose it can be done by general consent.

Mr. RIDGELY. It is hardly to be presumed that that general consent could be had. I should have no objection in the world to that course, if the house would give general consent. I think myself it would be the preferable course. But in view of the fact that this barrier interposes itself to the consideration of the proposition in that form, unless the gentleman can assure us that there will be general consent, (which I think is extremely problematical,) there is no other mode of reaching the end which the gentleman from Baltimore city (Mr. Audoun) has in view than the one he has proposed. If the sense of the house is that the existing judiciary system should be adopted, then they will vote for it in some form, perhaps by amending the instructions to the committee so as to make them conform to the sentiment of the house.

We are, of course, not obliged to adopt the proposition in the specific form offered by the gentleman from Baltimore city (Mr. Audoun.) It is like all other propositions, open to amendments and modifications. But if it be the object of the house to deliver itself from the interminable confusion in which it seems to be involved at this moment, by reason of the multiplicity of the propositions and amendments which encumber the subject as it is now before the house, this is a ready mode of reaching that end. If it is not prepared so to do by the specific instructions which accompany the motion made by the gentleman from Baltimore city, it can supersede those instructions by others. But I think sufficient has transpired here to satisfy the members of this convention that the report made by the committee on judiciary will not pass this house; that it cannot pass this house; that we shall be engaged here from day to day in discussing the subject, occupy a long period of time, and then, like our experience upon the usury question, perhaps get back finally to where we started from. Therefore, to avoid that delay, and to prevent the protraction of the session, it seems to me that the gentleman from Baltimore city (Mr. Audoun) has adopted a very wise plan to ask the house to recommit this report to the committee with instructions. If the house is prepared to instruct the committee to adopt the existing judiciary system, with such modifications as have been suggested, it can manifest it at once. I for one will vote for this recommitment with pleasure.

Mr. DANIEL. I rise to renew the motion to lay on the table. I wish to say that being a member of the committee on the judiciary——

The CHAIRMAN (Mr. Pugh.) The motion to lay on the table is not debatable.

Mr. THOMAS. I would inquire if we adopt this order of my colleague (Mr. Audoun,) and the judiciary committee should bring in a report in accordance with these instructions, are we bound by that report, and cut off from offering amendments to it?

Mr. RIDGELY. Certainly not.

Mr. DANIEL. That shows that this debate will all have to be gone over again.

Mr. CUSHING. We will get rid of pending amendments.

Mr. AUDOUN. I have conversed, I believe, with a majority of the members of this house, and I think they are anxious that this plan should be adopted. They are desirous to bring the session to a close, and to go home. And this is the only way that I see that can accomplish that.

Mr. DANIEL. That will be tested directly. My object is——

Mr. KENNARD. I hope my colleague (Mr. Daniel) after speaking on this question himself as much as he desires, will not insist upon his motion to lay upon the table, as there may be other gentlemen who desire to speak upon this question.

Mr. DANIEL. Well, I will not make that motion now, I will say what I said before, and what, as a member of this committee, I know to be true; that this recommitment will cause a great deal more delay. There will be great difficulty I think in getting that committee together, and getting them to act sufficiently to draw up an entirely new system.

And what work is there left for this house to do? There is one little report, the report of the military committee. Here we are with a full house, having sessions night and day. I think this house can perfect this judiciary system a great deal quicker than the judiciary committee can. I am as anxious to save time as is my colleague (Mr. Audoun.) But I think this house has come pretty much to the conclusion to adhere to the old judiciary system in a great measure, and if it has I do not see how there can be much debate or difficulty about the matter. If the house has come to the conclusion that the old system is the best one, then why send this matter back to the committee, and have it come back to the house, and have all the discussion over it?

I think that by a few decisive votes showing that the house is in favor of substituting the old system for the one reported by the committee, we will save pretty much all debate or amendment.

Mr. SCHLEY. I am sure no member of this convention is more deeply impressed with a desire to bring its labors to a close than myself. And I would cheerfully concur in any step that would accomplish that end. If I can be assured that the pending proposition is likely to bring our labors speedily to a conclusion, I will gladly concur in it.

But my object in rising now is to ask how much does this order comprehend? Does it mean that all this matter of the court of appeals, all that portion of the report of the judiciary committee anterior to part third, is to be gone over again in committee? Or is that to stand as the convention has determined it? I believe we have perfected the report up to part third—and I suppose that being the work of the convention to that extent the convention is satisfied with it, and not disposed to reconsider it. If the gentleman from Baltimore city (Mr. Audoun) will amend his order so as to refer only that portion of the report which remains unacted upon, for instance, the part relating to the circuit courts, the orphans' courts, the courts of Baltimore city, &c., with instructions to report at a specified time, or if he pleases to report the old system substantially, and to take before it the amendments proposed to be printed, then I will support his proposition. Perhaps such a reference, with instructions to report by a given time, to-morrow at noon, for instance, would facilitate the deliberations of the convention. I think it would, and I would cheerfully concur in such a proposition.

But if it is to take the whole report before the committee and have them go over all that we have already disposed of, then I for one will have to cast my vote against the order of reference. I understand that there will be at least four members of the judiciary committee absent to-morrow; one or two of them have got leave of absence to-day, and the others are now absent. So I am afraid that this reference will be unproductive of the good that its proposer anticipates.

Now I do not know how the convention is to progress more rapidly than by continuing the order of the day, as it has gone on with it up to this time, taking the proposed amendments into consideration, and substituting such of them for portions of the report as they may desire. And until I hear further from the mover of this order that he means to limit the work of this committee, or of a special committee, to this extent, I do not think I can support his order. If he will move to refer it to a special committee, or move that the committee on the judiciary be filled up temporarily so far as to supply the places of those who will necessarily be absent to-morrow, instruct them to report by noon to-morrow, and then move to take a recess until then, I will agree to it; otherwise I shall have to vote against it.

Mr. STIRLING. The proposition of my colleague (Mr. Audoun) strikes me very favorably; but I should like to have him make some modifications in it. It seems to me that it is one of the readiest modes of getting at this question; and I think if something of this sort is not adopted, we shall not soon arrive at a conclusion. I should prefer that that part of the report of the judiciary committee which we have already adopted should be left to stand. With that exception I entirely agree with the proposition to report the present judiciary system. I intended, when the time arrived, to propose an amendment altering the jurisdiction of the court of common pleas of Baltimore city, extending its jurisdiction to seven hundred and fifty dollars. With that exception I am willing to adopt the present system as it stands.

Mr. HEBB. I move the following as a substitute for the order proposed by the gentleman from Baltimore city (Mr. Audoun.)

Ordered, That the report of the committee on the judiciary department, with all the amendments proposed thereto, be recommitted to the committee, with instructions to report the judiciary system as embraced in the existing constitution, except so far as the same has been modified by the adoption of the article in the court of appeals, and excepting also to report nine judicial circuits instead of eight (erecting Baltimore county in a separate circuit,) and also, reporting a provision giving the general assembly the power to create additional circuits from time to time when required."

Mr. THRUSTON. I propose to save time by making the motion to substitute for the report by the committee on the judiciary, the present judiciary system of this State, except in so far as the same has been already modified by the action of the convention in considering the report of the committee That it seems to me will bring the question right before the house, and we can get along without any reference.

The CHAIRMAN (Mr. Pugh.) That motion cannot be entertained, because each section of the report of the committee must be taken up and considered by itself. The report of the committee is not now under consideration. The order of the gentleman from Baltimore city (Mr. Audoun) and the substitute proposed by the gentleman from Allegany (Mr. Hebb,) are now before the house.

Mr. MILLER. I should very much prefer, if this subject is to be recommitted to the committee with instructions, that they be instructed to reorganize the circuits according to the amendment offered the other day by the gentleman from Allegany (Mr. Hebb,) making I think twelve judicial circuits. One of the gentleman from Baltimore city (Mr. Audoun) says that he has consulted with a majority of the members of this house in reference to this matter, and that they have pretty much agreed to take the old judiciary system with the amendments which he has proposed. Now the substitute offered for the order he submitted provides very well for Baltimore county and perhaps for some other parts of the State. But we have four counties at present in our judicial circuit, and it is almost impossible for the judge to attend to the business of those four counties. I wish, if instructions are to be given at all, that the committee be instructed to report a system of circuits, making the number larger than either of the propositions now before the house; making at least twelve circuits. And I should hope also that we might get rid of the one-judge system, which we now have, and adopt something which will come near to having three judges upon the bench, a judge for each county in the circuit; and let that judge be a judge of the orphans' court.

I think, however, we can get along very well in considering the report of the committee, by offering amendments to each section as it comes up. The question of the consumption of time has been very much urged here. Every one of us is anxious to get through with our labors. But gentlemen must recollect that we are now considering the most important branch of our business here. I believe the people of the State desire a radical change in our judiciary system; that that question as much as anything else induced the people to call together this convention. And I think we shall not have performed our duty unless we give the people of this State as perfect a judiciary system as we can make. I do not think we should take into consideration the time necessary for that. We can afford to sit here a week or two longer for the sake of getting an improved judiciary system, even if we debate, and take vote after vote, upon the different amendments offered. I do not think the time will be wasted.

I hope, therefore, that this order will not be adopted; or that if it is adopted the amendment I have indicated will be made to the instructions. I know that the people of this circuit, and of other parts of the State, are very anxious for a radical change in the system of judges.

Mr. Ridgely. Power is proposed to be given to the legislature to re-arrange the circuits.

Mr. Miller. But not to increase the number of judges in the circuit.

Mr. Ridgely. Yes, sir.

Mr. Miller. I think we better provide for that in the constitution itself, as far as we can.

Mr. Negley. I am opposed to the substitute, and the proposition for which it is a substitute, principally upon the ground taken by the gentleman from Anne Arundel (Mr. Miller,) unless you embody in it instructions to report twelve judicial circuits, instead of what is now proposed. By that means you do get rid to a certain extent, if not fully, of two very serious objections to the present system. One is the present system of special judges. The operation of that system is a perfect nuisance in our portion of the State. And if Allegany, Washington, Frederick and Baltimore counties are arranged into separate judicial circuits we get rid of that nuisance to that extent. Besides, we get rid on the other hand, of the inconvenience attending the issuing of injunctions when the court is absent in another county.

Mr. Stirling. I wish to vote intelligently upon this subject. I have all along been friendly to the proposition of the gentleman from Allegany (Mr. Hebb.) But I understand that the counties of Washington and Frederick do not want to be separate judicial districts. If they want it, I am prepared to vote for it.

Mr. Negley. We want Washington county to be a separate district.

Mr. Stirling. Does the gentleman express the sense of his delegation?

Mr. Dellinger. Not mine.

Mr. Mayhugh. And not mine.

Mr. Negley. We are suffering from a want of justice from that cause now. We want Washington county created into a judicial circuit, and then one judge will do for us, and we should then avoid the necessity of having a law judge and an orphans' court bench. The entire State would be subjected to an increase of only four judges.—There are great abuses in our county, in reference to this system of special judges. As an illustration: we had a special judge up there; he got ten dollars a day. One of our lawyers went to him with three orders to sign. He could have signed them all in five minutes. But he said—"I will sign one today, one to-morrow, and one the day after tomorrow." And he signed one of those orders a day, and got his ten dollars for signing each of those orders. I think that very judge had got more than three thousand dollars from Washington county alone, for these little special cases. If we have the county erected into a judicial circuit, then we will get rid of that nuisance. And then we get rid of the trouble of getting into the stage and going off into Allegany county, to get the judge to issue an injunction, or sign some equity paper. That trouble will not all be obviated by the proposition of the gentleman from Allegany (Mr. Hebb,) but it will be lessened.

Mr. Edelen. I do not understand how the creation of additional districts, or the creation of Washington county into a separate judicial district will obviate the difficulty of special judges.

Mr. NEGLEY. I do not know as it will.—But still we certainly ought to change the law on that subject. And there ought to be certain instructions go to the committee to change this matter of special judges.

Mr. THOMAS. I would ask the gentleman from Washington county (Mr. Negley) what change he proposes to get rid of special judges? Suppose the circuit judge gets sick?

Mr. NEGLEY. Let the parties interested in the case select their own judge.

Mr. RIDGELY. That will be a special judge.

Mr. NEGLEY. And if they do not select their own judge, then the judge in the adjoining district will act. These frauds, as I conceive them to be, never have occurred in cases where the attorneys have been allowed to select the judge.

Mr. STIRLING. They can do that now.

Mr. NEGLEY. Where they have selected a special judge. But the judge of the adjoining district has appointed the special judge. The parties to the case not having exercised their privilege of designating the judge. The parties to the case ought to be compelled to select the judge; or some way to avoid this difficulty.

Mr. SANDS. Will the gentleman from Allegany (Mr. Hebb) accept an amendment to this substitute? Otherwise I must vote against it. His substitute as it stands leaves many of the circuits just in the condition in which they are now; and leaving them so, it leaves them subject to great difficulties. If the gentleman from Washington (Mr. Negley) wants a judge for his county, he does not want to go to Allegany, as he must do under this substitute. We have four counties in our circuit; and an amount of business too great for one man to attend to. Surely if he wants one judge for his county, we ought to have more than one judge for our four counties. I therefore suggest to my friend that he make such a modification of his substitute as will permit the committee to report such a number of judicial circuits as they may think best—subject of course to the subsequent action of this convention. I agree with my friend from Anne Arundel (Mr. Miller) that in our circuit, composed of four counties, Howard, Anne Arundel, Montgomery and Calvert, we do need relief; and I hope we will get it.

Mr. HEBB. I would prefer twelve districts of course; but I do not know that it will be carried.

Mr. RIDGELY. I hope the gentleman will not accept the amendment; let us vote upon his proposition.

Mr. PURNELL. Does the proposition of the gentleman from Allegany (Mr. Hebb) remodel the district in which I reside, Worcester, Somerset, and Dorchester, or does it leave it as it is now?

Mr. HEBB. My amendment to the proposition of the gentleman from Baltimore city (Mr. Audoun) leaves the district of the gentleman from Worcester (Mr. Purnell) exactly as it is now. Because I do not propose to change any district except the one now composed of Baltimore, Harford and Cecil counties. I propose to make Baltimore county into one circuit, and the other two counties will compose a circuit. The proposition I submitted the other day changed every circuit but the first, composed of St. Mary's, Charles, and Prince George's counties. I propose now to leave the committee to report such number of circuits as they may think proper, only to report the system which is in the present constitution.

Mr. PURNELL. I should prefer the arrangement as under the old system, composed of three counties. I should oppose any curtailment of our circuit by taking off the county of Dorchester. Let the district remain as it is, embracing the three counties.

Mr. STIRLING. I would suggest to the gentleman from Allegany (Mr. Hebb) that if he accepts the amendment of the gentleman from Howard (Mr. Sands,) it brings us back to the discussion of the merits of the question of the number of judicial districts. If we will agree to adopt either his substitute, or the proposition of my colleague (Mr. Audoun,) instructing the committee to report the present system, with these particular alterations agreed upon by the convention, we will get clear of everything before us, and will get a proposition which substantially meets the action of the convention. Then if the convention is in favor of increasing the circuits from nine to twelve it can easily be got at with one amendment. But if that amendment is to be brought in now, it raises the discussion at once as to the number of circuits, and no time is saved.

Mr. SANDS. If it is easy to put nine up to twelve, it is just as easy to put twelve down to nine. We only want some initiatory steps taken by which we can be sure of some reform. What is the objection? What does it amount to?

Mr. STIRLING. I have no objection to that whatever. As I said before, I am in favor of the proposition, but there are others here who are not. The course of remark of the gentleman from Howard (Mr. Sands,) and the gentleman from Anne Arundel (Mr. Miller,) shows that if we go on and add to this, it will lead to interminable discussion.

Mr. SANDS. This leaves it to the committee to fix it as they please. No matter how they may fix it, that does not hinder the convention from increasing or diminishing it. The committee would of course report a definite number, and it is just as easy to decrease the number, if they report ten or twelve districts, as it will be to increase it if they report seven or nine.

Mr. HEBB. As there is some objection to

my accepting the amendment, I do not accept it. But the gentleman can offer it as an amendment to my substitute, and have a vote upon it.

Mr. AUDOUN. I will accept the proposition of the gentleman from Allegany (Mr. Hebb) in lieu of the one I submitted.

The question was upon the order submitted by Mr. HEBB.

Mr. GALLOWAY. If this report, together with all the amendments that have been offered to it, is to be referred back to the committee, I think some time should be fixed for them to report it back again.

Mr. RIDGELY. That can be done after we have voted upon the order of reference.

Mr. GALLOWAY. As I understand, the chairman of that committee, and three or four of its members are absent. If this report is to go back to the committee, with all these amendments, the time may be far distant when we will ever hear from it again. I want some time mentioned.

Mr. STIRLING. I think it would be well, as the gentleman from Harford (Mr. Galloway) suggests, to insert a clause directing the committee to report by a certain day. And I would also suggest that so many of the committee as are present be authorized to act. And if they do not report by the day fixed, then that the matter be referr d to a special committee.

Mr. SMITH, of Carroll. If there was any unanimity of sentiment in reference to referring this report back to the committee, then I should think it would be well to act upon the suggestion of the gentleman from Baltimore city. But there is manifestly so wide a difference of opinion upon the subject, that it seems to me that it can only result in what the gentleman desires to avoid —a waste of time. We have barely a quorum present now, and it would be perfectly competent for a full house to-morrow to reconsider what we may do to-night. And even if the report goes back to the committee with certain instructions, it would be perfectly competent for the majority of the convention when they shall have again reported, to destroy the very effect of this recommitment. And the result will be, besides the difficulty that will be encountered of assembling a committee together, four or five of whose members are absent, we will start again just where we are now, and all this time will be lost. It seems to me the better plan would be to take up the several propositions already submitted and act upon them. One or two votes will determine the sense of this convention upon the general proposition, and then we can systematize the details as we may think proper.

Mr. THRUSTON. If this report is referred to the committee with instructions to make a certain report, any member of the committee present can make that report. It is not necessary for a majority or two-thirds of the members of the committee to be present to do it. It is a mere formal matter; the committee act under instructions; there is nothing whatever left to their discretion, and any number of the committee can make the report. Therefore I think the objection of the gentleman from Carroll (Mr. Smith) is not well taken.

Mr. SANDS. I move to amend the order of the gentleman from Allegany (Mr. Hebb) by striking out the words "nine judicial circuits, instead of eight," and inserting "such number of judicial circuits as the committee may deem necessary to meet the public necessities."

The question was upon the amendment submitted by Mr. SANDS.

Mr. STIRLING called the yeas and nays upon this question, and they were ordered.

The question being then taken, by yeas and nays, it resulted—yeas 39, nays 18—as follows:

Yeas—Messrs. Abbott, Billingsley, Blackiston, Briscoe, Brown, Chambers, Cunningham, Daniel, Dellinger, Dent, Earle, Ecker, Edelen, Gale, Galloway, Hebb, Hodson, Hollyday, Horsey, Lee, McComas, Mitchell, Miller, Morgan, Negley, Nyman, Parker, Parran, Pugh, Robinette, Russell, Sands, Smith, of Carroll, Swope, Sykes, Thomas, Thruston, Turner, Wooden—39.

Nays—Messrs. Annan, Audoun, Bond, Carter, Cushing, Hopper, Keefer, Kennard, King, Mayhugh, Mullikin, Murray, Purnell, Ridgely, Schley, Smith, of Worcester, Stirling, Wickard—18.

The amendment was accordingly adopted.

Mr. SMITH, of Carroll, when his name was called, said: While I am opposed to recommitting this report at all, believing that it will result in no good but only a waste of time, still I think the proposition made by the gentleman from Howard (Mr. Sands,) is more acceptable, and better in many respects, than any other offered, I therefore shall vote for it.

Mr. STIRLING. Now in order to prevent the committee having the right to go back to the one-judge system, I move to amend, by inserting after the words "judicial circuits" the words "not exceeding twelve."

The question being taken upon the amendment, upon a division—ayes 35, noes not counted—the amendment was adopted.

Mr STIRLING. I now move to add a clause to the order as amended, instructing the committee to report by Thursday next at twelve o'clock, M.

Mr. SCHLEY. I hope the gentleman will make it "to-morrow at one o'clock," and that the committee have leave to sit during the morning session of the convention.

Mr. STIRLING. I do not think that till day after to-morrow is too much time to give the committee. The whole report must be drawn up in some shape.

Mr. SCHLEY. Then I move to amend by instructing the committee to report to-morrow at one o'clock.

The CHAIRMAN (Mr. Pugh.) The question will be first taken upon the longest time.

The question was upon the amendment of Mr. STIRLING, instructing the committee to report by twelve o'clock, M., on Thursday next.

Mr. DANIEL. I think it would be better, and would save time, to refer this to a special committee at once. The chairman of the committee is away, and some four members of the committee have been excused from attending for a few days. I do not think any other member of the committee will take the responsibility of calling the committee together. I hope some friend of the measure will amend it so as to have a reference to a special committee.

Mr. SANDS. I do not know whether it would be a very respectful course towards the committee, who have taken a great deal of trouble to report a system, to oust the standing committee and appoint a special committee to take charge of the subject. I never heard of a procedure of that sort before, and I should hardly like to see it adopted here.

Mr. THRUSTON. I would like to state for the information of the house, that the chairman of the judiciary committee (Mr. Stockbridge) asked me to push the report as much as possible, and not mind his absence. He said he would like to see good progress made during his absence.

The question was then taken upon the motion of Mr. STIRLING to instruct the committee to report by twelve o'clock, M., on Thursday next; and, upon a division—ayes 29, noes 21—it was agreed to.

The question recurred upon the order as amended.

Mr. THOMAS. As I understand it, this order instructs the committee to report upon everything except the part relating to the court of appeals; it takes it for granted that that portion of the report is adopted. I find by reference to pages 489 and 490 of the journal of proceedings that section twelve of the judiciary report, being the first section in relation to the court of appeals, was adopted in so far as the amendment of the gentleman from Allegany (Mr. Thruston) was concerned. But there was an amendment offered by myself which was still pending at that time, which upon motion of the gentleman from Carroll (Mr. Smith,) was laid over informally. The inquiry I wish to make is whether this amendment of mine goes to this committee, and they are to report upon it also.

Mr. SANDS. I can explain to my friend how this matter stands. About the time we were passing this section, some one suggested that a substitute had been offered for it by the gentleman from Baltimore city (Mr. Thomas.) Then some gentleman on the floor stated that he had understood from the gentleman from Baltimore city, who moved that substitute, that he had no interest in pressing it, did not care to do so. He was absent sick, and unable to be in his place. And it was under these circumstances that the section was adopted.

Mr. THOMAS. The journal says that it was informally passed over. I understand on account of my absence. So far as my giving up my substitute is concerned, I never dreamed of such a thing; and furthermore I never said so to any person at any time.

Mr. SANDS. That was stated on this floor.

Mr. THOMAS. Then whoever said so, stated that which was not true.

Mr. MILLER. When the judiciary report comes up for action, will it be open to amendment so far as the part relating to the court appeals is concerned?

The CHAIRMAN (Mr. Pugh.) That is for the convention to determine.

Mr. MILLER. Then the vote already taken upon it is for nothing. I want to get back to the appointive system for the court of appeals.

Mr. STIRLING. The convention has passed upon that subject.

Mr. MILLER. The question I want to ask is this; when this report comes back from the committee, will it be open to amendment like a new report, and can you offer an amendment to any part of it?

Mr. RIDGELY. It will all be open to amendment.

Mr. BRISCOE. It seems to me that our object ought to be to make some progress. Our action here to-night, it seems to me, is very much like the action of a spavined horse; there is a great deal of movement, but no great amount of go about it. As I understand the sentiments of the judiciary committee, it is in favor of dividing the State of Maryland into eight judicial circuits. I do not understand that that conclusion upon the part of the committee has been changed since they submitted their report. And there has not been any expression of sentiment in this house, as heretofore expressed, so far as I understand it, that there shall be either a greater or less number of judicial circuits than the committee reported. And we are about to vote upon a proposition to send this subject back to the committee and ask them to report what kind of division they think should be made, when they have heretofore told us they wanted the State divided with eight judicial districts. And of course when they bring the report back again it will be with the very identical number of judicial districts it now contains.

Mr. STIRLING. That cannot be so, because the eight-district system was based upon the principle of having three judges to each circuit. This order cuts up the three-judge system, for it says the committee shall adopt the present judiciary system, which is a one-judge system. Therefore the committee cannot report three judges to each circuit; they must report one judge to a circuit. But they can alter the number of circuits, not exceeding twelve.

The question recurred upon adopting the order submitted by Mr. Hebb, which had been amended so as to read as follows:

"*Ordered*, That the report of the committee on the judiciary department, with all the amendments proposed thereto, be recommitted to the committee, with instructions to report the judiciary system as embraced in the existing constitution, except so far as the same has been modified by the adoption of the article in the court of appeals, and excepting also to report such number of judicial circuits, not exceeding twelve, as the committee may deem necessary to meet the public necessities, (erecting Baltimore county in a separate circuit,) and also, reporting a provision giving the general assembly the power to create additional circuits from time to time when required, and that the committee be instructed to report by Thursday next at twelve o'clock."

Upon this question Mr. Daniel asked for the yeas and nays, which were ordered.

The question was then taken, by yeas and nays, and resulted—yeas 20, nays 37—as follows:

Yeas—Messrs. Audoun, Cunningham, Cushing, Earle, Ecker, Hebb, Keefer, Kennard, King, Negley, Nyman, Parker, Pugh, Ridgely, Robinette, Stirling, Thomas, Thruston, Wickard, Wooden—20.

Nays—Messrs. Abbott, Annan, Billingsley, Blackiston, Bond, Briscoe, Brown, Carter, Chambers, Daniel, Dellinger, Dent, Edelen, Gale, Galloway, Hodson, Hollyday, Hopper, Horsey, Lee, Mayhugh, McComas, Mitchell, Miller, Morgan, Mullikin, Murray, Parran, Purnell, Russell, Sands, Schley, Smith, of Carroll, Smith, of Worcester, Swope, Sykes, Turner—37.

The order was accordingly rejected.

Mr. Abbott, when his name was called, said: When this proposition was first offered by my colleague (Mr. Audoun,) I was in favor of it. But after spending nearly an hour and a half in discussing this matter, and finding that there are hardly any two in the house, especially among the members of the legal profession, who think alike upon the subject, I shall vote against it. For if they once get this report in the committee, there is no telling when we shall get it back again, for committees do not always obey orders. The committee before was some three or four months in labor, and then brought forth a report which this house has already pronounced to be a mouse. I vote "no."

Mr. Ridgely. I now propose to submit an order much like the one just voted upon, but in a modified form. The objection was taken to the other order—and I understand it controlled the votes of a great many members—that the judiciary committee, by reason of the absence of several of its members, was not in a condition to consider this subject and report promptly to the house. I therefore submit the following order, which will remove that objection:

"*Ordered*, That the report of the committee on the judiciary department, with the amendments thereto, be referred to a select committee of five, with instructions to report a judiciary system as embraced in the present constitution, except that portion of the report which has been adopted by this body, and with further instructions to report such re-arrangement of the judicial circuits as they may deem necessary, not to exceed twelve, and that said committee report to-morrow at one o'clock."

Mr. Negley. The question has been asked whether this order excepts from the consideration of the committee that portion of the report relating to the court of appeals. Now the house has passed upon all that portion of the report except section twelve, or the first section relating to the court of appeals. The question has been asked whether those sections which have been acted upon and approved by the convention will be again open to amendment when the report comes back. I conceive that that cannot be so, because if we were now to go on and consider this report without referring it, that portion upon which the convention has acted, the part relating to the court of appeals, with the exception of the first section, is complete. It will be precisely in that condition when the special committee shall make its report. Otherwise we will find ourselves reduced to the absurd position of having passed one day through the second reading of a number of sections, and then the next day going over them again. I will vote for this order with the understanding that the portion of this report which has been read a second time shall be considered as having been finally passed upon, and that we are not to have the whole thing gone over again and argued. I consider that strictly, according to parliamentary law, that portion of the report cannot be gone over again.

Mr. Stirling. I suppose that all that part which is not referred to the committee for action will come back to the house precisely as it now stands.

Mr. Daniel. I do not want to speak upon this question. I simply rise to set myself right in reference to a matter to which allusion has been made here. In some remarks which I made the other night in reference to the postponement of section twelve of this report, I said that I had understood my colleague (Mr. Thomas) to say to me that he did not care much about the matter. Now I want to state exactly how that occurred, so that I may set myself right. After the house had adopted the amendment of the gentleman from Allegany (Mr. Thruston,) to elect the judges of the court of appeals upon general ticket, and the house had taken a recess, I passed by where my colleague (Mr. Thomas) was bundling up his papers, and said to him—"Well, I suppose that virtually defeats your amendment." He replied—"Well, I don't care much about it." Whether he understood me or not, I do not know. I did not say that he intended to withdraw his amendment, but merely not to press it. And I stated then that I did not wish that to have any influence upon the house.

Mr. MILLER. This order requires the special committee to report a judiciary system entire, including the court of appeals and everything else; the present judiciary system except such as has been adopted by this body. If they report under that order, they must go from A to Izzard, to get the whole thing in.

Mr. STIRLING. I would suggest to the gentleman from Baltimore county (Mr. Ridgely,) to strike out "which has been adopted by this body," and insert "relating to the court of appeals." That will then leave the part of the report relating to the court of appeals to stand just as it is now.

Mr. RIDGELY. I will modify the order in that way.

The question was upon the order as modified.

Mr. MAYHUGH. It seems to me that no two gentlemen in this house understand whether the whole of this report, or but a part of it, is to go to this special committee, for them to report upon as they please, or whether it is to be left subject to the action which the convention has had upon it already. In my own opinion, the business of the convention will be much facilitated by our progressing with this report as we have commenced. If this committee make a report to-morrow, it will be open to amendment just as the present one is. And in order to facilitate the business of the convention, I move that the order offered by the gentleman from Baltimore county (Mr. Ridgely) be laid upon the table.

Upon this question, Mr. RIDGELY called for the yeas and nays, which were ordered.

The question being taken, by yeas and nays, it resulted—yeas 34, nays 23—as follows:

Yeas—Messrs. Billingsley, Blackiston, Briscoe, Bond, Brown, Chambers, Cunningham, Daniel, Dellinger, Dent, Edelen, Gale, Hodson, Hollyday, Hopper, Horsey, Lee, Mayhugh, Mitchell, Miller, Morgan, Murray, Parran, Pugh, Purnell, Russell, Sands, Schley, Smith, of Carroll, Smith, of Worcester, Swope, Sykes, Thruston, Turner—34.

Nays—Messrs. Abbott, Annan, Audoun, Carter, Cushing, Earle, Ecker, Galloway, Hebb, Keefer, Kennard, King, McComas, Mullikin, Negley, Nyman, Parker, Ridgely, Robinette, Stirling, Thomas, Wooden, Wickard—23.

The motion to lay the order on the table was accordingly agreed to.

Mr. CHAMBERS moved that the convention do now adjourn.

Upon this question Mr. STIRLING called for the yeas and nays, which were ordered.

The question being then taken, by yeas and nays, it resulted—yeas 31, nays 23—as follows:

Yeas—Messrs. Billingsley, Blackiston, Brown, Chambers, Cunningham, Dellinger, Dent, Edelen, Gale, Hollyday, Hopper, Horsey, Kennard, King, Lee, Mayhugh, Mitchell, Miller, Morgan, Mullikin, Murray, Parker, Parran, Russell, Sands, Smith, of Carroll, Smith, of Worcester, Swope, Sykes, Thruston, Turner—31.

Nays—Messrs. Abbott, Annan, Audoun, Carter, Cushing, Daniel, Earle, Ecker, Galloway, Hebb, Keefer, McComas, Negley, Nyman, Pugh, Purnell, Ridgely, Robinette, Schley, Stirling, Thomas, Wickard, Wooden—23.

The motion was accordingly agreed to.

Mr. KENNARD, when his name was called, said: I would be perfectly willing to remain here if I thought it would promote the business of the convention. But I am convinced, from the discussion we have already had, that we can do nothing more here to-night. I therefore vote "aye."

Mr. THRUSTON, when his name was called, said: I would be perfectly willing to stay here, if I thought any good would result from a prolongation of our session to-night. But, judging from the temper of the house, I do not think any practical result can be obtained by remaining here longer, and therefore I vote "aye."

The convention accordingly adjourned.

EIGHTIETH DAY.

WEDNESDAY, August 24, 1864.

The convention met at ten o'clock, A. M., (Mr. PUGH in the chair.)

Prayer by the Rev. Mr. Owen.

The roll was called, and the following members answered to their names:

Messrs. Goldsborough, President; Abbott, Annan, Audoun, Belt, Billingsley, Blackiston, Bond, Briscoe, Brown, Carter, Cunningham, Cushing, Daniel, Dellinger, Dent, Duvall, Ecker, Edelen, Farrow, Gale, Galloway, Hatch, Hebb, Hodson, Hoffman Hollyday, Hopkins, Hopper, Horsey, Johnson, Jones, of Cecil, Keefer, Kennard, Larsh, Lee, Mayhugh, McComas, Mitchell, Miller, Morgan, Mullikin, Murray, Negley, Nyman, Parker, Parran, Pugh, Purnell, Ridgely, Robinette, Russell, Schley, Smith, of Carroll, Smith, of Worcester, Sneary, Stirling, Stockbridge, Swope, Sykes, Thomas, Thruston Turner, Valliant, Wickard, Wooden—66.

The journal of yesterday was read and approved.

LIMITATION OF DEBATE.

Mr. PURNELL moved to reconsider the order, found on page 748 of the journal of debates, adopted on the seventh of July, in relation to the limitation of debate.

The order read as follows:

"*Ordered*, That the time allowed each member for debate on any question before the convention be limited to thirty minutes; and that no extension of time be granted except by a vote of two-thirds of the members present."

The motion to reconsider was agreed to.

The question recurred upon adopting the order.

Mr. PURNELL moved to amend the order by striking out all after the word "that," in the first line, and inserting the words "the time allowed each member for debate on any question before the convention be limited to ten minutes; that no extension of time be granted except by a unanimous vote of the members present."

Mr. CUSHING. I move to amend the amendment by striking out the word "ten" and inserting the word "five."

Mr. PURNELL accepted the amendment.

Mr. BRISCOE. I move to strike out all that part of the order which relates to the unanimous consent of the convention for the time to be extended. It may be possible we may want some information some time, which cannot be given in five minutes.

Mr. DANIEL. I move to strike out the words "unanimous vote," and insert "the vote of two-thirds."

Mr. DENT. I move to insert "twenty" instead of "five." Five minutes is certainly too short a time to allow for any intelligent expression of views upon any subject of importance that may be presented to the consideration of this body. It would amount to a perfect stifling of debate. It seems to me we better adopt some order preventing all debate, rather than adopt the order which is proposed, and which would be a mere mockery. I do not suppose there are many subjects which would lead gentlemen to make extended speeches during the short period which we will remain in session. I was at least in hopes that we might be prepared to go on under the rule under which we have been acting for the last week or two. Very few persons have occupied so much time as has been allowed under the rule. There has not been much time consumed in debate. I think there is a general disposition to get away from here as soon as it can be done with credit to the body. I hope the debate will not be restricted to five minutes, but that at least twenty minutes will be allowed, which is a very short time.

Mr. DANIEL. I will move ten minutes, if that is voted down.

Mr. MILLER. I think that the twenty-minute rule ought to be adopted. The gentleman who moved to insert five minutes instead of ten, is, I believe, the only gentleman who has occupied the full time since the adoption of the thirty-minute rule.

Mr. THRUSTON moved the previous question, which was seconded.

The question was upon ordering the main question to be put.

Mr. CHAMBERS called for the yeas and nays upon this question, which were ordered.

The question was then taken, by yeas and nays, and resulted—yeas 34, nays 32—as follows:

Yeas—Messrs. Goldsborough, President; Abbott, Annan, Audoun, Carter, Cunningham, Cushing, Dellinger, Farrow, Galloway, Hatch, Hebb, Hopkins, Hopper, Jones, of Cecil, Keefer, Kennard, Mayhugh, McComas, Mullikin, Murray, Negley, Nyman, Parker, Pugh, Purnell, Robinette, Russell, Schley, Smith, of Worcester, Sneary, Stirling, Thruston, Wooden—34.

Nays—Messrs. Belt, Billingsley, Blackiston, Bond, Briscoe, Brown, Chambers, Daniel, Dent, Ecker, Edelen, Gale, Hodson, Hoffman, Hollyday, Horsey, Johnson, Larsh, Lee, Mitchell, Miller, Morgan, Parran, Ridgely, Smith, of Carroll, Stockbridge, Swope, Sykes, Thomas, Turner, Valliant, Wickard—32.

The main question was accordingly ordered.

Mr. SMITH, of Carroll, when his name was called, said: I do not think that five minutes is sufficient time for gentlemen to express their views upon the vital and important subjects which have been brought to the attention of this convention. We have occupied an immense deal of time in talking about inconsiderable matters in comparison with those before us, and there has been no objection to it. I think if gentlemen will confine their remarks to the subjects under discussion, and quit when they are done, we will get along much better. I think the order ought to be modified, and fifteen minutes ought to be inserted. And with a view to further amend the proposition which has been offered, I vote "no."

The question was upon the motion of Mr. DENT to insert "twenty minutes," as the limit of time for debate.

Upon this question Mr. MILLER called for the yeas and nays, which were ordered.

The question was then taken, by yeas and nays, and resulted—yeas 40, nays 27—as follows:

Yeas—Messrs. Goldsborough, President; Audoun, Belt, Billingsley, Blackiston, Bond, Briscoe, Brown, Carter, Chambers, Daniel, Dellinger, Dent, Duvall, Ecker, Edelen, Gale, Hodson, Hoffman, Hollyday, Hopkins, Horsey, Johnson, Larsh, Lee, Mayhugh, Mitchell, Miller, Morgan, Negley, Parker, Parran, Ridgely, Smith, of Carroll, Sneary, Swope, Sykes, Thomas, Turner, Valliant—40.

Nays—Messrs. Abbott, Annan, Cunningham, Cushing, Farrow, Galloway, Hatch, Hebb, Hopper, Jones, of Cecil, Keefer, Kennard, McComas, Mullikin, Murray, Nyman, Pugh, Purnell, Robinette, Russell, Schley, Smith, of Worcester, Stirling, Stockbridge, Thruston, Wickard, Wooden—27.

The amendment of Mr. Dent was accordingly adopted.

Mr. Daniel, when his name was called, said: I did not wish, if I could help it, to vote for either of the propositions submitted, because I would like to amend by inserting "ten minutes," which I think is long enough. But that amendment being cut off, I prefer twenty minutes to five, and therefore I vote "aye."

The question then recurred upon the amendment of Mr. Daniel, to extend the time of any member by a two-thirds instead of a unanimous vote.

Upon this question Mr. Wooden called for the yeas and nays, which were ordered.

The question was then taken, by yeas and nays, and resulted—yeas 35, nays 32—as follows:

Yeas—Messrs. Goldsborough, President; Abbott, Annan, Audoun, Belt, Billingsley, Blackiston, Bond, Briscoe, Brown, Chambers, Cunningham, Daniel, Dellinger, Dent, Duvall, Edelen, Gale, Hodson, Hoffman, Hollyday, Horsey, Johnson, Larsh, Lee, Mayhugh, Mitchell, Miller, Morgan, Negley, Parran, Ridgely, Sneary, Thomas, Turner—35.

Nays—Messrs. Carter, Cushing, Ecker, Farrow, Galloway, Hatch, Hebb, Hopkins, Hopper, Jones, of Cecil, Keefer, Kennard, McComas, Mullikin, Murray, Nyman, Parker, Pugh, Purnell, Robinette, Russell, Schley, Smith, of Carroll, Smith, of Worcester, Stirling, Stockbridge, Swope, Sykes, Thruston, Valliant, Wickard, Wooden—32.

The amendment was accordingly adopted.

The order as amended was then adopted, as follows:

"*Ordered*, That the time allowed each member for debate on any question before the convention be limited to twenty minutes; and that no extension of time be granted except by a vote of two-thirds of the members present."

MISCELLANEOUS.

Mr. Hopkins gave notice that at the proper time he would submit the following amendment to the report of the committee on the legislative department:

"The legislature shall foster and encourage moral, intellectual, scientific and agricultural improvement; they shall, when it may be practicable, make suitable provision for the blind, mute and insane, and for the organization of such institutions of learning as the best interests of the State may demand."

Mr. Audoun submitted the following order:

"*Ordered*, That the president appoint an assistant secretary to serve during the absence of Mr. Shaw, and that the secretary be allowed extra per diem for such time as he has been acting as assistant secretary."

Mr. Daniel. Does this order mean to exclude Mr. Shaw from his per diem?

Mr. Audoun. Certainly not. The secretary is now acting as secretary and assistant secretary both, and he should receive additional compensation.

Mr. Schley. I would move to amend the order by proposing to call one of the committee clerks to act as assistant secretary.

The President. The president has power to do that already. He has already called one of them on a former occasion to act as assistant secretary. If the convention desire it he will call another now.

Mr. Schley. I will not offer any amendment.

The question was then taken upon the order submitted by Mr. Audoun, and it was adopted.

The President, in pursuance of that order, appointed Mr. John McGarigle to act as assistant secretary, *pro. tem.*

Mr. Wickard submitted the following order:

"*Ordered*, That the assistant secretary be allowed extra pay for the time that he acted as secretary, in the absence of the secretary."

The President. Under a previous order the president had power to appoint an assistant secretary.

Mr. Hebb. The proposition is that Mr. Shaw, the assistant secretary, be allowed extra pay for the time he acted when Mr. Cole, the secretary, was absent. We have just passed an order allowing Mr. Cole extra pay for the time he acted in a double capacity, in the absence of Mr. Shaw.

The question was then taken upon the order, and it was adopted.

LEAVE OF ABSENCE.

Mr. Stockbridge. I ask permission to be absent from the convention until Friday morning. Nothing but imperious necessity would induce me to ask that permission at this time. The circumstances, I believe, are already known to the convention.

The leave of absence was accordingly granted.

JUDICIARY DEPARTMENT.

The convention then resumed the consideration of the report of the committee on the judiciary department, which was on its second reading.

Mr. Ridgely. With the consent of the house, I will take a moment to make a personal explanation. On page 513 of the journal of proceedings, will be found an order which I submitted last evening, and which, if unexplained, might subject me to the imputation of showing very great discourtesy to the committee on the judiciary. As I do not desire to occupy any such position, I will now take occasion to explain the circumstances which induced me to offer that order. An order had been submitted by my friend from Baltimore city (Mr. Audoun) to recommit the report of the judiciary committee with instructions to that committee. In the course of the debate upon that order, another gentleman from Baltimore city (Mr. Daniel,) a member of that committee, stated that in consequence of the absence of several members of that committee, it would be impossible for them to comply with the order then pending. A vote was taken, and the house refused to adopt the order. It was then suggested to me, by members all around the house, that the difficulty with the order grew out of the fact that the order could not be carried into effect if adopted, for the want of the presence of the members of the judiciary committee. Hence I offered the order that a special committee be substituted for the judiciary committee. I make this explanation for the purpose of acquitting myself from any purpose to show any disrespect for the committee on the judiciary, toward whom no member of the house has a higher respect than I have, and for whose members I feel under a profound obligation. And I will go so far as to say if it be not out of place, that I appreciate them so highly, that I would vote for the report they have made except for the fact that I have been deterred from so doing by considerations growing out of the magnitude of the expense which the system reported by them contemplates.

Mr. STIRLING. I move that the convention now proceed to consider the sections of this report which have been informally passed over.

The question being taken, the motion of Mr. STIRLING was agreed to.

The first section which had been informally passed over, being section three, was then read as follows:

"The judges shall be appointed, commissioned and designated as chief or associated justices, by the governor, with the advice and consent of the senate. Each judge shall hold his office during good behavior, or until he shall attain the age of sixty years, when, in the discretion of the governor, by and with the advice and consent of the senate, he may be re-appointed for a term not exceeding ten years, after which he shall not be re-appointed."

The pending question was upon the motion of Mr. THOMAS, [journal of proceedings, page 475,] to strike out all after the word "judges" in the first line, and insert,

"Of the several counties of this State, shall be elected by the qualified voters of the counties and the city of Baltimore, in the manner hereinafter prescribed."

Mr. ABBOTT submitted the following amendment:

Strike out the words "shall be appointed," and insert the words "when elected shall be."

Mr. BELT. Just at the time that we stopped discussion upon this report, I was trying to draw up an amendment which I proposed to offer, embodying what I would regard as a compromise of this question. It was to the effect that this report be recommitted to the committee with instructions from the convention to report a system of court of appeals, the judges of which shall be appointed by the governor. To that extent that would satisfy those who favor an appointive system. And also to report a system adapted to the counties, reserving to the people the privilege of electing their own judges. That I think would be a fair and proper compromise. I would rather have this report postponed for the present, in order to give me time to draw up a proposition in such a shape that I can get a vote of the convention upon it. I therefore move to postpone the further consideration of this report until to-morrow at 12 o'clock.

The question being taken upon the motion to postpone, it was not agreed to.

The question recurred upon the amendment submitted by Mr. ABBOTT.

Mr. STIRLING. The difficulty about that is, that there is nothing said in the report so far, except indirectly, that they shall be elected. There must be some indirect indication that they are to be elected. This section was intended by the committee to fix the mode of appointment.

Mr. HEBB. I move to strike out the words "shall be appointed, commissioned and designated as chief or associate justices by the governor, with the advice and consent of the senate," and insert in lieu thereof the following:

"Of the court of appeals shall be elected by the qualified voters of the State, and the governor, by and with the advice and consent of the senate, shall designate the chief justice, and the judge of the judicial circuits shall be elected by the qualified voters of their respective circuits."

Mr. THOMAS. That is exactly like my amendment, except a little change of phraseology. I therefore withdraw my amendment.

The amendment submitted by Mr. THOMAS was accordingly withdrawn.

Mr. ABBOTT also withdrew his amendment.

The question was then upon the amendment submitted by Mr. HEBB.

Mr. BELT. I propose to submit an amendment, which I have not drawn up in proper legal phraseology, for it is not in the form in which it ought to be submitted. It is a mere order that this particular branch of the report be recommitted to the committee with instructions. I think the committee will understand my phraseology, although from the haste in which I have drawn it I have not put it in the proper legal form in which I would like to have it. It will, however, at least test the sense of the convention upon the proposition. It is as follows:

"*Ordered*, That the report from the committee on the judiciary be recommitted to the committee on that subject, with the instruction of the convention to amend their report so as to embody the following principles, and to report on Friday at 11 o'clock.

"1. That there shall be a court of appeals to consist of —— judges, to be appointed by the governor from as many districts.

"2. That there shall be circuit courts, embracing three counties in each circuit, each county to elect one judge, but, as regards the more populous counties, the report of the committee must embrace the principle that a single judge in these counties shall, under laws to be passed, or rules of court to be adopted, have power to hold special terms of court as often as may be necessary to transact the business of those counties."

The PRESIDENT, The gentleman from Prince George's (Mr. Belt) can submit that as an independent proposition, not in the shape of an amendment to the report. The question now is upon the amendment of the gentleman from Allegany (Mr. Hebb.)

Mr. HEBB. The convention has already determined that the judges of the court of appeals shall be elected by the State at large. This proposition is to the same effect; it only contains the additional provision, permitting the governor in conformity with the provision in the present constitution, to designate by and with the advice and consent of the senate, which of the five judges shall be the chief justice. And it also proposes that the circuit judges shall be elected, as they now are by the people, instead of being appointed as provided by the section reported from the committee.

Mr. RIDGELY. Does the amendment prescribe any period of time for which these judges shall serve?

The PRESIDENT. That is left open.

Mr. THOMAS. By the twelfth section as reported from the committee, provision is made for the appointment of the judges of the court of appeals. When we reach that section we can determine how the judges are to be elected. I have submitted a substitute for that section which will be found on page 487 of the journal of proceedings, and which reads as follows:

"The court of appeals shall consist of a chief justice and four associate justices and for their selection the State shall be divided into four judicial districts. Allegany, Washington, Frederick, Carroll, Baltimore and Harford counties shall compose the first; Montgomery, Howard, Anne Arundel, Calvert, St. Mary's, Charles and Prince George's, the second; Baltimore city, the third; and Cecil, Kent, Queen Anne's, Talbot, Caroline, Dorchester, Somerset and Worcester, shall compose the fourth district; and the chief justice shall be elected by the qualified voters of the counties and the city of Baltimore on a general ticket.

"And one person from among those learned in the law, having been admitted to practice law in this State and who shall have been a citizen of this State at least five years, and above the age of thirty years at the time of his election, and a resident of the judicial district, or if chief justice a resident of the State as herein provided, shall be elected from each of said districts and the State, by the legal and qualified voters therein as a judge of said court of appeals, who shall hold his office for the term of fifteen years from the time of his election, or until he shall have attained the age of seventy years, whichever may first happen, and be re-eligible thereto until he shall have attained the age of seventy years, and not after, subject to removal for incompetency, wilful neglect of duty or misbehavior in office, on conviction in a court of law, or by the governor upon the address of the general assembly, two-thirds of the members of each house concurring in such address, and the salary of each of the judges of the court of appeals shall be four thousand dollars ($4,000) annually, and shall not be increased or diminished during their continuance in office, and no fees or perquisites of any kind shall be allowed by law to any of the said judges."

That substitute is still pending, as will be seen by reference to page 490 of the journal, where the following entry is made:

"The question then recurring upon the adoption of the amendment submitted by Mr. THOMAS,

"On motion of Mr. SMITH, of Carroll,

"The further consideration of section twelve was informally passed over."

It will be found, when we reach the portion of this report relating to the circuit courts that there is provision made in relation to the judges of the judicial circuits. It was for that reason I submitted the amendment to the third section, which was pending when this report was taken up this morning. I took it for granted that the convention by its action had already signified its intention to have an elective system of judiciary, and that when we reached those sections in their order we could provide for the election of the judges of the court of appeals for judicial districts, and the election of the judges of the circuit courts for their several circuits, or in any other mode the convention might prescribe. I therefore now move to strike out this third section.

Mr. HEBB. The convention has already stricken out the word "appointed" in the twelfth section, and inserted the words "elected by the qualified voters of the State."

Mr. THOMAS. I know that. But that was

done to perfect the section. My substitute for the entire section is still pending.

Mr. BELT. I desire to make a remark by way of personal explanation. I understand that the convention has decided generally as between an elective and an appointive system, to be applied to the whole judiciary of the State. I now make the inquiry of the chair for the purpose of obtaining information, if a vote can be had upon a proposition which shall compromise these two systems; allowing the judges of the court of appeals to be appointed and the other judges to be elected. I hold that that is the best system that we can adopt. I hold now, as I have always held, that the only evil connected with an elective system of the judiciary grows out of the large area to which the election applied. Generally in our State we have had the worst judges where they have had the largest constituencies. But if you adopt a system so as to embrace three counties in a circuit, and let each county elect its own judge——

Mr. STIRLING. I rise to a point of order. It will be found by reference to page 488 of the journal that the convention has determined that the judges of the court of appeals shall be elected by the qualified voters of the State on general ticket. I make the point that that vote must be reconsidered before the gentleman from Prince George's (Mr. Belt) will be in order with his proposition.

The PRESIDENT. The gentleman from Baltimore city (Mr. Stirling) is correct.

Mr. PARRAN. Is a motion to reconsider that vote now in order?

The PRESIDENT. Not at present. Section three is now under consideration, and must be disposed of in some way.

Mr. BELT. And the section being amendable is now open to any amendment which gentleman may choose to offer.

The PRESIDENT. Yes, sir. The question now is upon the amendment of the gentleman from Allegany (Mr. Hebb.)

Mr. CHAMBERS. And that very point is now decided. Is it in order to renew from time to time the very same proposition?

The PRESIDENT. If the convention choose they can affirm the same proposition in two places. The chair cannot control that.

Mr. CHAMBERS. Then I ask the yeas and nays upon the amendment. It brings up the question of appointment or election, and I want to be upon the record.

The yeas and nays were accordingly ordered.

Mr. BILLINGSLEY asked that the amendment be divided, which was ordered.

The first question was stated to be upon adopting the first branch of the amendment, as follows:

Insert after the word "judges" in the first line, the words "of the court of appeals shall be elected by the qualified voters of the State."

Mr. THOMAS. I desire to say a few words upon this question. If we are going to make a judicial system for the State which will be understood, it appears to me that the best way would be to divide this report into parts, under different headings, and then have all that relates to each part under its appropriate heading. For instance, have all relating to the court of appeals under the heading of "court of appeals;" everything relating to circuit courts under that heading; everything relating to the courts of Baltimore city, under that heading, &c. But the proposition of the gentleman from Allegany (Mr. Hebb) is a general proposition, applying not only to the court of appeals, but also to the circuit courts. He provides that the legal and qualified voters of the State shall elect the judges of the court of appeals; and the legal and qualified voters of the several circuits shall elect the judges of the respective circuits.

By reference to the present constitution you will find there no such provision as this third section. That article is divided into several parts, the sections relating to each part being under their appropriate heading, prescribing the qualifications of the judges, the tenure of office, salary, &c. Now, it appears to me, that that is the best and most simple way. When we come to the twelfth section of the report, the gentleman from Allegany (Mr. Hebb) can then get what he wants; for we can then provide whether the judges of the court of appeals shall be elected by the State at large, or by judicial districts; and when we come to the circuits, we can then determine whether the judges of the circuits shall be elected for ten years or for life, or during good behavior. But if we pass this general provision, we shall find ourselves all mixed up, and this report will have to be recommitted to the judiciary committee.

Mr. STIRLING. The views of my colleague (Mr. Thomas) would be very consistent with the action which the house refused to take last night. It was this difficulty which induced me last night to vote in favor of recommitting this report. The house having refused to do that, there is no other course now left except to amend the sections of this report as they stand. The judiciary committee, very wisely, I think, adopted a different arrangement from that in the present constitution. They have gone upon the principle of first grouping together all the general provisions of the judiciary system, and then arranged the special provisions under their appropriate headings.

If we adopt the principle of the present constitution, then we must have a recommitment. It is not now in order to offer a whole judiciary system as a substitute for this report. The section now under consideration, as reported by the committee, goes upon the basis of an appointive three-judge system, and generally prescribes the whole mode of the appointment of all the judges of the State. Following that precise mode of arrangement, and differing only in regard to the mode of selecting the judges, the gentleman from Allegany (Mr. Hebb) proposes to leave the general design of the committee in regard to the mode of arrangement to stand as it now is, but to make the section conform to the principle which the convention has adopted, by substituting the elective for the appointive system. If the convention wishes to adopt the arrangement of the present constitution, then they must adopt some way of getting rid of this whole report, and substituting something else in its place.

Mr. THOMAS. I desire to inquire whether the substitute which I offered for the twelfth section, and which will be found on page 487 of the journal, would be in order as a substitute for this section? It relates to the court of appeals, providing for dividing the State into districts, and confining the election of the judges to those districts respectively, instead of having them elected by the State at large as proposed by the gentleman from Allegany (Mr. Hebb.) The first branch of his proposition is that the judges of the court of appeals shall be elected by the qualified voters of the State.

The PRESIDENT. That has already been decided by a vote of the convention upon an amendment to the twelfth section.

Mr. THOMAS. Then why put it in here again?

The PRESIDENT. The chair has nothing to do with that.

Mr. STOCKBRIDGE. I suppose every one understood that it was necessary to make all the sections of this report correspond with the principle adopted by the convention. When we come to consider this third section, it is necessary to modify it. Although I do not agree to the policy of making our judiciary elective, yet as the convention has decided in favor of it, I do not propose to raise any objection to modifying the various sections so as to harmonize with the action of the convention.

The PRESIDENT. This is a mere general provision. It can make no difference if the general provisions are reasserted in the subdivisions.

Mr. SMITH, of Carroll. The convention has determined to elect the judges of the court of appeals by general ticket. But at the time that determination was expressed there was an amendment pending to that section. Therefore no final and determinate action has been taken upon that section by the convention; and when it comes up for final determination the amendment of the gentleman from Baltimore city (Mr. Thomas) will still be in order.

The PRESIDENT. Certainly; it will then be in order.

Mr NEGLEY. I suppose that any amendment that we should propose, which should contravene anything the convention has already determined upon, could not be received without a reconsideration of the action of the convention.

Mr. BERRY, of Prince George's. Would it be in order to move to postpone the section now under consideration until I can move a reconsideration of the vote by which the convention determined to elect the judges of the court of appeals on general ticket?

The PRESIDENT. It would be in order to move to pass over it informally.

Mr. BERRY, of Prince George's. Then I submit that motion.

The question was then taken upon the motion to pass over informally the third section of the report, and it was not agreed to.

The question then recurred upon the first branch of the amendment of Mr. HEBB.

Mr CHAMBERS. That involves two questions; first the principle of election, and next the election by the State at large. I am opposed to both.

The first branch of Mr. HEBB'S amendment is as follows:

Strike out all of the first sentence of the third section after the word "judges" and insert "of the court of appeals shall be elected by the qualified voters of the State."

Upon this question Mr. MILLER called for the yeas and nays, and they were ordered.

The question was then taken, by yeas and nays, and resulted—yeas 40, nays 24—as follows:

Yeas—Messrs. Abbott, Annan, Audoun, Cunningham, Cushing, Daniel, Dellinger, Ecker, Farrow, Galloway, Hebb, Hoffman, Hopkins, Hopper, Jones, of Cecil, Keefer, Larsh, Mayhugh, McComas, Mullikin, Murray, Negley, Nyman, Parker, Pugh, Purnell, Ridgely, Robinette, Russell, Schley, Smith, of Carroll, Sneary, Stirling, Swope, Sykes, Thomas, Thruston, Valliant, Wickard, Wooden—40.

Nays—Messrs. Goldsborough, President; Belt, Berry, of Prince George's, Billingsley, Blackiston, Bond, Briscoe, Brown, Chambers, Dent, Duvall, Edelen, Gale, Hodson, Hollyday, Horsey, Johnson, Lee, Mitchell, Miller, Morgan, Parran, Stockbridge, Turner—24.

The first branch of the amendment was accordingly adopted.

Pending the call of the yeas and nays, the following explanations were made by members, as their names were called:

Mr. BELT. I desire to say one word in explanation of my vote. I shall vote in the negative for the reason that being generally in favor of the appointive system of the judiciary, finding that this convention will not consent to the general appointment of the judges by the governor, I am willing to vote for the compromise plan which I submitted to the convention this morning, but which the chair has decided to be technically out of order. That plan is to have the judges of the court of appeals appointed by the governor, and the local judges elected by the people. For that reason I shall vote "no" upon this question.

Mr. BERRY, of Prince George's. Although I should much prefer to have all the judges elected by the people, yet I much prefer giving the power to the governor to appoint the judges than have them elected by the general vote of the State. I therefore vote "no."

Mr. CUSHING. Not having been present when the first vote was taken between an appointive and an elective judiciary, I wish to explain my vote on this question, and to say that I am entirely in favor of the appointive system throughout. But the house having decided by an overwhelming vote that it preferred the elective system, and not being at all desirous to disturb that result, I shall vote "aye" on this proposition, and shall vote for an elective system throughout, that question having been decided by the house.

Mr. DANIEL If the question was separated, and it simply the question of electing these judges, I should vote "no," because I am in favor of the appointive system for the court of appeals. But the two things being mixed up, and having to vote upon them both, I shall vote "aye," because if they are to be elected, I want them elected by general ticket.

Mr. PUGH. I am in favor of the appointive system. But the question between the appointive and the elective systems having been determined by the house, I shall interpose no objection to the perfecting of that system, and shall therefore vote "aye."

Mr. THOMAS. Being now, as I have always been, an advocate of the elective system for judges both of the court of appeals and the circuit courts, and being opposed, as I am, to the election of judges of the court of appeals by general ticket, I shall vote for the proposition of the gentleman from Allegany (Mr. Hebb,) because I do not want to vote against an elective system. But I do so with the understanding that I will meet the question concerning the court of appeals when the twelfth section comes up for consideration. I vote "aye."

Mr. THRUSTON. I am in favor of the appointive system throughout, but the house having decided in favor of an elective system, I shall no longer oppose it—and as the judges of the court of appeals are for and of the whole State, I think they should be elected by the voters of the whole State, I therefore vote "aye."

The question next being on the adoption of the second clause of the amendment, to wit:

"And the governor by and with the advice and consent of the senate, shall designate the chief justice."

It was adopted.

The question recurring upon the adoption of the third branch of the amendment, to wit:

"And the judge of the judicial circuits shall be elected by the qualified voters of their respective circuits."

It was adopted.

Mr. THOMAS. I move to strike out after the words "each judge shall hold his office" the words "during good behavior, or until he shall attain the age of sixty years, when, in the discretion of the governor, by and with the advice and consent of the senate, he may be re-appointed for a term not exceeding ten years, after which he shall not be re-appointed"—and insert the following in lieu thereof—"for ten years, removable for misbehavior, on conviction in a court of law, or by the governor upon the address of the general assembly, provided that two-thirds of the members of each house shall concur in such address."

Mr. STIRLING. The latter part of the amendment providing for removal of the judges, is provided for by section four of this report.

Mr. HEBB. I have an amendment which the gentleman from Baltimore city (Mr. Thomas) may accept. I move to strike out all after the words "each judge," and insert the following:

"Of the court of appeals, and of each judicial circuit shall hold his office for the term of ten years from the time of his election, or until he shall have attained the age of seventy years, whichever may first happen, and be re-eligible thereto until he shall have attained the age of seventy years and not after."

Mr. THOMAS. I will accept that amendment and withdraw the one I offered.

The question was upon the amendment of Mr. HEBB.

Mr. THRUSTON. I shall vote against that amendment, because I think the great evil of the elective system is the frequency of the election of judges. This bringing the judges frequently before the people to solicit a re-election, is I think the greatest objection to the old system. I prefer the provision of the report to this amendment

Mr. BERRY, of Prince George's. I move to strike out the word "ten" and insert the word "twenty" in the amendment.

Mr. STIRLING. I shall vote for the proposition of the gentleman from Prince George's (Mr. Berry) in preference to the proposition of the gentleman from Allegany (Mr. Hebb.) But I should certainly prefer to leave this matter as it now stands in the report. I have not been very fixed in my opinion in regard to the matter of appointing or electing our judges. I really do not think there is any great essential difference between the two systems. I think the vice of the systems is entirely in the tenure. Certainly, in courts having criminal jurisdiction, the result is that preceding an election the functions of the office bear directly upon a large class of persons who are interested in the re-election or the defeat of the judge. And there is a bonus offered to every judge to corrupt his moral integrity by administering the law to suit the people who he knows will have in their hands his nomination or election. There are a large class of persons, not criminals in the ordinary acceptation of the term, but who come under those provisions of law which are penal in their character, who wield a vast political influence. And it is a constant temptation to a judge to exercise the functions of his office just before an election so as to suit the views of those persons over whom he administers justice. It is true there may be just and pure men under such a system. But the system continually holds out temptations to corrupt their integrity. In other States that same thing has happened; and judges have studied the cases upon their dockets and allowed some of them to stand unprosecuted because they were seeking for votes at the approaching election. Now, if the people elect their own judges, there is no reason why the term of office should not be as provided in this report, so that the judge should be independent of any motive to exercise his functions without any reference to the views of the people.

I hardly suppose my view is going to prevail. But I wish to record my opinion upon this subject, and I shall vote in accordance with it.

Mr. Chambers. I am most happy to see some evidence of what I consider just sense upon the subject of judicial tenure. I shall consider it very much the happiest day that I have passed in this house, since the 27th of April, if the majority of this body could be brought to accord in the opinion, that the independent tenure of a judge, whether by appointment or election, during good behavior was the proper theory upon which to establish our judicial system. I do hope that reflection has brought to the minds of some gentlemen, a change of opinion upon this subject. With a view to ascertain that fact I propose to amend the proposition of the gentleman from Allegany (Mr. Hebb) now before the house, by striking out the tenure there contained, and inserting the words "during good behavior or until he shall attain the age of sixty-five years."

The President. That amendment is not now in order; there is already an amendment to an amendment pending.

Mr. Berry, of Prince George's. I propose to withdraw my amendment, so that the gentleman from Kent (Mr. Chambers) can submit the one he has indicated. I much prefer the life tenure, and will vote for it if I see the convention are in favor of it. But I am opposed to the judges being elected by the general ticket of the State. If that proposition is reconsidered, and the convention will allow each district of the State to elect its own judge by the vote of the district, I will go for the life tenure. I will withdraw my amendment for the present, so that the vote can be taken upon the amendment of the gentleman from Kent.

The amendment of Mr. Berry, of Prince George's, was accordingly withdrawn.

Mr. Chambers. I now submit the following amendment to the amendment of the gentleman from Allegany (Mr. Hebb:)

Strike out the words "for the term of ten years, from the time of his election, or until he shall have attained the age of seventy years, whichever shall first happen," and insert the words "during good behavior, or until he shall attain the age of sixty-five years."

Mr. Hebb. I desire to state why I offer the amendment which I have submitted. I have always been and am now in favor of an appointed judiciary system for the State. But the convention having determined in favor of the elective system, I thought it best that the judges of the court of appeals should be elected by general State ticket, one of the judges to come from each of the judicial districts. I offer this amendment because if the judges are to be elected by the people, I am opposed to their holding office for more than ten years; otherwise, if you happen to elect a bad judge you cannot get rid of him.

The question was upon the amendment of Mr. Chambers to the amendment of Mr. Hebb.

Mr. Thomas. In relation to the limitation of age, if this amendment should pass, I know at least one judge, one of the best judges upon the bench, who in the course of four or five years would be excluded from the bench. I do not consider that a man in growing old loses his mind, and becomes incapable of being a good judge. I think we have as many men of venerable age, who are good judges, as those who are young men. If it is the sense of the convention, I would vote to have no limitation in regard to age at all. If you elect your judges for ten years, if any one upon reaching the age of sixty or seventy years is not capable of fulfilling the duties of the office, the people need not re-elect him. I shall therefore support the proposition of the gentleman from Allegany (Mr. Hebb.) I think this matter of limiting the tenure of a judge because of age is wrong, not only in principle and theory, but in practice and experience. I have a letter in my possession now from a gentleman informing me that if this provision in relation to sixty or sixty-five years be adopted, one of the best judges we have in the State would thereby become incapacitated from serving on the bench.

Mr. Chambers. I ask the gentleman from

Baltimore city (Mr. Thomas,) whether in endeavoring to obtain the major proposition of independent tenure, it is not better to put it in such a shape as most likely to meet the apparent desire of the house. You must recollect one thing; some members object to going beyond sixty years. I am willing to fix the age just as gentleman please. The great purpose of my soul is to have an independent judiciary, a tenure during good behavior. The age is a secondary matter, which can be amended at any time. I will agree to seventy or ninety years, just as you please, so long as a man is fit for the position.

The question recurred upon the amendment of Mr. CHAMBERS to the amendment of Mr. HEBB.

Upon this question Mr. BERRY, of Prince George's, called for the yeas and nays, and they were ordered.

The question was then taken, by yeas and nays, and resulted—yeas 21, nays 44—as follows:

Yeas—Messrs. Berry, of Prince George's, Blackiston, Bond, Brown, Chambers, Cushing, Dent, Farrow, Hollyday, Hopkins, Horsey, Miller, Nyman, Parker, Pugh, Russell, Stirling, Stockbridge, Sykes, Thruston, Valliant —21.

Nays—Messrs. Goldsborough, President; Abbott, Annan, Audoun, Billingsley, Briscoe, Cunninghum, Daniel, Dellinger, Duvall, Ecker, Edelen, Gale, Galloway, Hatch, Hebb, Hoffman, Hopper, Johnson, Jones, of Cecil, Keefer, Kennard, Larsh, Lee, Mayhugh, Mitchell, Morgan, Mullikin, Murray, Negley, Parran, Purnell, Ridgely, Robinette, Schley, Smith, of Carroll, Smith, of Worcester, Sneary Swope, Thomas, Turner, Wickard, Wooden —44.

The amendment to the amendment was accordingly rejected.

Pending the call of the yeas and nays, the following explanations were made by members, as their names were called:

Mr. BILLINGSLEY. I am opposed to the general ticket system, although in favor of an elective system by districts. As a matter of compromise I would accept the proposition of the gentleman from Baltimore city (Mr. Thomas.) But I am utterly opposed to anything like a life tenure, and therefore vote "no" on this proposition.

Mr. BOND. I shall vote for the proposition limiting the term to sixty-five years, not because I think that is is a proper limitation, for my opinion is that men retain their mental and physical ability to seventy years of age perhaps as perfectly as to any other age.—I should therefore prefer the limitation to be seventy years. But inasmuch as sixty-five years approaches something near my views on that subject, I will vote "aye."

Mr. MAYHUGH. I am opposed to the appointive system, and to the life tenure. They are both obsolete ideas in this day; the people of this State preached their funeral sermon fourteen years ago. Being opposed to the appointive system, and seeing that those gentlemen who prefer that system are hanging on to whatever comes nearest to it, I shall vote "no."

Mr. BERRY, of Prince George's. I now renew my motion to strike out the word "ten," and insert the word "twenty" in the amendment of the gentleman from Allegany (Mr. Hebb.)

The question was upon the amendment to the amendment.

Mr. BERRY, of Prince George's, called for the yeas and nays upon this question, and they were ordered.

The question was then taken by yeas and nays, and resulted—yeas 25, nays 40—as follows:

Yeas—Messrs. Goldsborough, President; Abbott, Berry, of Prince George's, Blackiston, Bond, Chambers, Cushing, Daniel, Dent, Ecker, Farrow, Hodson, Hollyday, Hopkins, Horsey, Jones, of Cecil, Nyman, Parker, Pugh, Russell, Stirling, Stockbridge, Sykes, Thruston, Valliant—25.

Nays—Messrs. Annan, Billingsley, Briscoe, Brown, Cunningham, Dellinger, Duvall, Edelen, Gale, Galloway, Hatch, Hebb, Hoffman, Hopper, Johhson, Keefer, Kennard, Larsh, Lee, Mayhugh, McComas, Mitchell, Miller, Morgan, Mullikin, Murray, Negley, Parran, Purnell, Ridgely, Robinette, Schley, Smith, of Carroll, Smith, of Worcester, Sneary, Swope, Thomas, Turner, Wickard, Wooden—40.

The amendment to the amendment was accordingly rejected.

Pending the call of the yeas and nays, the following explanations were made by members, as their names were called:

Mr. MILLER. As I understand the proposition now before the house, it is an amendment to the proposition of the gentleman from Allegany (Mr. Hebb,) to make the tenure of office twenty years instead of ten. The vote will still have to be taken upon the proposition for ten years, if this is voted down. And if that proposition should be voted down, then the section would be left to stand as it now is; making the tenure of office of each judge during good behavior, or until he shall attain the age of sixty years.

The PRESIDENT. That is correct.

Mr. MILLER Then I vote "no."

Mr. NEGLEY. I agree that the too frequent election of judges is a great evil. I shall, therefore, vote for fifteen instead of ten years. I cannot vote for the proposition to make the tenure twenty years. I will vote for a proposition to make the tenure fifteen years, and that judges shall be ineligible for re-election. In that way you will take away all inducement to maladminister justice for political considerations. I therefore vote "no."

Mr. THRUSTON. I am in favor of a long

term of office, and therefore shall vote "aye" on this proposition. But if it is voted down I shall then submit an amendment to make the term six years; thinking the reason will apply with more force to six years than to ten years. If you elect a good judge you can re-elect him. If you elect a bad judge you can get rid of him. I vote "aye" on this proposition.

The question recurred upon the amendment of Mr. HEBB.

Mr. THRUSTON moved to amend the amendment by striking out "ten" and inserting "six."

Mr. STIRLING. I shall vote for that amendment. If it is rejected, then I shall move to insert "five" years. My opinion is that we should adopt the one extreme or the other.—If we are not to have a permanent tenure, then let us have a short one, so that we can put bad men out if they happen to get in.—We can induce a good man to take the office for six or five years, for if he should not be re-elected he can return to his practice. But ten years will be just enough to ruin his practice.

The question was upon the amendment of Mr. THRUSTON to the amendment of Mr. HEBB, to strike out "ten" and insert "six."

Upon this question Mr. CHAMBERS called for the yeas and nays, and they were ordered.

The question being then taken, by yeas and nays, it resulted—yeas 11, nays 53—as follows:

Yeas—Messrs. Annan, Carter, Cushing, Hodson, Keefer, Miller, Robinette, Stirling, Thruston, Turner, Wickard—11.

Nays—Messrs. Goldsborough, President; Abbott, Berry, of Prince George's, Billingsley, Blackiston, Bond, Briscoe, Brown, Chambers, Cunningham, Daniel, Dellinger, Dent, Duvall, Edelen, Farrow, Gale, Galloway, Hatch, Hebb, Hoffman, Hollyday, Hopkins, Hopper, Horsey, Johnson, Jones, of Cecil, Kennard, Larsh, Lee, Mayhugh, McComas, Mitchell, Morgan, Mullikin, Murray, Negley, Nyman, Parker, Parran, Pugh, Purnell, Ridgely, Russell, Schley, Smith, of Carroll, Smith, of Worcester, Sneary, Stockbridge, Swope, Sykes, Thomas, Valliant, Wooden—53.

The amendment to the amendment was accordingly rejected.

Mr. PUGH, when his name was called, said: I act upon principle, and try to get what I think is about right. After failing in that I am perfectly willing to take the best I can get. In the first place I tried to get a long tenure. Since I cannot get that I shall certainly vote "no" on this proposition.

The question again recurred upon the amendment of Mr. HEBB.

Mr. NEGLEY moved to amend the amendment by striking out the words "ten years from the time of his election, or until he shall have attained the age of seventy years, whichever may first happen, and be re-eligible thereto until he shall have attained the age of seventy years, and not after," and insert "fifteen years, and be ineligible for re-election."

Mr. BERRY, of Prince George's. There seems to be a diversity of opinion upon this subject. Every member of the convention seems to have his own peculiar ideas as to the proper tenure for the office of judge, how judges should be elected, and everything pertaining to that matter. I think we have voted upon a sufficient number of propositions now to indicate the sense of the convention upon those subjects. I therefore move that the whole report be referred back to the judiciary committee, with instructions to so amend the report as to meet the views of the convention, and to report by Tuesday next.

Mr. STIRLING. We spent two hours last night upon a similar proposition.

The PRESIDENT. The motion of the gentleman from Prince George's (Mr. Berry) cannot be entertained now without a suspension of the rules.

Mr. BERRY, of Prince George's. Then I move that the rules be suspended, in order to enable me to submit the motion to refer.

The question being taken, the motion to suspend the rules was not agreed to.

The question recurred upon the amendment of Mr. NEGLEY to the amendment of Mr. HEBB.

Mr. THRUSTON called for a division of the amendment to the amendment, which was ordered.

The first question was stated to be upon inserting the words "fifteen years," instead of "ten years."

Mr. PUGH. There seems to be a prevailing impression upon the minds of the majority of this convention, that we shall have an elective judiciary. To that I have no objection. But I think that the views of their constituents are not fully met by the adoption of that system by the convention. I do know that there are a great many people in the State of Maryland, and I know that all of the constituents whom I in part represent, with whom I have conversed, are in favor of the appointive system, for the reason that they think they can in that way better preserve the purity of the judiciary. It is with them, as it is with me, a very important matter to keep the judiciary as pure as possible. It is with them, as it is with me, a matter of conviction that one of the means by which the judiciary can be kept pure, is the extending their tenure, and removing them to that extent from the influences of political considerations.

Now I put the matter to gentlemen who have secured the elective system for their constituents, whether they cannot at least meet us half way upon this question, and extend the tenure of office to fifteen years. There can be no objection urged to that upon the ground that it is proper for the people to elect their judges; for they will still have that privilege, and then the views of those who think that the purity of the judiciary can be secured by a prolongation of the term of office, will to that extent at any rate, be met. For that reason I am in favor of the amendment submitted by the gentleman from Washington (Mr. Negley.)

Mr MILLER. Several gentlemen have got up here this morning, and said they were in favor of an appointed judiciary, and yet they voted for an elective judiciary. Yet enough members expressed themselves in favor of an appointed judiciary to have carried it, had they voted for it.

Mr. STIRLING. That remark applies to me to some extent, my preference being rather for an appointive system, though I have never been particular upon the subject. But I have been rather disposed to let the elective system stand, as I think it is the safest plan. Now the gentlemen on the minority side of the house, with very few exceptions, voted almost to a man for the elective system, and then turned around afterwards and voted for an appointed judiciary. Now I shall vote for an elective system hereafter altogether.

Mr. MILLER. Those remarks do not apply to me; I have voted for an appointive system out and out. And if those gentlemen who expressed themselves in favor of that system, and then, I do not care from what motive, voted against it, had voted for it, it would have been carried.

Mr. STIRLING. I do not impugn the motives of any one.

Mr. BERRY, of Prince George's. The remarks of the gentleman from Baltimore city (Mr. Stirling) apply to me. I assigned the reason why I changed my vote upon this question, and I thought gentlemen were satisfied about that. I am in favor of the election of the judges by the people, and in favor of the judges, both of the court of appeals and of the circuit courts being elected by the voters of the respective judicial districts and circuits. But I would sooner have an appointive system than have the judges of the court of appeals elected by a general ticket, and I shall vote for an appointive judiciary, rather than a system which elects those judges by the vote of the whole State, because the general ticket system would give the city of Baltimore with her large vote a controlling influence in the election of all the judges of that court.

Mr. CUSHING. The remarks of the gentleman from Anne Arundel (Mr. Miller) do very emphatically apply to me. I merely wish to say that my judgment upon the question of the number who would vote for the appointive system differs very widely from that of the gentleman. I exercised the right that I clearly possessed of not voting for that which I wished to have, when I did not think it would be carried.

Mr. PURNELL. I came here with the conviction upon my mind, and it has not been removed, that of the two the appointive was perhaps the best.

The PRESIDENT. This debate is proceeding in a manner not sanctioned by parliamentary law. Gentlemen must confine their remarks to the question before the house, unless they rise to a matter of personal explanation.

Mr. PURNELL. I only wish to define my position, so far as relates to the proposition now before the house, irrespective of what may have fallen from the gentleman from Anne Arundel (Mr. Miller) for his remarks have no personal application to myself. I was going on to say that I came here satisfied in my own mind that the appointive system was perhaps the true system.

The PRESIDENT. The gentleman is out of order. The appointive system is not now before the house. The question is upon the tenure of office.

Mr. PURNELL. I am willing to meet the gentleman from Cecil (Mr. Pugh,) and although I am in favor of limiting the tenure of office, and opposed *in toto* to the life tenure, yet if there is a disposition on the part of the convention to meet upon the basis of fifteen years, I am willing to forego my preference for ten years, and vote for the other. The chair rules me out of order so far as relates to the personal explanation; therefore I can say nothing upon that subject.

Mr. NEGLEY. The great objection that has always been urged against the elective system, is that by making a judge elective you hold out to him an inducement to maladminister justice, for the purpose of securing directly or indirectly, in some way, his re-election. Now if you make him ineligible for re-election you take away that temptation from him, and secure a system of judiciary as effectually free from political considerations as though you made it appointive. There is no difference so far as purity is concerned. Under the one system the judge is selected by the governor and the legislature, under the other he is selected immediately by the people. The one is that under which he holds his office by a life tenure; the other for fifteen years. I think fifteen years is not too long. It will take him four or five years before he will get properly into the harness, and I think the public interest would be subserved by keeping him there at least ten years after. If he is a bad judge, then that objection goes to the principle of electing judges at all. If you cannot trust the people to elect for fifteen years, neither can you trust them to elect for ten years. If the judge is bad he can be removed; there are ways provided for that in this constitution. So far as that objection is concerned, it does not reach this question.

Mr. THOMAS. I am opposed to the proposition of the gentleman from Washington

(Mr. Negley) and more especially the latter branch of it. The reasons he would give for voting for that proposition would be the reasons I should give for voting against it. He admits that the people are perfectly competent to elect a judge. If the people are competent to elect a judge once, they are competent to elect him twice. If they elect a competent judge, and he proves himself to be a competent judge at the end of the term, I am opposed to taking away from the people the right to re-elect him for another term. The whole of this power is lodged in the people. If the people go to work to elect a judge of your court, and elect an incompetent judge, at the end of his term they need not vote for him any more, and can turn him off the bench. If on the contrary they elect a good judge, whom perhaps at the time of his election they had not much confidence in, but who, from his position, and from the effect of listening to the argument of cases day after day, and from a latent ambition and determination to do his duty, has spurred himself up to make himself acquainted with the principles of law, and has become at the end of his term a good judge, the people have an undoubted right to re-elect him. But by the latter branch of the amendment of the gentleman from Washington county, the people would be prevented from re-electing him however good a judge he might prove to be at the end of his term.

Then I say that fifteen years is too long, if we should happen to elect a man who was not proper to be a judge—and I say that is nothing against the elective system, for it is just as likely that you would get an incompetent judge under the appointive system as under the elective system. I came here as a ten-year man; and I intend to stand by it. Of course if the convention choose to put it at fifteen years, subject to re-election, I shall be perfectly satisfied with it; but I am utterly opposed to the proposition to make him ineligible for re-election.

Mr. THRUSTON. I would like to throw out this suggestion, which may harmonize both sides; that we make the judge eligible for five years, and re-eligible for fifteen years thereafter; so that in case the judge should turn out to be a good judge, the people should have an opportunity of securing his services for twenty years; and if he was deficient in the qualities of a good judge, they would get rid of him in five years. I throw out the suggestion; and if it meets with favor I will move it as an amendment at the proper time.

Mr. NEGLEY demanded the yeas and nays, and they were ordered.

The question being taken, upon the first branch of the amendment—"fifteen years"—the result was—yeas 35, nays 30—as follows:

Yeas—Messrs. Goldsborough, President; Abbott, Belt, Blackiston, Bond, Brown, Carter, Chambers, Daniel, Dellinger, Farrow, Hoffman, Hollyday, Hopkins, Hopper, Horsey, Johnson, Jones, of Cecil, Larsh, Miller, Murray, Negley, Parker, Pugh, Purnell, Ridgely, Russell, Smith, of Carroll, Smith, of Worcester, Sneary, Stirling, Stockbridge, Sykes, Thruston, Valliant—35.

Nays—Messrs. Annan, Audoun, Billingsley, Briscoe, Cunningham, Dent, Duvall, Edelen, Gale, Galloway, Hatch, Hebb, Hodson, Keefer, Kennard, Lee, Mayhugh, McComas, Mitchell, Morgan, Mullikin, Nyman, Parran, Robinette, Swope, Thomas, Turner, Wickard, Wooden—30.

When their names were called,

Mr. BELT said: Being in favor of having the tenure for life or good behavior, I shall vote for "fifteen years" as the best we can get in the convention. I vote "aye."

Mr. MILLER said: Seeing very clearly from the indications that it is impossible to get a life tenure, or for good behavior, and that there is no prospect of that being carried, I vote "aye," not however committing myself to vote for the amendment after it shall be adopted.

The first branch of the amendment was accordingly adopted.

The question recurred upon the second branch of the amendment, "and be ineligible to re-election."

Mr. THOMAS demanded the yeas and nays, and they were ordered.

The question being taken, the result was—yeas 27, nays 37—as follows:

Yeas—Messrs. Abbott, Audoun, Billingsley, Briscoe, Brown, Chambers, Daniel, Ecker, Gale, Galloway, Hatch, Hodson, Hollyday, Hopper, Johnson, Jones, of Cecil, Mayhugh, McComas, Miller, Murray, Negley, Pugh, Purnell, Russell, Sneary, Turner, Valliant, Wickard—27.

Nays—Messrs. Goldsborough, President; Annan, Belt, Berry, of Prince George's, Blackiston, Bond, Carter, Cunningham, Dent, Duvall, Farrow, Hebb, Hoffman, Hopkins, Horsey, Keefer, Kennard, Larsh, Lee, Mitchell, Morgan, Mullikin, Nyman, Parker, Parran, Ridgely, Robinette, Schley, Smith, of Carroll, Smith, of Worcester, Stirling, Stockbridge, Swope, Sykes, Thomas, Thruston, Wooden—37.

The second branch of the amendment was accordingly rejected.

The question recurred upon the amendment submitted by Mr. HEBB as amended.

Mr. STIRLING moved to add the words "and until the election and qualification of his successor."

The amendment was agreed to.

Mr. THOMAS submitted the following amendment to the amendment:

Strike out the words "or until he shall have attained the age of seventy years, whichever may first happen."

The amendment was rejected.

The question then recurring upon the adoption of the amendment submitted by Mr. HEBB, as amended, it was agreed to.

No further amendment was offered to the third section.

OFFICERS OF THE COURTS.

The seventh section, which had been informally passed over, was read as follows:

"Sec. 7. The judge or judges of any court may appoint such subordinate officers for their respective courts as may be found necessary, but none other; and no crier shall be appointed in any court, but clerks or assistant clerks, sheriffs or their deputies, or bailiffs, as the court directs, shall, without additional compensation, perform the duties heretofore performed by criers."

Mr. STIRLING. I move to strike out that section. The court have the power to do that without this section; and the only effect of the section is to abolish the criers, which I really do not see any necessity for, while I see reasons against it. I think as a general principle that we ought not to turn people out of office.

Mr. STOCKBRIDGE. One word with reference to that, rather by way of explanation than argument; because I do not propose to argue any of these propositions. It is not the law of the State at this time, with reference to all the subordinate officers, that they are appointed by the judges; and in some of the counties they are appointed in a different manner. The first part of the section introduces a uniform system throughout the State, whereas it is not now uniform.

The second part strikes out of existence in this State an office which has become obsolete and useless, in the apprehension at least of a part of the committee. There was a time when that office was of much importance, in the early stages of the existence of the courts, when there were proclamations and calls, and when they had heralds and various paraphernalia that have now gone out of use. They are now utterly useless appendages to the court in every instance. They have been abolished utterly in nearly all the orphans' courts of this State already; although they are of as much importance and use there as elsewhere. I am not aware that there is a county in the State which retains a crier in its orphans' courts. I know of no reason why they should be retained in other courts more than in that. It is true that in one instance, in Kent county I believe, certain special duties, by act of assembly have been devolved upon the crier; he having been made keeper of the public buildings also; but that is an anomaly; and it is not so in other cases.

It is a very considerable expense, more or less, in all the counties. The lowest salary I am aware of, fixed for the crier of any court, is $75 a year. From that it ranges up, there being certain fees received also, until the highest salary received by law is $1,500 a year. I am not aware that the State, or that suitors in the courts get any equivalent for this expense. The expense of that office in the State must amount to some $12,000 or $15,000 a year; it cannot be under that; besides the perquisites of the crier not included in the fixed salary. Believing it is a sufficient object to save this amount of money, and to save also the fees charged to suitors, this section is reported as it stands. In my opinion, it ought to be adopted.

Mr. CHAMBERS. What is the salary of the crier in Baltimore city?

Mr. STOCKBRIDGE. It is impossible to answer precisely. The salary is $1,500 a year, and the fees. In the criminal court in Baltimore there is no fixed salary allowed. He draws his compensation, whatever it may be, from the city treasury, from time to time. It has ranged from $3,000 to upwards of $5,000. I have not the data to state the exact amount. It is more than that of the judge, uniformly; a good deal more.

Mr. BELT. I desire to say in connection with the remarks of the gentleman from Baltimore city, that I voted to strike this section out; not that I do not agree with my friend from Baltimore city, the chairman of the judiciary committee (Mr. Stockbridge,) that the office of crier ought to be abolished; but because I thought that this was a matter which would better be referred to the legislature; and because I am opposed to tying up the hands of the legislature as to the establishment and abolition of these petty offices. I think we shall do best to refer it there; and therefore I shall support the motion to strike this section from the constitution.

The motion to strike out the section was agreed to—ayes 31, noes 26.

TRIAL OF CAUSES.

The ninth section, which had been informally passed over, was taken up and read, as amended, as follows:

"Sec. 9. The legislature shall provide for the trial of causes in case of the disqualification of all of the judges of the circuit, but the parties to any cause may, by consent, appoint a proper person to try said cause, or may try any cause before the court without the intervention of a jury."

The pending question was stated upon the amendment submitted by Mr. NEGLEY, to strike out in line two "all of the judges," and to insert "any judge."

Mr. HEBB. That was taken up again in the evening, and on motion of Mr. THRUSTON the following section was substituted, as appears from page 479 of the journal:

"The general assembly shall provide for the trial of causes in case of the disqualification of all of the judges of the circuit to hear and determine the same, but in case of such disqualification, the parties thereto may, by consent, appoint a person to try the same; and the parties to any cause may submit the same to the court for determination without the aid of a jury."

Mr. STIRLING. That is correct. I recollect that it was decided that when we should have determined whether to have three judges or one, we would take it up again. That question has not yet been decided

Mr. NEGLEY. I move that it be informally passed over until we determine the number of judges.

The motion was agreed to.

COURT OF APPEALS.

The twelfth section which had been passed over informally, was taken up and read, as amended, as follows:

"Sec. 12. The court of appeals shall consist of a chief justice and four associate justices, and for their selection the State shall be divided into five judicial districts as follows, viz: Worcester, Somerset, Dorchester, Talbot, Caroline, Queen Anne, Kent, and Cecil counties, shall compose the first district; Harford and Baltimore counties, and the first seven wards of Baltimore city, shall compose the second district; Baltimore city, except the first seven wards, shall compose the third district; Allegany, Washington, Frederick, Howard and Carroll counties, shall compose the fourth district; St. Mary's, Charles, Anne Arundel, Calvert, Prince George's and Montgomery counties, shall compose the fifth district; and one of the judges of the court of appeals shall be elected from each of said districts, by the qualified voters of the whole State."

Mr. THOMAS. The pending question is upon my amendment to the section, contained on page 487 of the journal.

The amendment submitted by Mr. THOMAS was read as follows:

Strike out all after the word "the," in the first line, and insert the following:

"The court of appeals shall consist of a chief justice and four associate justices and for their selection the State shall be divided into four judicial districts. Allegany, Washington, Frederick, Carroll, Baltimore and Harford counties, shall compose the first; Montgomery, Howard, Anne Arundel, Calvert, St. Mary's, Charles and Prince George's, the second; Baltimore city, the third; and Cecil, Kent, Queen Anne's, Talbot, Caroline, Dorchester, Somerset and Worcester, shall compose the fourth district; and the chief justice shall be elected by the qualified voters of the counties and the city of Baltimore on a general ticket.

"And one person from among those learned in the law, having been admitted to practice law in this State and who shall have been a citizen of this State at least five years, and above the age of thirty years at the time of his election, and a resident of the judicial district, or if chief justice a resident of the State as herein provided, shall be elected from each of said districts and the State, by the legal and qualified voters therein as a judge of said court of appeals, who shall hold his office for the term of fifteen years from the time of his election or until he shall have attained the age of seventy years, whichever may first happen, and be re-eligible thereto until he shall have attained the age of seventy years, and not after, subject to removal for incompetency, wilful neglect of duty or misbehavior in office, on conviction in a court of law, or by the governor upon the address of the general assembly, two-thirds of the members of each house concurring in such address, and the salary of each of the judges of the court of appeals, shall be four thousand dollars ($4,000) annually, and shall not be increased or diminished during their continuance in office, and no fees or perquisites of any kind shall be allowed by law to any of the said judges."

The PRESIDENT. There is this difficulty, that the gentleman has embraced in his proposition what the convention has already passed upon in a different section. The latter branch of the proposition prescribes the tenure of office and the age of the judge. The convention has already passed upon that proposition in the third and fourth sections.

Mr. THOMAS. The latter part of it is embraced in the third section; but not the former part. I will omit the latter part, and modify my motion to strike out all after the word "the," in the first line and insert the following:

"Court of appeals shall consist of a chief justice and four associate justices and for their selection the State shall be divided into four judicial districts. Allegany, Washington, Frederick, Carroll, Baltimore and Harford counties, shall compose the first; Montgomery, Howard, Anne Arundel, Calvert, St. Mary's, Charles and Prince George's, the second; Baltimore city, the third; and Cecil, Kent, Queen Anne's, Talbot, Caroline, Dorchester, Somerset and Worcester, shall compose the fourth district; and the chief justice shall be elected by the qualified voters of the counties and the city of Baltimore on a general ticket."

That makes five judges of the court of appeals, the chief justice to be elected by general ticket, and the other four in their several districts.

Mr. BERRY, of Prince George's. I do not understand that the amendment states how the four judges shall be elected. It says that the chief justice shall be elected by the qualified voters of the counties and the city of Baltimore on a general ticket; but does not say how the associate judges shall be elected.

The PRESIDENT. The gentleman has stated that the associate judges will be elected from their several districts, and the chief justice on general ticket.

Mr. BERRY, of Prince George's. That is not so stated in the amendment.

The PRESIDENT. If the gentleman from Baltimore proposes to alter the mode of election, the convention having decided to elect all of the judges by the qualified voters of the whole State, it will be proper to reconsider that vote.

Mr. THOMAS. I will withdraw my amendment then.

Mr. BERRY, of Prince George's. I move to reconsider the vote by which it was determined that the judges should be elected by the people. I shall go for an appointive system. I certainly voted for the elective system.

The PRESIDENT. The gentleman can move to reconsider any part of this section, which is now pending.

Mr. BERRY, of Prince George's. Then I move to reconsider the vote that these judges should be elected by the qualified voters of the whole State.

Mr. DANIEL. The gentleman voted against that.

The PRESIDENT. The gentleman must have voted in the affirmative on the particular amendment he moves to reconsider.

Mr. DENT. He did vote in the affirmative on striking out "appointed" and inserting "elected."

Mr. BERRY, of Prince George's. I move to reconsider that vote.

The motion was duly seconded.

Mr. HEBB. If that is carried the gentleman will not effect his object; for the convention have decided in another section that judges shall be elected by general ticket.

Mr. BERRY, of Prince George's. I intend to follow up this motion.

Mr. STIRLING moved a call of the convention;

The motion being sustained,

The roll was called, and the following members responded:

Messrs. Goldsborough, President; Abbott, Annan, Audoun, Berry, of Prince George's, Billingsley, Blackiston, Briscoe, Brown, Carter, Chambers, Cunningham, Cushing, Daniel, Dellinger, Dent, Ecker, Farrow, Gale, Galloway, Hatch, Hebb, Hodson, Hoffman, Hollyday, Hopkins, Hopper, Horsey, Johnson, Jones, of Cecil, Keefer, Kennard, Larsh, Lee, Mayhugh, McComas, Mitchell, Miller, Morgan, Mullikin, Murray, Negley, Nyman, Parker, Parran, Pugh, Purnell, Ridgely, Robinette, Russell, Schley, Smith, of Carroll, Smith, of Worcester, Sneary, Stirling, Stockbridge, Swope, Sykes, Thomas, Thruston, Valliant, Wickard, Wooden—63.

On motion of Mr. GALLOWAY,

Further proceedings under the call were dispensed with.

The question then recurring upon the motion of Mr. BERRY, of Prince George's, to reconsider.

Mr. BERRY, of Prince George's demanded the yeas and nays, and they were ordered.

The question being taken, the result was —yeas 23, nays 43—as follows:

Yeas—Messrs. Belt, Berry, of Prince George's, Billingsley, Blackiston, Bond, Briscoe, Brown, Chambers Daniel, Dent, Edelen, Gale, Hodson, Hollyday, Horsey, Johnson, Lee, Mitchell, Miller, Morgan, Parran, Pugh, Turner—23.

Nays—Messrs. Goldsborough, President; Abbott, Annan, Audoun, Carter, Cunningham, Cushing, Dellinger, Duvall, Ecker, Farrow, Galloway, Hatch, Hebb, Hopkins, Hopper, Jones, of Cecil, Keefer, Kennard, Larsh, Mayhugh, McComas, Mullikin, Murray, Negley, Nyman, Parker, Purnell, Ridgely, Robinette, Russell, Schley, Smith, of Carroll, Smith, of Worcester, Sneary, Stirling, Swope, Sykes, Thomas, Thruston, Valliant, Wickard, Wooden—43.

When their names were called,

Mr. ABBOTT said: I was the mover, I believe, of the amendment to strike out "appointed," and insert "elected." I did it from principle; from the principle that our government consists of three separate and distinct branches, legislative, executive and judicial; and feeling that it was of the utmost importance to keep these as separate and distinct as possible from each other, I made that motion and voted for it; and I shall now vote against the reconsideration—"no."

Mr. AUDOUN said: I am here representing a portion of the people of Baltimore, instructed by them to vote for an elective system. As my course in life has been to obey the will of my constituents, I vote "no."

Mr. BILLINGSLEY said: I am here from St. Mary's, without any instructions. I was opposed to the appointment by the governor; but I am much more opposed to the general ticket system for the judiciary; and believing it a greater evil than the executive appointment, I shall vote to reconsider. I vote "aye."

Mr. DENT said: I voted for the motion to strike out "appointed" and insert "elected," when the motion was made, under the impression that the convention would allow each district to elect the judge which it was decided should come from that district. It was afterwards, however, so amended that the judges of all the districts were to be elected by general ticket throughout the State.—Preferring that there should be an appointment by the governor, rather than a general election by general ticket, I now vote for the reconsideration in order to substitute appointment in place of election by the people; "aye."

Mr. EDELEN said: The reasons stated by the gentleman from St. Mary's (Mr. Dent) are precisely those that govern me in voting "aye."

Mr. NEGLEY said: The members of the court of appeals being State officers, I have always believed that the State had a right to elect them by general ticket. This convention has solemnly so determined. I am willing to abide by that decision. I therefore vote "no."

Mr. PUGH. I am in favor of the appointive system for the judiciary. For that reason I vote for it, without any hope at all of its being carried. I willingly submit to the decision of the majority; but being in favor of that kind of system for the judiciary, I vote "aye."

The motion to reconsider did not prevail.

No further amendment was offered to section twelve.

OFFICERS OF THE COURTS.

Mr. RIDGELY. Before we pass away from part three, I desire to move as an additional section, the following:

"Section —. The judge or judges of any court may appoint such officers for their respective courts, as may be found necessary, and it shall be the duty of the general assembly to prescribe by law a fixed compensation for all such officers."

I do not desire to argue that amendment; but I will simply submit for the consideration of the house the reasons which induce me to offer the amendment. When the section which was stricken out, on the motion of the gentleman from Baltimore city (Mr. Stirling,) was under consideration, the gentleman from Prince George's suggested that it was an appropriate subject for legislation. With the view to meet that suggestion, I have made it the duty, in the section I have offered, of the general assembly to fix the compensation for these officers. In my own county there are officers appointed by the courts, whose fees of office are far greater than those of the judge himself, in my county. I consider the office very much a sinecure. At least there is comparatively no equivalent whatever for the service performed. I do not think it is right, as these expenses are to come out of our county treasury, as the counties have to levy for the expense of these officers, whose duties are comparatively very light, that they should be permitted to receive a compensation so far beyond the value of the services which they perform. I therefore propose that it shall be the duty of the legislature to fix the value of these services, and to prescribe by law what compensation this officer shall receive. I will not argue the matter; but simply ask that the yeas and nays be taken upon the proposed section.

The yeas and nays were ordered.

The question being taken, the result was —yeas 54, nays 11—as follows:

Yeas—Messrs. Goldsborough, President; Abbott, Annan, Audoun, Belt, Berry, of Prince George's, Billingsley, Blackiston, Bond, Carter, Chambers, Cunningham, Daniel, Dent, Duvall, Ecker, Edelen, Farrow, Galloway, Hatch, Hebb, Hodson, Hoffman, Hollyday, Hopkins, Hopper, Horsey, Johnson, Jones, of Cecil, Kennard, Larsh, Mayhugh, McComas, Mitchell, Miller, Morgan, Murray, Negley, Nyman, Parker, Pugh, Purnell, Ridgely, Russell, Smith, of Carroll, Smith, of Worcester, Snearr, Swope, Sykes, Thomas, Turner, Valliant, Wickard, Wooden—54.

Nays—Messrs. Briscoe, Brown, Cushing, Keefer, Lee, Mullikin, Parran, Robinette, Schley, Stirling, Thruston—11.

The section was accordingly adopted.

LEAVE OF ABSENCE.

Mr. DANIEL. I ask leave of absence for this evening, having important business in Baltimore.

Leave was granted.

Mr RIDGELY. I ask similar leave for this night only.

Leave was granted.

Mr. BERRY, of Prince George's. I ask leave of absence for a few days. I am unwell.

Leave was granted

Mr. WICKARD. I ask leave of absence for to-night.

Leave was granted.

Mr. STOCKBRIDGE asked leave of absence for a few days.

Leave was granted.

Mr. MULLIKIN subsequently asked leave of absence for to-morrow.

Leave was granted.

FILING WRITTEN OPINIONS.

Mr. MILLER. I move that the convention recur to section fifteen.

The motion was agreed to, and the section was read as follows:

"Section 15. Any three of the judges of the court of appeals may constitute a quorum, but no cause shall be decided without the concurrence of at least three judges in the decision, and in every case decided, an opinion in writing shall be filed within six months after the argument or submission of the cause, and the judgment of the court shall be final and conclusive."

Mr. MILLER. I move to amend the fourth line by striking out "six" and inserting "three;" so that the judges of the court of appeals may be required to furnish an opinion in writing within three months after the argument.

Mr. THRUSTON. I am in favor of that motion. I think three months is abundant time.

The amendment was agreed to.

CIRCUIT COURTS.

The convention resumed the consideration of section nineteen, which had been passed over informally, and which was read as follows:

"Sec. 19. The State shall be divided into eight judicial circuits, in manner following: The counties of St. Mary's, Charles and Prince George's shall constitute the first circuit. The counties of Calvert, Anne Arundel and Montgomery, the second. The counties of Allegany, Washington and Frederick, the third. The counties of Baltimore, Howard and Carroll, the fourth. The counties of Harford, Cecil and Kent, the fifth. The counties of Queen Anne's, Talbot and Caroline, the sixth. The counties of Dorchester, Somerset and Worcester, the seventh. And the city of Baltimore, the eighth."

The pending question was upon the following amendment submitted by Mr. Hebb:

Strike out all after the word "the," in the first line and insert:

"State shall be divided into twelve judicial circuits, in manner following: The counties of St. Mary's, Charles and Prince George's, shall constitute the first circuit; the counties of Anne Arundel, Calvert and Montgomery, the second; the county of Frederick, the third; the county of Washington, the fourth; the county of Allegany, the fifth; the counties of Carroll and Howard, the sixth; the county of Baltimore, the seventh; the counties of Harford and Cecil, the eighth; the counties of Kent, Queen Anne's and Talbot, the ninth; the counties of Caroline and Dorchester, the tenth; the counties of Somerset and Worcester, the eleventh; and the city of Baltimore, the twelfth."

Mr. Miller. Mr. President——

Mr. Thomas. I move the amendment on page one of the printed amendments.

Mr. Miller. I move to strike out the section and to insert the provision on page 18 of the amendments.

Mr. Thomas. I submit that my amendment was offered first. The only difference between the amendment of the gentleman from Allegany and my own is that he strikes out all after the word "the" in the first line, while my amendment is to strike out and insert. He makes twelve circuits, and my amendment makes nine.

The amendment was as follows:

Strike out the nineteenth section and insert the following:

"Sec. 19. The State shall be divided into nine judicial circuits, in manner and form following, to wit: St. Mary's, Charles and Prince George's shall be the first; Anne Arundel, Howard, Calvert and Montgomery shall be the second; Frederick and Carroll shall be the third; Washington and Allegany shall be the fourth; Baltimore city shall be the fifth; Baltimore county shall be the sixth; Harford, Cecil and Kent shall be the seventh; Queen Anne's, Talbot and Caroline shall be the eighth; Dorchester, Somerset and Worcester shall be the ninth; and there shall be elected as hereinafter directed for each of said judicial circuits, except the fifth, one person from among those learned in the law, and shall have been a citizen of the State at least five years, and above the age of thirty years, at the time of his election, and a resident of the judicial circuit, to be judge thereof, and the said judges shall be styled circuit judges, and shall respectively hold a term of their courts at least twice in each year, or oftener if required by law, in each county composing their respective circuits, and said courts shall be called circuit courts for the county in which they may be held, and shall have and exercise in the counties of this State, all power, authority and jurisdiction which the circuit courts of this State now have and exercise, or which may hereafter be prescribed by law, and the said judges in their respective circuits shall have and exercise all the power, authority and jurisdiction of a court of chancery."

Mr. Miller. I propose mine as a substitute for the whole section.

The President. The chair first recognized the gentleman from Anne Arundel (Mr. Miller,) whose amendment is first in order.

The amendment submitted by Mr. Miller, of which notice had been given by Mr. Clarke, was read as follows:

Strike out section 19, and insert:

"Sec. 19. There shall be a judge for each county in the State, who shall be elected by the legal and qualified voters of the several counties. He shall be a resident for one year in the county for which he may be elected next before the time of his election, and shall reside in the county for which he is elected, while he continues to act as judge."

Mr. Thomas. That brings up the question whether there shall be one judge in each county in the State. I have no remarks to submit on that subject, with the exception of this, that I am opposed to the election of one judge in each county. I think the system will be too expensive, and I do not think the counties want one judge in each county. In some counties I do not think there is business enough for one judge. I think it is better to break up the State into circuits. Some circuits may be too large and others too small; but we can enlarge those that are not large enough, and contract those that are too large.

Mr. Berry, of Prince George's. I am in favor of the amendments proposed by my colleague (Mr. Clarke.) I understand that it is proposed to have one judge in each county, who shall be chief judge of the orphans' court and shall have equity jurisdiction in the county, and preside with three other judges of his district to discharge the common law business of the several counties composing the circuit. I think it would be highly proper that we should have this change. It would be the means of facilitating the business in the various counties of the State. As to the cost, I will state to gentlemen that if Baltimore city will undertake to pay the costs of her judicial system, each county in the State will undertake to pay the cost of its judicial system. I do not consider that that question ought to be brought into consideration at all, when we consider the importance of the matter upon which we are now deliberating. It is a matter in which the citizens of the several counties in the State are deeply interested.

As we are now organized, in our circuit composed of the counties of Charles, St. Mary's and Prince George's, we have only one judge on our bench. He has jurisdiction not only of the common law but the equity business of the several counties. He holds two common law terms in each county, and two equity terms. We have then three judges elected for the orphans' court of the several counties, from the people. My experience in the practice of the law has been that the orphans' courts in the several counties are the most important courts we have. Cases arise in the orphans' courts of the counties, involving more indirect points of law, than arise in the circuit court in the trial of cases of *nisi prius*.

I have known cases to arise, where we in Prince George's county wanted to secure an injunction to prevent a sale, or to prevent a trespass, such as could not be remedied by an action of damages. I have had myself to ride some forty odd miles in the winter season to procure an injunction in an important case. Give us a judge for each county, and vest him with equity jurisdiction, and make him chief judge of the orphans' court, and associate judge of the circuit court of the district, and then you bring justice home to the people. If you require him to reside in or about the county town, he is accessible to every citizen of the county whenever a case of emergency may arise.

I had proposed to let Baltimore city settle upon her own judicial system. I thought it was a matter of so much importance to the gentlemen of Baltimore city, that they would be willing that the counties should agree what system they should have.

Mr. Thomas. I am willing.

Mr. Berry, of Prince George's. If the gentlemen from Baltimore city will select their own judicial system, suited to their own people, I am willing to go for it; and I think the same principle should actuate them toward the counties. We ought to have a change in the system. I say that it is almost a denial of justice to the people of the several counties, in many cases, as it now is. This is a highly important change; and I do hope that the members of this convention will consider it. Particularly do I address myself to the members of the various counties of the State. I know there are many members representing counties much more thickly populated than mine. But in my small county I have seen the workings of the present system to be injurious to the people. If you give us one judge, the legislature may prescribe that they may hold four terms in common law.—They may sit in chambers in the discharge of equity business, and act as the old chancellor did in the passage of orders, and trial of cases of injunction, matters most important to the citizen.

I say that the members of the various counties ought to take it into consideration; and I think if they will think of it properly they will determine with me that the change is an important and a proper one. Give us a judge for each county of the State. Give him equity jurisdiction in the county. Make him the presiding judge of the orphans' court of the county; and let him preside as associate judge of the circuit. Then he will not only have enough to do, but the wants of the citizens of the county will be fully supplied. I do hope that gentlemen from the city of Baltimore will not oppose the wants of the people of the counties in this respect. We are willing to give them their own system. The question of cost should not be taken into consideration at all. If it is, I tell them that the counties are willing to pay the cost of their own system if Baltimore city will do the same. I hope that this amendment will be adopted. I think it is a change that meets the wants of the people, and will be a great improvement upon the present system. I want the convention to understand that these are mere suggestions of mine. I said the other day I should say nothing except in the way of suggestion; and I hope they will take it as suggestion.

Mr. Bond. I think there can be no question that a judge in each county would be a great convenience to the people. The only objection in the world there can be to it is the additional expense. Upon the question of the judge having employment, if he is given the whole jurisdiction of testamentary affairs, and the orphans' court entirely abolished, as I think it ought to be, the whole equity jurisdiction, the whole testamentary jurisdiction, and the whole common law jurisdiction will furnish employment enough even in the small counties for any one judge. In fact a great deal of expense will be saved by having a judge resident in the counties. There are numerous cases where men are arrested and committed to prison and obliged to remain there a considerable length of time because there is no judge there to hear their case. I know that in some counties large costs have arisen in that way, which would not arise if there were a judge resident in the county, for there would be no delay whatever.

Upon the question of giving to the judge in the counties orphans' court jurisdiction, testamentary jurisdiction, I know there are very many in the State who are in favor of this old institution of the orphans' court. My own experience is this, that unless it is in some few cases where the gentleman elected or appointed orphans' court judge has been a long time in office, or repeatedly appointed, the register of wills is almost uniformly the judge of the orphans' court. In the transaction of business, and even in matters where he has no jurisdiction by law, the judges of the orphans' court constantly appeal to the register of wills to know what they shall do in this case or in that case; so that in fact they are in most cases a mere fifth wheel to a coach. If the orphans' court is abolished, it will be a large saving of expense, so far as their salary is concerned. If the judge is resident in the county, there will be a large saving of expense in the item I have mentioned, in regard to the speedy hearing of criminal cases.

The legislature might provide for these matters; and might even provide, if necessary for extending the jurisdiction of the register of wills. He might be given jurisdiction in all matters relating to apprentices and some other matters, that would render the orphans' court totally insignificant. As we all know, unless they have had any considerable experience, the register of wills is judge of the orphans' court *per se*, because they are obliged to rely upon him. If we make the judge of the circuit court judge of the orphans' court, there is no necessity for associate judges of the orphans' court. In this way the expense would be in some measure compensated for in giving a judge to each county.

Besides the argument mentioned by my friend from Prince George's (Mr. Berry,) it is a great convenience to the people to have a judge resident on the spot, in a case of *mandamus*, or cases of that sort. These are my reasons for advocating, at the proper time and place, the abolishment of the orphans' court, and the extension of the jurisdiction of the register of wills. I think we shall have abundant employment for a judge in each county.

Mr. Mayhugh. It would appear from the efforts made here to create new offices in the judiciary system of the State, that the people were really wild upon the subject in the counties and the city of Baltimore. It would really appear to the stranger coming into this convention, that the people were holding meetings and sending memorials to this convention to induce us to make important changes. In my county the question has been scarcely mooted in my presence. Now and then you would hear a man speaking of the judiciary system, and some little alterations or changes that ought to be made in it; but as a whole, the people of the county have rested perfectly satisfied with the judiciary under the old system. In my own opinion, it is a question of extravagance, and not of the retrenchment which should be made at the proper time. I believe that the people have no desire to create new offices, or to go into extravagance in this state of chaos and confusion. The people are already burdened with taxes. If we adopt the amendment under consideration, by which we create from twenty to twenty-five new offices, having already created five, making thirty, the convention will have incurred an expense of at least fifty or seventy-five thousand dollars annually. It is upon this ground that I oppose the amendment.

And not only upon that; for it is paying men, really, for doing nothing. The judges of the judicial districts in all the counties have been doing the work. They are able and competent for the task. Why then should we separate the judicial districts, and give one judge to each county, doubling the expense, when there is no more labor to be performed?

I oppose the amendment upon these two grounds; in the first place, I say it is extravagant; and in the second place, I say it is absolutely paying men for doing nothing. If you will decrease their salaries to $1,000 each, it might meet that objection; but that you could not do simply because you could not secure the learning, talent and ability, necessary for the position. Therefore I oppose the amendment, and hope there is no disposition upon the part of the convention to pass such an amendment.

Mr. Schley. I understood the gentleman from Prince George's who addressed the convention just now (Mr. Berry,) to express a willingness that the counties should pay the expenses of their courts I therefore wish to offer an amendment to the proposed amendment, to be added to the end thereof, in the following words:

"The salary of the circuit judges shall be levied and paid by the respective counties in which they act."

My object in doing so has been already indicated by some of the gentlemen who have addressed the convention. The great objection to the multiplication of the number of the judges, has been the enormous expense that is imposed upon the State. I find by statement A, of the comptroller's report, for illustration, taking several of the amounts of the levy of 1863 for the different counties, that the total assessment or levy upon the assessed value of the real and personal property of St. Mary's county, is $9,028.71; while in my county there is an assessment of $54,822.95; showing a disproportion in the ratio of six to one in the revenue levied by the State. It is manifest that we are paying five-sixths of the salary of the judges in the county of St. Mary's. A like disparity exists between other counties. In Prince George's the assessment is $22,923.94; and in Baltimore county $53,791.68; showing a disparity, not so wide as that I have already mentioned, but more than two and a half to one. Of the total amount of assessment upon the State, I find that my county pays nearly one-twelfth. So that if we have twenty-two judges in the State, we shall have to pay not only the salary of our own judge, but that of the judge of another county also. The same thing holds true with regard to Baltimore county, and is approximately true with regard to some of the other of the larger and upper counties of the State. For this reason I offer the amendment which I have read, and sent to the clerk's desk.

What has been stated as a further reason for multiplying these judges, is with me an objection. It is that the judge of the county may act as judge of the orphans' court. I will say just here that I shall persistently oppose any change in the present system of the orphans' court. I have no idea of providing for a judge of legal attainments upon the bench of the orphans' court. The system, in my opinion, works very well as it is, giving satisfactory justice and accessible justice; while the amendment by placing a legal judge upon the bench will lead, I fear, to litigation and endless strife.

There being already an amendment pending in the second degree, the amendment submitted by Mr. SCHLEY was ruled out of order.

Mr STOCKBRIDGE. I wish merely to give one word of explanation with reference to what seems to be a misapprehension of the system as reported and as now before the convention. The system creates just one new officer and no more. It adds one judge to the court of appeals. That is all the difference in the number of officers between the present system and the system as reported by the committee.

Mr. SCHLEY. I was speaking of the amendment.

Mr. STOCKBRIDGE. And the amendment of the gentleman from Prince George's (Mr. Clarke) is the same.

Mr. SCHLEY. It makes one judge to each county.

Mr. STOCKBRIDGE. It makes a judge to each county, but it takes away a judge in each county; substituting, in other words, a judge of the circuit court of the county for the judge of the orphans' court of the county.—So that in point of fact, instead of increasing the number of officers it diminishes them by just one less than the entire number of circuit judges in the State. The aggregate number of officers, when you come to count them, is less under the system reported by the committee than under the existing system. It is simply the character, the quality and position of the judge, which is changed.

Upon that I wish to give another word of explanation. I am aware that there is not very much cause of complaint of dishonesty in the orphans' court system, as it exists in our State. That court has been constituted in such a manner, as, for most of the matters that come before it, the generality of them, to do substantial justice, and to do it without much delay, and to do it honestly, so far as guarding the interests of those having business there was concerned. At the same time there has been a great clamor throughout the State, or a great desire expressed everywhere, to have an arrangement made by which the orphans' court could not only settle and close the personal but the real estates of persons of moderate means without an appeal to the equity courts as is always necessary now. That call has come up on all sides. Orders have been offered here from several counties looking to that very thing. In order to carry that out, it involved the imperative necessity of having a judge upon the bench of the orphans' court somewhat conversant at least with the rules and practice of the equity courts.

It was thought therefore that all the valuable features of the existing orphans' courts might be preserved, keeping there as a majority of that court men selected precisely as the judges are now selected from the masses of the people, from the honest and intelligent yeomanry, placing upon the bench one judge, who should be there at all times if possible, at least at all times when matters involving equity considerations or litigation or contest should be before them, who would be familiar with the practice of the courts, and especially with their equity powers. This system then proposed that the resident judge in each county should be the chief judge of the orphans' court. He could then supervise, precisely as if he were sitting in equity, the distribution and administration of estates, where real estate was concerned.

The system then embraced these changes; that there should be a judge resident in the county, subject at all times to the discharge of equity business, and who should there sit as chief judge of the orphans' court; and who should in the circuit sit in contested matters in that or the other counties of the circuit.

A single word with reference to the expense. The expense to the State of the judicial system as it now stands is a little more than $40,000 a year. I have heard but one expression of opinion upon this point, that some increase of the salaries is necessary. I believe gentlemen on all sides of the house concede that that is necessary. It is also conceded, and is not in question here, that there is a necessity for adding one judge to the court of appeals. These are necessary increases of the expense, which must be incurred under any system. The system here proposed will also increase the expense by the salary of the additional circuit judges, diminished however by the amount paid by the several counties to one judge of the orphans' courts. That will be the real difference between the systems. The system as reported may cost the State not far from $100,000 a year. The present system, modified as I have suggested that it must be, will necessarily cost the State a little more than $50,000 a year. These are the differences in the systems.

If it were proper to draw the analogy, we have had the proposition before the convention this morning, and the convention has deliberately stricken out one item, one section, which would have saved the State in its various departments more than $10,000 a year, upon an entirely unnecessary and mere ornamental appendage to the courts. If consistency be the aim of gentlemen, I do not see the consistency of striking out that section, and then insisting upon retrenchment where retrenchment is necessarily attended with a weakening of the judicial power all over the State. I do not know that there is a single county that is an exception, from which the cry has not come up that their equity business particularly was not attended to. In the county where the judge chanced to reside, usually the equity business was kept along with something like order and proper shape; but in all the other counties there was great inattention to it.

I might instance particular counties. The judge goes to a county on the occasion of holding his semi-annual term of the court. He attends, usually, in the first place, to the trial of the criminal business, giving that the precedence, and making a sort of general jail delivery. As soon as he gets through that, then attends to magistrates' cases, and then to the civil docket. By the time he gets through these cases, civil and criminal, his trunk is packed to go to the next circuit, and it is almost always an impossibility to induce him to remain to take up and dispose of the equity matters which are pending. He has usually an intermediate term for equity business. Sometimes he is there. Quite as often, I believe in the experience over the State, he is not there. If he is there it is still almost an impossibility to get matters attended to. I know in my own practice, of cases which should have been tried long ago in some counties, which have been standing four or five years untried, although every effort has been made to get a hearing before the judge, it has never been successful.

Now I lay down this proposition. As between a system that administers justice, and one that denies justice, the question of economy ought not to have any weight in this convention. If under the system as reported, or under the system as it is proposed to be modified, we can get this business done in the counties, and under the present system we cannot get it done, it is certainly the interest of the State, and of all the citizens of the State, that the more effective system should be adopted although it may be more expensive. It is no economy to leave the business undone. There are suitors in this State, now suffering a greater loss twice over from the neglect of their business and the utter impossibility of getting it done, than the difference between the two systems proposed. I therefore trust this convention will adopt some system which shall secure the result of the transaction of the business. I do not desire that there shall be one cent of expense beyond what is necessary to secure that. If gentlemen are satisfied that the business can be done without this additional expense, very well. I shall be glad to vote for it. But I do not see the possibility.

Gentlemen have said here that there has been no clamor upon this point. I grant it; and there never will be a clamor upon this point; because the great mass of the people are not litigants. They are not in the courts. They have not equity cases there. But those who are so unfortunate as to have cases in court, business men who want transactions of this sort, who are charged with the management of estates, who have business in the equity court to be adjusted and settled, do complain, and complain most loudly. The legal profession, who are connected with these cases throughout the State, complain. They are cursed by their clients for neglecting their business and not forcing it to a conclusion, when they know perfectly well that the fault does not lie with them; that it is an impossibility to obtain a hearing from the judge in these cases; that it is an impossibility for the judge, pressed as he is, to attend to them, to give them a practical hearing.

I trust therefore that this will be the first question, and take precedence of the question of economy. How can the business best be done? How can the ends of justice be secured? How can we prevent persons from being incarcerated in jail for the want of the presence of a judge to hear their cases or to take bail, in some instances longer than the term for which they could have been sentenced, even if tried when first arrested and found guilty? Such cases have occurred, and yet at the trial they have after all been acquitted. This is not just. It is an utter denial of justice. It is time the convention should take this matter in hand, and make this its first grand object. Let justice be done.

On motion of Mr. PURNELL,

The convention took a recess until eight o'clock, P. M.

EVENING SESSION.

The convention met at eight o'clock, P. M.

The roll was called, and the following members answered to their names:

Messrs. Goldsborough, President; Abbott, Annan, Belt, Berry, of Prince George's, Billingsley; Blackiston, Briscoe, Brown, Chambers, Crawford, Cunningham, Cushing, Dellinger, Dent, Duvall, Ecker, Edelen, Farrow, Gale, Galloway, Hebb, Hodson, Hoffman, Hollyday, Hopkins, Hopper, Horsey, Johnson, Keefer, Kennard, King, Lansdale, Lee,

Maybugh, McComas, Mitchell, Miller, Morgan, Mullikin, Murray, Negley, Nyman, Parker, Parran, Pugh, Purnell, Robinette, Russell, Sands, Schley, Smith, of Carroll, Smith, of Worcester, Stirling, Swope, Sykes, Thomas, Thruston, Turner, Wooden—60.

CIRCUIT COURTS.

The convention resumed the consideration of the report of the committee on the judiciary department on its second reading.

The pending section was the following:

"Sec 19. The State shall be divided into eight judicial circuits, in manner following: The counties of St. Mary's, Charles and Prince George's, shall constitute the first circuit. The counties of Calvert, Anne Arundel and Montgomery, the second. The counties of Allegany, Washington, and Frederick, the third. The counties of Baltimore, Howard and Carroll, the fourth. The counties of Harford, Cecil and Kent, the fifth. The counties of Queen Anne's, Talbot and Caroline, the sixth. The counties of Dorchester, Somerset and Worcester, the seventh. And the city of Baltimore, the eighth."

To which Mr. HEBB had submitted the following amendment:

Strike out all after the word "the," in the first line, and insert:

"State shall be divided into twelve judicial circuits, in manner following: The counties of St. Mary's, Charles and Prince George's shall constitute the first circuit; the counties of Anne Arundel Calvert and Montgomery, the second; the county of Frederick, the third; the county of Washington, the fourth; the county of Allegany, the fifth; the counties of Carroll and Howard, the sixth; the county of Baltimore, the seventh; the counties of Harford and Cecil, the eighth; the counties of Kent, Queen Anne's and Talbot, the ninth; the counties of Caroline and Dorchester, the tenth; the counties of Somerset and Worcester the eleventh; and the city of Baltimore, the twelfth."

To which Mr. MILLER had submitted the following amendment:

Strike out section 19, and insert:

"Sec. 19. There shall be a judge for each county in the State, who shall be elected by the legal and qualified voters of the several counties. He shall be a resident for one year in the county for which he may be elected next before the time of his election, and shall reside in the county for which he is elected, while he continues to act as judge."

Mr. MILLER. I am sorry that the chairman of the committee (Mr. Stockbridge) is not present this evening, and also that the gentleman from Baltimore county, who seemed to take a great deal of interest in this matter when the convention adjourned this morning, is absent. I thought he was inclined, although he made an objection to the additional expense of this system as reported by the committee, after the very able remarks made by the gentleman from Baltimore city, to think that we ought to adopt this system I have proposed, of having one judge to each county, or the system as reported by the committee.

This question of additional expense is one we ought to look at calmly and dispassionately. If there is to be any enormous increase of expenditure from this judicial system, we ought to take that into consideration and give it a fair weight. But let us look at it in the first place in the light figures will present it. Adopting the same increase of salaries, and increase in the number of the judges of the court of appeals, which would be necessary in any event, I think I shall be able to show conclusively to the convention that the actual increase in the expense will not be more than twelve or fourteen thousand dollars per year. In comparing the two systems together, as was said by the gentleman from Baltimore city (Mr. Stockbridge,) we must look to what will be the system as modified, if we take the old system and give these judges such increase of salary as is necessary to be given to them in order to make up their salaries to what we have given other officers, and what is conceded on all hands to be necessary. There is to be one more judge of the court of appeals. That is conceded on all hands to be necessary whether we adopt the present system or the old system. That will give an increase of $3,000 dollars a year. That is not to be attributed to the new system at all. Then we must increase the salaries of these judges $500 per year. We have fixed the salaries of the judges now at $3,000, an increase of $500 to each of them over and above what the present constitution fixes it at. That will make for the five judges of the court of appeals alone, $2,500 a year. Then if we increase the salaries of the circuit judges in the same way, if we adopt the present system of circuit judges, giving them an increase of $500 each, would be an increase of $4,000. And then the increase in the salaries of the judges of Baltimore city, if we increase them, as we probably shall, and as in justice we are bound to increase them, that will be $2,000 more. That will amount to $11,500 increase, which we must have if we take the old system. I do not suppose there is a member of this convention that does not see that if we adopt the old system there must be an increase of $11,500 in the salaries of the judges.

Now the actual salary of the judges under the present system is $33,500. This will make the cost of the system of judges $45,000, if we take the old system and modify it as we have modified the salaries of all the other officers, and which is not to be attributed to the additional expense of the new system the committee propose.

In addition to that, a report made to the

convention shows that we have been paying nearly $3,000 a year for the services of special judges. That will be gotten rid of in a very great measure by the new system. But it is a part of the cost of the existing system; and will continue to be a part of the cost of any system which takes that as a basis, and makes any such mere modification of it as has been proposed. This will give an annual cost of $48,000 for the judicial system, taking the basis of the old system as it stands.

Let us see how much we increase that by adopting this system of having a judge for each county. We have five judges of the court of appeals, whose salary we have fixed at $3,000 a year, making $15,000. Then we have twenty circuit judges, whose salary will amount, if we take the basis of the other salaries, to $2,500 each, amounting to $50,000. Then there are six judges of Baltimore city at $3,000 a year, reported at $3,500, and estimated at $500 less, as we have stricken down the salary of the judges of the court of appeals $500 below what was reported for them—amounting to $18,000 for these six judges. This makes the system cost $83,000 a year.

The difference between that and $48,000, which the present system costs, is $35,000. But what do we save in the operation? It is fair and just to take into account what is saved by the adoption of this system. In the first place, we save the salary and the expenses which the counties have to pay to twenty judges of the orphans' court; which would be fairly estimated at $500 a year, on the average. That will be a saving of $10,000 a year, in the matter of the orphans' court judges alone. Then we shall save the salary of the special judges; the amount of money paid every year for the salary of special judges, now amounting to about $3,000 a year. Then we shall save in the matter of criminal expenses alone in the counties, the expense of keeping criminals in jail until the time comes round for the trial of criminal cases, and delays that attend the present system in trying criminal cases, at least $300 per year for each county. I think that would be a fair estimate of the cost in each county of keeping criminals in jail until we could get a trial under the present system; which would be a saving of $6,000 more. Putting these three items together, they amount to $19,000 a year saved by the adoption of this system. Then the difference between the $19,000 and the $35,000 which the new system would cost over and above the present system, would be only $16,000. But if the system of four judges for the city of Baltimore is left as seems to be the desire of the convention the difference between the two systems will be only about $12,000 a year.

That seems to me to be a fair estimate of the cost of the two systems when compared together. It will be only about twelve or fifteen thousand dollars, and cannot exceed twenty thousand dollars a year.

Then what do we gain by the adoption of this? In the first place we gain this one great thing. We bring justice home to every man's door. We carry out in good faith that declaration in our bill of rights that every man for every injury done to his person or his property, shall have justice speedily without delay. That item alone, it seems to me, will be worth the whole difference between these two systems.

Then again we save expense by the speedy trial of all causes which may come before the judges in civil and equity cases. We save vastly in the amount of cost and expense in that way.

Then we have upon the bench three judges to determine all causes in which appeals can be taken to the court of appeals, except equity cases. All other civil cases will be decided by putting three adjoining counties into a circuit and letting the three judges sit as a bench, going back to the old system of letting three men decide every case instead of one; so that we shall have less appeals taken to the court of appeals; and the saving of expense to the people of the State will be very large in that way.

Then I say the saving in the cost of equity cases, and lessening the fees, is an item which should be taken into consideration when we compare these two systems.

If we would make our economy apply where it ought to apply practically, we should strike from the court some of the supernumerary officers who are now attached to the courts and now receive a large amount of fees, and perquisites, and *per diem;* and we might save a large sum in that respect. The gentleman from Baltimore city, the chairman of the committee (Mr. Stockbridge,) says that we should save twelve thousand dollars a year in that item alone.

Mr. STIRLING (in his seat.) He is mistaken in the facts.

Mr. MILLER. There is no mode I have of estimating the amount; but I know that in our county there would be a considerable saving; and I know that in the counties of this judicial circuit, were county courts organized, it might be effected, and would be effected by the judge in this county. We would get rid of the offices of criers and other mere ornaments of the court, who loaf about the court and do nothing but take their fees and get their pay. We should turn our economy in that direction; and let the great object which we have in view be to bring home the administration of justice to every man's door, and obtain a speedy trial of causes. If we can obtain that, I say that an additional cost of twelve or fifteen thousand dollars a year ought not to weigh in the estimation of the convention.

Let us compare this with some other things

that we have done. For the system of common school education we have raised four hundred and fifty thousand dollars a year. We have increased the taxation for the purpose of supporting common schools, over and above what we have heretofore been in the habit of paying, much more than the judicial system is proposed to be increased. While I do not disparage at all the importance of common school education, I think if we are to be liberal in these matters, it becomes us in the administration of justice to be a little liberal also. Let us manfully take it on ourselves to say that we will have justice administered speedily without delay; that we shall have at every man's door ready access to a judge; that courts shall be frequently held; and that the judge shall sit on our orphans' court bench and try the cases there which may be important in reference to matters of law.

Mr. PURNELL. I should like to ask the gentleman a question. In the system you advocate is it proposed to retain two judges of the orphans' court?

Mr. MILLER. Yes, sir; to preside with the judge of the county.

Mr. PURNELL. Did you deduct the amount of salary paid to this one judge?

Mr. MILLER. I did.

Mr. PURNELL. And what difference do you make in the expense?

Mr. MILLER. It makes a difference of about sixteen thousand dollars a year only. I think if we could adopt this system it would do more to benefit the people of the State than we shall do by almost any act that we have done from the beginning. That is a fair, it seems to me, and a candid statement of the matter; and I appeal to gentlemen not to let this small item of additional expense weigh in comparison with the great benefit and great advantages we shall attain by the adoption of this system.

Mr. THRUSTON. I have no doubt that it would add very much to the economy of certain classes of suitors to have a judge in each county in the State; and if the difference is to be trifling, only fifteen or twenty thousand dollars a year, I think it will be more than saved by the convenience to the community derived from having a judge always at hand. I know that under our present system, in cases where injunctions are wanted, we frequently have to go to an adjoining county to get an injunction; and sometimes it takes three or four days. In our present state of affairs we could not communicate with an adjoining county sometimes for ten days or two week. If it is only to make a difference of fifteen or twenty thousand dollars distributed over the whole State, it ought not to weigh a feather with the convention in regard to giving each county a judge; for there are cases where bail is to be given in criminal cases, there are cases of injunction, and other cases of that kind, which require immediate attention.

But there is another view to be taken of it, more important in my mind than even that; and it is this: the vast importance of having a bench of three judges to decide on important cases, especially if you have low priced judges, as you will have with the salaries provided now. There is a greater safety in having three judges. With three minds, there is a much better chance of having correct decisions than with one. We shall therefore have fewer appeals.

There is also another advantage in the system advocated, and which is I believe substantially that reported by the committee; and that is that we shall have the benefit of a legal man on the orphans' court bench, assisted by two judges to be elected by the people as heretofore. I think in that way economy will be subserved, by having a legal man on the orphans' court bench. I am in favor of this system decidedly, if there is but that small difference in the cost. I think it is the system reported by the committee on the judiciary.

Mr. MILLER. Substantially.

Mr. THRUSTON. I do not think we ought to hesitate one single moment, to gain the advantages we shall gain by this system at an expense of twenty thousand dollars; for we shall save it ten times over in the correctness of the decisions, and in the convenience of having access to judges always at hand, a judge residing in each county. I am therefore very much in favor of this system.

The question was stated upon Mr. MILLER's amendment.

Mr. ABBOTT. I should like to inquire what became of the amendment offered by the gentleman from Frederick (Mr. Schley,) this morning?

Mr. BERRY, of Prince George's. I would suggest to my friend from Frederick to include Baltimore city in his amendment.

Mr. STIRLING. It is perfectly proper as it is, for this section has nothing to do with Baltimore city. It relates entirely to the courts of the counties. Still I have no objection, if each county is to pay the expense of its own courts, to have the same principle applied to Baltimore city. We shall save a great deal of money by it.

The PRESIDENT. There were two amendments already pending; and the amendment was not in order. The question is upon the amendment submitted by the gentleman from Anne Arundel (Mr. Miller) to the amendment submitted by the gentleman from Allegany (Mr. Hebb.)

Mr. BELT. Before the vote is taken upon this question, I wish to make an inquiry of the chair with regard to the motion I proposed to offer this morning. I proposed to recommit this report with the view of having it reported on Friday evening, after deciding certain principles with regard to the court of appeals, and the courts of the counties. Will it be allowable to make that motion, if this amendment is voted upon?

The PRESIDENT. It will be in order to move to recommit the report.

Mr. MAYHUGH demanded the yeas and nays, and they were ordered.

The question being taken, the result was—yeas 29, nays 28—as follows:

Yeas—Messrs. Belt, Berrry, of Prince George's, Billingsley, Blackiston, Briscoe, Brown, Chambers, Crawford, Dent, Duvall, Edelen, Gale, Hollyday, Horsey, Johnson, Lansdale, Lee, Mitchell, Miller, Morgan, Negley, Nyman, Parran, Purnell, Smith, of Carroll, Smith, of Worcester, Swope, Thruston, Turner—29.

Nays—Messrs. Goldsborough, President Abbott, Annan, Cunningham, Cushing, Ecker, Farrow, Galloway, Hebb, Hoffman, Hopkins, Hopper, Keefer, Kennard, King, Mayhugh, McComas, Mullikin, Parker, Pugh, Robinette, Russell, Sands, Schley, Stirling, Sykes, Thomas, Wooden—28.

When their names were called,

Mr. SANDS said: As a member of the committee I should like to say a word in explanation of my vote The theory of the report is unexceptionable. The arguments advanced in its support by the gentleman from Allegany (Mr. Thruston) are in almost all respects unanswerable. I would not myself regard the expense of the system. It is scarcely an item in the account. But I do see great difficulties in the practical operation of our excellent theory. Some of our counties thrown together by it are very large—Allegany, Washington and Frederick, I doubt much if any one court could transact the business of that circuit. Again, some of the counties are very small. They would not have business enough to occupy the court. If there is a disposition to add to this proposition an amendment to the effect that every county shall pay its own judge, I feel certain that if this amendment should prevail it would array all the smaller counties against us. For these, among other reasons, as at present advised, I must vote "no."

Mr. STIRLING said: I will say that my feelings, so far as they are concerned, are in favor of the proposition; but it does not meet with sufficient unanimity and support from those interested in it to make it in my judgment safe for us to support it. If I saw any considerable part of our friends in the counties disposed to favor it, I should vote for it; but at present I must vote "no."

The amendment to the amendment was accordingly adopted.

Mr. HEBB. It is not adopted as an amendment to the section yet.

The question recurred on the adoption of the amendment to the section, as amended on motion of Mr. MILLER.

Mr. BELT. I take it for granted from the vote just taken that the matter is settled. I am willing when by a decided vote a principle is settled, that it shall then rest; and I hope there is no intention on the part of the gentleman from Allegany (Mr. Hebb) by a second vote to draw the house to a different judgment.

Mr. STIRLING. I will inform the gentleman from Prince George's (Mr. Belt) that I do not consider it settled; for I am satisfied that there is a large majority against it.

Mr. BELT. I have no doubt the result was as much a matter of surprise to the gentleman from Baltimore city (Mr. Stirling) as to the gentleman from Allegany (Mr. Hebb.) But the matter having been settled by the vote of the convention, I trust the same courtesy will be extended to the majority upon this question as upon every other.

Mr. STIRLING. I do not intend to discuss this proposition; but if you will analyze this vote it appears that the counties that have the least necessity for the one-judge system of judges have voted for the one-judge system; while the counties in which there is the greatest necessity for a one-judge system have mostly voted against it. The fact is, as I said before, that the vote does not show that there is that amount of unanimity among the convention itself, although there is a majority of one for it to-night, there is not that unanimity in point of strength and interest, that a proposition of that kind ought to command.

I do not wish to introduce into the decision of this question any matter at all political in its character; but in order to carry out this system we have got to have it adopted by the people. Now the counties that voted for it are not going to help to carry the constitution; while the counties that voted against it, as a general thing, are the counties that will help to carry the constitution among the people. If the gentlemen from these counties will tell me that they are in favor of adopting it before the people, I will vote for it. But I do not think it is proper to make a change in our judicial system that does not meet the support of that part of the convention that will endeavor to carry this constitution.

It seems to me that our present system, by enlarging the number of districts, and putting fewer counties in the districts, will accomplish everything that is necessary. I cannot see why Calvert needs a single judge; and there are one or two other counties in the same position where there certainly cannot be a necessity for that system. I am perfectly willing to vote for a large number of circuits, so that there may not be three or four counties together. But when I see that the large counties themselves are unwilling to take this proposition, whose constituents are so much more numerous than the constituents of the gentlemen who voted for it, it seems to me evident that it will not help the constitution before the people of the State.

Mr. BRISCOE. The line of argument pursued by the gentleman from Baltimore city is certainly a very extraordinary one. He has very clearly indicated that if he had a right to expect that certain sections of the State would come up and sustain the constitution, very likely he might be induced to pursue a certain course on this judiciary question, and might be willing to accommodate some of the counties. All that I have to say with regard to this question is that I am very sorry that any question, extraneous in its character should be brought into the settlement of a question like this. It is one in which the people of the whole State, the people of every section of it, are deeply concerned. It is one having no political bearing, involving none.

The gentleman from Baltimore seems to have forgotten that at least one member from Carroll county agreed with us that in every section of the State each county is entitled to a judge. One of the gentlemen from Allegany (Mr. Thruston) entertains the same opinion with regard to that question. So far as that is concerned the gentleman is at fault in his conclusions.

So far as regards the question of having a judge for the county I represent, I have simply to say that if this system is adopted as now before the convention, giving the judge of the county jurisdiction in all questions of equity, and giving him orphans' court jurisdiction, in addition to the duties in the circuit court, these duties will necessarily occupy the judge in each one of these counties for a very large portion of the year. So far as the duties of the orphans' court are concerned, we know that the responsibilities attached to it, and the great interests of the community at large involved in it, most clearly indicate to every man that it is one of the most important portions of the judicial system of Maryland. So far as my own section of the State is concerned, and I believe in every section of it, there is a necessity for a radical reform with regard to the orphans' court. When we combine the jurisdiction and duties of the equity judge, and judge of the orphans' court with the circuit court business, it seems to me that such duties will be imposed by such a system as will be sufficient to justify us in the employment of a judge.

But the great question is, as stated by the gentleman from Anne Arundel (Mr. Miller,) how to bring home justice, the speedy and efficient administration of justice to the door of every man in the community. I know from the experience in my section of the State of a judicial circuit where there are some four or five counties, that the duties of the circuit judge necessarily keep him constantly employed. If any case of emergency arises in our county, and we want an injunction, we have to go to the city of Baltimore, and then go to the city of Annapolis, and in nine cases out of ten we find our presiding judge attending some court in Montgomery county or Howard county, so that it is sometimes utterly impossible for us to reach him. Looking at it in this light, as a matter of necessity for us, I think there can be no just argument raised here against the adoption of that system.

I have only this to say, and to throw it out to gentlemen here, and they can put what value they please upon it, that if this system is adopted, I believe in my section of the State it will tend more to commend this work which we have done, as objectionable as I must be candid in saying it has appeared to be in the past, it will tend more to commend it to the approval of my people than any measure this convention has acted on in the past

Mr. STIRLING. I do not know but what some provision of this kind might have some effect upon the constitution in the portion of the State the gentleman comes from; but it must be very slight, and whatever effect it can produce, can just as well be produced by a modification of the circuits, giving a large degree of practical relief without going to the extent that the amendment goes to. I can say to the gentleman from Calvert county (Mr. Briscoe) that the case of that district ought to be remedied, and I am perfectly willing to vote for a remedy which will accomplish everything that is necessary, and I believe will satisfy the people there as well as this plan of having one judge to each county.

In breaking up our present orphans' court system, we run a great risk of making an unpopular change. The people do not want a change in the orphans' court, and if we have one judge in each county that will make a change in the orphans' court, and that is an additional reason for my voting against it. I shall vote against any change in the orphans' court. I believe it would be a great deal more dangerous to disturb that, than even to disturb the election of judges by the people. The counties which oppose this amendment represent a large vote, and we must take it into consideration that the more populous part of the State votes against this proposition, and the less populous part of the State votes for it. I submit to those gentlemen who care anything for this consideration that this does indicate a dangerous state of things. It indicates that there is no certainty that this one-judge system meets the wishes of the majority of the people.

Mr. BRISCOE. That section of the State has not been inconvenienced by the operation of the present system, and for that reason may not require a change. We do in our portion of the State require it, and there is an eminent necessity for it. In Allegany and the larger counties there is not that inconvenience under the present system. That is the reason I presume that these gentlemen are divided upon that question.

Mr. THRUSTON. I understand that the gentleman from Calvert alluded to me in his remarks just now. I did not hear his remarks.

Mr. BRISCOE. I alluded to the gentleman from Allegany as having voted for the substitute of the gentleman from Anne Arundel (Mr. Miller.)

Mr. THRUSTON. Yes, sir. I voted with the majority; but I would like to know what the gentleman said upon the subject.

Mr. STIRLING. It was in answer to my argument.

Mr. THRUSTON. Very well. I say this: It does not disturb the orphans' court. The judge elected is elected by the people as much as any member of the orphans' court is now elected by the people. If gentlemen come here to get their opinions of the popularity or unpopularity of certain measures, they will all differ. I think it will make this popular. I know that our people will suffer inconvenience under the old system, and I think this will commend the constitution to the people rather than the reverse. Where we differ upon these questions the right way is to look at the measure itself, and see whether it conduces to the public weal. If it does we should vote for it, unless we are positively certain that it will have a damnifying effect. If it is conducive to the public good, we have a right to presume that the public will see that and appreciate it. Therefore I think we ought not to give such considerations any weight whatever.

Mr. NEGLEY. I voted for this proposition of the gentleman from Anne Arundel (Mr. Miller,) and I will continue to vote for it. I believe that instead of damaging the constitution, it will have a great tendency to bring to its support a large number of persons. There was a large class of people in Washington county that were favorable to the old system, the appointive and three-judge system. This is a compromise between the old three-judge system and the appointive system, and the elective system with one judge. We have the elective feature. We have the three-judge characteristic. And I do believe that friends of the constitution that might have been prejudiced against it, under the elective system merely will be induced under the three-judge system to vote for it.

It does correct two evils we have labored under. We have labored under the curse of a special judge system. I have in my pocket a letter I received from one of the first citizens of the county asking that something might be done to give some relief from the curse of the special-judge system. He happened to be one of those who had business in court, and saw how it operated. By electing one judge in each county, we get rid of the expense and the nuisance of appointing special judges. And we get rid too of the trouble and difficulty of sending from Washington county, sixty-six miles to have an injunction issued, or to have some equity paper signed. These are two, and the only two grievances in regard to the operation of the present system that our people have complained of. Any system that will relieve our people of these grievances, I am sure will meet with their approbation, when it does not increase the expense to the State over fifteen or twenty thousand dollars, which is its utmost limit of increase in expense over the present judiciary system, and for this little additional expense I think the people of the State will be largely repaid. I am decidedly in favor of it, because I feel absolutely certain that unless we get this system, the convention will go back to the present system, and we shall still be forced to put up with these manifold inconveniences.

Mr. KEEFER moved that the convention do now adjourn.

Mr. SMITH, of Carroll, demanded the yeas and nays, which were ordered.

The question being taken the result was—yeas 21, nays 39—as follows:

Yeas—Messrs. Abbott, Chambers, Crawford, Cunningham, Cushing, Dellinger, Gale, Galloway, Hoffman, Hopper, Horsey, Keefer, Kennard, King, Mayhugh, McComas, Mullikin, Schley, Stirling, Thomas, Wooden—21.

Nays—Messrs. Goldsborough, President; Annan, Belt, Berry, of Prince George's, Billingsley, Blackiston, Briscoe, Brown, Dent, Duvall, Ecker, Edelen, Farrow, Hebb, Hodson, Hollyday, Hopkins, Johnson, Lansdale, Lee, Mitchell, Miller, Morgan, Murray, Negley, Nyman, Parker, Parran, Pugh, Purnell, Robinette, Russell, Sands, Smith, of Carroll, Smith, of Worcester, Swope, Sykes, Thruston, Turner—39.

The convention accordingly refused to adjourn. The question recurred upon the adoption of Mr. MILLER's amendment as an amendment to the original section reported by the committee.

Mr. THOMAS. I desire to submit but one remark in relation to this proposition. Were it not for the fact that I represent a constituency that I know will be obliged to pay for this new judicial system that is proposed to be inaugurated in the State, at least the greater part of it, I would not trouble the convention by making any remarks upon it. But I say now that unless the counties will agree to pay for this luxury they intend to have, there are thousands of people in my city that will not support your constitution. They have been taxed enough. The gentleman from Anne Arundel (Mr. Miller) seeks to convince this convention that by adopting this system you get rid of special judges. I will ask the gentleman from Anne Arundel how he proposes to get rid of special judges by electing one judge from each county.

Mr. MILLER. I will tell the gentleman. Under the present system there is only one judge in the circuit, and the court is composed of one judge only. Under this system the court is composed of three judges, and it is almost impossible that all three of the judges should be engaged in the same case or related to the same parties, so that there could still be enough to hear the case. That is the way in which it is possible to get rid of the special judges, and that is the way it will be done.

Mr. THOMAS. Does the gentleman pretend to say that when some of the judges may get sick, and there is a proposition put in this very bill that a man is entitled to two judges to try his case? And then you must consider that you deprive the people of the election of one of the people as one of the judges of the orphans' court, because the chief justice of the orphans' court is to be a man learned in the law, a professional gentleman, a member of the bar, which is not as it is at present, for now the judges of the orphans' court all come right from the people. Knowing as well as I do the people, I am perfectly satisfied that they are not willing to give up the system of electing their own orphans' court. So far as I understood the remarks of the gentleman he places to the credit side of his system the speedy trial of criminal cases, and then he goes to work and calculates the number of jail-birds that will be released by this system. How can this system try any more men with three judges than with one judge?

Mr. MILLER. I made no such calculation. I spoke of the cost in criminal cases of keeping them before their trial. I made no such argument as to the number of jail birds released.

Mr. THOMAS. How does he arrive at that? How does he know how many will be tried under the new system more than are now tried under the present system?

Mr. MILLER. It was the keeping before trial that I spoke of.

Mr. THRUSTON. Will the gentleman from Baltimore city allow me to ask him a question. If you have a case before the orphans' court for trial would you go as one of the people to try it?

Mr. THOMAS. I would go before the judge of the orphans' court. I do not understand the question.

Mr. THRUSTON. Would you employ a lawyer or one of the people to take charge of the case?

Mr. THOMAS. That would depend very much on the case. If I was one of the people and not a lawyer, whether I would employ a lawyer or not. There are a great many men in the counties that never employ lawyers.

Mr. THRUSTON. Try their own cases, do you mean?

Mr. THOMAS. Yes, sir. A great many go there and plead their own cases and have their own accounts passed in the orphans' court.

Mr. NEGLEY. Will the gentleman allow me to ask him another question? Is not the circuit court of the district as much the production of the people as the orphans' court?

Mr. THOMAS. No, sir.

Mr. NEGLEY. Have not they as much interest in it?

Mr. THOMAS. Yes; they have as much interest in it; but they do not take the same interest in it.

Mr. NEGLEY. Does it not belong to the people as much as the orphans' court?

Mr. THOMAS. Certainly it does; but they are a different kind of people. Lawyers are a very different kind of men from farmers. According to the present system you can take three farmers and put them on the orphans' court bench, but according to the proposed system you must take one lawyer and give him the same salary as one of the judges of the circuit court. Suppose your circuit court is in session, and your orphans' court wants to be in session. You have got to take the chief justice of the orphans' court and put him on the orphans' court bench, and leave the two associate judges of the circuit court to try the cases there.

Mr. BELT. How often do you suppose that will occur?

Mr. THOMAS. I do not know how often it will occur. But suppose you have two terms a year, and now have two terms a year, how can you do more business in your circuit court with three judges than you now do with one? And as to this matter of injunctions, the gentleman coming from Calvert county to Anne Arundel for a judge, and finding that he is attending a court in Montgomery or Howard, that is their own fault. As lawyers they ought to know where to find the judge. If they come down here after Judge Brewer when he is in Montgomery county, they ought to know that the court is in session in Montgomery county, and that it is Judge Brewer's business to be there, and they ought to have gone there in the first place instead of coming down to Anne Arundel.

Besides, in the matter of issuing injunctions three judges will be just as liable to be out of the county when gentlemen want injunctions as one judge. You cannot tie a circuit judge down to the county where he resides for the purpose of being there to issue injunctions whenever you want one. You cannot tie the man to his house or the court room. Very frequently with our four courts in Baltimore city when we want injunctions we go and find both of our equity judges gone; and I have frequently been under the necessity of sending to Saratoga or Bedford Springs in the summer time, for the purpose of getting an injunction, and the same way as to writs of *habeas corpus* or similar papers. Human nature is the same in three judges as it is in one. The mere fact of electing one judge from each county will not keep the judge in that county if he does not choose to stay there. And you cannot make him hold more terms of his court than are provided for by the constitution or the law, and whenever a judge chooses to adjourn his court he can do it.

These are my views of this subject. I do hope the convention will take a step back from the one they have just taken, and go over to our present system.

Mr. BERRY, of Prince George's. I am sorry to see evinced by our friend from Baltimore city (Mr. Thomas) an evidence of opposition to a measure which we regard as a matter of justice to the people in the several counties of the State. More particularly am I sorry for it as we are perfectly willing that Baltimore city shall fix her own system, and we are willing to vote for any system they may think the most advantageous to their people. I have had a great deal of practical experience since I have been at the bar, as to the inconvenience of the present system. I know of two cases that have arisen within the last two years in my county, in one of which the party was committed to jail for a very small offence against the criminal law, for which if convicted he could not have been sent to the penitentiary, but for which he was committed by a justice of the peace; and the means of getting that man out of jail was by *habeas corpus;* and he had to stay there six months because we could not get a judge there to try the *habeas corpus* in order to deliver him. In the other case a man was committed for an offence for which he would not have been sent to the penitentiary if found guilty, and when the case was tried he was acquitted. The judge rode thirty-seven miles in the inclemency of the weather of the winter season to try the case, and the man was acquitted after he had been kept in jail six months.

Mr. STIRLING. I admit all that; but I ask the gentleman from Prince George's if it would not be remedied by dividing the circuit in which Prince George's county is contained into two parts.

Mr. BERRY, of Prince George's. I answer it would for Charles and St. Mary's, the two lower counties, where the judge now lives.—Unless you give us in Prince George's a circuit, the judge lives as near as——

Mr. STIRLING. Suppose you make Prince George's one circuit, and put Charles and St. Mary's together.

Mr. BERRY, of Prince George's. It would remedy it so far as we are concerned; but would not for Charles and St. Mary's; for Charles and St. Mary's are two quite large counties.

There is another reason I will assign for this system. It is proposed by this system that the judge elected from the county shall preside as the chief justice of the orphans' court. I do think if there is any court known to the law where a lawyer should preside, it is the orphans' court. I have known most important cases arise in the orphans' courts; more so than in the circuit court of the county. I have known cases of this sort. I was counsel in a case where we presented the will of a party. It was in few words—I want A B to administer my estate. The judge said it was not a testamentary appointment; and I had to bring it to the court of appeals. The court of appeals declared it was a testamentary appointment. I carried it back; and they raised another objection, and decided against me on that. I carried that up to the court of appeals and they reversed that. The result was that before the letters testamentary were taken out, nearly the whole estate was wasted. In very many cases there are questions of law alone; and therefore there is a necessity of having at the head of the court a judge who knows something about the law.

Mr. STIRLING. Is it not perfectly possible with some indifferent judge, that you might have had the same decisions?

Mr. BERRY, of Prince George's. I do not think he could if he had read the hornbooks of the law. Any treatise on that branch of the law would have determined that that was a will.

Mr. SMITH, of Carroll. The proposition before the convention, as I understand it, is a simple one, standing entirely by itself. Every gentleman who has addressed the convention has confused it, it seems to me, by associating it with other provisions which do not necessarily attach to it. The simple proposition is whether there shall be or shall not be a judge in each county. Most of the gentlemen have connected with it that the duties of chief judge of the orphans' court are to be discharged by the judge of the circuit court in the county; and they have connected with it also the fact, assuming it as a necessary consequence of this vote, that there must be three counties in a circuit. I am, for one, entirely opposed to interfering in the slightest degree with the orphans' court as it now exists; and I cannot and shall not vote for it. This proposition is an isolated substantive proposition with no sort of connection with anything else. I have listened attentively to the statements made here; and in my mind they are conclusive as to the necessity of having a judge resident in each county in the State.

I am not so fortunate as the gentleman from Baltimore city (Mr. Thomas,) in understanding my constituents upon this or other subjects. I believe they have done very well so far; and I am perfectly willing to trust them hereafter. I believe they will look at this proposition as I look at it; as one eminently just, as one which will in the end be productive of no additional taxation at all commensurate with the convenience and advantage which this will afford. But even if the people do not so regard it; if the majority of my constituents were to oppose it—I have no means of knowing it—sti l I would not feel myself obligated to vote against it, unless there was some other reason than the sentiment of the people; for if I felt convinced that they were mistaken with regard to its practicable working if put in operation, I should feel myself justified in voting for it as I have done. I have a better opinion of the people of Baltimore than has been expressed here again and again by its immediate representatives. Whenever anything is done which any one of the gentlemen from Baltimore city seems to think will run counter to the feelings and wishes of any particular section of that city, they come here and appeal to the majority to vote against it because it may possibly lose votes for the constitution.

Mr. STIRLING. I hope the gentleman will except me from that remark. I do not intend to make any such appeals in behalf of Baltimore city. My own impression is that the vote of the city of Baltimore will not have the slightest effect in adopting the constitution. I referred in my remarks to the counties in the western and northern part of the State.

Mr. SMITH, of Carroll. I understood the gentleman, if not to-night, certainly on frequent occasions, to advocate this doctrine, which to me has no practical force whatever. I believe if the people of Baltimore city, or any large portion of them, vote against this proposition as a whole, because some few of its provisions do not meet their wishes, it would be weakness and cowardice in us, that it would be slavish in us to yield to such wishes and such mandates. I for one shall certainly not do so. I am acting on my own individual responsibility; doing in this matter as I have done heretofore, what I think is best for the whole people; and from that course I shall not turn.

It appears to me that there is manifest and glaring inconsistency in the conduct of the gentlemen from Baltimore city and others acting in that view, in this matter, compared with that upon another part of this report. It is well known that the convention determined, by a considerable vote it is true, that the elective system should prevail in the selection of the judiciary; and further, that it was determined also by a not very decisive vote, but by a very small majority, that the judges of the court of appeals should be elected by general ticket and not by districts. My friend from Baltimore city (Mr. Thomas) had an amendment pending. The question had not been finally determined. The section was open for consideration. On my motion the further consideration of it was postponed in order to furnish the gentleman an opportunity to express his opinions, and to invite the attention of the convention to it fairly, candidly and fully. The gentleman from Baltimore city and others, this morning, insisted that the convention having determined, not by a decisive vote, but by a small majority, as the journal showed, that the judges of the court of appeals should be elected by general ticket, and not by the qualified voters of the several districts respectively; it was not proper for the convention further to investigate the matter; that it was not proper that there should be a reconsideration. While I was willing that that matter should come up; while I believed, and believe now, that the better and fairer proposition in the end would have been, and that after years would have demonstrated it as I candidly believe, that the people should select from the several districts respectively the four associate judges, and the chief justice from the whole State, yet I yielded to my friend from Baltimore city so far that I did not press the amendment against the wishes of those gentlemen who expressed the opinion that it should not be considered. Now the convention having determined in precisely the same way that there shall be a judge in each county in the State, the gentleman has expressed his surprise, his consternation almost, that there should have been such a vote by a majority of this house, and that they should have dared to differ with him in this matter.

It may be a misfortune, but it is the fact, that we cannot all look at things in the same light. While differing from the gentleman upon this or any other proposition, I claim to do it fairly, candidly and conscientiously, with as much concern for the success of this constitution as he can himself entertain. I do not ask himself or any one else how I shall vote. I consult my own judgment. It is frail, imperfect, human; still it is the best guide I have. And if defeated in a measure, I will try to set an example which the gentleman may well follow, to yield pleasantly, and to retire as gracefully as I can. I shall not attempt by direction or by indirection to make it appear that those who have differed from me are not as competent to judge as I am.

Now, sir, coming back to first principles, I say that this proposition of itself meets my hearty approbation. It is not connected at all with the other matters which have been debated with it. We may pass this provision in the report, and adopt it as a section of the report; and yet we may with perfect consistency refuse to interfere in the slightest degree with the orphans' courts as they now exist, or to throw three counties into a circuit. This stands alone by itself; and I do not propose now, as it seems to me improper and out of place to discuss any of the other propositions which may come up in their turn.

Mr. SANDS. No one has a higher appreciation of the fairness of the gentleman from Carroll (Mr. Smith,) than I have. No one appreciates more highly his honest earnestness in any matter which he advocates. Still eloquent as he is, he has not entirely cleared up some very weighty objections in my mind. If I believed this was the last opportunity that the people of Maryland were going to have to reform the judiciary, I should be disposed to make great sacrifices looking to that end; but when it is a fact notorious to every gentleman in this convention that this constitution will provide for its own constant amendment according to the will and wishes of the people, I put it to gentlemen of the majority of this house whether we have a moral right to touch any provision of this constitution we are sure will make it unpalatable to a large portion of the people of the State.

I will say to my friends that they need not have any delusive hope about getting support for this constitution on account of any judiciary system they may frame or incorporate in it. I have no doubt but that if the simple question was before the people whether they would retain their present judiciary system, or adopt that indicated in this amendment, my friends would go before the people and urge it there quite as eloquently and as pertinently as they have done it here, and would vote with as great unanimity as they do now. But they will excuse me for the belief and the conviction that above this question of the judiciary of the State there are issues in the coming election upon this constitution which are going to be final and conclusive with each and every one of them. They may be willing, and doubtless are anxious that this system of their liking and of my personal liking, shall be attached to the constitution with the hope that if the constitution shall prevail this will be one benefit to them. Of course I believe they are entirely sincere in that. But I repeat again to my friends, that they must not look for one vote for this constitution from the opposition ranks. If one gentleman of the opposition would rise in his place to-night and say, "I will vote for this constitution, if that is put in it, and will urge my people to do it," God knows how gladly I would vote with him to put it in.

Mr. BELT. Will my friend allow me to ask him one question? Do I understand the gentleman from Howard to say that his vote upon the question how the judiciary system shall be established, will be controlled by his view of the probable vote upon the adoption of the constitution?

Mr. SANDS. I will answer that question very plainly. If I believed my vote for the judiciary system as proposed by the committee was going to lose this constitution before the people, or endanger its acceptance, I would sooner lose my right hand than to vote for it.

Mr. BELT. Then it is a secondary consideration whether it is a desirable system. But I do not understand my friend from Howard to impute to any gentleman upon this side of the house that his vote is guided by any such considerations, and until that is avowed it is unnecessary for me——

Mr. SANDS. No, sir; I think my proposition is a very plain one; and it is not intended to give personal umbrage to any one. I do not believe this constitution if we adopt the judiciary system spoken of, is going to get a single vote from a single gentleman of the opposition upon this floor.

Mr. BERRY, of Prince George's. While I shall oppose the constitution on other grounds, I will tell the gentleman this; that I will offer the same arguments before the people in approval of the judiciary system, if it shall be adopted, that I have done to-night.

Mr. SANDS. That amounts precisely to what I said. If they can get this judiciary system in the constitution, it is a God-send to them; but they are not going to vote for your constitution and mine, the constitution framed by the majority of this house to get all the judiciary systems on earth rammed into one and given to them.

Mr. CHAMBERS. Not with the negro in it?

Mr. SANDS. No; "not with the negro in it." Gentleman may as well know where the opposition stand with regard to it. Not while the negro is in it, will you ever get one of their votes.

Mr. BELT. Not mine.

Mr. SANDS. No; "not mine," I suppose might be repeated all round.

Now I want to ask my friend from Washington county (Mr. Negley,) turning from political considerations to legal considerations, whether he believes that such a provision as that proposed is practicable; whether he believes that the business of Allegany, Washington, and Frederick counties, can be discharged by any one court? Because, mark you, according to the experience of the oldest and the ablest judges who now occupy the bench, while the three-judge system is good in itself, because you had a chance to get a better and safer opinion from the court, upon which you could more surely rely, the very consultation necessary to make up that opinion so far delayed the progress of the business of the court. It has been found, in the experience of judges now upon the bench, and I have it from the lips of some of the best of them, that business is more rapidly transacted under one-judge. I am sorry I have not at hand a communication I received in my place from his honor, Judge Brewer, giving his experience for nearly thirty years. But I say that is the plain common sense view of the matter, that three judges upon the bench will delay the business of the court more than one will, because of the very time consumed in consultation about the propositions submitted before they can decide upon them.

I do not think that with the most energetic men in the State of Maryland upon the bench of the circuit, that would be formed of Allegany, Washington and Frederick counties they could discharge the duties of that court with three judges upon the bench.

So far as this matter of injunctions and writs of *habeas corpus* is concerned, what different state of things do you have under this system from that under the one-judge system? The court is sitting in Allegany county, for instance. Must not the three judges be there? Have not we placed the three judges upon the same bench? Would not the citizens of Washington county or Frederick county, if they wanted an injunction, have to go to Allegany county for it? And when the court go from Allegany to Washington county, in their circuit, would not the three judges all be there, and if the people of Allegany or Frederick wanted writs of *habeas corpus* or injunctions, would they not have to go to Washington county for them? And when the court went to Frederick county, would not the citizens of Washington and Allegany have the trouble of coming over the mountains to Frederick for these purposes? The objections urged to the one-judge system have no foundation so far as this matter is concerned; for you would have to follow the court in its circuit, whether there were three judges or one. You have to follow the court as a unit. If it is one, you have to follow it; if it is two, you have to follow it; and if it is three, it is still a unit, and that one court you have to follow.

Mr. Miller. Does not the gentleman know that issuing the writ of *habeas corpus* is a duty which pertains to the judge and not to the court?

Mr. Sands. I know that. But would not that judge be a part of the court? and would you not have to go to the court to find the judge, whether in Frederick, Washington or Allegany?

Mr. Miller. No, sir; not if one judge is all you want.

Mr. Sands. If three judges constitute the court, the three judges will always be where the court is, whether in Frederick, Washington or Allegany. Now I ask my friend from Washington whether he believes that the court could discharge the business of that circuit? I ask the gentlemen advocating this amendment whether they believe that if the convention adopt the theory, the theory is at all practicable? I do not believe it is. I do not believe the gentlemen can answer this in the affirmative.

Something has been said about the wishes of the people, and how far we ought to consult them, or not to consult them. I do not know how the delegation from Washington stands. I believe they are divided. I am sure that the delegation from Frederick, large and populous as a county, and numerous in its representation here, are a unit in opposition to this system; and I understand that out of the delegation from Allegany—while of course I do not mean to impugn the right of any one member to urge his own views of the matter—but one single member forms it. There are only two or three gentlemen on this floor from Western Maryland who indorse this system. And it is practically true that to the public sentiment of that part of the State, large and populous as it is, we must look for the votes for this constitution. And votes are vital; for if the constitution is lost this pet judiciary system is gone. You get neither one system nor the other. You resign both by clinging pertinaciously to one.

I would myself be glad to oblige gentlemen of the opposition by advocating this measure. I am perfectly plain and honest in telling them that I do not do it for the reason I have stated, that I believe it will endanger the constitution before the people, and I will do nothing that will do that. I like it for the same reason that some gentlemen dislike it; because the negro is in it, and I want him out of the way; and I will give my vote for a judiciary system or anything else likely to help us in getting him out of the way.

Mr. Kennard moved that the convention do now adjourn.

Mr. Miller. You cannot make that motion without intervening business.

Mr. Hebb moved a call of the convention.

The motion was rejected.

Mr. Hebb moved that the convention do now adjourn.

Mr. Negley demanded the yeas and nays, and they were ordered.

The question being taken, the result was—yeas 35, nays 25—as follows:

Yeas—Messrs. Abbott, Annan, Cunningham, Cushing, Dellinger, Ecker, Farrow, Galloway, Hebb, Hoffman, Hopper, Horsey, Johnson, Keefer, Kennard, King, Mayhugh, McComas, Mullikin, Murray, Nyman, Parker, Pugh, Purnell, Robinette, Russell, Sands, Schley, Smith, of Carroll, Smith, of Worcester, Stirling, Swope, Sykes, Thomas, Wooden—35.

Nays—Messrs. Goldsborough, President; Belt, Berry, of Prince George's, Billingsley, Blackiston, Briscoe, Brown, Chambers, Crawford, Dent, Duvall, Edelen, Gale, Hodson, Hollyday, Hopkins, Lansdale, Lee, Mitchell, Miller, Morgan, Negley, Parran, Thruston, Turner—25.

When their names were called,

Mr. Chambers said: I have invariably voted for an adjournment at night. I did so a while ago. But believing this an attempt at coercion, I vote "no."

Mr. Ecker said: For the reason assigned

by the gentleman from Kent (Mr. Chambers,) I am constrained, for the first time in my life upon this question, to vote "aye."

Mr. HEBB said: Deeming the proposition carried by the convention to-night one that could not be carried in a full house, and believing this an attempt at coercion by the minority now present, I vote "aye."

Mr. SMITH, of Carroll. While I perfectly understand the object of the motion to adjourn, I am not so wedded to any theory of my own as to desire a small majority to decide it. Believing that this proposition is one for the public good, and one which ought to commend itself to a majority of a full convention, and that it may be carried to-morrow by a larger vote than to-night, I vote "aye."

Mr. STIRLING. I vote to adjourn because there are eight or ten members absent to-night who I think may be here to-morrow, and I do not wish a vote taken to-night. I vote "aye."

Mr. THRUSTON. Believing that this is the best judicial system suggested, and that it will meet the views of the majority, I vote "no."

The convention accordingly adjourned.

EIGHTY-FIRST DAY.

THURSDAY, August 25, 1864.

The convention met at 10 o'clock, A. M.

Prayer by Rev. Mr. Owen.

The roll was called, and the following members answered to their names:

Messrs. Goldsborough, President; Abbott, Annan, Audoun, Billingsley, Blackiston, Bond, Briscoe, Brooks, Brown, Carter, Chambers, Crawford, Cunningham, Cushing, Daniel, Davis, of Washington, Dellinger, Dent, Duvall, Ecker, Edelen, Farrow, Gale, Galloway, Greene, Hatch, Hebb, Hodson, Hoffman, Hollyday, Hopkins, Hopper, Horsey, Johnson, Keefer, Kennard, King, Lansdale, Larsh, Lee, Markey, Mayhugh, McComas, Mitchell, Miller, Morgan, Murray, Negley, Nyman, Parker, Parran, Peter, Pugh, Purnell, Ridgely, Robinette, Russell, Sands, Schley, Schlosser, Smith, of Carroll, Smith, of Dorchester, Smith, of Worcester, Sneary, Stirling, Swope, Sykes, Thomas, Thruston, Todd, Turner, Wickard, Wilmer, Wooden—75.

The proceedings of yesterday were read and approved.

USURY LAWS.

Mr. WICKARD, moved to reconsider the vote by which the report on interest and usury laws was ordered to be engrossed for a third reading.

Mr. THOMAS. I would like to hear from the gentleman from Allegany the reason which induces him to move a reconsideration.

Mr. WICKARD. Because I greatly prefer the report of the committee. I am in favor of the parties making their own contracts; and at the same time I would have the legal rate of interest fixed.

The motion was not agreed to.

CIRCUIT COURTS.

The convention resumed the consideration of the report of the judiciary committee, on its second reading. The pending section was as follows:

"Sec. 19. The State shall be divided into eight judicial circuits, in manner following: The counties of St. Mary's, Charles and Prince George's, shall constitute the first circuit; the counties of Calvert, Anne Arundel and Montgomery, the second; the counties of Allegany, Washington and Frederick, the third; the counties of Baltimore, Howard and Carroll, the fourth; the counties of Harford, Cecil and Kent, the fifth; the counties of Queen Anne's, Talbot and Caroline, the sixth; the counties of Dorchester, Somerset and Worcester, the seventh; and the city of Baltimore, the eighth."

The question was upon the following amendment, being the amendment of Mr. HEBB as amended by the adoption of the substitute submitted by Mr. MILLER:

"Section 19. There shall be a judge for each county in the State, who shall be elected by the legal and qualified voters of the several counties. He shall be a resident for one year in the county for which he may be elected next before the time of his election, and shall reside in the county for which he is elected while he continues to act as judge."

Mr. SCHLEY submitted the following amendment to the amendment:

Add to the amendment the words "the salary of the circuit judges shall be levied and paid by the respective counties, in which they act."

Mr. STIRLING. I shall vote for this amendment, because upon the examination I have made since last night, I find that the entire taxation of some of the counties is not equal to the salary of the judge. If they want a judge, let them pay for it by local taxation. Otherwise the whole State revenue will be absorbed by the judiciary.

Mr. CHAMBERS. I hear with great surprise the proposition made and receiving a second, which is now before the house. I ask every member of this body if he ever heard of such a state of things; the government providing a judicial system for the State, and looking to each county to pay the costs of that system? Such a thing never was heard of in the State. I say there has never been such a proposition before.

Mr. STIRLING. The judge of the orphans' court is paid by the counties. Is not that a part of the judicial system?

Mr. CHAMBERS. Yes, sir; but I am not speaking of the orphans' court. I challenge the gentleman to show me that any statesman of the State of Maryland has ever suggested the idea, even thought of or dreamed of the idea of paying the judges of the court of appeals, for instance, out of the treasury of the particular district from which they come. The gentlemen from Baltimore have talked very freely of the expense to their particular portion of the State. Why, sir, where does Baltimore get her money from? Where do the profits come from which are made in the city of Baltimore? How is it sustained? Is justice sold to each county according to its means? I say there is no precedent for such a state of things. If you go for this, you should let the county regulate its own affairs, adjust the salaries and arrange the whole concern. Are you going to cut up the administration of justice into slices, and divide it among the counties according to their means? I think that we are coming to strange times indeed. Novelties involving the very peace of our communities have been most abundant, from the very day of our coming here. Gentlemen from the city of Baltimore should recollect how much the counties have contributed to build the canals and the railroads that have made her what she is.

Mr. CUSHING. The gentleman from Prince George's (Mr. Berry) made the suggestion to the house yesterday, that the counties wanted to pay for them.

Mr. CHAMBERS. Mr. Berry is not here to answer for himself. I heard no such suggestion from him. But I do not care where it comes from; it is a heresy; and I think it shows an enlargement of imagination that I did not suppose Mr. Berry possessed. I protest against it in the strongest terms, as an infringement of the rule of propriety adopted everywhere. The idea that justice is thus to be sliced up and parcelled out, made the subject of bargain and sale to the different counties of the State—I say it is a heresy of the very highest character. I should be exceedingly pleased to see it receive the marked discountenance of this body. I refrain from saying more at this time; for I believe that it cannot find very many advocates here.

Mr. AUDOUN demanded the yeas and nays, and they were ordered.

The question being taken, the result was —yeas 36, nays 40—as follows:

Yeas—Messrs. Abbott, Annan, Audoun, Brooks, Cunningham, Cushing, Daniel, Davis, of Washington, Dellinger, Ecker, Galloway, Greene, Hatch, Hebb, Hoffman, Hopkins, Hopper, Keefer, Kennard, King, Larsh, Markey, McComas, Nyman, Robinette, Russell, Sands, Schley, Smith, of Carroll, Sneary, Stirling, Swope, Sykes, Thomas, Wickard, Wooden—36.

Nays—Messrs. Goldsborough, President; Billingsley, Blackiston, Bond, Briscoe, Brown, Carter, Chambers, Crawford, Dennis, Dent, Duvall, Edelen, Farrow, Gale, Henkle, Hollyday, Horsey, Johnson, Landsdale, Lee, Mayhugh, Mitchell, Miller, Morgan, Murray, Negley, Parker, Parran, Peter, Pugh, Purnell, Ridgely, Schlosser, Smith, of Dorchester, Smith, of Worcester, Thruston, Todd, Turner, Wilmer—40.

When their names were called,

Mr. NEGLEY said: The first reason why I cannot vote for this is that the county courts are very often used for the collection of debts by persons living in Baltimore; and the second reason is that the State fixes the salary and mode of payment. If they will allow the counties to make their own contract with their own judge, I might vote for it; otherwise I cannot. I vote "no."

Mr. SANDS said: I vote for this proposition because Howard county does not want a judge for itself, and if it did would be willing to pay for it. I vote "aye."

The amedment was accordingly rejected.

The question recurred on Mr. MILLER'S amendment.

Mr. KEEFER moved to amend the amendment by striking out the words "several counties," in line two, and inserting "State at large."

Mr. MILLER. We have adopted this as an amendment; and the ruling of the chair has been heretofore that although you may amend by adding you cannot strike out.

The PRESIDENT. This section is not perfected yet. The question is yet to be taken on the amendment of the gentleman from Allegany as amended; and it may be still further amended.

The amendment to the amendment was rejected.

The question again recurred on the adoption of Mr. HEBB'S amendment as amended by adopting Mr. MILLER'S substitute.

Mr. PUGH demanded the yeas and nays, and they were ordered.

The question being taken, the result was —yeas 33, nays 44—as follows:

Yeas—Messrs. Billingsley, Blackiston, Bond, Briscoe, Brown, Chambers, Crawford, Dennis, Dent, Duvall, Edelen, Gale, Henkle, Hodson, Hollyday, Horsey, Johnson, Lansdale, Lee, Mitchell, Miller, Morgan, Negley Parran, Peter, Smith, of Carroll, Smith, of Dorchester, Smith, of Worcester, Swope, Thruston, Todd, Turner, Wilmer—33.

Nays—Messrs. Goldsborough, President; Abbott, Annan, Audoun, Brooks, Carter, Cunningham, Cushing, Daniel, Davis, of Washington, Dellinger, Ecker, Farrow, Galloway, Greene, Hatch, Hebb, Hoffman, Hopkins, Hopper, Keefer, Kennard, King, Larsh, Markey, Mayhugh, McComas, Murray, Nyman, Parker, Pugh, Purnell, Ridgely, Robinette, Russell, Sands, Schley, Schlosser, Sneary, Stirling, Sykes, Thomas, Wickard, Wooden—44.

The amendment as amended was accordingly rejected.

Mr. HEBB submitted the following amendment to the section :

Strike out all after the word "the," in the first line, and insert:

"State shall be divided into thirteen judicial circuits, in manner following: The counties of St. Mary's and Charles, shall constitute the first circuit; the counties of Anne Arundel and Calvert, the second; the counties of Prince George's and Montgomery the third; the county of Frederick, the fourth; the county of Washington, the fifth; the county of Allegany, the sixth; the counties of Carroll and Howard, the seventh; the county of Baltimore, the eighth; the counties of Harford and Cecil, the ninth; the counties of Kent and Queen Anne's, the tenth; the counties of Talbot and Caroline, the eleventh; the counties of Dorchester, Somerset and Worcester, the twelfth; and the city of Baltimore, the thirteenth.

Mr. STIRLING. I shall very cheerfully support this amendment. I have all the time opposed giving to each county one judge; but I am decidedly in favor of increasing the facilities of all parts of the State under the present system. And I think this amendment, putting not more than two counties together, except in one instance, and giving the large counties one judge, very properly meets the whole difficulty. It puts the smaller counties in a vastly better position than they are in at present, and I hope will be accepted by them. I think it will to some extent ameliorate the difficulties of our present system; and I hope it will be adopted.

Mr. BILLINGSLEY. Does that give to each county in the judicial district a judge?

The PRESIDENT.. No, sir.

Mr. BILLINGSLEY. I thought the question of one judge to each county had been decided?

The PRESIDENT. No, sir; it was carried last night and rejected this morning.

Mr. PETER. The great object to be attained by having one judge for each county was that there might be some remedy for the system as it existed in our courts. At the same time I thought it would be a great advantage to the people, not only residing in our counties, but throughout the State, to have their business attended to at once, especially in the chancery practice in our courts. How is it now in our courts? We have two chancery courts appointed in the year. Our judge has more chancery business than almost any two judges can attend to. The consequence is that we have but one chancery court in the year, and the disputed cases occupy the time. The court cannot get a trial and a decision for two years. Our judge labors, I will admit, almost day and night under the necessities of the case.

Now I appeal to this convention whether it is right to designate certain counties of this State, and give them the advantage of a judge, and give their lawyers this advantage in their practice, that they can always have a judge sitting at their elbows, while in other portions of the State the lawyers have to travel forty to sixty miles to get a little order passed in chancery.

Gentlemen seem to forget that it is not merely in chancery or in the common law business of our courts that there is a great advantage in having a judge present; but the orphans' court is pressed with business. Once if a gentleman thought proper he could go to that court to get business transacted when it was a plain matter of the settlement of an account. How is it now? Very often an orphans' court is so crowded, meeting one day in the week, that business is postponed week after week until it hangs for years before we can get even a simple account adjusted.

I thought the great object to be attained by this one-judge system was to have a judge in each county that could transact the business of the orphans' court; that it would save time; that lawyers throughout the State might have equal advantages in the transaction of their other business. I do not see the fairness of the gentleman's proposition at all. If Frederick county is entitled to one judge, why not Montgomery? Why not have the same system throughout the State?

I admit that the city of Baltimore is so large that it would take one judge to transact the whole business; but if the judge is not to attend to the business of the orphans' court, why not put Frederick and Washington county together? One judge could probably transact the business of those two counties. How is it now in our judicial division. We have Howard, Calvert, Anne Arundel and Montgomery, all combined. I will admit that one judge is not able to transact the business of those counties; but I unhesitatingly say that if the judge is not to transact the orphans' court business of the counties, let us divide up the State and hitch on Frederick to Washington, or put Allegany and Washington together. If that is to be the plan, that the judge is not to transact the orphans' court business, let us put the lower counties together. If we are going to bring down the expense, let us bring it down where it ought to be, and give the judge as much as he can do, or as much as he ought to do. If we are not to derive benefits adequate to the increase of the expense, let us curtail the expense as much as possible.

Mr. DENNIS. I move to amend the amendment by transposing Dorchester county from the twelfth circuit to the eleventh circuit, with Talbot and Caroline counties. I make that motion for this reason. Worcester, Somerset and Dorchester are put together. I take from the census the total free population of those counties.

TWELFTH DISTRICT.		ELEVENTH DISTRICT.	
Worcester......	17,013	Talbot	11,070
Somerset.......	19,903	Caroline.........	10,390
Dorchester.....	16,338		
Total.........	53,254	Total..........	21,460

So it seems that as arranged in this amendment the twelfth district has about two and a half times as large a population as the eleventh. There is a great impropriety in that, as the convention will see. In order to equalize it, I move to transfer Dorchester county to the eleventh district.

Mr. SANDS. I wish to make a remark in reply to the suggestion of my friend from Montgomery (Mr. Peter) about the fairness of this proposition. I am in the same judicial circuit with my friend; and I know what difficulties we have under the present arrangement. But I remind the gentleman that this amendment proposes at least to divide the difficulty and leave us only half the difficulty we have had heretofore. My friend asks on what principle of justice we can give to Baltimore city and Frederick county and Allegany county one judge each, and not give to Montgomery one judge. If my friend will just look at the last census, at the number of people over whom these judges are to preside, whose affairs they are to regulate, he will see the even handed justice of this proposition. For instance, Baltimore county, according to the census, has a white population of forty-seven thousand souls, and Montgomery county of eleven thousand. So Baltimore county has four times the amount of white population, the number of people who are to go into the courts as suitors, that Montgomery has. Is there no justice then in saying that Baltimore county shall have a judge, and that Montgomery county, not having near the population of Baltimore county, shall have with another county a judge to preside over the same number of people and to transact the same amount of business?

Mr. STIRLING. There is an additional reason for a judge in Baltimore county, that its situation brings into that county a large amount of business from Baltimore city.

Mr. SANDS. I was about to say that. Applying this principle also to Allegany county, we find that Allegany county has more than twice the population of Montgomery county. Is there no justice in giving Allegany a judge, with twice the amount of population, and four times the amount of litigation from the peculiar circumstances of the case? I think that the proposition is eminently fair. It divides the people of the State into districts containing about the same amount of population in each; and says that you shall have a judge for twenty or twenty-five or thirty thousand; and if there are not so many in one county, to transact business in that court, two or three counties may be put together.

If the theory contained in the judiciary report was a practicable one; if you could carry it out, I should advocate it here. But I see insuperable difficulties in the way of rendering that theory effective. Believing then that that is not one that can practically operate in Maryland, I go for what next promotes the public interest and convenience; so increasing the number of your circuits, and so constituting your judicial districts in circuits that twenty or twenty-five thousand people, or even less—far less as the gentleman will see by taking the census, for in some districts it is not fifteen thousand, and hardly ten thousand white inhabitants—may have a judge. I am willing to go so far, that ten, fifteen, or twenty thousand white inhabitants shall have a judge to transact their legal business.

I think that this is a proposition which our friends upon the other side can accept as a compromise in this matter, embodying a large step in advance of the previously entertained opinion of the majority of this house. I believe a large majority of those with whom I act, were in favor, in the first instance, of adopting the present system without change. Now we have nearly double the number of circuits. Is not that a long step in the way of compromise which the majority of this house to-day holds out to the minority? I hold on to the principle, definite, ascertained, infallible, that wherever as many as twenty thousand white people are congregated together in any municipal or other capacity, they shall have a judge, to attend to and decide on all matters that arise in litigation between citizen and citizen. I do hope, as the majority have made this long step toward a compromise, to see some gentlemen on the opposite side meeting it in the spirit in which it is made; and that we may at once, in some manner, have a certain degree of unanimity.

Mr. PURNELL. I am entirely opposed to making the change in the circuit which embraces the counties of Somerset, Worcester and Dorchester, contemplated by the gentleman from Somerset (Mr. Dennis.) While there may be some disproportion in population, and in territory, the business of that circuit is not of such magnitude as to require any change whatever. On the contrary, the judge can attend to the business of the three counties with very moderate labor. By the change contemplated we should lose the judge, Judge Spence, who is now the judge of that district, and resides in Cambridge, Dorchester county. A better circuit judge is nowhere to be found in this State I repeat, without fear of contradiction, that a better circuit judge cannot be found anywhere than Judge Spence, who now presides with so much dignity and character in that circuit.

If he were overburdened with business; if he could not get through with the business; if justice could not be dispensed to every citizen of the county, I would readily yield to the change contemplated by the gentleman from Somerset. But really it is not the fact. I speak with reference to my own county; and I believe the same parity of reasoning will apply to the other counties.

In the county of Worcester the court rarely sits more than a week, twice a year, there not being business enough to engage the court longer, criminal, common law and chancery business all combined. That shows that it would be utterly inexpedient to make any change. It is true that we have four terms during the year, a spring and fall term, and two intermediate terms; but the latter are merely formal assemblings of the court, there being no jury, and of course no jury trials. A few traverses before the court, and a little chancery business, constitute the whole business of the intermediate term.

I can see no reason then for the change. Our people do not require it; for I think I understand their views on that subject.

Therefore I shall oppose the amendment as proposed by the gentleman from Somerset, on the ground of inexpediency. I do not think the exigencies of the occasion require any such change. Under the old system the county of Caroline belonged to our circuit; but even then the business was despatched with facility without imposing any great labor upon the judges, under the old system of three judges. Since the change of 1850, when the labors have devolved upon one, he has with equal facility and promptitude and satisfaction, and in a manner entirely creditable to him, despatched the business, so as to meet the convenience and the interests of the people. Under these circumstances, I oppose this amendment; and I will add that our delegation are unanimous in that conclusion.

Mr. Thomas. When I submitted a proposition as an amendment to the nineteenth section of this report, I was under the impression that that would meet the views of the majority of the convention; that the only change that was necessary was to put Baltimore county into a separate and distinct circuit. I am perfectly satisfied from what I have heard from the western counties, that Allegany, and Washington, and Frederick, require themselves to be erected into separate circuits; and for that reason I am perfectly willing and satisfied to vote for the proposition of the gentleman from Allegany (Mr. Hebb.) I think his proposition is better than the one offered by the gentleman from Anne Arundel (Mr. Miller,) for more reasons than the one which I have given. The arrangement is not only better, less complex than the one submitted by the gentleman from Anne Arundel, but since this convention has shown that it does not intend that the counties shall pay for their own judicial systems, but that the State shall, it rids Baltimore city of that additional taxation which she would be obliged to pay in case the one-judge system were adopted.

There is another reason why I shall support it; and that is that it leaves the orphans' court just where it is, and where it should remain. And I think that those gentlemen who have been voting with us upon these propositions should come in now and sustain the proposition of the gentleman from Allegany, believing, as I do, that it is satisfactory to a large majority of the representatives of the State, and will be perfectly satisfactory to the people.

Mr. Dennis. I have but one word to say in response to the gentleman from Worcester (Mr. Purnell;) and it is that this is not a question as to how the judicial duties of the Worcester district have been performed. I concede to the gentlemen that the present occupant of that bench is one of whom any man in the limits of this land may well be proud. But the gentleman has a queer way of showing his love for his own people, and has a most astonishing way of showing his extreme friendship for the judge of whom he is so very proud. He is for imposing upon that judge the discharge of duties where 53,254 people are concerned, and leaving the adjoining district with 21,460. One ought not by any means to be burdened with a duty so much heavier than another man. The convention must see at once that it is desirable to equalize these districts. The amendment I propose separates Dorchester from the twelfth district, and leaves the two districts thus equalized:

TWELFTH DISTRICT.		ELEVENTH DISTRICT.	
Worcester	17,013	Talbot	11,070
Somerset	19,903	Caroline	10,390
		Dorchester	16,338
Total	36,918	Total	37,798

This brings the population very nearly equal; while, as provided by the amendment, the twelfth district will have 2½ times as many as the other. I leave the convention to say which is the best.

Mr. Chambers. I have but little to say on the subject of the proposed amendment, and probably should not have said a word but for the recurrence to the question of expense. Do gentlemen recollect that 19-20ths of the business of the court of appeals is from the city of Baltimore? When they open an account of that sort they ought to pay 19-20ths of the salaries of the court of appeals, upon a mere arithmetical calculation, disregarding everything like the principles which should regulate the administration of justice by the organic law of the State.

With regard to this amendment, I personally have no concern with it. I have only to say that the majority of this house will do what they please in regard to this matter. We prefer the arrangement of the committee; next to that, we prefer the arrangement we had adopted last evening, of one judge for each county to be elected. We can only say that the nearest approach the majority may make to any theory put forth by them, we shall certainly accept as a matter of necessity. For one I stand upon the record as opposed to the system, opposed on principle. I stand further opposed to it in detail; as I think the counties should each have a judge. I think that fitness in every respect required that we should adhere to the proposition adopted over night; but the gentleman from Baltimore has rallied his forces this morning, and it is rejected. I am therefore prepared to accept submissively whatever the majority of this body may think proper to allow.

Mr. STIRLING. I think the gentleman from Kent will believe me when I assure him that I have not made the slightest attempt to organize the majority of the house upon this question in any shape or form. I have had no consultation with them, except with two or three members in the casual intercourse around the State house this morning.

Mr. CHAMBERS. Then the gentleman pays himself a still higher compliment; for it seems to have resulted from his attempt to rally them last night, and I did not think any one member had so much power over the majority.

Mr. STIRLING. No, sir; it is simply because gentlemen are here who were not here last night.

Mr. BRISCOE. If I understood the convention that the report of the committee was not to be entertained with any favor in this house, and not likely to be passed, I could very readily determine how I should vote upon a proposition of the kind before this body. Compared with the present judiciary system of the State, I infinitely prefer the amendment of the gentleman from Allegany; but compared with the report of the judiciary committee, I am perfectly decided that I prefer the report of the committee. If I am bound to vote upon this amendment, as it now stands, although I prefer it to our present system, I am bound to vote against its adoption because I prefer the original report. That report reaches sooner the objects designed by the substitute offered by the gentleman from Prince George's (Mr. Clarke,) giving a judge to each one of the counties of the State. The report of the committee provides for a resident judge in each of the counties, and that report divides the State into judicial circuits.

So far as the question of economy is concerned, I do not see much difference between the report of the committee and the amendment of the gentleman from Allegany. This question of economy is one to which I wish to direct the attention of the convention. I understood from the chairman of the committee on the judiciary (Mr. Stockbridge) that if his report was adopted, the cost of the administration of the judiciary system would be increased above that of the present system only by a very small amount. I should like to learn from the gentleman from Allegany what would be the cost of his system, if he has made any calculation.

Mr. HEBB. I have made no calculation; but the system proposed by this amendment has eight districts less than as proposed by the committee. Therefore it will cost about $20,000 less than that, and about $10,000 more than the present system.

Mr. BRISCOE. Under the report of the committee, as I understand it, this is to be followed up by requiring one of the judges of the circuit to act as judge of the orphans' court in conjunction with two associate judges of the orphans' court elected by the people. So far as the question of economy is concerned, when we look to that view of it, I think the advantage of economy is with the report of the committee as it was brought before us originally. It seems to me that this is a proposition of the gentleman from Allegany, offered on the spur of the moment. The report of the committee on the judiciary, composed as that committee has been, I presume, of gentlemen representing every part of the State, who have conferred with the ablest counsel of the State, and looked to the interests of the State, goes over the whole subject carefully; and I think that their conclusions are entitled to more consideration by the house than the proposition of the gentleman from Allegany. Other things being equal I am disposed to favor the report of the committee, because, so far as the question of economy is concerned, I think the original report has the advantage in that respect over the gentleman's proposition.

If we adopt that we reach the important object, that we have a judge, although elected by a judicial circuit, resident in each one of the counties of the State. Looking to it in that light, I prefer the report as originally presented to this convention. This whole question about the cost and the expenditure, and who shall pay the cost of this judicial system, is one in which I think the whole State of Maryland is equally concerned, one section as much as another. So far as any effort is concerned to confine the payment of the expenditures of this system to the locality, I think it is unjust to the whole State and particularly to the city of Baltimore. The citizens of Baltimore will see that their interests are as much involved in the efficient administration of justice in the counties as in their own city. And if they look at it in that light, it seems to me that they will not hesitate on account of the expenditure of a few thousand dollars to adopt the best system. In that view of it, taking this as an alternative between this amendment and the report of the committee. I shall vote against the amendment offered by the gentleman from Allegany.

The amendment submitted by Mr. DENNIS was rejected.

The question recurred upon the amendment submitted by Mr. HEBB.

Mr. HEBB. I desire to state to those members who desire one judge for each county that it is impossible to carry that system. The largest number of circuits that can possibly be carried will be thirteen. If this is not adopted, an effort will be made to reduce the system to ten circuits.

Mr. BELT. I move to transfer Prince George's county from the third district to the first district so that Prince George's, Charles and St. Mary's shall constitute one circuit as they now do. These three counties lying together in the peninsula have been associated in the judicial system from the first foundation of the State. There is not business enough in the two lower counties, St. Mary's and Charles, to constitute one circuit. I think that will be testified to by the members of those counties here. Prince George's can well be connected with them, although it is a matter of fact that there is perhaps twice as much business in Prince George's county as in both the others put together. I think it leads to unnecessary expense and an unnecessary multiplication of the circuits, besides disconnecting our people from those with whom we have been associated in this way, and breaking up professional and personal intercourse, which I am in favor of preserving as long as possible. Of course I have no objection to associating with the people of Montgomery, but we have been connected with the lower counties and are used to it, and I hope that the convention will have no objection to make the alteration.

The amendment was rejected.

The question recurred upon the amendment submitted by Mr. HEBB.

Mr. DANIEL. I confess that I have had and have now some difficulty in determining how to vote upon the proposition now before the convention. As a member of the judiciary committee I agreed to that report, believing it was the best. I would have preferred the one judge to have done all the orphans' court business as well as the other business of the counties. It was thought better, on agreement, to compromise in committee, to have him sit with two associate judges, so as not to destroy the present orphans' court system, and array opposition to it. For the reasons assigned by my colleague on yesterday, I prefer the report of the judiciary committee, and the main reason is, that it is greatly desired by this house, and I believe will be determined, to confer additional equity jurisdiction upon the orphans' court of the State. That involves, I think, a great deal of strictly legal matter which has not been confided to the orphans' courts before, if estates real and personal are to be settled up in the orphans' court. It is a large power of chancery jurisdiction which has heretofore been confined to the circuit judge. If that is transferred I believe it will be proper to have a judge in that orphans' court. Seeing no other way to have a judge there except by the report of the committee, something like the one-judge system, I feel constrained to vote against all amendments that I may have an opportunity to vote for the report of the committee.

Mr. STIRLING. It seems to me that we are not coming to any definite conclusion. Gentlemen who like this better than something else will vote against it, and the proposition will be killed while a majority of the house is in favor of it. I suggest that the better means of reaching a definite result will be to take the question on the section reported by the committee, and I will move that the section reported by the committee be stricken out.

The PRESIDENT. The question is upon the amendment of the gentleman from Allegany (Mr. Hebb.)

Mr. HEBB. I have no objection to withdraw the proposition and take the vote upon striking out the section altogether.

The PRESIDENT. That will bring confusion again.

Mr. HEBB. I can only withdraw it with that understanding.

The PRESIDENT. The chair cannot recognize any understanding. If the gentleman withdraws his proposition the chair will take no further notice of it. Does the gentleman withdraw his proposition?

Mr. HEBB. No, sir.

Mr. DENNIS demanded the yeas and nays, and they were ordered.

The question being taken, the result was—yeas 52, nays 24—as follows:

Yeas—Messrs. Goldsborough, President; Abbott, Audoun, Blackiston, Bond, Brooks, Carter, Chambers, Cunningham, Cushing, Davis, of Washington, Dellinger, Duvall, Ecker, Galloway, Greene, Hatch, Hebb, Henkle, Hoffman, Hopkins, Hopper, Johnson, Keefer, Kennard, King, Larsh, Markey, McComas, Miller, Murray, Negley, Nyman, Parker, Parran, Pugh, Purnell, Ridgely, Robinette, Russell, Sands, Schley, Smith, of Dorchester, Smith, of Worcester, Sneary, Sykes, Thomas, Thruston, Todd, Wickard, Wooden—52.

Nays—Messrs. Annan, Belt, Billingsley, Briscoe, Brown, Crawford, Daniel, Dennis, Dent, Edelin, Farrow, Gale, Hodson, Hollyday, Horsey, Lansdale, Lee, Mitchell, Morgan, Peter, Schlosser, Smith, of Carroll, Swope, Turner—24.

When their names were called,

Mr. ABBOTT said: It was my opinion that it was not proper for this convention to make any change in its judiciary system, except perhaps to make one more district for Baltimore county, that county having a large accession of population; but inasmuch as it seems to be the desire of so many members of other counties that there should be a further change, and as this system seems to be the best that is offered, I vote "aye."

Mr. BOND said: As the proposition of the gentleman from Allegany approximates as nearly as any other to what I desire, I am very much inclined, in a spirit of compromise, to vote "aye."

Mr. CHAMBERS said: Believing this to be the best system which it will be the disposition of this house to furnish the State, I take this rather than incur the hazard of getting a worse one. I therefore vote "aye."

Mr. KING said: I rather look upon this as a compromise than anything else, giving an additional district to Baltimore county which has had such an influx of population, and I vote "aye."

Mr. MILLER said: I believe this to be the best thing we can get, and if we do not get this we shall get something worse. I therefore vote "aye."

Mr. NEGLEY said: I should have preferred the section as reported by the committee, but as indicated by the vote of the convention this morning, I think that is unattainable in any shape or form. As the nearest approximation to that system, and as being calculated to remedy in part at least the evils of the present system, I take this as the next best, and vote "aye."

Mr. SCHLEY said: The existing judicial system of the State answers the purposes of the constituency which I represent. I am sure that an alteration giving Baltimore county a separate judicial district would meet the wants and wishes completely of that district. We do not want any change. I believe on account of the increased cost of all the necessaries of life, that the people of my county and district are willing and desirous to increase the salaries of the judges above what is at present allowed by law; but they would with marked reluctance accede to any such increase if the multiplication of the number of the judges was so great as to make it an onerous burden to pay them. This is one reason why I proposed that every county desiring a judge should pay the expense of that judge. I wish to say on the pending question that I prefer the proposition of the gentleman from Allegany very much to the report of the committee, but I do not like it as much as the present system with the amendment I have indicated. Believing, however, that there is no chance of getting anything better, in the temper of the convention, or anything more accordant with the views I entertain, I vote "aye."

Mr. THOMAS said: I came to this convention under the impression that the only alteration or change required in the judicial system was to erect Baltimore county into a separate circuit. Feeling satisfied, as I do, from the vote of this convention that the counties desire separate circuits formed for some of them, I feel constrained to vote for this proposition "aye."

Mr. TODD said: After much deliberation I would have preferred the system reported by the committee. Believing it impossible to get that I shall vote for this proposition as the best we can do. I vote "aye."

The amendment of Mr. HEBB, creating thirteen judicial districts, was accordingly agreed to.

Mr. THRUSTON. I move to add the following:

"And the general assembly may from time to time increase the number of such judicial circuits, if the public convenience and interests require it."

I will merely say in advocacy of that amendment, that it may be a long time before we have another convention to change the constitution, and that various portions of the State may increase very largely in population, business, &c. I think it would be prudent to give the legislature that power. I do not see any harm that can possibly arise from it. I think it is nothing more than enabling the legislature to conform to the increase of population.

Mr. AUDOUN. I will suggest to the gentleman to use the words "alter or increase."

Mr. THRUSTON. I have no objection in the world to that.

Mr. SANDS. This word "alter," now in the amendment, seems to me not precisely a proper one, because the constitution provides for its own amendment in this respect as in others. If ten or twelve years hence we want another judge, all we have to do is to say so. But if we leave it to the legislature to be constantly altering the circuits, we shall have judges elected and ousted from their position, and at almost every meeting of the legislature there will be some change. As the necessity is provided for by the facility with which the constitution itself can be altered or amended, I think it is better to let it stand as it is. It is hardly proper to leave the judiciary system to be remoulded and remodelled by every legislature. One legislature will be democratic and will remodel and remould to suit their views. The next may be of some other politics, and may remodel and remould to suit theirs. I think it would be very unwise to make this a subject over which party politics could have any jurisdiction.

Mr. THRUSTON. I will merely say that the word "increase" necessarily implies the right to alter, because it cannot be increased without being altered.

Mr. SANDS. If it merely gives the right to increase the number of circuits, it will somewhat diminish my objection but not remove it entirely.

The next legislature may choose to increase the number to twenty-one, the very thing this convention has by a decided vote put the seal of its condemnation upon. I think the mode provided for the amendment of the constitution will meet the wants of the people whenever those wants arise. I think it would be better to let the thing rest; and not subject the matter to the changes of public opinion which may rule this way one year and another the next. I am very well convinced of the impropriety of this amendment.

Mr. THOMAS. It appears to me that there is another objection that may be suggested in relation to the proposition of the gentleman from Allegany, and it is this: If it gives power to the legislature to alter the judicial districts, you must at the same time give them power to provide for the election of new judges. There is already a power under our new constitution by which the legislature may change the judicial districts whenever the time shall come that the people may really desire it, by amending the constitution. If the people require the change they will ratify the amendment. Two successive legislatures can pass the amendment and submit it to the people, and the people can adopt it. It appears to me an unwise provision to give power to the legislature to undo exactly what we are doing, in our attempt to fix these judicial districts permanently.

Mr. THRUSTON. There seems to be so much objection to this amendment that I withdraw it.

No further amendment was offered to the nineteenth section.

The next section was read as follows:

"Sec. 20. In each of the above-named circuits, except the eighth, there shall be three courts, one to be held in each county; they shall be called circuit courts for the county in which they may be held, and shall have and exercise all the power, authority, and jurisdiction, original and appellate, which the present circuit courts of this State now have and exercise, or which may hereafter be prescribed by law."

Mr. HEBB submitted the following amendment:

Strike out section twenty and insert:

"Sec. 20. One court shall be held in each county of the State; the said courts shall be called circuit courts for the county in which they may be held, and shall have and exercise all the power, authority and jurisdiction, original and appellate, which the present circuit courts of this State now have and exercise, or which may hereafter be prescribed by law."

Mr. THOMAS. It appears to me that striking out "three" in the second line of the report of the committee we arrive at the same result.

The amendment of Mr. HEBB was agreed to.

No further amendment was offered.

The next section was read as follows:

"Sec. 21. For each circuit (the eighth excepted) there shall be three judges, who shall be styled circuit judges, one of said judges, during his term of office, shall reside in each county of the circuit; the said judges shall hold a term of their courts in each of the counties composing their respective circuits at such times as now are or may hereafter be fixed by law, such terms to be never less than two in each year in each county; special terms may be held by said judges, in their discretion, whenever the business of their several counties renders such terms necessary; a single judge may hold sessions of the circuit court for the disposal of all equity business, all business merely formal and uncontested, appeals from the decisions of justices of the peace (but no other appeals) and such causes civil or criminal as the parties litigant shall consent to try before a single judge."

Mr. AUDOUN submitted the following amendment:

Amend by striking out all after the word "for," in the first line, and insert:

"Each circuit (the thirteenth excepted) there shall be one judge, who shall be styled circuit judge, who during his term of office, shall reside in one of the counties composing the circuit for which he may be elected, the said judges shall hold a term of their courts in each of the counties composing their respective circuits at such times as now are or may hereafter be fixed by law, such terms to be never less than two in each year in each county; special terms may be held by said judges in their discretion, whenever the business of their several counties renders such terms necessary."

The amendment was agreed to.

Mr. PETER submitted the following amendment:

Add to the section the following:

"It shall be the duty of the judge elected for any circuit embracing more than one county to divide his time equally between each county, and he shall be required to reside at the county town one half of his time, in each county where the circuit embraces two counties, and one-third of his time in each county where the circuit embraces three counties."

The amendment was rejected.

No further amendment was offered.

COMMITTEE ON ACCOUNTS.

Mr. GALLOWAY. Before the convention proceeds further with the judiciary report, I ask that the rules be suspended to enable me to offer the following order:

Ordered, That the committee on accounts be instructed not to issue any more certificates for payment of members or officers of this convention until after its adjournment *sine die.*

The object is to give the committee an opportunity to close up accounts at the bank, and have them adjusted, so as to have no difficulty at the close of the session.

Mr. PUGH. It is customary to pass such an order.

The rules were suspended, on division—ayes 45, noes 20.

The order was adopted, on division—ayes 35, noes 30.

CIRCUIT COURTS.

The convention resumed the consideration of the report of the committee on the judiciary department.

The next section was read as follows:

"Sec. 22. The salary of each judge of the circuit court shall be three thousand dollars per annum, payable quarterly, and shall not be increased or diminished during his continuance in office."

No amendment being offered, the next section was read as follows:

"Sec. 23. There shall be a clerk of the circuit court for each county, who shall be elected by a plurality vote of the qualified voters of said county; he shall hold his office for the term of six years from the time of his election, and until a new election is held and his successor duly qualified; he shall be re-eligible at the end of his term, and shall at any time be subject to removal for wilful neglect of duty, or other misdemeanor in office, on conviction in a court of law.

Mr. PETER moved to strike out "six" in line four, and insert "ten."

Mr. MILLER moved to strike out "six" and insert "fifteen."

Mr. MILLER'S amendment was rejected.

Mr. PETER'S amendment was rejected.

SALARY OF CIRCUIT JUDGES.

Mr. ABBOTT moved to recur to the 22d section.

The motion was agreed to.

The twenty-second section was read as follows:

"Sec. 22. The salary of each judge of the circuit court shall be three thousand dollars per annum, payable quarterly, and shall not be increase or diminished during his continuance in office."

Mr. ABBOTT moved to strike out "three" and insert "two" in the second line, to make the salary $2,000.

Mr. SANDS moved to strike out "$3,000" and insert "$2,500."

The question being stated on the latter amendment, containing the largest sum,

Mr. ABBOTT demanded the yeas and nays, and they were ordered.

The question being taken, the result was—yeas 43, nays 28—as follows:

Yeas—Messrs. Goldsborough, President; Abbott, Billingsley, Briscoe, Chambers, Cunningham, Daniel, Davis, of Washington, Dellinger, Ecker, Edelen, Farrow, Galloway, Greene, Hebb, Hoffman, Hollyday, Hopkins, Hopper, Horsey, Johnson, Keefer, King, Lansdale, Larsh, Markey, McComas, Mitchell, Morgan, Negley, Nyman, Parran, Russell, Sands, Schley, Schlosser, Smith, of Carroll, Sneary, Swope, Sykes, Thruston, Todd, Wooden—43.

Nays—Messrs. Annan, Audoun, Blackiston, Bond, Brooks, Brown, Cushing, Dennis, Dent, Duvall, Gale, Hatch, Henkle, Kennard, Lee, Miller, Murray, Parker, Peter, Pugh, Purnell, Ridgely, Robinette, Smith, of Dorchester, Smith, of Worcester, Stirling, Thomas, Wickard—28.

When their names were called,

Mr. CHAMBERS said: I vote "aye," preferring $2,500 to $2,000.

Mr. HEBB said: I vote "aye," preferring $2,500 to $3,000.

Mr. PUGH said: I shall vote against this amendment because I prefer $3,000. I like to stick to my principles. I am not in favor of cheap justices, nor cheap instructors for our children. I shall vote to keep up the salaries to what I consider a fair value. I vote "no."

Mr. PURNELL said: I feel entirely disposed to compensate any officer of the State for the services he may render. But events connected with this particular service show at least to my mind very conclusively that there is no particular reason for increasing the salary at this time. Under the old system the chief justice received $2,200, and the associate justices $1,400. They seemed to be satisfied with it. At all events I never heard of any resignations, and they held office during life. In 1850 we raised the salary to $2,000; and I have heard of no resignations occurring since then on account of the inadequateness of the salary. The labors have not been increased since then, and I can see no reason why the compensation should be increased. I vote "no."

Mr. RIDGELY said: I shall vote against this proposition for the reason that I consider a judge who is upon the bench ten or eleven months in the year continuously entitled to a much larger salary than the judge who perhaps may not be occupied more than three, or four, or five months in the year. The judges of Baltimore city, and the judge of Baltimore county are occupied through the year; and I do not consider $2,500 any compensation for that service. I therefore vote "no."

Mr. THRUSTON. I vote "aye," though I am in favor of $3,000, because I cannot get more.

The amendment was accordingly agreed to.

Mr. DANIEL moved to insert after "annum" in line two, the words "except the judges of the thirteenth and eighth circuits, who shall receive $3,000 per annum."

Mr. STIRLING. Those are fixed in a separate section of the report. That may as well be left until that section comes up.

Mr. DANIEL withdrew the amendment.

Mr. DUVALL moved to amend by inserting after "annum," in line two, the words "except in those counties constituting special districts, wherein the salaries shall be $2,000 per annum."

Mr. PETER. The reason why I advocate that amendment is that I think it is just and right. In a district composed of three counties, look at the labor which the judge has to undergo, and look at the expense which he is put to. For instance, as the judicial circuits are now arranged, the judge elected for Prince George's county will have to visit Montgomery county and remain there some three months in the year to transact our business, which will subject him to great additional expense. His board would absolutely absorb the $500 additional, besides the labor he would undergo in visiting our county. How is it in Baltimore city, where a judge is elected for that city alone? He is at home all the time, from the commencement of the year to the end of the year. He is put to no additional expense for board. He has not this additional labor and toil. I think it is fair and right, if there is to be any difference whatever made in the compensation, that it should be in that ratio. Where the judges remain at home, and their districts consist of but one county, they should receive less, because they are not put to additional expense. Instead of that I see the idea is that the gentleman from Baltimore county, and the gentleman from Baltimore city shall have a larger salary. I can see no just reason for that. The services of a lawyer acting as judge are worth as much in the county as in the city. Are they better there, that they must be paid more? I see no reason for it. On the contrary I see urgent reason for paying them less.

Mr. DUVALL modified his amendment to read as follows:

"Insert after the words 'per annum,' in the second line, the words 'except in those circuits composed of one county, wherein the salary shall be two thousand dollars.'"

Mr. MILLER. There is fairness about that proposition, and I think it ought to be adopted. The gentleman from Baltimore city is ready to take care of his judge. We wish also in other parts of the State to take care of our judges. Judge Price, in Baltimore county, has now in his circuit Baltimore, Harford and Cecil counties—three counties. He has to travel over these counties, and perform his duties, holding terms of the court in each of these counties twice a year. He receives now but $2,000 a year. By this system he will be relieved of all duty in Harford and Cecil counties, and will have no travelling expenses at all. He will reside in Baltimore county.

Mr. STIRLING. He resides in Harford county.

Mr. MILLER. Then he will have to remove his residence to Baltimore county. He will have to live in Baltimore county.

Mr. THOMAS. There will be a new election in Baltimore county.

Mr. MILLER. Then a new judge will be elected in Baltimore county, and that new judge will be relieved of all travelling expenses, which I suppose in the course of the year must amount to $500. There is a separate system for Baltimore city. This is merely a matter for the counties. I am opposed to cutting down the salaries, but if it is to be done this proposition is a fair one.

Mr. SCHLEY. I cannot allow so unfair and monstrous a proposition to go here unanswered. I scarcely supposed that anything so manifestly unjust as this, could find an advocate in this house. How does the gentleman's own district compare in population, in taxation, or in extent of territory, with some of the large counties? Taking Prince George's and Montgomery, the largest perhaps, and the wealthiest district, which has more than one county to compose it, how does it compare with the large counties?

Mr. PETER. Will the gentleman allow me to interrupt him for one moment? How does the district of Montgomery and Prince George's compare with Allegany county?

Mr. SCHLEY. In white population it is some seven thousand inferior. In taxation, I think it is about one-half. And in extent of territory I do not think it will compare favorably with Allegany at all. There are no two parts of that district so remote from each other as the extremities of the county of Allegany, and not half so remote from their county seat in either county as the distant portions of Allegany. Then, sir, comparing them with my own county, I find that the white population of those two counties is little more than one-half of the population of Frederick, while the taxes are about the same. The cost of living is less in those two counties, the population being not so dense. I think that quite as much labor will be performed, while the cost of living is greater in the counties forming separate districts. For that reason I think a higher salary ought to be allowed in Baltimore.

Mr. SANDS. I have examined the statistics, and I will inform my friend that Allegany has exactly one thousand more white inhabitants than Prince George's and Montgomery combined.

Mr. PETER demanded the yeas and nays, and they were ordered.

The question being taken, the result was —yeas 19, nays 50—as follows:

Yeas—Messrs. Abbott, Billingsley, Briscoe, Dennis, Dent, Duvall, Edelen, Gale, Hatch, Henkle, Hodson, Horsey, Johnson, Lansdale, Mitchell, Miller, Morgan, Parran, Peter—19.

Nays—Messrs. Goldsborough, President; Annan, Audoun, Blackiston, Bond, Brooks, Brown, Carter, Chambers, Cunningham, Cushing, Daniel, Davis, of Washington, Dellinger, Farrow, Galloway, Greene, Hebb, Hoffman, Hollyday, Hopkins, Hopper, Keefer, Kennard, King, Lee, Markey, McComas, Murray, Nyman, Parker, Pugh, Purnell, Ridgely, Robinette, Russell, Sands, Schley, Schlosser, Smith, of Carroll, Smith, of Worcester, Stirling, Swope, Sykes, Thomas, Thruston, Todd, Wickard, Wilmer, Wooden —50.

When his name was called,

Mr. Abbott said: My motion was for $2,000 all round, and I shall therefore vote "aye."

The amendment was accordingly rejected.

No further amendment was offered.

The convention resumed the consideration of the twenty-third section as follows:

"Sec. 23. There shall be a clerk of the circuit court for each county, who shall be elected by a plurality vote of the qualified voters of said county; he shall hold his office for the term of six years from the time of his election, and until a new election is held and his successor duly qualified; he shall be re-eligible at the end of his term, and shall at any time be subject to removal for wilful neglect of duty, or other misdemeanor in office, on conviction in a court of law."

Mr. Thruston. I move to add the words, "He shall give his personal attention exclusively to the duties of said office." I wish to prevent offices from being farmed out.

Mr. Edelen. What does the gentleman mean by the word "exclusively?"

Mr. Thruston. That he shall not attend to any other trade; that that shall be his occupation.

Mr. Edelen. And that a man becoming a clerk shall give up all other business?

Mr. Thruston. Yes, sir; and attend to the duties of his office daily, and not carry on another business, and farm his office out to deputies.

Mr. Thomas. Suppose the clerk happens to be a farmer. This would preclude him from attending to his farm. Suppose he owns a store, he cannot attend to that.

Mr. Thruston. It only excludes him during the time he is required to attend to the duties of his office.

Mr. Thomas. I should think it did.

Mr. Miller. I think the amendment is a good one, and ought to be adopted. Men in the counties get elected to the office of clerk or register, and they never see the office from the time they are elected until their term expires. They just hire somebody to go there and do their duty for them.

Mr. Thruston. I put in the word "exclusively" for this purpose. He might go and stay there half an hour a day, and give his personal attention for that time, and direct his deputy, and never take a pen in his hand.

The President. Why not say "during office hours?"

Mr. Thruston. I will add "during business hours."

Mr. Thomas What is the necessity of putting it in at all? What if the clerk does appoint a deputy, who does the work properly?

Mr. Thruston. The people do not elect the deputy but the clerk. He is the man they want, and not any one that he may choose to take his place.

Mr. Thomas. He might get sick sometimes.

Mr. Briscoe. I should be very willing to sustain the proposition of the gentleman over the way, but that I believe the purposes of the proposition can be better accomplished by legislative action. I believe there is already an act of assembly requiring the clerks of each county to attend so many days in the week to the duties of their office; but whether there be or not, I think it is perfectly competent for the legislature to pass such a law; and it is hardly necessary to incorporate it here. I should be in favor of a proposition of that kind, making the bondman of the clerk responsible for his personal attendance to his duties.

Mr. Thruston. My object was this: The latter part of the section is that "he shall be subject to removal by the said court for incompetency, neglect of duty, misdemeanor in office, or such other cause or causes as may be prescribed by law." I want to impose the duties upon him personally in such a way that it shall be a wilful neglect of duty for him to transfer them to another person. I think this is the proper place for it.

Mr. Pugh. I think this is more properly a question between the officer who is elected and the people who elect him. The great difficulty in the constitution is in adopting phraseology that is liable to some misinterpretation. The gentleman has varied his amendment, so as to read not only "exclusively," but "during business hours." That is liable to objection; because if the officer was not there during all the business hours, he would not fulfil the constitutional provision. I do not see how it is possible to prevent it from being objectionable in that respect. If the people think a man does not attend to his duty, that he is an unfaithful public servant, they should not vote for him. I shall always be careful to vote for men whom I expect faithfully to discharge their duties. I do not intend to vote for a man who will avoid the duties of his office. It seems to me that being elected to an office like this, it is properly a question between the officer and the people.

Mr. Thomas. I would suggest that a proposition came from my colleague from Baltimore city the other day, to attach an amendment to the provision in relation to the attorney general to make him attend exclusively to the duties of his office and not to any other business. There was hardly a lawyer in the convention but voted against it on the ground that it was utterly impossible to get an attorney general to take the office under such circumstances. The objection applies with the same force to the clerk of the county courts.

Mr. SANDS. I think we have some legislation upon this subject, but the very phraseology of that legislation is a reason why the views of the gentleman from Allegany (Mr. Thruston,) which are very proper, are not now required by the law of this State.— Section two of article eighteen of the code is as follows:

"Every clerk shall attend at his office for the transaction of the business thereof, every day except Sundays, either in person or by deputy, unless prevented by sickness, accident or necessity."

If the words "or by deputy" were stricken out of this section, and it was offered by the gentleman from Allegany (Mr. Thruston) as an amendment to the section under consideration, I think it would meet the case, and very properly meet it. For the office of clerk in many of the counties of the State is worth more than that of the judge of the court.— The fees of the office go over, three thousand dollars, and in that case the office of clerk is worth three thousand dollars.

Mr. STIRLING. The constitution limits it to twenty-five hundred dollars.

Mr. SANDS. Well, twenty-five hundred dollars, then. They are then paid salaries equal to the salaries of the judges of the courts. Now we know what is the custom. I know what it is with us. A gentleman is elected clerk who is a farmer. Now farming his land is the grand consideration with him, while he farms out his clerkship to a deputy, and very frequently when you go to the office on business, you find no one there to transact your business but the deputy or a minor son. Now I think when a gentleman who has a farm, becomes a candidate for the office of clerk, and is elected by the people to that office, he ought to farm out his farm to somebody else, and stay at his office. What business has he away from his office, any more than the day laborer has away from the handles of the plough when paid for his work?

Mr. RIDGELY. I would ask the gentleman whether there is not most ample provision in this section, as it now stands, to protect the public against such maladministration of office of which he speaks, in that portion of it which renders him liable to indictment and removal for wilful neglect of duty?

Mr. SANDS. We all know what that all amounts to; it amounts to just nothing at all. Under the provision now, when the fees go largely over twenty-five hundred dollars, the clerk is allowed to pay a deputy for transacting the business of the office, and still receives himself annually twenty-five hundred dollars when he is not in his office one day in seven. I have had some observation and experience upon this subject. I know how important it is that you should confine these officials to their duties, and not have the clerkship regarded as something to be bid for in a nominating convention, and then when obtained farmed out perhaps to incompetent people, while the other pockets the salary. It is so in our register's office, and I think when we come to that matter it would be well to change that. We have statutory law requiring the register to be in his office certain hours, and yet he is not there on the average one day in the week And if a party owning a farm, or store, or anything else, wants the clerkship, then let him farm out his store or farm, instead of the clerkship, which is a public office vital to the interests of the people, and which at all times should be open to their inspection and accommodation in any way.

Mr. DENNIS. It really seems to me that all this is "much ado about nothing." It does seem to me that there are ideas prevailing in this convention practically reversing all the old doctrines about office. I had supposed that offices were created for the good of the community. But the prominent idea here seems to be that the office-holders are the exclusive beneficiaries, and you are so to arrange matters that they shall reap all the benefit of the offices without any regard to the community at all.

Now where is the necessity for the proposed amendment? You provide in the section that if the duties of the office are not properly discharged, the incumbent shall be subject to removal. What more do you want? Is not that sufficient? If the duties of the office are not discharged, either by him or his deputy, then he is subject to removal. I think it is eminently wise and proper that you should have the office open to deputies. My experience is that very frequently incompetent men are elected to this office, not unfrequently some cross-road politician who knows how to hurrah for bumcombe, but who is entirely ignorant of the duties of the office. And it is well enough to have some competent deputy to discharge the duties of the office.

Mr. STIRLING. It strikes me that this is a very strange proposition. It involves the idea that the clerk of the court is supposed to perform the duties of clerk himself. Now I submit that it is not expected that the clerk of the court shall perform the duties of the office himself. It may be proper for him, if the fees of the office are not sufficient to enable him to employ a number of deputies, to reduce the expenses by performing the duties himself. The gentleman from Somerset (Mr. Dennis) says the people have the right to elect whom they please. Suppose a man is elected who does not know how to make the entries; will you force him to do it. A large proportion of the clerks in the State do not know how to make the entries properly. All that they are expected to do is to give their supervision to the office, and to be responsible upon their bonds for the proper persons to perform the duties. If you say that no man shall be elected clerk except one who is a practical clerk, then you will have to take persons who cannot give the necessary bonds. If a clerk is responsible for what is done, and gives a reasonable amount of attention to seeing that the duties of the office are properly discharged, that is all that is expected.

And who is to take the place upon the terms proposed by this amendment? No one, except some man who has acquired the manual experience and execution sufficient to enable him to write up the entries, and yet is not able to give the necessary bonds; or some man who is broken down in his other business and relies upon his friends to give the bonds. One great part of the business of the clerk is to receive the public money, the license fees, etc., and he must give heavy bonds for the faithful discharge of that duty. A great part of his bond, is for the performance of that duty. You do not expect a man, who may be qualified to do that, to be thoroughly read up in "Harrison's Entries," and to know how to enter all proceedings in court.

Mr. THRUSTON. There is so much objection to my amendment that I will withdraw it.

The amendment was accordingly withdrawn.

Mr. AUDOUN. The section as it now stands provides for the removal of the clerk, but it does not provide for the filling the vacancy created by the removal. I therefore propose to amend the section by adding "and vacancies in said office of clerk by death, resignation or removal from office, shall be filled by the judge of the counties or city respectively, for the residue of the term thus made vacant."

Mr. THOMAS. I would suggest to my colleague (Mr. Audoun,) to add after the words "removal from office" the words "or other disqualification."

Mr. THRUSTON. That amendment might take away from the people for three, four or five years, the right to elect their clerk.

The PRESIDENT. The incumbent is to hold his office for six years, or until his successor is elected and qualified. You must strike out that provision.

Mr. AUDOUN. Not necessarily so. There is no provision in this section, as it now stands, to fill the office of clerk should he be removed from office.

Mr. HEBB. I am opposed to this proposition. In the section in relation to the register of wills, provision is made that in case of vacancy the judges of the orphans' court shall fill the vacancy until the next election. I would prefer a provision of that kind to this amendment, and have the new clerk elected for six years at the next general election for county officers.

The question was then taken upon the amendment of Mr. AUDOUN, and it was rejected.

Mr. PARRAN submitted the following amendment:

Add to the end of section twenty-three, the following:

"In the event of any vacancy in the office of the clerk of any of the circuit courts, said vacancy shall be filled by the judge of said circuit in which said vacancy occurs until the next general election when a clerk of said circuit court shall be elected to serve for six years thereafter."

Mr. HEBB. I would suggest to the gentleman to make it "until the next general election for county officers."

Mr. PARRAN. I will accept the amendment.

The amendment as modified was then adopted.

Mr. ABBOTT. I offer the following as an additional section:

"Sec. 24. The election for all judiciary officers shall be held on the third Wednesday of May in each year, that such officers may be required to be elected, and no other officers except a judicial one shall be elected at the same time."

I offer this section for the purpose of separating the election of judicial officers from other elections, and having it held in a season of the year when there are none of those political gatherings and troubles that there are frequently in the fall of the year. This will in a great measure satisfy many of those who are in favor of an appointive judiciary system, because it takes it out of the bustle of the elections for members of the legislature, State officers, and members of Congress, and makes it a separate and distinct election.

Mr. THOMAS. I would suggest to my colleague (Mr. Abbott) that he except from the operation of that section, the judges to be elected for the new judicial districts. It seems to me that they should be elected as soon as possible after the adoption of this constitution.

Mr. ABBOTT. Provision can be made for that hereafter; this is only to establish the general rule.

Mr. STIRLING. The only difficulty I have about this proposed section is that this report makes no provision at all for the time of electing the judges, having been based upon the appointive system. I think some provision should be adopted to apply to all elections of judges.

Mr. THOMAS. I think myself that the whole thing should be left to the committee on the schedule, and let them fix it.

The question was upon adopting the section as proposed by Mr. ABBOTT.

Upon this question Mr. ABBOTT called for the yeas and nays, but they were not ordered.

The question was then taken, and the section was rejected.

Mr. THOMAS. There is no provision made in this report in relation to filling vacancies occasioned by the death, resignation or other disqualification of the judges. It is necessary that some provision should be made for that; I therefore move the following additional section be adopted:

"Section 24. In case of the death, resignation, removal or other disqualification of a judge by the courts of this State, the governor, by and with the advice and consent of the senate, shall thereupon appoint a person duly qualified, to fill said office until the next general election for members to the general assembly thereafter, at which time an election shall be held as herein prescribed, for a judge, who shall hold said office for the term of fifteen years, and until the election and qualification of his successor."

Mr. STIRLING. I approve of this proposition, but I cannot vote for it any more than I could for the other. Simply for the reason that it meets only one branch of the question. Some provision must be made in relation to judges holding over, elections of judges of new circuits, and the filling of vacancies.—This provides for the filling of vacancies, and nothing else.

The PRESIDENT. This can be followed up.

Mr. STIRLING. I think we better let the whole matter lay over. This can be put in the schedule.

Mr. CHAMBERS. This is a proper subject for a permanent constitutional provision.—The schedule is only temporary, for the purpose of carrying the constitution into effect. As to the filling of vacancies for all time to come, that is a proper subject for the constitution. I can see no objection to it.

The question was then taken upon adopting the additional section proposed by Mr. THOMAS, and upon a division—ayes 41, noes not counted—it was adopted.

ORPHANS' COURTS.

Section twenty-four of the report was then read, as follows:

"Section 24. There shall be an orphans' court in each of the counties of the State, and the city of Baltimore, and the circuit judge resident in any county shall be ex-officio chief judge of the orphans' court of each county, and one of the judges of the circuit court of Baltimore city shall sit as chief judge of the orphans' court of said city; the qualified voters of the city of Baltimore and of the several counties of the State shall, on Tuesday next after the first Monday in the month of November eighteen hundred and sixty-seven, and on the same day of the same month in every fourth year thereafter, elect two men to be associate judges of the orphans' court of said city and counties respectively; no person shall be elected associate judge of the orphans' court unless he be a citizen of the State of Maryland, and resident in the city or county for which he may be elected at the time of his election; each of said associate judges shall be paid at a per diem rate for the time they are in session, to be fixed by the legislature, and paid by the said counties and city respectively."

Mr. THOMAS submitted the following as a substitute for the section:

"Section 24. The qualified voters of the city of Baltimore, and of the several counties of the State, shall, on Tuesday next after the first Monday in November, 1867, and on the same day in the same month in every fourth year thereafter, elect three men to be judges of the orphans' court of said city and counties respectively, who shall be citizens of the State of Maryland and citizens of the city or county for which they may be severally elected, at the time of their election; the judges of the orphans' court for the city of Baltimore, shall receive an annual salary of ——— hundred dollars, to be paid by said city.—The judges in the several counties shall receive a per diem, and be paid by the said counties."

Mr. HEBB. Before the question is taken upon the substitute, I move to amend the original section by striking out all after the word "Baltimore" where it first occurs, and insert the following:

"And the qualified voters of the city of Baltimore and of the several counties of the State shall, on Tuesday next after the first Monday in November, eighteen hundred and sixty-seven, elect three men to be judges of the orphans' court of said city and counties respectively; one of the said judges first elected shall hold his office for two years, one for four years and the other for six years; and at the first meeting after their election and qualification, or as soon thereafter as practicable, they shall determine by lot, which one of their number shall hold his office for two, four and six years respectively, and thereafter there shall be elected as aforesaid, at each general election for county officers, one judge to serve for the term of six years. No person shall be elected judge of the orphans' court unless he be a citizen of the State of Maryland, and a citizen of the city or county for which he may be elected, at the time of his election; each of said judges shall be paid at a per diem rate for the time they are in session, to be fixed by the general assembly, and paid by the said counties and city respectively."

The question was stated to be first upon the amendment of Mr. HEBB.

Mr. HEBB. The difference between the amendment offered by myself, and the one offered by the gentleman from Baltimore city (Mr. Thomas) is this: He proposes that the judges of the orphans' court shall be elected for four years; the proposition I submit is that, at the expiration of the terms of the present judges of the orphans' court, three men shall be elected in each county to serve respectively two, four and six years. So that at each county election held thereafter, there shall be one judge of the orphans' court elected for six years. The object of that amendment is that the judges of the orphans' court shall not all be elected at the same time. In our county last year three intelligent men were elected judges, and a register elected, all men new to the office, and entirely unacquainted with their duties. After the first election, under my amendment, there will always be two old judges holding over at each election.

Mr. STIRLING. There is one thing which strikes me in regard to this matter. The present constitution, as well as this amendment, says that these judges shall be citizens of Maryland, and citizens of the city or county in which they are elected. There is nothing said about his being a citizen of the United States.

Mr. HEBB. I think the gentleman will find that the general provisions already adopted provide for that; I am not certain.

Mr. STIRLING. The orphans' court is excepted.

Mr. HEBB. My amendment requires the judge to be a resident of the county.

Mr. STIRLING. I think the gentleman better say that he shall be a citizen of the United States, and a resident of the county twelve months before his election.

Mr. HEBB. I have no objection to that. I followed the phraseology of the present constitution, which does not require that.

The amendment of Mr. HEBB was modified accordingly.

Mr. THOMAS. The amendment of the gentleman from Allegany (Mr. Hebb) is all very well, so far as it provides for old judges holding over. I would be willing to accept his amendment, provided he would put in a clause that the judges of the orphans' court of the city of Baltimore shall receive a salary of not less than fifteen hundred dollars a year, to be paid by the city mayor and council, as city salaries are paid. Each judge now gets twelve hundred dollars a year, and is at his office every day from ten until three o'clock They can transact no other business, and it appears to me that fifteen hundred dollars a year is little enough for their services.

Mr. STIRLING. I would suggest to the gentleman from Allegany (Mr. Hebb) that he should say that they shall receive such per diem compensation as is now or may hereafter be fixed by the general assembly. That will leave the matter to stand as it is now. The act of the general assembly gives our judges such a per diem that they receive twelve hundred dollars a year.

Mr. BOND. I move to amend section twenty-four of the report by striking out the words "the qualified voters of the city of Baltimore, and of the several counties of the State," &c., to the end of the section, and insert the following: "business and duties of the orphans' court shall be performed by the judge of the circuit court for the district, except so far as the several registers of wills may be authorized by law to perform part of said duties."

The object of that amendment is to test the sense of the house upon the question of abolishing the orphans' court system altogether. It is not intended necessarily to apply to the city of Baltimore; perhaps a separate section would be necessary for that. Since the circuits have been diminished in size, and the duties of the circuit judges very much lessened, it does appear to me not only that the duties of the orphans' court could be better performed by requiring the circuit judge to sit as an orphans' court, for instance once a week, but in this way the whole orphans' court system might be got rid of.

My theory is that the orphans' court is a useless tribunal; that is to say, all or nearly all the duties are performed by the register of wills. I know it is the constant habit of the judges of the orphans' court to appeal to the register of wills in almost every case, as to their duties, what they shall do, how their duties shall be performed. and how it has been performed theretofore. I do not speak of gentlemen who have served in the orphans' court for several years. But as a general rule I assert that the orphans' court is a useless tribunal. The duties would be far better done by the judge of the circuit court. The orphans' court tends to complicate the judiciary machinery of the State, and increases the expenses heavily. I am certain that since the districts have been diminished, the judicial duties of the circuit judges have been lessened, and they can perform these duties. I am willing to except from the operation of my amendment the city of Baltimore, where the judges are constantly employed every day. There may be a judicial system established for the city of Baltimore, so as to enable the circuit judges there to attend to these duties. I offer this amendment now for the purpose of testing the sense of the convention upon the question of abolishing the orphans' court.

The PRESIDENT. As there is already an amendment to the section pending, the gentleman from Anne Arundel (Mr. Bond) must move his proposition as an amendment to the amendment.

Mr. BOND. Then I move to amend the amendment by striking out all after the word "the" in the first line, and inserting, "business and duties of the orphans' court shall be performed by the judge of the circuit court for the district, except so far as the several registers of wills may be authorized by law to perform part of said duties."

The question was then taken upon the amendment to the amendment, and it was rejected.

The question recurred upon the amendment of Mr. HEBB.

Mr. THOMAS moved to amend the amendment by adding thereto the following:

"Provided, the judges of the orphans court of Baltimore city shall receive an annual salary of fifteen hundred dollars to be paid by the mayor and city council of Baltimore, as city officers are paid."

Mr. NEGLEY. I cannot understand why the salaries of the judges of the orphans' court in the city of Baltimore should be fixed in the constitution, and the salaries of the judges of the orphans' court in the counties be left open to the legislature. I cannot see why the legislature is not as competent to fix the salaries of the judges of the orphans' court in the city of Baltimore, as it is to fix them in the counties. If you fix in the constitution the salaries of the judges of the orphans' court in the city of Baltimore, I do not see why you should not go to work and fix the salaries or per diem of the judges in the counties. Is the gentleman afraid that the legislature will not give them as much as this convention is disposed to give? Or is he afraid to trust the legislature hereafter on that subject? I do not see why this distinction should be made at all. I shall vote against the amendment. I am for uniform legislation.

Mr. DANIEL. I am rather opposed to the amendment in its present form. The legislature has heretofore regulated this matter. It increased the salaries of the judges last winter, and it will increase them again, I suppose, if necessary. I think it is rather bad policy to fix a certain salary in the constitution. I should rather see it remain as it now is, to be altered by the legislature as they may think proper.

Mr. THOMAS. If the counties desire to have the constitution fix the per diem of the judges of the orphans' court, I am perfectly willing to vote for any proposition they may offer to that effect. But the desire upon the part of county members appears to be that the county commissioners shall have control over that subject. But we prefer that the salaries of the judges of the orphans' court for Baltimore city shall be fixed. Last winter the salaries of those judges were raised to twelve hundred dollars a year. There was a general disposition on the part of the members of the legislature to fix it at fifteen hundred dollars a year; but on account of one gentleman opposing it, that proposition was defeated. We had great difficulty in getting it, for the simple reason that there was a clause in the constitution which said that the salary of no officer should be increased or diminished while he was in office. But after a long and full argument they overcame their constitutional scruples, and agreed to give the judges of the orphans' court what they considered a better salary than they had been getting before.—The duties of the judges of our orphans' court are as onerous as the duties of some of the judges of the circuit court. They are in session every day; they have to hear very frequently long litigated cases on the probate of wills. They can transact no other business. And it appears to me that while you give the judges of your small circuits twenty five hundred dollars a year, a salary of fifteen hundred dollars a year is little enough for the judges of the orphans' court for Baltimore city, whose duties require them to be in session every day in the week except Sundays.

Mr. STIRLING. In addition to what my colleague (Mr. Thomas) has said, I will state that it is impossible to fix in the constitution the compensation of the judges of the orphans' court in the counties, because there are no two counties in which the same services are rendered; their compensation must be a per diem. But the orphans' court in the city of Baltimore is organized upon a different principle. The judge there attends every day, and there is a reason why the per diem should be abolished and a proper fixed compensation given. I have not consulted all the delegates, but so far as the most of us are concerned, we think that a salary of fifteen hundred dollars is not too much, and as it comes out of the city treasury I do not suppose the county members are very much interested in the subject.

Mr. DANIEL. I feel great delicacy in again opposing this matter. But really it seems to me that I cannot see any reason for a different rule being established in the city from the one in the country. I believe that the practice in the city is to sit pretty much every day, but to meet at eleven o'clock and adjourn at one. And the judges can have time to attend to their other business either before or after those hours. And the legislature having, in view of the high prices and everything, fixed the salary at twelve hundred dollars, I really am opposed to fifteen hundred dollars at this time.

Mr. MILLER. I cannot see why a day's work in the orphans' court in the county is not worth just as much as in the city of Baltimore. We have just as good judges in our orphans' court, and they are worth just as much. And if you leave it to the legislature to fix their compensation they will fix it fairly and uniformly.

The question was then taken upon the amendment of Mr. THOMAS, and it was rejected.

The question again recurred upon the amendment of Mr. Hebb.

Mr. STIRLING. I move to amend the amendment as follows: Strike out the words "shall be paid at a per diem rate for the time they are in session, to be fixed by the general assembly, and paid by the said counties and city respectively," and insert "shall receive such compensation, to be paid by the said counties and city respectively, as is now or may hereafter be fixed by the general assembly."

Mr. HEBB. I accept that amendment.

The amendment of Mr. HEBB, as modified, was as follows: strike out all after the word "Baltimore" where it first occurs in section twenty-four, and insert "the qualified voters of the city of Baltimore and of the several counties of the State shall, on Tuesday next after the first Monday in the month of November, eighteen hundred and sixty-seven, elect three men to be judges of the orphans' court of said city and counties respectively; one of the said judges first elected shall hold his office for two years, one for four years and the other for six years; and at the first meeting after their election and qualification, or as soon thereafter as practicable, they shall determine by lot, which one of their number shall hold his office for two, four, and six years respectively, and thereafter there shall be elected as aforesaid, at each general election for county officers, one judge to serve for the term of six years. No person shall be elected judge of the orphans' court unless he be a citizen of the United States, and resident for twelve months in the city or county for which he may be elected at the time of his election; each of said judges shall receive such compensation, to be paid by the said counties and city respectively, as is now or may hereafter be fixed by the general assembly."

The question was taken upon the amendment and it was adopted.

The substitute for the section, offered by Mr. THOMAS, was withdrawn.

No further amendment was offered to the section.

Section twenty-five was then read as follows:

Sec. 25. The said orphans' courts shall have all the powers now vested in the orphans' courts of this State, subject to such changes therein as the legislature may prescribe; and in addition to the jurisdiction now exercised by the said courts, they shall have and exercise in relation to the real estate of deceased persons concurrent jurisdiction with the circuit courts sitting as courts of equity, and it shall be the duty of the legislature to make such modifications of existing laws as may be requisite to give full power and effect to this provision.

Mr. STIRLING. I move to strike out the words "and in addition to the jurisdiction now exercised by said courts," &c., to the end of the section. I think this was based upon a different idea from that which we have adopted. The committee, in framing this section, had in view a small number of circuits, with three judges to each circuit, and a different system of orphans' court. We have provided a large number of circuits, and left the old system of orphans' court to stand. The reasons, therefore, for putting this provision in the section do not now exist.

The question was upon the amendment of Mr. STIRLING.

Upon this question Mr. WICKARD called for the yeas and nays, which were ordered.

The question was then taken, by yeas and nays, and resulted—yeas 34, nays 37—as follows:

Yeas—Messrs. Goldsborough, President; Billingsley, Blackiston, Bond, Briscoe, Chambers, Crawford, Cushing, Daniel, Dennis, Dent, Duvall. Edelen, Farrow, Gale, Greene, Hodson, Hollyday, Hopkins, Horsey, Kennard, Lansdale, Mitchell, Miller, Morgan, Murray, Parker, Parran, Peter, Purnell, Ridgely, Sands, Stirling, Thomas—34.

Nays—Messrs. Abbott, Annan, Audoun, Brown, Carter, Cunningham Davis, of Washington, Dellinger, Ecker, Galloway, Hatch, Hoffman, Hopper, Johnson, Keefer, King, Larsh, Lee, Markey, Mayhugh, McComas, Negley, Nyman, Pugh, Robinette, Russell, Schley, Schlosser, Smith, of Carroll, Smith, of Dorchester, Sneary, Swope, Sykes, Todd, Wickard, Wilmer, Wooden—37.

The amendment was accordingly rejected.

Mr. SANDS, when his name was called, said: I shall vote "aye" because this provision would require the judge of the orphans' court to be a man versed in equity law and practice, and that he cannot be without study and experience. No man taken from among the people is fit to exercise the equity jurisdiction of the State. I therefore vote "aye."

Mr. THOMAS. I move to amend by inserting after the words "real estate of deceased persons" the words "not to exceed the value of one thousand dollars." That would give the orphans' court jurisdiction in relation to the real estate of deceased persons not to exceed the value of one thousand dollars. It appears to me that if we give any jurisdiction to the orphans' court in relation to the real estate of deceased persons, it should not exceed the sum of one thousand dollars. That sum would cover the real estate of nine-tenths of the persons whose estates would go into the orphans' court. Those interested in the estates of poor men, of men who die with only a thousand dollars worth of real estate, would go there But those interested in other estates of larger amount would take the other horn of the dilemma and go into the equity courts. This does not deprive the equity court of concurrent jurisdiction. And I would much rather go to an equity court to wind up a large estate.

Mr. PUGH. My objection to the amendment is this; it seems to me it would defeat the very object for which this section was drawn. Persons with very large estates have the privilege of going into the equity courts.

Mr. Stirling. The two courts are to have concurrent jurisdiction.

Mr. Pugh. I understand that. I do not pretend to understand this matter thoroughly, but so far as I know anything about it, this provision is for the purpose of avoiding expense—it is for the purpose of avoiding the entailing upon the heirs of deceased persons the heavy expenses of equity courts. If they choose to submit to the decision of the orphans' court, by the provision as it now stands, they will have the privilege of doing so, and not be subjected to all that expense. And without the amendment of the gentleman from Baltimore city (Mr. Thomas,) they have the privilege of taking their chances in a court of equity, if they see fit to do so. The whole object of this section can be secured in no other way than by leaving it optional with persons having charge of estates, to select either the orphans' court, or the equity court.

Mr. Stirling. I think my friend from Cecil (Mr. Pugh,) and I am afraid some other members of the convention have not contemplated the extent to which this section goes. I have no objection in the world to giving the orphans' court concurrent jurisdiction to some extent. But this section was framed upon the idea that the circuit judge should have the jurisdiction of the orphans' court. As the section now stands it amounts to giving the orphans' court absolute concurrent jurisdiction over the estates of deceased persons. So that if a man owns real estate of the value of $100,000, and it is mortgaged for $50,000, the mortgagers can force the heirs to go into the orphans' court to settle up the estate. It takes away from them the privilege of going into the equity court. For although it says "concurrent jurisdiction," the principle of law is plain that the court that first gets jurisdiction must have the entire jurisdiction of the case. And all that is necessary to be done is for anybody interested to make the slightest motion towards the orphans' court, and that takes away the right to go into the court of equity. And all these complicated questions of equity must be taken into a court which, in the counties, does not sit two days in the week. It will not be so bad in the city of Baltimore where the court is in session all the time, but in the counties they do not sit more than two days in the week.

The interests of other people are involved in the estates of deceased parties, and not only that, but questions of real estate law are very eminently technical. And judges of the orphans' court, with all their ability to discharge their ordinary duties, must necessarily be ignorant how to decide upon these technical questions. So far as the mere power of appointing guardians to sell or lease real estate, I have no objection to vesting that in the orphans' court. That is all that has ever been asked for them before, and the legislature has not been willing to give that. Yet after the legislature has absolutely refused to allow the orphans' court to authorize guardians to lease real estate, it is now proposed by this section to give them concurrent jurisdiction to administer the whole estate of deceased parties.

I hope the convention will re-consider what it has adopted I do not think members understood it properly, doubtless thinking it only gave the power which was asked in an order introduced into this body some time ago. This section was framed upon a different principle from the one which has been adopted by the convention. There should at least be some amendment made, limiting the jurisdiction of the orphans' court to a particular amount.

Mr. Miller. In addition to what has been said by the gentleman from Baltimore city (Mr. Stirling,) I would say that this is a very important question. I ask gentlemen to reflect that in our State we have always had a system of equity jurisprudence distinct from common law jurisdiction. If you adopt this section as it now stands it will amount almost to striking down those several jurisdictions. I know that in a great many of the northern States their probate courts have jurisdiction to distribute the real estate of deceased parties. But they have there an entirely different system from that which has prevailed in the State of Maryland, and which it is proposed to continue under this new constitution. They have no separate equity jurisdiction whatever. And in the New England States the probate courts administer all the estates of deceased parties.

And there is another consideration. In this State the title to real estate is a very important matter. Now, if this section is adopted, we shall have to go into the orphans' court, where the records are probably loosely kept, to find out where the title is; and we shall also go into the equity court—the circuit court, and the court of appeals—to find out the title to land. And there will be a complication of views upon that subject.

Now in reference to the cost of the matter. This section does not diminish the expense at all. And I should like to know how under this provision a man is going to close up and distribute the estate of deceased parties. It is to be concurrent jurisdiction. And he must file a bill in the orphans' court the same as in the equity court. The same costs will necessarily attend the distribution of an estate in the orphans' court as in the other. Lawyers must be employed to attend to it, and a decree must be passed by the orphans' court, as in the equity court, to direct the sale. I rather think the actual costs will be increased by this system.

There seems to be an idea abroad in the community that if you give the orphans' court this power, you will get rid of the necessity of employing lawyers. But that is not the case. You must employ your lawyers in the orphans' court as well as in any other court. You must have a bill regularly filed; all the parties having interest in the estate, whether as heirs, mortgagees, or anything else, will have to file their responses, as now in an equity court, and the distribution will have to be made by a decree of partition or of sale. As to the matter of expense, it will not be diminished one cent. But as a matter of convenience in reference to the fixing a place where the titles are to be searched for, it will be a great inconvenience to both sides, to have the system proposed in this section adopted.

And besides all that, you will find that these lay judges upon the orphans' court bench will make such decisions in regard to matters of equity jurisprudence, that it will compel appeals to be taken to the court of appeals in almost every case, because those judges will not be acquainted with equity jurisdiction. In reference to the personal estate it is very important that laymen should appoint appraisers to see to its value and distribution, because in reference to personal estate the title goes with the possession. There is not that great difficulty in regard to a pure and perfect title in reference to personal estate, that there is in regard to real estate. If any such system as this is adopted you will hereafter have your real estate titles in this State in the utmost confusion.

Mr. ABBOTT. I do not understand that there is anything in the constitution or any disposition to put anything in the constitution to prevent the people selecting such men as they see proper to act as judges of the orphans' court. Gentlemen speak here about "laymen." If the people want a lawyer to act as judge of the orphans' court, they will put him there. But we do not want to make a provision here to compel them to put a lawyer, or anybody else there, unless they want him. Let them put in whom they please.

Mr. DAVIS, of Washington. I move to amend the amendment of the gentleman from Baltimore city (Mr. Thomas) by striking out the words "one thousand," and inserting the words "three thousand."

The question was on the amendment to the amendment.

Mr. PUGH. I only want to act advisedly in regard to this matter. And I wish to ask the gentlemen from Baltimore city (Messrs. Thomas and Stirling,) and others here who are lawyers, some few questions in order to enable me to act advisedly. I am opposed to the amendment of the gentleman from Washington (Mr. Davis) for the same reason that I am opposed to the amendment of the gentleman from Baltimore city (Mr. Thomas.) The gentleman from Baltimore city (Mr. Stirling) referred to the case of real estate to the amount of $50,000 or $100,000. Now I would ask whether a party interested in that estate in its distribution, administration, or interested in it in any other way, has not the privilege of selecting which court he may prefer?

Mr. THOMAS. Certainly they have; that is exactly the difficulty. Some one party interested in that enormous estate might select the orphans' court, and then when the orphans' court once got jurisdiction, the court of equity could never obtain jurisdiction over it. The practice is different in the two courts. A man dies owing thirty or forty thousand dollars. You go into a court of equity to obtain a decree to sell the real estate, the personal estate not being sufficient. According to the principles of equity the mortgagees have the right to come in and claim their portion of the estate. And you must go through a regular routine for the purpose of having the accounts audited; taking testimony before commissioners, proving claims, etc. If this section is adopted, you must establish an entirely new system of procedure for the orphans' court.

Mr. PUGH. If the estate is of the peculiar character the gentleman mentions, insolvent as far as the personal estate is concerned, that not being sufficient to pay the debts of the estate, and thus necessitating the falling back upon the real estate, which is encumbered with mortgages, and about the title of which there may be difficulty; would not the executor or administrator, being responsible and having given bonds for the proper administration of that estate, select the proper course to let him out of the difficulty? In the case of a complicated estate, any executor or administrator, being responsible for the full value of the estate upon which he is administering, will protect himself; and in order to protect himself he will select that course of proceeding which will be most likely to secure his protection. If the gentleman or myself were the administrator of an estate, we would certainly secure our safety by selecting that court which would probably lead us most safely through all these difficulties.

Mr. THOMAS. Under the provisions of this section, it will not always be in the power of the executor or administrator to select which jurisdiction he will have. If the gentleman from Cecil (Mr. Pugh) is the executor of a large estate, and I am one of the creditors, I can take time by the forelock and go into the orphans' court before he knows anything about it, and acquire jurisdiction there. There is the great difficulty by giving the orphans' court this jurisdiction.

Mr. PUGH. I do not admit the statement of the gentleman that he as a creditor can obtain jurisdiction before I can do so as executor or administrator. But these objections do not reach the ground which I intend to take in this matter. I admit the difficulty in regard to complicated estates. But I do not admit—

of course I will admit what the lawyers say—I do not admit that it might not happen that the executor might have something to do with the real estate in a case where he acts as guardian for the heirs during the time he is executor or administrator.

Mr. MILLER. The executor does not act as guardian.

Mr. PUGH. Is not the executor the guardian of the heirs?

Mr. MILLER. No, sir; he administers the estate. The business of the executor is to realize as much out of the estate as possible.

Mr. PUGH. The executor during the time he is executor, and until a guardian is appointed and qualified acts in the capacity of executor and guardian.

Mr. STIRLING. Not at all. It is an ordinary principle of law that where a man dies his real estate goes to his heirs. And if his executor is appointed trustee of the real estate, then as trustee, but not as executor, he can go into a court of equity.

Mr. PUGH. I will admit, as I said before, that when an estate is complicated in this way there may be some difficulty about it. But in that case the parties interested in the estate can select the better jurisdiction. Now I claim, in order to avoid entailing upon the estate all the expenses which necessarily accrue from going into an equity court, that executors should have the right to settle up the real estate as well as the personal property of the parties whose estates they have control of. Much has been said here about getting rid of the lawyers. I do not intend to state that it is our object to get rid of lawyers where they are necessary. But where lawyers are altogether unnecessary, I claim that persons who are settling up the estates committed to their care, shall have the privilege of doing so without incurring the expense of lawyers, for the mere formalities which have been made necessary by the present system for the settling up of real estate in connection with the personal estate. That is all that has ever been claimed by those who are in favor of adopting this section as it stands; simply that those having charge of estates, shall have the choice of selecting the least expensive mode of settling up the estates committed to their care.

It is notorious that now no question at all can be raised in regard to real estate of a party deceased, without making it necessary to go into an equity court. And what is the result? First you make up a case for the circuit court—I do not know the legal terms, but I know the result. The first thing you know somebody is appointed trustee—I do not say he is always a lawyer, but that has always been my experience—who is not at all interested in the estate; having no interest whatever in it in any possible way. The result is the estate loses to that extent; the fees of the trustee are taken out; that slice is lost to these orphans, for the protection of whom the orphans' court was instituted. I know the practical result from my own experience; I have seen it worked out. And I know there is no possible way to avoid it under the present system, even when all the parties interested in the estate are united as to what is best to be done. The heirs, if they are old enough to know what is best, and everybody else interested in the estate, may come forward and say—"It is a perfectly plain matter, and we want it settled so and so." But that cannot now be done without going into an equity court, and in going into an equity court you must entail all these expenses upon the estate.

Mr. MILLER. If the heirs are of age they can settle it without going into court.

Mr. PUGH I say if they are old enough to know for themselves what is best, and to come forward and say that they are willing to have the estate settled in this manner. There are plenty of heirs who are under age, and yet who are old enough to know very well it is better for them to submit to a certain settlement suggested to them, and to which they agree. It is to such heirs that I referred; to a case where all the parties interested in the estate are satisfied with a certain plan of settlement, and who if permitted could settle the whole matter in a quarter of an hour.

Mr. STIRLING. How can they do that without giving some notice to creditors? The heirs do not own the whole estate.

Mr. PUGH. I refer to cases where there are no creditors.

Mr. STIRLING. The court cannot take it for granted that there are no creditors.

Mr. PUGH. The orphans' court has knowledge of all the circumstances of the estate, and can give notice to the creditors, if there are any, to file their accounts.

Mr. THRUSTON. If the heirs are under age, can the orphans' court make a different settlement from a court of equity?

Mr. PUGH. I do not say that.

Mr. THRUSTON. Can it release the executor?

Mr. PUGH. I do not say that.

Mr. THRUSTON. Then what will it amount to?

Mr. PUGH. It will not amount to anything as the law now stands. But it will amount to something if the orphans' court had the power to do what we wish them to do.

Mr. THRUSTON. They will have no power to do so; they must do the same as now.

Mr. PUGH As I stated in the outset, all I want in this matter is, if possible, to avoid expense to persons interested in an estate. I know that all the lawyers think differently about this matter, and favor the present system of filing a bill, having a trustee appointed, and that trustee one of the craft, who will come in and get his share of the estate.

If there is any way to avoid all that, I want it. I say that the executor, until a guardian is appointed, is in the capacity of executory guardian to the heirs.

Mr. Ridgely. There is a way out of the difficulty, as I will state to my honorable friend from Cecil (Mr. Pugh,) and that is by making this court a court to be presided over by one who is competent to discharge the functions of that court.

Mr. Pugh. I was in favor of that.

Mr Ridgely. There is no other way out of it. I am very sure that the course of argument taken by the gentleman from Cecil (Mr. Pugh) is sufficient of itself to satisfy this whole body of the utter impracticability of the provision made by the committee for a very different set of circumstances—would this convention for one moment entertain the proposition to give the criminal and civil jurisdiction of the State to the orphans' court? And yet that would be no more remarkable a proposition—not so remarkable a proposition as to give the equity jurisdiction of the State to the orphans' court. Because the equity jurisdiction of the State involves questions far more profound, difficult and complex than the criminal jurisdiction; questions arising out of real estate which are the most difficult questions that arise in the practice of law. We are now called upon to submit questions to laymen—I use that expression without meaning any reflection at all, merely to discriminate between those who are educated to the profession of law, and those who are not—we are called upon to submit questions of the most difficult and complicated character, arising out of the various interests in real estate, to a tribunal which is wholly uneducated to consider them; whose discipline and training of mind is in another direction entirely. The only effect of this would be to multiply peals.

Now these courts, ever since their formation, have been considered mere statutory courts; courts created with very limited powers, and denied all constructive or inferential powers. Every possible restriction has been imposed upon them by the law, in view of the fact that they are law courts, and not constituted with a view to consider and determine questions of law or equity. I hope the convention will not think of engrafting upon the constitution a provision which would be so very prejudicial to all the interests of every one—not of lawyers, but of heirs, creditors, and everybody else interested in the administration of real estate. It is impossible to confer such a distinction without involving common interests in confusion and difficulty.

Mr. Sands. I would just say, in addition to what has been said in regard to this matter by the gentleman from Baltimore county (Mr. Ridgely,) that if I wanted to promote the interests of lawyers as a class, I should certainly vote for this section as it stands here. Because then where I now go to the court of appeals once, I would go a dozen times.

Now my friend from Cecil (Mr. Pugh,) not being a lawyer, but being a man of high intelligence in other respects, has in the course of a few minutes demonstrated the wrong we would commit in permittting men ignorant in the law to decide questions of law. For instance, the question would come up before him, as judge of the orphans' court, whether by virtue of the office of executor or administrator a man was guardian to the minor heirs, notwithstanding the fact that there might be a guardian appointed by last will and testament. How would he decide that question? According to his view of the law as expressed here to-day, he would decide that he was such guardian by virtue of his office as executor. Yet the law is plain, as it stands in article 93, section 151 of the code, that that was not the legal view of the case. How would that affect me as a lawyer? In addition to my fees in the orphans' court, I would make my fees here, for I would at once bring the case to the court of appeals, where they would immediately decide that that was not the law—and in section 152 of the same article of the code, it is expressly provided that after a certain time he shall not act as guardian of the minor heir, even by virtue of his office as executor, where no guardian is appointed by last will and testament. That is the law. But how shall a man ignorant of the law know it to be the law; as a lawyer I go to the proper title in the code, and in article 93, sections 151 and 152, I find the law to be as follows:

"Whenever any person shall die seized or possessed of any lands, tenements, or hereditaments lying within this State, and any of the persons entitled thereto or any part thereof, shall be under age, and without a guardian appointed by last will and testament, or by the orphans' court, the administrator of the decedent, as soon as administration shall be committed to him, and not before, shall take possession of such estate, and discharge and fulfil all the duties of guardian to such infant, and shall account with the court in like manner as guardians are required by law to account, and subject to the like control and authority of the court, in all respects whatever."

"No administrator shall be bound in any manner to discharge and fulfil the duties of guardian after the close of his administration, or after three years from the granting such administration, nor after a guardian shall be appointed by the orphans' court."

By very lapse of time, where there is no guardian appointed by last will and testament, the heirs to the estate would be without a guardian, without any one to have legal charge of their interests in this matter.

Mr. Pugh. The gentleman admits that the executor is guardian for three years.

Mr. SANDS. Where there is none appointed by last will and testament.

Mr. PUGH. That is what I said.

Mr. SANDS. I go farther and say that even where, by virtue of his office, the executor is guardian of the minor heir, it is only for three years, and after that period the minor is without a guardian, unless one is appointed by the orphans' court.

Mr. PUGH. I never said he was so forever; but only that he was so.

Mr. SANDS. There was no limitation to the expression of the gentleman. The legal construction of his statement would be that the executor was guardian forever.

Mr. ABBOTT. Does not the latter portion of that section provide for all that?

Mr. SANDS. I tell you non-professional gentleman that your interests are vastly more at stake in this matter than those of the lawyers, although I am an humble member of that much abused fraternity. Your interests are at stake instead of mine. For if this section is adopted, where I now have one case going to the court of appeals from the orphans' court, I should then have a dozen. But the people who are not lawyers, and who would be put into the hands of men not lawyers to decide law issues, would be the sole sufferers.

I make these remarks to show that we might go to gentlemen of high intelligence in the orphans' court, and ask them to decide questions of law, and then we should have to go into the court-house to have their decisions reviewed and corrected. It is a most dangerous thing, and one that will be fraught with evil consequences, to put men not lawyers to decide law issues.

The question recurred upon the motion of Mr. DAVIS, of Washington, to amend the amendment of Mr. THOMAS, by striking out the words "one thousand" and inserting the words "three thousand" as the limit of the jurisdiction of the orphans' court over the real estate of deceased parties.

Mr. SWOPE called the yeas and nays on this question, which were ordered.

The question was then taken, by yeas and nays, and resulted—yeas 28, nays 41—as follows:

Yeas—Messrs. Annan, Audoun, Brown, Carter, Cunningham, Davis, of Washington, Dellinger, Dennis, Ecker, Gale, Hatch, Hopper, Johnson, Keefer, Markey, Mayhugh, McComas, Nyman, Pugh, Robinette, Russell, Schlosser, Smith, of Dorchester, Sneary, Swope, Sykes, Todd, Wickard—28.

Nays—Messrs. Goldsborough, President; Abbott, Billingsley, Blackiston, Briscoe, Chambers, Cushing, Daniel, Dent, Duvall, Edelen, Farrow, Galloway, Greene, Hebb, Hoffman, Hollyday, Hopkins, Horsey, Kennard, King, Lansdale, Larsh, Mitchell, Miller, Morgan, Murray, Negley, Parker, Parran, Peter, Purnell, Ridgely, Sands, Schley, Smith, of Carroll, Stirling, Thomas, Thruston, Wilmer, Wooden—41.

The amendment to the amendment was accordingly rejected.

Mr. CUSHING, when his name was called, said: I am willing to vote for the proposition allowing the orphans' court jurisdiction to the amount of one thousand dollars. But I am not willing to increase that amount, because it strikes me, though not a lawyer, that there will come up before the orphans' court questions concerning real estate that may be very embarrassing, and which in the end will lead to great litigation. I am willing to vote for one thousand dollars, to meet cases involving small estates. But where larger estates are involved, I think questions will arise which will govern the action of the other court. I therefore vote "no."

The question then recurred upon the amendment of Mr. THOMAS, to insert after the words "real estate of deceased persons" in the twenty-fifth section of the report, the words "not to exceed the value of one thousand dollars."

Upon this question Mr. WOODEN called for the yeas and nays, and they were ordered.

The question was then taken, by yeas and nays, and resulted—yeas 46, nays 26—as follows:

Yeas—Messrs. Goldsborough, President; Annan, Belt, Billingsley, Blackiston, Brooks, Brown, Chambers, Cunningham, Cushing, Daniel, Dellinger, Dent, Duvall, Ecker, Edelen, Farrow, Galloway, Greene, Hebb, Henkle, Hoffman, Hollyday, Hopkins, Hopper, Horsey, Kennard, Lansdale, Larsh, McComas, Mitchell, Morgan, Negley, Parran, Purnell, Robinette, Russell, Sands, Schley, Smith, of Carroll, Sneary, Swope, Sykes, Thomas, Wilmer, Wooden—46.

Nays—Messrs. Abbott, Audoun, Briscoe, Carter, Davis, of Washington, Dennis, Gale, Hatch, Johnson, Keefer, King, Markey, Miller, Murray, Nyman, Parker, Peter, Pugh, Ridgely, Schlosser, Smith, of Dorchester, Stirling, Thruston, Todd, Turner, Wickard—26.

The amendment was accordingly adopted.

Pending the call of the yeas and nays, the following explanations were made by members, when their names were called:

Mr. ABBOTT. Believing that the people are fully competent to select such men as they choose to transact their business, and being opposed to putting any limit upon them in that respect, I vote "no."

Mr. CHAMBERS. I do not think this orphans' court is the jurisdiction by which this real estate should be administered. I think it is altogether foreign to its character and mode of doing business. But I shall vote "aye" upon this proposition, upon the principle that the less mischief done the better.

Mr. PUGH. I shall vote against this proposition for reasons I have already stated. If the jurisdiction over real estate is limited to one thousand dollars, you might as well have no provision in regard to the matter, for it is almost impossible to conceive, in these times, of real estate worth so small a sum as one thousand dollars. I vote "no."

Mr. STIRLING. I hardly know how to vote upon this proposition. I am as much opposed to this as to the other. If the convention thinks it wise to adopt this policy, I have no objection in the world to it. But if it is to be adopted, I do not see why it should be limited to one thousand dollars more than any other amount. I vote "no."

Mr. THOMAS. In explanation of my vote, I will say that I am totally opposed to giving this jurisdiction to the orphans' court even to the value of one cent. I vote for this proposition only because I think it is the best we can do under the circumstances; it is the least of two evils. I therefore vote "aye."

Mr. RIDGELY. I propose the following as a substitute for the entire section:

"Sec. 25. The said orphans' courts shall have all the powers now vested by law in the orphans' courts of this State, subject to such changes as the general assembly may prescribe, and shall have such other jurisdiction as may from time to time be provided by law."

I will make one word of explanation of this amendment. If it is desirable that this jurisdiction shall be conferred upon the orphans' court, it can be conferred by the general assembly. And if it should be found, as we think it will, to work injuriously to the public interest, it can be modified or repealed by the general assembly. If it is incorporated into the organic law, it then becomes permanent during the continuance of the constitution, and cannot be changed by the general assembly even if it should be found to work injuriously. I propose, by the substitute I have offered, to confer the power upon the general assembly to enlarge the jurisdiction of the orphans' court, if in their judgment the public interest demands it. The difference between the two propositions is this: mine gives the control of the subject to the general assembly, while the other by putting it in the constitution places it beyond the control of any human power during the continuance of that constitution.

Mr. DANIEL moved that the convention take a recess, but withdrew the motion at the request of

Mr. RIDGELY, who submitted the following:

"*Ordered*, That the order for recess for evening sessions be suspended for this evening."

The question being taken, the order was adopted.

LEAVE OF ABSENCE.

Mr. THRUSTON asked and obtained leave of absence for a few days.

Mr. BROWN asked and obtained leave of ab sence for a few days.

Mr. DENT asked and obtained leave of absence for a few days.

Mr. GALE asked and obtained leave of absence for a few days.

Mr. ROBINETTE asked and obtained leave of absence for a few days.

On motion of Mr. CHAMBERS,

The convention then adjourned.

EIGHTY-SECOND DAY.

FRIDAY, August 26, 1864.

The convention met at ten o'clock, A. M.

Prayer by the Rev. Mr. Todd.

The roll was called, and the following members answered to their names:

Messrs. Goldsborough, President; Abbott, Annan, Audoun, Belt, Billingsley, Blackiston, Bond, Briscoe, Brooks, Chambers, Crawford, Cunningham, Cushing, Daniel, Davis, of Washington, Dellinger, Dent, Duvall, Ecker, Edelen, Farrow, Galloway, Greene, Hebb, Henkle, Hodson, Hoffman, Hollyday, Hopkins, Hopper, Horsey, Keefer, Kennard, King, Lansdale, Larsh, Lee, Markey, McComas, Mitchell, Miller, Morgan, Mullikin, Murray, Negley, Nyman, Parker, Parran, Peter, Pugh, Purnell, Ridgely, Russell, Sands, Schley, Schlosser, Smith, of Carroll, Smith, of Dorchester, Smith, of Worcester, Sneary, Stirling, Stockbridge, Swope, Sykes, Thomas, Todd, Turner, Valliant, Wickard, Wilmer, Wooden—72.

The journal of yesterday was read and approved.

ABSENT MEMBERS.

On motion of Mr. PUGH,

It was ordered to be entered on the journal that Mr. Scott, of Cecil, is detained from his seat on account of sickness.

On motion of Mr. DELLINGER,

It was ordered to be entered on the journal that Mr. Mayhugh is detained from his seat by indisposition.

JUDICIARY DEPARTMENT.

The convention then resumed the consideration of the report of the committee on the judiciary department, which was on its second reading.

ORPHANS' COURT.

The section under consideration was section twenty-five, which had been amended to read as follows:

"Sec. 25. The said orphans' courts shall have all the powers now vested in the orphans' courts of this State, subject to such changes therein as the legislature may prescribe; and in addition to the jurisdiction now exercised by the said courts, they shall have and exercise in relation to the real estate of deceased persons, not to exceed the value of one thousand dollars, concurrent jurisdiction with the circuit courts sitting as courts of equity, and it shall be the duty of the legislature to make such modifications of existing laws as may be requisite to give full power and effect to this provision."

The pending question was upon a substitute for the section, submitted by Mr. RIDGELY, as follows:

"Sec. 25. The said orphans' courts shall have all the powers now vested by law in the orphans' courts of this State, subject to such changes as the general assembly may prescribe, and shall have such other jurisdiction as may from time to time be provided by law."

Upon this question, Mr. PUGH called for the yeas and nays, and they were ordered.

The question was then taken, by yeas and nays, and resulted—yeas 43, nays 28—as follows:

Yeas—Messrs. Goldsborough, President; Billingsley, Blackiston, Bond, Briscoe, Chambers, Cushing, Daniel, Dent, Duvall, Edelen, Farrow, Galloway, Greene, Hebb, Henkle, Hodson, Hoffman, Hollyday, Hopkins, Horsey, Kennard, King, Lansdale, Larsh, Lee, Mitchell, Miller, Morgan, Murray, Negley, Parker, Parran, Peter, Purnell, Ridgely, Smith, of Worcester, Stirling, Stockbridge, Thomas, Turner, Valliant, Wilmer—43.

Nays—Messrs. Abbott, Annan, Audoun, Brooks, Crawford, Cunningham, Davis, of Washington, Dellinger, Ecker, Hopper, Keefer, Markey, McComas, Mullikin, Nyman, Pugh, Russell, Sands, Schley, Schlosser, Smith, of Carroll, Smith, of Dorchester, Sneary, Swope, Sykes, Todd, Wickard, Wooden—28.

The substitute was accordingly adopted.

No further amendment was offered to this section.

Section twenty-six was then read as follows:

"Sec. 26. There shall be a register of wills in each county of the State, and in the city of Baltimore, to be elected by the legal and qualified voters of said counties and city respectively, who shall hold his office for six years from the time of his election, and until his successor is elected and qualified; he shall be re-eligible, and subject at all times to removal for wilful neglect of duty, or misdemeanor in office, in the same manner that clerks of courts are removable. In the event of any vacancy in the office of register of wills, said vacancy shall be filled by the judges of the orphans' court in which such vacancy occurs, until the next general election of delegates to the general assembly, when a register shall be elected to serve for six years thereafter."

Mr. MILLER. There ought to be some provision here fixing the time of election.

Mr. STIRLING. There will be some difficulty in fixing the day of election. I do not think the registers of wills all go out at the same time. Our register of wills was elected last fall, and holds his office for six years. No election for register of wills will therefore be held in Baltimore for six years longer.

Mr. AUDOUN. I move to amend this section by inserting after the words "counties and city respectively," the words "on the Tuesday next after the first Monday in November, 1869."

Mr. TODD. There would appear to be some difficulty in adopting that amendment. The terms of some registers of wills expire before that time.

The PRESIDENT. The latter part of the section provides that the judges of the orphans' court shall be authorized to fill vacancies.

Mr. HEBB. There will be a general provision in the schedule that all these officers shall continue in office until their terms expire. This section provides that when a vacancy occurs it shall be filled by the judges of the orphans' court until the next election. I think the section is perfect as it is.

Mr. DANIEL. I do not think this amendment is necessary, as this matter is covered by the general provision.

Mr. STIRLING. If that amendment is adopted then the words "for delegates to the general assembly" ought to be stricken out near the close of the section, because there will be no election for members of the general assembly in any year which is parallel in point of enumeration to 1869. The elections for members to the general assembly will be held on even years. The section ought to be amended so as to read "the next general election for county officers." I make no objection to this amendment, but if adopted the change should be made I have suggested.

The question being taken upon the amendment of Mr. AUDOUN, it was rejected.

Mr. STIRLING. I now move to strike out the words "delegates to the general assembly," near the close of the section, and to insert the words "county officers." That will make this section conform to the action of the convention yesterday in regard to the orphans' court and clerks.

Mr. STOCKBRIDGE. I trust the gentleman will modify his amendment so as merely to strike out the words he has indicated, and insert none in their place.

Mr. STIRLING. That will not fix the day of election.

Mr. STOCKBRIDGE. It will be the next general election, whether for State or county officers.

Mr. STIRLING. I understand the convention has adopted the principle of electing county officers on alternate years to the election of State officers. It would be very odd to elect clerks and registers on general ticket for State officers one year, and the next year on the ticket for county officers. I think my amendment is the proper one.

The question being then taken upon the amendment of Mr. STIRLING, it was adopted.

Mr. DANIEL. In the sentence which now reads "until his successor is elected and qualified," I move to strike out the words "elected and." We provide in the section that the register may be removable for cause, and another appointed to fill the vacancy thus created. We ought not therefore to say "until his successor is elected and qualified," but "until his successor is qualified." I therefore move to strike out the words "elected and."

Mr. STIRLING. How can he come in any other way than by election?

Mr. DANIEL. By appointment to fill a vacancy.

Mr. STIRLING. This clause is to fix the term of office for a man elected by the people, which is to be for six years, and until his successor is elected and qualified. If he dies or is removed that takes the matter out of that provision entirely, and it comes under the next provision.

The question being taken on Mr. DANIEL's amendment, it was rejected.

No further amendment was offered to the section.

NEGRO APPRENTICESHIP.

Mr. TODD Before we pass from this part of the report I wish to call the attention of the convention to an amendment, of which I gave notice several days ago, and which I think would properly come under the part relating to orphans' court. I desire to move an additional section to come in before the section last adopted. It escaped my notice at the time, and I therefore offer it now. It is as follows:

"Sec —. It shall be the duty of the orphans' court of the several counties and the city of Baltimore, to duly apprentice to some business all negroes emancipated by the adoption of this constitution, who are minors, subject to such regulations as are now or may hereafter be prescribed by law; and in all cases the preference shall be given to their masters while in a state of slavery, when in the judgment of the said courts they are suitable persons to have charge of them."

Mr. STIRLING. I would suggest that it would be better to put this off until we get through with the organization of the courts. This breaks right in upon our work in that respect.

Mr. PUGH. I think we might as well take action on this matter now as at any other time.

Mr. TODD. I propose to modify my amendment by striking out the words "masters while in a state of slavery," and insert the words "former masters."

The amendment was modified accordingly.

Mr. PURNELL. I move to amend the clause which now reads "duly apprenticed to some business" by striking out the words "some business" and inserting the word "labor." I offer this amendment because as it now stands it might confuse the orphans' court in binding out this class of people; they might suppose it their duty to bind them out to artizans.

Mr. STIRLING. I move to postpone informally the further consideration of this proposed section.

Mr. MILLER. I hope that motion will not prevail. If we are to have any such provision as this, this is the proper place for it. It imposes a certain duty on the orphans' court, and we have those courts and their organization now under consideration. We have had from time to time promises given that some such amendment as this should be introduced. It was first proposed to be put in the article on the legislative department, but the objection was raised that the report on the judiciary department was the proper place for it. And now when it comes up as an amendment to the judiciary report it is moved to postpone it until some other department is considered, or until we get through this. I think this is the proper place and now is the proper time to consider and determine whether or not such a provision is to be inserted.

Mr. TODD. I do not see what is to be gained by postponing the consideration of this matter. It appears to me that we are as well prepared to act upon it to-day as we will be at any other time. The motion to postpone will only tend to delay the business of the convention. I hope the convention will act upon this matter now, and if they are disposed to vote it down, let them do so and have the matter settled.

The question being then taken upon the motion to postpone, it was not agreed to.

The question recurred upon the motion of Mr. PURNELL, to strike out the words "some business" and insert the word "labor."

Mr. TODD accepted the amendment, and the proposed section was modified accordingly.

Mr. SCHLEY. I move to amend by inserting after the words "in all cases the preference" the words "with the consent of the parents or next friend of such minor."

The question being taken, the amendment of Mr. SCHLEY was rejected.

Mr. GALLOWAY. I move to amend by striking out the words "duly apprenticed to labor" and insert "bind out, until they arrive at the age of twenty-one years for males, and eighteen years for females."

Mr. TODD. I have no objection to that amendment. I will accept it.

The section was modified accordingly.

Mr. TODD. Would it not be well to leave in the words "to labor?"

Mr. STOCKBRIDGE. I think you can trust the masters for that part of it. I move to amend by adding to the section the words "and said court shall bind all masters to whom any such apprentice shall be indentured, to cause said apprentice to be taught to read and write; and any violation of which obligation on the part of any master shall cancel the indenture of apprenticeship."

Mr. RIDGELY. I hope that amendment will not prevail. That is the existing law of the State of Maryland, and why should you put in the constitution a provision that belongs to the legislature, and which has been in operation for years? These covenants between apprentices and masters are all designed to protect the apprentice, and to obligate the master to perform his portion of the contract under existing laws. If we go on in this way we shall be codifying instead of making a constitution.

Mr. STOCKBRIDGE. I have proposed this amendment in good faith. I believe there is no necessity at all for incorporating this section in the constitution. I think the code already abundantly provides for this subject. But if it is to be incorporated in the constitution and an obligation imposed upon the courts to bind this class by wholesale in this manner, whether vagrants or not, whether the parents are able to maintain and educate them or not, bind them in ignorance and to ignorance—why we cannot take such a step without inflicting a severe blow upon the State. I thought it was conceded on all sides, when the article in reference to education was under consideration, that it was necessary for the State to make some provision that these persons now to be freed should not be freed in ignorance.

And in reply to the gentleman from Baltimore county (Mr. Ridgely,) I would say that I am not aware that where an uneducated colored person is bound out there is any obligation to teach that person to read or write. I know that even where white persons are bound out, if they are bound out without any instructions, there is not considered to be any such obligation. I think the amendment is an important one in reference to the future welfare of the State, and I hope it will be adopted.

Mr. STIRLING. I do not wish to debate this question. I shall certainly vote against this section as proposed by the gentleman from Caroline (Mr. Todd.) If the convention chooses to adopt it, it can do so. I have no doubt whatever that my friend from Caroline (Mr. Todd) thinks this provision will accomplish some good. And I know there are considerations which can be urged in its support. But the necessary effect of it will be to perpetuate slavery in Maryland for ten years longer. And holding the views I do upon that subject I cannot vote for it under any conceivable state of circumstances.

Now what does this section propose? It provides absolutely for the binding out of an entire class of persons, without any reference to the condition of the emancipated parents of these children, without any regard to the age of the children, whether they are eight or eighteen years of age, whether they are competent to earn a livelihood or not, even if the orphans' court thinks that they are able to support themselves, and will do so, they are as a class to be bound out. Now this section in its effect is not so much to provide for the custody of these people as it is to some extent to compensate the masters by giving them an additional furlough upon the time of their slaves.

I know the views of gentlemen who represent some of the counties upon the eastern shore, who are on my side of the house, have a great deal of force in them in regard to this matter. I do not wish to express my views upon that. They can exercise their own judgment about it. But I am perfectly willing to stand upon the existing system. And at the proper time I shall offer this substitute for the section:

"The orphans' court in the several counties, in apprenticing under the existing provisions of law any freed minors who shall have been slaves, shall give the preference in so apprenticing to those who were the masters of such minors at the time of the adoption of this constitution, where in the judgment of the court such masters shall be the proper persons to whom to apprentice such minors."

Mr. PUGH. I wish to move to strike out that portion of the section giving the preferenee to former masters.

The PRESIDENT. That is not now in order. The amendment of the gentleman from Baltimore city (Mr. Stockbridge) is now before the house.

Mr. SCHLEY. I hope the convention will in the first instance adopt the amendment offered by the gentleman from Baltimore city (Mr. Stockbridge,) which is very proper and needs no argument from me, it is so self-evident. But I do hope that this convention will pause long before they will accept any portion of the section of the gentleman from Caroline (Mr. Todd) to be incorporated into the organic law of the State. View it as you may, with every allowance for the humane motives of the proposer, it is nothing more nor less than modified slavery. It is nothing more nor less than undoing to a certain extent what we have already resolved to do—the abolition of slavery in the State of Maryland. It is nothing more nor less than to return to servitude and domestic slavery the minors whom your constitution makes free; and it will be so viewed by all who are interested in preserving the institution of slavery, by all who regard the institution as proper under our form of government to be placed upon the statute book of the State.

It is a very serious matter. The proposition to give a preference to their former masters is one that certainly looks humane; but the refusal to have the assent of the parents or next friends of those minors shows that there is something improper about it. If they were the proper persons to have the custody and the service of these minors, surely those most interested in their welfare ought to be the suitable persons to decide upon that. I have no doubt that in every case where the master has been humane that the attachment of the servant and his gratitude would incline him to select that master for the future master of his children during their minority. But we have upon the statute book a provision of law for all cases that can possibly arise here. Every necessity appears to be anticipated, and if there is a deficiency anywhere it can be supplied by statute better than by fundamental law.

Mr. Cushing. By the operation of this section as it is written here proposed by the gentleman from Caroline, I think its adoption would simply amount to postponing the emancipation of all minors until they arrive at the age of twenty-one years. I can hardly believe that to be the desire of this convention, many of whom I know have come here especially pledged against the adoption of any system of apprenticeship as a specific article in the constitution. The orphans' courts of the State will have power to apprentice any minors whose parents are unable to support them, and who are liable to be a burden to the community in which they live. There certainly can be no need of a provision to force the orphans' court to apprentice these minors when they are able to make their own living or when their parents are able and willing to support them. Many of the minors who must be apprenticed under the operation of this section will be fully competent to earn their own living. You apprentice men twenty years of age, under this section, quite capable of supporting themselves. You apprentice those of eighteen, seventeen, sixteen and fifteen, all of them fully capable of supporting themselves by their own labor. And you do this at a time when there is a demand for labor all over the State, when the cry is that there is not labor sufficient for the agricultural and mechanical operations of the State. And certainly the younger children can most of them be supported by their parents.

I regard this as a modified form of slavery, as a postponement of the emancipation of slaves in Maryland after the adoption of the constitution. I have no idea of voting for the adoption of an article which puts back into slavery all under twenty-one years of age. By the operation of this section all those between the ages of eighteen and twenty-one will be prevented from being taken into the army without compensation to their masters for interfering with the contract of their apprenticeship. I certainly hope it is not the intention of the convention to get rid of slavery, and then to put back into a modified form of slavery all slaves under twenty-one years of age.

As to myself, the delegation of Baltimore city are all instructed by our constituents upon this subject, and are definitely pledged not to vote for any law for colored apprenticeship; and certainly this is a proposition that none of us can entertain. And certainly in other parts of the State delegates were sent here for the purpose of emancipating the slaves, and it could not have been the will of their constituents that after their emancipation all persons under twenty-one years of age should be remanded to slavery.

The orphans' court has at present the undoubted power to apprentice all such as cannot support themselves, or whose parents cannot support them. While there is not the slightest doubt that in such cases the minors should be apprenticed that they may not become an expense to the community, and while they would always give their masters the preference, I am sure you need not give the orphans' court any more power than it now has under the present regulations and laws of the State. Certainly it will not at all aid in the adoption of your constitution in the western part of the State to put into it a section putting back into slavery all those under twenty-one years of age, who were previously emancipated by your bill of rights. I shall therefore be obliged to vote against everything which in the slightest degree looks to sanctioning in any way the proposition to put back into slavery all emancipated slaves under the age of twenty-one years.

Mr. Chambers. I regret to see the sad spectacle exhibited to us this morning. I had really hoped that this extravagantly violent animosity towards everything like the interest of the slaveholder, would ere this, by its own violence, have dissipated itself. It has been said that the most violent disease soonest terminates, either by cure or fatally. It would really seem that the expiration of time but adds fuel to the flame which has been so hotly burning against everything like the interest of the slave owner. We have had spectacles, I hope not of the sober feelings of the body generally, of gentlemen who have already been distinguished for the warmth of their opposition to everything like these slaveholding interests. I trust and am willing to believe they were not a fair specimen of the cool, calm, deliberate judgment of the majority of the house.

What is the proposition which has produced in the gentlemen's ideas, such an alarming apprehension that you are going to undo everything you have been doing. You have by one fell swoop manumitted men, women and children, old and young, firm, infirm and helpless; those who are as impotent as the child at the breast, and as incapable of maintaining themselves. You have left the master in a condition which imposes upon him the necessity of saying to those who have been brought into his family, those with whose parents he has been associated as members of the same family—you have brought the master to the absolute necessity of seeing these people perish for the want of food and clothing, or being at the expense of sustaining them.

Gentlemen have been asked, what are you to do with those so old as to be incompetent to maintain themselves, or these women and children so utterly helpless as to be incapable of providing for themselves. No answer has been given. No remedy has been suggested. Some gentlemen say that the legislature must provide. The legislature is not to meet until these people may rot in the streets, if they are left to starve according to the project of this convention. They require daily sustenance, constant protection from exposure to the weather. That is the reason suggested here for conferring this power; and we ask by what other process these people can be protected.

I take it for granted it has not been assumed, though it may be assumed, that the masters will sooner expend the last cent that they own than to allow these people to suffer extinction either by starvation or exposure. But when the proposition is offered by the gentleman from Caroline to do an act which I say, concerning nothing but the public interest, ought to be done, the fear is expressed that it will benefit the masters; that you are going to do some service to the masters; that you are going to entail slavery upon the servants. Is an apprentice a slave? You apprentice white people. Are they slaves? Is this process of universal emancipation to be postponed for twenty years because minor negroes are to be put out as apprentices in the same way exactly that white persons are apprenticed? The very moment a motion comes within sight of anything like a cent of remuneration, these gentlemen seem to take alarm, as if the country was going to be ruined by it, and their favorite scheme of universal emancipation interfered with or at least delayed. I regret exceedingly to see such a spirit prevail.

We are about to turn loose upon the community every minor negro in the State. Uneducated, unprepared for the condition of freedom, with no employment, no business, no avocation except that in which they must engage under the instruction of white people, as general laborers, entirely and exclusively accustomed to farming operations, thousands upon thousands are to be turned loose. To do what? I say the very best thing you can do with them is to place them under the guardianship, and direction, and guidance, and instruction of white persons, who can teach them how to take care of themselves. No; you cannot do that; their master will get some benefit from it. The gentleman from Baltimore city seems to have the utterly idle view that indenting him for ten years makes him a slave; that if you indent him from seven to twenty-one years of age, you make him a slave. We have had indentures all along; and who ever heard of an indented apprentice being considered a slave? How does it interfere with the rigid principle of universal emancipation for masters to have the preference in the guardianship of these minors?

I say again that I hope this exhibition of apprehension which seems to be entertained by gentlemen lest a dollar of compensation should be given to the masters who are stripped of their property, and not only that, but made to meet the expense of sustaining those who are impotent, those who must be sustained by them or perish, those for whom their friends do not profess to make provision, those who are here utterly neglected after being turned into the streets—the apprehension lest they should receive a dollar in return. I hope it does not reveal the feelings of all the gentlemen of the majority here, towards those upon whom their policy has brought ruin. I saw yesterday a letter from a gentleman, a warm supporter of the government, who was utterly ruined; and there are others in the same predicament; ruined by a sudden blow upon the part of the body selected for the protection of the people of the State in their persons, their property and their liberties, by a sudden blow inflicted at their hands, which in one sentence strikes down every dollars' worth of property they have. Is it to be a matter of regret that incidentally you should to some small extent remunerate these people, incidentally, under the operation of an act positively and actually useful to those who are to be emancipated by this body? I again appeal to the justice and equity and conscience of the majority of this house, not to carry out their ultra doctrines which I say manifest more a determined spirit of hostility to the slave owner, than a desire to benefit the slave.

Mr. PURNELL. My judgment inclines me to favor the proposition of the gentleman from Caroline (Mr. Todd.)

Mr. STOCKBRIDGE. I rise to a point of order. I did not wish to interrupt the gentleman from Kent (Mr. Chambers) during the progress of his lecture. But I submit that the amendment I proposed is the only thing now before the house, and that the merits of the proposition of the gentleman from Caroline (Mr. Todd) are not now under consideration.

Mr. CHAMBERS. I was merely answering the

arguments of other gentlemen. That is my apology for saying what I did.

The PRESIDENT. The usual course has been to permit the discussion of the entire subject. The chair has never taken the authority to restrict gentlemen strictly to the particular amendment under consideration.

Mr. PURNELL. My judgment inclines me to favor the proposition of the gentleman from Caroline (Mr. Todd,) not for the reasons assigned by my honorable friend from Kent (Mr. Chambers) but for considerations entirely my own. It is not so much for the purpose of protecting or seeking to protect the interests of the master in this connection, but for the purpose of ameliorating and improving the condition of the slave, the party on whom the provisions of this section must operate.

Now it seems to me that it is proper under the present circumstances, and under any circumstances, if you can improve the condition of any class of the community, either white or black, to do so. If by hiring out, or binding out, or apprenticing out this class of the community their condition will be ameliorated, and they will be brought in habits of industry and impressed with proper principles, no evil can result to them or to the community. And if incidentally some benefit may result to the master, that should not be an objection.

But I rise more particularly to address my remarks to the amendment offered by the gentleman from Baltimore city (Mr. Stockbridge,) in relation to providing for the education of this class. That gentleman, I know, understands very well the distinction between white and black apprentices. He understands that the legislature of Maryland a long time ago made vastly different provisions for the two classes. The one is provided with an education, and with other advantages; while in the case of binding out the other the articles of apprenticeship, or the indentures, are not required to express that the negro shall be educated, as is required in the other case. Now I will read for the benefit of the gentleman—hardly necessary for his benefit, for he knows it too well to require me to do that—but for the benefit of others whose attention has not been directed to that particular statute, the provision in relation to white apprenticeship, which says, [Code, article 6, section 15 :]

"Every child bound out under the provisions of this article shall, if a male, be bound until he arrives at the age of twenty-one years; or, if a female, the age of eighteen years. And the said courts shall in all cases, make it a part of the contract on the part of the master or mistress of such apprentice, that he or she shall give such apprentice reasonable education in reading, writing and arithmetic, to be particularized therein; and also teach such apprentice especially if a male, some useful art or trade; and in all cases supply clothing and maintenance."

That is for the white apprentice. In the same article of the code, section 36, will be found what is necessary, or rather what is unnecessary in all contracts of apprenticeship for the other race.

"It shall not be necessary in any such indenture, or in any indenture of a negro made by the trustees of the poor, to require that any education shall be given to such negro apprentice."

There is the distinction. Now I am not prepared to say that it is necessary to educate the negro, in order to make him useful to the community, and useful to himself, or to prepare him after he arrives at years of maturity to go and set up for himself, and to perform all the necessary duties that may devolve upon him as a citizen, occupying the sphere which he must necessarily occupy.

Does any one profess upon this floor that the negro will ever occupy the status of the white man? Is there any individual who can ever bring his mind to the conclusion that that degraded race will ever be raised to the degree of the white race? I mean exactly what I say; because that they are inferior to the white race there is no doubt. The God of nature when He created, stamped upon their forehead the mark as broad and lasting as the mark upon Cain. Is there any man who would elevate them to the degree of the white man? I cannot think so. The idea that the negro can ever elevate himself to the condition of the white man is preposterous. But unfortunately the white man can debase himself to the condition of the negro.

But I cannot support a proposition to elevate the negro to the sphere of the white man. While I am willing to see him bound to a master, to a kind and benevolent benefactor, who will raise him up to habits of industry, I am unwilling to educate him and prepare him for the higher walks of life—those which are occupied by his superiors, the white race. And in advocating this principle I do no violence to the principles upon which I was elected to this convention. I came here as an emancipationist; I voted for what is now the twenty-fourth article of the bill of rights, and I boast in that important act of my life, because I think it is for the benefit of the State of Maryland, though for a while it may subject us to some temporary inconvenience.—And I think the time will come when we all shall come to the conclusion that it is not alone for the benefit of the negro, and not to the prejudice of the master, but on the contrary it is to the advantage of the master, and the co-relative advantage of both master and slave.

I had other reasons which controlled my vote on that subject, which it is not now necessary to detail, having already in an humble way expressed them.

This subject of apprenticeship was never canvassed in my county; it was not the issue. But I am very well assured that the good sense of our people would have guided them to the same conclusion that now controls me; that they would have said that there is no harm whatever to result to the slave by placing him when freed in a condition where he will be impressed with habits of industry, and be reared up accustomed to labor, and thereby be better prepared when he arrives at maturity to go forth in the world upon his own resources, self-reliant.

I do not swerve one moment in a backward tendency in this matter. The remarks of my friend from Baltimore city (Mr. Cushing) certainly do not apply to me. We are not undoing what we have already done, but we let that stand as imperishable as marble, and as immovable as the rocks of Gibraltar. I consider that there is no violation of that principle in advocating this doctrine of apprenticeship, whereby we retain the negro in the hands of his master, if the orphans' court should consider him a judicious and proper person to be the custodian of the slave, if not, then some other one, who will impress him with like habits of industry. I shall therefore vote with great cheerfulness for the principles contained in the proposition of the gentleman from Caroline (Mr. Todd,) because I think the proposition is a good one; I think the principle is correct, and one which will ameliorate the condition of the negro, and there is no corresponding injury to the master.

Mr. Todd. I should have preferred that this convention should have voted upon this proposition without discussion, for the simple reason that I did not desire the time of the convention to be taken up in debate upon it. I thought the proposition had been long enough before them for every gentleman to understand it, and to make up his mind in regard to how he would act upon it. And I thought there was no necessity for a any member of this convention to attempt to throw additional light upon the subject. But from remarks that have fallen from the lips of gentlemen here, I feel constrained to utter a few words in defence of the proposition I have submitted to the convention.

Some gentlemen have said they are pledged to go against every such proposition. Of course I would not for a moment think of asking any gentleman to violate the pledges which he has made to his people. But I pledged myself to go for such a proposition, and the people whom I in part represent expect it of me. I go for it, not merely because I pledged myself to do so, but because I believe it to be right and proper. It has been said by the gentleman from Frederick (Mr. Schley) that the adoption of a proposition of this sort would be but the reduction of all these minors to a state of slavery. I do not so regard it. If that proposition be a correct one, then we ought to make it obligatory upon the legislature to blot out every particle of statutory law upon our books in relation to apprenticeship of any kind. For if this apprenticeship which I am advocating to-day is slavery, then all apprenticeship is slavery.

There is but one single difference between the proposition I have offered, and the law regarding apprenticeship as it exists upon our statute book. That difference is that the proposition which I have had the honor to submit makes it obligatory upon the orphans' court, when in their judgment the former owners of those minors are proper persons to have charge of them, to give to them the preference over other people. That is the one and only difference between the proposition I advocate here to-day, and the statute as it exists upon your statute book.

Now I am very far from doing, or desiring to do, anything that would look like remanding these negroes into a state of slavery. The one of my acts for which I expect always to be the proudest, is that act by which I cast my influence and my vote for the unconditional emancipation of all who have hitherto been held in bondage in this State. I shall ever look back to that period of my life with pride, whatever may be the consequences, whether this constitution be adopted by the people or not. I shall always glory in the position I then took, and by it I expect to stand or fall.

But it does seem to me that it is desirable that this convention should incorporate some such provision as this, which I have offered, in our organic law, for the purpose of protecting society. That is one reason I have for offering this proposition. If we throw out loose upon society the immense number of helpless minors who will be emancipated by the adoption of this constitution, we do not know to what extent society may suffer from it. It seems to me rather that we should take them into our arms, and throw around them this security, and in that way secure society. That we should provide for their interest by the adoption of a proposition of this character, as the gentleman from Worcester (Mr. Purnell,) has very well said, when they are apprenticed to suitable persons—and this proposition gives to the orphans' court the power to choose to whom to apprentice them—they will be taught principles of industry, they will be taught to labor, so that when they arrive at maturity they will be better prepared to go forth and earn their livelihood and become good and useful members of society, than if left to run wild at large, with none to protect them, and with no power to protect themselves, no disposition to take care of themselves, and prepare themselves for a state of freedom. So that it is not only desirable as a protection to society, but also desirable I think as a protection to the best interests, as providing for the best interests of these minors.

And it seems to me also to be an act of justice to those who have had the care of rearing them during a state of infancy. In that state they have been utterly unable to render any remuneration whatever to those who have had the charge of them. Now I am not one of those who believe that slavery in this State is, or ever was, or ever could be profitable even should it continue to exist. I believe that the expenses of the slaveholder in rearing his slaves, and in providing for them after they have passed the period of life in which they can be serviceable, far overbalances in many instances all the profits accruing from them while in a condition to render service. In the case of these minors, they have not been able to render any service; the majority of them are still in a state of infancy from one to ten and twelve years of age.—During that period the masters have had the care of them, have had to provide for their wants, to feed and clothe them. And it seems to me it would be but an act of justice to the masters to let them have their services until they arrive at the age of maturity, so as to remunerate them for the care they have exercised during their infancy.

I am not an advocate of State compensation; never have been. But I have thought that it would be prudent for the general government, and right for the general government to grant compensation. But the probability is that no such compensation ever will be granted. It seems to me, therefore, in view of that fact, in view of that probability, that we can afford to do at least this much, to give to the masters, when they are the proper persons to have charge of them, the services of these minors until they arrive at majority.

I will not at this time, trouble the convention with any further remarks, except to say in reference to the proposition of the gentleman from Baltimore city (Mr. Stockbridge,) concerning the education of these minors, that I have no objection whatever to the education of the negroes of this State. I hope the time will come when they will be educated, and be better prepared thereby to become useful members of society. But if gentlemen will look at the proposition I have submitted they will find that it provides for apprenticing them subject to such regulations as are now or may be hereafter prescribed by law. We expect to have a legislature who will make the necessary statutory law to carry out the principles embodied in the organic law which we are now framing. We expect them to conform that law in all respects not only to the letter but to the spirit of what we have done here. And I have no doubt that they will in regard to this special subject, enact a law that will make it obligatory upon masters of apprentices, whether white or black, and black as well as white, to teach them to read and write. Let us leave this matter then to the legislature, and not descend here to specific legislation; leave that to the body properly having charge of it.

Mr. Negley. If the amendment of the gentleman from Baltimore city (Mr. Stockbridge) were a practicable amendment, if the idea and the purposes which it contemplates could be practically realized in the community where it will and must necessarily be operative, I should not object to going for it. But I cannot see how, in the present state of society in the large slaveholding counties of this State, that proposition can be made of any practical benefit. There are no schools organized now for the education of these colored people. I cannot see how, without a great deal of preparatory legislation and work and arrangement this proposition of the gentleman from Massachusetts, [laughter]—I beg the gentleman's pardon; I really did not mean to say that; I meant "the gentleman from Baltimore city" (Mr. Stockbridge)—I do not see how it could possibly be carried out. I am in a general way, a friend of the education of both the black and the white. I believe that education is a means of lessening crime, and forwarding the progress of mankind, both black and white. But at this particular stage of the history of Maryland, I do not see how that possibly could be of any benefit; therefore I shall not vote for it.

I shall not vote for the amendment proposed by the gentleman from Baltimore city (Mr. Stockbridge.) But I shall vote for and support the section proposed by the gentleman from Caroline (Mr. Todd.) I think we have gone far enough—I do not see any necessity for us to go stark mad—upon this subject of emancipation. I do not see any necessity for us to run into the opposite extreme. There is always a tendency, when we leave one extreme to run into the opposite extreme. Can we not stop short of that? Can we not look a little to the good of the people of Maryland? Can we not look a little to the good of the emancipated negro? Can we not take into consideration the public welfare a little? Now if we emancipate these negroes, as we hope to emancipate them, and turn them loose in these large populous negro communities, what will be the effect? In the fall of the year, a mother and a father, with four or five or more helpless children, are turned loose. Provisions are scarce and immensely dear; clothing of all sorts is dear. I ask gentlemen how it will be possible for the parents of these negro children to carry them through the coming winter with comfort, or even without starvation?

Mr. Cushing. Cannot a man of eighteen or twenty years of age get through the winter?

Mr. Negley. I am not speaking about him.

Mr. Cushing. This proposition covers those of that age as well as all others.

Mr. Negley. I know it does.

Mr. Stirling. Does the gentleman suppose that masters will have bound to them children from one to five years of age? Will they not ask to have bound to them those that are from fifteen to twenty, and let those from one to five go? Is not that the principle of human nature everywhere?

Mr. Negley. I think the orphans' court will exercise a sound and humane discretion upon this subject. The gentleman's supposition is founded upon the idea that the orphans' court will be predetermined to do as much injury as possible to these emancipated negroes. It contemplates the binding out of these children over six years, at least. Now a negro child at the age of twelve years, is much more expensive to the parent or the master than a child of one or two years. And why? Because the child of twelve years will eat as much as a man, and will require a most as much clothing.

I do think it is for the good of society in these large slaveholding counties; it is for the happiness and welfare of the negro, and for the comfort of the master, that such a provision as that contemplated by the section of the gentleman from Caroline (Mr. Todd) should be incorporated into the constitution. This suddenly turning loose of immense quantities of negroes, utterly unused to, and unskilled, and uneducated in a single means of taking care of themselves—they will be like uncaged birds; they will not know how to manage, they will not know what to do. They cannot get houses to live in during the coming winter, and they would absolutely freeze and starve to death, if the humanity of their masters did not provide them with food and shelter

I am decidedly in favor both of doing good to the negro, and making some compensation to his former owner. I am not actuated by any ill-will or hatred towards the slaveholder; by no means. I have advocated the emancipation of the negro upon high moral grounds, and upon political grounds, uninfluenced by any feeling of bitterness towards the slaveholder, wherever he may be, and if I can consistently with my views of public duty, and with what I conceive to be for the public benefit, benefit the master also, it will be a source of gratification to me, rather than of disappointment and hate. I discard any such feelings at all. And for one I shall be very glad if they can have some compensation for the losses to which they will and must be necessarily subjected by the adoption of this constitution. Is not the injury they will suffer from the emancipation of all their slaves without compensation—is not that sufficient? Must you add another feather to the weight already on the camel's back?

Now I have gone about as far as I am inclined to go in that direction. And if I can, consistently with my ideas of public duty, do a good at the same time to the former slaveholder, and to the negro himself, I shall do it with great pleasure. And therefore I shall vote against this amendment of the gentleman from Baltimore city (Mr. Stockbridge,) because I consider it impracticable now. And I shall vote for the section proposed by the gentleman from Caroline (Mr. Todd,) because I believe it will do much good. I believe it will have a tendency to take away a little of that bitterness that is already too prevalent throughout this entire State. Let us try to get back a little towards common ground. We will have to live together in the future. Let us attempt now to make some approximation towards living together in brotherhood, and do each other a mutual kindness and good when we can do so without any sacrifice of principle.

Mr. Daniel. I have felt very much inclined heretofore to go for some provision of this sort; not considering it any special system of apprenticeship, but simply a binding out under existing laws, as I believe those laws would take hold of them, and bind them out if once freed. And I have thought it would be proper, where the masters were suitable persons, to give them the preference. But I think that matter is involved in a great deal of difficulty, especially if we look at the laws upon the statute book at present, and what has been the class of apprenticeship we have had in this State, almost since it has been a State. And I am really forced to the conclusion that the laws on the statute book are sufficient to regulate every case and matter that may arise of this sort.

Now there are some laws upon that book that I think we might come in conflict with, very much to the injury of this class of people, if we provide in the constitution in the direct and positive terms that is now proposed to be enacted here. It is proposed to enact here that the masters in every case, if suitable persons, shall have those children bound to them, without consulting the mother, without consulting anybody. I say that there may be cases possibly, in which the masters are not suitable persons, and yet it may be such a very delicate matter for the orphans' court to decide that, having established in the constitution a universal law that masters in all cases where they are suitable persons shall have the preference, it would result in every case pretty much in giving these apprentices to their masters. I shall therefore at the proper time, offer an amendment, which I think will prevent some of the fears that have been entertained of the consequences of these persons being thrown loosely out upon society, to be supported by their parents or others, or to get their living as they can by improper means. I think it will show an indication of the sentiment of this convention that these children shall be bound out under existing laws. And I believe there will be hardly one case in fifty where the orphans' court will not, as a matter of justice and right, give the masters and owners the preference, wherever they are suitable persons. And therefore it is not necessary for us to so positively provide for it, especially as we may run counter to some laws, and thus do injury. I propose to say simply:

"All minor slaves emancipated by this constitution, that is to say, males under the age of twenty-one, and females under the age eighteen years, shall be subject to the provisions of existing laws, or such as may hereafter be passed by the general assembly, relating to free negro apprenticeship."

Mr. CHAMBERS. Has that any meaning, sense, or operation whatever?

Mr. DANIEL. Yes, sir.

Mr. CHAMBERS. It is saying that the law shall exist; it is just exactly nothing at all.

Mr. DANIEL. Very well; I mean a little more. I have no doubt the gentleman would have it mean nothing, because he wants to get something else. I think it does mean something. It may be true that existing laws do, and I believe they would take hold of these people and bind them out. But a great deal has been said about these emancipated negroes being thrown out upon the community to get their own living, with nobody to take care of them. As I have said before, I want this convention to say in emphatic terms that it is their design that they shall be bound out, and that the provisions of existing laws simply, and nothing else, shall apply.

Now what are those provisions? Under the present laws, where they have parents living, a mother, for instance, the choice of that mother is selected. And yet the orphans' court is not bound by that choice. And if they believe that, under all the circumstances, that choice is unreasonable, they may override it notwithstanding, and bind to such persons as they may think proper. I think it would be rather a hardship to deprive the mother of all choice and selection in this matter. I believe, as I have said before, there may be some cases where it would not be proper to bind to the present masters. I have some in my own eye, where I know the mother and children have been cruelly treated; and I believe to bind them to their old masters would be saying that that system of cruelty should be continued. Therefore I do not wish to take away all choice from the parent. And, as I have said, as the orphans' court ultimately have the right to override the choice of the mother, I think the mother or the parents ought to select.

It is a provision under the old law that whenever the orphans' court may deem that the habits of the children would be improved by binding out, they shall have the right to have every such child brought before them and bound out. Is not that sufficient latitude? But, living in one of the counties of this State, I have seen that law as much abused as any law that I have ever seen upon the statute book. I have had something to do with it. I have seen certain parties wait until children were raised, so that they were able to earn a living. The fathers and mothers being left to take care of them until they were of some use, and then I have seen these constables and other parties go and inform the orphans' court that there were such persons living idle and lazy, boys of from twelve to fourteen, and girls of from ten to twelve, and have them brought up and bound out, just as they were able to render their fathers and mothers some service. The parents had taken care of them and raised them until they were able to be of some service, and then just at that very nick of time they were deprived of them, and the children were bound out to masters who got their services for the balance of the time, without being at any expense in raising them, or paying one cent for their services.

I say, therefore, that this system is liable to abuse. I confess that the objection does not apply in this case so strongly, because the masters are supposed to have raised them, and to have some title to their services. I am willing, and I think it best, to leave it to existing laws. And, as I have said before, I believe these children would be bound to their masters, wherever it would be right to do so. I think it would be proper to give the masters the preference in all cases, where they were suitable persons. I believe the orphans' court would very fully exercise that right, and I think it is useless to put in any more legislation upon the statute book in reference to the matter.

Mr. PUGH. I am astonished this morning in more ways than one. In the first place, I am astonished to find such difference in sentiment to-day in regard to the orphans' court, from that which was manifested here yesterday. It was only yesterday that there seemed to be a universal disposition not to let the orphans' court have too many duties to perform, especially where the interests of white orphans were concerned. Yet it is proposed here to-day, and very many of the legal profession are in favor of it, to give the orphans' court additional powers, at least where the interests of the black children of the State are concerned. I am astonished to see to-day that some of these legal gentlemen are in favor of increasing the powers of that court. However, I cannot say that I am so very much astonished, because we see a great many curious things as we pass along through the world, and I am ready for almost anything.

I have also heard remarks here to-day by

gentlemen so very different from remarks made by them on former occasions, that I am somewhat astonished for that reason. Now in regard to the gentleman from Worcester (Mr. Purnell,) I do not wish to answer his remarks for any other reason than this: I am afraid that if his remarks go unanswered to the people of the State, the impression might prevail that probably those of us who take a different view of this subject from what that gentleman does, were in favor of elevating the negro race; were in favor of something like negro equality; a rehash of that political, wishy-washy, meaningless talk which I think we met and effectually refuted in the canvass in this State. My only reason for noticing the remarks of the gentleman from Worcester is this: that he being known as a representative upon this floor of the Union party of the State, as it is called, and being opposed to us in this particular, if his remarks remain unanswered, the impression might prevail that those who opposed him did so for some such reason as that suggested; that is, we desired to elevate the negro race as compared with the white race; or rather, that we were in favor of this old idea of negro equality. For that reason, and that reason only, I wish to answer him.

And I wish to recall to the recollection of the gentleman some remarks made by him some time ago, which I heartily indorsed, and which when I did indorse them, I did not admit justified the idea that he or me were in favor of this policy of negro equality. I wish to recall to his recollection those remarks, because I indorsed them then, and indorse them now; and because I hold that in indorsing them now I do not indorse the idea of negro equality. The gentleman in his remarks on the article of the declaration of rights abolishing slavery, to be found on page 717 of the debates, said:

"I believe human nature is the same almost everywhere, and under almost any circumstances; although it may be covered with a black skin."

Mr. PURNELL. Read the connection.

Mr. PUGH. I will, for the connection is where the point is.

"It must be apparent to every man—though I speak more particularly to the farmer—who has employed slave labor and free labor, that free labor is incomparably more economical than slave labor."

Now the reason that justifies the latter clause of that quotation, is the same that justifies our course throughout this discussion, and our political course, as it is called, in the State. It is because we believe that free labor is a better system of labor than slave labor, that we are in favor of freeing the slaves of this State. It is not because we believe that when you free the slave you make him the equal of the white man. But it is simply for the reason suggested by the gentleman, that "human nature is the same almost everywhere, and under almost any circumstances; although it may be covered with a black skin."

Again, the gentleman says, on page 719 of the debates:

"I have seen the free Africans in the military service of Brazil. For at the time I was there Don Pedro was at war with Rosas, of the Buenos Ayrean dominions, and every day the soldiers were paraded upon the public square for the review of the emperor; and in that long line of soldiers you would find the Portuguese, the Indian, the half-breed African, and the full-blooded African, all in the same uniform. There was but little distinction to be observed between them. All seemed to be working in the service of their great master; all seemed to perform their services with alacrity and willingness, without any control except the authority exercised over them all by those who have a right to direct them."

The point is that these conditions follow necessarily from the principle stated by the gentleman in the quotation I first read. That is, that "human nature being the same almost everywhere, even although covered by a black skin," it will be better developed in a free state than in a slave state.

Now that brings me right to the point of my objection to the adoption of the apprentice system in the State of Maryland. It is because I do not believe that is the course of policy to properly develop the nation. It is not the proper course of policy in order to make the labor of the State the most valuable. That is one reason only.

I might state here why I am opposed, as I am opposed, to all systems of apprenticeship. They are generally opposed to all laws, and are never admitted excepting under certain extraordinary circumstances. It is not the best condition of labor, to produce the best results to the nation. It is only recognized to be a system of labor to be appealed to as the very last resort, when there is no other way; when the party to be apprenticed is unable to take care of himself, or herself, or when there are no parents and they are orphans cast loose upon the world. Then that system of labor is resorted to. It is only adopted through the force of peculiar circumstances, and not as a wise measure in itself.

The gentleman from Worcester (Mr. Purnell) objected to the amendment of the gentleman from Baltimore city (Mr. Stockbridge)—after having made the remarks from which I have quoted, and which I heartily indorse—because it contemplated the education of this laboring class. Now I submit to him, and I do not think he will take issue with me upon that point, whether he does not recognize the fact that it is better to have educated labor than uneducated labor?

It is perfectly proper to educate a horse; but it does not follow that you thereby make the horse the equal of a man.

Mr. CHAMBERS. To read and write?

Mr. PUGH. You can educate a horse in other ways than to read and write. But when it comes to a person who can be taught to read and write, I submit to the gentleman from Kent (Mr. Chambers,) that it would be better to do so. If you could teach a horse to read and write it would be a good thing; but you cannot do that. But you can teach the negro to read and write.

Mr. CHAMBERS. Not all of them.

Mr. PUGH. Well, some of them, then. You cannot teach some white men to read and write. But to the extent that you do teach all classes, white and black, to that extent you benefit the State. It is an obsolete idea that it is not better to educate all classes of the community. There is no human being so low that he cannot be improved to some extent by education. And I am astonished that the gentleman from Worcester (Mr. Purnel) should object to the amendment of the gentleman from Baltimore city (Mr. Stockbridge.) And I am also very much astonished that he sees in that amendment some evidence that we acknowledge that the negro is our equal. I have no such fear, and never had any such fear.

Mr. MILLER. Will the gentleman allow me to ask him a question?

Mr. PUGH. No, sir. I have allowed questions to be asked me heretofore, but I have not been allowed to ask some questions in return. Therefore I have come to the conclusion to permit none to be asked me.

The PRESIDENT. And the President will sustain you in that.

Mr. PUGH. Now I object to this notion that it makes the negro the equal of the white man to educate him. I have never had any such fear. The gentleman says, and says justly, that he is responsible for that statement for himself. I also say that the Almighty created the negro race our inferiors. I am not at all afraid of their becoming our equals, when the Almighty intended they should be our inferiors. I made use of an illustration upon a former occasion, and I will use it again here. If the Almighty made the white race the superior of the black race, can it be possible, if those two races are developed to their fullest extent, that in spite of the intention of the Almighty they can ever be made equals? Take two men, the one six feet high, and the other five feet high; that is their stature, so designed by the Almighty. Put them upon the same platform, the one by the side of the other. If they stand upright men, there is no way in which their two heads can be upon the same level, unless he who is the taller man should stoop. Now other gentlemen may do as they please; but we do not intend to stoop. I do not intend to indorse the idea that the white man should go down to the level of the black man. And I do not intend to indorse the idea that the negro shall be elevated to the level of the white man, since it is God's wisdom that it shall not be so.

But I claim from motives of political economy, as well as from motives of morality and of religion, that the negro shall be educated, shall be developed to the highest degree of which he is capable. I claim it, because it is the proper course to be pursued, in order to fully develop the resources of the nation; it is the proper course to be pursued, in order to make the labor of the nation the most available. For that reason I am in favor of educating everybody, of every color. And I will stand upon that platform everywhere. There is a want of equality in all society. And you might as well say it is not proper to educate a certain class of white people, because thereby you elevate them to a level with the aristocrats. By education you develop most fully all the resources of the people. And it is very well suggested by the gentleman from Harford, now sitting near me (Mr. McComas,) that the best way to save the community from crime is to educate the people.

Now I have objections besides those I have stated to this apprenticing of negroes, especially to their masters. I shall vote for the amendment of the gentleman from Baltimore city (Mr. Stockbridge,) but even if that is adopted, I shall not vote for the proposition of the gentleman from Caroline (Mr. Todd.) I am opposed to it because it gives the preference to and selects the former masters; to that extent it undoes the very work we have done. We have specially provided in our bill of rights that no man shall have any claim upon another by reason of the institution of slavery. Now if we acknowledge, as we shall do by adopting this proposed section, that the former master has the right to go into court and claim the first place in their consideration in apprenticing these negroes, to that extent we give the master control over his slave. I am opposed to recognizing even the faintest shadow of this institution, for reasons already given here in detail in this debate. I am not ashamed, nor am I at all backward in making the assertion, that I am opposed all the time, here and everywhere, from principle and from religious conviction, to the institution of slavery.

And I am opposed to it aside from those considerations. I am opposed to it, because from the bottom of my heart I believe that it has ever been an element of discord in this nation, and that it has brought this nation to the verge of ruin. I believe that as firmly as I believe in Almighty God. And believing that, I will not recognize anywhere, or in any way, the shadow of the shade of the existence of any right of the master over the slave he once held. I state that it is my belief that if you let this institution exist even in this mild form of apprenticeship, even in this almost half-dead form, the result will be that in those counties where the judges of the orphans' court are people of their selection, where the circuit court is a court of their creation, those gentlemen in those counties who entertain the idea that slavery is a benign and benevolent institution, will hang on to it by this slight thread as long as they possibly can; and hanging on to it they will keep up a political organization which it is just as important should be broken up, as it is that the institution itself should be broken up. They will keep good their political organization, and whatever disasters may befall us, they will unite under the banner of this institution, in this mild and almost dead form, and will hang on to it as long as they can. They show every disposition to do so, and in those counties where they have the courts, they will do so as long as possible.

I do not say this in bitterness of spirit, or because I have any hatred towards those people who own slaves. Some of the warmest friends I have in the world are men who own slaves. I do not say this out of any hatred or ill-will towards them. But I do say it out of an undying hatred to that system which, in my judgment, has brought my country to the verge of ruin. That is my judgment, and it is the judgment of many gentlemen in this house, that to that system, and to its existence in this country, we to-day owe all the evils that now surround us. And for that reason I am against recognizing its existence even by the shadow of its dying shade, in any manner, shape or form.

Mr. STIRLING. I had not intended to say anything in regard to this matter, when I read some time since a substitute for this section. But the course the debate has taken this morning, in my judgment renders it necessary that I should say something—not that it is necessary that I should inflict my views upon the house, but I wish to explain my own position.

I must confess that I have been very much surprised at this debate. In everything that I have said in this body, upon the subject of slavery, I have chosen to debate it upon political grounds only. I confess that I am surprised to hear gentlemen who have stood upon this floor and argued in eloquent language about the sinfulness of the institution of slavery, who have advocated before this convention as a proposition of law that every slave in this State was held by a thief's title, now get up here and advocate the holding out this proposition as a conciliatory measure to the disloyal element in this State, for the purpose of bringing about a more harmonious state of feeling. Now, while I have uttered no such language in reference to the sinfulness and illegality of slavery as has fallen from the lips of gentlemen upon this floor, still I am opposed to the provisions contained in this proposed section, because I believe they are counter to the political reasons which have brought us to adopt the policy we have already incorporated into this constitution. And representing a constituency which, so far as the portion I represent is concerned, is a unit upon this subject, I must stand up here, if it is but to utter a protest against this proposition.

I have no objection to allowing the matter to rest where the legislation of the State has placed it, severe as I regard that legislation to be. I have no objection to a provision which meets the views I have heard expressed upon this floor in regard to the custody of these minor children that are helpless, and in the hands of their masters to-day. But there is no reciprocity in this proposition. It is a proposition by which the master, if he chooses, can have bound to him those able-bodied males that constitute the great bulk of the labor of the slaveholding counties, and who are the very class upon which your policy of emancipation really operates; while, if he chooses, he can decline to have bound to him the helpless, whether young or old, who are unable to render the service he desires. I see no policy to be pursued in regard to those who are too old to take care of themselves. I see no proposition to have apprenticed to the master, or to any one else, those who are too young to take care of themselves. But I see a proposition that those who are able to take care of themselves, and to assist in taking care of those others, shall be re-enslaved to a certain extent for the purpose of providing compensation to those from whom they have been taken. I do say that if this policy is adopted it does break up part of what we have done, not upon a moral ground but upon a political ground; and it still keeps in what is actual slavery a large class of the population of the State, and still keeps the institution of slavery alive.

Gentlemen say it is nothing but apprenticeship. And what is apprenticeship, and what are the laws about apprentices? By the consent of the parents children may be apprenticed. And if children are vagrants and there is nobody to take care of them, they are to be apprenticed without the consent of the parents. This is a proposition to apprentice all persons of a certain class, whether they have parents or not, whether they can take care of themselves or not, whether there are those who can and will take care of them or not—they are all to be apprenticed without the consent of their parents, or without the consent of any one for them. What is this but a modified system of slavery? When you take these persons who have been held as slaves, and say that as a class they shall all be apprenticed to the same people who formerly held them as slaves; in a political point of view, what is that but continuing the existence of slavery for ten or more years?

What are the provisions of the law as it stands at present, in relation to the apprenticing of colored persons? The orphans' court has the power to bind out the children of any free colored person, if in the opinion of the court it will better their condition. They have the absolute discretion over the matter now. In my opinion it is an extreme power. It amounts to saying that even if the child is old enough to work for his own living or the parents are able and willing to support him, still if in the judgment of the orphans' court it is better to put him somewhere else, under other control than that of his parents, they shall have the power to do so.

Now the effect of the proposition before us is to neutralize the proposition which we have incorporated in this organic law, and in which we have said that this class of involuntary servitude shall no longer exist in this State—to neutralize it by another provision in the same organic law, which cannot be removed except by a constitutional amendment. What do gentlemen mean by saying that there shall be no involuntary servitude in this State? If without the consent of either parents or children you apprentice a whole class of people by a broad general description, what is that but involuntary servitude? And what is the difference between that involuntary servitude and slavery? What was the reason for putting in the twenty-fourth article of the declaration of rights, the words "involuntary servitude" in addition to the word "slavery?" That article says "there shall be neither slavery nor involuntary servitude." What does that mean?

Now, while I will consent to leave the law as it stands upon the statute book, I cannot consent to adopt any such provision as this. What is the actual state of facts? I do not pretend to deny that if a master has been left by this emancipation clause in the possession of helpless children two or three years of age, and he undertakes to support them and rear them, I admit that there is some reason in their remaining with him and rendering service until they are twenty-one years of age. But that is not the scope of this proposition; it is not confined to that class, but embraces those who are just as able to take care of themselves as is anybody else. And what is to become of the parents? If the master does not choose to employ the parents, and you take away the children who are able to support the parents, then the parents must go upon the county, if they from any cause are unable to support themselves. If not that, then what does it amount to? You not only force the minor who is emancipated to remain in the custody of the same man who before held him as a slave, but you force the parents to stay there also. Because if they have no support except from the child, then they must remain with the child; so that both parents and children will be put back into the same condition practically as before.

The whole scope and effect of this proposition is to keep from disturbing to some extent the foundations of that great deep which we have broken up. Now as I am opposed to anything that is reaction, as I am in favor of going straight forward in the work we have begun, I cannot support this proposition. With all due deference to the views of my friends here who support this measure, I honestly believe that if at this late day we put this into our constitution, it will be regarded as an evidence of a reactionary feeling in this convention. It will be considered as evidence that we have begun to quail before the work we have undertaken to accomplish; that as our State has been invaded, that as the threats of collision and demands for peace are resounding through the atmosphere, we, the representatives of the people of Maryland, in our halls of legislation, upon the soil of our native State, begin to hesitate about carrying out our great work. It will be so understood from one corner of the State to the other, by those men upon whom we must rely to carry this constitution. You can get no support by this or any other similar measure from the other classes. You must carry this constitution through upon the broad shoulders of those men who have looked the future in the face, and who are willing, under the providence of God, to abide by that future. And if they do not support it, then your constitution will go down with the weight attached to it, and which will sink it so deep that no hand of resurrection can ever raise it again.

Now I hope to put this constitution before the people of Maryland, and invite and be able to obtain the support of all of our people who are prepared for the emergencies of the future. And I expect no other support than theirs. And if they are not able to carry through this constitution it will go down only to be raised by some other state of circumstances, which I fear, if this constitution is defeated, will never occur.

I have said about all I wish to say upon this subject. I have made these remarks without any disrespect to any gentleman who differs from me. I see and I appreciate the motives which have induced them, I think mistakenly, to support this measure. But I do submit that such will be the tendency and effect of it. This is its political effect. As my friend from Cecil (Mr. Pugh) has said, it is to give something to which the political managers upon the other side can cling for the purpose of maintaining their political organization; something which is to form the basis for this great reconstruction which we are told is to be accomplished. Now I want nothing to do with any such reconstruction. I am not afraid of revolution. I believe the best reforms are always accomplished in revolutions.

It is said, what are you going to do with this class of people? Do with them? Let anybody go out on this railroad to Camp Parole, and if he does not see more greenbacks in the pockets of some of the wenches and other negroes travelling on that road than are in the pockets of many of the white people, I will confess myself greatly mistaken. Everybody knows that these people are now abundantly able to make their own living. It is true that gentlemen say they make it at the expense of their masters, at the expense of those who own them. But how can we with any consistency say that, when in addition to the practical emancipation accomplished by this war we have added legal emancipation? We cannot say it is unjust to the masters that these negroes make their own living. And will anybody say that any negro boy sixteen years of age, or even twelve years of age, is not able to make his own living now? You cannot get labor, black or white, though you cry for it. Old colored men are now getting wages in this State at the rate of two dollars and a half a day. A gentleman told me the other day that he paid two dollars and a half a day to an old colored man for whitewashing a wall, and could not get him for less.

Gentlemen talk about protecting these poor helpless negroes. The negro has no apprehension on the subject; they feel no difficulty about the future. Let them take care of themselves, if they are satisfied to do it.

In conclusion, let me say that the existing legislation remedies all the practical evils which ought to be remedied. Those masters who now have negro children in their infancy can be fully protected under the existing system. But this proposed section, if adopted, would place in the constitution beyond the control of the legislature any opportunity to alter that system, however necessary and important any such alteration may become. And I say again, it puts into the constitution something which looks inconsistent with what we have already done, and which must be accepted by the people in that light.

Mr. STOCKBRIDGE. The amendment which I submitted to the convention has provoked much more discussion than I anticipated; discussion not confined to the amendment itself, but going over the whole ground covered by the proposition of the gentleman from Caroline (Mr. Todd.) And it has been met not only by arguments, but by assumptions the most unwarranted, and in at least one instance, by a sneer that would have been contemptible in defence of any other than so worthless a cause as this.

I propose to say a few words in opposition to the proposition of the gentleman from Caroline (Mr. Todd,) and in advocacy of my own. It is well perhaps at the outset to see where we shall stand if the proposition of the gentleman from Caroline should not be adopted, and where we shall be placed in the event of its adoption. The law as it now stands upon our statute book makes abundant provision for all possible cases which can arise. And it does it with all the fulness of detail which in an act of assembly is perfectly proper, but which you cannot incorporate into a constitution provision. It provides, Code, article 6, section, 31:

"The several orphans' courts of this State shall, upon information being given to them, summon before them the child of any free negro, and if it shall appear upon examination before such court that it would be better for the habits and comfort of such child that it should be bound as an apprentice to some white person to learn to labor, the court shall bind such child as an apprentice to some white person, if a male, till he is of the age of twenty-one years, or if a female, till she is of the age of eighteen years."

Wherever the comfort and habits of such child require that such binding shall take place, it is obligatory upon the court to so bind it. But this most monstrous proposition of the gentleman from Caroline proposes that the orphans' courts shall take all negroes who are minors, without an exception, and bind them out as apprentices. And now upon what ground? Is it on the ground that it is for the good of the minors? Let gentlemen take up and examine the principle upon which they have founded their previous action. That principle, if I understand it, is that all men have some rights; and if there be one right common to all men which is more sacred than another, it is the right of the parent to foster and educate the child; and the obligation of the child to support and soothe the declining years of his parents is not more binding or obligatory. It is the right of the parents, wherever their character is such that they are capable of taking care of their children, to guide them in their early years.

Now what is proposed by the gentleman from Caroline (Mr. Todd) to be done? It is proposed to take, without a single exception, every female child who shall be emancipated by the operation of this constitution, who shall be under eighteen years of age, from her parents, whatever may be their condition, however able and willing they may be to support her, and bind her in unwilling servitude until she shall have attained the age of eighteen years; and to take every male child in the same way until he shall have reached the age of twenty-one years. Now where is the right, the justice, aye, the decency of such a provision? And more, it is proposed by these same gentlemen to bind them in an iggorance which shall be life-long. For the very advocates of this proposition oppose the amendment which I have offered, that these people shall, in this involuntary servitude, be prepared by some of the rudiments of education for that which is before them in their after years of freedom.

And gentlemen have sprung up in alarm as though the proposition that these people shall be educated was a proposition to place them upon an equality with the white race. Sir, I have no sympathy, no respect, even, for that feeling, or that fear, whatever it may be, that is so eternally afraid of negro equality. If, with generations that start, with the education we have already received, we cannot maintain the race with them, then in all conscience let us give them the track. It is not equality; they must be infinitely the superior of the white race, if, with the brand upon them, the degradation of generations of servitude, the stupidity and ignorance begotten of that servitude, they can rise to be socially and intellectually the equal of the white race, simply because it is proposed to embody in this section the provision that these negro apprentices shall be taught to read and write. What is intellectual equality? Was such a thing ever known as any negro becoming intellectually the equal of the white man, save in those occasional, those rare, those sporadic cases which every one looks upon as a phenomenon, like some rare musical genius, where it seems to be rather an intuition, an instinct, than the result of intellectual power? There are such cases; we have heard of blind Tom, the wonderful musician; of some rare mathematician, who performs processes he does not know how. But who ever talks of any such a one being the equal of anybody else. It argues nothing.

All that is proposed is that those who are the descendants of slaves, who were themselves born in slavery, but who are destined, as sure as the sun continues to rise and set, to be free, shall have some little preparation for freedom. What has been the cry on all sides here, what has been the clamor all through the discussion of this question of emancipation, but that we were throwing out upon the world a class of people who were unprepared for freedom? And now when it is proposed that those people shall be continued in servitude, we propose to add that during that servitude they shall have some sort of preparation for their coming freedom. And that raises all this clamor of negro equality. Was ever anything under the high heaven more absurd?

Now the purpose of the proposition of the gentleman from Caroline (Mr. Todd) is not to benefit the persons whom it is proposed to retain in slavery for this limited time. If that were the object, there is already law enough upon the statute book to accomplish that purpose. But it is for something else. It has been said that it is a sort of compensation to the masters. And gentlemen get up here, and express great regret, and lecture us as though they thought we were actuated by some malice upon this subject towards masters. I feel none whatever. But we have acted here, and such is the record of this convention with regard to what are the rights of men. We do not hurt the master. We adjudicate between the master claiming certain rights from a person, and the person himself who claims that those rights are his, and our decision is that he who claimed himself had a better right to himself than he who claimed to own him as his own. Now if that decision of ours was right, then I beg to ask why is this offer of compensation proposed? Let gentlemen be consistent upon this subject. If the principle of that decision was right, then the principle of this proposition is wrong—the two principles do not, and cannot be made to harmonize. I would not harm a hair of the head of any person who has owned a slave. I would not deprive him of one cent of his lawful property. But when we adjudicate upon the rights of men, we say that regardless of character and condition, these people shall no longer be deprived of those rights to which they are entitled.

Then, as my colleague (Mr. Stirling) has justly remarked, if, as it has been said, this is a beneficent provision for the good of the negro, what is to become of those who may be dependent upon those whom we propose to re-enslave? Will you add all the details of legislation here? You have said that the orphans' court shall bind all these negroes who are minors. But how? Here is a decrepid and sickly child; it is the duty of the orphans' court to bind it to a white person. But the white person chooses not to have it bound to him, and if every white person says, "I will not have this child bound to me," the orphans' court has no power to bind it out. Here is an infant. The orphans' court, in the discharge of its obligation, proposes to bind that infant to its former owner. But he and and everybody else says, "I will not take that infant." Then you throw upon the emancipated mother the charge of that infant until it is ten or twelve years old. And then, when it is old enough to render some assistance to its mother, to repay to some extent the care and trouble the mother has expended upon it, the orphans' court, without the consent of the mother, upon the application of some outside party, the former owner perhaps, steps in and binds that child ten years of age, for eleven years thereafter. Where is the justice in all this? Gentlemen, see how it will operate.

The orphans' court under existing law can bind out the child, provided they think it would be better for the habits and comfort of that child that it should be done. But it is not to be done on the motion of the orphans' court. Information must be given to the orphans' court, before it can be done, under existing law. But under this proposition you make the orphans' court itself the jury of inquest; and you bind it by its oath to support the constitution, to cause to be hunted up every child, and to bind it out if it can get anybody to accept the indentures. If not now, then eight or ten years hence, when the child shall have advanced in years, and shall have become able to take care of itself, and repay its decrepid parent some of the expense it has been, then you permit any one to come in and plunder that parent, who has thus reared the child during its years of infancy and dependence, of the succeeding years when it could be of some service, and you thus plunder the parent, without imposing any obligation whatever upon the master, during the years when the character of the child is to be formed, to teach it even so much as to know crooked s from straight l. That is the proposition before the convention. In all these cases, those who alone are to be benefited by the operation of this provision, are to judge for those who are to be despoiled by the operation. I do not say the individual; I mean the class. The class that is to be benefited, the very men who are interested in establishing the rule, are to judge that this, that, and the other is the proper form for enforcing this regulation.

Now I profess in all this to be actuated by but one principle. I do not recognize any special pledges as binding me to anything. I gave no pledges other than what are implied by my known reg rd for justice and for the obligations of right. But there are gentlemen in this convention who have given pledges, and I trust they will redeem them. I hold in my hand a resolution in these words:

"*Resolved*, That the delegates to the constitutional convention, nominated by this convention, are hereby pledged to vote first, last, and all the time for the immediate abolition of slavery in Maryland, *and against any system of apprenticeship to perpetuate its lingering existence in our midst*, and against State compensation for slaves."

I suppose the gentlemen from Washington county who were elected on such a platform, are bound by its obligations, or they would not have been elected to come to this convention.

Mr. NEGLEY. Will the gentleman allow me a word?

Mr. STOCKBRIDGE. Not now; I am nearly done. I say that upon this measure, as upon all others, I vote and act upon principle; from a sense of right and justice, and not because I feel hampered or bound by any pledge. I am bound here and everywhere to do justice to my fellow-man, and to do right before God. And with that obligation resting upon me, I will not vote for any such atrocious measure as this, wholly depriving the parent of all rights over the child, and wholly depriving the child growing up to freedom hereafter of all right to receive at least the rudiments of an education.

Mr. NEGLEY. The gentleman from Baltimore city (Mr. Stockbridge) has reference, I suppose, to myself. Now, sir, that resolution which he has read——

Mr. ECKER. I rise to a point of order. The gentlemen has already spoken twice.

Mr. NEGLEY. I rise to a personal explanation.

The CHAIRMAN (Mr. Daniel.) The gentleman from Washington (Mr. Negley) is in order for the purpose of a personal explanation.

Mr. NEGLEY. I drew that resolution myself, and therefore it is to be presumed that I knew what I meant by it. The proposition offered by the gentleman from Caroline (Mr. Todd) in my judgment provides for no apprenticeship at all. It is making provision for the benefit of these poor, helpless and defenceless negroes, for a specified time. It has not the idea or the intention of an apprenticeship. Negro apprenticeship, as provided for in the West India Islands, is something entirely different from what this proposition contemplates. That is a species of slavery.

Mr. CUSHING. Will the gentleman allow me to ask him a question?

Mr. NEGLEY. I will vote for this proposition on the ground not of any benefit to anybody in particular except the negroes themselves. The laws in regard to the orphans' court now make provision for binding out poor defenceless white children. Is that slavery in the eye of the constitution, which we have abrogated? We have stricken the shackles from the slave, and this proposition contemplates a vastly different relation. It is not slavery in the least, any more than it is slavery for the orphans' court to bind out the child of a white person. What does this proposition say? "According to the rules and regulations now governing the orphans' court." It is not slavery any more than it is to bind out a white child. It is to prevent a great public calamity; it is for the benefit of the negro, and for the good of society.

I find upon examination that there ought to be some limitation to this proposition. I do not think the provisions of this section should be in operation more than a year. And I do not think the binding out should be without the consent of the parent first had and obtained, and when the proper time comes, I will offer an amendment to that effect.

Mr. PURNELL. I feel no disposition to prolong this discussion and should have contented myself with voting upon the proposition without adding a single remark, but for the remarks that have fallen from my worthy friend from Cecil (Mr. Pugh,) who was about as unfortunate in defining my position as he was in the interpretation of the law of the orphans' court yesterday; and I think that was fully answered by the gentleman from Howard (Mr. Sands.) Those who heard the gentleman's interpretation of the orphans' court law yesterday, can very well appreciate his remarks upon my consistency. If any gentleman in this house will take the pains to read my remarks, or shall have the curiosity to do so, he may take them from beginning to end, and if he will find a solitary inconsistency between the remarks upon the pages of these debates and those which I made this morning, I will yield that I have been inconsistent.

Inconsistent in what? Have I changed my views as an unconditional emancipationists? I say not. I occupy the same position I did when my constituents sent me here. They sent me here as an emancipationist; and when I return to them I shall tell them exactly what I have done; and if I cannot vindicate myself before my constituents, it is for them to censure me for not having conformed to their will. I occupy now the same ground precisely that I have from the time they sent me here. In voting, as I conceive, to ameliorate the condition of this class by indenting them for a limited period, which at most cannot be more than ten or twelve years, I think I violate no principle contained in the bill of rights, or upon which I was elected to this convention.

As I observed before, the question of apprenticeship was not an issue in my county. I am unprepared to point to a single individual who ever mentioned the subject to me. I came here perfectly untrammeled so far as that question is concerned. The only and the absorbing question before them was the question of emancipation. It has been upon our statute books from the earliest history of our State that apprenticeship ought to exist. White apprentices are bound out annually, monthly, daily, in the various counties of the State. The law limits the treatment of them by their masters; and it is the duty of the masters to provide for educating them in certain branches. From the negro that privilege has been withheld. That seems to be the policy of the State; for what purpose I am not prepared to say. Nevertheless the provisions of law seem to indicate that that was the policy. I feel no disposition at this time to invade upon that policy. If the condition of the minor negroes can be improved by this system, I think it is our duty to do it. I think it is a benevolent duty. As their benefactors we ought to do it.

What hardship does it impose upon their parents, their father and mother? They are disencumbered of their board, maintenance, clothing, and of all care and solicitude in the matter. It is placed in other hands. The adult can go forth in the world and improve his own condition, and accumulate means, and is not subject to the incumbrance which would be otherwise imposed upon him of rearing up his minor children to their manhood. I am entirely satisfied in my own mind that it is a benevolent duty we owe to this class of people without in any degree infringing upon their rights.

Mr. RIDGELY. As I shall vote for this proposition with some modification which I shall propose, when an opportunity is offered, modified so as to put it under the theory which I understand the gentleman from Caroline (Mr. Todd) proposes to occupy, that is, precisely the theory of the existing laws of the State in relation to free negroes, I take this opportunity to say a word in explanation of the vote which I shall give.

A proposition which appears to me to be a very simple one has been made to occupy a character and position entirely different from its purpose; and I hope it has not been made to occupy such a position for the purpose merely of its defeat; but that gentlemen who have given that definition of it have come to the honest judgment that such was the meaning of the proposition. But it means anything else in the world, according to my interpretation of it, than that which the gentleman from Baltimore city (Mr. Stockbridge and Mr. Stirling) have given to it.

This is no proposition to enslave a free man; and it requires a most extraordinary stretch of imagination, in my judgment, for any mind to reach any such conclusion, or to engraft any such interpretation upon the proposition. What is the proposition? If it had read thus, that the jurisdiction of the orphans' court touching free negroes and mulattoes, as now exercised by law, or as hereafter may be prescribed by law, shall be so extended as to authorize them to give the preference in apprenticing such negroes and mulattoes, to their former masters, the whole proposition would have been comprehended. That is all it means. It means nothing more and nothing less. In the exercise of the present jurisdiction, of the power now conferred by law, over free negroes and mulattoes, the orphans' court shall be required to give a preference to the masters, and so indent these free negroes or mulattoes, if they believe them to be competent persons to hold such relations to them. It means nothing more and nothing less.

This ghost of slavery that has been invoked—I will not say invoked for the purpose of killing this proposition—has the effect of intimidating those who from convictions of duty are seeking to emancipate the enslaved race in this State. The orphans' court have the right now to bind over free negroes and mulattoes in this State; that is vagrants, any class of persons who are not capable of self-support. When your constitution takes effect, and emancipation becomes a law by the ratification of the people of the State, these people now slaves will all be free negroes and mulattoes. The laws of your State will attend to them, which pertain to free negroes and mulattoes.

I vote for this proposition merely to extend the jurisdiction of the orphans' court; merely to suggest to the orphans' court that there is some propriety in giving the preference to their former masters, a propriety as suggested by the gentleman from Baltimore city in view of the relations which exist between these parties, and not for any purpose of enslaving the apprentice, not for the purpose of caring for the interests of the master, but because you cannot get rid of the fact that you throw upon the community a large number of these people who are helpless, both from youth and from age. I have heard no proposition from any quarter of this house to extend the liberality of the State to the benefit of this class of people. They are to be thrown upon their own resources, helpless and uneducated as they are, upon their own providence.

I vote for this proposition because it simply adopts one single principle and no more. The only question before the house is this, will you give a preference to the master over a stranger in apprenticing a free negro or mulatto? There is no other question in this matter. There must be apprenticeship. They must be bound out, unless the acts of assembly are repealed or modified, for this provision is the same as the law now is in that respect. There is a certain class of vagrants, and the orphans' court have an arbitrary power to bind them. There is another class over whom, with the consent of their parents, they exercise that power. There is another class that can take care of themselves whom the orphans' court have power to bind out under your code. Now I propose that in the exercise of their power they shall give the preference to their former masters.

Mr. Sands If they are not vagrants they cannot be bound out.

Mr. Ridgely. They must be vagrants under the existing law, having no domiciles. If all vagrants must be bound out, under the law, as they belong to that class they must be bound out. And the orphans' courts have power to exercise a discretion over the cases, and to be controlled by the circumstances in binding them out. Do the orphans' court bind out people twenty years of age? Do they bind out girls of seventeen or boys of nineteen years of age? The uniform rule is to bind them when they are young. They are taken when they are young—and it is not expected that their services will be of much value during that period of their life—in the expectation that as they progress in years they will be some sort of equivalent for the care of them in their earlier years.

These are the reasons I stand by my vote upon emancipation. As the gentleman from Baltimore city says, I stand or fall by it. I gave that vote deliberately, from a conviction of duty. I would not swerve from it to the right or to the left. But I cannot be persuaded to believe that I am in the slightest degree derelict from that position in caring, to the best of my judgment, for these helpless creatures, large numbers of whom I know are improvident, and who may be thrown upon the world without means of support. If any member will suggest to the convention any means by which that object can be secured without such interposition, I should like to have them. For these reasons I shall vote for the proposition with a slight modification to put it beyond all doubt that the party to be bound out shall occupy precisely the same position that the free negroes and mulattoes now occupy, that there shall be no obligation to bind them out indiscriminately, but that in all the category of free negroes and mulattoes now known to the law, when bound out, the masters shall have the preference to others, if the court think proper. So far I will go, but no further.

Mr. Pugh. I ask simply the privilege of putting on the record two sections in the code which misled me, if I was misled, with regard to the law:

"151. Wherever any person shall die seized or possessed of any lands, tenements, or hereditaments lying within this State, and any of the persons entitled thereto or any part thereof, shall be under age, and without a guardian appointed by last will and testament, or by the orphans' court, the administrator of the decedent, as soon as administration shall be committed to him, and not before, shall take possession of such estate, and discharge and fulfil all the duties of *guardian* to such infant, and shall account with the court in like manner as guardians are required by law to account and subject to the like control and authority of the court in all respects whatever.

"152. No administrator shall be *bound* in any manner to discharge and fulfil the duties of guardian after the close of his administration or after the end of three years from the granting such administration, nor after a guardian shall be appointed by the orphans' court."

I submit that although he is not bound to act as guardian after the expiration of three years, nevertheless he can be I also submit that I was about right in another view of the orphans' court. The gentleman from Baltimore county (Mr. Ridgely) is in favor of the jurisdiction of the orphans' court for the benefit of poor white people. I was in favor of it yesterday not only for benefitting poor white children, but poor white orphan children.

Mr. Schley. I desire to make one or two statements of facts contained in the last census. Preliminary to that, however, I desire to say upon the proposition contained in this section, that I know of nothing which tends one particle to confuse my judgment of the practical operation of this section, if it be adopted by the convention. The apology for restoring free colored minors to practical slavery, under the guise of benevolence to them, is abominable.

It appears from the last census that of negro slaves, male and female, under the ages of twenty-one for males and eighteen for females, there were in 1860, in Maryland, 48,623. These are they who are included in the language of this section, all of whom, emancipated by this constitution, are to be restored to practical slavery under the guise of benevolence. In addition to that, I find that there are over the age of sixty-five and under the age of seven, of males and females, an aggregate of 21,605. Now the gentleman from Baltimore county who last addressed the convention (Mr. Ridgely,) said that it was to provide for the helpless by indenting them to their former masters. I wonder if anybody ever supposed that the former masters want the helpless and very young children. No, sir; it is when they begin to become useful, when they can be of service to their former masters, that they will take them. If you take out of those whom we intend to emancipate from slavery by the 23rd article of the bill of rights, and who may be apprenticed under this provision, those under the age of seven, there will be 29,557 who will practically come under this provision; and if you take out from the total number of slaves, those under the ages of twenty-one for males and eighteen for females, and over the age of sixty-five, there remains an aggregate of only 36,027.

Now we have heard gentleman upon this floor speaking of the thousands who have been taken and put into the military service of the United States; and we know that a large number between those ages have taken leg bail and walked off, and we have heard the clamor of the families taken off by the military and removed from their homes. Making a reasonable deduction, upon the lowest basis you please, and you cannot put it at less than fifty per cent. of the ages last mentioned taken away by these various causes, which would leave about 18,000 whom we propose to emancipate by the 23rd article of the bill of rights.

Much stress has been laid upon the benevolence of this proposition of the gentleman from Caroline (Mr. Todd;) but I confess my surprise that a minister of the gospel should never have said, in all his views of that unfortunate race, one word in advocacy of their being educated in this transition state—not one word.

It has also been said that a preference should be given to their former masters. I deny the proposition. I think they of all men have the least claim upon any ground to the apprenticeship of these freed minors. Why? Because there is a great deal of difference between the master of an apprentice as contemplated under the apprentice system heretofore existing in this State, and the slave master, who must of necessity feel some desire to perpetuate the feeling of dominion which he has been accustomed to exercise.

So far from the friends of this section being actuated by feelings of benevolence, I have seen no evidence yet that they are disposed to take the helpless adults or the helpless infants, and provide for either of them; but those who are just coming into usefulness, who are at an age when education is desirable, as I maintain it is, and who can pay by their labor for their support, are to be sent back to their former masters.

If this proposition contained a provision that the consent of the parents should be obtained, which has been studiously avoided by the convention, I should think this plea of benevolence had some foundation. But so far from that, I have seen every one who is an advocate of this proposition, so far as I am aware, carefully voting to prohibit the assent of the parent, the natural guardian of these free minor children. If preference was due to their former master on the ground that his relation would incline him to greater humanity than any other person, and if that is the reason for the preference, I ask who would be more likely to appreciate that than the parents, the natural guardians of the parties interested?

Again, sir, I find from the statistics of the State—and I will not go through all the figures—that taking the value of the labor of the males between the ages of twenty-one and sixty-five at $100 per annum, and taking the value of the labor of the females between the ages of eighteen and sixty-five at $50, and taking the numbers from the census of 1860, the aggregate value of their labor was $44,326,616.67 in exact figures. That, sir, for forty years, was I suppose about the average value of the labor that they rendered without one cent of wages being paid. Now why do you propose to continue the labor of a portion of this race for ten or fifteen years, without any remuneration? What is unrequitted labor but slavery?

The gentleman from Baltimore county who last addressed the convention, says that the State law is identical in its purview and object with the proposal of the gentleman from Caroline. I have no objection to that; if we were satisfied with that there would be no necessity at all of introducing an article which contains such dangerous elements as the one before us. I am not at all deceived by any arguments made in advocacy of this proposition. I can see in it a partial slavery, a practical slavery to which I will never consent.—And I will further say that such a proposition was anticipated early in the campaign in my county; and one of the resolutions adopted in our county convention pledged us faithfully to resist any attempt at negro apprenticeship in this State.

Mr. Markey. Adult; not minor.

Mr. Schley. I believe it was; but the principle is the same.

Mr. Cushing. I give notice that at the proper time I shall offer the following substitute for the section:

"The orphans' court of this State shall in binding out as apprentices, negro or mulatto minors emancipated by the provisions of this constitution, give the preference to the former owners, if such persons are suitable persons; but no such minors shall be bound out if their parents are able to support them; nor shall any such minor over ten years of age be subject to such apprenticeship unless he or she be a common vagrant."

My object in offering this is that I am sorry to see this morning a movement in approval of what has been the curse of our country, for the last three years, and to aid in undoing what has been done. The idea is announced by the gentleman from Washington county (Mr. Negley,) that he was willing to come here and emancipate the slaves, to declare in our bill of rights that every man had a right to the proceeds of his own labor; and then, as the gentleman himself announced, for the purpose of giving some compensation to the man from whom these slaves were taken, that he was willing to ignore the provisions of that bill of rights, and up to the age of twenty-one years deprive every such negro of the right to the proceeds of his own labor. It has been announced on the floor of this house in eloquent terms by the gentleman from Caroline (Mr. Todd,) that slavery was a sin in the sight of God, and proved from holy writ.

What is slavery? The gentlemen of the opposition told you what slavery was, when they told you that it was a thing protected by the constitution of the United States, which tells you that slaves are persons held to service for a term of years. Gentlemen have argued in favor of the right, regarding it as guaranteed by the constitution of the United States, to hold persons to labor for a term of years. Yet the gentleman from Kent (Mr. Chambers) asks you this morning, how holding men to service for a term of years can be called slavery, and denies that it is slavery.— If it is not slavery what becomes of the argument of the gentleman of the opposition that in emancipating the slaves we interfere with the right of the masters under the constitution of the United States. The wording is identical. Holding to service for a term of years, is merely making slavery extend until the man is twenty-one years of age; it is to take away from him his whole youth; it is to deprive him of the opportunity of providing for his aged parents. It is to crush his life out of him for his whole youth, and then throw him upon the community with his best powers exhausted. We have been told that we were throwing upon the community helpless women and children. By this very section it is proposed to take away the bone and sinew which might have helped to support the women and children. Having made a provision in accordance with the highest claims of justice for emancipating a man, and after declaring in the bill of rights that he is entitled to the proceeds of his own labor, you deprive him even of the satisfaction of supporting his aged father and mother who have been released from slavery. You take the able-bodied man of nineteen before your orphans' court and bind him for two years an apprentice to his former master, and he goes to his master's quarter, while his father and mother go to the almshouse of the county.— Under the operation of this section, you take the whole class of men and select from among them the men that would contribute to support the old, and aid to provide for the whole class, you take away all its young men and young women, all the able-bodied, and leave the old and infirm. On what principles of justice or right can this be urged?

Mr. President, I tell you, and gentlemen of the convention I tell you, that it is the one thing that has cursed the emancipation party of this country; the one thing that has cursed the Union party of this land, from the beginning until now; that it has never gone one step forward but straightway it made haste to go two back. We have gone to men with the knife at our throat, or with the bowie knife at our bosom, and begged them for God's sake to take some sort of conciliation. Detesting and scorning it, we dare not touch the sacred thing of slavery, but we must make peace and stultify ourselves. That is the operation and that alone. I doubt if the provision in this section accomplishes any other single thing more surely than to tell the people of Maryland, as my colleague has said, that we have sat here and heard the thunder of the cannon on the border, and we have heard the cries rising up from burning Chambersburg, and we are scared. If it means anything, it means, go to the people of the State who sent you here bound by a solemn oath to do your duty, who have said that negro apprenticeship under any special provision is a thing abhorred by them, and tell them that you found it inexpedient to do what they required; that you were afraid of pressing the emancipation principle in Maryland to the wall.

The gentleman from Washington thought proper in his second remarks to this house to take back the assertion that he did this for the sake of compensation to the slaveowners, by telling us that he did it for no one in particular. If then it is for the interest of nobody—for no man can seriously get up and argue that it is for the interest of the black man, of the slave we have set free to put them back—if the gentlemen who intend to vote for it do not intend it for the interest of the slaveholder, to whom they give this able-bodied labor during the term of their appren ticeship, in the name of almighty God, I ask why do they do it? The Union men and emancipationists of the State thought this convention had left behind the old things and were pressing forward to the new, on the day they declared all men within the borders of Maryland, and held to involuntary servitude, save for crime, free; and proceeding further, declared that all men had certain inalienable rights, and that among these were the right to the proceeds of their own labor; and still further, that slavery was a thing which had in Maryland no claim for compensation and forever prohibited the legislature of the State from granting compensation. We thought the thing was all foreclosed.

We little thought that upon the side of the majority of this house there would be evidenced an eagerness to take back the principle of this thing; not to put back all the blacks into slavery, but to put the bone and sinew of the race into slavery again, and throw upon the community the helpless and infirm. It is left, as my colleague (Mr. Stirling) told you, to the discrimination of the men who hold the slaves; for he only takes those he desires.—He will leave them a burden upon the State until they have attained such an age as to be profitable; and then all the profitable years of the young life of these negroes are to be given to the benefit of the master.

Believing as I do that slavery is injurious to the State of Maryland; believing that it has cursed the State of Maryland from the beginning of its history until now; believing as I do and as I have told you before upon the floor of this house that slavery has brought on this war; believing that slavery has charged this country with a debt of 1,800,000,000, and placed under the sod 500,000 human lives from the north alone; believing that for every single slave in the length and breadth of the land a price has been paid to the slaveowner: that for every slave in Maryland freed by this constitution, five men from the north have gone beneath the sod; believing that the price of blood has been paid for every slave, and that the blood alone shed upon the soil of this State is enough to have washed away every remnant of slavery; I am unwilling that there should be placed in the constitution of Maryland a provision beyond that which stands upon the statute book to-day.

Therefore I offer this proposition which I think is fair, and licensed in some degree by the weight of the laws now existing in this State. I think it is certainly all that any member of the majority of this house should vote for.

It is very easy for the charge to be made upon the floor of this house that men are instigated by hate of the slaveholders. It is a charge easily made, because every man is prone to make and believe such a charge who is injuriously affected by the operation of the acts we have passed. But the question of the slaveholder has hardly come into my mind. I do abhor from the bottom of my soul the system of slavery, because it has brought this tide of war upon the land. I do abhor from the bottom of my soul, slavery, because it has depressed and degraded the whole white population of the country in which we live. I do abhor slavery, because it has cursed my native State, and has rendered her far behind the other States of the Union which are free from it, in the race of improvement. And finally, sir, I do abhor slavery that we could never upon the floor of this house advance any proposition looking to the amelioration of the condition of the enslaved race, without members being startled from their propriety by some idea of negro equality. Slavery for years in Maryland has bound down human souls without one human right. In Maryland to-day nearly a hundred thousand men woman and children are held as beasts.

I wonder that after the eloquent argument of the gentleman from Caroline (Mr. Todd) upon this subject, pouring down from high heaven the indignation of an Omnipotent God upon such foul wrong, and the thunders of the Almighty upon those who have made it the occasion of civil war—I wonder that after proving to us by scriptural quotations that this was a crime with which God could have no sympathy, in the face of all that he could come and ask us to put back into the constitution of this State slavery up to the age of twenty-one years.

This proposition forces the orphans' court to put back into slavery every minor freed by this constitution. There is no discretion of age, no discretion of condition. Under the code of Maryland as it now is, the mere fact of the black man being able to support himself does not free him from the action of the apprenticeship laws of Maryland. I submit that it is simply absurd that there should be a law of Maryland which forces a man abundantly able to maintain himself back into the condition of an apprentice, to serve a master and to receive no wages.

The gentleman from Washington (Mr. Negley) inquired what was to be done with these people. A hundred thousand free blacks in Maryland support themselves now. The experience of counties and of the city of Baltimore tells you that there is no more prosperous class of labor in the State of Maryland to-day than the free black labor. They are abundantly able to support themselves by their own exertions. There are no more of them in the almshouses than of white people. The other hundred thousand can equally do it. What are the gentlemen of the lower counties to do for labor? The slaves being freed they must of necessity hire them or do without labor. Human nature is human nature, and although I can understand how, [illegible] a man may not desire in the first ill-feeling to hire his own slave, taken from him, yet I believe he will act under the strong necessity to hire another man in his place if he comes to labor. If the gentlemen in the lower counties do not wish for labor—if they prefer that their whole agricultural operations should stop, there is more than demand enough for all these free negroes in the other parts of the State. And if there is no demand for them there the army of the United States can take them from eighteen to twenty-one, and pay them such wages as will enable them to support their families at home. There is some way of providing for them. If the men that owned them will not use them, the men in the rest of the State will use them. And I should suppose that the army of the United States would take so many of them that their wages would support their families.

Mr. TODD. I wish to say with reference to the remarks of the gentleman who has just taken his seat, that I do not see any inconsistency between the course I pursued on a former occasion, when the twenty-third article of the bill of rights was under discussion, and the course I have pursued to-day in offering the section now under consideration. If the gentleman by his eloquence could convince me that apprenticeship is slavery, then I should offer a different section. I would offer a section forever hereafter prohibiting any apprenticeship in the State of Maryland, upon any terms, anywhere, or under any conditions. But I do not see it in that light; and therefore I think no extended remarks are necessary as a vindication of my course upon the ground of inconsistency. I feel myself that my course to-day is perfectly consistent with my course heretofore.

I have, however, drawn up an amendment to my proposition which I hope I will have leave to offer, which will modify it, though I prefer the proposition as it was originally offered by myself, with the modifications I have already accepted, yet, as a compromise measure, I propose the following modification: to insert after the word "minors" in the fourth line, the words, "incapable in the estimation of said courts of maintaining themselves."

Mr. HEBB. I would suggest to the gentleman to add, "and whose parents are unable to maintain them."

Mr. TODD. I would much prefer the modification as offered by myself.

Mr. RIDGELY. I hope the gentleman from Caroline will accept that.

Mr. TODD adopted the suggestion, and modified his proposition by inserting "incapable of supporting themselves, or whose parents are unable to maintain them."

Mr. SANDS. I give notice that at the proper time I will move the following substitute:

"In the indenturing of any negro apprentice under the laws of this State, the orphans' court shall give the preference to the former master of the apprentice, if there be such, and if he shall be a proper person to have the custody of the said apprentice."

I propose to make a very few remarks upon this question. I had hoped that I had said my last word here on this long-vexed question of slavery, or on any other subject that bore to it so close a resemblance. I had hoped that my share of the labors of this convention would be discharged, and I should go home without the necessity of again even alluding to this matter. But the course events have taken here this morning, very unexpectedly to myself, compels me, in simple justice to what I have said and done heretofore, to state my position with regard to this matter.

In conversation with many gentlemen of the opposition side of the house, I had expressed the hope that this question of apprenticeship would be allowed to rest where the law had placed it; allowed to rest in the administration of the orphans' courts of the several counties, which would, as a matter of course, exercise their best discretion in providing for the wants of minor negroes liberated under the twenty-third section of the bill of rights. I am sorry that I was disappointed in my expectation. I am sorry that the matter has been thrown again into this hall, to be the subject of long hours of debate. But there are some reasons, both on the master's account and on the slave's or the freedman's account, as well as my own, which force me to express the views which I entertain upon this subject as briefly as I can.

First and foremost, I consider myself pledged against the creation of any system of slavery by this constitution. I shall vote against the proposition, unless it be amended to meet the views I entertain, for the reason not only that I was thus pledged on this subject to the people who sent me here, but because my whole course since I have been a member of this convention is entirely inconsistent with the idea that I should favor the creation of an apprenticeship system. The reasons why I oppose it are these:

I put it to gentlemen on the opposition side of the house, and especially from southern Maryland, if negro labor is not a great necessity to them. A strong argument urged against the twenty-third article of the bill of rights was that this labor was absolutely necessary to their existence. Now I put the question whether they desire to drive this labor from their midst; because, in my opinion, they can adopt no more vigorous means of driving labor from their midst than adopting this section. Why? Because the twenty-third article, if the people adopt our constitution, liberates all adults, male and female; all over lawful age. Do you believe that the father and mother, the free man and free woman, are going to sit down quietly in their midst and leave their children in at least a state of half-slavery? Not one out of twenty will do it; but day and night they will be going off and carrying their little ones with them. You lose the labor you now have.

Another reason why I oppose the creation of this system is this: You are going to turn loose upon your State thousands and tens of thousands of men and women. You are giving them motives of industry and sobriety, and correct habits. How do you give them these motives? By robbing their homes of all that makes home pleasant and agreeable, loving and endearing? Will you say to the man and woman, you can go off in freedom, but your children must remain in servitude? What is the consequence? Dissatisfaction among them as a class. They have no object for which to labor; no child to educate; no pride to take in their children; nothing to live for save each other. What is to be the result of that? They will be idle. Idleness will beget intemperance in them. You know how wretchedly the negro goes through any trouble. Idleness will follow; universal pauperism will follow. And these people, instead of being an element of strength and prosperity in the State, will become its curse, simply because we have taken from them all motive for honest and honorable exercise. Is not that going to be so?

Try its effect by its application to your own feelings and your own consciences. What is the great spur to the exertions of every man? We have children. For them we toil. For them we spend. For them we labor early and late. For them we are sober, discreet, temperate, all that a man should be. Is it not so with this race? They have their human feelings, their human sympathies. Give them some motive for exertion if you do not want them to curse you, and curse the community, and curse the country.

What will follow? If they do not, now that they have an opportunity to labor for themselves, and to enjoy the fruits of their labor, become good, sober, honest citizens, or residents, if you do not like the term citizens, of the community, the law as it stands to-day, and as I propose to embody it in my substitute, will enable you to go into the orphans' court and require of the court that they apprentice to you in preference these children. That is right. We do not want vagrancy. I will go as far as any gentleman in this hall to guard against negro vagrancy. I never want to see it. I will be willing to resort to anything in the world to prevent it. But, in my humble opinion, the only way to prevent this class from becoming vagrants as a class, is to give them proper motives for exertion, labor, sobriety, and every virtue they ought to practice.

I hope there will be a disposition on all sides of this house to accept in a spirit of conciliation and compromise the offer made here to meet on the basis of the existing laws of the State; not requiring us, who are pledged to the contrary course, to create a new system, but to meet on the existing laws of the State, simply declaring in this section of our constitution that it shall be the duty of the orphans' court to give a preference to the master in all cases where apprentices must be indented. For that proposition I will vote with all my heart, and against the proposition as originally presented, I must as earnestly enter my protest, believing as I do that the acceptance of that proposition would work harm to the present master, to the negro and to the State; because I do believe that if the negro population of the State to-day had any idea that you intended to deprive their children of the benefits of the emancipation promised them by this convention, they would go from you in a month in swarms.

Before we passed our twenty-third article, it was directly met by gentlemen in our section of the country who owned negroes, and who urged immediate and speedy action in this matter on the very ground that the negroes were deserting them and going off in crowds. It will be so again. If you talk of the creation of an apprenticeship system, they will go from your land in swarms, as the Hebrews went from Egypt, and depopulate your State, take away from you the labor you say you want, and leave us then to till the soil with our own hands or to starve.

I tender again to gentlemen on the opposite side the olive branch which I hold out in the substitute I propose to offer, that these negroes shall be indentured under the laws of the State as they exist this day, and that in thus indenturing them, their masters, where they are proper persons to have them, shall have the preference. So far I will go. For that proposition I will vote with all my heart; and against the other I must as clearly enter my protest.

Mr. Purnell. I would like to ask the gentleman the question whether by the act of emancipation all indented negroes are set free? Does that liberate all the apprenticed negroes, the free negroes now in the State?

Mr. Sands. How can it free a negro that has never been a slave?

Mr. Purnell. I should like to have a categorical answer, yes or no, whether they are liberated who are held in apprenticeship?

Mr. Sands. I will read the article and the gentleman will see.

Mr. Purnell. I have it before me and can read it for myself; I wish to hear from you.

Mr. Sands. I should like to know what construction of it justifies that view of the case?

Mr. Purnell. Then I understand the gentleman to say that the passage of that article does not alter the present relation of the apprenticed free negroes.

Mr. SANDS. How could it?

Mr. PURNELL. That is not the question — That is all I wanted.

Mr. RIDGELY. That question may be followed up by another question: If the act of emancipation does not disturb the relation of an apprentice, can we by this section enslave a man by making him an apprentice?

Mr. SANDS. I have no doubt about the matter. What is the section?

"It shall be the duty of the orphans' court of the several counties and the city of Baltimore to bind out, until they arrive at the age of twenty-one years for males, and eighteen years for females, all negroes emancipated by the adoption of this constitution."

You ordain the emancipation first; and as soon as that takes effect freedom attaches to them. Then after giving them freedom you propose to take it from them again, putting it back into the condition of a slave.

Mr. CHAMBERS (in his seat.) Apprenticing does not take away freedom.

Mr. RIDGELY. That is not my view at all. I stated that with modifications by which the condition of apprenticeship would be put precisely in the category in which the act of assembly now puts it, I was in favor of the proposition. That is not the proposition of which you are speaking. That is not the proposition now before the house. It has been modified by the consent of the mover.

Mr. SANDS. I am speaking of the proposition before the house, the proposition to apprentice the whole class as the condition of their emancipation, although it does not bring them under the law of slavery in fact. Now as to this question asked by the gentleman from Worcester (Mr. Purnell,) how does the twenty-third article of the bill of rights at all interfere with the relation between master and apprentice? How could a man after reading this plain article ask that question?

"Article 23. That hereafter, in this State, there shall be neither slavery nor involuntary servitude, except in punishment of crime whereof the party shall have been duly convicted; and all persons held to service or labor as slaves are hereby declared free."

"Persons held to service or labor"—how? As apprentices, or indentured servants? No, sir; the plain language is "as slaves." If the article had read, "all persons held to service or labor as slaves or apprentices, are hereby declared free," I suppose in that case the gentleman's views would have been met.

Mr. PURNELL. I would like to ask one other question. What attitude will the slave now proposed to be freed under the twenty-third article occupy? Will they not occupy the same attitude or status that the free negroes now occupy?

Mr. SANDS. Unquestionably. Upon what principles is he to treat them? Just as you do the free negroes now, unquestionably; and not as the proposition offered here proposes to do. The law as it stands now allows the indenting of the children of vagrant and indigent parents. That is the difference. The proposition offered here commands the apprenticeship of the whole class. And I will tell my friends another distinction in this matter. The law as we have it requires the assent of the parent.

Mr. RIDGELY (in his seat.) Sometimes.

Mr. SANDS. The orphans' courts, now by law, is compelled to give the parent a say in the matter, and to act under that say unless there is a sufficient reason for doing otherwise. This section takes away from the parent all right to have a say in the matter whether the party is a proper person or not. Who knows so well as the parent who may have served that man thirty or forty years? He may be a good, kind master; and then he may be a bad master, a hard master, a cruel master; and yet the father and mother of the child, the persons best acquainted with the habits of the master, are not allowed to come into court, under the section as offered, and to say: "That is a hard master; do not give my child to him; he is a bad master, a cruel master; do not give my child to him."

I say again that I am perfectly willing to incorporate a section here which shall place all emancipated negroes precisely on a footing with the present free negroes, and liable to be indentured in the same way under the supervision of the orphans' court. I go further in that substitute, and provide that the master shall have the first offer of such indenture. I am willing to go that far. I am not willing to go any farther; simply because in doing that you take away from these colored people all inducements for honorable exertion, and you drive them in masses out of the State. You do them injustice in first setting them free as a class, and then as a class forcing them back into involuntary servitude; for, mark you, that is the term by which slavery is defined in the constitution of the United States, and that is the way it is defined in the twenty-third article of the bill of rights. "There shall be neither slavery nor involuntary servitude except for crime." I doubt whether, if that question were raised, in one of your courts, they would not decide that there was an entire conflict between the twenty-third article of the bill of rights and the present section proposed to be incorporated into the constitution; because you release them from involuntary servitude by the bill of rights, and then by this section you again force them into involuntary servitude.

Mr. CHAMBERS. The relation of husband and wife is an involuntary servitude.

Mr. SANDS. That is a very different thing. The great cry always is—don't white men apprentice their children? Of course they do, and choose their masters too, and they do it with the hope of affording the child that sort of education, and teaching him that sort of handicraft, which will make him a good citizen in the future. I am perfectly willing to guard the master; but I think that fairness and justice require us to go no further than the proposition I offer. And I hope the majority of this house, who have hitherto borne the heat and the burden of the day in this struggle for emancipation, are not going to mar their work. I hope they will not go beyond what is fair and right. I know that the sun has its spots; and this constitution——

(At this moment the hammer fell.)

Mr. SWOPE moved the previous question.

Mr. CHAMBERS demanded the yeas and nays, and they were ordered.

The question being taken upon sustaining the demand for the previous question, the result was—yeas 33, nays 36—as follows:

Yeas—Messrs. Abbott, Annan, Belt, Bond, Brooks, Cunningham, Cushing, Davis, of Wash'gton, Ecker, Farrow, Galloway, Greene, Hebb, Hoffman, Hopkins, Keefer, Kennard, King, Murray, Negley, Nyman, Pugh, Ridgely, Russell, Schley, Schlosser, Smith, of Carroll, Smith, of Worcester, Sneary, Swope, Sykes, Wickard, Wooden—33.

Nays—Messrs. Goldsborough, President; Audoun, Billingsley, Blackiston, Briscoe, Crawford, Daniel, Dellinger, Dent, Duvall, Edelen, Hodson, Hollyday, Hopper, Horsey, Lansdale, Larsh, Lee, Markey, McComas, Mitchell, Miller, Morgan, Mullikin, Parker, Parran, Peter, Purnell, Smith, of Dorchester, Stirling, Stockbridge, Thomas, Todd, Turner, Valliant, Wilmer—36.

The call for the previous question therefore was not sustained.

Mr. McCOMAS moved to reconsider the vote last taken.

Mr. MILLER and Mr. AUDOUN seconded the motion.

Mr. KENNARD. Is that motion in order?

Mr. HEBB. I rise to a question of order.—The object of moving the previous question is to ascertain whether the house is ready to take a vote on the question. If the question had been decided affirmatively there would have been some propriety in it.

The CHAIRMAN (Mr. Daniel.) It is the decision of the chair that any vote of the house can be reconsidered. A conclusion in the negative is as much a conclusion as if it were in the affirmative. The motion to reconsider is in order.

Mr. WOODEN demanded the yeas and nays, and they were ordered.

The question being taken upon reconsideration, the result was—yeas 45, nays 23—as follows:

Yeas—Messrs. Abbott, Annan, Bond, Briscoe, Chambers, Crawford, Cunningham, Cushing, Davis, of Washing'n, Duvall, Edelen, Galloway, Greene, Hebb, Henkle, Hollyday, Hopkins, Hopper, Horsey, Keefer, Kennard, King, Lansdale, Larsh, McComas, Miller, Mullikin, Murray, Negley, Nyman, Parran, Peter, Pugh, Ridgely, Russell, Schley, Schlosser, Smith, of Carroll, Sneary, Stirling, Swope, Sykes, Valliant, Wickard, Wooden—45.

Nays—Messrs. Goldsborough, President; Audoun, Billingsley, Blackiston, Brooks, Daniel, Dellinger, Dent, Farrow, Hodson, Lee, Markey, Mitchell, Morgan, Parker, Purnell, Sands, Smith, of Dorchester Smith, of Worcester, Stockbridge, Todd, Turner, Wilmer—23.

The motion to reconsider accordingly prevailed.

The question recurring upon sustaining the call for the previous question, the call was sustained.

The question recurred on the adoption of the amendment submitted by Mr. STOCKBRIDGE to the section submitted by Mr. TODD.

Mr. MORGAN demanded the yeas and nays, and they were ordered.

The question being taken, the result was—yeas 31, nays 39—as follows:

Yeas—Messrs. Abbott, Annan, Audoun, Brooks, Cunninghan, Cushing, Daniel, Davis, of Washington, Dellinger, Ecker, Farrow, Greene, Hebb, Hopkins, Hopper, Keefer, Kennard, McComas, Murray, Nyman, Pugh, Russell, Sands, Schley, Schlosser, Smith, of Carroll, Stirling, Stockbridge, Sykes, Thomas, Wickard—31.

Nays—Messrs. Goldsborough, Pres't.; Belt, Billingsley, Blackiston, Bond Briscoe, Chambers, Crawford, Dent, Duvall, Edelen, Galloway, Henkle, Hodson, Hoffman, Hollyday, Horsey, King, Lansdale, Larsh, Lee, Markey, Mitchell, Miller, Morgan, Negley, Parker, Parran, Peter, Purnell, Ridgely, Smith, of Dorchester, Smith, of Worcester, Sneary, Swope, Todd, Turner, Valliant, Wilmer, Wooden—39.

When their names were called,

Mr. NEGLEY said: If I could see any practical mode of carrying this amendment into effect, I should vote for it; but under the existing state of society, or the state of society that will be introduced by the liberation of the negroes for the next five or ten years, I see the utter impossibility of carrying this thing out. It must go over to the legislature. The legislature will have control over it. I therefore vote "no."

Mr. THOMAS said: While I am opposed, for the reasons given by me on a former occasion, to the free negroes emancipated by this constitution, from being educated by the general school system of the State, still, if this proposition is to be carried in relation to negro apprenticeship, I am in favor of these negro apprentices being educated by their masters. I therefore vote "aye."

Mr. VALLIANT said: I am in favor of the

principle contained in the proposition submitted by the gentleman from Baltimore city; but for the reason assigned by the gentleman from Washington (Mr. Negley,) I shall be compelled to vote against it. If there was any provision made for the education of the negro, I should have no objection to it. It would be impracticable in Talbot county. For that reason only, I vote "no."

The amendment was accordingly rejected.

The question recurring upon the adoption of the amendment submitted by Mr. TODD;

On motion of Mr. PUGH,

The subject was divided.

The question then being on the first clause of the amendment, as follows:

"It shall be the duty of the orphans' court of the several counties and the city of Baltimore to bind, until they arrive at the age of twenty-one years for males and eighteen years for females, all negroes emancipated by the adoption of this constitution, who are minors, and incapable of supporting themselves, or whose parents are unable to maintain them, subject to such regulations as are now or may hereafter be prescribed by law."

Mr. PUGH demanded the yeas and nays, and they were ordered.

The question being taken, the result was —yeas 51, nays 20—as follows:

Yeas—Messrs. Goldsborough, President; Annan, Belt, Billingsley, Blackiston, Bond, Briscoe, Chambers, Crawford, Cunningham, Daniel, Davis, of Washington, Dent, Duvall, Farrow, Galloway, Greene, Hebb, Henkle, Hodson, Hoffman, Hollyday, Hopper, Horsey, King, Lansdale, Larsh, Lee, Markey, McComas, Mitchell, Miller, Morgan, Mullikin, Negley, Nyman Parran, Peter, Purnell, Ridgely, Sands, Smith, of Carroll, Smith, of Dorchester, Smith, of Worcester, Sneary, Swope, Sykes, Todd, Turner, Valliant, Wilmer—51.

Nays—Messrs. Abbott, Audoun, Brooks, Cushing, Dellinger, Ecker, Hopkins, Keefer, Kennard, Murray, Parker, Pugh, Russell, Schley, Schlosser, Stirling, Stockbridge, Thomas, Wickard, Wooden—20.

When their names were called,

Mr. AUDOUN said: I shall vote against every proposition looking to placing in the organic law of this State anything which tends towards slavery of any kind. There is sufficient law now upon the statute books to provide for negro apprenticeship. I voted against open unvarnished slavery; I now vote against slavery whitewashed. I vote "no."

Mr. ECKER said: As I have not had an opportunity to speak on this question during its discussion before the house, I would take this opportunity to explain my vote. When the proposition of my friend from Caroline (Mr. Todd) was introduced, I was favorably impressed with it, and was inclined to vote for it, but on examination I find in the Code all laws necessary in the case And after hearing a number of speeches from gentlemen on both sides, and also observing that it had created quite a sensation with the opposition, they put me in mind of trout fishing on a warm summer's day; for no sooner was the "*bait*" thrown out, than every one caught at it. I vote "no."

Mr. NEGLEY said: Regarding this as no system of slavery whatever, being as distinct from it as light is from darkness, regarding it as a measure for the good of the free negro himself, and not at all reinstating him in any condition of slavery, not affecting his status of freedom under the 23d article of the bill of rights, but calculated to operate for the benefit of the section of the State where it will exist, I vote "aye."

Mr. PUGH said: I called for a division of this question simply because it contained two distinct substantive propositions. I do not intend to support either. I vote "no."

Mr. SANDS said: The proposition as modified is exactly in substance that which I offered as a substitute. For that reason I vote "aye."

Mr. SCHLEY said: I have no objection to the proposition as it stands; but deeming it superfluous, I vote "no."

The first branch of the section was accordingly adopted.

The question recurring upon the second clause of the amendment, to wit: "and in all cases the preference shall be given to their former masters, when in the judgment of said courts they are suitable persons to have charge of them."

Mr. PUGH demanded the yeas and nays, and they were ordered.

The question being taken, the result was —yeas 45, nays 27—as follows:

Yeas—Messrs. Goldsborough, President; Annan, Belt, Billingsley, Blackiston, Bond, Briscoe, Chambers, Crawford, Cunningham, Dent, Duvall, Edelen, Galloway, Henkle, Hodson, Hoffman, Hollyday, Horsey, King, Lansdale, Larsh, Lee, Markey, McComas, Mitchell, Miller, Morgan, Mullikin, Negley, Nyman, Parran, Peter, Purnell, Ridgely, Smith, of Carroll, Smith, of Dorchester, Smith, of Worcester, Sneary, Swope, Sykes, Todd, Turner, Valliant, Wilmer—45.

Nays—Messrs. Abbott, Audoun, Brooks, Cushing, Daniel, Davis, of Washington, Dellinger, Ecker, Farrow, Greene, Hebb, Hopkins, Hopper, Keefer, Kennard, Murray, Parker, Pugh, Russell, Sands, Schley, Schlosser, Stirling, Stockbridge, Thomas, Wickard, Wooden—27.

When their names were called,

Mr. HEBB said: I prefer leaving it to the discretion of the courts, and I vote "no."

Mr. NEGLEY said: Seeing no reason why the former owner of the indentured negro should not have the benefit of his services, if in the opinion of the orphans' court he is a suitable person to have them, I shall certainly vote "aye."

Mr. SANDS said: For fear I might seem inconsistent in my two votes, I shall give my reasons for voting in the negative upon this proposition. I do not think they ought to be in charge of those who declare against their emancipation. If I were on the bench of the orphans' court, and application were made for the services of a negro apprentice, and the master should tell me he ought not to have been set free, I should tell him he was not a suitable person to have the custody of a negro, and he should not have it. I therefore, on this branch of the proposition, vote "no."

Mr. THOMAS said: When I consented to come here to this convention, I stood pledged before my constituents to vote against any system of negro apprenticeship, and to vote in favor of unconditional and immediate emancipation, and to vote in favor of representation according to population. I have redeemed every single one of these pledges. I do not intend to violate a single pledge that I made. In consideration of that pledge, and in consideration furthermore, that I consider that the laws and the statutes of the State are already sufficient to meet the cases of all free negroes, as well those emancipated as those who are free now, I am opposed to putting anything in the organic law which is to provide for that; and more especially am I opposed to the proposition to give these slaves to their masters. I am in favor of allowing the law to remain just as it is, to allow the orphans' court to use their discretion. I therefore vote "no."

Mr. VALLIANT said: I do not rise to give all my reasons for my vote upon this branch of the amendment; but I rise simply to say that I shall vote under this apprehension, that the words "in all cases," have exclusive reference to such minors only as are incapable of supporting themselves, and has no reference to the whole mass of the negro minors emancipated by the 23d article of the bill of rights. Under that apprehension I vote "aye,"

The second branch of the section was accordingly agreed to.

Mr. GALLOWAY asked and obtained leave of absence for Mr. Gorrell, committee clerk.

Messrs. Hopkins, Edelen and McComas were excused from attending the sessions of the convention until Monday.

On motion of Mr. STIRLING,

The convention took a recess until 8 o'clock.

EVENING SESSION.

The roll was called, and the following members answered to their names:

Messrs. Goldsborough, President; Abbott, Annan, Audoun, Cunningham, Cushing, Daniel, Davis, of Washington, Dellinger, Ecker, Farrow, Galloway, Greene, Hebb, Hoffman, Hollyday, Hopper, Horsey, Keefer, King, Lansdale, Markey, Mitchell, Morgan, Mullikin, Murray, Negley, Nyman, Parker, Pugh, Purnell, Ridgely, Russell, Sands, Schley, Schlosser, Scott, Smith, of Carroll, Smith, of Worcester, Stirling, Stockbridge, Swope, Sykes, Thomas, Todd, Wooden—46.

There being no quorum present,

Mr. AUDOUN moved a call of the convention;

The motion being sustained,

The roll was called, and the following members responded:

Messrs. Goldsborough, President; Abbott, Annan, Audoun, Cunningham, Cushing, Daniel, Davis, of Washington, Dellinger, Ecker, Farrow, Galloway, Greene, Hebb, Hoffman, Hollyday, Hopper, Horsey, Keefer, King, Lansdale, Markey, Mitchell, Morgan, Mullikin, Murray, Negley, Nyman, Parker, Pugh, Purnell, Ridgely, Russell, Sands, Schley, Schlosser, Scott, Smith, of Carroll, Smith, of Worcester, Stirling, Stockbridge, Swope, Sykes, Thomas, Todd Wooden—46.

On motion of Mr. AUDOUN,

The sergeant-at-arms was sent after absent members.

Subsequently the sergeant-at-arms returned and reported that he could find but one absentee in the city, Mr. Chambers, who was indisposed.

On motion of Mr. PUGH,

The convention adjourned.

EIGHTY-THIRD DAY.

SATURDAY, August 27, 1864.

The convention met at 10 o'clock, A. M.

Prayer by Rev. Mr. Patterson,

The roll was called, and the following members answered to their names:

Messrs. Goldsborough, President; Abbott, Annan, Audoun, Blackiston, Brooks, Carter, Chambers, Crawford, Cunningham, Cushing, Daniel, Davis, of Washington, Dellinger, Duvall, Ecker, Farrow, Galloway, Greene, Hatch, Hebb, Hodson, Hoffman, Hollyday, Hopper, Horsey, King, Lansdale, Lee, Markey, Mitchell, Morgan, Mullikin, Murray, Negley, Nyman, Parker, Parran, Pugh, Purnell, Ridgely, Russell, Sands, Schley, Schlosser, Scott, Smith, of Dorchester, Smith, of Worcester, Sneary, Stirling, Stockbridge, Swope, Sykes, Thomas, Todd, Wickard, Wilmer, Wooden—58.

The journal of yesterday was read and approved.

ABSENT MEMBERS.

On motion of Mr. MULLIKIN,

It was ordered to be entered on the journal that James Valliant is detained from his seat to-day in consequence of attention to business as chairman of the committee on printing and reporting, with the printer in Baltimore.

On motion of Mr. HATCH,

It was ordered to be entered on the journal that had Mr. Hatch been in his seat yesterday he would have voted against the section added to the judiciary article, providing a system of involuntary apprenticeship, and in favor of the amendment which was offered thereto designed to secure such apprentices education so as to enable them to read and write.

Mr. ABBOTT submitted the following resolution:

Resolved, That in view of the uncertain condition of affairs in this State, owing to the possibility of an invasion by the public enemy, which may interfere with the expression of the popular will on the day to be fixed for voting on this constitution, that this convention, when it adjourns without day, will be adjourned subject to the call of the president, and in case of the death or disqualification of the president (H. H Goldsborough,) Frederick Schley, of Frederick county, Joseph B. Pugh, of Cecil county, Henry Stockbridge, of Baltimore city, Wm T. Purnell, of Worcester county, be and they are hereby authorized, in the order in which they are named, to act as president, and call the convention together;

Which was read the first time.

Mr. RIDGELY, from the committee on the schedule, submitted the following report, which was read the first time:

The committee on the schedule ask leave respectfully to make the following report:

ARTICLE —.

Schedule.

Section 1. Every officer of the State, the entire amount of whose pay, or compensation received for the discharge of his official duties, shall exceed the yearly sum of three thousand dollars, except wherein otherwise provided by this constitution, shall keep a book, in which shall be entered every sum or sums of money received by him, or on his account, as a payment, or compensation for his performance of official duties, a copy of which entries in said book, verified by the oath of the officer, by whom it is directed to be kept, shall be returned yearly to the treasurer of the State, for his inspection and that of the general assembly of the State, and each of said officers, when the amount received by him for the year shall exceed three thousand dollars, shall yearly pay over to the treasurer of the State, the amount of such excess by him received, subject to such disposition thereof as the general assembly may direct. Any such officer failing to comply with this requisition, shall be deemed to have vacated his office, and be subject to suit by the State, for the amount that ought to be paid into the treasury.

Sec. 2. The common law and statute law now in force, and not repugnant to this constitution, shall remain in force, until they expire by their own limitation, or are altered by the general assembly.

Sec. 3. The several courts, except as herein otherwise provided, shall continue with like powers and jurisdiction, both at law and in equity, as if this constitution had not been adopted and until the organization of the judicial department, provided by this constitution.

Sec. 4. The general assembly shall have power to pass all such laws as may be necessary and proper for carrying into execution the powers vested by this constitution, in any department or office of the government, and the duties imposed upon them thereby.

Sec. 5. If on any election directed by this constitution, any two or more candidates shall have the highest and equal number of votes, a new election shall be ordered, except in cases specially otherwise provided by this constitution.

Sec. 6. In the trial of all criminal cases, the jury may be the judges of law as well as fact.

Sec. 7. The trial by jury of all issues of fact in civil proceedings, in the several courts of this State, where the amount exceeds the sum of five dollars, shall be inviolably preserved.

Sec. 8. The general assembly shall have power to regulate by law, not inconsistent with this constitution, all matters which relate to the judges of election, time, place, and manner of holding elections in this State, and of making return thereof.

Sec. 9. All officers, civil and military, now holding office, whether by election, or appointment under the State, shall continue to hold and exercise their offices according to their present tenure, unless otherwise provided in this constitution, until they shall be superseded pursuant to its provisions and until their successors be duly qualified, and the compensation of such officers which has been increased by this constitution, shall take effect from the first day of January, 1865.

VOTE ON THE CONSTITUTION.

Section 1 For the purpose of ascertaining the sense of the people of this State, in regard to the adoption or rejection of this constitution, the Governor shall issue his proclamation within five days after the adjournment of this convention directed to the sheriff of the city of Baltimore, and to the sheriffs of the several counties of this State commanding them to give notice in the manner now prescribed by law, that an election will be held in the city of Baltimore and in the several counties of the State, at the usual places of holding elections in said city and counties, for the adoption or rejection of this constitution, on the twelfth day of October, in the year eighteen hundred and sixty-four, which election shall be held between the hours of eight o'clock, A. M., and six o'clock, P. M., and the judges of election of said city, and of the several counties of the State, shall receive at said election the votes only of such electors as are qualified according to the provisions of this constitution, who may offer to vote at such election, and the said sheriffs shall also give notice on or after the twelfth day of October, eighteen hundred and sixty-four, for all elections provided by this constitution, to be held during that year.

Sec. 2. At the said election, the vote shall be by ballot, and each ballot shall describe thereon the words "for the constitution," or "against the constitution," as the voter may elect, and it shall be conducted in all respects as the general elections of this State are now conducted. The judges of election shall administer to every person offering to vote, the oath or affirmation prescribed by this constitution, and should any person offering to vote refuse or decline to take said oath, he shall not be permitted to vote at such election, but the taking of such oath or affirmation, shall not be deemed conclusive evidence of the right of such person to vote; and it shall be the duty of the return judges of said city, and of the several counties of the State, having counted the votes given for or against the adoption of this constitution, to certify the result thereof in the manner now prescribed by law, accompanied with a special statement, that every person, who has voted, has taken the oath or affirmation prescribed by the constitution; and the Governor upon receiving such result and ascertaining the aggregate vote throughout the State, shall by his proclamation make known the same, and if a majority of the votes cast shall be for the adoption of the constitution, it shall go into effect on the first day of November, eighteen hundred and sixty-four.

SOLDIERS' VOTE.

Section 1. Any of the qualified voters of this State, who shall be absent from the county or city of his residence by reason of being in the military service of the United States so as not to be able to vote at home, on the adoption or rejection of this constitution, or for all State officers elected on general ticket, and for Presidential electors, and for members of Congress, at the election to be held on the Tuesday next after the first Monday in November, eighteen hundred and sixty-four, shall be entitled to vote at such elections as follows: A poll shall be opened in each company of every Maryland regiment in the service of the United States, or of this State, on the day appointed by this convention, for taking the vote on the new constitution, or on some day not more than five days thereafter, at the quarters of the commanding officer thereof, and voters of this State belonging to such company who shall be within ten miles of such quarters on the day of election, may vote at such poll; the polls shall be opened at eight o'clock, A. M., and close at six o'clock, P. M.; the commissioned officers of such company or such of them as are present at the opening of the polls, shall act as judges, and any one officer, shall be competent so to act, and if no officer be present, then the voters in such company present, shall elect two of the voters present to act as judges of the election; before any votes are received, each of the judges shall take an oath or affirmation, that he will perform the duties of judge according to law, will prevent fraud and observe and make proper return thereof, and such oath the judges may administer to each other; the election shall be by ballot, and any voter may vote in writing either "for the new constitution or against the new constitution."

Sec. 2. The judges may swear any one offering to vote, or to his being a legal voter of this State. The judges shall take down on a poll-book or list the names of all the voters as their votes are taken, and the tickets shall be placed in a box as taken; after the polls are closed, the tickets shall be counted and strung on a thread, and the judges shall make out a certificate, which they shall sign, addressed to the Governor, in which they shall state that they have taken the oath hereby prescribed, and shall certify the number of votes taken, and the number of votes for and against the constitution, the said certificates shall be accompanied with the names of the voters, and shall be plainly expressed, but no particular words shall be required.

Sec. 3. The judges shall, as soon as possible, transmit said returns, with the tickets so strung, to the Governor, who shall receive the returns of the soldiers' vote, and shall cast up the same, and judge of the genuineness and correctness of the returns, and may recount the threaded tickets, so as to satisfy himself, and the Governor shall count said vote with the aggregate vote of the State on the adoption or rejection of this constitution, and shall wait for fifteen days after the day on which the State vote is taken, so as to allow the returns of the soldiers' vote to be made, before the result of the whole vote is announced. The Governor shall receive the returns of the soldiers' vote on said election for State officers, Presidential electors, and members of Congress, and shall count the same with the aggregate home vote on State officers and the aggregate home vote in each district respectively for members of Congress.

Sec. 4. The Governor shall make known to the officers of the State regiments the provisions of this article of the schedule, and request them to exercise the right hereby conferred upon them, and shall take all means proper to secure the soldiers' vote; and the general assembly, at its first session after the adoption of this constitution, shall make proper appropriation to pay any expense that may arise herein.

Sec. 5. If this constitution shall be adopted

by the people, the provisions contained herein for taking the soldiers' vote on the adoption of the constitution, shall apply to all elections to be held in this State, until the general assembly shall otherwise provide.

JAS. L. RIDGELY,
Chairman,
JOHN A. HOPPER,
PETER G. SCHLOSSER,
JOEL HOPKINS.

NEGRO APPRENTICESHIP.

The convention proceeded to the consideration of the report of the committee on the judiciary department.

Mr. AUDOUN submitted the following amendment:

"Section —. It shall be the duty of the judges of the several orphans' courts of this State, before they shall proceed to bind any negroes as apprentices, to administer to the party to whom he or she is to be bound, the same oath as prescribed for voters by this constitution, in the article on the elective franchise, and upon the refusal of the said party to take and subscribe to said oath, the said courts shall hold the person so refusing to be an unsuitable person to have charge of such negro."

Mr. CUSHING moved to add the following:

"And the fact of such oath having been taken by the party to whom such negro has been bound, shall be expressed in the indenture."

Mr. AUDOUN accepted the amendment.

Mr. RIDGELY. That proposition comes up in a very small house. The principle decided yesterday was decided by an unusually large house. We are called upon in this condition of things to vote upon it. I move that this section be informally postponed; and on that question I ask for the yeas and nays.

The yeas and nays were ordered.

The question being taken, the result was—yeas 20, nays 37—as follows:

Yeas—Messrs. Blackiston, Crawford, Duvall, Hodson, Hollyday, Horsey, King, Lansdale, Lee, Markey, Mitchell, Morgan, Parran, Ridgely, Smith, of Dorchester, Smith, of Worcester, Stockbridge, Thomas, Todd, Wilmer—20.

Nays—Messrs. Goldsborough, President; Abbott, Annan, Audoun, Brooks, Carter, Cunningham, Cushing, Daniel, Davis, of Washington, Dellinger, Ecker, Farrow, Galloway, Greene, Hatch, Hebb, Hoffman, Hopper, Mullikin, Murray, Negley, Nyman, Parker, Pugh, Purnell, Russell, Sands, Schley, Schlosser, Scott, Sneary, Stirling, Swope, Sykes, Wickard, Wooden—37.

The motion to postpone was accordingly rejected.

The question recurred on the adoption of the section submitted by Mr. AUDOUN.

Mr. AUDOUN demanded the yeas and nays, and they were ordered.

The question being taken, the result was—yeas 44, nays 13—as follows:

Yeas—Messrs. Goldsborough, President; Abbott, Annan, Audoun, Brooks, Carter, Cunningham, Cushing, Daniel, Davis, of Washington, Dellinger, Ecker, Farrow, Galloway, Greene, Hatch, Hebb, Hoffman, Hopper, King, Markey, Mullikin, Murray, Negley, Nyman, Parker, Pugh, Purnell, Ridgely, Russell, Sands, Schley, Schlosser, Scott, Smith, of Worcester, Sneary, Stirling, Stockbridge, Swope, Sykes, Thomas, Todd, Wickard, Wooden—44.

Nays—Messrs. Blackiston, Crawford, Duvall, Hodson, Hollyday, Horsey, Lansdale, Lee, Mitchell, Morgan, Parran, Smith, of Dorchester, Wilmer—13.

The section was accordingly adopted.

DETENTION IN SLAVERY.

Mr. STIRLING submitted the following amendment to the report.

"Section —. Any person who shall, after this constitution shall have gone into effect, detain in slavery any person so emancipated by the provisions of this constitution, shall, on conviction, be fined not less than five hundred dollars, nor more than five thousand dollars, or be imprisoned not more than five years; and any of the judges of this State shall discharge, on habeas corpus, any person so detained in slavery."

Mr. RIDGELY. How can anybody be detained in slavery against the law?

The PRESIDENT. He can be forcibly held in slavery.

Mr. RIDGELY. They have the same rights that I have.

Mr. SANDS. What are petitions for freedom for?

Mr. STIRLING. This section cannot possibly do any harm; and while I do not think there is any absolute necessity for it, and do not offer it because I think it is necessary for the final abolition of slavery, yet somebody might be disposed to exercise the practical physical power of keeping a person in slavery who is legally emancipated. He may have the physical power to prevent a person from asserting the rights this constitution gives. While I do not think any j dge on the bench would make such a decision, yet by previous legislation it requires a petition for freedom to establish the right of emancipation; and I want to provide for the punishment of any man who shall undertake to detain in slavery those who are freed, and to resist the law we have undertaken to enact; and I want to provide for a discharge by a judge upon *habeas corpus*, without the formality of a petition for freedom.

Mr. WILMER demanded the yeas and nays, and they were ordered.

The question being taken, the result was—yeas 42, nays 13—as follows:

Yeas—Messrs. Goldsborough, Pesidrent;

Abbott, Annan, Audoun, Brooks, Carter, Cunningham, Cushing, Daniel, Davis, of Washington, Dellinger, Ecker, Galloway, Greene, Hatch, Hebb, Hoffman, Hopper, King, Markey, Mullikin, Murray, Negley, Nyman, Parker, Pugh, Purnell, Ridgely, Russell, Sands, Schley, Schlosser, Scott, Smith, of Worcester, Sneary, Stirling, Swope, Sykes, Thomas, Todd, Wickard, Wooden—42.

Nays — Messrs. Blackiston, Chambers, Crawford, Duvall, Hollyday, Horsey, Lansdale, Lee, Mitchell, Morgan, Parran, Smith, of Dorchester, Wilmer—13.

When his name was called,

Mr. HODSON did not vote.

The PRESIDENT. If the gentleman from Dorchester refuses to vote, the chair will order it to be so entered on the journal.

Mr. HODSON. I should prefer to have it so entered upon the journal.

The section was accordingly adopted.

No further amendments being offered to part IV, the next section was read as follows:

PART V.

Courts of Baltimore city.

"Section 27. There shall be in the eighth judicial circuit two courts, to be styled the superior court of Baltimore city and the circuit court of Baltimore city; each court to consist of three judges, who shall be appointed in the same manner, hold their offices for the same time, and have the same general powers and duties as are herein prescribed for other judges of courts of record in this State."

Mr. THOMAS submitted the following amendment:

Section 27. Strike out all after the word "the," in the first line, and insert the following:

"Thirteenth judicial circuit four courts, to be styled the 'superior court of Baltimore city;' the 'court of common pleas;' the 'circuit court of Baltimore city;' and the 'criminal court of Baltimore;' each court shall consist of one judge, who shall be elected by the legal and qualified voters of said city, and shall hold their offices for the term of fifteen years, subject to the provisions of this constitution with regard to the election and qualification of judges and their removal from office, and shall exercise the jurisdiction hereinafter specified."

Mr. THOMAS said: After I drew up the section on the fifth page of the amendments as printed, I found a section in the report in relation to the salary of officers; and I therefore leave that out of this section, and will offer it when the proper time comes.

Mr. STOCKBRIDGE. The practical operation of the adoption of the amendment is to retain the judicial system in Baltimore precisely as it is at present organized, with the single exception that one of the courts now is a court created by act of assembly instead of by the constitution itself. The courts are the same, and the judicial power on the bench will be the same under this amendment as that which at present exists; and the distribution of the duties and the jurisdiction of the courts is precisely the same as at present exists. I do not think any one familiar with the operation and practical working of these courts but will be satisfied on a little reflection that they are inadequate to the discharge, even at the present time, of the judicial duties which ought to be discharged in that city; besides which the litigation, the business of the courts, is constantly and rapidly increasing, the result of which is practically there, as it was complained of throughout the counties, the delay of justice to such a degree as almost to amount to a denial of justice. There is one advantage which the courts there have over the courts in the counties, that although there is but one judge on the bench, yet ordinarily the judges are always accessible. They are there; and in any case of great emergency which addresses itself with sufficient force to the discretion of the judges, they can give it prompt attention. But when their dockets are overcowded, a thousand to twelve hundred cases on the docket going over from one term to another, in spite of the utmost diligence on the part of the justice, I say it amounts practically to a denial of justice to provide a system by which there shall be no increased judicial force in that city.

In view of that fact, and to obviate another difficulty, the committee have reported a system somewhat different. They have consolidated the four courts into two, but have provided three judges on the bench in each of these courts; so that in fact, while there are but two courts, there are six judges; whereas under the system proposed by the amendment there are four courts and yet but four judges. The operation of that, with the other part subsequently given in the report of the committee, is to provide that practically there may be six courts sitting at a time. There being six judges, it is provided that they shall sit on the bench as a full bench in the hearing of important trials, in the hearing of motions, and in the distribution of business among themselves; yet they may sit in different departments of their business separately and thus transact their business. I am satisfied that the report, as it comes from the committee, will promote very much more the ends of justice in the city of Baltimore than is possible to be attained under the system proposed by the amendment. I hope therefore that the amendment will not prevail.

I have but one purpose in advocating the amendment; and that is to secure prompt justice and the speedy trial of all causes in the courts of that city, which affects any citizen of that great commercial and mercantile community to an extent which it is almost impossible for gentlemen of the counties who have not been familiar with the amount of important and pressing business there, adequately to understand. It is in behalf of that commercial and mercantile interest that I speak. I say that there business is embarrassed. It is accumulated; and it is impossible for them to discharge it. The utmost diligence on the part of the judges is insufficient to clear their dockets. It is so in both courts. In one of the courts the equity business is effectually blocked; cases standing there which have been standing there for years and years, so that it is impossible to get equity business transacted. I trust this convention will give the city of Baltimore more judicial force. They have done it for the counties, not to the extent the committee reported and thought desirable, but to some extent. If justice is to be administered in the city of Baltimore they must do it there. If they do not consent to do it, justice cannot be administered in those courts.

Mr. Abbott. I should like to have the gentleman explain to us how it is that two courts can transact more business than four.

Mr. Stockbridge. I fear my colleague has not read the report of the committee. If he had he would have discovered in the twenty-eighth and thirtieth sections that it is made competent for the three judges of each court, provided for in this section, so to "apportion and distribute the business of their courts as shall best facilitate the despatch of business and promote the ends of justice." To illustrate: that it may be evident that one court with three judges acting in that way may do more than two courts sitting with one judge each according to the other system. On the bench of the superior court there are three judges. They have the jurisdiction of all civil matters, equity not being included; that is, appeals from magistrates' decisions, and all original suits brought from one hundred dollars upward. In the distribution of their business they may assign one judge who shall go on trying appeals from magistrates' decisions; they may assign one judge who shall go on trying cases where the amount in dispute ranges from one to five or to seven hundred dollars; and the third judge may hear those cases above five or seven hundred dollars. So that practically the superior court may be sitting in three places and transacting business by three judges at once. Thus you get what is under the other system a force of three judges. Under the other system, you have given this jurisdiction to two courts; but you have only given it to two men, who consequently, to do their utmost, can only sit in the trial of causes in two places at once; while under the system reported by the committee, they can hear them in three places at once.

Precisely the same is it in the circuit court, in which is placed the equity jurisdiction of the present circuit court, and the jurisdiction of the present criminal court. For the three judges together have power to apportion and distribute the business among themselves.

They may make such an apportionment as to sit in three places at the same time; while under the amendment as proposed, this jurisdiction and labor is placed in two courts, but confined to two judges, and they can only sit in two places.

Mr. Abbott. The effect of it will be to give us six courts instead of four.

Mr. Stockbridge. Practically; but not all the time. It provides that where a suitor chooses, and where he thinks that one judge is not sufficient, he may demand a bench, and require that at least two of the judges shall sit in the trial of the case, so that he may have the benefit of two judges if there are important legal points involved. But the great bulk of the time there may be six men sitting in effect in as many different courts, but really in two.

Mr. Thomas. I desire to say a few words in relation to what has fallen from my colleague. As has been stated by him, the system proposed by this amendment is the present system, as practiced in the city of Baltimore, establishing four courts. The reason which is given by the gentleman for the increase of judges in the courts of Baltimore city, is that the courts, as established by the report of the committee, can greatly facilitate business, and that the courts now established cannot possibly perform the duties required of them. I have only to say in reply to that that the superior court of Baltimore city, having now jurisdiction over all sums where the debt or damage claimed is above five hundred dollars, if there are a great many cases on the dockets of the superior court, it is not owing to the jurisdiction of the court. I will venture to assert that if any gentleman of this convention will go into the superior court on the first three days of any term, and listen to the calling of the docket, he will find that two-thirds of the cases are postponed or continued by the lawyers themselves. The judge of that court has repeatedly complained in my hearing that the lawyers will not come up and try their cases. But we propose by further amendments to avoid the superior court having so much business, by increasing the jurisdiction of the court of common pleas from five hundred up to a thousand dollars, which will throw all these small cases, which are nine-tenths of the cases which give trouble in the superior court, into the court of common pleas.

How then does the court of common pleas stand in relation to its business? I will venture to assert that the court of common pleas, when it meets, on the second Monday of every term, is not in session two months in the term. This last term of the court, Judge King adjourned his court over a month ago, because he had not enough business to transact. We propose also to give the court of common pleas additional facilities for the performance of these additional duties. We take away from the court of common pleas the appeals from magistrates in relation to criminal cases. According to the present constitution, appeals from the magistrates in all cases go up to the court of common pleas.

Mr. STOCKBRIDGE. Not in all.

Mr. THOMAS. Yes, they do, except in the case of violation of the city ordinances. There are hundreds of cases every year in that court, involving the recovery of fines, penalties, and forfeitures, under the State laws, *quasi* criminal cases, which should properly go to a criminal court. We propose to give these cases to the criminal court, so that you will have the common law jurisdiction confined to two courts, which will increase their facilities, and the whole criminal jurisdiction will be confined to one court, and the equity jurisdiction will be divided between the present circuit court of Baltimore city and the equity court of Baltimore city, which will give them additional facilities for the performance of the duties assigned.

This system has been in operation for fourteen years, and there is no complaint yet in the city of Baltimore in relation to its courts; and it appears to me that the city of Baltimore is entitled to have her courts just as they now stand; because, I contend, they will be more acceptable to the people. I contend too that the report of this committee renders it more complicated than it now is. For instance, it is proposed by this report to give to the judges of the circuit court, which is to be composed of the present criminal court and the circuit court, both equity and criminal jurisdiction, and also to make one of the judges of that court the chief justice of the orphans' court. This convention has already decided that the orphans' court system shall remain just as it is. If you adopt the system as proposed by the committee in relation to the courts of Baltimore city, you have got to break up the orphans' court system, which you have already established and made uniform throughout the State.

Then in relation to the three-judge system as proposed by the committee, it will work badly in this way. There is a provision that whenever a man wants a case tried he shall be entitled to three judges.

Mr. STOCKBRIDGE. There is no such provision.

Mr. THOMAS. Two judges, then. Now suppose one of the judges is on the bench of the orphans' court. Another one sits every day to try cases. A lawyer comes in and wants to postpone a case. He sees one judge upon the bench, and knows that another one is sick, for you cannot prevent sickness, and he claims two judges, and is entitled to the postponement of his case. According to the practice now he is not entitled to the postponement of the case unless the parties agree, or unless he has a legal ground of continuance under the law. I say that so far as the trial of cases is concerned, the system is better and more expeditious under the present system than it would be under three judges.

Mr. STIRLING. I shall support the amendment my colleague has offered; and I desire very briefly to assign my reasons for doing so, because I regret to differ from my colleague who introduced this report, who has had a great deal of experience in these matters, and whose opinion with regard to them is worth a good deal. Upon careful examination I have not been able to agree with him, and I desire very briefly to state my reasons for differing.

The system which has been reported by the committee has already been so far altered with regard to the counties that the proposition would now apply to Baltimore city a condition of courts entirely different from the courts of the counties. It would establish a one-judge system in the counties, and a three-judge system in the city. It strikes me that there is something anomalous in that provision. There is one great advantage in the courts as we now have them in Baltimore. It is the advantage of perfect and entire simplicity. There is one judge for equity business; and under the substitute system there may be three judges for equity business who are to alternate or distribute themselves; and the consequence will be that where you now have one certain man you will have two or three uncertain men. The judges will be obliged either to assign some one permanently to transact the equity business, which will not be very easy consistently with the provision allowing a party to require two judges upon the bench, or they will have to distribute it among themselves.

The people are accustomed to the systems we have now; and this system produces a radical change in the whole system of the courts. I should be indisposed to adopt it without strong reasons for so doing. In investigating this subject, I have made it my business to inquire of the judges; and I state it as a matter of fact, which is certainly entitled to very great weight, that the judges of the courts of Baltimore city are unanimously opposed to the changes proposed. If their judgment is that this change is not wise,—they have no interest in the matter, for it is not proposed to disturb their offices—they are gentlemen whose opinion is entitled to great weight. They have told me, without exception, that they do not approve of the change introduced by the report of the committee.

With regard to the fact stated by colleague (Mr. Thomas,) with regard to the court of common pleas, it is true that Judge King not only attends to all the business of that court but has time to spare, abundant time to spare. Where is the press of business? There is some press in certain courts with reference to the administration of the chancery jurisdiction; and it would be well to relieve the superior court of part of its jurisdiction and give it to the court of common pleas which has not jurisdiction, and thus equalize that business and prevent delay.

My colleague (Mr. Stockbridge) speaks of the great difficulty in getting cases tried. I know that Judge Martin frequently sits there day after day with no company but the jurors and bailiffs, ready to entertain motions at law, because he occasionally stays on the bench when there is no necessity for it, sitting there frequently with no business and no company but his bailiffs. That his docket is so full, arises from the old cases upon it which have been retained simply because the counsel have a right to compel a continuance, the law divesting the judge of any control over them. The counsel continue cases by consent, and have got into a chronic condition of laziness. The old cases on the docket have been there so long that they hate to try them. I believe if the judges had power to compel the trial of a case, the docket would be disposed of. I know that Judge Martin devotes sufficient time to the work, because I know he sits there with nothing to do; and he says himself that he is able to transact the business.

The circuit court and the chancery court are more obnoxious to the charge of delay than any others. But if you relieve Judge Martin of a part of his jurisdiction, and still give him an equity jurisdiction, it will take equity business off the hands of the circuit court and relieve the docket of the circuit. The reason Judge Martin has no more time to spare for equity business is because he has so many of the small cases on his docket; but if you strike off all the $500 cases up to $1,000, he will have time to spare. I think he told me that he had a recess in his court amounting to certainly eight weeks in the year, and I think sometimes twelve weeks. That certainly is time enough for transacting the business.

I know that so far as the criminal court is concerned, the judge of that court works very hard; but because he works hard he gets through his docket. The criminal court frequently transacts its business in three days in the week, sitting there from ten till five o'clock. The judge says he would rather work very hard on three days than work moderately on four. Some other judges do not prefer that mode of business. They prefer to work from ten to half-past two on three days, than from ten to five or six on one day. The business is transacted, and there is time to spare. There are no cases continued in the criminal court. All the cases on the docket are called, and that docket has been kept clean ever since it has been under the administration of Judge Bond.

I am not in favor of making this change. It does unquestionably run against prejudice, and it runs against interest in a great measure, although I do not regard that as of much importance. I do regard the change as doubtful. I do not wish to say any more upon it. I will leave it to the decision of the convention. I believe so far as I have ascertained their views, it meets the concurrence of possibly the entire delegation with the exception of my colleague the chairman of the committee (Mr. Stockbridge.) I have not been able to ascertain the sentiments of a very large number of the members of our bar, but so far as I have been able to learn it meets with their concurrence; and I think the system reported by the majority of the committee is not acceptable to the majority of our people.

There is another consideration that occurs to me. There is one subject I hoped to be able in connection with this subject to bring before the convention; and it is the fact that the salary of the judges of Baltimore city, under the present system, in consequence of the alteration of prices that has taken place, has become so small that I know as a matter of fact that one-half, if not three out of four judges of that court are contemplating the resignation of their places and going back to the practice of the law. We have had great difficulty in getting good men upon the bench. We have in Baltimore now as good a judiciary as ever was upon the bench. We are reluctant to lose them. I know they will not stay there at the present rate of their salaries. I know that some of these gentlemen have been forced to borrow money to live, since these troubles have come upon us. With the expenses that prevail in Baltimore, the high price of fuel, the high price of everything, the enormous rise of everything, it is impossible for any man to occupy the position these men do, most of them men in the maturity of life with families around them, one of them with no family of his own but a family dependent upon him for support. What salaries can you afford to give if you increase the number of judges from four to six?

Then I cannot see how the system of three judges is going to gain anything, with the policy of allowing any party to demand two judges. If you give people the right to a bench, they will have it. No man will try his case before a single judge, if he has a chance to require two judges. As a practical thing, in every case there will be two judges upon the bench of the superior court.

There is another feature in this report. If there is any court in Baltimore which is acceptable to the people of that city at this present time, it is the criminal court. You want in the criminal court not merely legal ability, but executive force and unity of purpose. If you do not have unity of purpose the court is worthless, however much legal ability in the abstract may be upon the bench. You distract the judge of that court by requiring him to exercise chancery jurisdiction; and you disturb that unity of purpose by putting judge of the chancery court upon the bench of the criminal court. I say that the people of the city of Baltimore, so far as that court is concerned, are unanimously opposed to displacing the present judge of the criminal court. Yet this provision practically destroys his power by forcing him to act with an associate. It makes a two-judge system practically in the criminal court, and a two-judge system is the very worst kind of a system of criminal jurisdiction because it destroys practically all unity of purpose and executive force, while the great business of that court is to administer a jurisdiction which is *quasi* executive. The smaller cases are more to be regulated by a uniform policy than by any other principle. If there are two courts, the practice of which is inconsistent, they are the chancery and criminal courts. There is certainly more similarity between common law and equity than between criminal cases and chancery cases. The civil and criminal law are frequently blended in one court; but certainly chancery powers have not been often blended with the powers of criminal courts, except where one man is forced to administer all, and the criminal docket amounts to scarcely anything.

This last feature is my greatest objection to the report. I certainly would never consent to the destruction of the criminal court as it at present exists; and if there were no other objection to the report than that, I should oppose it; and I believe that I represent the sentiments of ninety-nine out of a hundred of those who sent me here in expressing these views with regard to the criminal court. I shall support this proposition. But I intend to support an amendment to the subsequent section to increase the jurisdiction of the court of common pleas from $500 up to $800 or $1,000.

Mr. Stockbridge. I wish to say a few words in reply to the remarks of my colleague. It is true, as has been said, that the present system has the merit of simplicity. There has scarcely ever been a question raised since the system was established in the city of Baltimore as to the jurisdiction of the courts, so far as the one comes in conflict or in contact with the other. The line is drawn very clearly, distinctly, and positively. That feature of the system it is certainly desirable, so far as possible, to retain. But that is the only recommendation of the present system; and I hold that, in view of all the circumstances which hang around it, it is not sufficient to retain it, practically denying justice, as it does, to suitors of the business community.

Gentlemen have argued this question as if they supposed this constitution was to be taken without any regulation or rule of the courts, but that the three judges were thrown together in hodge-podge, and out of that justice was to be administered, if at all, in some hap-hazard way. The report expressly provides that it shall be regulated by a rule of the court:

"It shall be the right of any party to an original cause pending in said court, under such rules and regulations as the court may prescribe, to require the presence of at least two of the judges of said court at the trial thereof."

That was thrown in with the full purpose of preventing the very evil which my colleague seems to anticipate, that a man will watch his time and wait until he discovers that a full bench of two cannot be had, and then demand a full bench to try his case. The rules and regulations are to arrange all that. They are to be required to make the demand at a certain time, upon the call of the docket, or at such time as shall seem to the court equitable and right, so that it shall not be made the means of defeating the ends of justice, and delaying the business of the court.

It is provided, too, that they are to distribute and apportion the business between them. My colleague, who has just taken his seat, draws a picture of a judge of the criminal court sitting in equity, or a judge in equity sitting upon the criminal bench and conducting the powers there. This is all to be done under a distinct division of the exercise of the jurisdiction conferred upon the judges.

Mr. Stirling. Will my colleague allow me to make a suggestion. There are three judges upon the bench, and the other two may assign to the one now in the criminal court duties in equity and put a new man in his place on the criminal bench. So that it is in the power of one of the present judges, together with one of the new judges to be elected, to oust the present occupant of the bench of the criminal court.

Mr. Stockbridge. "If the sky falls we may catch larks." It is possible that that judge may die to-morrow, and that we may have to provide for a vacancy upon that bench. It is possible that he may become disqualified, from sickness or otherwise, and we may have to provide for a special judge; and I will say here in passing, that this is another of the advantages of the system reported by the committee that it obviates entirely the necessity for special judges which we have sometimes had on one or another of the benches month after month at an additional expense to the State.

Now, in domestic economy, I grant that it is sometimes best to decide how much money we can spend, and then go on and devise how to make that meet the wants. But I submit that in the arrangement of judges the principle is a bad one to apply. The first question to be decided is, how can the ends of justice be obtained. When that is settled, manage so as to attain the ends of justice, and to make it as little expensive as possible to the State and to suitors.

I am not accustomed to make vague statements as to what my constituents want in any matter, or what are their sentiments, or that sort of thing. I come here to use my best judgment, and I propose to do it. And, although I have had interviews with judges, attorneys, and citizens, I do not think this a proper place to detail such private conversation. Had I no reason to sustain my position, I might fall back upon that. At present, I shall not. It is true, I have no doubt, that a judge who has done business in a particular way, who has settled into a particular rut, may prefer to continue in that cider-mill round, to going out of it and taking a different course. I know that office-holders all over the State have a desire, almost without exception, that we shall make no invasion upon their particular offices, save to increase their salaries. But I submit that it is not a sufficient ground for the retention of the present system.

It is true that equity business—I will not make it a personal matter with the present judge—cannot be done in the superior court of Baltimore city. My colleague in one breath said the reason was that the judge of that court had other business which engrossed his time, and in the very next breath he said the judge sat there with his bailiffs only and nothing to do.

Mr. Stirling. I can explain that perfectly well, if the gentleman will allow me. I was stating the facts.

Mr. Stockbridge. So am I stating facts. I will make the explanation myself. I do not require the gentleman's help. The jurisdiction conferred upon that court, its equity jurisdiction, is entirely concurrent with the circuit court. In every case which can go to the circuit court it is optional with the person bringing the suit to go into the circuit court or into the superior court. It has then jurisdiction in all replevin cases where the value of the article replevied is above $100, and in all magistrates' lien cases be the matter small or great, from $5 up to $50,000; and in all civil cases where the amount involved is above $500.

Let any gentleman, however, urgent his business, apply to that court for an injunction; and what is the result? The judge can say, and since this constitution has been in operation judges have said in most important and pressing cases: "Certainly you have the right to ask me to attend to this business if you choose, instead of going to the other court; and I am bound to attend to it; but I must attend to it when I can. I am in the trial of a case, and I may get through it next week or week after next; and then I will attend to your injunction matter." What is the result? Practically I say that is a denial of justice.

Then again, an attorney has an equity case in the circuit court which he wishes to bury up forever. What course shall he pursue to prevent its coming to trial? Time is the object for which he is fighting. He transfers it to the superior court. There are cases now buried up in that superior court just in that way, by persons desirous of getting them disposed of and transferred to that court for no other reason than to give them a sepulture almost without hope of resurrection before the crack of doom. If you are to try them you have to go through the same form, and the same amount of formality as in the court of appeals; have the record printed, have your brief prepared and printed, and go through the first trial from printed notes and a printed brief, and the delay and expense thereof, provided you can ever get the judge to consent to enter the trial of that cause.

I say, and I submit it to the calm judgment of gentlemen, that the system proposed is infinitely better than this. Where is the difficulty in assigning the entire equity jurisdiction to a single court which has indeed three judges, which will apportion the business, saying to A, yours is the administration of the criminal business of this court; and to B and to C, if you please, yours is the administration of the equity business?

It is inconceivable but they will adopt certain rules and regulations by which suitors coming on pressing business shall not go to B, and failing to get a reply from him, go to C, to dodge between the two courts and get a divided ruling on the subject. I cannot conceive of any judge fit to be upon the bench, that has not system, dignity, and character enough to prevent such a state of things.

Then as to coupling these jurisdictions, I am free to say it was for convenience only. It was the only coupling which did not seem to render more courts necessary. And I will say here that some of the most reputable and highly respectable members of the profession in the city of Baltimore have urged that all should be consolidated into one court. Only yesterday I received a letter from a highly intelligent gentleman who apologized for obtruding his advice, and urged in the most strenuous manner the importance of putting it all into one court with the same power of apportioning and distributing the business. What is the incongruity of coupling together these two jurisdictions? Every circuit judge throughout the State, outside the city of Baltimore, has both these jurisdictions, and in addition to that all the jurisdiction that is given to the other courts, in replevins, liens, and in all civil controversies, and actions for debt or damage, all of them are put into one hand. Here they are put into two distinct courts; and these courts are redivided, so that it is only when counsel is desired, and it is thought best to have conference, that another judge is called in.

This additional judge provides too against the contingency of there being left a vacancy upon the bench, and an inexperienced special judge being called in to decide it may be the most important matters. I am fully persuaded that while justice is not administered under the present system, it will be under the system as it is reported by the committee, if the convention see fit to adopt it. I do not believe it is possible so to arrange it that it can be administered otherwise. I am absolutely sure that if the jurisdiction of the court of common pleas be increased to $1,000, it will be utterly impossible for any judge, however diligent, and although he may have a constitution of cast iron, to discharge the business, and survive three years. It cannot be done. It is an absolute impossibility. It will require his labor night and day, and without any intermission from year's end to year's end.

Mr. AUDOUN demanded the yeas and nays, and they were ordered.

The question being taken, the result was—yeas 34, nays 20—as follows:

Yeas—Messrs. Goldsborough, President; Abbott, Annan, Audoun, Brooks, Carter, Cunningham, Cushing, Daniel, Davis, of Washington, Ecker, Farrow, Galloway, Hatch, Hebb, Hopper, King, Markey, Morgan, Mullikin, Murray, Pugh, Purnell, Ridgely, Sands, Schley, Schlosser, Sneary, Stirling, Swope, Thomas, Todd, Wickard, Wooden—34.

Nays—Messrs. Blackiston, Chambers, Crawford, Dellinger, Duvall, Hoffman, Hollyday, Horsey, Lansdale, Lee, Mitchell, Negley, Nyman, Parker, Russell, Scott, Smith, of Dorchester, Smith, of Worcester, Stockbridge, Wilmer—20.

When their names were called,

Mr. ABBOTT said: I have the very highest regard for the opinions of my colleague, the chairman of this committee; but it seems to me that the change he proposes is too great a one for our people just at this time. I am afraid it would be no benefit to us yet. I vote "aye."

Mr. DANIEL said: This is a matter of some delicacy, and I have some doubt about it; and I should like to be excused from voting.

The convention refused to excuse him; whereupon,

Mr. DANIEL said: Then I want to say in explanation of my vote that I agreed to this report in committee, expecting to sustain it. But from the opposition, as has been stated here, by the judges themselves, and others of the profession in the city of Baltimore, I have been led to change my views somewhat. Therefore I am forced to the conclusion that the present system is perhaps the best under all the circumstances. I therefore vote "aye."

Mr. PUGH said: I am free to confess that I am more singularly influenced on this occasion in my vote than any other vote I have cast in this convention. I vote as I do simply because it seems to me that the majority of the representatives of Baltimore want this peculiar system. If they do want it, I have no objection to their having it. I therefore vote "aye."

The amendment was accordingly agreed to.

No further amendment being offered, the next section was read as follows:

"Sec. 28. The superior court of Baltimore city shall have all the power and jurisdiction heretofore conferred upon and exercised by the superior court and the court of common pleas of Baltimore city (except the equity powers of the superior court,) subject to such modifications as may be made by law, and the judges shall so apportion and distribute the business of their court as shall best facilitate the despatch of business and promote the ends of justice."

Mr. DANIEL submitted the following amendment:

Strike out the twenty-eighth section and insert:

"Sec. 28. The superior court of Baltimore city, shall have jurisdiction over all suits where the debt or damage claimed shall exceed the sum of one thousand dollars, and in case any plaintiff or plaintiffs shall recover less than the sum or value of one thousand dollars, he or they shall be allowed or adjudged to pay costs in the discretion of the court. The said court shall also have jurisdiction as a court of equity within the limits of the said city, and in all other civil cases which are not hereinafter assigned to the court of common pleas."

Mr. THOMAS. I move to add the following amendment to the amendment:

"Provided all cases now pending on the law side of said court, where the debt or damage claimed is less than one thousand dollars, shall be prosecuted to final judgment in said court, as though its jurisdiction had not been changed."

Mr. DANIEL. I accept that.

Mr. ABBOTT moved to amend the amendment by striking out "one thousand" and inserting "eight hundred."

Mr. STOCKBRIDGE. I hope that amendment will not prevail, or that it will be voted down, and that an amendment will prevail to strike out "one thousand" and insert "five hundred." I am satisfied that with $800 the court of common pleas can never do the business—never.

Mr. DANIEL. The convention has just had a statement from my colleague upon this floor, coming from Judge King himself, and I know it to be correct from my own experience, that he has frequently eight weeks or more of leisure after finishing all the business ready for trial. On the other hand, in Judge Martin's court, as has been stated by my colleague, a thousand or twelve hundred cases go over pretty much every term, he not being able or if able not being willing to try them. This amendment gives to Judge King's court a jurisdiction $500 greater. It now comes up to $500; and I propose to increase it to $1,000; which takes out of Judge Martin's court all the cases between $500 and $1,000 and places them in Judge King's. Judge Martin's court has jurisdiction over all cases of replevin, no matter what the amount.

Mr. STOCKBRIDGE. Not if it is under $100.

Mr. DANIEL. That is a matter of small importance. They generally go before a magistrate. Judge King, I believe, never has a replevin in his court. I think he has no jurisdiction over replevins at all. He simply has the decision of cases under $500, and appeal cases, and insolvent cases. I think even with this distribution as proposed, to continue Judge Martin's jurisdiction over equity as well as common law just as it now exists, if we give Judge King this increased jurisdiction, Judge Martin's court will still be much more crowded with business than Judge King's court will be, and that the court of common pleas will easily get through its business up to $1,000; and that the business in the superior court will be much facilitated. I therefore think the amendment proper as I have offered it, and hope the amendment to the amendment will not prevail.

Mr. STOCKBRIDGE. The gentleman from Baltimore city (Mr. Stirling) said that the court of common pleas usually adjourns for eight weeks before the end of the term.

Mr. DANIEL. No, sir; my colleague said that it had frequently eight weeks leisure, and sometimes more.

Mr. STOCKBRIDGE. Eight weeks sounds very big; but everybody connected with law business in the city of Baltimore knows that all business is practically suspended from about the first of July until the September term of the court. There are your eight weeks. That is in fact nine weeks.

Mr. STIRLING. I mean independent of the usual summer vacation. I know that Judge King adjourns his court every day at half past one o'clock; and I could give a reason for it if it was proper.

Mr. ABBOTT. My colleagues know more about the workings of the courts than I do. Yet I have been so unfortunate as to have been in the courts and to have spent considerable time there as juror, and occasionally as a witness. The reason why I made this proposition to amend is that I thought this was going too far; that it was taking away too much from the superior court, and putting too much into Judge King's court. You double the sum; and as a matter of course you double the amount of business. The great bulk of the cases that are tried are between five hundred and one thousand dollars.

Mr. THOMAS. By another amendment which will be offered in relation to the court of common pleas, we should take from the jurisdiction of the court of common pleas all magistrate's cases of a criminal nature, or embracing fines, penalties or forfeitures. My colleague who once held the same position I now do (Mr. Stirling,) knows that that amounts to considerable in the course of a year.

Mr. ABBOTT. If you propose to cure the difficulty in another way, I withdraw the amendment.

Mr. STOCKBRIDGE. I now move to amend by striking out "one thousand" and inserting "five hundred," and upon that I hope a vote will be taken. But I wish to say one word before the vote is taken. Gentlemen are referring to private conversations with judges, and all that sort of thing, the amount of which is, that the judges on a certain occasion in the street made no objection to such a modification. I should have thought it very stupid in him if he had. No such thing was seriously proposed; and he might not have thought he could control the convention if he had opposed it. Some other judge might as well attempt to restrain us by an injunction. My colleague has been speaking of his private conversations with the judges, and of their approval of the present system. Did not they include the jurisdiction as well as other things. I wish my colleague would tell me that now; when the judges were in favor of retaining the existing system, did not they wish the jurisdiction retained too?

Mr. STIRLING. So far as I had conversation with them, it was with regard to the proposition in the report, and the general features of the present system. I have a very decided impression what the views of the judges are; but I had no specific conversation.

Mr. STOCKBRIDGE. I state as a fact that I have on more than one occasion heard every judge there complain of being overworked as it now stands. The judge whose jurisdiction you now propose to much more than double, has now original jurisdiction from one to five hundred dollars, a range of four hundred dollars. You propose to add to that a range of five hundred dollars more. My observation is, and I think it will be sustained by that of every gentleman present, that during the general course of the year, four-fifths of the civil business in the courts of Baltimore city is between five hundred and one thousand dollars.

Mr. STIRLING. I think about one-half.

Mr. STOCKBRIDGE. I think at least four-fifths. But according to the estimate of my colleague, you propose to take one-half of the business of the superior court and put it into the court of common pleas, in addition to what they have now, and to leave the other half in the superior court. The practical effect of that is going to be to arrange the business much worse than before. But I do not propose to argue it. I am opposed to the system, and this will only aggravate it. I hope my amendment will prevail to retain the jurisdiction of the superior court where it is.

The amendment was rejected.

Mr. STOCKBRIDGE. I have another amendment, the purpose of which is to make a little more clear and distinct the line of demarcation between the superior court and the court of common pleas. I move to insert in the second line, after the word "claimed," the words "exclusive of interest."

Mr. STIRLING. That is all right.

Mr. STOCKBRIDGE. There is often a matter of doubt as to which court a suit shall be brought in. This will make it more clear.

The amendment was agreed to.

Mr. STOCKBRIDGE. I wish to ask a question. These gentlemen are making an effort to harmonize and systematize things. There is a class of cases most anomalously assigned heretofore to the criminal court of Baltimore city; and I should like to understand whether it is proposed to retain them there or to give jurisdiction over them to the superior court or the court of common pleas. It has always seemed to me that it really belonged to the superior court; but before the amendment is acted upon, I thought it would be well to call attention to it. I refer to the class of cases in the criminal court with reference to opening streets, and things of that sort in the city of Baltimore. The amounts involved are large, and often take up a great deal of the time of the court, causing juries to be delayed there sometimes two to four weeks. Hundreds of thousands of dollars are involved; and these cases are in no way connected with the criminal jurisdiction of the city. It has always belonged to one of the civil courts, but it never has been there. I wish to know whether it is proposed to take that there, or to leave it where it is.

Mr. STIRLING. I have no objection to that proposition, if the gentleman thinks it necessary to make any change. What my colleague says is correct. As we are relieving the superior court somewhat, I have no objection to taking the street cases and putting them into the superior court. The only reason why it did not suggest itself to me to change it, is that it has been in the criminal court so long, and the records are all there; and it does not take up a great deal of time. But it is a jurisdiction which is not properly in the criminal court system. It is a civil jurisdiction. As we are relieving the docket of the superior court I have no objection to transfer it to that.

Mr. ABBOTT. I hope that at the proper time that will be done.

Mr. STOCKBRIDGE. Under the old constitution there was a good reason for placing it where it is. It was then not a criminal court merely, but the city court, to attend to what was properly city business. When Baltimore city was a part of Baltimore county, the civil business not belonging to the county was thrown into the city court. It was then perfectly proper; but that reason has long gone by; and it is certainly desirable to remove it now.

The PRESIDENT. Gentlemen are reminded that they are debating an abstract proposition and not an amendment before the convention.

Mr. STIRLING. I will move to amend the amendment by inserting next before the proviso accepted by my colleague, the words "and shall also have jurisdiction in all cases of appeals from the commissioner for opening streets."

Mr. DANIEL. I will accept that.

Mr. STOCKBRIDGE. I now move to strike out the clause, "as a court of equity within the limits of the said city, and." My reason for moving that is, that we have one court charged with nothing else, that does nothing else, that is purely a chancery court. There is no special reason that I can see, if we are to divide things by subjects, why the two should be united in this court more than in the criminal court or the court of common pleas The rules and regulations which prevail in this court are such that it is a final burying up of things when they once get into chancery there, and passing them over to our children and great grand children. I hope the amendment will prevail.

Mr. DANIEL. I want gentlemen to understand that in doing this we are altering the jurisdiction of the superior court as it now stands. This is copied exactly from the constitution. Ever since the organization of that court it has had equity jurisdiction. Ever since the organization of the circuit court they have had concurrent jurisdiction in all equity matters. Suitors frequently find it convenient to exercise a choice between these courts; and I think it would be a very radical change to take away that choice, and that portion of equity business, a large amount of which is already pending in the superior court of Baltimore city. I think therefore that the change is sufficient which we have thus far made, in which we have taken away from the superior court $500 of its jurisdiction, which my colleague the chairman of the committee has stated to the house constitutes four-fifths of the jurisdiction, in which I differ with him except as to the amount of civil business; but if it includes in the equity business the lien business, and the replevin business over which the court of common pleas has no jurisdiction, I do not think we have transferred anything like that amount. But now my colleague proposes, having stated to the house that four-fifths of the jurisdiction has been taken away and given to the court of common pleas by the amendment I made, necessarily burdening the court of common pleas by so much and relieving the superior court by so much, to take away all equity jurisdiction from the superior court and still further disencumber it and put the duties upon another court. I think with the $500 taken from its jurisdiction, this court can easily transact its business; and I think it is a fair distribution. Judge King I have no doubt can get through with his business. He always has time to spare, and is always obliging to attorneys, ready to try their cases when they are ready, with nothing else to do. I think this would relieve the superior court of so much of its jurisdiction that at any rate I am utterly opposed to taking from the superior court the equity jurisdiction which it has had ever since there has been a court in the city of Baltimore.

The amendment was rejected.

The amendment submitted by Mr. DANIEL, as modified by him, and amended, was adopted in the following form:

"Section 28. The superior court of Baltimore city shall have jurisdiction over all suits where the debt or damage claimed, exclusive of interest, shall exceed the sum of one thousand dollars, and in case any plaintiff or plaintiffs shall recover less than the sum or value of one thousand dollars, he or they shall be allowed or adjudged to pay costs in the discretion of the court. The said court shall also have jurisdiction as a court of equity within the limits of the said city, and in all other civil cases which are not hereinafter assigned to the court of common pleas, and shall also have jurisdiction in all cases of appeals from the commissioner for opening streets; provided, all cases now pending on the law side of said court, where the debt or damage claimed is less than one thousand dollars, shall be prosecuted to final judgment in said court, as though its jurisdiction had not been changed."

No further amendment was offered.

The next section was read as follows:

"Section 29. Either of said judges may sit alone for the trial of causes appealed from the decisions of justices of the peace, for the disposition of all formal and uncontested business, and such other business as the parties litigant shall consent to try before a single judge; but it shall be the right of any party to an original cause pending in said court under such rules and regulations as the court may prescribe, to require the presence of at least two of the judges of said court at the trial thereof."

Mr. THOMAS submitted the following amendment:

Strike out the section and insert the following:

"Section 29. The court of common pleas shall have civil jurisdiction in all suits where the debt or damage claimed, exclusive of interest, shall be over one hundred dollars, and shall not exceed one thousand dollars; and shall also have jurisdiction in all cases of appeal in civil cases from the judgment of justices of the peace in the said city, and shall have jurisdiction in all applications for the benefit of the insolvent laws of this State, and the supervision and control of the trustees thereof."

Mr. STOCKBRIDGE. That amendment seems to differ a good deal from the printed amendment. That provides for jurisdiction in cases of replevin.

Mr. THOMAS. Yes, sir; I struck that out for this reason. I was afraid if we gave the court of common pleas jurisdiction in replevin cases over one hundred dollars, perhaps it would increase its jurisdiction too much; and I thought it might be better to let the jurisdiction of the superior court over replevin cases remain where it is.

Mr. STOCKBRIDGE. I cannot see any sense in making the limit in the superior court $100 in one thing and $1000 in everything else. There is another anomaly about it. That is in the matter of lien cases, under the mechanics' lien laws.

Mr. STIRLING. I do not see any harm in that. Under the old constitution the superior court was made a sort of residuary legatee for all jurisdiction not carved out elsewhere. It has jurisdiction in any case where it has not been specially taken away from them. All jurisdiction except that given to the court of common pleas specially embraced between $100 and $500, goes under the general clause to the superior court, and in consequence of that the court of appeals have decided that all replevin suits, all suits for the enforcement of magistrates' liens, and all special cases like that, went to the superior court. It seems to me there is some reason about it. It is better to have the law of replevin, or the magistrates' lien law, administered in one court than two; and for this reason. Magistrates' liens are a matter of record. It is in the land record office, which is exercised by the clerk of the superior court. If you take that jurisdiction away from the superior court, and give it to the court of common pleas, it will involve a change of the records from the land record office.

Mr. STOCKBRIDGE. I do not see the force of the last objection; for to ascertain whether there is any incumbrance, it is necessary to examine the records of both courts, one as much as the other.

Mr. STIRLING. You have to find out whether there is any judgment against the man; and to find liens against the estate you would have to look in two records. You can very often satisfy yourself whether there is a judgment against a man from a knowledge of his personal character.

Mr. STOCKBRIDGE. I am aware that this matter was left very loosely by the former constitutional convention. It was supposed by everybody that jurisdiction in replevin matters, and in mechanics' lien matters, under $500, was conferred upon the court of common pleas; and for years where the claim of the mechanic who filed the lien was under $500, he filed it in the court of common pleas. Then somebody became affected with an uneasy doubt, and for a long time they recorded them in both courts; and after a long time a case was brought up to the court of appeals, and they decided that the superior court had jurisdiction, and that the court of common pleas had not; and then for the first time they ceased to file them in the court of common pleas. It was I think full half the time from the adoption of the constitution to the present time, before that decision was obtained.

Replevins also took the same course. In many cases jurisdiction was entertained and the cases were decided in the court of common pleas before there was an appeal which ousted them from their jurisdiction. Then, of course, a large number of cases on the docket had to go by default. I should be glad to see this freed from all doubt. One of these is called the superior court, and it was supposed there was to be some little superior learning, some better qualifications upon the bench of that court to which is given the jurisdiction of larger matters, in one particular class of cases or in all. We might say that they might take original jurisdiction in all cases of mechanics' liens where five dollars were involved, and from that up, and thus send them all to the superior court. Anywhere from five to five hundred dollars this court has jurisdiction; but if you say that it shall only have jurisdiction in replevin cases up to one hundred dollars, I do not see the propriety of it. I think if there is any reason for dividing the jurisdiction it should be divided by the same line with regard to everything.

Mr. STIRLING. My colleague has already said that we have put so much upon the court of common pleas that no mortal man can discharge the duties, and I see no reason for giving them still more.

Mr. THOMAS. The court of appeals has already decided the case, and the duties of the superior court are just as ascertained and distinct now as they would be if we put it into the constitution. This leaves it just where it is, and there is not a lawyer in Baltimore who does not know which court has jurisdiction in all lien cases and all replevin cases over and above one hundred dollars.

The question being taken on the amendment, no quorum voted.

Mr. SANDS moved a call of the house, but the motion was not sustained.

The question being again taken, the amendment was adopted.

No further amendment was offered.

The next section was read as follows:

"Sec. 30. The circuit court of Baltimore city shall have all the jurisdiction and authority heretofore exercised by the criminal court and the circuit court of Baltimore city, or which may hereafter be prescribed by law; and the judges shall apportion and distribute the business of their court in such a manner as shall best facilitate the despatch of business and promote the ends of justice."

Mr. THOMAS submitted the following amendment.

Strike out all after the word "shall" in the first line, and insert the following:

"Have jurisdiction concurrent with the superior court of Baltimore city in all cases in equity, in cases arising under the act to direct descents and its supplements, and shall exercise all the power that is now or may be hereafter conferred by law; provided, said court shall not have jurisdiction in applications for the writ of *habeas corpus*."

Mr. STIRLING moved to amend the amendment by adding "in cases of persons charged with criminal offences."

Mr. THOMAS accepted the amendment.

Mr. STOCKBRIDGE. This amendment differs entirely from the printed amendment, and I can hardly see the effect of it from hearing it read.

Mr. THOMAS. After I drew up the amendment, which was printed, I consulted the act of 1853 which organized the present circuit court, and I found that section two, which confers jurisdiction upon the circuit court, says that the said circuit court shall have concurrent jurisdiction with the superior court of Baltimore in all cases of equity, in cases arising from the act in relation to *habeas corpus*, and generally such as have heretofore been conferred upon the chancellor of the fifth judicial circuit. The only alteration I have made in it is to take away from the circuit court jurisdiction over writs of *habeas corpus*, which I do not consider properly belonging to that court, and which frequently embarrass that court. I know, myself, that frequently applications are made to the judge of that court in the absence of the judge of the criminal court, upon writs of *habeas corpus*, and the prosecuting officer has been made to go into that court to try these cases, thereby postponing highly important equity cases then on trial, on account of the peculiarity of the law which gives to *habeas corpus* cases the privilege of being heard first. That was my reason for taking away from this court this jurisdiction. I accepted the amendment of my colleague to leave the court jurisdiction over writs of *habeas corpus* in others than criminal cases for this reason: It oftentimes happens that inasmuch as the equity court has jurisdiction over wards, applications are made to take a ward out of the possession of some persons not entitled to have custody, or by a husband to get his wife, and such cases; and I think in such cases the jurisdiction ought to be retained.

Mr. STOCKBRIDGE. Permit me to inquire whether the twenty-seventh section as we adopted it, providing for the courts, styles that court the equity court or the circuit court?

Mr. THOMAS. The reason why we changed the name from the equity court to the circuit court is this. It has been known by that name for years, and everybody knows the circuit court of Baltimore city to be the equity court. I think on that account that the name would better remain as it is.

Mr. STOCKBRIDGE. I only desired to know whether the change had been made. I wish now to inquire with reference to the matter of the *habeas corpus*, in reference to the denial of the right of *habeas corpus* as embodied in this thirtieth section in cases where the judge of the criminal court is absent. The point of my inquiry is this: Whether it is designed that that judge alone shall have jurisdiction in these cases of *habeas corpus*, or whether it will be shared by other judges, and if so by what other judges?

Mr. THOMAS. I think the judge of the superior court and of the criminal court have jurisdiction. I am not satisfied whether the judge of the court of common pleas has or not. I think he has not.

Mr. STOCKBRIDGE. I merely wanted to know if we deny the power to this judge, where it was to be vested?

Mr. STIRLING. "And shall exercise all the power that is now or may hereafter be conferred by law." That would give the legislature power to control the whole subject. I move to strike out the words "or may be hereafter."

The amendment to the amendment was agreed to.

The amendment as amended was adopted.

No further amendment was offered.

The next section was read as follows:

"Sec. 31. One of the judges of said court shall sit as chief judge of the orphans' court of the city of Baltimore, and either of the judges may sit alone in either department of the business of said court, but it shall be the right of any party to an issue pending in said court, under such rules as the court shall fix, to require the presence of at least two of the judges at the trial thereof; and no order for an injunction or the appointment of a receiver shall be passed without the concurrence of at least two of the judges therein."

On motion of Mr. DANIEL,

The section was stricken out.

On motion of Mr. THOMAS,

The following section was inserted as section thirty-one:

"Sec. 31. The criminal court of Baltimore city shall have and exercise all the jurisdiction now held and exercised by the criminal court of Baltimore, except in cases of appeals from commissioners for opening streets, and shall have jurisdiction in all cases of appeals from justices of the peace in said city for the recovery of fines, penalties and forfeitures."

SALARY OF CITY JUDGES.

The next section was read as follows:

Sec. 32. Each of said judges shall receive an annual salary of three thousand five hundred dollars, payable quarterly.

Mr. ABBOTT. I move to strike out "five hundred." The salary of the other judges throughout the State was increased five hundred dollars, and I am sure that is enough for these. The judge of the criminal court has always had a salary five hundred dollars less than that of the other courts, which the people of our city think is very improper. We think he should have the same salary as the judges of the other courts. His salary now is only two thousand dollars, and that of the other judges is twenty-five hundred dollars. It seems no more than right and proper that the judges should all receive the same salary, and I move to make it uniform at three thousand dollars.

Mr. SANDS. The judges of the court of appeals are to receive three thousand dollars, and I hope the amendment will prevail. I hope we shall not give the circuit judges a higher salary than that of judges of the court of appeals.

Mr. THOMAS. I think instead of decreasing these it would be better to increase the salary of the court of appeals.

Mr. SANDS. It would be rather anomalous to fix the salary of these judges below that which we have fixed upon for the court of appeals.

Mr. STIRLING. I will merely suggest that my friend from Howard (Mr. Sands) leaves out of view altogether the fact that there is a manifest difference between the city of Baltimore and the counties with regard to the amount of money it takes a man to live. I have very little to say on the matter. I do not profess to be a great man myself; but if I should be offered one of these places, I should not consider it much of an offer.

The PRESIDENT. Living in the city of Annapolis is about as dear as anywhere else.

Mr. STIRLING. They do not have to live here all the time; and it is the question of their general expenses. I know there is not a man of family occupying the position of judge in Baltimore city, who can live to save his life on $3,000 a year. I know he cannot live on that. I am not a very extravagant man; I do not live in any very great splendor, and I cannot.

Mr. Pugh. I want some information with regard to this matter. I am in favor, and have been all the time, of paying judges liberally. I am therefore perfectly willing to vote to pay the judges of Baltimore city $3,-500; but it suggested itself to me the moment I heard the section read that we had fixed the salary of the judges of the court of appeals at $3,000. I wish to know if there is any way of getting that subject up and increasing the salaries of the judges of the court of appeals. It would certainly be improper to put them in an inferior position in respect to salary than the judges of the lower courts, in Baltimore city. I am in favor of giving such salaries as will secure the best men for such positions. I wish to vote in favor of making the salary of the judges in the city of Baltimore $3,500; but I would not like to do so unless we reconsider our action with regard to the court of appeals.

Mr. Daniel. I think one way of judging what salaries the judges ought to receive is to look at the men and the object, which is to get good men in the practice of the profession. Now compare the practice of lawyers in the city of Baltimore with that of lawyers in the counties; and you will find on account of the greater amount of business more than double, treble the average practice of lawyers in the counties. Therefore, in order to secure a good lawyer upon the bench in the city, you must necessarily pay more than you would pay in the counties.

Besides, sir, they have a great deal more work to do in the city. Our courts sit nine or ten months in the year constantly; whereas in most of the counties, they sit far less time, and in a few they do not occupy four months in the year. We have double the amount of work to do in the city. And there is scarcely any man in the city of Baltimore competent to take the place of judge, who does not receive from his practice at least $5,000 a year.

In reference to the court of appeals, I would like to see the salary increased; but it is known that a number of these judges of the court of appeals are taken outside of the city of Baltimore, where their practice has nothing like the range of successful practice in the city of Baltimore. Therefore it is not so great a sacrifice for gentlemen of the court of appeals taken outside of the city of Baltimore as to gentlemen in the city of Baltimore. I think that is an important consideration to look at, what lawyers in good practice get in the particular location where you propose to make them judges. If their practice in the counties is only $2,500 a year for the best lawyers; they can very well afford to go on the bench fifteen years for that salary. But when the practice is $5,000 or $10,000 a year, as it is in the city of Baltimore, they can ill afford and will not give up that practice to go upon the bench at $3,000 a year. I think this is an important consideration.

Mr. Ridgely. In relation to the last observation made by the gentleman from Baltimore city, my experience is the very reverse. I grant that we have got excellent judges, the very best judges perhaps that could be obtained; and yet not one of them had, in my opinion, a practice of $5,000 a year. I know the very best judge we have got did not practice at all, and I think the same observations will apply to other portions of the State.

Now I have no objection at all to giving the judges of Baltimore city $3,500 a year, if even-handed justice is done to all parts of the State. In Baltimore county the judge will have to hold the court continuously every month in the year, and he will be employed every day in the year, and he will have to break up his establishment at home, and come to reside at Towsontown, the county seat, and will have to pay as high there for living as he would in Baltimore city.

Mr. Stirling. How much will it take to rent a house there?

Mr. Ridgely. I do not know about that. It will cost as much to live at a hotel there, as in Baltimore city. I am opposed to increasing the compensation.

Mr. Abbott. The gentleman from Baltimore county (Mr. Ridgely) has expressed the views I entertain. In answer to the remarks of my colleague (Mr. Stirling,) I will say that there is not a city in the Union where living is so cheap as in Baltimore city.

Mr. Stirling. Is it not high everywhere?

Mr. Abbott. We are making a constitution for all time, not for a few years. I know my income has not increased according to the increase of prices. I hope soon to see things settling down again. The increase that is proposed to be given now, making the salary $3,000, is I think all that should be asked.—I hope the gentlemen from the counties who have to pay a portion of this tax will consider these things well, before they vote for this proposition.

Mr. Stockbridge. Gentlemen can get judges for less than $3,000 dollars a year.

Mr. Stirling. I have no doubt some could be got for $500 a year.

Mr. Negley. Why should there be a discrimination made in favor of the judges of Baltimore city and against those of the counties? I believe the work of the judge of the court in Baltimore county will be as continuous and onerous, as that of the judge of any court in Baltimore city. And everything in Baltimore county will be nearly if not quite as high as in Baltimore city, and so in Frederick county; and I know that in Washington county it will be pretty nearly so. Then why make a distinction in favor of one and against another. It has been said that the cost of living in Baltimore city is higher than it is in the counties. Admit it: but then they get a *quid pro quo* for it. They get additional comforts and conveniences, and all that. They get more in return for what they pay. And I do not think there is any reason why this discrimination should be made. I am in favor of a uniform system. There is no reason for this discrimination, and I will vote against it. And at the proper time I will move to insert $2,500 instead of $3,000.

Mr. ABBOTT. They get $3,000 now, all except the judge of the criminal court.

Mr. CUSHING. I was very much surprised to hear my colleague (Mr. Abbott) bringing into the argument upon this question of salaries for judges, and using it as an argument against it that his personal income had not increased in proportion to the increase in the value of articles of various kinds. Why the gentleman should bring that in, unless he intended to state to the convention that his income did not amount to $3,000 a year, and consequently no man should have more than that, I cannot opine. Unless the gentleman says he can live abundantly on less than that in the city of Baltimore, it is without point.

I utterly deny that three thousand dollars a year is at all adequate to keeping up a proper style of living for a judge in Baltimore city. I deny that three thousand dollars a year is a fair compensation for any man in Baltimore city who has legal capacity to qualify him for a seat on the bench. I have voted consistently in this convention to make the salaries in the counties three thousand dollars a year. And I desire that the salaries of the Baltimore city judges should be from four to five thousand a year; nor do I think that that increase would be too much. And when you take a man from the bar to be a judge, and prohibit him from having any other occupation by which he could increase the amount of his compensation, three thousand dollars a year I think is too little. You do not allow him the same privilege that you allow any man outside of an official position of this kind, to increase the amount of his compensation. You cut him off from any fees from his practice, and tie him down to this amount. No matter what may have been the previous style of his living, he must at once conform it to the salary you give him. There is no equity in this at all. There is no reason why, if you want a man to act as judge, you should not give him a fair compensation.

And I do not understand on what plea a reduction is urged of every salary that has been proposed to this house. There has not been a salary reported to this house by any committee, after long consideration, that has not been reduced five hundred dollars. The question what it will cost a man to live in the place where he will have to live, and the fact that he can make nothing but his salary, are not considered at all. But it is from a vague idea that because you give a man enough, the people will say that you are imposing a heavy tax upon the State. The people are more willing to pay ample salaries for the work they want to have done, than their representatives in this convention are to vote them. Gold cannot be bought for the price of copper. The people know that if you give an inadequate salary, you cannot find a man of the requisite ability to take the position.

I have now a letter from one of the judges of the courts in Baltimore, who assures me that with the salary at present given him he must resign, for he cannot live on the salary now paid him. Whatever may be the bearing of the statement of my colleague (Mr. Abbott,) that his income has not increased in proportion to the increase of prices, here is an actual fact, that the judges of the courts in Baltimore cannot live upon the salaries now given. There is no complaint that these judges are not competent, that they have not done their work. And if they do their work, they are entitled to proper compensation for it. It is a simple question of justice, whether, when you require certain qualifications of a man to perform certain duties, he is worthy to receive a fair compensation.

The question is asked me whether we always have candidates enough at the present salary. Certainly, we have candidates, as I have no doubt we would have, if the salary was as low as one thousand dollars a year.—And I would guarantee that the man who would take the place of judge at one thousand dollars a year would make fifteen thousand dollars a year. I will guarantee to furnish you in Baltimore city with judges at one hundred dollars a year, and I will then guarantee that they will make from ten to fifteen thousand dollars a year.

What did the judges get under the old system? The judges of Baltimore city, under the old system, being allowed fees, got from five to six thousand a year. That system was one contrary to justice, not right. We have had good judges under our present constitution, but it was with a very different style of living from now. Prices have changed very much and very materially. They are going to be very much higher for a great many years to come. If gentlemen think that things are going to settle down to their old condition within the time of the judges under the present constitution, they are very much mistaken. You are making a provision in your constitution which will last only some twenty years at the furthest; probably the legislature, with power to submit amendments to the people at any time, may change it sooner. And the salary of $3,500 a year would not last perhaps for five years.

I have never seen the time in this State when $3,500 was too much salary for a judge in Baltimore city, or $3,000 too much for a judge in the counties. I am perfectly willing, so far as I myself am concerned, if the convention will fix the salaries of the judges in Baltimore city at $4,000 a year, to provide that the city of Baltimore shall pay the difference between that and the sum proposed to be paid them by the State. But I do not like this unwise economy. Pay good judges good salaries.

The question recurred upon the motion of Mr. ABBOTT, to amend section thirty-two by striking out the words "five hundred," so as to leave the salaries of judges in the city of Baltimore three thousand dollars

Upon this question Mr. ABBOTT called for the yeas and nays, which were ordered.

The question was then taken, by yeas and nays, and resulted—yeas 39, nays 12—as follows:

Yeas—Messrs. Goldsborough, President; Abbott, Annan, Audoun, Blackiston, Brooks, Chambers, Cushing, Daniel, Davis, of Washington, Dellinger, Ecker, Farrow, Galloway, Greene, Hebb, Hoffman, Hollyday, Hopper, Horsey, Lansdale, Lee, Markey, Mitchell, Mullikin, Murray, Nyman, Pugh, Purnell, Russell, Sands, Scott, Smith, of Worcester, Sneary, Stirling, Sykes, Thomas, Todd, Wilmer—39.

Nays—Messrs. Cunningham, Duvall, Hatch, King, Negley, Parker, Ridgely, Smith, of Dorchester, Stockbridge, Swope, Wickard, Wooden—12.

The amendment was accordingly adopted.

Mr. RIDGELY, when his name was called, said: I shall vote "no" on this proposition for the reason that I am in favor of increasing uniformly the salaries of all the judges throughout the State to $500. That would give the judges of Baltimore city $3,000, except the judge of the criminal court, who would get $2,500. This is increasing the salary of one of these judges $1,000. I vote "no."

Mr. STIRLING, when his name was called, said: I shall support this amendment, not because I think the salary is enough, but because I think it is about as much as the convention is disposed to allow. And in deference to the judgment of the convention I want to come as near the temper and disposition of the house as I can. I vote "aye."

Mr. THOMAS. I move to amend the section by adding the following:

"Provided the mayor and city council of Baltimore shall have the power to add the additional sum of one thousand dollars to the salaries of each of said judges, to be paid by the mayor and city council of Baltimore."

Mr. ABBOTT. I do hope that amendment will not prevail. If it does we shall have three hundred and seventy lawyers eternally boring the city council to get higher salaries for the judges. It would be impossible for us to get good men to serve as members of the city council under such circumstances as that.

Mr. STIRLING. What interest have the lawyers of Baltimore in increasing the salaries of the judges? It is none of their business. It would be for the interest of those who wanted their places to try and turn them out.

The question was taken upon the amendment of Mr. THOMAS, and it was rejected.

Mr. STIRLING. Gentlemen will not pay good salaries to our judges out of the State treasury, nor let us do so if we desire.

Mr. CUSHING. I move to amend by adding the following:

"Provided, the mayor and city council of Baltimore shall add the additional sum of one thousand dollars to the salaries of each of said judges, to be paid by the mayor and city council."

I do not see why the counties should not be perfectly willing to allow the city of Baltimore to pay this extra sum, which does not affect the State in any way. I desire to make it obligatory upon the city, in order to prevent the question going before the city council, as my colleague (Mr. Abbott) so much apprehends, and thus bring the question of the salaries of the judges into politics, thus rendering the judge dependent in some degree upon his agreement of political views with those of the majority of the city council. My amendment avoids that; and the question of the agreement of the personal politics of any judge with those of the mayor and city council will not enter into the question.

Mr. RIDGELY. I would desire to be informed where we derive our power to vote money out of the city treasury of Baltimore?

Mr. CUSHING. If the legislature of Maryland, coming from the people, has the power to vote money out of the treasury of the city of Baltimore for police, &c., certainly the people of the State, and the people of the city of Baltimore in voting for the constitution, have exactly the same right to vote money from the city of Baltimore. The power resides in the people, and the people exercise it. If the people can do it through their legislature, they certainly can do it through their convention. If this convention has any power to make any legislation at all affecting the city of Baltimore, it has also the power to make the city of Baltimore provide for its share of that legislation. There is certainly no question that if the gentlemen of the counties brought in a proposition here that their counties should pay an additional sum to their judges, there would be no objection to it. There was a proposition made by a gentleman upon the floor of this house, and it met with the concurrence of a number of members, that if we adopted the system of taking a judge from each county, the county should pay its own judge. There was no objection made then that this convention had no power to insert such a provision as that in the constitution. There is no question that this convention has the right, if it pleases, to make the respective counties and the city of Baltimore pay the salaries of their judges, and of all their officers. This convention does provide that the State's attorneys should be paid, as far as possible, by the counties out of the fees. I do not think the question of the power of the convention to act on this amendment need cause any gentleman to hesitate. Nor do I see why any gentleman of the counties can hesitate to let the city of Baltimore pay this sum to her judges.

Mr. SANDS. I for one will not vote to place the county I represent in this position. It would be saying that while providing for the general administration of justice, she was not with other counties willing to make provision out of the general fund of the State, but required Baltimore city, through her municipal government to provide for justice within her own borders. I cannot vote to place the constituency I represent in this convention in any such attitude. Nor do I see how any other county member can vote for it. It would appear upon the record that in setting up the judiciary of the State, we were convinced that Baltimore ought to have certain matters, but we would not pay for them out of the public treasury.

Mr. STIRLING. It will represent the fact that the convention does not think this ought to be paid, but the city of Baltimore does.

Mr. ABBOTT. The city of Baltimore don't think any such thing.

Mr. SANDS. Then we are to be put into the position of giving way in the convention to a portion of the members. What does the action of the convention signify in striking out $3,500 and putting in $3,000? Does it signify that the convention is unwilling to allow a fair salary for these judges? If it does, then I am ashamed of it. I as one of the members of the counties am ashamed of the fact that we voted upon the ground simply of $500 additional out of the treasury of the State to fix the salary of the judges of Baltimore city. I did not vote upon any such ground. But I say the fair interpretation of any vote now by this body in favor of the proposition of the gentleman from Baltimore city (Mr. Cushing) will not only be to that effect, but that is the inevitable conclusion. We would not vote to pay the Baltimore city judges $3,500 when it was proposed for the State to pay it, but we were perfectly willing to vote that the Baltimore city judges should be paid $4,000 when the city of Baltimore is to pay it. The members of the counties, I think, have too clear an appreciation of the honor of their constituencies to consent to be put in any such false position as that.

If I thought the judges of the city of Baltimore should be paid $3,000 by the State and $1,000 by the people of Baltimore, I never would have voted to strike out the $3,500 reported by the committee and put in $3,000. I voted to strike it out simply because it was an anomaly, something which I suppose does not appear in any constitution in the Union, that the judges of an inferior court should receive a larger salary than the judges of a superior court. I voted for it that the people of the State and the people of the city of Baltimore should have no unfair or undue discrimination in favor of certain localities. I do not see how any county member upon this floor can vote to place his constituents in the attitude of saying they were not willing that the Baltimore city judges should be paid $3,500 out of the treasury of the State, but they are willing they should be paid $4,000, if $1,000 of that amount came out of the city of Baltimore. I earnestly trust this amendment will not prevail.

Mr. NEGLEY. I would like to know what right a delegate from Washington county, has to vote money out of the treasury of the city of Baltimore. It would be indecent and improper. We voted to fix the salaries of the judges all over the State. We voted to give Baltimore city judges five hundred dollars more than we give the county judges. But it was in the exercise of a general principle, and to take the amount to be paid out of the common treasury of the State. And it was because this three thousand five hundred dollars or three thousand dollars was to be paid out of the common treasury of the State that we had any right as the representatives of the common State to vote upon the subject at all. And when we did fix the salary at three thousand dollars, we exhausted all the right we had.

Now I am opposed to this special act, to putting this special provision in here, to determine this question of voting money out of the treasury of the city of Baltimore to pay these judges. How do we know that the city wants it? They are divided among themselves. One party says they do want it, the other party says they do not. They are absolutely afraid to trust their own representatives with this question.

Mr. STIRLING. Not a bit. We voted it down, so far as our vote was concerned.

Mr. NEGLEY. We do not ask the city of Baltimore to authorize us to give the judges of Washington county an additional sum; we will settle that ourselves. If we think his salary is insufficient, and we choose to give him more, that is a matter for us; we do not want anybody else to vote away our money for us. Let the city council itself, if it thinks proper, apply to the legislature for power to do this, if they do not have it now. I cannot vote for this proposition, because the people of Baltimore are competent to settle it.

Mr. ABBOTT. The people of the city have

a perfect right to vote any amount of money to these judges that they see fit.

Mr. STIRLING. This provision says the judges shall not have any more.

Mr. ABBOTT. Out of the State treasury.

Mr. STOCKBRIDGE. I rise simply to correct a statement of fact by the gentleman from Howard (Mr. Sands,) who says that such an anomaly was not before known of judges of an inferior court receiving a larger salary than judges of a superior court.

Mr. SANDS. So far as I know.

Mr. STOCKBRIDGE. Well, the gentleman will know more in a moment. The judges of the court of appeals of the State of New York receive a salary of three thousand five hundred dollars a year. The governor of that State receives a salary of four thousand dollars a year. The judges of the superior court, and the judges of the court of common pleas for the city of New York receive five thousand dollars a year salary; a thousand dollars more than the governor, and fifteen hundred more than the judges of the court of appeals of that State. I wanted to correct the gentleman as to that matter of fact.

Mr. SANDS. Is there any other case? I should like to know all these cases. New York may have done this thing. I want to know if there is any other case.

Mr. STOCKBRIDGE. We will instruct the gentleman in facts as we go on. It is nothing unusual for this convention to say the counties shall pay so and so. We have done it all through the constitution. We have said that the judges of the orphans' court shall be paid by the counties. Gentlemen know that if they know at all what we have done in this convention. We have provided that certain fees shall be paid by certain suitors.

I am very much pleased with this rage of economy. I like to see money saved to the State and to the citizens of the State. I wish this rage had prevailed when we had the seventh section of this judiciary report before us. Yet gentlemen deliberately struck out a provision which proposed to cut off a useless appendage of the judicial department, and which costs the State more than ten thousand dollars a year.

The PRESIDENT. The convention reinstated it.

Mr. STOCKBRIDGE. Not so. The proposition of the committee on judiciary was to strike out and abolish a certain office, which was good for nothing but to draw money, and which did draw money pretty freely. That proposition was stricken out. Then an amendment was made, upon the motion of the gentleman from Baltimore county (Mr. Ridgely,) which simply made the salary of that officer fixable by the general assembly. But until they do fix it, of course it stands as it does now, ranging from seventy-five dollars in the small counties up to fifteen hundred dollars and fees, and so on up to four or five thousand dollars and fees. So that that good for nothing officer is really receiving two thousand dollars a year more than gentlemen are willing to allow to our judges. I congratulate them on this streak of economy.

Mr. ABBOTT. We are paying for judges now more than we are paying for any other officer in the State, except the governor. I do not see that there is any room for the gentleman to find fault.

Mr. STOCKBRIDGE. I did not say I found fault; I approved this economy highly.

The question was then taken upon the question of Mr. CUSHING, and it was rejected.

Mr. SANDS. Some of us who want to get home must start in the half past two o'clock train. I therefore move that the convention now adjourn.

The motion to adjourn was withdrawn by Mr. SANDS, at the request of

Mr. CUNNINGHAM, who moved that when this convention adjourn to-day it stand adjourned to Monday next at twelve o'clock.

Mr. CUSHING moved to amend by making it half past twelve o'clock.

Mr. CUNNINGHAM accepted the amendment.

The question was then taken upon the motion of Mr. CUNNINGHAM, as modified, and it was rejected.

SCHEDULE.—MINORITY REPORT.

Mr. LANSDALE, from the minority of the committee on schedule, submitted the following report, which was read:

The undersigned, a minority of the members of the committee on provisions and ordinances as may be desirable to carry into effect amendments to the constitution, report that they dissent from the report submitted by the majority of the committee.

First. Because they believe the authority given to soldiers in camp to vote at all elections, will utterly fail to have the effect proposed by those who advocate the measure; on the contrary, as the undersigned believe, it will enable the officers who command the soldiers, to control the votes of those who feel and know the power of their officers, to make them suffer in various ways the penalty of disobedience to their wishes. To a soldier on duty, the first great lesson taught, is obedience to his commanding officer. Military necessity requires a rigid exaction of this duty; it allows of no discussion or discretion. To fail in the smallest respect insures harsh treatment, even in cases where martial law prescribes no specific penalty. It will not be doubted that the only safe approach to the favor of an officer is to gratify his wishes by voting his ticket.

Second. But whatever may be the propriety of taking the votes of soldiers or their officers, the undersigned cannot permit themselves to doubt of the concurrence of the convention in their determined opposition to so much of the report of the majority as provides for the immediate operation of portions of the constitution before its adoption by the people. Surely if any one proposition, in regard to our proceedings was universally accepted by all who voted, whether for or against a convention, it was this, that its work was to be submitted to and accepted by the people of the State before it should have any effect. Yet the majority propose that now at the very moment when the question of adoption is being taken, in the very act of taking that question, the people shall be bound and governed by it, so far as it relates to some of its most important and vital changes of the existing system of government. What a strange spectacle would be exhibited if the provisions now proposed should be enforced as part of the new constitution, in direct opposition to the existing constitution, and yet the result show that the people will not accept the new constitution? The present constitution exists until the new one is adopted. How then can the provisions of the present constitution be violated, or interfered with, until the new one has an existence by the adoption of the people? The great purpose of the majority seems to be, to deprive those who form the constituency of this convention of the privilege secured to them by the present constitution of passing upon the work of this body, and to this end, by newly contrived oaths and by the aid of the military, to confirm their proceedings. For these amongst other reasons, the undersigned protest against the report in the particulars mentioned. All which is respectfully submitted, &c.

THOS. LANSDALE,
A. J. CRAWFORD.

On motion of Mr. CUNNINGHAM, it was

Ordered, That when the convention adjourn to-day, it stand adjourned until Monday next at twelve o'clock, M.

On motion of Mr. CUSHING,

The convention then adjourned.

EIGHTY-FOURTH DAY.

MONDAY, August 29, 1864.

The convention met at 12 o'clock, M.

Prayer by Rev. Mr. McNemar.

The roll was called, and the following members answered to their names:

Messrs. Goldsborough, President; Abbott, Annan, Audoun, Baker, Billingsley, Blackiston, Bond, Briscoe, Brooks, Carter, Chambers, Cunningham, Cushing, Daniel, Davis, of Charles, Davis, of Washington, Dellinger, Dennis, Duvall, Earle, Ecker, Farrow, Galloway, Greene, Hatch, Hebb, Hodson, Hoffman, Hollyday, Hopkins, Hopper, Keefer, Kennard, King, Larsh, Lee, Markey, McComas, Miller, Morgan, Mullikin, Murray, Negley, Nyman, Parker, Parran, Purnell, Russell, Schley, Scott, Smith, of Worcester, Sneary, Stirling, Stockbridge, Swope, Sykes, Thomas, Todd, Turner, Valliant, Wickard, Wilmer, Wooden—64.

The proceedings of Saturday were read and approved.

On motion of Mr. VALLIANT,

It was ordered to be entered on the journal that Mr. George W. Sands, is detained from his seat in the convention by business connected with the coming draft.

THREE SESSIONS DAILY.

Mr. MULLIKIN submitted the following order:

Ordered, That until the final adjournment of the convention, three sessions daily shall be held, commencing at half-past nine o'clock, A. M., half-past three o'clock, P. M., and eight o'clock, P. M.

Mr. AUDOUN moved to lay the order on the table.

Mr. HEBB demanded the yeas and nays, and they were ordered.

The question being taken, the result was—yeas 27, nays 34—as follows:

Yeas—Messrs. Audoun, Billingsley, Blackiston, Bond, Briscoe, Carter, Cunningham, Davis, of Charles, Dennis, Duvall, Hodson, Hoffman, Hollyday, King, Larsh, Lee, Miller, Nyman, Parker, Parran, Sneary, Stirling, Stockbridge, Sykes, Todd, Valliant, Wilmer—27.

Nays—Messrs. Goldsborough, President; Abbott, Annan, Baker, Brooks, Cushing, Daniel, Davis, of Washington, Dellinger, Earle, Ecker, Farrow, Galloway, Greene, Hatch, Hebb, Hopkins, Hopper, Keefer, Kennard, Markey, McComas, Mullikin, Murray, Negley, Purnell, Russell, Schley, Scott, Smith, of Worcester, Swope, Thomas, Wickard, Wooden—34.

The convention accordingly refused to lay the order on the table.

The question recurring upon the adoption of the order,

Mr. MULLIKIN demanded the yeas and nays, and they were ordered.

The question being taken, the result was—yeas 32, nays 31—as follows:

Yeas—Messrs. Goldsborough, President; Abbott, Annan, Baker, Daniel, Davis, of Washington, Dellinger, Earle, Ecker, Farrow, Galloway, Greene, Hatch, Hebb, Hopkins, Hopper, Keefer, Kennard, Markey, McComas, Mullikin, Murray, Negley, Purnell, Russell, Schley, Scott, Smith, of Worcester, Stockbridge, Swope, Wickard, Wooden—32.

Nays—Messrs. Audoun, Billingsley, Blackiston, Bond, Brisc e, Brooks, Carter, Cunningham, Cushing, Davis, of Charles, Dennis, Duvall, Hodson, Hoffman, Hollyday, King, Larsh, Lee, Miller, Morgan, Nyman, Parker, Parran, Sneary, Stirling, Sykes, Thomas, Todd, Turner, Valliant, Wilmer—31.

The order was accordingly adopted.

PRINTING THE NEW CONSTITUTION.

Mr. VALLIANT submitted the following order:

Ordered, That the comptroller of the treasury be, and is hereby authorized and empowered to contract for the printing of six thousand copies of the constitution, and that the librarian be directed to distribute the same among the members, as early as practicable after the adjournment without day of the convention, and that the cost of said distribution be paid by the comptroller.

Mr. VALLIANT said: I have provided by this order for the distribution of the constitution among the members, because I thought the members would be more likely to distribute them among the people early than any one else. I have also added a clause that the cost of the distribution be paid by the comptroller, deeming it better that the actual cost of the distribution should be paid by the government. A very trifling matter has given rise to some discussion here, about the distribution of documents by the librarian, for which the legislature appropriated $150, while it seems it did not cost quite that.

Mr. STOCKBRIDGE. I move that the consideration of this order be postponed until to-morrow. It seems to me that the order in its present form is not a proper one to accomplish the purpose which the gentleman designs to accomplish by it. If the purpose be, as I take it to be, to distribute the new constitution broadcast throughout the State preparatory to a vote upon it by the people, six thousand copies are not sufficient. If I recollect aright the former State convention made provision for publishing it in extras in all or nearly all the newspapers throughout the State, so that it might be scattered wherever a newspaper went. It seems to me that something of that sort is far preferable to this. It is for that reason that I move the postponement of the consideration of this order until to-morrow, that we may see what is the best form to secure the distribution of the constitution.

The motion to postpone was agreed to.

COURTS OF BALTIMORE CITY.

The convention resumed the consideration of the report of the judiciary committee, which was on its second reading.

The next section in order was read as follows:

"Sec. 33. There shall be a clerk of the superior court and a clerk of the circuit court of Baltimore city, who shall be elected by the qualified voters of the city of Baltimore, hold their respective offices for the term of six years, and until a new election is held and his successor duly qualified, and be re-eligible thereto, but removable by the judges of the court of which they are respectively clerks, for incompetency, wilful neglect of duty, misdemeanor in office, and such other causes as may be prescribed by law."

Mr. THOMAS submitted the following amendment:

Strike out section thirty-three, and insert:

"Section 33. There shall be a clerk of the superior court of Baltimore city, and a clerk of the circuit court of Baltimore city, and a clerk of the court of common pleas in Baltimore city, and a clerk of the criminal court of Baltimore city, and each of the said clerks shall be elected by the legal and qualified voters of said city, and shall hold his office for six years from the first day of January succeeding his election, and until his successor is elected and qualified, and be re-eligible thereto, subject to be removed for wilful neglect of duty or other misdemeanor in office on conviction in a court of law. In case of a vacancy in the office of a clerk of any of said courts the judge of the court of which he was clerk, shall have the power to appoint a clerk until the general election for county officers held next thereafter, when a clerk shall be elected for the residue of the term thus made vacant."

Mr. DANIEL moved to amend by striking out the last clause, "when a clerk shall be elected for the residue of the term thus made vacant."

Mr. THOMAS accepted the amendment.

The amendment, as amended, was agreed to.

No further amendment being offered, the next section was read as follows:

"Sec. 34. The judges of the superior court as herein constitued, shall designate as clerk of said court, in their discretion, either the clerk of the present superior court, or the clerk of the court of common pleas, and the person so designated as clerk shall continue to act as such until the end of the time for which he was elected; the other of said clerks shall, until the end of the time for which he was elected, continue to act as clerk in that department of the business of the superior court which in the judgment of the judges of said court, nearest corresponds to the business of the court of which he was elected clerk, and shall receive the fees and emoluments pertaining thereto as he would have done if said court had continued an independent court, and the judges of said superior court shall make such rules and regulations as may be found necessary to give full force and effect to this provision."

Mr. THOMAS submitted the following amendment:

Strike out section thirty-four, and insert the following:

"Sec. 34. The present clerk of the superior court of Baltimore city, and of the court of common pleas in Baltimore city, and of the criminal court of Baltimore, shall continue to act as clerks of said courts respectively, during the time for which they were severally elected, and in case of the death, resignation or disqualification of either of said clerks before the expiration of the time for which they were elected, the judge of the court, where such death, resignation or other disqualification may occur, shall have the power to appoint a clerk as provided by the thirty-third section of this article. The present clerk of the circuit court of Baltimore city shall continue to act as clerk of said court, until the first election for members of the general assembly next after the adoption of this constitution, when a clerk of said court shall be elected in the same manner, and hold his office for the same time, and be subject to the same provisions of this constitution as the clerks of the courts in said city."

Mr. STIRLING. I suggest to my colleague to strike out "members of the general assembly" and insert "county officers."

Mr. THOMAS modified his amendment accordingly.

Mr. STOCKBRIDGE As it stands it seems to me that there ought to be a verbal modification made in it. There are no county officers elected in Baltimore city of course. I suppose that means county officers throughout the State; and I would suggest that it be modified so as to read "until the first election for county officers in the State."

Mr. STIRLING. My impression is that it is perfectly correct as it stands. The city of Baltimore so far as the clerks of the courts and the sheriffs are concerned is one of the counties in the State. The mayor and city council of Baltimore are a municipal corporation; and it is only a municipality so far as they are concerned.

The amendment was agreed to.

No further amendment being offered, the next section was read, as follows:

"Sec. 35. The clerk of the superior court shall have the custody of all dockets, records, and papers now in the custody of the clerk of the superior court or court of common pleas, and of all such other dockets, records and papers as he may hereafter be required by law or by the judges of the said court to take custody of, and shall receive and record all deeds and other papers required by law to be recorded in said city, and not otherwise provided for; he shall, unless the general assembly shall provide a different mode, issue all marriage and other licenses required by law, and discharge all the duties and be subject to all the obligations heretofore discharged by or imposed upon the clerk of the superior court and the clerk of the court of common pleas, subject to such modifications thereof as may be made by law or by the judges of his said court."

Mr. THOMAS submitted the following amendment:

Strike out section 35, and insert:

"Sec. 35. That the clerk of the court of common pleas shall have authority to issue within said city, all marriage and other licences required by law, subject to such provisions as the legislature have now or may hereafter prescribe, and the clerk of the superior court of said city shall have the custody of all deeds, conveyances and other papers now remaining in the office of said court, and shall hereafter receive and record all deeds, conveyances and other papers which are required by law to be recorded in said city. He shall also have custody of all other papers connected with the proceedings on the law or equity side of Baltimore county court, and of the dockets thereof so far as the same have relation to the city of Baltimore."

Mr. THOMAS said: This is the same provision that is contained in the present constitution, including the provisions the legislature have already prescribed as well as those which they may hereafter prescribe.

The amendment was agreed to.

No further amendment being offered, the next section was read as follows:

"Sec. 36. The clerk of the circuit court of Baltimore city shall have the custody of all the dockets, records and papers now in the office and custody of the clerk of the circuit court of Baltimore city, and of the clerk of the criminal court of Baltimore city, and of all dockets, records and papers hereafter pertaining to the business of the said circuit court as hereby constituted, or which he may be required by law, or by the judges of said court to take custody of. He shall discharge all the duties pertaining to the office of clerk of said court, or which have heretofore been imposed by law upon the clerks of the circuit or criminal court of Baltimore city, or which may hereafter be imposed by law, or required by the judges of his said court. And the present clerk of the criminal court of Baltimore city shall be clerk of the circuit court as hereby constituted until the end of the time for which he was elected clerk of said criminal court."

Mr. THOMAS moved to strike out this section.

Mr. STIRLING. This section is useless unless the convention reconsider the action taken on Saturday.

The motion was agreed to.

JUDGES OF CIRCUIT COURTS.

Mr. THOMAS submitted the following as an additional section:

"Sec. —. There shall be elected by the legal and qualified voters of the third, sixth, seventh, eighth and eleventh judicial circuits on Tuesday next after the first Monday in the month of November, 1864, (eighteen hundred and sixty-four) one person to be judge of each of said judicial circuits respectively, who shall possess the same qualifications, exercise the same powers, receive the same salaries, and serve for the same term, as prescribed by this constitution for the judges of the several circuits; and the present judge of the first judicial circuit shall continue to act as the judge of the first judicial circuit, and the present judge of the second judicial circuit shall continue to act as judge of the second judicial circuit, and the present judge of the third judicial circuit shall continue to act as the judge of the fourth judicial circuit, and the present judge of the fourth judicial circuit shall continue to act as the judge of the fifth judicial circuit, and the present judge of the sixth judicial circuit shall continue to act as the judge of the ninth judicial circuit, and the present judge of the seventh judicial circuit shall continue to act as the judge of the tenth judicial circuit, and the present judge of the eighth judicial circuit shall continue to act the judge of the twelfth judicial circuit, and the present judges of the several courts of the fifth judicial circuit shall continue to act as the judges of the several courts of the nineteenth judicial circuit, until the expiration of the time for which they have been severally elected, or until they shall have attained the age of seventy years, whichever shall first happen, and until their successors are elected and qualified. And in case of the death, resignation, removal or other disqualification of any of the judges hereby continued in office, the governor, by and with the advice and consent of the senate, shall appoint a person duly qualified, according to the terms of this constitution, to fill said office, until the next general election for county officers thereafter; at which time an election shall be held as herein before prescribed for a judge, who shall hold his office for fifteen years, according to the provisions of this constitution, as to the qualification and removal of judges."

Mr. HEBB. Some of these provisions are already embraced in the report on the tenure of office, &c. I have prepared an amendment which I think will answer the purpose, and which I designed to offer to the come in at the end of Part III.

Mr. THOMAS withdrew his amendment.

Mr. HEBB submitted the following amendment:

Insert as an additional section, to follow section twenty-one, the following:

"The present judges of the circuit courts shall continue to act as judges of the respective circuit courts within the judicial circuits in which they respectively reside, until the expiration of the term for which they were respectively elected, and until their successors are elected and qualified, viz: the present judges of the first, second, third, fourth, sixth and eighth judicial circuits, as organized at the time of the adoption of this constitution, shall continue to act as judges respectively of the first, second, fourth, fifth, ninth and twelfth judicial circuits, as organized under this constitution; and an election for judges of the third, sixth, seventh, eighth, tenth and eleventh judicial circuits shall be held on Tuesday next after the first Monday of November, eighteen hundred and sixty-four."

Mr. THOMAS. I will suggest that the gentleman includes the tenth judicial circuit.—Judge Ricaud was only appointed last year; and according to the rules he would not be elected until a year from next fall.

Mr. STIRLING. It strikes me that the judge would have held over a year more if the convention had not been held; and you ought not to displace him and require an election to be held in that district sooner than it would otherwise have been held. There is no necessity for holding an election in that district for judge until a year from next fall. I move that the further consideration of this section be informally passed over. It occurs to me that that makes no provision with reference to the court of appeals; and I think there ought to be some provision made there.

Mr. HEBB. I have made provision for that in another amendment With regard to the judge of the tenth judicial circuit I will state that the election of all these judges is provided for to take place at the next general election of members of the general assembly.—The election next year is for county officers; and if the convention choose to reconsider what they have already decided, and say they may be elected at the election either of members of the general assembly or of county officers, then it will be proper to provide that the election of the judge of that district shall take place next year.

Mr. STIRLING. Some provision will have to be made with regard to that; for the convention have determined that the judges shall hold for fifteen years, a term which will inevitably require a change in the time of election, or make this an anomalous provision. I do not, however, propose to change this, for I want these elections to be kept separate as far as possible from party politics.

The motion to postpone was agreed to.

ANOTHER COURT IN BALTIMORE.

Mr THOMAS submitted the following amendment:

"SEC. —. The legislature shall, whenever it may think the same proper and expedient, provide by law another court for the city of Baltimore, to consist of one judge, to be elected by the legal and qualified voters of said city, who shall be subject to the same constitutional provisions, hold his office for the same term of years, and receive the same compensation as the judge of the superior court of said city, and said court shall have such jurisdiction and powers as may be prescribed by law; and the general assembly may reapportion the civil jurisdiction among the several courts in Baltimore city, from time to time, as in their judgments the public interest and convenience may require."

Mr. THOMAS said: I will state that that is an exact copy, with a very slight variation in the latter part of it, of the provision in the present constitution.

Mr. STIRLING. My colleague, the chairman of the committee (Mr. Stockbridge,) has objected to the system we have adopted that it crowds the jurisdiction of the court of common pleas. The object of this is to give the legislature power, if the jurisdiction can be better apportioned among the several courts, to reapportion it. It can certainly do no harm. The legislature may take part of the jurisdiction from that court and give it to another, if they think it necessary.

Mr. MILLER. I should like to learn from some gentleman what necessity there is for a new court in Baltimore city. There are four now. The provision of the old constitution was for three courts; and this was for a fourth if three were not sufficient.

Mr. THOMAS. There is no necessity now; but before the constitution is revised again the commercial interests of Baltimore may have so increased that it may become necessary to have another court.

Mr. STIRLING. It cannot be organized unless the general assembly provide for it; and if there is no necessity for it they certainly will not do it.

Mr. STOCKBRIDGE. I have no objection at all to the latter part of the section. The latter part of it I think is really important, that there should exist some such power somewhere. But I do not see the necessity for a provision to multiply the courts. If it were put in the alternative that they might establish an additional court or increase the judicial power of the existing courts by adding a judge, if they should find it necessary for the transaction of the business, I should have no objection whatever to the section. It might be decidedly better than to establish a new court, that two judges should be placed in charge of an existing court, with power to apportion their business. It seems to me that the multiplicity of courts covering the same territory is certainly going to operate very badly indeed. I would greatly have preferred to see the judicial power of the city vested in a single court, with sufficient judicial power, and with a sufficient number of judges to transact all the business. I am satisfied that it would work much better than arbitrarily making each court a Procrustean bed, for one man to fill, who may know very little about these particular duties, while you cannot change his jurisdiction from one court to another. I trust the amendment will be modified as I have suggested.

Mr. THOMAS. It appears to me a great deal better to have a multiplicity of courts than a multiplicity of judges; because, in the first place, it is more simple and less complex to have more courts than it is to have more judges. I am perfectly aware that Baltimore city does not require any other court or more judges than it has at the present time. But we are making this constitution for years to come, I hope. We do not know but in the course of five or six years it may be absolutely necessary for the commerce of Baltimore to have another court; and it is a great deal better, if it were necessary, to have another court rather than to have an increase of judges in the present courts. I think this was a wise provision put into the constitution under which we live; and it was the origin of one of the most useful courts within the limits of Baltimore city. I think it will be wise now to give the same discretion to the legislature. Most certainly, as has been well said by my colleague (Mr. Stirling,) if the wants of the people and the mercantile interests of Baltimore require it, we ought to have it; and if they do not, the legislature will not provide for another court.

Mr. DANIEL. If my colleague (Mr. Stockbridge) will prepare an amendment so as to give the legislature the alternative he has suggested, I should prefer it to an increase of the courts, so that the legislature may either increase the courts or the judges as they think proper. In the absence of that I shall vote for the proposition as it is.

Mr. THOMAS. If you have an increase of the judges, the legislature might go on and increase the number of judges in every single court, in all the four courts, which would be a very heavy expense; whereas if you adopt this amendment, we can only have one more court, to be limited to one judge.

The question being taken on the adoption of the amendment, the result was—ayes 32, noes 14—no quorum voting.

The question being again taken, the result was—ayes 35, noes 18. The amendment was accordingly adopted.

The next section was read as follows:

PART VI.

Justices of the Peace.

"Sec. 37. The judges of the circuit courts shall appoint in each election district of the several counties composing their respective circuits, and the judges of the superior court and of the circuit court of Baltimore city, by concurrent action, shall appoint in the city of Baltimore such number of justices of the peace as the wants and interests of the people may require. They shall certify their appointment so made to the governor, by whom the appointees shall be commissioned as justices of the peace of the State of Maryland, in and for ——— county and city. The justices so appointed and commissioned shall be conservators of the peace, shall hold their office for two years, and shall have such jurisdiction, duties and compensation, subject to such right of appeal as hath been heretofore exercised or shall be hereafter prescribed by law."

Mr. AUDOUN submitted the following amendment:

Strike out section 37, and insert:

"Sec. 37. The general assembly, at its first session after the adoption of this constitution, shall fix the number of justices of the peace and constables for each ward of the city of Baltimore, and for each election district in the several counties, who shall be elected by the legal and qualified voters thereof, respectively, at the next general election for county officers thereafter, and shall hold their offices for two years from the time of their election, and until their successors in office are elected and qualified; and the general assembly may, from time to time, increase or diminish the number of justices of the peace and constables to be elected in the several wards and election districts, as the wants and interests of the people may require. They shall be, by virtue of their offices, conservators of the peace in the said counties and city respectively, and shall have such duties and compensation as now exist, or may be provided for by law. In the event of a vacancy in the office of a justice of the peace, the governor shall appoint a person to serve as justice of the peace until the next regular election of said officers, and in case of a vacancy in the office of constable, the county commissioners of the county in which a vacancy may occur, or the mayor and city council of Baltimore, as the case may be, shall appoint a person to serve as constable until the next regular election thereafter for said officers. An appeal shall lie in all civil cases from the judgment of a justice of the peace to the circuit court of the county, or to the court of common pleas of Baltimore city, as the case may be, and on all such appeals, either party shall be entitled to a trial by jury, according to the laws now existing, or which may be hereafter enacted; and the mayor and city council of Baltimore shall have the exclusive power to create, organize and govern such police force for the good government of said city as they may deem necessary."

Mr. Daniel. I would prefer that that section should be passed over informally; and I will make that motion and submit my reasons. The question now comes up as to the appointment or election of justices of the peace. It is not a question peculiar to the city of Baltimore at all; but I suppose the same law we enact for the State will prevail in Baltimore city. For myself I prefer very much that the magistrates and constables at least should be appointed. I think that the question is properly presented that this convention having determined to elect the judges instead of appointing them, a large number of the convention, and a large number I think of the people of the State, I will not say a majority, prefer that these officers should be appointed rather than elected. I think it would be fair to those who have yielded their preference and allowed the judges to be elected, fair to them and to their constituencies, that they should be allowed to have these minor officers, magistrates and constables, appointed by some power, if not by the judges as here proposed.

I think as I have already heretofore remarked upon this floor, that much greater evil arises from the election of these smaller officers, constables magistrates, and road supervisors, than from the election of judges; that the people will be a good deal more circumspect in the election of judges. It has been stated in the discussion of some other propositions in relation to this, that there is a disposition to swap off the first and highest officers of the State for the small and petty offices. I think this leads to a great deal of corruption, and is the principal cause of corruption in our elective system. As has been stated in reference to constables in Baltimore city, it is a known custom that men get themselves elected, who are busy running about the wards, and as soon as they are elected they go and sell the office to somebody else for one hundred or one hundred and fifty dollars, who becomes the constable instead of him. I think therefore that magistrates and constables ought to be appointed, as we have determined upon the election of the judges by the people. If this section is passed over until the other section comes up, I will move an amendment to it; and I therefore move to pass over this informally now.

Mr. Hebb. I hope the proposition to postpone the section will not be agreed to. We have had ample time to prepare amendments to the section.

The motion to postpone did not prevail.

Mr. Thomas moved to insert in the line after the words "as the case may be," the words "or if for the recovery of a fine, penalty or forfeiture, to the criminal court."

Mr. Audoun accepted the amendment.

Mr. Daniel. I move to strike out from the original section down to "action" in the fourth line, and to insert "the judges of the several courts shall appoint."

Mr. Stockbridge. It occurs to me, and I wish the convention would give attention to this point, that we are no longer upon the courts of the city of Baltimore, but legislating for the whole State; and the gentleman's amendment is defective in that it makes no provision except for the appointment of justices of the peace in Baltimore city. The article as it stands reported by the committee provides for the appointment of justices of the peace for the entire State, including the counties.

Mr. Daniel. I did not mean to do that. I will modify my amendment by striking out "superior court and of the circuit court," and inserting "several courts." It will then apply to the whole State.

Mr. Stockbridge. I had designed to offer an amendment, and I now prefer it to the amendment of my colleague. His amendment is that they shall be appointed by the judges of the several courts, whether in the four courts, or in five, including the orphans' court, may be indefinite. My amendment was to strike out the words "superior court and of the circuit court" and to insert "court of common pleas and of the criminal court," the two courts which review magistrates' decisions.

Mr. DANIEL. I will accept that.

Mr. HOFFMAN. I hope the amendment will be adopted that the justices of the peace may be elected by the people.

Mr. THOMAS. The only objection I have to the amendment moved by my colleague to the original section, is this. It appears to me to give too much power to one man. In your counties the circuit judge appoints all your magistrates. And the judges in Baltimore city appoint all the magistrates of the city, some twenty-five in all. It appears to me that taking that power out of the hands of the people and putting it into the hands of one or two men is giving too much power to one or two men.

Mr. BRISCOE gave notice that at the proper time he would submit the following amendment to the original section:

Strike out section 37 down to the word "require," in the sixth line and insert:

"The county commissioners of the several counties of this State shall appoint in each election district of the several counties, and the orphans' court of the city of Baltimore, shall appoint for the city of Baltimore, such number of justices of the peace, as the wants and interests of the people may require."

Mr. DANIEL. One word with regard to giving the judges the appointment in the counties of the State. I think he is an eminently proper person to appoint these magistrates, because it has been said that the judges review the decisions of the magistrates. It is known that under the old constitution the governor appointed. We have thought it better to put it into the hands of the judge, because the judge, being generally a resident of one county, and having intimate knowledge of the people of the counties, can easily appoint people capable of serving properly.—As he has to review their decisions, both criminal and civil, it will be for the interest of every judge sitting on the bench to appoint such men as magistrates as will do justice to both the civil and criminal jurisdiction given to them. The judge will necessarily have information, sitting in the county three or four terms every year; and especially as we are increasing the number of circuits, his knowledge will be almost as intimate as that of any man in the county; and besides he can call to his aid men whom he knows in the county. I think that it ought to be taken out of the hands of the people at this time, and indeed for all coming time they ought to be appointed instead of elected.

Mr. RUSSELL. I hope the section reported by the committee will be adopted. I think the people in the county I in part represent are perfectly sick of the election of magistrates and constables, and would like to see it changed. I think the plan of appointment by the judge a very good one, and I should like to see it adopted.

Mr. AUDOUN demanded the yeas and nays, but they were not ordered.

Mr. STIRLING. This amendment is perfectly proper. It does not decide anything at all, but is merely to perfect the original section. It is necessary to change the language of the section because it is inconsistent with what the house has already done.

Mr. AUDOUN. I desire to say to the house that this amendment instead of providing for the election of magistrates provides for their appointment.

Mr. STIRLING. No, sir; it does not provide either for their election or appointment. The report of the committee provides for their appointment, but this amendment is merely a verbal change in the report, striking out certain judges and inserting others; and has no effect whatever upon the question of their appointment.

The amendment submitted by Mr. STOCKBRIDGE, and accepted by Mr. DANIEL, was adopted.

Mr. BRISCOE submitted the following amendment:

Strike out section 37 down to the word "require," in the sixth line and insert:

"The county commissioners of the several counties of this State shall appoint in each election district of the several counties, and the mayor and city council of the city of Baltimore, shall appoint for the city of Baltimore, such number of justices of the peace as the wants and interests of the people may require."

Mr. BRISCOE said: I propose this amendment because I really believe that so far as the selection of justices of the peace is concerned, the appointment of the court could only be suitable in the community in which the judge resides. In the ordinary course of things the judges are not presumed to be acquainted with the people of their whole circuits. I think it is better therefore to leave it to the county commissioners, who are intimately acquainted with the men in every section of the county, and who I think could more efficiently perform the duty.

Mr. STOCKBRIDGE. At the time this report was made there was a report pending before us which provided for the appointment of constables in another way. As it now stands they are nowhere provided for. I suggest to the gentleman to insert the words "and constables" after the words "justices of the peace," so as to read "justices of the peace and constables."

Mr. BRISCOE modified his amendment accordingly.

Mr. DANIEL. I hope the amendment will be adopted.

The amendment was adopted—ayes 35, nays 17.

Mr. STIRLING submitted the following amendment:

Strike out the words "as the wants and interests of the people may require," and insert "as now are or may hereafter be fixed by the general assembly."

Mr. STIRLING said: I prefer to leave it to the legislature, for I think it is too large a discretion for the county commissioners to increase the number of justices of the peace and constables as they may choose.

The amendment was agreed to.

On motion of Mr. STOCKBRIDGE,

The words "and constables" were also inserted in line eight, after the words "justices of the peace."

Mr. THOMAS submitted the following amendment:

After the word "law," in the thirteenth line insert:

"And shall be subject to removal by the judge of the county or city having criminal jurisdiction, for wilful neglect of duty or misdemeanor in office, on conviction in a court of law."

Mr. THOMAS said: As the law now stands the magistrates and constables are the only two officers not removable for malfeasance. I have myself known them to be convicted of malfeasance in office, and pay their fines and go to work and perpetrate the same crime over again. Whether elected by the people or appointed the power should reside somewhere to remove them as we may remove judges. For that reason I offer this amendment.

The amendment was adopted.

Mr. KEEFER moved to amend the substitute by inserting in the fifteenth line, after the words "in the event of," the words "any two or more persons who shall have the highest and an equal number of votes or."

Mr. AUDOUN accepted the amendment.

Mr. KEEFER moved to amend the substitute by inserting in the eighteenth line, after the words "and in case," the same clause.

Mr. AUDOUN accepted the amendment.

Mr. STOCKBRIDGE. I ask the attention of the convention to an amendment which is in my judgment very important. I move to strike out from the substitute offered by my colleague (Mr. Audoun) the following words, at the close of the section:

"And the mayor and city council of Baltimore shall have the exclusive power to create, organize and govern such police force for the good government of said city as they may deem necessary."

In the first place, if such a principle is to be enunciated or is to be adopted by the convention, it does not belong to the section where it is placed. It is in a section relative to justices of the peace and constables of the State; and this has appended to it a clause with reference to the police force of the city of Baltimore. The first practical result of the adoption of that, which I can see, would be to inaugurate civil war in the city. It is evidently designed entirely to extinguish the existing police system of the city and to inaugurate a new force under new conditions, but it provides, rather loosely it seems to me, that they shall have "exclusive power to create, organize and govern such police force for the good government of said city as they may deem necessary." There is already there such a police force as the general assembly deem necessary. Are there to be two distinct systems in force in the city? That is the first effect of it, that it does not extinguish the present system, but authorizes, or rather makes imperative upon the mayor and city council of Baltimore to inaugurate such force as they may deem necessary. It is entirely different from the provision of the old constitution or of any constitution that ever existed. It will not, I am persuaded accomplish its purpose. I see nothing of value in it. I am perfectly willing to leave that matter in the control of the general assembly. I desire the convention to consider its practical effect. It seems to aim to effect in a covert way what could not be effected in an open way and standing by itself. It is smuggled in at the end of this very long section to which it does not belong, and I hope it will be stricken out.

Mr. AUDOUN. I am not in the habit of engaging in "smuggling." I think if my colleague will look at the present constitution he will find the same provision I have offered here as a substitute for this section contained in the present constitution. As a representative of the city of Baltimore, representing a certain portion of the people there, I only ask this convention to give them the control of their police; to give them what the counties have, the control of their police system. I ask nothing more. I had no other object in view at the time I offered this substitute.—I do not desire, nor do I think that this convention for a moment suspects me of smuggling anything into this convention or into this constitution.

Mr. STOCKBRIDGE. I wish merely to correct an error into which my colleague (Mr. Audoun) has fallen. He seems to suppose that this provision is the same as that in the existing constitution. I wish the convention to note the difference. The clause he offers is this:

"And the mayor and city council of Baltimore shall have the exclusive power to create, organize and govern such police force for the good government of said city as they may deem necessary."

The provision in the existing constitution reads:

"And the mayor and city council may provide, by ordinance, from time to time, for the creation and government of such temporary additional police, as they may deem necessary to preserve the public peace."

The reading of the two is all the comment I desire to make.

Mr. STIRLING. I wish to say a word in relation to the clause which it is proposed to strike out, resembling a provision on the same subject in the present constitution. I do not see any unfairness in the mode in which that is introduced; but I cannot vote for it, because although in the same place, it has a broader effect. It does unquestionably abolish the present police force in the city of Baltimore. I do not wish to argue the question of the present system. I am unable to say whether it is unpopular with a majority of the people. But at all events I do not think this is the time or place in the present constitution to undertake to abolish that system, and introduce a new system. The people of Baltimore have a right to appeal to the legislature to change it, if they think proper. They have never done so. I shall therefore vote for the motion to strike out, because I am indisposed to vote in this way to abolish the present police force of the city.

The motion to strike out the clause was agreed to.

Mr. THOMAS. I now move the same amendment after the word "law" in the fifteenth line of the substitute that I offered to the original section, to insert:

"And shall be subject to be removed by the judge of the county or city having criminal jurisdiction, for wilful neglect of duty or misdemeanor in office, on conviction in a court of law."

The amendment was adopted.

The question recurred upon the adoption of the amendment moved by Mr. AUDOUN, as amended.

Mr. MILLER. As I understand it the only difference between the two is that in one case these officers are elected by the people, and in the other they are appointed by the county commissioners of the several counties, subject to removal by the judge on conviction in a court of law. The convention by a very decided vote, has just adopted the system of appointment instead of election by the people. I hope the convention will adhere to that vote, and let the original section stand as it now is.

Mr. THOMAS. In what respect have we so decided? We have not taken any vote upon that.

Mr. MILLER. By adopting the amendment of the gentleman from Calvert (Mr. Briscoe.)

Mr. THOMAS. Oh, no. I voted for that myself.

Mr. MILLER. I do not want to take away any of the power of the people. I am willing that the principle of election by the people should be carried out. But we have taken away from the people the election of road supervisors; and it seems to me that the selection of magistrates and constables should be placed in some appointing power rather than left in the hands of the people; because as it has been frequently stated here, men will go to the polls and mix up these little matters of road supervisors, constables and magistrates, with the election of the most important officers of the State. I think that to cut off one from the other would do more to prevent corruption in our elections than anything else we can possibly do. I hope we shall hold on to the amendment we have adopted, and the section as amended, and give the appointment to the county commissioners.

Mr. PURNELL. I indorse entirely what my friend from Anne Arundel (Mr. Miller) has said in this connection. The only difference, I understand, between the original section as amended, and the substitute, is that the original section provides for appointment instead of the elective system. While I have no disposition whatever to curtail the elective franchise, yet I do think in relation to these particular offices, it would be much better that they should be appointed than that they should be elected. I think it would insure the selection of better officers, without having that disturbing element of politics referred to so properly by the gentleman from Anne Arundel. I shall move at the proper time for a division of this question. I think while they should be appointed, I should prefer their appointment by the judges of the circuit court, who I think are better qualified to judge of the competency of the officers than perhaps the county commissioners would be. It often occurs that the judges of the circuit courts have to review the judgments of magistrates, and they are better qualified to judge of their qualifications than those who occupy different spheres, and who have not had their attention directed to that particular line of duties. Hence I think it is better that the magistrates should be appointed by the judges of the circuit court, and in the city of Baltimore by the concurrent action of the city courts there. So far as relates to constables, I think it would be better to have them appointed by county commissioners. While the county commissioners might not be so well qualified to judge of the qualifications of justices of the peace, they would be and are qualified to judge of the competency of constables. So that at the proper time I shall ask that this be modified, although I prefer appointment for both offices.

Mr. AUDOUN. If I understand what I was sent here for by the people who sent me here, I believe I was sent here as their servant, and not as their master. I believe that I was sent here for the purpose of voting for such measures as would best advance their interests. With regard to the magistracy, they are the men who are to execute the laws, and I believe the majority of my people intended that I should come here and vote for the elective system, because they desire to have an opportunity to select their own rulers. I believe that if the gentlemen from the counties will think for a moment what are the wants of their people, they will find that they are in the same situation with myself to-day.

Mr. STIRLING. I shall vote against this amendment, not because I have made up my mind against the election of justices, but because this amendment embraces both justices and constables; and I think that the present system of electing constables is perfectly absurd. In the first place the idea that the number of constables should correspond with the number of districts, is an absurdity upon its face. Some wards and some election districts may require a greater number of constables than others. The difficulty with us is that there are too many constables. It is not easy to get a good constable. To become a good constable a man must make a business of it. And the present system requires so many that men cannot get a living at it. There are more constables than there is a necessity for. We do not want forty-eight constables. There is no necessity for it. They cannot live; and the office very often goes begging. Men submit to put their names on the tickets more for amusement than anything else. Half of them if they are elected never serve at all. I have made up my mind to vote for the report of the committee as it stands; but I must say that it is so great an alteration that I am rather inclined to vote for election.

Mr. THOMAS. It occurs to me that the suggestion of the gentleman from Worcester (Mr. Purnell) is a very proper one, and that while it would be very proper for the people to elect the justices of the peace, it would be very proper to give to the county commissioners and the mayor and city council of the city of Baltimore, as they now have in case of vacancy, the power to appoint the constables, and also to diminish the number of constables; to allow the county commissioners and the mayor and city council of Baltimore to fix the number of constables required. In order to take the sense of the convention on that, I move to strike out of the section offered by my colleague (Mr. Audoun) the words "and constables" wherever they occur.

The amendment was rejected.

Mr. STOCKBRIDGE moved to amend the substitute by inserting the word "incompetency" before the words "wilful neglect of duty."

The amendment was agreed to.

The question recurred on Mr. AUDOUN'S amendment as amended.

Mr. DANIEL demanded the yeas and nays, and they were ordered.

Mr. HEBB. This provides that the general assembly shall fix the number, and that they are to be elected at the next general election thereafter, so that they will be elected two years from this fall.

Mr. DANIEL. I will suggest that it is of no use to amend it further until we see whether we want it or not. If we vote this down the appointive system stands as the system.

The question being taken, the result was—yeas 21; nays 38—as follows:

Yeas—Messrs. Annan, Audoun, Blackiston, Brooks, Cunningham, Davis, of Washington, Dellinger, Ecker, Hatch, Hoffman, Keefer, Kennard, Larsh, Morgan, Nyman, Sneary, Stockbridge, Swope, Thomas, Wickard, Wooden—21.

Nays—Messrs. Goldsborough, President; Abbott, Baker, Billingsley, Briscoe, Carter, Chambers, Daniel, Davis, of Charles, Duvall, Earle, Farrow, Galloway, Greene, Hebb, Hollyday, Hopkins, Hopper, King, Lee, McComas, Miller, Mullikin, Murray, Negley, Parker, Parran, Purnell, Russell, Schley, Scott, Smith, of Worcester, Stirling, Sykes, Todd, Turner, Valliant, Wilmer—38.

The substitute moved by Mr. AUDOUN was accordingly rejected.

Mr. DANIEL submitted the following amendment to section 37:

Strike out the words "justices of the peace and," and insert after the word "constables," "and the judges of the circuit courts of the several counties, and the judges of the court of common pleas and the criminal court of Baltimore city, such a number of justices of the peace."

Mr. THOMAS. Has not that already been decided by the convention?

The PRESIDENT. This question has been once voted upon, and cannot be offered again.

Mr. DANIEL. I think that the proposition was to appoint both constables and justices of the peace. I move so to amend that the county commissioners shall appoint the constables, and the judges the justices of the peace.

The PRESIDENT. That proposition has not been distinctly voted upon by the convention, and is in order.

On motion of Mr. PURNELL,

The convention took a recess until half-past 3 o'clock, P. M.

AFTERNOON SESSION.

The convention met at half-past three o'clock, P. M.

The roll was called, and the following members responded to their names:

Messrs. Goldsborough, President; Abbott, Abbott, Annan, Baker, Cushing, Davis, of Charles, Davis, of Washington, Dellinger, Dennis, Duvall, Earle, Ecker, Farrow, Greene,

Hebb, Hoffman, Hollyday, Hopkins, Hopper, Keefer, Lee, McComas, Morgan, Murray, Negley, Nyman, Parran, Purnell, Russell, Schley, Scott, Smith, of Worcester, Sneary, Stirling, Stockbridge, Swope, Sykes, Thomas, Turner, Wooden—41.

There being no quorum present,

Mr. FARROW moved a call of the convention;

The motion being sustained,

The roll was called, and the following members responded:

Messrs. Goldsborough, President; Abbott, Annon, Baker, Blackiston, Cushing, Davis, of Charles, Davis, of Washington, Dellinger, Dennis, Duvall, Earle, Ecker, Farrow, Greene, Hebb, Hoffman, Hollyday, Hopkins, Hopper, Keefer, Lee, McComas, Morgan, Murray, Negley, Nyman, Parran, Purnell. Russell, Schley, Scott, Smith, of Worcester, Sneary, Stirling, Stockbridge, Swope, Sykes, Thomas, Turner, Wooden—39.

On motion of Mr. FARROW,

The sergeant-at-arms was sent after the absent members, and was ordered by the president to remain at the cars until they should depart from the city.

The PRESIDENT stated that Mr. Brooks had been allowed leave of absence, and would be permitted to leave.

The roll was again called, and the following members responded:

Messrs. Goldsborough, President; Abbott, Annan, Audoun, Baker, Billingsley, Blackiston, Bond, Briscoe, Carter, Chambers, Cunningham, Cushing, Dail, Daniel, Davis, of Charles, Davis, of Washington, Dellinger, Dennis, Duvall, Earle, Ecker, Farrow, Galoway, Greene, Hatch, Hebb, Hoffman, Hollyday, Hopkins, Hopper, Keefer, Kennard, King, Larsh, Lee, Markey, McComas, Morgan, Mullikin, Murray, Negley, Nyman, Parker, Parran, Purnell, Russell, Schley, Scott, Smith, of Worcester, Sneary, Stirling, Stockbridge, Swope, Sykes, Thomas, Todd, Turner, Valliant, Wickard, Wooden—60.

Mr. BILLINGSLEY moved to dispense with further proceedings under the call.

The motion was rejected.

Mr. STIRLING moved to suspend further proceedings under the call.

Ruled out of order, the mace not being returned.

The sergeant-at-arms returned and reported that he had notified all the absentees he could find in the city.

On motion of Mr. STOCKBRIDGE,

Further proceedings under the call were dispensed with.

JUSTICES OF THE PEACE AND CONSTABLES.

The convention resumed the consideration of the report of the committee on the judiciary department on its second reading.

The pending section was the 37th, which was read as amended, as follows:

"Section 37. The county commissioners of the several counties of this State shall appoint in each election district of the several counties, and the mayor and city council of the city of Baltimore, shall appoint for the city of Baltimore such number of justices of the peace and constables as now are or hereafter may be fixed by the general assembly. They shall certify their appointment so made to the governor, by whom the appointees shall be commissioned as justices of the peace and constables of the State of Maryland, in and for ——— county and city. The justices so appointed and commissioned shall be conservators of the peace, shall hold their office for two years, and shall have such jurisdiction, duties and compensation, subject to such right of appeal as hath been heretofore exercised, or shall be hereafter prescribed by law, and shall be subject to removal by the judge of the county or city having criminal jurisdiction, for wilful neglect of duty or misdemeanor in office, on conviction in a court of law."

The pending question was on the amendment submitted by Mr. DANIEL, as follows:

Strike out the words "justices of the peace and," and insert after the word "constables," "and the judges of the circuit courts of the several counties, and the judges of the court of common pleas and the criminal court of Baltimore city, such a number of justices of the peace."

Mr. THOMAS. I hope before the convention votes upon this proposition that they will hesitate and think. The proposition of my colleague has just been rejected by this convention. They have voted that in no case will they allow the judge of the courts to appoint magistrates and constables. They have voted in lieu thereof that that power shall be exercised by the county commissioners of the counties, and the mayor and city council of Baltimore. Now the proposition comes back again to undo just what the convention has done, to give to the courts of the respective counties and of the city the power to appoint your magistrates. All I have to say in relation to this proposition is, that if you want to make the judges of your courts huckstering shops for the purpose of dealing out the offices of justice of the peace, using them for political capital, then give the judges of your courts the appointment of your magistrates, and thus degrade the judiciary of your State beneath anything heretofore attempted in the State of Maryland. What has been the whole argument of the gentlemen who have favored the appointment of your judiciary? It was to keep your judiciary as pure as it could be kept. Suppose you give to the judges of your courts the power to appoint your magistrates, what will be the result? In the city of Baltimore we have some thirty odd magistrates, two in some wards and one in the others. The moment you give that power to your judges, that moment you are going to have your political cliques and caucuses got together to go to your two judges and get them to appoint this man or that man to office. What else do you do? You have already put a provision into the constitution electing judges for fifteen years. This gives power to the judges after they are elected to keep men on the bench as magistrates for that length of time.

I say if there is any truth in the principle that all government originates of right from the people, and the people have exercised this power in electing their magistrates, with all the other officers elected under the constitution, you have no more right to take away from the people the right to elect their magistrates and their constables than you have to take away the right to elect their judges. Where is the difference? Your magistrate's courts sit in cases to range from one cent up to $100; and therefore are more intimately acquainted with the people of your State than the judges of your circuit courts. I venture to assert that nine-tenths of the cases tried in your State are tried before these very magistrates' courts. Still it is proposed to take this away from the people, and give that right to one man in a circuit composed of two counties in some cases, and in others of one; and to two judges in a population of 250,000 souls in the city of Baltimore.

I do not say that the judges now in power would not exercise the power rightfully. I believe they would. But gentlemen must understand that we are making a constitution for all time; and if you give the judges elected under it the power to appoint the magistrates, those magistrates may band together in certain cliques and caucuses and keep certain men in office. You cannot tell how far the principle is going to be carried, nor what corruption will be used in obtaining these offices. Our present judges are good, upright men; but it may turn out hereafter that we may have bad men in office. I am opposed to giving this power to the judges which of right belongs to the people. I am opposed to the amendment already adopted by this convention; but I take that as the less of two evils. The county commissioners are elected by the people once in every two years. The mayor and city council of the city of Baltimore are elected by the people once in every two years. And, therefore, coming fresh from the people, they are a great deal more capable of judging as to the qualifications of those who shall be appointed magistrates and constables in their respective wards and districts, than the judges of the circuit, elected from the counties at large. These are the views which will induce me to give my vote against this proposition.

Mr. Daniel. It seems that my colleague is not so much opposed to the appointment of magistrates by the judges as to the adoption of the appointive system at all. The whole force of his argument goes to the fact that all these officers should be elected by the people, and that we are destroying vital rights by taking this away. Every member knows that there is a very great difference of opinion about the appointment or election of all these officers, judges as well as others. As I said before, this convention has determined to elect the judges, while a great portion of the people had their hearts set on the appointment of the judges; that is to say, so far as I know, a vast portion of the people I talk with. Other gentlemen think otherwise. But that point has been yielded and decided by the convention. Now you propose, for the very lowest and smallest officers, not to gratify this other portion of the people at all, that they shall be elected by the people. You give these people no chance to come in, on any principle of compromise, and vote for your constitution and sustain it.

I believe further that more mischief arises from the election of constables and magistrates, than of judges, a great deal. It is these little offices that control. It is a sort of under current that controls. And the question of swapping off a low office for a higher one, frequently defeats a proper election for the more important offices. I shall not therefore undertake to reply to the remarks of my colleague with regard to the appointive and elective systems. I leave that to the convention to decide. They did decide by this amendment, as I understand it, by a very large vote, that they would not substitute the elective system for these officers for the appointive system.

As to my colleague's argument that little cliques will be formed to procure appointment by the judges, I suppose if the appointment is placed in the hands of anybody, county commissioners, the governor, or any other officers, there are people who will appeal to their friends to aid them in getting appointed. You cannot keep them from it. The same objection applies to anybody into whose hands you may put it. I wonder if these little cliques will not come around the mayor's office, if it is left in his hands. Will they not come around the county commissioners if it is left in their hands? I wonder whether they will be freer from improper influences than the judges of your courts, in the appointment of such officers. I think the judges, elected as they are, for fifteen years, would be placed far higher above all these little petty considerations. Their offices would not depend upon it at all. Their election would not depend upon it. They are in for fifteen years already. They have to review the decisions of the magistrates, and knowing these persons in the counties and in the city of Baltimore—because as we have re-districted the State, we have in many counties a judge for each county, and in small counties a judge for two counties;—they would be beyond the control of political influence far more than the mayor and city council of the city of Baltimore, or the county commissioners of the counties, who are elected every two years from the people, and who would be looking forward to the men whom they could make use of in their re-election.

I think too that it would add dignity and importance to the office of justice of the peace, if they were appointed by the court. And as we have already said that the county commissioners shall appoint the road supervisors, and as I propose to leave in this section the provision that they shall appoint the constables, I think that the appointment of road supervisors and constables will be a pretty good duty; and that we may as well divide the work of appointment a little, and give the judges of the courts the appointment of justices of the peace. I think that would work better every way.

Mr. NEGLEY submitted the following amendment to the amendment

Strike out "judges of the circuit court of the several counties, and the judges of the court of common pleas and the criminal court of Baltimore city," and insert "the governor by and with the advice and consent of the senate."

Mr. MILLER. I would like to ask the gentleman from Baltimore city (Mr Daniel) how he proposes that the two judges shall act in case they differ about the appointment. There are two men to make the appointment; and, if they differ no justice of the peace could be appointed.

There is a great deal of force in what the gentleman from Baltimore city has said with regard to the importance of having the appointments made free from all political interference; for a justice of the peace is very much such an office as that of judge. For that reason at a previous session of the convention I voted against the election of justices of the peace. The governor has had in former times the appointment of all justices of the peace in the State. It is not in derogation of that principle in our declaration of rights that all government of right originates in the people, that the governor should have the appointment of these officers, because that was in our old constitution of 1776, and has been in our constitution down to the present time. Our government has been a government of the people from the revolution down, notwithstanding the fact that some of the officers came from the governor. It is very right, I think, if we take it away from the county commissioners and give it to anybody else, that it should go back to what is known in this country as the appointing power, the executive branch of the government, by and with the advice and consent of the senate.

The amendment to the amendment was agreed to.

The question recurred on the amendment as amended.

Mr. NEGLEY moved to reconsider the vote by which Mr. AUDOUN's amendment was rejected.

The PRESIDENT. The vote must first be taken on the pending amendment.

Mr. THOMAS. Will it be in order to reconsider afterwards?

The PRESIDENT. Yes, sir. The question is now upon the amendment of the gentleman from Baltimore city (Mr. Daniel,) as amended, to the amendment of the gentleman from Calvert (Mr. Briscoe.)

Mr. STIRLING. This amendment is not an amendment to the amendment of the gentleman from Calvert; for it proposes to strike out from that amendment words which are not in it.

Mr. DANIEL. No; I proposed to strike out "justices of the peace."

Mr. BRISCOE. The amendment which I offered to the original section was carried. It then became a part of the original section. Now the proposition is to amend the section as amended by the adoption of my proposition.

The PRESIDENT. Yes, sir; the amendment is to that part of the section amended on motion of the gentleman from Calvert (Mr. Briscoe.)

Mr. MORGAN demanded the yeas and nays, and they were ordered.

The question being taken on Mr. DANIEL'S amendment as amended, the result was—yeas 32, nays 27—as follows:

Yeas—Messrs. Annan, Baker, Bond, Chambers, Cunningham, Cushing, Daniel, Davis, of Washington, Earle, Galloway, Greene, Hebb, Hollyday, Hopkins, Hopper, Lee, McComas, Miller, Mullikin, Murray, Nyman, Parker, Purnell, Russell, Schley, Scott, Smith, of Worcester, Sneary, Stirling, Swope, Sykes, Todd—32.

Nays—Messrs. Goldsborough, President; Abbott, Audoun, Billingsley, Blackiston, Briscoe, Carter, Dellinger, Duvall, Ecker, Farrow, Hatch, Hoffman, Keefer, Kennard, King, Larsh, Markey, Morgan, Negley, Parran, Stockbridge, Thomas, Turner, Valliant, Wickard, Wooden—27.

When their names were called,

Mr. CUNNINGHAM asked to be excused from voting. Not being excused, he voted "aye."

Mr. ECKER said: I do not care which way it goes. I am inclined to think we shall be under the necessity of employing an attorney at any rate to explain this particular clause in the constitution if we want to know what it means; and in order to save that ten dollar note which must go into somebody's pocket, I vote "no."

Mr. NEGLEY said: I vote against this section because I want to move a reconsideration of the substitute offered by the gentleman from Baltimore city (Mr. Audoun,) and have that perfected if possible. I therefore vote "no."

Mr. STOCKBRIDGE. I am not prepared to vote understandingly upon this, not having these amendments before us. They have become so complicated that I do not know what is right and what is wrong. Not knowing what to do, it is best perhaps to do nothing; and I therefore vote "no."

The amendment as amended was accordingly agreed to.

The question recurred upon the section as amended.

Mr. MILLER moved to strike out the following words:

"They shall certify their appointment so made to the governor, by whom the appointees shall be commissioned as justices of the peace of the State of Maryland, in and for ——— county and city."

Mr. HEBB. I would suggest to the gentleman to transpose these words. The governor is to appoint the magistrates and the county commissioners the constables. Then the appointment of the constables should be certified to the governor. If it is necessary for the governor to commission the justices of the peace, when appointed by the judges of the courts, I should suppose it would be necessary to commission the constables to be appointed by the county commissioners.

Mr. MILLER. As perfect a *non sequiter* as ever I heard. The county commissioners are required to appoint constables as they would appoint a collector or anybody else. The governor has nothing to do with commissioning them. The governor appoints the justices of the peace, and these he can commission. We do not want the constables commissioned.

The amendment was agreed to.

Mr. STOCKBRIDGE. The clause moved by the gentleman from Baltimore city (Mr. Thomas) was placed in this section in exactly the same form as in the substitute which was subsequently rejected. In the substitute the convention upon my motion inserted the word "incompetency," and I now move to insert that word in the original section before the word "wilful."

The PRESIDENT. The journal has gone to the printers; but it is the impression of the chair that that amendment was only moved to the substitute which was rejected; that it was not placed in the original section.

Mr. STOCKBRIDGE. Then I will move to insert that amendment including the word "incompetency" at the end of the section, as follows:

"And shall be subject to removal by the judge having criminal jurisdiction in the county or city, for incompetency, wilful neglect of duty, or misdemeanor in office, on conviction in a court of law."

Mr. BRISCOE. I move to amend the amendment by striking out the word "incompetency." I hold that justices of the peace should be placed as far above all influences and power as any other judge in the land. I see nowhere in the constitution of Maryland, or in any other State constitution that a judge is removable for incompetency. I think that so far as regards wilful neglect of duty, or malfeasance in office, or misbehavior, he should be removable for those causes. But the question of incompetency reaches the head and not the heart of the judge. It has been well said, God forbid that we should undertake to confer the power to punish a man for a defect of understanding. He may make a decision. and may be indicted for having made that decision, and from mere prejudice may be brought up for conviction, and upon the opinion of twelve men that he is incompetent to act as judge he may be removed from the office. I see no necessity for putting that word there, and I therefore move to strike it out.

Mr. STOCKBRIDGE. I almost regretted having moved the insertion of that word after I did so, for I was assured by some gentlemen that there would be no justices of the peace left in their counties if the amendment was adopted. But I wish to remind my friend from Calvert county (Mr. Briscoe) that this is nothing either unusual or unprecedented. The existing constitution of the State provides with reference to the judges of the court of appeals precisely the same ground for removal. It says:

"* * * as a judge of the said court of appeals who shall hold his office for the term of ten years from the time of his election, or until he shall have attained the age of seventy years, whichever may first happen, and be re-eligible thereto until he shall have attained the age of seventy years, and not after; subject to removal for incompetency, wilful neglect of duty, or misbehavior in office, on conviction in a court of law," &c.

The terms are precisely the same as in this amendment.

Mr. BRISCOE. I referred to the judges of the circuit court. I have that provision before me, and it does not apply to them at any rate.

The amendment to the amendment was rejected.

The amendment was agreed to.

Mr. STIRLING moved to amend by inserting before the last amendment the words "justices of the peace and constables so appointed."

The amendment was agreed to.

Mr. HEBB moved that the section be transposed to read as follows:

"Sec. 37. The governor by and with the

advice and consent of the senate shall appoint such number of justices of the peace, and the county commissioners of the several counties, and the mayor and council of the city of Baltimore shall appoint such number of constables for the several election districts of the counties and wards of the city of Baltimore as are now or may hereafter be prescribed by law, and justices of peace and constables so appointed shall be subject to removal by the judge having criminal jurisdiction in the county or city, for incompetency, wilful neglect of duty, or misdemeanor in office, on conviction in a court of law. The justices of the peace and constables so appointed and commissioned shall be conservators of the peace, shall hold their office for two years, and shall have such jurisdiction, duties and compensation subject to such right of appeal as hath been heretofore exercised, or shall be hereafter prescribed by law."

The amendment was agreed to.

The question was stated upon the adoption of the section as amended.

Mr. THOMAS demanded the yeas and nays, and they were ordered.

The question being taken, the result was—yeas 38, nays 19—as follows:

Yeas—Messrs. Goldsborough, President; Abbott, Annan, Audoun, Baker, Bond, Chambers, Cunningham, Cushing, Daniel, Earle, Farrow, Galloway, Greene, Hatch, Hebb, Hollyday, Hopkins, Hopper, Lee, Markey, McComas, Miller, Mullikin, Murray, Nyman, Purnell, Russell, Schley, Scott, Smith, of Worcester, Stirling, Stockbridge, Swope, Sykes, Thomas, Todd, Valliant—38.

Nays—Messrs. Billingsley, Blackiston, Briscoe, Davis, of Washington, Duvall, Ecker, Hoffman, Keefer, Kennard, King, Larsh, Morgan, Negley, Parker, Parran, Sneary, Turner, Wickard, Wooden—19.

When his name was called,

Mr. THOMAS said: For the purpose of moving a reconsideration I vote "aye."

The section as amended was accordingly adopted.

Mr. TODD. I move that the convention adjourn.

Mr. MILLER. I move that the order providing for three sessions a day be rescinded. Our experience this afternoon has shown that we cannot get along without the journal before us. When we take a recess the journal goes into the hands of the printers.

Mr. STOCKBRIDGE. There are but two more sections in this report. It will take us but a few minutes to dispose of them.

Mr. THOMAS. I move that the convention take a recess.

The question being taken upon the motion to take a recess, it was rejected.

Mr. CHAMBERS. I ask for an explanation of the ruling upon the order about the adjournment. We have voted in every sort of way about adjournment. We have voted to adjourn from Friday to Monday in defiance of the order. We have voted to adjourn from one morning to the next morning in defiance of the order, and now I understand that the chair refuses to receive a motion to adjourn in consequence of the order.

The PRESIDENT. No, sir. The gentleman from Kent misunderstands. There were two motions pending—one to adjourn, carrying the convention over to to-morrow morning, and the other to take a recess, carrying the convention over until eight o'clock this evening. The latter motion the chair regarded as a privileged question, being in accordance with the order adopted by the house, and therefore took the vote on that question.

Mr. BRISCOE. I move that the convention adjourn.

Mr. STIRLING. What effect will that have?

The PRESIDENT. It will carry us over until to-morrow.

Mr. STIRLING. Is that in order?

The PRESIDENT. Yes, sir.

Mr. DANIEL. I thought that when we had solemnly adopted an order it had to be rescinded by another order.

The PRESIDENT. It is not a standing order of the house. The order is a determination of the house to hold three sessions a day. The house can now determine otherwise. The order is operative only so long as it is the pleasure of the house.

Mr. DANIEL. Can it be departed from by a mere motion?

The PRESIDENT. A motion to adjourn is equivalent to a motion to suspend the order for to-day and to adjourn. If the house desires to hold three sessions to-day it can do so.

Mr. MORGAN. I ask leave to offer an order.

Mr STOCKBRIDGE. Is that in order?

The PRESIDENT. Not without a suspension of the rules.

Several members objected.

Mr. DANIEL. Has not the chair decided that a motion to adjourn simply took us over to the evening session?

The PRESIDENT. Yes, sir. But the chair was in error at that time. A motion to adjourn is always in order, and it will take the house over until to-morrow morning.

Mr. ABBOTT. What becomes of the order to hold an evening session if the house adjourns?

The PRESIDENT. It is suspended *pro tanto*, only for that evening. It does not prevent the operation of the order to-morrow. It still stands to-morrow just as operative as it is to-day. To rescind the order would require a notice of one day.

Mr. DANIEL. I give notice that if the motion to adjourn shall be voted down, I shall move to take a recess until eight o'clock.

Mr. HEBB. I move that the convention now take a recess.

Mr. VALLIANT. We have just voted that down only five minutes ago.

The PRESIDENT. The motion to take a recess is a privileged question, being in conformity with the order of the house. The motion to adjourn having intervened, the motion to take a recess can be renewed.

The motion was agreed to—ayes 32, noes 28.

The convention accordingly took a recess until 8 o'clock, P. M.

EVENING SESSION.

The convention met at 8 o'clock, P. M.

The roll was called, and the following members answered to their names.

Messrs. Goldsborough, President; Abbott, Annan, Audoun, Baker, Carter, Cunningham, Cushing, Daniel, Davis, of Washington, Dellinger, Earle, Ecker, Farrow, Galloway, Greene, Hatch, Hebb, Hoffman, Hollyday, Hopkins, Hopper, Keefer, Kennard, King, Larsh, Markey, McComas, Mullikin, Murray, Negley, Nyman, Parker, Pugh, Purnell, Russell, Sands, Schley, Scott, Smith, of Worcester, Sneary, Stirling, Stockbridge, Swope, Sykes, Thomas, Todd, Valliant, Wickard, Wooden—50.

JUDICIARY DEPARTMENT.

The convention resumed the consideration of the report of the committee on the judiciary department, which was on its second reading.

The next section was read as follows:

PART VII.

Sheriffs, &c.

"Section 38. There shall be elected in each county and the city of Baltimore, in every second year, one person resident in said county or city, above the age of twenty-five years, and at least five years preceding his election a citizen of this State, to the office of sheriff. He shall hold his office for two years and until his successor is duly qualified, and shall be ineligible for two years thereafter, shall give such bond, exercise such powers, and perform such duties as now are or may hereafter be fixed by law. In case of a vacancy by death, refusal to serve or neglect to qualify or give bond, by disqualification or removal from the county or city, the circuit court shall appoint a person to be sheriff for the remainder of the official term."

Mr. THOMAS. I move to strike out in the sixth line the words "and shall be ineligible for two years thereafter." The object of that amendment is to bring up the question whether sheriffs shall be eligible or ineligible to re-election. It seems to me that there is no necessity for this clause in the constitution any longer. I hold that the reason of it, at the time it was introduced, was, that the sheriffs of the several counties were collectors of the taxes; and it was therefore very proper that they should be ineligible. Now the sheriffs are not collectors of taxes; and about the time the sheriff begins to understand his duty this requires him to go out of office. If the people find that they have got a good sheriff, after two years service, I think they ought to have the power to re-elect him if they think proper.

The amendment was agreed to.

Mr. NEGLEY moved to amend by striking out "two" in the fifth line, and inserting "four."

Mr. SCHLEY. I hope the convention will not hastily adopt these changes. It seems to me that they are very important. It seems to me that to strike out "two" and insert "four," and to strike out "and shall be ineligible for two years thereafter," which has been done, but I did not imagine it would be done or I should have spoken upon it before, are important changes. For a long time this has been the custom in this State, and why it should be changed now, I am at a loss to conjecture. I hope before this is acted upon some further consideration will be given to it. For myself I shall oppose this amendment.

Mr. SANDS. I agree entirely with the sentiments expressed by the gentleman from Frederick (Mr. Schley,) and I will state very valid reasons that ought to commend themselves to the judgment of this body. If it were proper to do so I would also suggest to some gentlemen who voted for it, reasons why, upon mature deliberation they should move a reconsideration of the vote agreeing to the motion of the gentleman from Baltimore city, by which this section has already been amended. The reason for that clause being incorporated in the section originally was not merely that sheriffs were collectors of taxes. I know of no office in which a man can wield more political power than as sheriff of your city or county. From the nature of his official duties, he wields such a tremendous power over the people that he can exercise more influence over the community at large than the judge on the bench or any other officer of the State. I believe that this interval between the terms of a sheriff was provided, simply that they might be deprived of the power of holding the rod over any man's head about election time, saying, "I will make my levy, or I will hold on and will not make my levy; what will you do on an election day?"

Another reason, which is a very strong one. We know that the disease of sheriff's indulging the people, even when there is to be an interval of terms, has grown to be chronic. How many sheriffs in the State of Maryland ever complete their business up to the end of their two years—sheriffs or collectors either? Is it not a matter of public notoriety how much the sureties of sheriffs all over the State have suffered from their dereliction. It is true that now and then you find a punctual man, who at the end of his sheriffalty, will be able to settle up his business But where you find one such man, I will venture to assert it as a fact known to many members of this body, you will find a score that are just the reverse. Now if you lengthen this term, and make the sheriff believe that instead of squaring up at the end of two years he can wait for four years, the interests of the public are immeasurably made to suffer, because you have taken away the spur to urge him to the discharge of his duties.

I have had an opportunity, as many other gentlemen have had, of watching this, and seeing its practical operation. And I say that for the good of the community, in the respects to which I have alluded, this office, so powerful over the people, should be cut off from politics as much as possible; and the officer holding that position should be cut off as much as possible from the power of using his office for his own individual benefit. That I believe to have been the true and the real reason why, when the constitution was framed, and in all our previous practice, we have required an interregnum, so that the man who was executing the writs of your court, might not have it in his power to hold them in his hands as rods over the heads of other men, and say to them, "How will you vote to-morrow, or the next day, or at the next election? I am a candidate again, and I can indulge you. I will either indulge you or press the matter according as I am satisfied what will be your action." I suggest this for the reflection of gentlemen. I do trust they will give these matters that serious and earnest attention which they so pre-eminently deserve.

This is not a mere question whether a man shall hold an office for two years or four, or whether he shall be re-eligible or not; but it is the question how to protect the public against the improper use of the offices of the State; how to protect them against the abuse that will inevitably grow out of the long term of the office of sheriff. These are very grave considerations. I have really concluded in my own mind, since I have heard this matter talked about, that we could do scarcely anything more deleterious to the public, more dangerous to the very men themselves who hold these offices, than to lengthen the term to any extent, or to make them immediately re-eligible. These are some of the views I entertain on the subject, and I would like that the matter should be well weighed before it is voted upon.

Mr. Thomas I must confess that I do not see this as the gentleman from Howard (Mr. Sands) does. The same reasons which influence his mind to oppose the re-election of sheriffs induced me to vote in favor of this amendment. The gentleman conjures up in his imagination that if a sheriff is re-eligible to office, having in his hands a great number of executions, and papers of that kind, he will go to the men against whom the executions are issued, and threaten them that if they do not go to the polls at the next election and vote for him he will levy his executions. The gentleman knows as well as I do that the sheriff of the city or county is a mere executory officer.

Mr. Sands (in his seat.) I know that.

Mr. Thomas. When a writ is issued in court and put into the hands of a sheriff to execute it, he is bound to execute that writ within a certain number of days, or he is mulct in damages. Is there a sheriff who will go to the debtor and say, "I have an execution against you which I will levy if you don't go to the polls and vote for me," when he has the provision of law staring him in the face that he may be brought up before the court of justice for malfeasance in office, if he does not levy?

Mr. Sands. I did not intend to be understood to argue that he would go to the man's face and say these things to him.

Mr. Thomas. How will he get his vote without going to him?

Mr. Sands. There are plenty of ways to make a man feel it without saying it.

Mr. Thomas. I suggest that if he keeps his execution in a pigeon hole and says nothing about it at all, it would not have much influence in getting him re elected. He must have some influence over him by that execution, to make the gentleman's argument good; and I say that the sheriff dare not do it because the law says he shall not do it. The law compels him to return his execution in a certain time. If he returns *nullum bonum* as a reason for not making a levy, and if it is a false return, if he returns that there were no goods when there were goods, he is responsible on his bond. Therefore I do not see that the re-eligibility of the sheriff is to have any of the bad effects prophesied of by the gentleman from Howard.

It appears to me that when the people have a right to elect an officer, if he turns out to be a good officer, this interregnum of two years in which the people cannot re-elect him is utter nonsense. Besides, he can be elected at the end of the next two years, after having served two years and there has been an interval of two years; and he can make the same promises, "I will not serve these executions if you will vote for me two years hence;" and the argument has the same force to prevent his being re-eligible at the end of two years as to prevent his being re-eligible immediately upon the expiration of his first term.

Mr. Negley. I cannot see the force of the reasoning of the gentleman from Howard (Mr. Sands.) I am opposed to these extremely short terms of office in any case, because the incumbent scarcely gets warm in his position, scarcely gets familiar with the duties of his office, before his term expires. I cannot see how this is to prevent the settling up of the sheriff's accounts. I am satisfied that if you were to abbreviate his term still more, and instead of putting in the sheriff for two years, were to put him in for six months, so that instead of having one sheriff appointed for two years you would have four sheriffs appointed in the same length of time, it would not facilitate the settlement of the accounts. If you make it four years, instead of having two sheriffs appointed in four years, you will have only one.

As to the clause to prevent re-election, I think it is hardly necessary to put it there, for this reason. I have scarcely ever known any disposition in our county to re-elect a sheriff, and I have never known a sheriff to be re-elected or re-appointed. I do think that is not much of an evil, if it is an evil.

I do not think any bad result will follow from extending his office for four years. We have lengthened the term of a good many other officers, and I do not see why we should not this. As to the terrible, tremendous, overwhelming, and irresistible influence of the sheriff, of the exercise of which the gentleman from Howard speaks, I cannot conceive of it. It exists more in the fertile imagination of the gentleman than in the actual fact. I cannot conceive what terrible, crushing influence he can exercise as an executive officer in any case. I do not want to revolutionize society, or overturn its foundations, or endanger public justice. Not at all. Yet the gentleman speaks as though it were something terrible to lengthen his term of office. I do not so think.

Mr. Stirling. I shall certainly vote against this amendment. I certainly think this is bad enough as it is, and I shall not vote to make it worse. It strikes me that the provision in the constitution, which has been there for so long a period of time, must have been put there for some reason. Sheriffs have been elected before any other subordinate officer, way back for a period of thirty or forty years past; elected by the people. Yet in every constitution this same provision has been retained of election for two years, and forbidding re-election. That alone carries with it the conviction that there must have been some reason for it. The position taken by the gentleman from Howard (Mr. Sands,) it seems to me, is not entitled to be treated as a matter of imagination at all. A sheriff has power distinct from everybody else. He may have writs of execution, on the person or property of three or four hundred citizens of the county.—What sort of a man is that to go before the people for re-election, with a large part of the voters of the county subject to his control, when he can put them in jail or sell their property at auction? It strikes me that that provision was put into the constitution because it was thought it was not fair to give a man that power, allowing him to put himself up as a candidate for office; it was because of the temptation to the sheriff constantly to exercise his office for his own immediate emolument. The powers and influences of the other officers are indirect powers to a very great extent; but this is an absolute, fixed, definite, personal control over A, B and C.

It is of no use to say that the sheriff is bound to make a return in a certain number of days. It is a fact that he does not make it in a certain number of days. They are often allowed to grant time, and are often instructed by the persons who have the judgments to obtain money by compromise. Nobody complained of the constitution as it stood. It was a part of the constitution of 1836, and of the constitution of 1850, and I heard no complaint about it. I certainly see no reason why we should extend the term beyond two years. It will not be a popular provision.—Certainly when the sheriff has been in two years making money, there are plenty of people who want him to give way to somebody else. Certainly some sheriffs make an independent fortune out of the office; and there is no reason for continuing them in it.

Mr. Schley. Before the convention votes on this amendment I should like to call their attention to what has been the practice in this State. Not dreaming that such a thing would be proposed here, I am not prepared to give all the reasons for the law as it now stands. I find, on referring to the constitution of 1776, that the sheriff was elected every third year in this State. So that we had a term of three years, which, when we came to reform the constitution in 1850, was deemed to be too long a period. In both constitutions the disqualification for the succeeding term was incorporated in the organic law.—I am sure the convention must admit the validity of the reasons adduced by the gentlemen from Howard (Mr. Sands) and Baltimore city (Mr. Stirling) in behalf of retaining this qualification. I hope some gentleman who voted in the affirmative upon that proposition will move its reconsideration presently.

From three years the term was reduced to two. I have never heard any one complain that that term was too brief. In my own experience, in my own county, I find that every incumbent of that office has made a fortune for himself in two years. I say a "fortune," which is a comparative term. I have never known a man within my recollection, to retire from the office of sheriff, in Frederick county, after serving in it for two years, with less than seven thousand dollars clear earnings; and I have heard that it has ranged up as high as twenty thousand. I regard either of these sums as a fortune. I have not heard any reason why the term should be prolonged to four years; but I can very well conceive reasons why it should be limited to two. If there were no other reason, the very fact that there is no apparent necessity for prolonging the time of which there is no complaint is sufficient to induce me to vote for retaining the present term of two years.

Mr. DANIEL. I wish to express my approbation of what has been so well said by the gentleman from Howard, as well as the gentlemen from Baltimore city and Frederick.—If we look at deputy sheriffs who expect to be elected as sheriffs at the next term, and a great many of them are electioneering for it, there is a temptation to these men very frequently not to make their collections as they ought to do. I think the same reason would operate as well as the reasons which have been assigned, upon the sheriffs; that there would be every inducement for them to delay their executions, if they have held out to them by these very men from whom they are to collect, that they will support them at the next election.

In addition to that, this office is a very remunerative one in every county and the city of Baltimore; because in nearly every county, if not in every county, they have the taxes to collect in addition to the regular amount of the sheriff's duties. This makes it an important office. Not only the sheriffs themselves are interested in this, but their bondsmen. I apprehend that if you prolong the term to four years, and put the collection of taxes in the hands of the sheriff, he will find it very difficult, for a term of four or eight years, to get bondsmen. My experience is that nearly every sheriff in the State comes here and asks additional time to make his collections after he has gone out of office. Hardly a sheriff finishes up his work without asking additional time. And yet you propose to put him in another term, and to make the term four years.

It is a significant fact that where the sheriff is appointed, he is appointed annually; showing that there is some good reason for making the term short; and the reason is this, that they should make up their collections, and relieve their bondsmen, and go out of office for a term; and then if they have been good sheriffs they can be put in again.

The amendment was rejected.

On motion of Mr. McCOMAS, (seconded by Messrs. ANNAN and ABBOTT,)

The vote by which the amendment submitted by Mr. THOMAS was adopted, was reconsidered.

The question recurring upon the adoption of the amendment submitted by Mr. THOMAS, to strike out the words "and shall be ineligible for two years thereafter,"

It was rejected; leaving the section as reported by the committee.

No further amendment was offered.

The next section was read as follows:

Section 39. Coroners, elisors and notaries public may be appointed for each county and the city of Baltimore, in the manner, for the purposes, and with the powers now fixed or which may hereafter be prescribed by law.

No amendment was offered.

Mr. HEBB submitted the following amendment:

At the end of the twelfth section insert:

"The present chief justice and associate justices of the court of appeals shall continue to act as such until the expiration of the term for which they were respectively elected, and until their successors are elected and qualified; and an election for a judge of the court of appeals, to be taken from the fourth judicial district shall be held on Tuesday next after the first Monday of November, eighteen hundred and sixty-four."

The amendment was adopted.

Mr. HEBB submitted the following amendment:

Insert as an additional section the following:

"Section 24. In case of the death, resignation, removal or other disqualification of a judge of an orphans' court, the governor, by and with the advice and consent of the senate, shall appoint a person duly qualified to fill said office for the residue of the term thus made vacant."

The PRESIDENT. It is my impression that a provision of that sort has been already adopted.

Mr. HEBB. No, sir; not for the orphans' court. This is to provide for filling a vacancy in the orphans' court.

Mr. THOMAS. On page 535 of the journal the gentleman will find that a section submitted by myself was adopted:

"Mr. THOMAS submitted the following amendment:

"Insert as an additional section the following:

"Section 24. In case of the death, resignation, removal or other disqualification of a judge by the courts of this State, the governor, by and with the advice and consent of the senate, shall thereupon appoint a person duly qualified to fill said office until the next general election for members to the general assembly thereafter, at which time an election shall be held as herein prescribed, for a judge who shall hold said office for the term of fifteen years, and until the election and qualification of his successor."

"Decided in the affirmative."

Mr. HEBB. That provides for a judge to be elected for fifteen years. I hardly suppose we want a judge of the orphans' court to be elected for fifteen years.

Mr. SCHLEY. I will call the attention of the convention to a clause in the article on the executive department, authorizing the governor to appoint, by and with the advice and consent of the senate, all civil and military officers whose appointment or election is not otherwise herein provided for, unless a different mode shall be prescribed by the law creating the office. I see however that that does not apply to vacancies.

Mr. SANDS. I will suggest merely that our work may be symmetric and systematic, that this should more properly come in between the twenty-fifth and twenty sixth sections.—The first section creates the orphans' court and the second section defines its jurisdiction; and it seems to me more proper that we should there provide for vacancies.

Mr. HEBB. The committee on revision can arrange that.

The amendment was adopted.

On motion of Mr. STOCKBRIDGE,

The further consideration of the report was postponed until to-morrow.

THE MILITIA.

On motion of Mr. STOCKBRIDGE,

The convention proceeded to the consideration of the report of the committee on the militia and military affairs, which was on its second reading.

The first section was read as follows:

"Section 1. The militia shall be composed of all able-bodied male citizens, residents of this State, being eighteen years of age, and under the age of forty-five years, who shall be enrolled in the militia, and perform military duty in such manner not incompatible with the constitution and laws of the United States, as may be prescribed by the general assembly of Maryland."

Mr. RUSSELL submitted the following amendment:

Section 1. Add at the end, "but persons whose religious opinions or conscientious scruples forbid them to bear arms shall be relieved from doing so on producing to the proper authorities satisfactory proof that they are thus conscientious."

Mr. AUDOUN. I beg leave to call the attention of my friend to the second section of the minority report, which provides for the class of persons to whom he alludes. It is this:

"Sec. 2. Persons whose religious opinions or conscientious scruples forbid them to bear arms shall not be compelled to do so in time of peace, but shall pay an equivalent for such personal service."

Mr. PUGH. There is nothing there to provide for producing satisfactory proof.

Mr. RUSSELL. The object of the amendment I have introduced was to relieve a class of persons who are conscientiously opposed to bearing arms. They have heretofore under former laws of the State, with the exception of the militia law passed by the last legislature, had that privilege. There is a class of persons in this State that are really and truly conscientious against bearing arms, and it is for their relief that I have offered this amendment. It is not for the benefit of those who would counterfeit peace principles or manufacture them for the occasion. It is for those who truly entertain peace principles, and who have heretofore been relieved under former laws or constitutional enactments, and for them only that I have offered this amendment. It has been very carefully drawn up, so as to require the production of satisfactory proof that they are thus conscientious, and would not include those who are conscientiously opposed to this war in preference to any other, but only those who are really and truly conscientious with regard to all war.

Mr. SCHLEY moved to amend the amendment by adding the words "in time of peace, but shall pay such equivalent for military service as the general assembly may prescribe."

Mr. RUSSELL. That will destroy the whole object I had in view. They cannot render any equivalent at all. You may as well let the whole thing go, as to incorporate that amendment.

Mr. STIRLING. I hope that amendment will not be adopted. The law of this State as it stood previous to the adoption of the act of the last session exempted the Society of Friends from bearing arms; and it has been a provision that has been inserted in most of the militia laws of this State. There are in this State a large number of persons belonging to the Society of Friends, and the society of people called Dunkers, who are sincerely conscientious upon this subject. There is no good to be accomplished by forcing them to bear arms, and a vast amount of harm might be done by requiring them to do it. The amendment which proposes a commutation is not right. If it is right that they should bear arms they should be made to bear arms. If they have conscientious scruples against bearing arms, I suppose they will be equally strong against paying a commutation for the service. It is a serious matter for the friends of the constitution to settle. It is not improper for me to state that the entire body of the people who desire to be protected in their religious scruples by the amendment of the gentleman from Harford (Mr. Russell) are friends of this constitution; and their religious prejudices, feelings, or wishes, ought to be consulted for that reason if for no other. I am therefore both from policy and from principle desirous that the amendment of the gentleman from Harford should prevail. It may possibly require some changes; but I think that substantially as it is it ought to be passed. I should prefer that the word "religious" should be inserted before "conscientious." Will the secretary read the amendment offered to the section by the gentleman from Harford?

The secretary read the amendment.

Mr. STIRLING. I think that is all right; and I hope that amendment will be adopted.

Mr. SCHLEY. I think that every citizen is bound to bear arms in time of war; but I see the force of the objection made by the gentleman from Baltimore city (Mr. Stirling,) and knowing that the object I have in view is attained by the federal law, I withdraw the amendment that I offered.

Mr. SANDS. I will suggest that in its present form the amendment will not only exempt persons whose faith has always heretofore exempted them, but being in the disjunctive, "whose religious opinions or conscientious scruples forbid them to bear arms," it will take in all people all over the State who are conscientiously opposed to bearing arms.

Mr. STIRLING. They have got to prove it.

Mr. SANDS. I saw a case of this sort in the court room. A gentleman came in and was put upon the witness' stand. The judge said, "Swear him." "No, sir; I do not swear; I affirm." "Are you a Quaker?" Well, he laughed and said he was a kind of one. "Are you in full standing in the Quaker church?" "No, sir." He had married a Catholic lady and could not say he was. "Swear him," said the judge. I am perfectly willing that those belonging to religious societies, who have professed and whose fathers before them professed conscientious scruples against bearing arms, should be exempted; but I think it would better be done by name. If you put in this amendment "religious opinions or conscientious scruples" you will have nine-tenths——

Mr. STIRLING. If the gentleman will allow me, I move to strike out "or" and insert "and."

Mr. RUSSELL. I accept that amendment.

Mr. SANDS. I know that these people and their fathers have always held this faith and borne their testimony against arms-bearing; and I want to see them relieved; although I very much admired the spirit of the Quaker gentleman in a village store who was aiding in raising a cavalry company, and who, when reproached with violating his peace principles, said, "Well, brother, I have declined until after the war." I admired that Quaker.

Mr. ECKER. That story sounds very doubtful, because they do not generally call each other "brother." They do not use that term at all.

I hope the amendment of the gentleman from Harford will pass. The people up in our section are very much interested in the matter. We have some Friends there. We have a good many there who are conscientious in the matter; and we do not ask anything excepting of those who are really conscientious, and who can prove that fact before the proper authorities. I know a case that I will cite, as the gentleman has cited one. A young man about the time the draft was going on, wanted to be exempted, and said, "I am conscientious about this; I belong to the Dunker church." "But you are not a member of the Society of Friends; and we cannot do anything for you." He had been a full member of the Dunker church and was really conscientious; and there was an effort made to exempt him. If any member is not conscientious on the subject, of course it will be known to the society. It will be known by the society to which they belong whether they are conscientious or not. That is as far as we want to go. I have the honor of being a kind of birthright Friend myself, although I do not object to fighting in this war.

Mr. PUGH. The principal reason why I am in favor of the amendment of the gentleman from Harford is because it makes a distinction between the members of the same religious body. There are a great many Quakers who are not conscientiously opposed to bearing arms, and I have no doubt it was for that reason that the gentleman from Harford drew up his amendment in this form. It might have been proper to exempt the whole class of people called Quakers, and the whole class of people called Dunkers; but there are whole regiments of men now in the armies, who have been Quakers, and who are Quakers in all other respects except so far as this war is concerned. They had no conscientious scruples about going into this fight. And there is no religious society better represented in this war, so far as Pennsylvania is concerned, than the religious society of Quakers. This amendment is only to exempt those who even in this war still feel it their duty to bear the testimony the society has always borne against all wars at all times.

Mr. AUDOUN. I should be perfectly willing to vote for the amendment offered by my friend from Harford, if he would insert this language:

"Persons whose religious opinions or conscientious scruples forbid them to bear arms, shall not be compelled to do so in time of war, but shall pay an equivalent for such personal service."

While these gentlemen do not desire to enter into military service, I should like to see them willing to do something to assist the government.

Mr. PUGH. Will the gentleman permit me to explain? If they were to pay an equivalent, it would only be a public acknowledgment of their cowardice. It is not because they are cowards. They have given positive evidence that they are not. It is not that being unwilling to expose their precious bodies they will pay for exemption. That would be an acknowledgment that they are cowards. It is not because they are afraid; but these men are conscientiously opposed to bearing arms; and if they were not they would certainly go and fight.

Mr. AUDOUN. Then I desire to ask the gentleman one question. Do they desire to be exempt from military service, and exempt from paying for carrying on this war, and yet do they desire to be protected by this government and to exercise all the rights of a citizen under it?

Mr. PUGH. They pay all their taxes.

Mr. AUDOUN. Why should they have more protection than others?

Mr. NEGLEY. I cannot see the justice of this proposed distinction among our citizens. Suppose all the men in Maryland were to be of the denominations of Quakers, Dunkers, and Menonists. What becomes of your military law? Would there be any men to bear arms in this State in case of an invasion? The State of Maryland might be overrun and trodden under foot, and there would not be a citizen within its borders to lift his arm in its defence. I cannot conceive why any class of men should ask to be exempt. Is it not a part of morals that a man's first duty is to his God, his second to his country, and his last to himself? Why then should this distinction be made? If you exonerate one class of religious people, why should not you excuse other classes? I say that individual scrupulousness has not a right to come into opposition to the law. If your country has a right to demand your services, it is your bounden duty to pay it; and no man has a right to interpose individual scruples against the demands of his country. If the State of Maryland has a right, moral and political, to demand of its citizens military service, no individual, I care not what his religious opinions may be, has a right to interpose these scruples between the proper performance of his duty and his State. I do not concede the principle that it is at all right. It has been done in the past; but the federal government do not recognize this and never will recognize it.

Mr. STIRLING. The gentleman is entirely incorrect in his fact, for the last enrolment does recognize it.

Mr. NEGLEY. Does the constitution of the United States recognize it?

Mr. STIRLING. No, sir; the constitution of the United States does not say anything about it.

Mr. NEGLEY. Does the present draft recognize it?

Mr. STIRLING. Yes, sir; the present draft does.

The PRESIDENT. They have to pay a commutation.

Mr. STIRLING. No, sir; he is to perform no duty excepting to attend to the sick in the hospital. That is the law now.

Mr. SCHLEY. They pay a commutation and that is set apart as a separate fund.

Mr. STIRLING. That is the former act.

Mr. SCHLEY. No, sir; that is the provision in the present draft. I am the receiver of commutation money in Frederick county, and these are my instructions.

Mr. PUGH. They pay commutation for a purpose, and that purpose is the hospital and not the army. That is what they pay the money for. It is not paying an equivalent for bearing arms, but only for hospital purposes.

Mr. NEGLEY resumed: That is a distinction without a difference. It is for hospital purposes. I wonder if it is not for the army—for the wounded soldiers of the army. You may as well give it for the purposes of the army as for anything else. Still I do not concede that the principle is right to the rest of the citizens of the State. I respect their conscientious scruples. I say that there is not a more deserving class of citizens in the State. But I have always doubted, and I always will doubt the principle, whether it is right that that class of citizens should have the right to demand exemption from the performance of the duties of citizens in any direction. They live under our government. They receive its protection. I think it is a duty in correct morals, a religious duty that they owe, to be dutiful to "the powers that be," to "render unto Cæsar the things that are Cæsar's;" and that includes the proper discharge of the individual duty to the government if it means anything at all. I have always doubted the propriety of granting to a part of the State this exemption from military duty; because if the government has a right to claim the obedience and military service of any portion of its citizens, it has certainly *cetens paribus*, an equal right to claim the services of all its citizens. And if the government releases any portion of its citizens from military duty, on the same principle it ought to release all. For one, on strict political principles, I cannot vote for it.

Mr CUSHING. While I would not deny. that the views of the gentleman from Washington have a great deal in them at first sight, because there is a strong feeling with most of us that all classes of men in a time of public danger should do their part toward the common defence, yet I think that upon the question of expediency alone it might be well for gentlemen to consider whether the services of men conscientiously opposed to bearing arms, who have for many years of history suffered oppression and suffered death rather than to resort to defending themselves by arms, if forced into your military service, would avail anything. Would not they be merely men taken to the slaughter? They are men forbidden by what they believe to be a high religious principle, by what they think to be, as the gentleman from Washington county put it, their first duty, their duty to their God, from bearing arms; believing the bearing of arms to be inconsistent with their duty to their God. Would they not be merely inefficient soldiers, men taken into your military ranks simply to be slaughtered?

There is no question but these men have not only in this war, but in all previous wars done much for the cause of the country, though they have not borne arms. They have given of their money cheerfully and without stint. They have been found wherever you go, visiting our hospitals, caring for the wounded and sick soldiers; they have been found working for the good of those who have been wounded in the common defence, and aiding the widows and orphans who have been deprived of their protectors by the fortunes of war. Their position is not a new one. If it were a thing brought here to-day for the purpose of escaping the disastrous effects of this war, in their own person, the argument that every citizen ought to aid in the common defence, would be good and unanswerable. But when we find that these people have segregated themselves from the world upon that main ground that they conscientiously believed that the triumph of the doctrines of their denomination and of pure religion was a work of moral means and not of force; when we find that they have taken as one great theory of their religious views that the time of the millenium, so to speak, upon the earth, is to be brought about by abstaining from all contentions by arms; when we find that they have passed through all cases of tyranny merely by moral quiescent force, *vis inertiæ*, and have succeeded time and again in accomplishing their ends by the very sublimity of the spectacle of men who from principle, rather than resort to means of force which were within their reach, have quietly endured all that could be done against them, have quietly suffered and quietly died; the imputation of cowardice cannot lie against them, or the imputation that in this particular case it is an effort to evade their public duties; but it is simply carrying out what for long years they have persistently maintained to be their religious duty. And we find too that in all civilized and christian countries, it has been found necessary, and it has been sustained by the moral sense of the rest of the community, to provide that those having such conscientious scruples should not be forced to bear arms.

Mr. Pugh. I will remind the gentleman that even the last rebel Congress exempted them.

Mr. Cushing. Gentlemen will remember that in the valley of Virginia a thrill of indignation went through the whole community because an old Quaker by the name of Daniel had been forced into the military service by the rebel forces. His grey hairs were disregarded, and his religious principles met with derision from those men. I heard it said day after day that the cause which required them to force such men into their army, contrary to the sentiment of the civilized world, could not meet with success.

There comes a time in every crisis of history, in every case of war, when, if in order to carry on the war you have not strength enough to allow fair play to strong religious convictions, convictions which you have recognized in all the antecedent portion of your history, you must fail. To attempt to force these men into arms in defence of the country is a confession which you would better not put into your constitution. It is a confession that you fear that without these men you cannot defend your State. This we know is not so.

It has been argued here that these men ask you to protect them, and are unwilling to protect themselves. There never has been an instance in which these men have asked you to protect them by force of arms. The ordinary protection against violence they pay for in their taxes, and you are bound to furnish them. They have never made a request for any organized military force to protect them. They have always taken the consequences.—They have always said, these are our principles, and we are willing to stand our lot and take the result.

They have been exempted by the federal government in the last draft from all military service. Those of them who were drawn were not to be required in any single way to bear arms or to yield military service; all the service to be required of them is to attend the sick and minister to the wounded. Even in this time of calamity, in this time of national distress, when it has called upon all other classes of men, and when not even the ministers of other christian denominations have been exempt from the provisions of this law, it is put on record as the result of the experience of this war, and as the opinion of the military authorities that it is more advisable not to force these men to arms; and they have not done it.

In the whole history of our State they have been practically exempt. I think, as my colleague urged, that a great deal is due to them for their unfaltering loyalty to the principle that our constitution announces. We have put things into this constitution not so much from principle as because they would please the loyal men in our midst. Here is a thing which we are asked to put in, upon the ground of principle, to relieve these men from violating their principles, rather than to violate which they will die. I ask you if the prejudices of these men in this matter are not quite as much to be regarded as the prejudices of a county or city as to the election of a sheriff, or the tenure of office of a sheriff, or as to the emolument of a judge.

Under this provision, as proposed by the gentleman from Harford, testimony can be taken whether they have been known in the communities in which they live, to be men who have born consistent testimony against the bearing of arms, or whether they have not. That is the reason I object to the suggestion of the gentleman from Howard (Mr. Sands) to put in their names. The gentleman from Cecil (Mr. Pugh) told you that there are many who are members of the Society of Friends who do fight, who are not opposed to fighting. I do not wish to deprive the militia of the advantage of the services of those who are willing to fight. But I think we should relieve those who are conscientiously opposed to bearing arms. I shall with great pleasure give my vote for this amendment to the section, and I hope the convention will view it in the same light.

Mr. AUDOUN. I have but one question to ask; and that is, while this country is shaking to its very foundation, will these gentlemen come into this convention and ask to be excused from assisting that government which has given them protection from their infancy up to the present day? That is the only question I have to ask them.

Mr. STIRLING. I merely wish to cite the law. The last act of assembly, certainly without intending to do so, departed from the language of the code, which is simply in these words:

"Except ministers of the gospel, &c., and all persons conscientiously scrupulous of bearing arms, who shall produce to the captain or commanding officer proof of being so conscientious."

That has been the law ever since the original militia law passed; certainly thirty or forty years.

Mr. SANDS. My very excellent friend from Carroll (Mr. Ecker) and some other gentlemen seem to have misunderstood my remarks so far as to construe them into an unwillingness to exempt the Friends. I expressly declared that I was in favor of their exemption from military duty. All I desired was that the phraseology of this amendment might be such as would prevent other classes from taking advantage of it. Therefore I shall give my vote for the amendment as amended on the motion of my friend from Baltimore city (Mr. Stirling,) by striking out the disjunctive "or" and inserting "and." I shall vote for it with the greatest pleasure.

Mr. PUGH. I wish to answer the gentleman from Baltimore city (Mr. Audoun) as to their coming into this convention and asking to be exempt. It is only that certain members of this convention desire to keep the record now as it always has been. I wish to call the attention of the convention to the fact that it does not make a particle of difference what we do; for this class of people have suffered all their lives, and will continue to do so rather than violate their principles. We shall only be putting ourselves in the anomalous position of endeavoring to enforce a law which has never been enforced. Whenever their conscientious convictions come in the way, they simply die That is their whole history. They simply die; and have always done so. That is their whole history.

Mr. GALLOWAY. I would say to those who seem disposed to oppose this amendment, and who seem to think that no other men are required for this war than those who are to bear arms, that there are almost as many men required to aid in putting down this rebellion, or in relieving the suffering occasioned by it, without bearing arms, as are required for bearing arms. I will state one fact, which I hope may assist in passing the amendment offered by my colleague (Mr. Russell;) that after every hard fought battle within reach of my neighborhood, the Friends in that county have been the first who have gone to aid suffering humanity. After the battle of Gettysburg, where there was so much suffering, not only of our own forces but of those of our enemies, the Friends of our neighborhood went there as nurses, and provided everything calculated to relieve their sufferings. They were the first to start in the march to that place.—They are conscientiously opposed to bearing arms; but they are not conscientiously opposed to relieving the wants of the suffering. I hope the convention will pass the amendment of my colleague; and I assure the convention that it will give votes to the constitution in my county.

The amendment was adopted.

Mr. TODD moved that the convention do now adjourn.

Mr. WOODEN demanded the yeas and nays, and they were ordered.

The question being taken, the result was—yeas 15, nays 34—as follows:

Yeas—Messrs. Audoun, Carter, Cunningham, Davis, of Washington, Dellinger, Hollyday, King, Negley. Nyman, Parker, Sands, Scott, Smith, of Worcester, Sneary, Todd—15.

Nays—Messrs. Goldsborough, President; Abbott, Annan, Baker, Cushing, Daniel, Earle, Ecker, Farrow, Galloway, Greene, Hatch, Hebb, Hoffman, Hopkins, Hopper, Keefer, Kennard, Larsh, McComas, Mullikin, Murray, Pugh, Purnell, Russell. Schley, Stirling, Stockbridge, Swope, Sykes, Thomas, Valliant, Wickard, Wooden—34.

When his name was called,

Mr. TODD said: I wish to say that I did not expect to come here to-night, as I was suffering from indisposition; but I came in order that the convention might not be retarded in its work from the want of a quorum, on account of my absence, when my presence would constitute a bare quorum. I am now suffering and others are suffering. I hope the convention will adjourn. If not, there are some of us who will be obliged to leave.

The convention accordingly refused to adjourn

No quorum having voted,

Mr. SCHLEY moved a call of the house.

The motion was not sustained.

On motion of Mr. STIRLING,

The convention adjourned.

EIGHTY-FIFTH DAY.

TUESDAY, August 30, 1864.

The convention met at half-past 9 o'clock, A. M.

Prayer by Rev. Mr. Owen.

The roll was called, and the following members answered to their names:

Messrs. Goldsborough, President; Abbott, Annan, Audoun, Baker, Barron, Billingsley, Blackiston, Bond, Briscoe, Brooks, Carter, Cunningham, Cushing, Daniel, Davis, of Washington, Dellinger, Dennis, Duvall, Earle, Ecker, Farrow, Galloway, Greene, Hatch, Hebb, Hodson, Hoffman, Hollyday, Hopkins, Hopper, Horsey, Jones, of Cecil, Keefer, Kennard, King, Larsh, Lee, Markey, Mayhugh, McComas, Miller, Morgan, Mullikin, Murray, Negley, Nyman, Parker, Parran, Pugh, Purnell, Russell, Sands, Schley, Scott, Smith, of Carroll, Smith, of Dorchester, Smith, of Worcester, Stirling, Stockbridge, Swope, Sykes, Thomas, Todd, Turner, Valiant, Wickard, Wooden—68.

The proceedings of yesterday were read and approved.

STATE LIBRARIAN.

Mr. THOMAS submitted the following order.

Ordered, That the committee on accounts issue a certificate in favor of the State librarian for two hundred dollars, for his services rendered this convention, in obedience to an appointment by the general assembly of Maryland, at its last session, in purchasing the necessary stationery for the convention, and other extra services rendered the convention during the session.

Mr. THOMAS said: By reference to the journal of the senate for 1864, page 838, it will be found that the general assembly appointed the State librarian to procure the necessary stationery for the convention. It will be found also by reference to the proceedings of the last constitutional convention, page 740, that that convention passed a resolution at the end of the session which provided that the librarian be paid such sum for his services in purchasing stationery, &c., as the committee of accounts may certify to the president ought to be allowed.

With reference to this order it is only necessary for one to say that the State librarian has spent a great deal of time in purchasing paper and stationery and in the distribution of it to the members of the convention.

There was also a resolution of 1864, providing that the secretary of the senate should be authorized to fit up the rooms, &c. That was done, and the secretary of the senate was paid for his services.

I learn that in 1850 the State librarian received the sum of $400 for his services, and I think $200 is little enough to pay him now. I hope the convention will pass the order. It is known to every member of the convention that the State librarian has been very kind to the members; that he has been at all hours in the library to furnish books and paper of all kinds to members; and he has been very efficient in hunting up the books necessary to use in the debate.

Mr. ANNAN demanded the yeas and nays, which were ordered.

The question being taken, the result was—yeas 42, nays 29—as follows:

Yeas—Messrs. Abbott, Audoun, Barron, Belt, Billingsley, Blackiston, Briscoe, Brooks, Carter, Cushing, Daniel, Dellinger, Duvall, Earle, Farrow, Greene, Hatch, Hebb, Hodson, Hollyday, Kennard, Larsh, Lee, Markey, McComas, Miller, Morgan, Mullikin, Murray, Parran, Purnell, Ridgely, Sands, Schley, Smith, of Dorchester, Smith, of Worcester, Stirling, Swope, Sykes, Thomas, Todd, Turner—42.

Nays—Messrs. Goldsborough, President; Annan, Baker, Bond, Cunningham, Davis, of Washington, Dennis, Ecker, Galloway, Hoffman, Hopkins, Hopper, Horsey, Jones, of Cecil, Keefer, King, Mayhugh, Negley, Nyman, Parker, Pugh, Russell, Scott, Smith, of Carroll, Stockbridge, Valiant, Wickard, Wooden—29.

When their names were called,

Mr. ABBOTT said: As this has been the custom heretofore, I vote "aye."

Mr. NEGLEY said: Does this come out of the fund provided for the convention?

The PRESIDENT. I do not know what fund it comes out of. I do not see under what authority it is appropriated.

Mr. THOMAS. From the same fund from which heretofore we have paid for extra services performed by our committee clerks.

The PRESIDENT. I do not think any order has been passed for extra services of committee clerks.

Mr. THOMAS. I know that I voted for an order last week to pay the clerk and assistant clerk of this convention.

The PRESIDENT. That was when they were required to perform double duty—duty in two capacities.

Mr. NEGLEY. I cannot vote for this. I vote "no."

Mr. PUGH said: I shall vote against this order with the intention, if it is voted down, to move to refer this subject to the committee on accounts. I do not pretend to understand the subject, and I think the proper way would be to refer it to the committee on accounts, and have them report upon it. I vote "no."

Mr. STOCKBRIDGE said: I prefer to vote upon the recommendation of some committee that we may act understandingly, and therefore at this time, I shall vote "no."

Mr. BROOKS said: I have ascertained that at the time of the last convention the State librarian received $500 for the same services. I therefore desire to change my vote, and will vote "aye."

The order was accordingly agreed to.

ORDERS.

Mr. VALLIANT submitted the following order:

Ordered, That the president of this convention shall be authorized, after the final adjournment of this convention, to make order for the payment of all bills remaining unpaid in connection with the reporting and printing of the journal of debates, whenever the same shall be presented to him duly certified as correct by Mr. Joseph H. Audoun, or some other member of the committee on reporting and printing.

On motion of Mr. ECKER,

The order was referred to the committee on accounts.

On motion of Mr. BARRON,

It was ordered to be entered on the journal, that had John Barron been in his seat on Friday, 26th instant, he would have voted against the section added to the judiciary article, providing a system of involuntary apprenticeship; and in favor of the amendment which was offered thereto designed to secure such apprentices education so as to enable them to read and write.

On motion of Mr. SMITH, of Dorchester,

It was ordered to be entered on the journal, that Alward Johnson is absent from his seat in the convention, in consequence of sickness.

On motion of Mr. TODD,

It was ordered to be entered that the continued absence of T. S. Noble, of Caroline county, from his seat in this convention is occasioned by a protracted illness.

THE NEW CONSTITUTION.

The convention proceeded to the consideration of the following order submitted yesterday by Mr. VALLIANT:

Ordered, That the comptroller of the treasury be, and is hereby authorized and empowered to contract for the printing of six thousand copies of the constitution, and that the librarian be directed to distribute the same among the members, as early as practicable after the adjournment without day of the convention, and that the cost of said distribution be paid by the comptroller.

Mr. TODD moved to strike out "six" and insert "ten," so as to order ten thousand copies to be printed.

Mr. PUGH moved to insert "twenty."

Mr. WICKARD moved to insert "thirty," and after the word "constitution" to insert "five thousand to be in the German language."

Mr. BRISCOE. I hardly think these extra copies of the constitution will be printed and distributed throughout the State before the vote is taken. If a copy of the constitution adopted by the convention could be printed in the public journals of the State, they would be sufficiently distributed among the people of the State by that time. These copies to be distributed will hardly reach members before the vote on the adoption of this constitution. They are pamphlet copies, and it may be that they will be, I hope they will be, of no material use to anybody.

Mr. STOCKBRIDGE. I have two objections to the order. I understand the purpose to be to distribute the new constitution so that it may be intelligently adopted by the people. In the first place, it seems to me that the machinery suggested is too slow; and in the second place, that there will not be enough copies published, even at the largest estimate which has been made.

It will be slow work to set up and print off the constitution, taking perhaps a week or ten days; and as much longer for members to distribute them, if they ever do it, which may be a matter of doubt with regard to some members, if we leave it to them.

I find upon the journal of proceedings of the last convention that the gentleman from Baltimore county (Mr. Ridgely) offered the following order:

"*Ordered*, That the chair appoint a committee of three to contract with the Baltimore Sun, or some other newspaper in the city of Baltimore for the publication of the constitution entire, in extra newspaper form, and for supplying fifty thousand copies to be distributed as follows: to the various county newspapers in the State, in proportion as near as may be, to their respective subscription lists, and two hundred copies to be furnished to each member of the convention, the contract to be executed within one week after the close of the session."

Published in that form, and sent out as extra sheets of these papers, they reach every subscriber throughout the State within a week or ten days from the time the convention adjourns. I should greatly prefer that we should adopt something similar in form to the plan adopted by the last convention.

The question being taken upon Mr. WICKARD's amendment, it was rejected.

Mr. RIDGELY moved to insert "fifty," and the words "ten thousand copies to be printed in the German language."

The amendment was agreed to.

Mr. STOCKBRIDGE submitted the following amendment:

Strike out all after the word "that" in the first line, and insert:

"The chair appoint a committee of three to contract with the Baltimore American or some other newspaper or newspapers, for the publication of the constitution entire in extra newspaper form, 5,000 copies in the German language and 50,000 in the English, to be distributed as follows: two hundred copies to be furnished to each member of the convention and the remainder to be equally distributed by said committee among the various county newspapers and postmasters who will promptly distribute the same among the people, the copies to be furnished by the contractor for printing the same within one week after the final adjournment of this convention."

Mr. VALLIANT. It seems to me that the pamphlet form is decidedly the best form for the distribution of the new constitution. If distributed in sheet form, they will not be preserved longer than the first week; while if distributed in pamphlet form, every man will like to be in possession of a copy of the constitution, although every man does not like to incur the expense of paying for it. So that if printed in pamphlet form they will be much more likely to continue in the possession of the people of the State.

As to the cost there will be no material difference. If there is any it will be very trifling indeed. And the distribution can be made in the form prescribed by the gentleman. I see no reason why we should print it in newspaper form, when we can print it in pamphlet form, suitable for preservation, at the same cost, or very nearly the same.

Mr. WICKARD. I think that 5,000 German copies will not be sufficient. I move to increase the number to 10,000.

The amendment was agreed to.

The question recurred upon Mr. STOCKBRIDGE's amendment, and it was agreed to—ayes 40, nays 21.

The order as amended was agreed to.

RECALL OF CONVENTION.

The convention proceeded to the consideration of the following resolution submitted by Mr. ABBOTT on Saturday:

Resolved, That in view of the uncertain condition of affairs in this State, owing to the possibility of an invasion by the public enemy, which may interfere with the expression of the popular will on the day to be fixed for voting on this constitution, that this convention, when it adjourns without day, will be adjourned subject to the call of the president, and in case of the death or disqualification of the president, (H. H. Goldsborough,) Frederick Schley, of Frederick county, Joseph B. Pugh, of Cecil county, Henry Stockbridge, of Baltimore city, Wm. T. Purnell, of Worcester county, be and they are hereby authorized, in the order in which they are named, to act as president, and call the convention together."

Mr. ABBOTT modified his resolution so as to read:

Resolved, That in view of the uncertain condition of affairs in this State, owing to the possibility of an invasion by the public enemy, which may interfere with the expression of the popular will on the day to be fixed for voting on this constitution, that this convention when it adjourns, for the purpose of taking the sense of the people on this constitution, stand adjourned subject to the call of the president, and in case of the death or disqualification of the president, (H. H. Goldsborough,) Frederick Schley, of Frederick county, Joseph B. Pugh, of Cecil county, Henry Stockbridge, of Baltimore city, Wm. T. Purnell, of Worcester county, be and they are hereby authorized, in the order in which they are named, to act as president, and call the convention together; but should the day appointed for the adoption or rejection of this constitution pass without interruption, then the president shall declare, through the public press, the final adjournment without day of this convention.

Mr. RIDGELY. What effect will that have upon the question of the *per diem* of members? Would members draw their *per diem* for the interim?

Mr. CUSHING. It would cease on the adjournment.

Mr. RIDGELY. But the convention does not adjourn. It is still a convention. It is doubtful, in my mind, whether there would not be such an obligation to pay members; although I have no idea that that formed any part of the gentleman's intention.

Mr. ABBOTT. No, sir. I will add the words, "and no per diem shall be allowed for the recess"

Mr. DENNIS. I confess that I do not see clearly the reason for this. The resolution as it now stands differs from the form in which it was originally submitted. I feel some curiosity to learn from the gentleman from Baltimore who offered this resolution (Mr. Abbott,) how it was that we could adjourn *sine die* subject to a future call. But that part of it is changed.

Mr. ABBOTT. The resolution was drawn up very hastily.

Mr. DENNIS. It is to be hoped that such a resolution as that was drawn hastily. But as it now stands I do not understand why this body should continue in session. The legislature meets, performs its work, and adjourns subject to the constitutional limitations and provisions. The convention which has met here has been in session for four months performing its work, made its constitution, printed it in the English, German, High Dutch and Low Dutch, and put it before the people; and yet it seems that this body is still to be continued, *cui bono?* Why is it to be continued? Is it on account of interruption on the day of taking the vote? What kind of interruption? Where is the interruption? How is it to take place? Is it to be from a foreign enemy, or from a domestic foe? Is it to be from rebels abroad or from traitors in our midst? Is it to be from a drunken spree? Or what is to be the interference which is to require six, eight, or a dozen gentlemen seriatim to be authorized to call the convention together again? And when called together again, for what purpose is it? To revise and amend the new constitution and put it again before the people? Is that the purpose for which it is to be called together. The gentleman has amended the *sine die* clause, but still I should like to learn the reasons why this should be adopted.

Mr. ABBOTT. The resolution carries its own explanation upon its face. If the gentleman cannot understand it, he cannot understand the English language.

Mr. DENNIS. I confess there are a great many things the gentleman does that I cannot understand. I call for the yeas and nays on the resolution.

The yeas and nays were ordered.

The question being taken, the result was—yeas 51, nays 18—as follows:

Yeas—Messrs. Goldsborough, President; Abbott, Annan, Audoun, Baker, Carter, Cunningham, Cushing, Daniel, Davis, of Washington, Dellinger, Earle, Ecker, Farrow, Galloway, Greene, Hatch, Hebb, Hoffman, Hopkins, Hopper, Jones, of Cecil, Keefer, Kennard, King, Larsh, Markey, Mayhugh, McComas, Mulligan, Murray, Negley, Nyman, Parker, Pugh Purnell, Ridgely, Russell, Sands, Schley, Scott, Smith, of Worcester, Stirling, Stockbridge, Swope, Sykes, Thomas, Todd, Valiant, Wickard, Wooden—51.

Nays—Messrs. Billingsley, Blackiston, Bond, Briscoe, Brown, Chambers, Dennis, Dent, Duvall, Hodson, Hollyday, Horsey, Lee, Miller, Morgan, Parran, Smith, of Dorchester, Turner—18.

The resolution was accordingly adopted.

THIRD READING OF REPORTS.

Mr. STOCKBRIDGE. I move that we proceed this morning to take up reports upon their third reading; and I first move to take up report No. 12, upon the elective franchise. I make this motion in order that they may go into the hands of the committee on revision.

Mr. PUGH. I second that motion because the committee on revision cannot get along until these reports are passed.

The motion was agreed to.

ELECTIVE FRANCHISE.

The convention accordingly proceeded to the third reading of the article on the elective franchise, and section first was read as follows:

Section 1. All elections shall be by ballot, and every white male citizen of the United States of the age of twenty-one years or upwards, who shall have resided in the State one year next preceding the election, and six months in the city of Baltimore or in any county, shall be entitled to be registered as a legal voter; and such registration made in accordance with such provisions as the general assembly may prescribe, together with the muster rolls of all such soldiers as may be entitled to be registered in the State, and who may be serving in the army of the United States, shall be held and taken as the only evidence of qualification to vote at any election hereafter, and the general assembly shall by law provide for taking the votes of soldiers serving in the army of the United States, in the field; and in case any county or city shall be so divided as to form portions of different electoral districts for the election of congressmen, senator, delegate, or other officer or officers, then to entitle a person to vote for such officer, he must have been a resident of that part of the county or city which shall form a part of the electoral district in which he offers to vote, for six months next preceding the election; but a person who shall not have acquired a residence in such county or city, entitling him to vote at any such election, shall be entitled to vote in the election district from which he removed, until he shall have acquired a residence in the part of the county or city to which he has removed.

Mr. HEBB. That word "not" should not be in the nineteenth line of this section. It should be "but a person who shall have acquired a residence." It was not in the old constitution.

Mr. SANDS. That very word "not" heals the ambiguity of the section in the old constitution.

Mr. HEBB. If it meant one thing in the old constitution without the word "not," it must mean a different thing here with it.

Mr. SANDS. It was a clerical error in the old constitution, and the committee inserted it for the very reason that it cleared up the ambiguity.

Mr. STIRLING. It strikes me upon reading it precisely as it struck the gentleman from Allegany (Mr. Hebb.) The clause now says that a man who has not acquired a residence shall be entitled to vote.

Mr. SANDS. Certainly; if he has not acquired it there, he shall be entitled to vote in the election district from which he removed.

Mr. STIRLING. The provision in the old constitution was this: that a man may go back to the election district in which he resided before his removal to another district, if he has not resided for six months in the district in which he now lives. But it never allowed a man to go from one county to another county to vote because he had not resided in the new county for six months.

Mr. SANDS. The gentleman utterly mistakes the purport of it. It is not to go from one county to another, but to go from one district to another.

Mr. STIRLING. The interpretation put upon it in the city of Baltimore is different. Without this provision, according to the opinion of Reverdy Johnson and other eminent lawyers, it required a six months residence in moving from ward to ward

Mr. ABBOTT. I myself happen to have been a judge of elections for the last two years, and

I have invariably sent men back to the wards they moved from in such cases.

Mr. STIRLING. Certainly; that is exactly what I say.

Mr. SANDS. I think it is important that the convention should understand this matter. If they will look at the old constitution they will see that it was intended to secure a vote to the citizen of the State wherever he might be. It was meant to secure to him the privilege of voting wherever he might be. If he had gone out of one county into another, and had not been in the new county the six months required to give him a residence there, he could go back to the county from which he moved and vote there, the counties being in the same congressional district. A gentleman from Baltimore county moves over into Howard county, in the same congressional district, and not having been in Howard county six months, he cannot vote there; but this article of the old constitution enabled him to go back and vote in Baltimore county for the congressman in the same congressional district with himself. The only difficulty that ever arose was from the ambiguity from the omission of this very word "not." The committee after full discussion of this matter put in this word as healing the ambiguity and making perfectly plain that which was not plain before.

Mr. STIRLING. It applies to the case of a man moving into a different district.

Mr. SANDS. No, sir; twenty-four hours gives a residence in the district. You may go from number one to number two, and vote in twenty-four hours.

Mr. STIRLING. In the city of Baltimore the wards are divisions into election districts; and it has been decided that in order to enable a man to vote for a constable or a magistrate even, he must have six months residence in the ward.

Mr. SANDS. Any amendment that may be required to meet the wants of Baltimore city, I shall be satisfied with.

Mr. STIRLING. The constitution expressly says that a man must reside six months in the district; and if in the election of constables and magistrates the divisions of the county are not districts, I do not know what are.

Mr HEBB. In my opinion the phraseology of the old constitution is the correct one. The first part of the sentence is:

"And in case any county or city shall be so divided as to form portions of different electoral districts for the election of congressmen, senator, delegate or other officer or officers, then to entitle a person to vote for such officer, he must have been a resident of that part of the county or city which shall form a part of the electoral district in which he offers to vote, for six months next preceding the election;"

Then it stops there, with a semicolon, and proceeds:—"but a person who shall have acquired a residence in such county or city, entitling him to vote at any such election, shall be entitled to vote in the election district from which he removed, until he shall have acquired a residence in the part of the county or city to which he has removed."

The first part of the paragraph refers to the dividing of a county so as to form portions of different electoral districts, one distinct subject matter; the latter portion of the paragraph refers to the election districts of a county. It provides that if a person shall have resided three months in one election district, and then removed to another election district in the same county and resided there three months, having resided six months in the county, and thus acquired a residence in such county, he shall be entitled to a vote in the election district from which he removed; and may vote there until he shall have resided full six months in the election district to which he has removed. That is the meaning of it; and I think the word "not" which the committee have inserted, destroys the sense.

Mr. STIRLING. I have always understood it that way, certainly. If a man has been six months in a county it fixes his right to vote somewhere; and if he has acquired a residence in a county, and has moved into a different district in the same county, he must go back to vote to the place from which he came, until he acquires a residence in the election district to which he goes.

The PRESIDENT. I can only say that the interpretation in my county has been very different from that. A man living in one district moving into another, is there but a single day; he can vote in the old district within the rule. A man who goes from Caroline to Talbot, who has been in Talbot five months can go back to Caroline and vote, under the interpretation that has been given to this constitution. He cannot vote now in Talbot county, for he has not acquired a residence there; but he has not lost his residence in Caroline.

Mr. STIRLING. The constitution never meant anything of the sort. It never meant that a man should have the right to go back from one county to another.

The PRESIDENT. I always understood that to be the interpretation given to it by the last convention. I have understood that that was the unanimous opinion of the last convention. I will ask the gentleman from Baltimore county, who was a member of that convention.

Mr. RIDGELY That has been the practice under that understanding in my county.

Mr. MAYHUGH called for the previous question.

The PRESIDENT ruled the call not to be in order.

Mr. STIRLING. I shall certainly vote to strike out the word "not" if the amendment is offered.

Mr. Hebb. I move to strike out the word "not" in the nineteenth line of this section.

Mr. Chambers. I understand that the difficulty is the question whether the word "not" should be in or out. It seems to me to be a plain question. The intention of this last paragraph is to give a vote to a certain individual. What is to be the category of that individual. Let us illustrate it by a man residing in Queen Anne's county until he shall have become entitled to vote. It is intended to secure to him, if he shall remove to Kent within less than six months prior to the day of election, not being entitled to vote in Kent, the right to vote in Queen Anne's. It is necessary to assume that he was entitled to vote in Queen Anne's, whence he removed. A man therefore entitled to vote, and removing, is entitled to go back and vote in the county from which he removed until he has gained a residence.

But what does this say? It says a man who is "not" entitled to vote. It therefore gives the right to a man from Queen Anne's to go back there and vote, provided he is not entitled to vote there.

The President. Not entitled in point of residence.

Mr. Chambers. He must be entitled to vote where he formerly resided; and this says he must be not entitled to vote there.

The President The gentleman will see that the word "not" does not apply to entitling him to vote, but to acquiring a residence.

Mr. Chambers. Well, sir, he must acquire a residence in order to be entitled to vote.

Mr. Abbott. I understand that a voter never loses his right to vote. If in any city or county he has not resided there six months and is therefore not entitled to vote there, he must go back to the county from which he came, or to the city if he went from Baltimore.

Mr. Stirling. The interpretation I have always seen placed upon this section is this. The gentleman from Kent seems to think it refers to residence in the county. If it did, then there would be no necessity for all this phraseology about the different election districts. It says:

"And in case any county or city shall be so divided as to form portions of different electoral districts for the election of congressmen, senator, delegate, or other officer or officers, then to entitle a person to vote for such officer, he must have been a resident of that part of the county or city which shall form a part of the electoral district in which he offers to vote, for six months next preceding the election."

Now the city of Baltimore is so divided as to form portions of different electoral districts. If a man resides in the city of Baltimore, and moves out of the portion of the city which forms the third congressional district into the portion which forms the second, he may go back to the third district to vote, if he shall have resided six months in the city. I never heard that a man who moved out of Baltimore could come back to vote in the congressional district in which he had lived at any time within six months after he left the city. He may go back to the congressional district in which he lived, provided he is entitled to vote in Baltimore city, having resided there for six months. That is the reason why the word "not" should be left out. It was intended that a man should not vote at all who had not been somewhere in the county for six months; but this change enables a man to vote in a county if he has not been there six months.

Mr. Sands. Certainly not.

Mr. Stirling. Unquestionably.

Mr. Sands. I never heard any statement like that.

Mr. Stirling. I do not think it is intended to apply to different counties at all, but to different electoral districts.

Mr. Stockbridge. I have had some little practical experience under the constitution, and I know that a great many judges of election have found a practical difficulty. They have found it easy enough to arrange where the removals where in the county to different parts forming different election districts; but they have found it a *casus omissus* where the removal was from one county into another. A person under the old constitution must be a resident in the county where he proposes to vote, and must have resided there for six months. Consequently if he had removed his house, as is a frequent case, from Baltimore county to Baltimore city less than six months before the election, not having resided in Baltimore city six months, he was not entitled to vote there, and not being on the day of election a resident in Baltimore county he was not entitled to vote there; and he could vote in neither place. This was the case when he had moved from the county to the city, or *vice versa*. I have seen persons go by the score from the polls where they wished to vote, where the judges of election wished their votes to be deposited, because under the constitution their votes could not be received.

If gentlemen wish to provide for that which was a *casus omissus* under the old constitution, it is very easy to do it by striking out "not," and then adding "or any voter removing from one county to another may vote in the county from which he removed until he shall have acquired a residence in the county to which he removed." In that way both cases will be provided for. As I look at this, it will leave the same *casus omissus* as under the old constitution.

Mr. Stirling. A man has no more right to go back from one county to vote than he has to go back to Pennsylvania and vote when he has been here only eleven months. A man must have been six months in the county where he offers to vote.

Mr. SANDS. Of course this is intended to apply to people who have a county residence, that is a residence of six months. Suppose Baltimore county is put into one congressional district, and suppose a man who has been living in Baltimore county had no residence there and came over into Howard county and offered to vote, and then went back to Baltimore county and offered to vote. Would my construction enable him to vote? Certainly not. He must have lived in Baltimore county six months, or he could not go back there and vote. The six months residence must be in the county where he votes.

The PRESIDENT. I may be mistaken, but under this provision as I have always regarded it, a man does not lose his residence.

Mr. SANDS. I think the plain intent is to secure the individual his vote, that he may not lose his representation in the federal Congress simply from moving from one county to another, that he may not lose his county residence.

Mr. STIRLING. He is required to have the same residence in voting for a member of Congress as in voting for a county officer.

Mr. MILLER. One word with regard to the idea that a man removing from one county to another has the right to go back into his county to vote until he obtains a residence in another county. The constitution declares that he must have resided one year next preceding the election in the State, and six months next preceding the election in the county in which he offers to vote. If he has gone away and left a county with the intention of taking up his residence in another county for four months, how can he be resident there for six months next preceding the election? It seems to me that the construction the gentleman from Baltimore city (Mr. Stirling) has put upon this section is perfectly proper; that the word "not" should be stricken out in order to cover the case he mentions; and then if we want to allow a man to go back to another county to vote, you ought to make a special provision for it. If you allow the word "not" to remain, you let a man vote where he has not resided for six months next preceding the election.

Mr. SCOTT. I am right glad to be present at this grammar school. This very same question was taken up in committee, and I took the same ground then, that the word "not" ought to be left out; but I was overruled in the committee, and not being present when this was acted upon, my attention was not called to it in the convention. I am of opinion that it ought to be stricken out.

Mr. SCHLEY. It is very evident that the word "not" is out of place. The whole context of this section applies to the division and subdivision of counties in the State into different electoral districts. There is some ambiguity in the whole phraseology of the section; because it speaks of the electoral districts in the eighteenth line, and election districts in the twenty-first line, meaning different things.

Let me suppose a case which might occur under the constitution. It was proposed to give Baltimore county two senators in the general assembly of the State. Now suppose Baltimore county had been divided into two senatorial districts, and that the northern portion had formed the first. A, living in the southern part, removes to the northern part antecedent to the election. This provision—A having moved into the northern part of Baltimore county—says in the sixteenth line that he must have been a resident of that part of the county in which he offers to vote for six months next preceding the election, and not having been in the northern part of the county for six months, he cannot vote there. But having been a resident of Baltimore county all his life, he feels that he is entitled to vote for a senator in the general assembly of the State; and the subsequent part of this section gives him the power, because it says that having acquired a residence in Baltimore county, having resided there more than six months, he shall be entitled to vote in the election district from which he removed.

I apprehend this is the object, and the only object of this part of the section. It might have been expressed more clearly; but that is the exact language, excepting this word "not," as I understand, of the old constitution. I think that in this view of the case it is very clear that the word "not" is out of place, and ought to be stricken out.

The PRESIDENT. The motion should be to open the section for the amendment, under the fifty-third rule.

Mr. HEBB. I make that motion.

The question being taken, the result was—ayes 30, noes 28.

Less than a majority of the members elected to the convention having voted in the affirmative, the motion was rejected.

Section two, containing the oath to be taken by voters, having been read,

Mr. SANDS moved to open the section for amendment by inserting "mental" in line fortieth, so as to read: "and I swear this without any mental reservation or evasion."

The motion was rejected.

Mr. BRISCOE moved to open section two, for amendment, in order to insert in the thirty-eighth line in the oath, after the word "notwithstanding," the words: "and that I am now and have heretofore been in favor of the restoration of the Union as it was and the constitution as it is." Upon that motion he demanded the yeas and nays.

The yeas and nays were ordered.

Mr. PUGH. If the section is opened to amendment does it open it to all amendments?

The PRESIDENT. It does not; only to the amendment proposed.

The question being taken, the result was—yeas 17, nays 51—as follows:

Yeas—Messrs. Billingsley, Blackiston, Bond, Briscoe, Brown, Chambers, Clarke, Dennis, Dent, Hollyday, Horsey, Lee, Miller, Morgan, Parran, Smith, of Dorchester, Turner—17.

Nays—Messrs. Goldsborough, President; Abbott, Annan, Baker, Barron, Brooks, Carter, Cunningham, Cushing, Daniel, Davis, of Washington, Dellinger, Earle, Ecker, Farrow, Galloway, Greene, Hebb, Hoffman, Hopkins, Hopper, Jones, of Cecil, Keefer, Kennard, Larsh, Markey, Mayhugh, McComas, Mullikin, Murray, Negley, Nyman, Parker, Pugh, Purnell, Ridgely, Russell, Sands, Schley, Scott, Smith of Carroll, Smith, of Worcester, Stirling, Stockbridge, Swope, Sykes, Thomas, Todd, Valliant, Wickard, Wooden—51.

When his name was called,

Mr. SANDS said: If the gentleman from Calvert or the convention would accept an amendment to the amendment I would certainly vote for it. It is to add: "And I do especially denounce and disclaim that violation of the constitution of the United States which resulted in armed rebellion against the Union of the United States. I vote "no."

The motion was accordingly rejected.

The bill having been read through,

The question being then taken upon the final adoption of the report, by yeas and nays, under rule forty-third, the result was—yeas 50, nays 17—as follows:

Yeas—Messrs. Goldsborough, President; Abbott, Annan, Baker, Barron, Brooks, Carter, Cunningham, Cushing, Daniel, Davis, of Washington, Dellinger, Earle, Ecker, Farrow, Galloway, Greene, Hebb, Hoffman, Hopkins, Hopper, Jones, of Cecil, Keefer, Kennard, Larsh, Markey, Mayhugh, McComas, Mullikin, Murray, Negley, Nyman, Parker, Pugh, Purnell, Ridgely, Russell, Sands, Schley, Scott, Smith, of Carroll, Smith, of Worcester, Stirling, Stockbridge, Swope, Sykes, Todd, Valliant, Wickard, Wooden—50.

Nays—Messrs. Billingsley, Blackiston, Bond, Briscoe, Brown, Chambers, Clarke, Dennis, Dent, Hollyday, Horsey, Lee, Miller, Morgan, Parran, Smith, of Dorchester, Turner—17.

The article on the elective franchise was accordingly passed.

EXECUTIVE DEPARTMENT.

On motion of Mr. STOCKBRIDGE,

The report of the committee on the executive department was taken up and read the third time.

Mr. STOCKBRIDGE called attention to the accidental omission of a word in section fourteen, line one; which was corrected by inserting the word "of," so as to read "in case of any vacancy," &c.

Mr. HEBB called attention to the fact that the word "legislature" occurred in several places.

The PRESIDENT stated that there was an amendment adopted to strike out "legislature" wherever it should occur and insert "general assembly," and that the correction would accordingly be made.

Mr. STOCKBRIDGE called attention to the twenty-fourth section, "he shall carefully keep," &c., which should read "the secretary of State shall carefully keep," &c.

Mr. EARLE. Both these amendments have been made. They are upon the journal, page 460.

The question being then taken upon the final adoption of the report, by yeas and nays, the result was—yeas 54, nays 16—as follows:

Yeas—Messrs. Goldsborough, President; Abbott, Annan, Audoun, Baker, Barron, Brooks, Carter, Cunningham, Cushing, Daniel, Davis, of Washington, Dellinger, Earle, Ecker, Farrow, Galloway, Greene, Hatch, Hebb, Hoffman, Hopkins, Hopper, Jones, of Cecil, Keefer, Kennard, King, Larsh, Markey, Mayhugh, McComas, Mullikin, Murray, Negley, Nyman, Parker, Pugh, Purnell, Ridgely, Russell, Sands, Schley, Scott, Smith, of Carroll, Smith, of Worcester, Stirling, Stockbridge, Swope, Sykes, Thomas, Todd, Valliant, Wickard, Wooden—54.

Nays—Messrs. Belt, Billingsley, Blackiston, Briscoe, Brown, Chambers, Clarke, Dennis, Dent, Duvall, Hollyday, Horsey, Lee, Morgan, Parran, Smith, of Dorchester—16.

When his name was called,

Mr. CHAMBERS said: I was not here when the provision for a lieutenant governor was acted upon. It is an office perfectly useless and quite expensive; and I vote "no."

The article on the executive department was accordingly passed.

LEGISLATIVE DEPARTMENT.

On motion of Mr. STOCKBRIDGE,

The report of the committee on the legislative department was taken up and read the third time.

The question being taken upon the final adoption of the report, the result was—yeas 51, nays 16—as follows:

Yeas—Messrs. Goldsborough, President; Abbott, Annan, Audoun, Baker, Barron, Brooks, Carter, Cunningham, Cushing, Daniel, Daniel, Davis, of Washington, Dellinger, Earle, Ecker, Farrow, Galloway, Greene, Hotch, Hebb, Hoffman, Hopkins, Hopper, Jones, of Cecil, Keefer, Kennard, King, Larsh, Markey, Mayhugh, McComas, Mullikin, Murray, Negley, Parker, Pugh, Purnell,

Ridgely, Russell, Sands, Schley, Smith, of Worcester, Stirling, Stockbridge, Swope, Sykes, Thomas, Todd, Valliant, Wickard, Wooder—51.

Nays—Messrs. Belt, Billingsley, Blackiston, Briscoe, Brown, Chambers, Clarke, Dennis, Dent, Duvall, Hollyday, Horsey, Lee, Morgan, Parran, Smith, of Dorchester —16.

The report of the committee on the legislative department was accordingly passed.

BASIS OF REPRESENTATION.

On motion of Mr. STOCKBRIDGE,

The report of the committee on the basis of representation was taken up and read the third time by its title.

Mr. CUSHING moved that so much be considered the third reading of the report.

Mr. BILLINGSLEY objected.

Mr. CUSHING. I make that motion, and ask that the question be taken.

Mr. CHAMBERS. Will it be in order to adopt that course? Is a matter of such vital interest, embracing a portion of the article on the legislative department, to be taken up and disposed of without having a single section of it read? Are we to have no chance to consider the question of the basis of representation? When gentlemen are sensible that injury is done to my own county by the system, are they to take up the system and drive it through without a word? To us it is a serious affair. The constitution is to operate nominally for all time. It is to effect all classes of people, in a way that cannot be avoided except by calling another convention or some such trouble. If we here are not able to devote half an hour to understanding whether an article that is to be passed, and which has occupied days upon days, and nights, too, I may say, is just to all parts of the State, I protest against such a mode of proceeding. I hope it will not be sanctioned by the convention.

Mr. BRISCOE demanded the yeas and nays, and they were ordered.

Mr. HEBB. I hope the gentleman will withdraw the motion. It will take as long to call the yeas and nays as to read the report.

Mr. CUSHING. I decline to withdraw it, because if the report is read through there will be motions made to amend, and there will be two votes to be taken upon which the yeas and nays will be called where we shall have one now.

The question being taken, the result was—yeas 13, nays 52—as follows:

Yeas—Messrs. Goldsborough, President; Audoun, Baker, Barron, Brooks, Cushing, Farrow, Hatch, Hebb, Kennard, McComas, Mullikin, Swope—13.

Nays—Messrs. Abbott, Belt, Billingsley, Blackiston, Briscoe, Brown, Chambers, Clarke, Cunningham, Daniel, Davis, of Washington, Dellinger, Dennis, Dent, Duvall, Earle, Ecker, Galloway, Greene, Hoffman, Hollyday, Hopkins, Hopper, Horsey, Jones, of Cecil, Keefer, King, Larsh, Lee, Markey, Mayhugh, Morgan, Murray, Negley, Parker, Parran, Pugh, Purnell, Ridgely, Russell, Sands, Schley, Smith, of Dorchester, Smith, of Worcester, Stirling, Stockbridge, Sykes, Thomas, Todd, Valliant, Wickard, Wooden—52.

When their names were called,

Mr. DANIEL said: As I think it is sometimes absolutely necessary for us to make corrections in these reports, I think they ought to be read through, and I therefore vote "no."

Mr. MAYHUGH said: The people of all parts of the State are interested in this. Besides, I think it is proper and right that all these reports should be read through the third time. There might as well be no such thing as a third reading if all the reports are to be hastily passed through in this manner. Some members might suggest something which requires alteration. It would take no more time to read it than to call the yeas and nays. I vote "no."

The motion was accordingly rejected.

The report was read the third time.

Mr. HOLLYDAY. I move to amend the report so as to give Kent county two representatives instead of one. We are now paying a much larger tax than Caroline county, which has two, and our income tax is much greater. We have a larger number of votes, I think, and still we only have one representative. I think we are entitled to two representatives, and I hope the convention will give us that number.

Mr. SANDS. I would be glad, from the facts which have come to my knowledge since the adoption of this report by the convention upon its second reading, if the convention would consider favorably the amendment made by the gentleman from Kent (Mr. Hollyday.) The county stands now, as our statistics show us, within one hundred or so of being entitled to two representatives in point of population, and as stated by my friend in other matters, in point of property, so far as that has a right to representation, she is rather in advance of some other counties that now have two representatives. I know we have a great many friends in Kent who would esteem it as an act of great injustice if we were to leave them with a single representative.

I am not sure that any county should have less than two, because the sickness or inevitable absence of a single member would always leave the county unrepresented. Especially as the county of Kent approaches so very near the number which would entitle her to two, it may be less than a year, or six months before she will be entitled in point of numbers to two—I would like it if our friends would give this matter a liberal consideration, and vote accordingly. It cannot do any harm to the State for one more or less member to sit upon this floor, and it might do good to us. It certainly, I think, would do scarcely less than justice to that county. If she were hundreds or thousands away from the quota, I would not be an advocate of the change, but would say, let her wait.

Mr. DENNIS. You say "it might do good to us." Whom do you mean by "us."

Mr. SANDS. The people of the State, of whom I am one. That is what I mean by "us," speaking collectively. It cannot do any harm to the people of the State of Maryland to vote an additional member to these people when their population so nearly approaches the proper number. I think they can well appeal to the majority of this house, and that we ought to listen to that appeal. I know we have large numbers of friends in Kent county who would be greatly disappointed and much embittered if something is not done in this matter. Both as a matter of justice and of policy I would like to see our friends adopt it. As I said, it can do us, meaning the people of the State, no harm to give an additional member here, and it may be doing simple justice. I hope the motion will prevail.

Mr. TODD. I was myself on the point of making the same motion made by the gentleman from Kent (Mr. Hollyday.) For the reasons that have been very well expressed by the gentleman from Howard (Mr. Sands,) I hope this convention will reconsider its action and give Kent county two representatives.

Mr. BILLINGSLEY. I shall make the same motion for St. Mary's county. I was not here when the basis of representation was established, but there is one fact which I think has escaped the consideration of this body that ought to make a very deep impression upon them in regard to this matter. It is that St. Mary's county is the mother of all the counties; that it was there that religious liberty was first inaugurated, and that it is due to her position as the mother of the counties, and as having inaugurated civil and religious liberty, if she has not the numbers under this ratio to entitle her to an additional representative; and I therefore hope the convention will be liberal enough to give us one more representative.

Mr. STIRLING. I shall support the amendment of the gentleman from Kent (Mr. Hollyday.) After considerable reflection, I have become convinced that it is wise and politic to do so. I think in fact it is only 150 short; and that her voting population is even larger than that of Caroline, which has two representatives. That is the reason why I will make this exception. But I cannot accede to the request of my friend who sits behind me, (Mr. Billingsley,) because upon the principle we have established St. Mary's county, if allowed two representatives, will be in an unequal position, even as compared with Kent; for it will be giving Kent county with a population of 10,000 two representatives, and St. Mary's the same number with a population of about 5,000. Certainly there is no justice in this. Kent county has nearly enough for two representatives.

Mr. BILLINGSLEY. I think that the fact which the honorable gentleman has stated should be to this convention an additional consideration for giving us what we claim. By whom have we lost our property?

Mr. STIRLING. I referred to the free population.

Mr. NEGLEY. I hope the house will not disturb the principle adopted in this report. If you open it at all in one instance, and deviate from the vital principle upon which it was established, you will be asked to open it in others; and if you open it in one instance, I say there is no reason why we should not open it in others. There is great complaint by our friends from Baltimore county, that the report operates unjustly upon them; and they have an equal right with Kent and St. Mary's to come here and ask that they have one additional member. You will open this entirely. You will destroy its symmetry. You will destroy the very fundamental principle upon which the apportionment is made.

Have the people of Kent county a right to complain? Is it not made a principle that every 5,000 white persons or fraction thereof over one-half shall be entitled to one representative? This is a principle that operates upon all the counties alike; and if you disturb it at all, you disturb the whole entire principle. It is like knocking away the foundations upon which a superstructure is built. The whole thing topples to the ground. If you violate the principle in this solitary instance, it destroys the validity of the rule *in toto*. There is no sense or reason in it. Baltimore county has a better right to come forward and ask for two additional representatives than Kent or St. Mary's for one. The provision is made that as soon as a county has a fractional part over the half of 5,000, she may go before the legislature and ask an enumeration of the State, and get her additional representative. All the small counties can do so.

It will be departing from the principle; and if you open the report in this one instance, you will have applications from other counties. You will destroy the whole report, and be at sea again; and perhaps it will take days and days before it is finally settled. If you open this report at all to give Kent county one more, I shall claim and I shall vote to give Baltimore county one or two additional representatives, and Frederick county, too, and for my own county I shall put in a claim.

Mr. DANIEL. There is no rule without its exceptions. It is said that the exceptions are necessary to constitute the rule. Now I think this is such a slight exception to the rule, and I think the equity of the case and the circumstances appeal to us so strongly to deviate from the strict rule we have made in this matter, that I shall vote very cheerfully for opening the report to allow this additional representative to be given to Kent county. As it has already been said, not only in point of population, they are so near, but they are ahead of a good many other counties that have additional representation, in point of wealth and other circumstances.

Mr. NEGLEY. Wealth is not the basis of representation.

Mr. DANIEL continued: As to the objection raised by the gentleman from Washington, that if we open this, the whole structure topples, and we must necessarily open it, and necessarily amend it for everybody who asks it, I cannot see the force of the reasoning. But I say to him that we will judge of every case upon its own merits. When the appeal comes from St. Mary's or Baltimore county, if they apply, we will judge of each case upon its own merits, taking up one at a time, and judge of it upon its own merits. I am for opening the report and granting an additional member; and when the other cases come up, if other applications shall be made, I will judge of those. I am free to say that the application of St. Mary's I shall not vote for, and I shall vote against every other that has not stronger claims than St. Mary's; but this having a great deal stronger claim, I shall vote for it.

Mr. HOFFMAN. The gentleman from Washington (Mr. Negley) has referred to the claims of Baltimore county. Our people are complaining very bitterly that, with a population twice that of Carroll county, we have only one additional representative. I hope this will be opened, and that the gentleman from Kent will be allowed one more, and that Baltimore county will get one or two more.

Mr. PUGH. I have only to say that the reason why I shall vote for giving to Kent an additional representative is that I do not think that, in point of fact, the principle is violated by our doing so. I think, in point of fact, that the language used in this section would be applicable to the county of Kent. Although we confined the number to one, upon the census of 1860, yet I think that, in point of fact, Kent is to-day entitled to two representatives, because I think that there are to-day far more than this small fraction of white people that are required in order to entitle the county to two.

But with regard to Baltimore county, I do not believe that, according to the principle adopted, Baltimore county is entitled to additional representatives; nor do I believe any other county is entitled to more than we have allowed it. I certainly intend to support the amendment proposed by the gentleman from Kent, for the reason that I now state, that I believe that that particular county is to-day, on account of the white people that are in the county, entitled to two representatives. It is a peculiar case, unlike the case of any other county. She only lacks a very few by the census, and, as I have said before, I believe the principle applied to the number as it exists there to-day, would give to Kent county an additional representative.

Mr. CLARKE. I merely rise to say that upon the pending proposition I shall vote with pleasure to increase the representation of Kent county to two members. And I will say that if a similar proposition is offered to increase the representation of the other counties cut down to one member, I shall vote for such an amendment to the present report; and, to a great extent, upon this ground, that by cutting down any of the counties to one member, having only one senator, in the event of the sickness or necessary absence of the member during that session of the legislature, you must necessarily have, even upon the floor of this house, a county without any representation whatever.

I think it further necessary to make one allusion to the question of principle being involved in the adoption of the amendment. Gentlemen forget that there is no principle involved in it at all. We see to-day that we hear complaints from Washington county; we hear complaints from Baltimore county; we hear complaints from Kent; we hear them from all parts of the State. And why? Because in the adoption of this representative system you have not gone upon principle; but have merely adopted the arbitrary rule that for every 5,000, to a certain extent, you will give one member; and then you go on according to a certain other rule, changing the rule with the increase of population. If it was principle involved in this case, the principle would work right and justice everywhere, and give satisfaction to every portion of the State. You have just as much right to say you will give one member for every 3,000 as for every 5,000 or 10,000. It is a mere arbitrary standard; a rule which you choose to adopt; and no principle is involved; and hence the result is complaint from every side.

Now I say that there being no principle involved in the case, but only an arbitrary rule, I go for extending this arbitrary rule further, and giving to every county of the State at least two members upon this floor; so that the small counties shall not be left during a great portion of the time without representation.

One other remark I wish to make upon this question. I was not here when the vote was taken upon this question upon the second reading of this report. I think it was intimated by the gentleman from Baltimore city that the proposition offered by my colleague and myself to have representation according to population throughout the State was right; but it was voted down, and the gentleman could not vote for it on the ground that it could not be adopted. The result is that, acknowledging the principle to be right, they will not vote for it, and it cannot be adopted, and they cannot agree upon any proposition. Now is the appointed time for the house to consider——

Mr. CHAMBERS. Will the gentleman allow me to suggest to him that if he will give way I think we may take the vote.

Mr. CLARKE. Very well; I will give way.

Mr. ABBOTT. The gentleman speaks of this as an arbitrary rule. The committee on representation spent a great deal of time over this subject, and came here, so far as the majority are concerned, making a unanimous report. This report has been adopted by the house by a large vote, being based upon a principle.—The only way we can have a republican form of government is to have a representation based upon some firm and fixed principle. There is a provision that a census may be taken by the legislature at any time. Our next legislature can order a census to be taken in the State, and the basis changed or altered in proportion to the number of white inhabitants that they have. I hope that the report will not be opened at all. But if it is to be opened, let the proposition be made at once by every county asking for what it wants, and then let us take one vote upon the whole. If we are going to break the rule at all, we may as well break it all to pieces as to break out one piece at a time.

The same rule holds good now that was good when we acted upon this subject before. I find that Kent county lacks 2,653 of the number for two representatives, which is 10,000. The rule we adopted allows a representative for a fraction equal to one-half the number for a representative, which we fixed upon as a sufficient deviation from the strict rule. Kent county has a white population of 2,347 by the last census over the number required for one member.

Mr. HEBB. That is 153 less than one-half of 5,000.

The PRESIDENT. If she had 154 more, she would be entitled to another representative.

Mr. ABBOTT. The next legislature if they deem it necessary may take a new census of the State; then if the people of Kent have the requisite number they can have a representation according to their population, observing the rule, and have two members. I hope the house will not break the rule unless they intend to give every county, Baltimore county, Frederick county, Howard county, and every county in the State, including Baltimore city, an additional representative.

Mr. MAYHUGH. I trust the report will not be disturbed by increasing the number of members for any county. I was a good deal opposed to the representation allowed to Baltimore city, and the counties generally were opposed to it. But the report being made on principle, I fully concurred in that report.—The gentleman from Prince George's (Mr. Clarke) has said that there are calls from all the counties, from every portion of the State in regard to this matter; that it is a violation of justice, and an arbitrary principle, and you might as well go indiscriminately and give so many to each county without any basis at all. If that be the case, then every county will be seeking for amendments, and the city of Baltimore will claim that she has a right to be represented according to population. I appeal to the judgment of any gentleman in this house, whether any report could have been framed upon a more just and equitable principle. The State being a small one, it was necessary to curb the representation of Baltimore city. Otherwise she would have the whole power of the State in her own hands. And in doing so, it has been done upon principles of justice, cutting down the larger counties on the same principle.

Now a gentleman has made a motion to increase the number of members for Kent county. Although I was opposed to the present representation for Baltimore city, yet having agreed to the report and concurred in the principle, I say to vary from it would be sheer injustice. Upon any principle that I could conceive to be right, I was ready to give another representative to Kent; but it would be sheer injustice to Baltimore county and every other county in the State to give it now, because it violates every principle upon which this report is founded; and I conceive we could make no apportionment upon a principle more just to every portion of the State than that of this report. Surely if you award another representative to one county, you must award it to every county, and you must award it to Baltimore city; and if this motion prevails I shall strive with every power I possess to increase our representation.

Mr. STIRLING. The reason I advocate this amendment, is because, as the gentleman from Cecil (Mr. Pugh) said, it is no deviation from the principle. It is only a variation of a few hundred, and so near the principle that it amounts actually to the same thing. I do not see why giving this representative to Kent is any reason for giving further representation to the large counties, unless we are to adopt the principle advocated by the gentleman from Prince George's (Mr. Clark) to give to the people of the whole State an absolute representation of one delegate for 5,000 people; and I do not care who gets the power under that basis. If the majority are entitled to the power, nobody pretends to say why a party of people living inside of Baltimore city are not as much entitled to representation as they would be if living in Prince George's or Calvert county. They cast as many votes; and they are entitled to the same representation upon the republican principle. But the people of this State have not reached that principle of justice yet; and therefore I am not prepared to make a fool of myself by trying to get it. The principle established by this report is the best principle, and comes the nearest to the absolutely just principle that every white man is entitled to be represented, the only proper system of representation that can be adopted now. So far as the principle is correct, it is perfectly satisfactory. It proceeds upon the principle of giving to every county a representation to a certain extent according to numbers; but when it comes up to the large counties and the city of Baltimore, one delegate is to represent more people than in the small counties. That is the theory upon which it goes; and the report is perfectly equal so far as the theory is correct. I would be willing to accept the principle that gives the voter everywhere the same representation, whether he resides among great houses or lives out in the fields. The only reason why I favor this particular amendment is that I do not regard it as violating the principle of the report in fact. I do not care much about it.—I shall not press it; and as to any other amendment to the report, if it shall be offered, I shall vote against it.

Mr. RIDGELY. I shall vote for this proposition of the gentleman from Kent; and I shall be very frank in stating the reasons why I shall vote for it. I shall vote for it because I believe it will help the constitution in Kent county; and I will vote for any proposition founded upon justice which has such a feature incident to the administration of such justice.

But I shall vote for the proposition to open this article for another reason; that while I believe the rule adopted works in general very equitably, I have never yet known of any rule which was free from exceptions; and I believe exceptional cases will justly arise under any rule that we can devise. If any county can show a case of equity and justice, even though it may contradict the strict letter of the rule, I will vote to enlarge the representation of such county, upon the theory just stated, that it is a case properly of exception to the general rule.

Now I will say with regard to my county, and my whole delegation concur with me, that it will be difficult to sustain ourselves at all with our people. We have been flooded with letters from every quarter of our county, and every county paper has been assailing us and assailing the convention ever since we adopted it. I believe if we had one more in our county it would help our constitution very much; and therefore, while I will vote for one more representative for Kent county, I shall ask my friends to vote for one more for Baltimore county upon the same principle.

Mr. SCHLEY. After very mature deliberation and considerable debate, this report, No. 4, passed through its second reading. All that I have heard since the motion of the gentleman from Kent (Mr. Hollyday) was made, only induces me to believe that it will lead to a repetition of that debate, and a prolongation and delay, if this question is opened again. I believe the rule of this apportionment is equitable; and I am prepared to defend it. I confess, however, that in the case of Kent county, I feel a strong disposition to depart from the strict letter of the provision of the section, for reasons which it is unnecessary for me to recapitulate, but which are very well known to every member of the convention. The opinion prevailed to a great extent I am sure, among those who voted for this section, that Kent county might without any real departure from the rule be awarded two delegates.

I think it probable that since the census was taken, one hundred and fifty-three white persons have settled in Kent; and I think it very probable that if the census were to be taken to-day, she would be entitled to another representative. I believe that that consideration will have great weight with the counties generally; and that they will order at an early day an enumeration of the inhabitants of the State to be made; so that although Kent may complain that in strict justice it is this day entitled to two members, her privation will not be of long duration if we adhere to the rule. I shall not only vote against giving to Kent county an additional member for this reason, but because I believe it would induce a very unnecessary prolongation of the session and a renewal of the old debate we have already gone through.

Mr. BRISCOE. One word; and I beg pardon of my friend from Kent for undertaking to say a single word in favor of his proposition when the result may very likely be to kill that proposition; as it seems that members of the minority do sometimes kill a proposition by talking it down.

I recollect that when this matter was before the convention, I was about to offer a proposition that no county should have a less representation in the house of delegates than two members; but the previous question was sprung upon me, and I had no opportunity to offer that proposition. Of course that includes the amendment of my friend from Kent, to give his county two representatives.

Gentlemen have talked in this convention about arbitrary rule and about principle. I defy any member of this convention to show me in the representation of any State of this Union, any State which has ever been able to bring down its representation to a mathematical principle. They almost always have a fraction either diminishing or increasing that representation. And the gentleman from Baltimore (Mr. Stirling) does not apply even to his own section of the State, and to the city of Baltimore the naked principle of representation according to population, and is unwilling to make an application to apply that principle; but he is in favor of an arbitrary rule, and its relaxation in a single county of the State. He has intimated that he should like to know why a man in the city of Baltimore is not equal to the man that lives in the old fields in the county of Prince George's or of Calvert. Now, sir, some wise men have said, and I believe it to be a solemn and indisputable truth, it was no less a statesman than Thomas Jefferson who said it, that in a republic, large cities are sores upon the body politic. He has displayed wisdom in other things. I leave that question between the gentleman from Baltimore city and Mr. Jefferson.

I will tell the gentleman why I hold that a man in the city of Baltimore is not entitled to be fully represented here in population the same as a citizen of my own county or the county of Prince George's. There is no State in the Union situated like the State of Maryland. We have here a small State, in population and territory, and a large, progressive, and powerful city. I am in many things proud of that city. I am willing, so far as I am concerned, when participating in the legislation of the State, and I think what I have done in the past will bear me out in the assertion, to contribute, so far as I think consistent with the public welfare, to the advancement of that great city. But when you come to the question of representative power; when the gentleman asks me why the men in the city of Baltimore should not in representative power in the State rank head by head with the men in the rural districts of the State, I will tell him that the citizen in the rural districts of the State is a permanent inhabitant; but when you come to a large city like the city of Baltimore, there is always a floating population passing away, migrating, having in fact no identity of interest with the population of the State. I have nothing to say to the suggestion of the gentleman who drew a comparison between men living in the city and in old fields, further than to say to him that there are some other sections of the State besides old fields. I leave it to the sound judgment and good sense of the convention to determine whether, these things being so, as they are undeniably, I think, it would not be fair in making this rule, because you have not adopted a principle, for us to permit the counties to protect themselves in their apportionment.

The principle, which is no principle but an arbitrary rule, which you have established, gives to the city of Baltimore eighteen representatives. The gentleman has very frankly said that is all he can get, and he is satisfied. They took particular pains however to exclude some three or four of the counties from what they said was the rule or principle. They departed from the rule or principle for the city of Baltimore.

Mr. Stirling. We restricted it.

Mr. Briscoe. They restricted the rule, and made the representation less than the rule required; and when they came to my county, the small county of Calvert, they restricted it to one delegate. I was about to offer a proposition to the convention that no county should have less than two, but the previous question cut me off. Now I say that so far as the rule applies to any theory of representation, under no government on God's earth can you reach a true and exact representation as to numbers. Under the rule here, an excess of 2,500 over the 5,000 will allow an additional representative. We have a white population of upwards of 6,000.

Mr. Stockbridge. The census says 3,997; three less than 4,000.

Mr. Briscoe. Very well; that is the standard so far as the principle of representation is concerned; but I know the population is about 6,000. This matter of representation has never under our government been reduced to any well settled principle. And if the principle always has been departed from, I think you cannot make a rule which will not require to be restricted in some particular instances. I ask if there is a State in the Union which has established a rule, from which they have not departed for the protection of some section or the smaller counties of the State? I think that the gentlemen representing the counties should look to it that in the advancing stride of power in the city of Baltimore, it does not absorb all the political power of the State. I do not believe the people of the city of Baltimore demand, and I do not presume these gentlemen came here prepared to demand for them, or to say that we have any authentic voice from the city of Baltimore demanding a representation according to their numbers.

Mr. Stirling. I should like to ask the gentleman whether every political party representing the city of Baltimore in this hall does not express the same thing? I should like to hear the gentleman say whether he conceives that his political friends in Baltimore are opposed to being represented here?

Mr. Briscoe. I know that they opposed it in 1850; for in the convention which met here, we had the power, and they did not then demand representation according to population. That is a historical fact in which the proceedings of that convention will bear me out.

Mr. Stirling. They were in the same position that we are—not fools enough to demand what they knew they could not obtain.

Mr. Briscoe. You may imagine that; but I refer to the remarks of Mr. Brent, of the city of Baltimore, who was *par excellence* the leader of the idea that representation according to population was the just theory, and even he did not demand it.

Now the question is, as you have not got a principle by which you can govern this, is it fair and right and proper, when you have no demand from the city of Baltimore, as I believe, to give her this representation? I have heard a great many wise men and intelligent men with whom I have conversed, from the city of Baltimore, say that they believed that when Baltimore city was represented by two intelligent men from that city in the olden time, they controlled more moral power in the legislative halls of your government than all your representatives at present.

I say then, looking at the results, that you have adopted no principle. I have stated why I shall vote for the proposition of the gentleman from Kent, that I want all the small counties to be placed in the same category and to have two representatives each.—I wanted to give my reasons, although what I might say here might very likely have some effect in causing the proposition to be voted down. I leave gentlemen to determine it upon its merits. I had thought that in these families of counties, although I have asked very few things of this convention, that the small people of a family were generally pets; but I have found it otherwise here. The principle of concession that the smaller children of a family are generally treated with more favor than the larger ones, runs through this patriarchal system at any rate. I see no rule by which you have a right to stand up and claim as a matter of right and justice to deny my county two representatives, to send here, that in the contingency of one man being absent, my county may not be for months at a time wholly unrepresented.

Mr. Cushing. How is it in Delaware in Congress?

Mr. Briscoe. I say that the rule of representation is adopted in no State in the Union with less exception than in the State of Maryland. So far as the question of representative power of the city of Baltimore is concerned, I know very well that even when Baltimore city was part of a county, with a large rural district attached to her, there was great concern lest she should obtain the control of the State, and the city of Baltimore should become in the State of Maryland what Paris is in France. I have no distrust of her power. I am willing to trust her, if she is willing to accord to me what I believe to be fair and right. See the tendency of this. Thirty to fifty years ago, we gave to Baltimore but few representatives in this hall. She has come here through the counties which have been built up through her prosperity. We have met their representatives in the legislative halls of the State, and we have conceded from time to time to her demands. First she had two representatives; then some six, and then it went up to ten; and now Baltimore city is here again demanding and asking for political power in this State. I believe that in the end it will result dangerously to the interests of the State of Maryland. I believe it in my heart. I believe that if we go so far in this convention as to make Baltimore the stronghold of political power in this State, controlling the popular elections of the State, we shall live to see the day that we will regret it.

There is always a conflict between labor and capital. It existed under the old government. It has been the subject of much attention; the conflict between labor, or the producing interests of the State, and the capital of the State.

Mr. Stirling. Is there no labor in the city of Baltimore? Is it all capital?

Mr. Briscoe. I am speaking of the agricultural labor of the State. Those who are engaged in the agricultural department of your State are in opposition to them. I do not say that if principle is properly directed and talent properly controlled, it will lead to evil. But wise men, statesmen, men with the eye of prophecy, never will agree to come under the influence of any one particular class of labor in the State, and to give it an inordinate and overwhelming control in the legislation of the State. For that reason I say that when these gentlemen do not apply the rule of justice to themselves, they should not exclude Kent county and the county of Calvert from the boon we are asking of them.—I think that there should be no representation here for any county, upon grounds of expediency, efficiency, and above all from principles of self-protection, less than two representatives. I do not propose to offer this as an amendment to the proposition of my friend from Kent (Mr. Hollyday,) for I say I am willing to vote for it. But if you adopt that, I hope the convention will permit me to offer this amendment and place myself right on the record. It was ruled out before on the adoption of the previous question, and I had no opportunity to offer it. I do not suppose it will be adopted; but I desire to offer it, to present my claims for my own county, and to represent my own views.

Mr. Cushing. I moved that so much be considered the third reading of the report, because I knew this amendment would be thrown in upon the house. We have consumed nearly two hours in discussing the question whether this report shall be opened to amendment. The majority of this house, after a long consideration, when the question was open to argument, when the report went through its second reading, section by section, accepted this report as it now stands; and I ask if it is advisable for the majority of this house in any way to amend the report. I have heard no new reason urged for opening it; no fact which was not before us when it was upon its second reading. Remember that two hours have passed simply in the discussion of the proposition to admit one amendment. The amendment itself, if admitted, may be debated for the Lord knows how many hours more. Then comes another proposition which may take two hours more. We would better have no second reading of a report at all, if when the house has upon the second reading of a report decided by a unanimous vote of the majority of the house that the report shall stand as it is, it can be brought before the house again and leave asked to open the report and change it upon the third reading, because the yeas and nays take up time, and if the matter meets with any opposition we may spend two hours or more upon the simple question whether the report shall be opened for amendment. If reports which have been before the house for weeks, and which have finall gone through, are to come up again, and have the whole question opened, every report we have gone through may be taken up in the same way. If a proposition is made to this house which meets the view of the majority, I think the better way is to refer it to the committee on revision, and let the question be decided at once and without debate. Then let the committee on revision report the amendment back to the house.

I want to apologize to the house for being a member from the city of Baltimore. After the eloquent remarks of the gentleman from Calvert (Mr. Briscoe,) I think if the report should be opened by the convention for amendment, the convention would better take away the eighteen members allotted to the city of Baltimore and give them to Calvert county, so that the State may be well ruled, and one given to Baltimore. I never was so ashamed of anything in my life, as I am of having come here from the city of Baltimore, after the eloquent remarks of the gentleman from Calvert. I am led to believe that there is no virtue, nothing to benefit the State, which the counties can expect from Baltimore, that the counties have built up Baltimore, while she has done nothing but devour them; and I am exceedingly sorry that I should have been placed in the position of being a member from so contemptible a place. I wish to apologize to the convention for it, and to assure them that it was not my fault. I should have preferred to have been from among the agricultural people of the State, down in Calvert county.

Mr. Holliday. I hope my motion will not be prejudiced before the convention by any amendment to that now offered. I would not have offered it, had not Kent county been so near the number that is required by the report for two members; and I thought it would meet the sense of the convention today to give that number to the county. I would greatly desire, if the convention would do so, that two representatives should be given to every county; so that if one member should be unable to attend, the county should not be entirely unrepresented. It will be remembered that a member of this convention was sick and unable to be here for three months; and the same thing might occur in any of the small counties; and then they would have no representative at all.

In Kent county, as I said before, we pay a tax more than equal to Caroline; and we are paying an income tax of one thousand dollars more than Caroline, I believe. I hope the convention in considertion of these matters will give us two members.

Mr. Scott. I happen to have some business acquaintance with our neighbors of Kent county; and I hope that as a matter of justice two representatives will be allowed to her. I have no doubt from the thrifty and enterprising character of her people, and the number of men necessary to carry out her various improvements, and particularly in preparing timber, that she has now more than the additional number, if a census were to be taken to-day, which would entitle her to an additional delegate. I know it has acquired a vast influx of white labor to get all the timber which comes from that county, and there are other pursuits also requiring additional labor. I think it would be no injustice, but perfectly in accordance with the principles laid down in the report.

Mr. Abbott. I desire to say one word, being chairman of the committee. Like my colleague (Mr. Cushing,) I feel that I ought to apologize to the convention, after the views that have been expressed here, for being a member from that great sore and ulcer upon the body politic, disfiguring the State.

I believe, sir, that we have four separate and distinct classes of people that make up the great mass requiring representation. First, is the producing, the working class; the farmers and miners; all that produce anything, or cause anything to be produced from the earth. Next is the mechanic; next the manufacturer; and next the merchant. These constitute the four great quarters of our political community; they are the ones to be legislated for, and who should be represented. I never dreamed that the city of Baltimore, where a large portion of the inhabitants of the State are congregated, ought to be subdivided, and made as so many adjoining counties. It seems to be supposed here that the city of Baltimore will be represented by one separate and distinct class of people. We have heard a great deal upon this floor about the mercantile interests of Baltimore and the producing interests of the State. Day after day has passed, in which the name of mechanic or manufacturer has never been heard in these halls. They are two equally important branches of our community, and equally require representation. They are congregated mostly in the city of Baltimore. The subdivision of the city into three counties of the State, induces the hope that hereafter the mercantile, the manufacturing, and the mechanical interests will all be represented upon this floor as separate and distinct classes. While the men of the State outside of the city of Baltimore are producers, and come here in a solid body for their interests, and advocate their interests, the city of Baltimore has had two at one time, and finally ten representatives upon this floor, and they have only represented the interests of the mercantile and monetary community.

I hope that the system which has been established here will not be disturbed. Although there may be but one member for some counties, these counties, particularly after the adoption of certain sections in the constitution prohibiting local legislation, will not suffer the inconvenienee they have heretofore if their delegate is not here to represent them. I think that the report ought to remain as it is, in order that all parts of the State may have a fair representation.

Mr. NEGLEY. I hope the convention will not disturb this report. If the majority of the house by whom it has been carried heretofore disturb it now, you will have to reorganize the entire thing; because not a single feature in it will be applicable to it when once disturbed. The whole theory is based upon what it is now; and the nature of the provisions for future additions in the representation of the State will be entirely destroyed, and you will have to refer the whole thing back to another committee, or will have to go into committee of the whole to reconsider and reorganize and reform the entire plan. Have not we spent time enough over this? Have not we considered it fully? There is no system at all that you can possibly form, containing so many elements of compromise as this one system which was maturely and deliberately considered by the committee, and by the convention upon its second reading. If it be disturbed at all, we come back to first principles, and we must reorganize it from its foundation. And where shall we end? The temper of the house is not such as to be able to take up such a question and act upon it with deliberation, as when it was before us upon its second reading. We are just on the eve of adjournment. We are all in a hurry, anxious to get away; and the danger will be that if we disturb this report, we shall make it infinitely worse than it is now before we can agree upon it. I think we would better stand by the report as it is.

Mr. BARRON called for the previous question.

Mr. BRISCOE. I understand my proposition to be before the convention, as I have sent it to the table.

The PRESIDENT. The previous question does not apply in this case.

Mr. STIRLING. This is a question independent of the question of adopting the report; and upon that the previous question is called.

The PRESIDENT. The previous question applies to the entire report.

Mr. CHAMBERS. I rise to a question of order. I find by the rules and orders that a motion to amend may be made at the third reading as well as at any other time. The chair has ruled several times that that is not the order of proceeding, but that the question should be, shall the article be opened for amendment. I do not find anything about opening it.

The PRESIDENT. It is the fifty-third rule.

Mr. CHAMBERS. That rule is as follows:

Rule 53. "After a report of any committee (embodying proposed provisions for the constitution) has passed through its second reading, the question shall then be put by the president of the convention, "Shall this report be engrossed for a third reading?" After any report of a committee has passed to a third reading, it shall not be in order to amend the same, except by the consent of the majority of the members elected to the convention."

But by the consent of that majority it may be amended; and the question of amendment is just like any other amendment, I take it.

The PRESIDENT. No, sir.

Mr. CHAMBERS. My colleague moves to amend this report. That motion cannot prevail except by the consent of the majority of the members elected to the convention; but it is a proper motion.

The PRESIDENT. I will remark to the gentleman from Kent (Mr. Chambers,) that under the parliamentary rule a report upon the third reading connot be amended. That is a general principle of parliamentary law, and of course there must be a motion to dispense with that rule of parliamentary law before the convention can get at the provision in this rule.

Mr. CHAMBERS. The fifty-third rule controls that, and expressly says that it may be amended on the third reading.

The PRESIDENT. The convention is to be consulted whether, upon a consideration of the entire report they will permit that amendment to be introduced. If the convention permits the amendment to be introduced then it will be in order to submit the amendment.

Mr. BARRON. Has there been any question before the house for the last two hours?

The PRESIDENT. Yes, sir; the simple question whether the convention will order the report to be opened for an amendment. Under the general principles of parliamentary law, the report could not be opened upon the third reading. It is the question whether the convention will open it.

Mr. SANDS. I would like to say a single word by way of appeal to our friends in this house. It will be very brief, and if members do not choose to listen to it, they can do as they please.

The PRESIDENT. The convention will come to order. Members will take their seats.

Mr. SANDS resumed : I was just going to say I hope our friends will not exhibit so much of the spirit of the late Charleston convention here ; that if they cannot have matters entirely their own way, they will not threaten to fly off and request something else unreasonable. Here is Kent county nearly up to the standard. My friend from Frederick proposes to leave it to the next legislature; so that we shall be necessitated to have an entire State enumeration, simply to give Kent an additional member. Is that wise? I shall vote to give another member to Kent county, and another to Baltimore county, and there I shall stop ; believing that these two counties are actual cases of hardship.

This rule of adopting the absolute ratio of population does very well in the large cities ; but how does it operate upon the counties? It goes right out of Baltimore city, and applies city rules, based upon a large floating population, to the large counties, so as to bring down a population of fifty or sixty thousand souls almost upon a level with a population of twenty-five thousand. I do not think we ought to hold on to any such arbitrary rules, where they work injustice.—I shall with great pleasure vote for the motion of the gentleman from Kent (Mr. Hollyday,) and if Baltimore county makes a claim for another member I will vote for that; but I do not believe that any other county is in a condition to urge any claim for another.

Mr. MAYHUGH demanded the yeas and nays.

Mr. CLARKE. Is the question upon opening the section?

The PRESIDENT. The question is upon opening the section for the purpose of making the amendment proposed by the gentleman from Kent (Mr. Hollyday) to give Kent county an additional member.

The yeas and nays were ordered.

Mr. RIDGELY. Is the proposition before the house subject to enlargement or amendment?

The PRESIDENT. I rather think not.

Mr. STIRLING. Any other amendment can be offered afterwards.

The PRESIDENT. Any amendment can be offered to this amendment for the purpose of perfecting it.

Mr STIRLING. If the house decides not to let this amendment in, any other member can move to open it for any other amendment, and it can be opened for that, if the house consent to it.

The PRESIDENT. Yes, sir; they must consent to each amendment.

Mr. CLARKE. Is it not in order to amend the amendment of the gentleman from Kent, so as to extend the proposition to all the counties having one representative?

The PRESIDENT. No, sir; it must be an amendment to the particular proposition of the gentleman from Kent.

Mr. RIDGELY. We can make a similar proposition for another county, I understand, only through a similar motion.

The PRESIDENT. Yes, sir; the gentleman from Kent (Mr. Hollyday) moves to open the report for a particular purpose. No other amendment than to accomplish that particular purpose will be admitted.

The question being taken, the result was—yeas 45, nays 24—as follows :

Yeas—Messrs. Goldsborough, President; Billingsley, Blackiston, Bond, Briscoe, Brown, Carter, Chambers, Daniel, Dellinger, Dennis, Dent, Duvall, Earle, Ecker, Greene, Hodson, Hoffman, Hollyday, Hopkins, Hopper, Horsey, Jones, of Cecil, Kennard, King, Larsh, Lee, Markey, Miller, Morgan, Mullikin, Nyman, Parker, Parran, Pugh, Purnell, Ridgely, Sands, Scott, Smith, of Dorchester, Smith, of Worcester, Stirling, Swope, Sykes, Todd—45.

Nays—Messrs. Abbott, Annan, Audoun, Baker, Barron, Belt Brooks, Clarke, Cunningham, Cushing, Davis, of Washington, Farrow, Galloway, Hatch, Hebb, Keefer, Mayhugh, McComas, Murray, Negley, Russell, Schley, Valliant, Wickard—24.

The PRESIDENT. Under the fifty-third rule the consent of the majority of the menbers elected to the convention is required. The motion therefore is lost.

Mr. PUGH. I move a reconsideration of the vote; I voted in the majority.

The motion was seconded by Messrs. SANDS and TODD.

Mr. MAYHUGH demanded the yeas and nays on the question of reconsideration ; and they were ordered.

The question being taken, the result was—yeas 49, nays 22—as follows :

Yeas—Messrs. Goldsborough, President; Belt, Billingsley, Blackiston, Bond, Briscoe, Brown, Carter, Chambers, Clarke, Daniel, Dellinger, Dennis, Dent, Duvall, Earle, Ecker, Galloway, Greene, Hodson, Hoffman, Hollyday, Hopkins, Hopper, Horsey, Jones, of Cecil, Kennard, King, Larsh, Lee, Markey, Miller, Morgan, Nyman, Parker, Parran, Pugh, Purnell, Ridgely, Sands, Scott, Smith, of Dorchester, Smith, of Worcester, Stirling, Swope, Sykes, Todd, Valliant, Wooden—49.

Nays—Messrs. Abbott, Annan, Audoun, Baker, Barron, Brooks, Cunningham, Cushing, Davis, of Washington, Farrow, Hatch, Hebb, Keefer, Mayhugh, McComas, Mullikin, Murray, Negley, Russell, Schley, Stockbridge, Wickard—22.

The vote was accordingly reconsidered.

The question recurred upon the motion to open the section for the amendment proposed by the gentleman from Kent (Mr. Hollyday.)

Mr. PUGH. I move to suspend the fifty-third rule.

The PRESIDENT. That is not in order.

Mr. PUGH. We are now in precisely the same position that we were before we took the vote upon the motion. We are about to take the vote; and before the vote is taken I move to suspend the fifty-third rule.

The PRESIDENT. It is not in order to suspend that rule.

Mr. PUGH. I call the attention of the chair to the forty-ninth rule:

Rule 49. The rules may be suspended when demanded by three-fifths of the members present.

The PRESIDENT. That is a suspension of the rules of the convention. The suspension of the rules is to avoid their operation for a particular time for a particular purpose. You cannot suspend the operation of this rule here.

Mr. PUGH. The purpose I have is very plain. A large majority are in favor of doing a certain thing, and their recorded votes say so. It is because I am in favor of the democratic principle of the rule of the majority that I move to suspend the fifty-third rule, to allow the majority of the house, being in favor of doing a certain thing, to have that privilege. I ask the gentleman from Kent to withdraw his motion in order that I may make the motion to suspend the rules.

The PRESIDENT. What is the object of suspending the rule?

Mr. PUGH. To give the majority of the house the power to do as they have decided by their vote that they will do.

The PRESIDENT. That amounts to rescinding the rule.

Mr. PUGH. While it is suspended it is not in operation.

Mr. SANDS. Many of us voted for this proposition who were anxious to obtain the object; but we will not do so outside of our regular rules, and will vote against any suspension of the rules. I voted for the proposition as a measure of fairness; but I will not vote to rescind or violate our rules in order to pass it.

Mr. PUGH. I do not regard it as a violation of the rules. Under the 49th rule, which I have read, I have a perfect right to make this motion. I have as much right to ask for action under the 49th rule, as any gentleman under the 53d rule.

The PRESIDENT. The gentleman mistakes the character of the suspension of the rules. It is only done for the purpose of progressing in the business of the convention. It is not that any vote or action of the convention shall be changed thereby. The rules could be suspended at any time, and the majority could do anything they pleased.

Mr. PUGH. That is my idea; and the reason for my motion.

The PRESIDENT. The convention can rescind the rule upon one day's notice. If this proposition is voted down now, it does not preclude the reconsideration of it at any time.

Mr. CHAMBERS. I understand the chair to have intimated that the fifty-third rule covered the question of the amendment proposed by my colleague. If I understand the state of the case, there is nothing to require more than a majority of the votes of the members present to carry the proposition except so far as the fifty-third rule provides to the contrary. The fifty-third rule says that it shall require a majority of the members elected to the convention to amend upon the third reading; but if this rule does not operate, the majority carry the question. If the rule is suspended, how can it operate? The rules, as I understand the practice in congress, are suspended for the purpose of taking a particular vote, a vote upon a particular question. The very motion of the gentleman from Cecil (Mr. Pugh) is that the fifty-third rule shall not operate *quoad hoc*, so far as the vote upon this question is concerned. If the fifty-third rule be suspended it does not operate. If it does not operate, the majority carries the vote. That is the view I take of the matter. I cannot see how, if the rule is suspended, it can yet be in force to require a larger vote than a majority. The rule being suspended is silenced; and the rule being silenced the majority carries it. I submit it to the chair that this is a proper consideration.

Mr. NEGLEY. We have attempted on previous occasions to alter the rules; and that motion must lie over.

Mr. CLARKE. Will the gentleman yield the floor to enable me to make a suggestion? I had not looked at the fifty-third rule at the time the chair made the decision that the motion was not adopted. Upon reading the rule, I take the liberty to call the attention of the chair to it, with a view to a modification of his decision. It reads in this way:

"After any report of a committee has passed to a third reading, it shall not be in order to amend the same, except by the consent of the majority of the members elected to the convention."

This rule therefore applies to the question whether it shall be in order to amend the report on its third reading; in other words whether the report shall be opened upon its third reading to amendment That was passed upon by the house without the yeas and nays being called; and they determined that this amendment might be offered.

The PRESIDENT. No, sir; the reverse. The yeas and nays were called upon that question, and a majority of the members elected did not vote for it.

Mr. CLARKE. I voted upon the question understanding it to be the question whether or not this amendment should be embodied in the report.

On motion of Mr. ANNAN,

The convention took a recess until half past 3 o'clock, P. M.

AFTERNOON SESSION.

The convention met at half past 3 o'clock, P. M.

The roll was called, and the following members answered to their names:

Messrs. Goldsborough, President; Abbott, Annan, Audoun, Baker, Barron, Billingsley, Blackiston, Bond, Brooks, Carter, Chambers, Cunningham, Cushing, Daniel, Davis, of Washington, Dellinger, Dennis, Dent, Duvall, Earle, Ecker, Farrow, Galloway, Greene, Hatch, Hebb, Hoffman, Hollyday, Hopkins, Horsey, Keefer, Kennard, King, Larsh, Lee, Markey, Mayhugh, McComas, Miller, Morgan, Mullikin, Murray, Negley, Nyman, Parker, Parran, Pugh, Purnell, Ridgely, Russell, Sands, Schley, Scott, Smith, of Carroll, Smith, of Dorchester, Smith, of Worcester, Stirling, Stockbridge, Swope, Sykes, Thomas, Todd, Turner, Wickard, Wooden—66.

Mr. SCOTT. I move that the fiftieth rule be put in force.

Mr. STIRLING. I should like to know the object of that. We have sixty members here; and it will delay the progress of the house. It interferes with the progress of the business.

Mr. SCOTT withdrew the motion.

BASIS OF REPRESENTATION.

The convention resumed the consideration of the report of the committee on the basis of representation, on its third reading; the pending question being the motion of Mr. HOLLYDAY to open the report for the purpose of so amending it as to allow Kent county two representatives.

The PRESIDENT. At the time the gentleman from Cecil (Mr. Pugh) moved to suspend the fifty-third rule, the chair was under the impression that at that stage of the proceedings the motion was not in order. The chair is now of opinion that it is competent to suspend the rule; but that it requires a vote of three-fifths of the members present, as required by the forty-ninth rule.

Mr. PUGH renewed the motion to suspend the fifty-third rule.

Mr. ABBOTT demanded the yeas and nays, and they were ordered.

The question being taken, the result was—yeas 40, nays 26—as follows:

Yeas—Messrs. Goldsborough, President; Billingsley, Blackiston, Bond, Briscoe, Daniel, Dennis, Dent, Duvall, Earle, Galloway, Greene, Hoffman, Hollyday, Hopkins, Horsey, King, Larsh, Lee, Markey, Miller, Morgan, Mullikin, Nyman, Parker, Parran, Pugh, Purnell, Ridgely, Sands, Scott, Smith, of Carroll, Smith, of Dorchester, Smith, of Worcester, Stirling, Swope, Sykes, Thomas, Todd, Turner—40.

Nays—Messrs. Abbott, Annan, Audoun, Baker, Barron, Brooks, Carter, Cunningham, Cushing, Davis, of Washington, Dellinger, Ecker, Farrow, Hatch, Hebb, Keefer, Kennard, Mayhugh, McComas, Murray, Negley, Russell, Schley, Stockbridge, Wickard, Wooden—26.

The fifty-third rule was accordingly suspended, three-fifths of the members present having voted for its suspension.

The question recurred upon the motion to open the report to the amendment moved by Mr. HOLLYDAY.

The question being taken, the result was—ayes 37, noes not counted.

The motion was accordingly declared adopted.

Mr. HOLLYDAY moved to amend the third section of the report by striking out "one," in the eighteenth line and inserting "two," so as to give Kent county two representatives.

Mr. CUSHING. I wish to inquire whether, the fifty-third rule having been suspended, this report can be amended, in parliamentary law, upon the third reading, excepting by unanimous consent. Is there any rule authorizing the amendment upon the third reading except the fifty-third rule, which we have suspended?

The PRESIDENT. The fifty-third rule was only suspended for this particular occasion.

Mr. CUSHING. But being suspended for this particular occasion we fall back upon the general parliamentary practice, which is that the report cannot be amended upon the third reading. In congress, for instance, no bill can be amended upon its third reading.

Mr. PUGH. I will answer the gentleman, so far as I understand this matter. My impression is that this is a convention assembled here to make a constitution. Among other things it adopted for its government a certain set of rules. One of those rules provides that for the accomplishment of any special purpose the convention may, independent of all parliamentary law, suspend one of its rules or all of its rules. The convention under that rule has suspended another rule for a special purpose, in conformity with the rules and not outside of the rules. My objection to the argument of the gentleman from Baltimore city (Mr. Cushing) is just this. He claims, or suggests to the chair that we have gone beyond the pale of the rules—that we are beyond the working of the rules—that having suspended this rule we are thrown back upon parliamentary law. My answer is that we are acting strictly in conformity with the rules. Under one of the rules adopted by this body we suspend another rule for a special purpose. In conformity with the rules we have suspended one of them. The ground taken by the gentleman from Baltimore city is that we are not now acting under the operation of these rules because we have suspended one of them. The ground I take is that we are acting under these rules, because we have acted in obedience to the rules in suspending this fifty-third rule.

Mr. CUSHING. I am indebted to my colleague for the suggestion that the gentleman from Cecil (Mr. Pugh) wants to eat his cake and have it. He has suspended the fifty-third rule and yet he wishes it to be operative. The forty-seventh rule is:

"*Rule* 47. The rules of parliamentary practice shall govern the convention in all cases to which they are applicable, and in which they are not inconsistent with the standing rules and orders of the convention."

The only rule in reference to amending a report upon the third reading which is inconsistent with the parliamentary practice is the fifty-third rule, which in the present case does not exist because it has been suspended in its operation. I hope and trust that the gentleman from Cecil having made the motion to suspend the rule in order that this question might be settled, the convention will settle it according to the parliamentary law, and will pass the report in exactly the form it was agreed upon on its second reading and admit no amendment whatever.

Mr. STOCKBRIDGE. I rise to a question of order, that a point of order is not debatable.

The PRESIDENT. The chair can permit the disc ssion to go on.

Mr. CUSHING resumed: Therefore I say that the fifty-third rule being suspended no longer operates, and therefore the convention is thrown back upon the forty-seventh rule which confines us to parliamentary practice. Now, in parliamentary practice, I can only go to the highest authority in this country—the house of congress—which do not allow a bill to be amended upon its third reading. We have suspended the only rule which made our practice different from that of congress. We fall back upon the forty-seventh rule, which refers us back to parliamentary practice. I rise therefore to the point of order that the proposition being to amend upon the third reading, and the fifty-third rule being suspended, it is not in order.

Mr. NEGLEY. I think the point taken by the gentleman from Baltimore city (Mr. Cushing) is perfectly clear. By what authority or power do you take up this report and amend it upon the third reading? Is it by general parliamentary law—by authority outside of our rules? No, sir. It is by the fifty-third rule. That is the only power in the rules of this house by which you can amend a report upon its third reading. There is no other rule or rules in this whole body of rules by which you can touch a report upon its third reading for the purpose of emendation. What have we done? We have suspended the very rule which gives us the power of emendation. Where is the power then? If we have it anywhere it is in the general parliamentary law. By the forty-seventh rule you are not only governed as a general principle by parliamentary law, but that rule expressly says that you shall fall back upon parliamentary law, and that parliamentary law is that you cannot amend a report upon its third reading.

Mr. CHAMBERS. It seems to me that the ingenuity of the gentleman from Baltimore (Mr. Cushing) has had the effect to obfuscate this business. There are certain parliamentary rules, and where nothing is said upon a particular point legislative bodies choose to regulate themselves by those rules. That is a conventional affair. They may do so or they may not, as they please. With regard to this matter this body has made its selection. There are certain rules of parliamentary law, but we have adopted a different law.

Mr. CUSHING. We have suspended it.

Mr. CHAMBERS. We have not done such a thing. We have not suspended the whole. The gentleman has talked himself into a fog, but I do not think he can talk us into it. What is the history of this particular parliamentary rule? We have said distinctly that we will not adopt it—we will adopt another rule. The parliamentary rule is that you cannot suspend a rule without a vote of two-thirds. We have no such rule. We have repudiated that parliamentary rule. We have adopted another rule for our government, and we say, taking this rule and the rule for suspension together, that except in cases where we suspend this rule we will require a majority of the whole number of votes to pass an amendment. But we have repudiated the parliamentary rule. We have declared as perfectly and effectually as if it had been in words that we will not adopt the parliamentary rule of requiring two-thirds to suspend the rule. We have suspended the operation of one of these rules. To suspend it is not to destroy it or to remove it. We merely say that as to this particular vote it shall be suspended. Then you bring it back to parliamentary rule, and what is the result? You have the parliamentary law hanging over you, and you have a suspended rule directly in opposition to it—two rules upon this subject—one in a state of suspense, and the other in the state of adoption. It seems to me that it is a very clear thing that the rule cannot be destroyed by a vote not mentioning it, relating to it, or referring to it. The parliamentary rule has no existence in this body in this case. When we adopted the other rule we virtually discarded it as fully as if we had said so in so many words.

Mr. DANIEL. It seems to me that the forty-second rule will control this. It says:

"All questions except those otherwise herein provided for, shall be determined by a majority of the members present."

This is a question not otherwise provided

for. We have allowed the majority of the members present, except in certain cases, to determine everything. That is the rule of all bodies of this sort. Besides, if we submit the constitution to the people, and if they ratify it, I say it cures all that is behind it.

Mr. GREENE. I move to reconsider the vote by which the fifty-third rule was adopted; and if that motion prevails I shall immediately move to strike out the provision that a majority of the members elected shall be necessary to amend a report upon its third reading. I think that will obviate the difficulty.

Mr. PUGH. I intended to suggest that that is in effect the motion I made; because at the time the object for which the rule was to be suspended was distinctly stated. The object was stated to be in relation to action upon this amendment.

The PRESIDENT. The chair cannot entertain a motion while the point of order is pending.

Mr. PUGH. We are acting under the rule which allows the convention to suspend any rule which interferes with the action of the body. That is the object for which the forty-ninth rule was adopted. That was the intention of the framers of that rule, undoubtedly, that three-fifths of the members assembled in this convention should determine that for the time being, in order to accomplish a certain stated purpose, a certain rule should not operate. They have so determined by one of their rules, just as binding as any other rule, and you must take the thing as a whole, for we are acting under the rules and in conformity with one of them. The convention have determined that for the time being, for a specific purpose stated, the fifty-third rule shall not operate. I submit this point that in conformity to the rules as a whole, this body have the right, by a vote of three-fifths of the members present, to suspend the rules for any purpose; and having determined to do that, I submit that there can be nothing in the rules to conflict with that action.

The PRESIDENT. The gentleman from Cecil (Mr. Pugh) has moved to suspend the fifty-third rule. That fifty-third rule requires that a motion to alter or amend a report upon its third reading should receive the sanction of the majority of the members elected to the convention, in order to prevail. After that rule has been suspended it throws us back upon the general principles of parliamentary law, if those general principles are not in conflict with any other standing rules of the house. If that general principle of parliamentary law is in conflict with any other standing rule of the house, of course the parliamentary law must give way to the rule adopted by the convention.

The convention has decided under the forty-second rule that all questions without any limitation, shall be decided by a majority of the members present, except in the cases provided for. The fifty-third rule is one of those cases provided for. Therefore it was necessary to suspend that rule in order to enable the majority to control this question The parliamentary practice standing in direct opposition to the forty-second rule is also controlled by the forty-second rule. So that when you suspend the rule requiring more than a majority, the forty-second rule puts it in the power of the majority of the members present to control the question. That is the judgment of the chair. The amendment is therefore in order.

Mr. SCHLEY. I move to amend the amendment so as to strike out "seventy-nine" and insert "eighty."

The PRESIDENT The section was opened, under the fifty-third rule to the specific amendment indicated.

Mr. SCHLEY. This is a part of the amendment, or the consequence of it.

The PRESIDENT. The gentleman only moved to open the report to give Kent county two members instead of one.

Mr. CUSHING demanded the yeas and nays on the amendment submitted by Mr. HOLLYDAY, and they were ordered.

The question being taken, the result was—yeas 46, nays 19—as follows:

Yeas—Messrs. Goldsborough, President; Belt, Billingsley, Blackiston, Bond, Briscoe, Carter, Chambers, Clarke, Daniel, Dellinger, Dent, Duvall, Earle, Ecker, Galloway, Greene, Hoffman, Hollyday, Hopkins, Hopper, Horsey, Kennard, King, Larsh, Lee, Markey, Miller, Mullikin, Nyman, Parker, Parran, Pugh, Purnell, Ridgely, Sands, Scott, Smith, of Carroll, Smith, of Worcester, Stirling, Swope, Sykes, Thomas, Todd, Turner, Wooden—46.

Nays—Messrs. Abbott, Annan, Audoun, Baker, Barron, Cunningham, Cushing, Davis, of Washington, Farrow, Hebb, Keefer, Mayhugh, McComas, Murray, Negley, Russell, Schley, Stockbridge, Wickard—19.

When their names were called,

Mr. BELT said: I was in favor of the proposition supported by my colleague (Mr. Clarke,) who introduced into this house what I regard as the only true principle of representation, that you should place it upon the sound basis of population, and district the State, dividing it so that every man in it, every resident voter, should vote for one man. That not being adopted, the convention having decided to come down to a more arbitrary standard, my preference was to have the standard fixed as it is in the present constitution. Seeing that that will not be done, and that giving to Kent county one other member is an approach to it, I shall, simply on that theory vote for it, and upon no other ground. I have strong objections to the proposition as at first announced, giving an addition to Kent that is not extended to Charles, St. Mary's, and other counties, but that is excluded from the question; and as an approach to what I regard as right I vote for this proposition, "aye."

Mr. HEBB said: The majority of this house having solemnly decided heretofore that this report should stand as it is, I feel bound to vote against all changes; and I vote "no."

Mr. MAYHUGH said: I have not heard a single argument in favor of this amendment, and no argument can be adduced in favor of it; and I therefore must vote "no."

Mr. NEGLEY said: As it would disturb the foundation upon which this whole apportionment is based, and violate it in one particular, and I do not see why you might not as well violate it in a thousand, I vote "no."

Mr. SCHLEY said: I felt strongly tempted to vote for the proposition of the gentleman from Kent, but am restrained by two considerations; first, an unwillingness to violate the principle adopted here, and secondly, a desire to stand by the action of the majority as the report was agreed upon. I vote "no."

The amendment was accordingly adopted.

BALTIMORE COUNTY.

Mr. HOFFMAN. I move to suspend the fifty-third rule for the purpose of making a motion to open the report of the committee for the purpose of amending it in reference to Baltimore county by adding one to her delegation, giving her "seven" delegates instead of "six."

Mr. BRISCOE. I understand my proposition that I offered this morning to be pending.

The PRESIDENT. But one proposition can be entertained at a time.

Mr. BRISCOE. I made the motion notwithstanding.

The PRESIDENT. The gentleman was not in order if he did make the motion.

Mr. CLARKE. Before voting upon the motion of the gentleman from Baltimore county, I should like to have some explanation upon what ground the proposition is based. We had from the gentleman from Kent (Mr. Hollyday) some reason for his proposition.

Mr. RIDGELY. We have a population of 46,722, and under this apportionment we get but six delegates; while Carroll county, with a population of 22,525, gets five delegates. Our people are complaining very much about this apportionment. We think the rule works very unjustly to us; and that it has been arbitrarily fixed in this respect. We hope the convention will grant us this one; and we shall not then be represented according to population as fully as other counties. I hope the convention will grant us this one member, for the sake of the constitution; for the sake of satisfying our constituents. We want them to vote for this constitution, and to give a strong majority for it.

Mr. MILLER. I hope that motion will not prevail. When the minority report of the committee on the basis of representation was before the body, Baltimore county was represented in that by eight delegates. She chose, however, not to accept that apportionment which would give her eight delegates, and give to some other counties one more delegate; but she chose to adopt this principle, arbitrary rule—call it what you choose—cutting down my county, Anne Arundel, one representative, and cutting down other counties in the State, and giving her six delegates. I say now let Baltimore county stand or fall upon that. What claim has she, according to the basis fixed in this report of her own adoption, for other counties, to another member? The basis of 5,000 for each delegate up to a population of 25,000 will give her five delegates. Then the principle or arbitrary rule which they saw fit to adopt, has cut them down, and has cut down Baltimore city. In order to prevent the too large delegation which would result in Baltimore city, they have chosen to say that the next 20,000 shall give her one more delegate. Then that will give her the sixth delegate, and will leave only 1,722 for the fraction over. For that fraction I do not think she has the least claim upon the principle or the rule to ask for another delegate.

Mr. SANDS. Mr. President——

The PRESIDENT. The question of suspending the 53d rule is not debatable.

Mr. RIDGELY demanded the yeas and nays, and they were ordered.

The question being taken, the result was—yeas 35, nays 29—as follows:

Yeas—Messrs. Goldsborough, President; Barron, Briscoe, Carter, Chambers, Cunningham, Daniel, Earle, Ecker, Galloway, Greene, Hoffman, Hollyday, Hopkins, Hopper, Kennard, King, Larsh, McComas, Mullikin, Parker, Pugh, Purnell, Ridgely, Sands, Scott, Smith, of Carroll, Smith, of Worcester, Stirling, Stockbridge, Swope, Sykes, Thomas, Wickard, Wooden—35.

Nays—Messrs. Abbott, Annan, Baker, Belt, Billingsley, Blackiston, Bond, Clarke, Cushing, Davis, of Washington, Dellinger, Dent, Duvall, Farrow, Hebb, Horsey, Keefer, Lee, Markey, Mayhugh, 'Miller, Murray, Negley, Nyman, Parran, Russell, Schley, Todd, Turner—29.

When their names were called,

Mr. CLARKE said: I have one word to say with reference to the vote I shall give upon this proposition. I voted in favor of the proposition to amend so as to give Kent county two delegates instead of one. It was with great hesitation that I was brought to vote for that amendment; and it was simply upon this ground: I was opposed, when the convention had adopted a basis of representation here, to departing one iota from the actual operation of the rule—for I will not call it a principle. I yielded only upon the assertion of the gentlemen that Kent county really had population enough to be entitled to two members.

Now the proposition is to go further, and having adopted a principle, to tinker up the basis of representation just to suit localities, and make it popu'ar here and there. If the gentleman from Baltimore county can in any way satisfy me that, under the rule adopted here, his county is entitled to this additional representative, I will vote to open the report. That is the only ground upon which I voted for the amendment giving a member to Kent county, that it was actually entitled, by its population, according to the rule, to have two members. I am not now satisfied of that, so far as regards Baltimore co nty; and I therefore vote "no."

Mr. DENT said: When I voted for the suspension of this same rule a short time ago, I did so under the impression that I was opening the matter to any amendment that might be offered, not supposing it was confined to the special amendment indicated by the gentleman from Kent. But since it appears that it is necessary to suspend in order to move any and every amendment that requires a special motion, I shall vote against any further suspension, unless it have a general application to other amendments to be offered on the same subject. I vote "no."

Mr. MCCOMAS said: I voted "no" upon the last proposition, because I was opposed to any departure from the principle established in the bill. I shall vote "aye" upon this, because the convention, by a large majority, has concluded to depart from the principle established. I do not see why Kent county should have two delegates for 7,000, and Baltimore county six delegates for 46,000. They are both agricultural districts, under the same circumstances. There may be justifiable grounds for discriminating between the city and the counties, but I see none for discriminating between counties. I vote "aye."

Mr. RIDGELY. As one of the delegates from Baltimore county, I will say a word in reply to the question asked here by the gentleman from Anne Arundel (Mr. Miller,) why Baltimore county refused eight delegates upon the theory of representation suggested by the other side of the house, but went for a proposition which reduced the amount of her delegation, and now asks for an increase of her delegation. I have but a very short answer to make to that, and it is this: *Timeo Danaos et dona ferentes*.

Now, sir, in relation to the remark of the gentleman from Prince George's (Mr. Clarke,) who suggested as a reason why he should discriminate and give an additional member to Kent county and refuse it to Baltimore county, that he had been assured by the declaration of some member of this house that there was a sufficient population in Kent county to bring it within the rules, I ask him as a lawyer, whether, in the course of his professional career, he ever permits himself to be assured by declarations founded upon mere judgment, of any fact?

Mr. CLARKE. As the gentleman has put the question——

SEVERAL MEMBERS. Order; order.

The PRESIDENT. The chair cannot permit discussion.

Mr. RIDGELY. I desire to say that I vote for the proposition now before the house upon this theory—I want to explain my vote—that the strict operation of the rule excluded my county from another delegate, and also excluded Kent; and what is fish for one is flesh for the other.

The PRESIDENT. The gentleman appears to be transcending the rule, to state concisely the reasons for his vote. The chair cannot permit discussion at this stage of the case.

Mr. CLARKE. When the vote is over, I hope I shall be permitted to make a personal explanation.

Mr. BELT. I move that the gentleman be permitted ——

The PRESIDENT. It is not in order now.

Mr. RIDGELY voted "aye."

Mr. SCHLEY said: When the question was up before, I voted "no," because I believed this was wrong. I have not changed my opinion in that respect; and therefore I again vote "no."

Mr. THOMAS said: I desire to say in explanation of my vote, that when I cast my vote in favor of Kent county having an additional delegate, I did it in good faith; and I did it with the understanding that it was to be a compromise between those two sections; and that while this convention would give to Kent county her rights, they would not refuse to Baltimore county, the largest county in the State, hers. But, to my utter surprise, I find that gentlemen have gone back from their promises.

The PRESIDENT. The gentleman is not in order.

Mr. THOMAS. I am trying to explain my vote; and I am opposed to this more especially as gentlemen of the majority of this house have given to the minority one more delegate, and have refused to give the majority one more delegate that they are entitled to receive. I think it is no more than just and right that Baltimore county should have an additional delegate. She gets but six delegates for 46,000 souls ——

Mr. CLARKE. I call the gentleman to order.

Mr. THOMAS. I am explaining my vote. I say that Baltimore county is more entitled to seven delegates than Kent county to two. I voted for two for Kent county; and I vote for Baltimore county to have an additional delegate as a compromise. I therefore vote "aye."

The rule requiring a three-fifths vote, the motion was rejected.

Mr. STOCKBRIDGE. I ask permission to move to strike out "79" and insert "80."

Mr. Briscoe. It is very likely that the matter may have to be changed again. I have a motion to make.

Mr. Stockbridge. I will give way for the present.

Mr. Briscoe. I move to suspend the 53d rule to enable me to move to strike out "one" after Calvert, Charles and St. Mary's, and to insert the word "two" in each place, so as to give each county of the State two delegates at least. I was somewhat surprised a few moments ago to hear the gentleman from Baltimore city (Mr. Thomas) say that there had been an outside understanding that this thing, so far as the increase for the county of Baltimore was concerned, was to be considered ——

The President. The motion to suspend is not debatable.

Mr. Briscoe. I will move to add one to Baltimore county at the same time.

The motion to suspend the 53d rule was rejected.

KENT COUNTY.

Mr. Thomas moved to reconsider the vote by which the amendment submitted by Mr. Hollyday to increase the representation of Kent county was adopted.

Mr. Hollyday. I hope that motion will not prevail. The gentleman from Baltimore city (Mr. Thomas) stated that there had been a promise made if another representative was given to Kent, to give another one to Baltimore county. I should like to know from whom that promise came; for I have not understood that there was such a promise.

Mr. Thomas. I will say to the gentleman that I thought it was generally understood. I would not have come up to the house this afternoon, sick as I am, if I did not think from what I heard outside of this house that Baltimore county was to have one more delegate. I told the gentleman at dinner I would be here.

Mr. Hollyday. I can only say with regard to that matter that I never promised anybody. I told them I had no objection at all to giving one to Baltimore county; but I never said that I would vote for it. I am one of those who never make an araangement of that kind. I told them that I would not bind myself to vote for Baltimore county or any other county.

Mr. Chambers. In explanation of my position I solemnly protest that I not only never heard of the compromises, but never heard that it was designed to move, if Kent obtained a member, that Baltimore county should have another, until I heard it from gentlemen upon this floor since the vote was taken.

Mr. Barron. I will state that this morning it was mentioned that Kent wanted a member, and Baltimore county a member, and I said: put them both together and I will vote for them. I was willing to vote for Baltimore county every day in the week; but I saw that as soon as they got the member for Kent, they were satisfied to go back.

Mr. Clarke. This is a motion to reconsider, and I regard it now in order in debating the matter whether or not we should reconsider the vote, to call the attention of the convention to the difference of the ground upon which Kent county appealed to the convention, and that upon which Baltimore county has appealed to the convention. I will state, as I stated before, that I voted this morning at first against the increase to Kent county upon the ground that the convention having determined upon an arbitrary rule by which representation should be apportioned in the State, the basis of that rule should be applied and carried out to its consequences, and that there should be no departure from it for the purpose of conciliating anywhere any local feeling, or any local dissatisfaction; because after the principle was adopted it must work equally everywhere if that was to be the rule of representation.

I stated further, as a reason for my subsequent vote upon the proposition to increase the delegation from Kent county, and as a reason for my vote in opposition to the increase of the delegation from Baltimore county in order to reconcile the two votes, that I did it simply upon this ground; that I had heard it stated by gentlemen in whose word I placed implicit confidence, upon this floor, that Kent county possessed a white population which entitled her to two members. The gentleman from Cecil said he knew that the population of Kent since 1860 had largely increased, and by the census of 1860 Kent county only wanted about one hundred and fifty additional white population to entitle her to another member. And other gentlemen stated positively that they were sure that if the population of Kent county were now to be taken, she would have a population which would entitle her to two representatives.

Now the gentleman from Baltimore county (Mr. Ridgely) inquires whether I, as a lawyer, would take hear-say evidence. I do not take hear-say evidence at all. That was not a hear-say state of evidence. It was the testimony of honorable gentlemen upon this floor, asserting from their knowledge of the fact that she was entitled to this representation. And I would ask him, or any gentleman upon this floor, if honorable members here make an assertion, acting under their oaths, and their duties to the State of Maryland, other members have not a right to act upon it. That fixes my vote for Kent county. Now I will come to Baltimore county.

Baltimore county had under this apportionment five members, one for each five thousand white inhabitants, up to twenty-five thousand. Then the convention say that they will only give one more member for every additional twenty thousand. At the rate of one to every five thousand you come up to the population of twenty-five thousand. Then giving Baltimore county one more for twenty thousand, that brings it up to forty-five thousand, and the population of Baltimore county is forty-six thousand. I will read from the report:

"For every five thousand persons, or a fractional part thereof above one-half, one delegate shall be chosen until the number of delegates in each county and district of the city of Baltimore shall reach five."

That will bring up the population to twenty-five thousand. Then it says:

"Above that number one delegate shall be chosen for every twenty thousand persons, or a fractional portion over one-half thereof, until the whole number of delegates from each county, and district of the city of Baltimore, shall reach ten."

You then give Baltimore county another delegate for twenty thousand, bringing up the population of Baltimore county to forty-five thousand. Now Baltimore county comes forward and claims for sixteen hundred additional people. When your rule adopted gives one additional member for twenty thousand people, they come here and ask for sixteen hundred people an additional member. Where is the position of justice before this convention in the appeal of Baltimore county compared with that of Kent county? Kent county comes with the assertion of facts, and I believe those facts can be substantiated by evidence, by which she is entitled to another member. Baltimore county has forty-five thousand citizens represented here by six members, and then she has sixteen hundred more people, and your rule says that she must have twenty thousand more to claim another delegate. What justice, what right is there in the claim? If Baltimore county is to have an additional member, when the rule requires twenty thousand people, and they have but sixteen hundred upon which to base that claim, I may ask, great God! what shall be done with the people of these smaller counties cut down, some to one, and others to two, where the inequality is greater?

The truth of the matter is, that it would be said that this was an arbitrary rule, and that you might just as well say at the outset that you would have one for every three thousand up to five members. While that would have given my county her three members, it would have given Calvert her two members. Again, should we preserve the present basis, there would have been just as much reason for adopting one for every three thousand up to five, as one to every five thousand, and then going on to twenty thousand. That shows the arbitrariness of the rule; that the rule was adopted and carried out as an arbitrary rule. If it works against certain portions of the State it is wrong. I regard it as wrong because it was no principle. But the convention have determined to adopt it, and I say let it go on and work out its legitimate results.

I will maintain it in its legitimate results. And least of all will I be placed in an inconsistent position for giving Kent county two because it is entitled to two, and then not giving Baltimore county two when she is not entitled to it, having an additional number of only sixteen hundred out of twenty thousand to entitle her to it. And because we do not under these circumstances vote for another representative for Baltimore county, gentlemen talk about "promises," and making "fish of one and flesh of the other." I must profess, that on one side or the other, I have made no promises. I have no pledges to redeem one way or the other. I have acted throughout upon what I regarded as justice to all portions of the State. If our views had been carried out, every white man in the State would, when this constitution went forth before the people, have stood equal under the laws and the constitution which is to govern us. If they do not stand equal here, it is not because of the position taken here by the opposition of this house. If this constitution should be adopted under the provisions under which it is to be voted for, I thank God there will be one provision here for an organization to rest upon to cry unto the people to rise in their majesty and amend it, and to give equality to every white man under the law, and the right of representation according to population. That is just and right; and even the last convention came up to it except solely in the case of Baltimore city, which they restricted for certain reasons below a representation corresponding to that of the counties. The State of Maryland has been travelling up to it, and in the present constitution had adopted the principle of representation according to population, with that single exception. But this question has taken the back track upon the question of representation.

Gentlemen have told us upon this question of representation, that they were elected to carry out the views of the people. I ask what was the doctrine which the "American," the organ of this body, preached and heralded through the State, if it was not representation according to population. Article after article of that paper went before the people calling that the only true theory or principle. If gentlemen say that in calling this convention or adopting it, the people voted for emancipation, they just as much voted for representation according to population. And these gentlemen, I contend, have violated the instructions of the people.

I have said these things in vindication of the course I have taken, and which my colleagues have taken upon this question, to relieve ourselves of the positions in which it has been attempted to place us, as if we were governed by partisan motives upon these questions of Kent and Baltimore counties. There is no question of partisanship involved in it. Unless I had been satisfied from the assertions of gentlemen upon this floor, that Kent county had a population entitling her to two representatives, I should never have voted for it, although represented here by gentlemen of my own political complexion. Having adopted the rule, I will carry it out to its legitimate principles, let it work what wrong it may, for I know it can only work wrong.

Mr. SANDS. I am one of those gentlemen upon this floor who voted to give Kent two members, and I believed that from the sense of fairness and liberality on the part of other gentlemen, a claim so just as that urged by Baltimore county would be met in the same spirit with which I met their claim. But I now heartily second the motion for the reconsideration of that vote, because I find that that is not so. Heartily do I second that motion, and if there is a Union man in this house to whom I can say one word that can reach his heart or his head, that may carry us back where this report found us, I hope he will listen.

"Representation according to population." They are going to raise a cry about that, are they? I wish they would come to my county and raise the cry. They did raise a cry last spring; but what was the cry? "Why, you are one of those radical fellows that is for representation according to population, and you want the counties swamped by the great city of Baltimore." That was the terrible bug-a-boo which we had to meet and fight at every cross-roads, as gentlemen in our county know. I wish the gentlemen would come and raise that cry. I will raise stands from which to raise it, and I will get crowds together to listen to it. Then perhaps we may come back here and get representation according to population, Baltimore city and all included. I assure the gentlemen that if they will only raise that cry, if they will sound it clarion-like, and convince the people that the true theory is representation according to population, it will get my hearty vote. They did not do it. The whole theory of the fight last spring when the people were electing us from the counties, was the very contrary to what the gentleman urges here.

Mr. CLARKE. Will the gentleman allow me one moment?

Mr. SANDS. I would prefer not.

Mr. CLARKE. Well, the gentleman's opponent ran against him, and he was elected. I do not know what he ran on.

Mr. SANDS. I will tell you what I ran on. I was not afraid to say to the people, even in the face of the demagogue cry that the counties were going to be swamped by Baltimore city, "I am for a fair and liberal representation for Baltimore city; but I pledge you my word, men of Howard county, that I am not going to bring you into the difficulty. These people talk about swamping you under the influence of the great commercial emporium." The gentlemen who declaimed against representation according to population were the very gentlemen who were in party affiliation and sympathy with the gentleman who last addressed the convention. This convention is not going to take back tracks. I will tell you what it will do. It will wipe out any of those tracks that have been made in the wrong direction, believing that those who made the tracks would be met with equal liberality elsewhere. I am going to wipe out my tracks now. Other members may do as they please about it.

Now about the fairness of this thing, of the gentlemen of the minority going to Baltimore county, and telling them that they had offered them seven members upon this floor, and that Baltimore county had voted against it——

Mr. CLARKE. We offered them eight members.

Mr. SANDS. And because you could not give her eight, you wanted to tie her down to six, and would not give her seven. That is consistent, I must say.

Mr. RIDGELY. In order that they themselves might get four.

Mr. SANDS. How about the fairness of the representation given to Prince George's, and the representation given to Baltimore county. Let us see about that. Prince George's has a little over 9,000 free white inhabitants. Representation is based upon the basis of free white population.

Mr. CLARKE. That is what we object to.—Our basis was according to the entire population.

Mr. SANDS. I know that, including the negro population; and that is what we did not want. Now let us look at the figures. Let me proceed with the examination of the representation allotted to Prince George's county, and the representation allotted to Baltimore county. According to the tables of the census of 1860, Prince George's county has a little over 9,000 white inhabitants, while Baltimore county has considerably more that four times that number of white inhabitants.—Prince George's county has been allowed two representatives. According to that is not Baltimore county, with more than four times the number of white inhabitants that Prince George's county has, entitled to eight representatives? O! no! cry the gentlemen; you have adopted a rule, and we stick to it. Now it was argued here this morning on that side of the house, and very properly, that there were no rules without exceptions; that the exceptions proved the value of the rule. But they are now agreed to act in this matter as if there was but one single exception, and that was on their side, and that there was no other to counterbalance it. I say it is but just to Baltimore county that she should have this additional member.

Gentlemen talk about the increase of population in Kent county since 1860. Do not they suppose that the larger, populous and rapidly growing county of Baltimore has increased its thousands also since then? To be sure it has, and gentlemen must know it as well as I do. They can in their calculations and arguments make allowance for the growth of the little county of Kent, and can assert that they have no doubt in the world that she has a number of people that did not appear upon the face of the census table of 1860, and then they shut their eyes most persistently to the fact that Baltimore county, from her position, size, population, and everything that goes to favor an increase, must have increased at least ten to one to what Kent has.

Now let gentleman act consistently in this matter. Let them either bind themselves down to a rule and adhere to it, and say—"I take what is nominated in the bond; I ask no more;" or if they vary from the rule let them be as consistent about it as they can.—Do not come to the conclusion that Kent has more inhabitants than appear upon the census, and then when you come to the case of Baltimore county, utterly ignore the fact that her increase must have been at least ten for every one that Kent has increased.

There have always been a class of politicians in the country who have been ready to raise some cry whenever there is a popular election. There is always some catchword invented to be thrown out among the people to confuse and mislead them. The gentleman could not serve our people that way. He might come among them and raise the cry of "representation according to population," and then if he asked them for their votes, they would tell him they had not yet advanced quite that far in their political education. I am sure the cry raised in Baltimore county would not benefit him or his party, when it was known that they had here to-day refused Baltimore county her moral and political right.

We have, as far as we can, to adopt some rule, as we have a large city, with more than one-third of the population of the State in it, we have to adopt some rule which is progressive in regard to this matter of representation. But when you come to a county situated as Baltimore county is, with 40,000 and more inhabitants to-day, you cannot tie her down arbitrarily to an iron rule, in the face of all her strength, wealth, population and intelligence. That would work her great harm. Still gentleman cry—"It is so nominated in the bond" But when it comes to Kent county, or some other little place whose political sympathies are different from those of Baltimore county, then the rule is a withe of straw, and will go by the board.

Now I hope the Union men of this house will not do Baltimore county the injustice, after first saying that Kent county shall be benefited outside the rule, then tying Baltimore county down to the rule. I trust they will not so far forget their duty to themselves, to Baltimore county, and to the majority of the people of the State who sent them here, as to give up their rule when it works against them, and refuse to relax it when it will work in their favor.

Mr. STIRLING moved the previous question, which was seconded.

The question was then taken upon ordering the main question, and upon a division—ayes 37, noes not counted—the main question was ordered.

Mr. BRISCOE moved a call of the house, which was ordered.

Pending the call of the roll,

On motion of Mr. CUSHING,

Further proceedings under the call were dispensed with.

The question recurred upon the motion of Mr. THOMAS, to reconsider the vote by which the amendment of Mr. HOLLYDAY was adopted, giving Kent county two delegates instead of one.

Upon this question Mr. ABBOTT called for the yeas and nays, and they were ordered.

The question was then taken, by yeas and nays, and resulted—yeas 30, nays 35—as follows:

Yeas—Messrs. Goldsborough, President; Abbott, Annan, Audoun, Baker, Barron, Cunningham, Cushing, Davis, of Washington, Dellinger, Ecker, Farrow, Galloway, Hebb, Hoffman, Keefer, King, Larsh, Mayhugh, McComas, Murray, Negley, Parker, Ridgely, Russell, Sands, Schley, Thomas, Wickard, Wooden—30.

Nays—Messrs. Belt, Billingsley, Blackiston, Bond, Briscoe, Brown, Carter, Chambers, Clarke, Daniel, Dent, Duvall, Earle, Greene, Hollyday, Hopkins, Hopper, Horsey, Kennard, Lee, Markey, Miller, Mullikin, Nyman, Parran, Pugh, Purnell, Scott, Smith, of Carroll, Smith, of Worcester, Stirling, Stockbridge, Swope, Sykes, Todd—35.

The motion to reconsider was accordingly not agreed to.

Pending the call of the roll, the following explanations were made by members, as their names were called.

Mr. CHAMBERS. Gentlemen assert here that a compromise was proposed by which Kent county was to obtain an additional member. The import of the statement would naturally be that Kent county had compromised herself on that subject to some extent. There does not seem to be a shadow of foundation for such a thing. I demand of gentlemen to say whether Kent county has been a party to any such arrangement.

Mr. THOMAS. I would relieve the gentleman from Kent (Mr. Chambers) by saying——

The PRESIDENT. No explanations are in order except strictly to explain votes.

Mr. CHAMBERS. I vote "no."

Mr. DANIEL. After having voted for this amendment in the beginning, because I believed the principle was right, without any reference to any compromise or promise of any sort; and not having seen any reason to change that opinion, though I am somewhat sorely tempted to change my vote, on account of the speeches of gentlemen here, and the attacks upon Baltimore, still I vote "no" upon the reconsideration.

Mr. DENT. I desire only to say that I heard here to-day for the first time that there had been any pledge made, by those who voted to give Kent county an additional delegate, to give any to any other county. Nor did I ever hear that it was contemplated by Baltimore county to ask for an additional delegate, until the member from that county (Mr. Ridgely) made the motion here. So I do not vote in reference to any such agreement, never having heard it from any source, until I heard it announced on the floor here. I voted for the additional delegate to Kent county and did so in good faith, although I did not care much about it, because I did not think it would make a great deal of difference. On this motion to reconsider I vote "no."

Mr. HOLLYDAY. I will state that if there was any arrangement made, such as has been spoken of here, I do not know with whom it was made. I made no arrangement with anybody. I told gentlemen that I wished to have another delegate for Kent county. The gentleman from Howard (Mr. Sands) told me that he thought we were entitled to it, and that he would do all he could to get it for us. As for any promises to vote for any other county, I never made any. As I think we are really entitled to, and as I said before I think we have more than the number required should a census be taken to-morrow, I shall vote "no" on this question.

Mr. MAYHUGH. I saw the humbug of this thing, when we started out. It was a great deal like the fable of the spider and the fly.—The spider has got the fly now, and is trying to get away. I think gentlemen should have considered this matter before they voted it through. I most sincerely hope this vote may be reconsidered, for I think it is unjust. I vote "aye."

Mr. MILLER. In explanation of the vote I shall give, I will say this: In the debate upon this report while on its second reading, I pointed out as one of the great matters of injustice wrought by this arbitrary rule, that it gave Kent county but one delegate, when she lacked but one hundred and fifty-three white inhabitants to bring her within the rule allowing two delegates, while Caroline county with only two hundred and forty-seven more white inhabitants than Kent county, was allowed two delegates. I voted to give Kent county the additional delegate upon the assurance of gentlemen that she now had inhabitants enough to bring her within the rule. I vote "no" on this question.

Mr. PUGH. I generally try to vote upon every question upon its merits. I may fail to do so sometimes, but I try to do so. I voted to give Kent county two delegates, because in my opinion I was not thereby violating the practical application of this rule, and I am not disposed now to retrace my steps. I vote "no."

Mr. SANDS. I deem a word necessary in justification of myself, in reply to remarks made by my friend from Kent (Mr. Hollyday,) and he will bear witness to the truth of what I say. I do not think we ever had a conversation about this matter of Kent county, that I did not also instance Baltimore county, and say that I was in favor of giving each of them an additional delegate. And I did vote —without there being any compact at all, which I distinctly declare there was not so far as I am concerned—I did certainly vote for Kent county, with the full conviction made upon my mind by the conversation I had in regard to it, that Baltimore county had equal claims. I endeavor to act out my views fairly and deliberately, and I must then be allowed to judge what is my proper course of conduct, when having performed my share of the work. I find gentlemen on the other side of the house failing in what I expected of them. I vote "aye" on the question of reconsideration.

Mr. SCOTT. I generally leave my votes to explain themselves. But in explanation of this vote, I will say that having voted in good faith for an additional member to Kent county, because I believed that if a new enumeration were made to-day she would be found to have the population to entitle her to it, I shall vote "no" on this question.

Mr. THOMAS. I desire to say in explanation of my vote, that when this question of representation first came before the convention, I voted for the report, as it was originally made, under protest. The recollection of members of this convention, and the record of debates will bear me out in that statement. Coming here as I did to get representation according to population, I strove my best to get it, and then took what I did as the best I could get.

So far as any pledges from the gentleman from Kent (Mr. Hollyday) were concerned, I will say that he never did pledge himself to me to vote to give another delegate to Baltimore county, nor did the other gentleman from Kent (Mr. Chambers.)

Mr. CHAMBERS. Or converse upon the subject.

Mr. THOMAS. The gentleman from Kent, (Mr. Hollyday) across the way, did converse with me frequently upon the subject.

The PRESIDENT. The gentleman must state concisely the reasons for his vote.

Mr. THOMAS. I am stating my reasons.—The reason that induced me to move this reconsideration is that I do not think it is fair to give Kent county a delegate in addition to the one she already has, and not give Baltimore county an additional delegate for the large number of voters she has. I then vote "aye."

Mr. STOCKBRIDGE. I now move to amend this section by striking out "seventy-nine" and inserting "eighty," to make it correspond with this action.

The PRESIDENT. If there is no objection that will be done.

Mr. ABBOTT. I object.

Mr. STOCKBRIDGE. Then I move to suspend the rules, so that the section can be so amended.

The motion to suspend the rules was agreed to, and the section amended accordingly.

Mr. BELT. Before we adopt this report finally, before we present to the people of Maryland, this merely arbitrary system of representation, as a test question I will move that the rules be suspended, so as to enable me to again present to the house the proposition that I and my colleague (Mr. Clarke) formerly presented: that the basis of representation shall be the entire population of each county; and the State shall be districted into as many districts, as there may be members of the house of delegates.

The immediate effect of that proposition will be to give to Baltimare city twenty-nine members—I think that was the calculation; twenty-eight or twenty-nine: to Baltimore county eight members, while it leaves the small counties as they stood before.

I wish to say in reference to a remark which was made in the course of the debate when this subject was up before, and which I then had no opportunity to answer, that this proposition was not drawn by us as any catch, or threat, or anything of that sort. But it is the view I have always held; I have never held any other, as my colleagues can testify It is in opposition to the views held by a great many gentlemen in my own county. I maintain it now as I have always maintained it, in the face of all opposition. I say it is the correct doctrine, and I want it to be recorded here upon the record of debates, that I have offered this proposition in good faith. I do not want it said that I came in here and offered anything that I did not heartily indorse, and truly and sincerely approve of. I do regard it as the true theory upon which this matter ought to be settled; to have the whole State represented upon the basis of the total population, and have each county and the city of Baltimore, divided into as many districts as they may respectively be entitled to delegates in the legislature; so that no man in Baltimore county shall vote for six members, and in Baltimore city for six or seven, while I can vote for but one or two.

If there is any question in regard to its popularity before the people, I shall be most happy to meet the gentleman from Howard (Mr. Sands,) or any other gentleman before the people anywhere upon a question of this sort. Because there is not a county in this State, let alone the city, where there has not been a sufficient degree of the influence of the court-house clique in the county town to disgust the people, and lead them to want to have the county districted, in order to get rid of it. It is so in all the counties; it is so with us. And it will prove to be so when you bring this question to a practical test before the people.

The question was then taken upon the motion of Mr. BELT to suspend the rules for the purpose of amending the report, and it was not agreed to.

The report having been read the third time was then adopted, by yeas and nays (under rule forty-three,)—yeas 48, nays 14—as follows:

Yeas—Messrs. Goldsborough, President; Abbott, Annan, Audoun, Baker, Barron, Carter, Cunningham, Cushing, Daniel, Davis, of Washington, Dellinger, Earle, Ecker, Farrow, Galloway, Greene, Hebb, Hoffman, Hopkins, Hopper, Keefer, Kennard, King, Larsh, Markey, Mayhugh, McComas, Mullikin, Murray, Negley, Nyman, Parker, Pugh, Purnell, Ridgely, Russell, Sands, Schley, Scott, Smith, of Carroll, Smith, of Worcester, Stirling, Stockbridge, Swope, Sykes, Thomas, Todd, Wooden—48.

Nays—Messrs. Belt, Billingsley, Bond, Briscoe, Brown, Chambers. Clarke, Dent, Duvall, Horsey, Lee, Miller, Parran, Wickard—14.

Mr. SCOTT, when his name was called, said: I was not here when this report was under discussion on its second reading. If I had been here at that time, I should have moved to amend it by substituting a proposition to divide the whole State into representative districts, each district to elect one member, which I consider the proper and the only correct and republican system of representation. But as this is the plan which has been decided upon by the convention, I shall vote "aye," as being the best I can get

Mr. WICKARD. I seldom rise to explain my vote, and I do not think I shall do so now. When I return to my constituents, and they ask me in a respectful and proper manner, I will take occasion to tell them why I vote as I do. I vote "no."

On motion of Mr. STIRLING,

The convention then took a recess until 8 o'clock, P. M.

EVENING SESSION.

The convention reassembled at 8 o'clock, P. M.

The roll was called, and the following members answered to their names:

Messrs. Goldsborough, President; Abbott, Annan, Audoun, Baker, Barron, Belt, Billingsley, Blackiston, Brown, Carter, Clarke, Cunningham, Cushing, Daniel, Davis, of Washington, Dellinger, Dent, Duvall, Earle, Ecker, Farrow, Galloway, Greene, Hebb, Henkle, Hoffman, Hollyday, Hopkins, Hopper, Horsey, Keefer, Kennard, King, Lansdale, Larsh, Lee, Marbury, Markey, Mayhugh, McComas, Miller, Morgan, Mullikin, Murray, Negley, Nyman, Parker, Parran, Pugh, Purnell, Ridgely, Russell, Sands, Schley, Schlosser, Scott, Smith, of Carroll, Smith, of Worcester, Sneary, Stirling, Stockbridge, Swope, Sykes, Thomas, Todd, Turner, Wickard, Wooden—69.

On motion of Mr. EARLE,

The committee on engrossment and revision were permitted to meet during the sessions of the convention.

MILITIA AND MILITARY AFFAIRS.

On motion of Mr. STOCKBRIDGE,

The convention then resumed the consideration of the report of the committee on militia affairs, which was on its second reading.

Section one was under consideration, having been amended to read as follows:

"Sec. 1. The militia shall be composed of all able-bodied male citizens, residents of this State, being eighteen years of age, and under the age of forty-five years, who shall be enroled in the militia, and perform military duty in such manner, not incompatible with the constitution and laws of the United States, as may be prescribed by the general assembly of Maryland, but persons whose religious opinions and conscientious scruples forbid them to bear arms, shall be relieved from doing so on producing to the proper authorities satisfactory proof that they are thus conscientious."

Mr. NEGLEY. I do not see why one class of our citizens should be exempted from military duty, any more than another. I therefore move to amend the section by adding the following:

"All married men between the ages of eighteen and forty-five years, who support their families by their daily labor, shall be placed upon the same footing of exemption, as persons whose religious opinions and conscientious scruples forbid them to bear arms."

Mr. PUGH. I rise to a point of order. It occurs to me that this amendment is inconsistent with the action already taken by the convention upon this subject.

The PRESIDENT. That is for the convention to determine.

Mr. NEGLEY. I have no doubt it is extremely inconsistent with the gentleman's ideas of what should be there. I do not see what right the State of Maryland, or any other State, has to make any distinction in favor of one class of its citizens or another, upon the ground of religious opinions or scruples. I would ask the convention whether there is not a very large class of people in the State of Maryland whose families are dependent upon their daily labor for their support? Whether it is not a matter of conscience with those men to support their wives and little ones? Yet by the action of this house this class of our citizens can be torn away from their families and dragged into military service, while another class, who are perhaps a great deal better off in respect to this world's goods, or are perhaps a great deal better able to perform military duty, are exempted. Now, I know that in many portions of the county in which I live, there are numbers of stalwart young men who, under the operation of this section, would be exempt from military duty, and the State would not be able to call for their services under any circumstances. Yet there is another class whose families, and whose children depend upon their daily exertion for their support. You take them away, but allow the others to go free. I do not think this is fair, that it is just. I think it is the duty of every person to render that duty to his country which the country demands. I do not believe in the doctrine of exempting one class of citizens from duty, and compelling another class to perform that duty.

If this matter of individual conscience is to exempt a man, then every man might have conscientious scruples about shedding human blood. And you would have no man in the service of the State; the State would not possibly get any man to serve it. And as a matter of principle it is not right. Last night we inserted that in our constitution which is not in our present constitution. Why were you not content to leave the matter as it was in the old constitution? There are only two sections about the military, and there is not one word about exempting any class of citizens from military duty. Why was not this convention content to let the matter rest where the old constitution left it? There is legislation on the subject, and why not leave it there?

Mr. STIRLING. Did not this report, as it came from the committee, provide that every able-bodied citizen should be liable to bear arms?

Mr. NEGLEY. It was possible to amend that so as to conform to the law as it now stands, or to the constitution, and leave the whole matter in the hands of the legislature, where it ought to be. Just look at the operation of this law. In the war of 1812, I believe, and in the war with Mexico, the federal government called upon the State for troops, not like it does now, but through its executive officer, and the State then got volunteers in the Mexican war; but in the war of 1812 it called out its militia. And there is a large class of your citizens who say that was the proper way for our government to have done, and that it was a violation of State's rights to draft directly; that the federal government ought to have called upon the several States for their respective quotas, and those States ought to have supplied them to the federal government. Now if the federal government were to call upon the governor of the State of Maryland for a portion of its militia, would these men be reached at all? You could not get this exempted class of citizens into the service even of the United States. It was said last night that the federal government would cure this difficulty; that they would reach this class of our citizens, and there was no necessity for us to endanger the passage of the constitution by refusing this concession. I think it is unmanly and mean to throw upon the shoulders of the federal government that which you are unwilling to stand up to yourselves. If you are not willing to stand up to a principle yourself, it is unmanly to take shelter behind the shoulders of the federal government. If it is right for the federal government to call upon this class of citizens in times of distress and necessity, to enforce its laws, then it is right for you to recognize that principle in your constitution. If it is improper in morals and in politics for a State to call upon all classes of its citizens, without distinction, to render military service in times of need, then you should not throw upon the shoulders of the federal government the duty of calling these men out.

Now the federal government has not exempted this class of citizens. Under the draft which is to take place on the fifth of September no one is exempted, not even ministers of the gospel are exempted. The only concession the federal government makes is this—that this class of persons who have conscientious scruples about performing military duty, those ministers of the gospel who have some conscientious scruples about violating their vows, are placed in the hospital service of the country. Now I think it is very improper to make the distinction proposed here, and put it in the fundamental law of the State, thereby taking away from the legislature of Maryland all power to change it. Suppose you establish a military system in the State of Maryland. Your militia, to be worth one cent, will require these men to be drilled, to be called out once a week, or once a month at least. What will be the result? You force a large class of men away from their work, who can illy spare the time, make them go through military evolutions, discipline them in the art of bearing arms; while you exempt another large class, and leave them free to go and make money, and carry on their business, without even paying a fine. Is that just?—Yet this section that you are about to pass contemplates this very thing. You compel a large class of our citizens to come into this thing; you make them discipline themselves by meeting in companies and in brigades.—And then you exempt entirely another large class. Is that equal-handed justice? Is it not fair that you should treat all your citizens alike? Should you make any distinction between them?

Gentlemen talk about endangering the passage of the constitution. I say this is a two-edged sword; it will cut both ways. Do you suppose men whose families are dependent upon their efforts for support, are so stolid and stupid as not to see the injustice of this matter? It is a dangerous thing to let it become known in the settled portions of this State that this injustice is done to a large class of citizens, and they will vote against your constitution. I believe there are numbers in the town of Hagerstown, who, if they once understood this gross injustice, would not touch your constitution. I say it is a dangerous thing. Be governed by principle; do what is right and just, and do not bind your legislation to a miserable policy, that does not bottom itself upon firm and just legislation. It is a miserable thing at best, and in the end is bound to fail. Let all your legislation be enlightened; let it be founded on just and fair principles, principles that no man can gainsay, that will stand the test. Any other species of legislation is false, and is bound to do more injury than good in the end.

The question was upon the amendment of Mr. NEGLEY to the first section.

Upon this question Mr. NEGLEY called for the yeas and nays, and they were ordered.

The question was then taken by yeas and nays, and resulted—yeas 11, nays 48—as follows:

Yeas—Messrs. Belt, Billingsley, Dent, Henkle, Lansdale, Lee, Marbury, Mayhugh, Miller, Negley, Smith, of Carroll—11.

Nays—Messrs. Goldsborough, President; Abbott, Annan, Baker, Barron, Blackiston, Brown, Carter, Clarke, Cunningham, Cushing, Daniel, Davis, of Washington, Ecker, Farrow, Galloway, Greene, Hebb, Hoffman, Hollyday, Hopkins, Hopper, Horsey, Keefer, Kennard, Larsh, Markey, McComas, Mullikin, Parker, Pugh, Purnell, Ridgely, Russell, Sands, Schley, Schlosser, Scott, Smith, of Worcester, Sneary, Stirling, Stockbridge, Swope, Sykes, Thomas, Todd, Wickard, Wooden—48.

The amendment was accordingly rejected.

Mr. LANSDALE moved to amend by inserting the word "white" before the words "male citizens."

Upon this question Mr. LANSDALE called for the yeas and nays, and they were ordered.

The question was then taken by yeas and nays, and resulted—yeas 15, nays 48—as follows:

Yeas—Messrs. Belt, Billingsley, Blackiston, Brown, Chambers, Clarke, Dent, Duvall, Henkle, Hollyday, Horsey, Lansdale, Lee, Marbury, Miller—15.

Nays—Messrs. Goldsborough, President; Abbott, Annan, Audoun, Baker, Barron, Carter, Cunningham, Cushing, Daniel, Davis, of Washington, Dellinger, Ecker, Farrow, Greene, Galloway, Hebb, Hoffman, Hopkins, Hopper, Keefer, Kennard, Larsh, Markey, Mayhugh, McComas, Mullikin, Negley, Parker, Pugh, Purnell, Ridgely, Russell, Sands, Schley, Schlosser, Scott, Smith, of Carroll, Smith, of Worcester, Sneary, Stirling, Stockbridge, Swope, Sykes, Thomas, Todd, Wickard, Wooden—48.

The amendment was accordingly rejected.

Mr. DAVIS, of Washington. I move to strike out the words "forty-five" and insert the words "sixty-five." I do this for the benefit of my colleague (Mr. Negley.) Under the section as it now stands he is exempt from military duty. And as he is very anxious that everybody shall perform military duty, I am sure he will vote for my amendment.

The question was then taken upon the amendment of Mr. DAVIS, of Washington, and it was rejected.

Mr. BELT. I move to amend the section by adding the following:

"Provided, however, that no one shall be regarded as being capable of serving in the militia of this State, unless he shall first take the oath prescribed in this constitution for civil officers under the same."

Mr. HEBB moved the previous question on the section, which was seconded and the main question ordered.

The first question was upon the amendment of Mr. BELT, and being taken the amendment was rejected.

The question was then upon agreeing to the section as amended.

Upon this question Mr. DENT called for the yeas and nays, and they were ordered.

The question was then taken by yeas and nays, and resulted—yeas 47, nays 15—as follows:

Yeas—Messrs. Goldsborough, President; Abbott, Annan, Audoun, Baker, Barron, Carter, Cunningham, Cushing, Daniel, Davis, of Washington, Dellinger, Ecker, Farrow, Galloway, Greene, Hebb, Hoffman, Hopkins, Hopper, Keefer, Kennard, Markey, Mayhugh, McComas, Mullikin, Negley, Parker, Pugh, Purnell, Ridgely, Russell, Sands, Schley, Schlosser, Scott, Smith, of Carroll, Smith, of Worcester, Sneary, Stirling, Stockbridge, Swope, Sykes, Thomas, Todd, Wickard, Wooden—47.

Nays—Messrs. Belt, Billingsley, Blackiston, Brown, Chambers, Clarke, Dent, Duvall, Henkle, Hollyday, Horsey, Lansdale, Lee, Marbury, Miller—15.

The section as amended was accordingly adopted.

Section two was then read as follows:

"Section 2. It shall be the duty of the general assembly to provide for and perfect from time to time the enrolment of the militia, and also for its effectual organization, and to make for this purpose such a division of the State into military districts as may secure these results, and in so doing to especially pass such laws as shall promote the formation of volunteer militia associations in the city of Baltimore, and every county, and to secure to them such privileges or assistance as may afford them effectual encouragement."

Mr. WICKARD. I move the following, which is section three of the minority report, as a substitute for this section:

"The general assembly shall provide for organizing, equipping, and disciplining the militia, in such manner as shall be most effective to repel invasion and suppress insurrection, not incompatible with the laws of the United States."

The question being taken upon the substitute, upon a division—ayes 45, noes not counted—it was adopted.

Mr. RIDGELY. I move to further amend this section by inserting after the words "the general assembly shall provide", the words "at its first session after the adoption of this constitution."

Mr. STOCKBRIDGE. I hope that amendment will not be adopted, unless there is something else put with it. It imposes an obligation upon the general assembly at its first session but none thereafter. Practical defects by the thousand may be developed as the system progresses, but this amendment imposes no obligation upon the general assembly to rectify them. I hope the amendment will be so changed as to impose a lasting obligation upon the general assembly.

Mr. RIDGELY. I will modify the amendment, so that it shall read "at its first session after the adoption of this constitution, and from time to time thereafter as the exigency may require."

The amendment as modified was then adopted.

Mr. STOCKBRIDGE. I move to amend the section by transposing the words "not incompatible with the laws of the United States," at the end of the section, to after the words "in such manner."

The amendment was adopted.

Mr. BELT. I desire to offer an amendment, and I wish to say a word or two on it before the vote is taken. I have no objection in the world, excepting the general objection I have stated here so often, to have a clause inserted in the constitution, directing the legislature to provide for organizing the militia of the

State. I am opposed to that upon general principles, because I am oppose to restricting the legislature in any way. If a constitutional provision of this sort should be adopted, one of the most important rights and privileges of the people of Maryland will be to be organized in their respective districts, just as is now done under the operation of the law. I do not suppose that anybody who lives in Prince George's county wants to be jerked out of there and carried to Allegany county for the purpose of being equipped and drilled under a militia system in Allegany county. I therefore move to amend this section by inserting after the words "disciplining the militia," the words "in the city of Baltimore, and in every county."

The question being taken upon the amendment, it was rejected.

Mr. AUDOUN. I move to amend this section by adding the words "and shall pass such laws as shall promote the formation of volunteer militia associations in the city of Baltimore, and every county, and secure to them such privileges or assistance as may afford them effectual encouragement."

The question being taken upon the amendment, upon a division—ayes 24, noes 26—it was not agreed to.

No further amendment was offered to this section.

Mr. PURNELL. I offer the following as a new section:

"The governor shall have power to call forth the militia to execute the laws of the State, suppress insurrection, and repel invasion."

There was a law passed at the last session of the legislature, which perhaps gave the governor that power. But it was gotten up very hastily, and the system then arranged was very imperfect, and will have to undergo revision. I propose to place it in a more permanent form, by putting it into the constitution, and not leaving it to the legislature at all.

Mr. SCOTT. That power is already given to the executive, in the article on the executive department.

Mr. STOCKBRIDGE. The eleventh section of the article on the executive department, which we adopted to-day, reads as follows:

"SEC. 11. The governor shall be commander-in-chief of the land and naval forces of the State, and may call out the militia to repel invasions, suppress insurrections and enforce the execution of the laws; but shall not take the command in person without the consent of the general assembly."

Mr. PURNELL. I will withdraw my amendment under these circumstances.

The amendment was accordingly withdrawn.

Section three was then read as follows:

"SEC. 3. The adjutant general shall be appointed by the governor, by and with the advice and consent of the senate. He shall hold his office for the term of ——— years, and receive for his services an annual salary of ——— dollars."

Mr. THOMAS moved to fill up the first blank with the word "four."

Mr. STIRLING. I move to strike out the words "for the term of ——— years," and insert "during the pleasure of the governor." It would work very badly if the governor and the adjutant general did not agree. He is a sort of staff officer to the governor, and ought to be subject to his absolute control, and not be independent of him.

Mr. THOMAS. My object in moving to make it four years was to make it correspond to the term of the governor. I would have no objection to inserting after the word "years" the words "or during the pleasure of the governor."

Mr. STIRLING. A man who was really worth anything would not want to stay in the office if the governor did not want him there.

The question was then taken upon the amendment of Mr. STIRLING, and it was adopted.

Mr. STIRLING. I now move to strike out the words "an annual salary of ——— dollars," and insert "such compensation as is now or may be hereafter fixed by law."

The PRESIDENT. The adjutant general now draws two thousand dollars."

Mr. STIRLING. He does not draw that as adjutant general.

Mr. STOCKBRIDGE. Section 12, chapter 284 of the laws of the last session of the legislature provides:

"That the salaries of the several department officers shall be as follows, to-wit: The adjutant general shall receive, so long as he discharges the duties of quartermaster general, inspector general and commissary general, as herein before provided, the pay of two thousand dollars per annum, payable as heretofore," &c.

Mr. STIRLING. He draws that as long as the legislature allows him to perform those other duties, but not as adjutant general.

Mr. STOCKBRIDGE. He is *ex officio* all this; but he performs no additional duties so long as there is no militia under arms.

Mr. DANIEL. I believe the adjutant general only got one thousand dollars before that last law was passed. And I think he did not get that much until within a recent period. I believe five hundred dollars a year was all he got for a long time. I want to know whether these additional duties are so onerous as to be deserving of a thousand dollars extra pay, or whether they are not put on so as to lug in the extra thousand dollars. I think one thousand dollars is enough, and that we better fix it at that.

Mr. STIRLING. As far as I am concerned, I do not know how to vote on the amount of compensation. It may be that the legislature might fix it in such a way that it would not require even one thousand dollars to be paid. I think the legislature can be trusted to fix this compensation. If you put "one thousand dollars" in the constitution, it may be too little, or it may be too much. If they provide that, when the militia system is in operation, the adjutant general may be relieved of many of these duties, and be left to perform only some slight duties. In that case a thousand dollars a year is too much compensation.

The question was then taken upon the amendment of Mr. STIRLING, and it was adopted.

No further amendment was offered to this section.

Mr. WICKARD. I now move as an additional section, the following from the minority report:

"Section 4. The militia officers shall be chosen or appointed as follows: Captains, subalterns and non-commissioned officers shall be chosen by the written votes of the members of their respective companies; field officers of regiments and separate battalions by the written votes of the commissioned officers of their respective regiments and separate battalions to which they belong; brigadier generals and brigade inspectors by the field officers of their respective brigades; major generals, brigadier generals, and commanding officers of regiments or separate battalions, shall appoint the staff officers of their respective divisions, brigades, regiments or separate battalions."

Mr. RIDGELY. We have already provided, by adopting section three of the minority report, that "the general assembly shall provide for organizing, equipping and disciplining the militia, in such manner as shall be most effective to repel invasion and suppress insurrection, not inconpatible with the laws of the United States." It appears to me that we have devolved upon the legislature the general power of organizing a militia system. I do not, therefore, think it proper that this convention should enter into the details of what that system shall be. The general power is conferred upon the legislature, and there I think it should be permitted to rest.

Mr. WICKARD. I will state that this section is drawn up in accordance with the constitutions of other States. The power is given to the militia of every State to elect their own officers.

Mr. STIRLING. I merely wish to say that I think it is a great deal better for the constitution to be silent upon this subject, and let the legislature, from time to time, provide whatever may be necessary. This State and this country are in a very anomalous condition at this time. I am not willing to fetter the legislature, and to decide now that the militia shall elect their own officers. I am willing to let the legislature say so, if they choose. But there may be men called out to serve who are entirely hostile to the government that calls them out. And I am not willing to intrust such men with the selection of their own officers.

The question was upon agreeing to the amendment of Mr. WICKARD.

Upon this question Mr. WICKARD called for the yeas and nays, and they were ordered.

The question was then taken, by yeas and nays, and resulted—yeas 27, nays 35—as follows:

Yeas—Messrs. Abbott, Audoun, Baker, Barron, Belt, Billingsley, Blackiston, Brown, Chambers, Clarke, Dent, Duvall, Ecker, Greene, Hebb, Hollyday, Horsey, Keefer, Lansdale, Lee, Marbury, Markey, Miller, Negley, Schlosser, Sneary, Wickard—27.

Nays—Messrs. Goldsborough, President; Annan, Carter, Cunningham, Cushing, Daniel, Davis, of Washington, Dellinger, Farrow, Galloway, Hoffman, Hopkins, Hopper, Kennard, Larsh, Mayhugh, McComas, Mullikin, Parker, Pugh, Purnell, Ridgely, Russell, Sands, Schley, Scott, Smith, of Carroll, Smith, of Worcester, Stirling, Stockbridge, Swope, Sykes, Thomas, Todd, Wooden—35.

The amendment was accordingly rejected.

Mr PUGH. I move to reconsider the vote by which the amendment to the second section, proposed by the gentleman from Baltimore city (Mr. Audoun) was rejected. The amendment was to add to the section the following:

"And shall pass such laws as shall promote the formation of volunteer militia associations in the city of Baltimore, and every county, and secure to them such privileges or assistance as may afford them effectual encouragement."

I voted against it under a misapprehension. My impression at the time was that, by adoption of the section of the minority report, the legislature was authorized to make all these necessary arrangements. But I have been informed that they have so far failed to do so. They have hitherto failed to encourage the formation of volunteer companies throughout the State; and the inference is that they may so fail in the future.

The question was then taken upon the motion to reconsider, and it was agreed to.

The question recurred upon the amendment, and being taken, it was adopted.

No further amendment being offered to the report, the same as amended was then ordered to be engrossed for a third reading.

Mr. RIDGELY moved to suspend the rules, in order that the report might now be put upon its passage.

Mr. DENT. It occurs to me that it is rather premature to put this report upon its third reading now. The amendments have not been incorporated into the original report, and it will require some care to incorporate them properly. It is better that the report as amended should be engrossed and read in full before this body on its final passage; it will not take much time.

The question was then taken upon the motion to suspend the rules, and upon a division—ayes 35, noes 28—it was not agreed to, three-fifths not voting in the affirmative.

MISCELLANEOUS.

Mr. HOPKINS. It will be found by reference to page 517 of the journal that I gave notice that at the proper time I would submit the following amendment to the report of the committee on the legislative department:

"The legislature shall foster and encourage moral, intellectual, scientific and agricultural improvement; they shall when it may be practicable, make suitable provision for the blind, mute and insane, and for the organization of such institutions of learning as the best interests of the State may demand."

I would inquire what has become of that amendment.

The PRESIDENT. The article on the legislative article was passed this morning.

Mr. HEBB. I would suggest that the gentleman can accomplish his purpose by referring it to the committee on revision, with instructions to inquire into the expediency of inserting this in the legislative article.

The PRESIDENT. The gentleman from Howard (Mr. Hopkins) can move to add it to that portion of the article on the legislative department not yet acted upon, in relation to interest and usury laws.

Mr. STOCKBRIDGE. I would suggest that the subject-matter of the proposition of the gentleman from Howard, would come as properly in the article on education, as the article on the legislative department.

Mr. BROWN moved that the convention adjourn—not agreed to.

Mr. PURNELL moved to suspend the rules, in order to submit a motion to reconsider the order limiting debate.

The question being taken, the motion to suspend the rules was not agreed to.

Mr. DELLINGER. I believe the majority of the convention are about as tired as I am; I therefore move that we adjourn.

The question being taken, upon a division—ayes 35, noes 25—the motion was agreed to.

And the convention accordingly adjourned.

EIGHTY-SIXTH DAY.

WEDNESDAY, August 31, 1864.

The convention met at 9½ o'clock, A. M.

Prayer by the Rev. Mr. Patterson.

The roll was called, and the following members answered to their names:

Messrs. Goldsborough, President; Abbott, Annan, Audoun, Baker, Barron, Billingsley, Blackiston, Bond, Briscoe, Brooks, Brown, Carter, Chambers, Cunningham, Cushing, Daniel, Davis, of Charles, Davis, of Washington, Dellinger, Dent, Duvall, Earle, Ecker, Farrow, Galloway, Greene, Hatch, Hebb, Henkle, Hodson, Hoffman, Hollyday, Hopkins, Hopper, Horsey, Keefer, Kennard, King, Lansdale, Larsh, Lee, Marbury, Markey, Mayhugh, McComas, Miller, Morgan, Mullikin, Murray, Negley, Nyman, Parker, Parran, Peter, Pugh, Purnell, Ridgely, Russell, Sands, Schlosser, Scott, Smith, of Carroll, Smith, of Dorchester, Smith, of Worcester, Sneary, Stirling, Stockbridge, Swope, Sykes, Thomas, Todd, Turner, Valliant, Wickard, Wooden—76.

The journal of yesterday was read and approved.

PAY OF CHAPLAINS.

Mr. HOFFMAN submitted the following order:

Ordered, That the committee on accounts be instructed to pay to Rev. Mr. Owen, Patterson, Davenport and McNamar, one hundred dollars each, for services rendered as chaplains to this convention.

Mr. SCHLOSSER moved to strike out "one hundred," and insert "one hundred and fifty."

The question being taken on the motion of Mr. SCHLOSSER, it was not agreed to.

Mr. NEGLEY moved to amend so as to give the chaplains the same per diem for each day they officiated, that is paid to members of the convention.

The question being taken on the amendment of Mr. NEGLEY, it was not agreed to.

The original order was then adopted.

FORWARDING THE DEBATES TO MEMBERS.

Mr. TODD. I offer the following order:

"*Ordered*, That Collins Tatman, one of the folders of this convention, shall be continued in office until all the debates of this convention have been printed, and that he be directed to send the same to the members of this convention, and that he shall receive his per diem while so employed."

I have only a few words to say in reference to that order. I suppose it is unnecessary to say that it will be necessary for this convention to make some provision by which the debates of this body, which shall be printed after our final adjournment, may be forwarded to members at their homes, and I think it proper that Mr. Tatman, being one of the folders, should be appointed for that purpose.

It is unnecessary for me to call the attention of the convention to the manner in which Mr. Tatman has discharged the duties of his office, further than to say that, as far as I have heard, he has discharged them to the entire satisfaction of this body. He has for the last two or three weeks worked alone, and worked day and night in order to keep the work of the convention up. He has been a faithful and meritorious officer, and is deserving of this manifestation of our regard. I think I can safely guarantee to the members of this body that the work will be diligently attended to, and that he will take no advantage whatever of the license thus given.

Mr. HEBB. I offer the following as a substitute for the order of the gentleman from Caroline (Mr. Todd:)

"*Ordered*, That the secretary be directed to forward to the several members of the convention after its adjournment, their copies of the journal of debates until it shall have been completed—and the president is requested to issue his certificate for the usual per diem so long as he shall be so employed."

The order I have offered contemplates that this duty shall be performed by the secretary; as it has always been customary for the secretary to continue over for the purpose of performing this duty. The last convention passed an order requiring the secretary of the convention to perform this duty, and our secretary has prepared a book, in which the members have written the names of those to whom they desire to have these debates sent. It is quite a laborious duty, and one which I think properly belongs to the secretary of the convention.

Mr. TODD. I should like to hear the gentleman give some reason why this should be the business of one officer, instead of another, especially since that other has been employed as folder for this convention. It seems to me that this is his legitimate business.

Mr. KING. How has this been done heretofore? I am not much acquainted with this business, but I have understood that heretofore it has been considered as part of the duty of the secretary.

Mr. THOMAS. I will state to the gentleman from Baltimore county (Mr. King) that by reference to the journal of debates, and the journal of proceedings of the last convention, it will appear that the secretary of that convention was authorized to do the very work which the gentleman from Caroline (Mr. Todd) now desires to have the folder do.

Mr. KING. It is a part of the duties of the secretary.

Mr. THOMAS. Not a part of his regular duty, but a duty especially assigned to him after the adjournment of the convention. Of course the convention would not expect the secretary and folder to remain here at their own expense after the adjournment of the convention, and forward these debates. Somebody must stay here, and whoever stays must be paid.

Mr. KING. I thought it was part of the duties of the secretary to remain here and wind up the business of the convention, and that this devolved upon him.

Mr. THOMAS. Yes, sir.

Mr. TODD. I do not know what the precedents are in this case; but admitting that they are as the gentleman from Baltimore city (Mr. Thomas) has stated, I do not see that we are under any obligation to follow any precedent set ten, fifteen, or twenty years ago, by any other convention. We are to act for ourselves, as we may think best.

Mr. DENT. It appears to me that there will be a great deal of labor to be performed, after this convention shall have adjourned, in the way of folding and forwarding the debates and documents necessary to be forwarded to members; and that it will keep one person pretty well employed. The secretary will have other duties to perform, and it seems to me quite proper that one person should be assigned to this especial duty, as proposed by the gentleman from Caroline (Mr. Todd.)

Mr. HEBB. It could be added to the order that one of the folders should be employed. It would be considerable work for a folder to fold one thousand sheets of these debates every day, and forward them.

Mr. MILLER. How will the secretary do it?

Mr. HEBB. He can fold them himself, or hire somebody to do it; or a folder can be appointed in addition to the secretary.

Mr. SANDS. I am very much opposed to ousting one man from an office to which he has been appointed, and taking another man from another office to which he has been appointed, and putting him in his place. We made this man our folder; that is, we said he should fold the journal of proceedings, and the journal of debates of this convention. Now, before his task is done, on account of the printer being behind with his work, we propose to take him from the post in which we have placed him. If the secretary has duties here, let him remain and be paid for his work. But I shall oppose the ousting another man from his place. If there has been any such precedent, then I think it is a very bad precedent, and ought not to be followed.

Mr. VALLIANT. I do not wish to debate this order, but my conscience will not allow me to withhold from the convention some information I have. The printer of the debates has offered to furnish the paper and mucilage, and fold the debates for three dollars a signature, or one thousand sheets.

Mr. SANDS. I move to amend the substitute by inserting after the word "secretary" the words "and Collins Tatman, folder."

Mr. HEBB. I will accept that amendment.

Mr. TODD. With that understanding I will accept the substitute in place of the order which I offered.

Mr. PUGH. Then I will call for a division of the question, which will amount to the same thing.

The question was upon the order of Mr. HEBB, as modified.

Mr. DAVIS, of Washington. I think there

is work enough for one person, but not for two. I therefore move to strike out the words "the secretary and."

Mr. VALLIANT. I offer the following as a substitute for the order:

"*Ordered*, That the comptroller be authorized to contract with the printer for the folding of the journal of debates and mailing the same after the adjournment of the convention."

I have made an estimate of what the expense will be if the offer of the printer is accepted. He offers to fold the debates for three dollars a signature, furnishing the paper and mucilage himself.

Mr. TODD. Not pay the postage.

Mr. VALLIANT. Is it proposed that the secretary, or the folder, shall do that? If so I will withdraw my substitute.

The PRESIDENT. The State will have to pay the postage.

Mr. VALLIANT. I was about to remark that the expense of getting the printer to do this will be from two dollars to two dollars and a half a day.

On motion of Mr. PUGH,

The further consideration of this subject was postponed until to-morrow.

LIMITATION OF DEBATE.

Mr. DANIEL submitted the following order:

Ordered, That the time allowed to each member for debate on any question before the convention be limited to five minutes; that no extension of time be granted except by a unanimous vote of the members present.

The PRESIDENT. The former order must be first reconsidered.

Mr. CUSHING. This is only amending the time allowed. I do not see any reason for reconsidering the order.

The PRESIDENT. If this order is adopted, it supersedes the other order.

Mr. CUSHING. Certainly, that is what we desire.

Mr. DENT. I do not think there has been any disposition to speak against time since the adoption of the order limiting debate to twenty minutes. And it is necessary that gentlemen should explain their views, in favor of or in opposition to propositions upon which they have to vote. And five minutes will not give any gentleman an opportunity of explaining intelligibly his views upon any important subject, so as to have them understood by his constituency or by the public. Twenty minutes is certainly a very short time in which to do it. But that has seldom been consumed by any one in our recent debates. I am sure it is the object and the desire of every member of this body to get through with the labors of this convention as speedily as possible. And there is no necessity of imposing upon members such checks and restraints as the limitation of debate to five minutes. It will work manifest injustice, for it will be almost impossible for any one to get the unanimous consent of the convention to express his views for a longer period than the time fixed. I hope the order will not be adopted.

Mr. SANDS. I move to amend the order by striking out "five" and inserting "ten." I am as anxious to get away as anybody. But really the views expressed by the gentleman from St. Mary's (Mr. Dent) have a great deal in them.

Mr. DANIEL. I have always heretofore voted for not cutting off the time to these short periods, so as to give members time for debate. I have gone for fifteen minutes, and I went for twenty minutes before. But I shall vote for this order as it is now. We have passed through the main subjects before this convention except one report. We are now approaching the close. I think any gentleman can explain what he has to explain in five minutes. I think some advantage has been taken of the time allowed, and by offering amendments and calling yeas and nays, in order to delay and consume time. I am therefore in favor of voting for the shortest time in reason. I will vote for five minutes, though I am willing ten should pass.

Mr. BILLINGSLEY. I think five minutes, or ten minutes, would be equivalent to allowing no debate at all, for it is too short a time to devote to a subject of paramount importance.

Mr. MAYHUGH moved to lay the order on the table.

On this question Mr. DANIEL called for the yeas and nays, and they were ordered.

The question was then taken, by yeas and nays, and resulted—yeas 39, nays 33—as follows:

Yeas—Messrs. Goldsborough, President; Audoun, Barron, Billingsley, Blackiston, Bond, Briscoe, Brooks, Brown, Chambers, Clarke, Crawford, Cunningham, Davis, of Charles, Davis, of Washington, Dellinger, Dent, Duvall, Henkle, Hodson, Hollyday, Horsey, Johnson, Lansdale, Lee, Marbury, Markey, Mayhugh, Miller, Morgan, Negley, Parran, Scott, Smith, of Dorchester, Sneary, Stockbridge, Sykes, Turner, Wilmer—39.

Nays—Messrs. Abbott, Annan, Baker, Cushing, Daniel, Ecker, Farrow, Galloway, Hatch, Hebb, Hoffman, Hopkins, Hopper, Keefer, Kennard, Larsh, McComas, Mullikin, Parker, Pugh, Purnell, Ridgely, Russell, Sands, Schlosser, Smith, of Carroll, Smith, of Worcester, Stirling, Swope, Thomas, Valliant, Wickard, Wooden—33.

The motion to lay the order on the table was accordingly adopted.

On motion of Mr. VALLIANT,

It was ordered to be entered on the journal that Melancthon Dodson, (page,) is detained from the convention by protracted sickness.

VOTE ON ADOPTING THE CONSTITUTION.

Mr. HENKLE submitted the following resolutions, which were read the first time:

Whereas, The subject about to be submitted to the people of the State of Maryland, at the coming election for the adoption of a new constitution, being simply a question of preference for the present or the proposed constitution, a question affecting vitally the interests of all our people and the future welfare of the State; and whereas, it is of the most paramount importance that the people should be thoroughly informed of the nature and tendency of the issues about to be decided in order that they may vote intelligently thereon; therefore,

Resolved, 1st. That the right of the people peaceably to assemble and publicly discuss questions of public interest, is an inalienable right and essential to their liberties, hence we desire that the people shall so peaceably assemble in public places, and fully, freely, fairly, and without any molestation whatever, discuss the questions now submitted to their consideration.

Resolved, 2d. That we recognize as a fundamental principle of liberty, that "all good government derives its authority from the consent of the governed," and to this end in the language of the fifth article of our bill of rights, "every free white male citizen, having the qualifications prescribed by the constitution, ought to have a right of suffrage."

INTEREST AND USURY.

Mr. STIRLING presented the following petition, which was read:

"*To the Honorable the Constitutional Convention of the State of Maryland:*

"Baltimore Corn and Flour Exchange have seen with regret that several substitutes have been offered for the report of the committee on interest and usury laws, and earnestly hope that the report of said committee, so much more in accordance with the liberal spirit and commercial wants of the day, may be adopted.

"We need scarcely remind the members of the convention that capital, like everything else, will always seek the highest market, and we can scarcely expect to retain it in our midst when it will readily command more in all our neighboring cities. It is an undisputed maxim in trade that no law so effectually and fairly regulates prices as the law of supply and demand; and money, as nothing more than an article of merchandise, responds as promptly to this law as any other article.

"The trade and business of the world illustrate this truth, and it has come now to be an axiom in political economy that in matters of finance and trade the legislative restrictions there are the better for all concerned, and that trade and commerce, if left to itself, would obey one of the great elements of nature and seek its own level.

"The Exchange, therefore, trust most earnestly that your honorable body will adopt the report of the committee, as being not only in conformity with the wants and wishes of our city, but identical with the true and permanent interests of our State.

"All of which is respectfully submitted,

WILLIAM CHESNUT,
President of the Corn Exchange."

REPORTING AND PRINTING THE DEBATES.

Mr. GALLOWAY, from the committee on accounts, made the following report, which was read the first time:

To the Honorable, the President of the Convention.

The committee on accounts, in compliance with the order passed the 30th instant, respectfully report that after a careful examination of said order, they recommend that the president of the convention pay all bills for reporting and printing of the journal of debates remaining unpaid after the adjournment of the said convention, when the same are duly certified as correct by Mr. Joseph H. Audoun, or some other member of the committee on reporting and printing.

All of which is respectfully submitted,

WM. GALLOWAY, Ch'n.
WM. S. WOODEN,
THOMAS RUSSELL,
H. BAKER,
E. L. PARKER.

JUDICIARY DEPARTMENT.

On motion of Mr. THOMAS,

The convention resumed the consideration of the report of the committee on the judiciary department, which was on its second reading.

The pending question was upon the motion to insert the following additional section, to come in after section twenty-one of the report.

"Sec. — The present judges of the circuit courts shall continue to act as judges of the respective circuit courts within the judicial circuits in which they respectively reside, until the expiration of the term for which they were respectively elected, and until their successors are elected and qualified, viz. the present judges of the first, second, third, fourth, sixth and eighth judicial circuits, as organized at the time of the adoption of this constitution, shall continue to act as judges respectively of the first, second, fourth, fifth, ninth and twelfth judicial circuits, as organized under this constitution; and an election for judges of the third, sixth, seventh eighth, tenth and eleventh judicial circuits shall be held on Tuesday next after the first Monday of November, eighteen hundred and sixty-four."

Mr. HEBB. This section merely provides that the present judges shall continue to act as circuit judges, in the districts in which they reside. And it then provides for the election of judges in those districts in which none now reside.

Mr. PARRAN moved to amend by inserting after the words "until their successors are elected and qualified," the words, "or until they shall have attained the age of seventy years."

The PRESIDENT. I think that provision is contained in the general provisions of this report.

Mr. MILLER. That does not apply to judges who hold over; only to those who may be elected under this new constitution. Under the present constitution there is no limitation in regard to age upon the circuit judges.

Mr. STIRLING. I at first felt inclined to vote for this amendment. But if there is no such restriction in the present constitution in regard to those judges who hold over, if we adopt this amendment we shall be imposing a restriction upon these judges, which did not exist when they were elected. I shall therefore not vote for this amendment.

Mr. CHAMBERS. An observation has been made here which requires correction. It has been said that the old constitution made no provision in regard to the age of the district judges. Now so far as the printed constitution is concerned that is true; but so far as the action of the convention is concerned that is not the fact. The convention did pass upon that subject; there is no mistake about it; the journal will show it. But in the hurry and confusion of winding up, and such a hurry and confusion as I suppose was seldom witnessed in a legislative body—in the great anxiety to get off by the particular day and hour appointed, the constitution was in point of fact left unfinished, in the hands of a committee; and this portion of it was omitted. That is the fact; this provision passed the convention without any sort of difficulty, by a majority equal to that which passed the provision in regard to the age of the other judges. But it was not inserted in the constitution.

The PRESIDENT. And therefore was not voted upon by the people.

Mr. CHAMBERS. And there is justly no precedent to be claimed on that subject.

Mr. STIRLING. It is a mere question as to what constitutes the constitution; whether what is to be found in the journal of the convention, or what is in the recorded copy of the constitution, is the law under which we are now living.

The PRESIDENT. The constitution as printed was that which was ratified by the people.

The question was then taken upon the motion of Mr. PARRAN, to insert the words, "or until they shall have attained the age of seventy years," and it was rejected.

The amendment was then taken upon the section as proposed by Mr. HEBB, and it was adopted.

Mr. THOMAS moved to insert the following as an additional section in relation to the judges of the courts of Baltimore city:

"Sec. —. The present judges of the several courts of Baltimore city shall continue to act as such until the expiration of the terms for which they were respectively elected, and until their successors are elected and qualified."

The question being taken upon the section, it was adopted.

Mr. HEBB. On one of the days when this report was under consideration, the following additional section was adopted, on motion of the gentleman from Baltimore city (Mr. Thomas:)

"Sec. 24. In case of the death, resignation, removal or other disqualification of a judge by the courts of this State, the governor by, and with the advice and consent of the senate, shall thereupon appoint a person duly qualified to fill said office, until the next general election for members to the general assembly thereafter, at which time an election shall be held as herein prescribed for a judge, who shall hold said office for the term of fifteen years, and until the election and qualification of his successor."

Under another section, which the convention subsequently adopted, the terms of some of the judges will expire on the year when county officers are elected. It will therefore be necessary to amend this section.

The PRESIDENT. As the section has already been adopted, it must be reconsidered before it can be amended.

On motion of Mr. HEBB,

The vote by which the foregoing section was adopted was reconsidered.

Mr. HEBB then moved to amend the section as follows: strike out the words "for members of the general assembly thereafter," and insert "thereafter whether for members of the general assembly or for county officers, which ever shall first occur."

The question being then taken on the amendment of Mr HEBB, it was adopted.

The section as amended was then adopted.

On motion of Mr. HEBB,

The following additional section was adopted:

"Sec. 38. In the event of a vacancy in the office of a justice of the peace, the governor shall appoint a person to serve as justice of the peace for the residue of the term; and in case of a vacancy in the office of constable, the county commissioners of the county in which the vacancy occurs, or the mayor and city council of Baltimore, as the case may be, shall appoint a person to serve as constable for the residue of the term."

Mr. GALLOWAY moved to reconsider the

vote by which the following section was adopted:

"Sec. 37. The governor by and with the advice and consent of the senate, shall appoint such number of justices of the peace, and the county commissioners of the several counties, and the mayor and city council of the city of Baltimore shall appoint such number of constables for the several election districts of the counties and wards of the city of Baltimore as are now or may hereafter be prescribed by law, and justices of peace and constables so appointed shall be subject to removal by the judge having criminal jurisdiction in the county or city, for incompetency, wilful neglect of duty, or misdemeanor in office, on conviction in a court of law. The justices of the peace and constables so appointed and commissioned, shall be conservators of the peace, shall hold their office for two years, and shall have such jurisdiction, duties and compensation, subject to such right of appeal, as hath been heretofore exercised, or shall be hereafter prescribed by law."

The motion to reconsider was seconded by Messrs. THOMAS and MARKEY.

Mr. BRISCOE. I would like to know what object gentlemen have in moving this reconsideration.

Mr. THOMAS. The motive I had in seconding the motion to reconsider was to have the justices of the peace elected by the people, and the constables appointed by the commissioners of the counties, and the mayor and city council of Baltimore. That is my object. And at the time I voted for the section, I stated that I did so for the purpose of moving a reconsideration when there was a full convention.

Mr. BRISCOE. The convention has expressed its desire not to have the justices of the peace elected by the people.

Mr. MILLER. There was a very decided vote in the convention on two different occasions in favor of having the justices of the peace appointed, instead of elected. At one time by a very decided vote they gave the appointment to the commissioners. But upon further reflection, they amended that so as to give the appointment of justices of the peace to the governor, by and with the advice and consent of the senate. The vote by which the appointment was given to the governor stands recorded upon the journal as yeas 38, nays 19. Some of the gentlemen may have voted in the affirmative with a view to a reconsideration. But I do not think we have a much fuller house this morning than we had then.

It is not necessary to go over the arguments to the house in favor of the appointment of these officers. It was fully discussed and argued when it was under consideration before, and unless some extraordinary new light has shone in upon the minds of the members of this convention, I should suppose that the former discussion was sufficient to show that the proper course to be pursued was that which the convention determined upon. I hope the vote will not be reconsidered, because the object of the reconsideration is simply to put us back again, if possible, to the elective system, which we have got rid of by this section.

The question was upon the motion to reconsider.

Upon this question, Mr. SMITH, of Carroll, called for the yeas and nays, which were ordered.

The question was then taken, by yeas and nays, and resulted—yeas 38, nays 41—as follows:

Yeas—Messrs. Annan, Audoun, Baker, Barron, Billingsley, Briscoe, Brooks, Carter, Cunninghan, Davis, of Charles, Davis, of Washington, Dellinger, Duvall, Ecker, Galloway, Hatch, Hoffman, Johnson, Keefer, Kennard, King, Larsh, Markey, Mayhugh, Morgan, Negley, Parran, Ridgely, Sands, Schlosser, Smith, of Carroll, Smith, of Dorchester, Swope, Thomas, Todd, Turner, Wickard, Wooden—38.

Nays—Messrs. Goldsborough, President; Abbott, Blackiston, Bond, Brown, Chambers, Clarke Crawford, Cushing, Daniel, Dent, Earle, Farrow, Greene, Hebb, Henkle, Hollyday, Hopkins, Hopper, Horsey, Lansdale, Lee, Marbury, McComas, Miller, Mullikin, Murray, Nyman, Parker, Peter, Pugh, Purnell, Russell, Scott, Smith, of Worcester, Sneary, Stirling, Stockbridge, Sykes, Valliant, Wilmer—41.

The motion to reconsider was accordingly rejected.

On motion of Mr. THOMAS,

The following was adopted as an additional section in relation to Baltimore city courts:

"Sec. —. All causes pending in the several courts of Baltimore city, at the adoption of this constitution, shall be prosecuted to final judgment as though the jurisdiction of the several courts in which they may be pending had not been changed."

No further amendment was offered to the report.

The question was upon ordering the report as amended to be engrossed for its third reading.

Mr. STIRLING. If this report is ordered to be engrossed for its third reading, it cannot be altered in any respect, except by the consent of a majority of the members elected to this convention, or by a suspension of the rules, which will require a three-fifths vote. There may be some changes necessary, which can only be told when we have had an opportunity to examine it as amended, and as there is plenty of work for us to do, I move that this report as amended be printed, and that its further consideration be postponed for the present.

The motion was agreed to.

APPOINTMENT, TENURE OF OFFICE, &C.

On motion of Mr. STOCKBRIDGE,

The convention proceeded to consider the report of the committee on tenure of office, duties and compensation of civil officers, &c., which was on its third reading.

Section one was read as follows:

"The governor, the comptroller of the treasury and the treasurer, shall constitute the board of public works, who shall exercise a diligent and faithful supervision of all public works in which the State may be interested as stockholder or creditor, and shall appoint the directors in every railroad or canal company in which the State has the legal power to appoint directors, which said directors shall represent the State in all meetings of the stockholders of every railroad or canal company in which the State is a stockholder; said board of public works shall require the directors of all said public works, from time to time, and as often as there shall be any change in the rates of toll on any of said works, to furnish said board a schedule of such modified rates of toll, and shall use all legal powers which they may possess to obtain the establishment of rates of tolls, which may prevent an injurious competition with each other, to the detriment of the interests of the State, and so to adjust them as to promote the agriculture of the State; the said board of public works shall keep a journal of their proceedings, they shall hold regular sessions in the city of Annapolis, on the first Wednesday in January, the first Wednesday in April, the first Wednesday in July, and the first Wednesday in October, in each year, and oftener if necessary, at which sessions they shall hear and determine such matters as affect the public works of the State; and the general assembly may confer upon them the power to decide; they shall at each regular session of the general assembly, make a report to the general assembly and recommend such legislation as they shall deem necessary and requisite to promote or protect the interests of the State in the public works, and perform such other duties as may be hereafter prescribed by law; and a majority of them shall be competent to act; the governor, comptroller of the treasury and treasurer shall receive no additional salary for the services rendered as members of the board of public works."

Mr. THOMAS. I move to amend this section by inserting after the word "governor," in the first line the words "lieutenant governor, attorney general." I think it would be well to have those officers members of the board of public works. By reference to the constitution of the State of New York, I find that the treasury officers, together with the lieutenant governor, are all, by virtue of their offices, made commissioners of public works.

The question being taken on the amendment of Mr. THOMAS, it was rejected.

Section two of the report was then read as follows:

"There shall be a commissioner of the land office elected by the qualified voters of the State on Tuesday next after the first Monday in the month of November, in the year eighteen hundred and sixty-nine, and on the same day in every sixth year thereafter, who shall hold his office for the term of six years from the first day of January next after his election. The returns of said election shall be made to the governor, and in the event of a tie between any two or more candidates, the governor shall direct a new election to be held by writs to the sheriffs of the several counties, who shall hold said election after at least twenty days notice, exclusive of the day of election. He shall perform such duties as are now required of the commissioner of the land office or such as may hereafter be prescribed by law, and shall be keeper of the chancery records. He shall receive a salary of two thousand dollars per annum, to be paid out of the treasury, and shall charge such fees as are now or may be hereafter fixed by law. The said commissioner of the land office shall make a semi-annual report of all the fees of his office, both as commissioner of the land office and keeper of the chancery records, to the comptroller of the treasury, and shall pay the same semi-annually into the treasury."

Mr. STOCKBRIDGE. Before we pass from this section I would like to inquire of the chairman of the committee on the schedule (Mr. Ridgely,) whether any provision is embodied in the schedule which provides for any vacancy in the office of commissioner of the land office, or of the librarian? I observe that there is no such provision in this report, and it may be well to have one inserted.

Mr. RIDGELY. We have made no provision for vacancies; only for the continuance of those now in office until their terms have expired.

Mr. STOCKBRIDGE. Not to delay the convention then, I will now give notice that when we reach the report on the schedule I will offer a general provision in relation to vacancies.

The PRESIDENT. I do not think that there are any offices not provided for in that respect, except the two named by the gentleman from Baltimore city (Mr. Stockbridge.)

Mr. CLARKE. It was the understanding of the committee, I think, that there would be some general provision which would cover all cases not specially provided for. For that reason no provision of this character was put in this report.

Mr. STOCKBRIDGE. I move that the rules be suspended in order that I may offer an amendment to this section, as follows: add to the section the words "in case of vacancy from death, resignation, or any other cause, the governor shall fill such vacancy until the next general election in the State thereafter, when a commissioner shall be elected for a full term ensuing."

By general consent the rules were suspended and the amendment received.

The question was upon agreeing to the amendment.

Mr. STIRLING. I would suggest to my colleague (Mr. Stockbridge) to modify his amendment so that it shall read "until the next general election for members of the general assembly." There are two general elections provided for under this constitution.

Mr. STOCKBRIDGE. This article provides for his election at a general election which is not for members of the general assembly.

Mr. STIRLING. The amendment of my colleague is correct according to this report. But it strikes me that it would be proper to have the report corrected. It was provided that an election for this office should be held in 1869, because the term of the present incumbent expired at that time. But it is an anomaly to provide for the election of a general State officer at an election for county officers. If the amendment I propose is adopted, it will in effect extend the term of the present incumbent one year; but I see no objection to that. The house has already provided in the article on the treasury department that there shall be an election for comptroller and treasurer this fall, not to interfere with the terms of the present incumbents, but that the elections for those officers shall hereafter take place on the same day with the elections for governor and members of the legislature. That being the case, the election for commissioner of the land office ought to take place on the same day, as he is also a State officer. I therefore move to amend the amendment by inserting after the words "next general election" the words "for members of the general assembly."

The question being taken upon Mr. STIRLING's amendment to the amendment of Mr. STOCKBRIDGE, it was adopted.

The amendment as amended was then adopted.

Mr. STIRLING. In order to make the section conform to the amendment just adopted, I move to strike out the word "sixty-nine" near the beginning of the section, and insert the word "seventy."

The question being taken, the amendment of Mr. STIRLING was adopted.

The next section was then read as follows:

"Sec. 3. The State librarian shall be elected by joint vote of the two branches of the general assembly for four years, and until his successor shall be elected and qualified. His salary shall be fifteen hundred dollars per annum. The legislature shall pass no law whereby he shall receive an additional compensation. He shall perform such duties as are now or may hereafter be prescribed by law."

On motion of Mr. STOCKBRIDGE,

By general consent the section was amended by adding thereto the following:

"In case of a vacancy in the office of State librarian from death, resignation or any other cause, the governor shall fill such vacancy until the next meeting of the general assembly thereafter."

The next section was then read as follows:

"Sec. 4. The county commissioners shall be elected by general ticket by the voters of the several counties, on Tuesday next after the first Monday of November in the year eighteen hundred and sixty-five, and on the same day in every second year thereafter; said commissioners shall exercise such powers and perform such duties only as the legislature may from time to time prescribe; but such powers and duties shall be similar, and the tenure of office uniform throughout the State, and the legislature shall have power to pass such laws as may be necessary for determining the number for each county, fixing the salary, and ascertaining and defining the powers, duties and tenure of office of said commissioners; and the commissioners elected under this constitution shall have and exercise all the powers and duties in their respective counties now exercised by the county commissioners under the laws of the State, and they shall receive the same salary, and their present number in the several counties shall remain the same until changed by law."

Mr. RIDGELY. It will be observed that these county commissioners are to be elected on general ticket and not by districts, and for a period of two years. On motion of the gentleman from Allegany (Mr. Hebb,) a provision was adopted in relation to the judges of the orphans' court, by which the first judges elected are to serve respectively two, four and six years, and then a judge will be elected every two years for a period of six years. Now it strikes me that the same reasons which influenced the house to modify the present system in relation to the judges of the orphans' court, pre-eminently exist in relation to the board of county commissioners, and that great public benefit would result from adopting a system by which they should not all go out of office together.

Mr. HEBB. I fully concur in the remarks of the gentleman from Baltimore county (Mr. Ridgely.) And if the convention will consent to suspend the rules to enable me to offer such an amendment, I will do so.

Mr. SCOTT. I hope the convention will suspend the rules for that purpose. The county commissioners are actually the most important officers we elect. They come right down to the pockets of the people. The board is open for bogus claims, when they are all inexperienced, men coming in at the same time, and they are not unfrequently taken advantage of. And I think some arrangement of this kind is necessary in order to keep up a competent and efficient board of county commissioners.

The question being taken upon the motion to suspend the rules, it was agreed to.

Mr. Hebb moved to amend section four of the report by striking out the words "on Tuesday next after the first Monday of November, in the year 1865, and on the same day in every second year thereafter," and insert in lieu thereof the following:

"An election for county commissioners shall be held on Tuesday next after the first Monday of November, 1865; as nearly one-half as may be of said commissioners shall hold their office for two years, and the other half for four years, and at the first meeting after their election and qualification, or as soon thereafter as practicable, they shall determine by lot which of their number shall hold his office for two and four years respectively, and thereafter there shall be elected as aforesaid, at each general election for county officers, commissioners for four years to fill the places of those whose term has expired."

The question being taken, the amendment was adopted.

The remaining sections of the report were then read, but no other amendments, except some verbal ones, were made to the report.

The report having been read the third time, the question was upon its final passage.

The question was then taken by yeas and nays, under rule forty-three, and the report was adopted—yeas 41, nays 22—as follows:

Yeas—Messrs. Goldsborough, President; Abbott, Annan, Baker, Cunningham, Cushing, Daniel, Davis, of Washington, Dellinger, Ecker, Farrow, Galloway, Greene, Hebb, Hoffman, Hopkins, Hopper, Keefer, Kennard, Larsh, Markey, Mayhugh, McComas, Mullikin, Negley, Parker, Purnell, Ridgely, Russell, Sands, Schlosser, Scott, Smith, of Carroll, Smith of Worcester, Sneary, Stirling, Stockbridge, Swope, Thomas, Todd, Valliant, Wooden—41.

Nays—Messrs. Billingsley, Blackiston, Bond, Briscoe, Brown, Chambers, Clarke, Crawford, Dent, Duvall, Hodson, Hollyday, Horsey, Johnson, Lansdale, Lee, Marbury, Miller, Parran, Peter, Smith, of Dorchester, Wilmer—22.

Mr. Billingsley. Does not the rule require that every article on its final passage shall receive the votes of a majority of the members elected to this convention before it shall be declared adopted?

The Chairman (Mr. Daniel.) The rule was altered so as to require only the affirmative votes of a majority of the members present.

Mr. Billingsley. So that a minority of this body can pass any provision they think proper.

The Chairman (Mr. Daniel.) Certainly, if they constitute a majority of the members present.

EDUCATION.

On motion of Mr. Stockbridge,

The convention then proceeded to the consideration of the report of the committee on education, which was on its third reading.

Sections one and two were read, and no amendments offered thereto.

Section three was read as follows:

"Sec. 3. There shall be a State board of education, consisting of the governor of the State, the lieutenant governor, the president of the senate, the speaker of the house of delegates and the State's superintendent of public instruction, which board shall perform such duties as the general assembly may direct."

Mr. Stirling. I move to strike out the words "the president of the senate."

Mr. Thomas. Suppose the lieutenant governor should become governor, then the president of the senate could act upon this board.

Mr. Stirling. That is a contingency that might arise, it is true. But then this should be put in the alternative—"the lieutenant governor, or the president of the senate." However, I will withdraw my amendment.

The remaining sections of the report were then read, and no amendments offered thereto.

Mr. Hopkins. I offer the following as an additional section:

"The legislature shall foster and encourage moral, intellectual, scientific and agricultural improvement; they shall, when it may be practicable, make suitable provision for the blind, mute and insane, and for the organization of such institutions of learning as the best interests of the State may demand."

Mr. Stockbridge. I suppose no member of the convention can have any objection to the proposition of the gentleman from Howard (Mr. Hopkins.) But it has probably slipped his memory, for it has been some time since we acted upon it, that we have adopted precisely his idea, and almost his very language, in the declaration of rights. The forty-third article of the declaration of rights reads as follows:

"That the legislature ought to encourage the diffusion of knowledge and virtue, the extension of a judicious system of general education, the promotion of literature, the arts, science, agriculture, commerce and manufactures, and the general amelioration of the condition of the people."

That would seem to cover the very proposition of the gentleman, and part of it is in the very language of his proposition; and will probably obviate any necessity for incorporating his proposition in this report.

Mr. HOPKINS. Does it relate to the blind, deaf and dumb?

Mr. STOCKBRIDGE. They will be embraced under the last clause of the article, relating to "the general amelioration of the condition of the people."

Mr. HOPKINS withdrew his amendment.

The question was upon the passage of the report.

Mr. STOCKBRIDGE moved a call of the house, which was ordered.

Pending the calling of the roll,

Mr. STIRLING moved that further proceedings under the call be dispensed with.

The motion was not agreed to.

The calling of the roll was then completed, the following members answering to their names:

Messrs. Goldsborough, President; Abbott, Annan, Audoun, Baker, Barron, Billingsley, Blackiston, Briscoe, Brooks, Brown, Carter, Chambers, Clarke, Cunningham, Cushing, Daniel, Davis, of Charles, Davis, of Washington, Dellinger, Dent, Duvall, Ecker, Farrow, Galloway, Greene, Hatch, Hebb, Hodson, Hoffman, Hollyday, Hopkins, Hopper, Horsey, Johnson, Keefer, Kennard, Lansdale, Larsh, Lee, Marbury, Markey, Mayhugh, McComas, Mullikin, Negley, Parker, Peter, Pugh, Purnell, Ridgely, Russell, Sands, Schlosser, Scott, Smith, of Carroll, Smith, of Dorchester, Smith, of Worcester, Sneary, Stirling, Stockbridge, Swope, Sykes, Thomas, Todd, Valliant, Wickard, Wilmer, Wooden—68.

On motion of Mr. McCOMAS,

Further proceedings under the call were dispensed with.

The report of the committee on education was then passed, by yeas and nays, (under rule forty-three)—yeas 56, nays 18—as follows:

Yeas—Messrs. Goldsborough, President; Abbott, Annan, Audoun, Baker, Barron, Bond, Briscoe, Brooks, Carter, Cunningham, Cushing, Daniel, Davis, of Washington, Dellinger, Earle, Ecker, Farrow, Galloway, Greene, Hatch, Hebb, Hoffman, Hopkins, Hopper, Keefer, Kennard, King, Larsh, Markey, Mayhugh, McComas, Mullikin, Murray, Negley, Nyman, Parker, Pugh, Purnell, Ridgely, Russell, Sands, Schlosser, Scott, Smith, of Carroll, Smith, of Worcester, Sneary, Stirling, Stockbridge, Swope, Sykes, Thomas, Todd, Valliant, Wickard, Wooden—56.

Nays—Messrs. Billingsley, Blackiston, Brown, Chambers, Clarke, Davis, of Charles, Dent, Duvall, Hodson, Hollyday, Horsey, Johnson, Lansdale, Lee, Marbury, Peter, Smith, of Dorchester, Wilmer—18.

Mr. CLARKE, when his name was called said: I think this is an improper time to make changes in our constitution. And being opposed to the whole of the proceedings inaugurating a change in the constitution of Maryland at this time, I shall vote against this article, although there are many things in it to which I do not object. I vote "no."

TREASURY DEPARTMENT.

On motion of Mr. STOCKBRIDGE,

The convention proceeded to the consideration of the report of the committee on the treasury department, which was on its third reading.

The report was read the third time, and no amendments were offered thereto.

The report was then passed, by yeas and nays, (under rule forty-three)—yeas 53, nays 14—as follows:

Yeas—Messrs. Abbott, Annan, Audoun, Baker, Barron, Billingsley, Bond, Brooks, Carter, Chambers, Cushing, Daniel, Davis, of Washington, Dellinger, Dent, Earle, Ecker, Farrow, Galloway, Greene, Hatch, Hebb, Hoffman, Hollyday, Hopkins, Hopper, Johnson, Keefer, Kennard, Larsh, Markey, Mayhugh, Mullikin, Negley, Parker, Pugh, Purnell, Ridgely, Russell, Sands, Schlosser, Scott, Smith, of Carroll, Smith, of Worcester, Sneary, Stirling, Stockbridge, Swope, Sykes, Thomas, Todd, Valliant, Wooden—53.

Nays—Messrs. Blackiston, Briscoe, Brown, Davis, of Charles, Duvall, Hodson, Horsey, Lansdale, Lee, Marbury, Parran, Peter, Smith, of Dorchester, Wilmer—14.

JUDICIARY DEPARTMENT.

Mr. CHAMBERS. Before proceeding to any other report, I would ask the attention of the house for a moment. I received this morning from a very respectable source, a letter suggesting the propriety of a change in the report of the committee on the judiciary department, which has not yet passed. The only way in which I can respond to the wishes of my correspondent, which I wish to do, rather on his authority than my own, is to ask the house to adopt this order:

"*Ordered*, That the committee on the judiciary be directed to inquire into the expediency of inserting in the constitution a provision that in all cases in law or equity the parties may by agreement select some one learned in the law to act as judge in the cause, without expense to the State, and subject to such regulations as the legislature may provide."

It is simply a resolution of inquiry, and commits nobody to anything.

No objection being made, the order was received and adopted.

COUNTIES AND TOWNSHIPS.

On motion of Mr. STOCKBRIDGE,

The convention then proceeded to consider the report of the committee on the rights, duties, divisions and subdivisions of counties, which was on its third reading.

The first section was read as follows:

"The general assembly may provide for

organizing new counties, locating and removing county seats, and changing county lines, but no new county shall be organized without the consent of a majority of the legal voters residing within the limits about to form said county, nor shall any new county contain less than four hundred square miles, nor less than ten thousand white inhabitants, nor shall any county be reduced below that amount of square miles, nor below that number of white inhabitants.''

Mr. Ridgely. I move that the rules be suspended in order to enable me to offer an amendment. I desire to move to insert after the words "legal voters residing within the limits about to form said county," the words "nor shall the lines of any county be changed without the consent of a majority of the legal voters residing within the limits of the lines proposed to be changed."

Mr. Stirling. That proposition was offered by my colleague (Mr. Stockbridge) upon the second reading of this report, and it was voted down.

Mr. Ridgely. I cannot help that; I propose to offer it again.

The question being then taken upon the motion to suspend the rules, upon a division —ayes 44, noes 16—it was agreed to.

Mr. Ridgely. I now move to amend section one of this report by inserting after the words "about to form said county" the words "nor shall the lines of any county be changed without the consent of a majority of the legal voters, residing within the limits of the lines proposed to be changed."

I will in a very few words explain the object of that amendment. The previous part of the section provides that in the event of organizing a new county, the consent of the majority of the legal voters residing within the limits about to form said new county shall be first obtained. It is also proposed that any portion of the lines of a county may be changed; but there is no provision made to consult the residents within the limits of the lines proposed to be changed. Now I understand very well the effect of this provision about changing county lines, and I have no objection in the world to it. I am free to confess that Baltimore city must necessarily, by reason of its constantly accumulating population, find its way within the limits of Baltimore county. It is the result of that sort of law which nothing in the world can prevent. In time it must find its way there; and I do not propose to throw any obstacle in the way of that end.

But I simply ask that the people, residing within the limits of the district proposed to be included within the increased limits of Baltimore city, shall be consulted, for the same reason that you would consult the people residing within the limits of a new county that you propose to form. I ask that the same theory be applied to the people of Baltimore county, in relation to an increase of the limits of Baltimore city, that you would apply in relation to the organization of new counties in the State. I know that Baltimore city must increase and expand, until in process of time it shall absorb a large portion of the area of Baltimore county, and I say God-speed to it. I do not propose to throw any obstacles whatever in its way. But I simply ask that when they apply to the legislature for an extension of its boundaries, there shall be a limitation upon the power of the legislature to grant, which shall require the assent of the people residing in the portion of the county asked to be included within the limits of Baltimore city. It will have a very serious effect upon our county treasury. The very largest proportion of the taxes received by the county, is derived from the suburban population of Baltimore city; and the extension into Baltimore county of the limits of Baltimore city, of course very essentially affects the financial ability of that county to sustain itself.

And I ask, in view of its importance to our community, that you will at least put in here a provision that the people shall be consulted and their consent obtained before any such extension of boundary shall be granted to Baltimore city.

Mr. Stirling. So far as this matter applies to Baltimore city, I certainly have no desire that any thing should be done in respect to extending its limits, which would be unacceptable to the people interested in the matter; anything which would be unjust to Baltimore county. So far as I have any personal interest in the matter, it is rather against any increase of the city limits, than otherwise.

But this proposition affects all the counties of the State; it seems to me it is too broad. It says the legislature shall not change the lines of any county, except upon the consent of those who reside within the lines proposed to be changed. Now it may be necessary to change a county line for a few yards, or a few hundred yards. There might be but one or two people residing within the limits of the proposed change. One man might hold the whole of the land within those limits, and thus you would give to him the absolute control over the matter.

This applies more particularly, however, to Baltimore city. I do not suppose there is any prospect of any increase of the limits of Baltimore city for some time to come. It is not needed at present, although the city limits do run about on the line of the houses, and there are a great many streets laid out beyond the city limits. Still, if there should be any extension of the limits, it would not be much, not more than a half mile or so beyond where the limits now are. You could not embrace within the limits of Baltimore city whatever is suburban; only the portion where the streets are built out. Now, if the legislature should see fit to extend the city limits for a short distance, so as to include the paved streets, the built up streets outside the city, those who now receive all the benefits and protection of the city government, might vote that they would not come out of Baltimore county into the city, simply for the purpose of escaping that portion of the city taxes which they ought to bear. Men now go and build houses just outside of the city limits, where they get all the protection of the city government, all the benefits of living within a city, while they escape the taxes in the city. Now a man should not be allowed to exercise selfish interests in that way. If he wants to live in the county, let him move in the county; if he wants the benefits of a city, then let him pay for them.

This proposition practically puts it into the power of two or three landholders to decide the whole question of legislative policy in regard to this matter. I do not believe the legislature will do anything which will not be acceptable to the people. I know the people of the city of Baltimore will ask nothing against the interests of Baltimore county.

Mr. Ridgely. I do not place it upon that theory at all. I do not understand how the people of Baltimore county get any protection from the city of Baltimore. I do not understand that argument. This is a question of right, one which belongs to the people of the community to be consulted upon the subject. It is a question of the transfer of their relative political position; and I ask this house, upon that ground, to give them protection.

Mr. Stirling. What I meant by the people of Baltimore county receiving all the benefits of the city government, was this: not that those who belong *bona fide* to the county receive these benefits; but I refer to the people who transact all their business in town, who are in effect citizens of Baltimore, who go to our mass meetings, some of whom are made presidents of those meetings; some who, the moment you touch their real interests, are all Baltimoreans. They are merchants, mechanics, manufacturers, men who do business in Baltimore city, who belong there; men who have no interest in Baltimore county, who actually receive all the benefits of the city government in their business. These men go just outside of the city limits, on a street which runs continuously from the centre of the city out to their houses; they go there to escape their portion of the city burdens. They want to receive all the benefits of the city, and then evade their share of its burdens. I know men who are worth millions of dollars, who have put themselves in that position, and thereby escape taxes on their property to the amount of $500,000 or $600,000 annually. Wherever a man owns a farm, or a country-seat, or any property *bona fide* in the county, that is all well enough. But I am opposed to these Baltimore city people doing this, while they live on streets built out by the city, and occupy three-story brick houses on those streets, and who are not country men at all.

Mr. Ridgely. I only desire to observe that the class of people of whom the gentleman from Baltimore city (Mr. Stirling) speaks, is very small compared with the abiding, fixed, rural population of Baltimore county.

Mr. Stirling. I know that.

Mr. Ridgely. The number of Baltimore county people who transact business in Baltimore city is comparatively a very small number, alongside the great body of the people who have their fixed residence and agricultural pursuits outside of the limits of Baltimore city.

Mr. Hebb. My first impression was to vote for this amendment. But if it is not adopted, the legislature will have the right to alter the limits of Baltimore county and Baltimore city, as they may deem most expedient, and I think it is better to leave it in that way. Of course those parties who live just outside of Baltimore city will always vote to stay out to avoid the city taxes.

Mr. Stockbridge. So far as that is concerned, there is really a greater practical difficulty about this matter than any that has yet been stated. Everybody knows that taxation in every city of large size, which has to maintain a government like that of the city of Baltimore, is unavoidably higher than taxation in the county. Now there are many men who own whole rows of houses, and warehouses, in Baltimore city, and rent them, who have their own residences in the city of Baltimore, where they live six and eight months in the year, and yet who also have their country residences outside of the city. Now these men, in electing which they will have as their residence, having the opportunity, will select the county. The result of which is a practical saving to them of $10,000, $15,000 or $20,000 a year in taxes alone. Because all their personal property, all their floating property is taxed where they claim their residence, in the county. And while the city is protecting this property of theirs in town, while they are doing business there, and having all the benefits and protection of the city government for the great bulk of their property, they are paying only county taxation. This operates very gross injustice; and such men will never consent to change their place of residence from the county to the city, for the very obvious reason which I have stated. There are other practical objections and difficulties, but this to me is the insuperable objection, so far as the limits between Baltimore city and Baltimore county are concerned.

The question was upon agreeing to the amendment of Mr. Ridgely.

Upon this question Mr. STOCKBRIDGE called for the yeas and nays, which were ordered.

The question was then taken, by yeas and nays, and resulted—yeas 37, nays 33—as follows:

Yeas—Messrs. Annan, Baker, Billingsley, Blackiston, Bond, Briscoe, Carter, Chambers, Clarke, Crawford, Davis, of Charles, Dent, Duvall, Hoffman, Hollyday, Hopkins, Hopper, Horsey, Johnson, King, Lansdale, Larsh, Mayhugh, Negley, Parker, Parran, Peter, Ridgely, Smith of Carroll, Smith, of Dorchester, Sneary, Sykes, Todd, Turner, Valliant, Wilmer, Wooden—37.

Nays—Messrs. Goldsborough, President; Abbott, Audoun, Barron, Brooks, Brown, Cunningham, Cushing, Daniel, Dellinger, Ecker, Farrow, Galloway, Hatch, Hebb, Hodson, Keefer, Kennard, Lee, Markey, McComas, Mullikin, Pugh, Purnell, Russell, Schlosser, Scott, Smith, of Worcester, Stirling, Stockbridge, Swope, Thomas, Wickard—33.

The amendment was accordingly adopted.

Mr. ABBOTT, when his name was called, said: Believing that this is a matter entirely for the legislature, I vote "no."

Mr. DANIEL. I am alike interested in the county as the city. But believing that this amendment may do harm to the city, I shall vote "no."

No further amendment was offered to this section.

Section two was then read as follows:

"The general assembly shall provide, by general law, for dividing the counties into towns or permanent municipal corporations, in place of the existing election districts, prescribing their limits and confiding to them all powers necessary for the management of their public local concerns; and whenever the organization of these township corporations shall be perfected, all officers provided for in this constitution, but whose official functions shall have been superseded by such organizations, shall be dispensed with, and the affairs of such towns and of the counties as affected by the action of such towns, shall be transacted in such manner as the general assembly shall direct."

Mr. CHAMBERS. I find in this section the following:

"The general assembly shall provide, by general law, for dividing the counties into towns or permanent municipal corporations, in place of the existing election districts, prescribing their limits and confiding to them all powers necessary for the management of their public local concerns," etc.

This subject seems to have been acted upon while I was absent. I think it may not have attracted as much attention as it deserved. The consequences, perhaps, had not been regarded as seriously as they merit. From the early history of our State, we have been divided into counties and parishes. Many of our old acts of assembly have recognized those territorial divisions of the State, and many of their provisions necessarily connect themselves with that division. Subsequently election districts were introduced, and the whole State is now divided into election districts. Our people are familiar with this arrangement. I have not heard that it has produced the slightest inconvenience. We have had corporations that have transacted all our county, parish and district concerns, without the slightest exception being taken, so far as I have learned, to their efficiency.

But now the proposition is introduced to adopt the system which prevails in the northern States, converting all this into a different order of things, by the creation of townships. This system, I believe, universally prevails at the north, where each township is a sort of province by itself; where they do all their business, impose their taxes, and regulate all their concerns, as an independent, and to a certain extent a sort of sovereign community. Now all this is utterly unknown to our people. It does not comport at all with the habits of any who have been educated here. And gentlemen who come among us from the north, can very soon fall into our habits. I have heard of none of them objecting to our system, or failing to migrate here because of this difference in our organization.

Now if this proposition is adopted, you subvert the ideas of very many amongst us; you bring about a state of confusion, for which I do not perceive the slightest necessity upon the face of the earth. Why make this change? What is it to effect? How is it to promote the interests of the State? Who demands it? To what end is it to be brought about? Are gentlemen aware that this will require the whole State to be cut up in a different manner altogether, with a different style altogether of governing the State; a different set of officers altogether, just by this simple provision? A very few words comprise all this. But I tell gentlemen that those few words are of most tremendous import. It is the introduction of a new system of governing the State in its internal affairs. See what it provides:

"And dividing the counties into towns, or permanent municipal corporations, in place of the existing election districts, prescribing their limits, and confiding to them all powers necessary for the management of their public local concerns."

It is a complete revolution; an entire change, of course to be followed by the necessary consequences. Whenever these townships shall be perfected, then the officers provided for in this constitution, but whose official functions shall be superseded by such organization, as they all will be, your county commissioners and everything of that sort, will all be dispensed with. It so provides.

"And whenever the organization of these

township corporations shall be perfected, all officers provided for in this constitution, but whose official functions shall have been superseded by such organizations, shall be dispensed with, and the affairs of such towns and of the counties as affected by the action of such towns, shall be transacted in such manner as the general assembly shall direct."

Mr. BARRON. Will the gentleman allow me to ask him a question?

Mr. CHAMBERS. Yes, sir; two of them; any question but the previous question.

Mr. BARRON. Would the gentleman have any objection to having a town upon his farm?

Mr. CHAMBERS. I would not let it go there, if I could control the matter.

Mr. BARRON. Not if they paid you for it?

Mr. CHAMBERS. Not a town in this sense; these towns have no houses in them. If the gentleman means whether I would have a town there in the character of a city, that is another matter. But a township need not have a hut in it; the people may live in straw houses, or in huts quarried in the earth. Townships are to be erected. But the gentleman does not suppose that the legislature are to build houses in these towns. I will go for that.

Now, I submit to my friends that no party politics are involved in this matter at all. I hope gentlemen will not be alarmed because your humble servant proposes to offer an amendment, as unacceptable as my propositions generally are. But do you gentlemen, Marylanders, want to go to Boston, or Hartford, or any other section of the northern part of the country, to learn how to manage your own municipal affairs? Are you not satisfied with what you have always been in the habit of doing; with what your fathers have been in the habit of doing?

I would therefore in the most modest way, ask leave to move so to amend this section that it shall at least read, "The general assembly *may* provide, by general law, for dividing the counties into towns," &c., instead of having it read, "The general assembly *shall* provide," &c. Let the legislature have some discretion in the matter. We are receiving more northern men every day, and probably the time will arrive when we will have such a number of them that the State will be governed by them. I do not believe that the people of our State would now know how to manage townships of this sort. I ask permission therefore to open this section to amendment so far as to change "shall" to "may," so as to allow the legislature some discretion in this matter; not compel them, bind them, oblige them to make this change.

Mr. STOCKBRIDGE. Is it competent to propose that amendment, in case this section is opened to amendment? This report as it came from the hands of the committee read: "The general assembly *may* provide," &c. On its second reading the motion was made to strike out "may" and insert "shall," and the convention adopted that motion. I would suggest that it is not competent now to move to strike out that which the convention has put in.

The PRESIDENT. If the convention agrees to open the section for this amendment, it operates virtually as a reconsideration.

The question was upon the motion of Mr. CHAMBERS to suspend the rules.

On this question Mr. CHAMBERS called for the yeas and nays, which were ordered.

The question was then taken, by yeas and nays, and resulted—yeas 25, nays 42—as follows:

Yeas—Messrs. Billingsley, Blackiston, Bond, Brisc e, Brown, Chambers, Clarke, Crawford, Davis, of Charles, Dent, Duvall, Hoffman, Hollyday, Horsey, Johnson, Lansdale, Larsh, Lee, Marbury, Parran, Peter, Ridgely, Smith, of Dorchester, Sneary, Wilmer—25.

Nays—Messrs. Goldsborough, President; Abbott, Annan, Audoun, Baker, Barron, Brooks, Carter, Cunningham, Cushing, Daniel, Davis, of Washington, Ecker, Farrow, Galloway, Greene, Hatch, Hebb, Hopkins, Hopper, Keefer, Kennard, Markey, Mayhugh, McComas, Mullikin, Negley, Parker, Pugh, Purnell, Russell, Schlosser, Smith, of Carroll, Smith, of Worcester, Stirling, Stockbridge, Swope, Sykes, Todd, Valliant, Wickard, Wooden—42.

The motion to suspend the rules was therefore not agreed to.

Mr. STOCKBRIDGE. The words "towns" and "townships" are used interchangeably, or promiscuously in this section. I would therefore ask permission to move to strike out the word "town" where it occurs, and insert the word "township" so as to make this section uniform in that respect.

The PRESIDENT. That is a merely verbal alteration, which the chair will direct the secretary to make.

Mr. DAVIS, of Charles, moved to strike out the second section.

The question being taken, the motion to strike out was not agreed to.

The report having been read a third time, the question was upon its adoption.

The question was then taken, by yeas and nays (under rule forty-three,) and the report was adopted—yeas 48, nays 20—as follows:

Yeas—Messrs. Goldsborough, President; Abbott, Annan, Audoun, Baker, Barron, Brooks, Carter, Cunningham, Cushing, Daniel, Davis, of Washington, Dellinger, Ecker, Farrow, Galloway, Greene, Hatch, Hebb, Hoffman, Hopkins, Hopper, Keefer, Kennard, Larsh, Markey, Mayhugh, McComas, Mullikin, Negley, Parker, Pugh, Purnell, Ridgely, Russell, Schlosser, Smith, of Carroll, Smith, of Worcester, Sneary, Stirling, Stockbridge, Swope, Sykes, Thomas, Todd, Valliant, Wickard, Wooden—48.

Nays—Messrs. Billingsley, Blackiston, Bond, Brown Chambers, Clarke, Crawford, Davis, of Charles, Dent, Duvall, Hollyday, Horsey, Johnson, Lansdale, Lee, Marbury, Parran, Peter, Smith, of Dorchester, Wilmer—20.

LEAVE OF ABSENCE.

Mr. PUGH asked and obtained leave of absence until to-morrow.

Mr. HOPPER asked and obtained leave of absence until Friday next.

Mr. WICKARD asked and obtained leave of absence until to-morrow morning.

Mr. BLACKISTON asked and obtained leave of absence until to-morrow.

Mr. NEGLEY asked and obtained leave of absence for to-morrow, on account of important business.

On motion of Mr. DAVIS, of Charles,

The convention then took a recess until half-past three o'clock, P. M.

AFTERNOON SESSION.

The convention met at half-past 3 o'clock, P. M.

The roll was called, and the following members answered to their names:

Messrs. Goldsborough, President; Abbott, Annan, Audoun, Baker, Barron, Brooks, Brown, Carter, Chambers, Cunningham, Cushing, Daniel, Davis, of Charles, Davis, of Washington, Dellinger, Dent, Duvall, Earle, Ecker, Farrow, Galloway, Greene, Hatch, Hebb, Hoffman, Hollyday, Hopkins, Horsey, Keefer, Kennard, King, Lansdale, Lee, Markey, McComas, Morgan, Mullikin, Negley, Nyman, Parker, Parran, Purnell, Ridgely, Russell, Sands, Schlosser, Scott, Smith, of Carroll, Smith, of Worcester, Sneary, Stirling, Stockbridge, Swope, Sykes, Thomas, Todd, Turner, Valliant, Wickard, Wilmer, Wooden—62.

STATE'S ATTORNEYS.

On motion of Mr. STOCKBRIDGE,

The report of the committee on State's attorneys was taken up, read the third time and passed by yeas and nays—yeas 48, nays 4—as follows:

Yeas—Messrs. Goldsborough, President; Abbott, Annan, Audoun, Baker, Barron, Brooks, Carter, Chambers, Cunningham, Cushing, Daniel, Davis, of Washington, Dellinger, Dent, Duvall, Ecker, Farrow, Galloway, Greene, Hatch, Hebb, Hopkins Kennard, Markey, McComas, Morgan, Mullikin, Negley, Parker, Purnell, Ridgely, Russell, Sands, Schlosser, Scott, Smith of Carroll, Smith, of Worcester, Sneary, Stirling, Stockbridge, Swope, Sykes, Thomas, Todd, Valliant Wickard, Wooden—48.

Nays—Messrs. Brown, Hollyday, Horsey, Lee—4.

MILITIA.

On motion of Mr. STOCKBRIDGE,

The report of the committee on the militia and military affairs was taken up, read the third time, and passed by yeas and nays as follows:

Yeas—Messrs. Goldsborough, President; Abbott, Annan, Audoun, Baker, Barron, Brooks, Brown, Carter, Chambers, Cunningham, Cushing, Daniel, Davis, of Washington, Dellinger, Ecker, Farrow, Galloway, Greene, Hatch, Hebb, Hollyday, Kennard, Markey, McComas, Mullikin, Negley, Parker, Purnell, Ridgely, Russell, Sands, Schlosser, Scott, Smith, of Worcester, Sneary, Stirling, Stockbridge, Swope, Sykes, Thomas, Todd, Valliant, Wooden—44.

Nays—Messrs. Dent, Duvall, Horsey, Lee, Marbury, Morgan, Turner, Wickard—8.

PARCHMENT COPIES OF THE CONSTITUTION.

On motion of Mr. RIDGELY,

Ordered, That four copies of the constitution when finally adopted by the convention, be copied on parchment or detached sheets of bill paper, that the same be subscribed by the president and members of the convention, attested by the Secretary, and that one copy thereof be deposited with the executive, one copy with the clerk of the court of appeals, one copy with the comptroller, and one copy with the librarian.

THE SCHEDULE.

Mr. DANIEL moved that the convention proceed to the consideration of the report of the committee on the schedule, on its second reading.

Mr. CHAMBERS. I hope not. I hope that will be postponed until the morning session, when the house is full That report contains provisions which are most mischievous; but I forbear to characterize them. I ask the house to postpone the report until the house is full.

Mr. DENT. I wish to say a word or two in opposition to taking up this report at this time. The house is very thin; and the report contains provisions which certainly require close examination and scrutiny. I think it will be unfair to the minority, and I trust there is no disposition to deal unfairly with the minority by taking up that report at this time. Perhaps we can find something with which we can proceed more in harmony than we can with the schedule as reported. I have read the schedule, and I cannot express in words the feelings that it stirred up on reading it, the surprise that it engendered. I trust that it will be left for a later period of the session, especially as it provides or is intended to provide for the submission of our work to the people of the State. There are other reports still pending, upon which we can act, I suppose. But if there are not, let us wait for other reports to come in, and defer any action upon this at present. I do not like to express all that I feel on this occasion. I trust there will be no disposition to press or urge this matter so far as to make it seem to be expressly in opposition to the will of the minority, which I know is of very small account. Yet we wish and hope to be fairly treated in the consideration of this report, which we consider of such vital importance to the constituency which we represent.

Mr. STIRLING. I should be very much indisposed to do anything upon a matter of so much importance, which might seem to friends upon the other side to be going too fast; but I do not feel the force of the objection of the gentleman from St. Mary's for this reason. Although the house is not as full as it is sometimes, we have sixty members here, which is certainly a very considerable attendance. This report will take some time. It will take up the afternoon. We may have the afternoon and night session upon it. If we wait and take it up to-morrow, it might take up the whole day, which would throw us still further forward. I hope the convention will be able to adjourn by Friday, or at most by Saturday. We have all the reports of the committee on revision to consider, which are not ready yet. This report will take up some time. I cannot see the hardship of beginning upon it this afternoon. Gentlemen have all read it. The gentleman from St. Mary's (Mr. Dent) has expressly said that he has considered it so much as to form a very definite opinion upon it. I see here representatives of the minority who are abundantly able to take care of all their interests. If gentlemen wish to explain their views, they can do it just as well now as at any other time. There are enough gentlemen on the floor to take care of the interests of the minority. And besides, if gentlemen do not choose to attend, they have no right to expect us to delay our business upon their account.

Mr. DANIEL. If there was any advantage to be taken in this thing, I would certainly not press it. But, as has been said, our session is coming fast to a close. We have but a day or two left. The chairman of the committee informs me that it is probable he shall have to leave to-morrow afternoon; and I do not believe we shall get through this report in one day; especially if gentlemen are spreading themselves and have so much pent up wrath with reference to this schedule, as one of them tells you he has. I think it would be better to get clear of some of that this afternoon; and then they will not have so much on hand to-morrow. It does a man good sometimes to get clear of it. We know that these gentlemen vote against us on the most simple things. Gentlemen have opposed upon the third reading, reports which were exactly like the articles in the old constitution; upon the treasury department, and others which had nothing political in them. They are so afraid of us that they will not vote with us if they can help it. Anything we may say will not change the vote at all These gentlemen will all vote against us, and we shall all vote one way.

Mr. DENT. I hope not.

Mr. DANIEL. Yes we will. We shall come to an agreement, and our side of the house will vote one way and the other the other way. We have got enough present, I suppose, to carry out our views now; and if we wait for a fuller house, we shall only have a few more votes added to it. The gentlemen who are in the minority this evening, will be in the minority to-morrow just as much. I do not see that it will change the result a particle; and we may just as well go forward thus much with our work. We may as well go on with this report this afternoon and to-night.

Mr. CHAMBERS. It is very true that we are the minority; and it is very true that we shall be the minority to-morrow. But will any gentleman look at our empty seats, and then pretend to say in the face of this body, that we are not here without our friends?

Mr. DANIEL (in his seat.) Whose fault is it?

Mr. CHAMBERS continued: Any man with eyes must see it, and must acknowledge that they are absent. We hold, at least I do, that among all the enormities committed by this body towards the minority here and their constituency, there is nothing to be compared with this. That is the view I take of it. We are told that there are gentlemen here of the minority who can protect themselves. In a matter of the utmost importance, when we wish our friends to be here, at its consideration, are we to be treated as if it were a two-penny affair? It is said that we vote against all your bills, and make no distinctions. That is a fact so far as I am concerned; for I will not vote for your bills when I have no opportunity of knowing what they are, you go with such railroad speed. I shall not vote for them when I have not seen the contents of them. When gentlemen are making such political changes, I certainly am not ready to vote for your treasury reports or your attorney general reports, or anything else, which they may not see any harm in. They put political matters in a report, and do not presume that those political matters are offensive. Offensive? That is not a term which will half designate this report, in my judgment.

All I ask is to wait until our friends are here to-morrow; that you will not be in such hot haste in a matter of this sort. You drive us here from nine, three and eight o'clock. Gentlemen must have some time to themselves. My two neighbors have gone on business of urgent importance to Baltimore. My colleague's wife has been waiting there these two days on a matter of business of a domestic character but quite important. Other gentlemen are absent very unexpectedly on important business; and who would be sorry to be denied the privilege of being present. But we can only make known our wishes. If they are disregarded we cannot help it. I must say that I shall regard it as an act of oppression to refuse such a request as this.

Mr. SANDS. I cannot be still and hear myself, as one of the members of this house, charged with oppression. I cannot sit still patiently, and hear the house lectured for oppression; when evidently the complaint upon the other side is that their own members are not in their seats. What do they ask of us? To wait until their members are in their seats? Have we forced them out of their seats? Whose act is it by which they are not here to-day, but their own? Because they are not here in their places to-day, where their constituents who intrusted them with their interests commanded them to be, we are charged with oppression if we continue our work. The twenty-fifth rule of this body, one of our standing rules, is in this language:

"*Rule* 25. No member shall absent himself from the service of the convention unless he have leave, or be sick, or unable to attend."

That is the duty of gentlemen; and when they absent themselves without leave, it is in violation of a standing rule of the convention. They are absent to-day. The majority are here in force as full as ever, fifty to fifty-three members voting with us. Yet we are to be told that we are oppressors solely because these gentlemen of the minority are out of their seats. I cannot myself express the sentiments with which I listen to scoldings of this sort. It is time that they be ended. This house is here; we are here; I am here to discharge the duty my constituents sent me here to discharge. I am not going to pause in that duty because somebody else is absent, or sit still and be scolded because other people are not here.

Mr. CHAMBERS demanded the yeas and nays, and they were ordered.

The question being taken, the result was—yeas 42, nays 12—as follows:

Yeas—Messrs. Goldsborough, President; Abbott, Annan, Audoun, Baker, Barron, Brooks, Carter Cunningham, Cushing, Daniel, Davis, of Washington, Dellinger, Ecker, Farrow, Galloway, Greene, Hatch, Hebb, Kennard, Markey, McComas, Mullikin, Negley, Parker, Purnell, Ridgely, Russell, Sands, Schlosser, Scott, Smith, of Worcester, Sneary, Stirling, Stockbridge, Swope, Sykes, Thomas, Todd, Valliant, Wickard, Wooden—42.

Nays—Messrs. Brown, Chambers, Dent, Duvall, Hollyday, Horsey, Lansdale, Lee, Marbury, Miller, Morgan, Turner—12.

The convention accordingly proceeded to the second reading of the report on the schedule, and the first section was read as follows:

Section 1. Every officer of the State, the entire amount of whose pay or compensation received for the discharge of his official duties, shall exceed the yearly sum of three thousand dollars, except wherein otherwise provided by this constitution, shall keep a book in which shall be entered every sum or sums of money received by him, or on his account, as a payment, or compensation for his performance of official duties, a copy of which entries in said book, verified by the oath of the officer, by whom it is directed to be kept, shall be returned yearly to the treasurer of the State, for his inspection and that of the general assembly of the State, and each of said officers, when the amount received by him for the year shall exceed three thousand dollars, shall yearly pay over to the treasurer of the State, the amount of such excess by him received subject to such disposition thereof as the general assembly may direct. Any such officer failing to comply with this requisition, shall be deemed to have vacated his office, and be subject to suit by the State, for the amount that ought to be paid into the treasury.

Mr. STOCKBRIDGE submitted the following amendment: strike out "officer," in line one, and insert "person holding any office created by or exiting under the constitution or laws."

Mr. STOCKBRIDGE said: The term "every officer" of the State seems to be definite; but the history of the past is that there have been persons under that, holding office and receiving large salaries, who have not made any return at all.

The amendment was adopted.

Mr. STOCKBRIDGE. I am aware that this section is an exact copy of the old constitution; but still there is a mistake in it. I move to strike out the word "treasurer" in the ninth line, and to insert the word "comptroller."

Mr. RIDGELY. The committee intended to make that amendment and forgot it.

The amendment was adopted.

Mr. RIDGELY. I wish to call the attention of the gentleman from Baltimore city (Mr. Stockbridge) to the amendment he first offered. I am afraid it goes very much beyond what my colleague intends. The expression "every person holding any office created by, or existing under the constitution or laws of the State," includes all the municipal officers of the city of Baltimore, I think. If the city of Baltimore choose to pay them more than three thousand dollars it is no business of ours. If the city of Baltimore pays a man four thousand dollars, why should we take one thousand dollars out of his pocket and put it into the State treasury? It puts a restriction upon the city of Baltimore, that it shall not pay the city clerk or any other officer a higher salary than three thousand dollars. That is none of our business, if the people choose to pay more. They have not done so, so far as I am aware. I hope the house will reconsider its action on that amendment if the gentleman construes it as I do, to cover all municipal officers.

Mr. ABBOTT. The reason why I voted in favor of the amendment was that I was not aware in doing so that it would affect the corporation officers. If it does, I hope the gentleman will change the language of it.

Mr. STIRLING. It may be so construed, for the officers of Baltimore city are officers under the laws of this State.

Mr. STOCKBRIDGE. If it is in order to offer an explanation, I will tell exactly what I meant. There have been certain officers, I may instance certain clerks, sheriffs, criers, officers about the courts in the State of Maryland, who have received fees to an amount larger than three thousand dollars, year after year, and have said that they were not officers of the State; that they were officers of the court. Those, in my apprehension, are just the sort of persons designed to be reached by this. When persons have a fixed salary, it is known; but there are none that have a fixed salary by the State that are obnoxious to this, either in the former constitution or as modified by the amendment. It was designed to meet just such cases and no others, where the fees and contingent emoluments of the office amount to more than three thousand dollars. The design is that in all such cases the excess should go to the State.

I do not think that the article as it has been amended, is obnoxious to the objection that is made to it. "Every person holding any office created by or existing under the constitution or laws of this State." In one sense everything that exists in the State is under the constitution and laws of the State. They have a certain power and control over it. We establish a corporation. Inasmuch as we give a legal existence to that corporation, in that sense the officers of the corporation are under the laws of the State, no matter what the corporation is—the Baltimore and Ohio Railroad Company, the Gas Company, or any other manufacturing company. But then they receive no fees or emolument from the people contingent upon their holding a public office. So we establish a municipal corporation, the corporation of Baltimore or any other city. It is true we give it a legal existence. So far as it depends on the laws of the State, it is under the constitution and laws of the State. But we neither fix the salaries, fees, or anything else under the laws of the State. Though they derive them from the people, it is under certain ordinances which the corporation create. It seems to me that these are not under the laws of the State in any proper sense of the term. I think that no city officers will be reached by that. I am not aware that any officer is paid by fees.

Mr. STIRLING. There is nothing about fees. It is "pay or compensation."

Mr. STOCKBRIDGE. Fees are compensation. Salary is compensation. There is no fixed salary of any State official in the State of Maryland which amounts to three thousand dollars.

Mr. STIRLING. The mayor's salary is three thousand dollars.

Mr. STOCKBRIDGE. That is under the laws of the city. The city solicitor gets three thousand dollars.

Mr. ABBOTT. I understand my colleague to say that this does not contemplate any officer of any incorporated company.

Mr. STOCKBRIDGE. I do not understand it to do so, municipal or any other.

Mr. MILLER. It is unfortunate; but the gentleman's say-so is not a part of the constitution.

Mr. STOCKBRIDGE. I have offered an amendment which I considered a proper one, and it has been adopted. If anybody wishes to modify it, he can make the motion.

Mr. STIRLING. Officers of the courts will still say that they are officers of the courts, and do not hold office under the constitution or laws

Mr. THOMAS. I move to amend by striking out the words in the ninth and tenth lines, "treasurer of the State, for his inpection and that of the general assembly of the State," and inserting the words "county commissioners of the several counties, and to the register of the mayor and city council of Baltimore."

My object is this; that where there is an excess of fees paid by a county or city official, that excess of fees shall go back to the county or city taxed with the payment of the excess, and not to the State. I think the State is not entitled to any excess of fees that may accumulate in Baltimore county or Allegany county. If there is any excess of fees in the performance of official duties, it should go back to the tax payers that are taxed to pay those fees. If this amendment is carried, I shall move, in order to make it conform to this amendment, to amend so as to read "shall yearly pay over to the treasurers of the several counties, the amount of such excess by them received, subject to such disposition thereof as the county commissioners may direct."

Mr. STIRLING. I had not designed to vote for any amendment or to offer any to this section. I did not know there was any objection to it. But since it has been amended I wish to say a word with regard to this proposition of my colleague. I did not design to make the motion; but if I had wished to make a motion it would have been to strike out this section from the constitution; for the legislature has power to provide for it. In point of fact this clause of the constitution now covers scarcely any officer in the State; for almost every officer will say he does not come under it.

The PRESIDENT. The gentleman is mistaken in that respect. A very large revenue is derived from that source.

Mr. STIRLING. By the last report we received $5,000.

The PRESIDENT. The gentleman is mistaken. The county of Frederick produces more than that.

Mr. STIRLING. What office?

The PRESIDENT. Register in the county clerk's office.

Mr. STIRLING. That is exactly what I say. That is all provided for by law by another provision of the constitution. If the chair will allow me I will explain that. There are other sections providing that no clerk or register shall get more than $2,500, and that the excess shall be paid over. That is perfectly independent of this section. There are various acts of assembly making such provision. It is true that there are certain officers who have not complied with the provisions of this section; but if they have not complied, it has been the fault, not of the law, but of the practice under the law. The law as it stands works this public injustice. It takes out of the pockets of the several counties and the city of Baltimore, money drawn from their tax payers, and puts it into the treasury of the State. Take the office now held by my colleague (Mr. Thomas,) in the city of Baltimore. The fees of the State's attorney in Baltimore city are paid partly by those parties arrested and tried, and partly by the city of Baltimore, a very small portion by criminals, because criminals in general have very little money and do not pay the costs, but chiefly from the municipal treasury of the city of Baltimore. The fees altogether amount to four or five thousand dollars a year. The excess over $3,000 which the State's attorney receives, he is required under this provision to pay into the State treasury. It is a yearly taxation of the city of Baltimore to the extent of $1,500 or $2,000 as the case may be, for the benefit of the State treasury. The officer is first required to pay his own salary and the excess he is required to pay into the treasury of the State. So it is with the sheriffs. A large portion of their fees are paid by the county; but the excess is not paid into the county but into the State treasury. If there is an excess, it inures not to the benefit of the county but of the State. On what principle should the State thus tax its own municipalities and subdivisions? That is the result of this policy; for nine-tenths of all these fees come out of the treasury of the several counties. The fees of the clerks are different.

The PRESIDENT. If you change this you will have to increase the taxation by this amount.

Mr. STIRLING. At any rate the counties should have the right to retain what is raised from their own taxation. The tax-payers pay these fees, and they are paid over to the officer, and the officer pays them over to the State. I say this is robbing the counties for the benefit of the State treasury. The city and counties ought to pay their portion of the State tax uniformly. This is an unequal mode of raising taxes for the benefit of the State. But in the case of clerks and registers it is perfectly fair; for they get their fees out of suitors, and it is an indirect mode of State taxation, perfectly proper That is already covered by previous legislation. This section only embraces two or three classes of officers, and in these cases the city and county officers are taxed for the benefit of the State treasury. This money comes out of the pockets of the counties and of the city, and if you wish to provide that no officer shall receive more than $3 000, he ought to pay back the excess where he got the excess; and not receive the excess from the counties and pay it here. I shall therefore vote most unquestionably for the amendment of my colleague.

The amendment was rejected.

Mr. CLARKE. The amendment was in the ninth line; and that only raises the question where the returns shall be made. The twelfth line, I think, would be the proper place to offer the amendment to raise the question where the money should be paid.

Mr. RIDGELY. It is precisely the same question.

The PRESIDENT. One makes the return, and the other the payment.

Mr. THOMAS. I do not think it is the same question.

The PRESIDENT. No; it is not the same question.

Mr. STIRLING submitted the following amendment:

After the word "direct" in line 5, insert:

"But such portion of such excess as has been paid by any county or the city of Baltimore shall be paid over by the treasurer of the State to such county or city respectively.

Mr. STIRLING said: It is proper to account to the State, to show the State where the money came from; and then it is proper that the State treasurer should pay it back to the counties of the State from which he received it.

The PRESIDENT. I should think there was enough of that business already in that department. To receive money from the city of Baltimore, for instance, and pay it right back to the city is a work of perfect and entire supererogation. It only imposes upon the comptroller of the State a burden, from which the State does not get a tenth of a cent advantage.

Mr. STIRLING. No, sir; the State may get cheated, if it is not so.

The PRESIDENT If they would cheat the county authorities, they would cheat the State.

Mr. Miller. If that amendment prevails, we shall have to adopt another system of raising taxes, and increase the direct tax.

The amendment was rejected.

Mr. Clarke submitted the following amendment:

"Sec. 1. Strike out the words "treasurer of the State" in line 13, and insert "the county commissioners of the several counties and the register of the city of Baltimore."

Mr. Clarke said: The result is this. Under the amendment offered by the gentleman from Baltimore city all the excess was paid into the treasury; and the State would receive and have to pay back again these amounts to the treasurers of the various counties. The provision now proposed is that the return shall be made to the comptroller of the State, but that the amounts shall be paid over directly to the county commissioners and the register of the city of Baltimore. I think the principle is correct, that this should be done as indicated by the gentleman from Baltimore city. In other words the people of the various counties are taxed to pay the expenses exceeding $3,000, and the result is that this excess of taxation upon the people of the county is paid to the State. By a regular direct tax it is right to support the State; but if a county pays over and above the salary of these officers an excess, is it not right that that excess should be paid back to the county for its benefit, instead of requiring the county to pay a direct tax to the State, and also to make a payment towards the general expenses of the State over and above its proportion? In other words whatever the county, out of the pockets of its own people, pays by reason of the extra amount of work done in the counties, should not accrue to the benefit of the whole State, but should go back to the county, and to that extent the people should be relieved from county taxation. Unless you do that the result is that the county pays an excess. It not only pays a proportion of the State tax upon an equality with all the other counties, but money taken from their pockets also goes into the general fund. It seems to me a question of justice to the people of the counties, that if their business is such as to take out of their pockets this money over and above the amount necessary to pay the salaries of their officers, they should have that credited on the amount of their local taxation, and to that extent should be relieved from local taxation. In other words the money taken out of their pockets should go back to them, and not to the State generally. This seems to me so fair and just that I think the convention from considerations of justice ought to adopt this provision.

Mr. Ridgely. If I could concur with the argument of the gentleman from Prince George's (Mr. Clarke) in his premises, so far as this amendment is concerned, I would agree that this money should go back to the pockets of the people of the State. There we would not disagree; but unfortunately this money is not paid by the people of the county at large, as the taxes are. It is paid by the suitors independently of the county. What justice is there in paying into the county treasury funds arising from such a source as that? If there is any injustice, let the people be reached who pay it. Let the legislature make a new scale of fees, and reduce the fees, so that the people shall be relieved from this kind of taxation—so that suitors shall be relieved. If that were to be done, to relieve the parties engaged in litigation from the unnecessary payment of this money, that would be right and proper and I would go for it. But you cannot reach them in this form. The only mode in which that can be done is by legislative action, by a reduction of the scale of fees, so that there shall be no excess of fees. As it now stands, there is nothing clearer in the world than the position of the gentleman from Anne Arundel county (Mr. Miller) that if you abstract $10,000 or $20,000 for the State treasury, you have got to make it up by a direct tax upon the people at large.

The President. You would better say $50,000; and that would not cover it.

Mr. Clarke. The only point of difference between us is upon the question where the excess comes from. In my judgment the excess really comes from the pockets of the people of the counties. In the case of the register, all his fees are from property administered in the county and taxed in the county; so that all the excess of fees in the register's office comes out of the property of the county, because that is the only property that is administered there. Property outside of the county is not administered there. When you come to the case of the excess of fees derived from suits, the great bulk of the suits in which the expenses are paid by the parties, is the case of suits brought upon plain notes. There are very few contested cases between non-residents of the county and residents. The great bulk of these suits are plain cases. Who pay the costs? The defendants pay the costs. The plaintiffs who recover their costs are non-residents, but the residents really pay them. So that in the end, in the case of suits brought, and also in the case of register's fees, the money comes out of the counties. I know that in many counties an excess is very often paid into the treasury. I know that the register receives the excess from the people of the county; and in the case of suits, nearly every suit is upon a plain note, a note in Baltimore city, or an open account, and the defendants pay costs when judgment is rendered. Although the plaintiff may pay it first, they get back, and virtually it all comes from the residents of the county.

Mr. RIDGELY. From the particular parties of the particular transactions.

Mr. CLARKE. Certainly; but it comes out of the pockets of the residents of the county.

Mr. DANIEL. The gentleman says that it pretty much all comes out of the pockets of residents If plaintiffs always gained their suits, this might be so; but the plaintiffs as frequently lose as they gain, and then it comes out of the pockets of the plaintiffs, who may be citizens of Baltimore, or New York or Philadelphia. When the cases go against the plaintiffs, a great deal of the costs come out of the pockets of non-residents of the State. I fear the practical operation of this would be in the end to take so much out of the treasury, for I fear it would ultimately remain in the pocket of the officer who is to pay it, and now does pay it over to the State; because I fear that if it went to the counties and the city of Baltimore, there would be constant petitions to remit these moneys; and it would be much more likely to be remitted to the county officers or the city authorities if the change was made. The result would be therefore to take so much out of the treasury and to give it to the officers.

Mr. CHAMBERS. My friend from Prince George's (Mr. Clarke) seems to have forgotten one thing. While the surplus fees are paid into the State treasury, he does not seem to have recollected that there is but a small return for the excessive costs which are expended by the State in the creation of those offices. His county has one judge receiving $2,500 or $3,000.

Mr. CLARKE. We have not one judge.

Mr. CHAMBERS. The two counties then have a judge; and of course there is expended by the State in that county but half that sum. How much is expended in Baltimore, where the great bulk of these fees are? Will the fees pay it? Your county helps to pay it.—My county, everybody's county helps to pay these salaries. The resident of the counties pays these taxes. He pays a tax on his horse, a tax on his negro I was about to say, but that is a gone business, a tax on his land. This is all paid by the individuals in the counties, and it goes into the treasury of the State. There is no return of it to the parties, as the gentleman from Baltimore county (Mr. Ridgely) has shown. If it were to be returned to the parties, there might be some justice in it. But you do not return it to the parties. The man who never had a suit in his life gets as much benefit from the surplus being returned to his county as the man who helped to pay the fees. It seems to me that the only proper way, simply as an act of justice, is to pay it into the treasury of the State. We of the small counties are all taxed to help to pay the salaries of the judges; and when there is a return of a surplus of receipts, I think it ought to be to the treasury of the State. The last thing in the world that a delegate from the small counties would desire, would be to have it paid anywhere else but in the treasury of the State.

Mr. STIRLING. The gentleman seems to suppose that the State pays the expense of the courts. The State pays the salary of the judges, which is a very small proportion.—The counties pay the per diem of the judges of the orphans' courts from the county treasury, and pay the register of wills that portion of his fees which are not paid by suitors. The city of Baltimore pays eight thousand dollars to support the criminal court. The State pays for the judge $2,000, and the city of Baltimore pays the other expenses, $8,000. All the per diem of the bailiffs, all the expense of the witnesses, all the fees, and every contingent expense, the city pays; and it pays nearly the whole of the State's attorney's salary. That portion of his fees collected by the sheriff does not amount to more than $300; and when the State's attorney gets $4,500 he pays it all excepting $3,000 into the State treasury. Every fee on the books which the clerk certifies is not collected, must be paid out of the city treasury. I know that when I was State's attorney I took the identical money I had received from the city treasury, and paid it into bank, and drew upon it for the benefit of the State treasury. I say that is taking the money out of the pockets of the county and the city, and paying it for no equivalent into the treasury of the State. There is no justice or equity in it. It is not compensated for by paying the salary of judges. It is a taxation without principle.

The PRESIDENT. If you abstract from the revenue of the State a source of revenue yielding $50,000, how are you to replenish the treasury by that amount? It could only be by taxation. It amounts to the same thing.

Mr. MILLER. This is one of those cases of indirect taxation, which the State has always resorted to. I think if this provision in the old constitution had been properly enforced and thoroughly enforced, the State would have derived a much larger revenue than the report of the comptroller now shows. I hope that hereafter the provision will be enforced.—There was a species of officer alluded to the other day, who will be reached by it—the criers of the city of Baltimore who receive twelve or fifteen thousand dollars.

Mr. STIRLING. There is not a word of truth in that.

Mr. MILLER. We want the laws to be enforced as against all officers who come within the provisions of this section of the constitution. If it had been enforced as it ought to have been heretofore, I say the revenue of the State would have been greater, and the people to that extent would have been relieved from direct taxation. Abolish this source of revenue to the State, and we shall have to resort to other taxes, either direct or indirect, to obtain a revenue. It has come out in the debate that there are a great many officers in the city of Baltimore who are receiving a very much larger sum than three thousand dollars a year in fees which they ought to pay over under this provision of the constitution.

Mr. STIRLING demanded the yeas and nays, and they were ordered.

Mr. HEBB. If this amendment is adopted, what will become of the fees of State officers?

The PRESIDENT. They will go by the board.

The question being taken, the result was —yeas 15, nays 36—as follows:

Yeas—Messrs. Audoun, Brooks, Brown, Clarke, Cunningham, Cushing, Duvall, Hatch, Kennard, Marbury, Markey, Stirling, Stockbridge, Sykes, Thomas—15.

Nays—Messrs. Goldsborough, President; Abbott, Annan, Baker, Carter, Chambers, Daniel, Davis, of Washington, Dellinger, Dent, Ecker, Farrow, Galloway, Greene, Hebb, Hollyday, Horsey, King, Lansdale, Lee, McComas, Miller, Mullikin, Negley, Parker, Purnell, Ridgely, Russell, Scott, Smith, of Worcester, Sneary, Swope, Todd, Valliant, Wickard, Wooden—36

The amendment was accordingly rejected.

No further amendment was offered.

Mr. DELLINGER moved that the convention take a recess.

The motion was rejected—ayes 25, noes 26.

COMMON LAW.

The next section was read as follows:

"Sec. 2. The common law and statute law now in force, and not repugnant to this constitution, shall remain in force, until they expire by their own limitation, or are altered by the general assembly."

Mr. MILLER. I move to strike out that section. I do it for this reason: that I never heard before of a provision of any constitution, or of any writer on law, or any legal gentleman making the assertion that the common law expires by its own limitation. It is a provision that the common law, as well as the statute law now in force, and not repugnant to this constitution, shall remain in force until it expires by its own limitation. We have provided for all that in the bill of rights.— The way in which it should be put in, if it is to be put in the constitution at all, is that the common law, by which is meant the common law of England, shall prevail in the State of Maryland, and that the inhabitants of the State of Maryland shall be entitled to the benefits of the common law, and of such statutes of England changing their law as existed at the time of our revolution, and as were found applicable to our peculiar circumstances, not having been re-enacted by our legislature. That provision is contained in our bill of rights. The third article is:

"Art. 3. That the inhabitants of Maryland are entitled to the common law of England, and the trial by jury according to the course of that law, and to the benefit of such of the English statutes as existed on the fourth day of July, seventeen hundred and seventy-six, and which, by experience, have been found applicable to their local and other circumstances, and have been introduced, used and practiced by the courts of law or equity, and also of acts of assembly in force on the first day of June, eighteen hundred and sixty-four, except such as may have since expired or may be inconsistent with the provisions of this constitution, subject nevertheless, to the revision of and amendment or repeal by the legislature of this State; and the inhabitants of Maryland are also entitled to all property derived to them from or under the charter granted by his Majesty, Charles the First, to Cecilius Calvert, Baron of Baltimore."

Does this mean anything more than that? If it means that, it ought to have been expressed in such language. To say that the common law shall continue in force until it shall expire by its own limitation, appears to my mind a proposition that does not sound very proper to be expressed in a constitution. The common law continues in force. It is one of our birthrights, that we have inherited and received from our ancestors. It is properly expressed as among the rights of the people of the State of Maryland. It is not something to be provided for as something that shall continue, implying that it would not continue unless we declared by a special provision that it should continue. I think the section is altogether unnecessary.

Mr. RIDGELY. The gentleman has taken the ground that this is already provided for in the bill of rights. I shall not take any issue with him there. Then he expresses surprise that anybody should undertake to assert such a proposition as is implied in the language employed in this section, and says that nobody ever heard of such a proposition. Now I will take up this book of constitutions, and open to one of them. I find in the schedule attached to the constitution of Michigan this very language, and in all probability I took it from there. I have no recollection now whether I did or not—the only difference being that in that schedule the language is "the common law and the statute laws," putting the word in the plural, and that the final clause is, "or are altered or repealed by the legislature," from which I omitted the word "repealed." It is certainly not a very extraordinary provision. It is simply to declare that it shall continue until the legislature shall change it. If there is any harm in that proposition I cannot see it.

Mr. CHAMBERS. The gentleman will admit that to speak of the common law expiring is not a proper expression. You might as well talk about immortality coming to an end.

The amendment was rejected.

Mr. DANIEL moved to strike out "law," and insert "laws."

The amendment was agreed to.

Mr. MILLER submitted the following amendment:

Strike out section two and insert:

"Sec. 2. The common law now in force shall remain in force as heretofore until altered by the general assembly, and the statute laws now in force and not repugnant to this constitution shall remain in force until they expire or are altered by the general assembly."

The amendment was rejected.

No further amendment was offered.

THE COURTS—LEGISLATIVE ELECTIONS.

The next section was read, as follows:

"Sec. 3. The several courts, except as herein otherwise provided, shall continue with like powers and jurisdiction, both at law and in equity, as if this constitution had not been adopted and until the organization of the judicial department provided by this constitution."

No amendment being offered, the next section was read as follows:

"Sec. 4. The general assembly shall have power to pass all such laws as may be necessary and proper for carrying into execution the powers vested by this constitution, in any department or office of the government, and the duties imposed upon them thereby."

Mr DUVALL submitted the following amendment:

"Add to the end of section the words "provided such vested powers do not interfere or conflict with those rights guaranteed by the constitution of the United States."

The amendment was rejected.

No further amendment was offered.

Mr. TODD moved to take a recess.

The motion was rejected.

The next section was read as follows.

"Sec. 5. If on any election directed by this constitution, any two or more candidates shall have the highest and equal number of votes, a new election shall be ordered, except in cases specially otherwise provided by this constitution."

No amendment was offered.

RIGHTS OF JURY.

The next section was read as follows:

"Sec. 6. In the trial of all criminal cases, the jury may be the judges of law as well as fact."

Mr. RIDGELY. I move to strike out "may" and insert "shall." It is an error.

Mr. CHAMBERS. I shall move to strike out that section. It a very mischievous thing, adopted by the last convention in a moment of hurry, and with some difficulty. It has in my humble judgment produced mischief, and nothing else but mischief. Under the construction which it has obtained, I believe it does not materially alter the practice of the courts. For all time, so far as I am acquainted with the history of the bar, in the country from which we derive our judicial opinions and practice, it has been the privilege of the court to instruct the jury in all questions of law. It has always been considered the duty of the jury to pay respect to that instruction. That the jury at all times have had the privilege to bring in a general verdict, upon what grounds they please, is equally certain. I do not believe that it was the intention of those who passed this provision, and I will not believe that it is the desire of this convention. I do not suppose it can be the wish of any gentleman, or of the discreet portion of the community, to disarm the court of this privilege. I have heard it claimed in the face of the judge, in the face of statute law, read from an act of assembly just as plain as that two and two make four. I have heard counsel in a case where excitement had been produced from surrounding circumstances, say to the jury that they had a right to trample that law under their feet; that they had the constitutional right to disregard the law. I remember an able argument that the reason why they had the privilege was that in the improved state of the world, and especially this portion of it which we inhabit, intellectual improvement had prepared the way to submit to the jury, not only the construction of the law, not only the interpretation of the law, but the determination what the law ought to be. And I have had the discomfort of seeing such an argument prevail, and a verdict correspondingly rendered.

If the law be of any value; if there be any motive to institute a system of written law, it is that every man may have some certain standard by which his rights of property and all his rights may be measured and determined; some fixed, known, permanent standard of measurement. There never was a time according to the practice always prior to this period, at which the jury did not exercise all the prerogatives which I think they should claim for their own good, or the good of those who are litigants before them, or for the good of society at large. They have the right, because they have the power to find what verdict they please. Even now the courts set aside a verdict in a civil case, if the court misstates the law to the jury. Or if a jury now against a criminal, find a verdict contrary to the law as given in the instruction of the court, the court may set aside their verdict. This constitutional authority is not held as such that the court are bound to respect their verdict after they have determined the law. The language of it is simply calculated in my judgment to mislead and to do mischief. I know of no earthly good it will do. I never heard of a case. Our records may be searched. There is not a judgment to be found in which it has ever been held as a doctrine of this State that the jury could not give a verdict in a criminal case always as they please. The fact is established that they have practically all the power which it is desirable that they should have. The language of the section is:

"In the trial of all criminal cases, the jury may be the judges of law as well as fact."

With regard to the change of the language, I will only say as a lawyer, that "may" in that connection, is just as imperative as "shall." I suppose every lawyer in the house will confirm that idea. In all legal proceedings, where there is nothing to show the contrary, these terms are considered as equivalent. I think the interests of the State, in its judicial department, especially in its criminal jurisdiction, will be promoted, mischiefs will be obviated, difficulties will be obviated, and in all respects, benefits will result from striking out the sixth section.

The amendment to substitute "shall" for "may" was adopted.

Mr. Chambers moved to strike out the entire section.

Mr. Miller. I agree with a great deal that has been said by the gentleman from Kent (Mr. Chambers) with reference to this provision contained in our present constitution, and sought to be incorporated in the one we are about to offer to the people for their sanction. The system of trial of criminal cases in this State has always been different from that in most of the northern States. A criminal is brought to the bar here; his counsel are employed; and the State's attorney represents the State. Upon questions of the admissibility of evidence, the judge decides; and that is the only thing upon which the judge in our State does decide.

Mr. Chambers. Or ever did.

Mr. Miller continued: But in most of the northern States, after the counsel have closed on both sides, the judge "sums up," as they call it, to the jury, and gives his views both of the evidence and of the law. Now under this provision of the constitution we may get rid perhaps of a good deal of difficulty. If the judges, with this restriction taken away, should undertake to charge the jury, and state to the jury what the law is in reference to the crime of which the accused stands charged, the accused would have the right to except to that charge, and to take it before the higher tribunals to see whether the court has correctly pronounced the law of the case or not. We have never had in this State, such cases brought to the court of appeals. Our criminal appeals are all reduced to error of the record itself, matters in the indictment, demurrers to the indictment, or something of that kind. I do not know but a case in which the judge has undertaken to charge the jury, and has given instructions to the jury to which the criminal has taken exception, might go up to the court of appeals. This provision has prevented that being done; and we have had no difficulty of that kind.

Mr. Chambers. No exception lies but by statute; and the statute expressly says that exceptions shall lie in civil cases.

Mr. Miller. I am perfectly aware of that; but I very much doubt whether it would not be the right of the criminal, under the existing statute, if the judge should undertake to give his views of the law to the jury, and should lay down the law wrongly, to take exception to it, and to bring it up to the court of appeals. The circuit judges may be mistaken with regard to their construction of the law as well as the lawyers who are arguing it for either side before the jury. If you give the judge the power to charge the jury upon the law, the lawyer upon either side differing as to the construction of the law, then I say that the criminal ought in all cases to have the right of appeal He ought not, for his life or his liberty, to be left to the discretion and the charge of the judge without an appeal to the court of appeals. At present, in the argument before the jury, we have a right as lawyers defending, or as prosecutors prosecuting, to say that every construction of the law is say so, that the law means this and the law means that. It has been decided by the court of appeals that we can argue before the jury that a law is unconstitutional. That question is not beyond the power of the jury. Let a statute law be passed in regard to any offence, as it was passed in this town some years ago, prohibiting the selling or giving of spirituous or intoxicating liquors to a minor or person of color, or anything of that kind, and there are expressions in that law about which the lawyers may very well differ. I say then, in such a case as that, on the ground of mercy to the criminal, and the indulgence which the law allows in such a case as that, the jury should be the judges of the law as well as of the fact.

I know it has always been the practice in this State for the jury to render a general verdict. But let me put a case which frequently occurs. There is no earthly dispute about the facts; not the least in the world. The facts are proved by undisputed testimony, and no human being on either side would doubt them. The whole question is whether the law was intended to cover that state of facts. In such a case as that, this provision of the constitution interposes and says that that matter shall be decided by the jury and not by the court. The State has all the advantage which it needs in such a case as that. It has the closing argument in all criminal cases. The State's attorney can present his views of the law as well as of the facts to the jury in his closing argument, and review all that has been said by the counsel for the defence; so that the case comes fairly and squarely before the jury.

There have been times when this matter in England was a matter of grave doubt. It was a long while before it was settled in England that if a jury should undertake to bring in a verdict contrary to the instructions of the judge, upon the law, that the jury was not liable to be punished for so doing. It was not until the great libel case; when it was asserted and maintained with great power that it was the principle even under the common law that the jury were the judges of the law and of the fact. I ask how it would be in the case of the defence of a man honestly entertaining views of the law different from those of the judge; what lawyer would undertake to give his views of the law to the jury, if the court could put him down? He could not go on and argue it, as he can under this provision of the law, as it now stands. For these reasons I shall vote against striking out this section.

On motion of Mr. NEGLEY,

The convention took a recess until 8 o'clock, P. M.

EVENING SESSION.

The convention met at 8 o'clock, P. M.

The roll was called, and the following members answered to their names:

Messrs. Goldsborough, President; Abbott, Annan Audoun, Baker, Barron, Belt, Briscoe, Brooks, Brown, Carter, Chambers, Clarke, Cunningham, Cushing, Daniel, Davis, of Washington, Dellinger, Dent, Duvall, Earle, Ecker, Farrow, Galloway, Greene, Hatch, Hebb, Henkle, Hollyday, Horsey, Jones, of Cecil, Kennard, King, Lansdale, Lee, Marbury, McComas, Miller, Morgan, Mullikin, Murray, Negley, Nyman, Parker, Parran, Purnell, Ridgely, Russell, Sands, Schley, Schlosser, Scott, Smith, of Carroll, Smith, of Worcester, Sneary, Stirling, Stockbridge, Sykes, Thomas, Todd, Turner, Valliant, Wickard, Wooden—64.

THE SCHEDULE.

The convention resumed the consideration of the report of the committee on the schedule.

The question being on the adoption of the amendment submitted by Mr. CHAMBERS, to strike out the sixth section of the report, as amended as follows:

"Sec. 6. In the trial of all criminal cases, the jury shall be the judges of law as well as fact."

The amendment was rejected.

The next section was read as follows:

"Sec. 7. The trial by jury of all issues of fact in civil proceedings, in the several courts of this State, where the amount exceeds the sum of five dollars, shall be inviolably preserved."

No amendment being offered, the next section was read as follows:

"Sec. 8. The general assembly shall have power to regulate by law, not inconsistent with this constitution, all matters which relate to the judges of election, time, place, and manner of holding elections in this State, and of making return thereof."

Mr. DUVALL submitted the following amendment:

Amend by striking out "not inconsistent with this constitution," in the second line.

The amendment was rejected.

No further amendment was offered.

The next section was read as follows:

"Sec. 9. All officers, civil and military, now holding office, whether by election or appointment under the State, shall continue to hold and exercise their offices according to their present tenure, unless otherwise provided in this constitution, until they shall be superseded pursuant to its provisions and until their successors be duly qualified, and the compensation of such officers which has been increased by this constitution, shall take effect from the first day of January, 1865.

No amendment was offered.

COMMISSIONERS OF REVISION.

Mr. STOCKBRIDGE submitted the following amendment:

Insert as an additional section the following:

"Sec. 10. It shall be the duty of the governor immediately after the adoption of this constitution, to appoint two "commissioners of revision," whose duty it shall be to prepare and present to the general assembly at its first session thereafter, drafts of all bills which the general assembly are required by this constitution to pass, or which may be necessary to carry into effect its provisions.

The commissioners of revision shall also proceed with all reasonable despatch, to revise the code of the State, embodying in it all existing laws not now incorporated therein, omitting all superfluous words and enactments, and all such as have ceased to affect existing rights, condensing the whole into as concise a form as is consistent with a full and clear expression of the law, and suggesting any errors or omissions which may be found to exist therein, and the best mode of rectifying the same.

They shall report the code so revised, to the general assembly for its approval, and while the bills so prepared, and the code so revised by them, shall be under consideration, shall be entitled to seats upon the floor of the senate or house of delegates, and to take part in the discussions thereof, but without the right of voting thereon."

Mr. STOCKBRIDGE said: I will state in a few words the purpose of that amendment. The present constitution made provision for certain commissioners of revision to codify the law of the State. That work was done. The present constitution has no such provision in it; and at the same time we have made no extra provision, as the last constitutional convention did, for any extra session of the general assembly or prolongation of their first session, while we have made it obligatory upon them to pass certain laws to carry into effect provisions of the constitution. This section is designed to devolve the duty upon some persons selected by the governor to prepare drafts of all the laws we have made it obligatory upon the general assembly to pass, that they may be put in form ready for the general assembly to refer to their committees to act upon as soon as they come together.

Every gentleman knows that after the adoption of the last constitution, though it was made necessary for the legislature to pass certain laws at their first session, some of them were not passed until eight or ten years subsequent to the adoption of the constitution, and some of them have never been passed at all. This provides that certain men, qualified for the purpose, to be certified by the governor, shall in the first place prepare drafts of all such laws.

Since the adoption of the code, there have been a large number of laws passed, modifying the sections of the code. It is proposed further then that these commissioners shall then revise the code, and embody subsequent enactments in it; and shall do what the former commissioners of codification did not do, call the attention of the general assembly to such laws as have become inoperative and ceased to have effect, or need modification, to carry out the existing state of things, and to adopt the code to the existing state of things; that they shall thus prepare a new edition, a revision of the code, and present it to the general assembly as early as practicable. Of course it would not be practicable to do so at the first session of the general assembly, but they might do so at the second. I think the provision an important one; and I therefore offer that section.

Mr. RIDGELY. I would ask the gentleman from Baltimore city how he proposes that the commissioners shall be compensated.

Mr. STOCKBRIDGE. I take it for granted that they will be compensated for such services as they render, by the general assembly.

Mr. MILLER. We have had some experience in this matter. I suppose the last codification cost the State of Maryland over fifty thousand dollars. Besides that, the amendment provides that inasmuch as the legislature will be so weak and incompetent to perform its duties, and will not have the patriotism to stay here beyond the time they are paid for, will not stay without pay to carry out the great work they will have to do under this constitution, therefore the State must go to the expense of providing a couple of gentlemen to aid them in their work. That is a new idea at least. The gentleman is mistaken in saying that there is any limit to the sessions of the legislature under the provisions of the legislative article.

Mr. STOCKBRIDGE. I did not say there was.

Mr. MILLER. The gentleman said that this constitution does not provide any extension of the time.

Mr. STOCKBRIDGE. I say so still.

Mr. MILLER. I say that the first legislature need not adjourn by the 10th of March. They may hold on as long as they please. This proposed constitution allows the members to sit here from January to January if they please; and if the legislature has not enough of the spirit of patriotism to stay and carry out the directions of this constitution, even if it goes beyond the eighty days for which they receive pay, it does not speak very well for the great objects which we suppose will be carried out by this constitution if it shall be adopted. If they are so important that we must call for aid and expend a large sum of money for some other gentleman to help the legislature do their work, I think they might remain in session a little longer.

Mr. SCHLEY. I ask a division of the question. So far as the first object, the preparation of drafts of bills for the general assembly is concerned, I deem it of very great importance.

Mr. CHAMBERS. It occurs to me that in anticipation, at the time at which the code is to be made up, the legislature is to pass various laws, having a very material influence upon the character of our legislation; yet, if this proposition is passed, just before the passage of these laws the acts of assembly are to be codified. I suggest therefore whether this is not rather a precipitate movement; whether the laws should not first be passed, and then the code be made, and the system of laws be passed applicable to the new state of things. I suggest that the code be delayed until the legislature pass the laws which this constitution requires.

Mr. STOCKBRIDGE. I confess I do not appreciate the force of the objection urged by the gentleman from Kent (Mr. Chambers.) The amendment provides that two commissioners, who cannot be appointed earlier than the 1st of November, shall prepare a large number of important laws. The general assembly meet on the 1st of January. These laws are to be prepared as soon as practicable; and certainly these commissioners will have as much work in that line as they can do while the general assembly are in session the first time. That is the time when these important laws will be passed. They are then, as soon as practicable, to go on to revise the Code. Of course they will embody the laws just passed. It will be impossible of course to revise the laws at the first session of the general assembly. No one was crazy enough to dream of such a thing as that. If they prepare the laws for the general assembly to pass at its first session, it will be work enough.

Mr. CHAMBERS. And more than ever has been done yet.

Mr. NEGLEY. I cannot vote for this section as offered. What does it propose? It proposes to appoint two commissioners to do the work for which the people of Maryland elect the legislature. That is, they are to go to work to prepare laws; and when the next legislature comes here they are merely to ratify those laws. Is there not enough intelligence in the legislature of Maryland, and is there not enough discrimination among the voters of Maryland to send competent persons here and frame laws in accordance with the new order of things brought about by the constitution which we hope may be adopted? Has it come to this, that we must send here two men as guardians, as intelligent and legal guardians of the legislature of Maryland? It is an imputation upon the legal knowledge of the profession to which the gentleman belongs, and upon the general knowledge of the people of Maryland. I certainly cannot support any such proposition as that, that we are to put the legislature under guardianship.

Besides that; you pass this section, and appoint these commissioners. What is the history of the commission under the last codification of our laws? We have hardly a limit to the expenses to which this commission will go. They will linger and continue, and they will consume a year or eighteen months in doing that which I am certain the coming legislature will do as well and as thoroughly. And when the new legislature assembles again, they go to work and appoint a committee to do the very work which has been already done by the commissioners. Is it to be presumed that there will not be any legal ability in that legislature? Is it to be presumed that the committee will not have the time and capacity to do the work? I cannot think so, and therefore I cannot vote for it.

The question being on the first branch of the amendment, as follows:

"Sec. 10. It shall be the duty of the governor immediately after the adoption of this constitution, to appoint two "commissioners of revision," whose duty it shall be to prepare and present to the general assembly at its first session thereafter, drafts of all bills which the general assembly are required by this constitution to pass, or which may be necessary to carry into effect its provisions."

Mr. STOCKBRIDGE demanded the yeas and nays, and they were ordered.

The question being taken, the result was—yeas 22, nays 40—as follows:

Yeas—Messrs. Abbott, Annan, Audoun, Brooks, Daniel, Dellinger, Farrow, Greene, Hatch, Hebb, Jones, of Cecil, McComas, Ridgely, Russell, Sands, Schley, Scott, Stockbridge, Sykes, Thomas, Todd, Valliant—22.

Nays—Messrs. Goldsborough, President; Baker, Barron, Belt, Briscoe, Brown, Carter, Chambers, Clarke, Crawford, Cunningham, Cushing, Davis, of Washington, Dent, Duvall, Ecker, Galloway, Henkle, Hollyday, Horsey, Kennard, King, Lansdale, Lee, Marbury, Miller, Morgan, Mullikin, Negley, Parker, Purnell, Schlosser, Smith, of Carroll, Smith, of Worcester, Sneary, Stirling, Swope, Turner, Wickard, Wooden—40.

The first branch of the amendment was accordingly rejected.

The question recurred upon the second branch of the amendment, as follows:

"The commissioners of revision shall also proceed with all reasonable despatch, to revise the Code of the State, embodying in it all existing laws not now incorporated therein, omitting all superfluous words and enactments, and all such as have ceased to affect existing rights, condensing the whole into as concise a form as is consistent with a full and clear expression of the law, and suggesting any errors or omissions which may be found to exist therein, and the best mode of rectifying the same.

"They shall report the Code so revised to the general assembly for its approval, and while the bills so prepared, and the Code so revised by them, shall be under consideration. shall be entitled to seats upon the floor of the senate or house of delegates, and to take part in the discussions thereof, but without the right of voting thereon."

Mr. STOCKBRIDGE withdrew the second branch of the amendment.

The next section was read as follows:

VOTE ON THE CONSTITUTION.

"Section 1. For the purpose of ascertaining the sense of the people of this State, in regard to the adoption or rejection of this constitution, the governor shall issue his proclamation within five days after the adjournment of this convention directed to the sheriff of the city of Baltimore, and to the sheriffs of the several counties of this State, commanding them to give notice in the manner now prescribed by law, that an election will be held in the city of Baltimore and in the several counties of the State, at the usual places of holding elections in said city and counties, for the adoption or rejection of this constitution, on the twelfth day of October, in the year eighteen hundred and sixty-four, which election shall be held between the hours of eight o'clock, A. M., and six o'clock, P. M., and the judges of election of said city, and of the several counties of the State, shall receive at said election the votes only of such electors as are qualified according to the provisions of this constitution, who may offer to vote at such election, and the said sheriffs shall also give notice on or after the twelfth day of October, eighteen hundred and sixty-four, for all elections provided by this constitution, to be held during that year."

Mr. CHAMBERS. Against this I raise my voice, as being more in violation of the obligations due from this convention to the people of Maryland than any act which has been suggested in this body. I suppose that if there is one proposition in regard to which there will be no division of opinion among gentlemen of this body, one fact which will be universally conceded, it is that by those who voted for the assemblage of this body, whether for or against a convention, there was not one dissenting voice in regard to the proposition that it should be a dead letter until the people should act upon it. There is not a man that I have ever heard of in the State, who participated in the election, that has suggested, that, so far as I know, has ever dreamed of having a constitution until it was submitted to the people and sanctioned by them. I say again, I do not suppose there is upon this floor one individual who, if candid and sincere, will deny that it was the universal expectation that this should be a dead letter until sanctioned by the people.

Starting at that point, what do we witness? The old constitution is in force, perfectly in force, as much so as it was one hour after its adoption, until this new constitution is adopted by the people. In inevitable result, the old constitution, and all the rights and privileges which are by it secured to the citizens of the State, continue in full force and effect until this new constitution is sanctioned by the people.

In the face of this fact, this section proposes to violate that constitution; to deprive certain individuals of rights and privileges which are secured under that constitution; not only to take away the rights of those who have heretofore exercised the first and boasted privilege of freemen, the right to vote; but it undertakes presently, in strict conformity with the principle adopted in this section, to introduce a perfectly new class of voters unknown to that constitution. Is this possible? Is it possible that gentlemen propose, by an instrument of no force and effect until after a certain event, by an instrument thus hereafter to have validity infused into it, to operate such a monstrous result as to destroy constitutional prerogatives and privileges? Let us for one moment look at this. Who sent us here? Those who, under the constitution now existing and in full force, had the right to vote. At least that is the theory of this body. How far they participated in it, I am not here bound now to determine. But none other except those, and all those who choose to present themselves as candidates for the exercise of this privilege, were the constituency—the rightful constituency of this body; none other.

What is now proposed? That while that constitution is yet unrepealed, while it is yet in force, you are to send this constitution, not to that constituency whom we represent, not to be acted upon by those who sent us here, but by a different constituency altogether, those who are supposed to be opposed to it being restrained by further provisions and restrictions, and those who are supposed to be favorable to it being introduced into the arena as voters, never before known to any constitution which we have had. Is this the mode of erecting constitutions, to shuffle off the constituency which you have had, to deny the privileges which have been exercised? It is bad enough to allow the privilege to others, to extend it; but when we present ourselves here standing on the shoulders, and acting on the authority of a class of individuals, are we then to be told that in defiance of their constitutional rights they shall not vote unless they conform to additional restrictions which this constitution imposes?

Let us suppose for one moment, and no man has a right to say that such a supposition is at all impossible, that the people do not choose to adopt this constitution. What predicament are you in? It shall have then resulted that you have restrained persons constitutionally entitled to vote, by an enactment without a shadow of obligation. If this constitution is not adopted by the people, it has not a shadow of obligation; it has no more force or effect than a newspaper. As yet this paper which is conditionally and only conditionally to have any effect, is to deprive every individual of his right to vote, who besides the privilege secured by the constitution, besides the restrictions imposed by the constitution and existing law, shall not further in addition subject himself to the restrictions imposed by this present instrument. Is that a state of things which gentlemen can admire? Is it a state of things they can honestly desire? Is it a state of things it is supposed they will submit to? Is it a state of things becoming a government of freemen? Is it a treatment which our constituency deserve at our hands, to say that this session of the convention is the result of the voluntary action of the people of the State? What people? People who are voters under the constitution of 1851. Why not then let these people, this constituency, decide this question? The idea of having a piebald concern here, of having provisions intended to throw out some voters and bring in others, and to have effect while the other provisions are silent, is an anomaly unknown to any history we have of our proceedings. Is it a constitution or is it not? If it be so, boldly go in the face of the people and say so. If it be not, why attempt to impose these restrictions and fasten its obligations, when it is not a constitution? If it be not, what is it? What is the appellation, what is the title of this paper? A quasi constitution? A partial constitution? A contingent, conditional constitution? This sort of proceeding strikes me as violating every principle we owe to those who sent us here, every principle that could be expected at our hands to be adopted. I feel very unwilling to indulge in harsh expressions. I feel very unwilling to characterize such proceedings by terms which I think become it. It does strike me as a most monstrous encroachment upon the plainest rights that can possibly be claimed by a free people.

There are gentlemen here who profess to regard the act of assembly as obligatory. That has been the general sentiment, at least one very frequently expressed here. You are trampling upon that. What does that tell you? Your constitution, before it has any legal effect, before it can operate upon any one either to restrain his vote or to open the polls to him, before it can have any effect any how or anywhere or on any one, must be confirmed by the people. I repeat again that any voter in the State has said so; not by putting it on his ticket, not perhaps by open declaration, but in his own person, in his own mind, he has as fixedly so determined as he has to put his ticket in the ballot-box; without, I say again, a dissenting voice upon the subject. We talk sometimes very gravely about regarding the popular will, the rights of the people, their sovereignty, their possession of all power, being the source of all power, and of our obligation to regard their will and their wishes. I appeal to the people. I appeal to their wishes and their will. I say that has been violated in the person of every voter, if such a claim as this is suffered to be carried into effect. We have by the constitution as it exists a large class of citizens whose vote will probably be rejected under the provisions of this constitution. I have had occasion before to say that there are many persons in this State as innocent, in the category now made criminals for the first time, as any other person living. There are persons who make very free with the terms "rebel," "secessionist," and all that sort of thing, denouncing men as good and pure as themselves.

There are cases, I cite my own as one of them, where the language of this oath certainly would seem to apply. A man must never have given comfort, aid, countenance, or services to the rebels. I have issue of my own body, blood of my blood, bone of my bone, a man who was in the South long ago, a man who there enlisted with as firm a purpose upon his part to do right, as you or anybody else, with no thought of doing wrong; a person suffering from wound and disease. I have furnished him relief. How? Surreptitiously? Criminally? Violating any law in doing so? No, sir; by going to the officers of the government, officers wearing the uniform of the country, men who do their duty, and passing through their hands the necessary means to afford aid and comfort to that wounded and sick prisoner. Am I to be excluded? Is every principle of every law to be violated in my person? It is not only a law in violation of the will of the people when they voted upon this subject; not only such a law as your own bill of rights denounces, an *expost facto* law; but it is a law in violation of the dictates and the feelings which God Almighty has planted in every human breast, which has not become degraded. I am insensible however to any such act. The great God who has made us, made me at least of such materials that all the conventions, and all the oaths that human ingenuity can pour in my face, shall never prevent me from helping an afflicted, wounded, diseased grandson. I would do it though this convention should pronounce it a cause of death, and erect the gallows in the place where you sit.

These are my sentiments. I avow it. It seems that it has been brought within the criminal code. I think that is the language, nobody shall vote but one who shall swear by virtue of this constitution, no constitution before, no law before, nobody but he that shall swear that he has not furnished aid or comfort, or countenance to any individual in the rebel service.

Mr. President, I have expressed these sentiments, restraining myself within such terms as I hope have not been personally offensive to any gentleman upon this floor. I have before made appeals to the calm considerate reason of gentlemen. I have before deprecated the influence of party feeling, and party connection, by which gentlemen are induced to surrender their judgments to the control of political influences. I ask them in the name of every principle that is dear to freemen; in the name of every obligation they owe to their constituents, in the name of every principle which belongs to constitutional right, to political privilege, to forbear this last and final step. You have been brought here, the majority of this body, to frame certain propositions, and to submit them to the people of the State. There have been many of them very offensive to those of us who form the minority of this body. Your right to do so has not been impeached. It is a duty which you are to perform on the responsibility you owe to your God, to your constituents, and to yourselves. That is not the case in this matter. You are now taking a step, not to do that which you were sent here to do, not to do that which is a proposition which the people may accept or reject, not to propose a constitution to have effect or to have none according to the vote which shall pursue it. You are sent here for no such purpose as to deprive those who have enjoyed constitutional rights of the fair exercise of those rights in determining the question of acceptance or rejection. And you will in my humble judgment transcend your powers and your obligations, by venturing to go beyond your duty to introduce a system which can have no possible support from any obligation or any power or any authority which has been conferred upon you, and which, as I said before, in the event of the rejection of this constitution you will find to have been mere waste paper.

I submit, whether under these circumstances a majority of this house will persevere in the infliction of what at least I esteem the most aggravated outrage upon our rights which has been suggested by any member of this body. I say this without any purpose to offend the personal feeling of any gentleman upon this floor. I say it from a high sense of duty. I say it under the belief that this act, if consummated, will not fail to be regarded by a large portion of these people as oppression of the grossest character, without any warrant of authority.

Mr. Ridgely. I propose to occupy but a few moments of the time of this convention. A great deal that has been said by the honorable gentleman from Kent (Mr. Chambers,) in view of the tone and temper in which the sentiments have been expressed, sufficiently answers itself. It indicates to my mind at least that there has been much more feeling and excitement than deliberate judgment. I propose to vindicate this report upon the theories of law; and I propose in my humble way to acquit it of all the imputations of outrage and indignity and wrong which the gentleman has charged to be its purpose. I believe that all that we are charged by this proposition with doing, taking away from the people their rights, denying to them the exercise of their prerogative, is wholly without warrant or foundation, in view of the theories of the existence of this body.

I had occasion some weeks ago, when the question of the proper exposition of the convention bill was before the house, arising out of the question of the qualification of members of this body, to express my views upon the theories of that convention bill; and the gentleman from Kent took occasion to express his theory of the convention bill.

We differed *toto cœlo*. I but repeat what I then said when I again remark that I believe that that convention bill indorsed by the people, submitted to the people by the legislature, is the programme, or *projet*, by which this constitutional convention was to be assembled and organized, and by which its powers were to be exerted, and by virtue of the indorsement which the people gave to it, became the fundamental law; and that in exercising our prerogatives here, our functions here, we were controlled by the convention bill, not by reason of the fact that it was a mere act of the general assembly, but by reason of the fact that the people, the great sovereigns, the people, had indorsed it and gave to it organic life, so far as it described the powers which were to be exercised under it.

I have heard nothing which has induced me to believe that that theory was founded in error. I believe it is a sound theory. Although the honorable gentleman from Kent on that occasion confined the powers of the convention bill exclusively to the mere theory of indicating the process by which the body was to be assembled, and by which it was to be put in motion when assembled, and denied that even into that convention bill we could look for the qualifications of members, disregarding the qualifications of members as an inherent part of the machinery necessary to put the body in motion; yet I hold that the very admission that we were bound by the form and terms of the bill even in a single iota, admits the whole obligation; that if we were bound by the phraseology and terms of the convention bill, to adhere to it even in the organization of the house, the force of the obligation could not be restrained but that it became full and ample.

Under that theory of the law let us look at the convention bill, and see what it provides. I read from the sixth section:

"*And be it enacted*, That the constitution and form of government adopted by the said convention as aforesaid, shall be submitted to the legal and qualified voters of the State, for their adoption or rejection, at such time, in such manner, and subject to such rules and regulations as said convention may prescribe."

I pray you, gentlemen, is there any limitation as to the power of this body to prescribe rules and regulations? May you not prescribe the qualifications of the voter as well as fix the day of election? May you not prescribe the qualifications of the voter as well as the period of time within which the election shall be held? Who shall say how, when, or where this power is to be restrained? The legislature have not qualified it nor limited it, beyond the terms employed in the act itself; and the people have indorsed at the ballot box the *projet* of law submitted to them by virtue of the authority of the legislature. We are here then armed with the power of the people; and by the authority of the people are we exercising the function which we propose now to exercise, to submit this instrument to them for their adoption or their rejection, pursuant to the very terms which they themselves have prescribed.

I propose to confine my observations entirely to this theory of the law, to discuss this question as a question of law. I hold, therefore,—I may be wrong, but if wrong it is my honest judgment, and on that judgment I have framed this report—I hold that the convention bill, by virtue of the power inspired into it by the people, is the fundamental law, and I hold further that the constitution of the State, as it now is, only so far as it forms a part of the convention bill, is binding upon this body. I acknowledge,—nobody disputes the theory here—that the people are the source of all power. It would be the highest arrogance and presumption on the part of this body to assume to entrench in the slightest degree upon that high prerogative of the people. We do not come here to take away from the people. We come here to submit to them our work, as we believe, in conformity to their own commands, and the literal terms of the language which they have directed to us.

Under these conscientious convictions I am told that I am degrading myself; we are told here that we are sinking to the level of degradation; and in the same breath the honorable gentleman says, "I do not mean to offend, and I trust I shall not even be suspected of meaning to offend." Is it possible, Mr. President, that honorable gentlemen are to be spoken to in terms thus flippantly, thus arrogantly.

Mr. CHAMBERS I believe I did not use the term "degrading."

Mr. RIDGELY. I leave it to every gentleman in this house if he did not use it. But a large portion of the gentleman's argument was feeling rather than deliberate judgment. I leave the question to the convention, submitting my theory of the law, and my deliberate conviction that it is sound; and under those views of the law, I reiterate that the power of this body to pass this report is in strict conformity with the authority conferred upon us by the people.

Mr. CHAMBERS. I did not turn to the act of assembly. I did not suppose it would be necessary to make an argument. It says that the legal and qualified voters of the State are entitled to vote upon the constitution, subject to regulation of the time of voting, the place of voting, or any other regulations the convention may prescribe; regulations of what? Regulations of voters entitled under the constitution to vote? To regulate a thing is not to manufacture it.

Mr. MILLER. I have a word or two to say upon the very theory assumed by the gentleman from Baltimore county (Mr. Ridgely) He and I agree in regard to what this convention bill was, what was its purpose and object, and what force and effect it had over this body at the commencement of the sessions of this convention. Now he declares that by the vote of the people, in calling this convention, they made this convention bill a part of the fundamental and organic law under which we were acting. I agree with him; and I turn to the provisions of that bill; and I will show to this convention that the report of this committee is directly in conflict with the provisions of that bill.

He has referred to the sixth section of the law. The sixth section provides that this constitution shall be submitted to the people for its ratification. Now if we take the other theory, that this is a sovereign body, independent of all legislative enactment, why go through the farce of submitting this constitution to the people at all? Why not say at once that the constitution which we here adopt shall on or after a day upon which we fix, be the constitution and organic law of the State? If the theory of the absolute sovereignty of this convention is to prevail, then this convention has the right to do that.

But if the gentleman from Baltimore county adopts the other theory, and then says we will submit it to the people, and that this convention bill is the fundamental and organic law, then we must go to that bill and see what its provisions are. The question here is this. We have prescribed in this report, or shall if we adopt it, qualifications of the right of voting upon the adoption of this constitution, different from what the present constitution prescribes, and different from what the convention bill itself prescribes. What does the 6th section declare?

"Sec. 6. *And be it enacted*, That the constitution and form of government adopted by the said convention as aforesaid, shall be submitted to the legal and qualified voters of the State," &c.

To what does that refer, for the qualification of voters? This law was passed under the existing constitution of the State. The "legal and qualified voters" here meant, are those who under that constitution are legally qualified to vote; that is, a man who is a citizen of the United States, who is twenty-one years of age and upwards, who has resided a year within the State and six months within the county in which he offers to vote. Those are the "legal and qualified voters" to whom this section of the convention bill refers. No other sensible construction can be placed upon that language. Now what further?

—"for their adoption or rejection, at such time"—

This convention may fix any day it pleases upon which the "legal and qualified voters" are to vote.

—"in such manner"—

That is, they may require the voting of the "legal and qualified voters" to be in the manner they may adopt, either by ballot, or *viva voce*, or in any other mode they please. This refers to the manner of voting.

"and subject to such rules and regulations as said convention may prescribe;"—

That is, they may prescribe the rules and regulations under which the "legal and qualified voters" are to vote. The polls shall be opened at 9 o'clock in the morning, or if the convention choose to say so, shall be opened at ten o'clock, and closed at five; and they may vote on one, two, or three days, just as the convention see fit to prescribe.

That is what the law says on that subject.

That would be clear, perfectly clear, if there was not one word more in this section on the subject. But the gentleman from Balmore county (Mr. Ridgely) has carefully abstained from reading the concluding and conclusive portion of the section upon this subject. What is it?

—"and the provisions hereinbefore contained for the qualification of voters and the holding of elections, provided in the previous section of this act, shall be applicable to the election to be held under this section."

What is "the election to be held under this section?" It is the election to be held upon the adoption of this constitution which we are now framing; and no other election is to be held under this section except that. The qualifications of those who are to vote upon this question, as this sixth section prescribes, are to be the same which this law says shall be their qualifications.

—"and the provisions hereinbefore contained for the qualification of voters and the holding of elections, provided in the previous section of this act, shall be applicable to the election to be held under this section."

Human language could not express it in plainer terms. The qualifications of the people who are to vote upon the adoption of this constitution are those which are prescribed under the existing constitution and this law. This law added some new qualifications, or some new restrictions upon the right of suffrage, which were not embodied or embraced in the existing constitution of the State. What were they? We must go to the law to see what they were. In the first section it is provided:

"And the said judges of election shall at said election, administer the oath or affirmation to every person offering to vote, whose vote shall be challenged on the ground that such person has served in the rebel army, or has either directly or indirectly given aid, comfort, or encouragement to those in armed rebellion against the government of the United States, or is for any other reason not a legal voter, in the manner and form provided by section 21 of article 35 of the Code of public general laws relating to elections; and a judge or judges of election, failing to comply with the provisions of this act, shall be liable to the same penalties as he or they would be by the non-compliance with the existing election laws of this State."

Then these are the additional provisions, or qualifications, or restrictions, or whatever you may choose to call them, superadded by the law of 1864 to the qualifications contained in the constitution of the State. Under the provisions of the constitution of the State every free white man, twenty-one years of age, and a citizen of the United States, one year a resident of the Sate, and six months a resident of the county, had a right to go to the polls and vote, without challenge and unquestioned. Then this law comes in and says in addition to that, if he be challenged for any of the reasons specified in this law, the judges shall put the oath to him. It was under that law, and subject to the rules and regulations prescribed by the governor of Maryland in carrying out that law, in the interpretation which he placed upon it, that the people of the State did vote for this convention. And when we come to the sixth section, which prescribes the submission of the constitution to the people for ratification, it goes back precisely to the same constituency which voted under this law for the convention.

If the provisions of this report had stopped with the provisions of this law, and said nothing further; if it had prescribed that the voters upon this constitution should, when challenged for any of the reasons here set forth, take the oath as prescribed in the law, if the same regulations and rules were to prevail, I should have said that the report was in strict conformity with the law under which we are acting, the organic fundamental law, as the gentleman from Baltimore county says. But that is not the report. The report sends it back with a restriction upon the sight of suffrage, neither contained in the existing constitution nor in the law of 1864. It sends it back to the oath prescribed in the present constitution, which can have no effect in law until adopted by the people; and that oath is to be made operative on the day of election, before the constitution is ratified. That oath, as every gentleman in the convention knows, is an entirely different oath in its form and character, from that which we adopted and prescribed in the act of 1864. We are then undertaking to say that additional restrictions shall be put upon the right of suffrage at the election at which this constitution is to be adopted.

Furthermore, it is declared in another section of this report that those who could not vote at all under the present constitution, for the calling of this convention, who had no right of suffrage either under the constitution or under the convention bill, shall, at the election which is to decide the future fate of Maryland, and to decide in a great degree the future condition of the State of Maryland in reference to this important subject of emancipation, be entitled to vote; that people who could not vote to send men here to emancipate slaves, may, on the adoption of this constitution, vote to carry into effect the constitution which they had no power to send delegates here to frame.

On this construction of the law of 1864, and on the gentleman's own argument that that is the fundamental law for the government of this body, I say it is impossible for human reason to escape the conclusion that this report goes beyond them both.

Mr. STOCKBRIDGE. Will the gentleman explain to whom he refers, who had not the right to vote, and may vote now?

Mr. MILLER. The soldiers in the field.

Mr. STOCKBRIDGE. How is that?

Mr. MILLER. I say that it is by another section of this report. The gentleman from Baltimore city (Mr. Stirling) tried by act of assembly to provide for allowing soldiers to vote; but by a very large majority in the senate, after a full discussion of the subject, it was decided that under your present constitution you could not allow the vote of the soldier to be taken outside of the State of Maryland. They must come back into the State, into the county, and into the precinct or election district where they resided, before they could vote. That was the decision of the last legislature of the State It was attempted to be incorporated into this very convention bill, that the soldiers might vote; and it was voted down. I may be mistaken in saying that it was attempted to be put into this bill; but there was an act allowing your soldiers to vote upon the question of calling this convention or not, and the legislature voted it down because they had no constitutional power to pass it; and they could not have incorporated it into this bill, because it was the decision of the legislature at that time, clear and unquestioned upon the law. The supreme court of Pennsylvania had decided the same thing in reference to the provisions of their constitution. The supreme court of Connecticut had decided the same thing with reference to their constitution, and in New York the same thing. They had to amend their constitution before they could allow the soldiers out of the State to vote.

(The allotted time, twenty minutes, having expired, the hammer fell.)

Mr. SANDS. I feel it my duty to say a word or two in respect to some things that have been announced on this floor, both as matters of fact and as matters of law. The gentleman from Kent (Mr. Chambers) made a most effective appeal to this body on the subject of his personal connection with those who were in armed hostility to the United States. I think from my personal knowledge of the circumstances in that case, I can safely appeal to the gentleman from Kent, and ask him whether ever a prisoner of war was more humanely and kindly treated than his relative; if ever those who were discharging the functions of government and who were its friends, showed more disposition to give access to a prisoner by his friends, and in every way and manner possible to conduce to the comfort and welfare of such a prisoner?

Mr. CHAMBERS. I have not said one word to the contrary. On the contrary, I take pleasure in saying that those with whom I have conferred, officers to whom I have applied, invariably treated me with the utmost respect. They have not permitted me, but they have permitted members of my family to go and see this man, and have allowed me to furnish means of aiding and comfor ing him.

Mr. SANDS. That is the truth he has spoken, to the honor and credit of the government of the United States and its authorities. Its treatment of its prisoners of war has never been exceeded in kindness and liberality, and all that is noble and ennobling. It may do to talk about the gibbets being erected for our friends, when they are working for a particular view; but when they are called upon for the truth of the fact, out of the mouths of those most interested you have the truth. I thank God to-night that the government and its agents have been pre-eminently humane, kind, and liberal. I am sorry that the facts of to-day do not show that those who are in the control of the rebellion are acting in a like spirit of christian charity and kindness. The world knows the facts; and I do not choose to consume any more time in talking about them. But I want it plainly and distinctly understood that I listen with no degree of patience whatsoever to appeals, however eloquent, that set up the spectres of the gibbet between the grandfather and the grandchild, when it is but a spectre; when it is but the shadow of a shade; when it has no foundation whatever in reality.

Nor need the gentleman or any of his friends indulge in one moment's anxiety or apprehension that they are to be excluded from the ballot box because by the permission of the government and its authorities and through its agents, they have ministered to their friends. That is not adhering to, giving aid and comfort in its legal sense, or in the sense in which it stands embodied in this report. The gentleman knows that. It is a different thing from that. It is a secret, persistent, active sympathy and aid giving, not to the personal relative or the personal friend, which is aimed at. It is the energetic and persistent giving aid and comfort to rebellion, which is to disqualify; and I say under the law,—I say it to my friend who addressed this house, under the strict letter of the law, that is a disqualification from voting. The gentleman can find it in the very language that has been read. In this oath that was to be put by the judges of election, what do you find? This is the language, for a few words cover it all:

—"or has either directly or indirectly given aid, comfort, or encouragement to those in armed rebellion against the government of the United States."

Does the gentleman say that in these words, the conveying of intelligence useful to the public enemy and hurtful to the public cause, is not included? He can hardly make such a declaration as that here as his recorded opinion.

—"or is for any other reason not a legal voter in the manner and form provided," &c.

Now I will go back to the article in the present constitution and see whether it does not exactly follow and tally with the provisions of the convention bill, which have been quoted to-night. It is in the second section of the article on the elective franchise:

"Sec. 2. No person who has at any time been in armed hostility to the United States, or the lawful authorities thereof, or who has been in any manner in the service of the so-called "Confederate States of America;" and no person who has voluntarily left this State and gone within the military lines of the so-called Confederate States or armies with the purpose of adhering to said States or armies"—

Is not that giving them aid and comfort of a very material sort?

—"and no person who has given any aid, comfort, countenance or support to those engaged in armed hostility to the United States."

That is the very language of the act that called us together.

—"or in any manner adhered to the enemies of the United States, either by contributing to the enemies of the United States, or unlawfully sending within the lines of such enemies money or goods, or letters, or information, or who has disloyally held communication with the enemies of the United States, or who has advised any person to enter the service of the said enemies, or aided any person so to enter, or who has by any open deed or word declared his adhesion to the cause of the enemies of the United States, or his desire for the triumph of said enemies over the arms of the United States, shall ever be entitled to vote at any election to be held in this State."

Now I put it to gentlemen in common honor and honesty, and common sense too, whether the language of this act does not cover every provision of that section of the article on the elective franchise? No gentleman can seriously give a negative answer to this proposition.—As to the usual qualifications of voting, age, State and county residence, we know that these qualifications for voting were made for times of peace and not of civil war. Upon the theory of the gentleman from Anne Arundel, (Mr. Miller) see what might be the state of facts, I trust not the probable state of facts. Suppose that upon the day of election the State of Maryland were invaded by a confederate army. Large numbers of people from all these counties have gone into the confederate army. Suppose upon th t day Maryland was invaded by a confederate army. I say that upon the theory of the gentleman from Anne Arundel, every man among them who was formerly a citizen of Maryland, might go unchallenged to the polls and deposit his ballot, though he had winged the leaden messenger of death to some Union soldier's heart but the moment before. It would be a beautiful state of facts. It would be not even keeping up the law of Mr. Wigfall, who appealed from ballots to bullets; but it would be going back and using the very means from which he had appealed, and taking both ballot and bullet.

Now I can assure gentlemen that the loyal people of Maryland have made up their minds, that while they will in all things, while dealing with prisoners of war or others, follow the example of their government, he who wings the leaden bullet, or he who gives him aid and comfort, shall not deposit the ballot. The perils of the times are too imminent to allow of any half-way policy on this point. While I would go as far towards securing to every loyal man who has never given aid and comfort to the enemies of the government the right of voting, and would with him shoulder to shoulder battle for his rights, I will battle so long as God gives me life, by word and deed, against seeing the ballot box of Maryland polluted by the ballots of traitors.

As to the soldiers voting, that is not in this section, and I did not intend to say anything about it. I was not present here at the time of the discussions in the legislature upon that subject; but there are gentlemen here who were here then, and who took part in those discussions, and they will set the matter right. My friend overlooked the fact that the argument was that in its legislative capacity the legislature could not do this thing. My friend from Frederick, in the senate, voted against the soldiers voting, although he earnestly desired that they might vote; and what was the reason he assigned, and the reason that other gentlemen assigned? That they were here in a legislative capacity, and could not do it.—We are not here in any such capacity. We are here representing the sovereign people of Maryland, sent here to form their popular will into an organic law; and we mean to do it and abide the consequences.

Now in actual fact, as to the soldiers voting, who has a better right to vote than the soldier? I claim that he has as good a right to vote as any gentleman upon this floor. If he has not a right to vote as a soldier, I have not. In the bare letter of the law I have, but in its spirit I have not. He has taken his life in his hand and gone out to the battle-field to do or die if need be in the service of his country. He is a better man than I am; and I am proud to say so. If I can help him to vote, wherever he may be, on the weary march, in the camp, or on the field, God helping me, I will help him to do it; for he has a better right to vote than I have.

This is not so much a question whether the soldier shall have the right to vote or not, as how he shall vote. There is the pinch. A camp is a good school for political education. Your political meetings, your conventions, &c., where men make great harrangues, and the people shout, and all that sort of thing, are a good place to talk, a good place for buncombe; but I tell you it is the man who is facing death for his country who learns in a day what we might take years to learn.

I had no idea of detaining the convention. I did want to vindicate my country against the idea that she sets up gibbets between the grandfather and the grandson, when that grandson is a sick and wounded prisoner. I wanted to show in what a spirit of enlightened christian charity she had acted.. I wanted the world to know it. I wanted to say here, what gentlemen must know, that that is not the case pointed at in this section; that no one could exclude the gentleman from Kent upon such a ground, for ministering to the wants of a sick and wounded prisoner when the government allowed him to do it. That is a sufficient answer to any man sitting as judge of election. No man in his senses would dream of rejecting a ballot on that ground. Let us come down to the plain simple facts of the case. Let us set forth the cases meant to be reached by this law. Let gentlemen who have been their own avowed advocates upon this floor, instead of setting up imaginary cases and knocking them down, appealing to your feelings, set up the real facts of the case and appeal to your judgment.

I wanted to point out to my friend from Anne Arundel (Mr. Miller) how exactly the provisions of this section of the elective franchise article followed the very word and letter and spirit of the act that called us together; and I wanted, too, to point out the fact that we do not sit here to-day as a legislature with regard to this matter; but the people at the ballot-box this spring broke the legislative fetters and sent us here to carry out their will. That is the true state of the case.

Mr. NEGLEY. I wish to make a few remarks.

Mr. CHAMBERS (interposing.) My indisposition compels me to retire. I desire to hear the rest of this debate; and as it is now ten o'clock, with the consent of the gentleman I will move that the convention adjourn.

Mr. NEGLEY declined to yield the floor for the motion, and Mr. CHAMBERS thereupon retired from the hall.

Mr. NEGLEY resumed: The argument of the gentleman from Kent (Mr. Chambers) is this: that there is no power under the constitution of Maryland given even to the legislature or the constitutional convention to prescribe any other qualifications for the voter than those given and laid down in the constitution. The gentleman from Anne Arundel (Mr. Miller) takes the same view, and says there is no power conferred by the constitution, no power residing in the legislature of Maryland, no power in this constitutional convention to prescribe any other qualifications than those laid down in the constitution. Now I will call the attention of the gentleman from Kent (Mr. Chambers) to the law calling this constitutional convention. What does that do? That prescribes an additional qualification.—What is the qualification in the constitution of Maryland? It is that a voter shall be a citizen of the United States, shall be a resident of the State one year, shall reside in the county or city where he attempts to vote, and shall be a white man. These are the four elements of the qualification. The constitution of Maryland makes no provision for any oath. According to the theory of the gentleman, therefore, these are the only qualifications that can be prescribed; and no legislature and no constitutional convention can prescribe any others. Now what is the fact?

Did not the last legislature of Maryland prescribe an additional oath as a qualification for the voter who came forward to vote upon the call of this convention? Had they authority for that in the constitution? None whatever.

Mr. BRISCOE. I will tell the gentleman from Washington the position taken by the gentlemen who opposed that oath in the convention bill, that there was no constitutional power to incorporate that oath in the convention bill, and therefore that it was not binding.

Mr. STOCKBRIDGE. The majority were against you.

Mr. NEGLEY resumed: The position of the gentleman from Kent (Mr. Chambers) was that there was no power conferred by the constitution to prescribe any other constitutional qualification for the voter. Then if the legislature attempted to prescribe any other qualification, it was a usurpation, and it was illegal. If this constitutional convention attempted to prescribe any additional qualification, it was a usurpation and illegal. And the gentleman from Anne Arundel took the same position. Yet what was the fact? The legislature of Maryland last winter did absolutely attach an additional qualification to the elective franchise in the vote for this convention. What was that additional qualification? Here it is. It is an oath—the oath prescribed by the act calling this convention together. It is not necessary for me to read it. But it is not authorized in the constitution. It is outside of the constitution. It is an addition to the constitution.

Now I put this question. If the legislature of Maryland had the power to prescribe an additional oath, which did not exist in the constitution, has not this constitutional convention an equal right? The legislature did prescribe an oath. Now what do they say in the sixth section?

"Sec. 6. *And be it enacted*, That the constitution and form of government adopted by the said convention as aforesaid, shall be submitted to the legal and qualified voters of the State"——

That is the legal and qualified voters of the State as prescribed by the constitution.

——"for their adoption or rejection, at such time, in such manner, and subject to such rules and regulations as said convention may prescribe; and the provisions hereinbefore contained for the qualification of voters and the holding of elections provided in the previous section of this act, shall be applicable to the election to be held under this section."

They attach an additional qualification to the elective franchise in the very act calling the convention together, as clearly as the sun shines, because there is nothing in the constitution of Maryland which at all gives them the right to attach this additional qualification; and they say that in addition to the qualifications which the voter must have under the constitution of Maryland, he must come forward and take this oath which they prescribe. That, according to the gentleman from Kent, and the gentleman from Anne Arundel, is the additional qualification which they pronounce unconstitutional. They pronounce that additional qualification unconstitutional, and yet——

Mr. MILLER. I did not say any such thing. I did not say that was unconstitutional at all.

Mr. NEGLEY. You admit that that was constitutional then?

Mr. MILLER. I say that the provisions of the convention bill, having been adopted by the people by their vote, became, as the gentleman from Baltimore county (Mr. Ridgely) says, the fundamental law of this convention.

Mr. NEGLEY. Yes, sir; it becomes the fundamental law of this convention, and yet before that was submitted to the people, a qualification for the voter was prescribed in it, not recognized in the constitution of Maryland, the qualification of an oath; while the constitution of Maryland did not make any provision for such an oath as is prescribed in this constitutional convention law. This is an additional qualification; and they had no authority under the constitution for it. But the gentleman admits that that being submitted to the people, and the people having voted upon it, it is a part and parcel of the constitution of Maryland now, so far as we are acting under this convention law.

Now what do we propose to do? What did this sixth section say? It says that this additional provision, this qualification of voters, shall attach to the voter who votes upon the constitution which this convention may frame; that the additional qualification which this last legislature of Maryland fixed upon the exercise of the elective franchise in voting for the convention, shall attach to the party who votes for this constitution that is framed by this convention. According to the theory of the gentleman from Anne Arundel, that means the additional oath prescribed by the convention law, and gives us the power to prescribe that same oath in the adoption of this constitution by the people.

Then what does the sixth section further say? It goes on to say, as the gentleman from Baltimore county (Mr. Ridgely) properly declares, that it shall be submitted, "subject to such rules and regulations as the said convention may prescribe." That is a clear and unquestioned power granted to this convention to prescribe an additional oath; which we have done in this schedule. It is an unquestioned power given to this convention to make such additional rules, such additional regulations, and to throw such additional qualifications around the elective franchise as we may deem right and proper when we come to submit the constitution to the vote of the people. So that strictly and legally we have that clear unquestioned right; and we have not at all transcended any powers conferred; we have not assumed any. We have the power of the constitution; we have the authority of the law calling this convention together in the qualification which they prescribe; and we have the power clearly and indubitably conferred by the sixth section of the convention bill to prescribe such qualifications as we may deem proper. I shall vote for that under the firm and absolute conviction that it is all according to law, and all according to authority of the very highest kind; that we violate no law; that we strain no point; that we do nothing illegal at all in fixing this qualification.

Mr. DUVALL moved that the convention adjourn.

The question being taken, the result was—ayes 20, noes 22.

The motion was accordingly rejected.

No quorum having voted,

Mr. HEBB moved a call of the house, and the call was sustained.

The call of the roll having been commenced by the call of the president's name, and his response,

Mr. AUDOUN moved that further proceedings under the call be dispensed with.

The motion was agreed to.

Mr. ABBOTT called for the previous question.

The PRESIDENT. The motion to adjourn is not decided yet.

Mr. CUSHING. A quorum is not necessary to decide a motion to adjourn.

The question being again taken upon the motion to adjourn, it was rejected.

Mr. BRISCOE submitted the following amendment:

Add to the first section:

"And at said election a vote upon the adoption or rejection of the fortieth section of the article on the legislative department be submitted and taken separately and apart from all other sections therein, and if upon the casting up of the votes thereon it shall appear that a majority of the voters of this

State shall be opposed thereto, that the said article shall be inoperative and of no effect, otherwise to be and remain in full force and effect in law."

Mr. BRISCOE said: I do not propose to detain the convention by any extended discussion upon this amendment. From the opening of this convention I have eschewed all extended discussion upon the various matters appertaining to the subject of slavery. I hope that the convention will give to the people of Maryland a fair opportunity of determining, if this constitution is to prevail, by which it is proposed that the institution of slavery in this State shall be abolished; that no compensation shall be granted to the slaveholders, to those who will be deprived of their property by this constitution if it shall be adopted.

I knew very well when this convention assembled here, that there were certain things predetermined. I knew very well when the standard of abolitionism was first raised at the instance of the President of the United States, under his proclamation of the 10th of March, that there was a party then being organized in this State, sustained by all the power of the government, to carry out practically the recommendation of that proclamation. I confess that I have not been astonished that this convention has come to the conclusion to wipe out that institution. I came here with very little hope that the action of this convention would result in anything likely to continue it any longer as an institution of this State. But when I found that the convention had gone further, and had violated what I knew to be the wish of the President of the United States himself, that compensation should be granted to the slave owner, I must confess it struck me with astonishment. I simply offer this motion to test the sense of the house, and to give them an opportunity to say whether the people of Maryland in all time to come shall be deprived of the right here taken from them by an act, as I believe, of sheer and absolute despotism.

I came here, as I said in the beginning, determined to take very little part in the discussion in this convention. I was blessed in one respect. I expected very little from it, and therefore shall go away from it very little disappointed. I had learned in the past to look to the opinions of those men who foretold to us what would be the results when the element of abolitionism seized upon the popular mind. I had seen it proclaimed everywhere, and more particularly in the opinion of the great Clay, who with prophetic sagacity said if the abolitionists should assume the ascendency in the country:

"With them the rights of property are nothing; the deficiency of the powers of the general government are nothing; the acknowledged and incontestible powers of the States are nothing; civil war, a dissolution of the Union, and the overthrow of a government in which are concentrated the fondest hopes of the civilized world, are nothing. A single idea has taken possession of their minds and onward they pursue it, overlooking all barriers, reckless and regardless of all consequences."

We have seen the prophecy of Mr. Clay fulfilled. Within the last two years that party has assumed the control; and we have seen the result, not only in the condition of the country at large, but in the action of this convention. The great Webster, too, said of the same party—the abolitionists:

"Let these infernal fanatics get possession of the government, and they will treat the decisions of the supreme court with contempt; they will make laws to suit themselves; they will lay violent hands on all who disagree with them: they will bankrupt the whole country, and finally deluge it in blood."

When the President of the United States enunciated in his proclamation the necessity of wiping out this institution, and when I saw a party organization raised in this State for the purpose of accomplishing this recommendation, I ceased to have hope that any rights of mine, that any rights appertaining to the people of the State would be respected if they stood in the way of the accomplishment of that great purpose—the destruction of the institution of slavery.

These men who act with that party organization may be as conscientious and as sincere in their motives as I am in mine; but we see the prophecies of Clay and Webster illustrated to-day, and demonstrated all over the Union. These men, having obtained possession of your national government are seizing upon your State governments, and they are reckless and heedless of all consequences in accomplishing their great purpose, the purpose that gave this convention life and being, the putting to death of the institution of slavery.

I was prepared for the determination on the part of this convention to destroy that institution; but that they would deprive the people of Maryland of all opportunity to avail themselves of that returning sense of justice, which I believe sooner or later will come, passes all reason and common justice. But I will make no argument upon it. I simply ask that this question shall be determined by the people at the ballot-box, when the constitution shall be submitted to them for their rejection or adoption, that they may say whether or not the legislature shall be forever prohibited from making compensation for the slaves taken from them and set free by this constitution.

Mr. ABBOTT called for the previous question.

Mr. CLARKE demanded the yeas and nays, which were ordered.

The question being taken on sustaining

the call for the previous question, the result was—yeas 40, nays 16—as follows:

Yeas—Messrs. Goldsborough, President; Abbott, Annan, Audoun, Baker, Barron, Brooks, Carter, Cunninghom, Cushing, Daniel, Davis, of Washington, Dellinger, Ecker, Farrow, Galloway, Greene, Hatch, Hebb, Jones, of Cecil, Kennard, McComas, Mullikin, Nyman, Parker, Purnell, Russell, Sands, Schley, Schlosser, Scott, Smith, of Worcester, Sneary, Stirling, Swope, Sykes, Todd, Valliant, Wickard, Wooden—40.

Nays—Messrs. Belt, Briscoe, Clarke, Crawford, Dent, Duvall, Horsey, Lansdale, Marbury, Miller, Morgan, Negley, Parran, Ridgely, Stockbridge, Thomas—16.

When their names were called,

Mr. CLARKE said: I regard the pending section as the most important proposition which has been before the convention from its first organization until the present time; and I do hope that this convention upon the mere consideration of this section this evening, without giving opportunity to gentlemen to define their views upon it, will not press it to a decisive vote to-night by the call of the previous question. It is a question which affects not merely the political rights of parties, but lays the foundation of the fundamental principles of government and the fundamental principles of the social compact. I shall vote against the previous question; and if it is sustained I shall regard it as an indication of an intention on the part of this house which violates in my humble judgment, without even giving a chance for discussion and placing them properly before the people, their rights under the constitution of the State. I vote "no."

Mr. NEGLEY said: Having myself had an opportunity to speak upon this question, common decency and justice require that I should not vote to prohibit any other member from exercising a like privilege. I vote "no."

Mr. SANDS said: I do not agree with the gentleman from Washington (Mr. Negley,) that because I have spoken I cannot join the majority of the house in sustaining the previous question. It has been argued on both sides about equally; and I therefore vote "aye."

The call for the previous question was accordingly sustained.

The question being first upon the amendment submitted by Mr. BRISCOE to the section,

Mr. BRISCOE demanded the yeas and nays, and they were ordered.

The question being taken, the result was—yeas 12, nays 48—as follows:

Yeas—Messrs. Belt, Briscoe, Clarke, Crawford, Dent, Duvall, Horsey, Lansdale, Marbury, Miller, Morgan, Parran—12.

Nays—Messrs. Goldsborough, President; Abbott, Annan, Audoun, Baker, Barron, Brooks, Carter, Cunningham, Cushing, Daniel, Davis, of Washington, Dellinger, Earle, Ecker, Farrow, Galloway, Greene, Hatch, Hebb, Jones, of Cecil, Kennard, King, McComas, Mullikin, Murray, Negley, Nyman, Parker, Purnell, Ridgely, Russell, Sands, Schley, Schlosser, Scott, Smith, of Carroll, Smith, of Worcester, Sneary, Stirling, Stockbridge, Swope, Sykes, Thomas, Todd, Valliant, Wickard, Wooden—48.

When his name was called,

Mr. ABBOTT said: This question having already been decided by the people once, I do not feel disposed to insult them with it again; and I therefore vote "no."

The amendment was accordingly rejected.

Mr. DANIEL moved that the convention adjourn.

The motion was rejected.

Mr. DUVALL demanded the yeas and nays upon the section, and they were ordered.

The question being taken, the result was—yeas 47, nays 12—as follows:

Yeas—Messrs. Goldsborough, President; Abbott, Annan, Audoun, Baker, Barron, Brooks, Carter, Cunningham, Cushing, Daniel, Davis, of Washington, Dellinger, Ecker, Farrow, Galloway, Greene, Hatch, Hebb, Jones, of Cecil, Kennard, King, McComas, Mullikin, Murray, Negley, Nyman, Parker, Purnell, Ridgely, Russell, Sands, Schley, Schlosser, Scott, Smith, of Carroll, Smith, of Worcester, Sneary, Stirling, Stockbridge, Swope, Sykes, Thomas, Todd, Valliant, Wickard, Wooden—47.

Nays—Messrs. Belt, Briscoe, Clarke, Crawford, Dent, Duvall, Horsey, Lansdale, Marbury, Miller, Morgan, Parran—12.

When his name was called,

Mr. DUVALL said: Believing as I do that the requirements of this section are without authority, dangerous and wrong, violating every principle of right and justice, and a blow aimed at the liberties of the people, I vote "no."

The section was accordingly adopted.

On motion of Mr. PURNELL,

The convention adjourned.

EIGHTY-SEVENTH DAY.

THURSDAY, September 1, 1864.

The convention met at 9½ o'clock, A. M.

Prayer by the Rev. Mr. McNemar.

The roll was called, and the following members answered to their names:

Messrs. Goldsborough, President; Abbott, Annan, Baker, Barron, Belt, Blackiston, Briscoe, Brooks, Brown, Carter, Chambers, Clarke, Crawford, Cunningham, Cushing, Dail, Daniel, Davis, of Washington, Dellinger, Dent, Duvall, Earle, Ecker, Galloway, Greene, Hatch, Hebb, Henkle, Hodson, Hollyday, Horsey, Johnson, Jones, of Cecil, Kennard, King, Lansdale, Lee, Marbury, Markey, McComas, Miller, Morgan, Mullikin, Murray, Nyman, Parran, Pugh, Purnell, Ridgely, Russell,

Schlosser, Scott, Smith, of Carroll, Smith, of Dorchester, Smith, of Worcester, Sneary, Stirling, Stockbridge, Swope, Thomas, Todd, Valliant, Wickard, Wilmer, Wooden—66.

The proceedings of yesterday were read and approved.

On motion of Mr. McComas,

Ordered, That the folders and postmasters, and whoever shall have the authority to attend to their duties, after the adjournment of the convention, be instructed not to fold or frank any other printed matter than such as has been published by authority of the convention.

PERSONAL EXPLANATION.

Mr. Chambers. I rise to a matter of personal explanation. I have been intrusted by a gentleman from Talbot county, of high respectability, to state to this convention the facts in regard to a circumstance which a member now in his seat from Talbot (Mr. Valliant) has brought to the notice of this body. It seems that on a former occasion the member from Talbot was pleased to allude by name to this gentleman, Mr. Thomas P. Williams, amongst those whom I understand from the context that he charges with being secessionists, or unfaithful members of the community, disloyal men. He mentions the name of Mr. Thomas P. Williams, who, he asserts, had given money to a brother of the member, to induce him to go South and take up arms against the government. Mr. Williams considers himself as deeply injured by this, which he says is a misrepresentation. He has had strong southern sympathies. That he makes no concealment of. But he has always avoided any act by which any law of the United States or of the State of Maryland could in any shape be violated. He has avoided any act in conflict with those laws. His statement is that he did not furnish him money. This gentleman, Mr. George E. Valliant, has since returned from the South, and I hold in my hand his certificate, in these words:

State of Maryland,
St. Michael's, Aug. 29, 1864.

I, George Enos Valliant, of St. Michael's, do solemnly aver and declare that what my brother said in convention as regards Thomas P. Williams persuading "me, or any other person, so far as I know, to go down to Virginia, and there defend his native South from the inroads of northern Goths and Vandals, and offered to pay the expenses of ten young men to go and do as he urged my brother to do, and other things," is positively untrue.

[Signed] Geo. E. Valliant.

Signed in presence of
O. R. Sparks.

These are gentlemen known to you, and I suppose their signatures will not be contested. I rise here in the name of an injured individual, injured in a material way, but I hope undesignedly and by mistake; with a view of giving the member from Talbot an opportunity to retract this assertion in the presence in which it was made. I make no comments upon the subject. I have done this as an act of justice to a gentleman whom I have known and you have known to be one of the most respectable citizens of Talbot county, and a man whose conduct, so far as I know, is above impeachment.

Mr. Valliant. Mr. President——

Mr. Cushing. I wish to ask if these remarks will go upon the journal of debates. It is a personal matter entirely, concerning a gentleman in Maryland; and I wish to know whether the journal of debates of this convention is open for every gentleman in Maryland, who may consider himself aggrieved by remarks in this house to come here and defend himself upon that journal of debates?

Mr. Chambers. I ask for information, whether there is one individual man in this house so unkind—I use no strong expression now—as to desire that an imputation shall be made against an individual of a high crime and placed upon the journal, and to deny to that individual the privilege of placing there his contradiction of it? Is there a man in this house whose feelings will allow him to take this position?

Mr. Cushing. I am not objecting to it. I simply asked the question. I have never known that in Congress a man supposing himself to be injured by the debates there could so defend himself. I asked for information.

The President. I understand the gentleman from Baltimore city to make an inquiry of the chair whether an individual not connected with this body has a right to have his defence, of whatever character it may be, spread upon the journal of the debates and proceedings of this body. That is not a matter exclusively within the power or control of the president. The gentleman from Baltimore city has the right to call the attention of the convention to it; and the convention has the power to decide whether this matter shall be spread upon the journal or not. It would be a matter of assumption upon the part of the président to arrogate to himself the right to permit this to be placed upon the journal or to exclude it. The people are represented in this body. Every man in Maryland is represented here by some person or other. Of course if any one is aggrieved, it is for this body to judge whether it comes within the constitutional provision to permit their grievance to be laid before them, subject to any investigation they may choose to make. That is a matter exclusively within the province of the convention. The president is to decide points of order and other matters which may come before him for the regulation of this convention; but any matter outside of that is a matter for the deliberation and the judgment of the convention. If the gentleman from Baltimore city desires to make a motion, it will bring the question up properly before the convention, whether they will permit these remarks to be spread upon the journal of debates or not; whether they will act upon it before the member from Talbot has an opportunity of explaining himself. After the gentleman from Talbot shall have explained himself, the entire matter will be before the convention for their judgment.

Mr. CUSHING. I understand the chair that it would be an act of assumption for the president either to allow it to go upon the record of debates or to refuse it. Do I understand that it cannot go upon the debates without an order of the body?

The PRESIDENT. No, sir; everything that is transacted in this body is to be faithfully reported, unless the convention shall otherwise determine. The convention have the power to control their debates and proceedings. They have the power to expunge, if they choose, a portion of the journal, or say that a portion of the debates and proceedings shall not be entered upon the journal of debates and proceedings; and so far as that is concerned, to exclude it from public consideration. They have the entire control over this matter. The president has no control over this subject, further than to see that all proceedings of whatever nature, whether in the shape of personal matters or otherwise, shall be conducted in the forms prescribed by parliamentary law. It is for the convention to decide whether this matter shall be entered upon the journal. Of course the convention will not exclude the gentleman from Talbot (Mr. Valliant) from the privilege of making any personal explanation that he desires.

Mr. VALLIANT. I understand that the question as to whether or not any discussion that may arise between the gentleman from Kent and myself is to be entered upon the journal, is a question to be decided by this convention. I apprehend that if it be allowable that whatever explanations are necessary to be made, should be made, the explanations should first be made, and the question discussed afterwards whether or not it be entered upon the journal.

I understood the gentleman from Kent (Mr. Chambers) to say that I had said in my remarks made here on the twenty-third article of the declaration of rights some time in last June, that Mr. Williams had given money to my brother. Now, sir, here is the speech reported in the debates.

Mr. CHAMBERS. I wish to say that I was not here, and knew nothing about it, and professed to know nothing about it. I saw it so reported.

Mr. VALLIANT. I will read the remarks:

"And further, if we undertake to compensate the loyal slaveholder, we will soon have to compensate the disloyal also. It will be an easy matter for the disloyal a few years hence to come forward and prove by testimony, competent in law, that in 1864 they were loyal men—were opposed to the rebellion and never aided it by word or deed. Mr. Thomas P. Williams, of my county, who in the month of May, 1861, persuaded my boy brother, George Enos Valliant, then a boy but seventeen years old, to go down to Virginia and there defend his native south from the inroads of northern goths and vandals, and offered to pay the expenses of ten young men to go and do as he urged my brother to do, and other things too numerous to mention, will be able to bring some one to swear that he too has ever been loyal, and thereupon base a claim for compensation, and thus the State will be obliged to compensate the loyal and the disloyal alike, and will also be obliged to compensate the sufferers to whom I have alluded in the western counties, (which latter our legislature has already refused to do.) And in doing all this we seriously threaten our State with bankruptcy."

It is "and *offered* to pay," not that he did do it. My information is not that he did it, but that he did not do it. When my brother went and threw himself in the way of Mr. Thomas P. Williams, so that Mr. Thomas P. Williams could fulfil the obligation, and comply with the offer he had made to my brother, my brother said he did not pay him the money; but he said he *offered* to pay not only his expenses, but the expenses of nine other young men, and other things too numerous to mention. My hour had been consumed; but if it had been a matter of consequence that I should mention these things, I would have done it. And now that the matter has come up, I intend to mention these things, and they are things which in my county are a matter of public notoriety, known to every man in the county.

In the month of May, 1861, I was the guardian of my brother, who was then but seventeen years of age. He came to me and asked me for money sufficient to take him down south. He said all his sympathies were with the south. He believed that upon the great questions which had just been submitted to the arbitrament of the sword, the south was right. The northern people were going down to invade their rights, and he wished to go south and help defend their rights. "And I demand of you as my guardian," he said, "to furnish me the money to take me down there." I declined to do so. I declined to furnish him the money. Said he, "It don't make any difference; Mr. Williams says he will furnish the money, and I am independent of you anyhow." I am willing that the stenographer should take this down and to have the matter investigated in a court of law if necessary. Whenever this matter comes up before a court for trial, my brother comes as a witness upon the stand, if he is alive, and I will have him thoroughly interrogated. I am now willing to take a solemn affidavit that my brother did make that statement to me in the year 1861. I recollect it just as distinctly as I recollect that I arose this morning. There is no event of my whole life more deeply impressed upon my recollection than the statement my brother made to me that year.

"And other things too numerous to mention." What are they? Here is another thing I will make a solemn affidavit to. I was present. I had eyes to see and I saw. I had ears to hear and I heard. I recollect that on Saturday night—I never tried to remember the identical day, but I have been keeping a journal of my life, and every day making minutes, and I have got that down, and I cannot forget it—on the Saturday night prior to the 4th day of February, 1861—my colleagues will remember the 4th day of February, 1861, for it was a big day in our county, and there was a big thing done there on that day; we had an election—on the Saturday night prior to that 4th day of February, 1861, the gentleman whose name occurs in my speech here, was in my town, and made a speech in my town, and I heard that speech. It was not such a speech as we have been listening to from gentlemen who advocate southern rights here upon this floor. It was such a speech that if he were to dare to make it today, he would not be a free man twenty-four hours, and he knows it. I will take my solemn affidavit, and hold myself responsible to my Almighty God, and all creation, and every living man, for what I say, when I say that he advocated the immediate disruption of this confederacy. He said it ought to be done, and went on to give the most silly reasons I ever heard. This was his argument. I have not tried to recollect it. I recollected it because I could not help it. I wish I could forget that such a thing had been done in my town. and the man allowed to go scot free. I wish I could forget it. It was one of those "other things too numerous to mention."

Here is the argument he used to influence the people of that town—the oystermen of that town. Said he: "The southern people have heretofore been travelling up North in the summer season to spend a few months perhaps, or a few weeks at any rate, at such places as Saratoga, Newport, Cape May, &c., spending money there among those Yankees who are trying to infringe upon our rights for a long number of years. Now if Maryland will only consent to go south, they will stop at Mason and Dixon's line, and won't go any further. This little town is situated in a most beautiful district of the country, and has a great many attractions, and these large planters instead of going north will stop in this very identical town, and instead of spending their money at Saratoga, will spend it here." [Laughter.]

Yes, sir; I listened to that sort of argument, and I confess I got sick. I took a dose of tartar emetic once in my life, and it produced just the same effect. [Laughter.] Yes, sir; and he advised my people to defend their southern rights at the point of the bayonet. He told them we must separate, and we must maintain that separation by force of arms. That is what he said, and I heard it, and I will swear to it. Others heard it besides me. I do not know whether others can recollect it or not. Perhaps they can, and perhaps they cannot. I recollect it.

"Other things too numerous to mention." I reckon that my colleague in the chair (the president) can remember very well that on the Sunday succeeding the 19th of April, a certain steamboat left my county with one hundred persons on board to defend, as they said, the city of Baltimore from the inroads of northern bands. I reckon that my colleague and other gentlemen can distinctly remember who it was that chartered that boat. I was not present when the contract was made between Mr. Williams and the captain of that boat, if Mr. Williams was the man that chartered it. But this I do know, that as a matter of public notoriety in that county, he did charter that boat to go and assist these Baltimoreans to resist the passage of Massachusetts troops through that city. It has been asserted in my county, I suppose five hundred times in my hearing, and I have never once heard it denied, not even by his political friends. These are "other things."

Sir, I had a right to say this thing, because I was personally interested. This young man is my brother—both sons of the same mother and the same father. It may have been a little indiscreet, I will admit. It may be that I was governed a little too much by my feelings in making that statement. But let any gentleman in this convention place himself in my predicament. I had been one of the most unfortunate of men in my domestic relations. Just at the inception of these troubles I was unfortunate enough to have my domestic situation in life changed by the death of her who was to me dearer than life itself, a few days succeeding the election of Mr. Lincoln. I had then five brothers living, and three sisters. Every one of them sympathized with this infernal rebellion—every one of them. Of four brothers, three are now serving the rebel confederacy, and one now is at my house, after having served in the rebel confederacy twenty-seven months. At the beginning of these troubles I had seated at my table four or five brothers and two or three sisters every day. Less than a year ago my house was cleaned out. Not even a sister had I remaining; and I have since been living there alone. The disruption of my domestic happiness is to me exclusively attributable to these difficulties. I have been alone, and I have been an unhappy man. And, sir, I believe as firmly as I believe there is a

God, that the man whose name I have mentioned in these remarks is in part the cause of my unhappiness.

My brother was a boy seventeen years old. Think of it; seventeen years old. This gentleman is a man of mature age, whose head is silvered by the frosts of many winters; a man of mature judgment; a man who understands; a man of no ordinary intelligence; a man who understands thoroughly the history of this crisis; who understands thoroughly the history of the great quarrel which has separated, in feeling at least, the two great sections of this great empire. This individual comes to my brother, an unsophisticated boy, an ignorant boy, with nothing more than a common school education, perfectly ignorant of the history of these troubles, and offers to pay his expenses south. Now if he did offer to pay his expenses to go south, is it reasonable to suppose that he did that and nothing more? If there was a doubt remaining on my brother's mind as to whether or not he ought to go, is it or is it not likely that that gentleman tried to remove that doubt? The very fact of the offer was persuading him. I contend that the very offer to pay his expenses was of itself a persuasion to go.

Last fall my brother was captured, was arrested, and he lay four months at Fort McHenry. After a great deal of trouble I succeeded in getting him out. While he was lying there, wasting away with disease, lying there under an imputation disgraceful to him, and calculated to disgrace the social position of his family—the imputation of a spy—I could not do otherwise than feel sore. I feel sore now when I recollect the language my brother used to me in May, 1861, and I feel indignant. And when I remember that the influence then used by this gentleman, in part at least, was the cause of my brother's going south, entailing disgrace on himself and disgrace on his family, I cannot help feeling sore and feeling indignant. My feelings are mortified and wounded. It is the severest blow I ever received in my life. I have alluded to the unhappy event which occurred on the 14th of November, 1861; I mean unhappy to me, changing my position in life. But even that, though it wrung tears of blood from me, even that was not as violent a blow to my feelings as the course pursued by this brother of mine, influenced in part to pursue that course by this gentleman. No man can conceive what my feelings have been, unless he has been in that predicament. You may form some faint conception of what my feelings have been, but only a faint conception.

If I have been guilty of some little indiscretion, in a moment when my feelings may have had more control over me than they ought to have had, this convention at least will make some allowance for it. I do not make this acknowledgment as any apology. I have no apologies to make for one single solitary syllable uttered in that speech; none; none whatever, sir; none. I stand here as a wronged man. I was not only his brother, but his guardian, and to some extent responsible for what that boy did; not responsible perhaps in law, but I was responsible to the memory of his father, and to the memory of his mother; and I was responsible to his future history. I advised that boy not to go. I lectured him by the hour. And when my brother told me that Mr. Williams had offered to pay his expenses South, it was reasonable for me to conclude that all the lessons I had imparted to him, were done away with by the lessons of this gentleman. I do not know the extent of those lessons. I have not said in my speech that this gentleman lectured to him as I did. I only say that my brother told me in the month of May, 1861, that Mr. Williams did offer to pay his expenses; and I submit to gentlemen if it was not reasonable for me to conclude that these propositions did not end with simple air; if it was not reasonable for me to conclude that he had persuaded him to go otherwise than simply by making that offer.

I will not detain the convention longer. My feelings have perhaps taken a little more control of me on this occasion than they ought to have done; but gentlemen will make allowance for that. If I have trespassed longer upon their time and attention than I ought to have done, I am ready to apologize to the convention. I will apologize further, for asking the convention to listen to the statement of an aggrieved and an injured man.

Mr. Chambers. I have but a word to say. I know nothing of these matters. I beg to be considered as not asserting any one fact of my own knowledge. This respectable gentleman, who has been known to me for years as a man of high standing and position, has asked at my hands this favor. His statement to me is that for the first time on Saturday, he heard from the pamphlet speech or from some other source, the statement that he had persuaded this young gentleman and others to go South, as stated again now, and as copied precisely in this affidavit. This information came to him here on Saturday last. He knew nothing of these further charges and imputations. He instantly went in pursuit of Mr. George E. Valliant, the only name given here, the other persons not being known to him, and not being named in the speech, and he obtained from Mr. Valliant this certificate, the authenticity of which is not disputed, I understand, in which Mr. Valliant says that no such thing occurred. He did not persuade him. He did not persuade to his knowledge any other person. This gentleman further states to me that he holds himself perfectly able to prove that the gentleman, who is now in his seat, himself gave him the money to go South.

He states further that he is perfectly able to prove by as high and as distinguished men as can be found in the county of Talbot or elsewhere, that the speech which he made was not of the character described by the gentleman. The people of Talbot know the gentleman; they know the transactions; and it is befitting that these matters should there be settled. I have performed my duty by making the representation which I have received at the hands of Mr. Williams, and producing the certificate which may be examined by the gentleman if he desires it.

Mr. VALLIANT. I would like to reply to the additional charge; and I will do it in a moment.

Mr. CHAMBERS. One thing further, if the gentleman will allow me. I am desired by Mr. Williams to say that it would be gratifying to him to have a committee appointed by this body to inquire into the facts and report upon them. He is prepared for that.

Mr. VALLIANT. I am charged by the gentleman—I cannot say directly by the gentleman from Kent, for he takes it upon the assertion of his friend—with having furnished my brother with the money to go South. I remember distinctly giving my brother a draft upon a friend of mine for $25, not presuming that he was going to use it for that purpose. It was given sometime prior to his leaving. Immediately upon giving that order, I left my home, and was absent from home some ten days or two weeks; and it was during my absence that my brother left. I did not know at the time that he was going to use it for that purpose. I knew he wanted to go; that his inclinations were all that way. But when I left him at home I left with a tolerable hope that my brother would eventually decline going. But when I returned home I was unhappy enough to learn that he had gone. I knew my brother wanted money. He was at that time out of a situation, and had had no situation for some weeks. I knew he wanted money, and I gave him the small sum of $25, scarcely presuming that would be sufficient to take him down South, independent of the expenses and the difficulties he would be obliged to surmount after he got there. I gave it to him because it was due to him, and not to go South. On the contrary, when he asked for money to go South, I positively declined to furnish it; and it was my declining to give him money that led him to say that this gentleman would give him money and that he was independent of me. These are the facts of the case as exactly as I can state them.

FOLDING THE DEBATES.

Mr. VALLIANT withdrew the amendment submitted by him on yesterday to the order submitted by Mr. HEBB, in relation to folding and mailing the journal of debates after the adjournment of the convention.

DECLARATION OF RIGHTS.

On motion of Mr. HEBB,

The convention proceeded to the consideration of the report of the committee on revision and engrossment in reference to amendments to the declaration of rights, as follows:

"The committee on engrossment and revision report, that they have examined the engrossed copy of the declaration of rights.

"The word 'at' should be inserted after the word 'and' in the first line of the thirtieth article.

"And the word 'persons,' in the thirteenth line of the thirty-sixth article should be 'person.'

"The committee recommend that the forty-sixth article be united with the fortieth article.

"The fortieth article would then read, 'that the liberty of the press ought to be inviolably preserved, and every citizen ought to be allowed to speak, write and publish his sentiments, being responsible for the abuse of that liberty.'"

On motion of Mr. HEBB,

The report was concurred in.

THE SCHEDULE.

The convention resumed the consideration of the report of the committee on the schedule, on its second reading. The next section in order was the second section on voting on the constitution, which was read as follows:

"SEC. 2. At the said election, the vote shall be by ballot, and each ballot shall describe thereon the words 'for the constitution,' or 'against the constitution,' as the voter may elect, and it shall be conducted in all respects as the general elections of this State are now conducted. The judges of election shall administer to every person offering to vote, the oath or affirmation prescribed by this constitution, and should any person offering to vote refuse or decline to take said oath, he shall not be permitted to vote at such election, but the taking of such oath or affirmation, shall not be deemed conclusive evidence of the right of such person to vote; and it shall be the duty of the return judges of said city, and of the several counties of the State, having counted the votes given for or against the adoption of this constitution, to certify the result thereof in the manner now prescribed by law, accompanied with a special statement, that every person, who has voted, has taken the oath or affirmation prescribed by the constitution; and the governor upon receiving such result and ascertaining the aggregate vote throughout the State, shall by his proclamation make known the same, and if a majority of the votes cast shall be for the adoption of the constitution, it shall go into effect on the first day of November, 1864."

Mr. DUVALL. My remarks in explanation of my vote last night were intended to apply to this section. I supposed this was the one we were voting upon.

MILITARY INTERFERENCE WITH THE VOTE.

Mr. HENKLE submitted the following amendment:

Add at the end of the second section,

"And in case any organized military or armed force of the United States shall appear at the places where the polls shall be held, and shall interfere with said election, unless such military or armed force shall be called out by the judges of election or other civil authority charged with the preservation of the peace, the said judges of election shall under oath certify to the governor such unwarranted military interference with said election in such election district or precinct; and the governor shall immediately thereupon, order a new election after ten days notice, to be given by the sheriff as aforesaid, in such election district or precinct; and such new election shall be held and conducted in the manner and form hereinbefore provided, and the governor shall order a new election from time to time, as often as such illegal military or armed interference with the election shall be certified to him as aforesaid."

Mr. HENKLE demanded the yeas and nays on the adoption of the amendment, and they were ordered.

The question being taken, the result was—yeas 28, nays 39—as follows:

Yeas—Messrs. Belt, Blackiston, Briscoe, Brown, Chambers, Clarke, Crawford, Dail, Davis, of Charles, Dent, Duvall, Edelen, Henkle, Hodson, Hollyday, Horsey, Johnson, Lansdale, Lee, Marbury, Mitchell, Miller, Morgan, Parran, Peter, Smith, of Dorchester, Turner, Wilmer—28.

Nays—Messrs. Goldsborough, President; Abbott, Annan, Audoun, Baker, Barron, Brooks, Carter, Cunningham, Cushing, Daniel, Davis, of Washington, Dellinger, Galloway, Greene, Hatch, Hebb, Jones, of Cecil, Kennard, King, Markey, McComas, Mullikin, Parker, Pugh, Purnell, Ridgely, Russell, Schlosser, Scott, Sneary, Stirling, Stockbridge, Swope, Thomas, Todd, Valliant, Wickard, Wooden—39.

When his name was called,

Mr. BRISCOE said: So far as that is concerned, it is only repeating a provision in the convention bill. I understand that it is conceded on all sides that the convention bill, which gave life to this convention, which bill provides the law regulating the vote upon the adoption of this constitution, is still the binding law of this State. It matters not whether the report of this committee is in addition to that or not. I shall vote for the proposition of my friend from Anne Arundel (Mr. Henkle,) but it really seems to me that notwithstanding the adoption of that report the obligation is still binding upon the judges of election, by virtue of the act of assembly at its last session, calling for or providing for the assembling of this convention. In that view of it, I hope the convention, in order to clear up this matter, will adopt the amendment of my friend from Anne Arundel. I vote "aye."

The amendment was accordingly rejected.

THE TEST OATH.

Mr. DENT moved to strike out the following words:

"The judges of election shall administer to every person offering to vote the oath or affirmation prescribed by this constitution, and should any person offering to vote refuse or decline to take said oath, he shall not be permitted to vote at such election, but the taking of such oath or affirmation shall not be deemed conclusive evidence of the right of such person to vote."

Mr. DENT said: When yesterday I urged the postponement of the consideration of this schedule, on account of the sparse attendance of members in the hall, I said I believed, that I was surprised at the provisions incorporated in the schedule for the submission of the constitution to the people. I might have added, however, that if I had reflected for a moment on the acts of the past, there would have been no occasion for surprise. But, sir, I have a proneness to forget the acts of the past, for the moment, and am too much disposed to hope and believe that, notwithstanding what has transpired in the past, the future will go on smoothly and evenly as once before. In this hope I have been often disappointed, and I am learning now to hope no more from those who are in the ascendency in the government of this State and in the federal government; for, notwithstanding the plainest provisions of constitutional law—notwithstanding they are so plain that he who runs may read, we have gentlemen rising on this floor, and declaring that the act of the legislature by which this convention was assembled became, by the action of the people, the permanent law of the State—the fundamental law—the organic law. So far as that view is true, if it is true at all, it supersedes the constitution of the State of Maryland, which it is our duty to sustain.

If it be true that the enabling act—for it was barely an enabling act—became by the action of the people the organic law of the land, it contravenes the provisions of the constitution and thereby repeals it—an absurdity which I could scarcely have supposed would have obtained support or credence in the mind of any intelligent man. It shows plainly to my mind what straws people catch hold of to sustain a falling and sinking cause. For the want of something better they seize upon that—not as an argument, because it is not, but as a pretext for incorporating such a provision as that now under consideration in order to limit the exercise of the elective franchise, a right which has been so clearly defined by the constitution of the State of Maryland, and which this convention cannot limit or restrict in accordance with law, justice, or truth, except by a constitution which may supersede the old one. It is often spoken of as the old constitution, but I think it is still the constitution. It is not the old constitution. We have no other constitution than that which was adopted in 1851.

But I return to the proposition that the convention law, or that which is called the convention law, which was in fact merely an enabling act, has become the organic law of the land. Did the people vote for or against that convention bill? Was that the question submitted to the vote of the people, and upon which they gave their decision? I think not, sir. The question was "for or against a convention." That was the simple question propounded to the people at the election. By the return of the votes it appears that a majority were in favor of the call. While I admit that as an apparent fact, it has failed to convince me that a majority of the legal voters of the State were in favor of the call of the convention. I believe exactly the contrary. But for the limitation which was put upon the voting, but for the restrictions imposed in the convention bill, which were against and in violation of the constitution, but for the interposition of military interference with the free exercise of the most valuable of all rights, this convention, in my humble opinion, would not have been sitting here to-day. It would never have met. That, however, is a matter of opinion. I confess the results as they have been given to us by the returns of that election are against that opinion so far as concerns the number of votes cast.

But it must not be forgotten that on so vital a question as that of calling and electing a convention for the purpose of framing the organic law of the State, there was no free expression of opinion. The ballot-box was so hedged in by bayonets everywhere that it was but a farce, more calculated to excite indignation in the minds of the people than respect for the law, or the action of those who control these matters. It is useless for me to read the elective franchise as provided for in the constitution of this State. It has been so frequently read upon this floor, as well as so constantly within the reach of every member of this body, that if its action were to be influenced by the definition of a legal and qualified voter therein prescribed, we should not have before the convention the provision which I move to have stricken out. Article fifteenth of the bill of rights a part of the constitution of the State, and probably a part of the constitution which it is proposed soon to submit to the people, contains this provision:

"Art. 15. That retrospective laws, punishing acts committed before the existence of such laws, and by them only declared criminal, are oppressive, unjust, and incompatible with liberty; wherefore, no *ex post facto* law ought to be made."

I submit that the provision here, which is intended to be operative before the vote upon the constitution has been taken, is clearly in violation of that declaration, so plainly so as to be incontrovertible. It would seem that it were absurd to regard it as necessary even to call the attention of the convention to it.

Another article of the declaration of rights, I will read:

"Art. 21. That no free man ought to be taken or imprisoned, or disseized of his freehold, liberties or privileges, or outlawed, or exiled, or in any manner destroyed, or deprived of his life, liberty or property, but by the judgment of his peers and by the law of the land."

How does this affect the privilege, the exercise of the great inalienable right of suffrage, which can only be lost through crime, as declared by the constitution of the State? How can you clog the exercise of that right by such provisions as that under consideration? It cuts many of the citizens off from the privilege of voting; citizens the equals of any upon this floor; citizens as eminently patriotic as any that sit in this hall or have sat in it. Their opinions and feelings may be different from those of the majority here; but I trust they are not, in consequence of those feelings and opinions, to be treated as criminals, unworthy the exercise of that great right of suffrage, the only safeguard for free men. I trust they are not to be pushed away by the bayonet or by force, nor by any arbitrary provision that this constitution or this schedule of submission may make, from the exercise of that great right which is inherent to the citizens of the State, and of which they cannot be deprived legally except in the manner prescribed by the constitution.

Then, sir, I maintain that it is clearly an effort to arraign the citizen without a trial, and to impose a penalty upon him for certain opinions that he may entertain; and is therefore wrong, by every rule or principle of justice by which it may be examined or investigated. It is to impose a penalty for such a fact, without a trial, without an investigation. Its object is, in my opinion, evidently felonious. I think of no other word at this time calculated to express the effect, if not object, of the provision now under consideration. It seeks to disfranchise the voter without a trial. It is a test oath imposed for the purpose of restricting him in the exercise of his right of suffrage, unwarranted by any principle of law, equity or justice. It is well calculated to produce in the minds of the manly and independent citizens throughout the State, a feeling of hatred towards the powers that rule, and to engender in the heart a bitterness of venom which may break out some of these days, if persisted in, in something worse—something more gloomy and sad than anything which has occurred within the limits of our State. I would read a declaration of an illustrious citizen of the past; because we of the present day seem to have forgotten that such men ever existed in those days which tried men's souls. We seem to have forgotten the lessons which they taught us, and which the history of those days teaches us. We seem to have forgotten entirely the great principles upon which the government they established was founded. I read from a speech of John Hancock, delivered in Boston, as long ago as 1774:

"It is to the last degree vicious and infamous to attempt to support a government which manifestly tends to render the persons and property of the governed insecure. Some boast of being friends to government; I am a friend to righteous government, to a government founded on reason and justice; but I glory in publicly avowing my eternal enmity to tyranny."

Such, sir, may have to be the open declarations of some of our own fellow-citizens. I would avert anything of the kind if I had power to do it; but it seems impossible to stem or to check in the slightest degree the torrent of oppression which is sweeping down the rights of the citizens of the State, unless they fall into one current, that current represented by the majority controlling this convention.

"The paramount question," as has been asserted here over and over again, upon which the people of Maryland were called to decide, when voting for or against the convention, was the abolition of slavery. The abolition of slavery is a small loss to the citizens who sustain it, in comparison to the privation of the exercise of the elective franchise right.—But small as it is, there might have been something like a show of justice exhibited in the determination of that question by providing that those who had been deprived of their property might receive some compensation for it in the future, if there is an inability to do it in the present. The failure to do this calls to my mind the character of the abolitionists, as portrayed by the great Clay, as read by my friend on my left (Mr. Briscoe) last night. It cannot be too often repeated. Its truth has been verified. It has been realized so strongly in the present day that we are surprised at the prescience and foreknowledge of the great statesman who uttered these sentiments. I will read that paragraph again. It is from a speech delivered by Henry Clay against the insidious policy of the abolitionists:

"Abolitionism! With abolitionists the rights of property are nothing; the deficiency of the powers of the general government is nothing; the acknowledged and incontestable powers of the States are nothing; a dissolution of the Union and the overthrow of a government in which are concentrated the hopes of a civilized world are nothing. A single idea has taken possession of their minds, and onward they pursue it, overleaping all barriers, reckless and regardless of all consequences."

Such has been the history of abolitionism for the last few years Such is the history of abolitionism in its present stage. Such has been the history of abolitionism in the action of this convention. How well he understood their character this paragraph clearly shows. The effort upon the part of this convention at consolidation is so manifest, from the debates in the discussion of various questions, and from the acts of this body on various provisions incorporated in this constitution, that we are forewarned to look with fear and apprehension upon the consequences of such centralization of power as seems to be conceded to the federal government by the majority of this convention. This is but another step to that end.

There must be, I opine, some apprehension existing in the minds of gentlemen here that their work will not take so well with the people after all; and that therefore it is necessary to hedge them in, or to keep them out from the ballot-box, the great last refuge of the free man —not the last, I hope, but the great refuge of the free man; thereby to enable them the more securely to take the step towards centralization of power, as has been frequently indicated in the debate, and strongly indicated in some of the provisions of the constitution. It arises from a dread of a free people and a love of power. We should not forget that a free ballot, freedom of speech, and freedom of the press, as appeared to that great man, Jefferson, is formidable to tyrants only. They alone dread the effects of a free ballot, free speech and a free press. I am drawn to infer from the action of this convention—because I know it will be their conclusion, as we have been so advertised by a member upon this floor—that it is the operation of such apprehension that their work will fail to commend itself to the majority of the people of the State, which leads them to throw these restraints about the ballot-box, and prohibit the free exercise of that great right which I have been taught to esteem as a heritage inestimable in value, transmitted by a long line of ancestors, dating back to nearly two hundred years ago, and one which I had hoped to be able to transmit as a part of our constitution untarnished to those who may come after us.

[The twenty minutes having expired, the hammer fell.]

Mr. PETER. I regret that I was absent from

the convention last night during the debate on this first section. I must admit that I was not only surprised but disappointed when I first learned that such a proposition had been entertained in this convention. The question arises, under what law are the people in the State of Maryland now living, and under what constitution are they living? Can any part of the constitution which we now propose to adopt, in any wise or in any manner affect the people in this State until it is declared by the people of the State to be the constitution. If one part of this constitution can be made to affect the people of the State of Maryland before it is submitted to them, and before it receives a majority of the qualified voters of the State, why not at once declare it as the constitution of the State? If you can make one section of this constitution take effect upon the people of this State before you submit it to them, with equal propriety you can declare the whole at once the constitution and let it have all the force that you give to one part of it. What is the constitution under which we now live? Not the one we propose to adopt, but the constitution framed in 1850. It is the qualified voters of the State who now have the right to vote. Does any proposition or any clause passed by the legislature affect the old constitution? Will gentlemen in this house pretend to say that the last legislature could pass a law in direct contravention to the old constitution? Mr. President, I am astonished. What are constitutions made for? What are they? The constitution embodies the organic law of the State. The constitution as it now exists prescribes what shall be the qualifications of the voters of the State of Maryland. Even suppose that the last legislature had said in terms direct and explicit, that every man in the State of Maryland should be required to take this oath, have the legislature the power to destroy the constitution as it exists? Have they the power to destroy the fundamental law of the land?

I have been informed that men argue that they have a right to insert this test oath, because that is in the law under which the convention itself is called. Is there any court in the State of Maryland that would entertain a view of this kind? Suppose the legislature passes any unconstitutional law; how will courts treat it? I say that if the last legislature had said in terms as explicit and plain as they could have expressed it, that no man in the State should vote without taking this oath, no court would say that that law was constitutional. I assure gentlemen here that my people will stand by that constitution until it is set aside. The day is fast waning in the horizon when the rights of freemen can be trampled in the dust. The organic law of our land prescribes what shall be the qualifications of voters of this State; and I assure gentlemen that if I be the only man in my county, I will dare to approach the polls, and I will dare to say to those judges, here is my ballot under the law of my State, under the constitution as it now exists. I will dare further. If they refuse that vote I will prosecute them to the utmost limit of the law; and if there be no justice in the land outside of the courts, I hope there to bring them to justice, and I hope there to visit upon their heads that punishment which the law has prescribed, that punishment which they cannot escape from under the law which exists, of which this convention cannot alter one tittle nor one iota until it is approved by the people. And I believe that I am not the only free man in Montgomery county that will dare to adopt this course. I believe there are others there, greater than I am, yet who cherish the rights of freemen as dearly as I do, and they will dare to stand in the same place and assert our rights in the courts of the State as they now exist.

How is the organic law of this State to be changed? The law lays it down here that this convention shall assemble, that it shall adopt a new constitution, not a constitution to affect the people of the State of Maryland now, or that shall affect them in any time hereafter, until it shall first be submitted to the people, and until it shall receive the sanction of a majority of the qualified voters of the State. But before I dwell particularly upon that point I will make another.

If we have a right to require this oath, we have a right to require anything else. If this convention can incorporate into the organic law which they propose to the freemen of this State, an oath which must now directly bear upon the people of this State, why not at once require every man to swear that he will vote for this constitution, and say that unless he shall take that oath he shall not be permitted to vote at all? If they can do the one, they can do the other. I unhesitatingly say that any court of justice or any court of law will sustain me in this view. Why not say that no man, unless he is in favor of abolition, shall vote upon the constitution? If you propose to put anything of this kind into the constitution, which is to have any effect upon the people of this State, why not make it plain sailing? Why not cut all the timbers out of the road and make a highway for this party which seems to go upon the principle of rule or ruin? Why try to smoothe the matter over? Why try to cover it up with a little tinsel? Why try to give shape to that which has no shape, to give power to that which has no power, to give life to that which is dead and without life?

If we are to usurp powers here, and act out boldly and in defiance of the law and the constitution of this State as it now is, do not submit the matter to the people at all. Do not let us have a mere form of mockery; a form of godliness, I might say, while we deny its power. Sweep it out at once, and wipe your hands, and say the abolition party is the party of the State of Maryland, and no other man within the bounds of this State shall have the right to exercise that great privilege of freemen at the ballot-box.

Let us examine this law closely, which I understand gentlemen have relied upon for the power which they propose to exercise, the law calling this convention together; and let us see if it will bear any such interpretation.

In the first place, on whom does the requirement of the oath, as it is set forth in this call of the convention, rest? It does not rest on the voter of this State at all. I will refer to the fourth section :

"Sec. 4. *And be it enacted*, That before any member or officer of said convention shall enter upon the discharge of his duties, he shall take and subscribe before the governor of this State, who is hereby authorized to administer the same, the following oath or affirmation."

Does it say one word there to the effect that any man hereafter that may think proper to vote for or against this constitution, shall take this oath before he can vote? We must have had a grand set of fools in our last legislature if they could have supposed for one instant that they could have incorporated into this law such a complete violation of the constitution as it existed. I presume we had here men of some sense at least, who knew that in what they were doing they had no power to destroy the organic law of the State as it existed. The oath, as it exists in this law, was applicable alone to the members of this convention and its officers ; and to no person outside.

Having ascertained by the law to whom the oath was applicable as passed by the legislature, let us see what the legislature really did intend, and what they did do in the enactment of this law, which should have any effect upon the votes to be cast upon this constitution hereafter. That is to be found in the sixth section, which I will read :

"Section 6. *And be it enacted*, That the constitution and form of government adopted by the said convention as aforesaid, shall be submitted to the legal and qualified voters of the State, for their adoption or rejection, at such time, in such manner, and subject to such rules and regulations as said convention may prescribe; and the provisions hereinbefore contained for the qualification of voters and the holding of elections provided in the previous section of this act, shall be applicable to the election to be held under this section."

To understand the law properly we must take all its parts. We must not say that the sixth section shall have effect, and the first section have none. The sixth section refers to the "provisions hereinbefore contained for the qualification of voters, and the holding of elections provided in the previous section of this act." This refers back to the first section. Let us see then what the first section contains; because I think the legislature has made it so plain that the wayfaring man, though he be a fool, need not err therein.

"Section 1. *Be it enacted by the General Assembly of Maryland*, That on the first Wednesday of April next, at the same places where the polls are by law held in the several counties and the city of Baltimore, for the election of delegates to the general assembly, every person entitled to vote for delegates to the general assembly shall vote upon the question of the call of a convention to frame a new constitution and form of government, by expressing in writing, or in printed form, on the same ballot he may cast for delegates to said convention the words 'for a convention' or 'against a convention,' as the case may be," &c.

The only qualification in this first section then is that voters shall be "entitled to vote for delegates to the general assembly." I suppose gentlemen will say, "subject to such rules and regulations as said convention may prescribe." Has the convention any right to make any rules or regulations altering the organic law? Did the legislature of this State presume for one moment that this convention would attempt any such thing? No person dreamed of it; no person thought of it. It did not enter the mind, or cross the brain of one of the legislators who passed that law, that this convention would attempt to frame an organic law of this State to take effect upon the people of the State until it had been submitted to them, and until the legal voters, those properly qualified to vote for members of the general assembly, should have exercised the right to cast their votes for or against the proposed constitution.

Another question naturally arises in the minds of all of us. What are we to accomplish by test oaths? Whenever the morals of a people become so degraded, whenever a people are so debased that it is necessary to apply test oaths to them, to apply all the means that you can use, and put police detectives, and everything else around them, what are their oaths good for? If those oaths are for the prevention of crime, to have effect upon parties who but for them would be guilty of crime, would those parties regard the oath? If their morals are so debased that it would be necessary to apply test oaths to them, would they not be base enough to take the oath and to disregard it?

Mr. CLARKE. I hoped that some gentleman upon the other side would have been ready to speak upon the section now under consideration. I shall be very brief in the remarks which I shall make. I should not in fact now trespass upon the indulgence of the house, at this late stage of the session, except for the fact that I regard the proposition now before this body as more vital, more important, striking a deeper and deadlier blow at the rights of the people, than any proposition which has yet been submitted to the action of this convention.

This is not a mere question of the power of this convention; because when I approach that branch of the subject I think the power of the convention can be easily determined; but it is a question which affects the powers and the rights of the people. The people in 1851, on the theory that they were to assemble in the first place through their representatives to frame a constitution, and that the people then acting upon the principles of the social compact were to adopt the constitution, ratified the constitution under which we now live. That constitution secures to them, until they adopt another, all their rights, rights of property, rights of person, rights of speech, and the political franchise, the right of voting. Until that is altered, that is the watchword and the landmark of their rights; and there is no power, save the people's power, which can alter, which can modify, which can in any way affect the elective franchise, and these other sacred rights.

Has this constitution been changed yet? Is it changed before the people, by their vote, determine to change it? Surely it is not. This constitution, then, being the law, it defines the rights of the people. I will not read the provision, but it provides that every free white male citizen, having resided twelve months in the State, and being a citizen of the United States, shall be entitled to vote. It is said and argued by gentlemen on one side of this house, that it is not the constitution of the State to which you are to look, but you must look at the provisions of the convention bill; and that if this convention has this power under the provisions of the convention bill, then they have the right to prescribe this oath. I will not follow the argument of the gentleman from Anne Arundel (Mr. Miller) last night, to show that the provisions of this convention bill do not authorize the convention to prescribe such an oath.

The view I take of the power of the convention is this: This convention was called together to frame a new constitution or form of government. Was any power given them to adopt the organic law? Was any power given them to put the organic law, or any portion or provision of it, in operation? Not at all. The people were to vote on the question of the call of the convention to frame a new constitution or form of government by express writing or printing on the same ballot with the names of delegates. That was the sole power given, to frame the constitution; and therefore there was no power to adopt it. Hence, even if the sixth section requiring it to be submitted, had not been in the bill, this convention would have had no power to adopt it as the organic law of the State without submitting it to the vote of the people.

I contend therefore that the sole power of this convention is to frame, and after framing to submit it; and, further, I contend that the people in voting for or against the convention did not pass upon any provision in this convention bill; nor is the convention bill further the law of this body than of the people of the State. The convention has already decided that question. We have heard the gentleman from Baltimore city (Mr. Stirling) announce upon this floor, in regard to the first section of the bill, which says that "the legal voters of this State shall, by ballot, elect delegates to the said convention, whose qualifications shall be the same as those now required for a seat in the house of delegates," when State's attorneys and other officers are excluded from the house of delegates and occupy seats upon this floor, and have been decided by the convention to be entitled to these seats—the gentleman from Baltimore city announced as the political view of his party upon this floor that they did not regard the provisions of this bill as controlling the power of this convention.

Mr. STIRLING. No, sir; I did not say that. The gentleman must have misunderstood me.

Mr. CLARKE. I understood the gentleman to say that notwithstanding the provisions of the first section these gentlemen had a right to hold their seats here.

Mr. STIRLING. I said that even if the bill had made them ineligible, I would not then vote to turn any of them out; and I expressly waived that question there.

Mr. CLARKE. That is my argument, that by their action the gentlemen have practically assumed that position.

Mr. STIRLING. But I distinctly took the ground that those gentlemen were all perfectly qualified under the bill itself.

Mr. CLARKE. That being the sole power of this convention, to frame a constitution and to adopt nothing, I regard any provision which may be in the convention bill as entirely outside of the question; and we come now directly to the question, what are the rights of voters under the existing constitution of the State? That question is decided by the provision relating to the elective franchise. I hold therefore that this convention has no power to limit, qualify, alter, or in any shape to modify the provision which determines the right of the people of the State to vote upon the adoption of this constitution.

And I do it irrespective of the form of this oath. If the oath contained even the opposite of what is placed in it, and called upon the citizen to swear, "I have expressed my sympathy for the south, I have rendered aid and comfort," it would be equally obnoxious to me, because it would be a violation of the fundamental law and the rights of the people of the State. I attack it, independent of its provisions, because it is a violation of the rights of the people.

One word more in regard to what fell from the gentleman from Howard (Mr. Sands) last night, who contended that this was a case of civil war, and unless you put some such provision as this into this report, those who had left the State and gone into the southern army, in the event of an invasion of the State and the return of citizens of the State in the invading army, they would have the right to vote. I humbly conceive that that is not the case. Those who were formerly citizens of the State of Maryland, and who have left the State of Maryland and gone into the southern army, have abandoned their residence. Under the decision of the courts they have been declared to be alien enemies; and no one can pretend that an alien enemy can come here and vote. They have lost their right to vote under the decision of the supreme court of the United States; and no gentleman can contend for a moment that one who has gone into the territory declared to be in a state of warfare, and who has lived there, can come back and claim this right.

Mr. DANIEL. Is that your construction of the decision?

Mr. CLARKE. It is. It declares that every man in that territory is in a state of warfare with this government, and all that are there are alien enemies. The man residing there, whether loyal or not, is just as liable to be treated as an enemy, and his property treated as the property of an enemy, as if he were taken in arms against the government. It is a territorial war; and all within that territory are alien enemies. The decision is clear and plain. They have sworn allegiance to another government; and it is plain that they cannot claim to be citizens of Maryland. Hence there is no such necessity for this provision; and gentlemen really do not fear anything of the kind. The provision is directed, not against the armies fighting against the government, but against a class of men in Maryland, who have stood here and performed their duties under the constitution of the State of Maryland and the constitution of the United States; who have paid their taxes, borne the burden of the draft, and done everything which, as loyal citizens, they were required to do, save to bend the knee to every violation of the constitution of the United States, and to every dogma which is announced as a party dogma to be enforced in this State. It is done for the purpose of reaching that class of men who about the nineteenth of April were true, and desired to perpetuate the Union, who at that time, and I know many such, had southern sympathies, and were desirous of healing these difficulties, and thought there was only one way to settle them, by standing up and maintaining under the constitution their rights, who only saw that it could be done in that mode and manner. They did express their sympathies; but because they were true to their State, and the rights of property of the citizens, violating no law, is that any reason why they should now be disfranchised, because they have not supported this administration when they have seen such scenes going on, because they have not shouted hozannahs to those in power? Men who desired the preservation and perpetuation of the Union may have seen at certain stages of this controversy that if the other party had succeeded there would have been a death blow to the republican party; and felt that in that result there was more hope for the perpetuation of the freedom of the white citizens of this country. They may have expressed such views, and acted in good faith, desirous under the workings of Providence to accomplish a proper solution of our difficulties. Are they for a difference of opinion to be excluded?

Gentlemen may adopt this provision, but in my humble judgment if adopted, the action of the convention will not be authorized by any powers conferred upon them; and if they undertake to administer that oath, they will have no more legal power or authority, now that the present constitution is the rule of government, than if I were to administer an oath without any authority whatever. It is an illegal act; an act without authority. I do not know whether any such case will be tested or not, but if any one took the oath, there is no court of law, I believe, in the State, which would hold that he could be convicted under that oath for perjury; because judges have to swear to support the constitution; and this would be contrary to the constitution; not the constitution upon which the people are to vote, and which is not yet the law of the land, but the existing constitution. And unless the judges of election have power under the existing constitution to administer that oath, they are acting outside of their authority, and their act is null and void. Some may refuse to take the oath, if they think proper. Others may take it in good faith.—There are others probably who might not take it in good faith. But I say this, if they do take it, the result is that they are simply standing up and going through an idle form, which no court of law can recognize any authority for. I do hope that the people of the State will not be deluded by this action of the convention, undertaking without authority to impose such an oath.

The legislature admitted last winter that they had no right to impose an oath as a qualification for voting upon the question of the convention. And when the convention met here it was denounced on the other side of the house as unconstitutional, and it was said that you could not pass a law prescribing an oath as a qualification for voting upon the constitution. But it was arranged by some legerdemain to put language into the convention bill, which properly construed only entitles the judges of election to administer the oath which under the code and the constitution of the State they are now authorized to administer. It said that if any one put the question whether the person offering to vote had served in the rebel army, whether he had done this, that or the other, not that he should swear to this or that fact, but that he should put the oath under the section of the code; and the section of the code only authorizes the judges of election to put the oath as to their right of voting. The constitution determines the question of the right of voting.

I hope therefore, although it was necessary for me to say this in order to prevent this convention from exercising an unauthorized power, and placing themselves in that position, that if it is done the people will still hold on to this instrument, the constitution adopted in 1851, as the sheet-anchor of their rights; until by a vote of the people it is decided that that constitution shall be abolished, and another shall go into effect; and that they will claim all their rights and all their political franchises under this instrument, and trust to the courts and the authorities of the country. The country is now speaking through many standard-bearers, for the great rights of the people whom we have before us. Maryland this day assumes a new position in the struggle which is to take place. We have Fremont on the one hand, the standard-bearer of the political rights of the people at the ballot-box. We have another candidate, McClellan, representing another faction of the people, standing up for the rights of the people; and I believe, although his followers do not here in Maryland stand up for the rights of the people, even Abraham Lincoln will before the eighth of November. I believe he has already, so far as I have seen, countermanded this action of the military authorities, and that he will take that ground and will not dare to resist the power of the American people. I believe no power, no party, even with Abraham Lincoln at its head, will dare to resist the rights of free speech, a free press, and free political rights at the ballot-box. If any party on the eighth of November shall dare to come out and plant itself in opposition to these great principles, the American people will doom it to destruction and to annihilation.

Mr. Stockbridge. I did not quite understand one remark of the gentleman who has just taken his seat, whether he said McClellan and a "faction" of the people, or a "fraction" of the people.

Mr. Clarke. It is immaterial to me which you call it; they are all divided into fractions.

Mr. Stockbridge. I hope it will be a vulgar fraction, reduced to its lowest quantity, in a very few months.

I had not designed to take any part in the discussion which has sprung up on the question before the convention; but words so full of menace have fallen on our ears since it has been under discussion, that I feel that I should be false to those who sent me here if I should not offer a few words in reply. It does raise a great and important question; and I go as far as he who goes farthest to protect the ballot-box in its purity, to preserve the rights of the people under it; and that is the great thing which Union men have been struggling for in these United States for the last three years and a half. This whole infamous rebellion is a war upon the decision of the ballot-box, and nothing else. But yesterday, flashing over the wires from Chicago, comes another resolution admonishing us in advance of another war upon the decision of the ballot-box if the people shall dare to vote in such a way as to place the conclave there in the minority. Of that I may say a word before I conclude.

This report raises two questions in connection with the ballot-box. One objection brought against it is, that it allows those to vote who are not entitled to vote; and the other, that it deprives those of the privilege of voting who are entitled to vote. As I do not propose to occupy the attention of the convention more than once in reference to it, I beg leave to say a word upon the first of these propositions, although not now immediately before the house. It was discussed last evening by the gentleman from Anne Arundel county (Mr. Miller) and others. The gentleman in order to maintain his position is compelled to assume that when a man becomes a soldier of the nation he forfeits his right to vote. But, sir, soldiers as such do not cease to be legal voters. This section as reported by the committee says that any of the qualified voters of the State who shall be absent in the army shall have the right to vote. The legislature which passed the act under which we are sitting, and who refused to pass an act authorizing the soldiers to vote, never had any difficulty upon that point. They never supposed for an instant that a soldier ceased to be a voter by the act of becoming a soldier, and that when he placed his life at hazard for his country he forfeited the dearest rights of freemen; never. The difficulty arose on another point. If gentlemen knew anything about what passed, they would know more than they seem to know in the discussion of this question. The difficulty was this. The section reads:

"Sec. 1. Every free white male person of twenty-one years of age or upwards, who shall have been one year next preceding the election a resident of the State, and for six months a resident of the city of Baltimore, or of any county in which he may offer to vote and being at the time of the election a citizen of the United States, shall be entitled to vote *in the ward or election district in which he resides*, in all elections hereafter to be held," &c.

Hence it was argued that he had not the right, and that the legislature could not give him the right to vote anywhere, unless he actually deposited his ballot in the ward or election district in which he resided. That was the difficulty. I did not believe the objection a valid one, and do not now; but that was the grand bug-a-boo upon which certain gentlemen stuck, which defeated that action which would have given the soldier in the field his rights. But that legislature did give us the power to make provision for the soldiers, when they said as they did in the sixth section that the constitution should be "submitted to the legal and qualified voters of the State," the soldiers being included in that category, to vote "at such time, in such manner, and subject to such rules and regulations as said convention may prescribe." That has been ratified by the people who sent us here. I am surprised to hear certain gentlemen call in question the force of that decision of the people upon the question. Turning back in our debates to page 764, one gentleman (Mr. Chambers) uses this language:

"There could be no convention without the exercising of such a power on the part of the legislature. But they have not one atom of power beyond that. They can neither restrain the people in the choice of their representatives, nor can they restrain this body in the exercise of its legitimate power, the power to make the government what they please."

And thus he proceeds at great length; and again, on page 767, the same gentleman says:

"So I say here, when the constitution of the State directs the legislature to call a convention, if the people wish it, it confers upon them the necessary power, without which that could not be performed which is enjoined upon them. It conveys the necessary power to appoint time, manner, place of election, time and place of assemblage, &c. That being done, they may just as well undertake to control the winds that blow, as to control the action or power, either of the people in selecting, or of this convention in acting."

That is the law as it has been laid down here by one who acts with those whose opposition to the present section is so great. And that is all I propose to say, in the few moments I propose to occupy at this time, upon the powers of this convention. I say it is clearly the right of the soldiers to vote, and we have clearly the power to authorize them to do so.

Next comes the other question. Shall any person be excluded from the right? We are at this time somewhat singularly situated. We are a border State between two great sections of our country at war. Our legal position is with the national government. Hundreds of our men, natives here, are in arms, warring against the government of the nation, making predatory incursions into our State, robbing, plundering, bringing fire and sword within our borders. Have such men a right to vote? The gentleman who has preceded me (Mr. Clarke) has said that under the decision of the United States supreme court they have not that right. Pray tell me, how is it to be ascertained? Here is a man born in Maryland. In 1861 he joined the enemies of his country and did his utmost to uphold them, and for twenty-four months so continued. He is now returned and has been here twelve months. Admitting, for the sake of argument, that when he went over there it was with no design to return; that he went designing to make that his home. But now he has returned, and designs to make this his home. I ask any man to tell me, if this logic be correct, how it is possible for that man to be deprived of his vote, construing the phraseology of the law as you may? He is a native here. For the last twelve months this has been his home. What matters it where he was before that? How can you go back to the fact where he was or what he was doing? How does it appear that he was not a peaceable citizen of Ohio, Wisconsin, Minnesota, or Oregon, or that he was not with our army before Mobile, Charleston, or Richmond? Has he not, strictly construing it, every requisite for a voter, as the law stands upon the statute book? Can he vote? I say that it is not equitable and right; that you cannot allow him a vote without inaugurating civil war at the ballot-box. As a measure of precaution, it is not right that he should be allowed to vote.

Look at it. Remember what has passed since this convention commenced its sessions. Men here within the sound of my voice have had their pockets picked of their watches and their purses, their stables robbed of their horses, their corn cribs despoiled, their crops laid waste; and who has done it? We have places called Hagerstown and Williamsport, which have been bombarded since we have been staying here. Gentlemen may know that in the western part of the State there is a town called Cumberland. One fine morning in 1864, the commander of the United States forces received a note in these words:

"August 2, 1864.

"*To the commander of the forces in the block house:*

"You will surrender the block house and your forces at once. If you do not, you will not receive any terms.

"Bradley T. Johnson,
"Brig. Gen. Confederate forces."

And this Bradley T. Johnson, late chairman of the State democratic central committee of Maryland, if he is not now, is he to be allowed to vote? I cite him only as a more prominent actor in these scenes. Who commanded the rebel ram, the Tennessee? A Marylander, Buchanan. Who commanded the Alabama? The Marylander, Semmes. And who is now roaming over the ocean in the Tallahassee? The Marylander, Wood. Are these men to come back here and vote? I say it is our right and our duty to protect the ballot-box so that they shall be excluded.

I come to another point. Are these the only ones to be excluded? I refer in no spirit of unkindness to the gentleman behind me from Kent county (Mr. Chambers,) or to his grandson who has figured repeatedly in the debates upon this floor. I refer to it precisely as the gentleman has, as an illustration of a principle, and nothing else. That young man stands precisely in the category of those others. Now, the question is asked, he put it himself, shall he be disfranchised, deprived of the right to vote under this constitution, because he visited him and ministered to his wants when wounded and suffering? I beg leave to answer that question; and to say that that depends very much upon circumstances. If that young man joined the rebels who were warring upon our national government, and who came here to plunder our State, incited thereto by his venerable grandparent, and encouraged therein, and that grandparent giving him aid to accomplish this infernal purpose, then that grandparent is so far accessory to the act that he should be punished accordingly.

Mr. Chambers (interposing.) The grandfather tells you that he did no such thing. The young man for years had been a resident of the South, and I had neither seen him nor had correspondence with him. The gentleman talks about assuming a case for the sake of illustration. The gentleman has no right to assume a state of facts which are offensive.

Mr. Stockbridge. I believe on a former occasion the gentleman from Kent did state the facts which he now repeats; but it had escaped my memory. I shall refer to it in different terms. I will suppose that he had been residing in Kent county when the war commenced.

Mr. Chambers. You have no right to suppose it.

Mr. Stockbridge. I say, *suppose* that to have been the case, as it was the case with thousands, upon that hypothesis I will repeat every word I have uttered, because that is the case with many. But if that soldier wounded, if he had ceased to be an enemy, and was wounded and a prisoner, no one supposes for a moment that under the provisions of this article, he who administered to his wants would be any more obnoxious to any penalty than the surgeon who dressed his wounds, or the quartermaster who supplied his wants.—But there have been cases—we have known them—gentlemen here know them just as well as they know their own existence, where brothers and sons, fathers and grandfathers, have armed the hand that has been raised to strike the parricidal blow, have prepared the means with deliberate purpose and intent to pull down the pillars of our national edifice. I say that every right-minded man will concur with me that those who have done this act, inciting the young and more thoughtless to pursue this infamous course, are more guilty, more justly obnoxious, than those who have actually done the act and placed their lives in peril in doing it.

As I said at the outset, this is a war against the decision of the ballot-box which we want to maintain. It comes with very singular grace from gentlemen to be upholding and protecting the ballot-box with one hand, while with the other they wield the sword which shall destroy its decisions forever. I spoke of the resolution which came flashing from Chicago. I ask gentlemen to note its terms:

3d. *Resolved*, That the direct interference of the military authority of the United States in the recent elections held in Kentucky, MARYLAND, Missouri and Delaware was a shameful violation of the constitution, *and a repetition of such acts in the approaching elections will be held as revolutionary*, AND RESISTED WITH ALL THE MEANS AND POWER UNDER OUR CONTROL.

What does that amount to? Gentlemen talk about military interference. When? The gentleman whose seat is vacant here upon this floor to-day, (Mr. Jones, of Somerset,) is reported to have been sitting there at that time, and did not repel the slander. If there were any such interference, which is to justify this resistance hereafter to the decisions of the ballot-box if it should put us in the majority, it was either at the election in the fall of 1863, or at the election which sent us here. Was it in the election of the fall of 1863? Where were the contested elections of that year? It was easy enough to prove it. There was one sent here from Somerset county for adjudication; and how was it adjudicated? The very gentleman now holding his seat at Chicago (Mr. Jones, of Somerset,) was the very man who came here, and with all his influence and eloquence showed that it was a lawful and legal election. And where are the contested elections of this body? Gentlemen have talked here of military interference. Is not this convention law broad enough? Was there military interference in the State to justify this language? If there had been the judge was under obligation to send a certificate to that effect to the governor.

Mr. Stirling. They did in one instance.

Mr. PETER. In our county it was done, and a fresh election held.

Mr. STOCKBRIDGE. There was a fresh election in that district, and here are the men elected to represent that county. Then there has been no interference save in one election district, and that has been remedied, and here are the gentlemen as the result of it. Nobody has protested against it. Yet here is foreshadowed, and gentlemen's remarks this morning have foreshadowed precisely the same thing, their resistance if they happen to be in the minority, with all the means and power under their control? And what are the means and power under their control? Gentlemen will know, if they remember, that within the past few days, in Indiana, hundreds of thousands of rounds of fixed ammunition have been ferreted out, and thousands upon thousands of the best navy revolvers. These are some of the "means under our control" which are to be used in maintaining the purity of the ballot-box, and the fairness of elections.

I say then that the opposition to this article is not designed, and does not tend to promote the purity of the ballot. What is the pure ballot? Where the citizens of our State can declare their preference for the man of their choice. What did our fathers say when they formed their constitution, and how stood it in the constitution of Maryland always until 1850? They had no scruples on this point. They said in the convention of 1776:

"Art. 6 That the right in the people to participate in the legislature is the best security of liberty and the foundation of all free government; for this purpose elections ought to be free and frequent, and every man having property in and common interest with and an attachment to the community ought to have the right of suffrage."

They believed that an attachment to the community was essential to the right. But now men appeal to the bullet from the ballot. And then when defeated with the bullet also, they claim the right to appeal from the bullet back again to the ballot, and under conditions of their own dictation.

That same convention went further. Gentlemen say that we are tyrannizing. Let me read another order adopted in 1776 in this very hall:

"*Ordered*, That no person who has refused or neglected to subscribe to the association (unless from religious principles,) be permitted to come within the doors of this house during the sitting of the convention."

That shows the spirit of that day, when it was said, and said truly, that every man having an attachment to and an interest in the community, who designed by his vote to uphold the interest of the community, and he alone had the right to vote. But now men suppose that treason is to stand on an equal footing with loyalty to the laws and to the constitution of the country.

But, Mr. President, not only have we a clear right to adopt this as a means of self-defence, not only have we the revolutionary right, in the language of this resolution, and of members here, to meet revolution, if necessary, by counter-revolution, but we have at all times the right to maintain the government against revolutions. Men institute a revolution; appeal to bullets; and then complain if we do anything more than to fight. They set your house on fire, or come with the torch to do so, and then complain that you do not confine yourself to the legitimate business of pouring on water instead of striking down the hand that is applying the torch. Is there any doubt as to our right in this matter, that it is as much a duty to strike down the hand as it is to pour on the water? When all these great interests are at stake, we are bound to take efficient measures to protect ourselves against the repetition of these outrages. If gentlemen will resort to resistance "with all the means and power under our control," they can do so. I know not what effect it may have on others, but for one I am ready to meet whatever in that line may come.

SEVERAL MEMBERS. So am I; so am I.

Mr. STOCKBRIDGE continued: We have seen this resistance inaugurated. It is threatened now to be brought north of the Potomac and to be inaugurated elsewhere if the people shall presume to cast a majority of votes against the man of their choice. The instances which we have witnessed for the last few months, even while assembled here, and in our own State, show that all is fair and right if we get the majority, and all is wrong and a shameful violation of the constitution and to be resisted, if we fall into the minority. If that be the ground, let it come.

Mr. CUSHING moved the previous question.

Mr. MARBURY. Will the gentleman withdraw that motion for a few moments? There is one statement I want corrected.

Mr. CUSHING. I will withdraw the motion if the gentleman will renew it.

The CHAIRMAN (Mr. Daniel.) The gentleman from Prince George's (Mr. Marbury) had the floor before the motion for the previous question was seconded. The gentleman can proceed.

Mr. MARBURY. The gentleman from Baltimore city who has addressed the convention (Mr. Stockbridge) attempted to show this convention that in the various elections held in this State for the last two years there had been no military interference, and said he had not heard of any military interference whatever. Now I will inform him that at the last November election, which elected the legislature of which he was a prominent and distinguished member, at that election, in my own county, a company of military, under the command of Colonel Baker, a government detective and general military superintendent for our county, came down to our county seat, and was there until a late hour in the evening, and issued his order that no one should be allowed to vote there unless he took the oath—I do not know who framed it—an oath stuck up there and presented to everybody.—Hundreds of persons just as loyal as the gentleman himself, men who never did a disloyal act in their lives, and who never contemplated such an idea, men as perfectly pure and spotless as the gentleman himself, came to that town to offer their votes at the polls; and they were met with this oath and this military interference. Capt. Watkins, of the eastern shore, captain of another military company, remonstra- with Colonel Baker and his party; but Colonel Baker being the superior officer, he yielded to him. There was a committee of gentlemen appointed to go to Washington and investigate the affair. They were detained there until a late hour in the evening of the day of election, and when they returned they said it was without order.

When I went up to vote fifty soldiers stood in front of the polls, who stood there the whole day. I went up and offered to vote. They said "You will have to take the oath." I said, "There is nothing in your oath that I object to; I don't care what it is. I don't care what you put there on that subject; I would just as lief take one oath as to take another; but I am opposed to taking any oaths. You have no right to come here and require this oath." The captain, I will do him the justice to say, replied, "I agree with you. I am a Massachusetts man, but I agree with you. We have no right to put such oaths. But I am a soldier, and it is on my orders. Do you blame a soldier for doing his duty?" I said, "No, I do not." I put this question to the captain: "Captain, these judges here are sworn to execute the law of the State. That is their duty. Do you blame the judges for doing their duty?" He said, he did not. He wished that his orders were not the paramount orders, but he had to obey his orders.

I give this as an illustration to show that there was military interference. I know of a number of gentlemen here who can give a great many instances of that sort.

There is another subject which has been introduced here. It has been said over and over again, upon this floor, that there have been demagogues and conspirators in the State of Maryland. I have seen nothing and heard nothing coming from the minority like the appeals made here about the prisoners from the federal army held in the South. It has been said that they are dying inch by inch, and that the cruelty and barbarity that has been practiced upon those unfortunate men have never been equalled in the history of the world.

The CHAIRMAN (Mr. Daniel.) That is not in order.

Mr. MARBURY. It is a branch of the subject which has been introduced into this debate, and I wish merely to reply to it.

The CHAIRMAN. It is not germain to the subject under consideration.

Mr. MARBURY. Perfectly. I want it to be understood, Mr. President, that I have as much sympathy for those unfortunate soldiers as any man living.

The CHAIRMAN. The gentleman will come to order. The question under consideration is the amendment offered by the gentleman from St. Mary's (Mr. Dent,) to the second section with regard to administering the oath to voters.

Mr. MARBURY. With all deference to the judgment of the chair, I will say that the gentleman from Howard (Mr. Sands) alluded to this branch of the subject, and I wish to reply to that.

Mr. BRISCOE. I will make one suggestion to the chair. The whole subject-matter before the convention is one which appertains to the obstruction of the ballot-box, and we regard the imposition of this oath an obstruction of the ballot-box. The gentleman was discussing it in that connection.

The CHAIRMAN. What has the treatment of our prisoners in Richmond to do with the freedom of the ballot-box?

Mr. STIRLING. I move that the gentleman be allowed to proceed.

The CHAIRMAN. The gentleman may proceed.

Mr. MARBURY resumed: I was going on to say that I have as much sympathy with those soldiers as any man living. It may be true that they have suffered all that has been represented. I regret most deeply that it is so. It may be that they have been dying inch by inch. It may be that they have been brought here starved to death and not properly clad. That may be all so. But there is another side to the picture. If you will go to the captain of the boat that conveys these prisoners to and from City Point, he will tell you that comparing the miserable condition of those that go North with that of those that go South, so far as he is able to judge, it is identically the same.

Mr. PUGH. Who is the captain of that boat? I ask for information. Will the gentleman give us the authority for his statement?

Mr. BARRON. What is the captain's name?

The CHAIRMAN (Mr. Daniel.) The gentleman is entitled to the floor and must not be interrupted.

Mr. MARBURY resumed: The prisoners who have gone South have suffered all that they have suffered, and I regret it most deeply. But whose fault is it? That is the point. Who is to protect the citizen soldier? To whom shall he look for protection? Does he look to Jeff. Davis? Does the soldier of the United States federal army look to Jeff. Davis for protection? My God, sir, he is the man of all others whom he should last look to. He looks to his own government—to the power and duty of that government under the constitution to protect him. And, sir, tell me why it is, that those soldiers have lain so long in these dungeons of the South? It is because the secretary of war, with that arbitrary despotic power which he wields, has refused to enter into proper negotiations for the exchange of prisoners. One of the very first causes of this difficulty was the introduction of slaves into the army of the United States. It was said over and over again—it was said by the secretary of war and by some of the best military men in this country—it was said by some of the head men in the army, by some generals and major-generals, over and over again, and by governors of States throughout the North, that if you put negro slaves into the federal army to fight against the South you will raise the black flag. There will be no quarter shown—there will be no mercy to prisoners—there will be none of the considerations of humanity influencing these people. That was done contrary to the advice of all these gentlemen—contrary to the advice of some of the first intellects of this land. It was done, and the consequences that they predicted followed. It was seen that the man who had heretofore been merely considered as property in this country, who had not been put upon an equality with the white man, who had received all the benefits that the white man could bestow upon him, and who was still going on to receive these benefits, so far as he was capable of improving under them, was not in a condition at this time to be put upon an equality with the white man. It was denounced in the North as well as in the South. If the responsibility rests anywhere for the treatment of these prisoners, in my humble judgment, it rests with the administration of this government. They are responsible for it. Let them enter into proper negotiations. Let them consider the rights of the soldier. Let them place proper guards and protection around him. Had they done this, the exchange would have taken place long ago. Why should they have stood upon a punctilio? Why should not they have said, release these men at all hazards? I see only one reason. I may be wrong, but I can see no other. It was necessary to get up a hue and cry at the North. The war-fever was waning. Hopes for peace were springing up throughout the country, and everybody was anxious about peace. It became necessary to get up a hue and cry to arouse the spirit of the North, to revivify and invigorate the war feeling, and the only way that it could be done was by letting our soldiers stay down there suffering and dying inch by inch, to be heralded all over the country, and to be pictured in photographs. The telegraph was called in to carry the news that our soldiers were dying inch by inch, and then the photograph was resorted to to send their pictures through the country, and thus it was heralded through the North, and it had its effect. Did the poor soldier need to go down there—the poor prisoners who are dying inch by inch—that it should have aroused the spirit of the North? That the men who have risked their lives, property, and everything, and been made prisoners, should be made sufferers in order to make capital out of their unfortunate condition, I conceive to be unpardonable. Yet, in my humble judgment, that is the only conceivable construction that can be put upon the course pursued by the administration of this government which will in any conceivable degree justify their conduct. I think when these facts are thoroughly understood and demonstrated, we shall never hear anything more of this inhumanity and barbarity.

I intend to pass no eulogy upon these southern people. I intend to pass no eulogy upon anybody. But when I see that my country is going wrong, when I see that they are leading us to despotism, that they are exercising usurped powers, I consider it to be my duty to raise my humble voice in opposition to any such measures. As to the oath that is proposed here, I have on another occasion given more in full my views upon that subject. I have before stated that you might pile up your oaths as high as heaven, and they should never stand between me and my duty as a citizen of this State. I will resort to all honest, honorable and constitutional means in my power to enable me to secure my rights at the ballot box. I hope and trust that the people of the State of Maryland will not be intimidated, but will put their mind to the subject, and see that it is nothing more than a trap to drive off all who happen to be opposed to the party that is now ruling the State.

The gentleman from Baltimore city (Mr. Stockbridge) has alluded to something fiery that he said had come from the Chicago convention. Whatever that Chicago convention may do, if it is done by the advice and by the deliberative action of those true democrats of the north who have stood up for State's rights and the people's rights, through sunshine and through shade, through stormy and through peaceful times, I shall give it my hearty vote, and my hearty concurrence. These are men they have nominated who were in some respects objectionable to us. One of them has in former times exercised arbitrary power. Let bygones be bygones.

Mr. Abbott. I call the gentleman to order.

The Chairman (Mr. Daniel.) The house has allowed the gentleman to proceed.

Mr. Abbott. No vote was taken.

The Chairman. If the gentleman insists upon it, the chair must rule the speaker out of order.

Mr. Cushing. Other gentlemen will desire to go into the same discussion.

Mr. Stirling. I move that the gentleman be allowed to proceed.

The motion was agreed to.

Mr. Marbury resumed: I was about to say that at one time the gentleman who now seems to be the standard bearer of the democratic State's rights party of this country might seem to have been somewhat identified with this doctrine of arbitrary power, arbitrary arrests, &c. But if that was the case, he was then a subordinate officer. He was not exercising his own sense of justice. He was doing as the soldier of Massachusetts told me he was doing, obeying orders; and I do not blame men for obeying orders. But that gentleman now standing on the broad basis of his own rights, taking a wide survey of the whole field, seeing how the State's rights doctrines loom up as the true constitutional life-giving principles of the country today, is not a man shackled by foreign power, but he stands by the principles of constitutional liberty, and it is our duty, in my humble opinion, to give him our hearty and cheerful support.

Mr. Abbott. Is not he an officer in the army yet?

Mr. Davis, of Charles. I call the gentleman from Baltimore to order.

Mr. Marbury. Whether an officer of the army or not, that we can make him President of the United States is a fixed fact, if we give him our hearty support, just as certain as anything under heaven. I will give an illustration of it. I heard of a vote taken down in the navy yard—I do not know how many gentlemen were there, sick and wounded—and only about seventy of all that were there were not McClellan men, and those seventy said they were for McClellan but were afraid to say so. Now that is my experience of the army. I have seen a great many soldiers about Washington, and almost all of them are for McClellan. With his Napoleon spirit, his love of liberty, when he obtains the power to act freely, to act for himself, the first thing that he will strive to remedy will be the enormity of the acts of the present administration, in its unconstitutional interference with the rights of the citizens of this country.

Mr. Briscoe. I desire to say a few words upon the subject before the convention. And first I desire to say incidentally in reply to the gentlemen from the city of Baltimore (Mr. Stockbridge,) who seemed to have a holy horror of the effects of one of the Chicago resolutions, that the men who passed that resolution are constitution-loving men, and law-abiding citizens; and some of them from the State of which the gentleman himself is a native (Massachusetts.) When they said they would avail themselves of all their powers and means to protect the ballot-box, they meant they would avail themselves of all constitutional modes of protecting the ballot-box.

Mr. Stockbridge. They did not say so.

Mr. Briscoe. I wish to God I could say as much for the gentleman from the city of Baltimore. I wish to God that I could today say as much for the members of this convention, that they were prepared to stand by the constitution of their State, and willing to allow every man within its limits to vote, as that constitution says he has a right to vote, without any restriction. The democratic party sanction no such test oaths as are intimated in this section. They regard them, and have regarded them in all time past, in the language of a distinguished man, as "the first weapons that young oppression learns to handle; weapons the more odious that they are barbed and poisoned, requiring neither strength nor courage to wield them." I tell the gentleman from Baltimore, and I tell the majority of this house, that I would have more respect, and I believe the majority of the people of Maryland would have more respect for a constitution written by the pen of a military commander at Washington, or ordered by Secretary Stanton at the head of the war department, to be the organic law of Maryland, than for a constitution which shall demand of them this odious unconstitutional oath, this odious test that you here apply to the citizens of the State.

I say that it is grossly unconstitutional. I took that position in the Senate of Maryland when I opposed the incorporation of the oath in the bill which called you together. The constitution of the State unquestionably tells you in the plainest language, who is to be a voter at all elections to be held under it. One of the highest legal authorities of your land, Chief Justice Story, from whose commentaries I read, section 624, said:

"It would seem but fair, reasoning upon the plainest principles of interpretation, that when the constitution established certain qualifications as necessary for office, it meant to exclude all others as prerequisites. From the very nature of such a provision, the affirmation of these qualifications would seem to imply a negative of all others. * * * * * A power to add new qualifications is certainly equivalent to a power to vary them. It adds to the aggregate what changes the nature of the former requires."

You have as much a right to say that any man who has been a drunkard for the last six months, shall not be entitled to the right of suffrage at the coming election, as to say that he shall not vote without taking this test oath.

Again, in section 627, Judge Story says: "The people of the State by adopting the constitution have declared what their will is as to the qualifications for office. And here the maxim if ever must apply, "*Expressio unius est exclusio alterius*."

I had hoped that this convention would have permitted its work—a work of such grave and solemn importance—to go to the people of Maryland apart from partisan considerations to the decision of their free unstifled voice. But they fear that if they do so, if they leave this work to the decision of the free people of Maryland at the polls, they will tear to shreds the work of their hands, and reject it. They know that they do not even represent a respectable minority of the 90,000 voters of the State of Maryland. If a man who has read and seen what has transpired in the State of Maryland for the last two or three years does not know that, I have very little hope of his ever learning anything in the future.

As to what the gentleman from Baltimore city says in regard to the statutes passed by the State of Maryland striking at disloyalty, striking at men whom they conceived to be untrue to the country, he read a statute from the laws of Maryland, passed I believe before any constitution of the State of Maryland had been adopted. I call the attention of the gentleman to the fact that the men who passed that statute had no organic law, and it does seem to me from the course these gentlemen are pursuing, they have forgotten that they have such a thing as a constitution binding them in the State of Maryland.

We know the purposes of this. I tell the convention that they may do this work; they may submit this form of government to the people; but there is a higher authority, a sober second thought of the people of Maryland which will undo their work, and treat with contempt any effort emanating from any source to throttle the free expression of their will. You may pass this proposition, and the vote may be called in Maryland. You may, as you did upon the call of this convention, by your unconstitutional test oath, exclude forty thousand high-toned and conscientious men from the ballot-box. But there is a day of freedom to come. I thank God that the military arm of the government which intervened at the call of the legislature which brought you here, which made you; which gave you life and being, cannot live forever in this land. There is a returning day when the forty thousand disfranchised men of Maryland will speak in thunder tones and tear your work into shreds and scatter it to the four winds of heaven. If we could have had the opportunities that you had, without the restriction of the oath, we could have spoken with some degree of power. I tell these gentlemen that there is still power in the public voice, and the will of the people which, when peace and calmness comes upon the land, will return the judgment upon them.

There was a time, in 1856, when your State was lashed into a boiling cauldron by another element of proscription, that of the Catholic, by a war raised against that religion. And some men, floating upon that turbulent wave that had been lashed into fury by the storm, came to your legislative halls. They went back, and they never were heard of until another storm came, and again they are here. But they may see the hand writing on the wall These men who have been raised up, floating on the current, in the turmoil of the hour, will disappear (as the bubbles that children blow for amusement, before the returning sound sense of the majority of the people of the State of Maryland.

You may ask for military power to come here and aid you; you may arm your organizations of plug-uglies, or any other such clubs or associations, to give you temporary power at the ballot-box, but in vain. The people of the State of Maryland, thank God, love liberty, and will have it. They will have it in spite of your convention, in spite of the interference of the military, in spite of all obstructions. It will come sooner or later, and I warn these gentlemen. It has been said in the language of scripture that it is a fearful thing to fall into the hands of an offended God. So I tell some of these gentlemen, that so far as human punishment is concerned, it is a fearful thing to fall into the hands of an outraged and offended people. You may pursue this course; you may violate justice; you may perpetrate outrages; offences against the law and in violation of personal liberty may be committed; but the end will some day come.

A very few years ago, under the despotism of Austria, there was a man whose name is given to infamy and scorn for all time to come, Haynau, the Austrian butcher. He violated the sentiment of the civilized world. He violated the principles of liberty and justice; and what was his fate? I thank God that it was the privilege of a great American statesman to arraign him before the bar of the civilized world for his injustice and his butchery. He went, sir, finally, home to his infamy. And why? Because he violated the instincts of human right and human justice. He violated the instincts of mankind. And if you by your action here, violate the principles of justice, you will feel, sooner or later, the scorn and contempt of the civilized world.

I said last evening that I came to this convention with very little hope of accomplishing anything. I did not even participate in the sanguine feelings of some of my friends that we should be able by our intercourse with gentlemen of this convention, in their introducing the measures that they term reform, to produce this result, at least that it should not be that repulsive sort of reform which overrides all common justice. I did not participate in any such hopes. I had seen that the mandate had gone forth from the city of Washington, emanating from the President, following up his enunciation at Springfield, that this country could not stand divided, but must become all one thing or the other. In a few months after his inauguration he issued his proclamation telling the people of Maryland that this work is his peculiar work, and that it had been the philosophy of his life and must be accomplished. I happened to be in your legislative halls at that time. I resisted it then. In a very few months I saw the standard of abolitionism raised in Maryland. It hoisted its banners and called on the people, but in a few months after, on the 10th of March, 1862.

(The allotted time under the order, twenty minutes, having expired, the hammer fell.)

Mr. THOMAS. I had intended to say nothing on the subject before the convention; and I have sat quietly in my seat this morning and listened to sentiments, emanating from men of Maryland that have actually made my Maryland blood boil in my veins. The gentleman who has just taken his seat proclaims to this convention that he came here expecting nothing, and that he goes away not disappointed. In my humble judgment he could not have paid a higher compliment to the majority of this convention than when he uttered that sentiment. He expected nothing. I came here to abolish slavery; and thank God, my vote has helped to do it. I came here to rid the State of Maryland from this curse of slavery, because just such men as the gentleman who has just taken his seat had used the slave power to bring upon us the very troubles of which we are now endeavoring to rid our country. He thanks God that there is a time of vengeance that is to come.

Mr. BRISCOE. Not vengeance. I did not use that word.

Mr. THOMAS. At the time when the avenger comes, he will meet you and me, and give us our deserts. An outraged and indignant people will meet us at their bar of judgment, and they will mete out to us our deserts. What have we done, that an avenging God and an avenging people are to visit upon us the violence of their wrath? Have we deprived men of their liberty? We came here to give men liberty; and we have given it. Have we deprived men of their rights? We came here to give men their rights; and we have done our duty, thank God, nobly. In so far as the avenging judgment of God is concerned, I have an approving conscience in me that tells me that I have done right; and I can stand before the same bar of God and render up an account for the deeds that I have done, alongside of the gentleman from Calvert (Mr. Briscoe.) And in so far as standing before the bar of the people is concerned, I have got the same nerve to meet whatever fate the people choose to award to me as he has to meet the fate awarded to him. Threats coming from what quarter they may, cannot intimidate me in the honest discharge of my duty.

This constitution is to be submitted to the vote of the people of Maryland. I for one will never give my vote that that constitution shall be submitted to the disloyal people in Maryland. I want a loyal constitution. I have endeavored to make a loyal constitution. And so help me God, if the lightnings of heaven shall strike me down when I utter it, or if the knife of the assassin is to drink my blood hereafter because I have uttered it, no rebel, no man in armed rebellion against this government, no man who sympathizes either directly or indirectly, or who has given aid, comfort or encouragement to those in armed rebellion, shall by my consent ever vote upon this constitution. Am I right? If you are to have blood, drink in your blood. If you are to have peace, meet me half way and have peace. But am I to have peace when my brother has been murdered in cold blood by those hell-hounds who first brought on this war; desolating my happy home? And because gentlemen who dare to get up on this floor and express their sympathy for these men are not to be allowed to vote, that is sufficient cause for vengeance to be meted out to me.

Gentlemen have said here this day what I thank them for. They have said that George B. McClellan was their candidate. I am glad of it. The speech of the gentleman from Prince George's (Mr. Marbury) was made for the ears that will soon hear it, to be carried along to them at their camp-fires, to ask them to vote for this noble patriot. All I have to say to the soldier is to take up the speeches of the opposition of this convention, who have been giving their sympathy to those in armed rebellion; and then put alongside with them their indorsement of George B. McClellan, their adhesion to him as their candidate, and their determination to support him; and then let the soldiers consider upon how many battle-fields they have fought, how dearly their brothers and companions have spent their lives, what desolated homes and firesides they have left; and if they can then vote for the candidate that these gentlemen will vote for, then my confidence in Maryland soldiers is gone.

Gentlemen take exception to the test oath as to the adoption of this constitution, and say that the soldier has no right to vote for it. The more honest and brave of them tell us that they want the soldier to vote for their peace candidate. The soldier is not good enough to vote for your constitution, but he is good enough to vote for George B. McClellan. I had intended not to say one word upon this matter; but I would respectfully refer gentlemen to the speech of their own representative, delivered in this peace convention which nominated this pure patriot, whom they will now support, and see what Mr. Harris, of Maryland, said there about him. Here is his language:

"One was nominated here to-day who is a

tyrant! He it was who first initiated the policy by which our rights and liberties were stricken down. That man is George B. McClellan. Maryland, which has suffered so much at the hands of that man, will not submit to his nomination in silence. His offences shall be made known. This convention is a jury appointed by the people to pass upon the merits of the public men whose names would be presented for the support of the great democratic party. General McClellan, I repeat, is a tyrant. He stood here to indict him."

"Mr. Harris proceeded to say that General McClellan was an assassin of States rights, a usurper of our liberties, and if nominated he would be beaten everywhere, as he was at Antietam. He added that he could not go home and ask the members of the legislature of his State to vote for such a man. He would not himself vote for him." [Hisses.]

Yet that man, the tyrant and usurper in Maryland, is going to receive the support of these gentlemen; and soldiers wearing the uniform of the United States government, which is denounced day after day in this hall in unmeasured terms, are asked to support him.

All I have to say in conclusion is, that my work in this convention is nearly done. This is perhaps the last time that I shall utter my voice in this convention, except to vote upon these propositions. I give my vote for this section with the same feeling that I gave my vote in support of the declaration of emancipation. I gave it with a full determination that I was doing what was approved by my conscience and by my God. I gave it with a determination that those who shall come after me when this war shall have been ended, and peace shall have been brought back once more to this now distracted land, will honor me for it. And if I am to die, be it sooner or later, be it the death of a martyr, or be it any other death that Almighty God may ordain for me, I shall never regret that I have not only voted to allow Maryland soldiers to vote to adopt this constitution as the organic law of the land, but that I have voted to prevent every man who is in sympathy with, or who has given any aid, comfort or encouragement to those in armed rebellion against the government of the United States, from voting either in favor of or against the adoption of this constitution.

Mr. STIRLING. I desire, Mr. President, to express some views upon this proposition that is before the convention; and as the time is short, I will endeavor to confine myself to the question of authority which has been raised in the debate by gentlemen who have addressed the convention. I will merely observe in commencing that it certainly strikes me with some surprise that gentlemen can profess, in the first place, their entire loyalty, and the entire loyalty of their constituency, and then declaim, as they have declaimed here, against the effect of these obligations, even so far as to make the statement that they will disfranchise 40,000 of these very people that they loudly claim to be loyal patriots, highminded, and honorable gentlemen.

The gentleman from Prince George's (Mr. Clarke) has alluded to this subject. He has not been so specific with regard to general political matters as the gentleman who preceded him, and I may almost express the hope, from the very fair course he has pursued on several occasions, I may at last have the privilege before the presidential election, of standing upon the same platform with him in the support of Mr. Lincoln, for I recollect his saying once before that he should prefer him to either Fremont or McClellan. I do not know whether he has changed his views on that subject as he did upon the question of representation according to population.

I will merely allude to the gentleman from Calvert (Mr. Briscoe) now, as to the "hereafter" with which he threatens us, to say, that, so far as my people are concerned, we think *this* is the "hereafter." I will reply to him that the loyal men of Maryland have got past the day of their evil things, and the gentlemen the day of their good things; and I can say to him, in the language of scripture, as was said to the rich man after he had lived in purple and fine linen, and gone to the abodes of the damned, "Thou hast had thy good things, and likewise these people their evil things; and now they are comforted, and thou art tormented." [Applause and laughter, promptly suppressed by the President.]

What is the difficulty? Gentlemen say that this constitution can have no force until it is adopted. So far as relates to its permanent provisions, I admit that it cannot, until it is adopted, and the time arrives at which it goes into effect. But I declare the doctrine laid down by the gentleman from Kent (Mr. Chambers) in his speech last night, and the doctrine laid down by the gentleman from Anne Arundel (Mr. Miller,) that a proposed constitution must be submitted to the same constituency which elected the convention, is a doctrine that is not sustained either by the law or by the fact. I propose to prove that it is neither law nor fact. There are a great many constitutions, as they are contained in this book of "Constitutions," which do not give the provisions under which they were submitted.

Mr. CHAMBERS. I hope you do not attribute that doctrine to me?

Mr. STIRLING. I understood the gentleman to say that the same law which directed who should vote upon the convention, directed who should vote upon the constitution.

Mr. CHAMBERS. No; it had reference to

Maryland. I knew that in Virginia they had enlarged the vote, and had admitted the vote so enlarged.

Mr STIRLING. The gentleman makes a qualification which helps my argument; but I did not so understand him.

Mr. DAVIS, of Charles. I merely wish to understand the gentleman's argument. Does he mean to say that when the question is submitted to the people with regard to the calling of a convention, instead of submitting the constitution which is formed to the people for their action, they can make it valid by their own act?

Mr. STIRLING. No, sir. The power must come from the people, and if there is an understanding that it is to be submitted to the people, of course it must be submitted to the people. What I deny is that it must be submitted to the same identical constituency which elected it. The gentleman has alluded to Virginia. I will read what the constitution of Virginia says on this subject:

"And such officers"—alluding to the officers who are to open the polls—"keeping said polls open for the space of three days, shall then and there receive, and record in said poll-book, the votes for and against this constitution and schedule, of all persons qualified, under the existing or *amended* constitution, to exercise the right of suffrage."

The convention of Virginia recognizing the fact that they were bound to submit that constitution to the people, allowed the vote at that election of men who, under the existing constitution of Virginia, were not allowed to vote, and to whom the provisions of the amended constitution were about to extend the right of suffrage.

Now turn to the constitution of Tennessee. That is still stronger. The ordinance provides, "that no person shall be deemed a qualified voter in said election except such as are included within the provisions of the first section of the fourth article of this amended constitution."

Where are we to get constitutional law, if we do not get it from the practice of the States? The provisions of the constitution of Texas are almost identical, so far as I can see, with these. And they are the only provisions mentioned in this book to which I am referring.

We all know that there is a process to be gone through. The legislature provides for holding the convention; but the convention derives its power from the people to amend the constitution. Every matter which is necessary to put the constitution into force prior to its adoption, everything which is necessary to regulate the election under which it is to be adopted, is immediately in the power of the convention. So far has the doctrine gone in this country, that it has been claimed time and again that when the people desired a constitutional convention, they had a right to elect a constitutional convention, and that the convention could declare the constitution in force without submitting it to the people; and this was sustained by the authorities of the United States in regard to the State of Kansas.

I say that we are not bound under the laws of this State, under the doctrines of American constitutions, or under the peculiarity of this reforming process where a convention has at least *quasi* sovereignty, to submit the constitution to the same constituency of the country. I admit that this is a high moral power which ought to be exercised with great caution and a high sense of responsibility. But there is no sense in which this convention is absolutely bound, as a matter of law, to submit the constitution to the identical people who voted upon the convention.

Suppose that they were. What does this constitution undertake to do? It disqualifies nobody from voting except upon the ground that they have put themselves under such circumstances in point of fact as to disqualify them from the exercise of what the law gives them. And I say that even if we were bound to submit it to the same constituency, if we had no right to prescribe other qualifications, we have a right under the state of things now existing, to impose such a condition as to make those offering to vote prove that in fact they are entitled to cast their votes.

The gentleman from Calvert (Mr. Briscoe,) a little while ago, made some reference to the practice in this State, and said, I believe, that at the time a certain statute was adopted, there was no organic law in this State. That is not the fact. The people of this State in the year 1778 were acting under the constitution of 1776. That constitution goes on to declare that every freeman that possessed a certain amount of real estate or personal property should be entitled to vote for members of the house of delegates. Yet that constitution was passed during a state of civil war. It was passed at a time when a portion of the people described under that section, and holding the requisite amount of property, did not acknowledge the government that had been set up, but acknowledged their allegiance elsewhere and sympathized with the public enemy. What did the legislature do? Not at constitutional convention called to prepare a constitution in 1776, but the general assembly in 1778 acting under the constitution of 1776? They expressly say that every person up to a certain age shall take an oath of allegiance, and that any person who refuses or neglects to take that oath of allegiance shall never vote at any election thereafter to be held in this State. The constitution of 1776 provides:

"The house of delegates shall be chosen in the following manner. All freemen, residents of this State, above twenty-one years of age, having a freehold of fifty acres of land in the county, and having property in the State above the value of 30*l.*, having resided in the county one whole year preceding the election, shall have the right of suffrage in the election of delegates from the said county."

But then comes the act of 1778 of the legislature, "that every person chargeable with the triple tax as aforesaid," having refused or neglected to take the oath of allegiance, shall be disabled from doing certain things, among which is voting at any election of senators or delegates.

Now suppose this state of facts. Suppose that the constitution says that every man possessing certain qualifications is entitled to vote. Suppose there is an actual armed rebellion going on against the State government, and that there are in the several counties of the State men actually in arms against that government, endeavoring to tear down the constitution, and to usurp the executive power. Will any man pretend to tell me that because the constitution says that every man twenty-one years of age and possessing certain other qualifications shall be entitled to vote, that men in arms are entitled to lay down their muskets by the side of the ballot-box and put their votes in the ballot-box?

Mr. Briscoe. What right has the judge to reject them?

Mr. Stirling. The judge of elections may have no right to reject them; but the *people* can stop them from voting; and that is exactly what the people of 1778 did. They said that allegiance and protection are identical, and while the struggle goes on, and even after this war is concluded, if you do not acknowledge your obligations to this government, but sympathize with the public enemy, you are not in a condition to exercise the right of suffrage. Suffrage implies acquiescence in the result of the ballot; and if a man simply wishes to use the ballot-box as a machine to aid an armed revolution, he is not in a condition to vote, any more than the insane man in the hospital. If he does not hold himself amenable to the authority of the government, it does not concern him, and he is not in a condition to exercise the right of suffrage. All these provisions are simply to ascertain, in this civil tumult, the state of fact in which a man is.

Whom does it disfranchise? People talk about sympathy. The word "sympathy" is not in the law. It disfranchises men in arms against the government; men whose active agency is in fact in various ways an aid to these men. What sort of a position should we hold, if we did not exclude them? Is it not a matter of fact that there is an army seeking to invade this State, and that it is one of the hopes of that army to take this State out of that relation to the United States which its own constitution recognizes? Is it not a matter of fact, that a portion of the people of this State sympathize with that army? Will any man tell me that if the army of Jeff. Davis succeed in this State, this government would not supersede the actual government of this State in twenty-four hours after they get here? I say that the man who only waits until the army of his friends comes here to tear down this constitution and form of government and erect it into a form of government subordinate to a foreign nationality, the man who stands ready to aid the public enemy, and does not do it simply because he is too lazy to do it, is waiting to tear down the very ballot-box that he asks to place his vote in; and is in such a position that he can only mean to use his ballot for the purpose of cowardly, treacherous assassination against that which he does not dare to raise his arm against.

It excludes no man who is willing to submit, no man who is not in the position of a public enemy. He must not have expressed a desire for the success of the public enemy. Does a man want to vote under a government when he desires the enemies of that government to succeed? Does a man want to elect a governor when his desire is that an army may come and turn that governor out of his seat? Does a man want to vote for a constitution when he wants an enemy to come and aid him to tear down the constitution?

If people do honestly desire the preservation of this constitution and this form of government, as a constitution and form of government of a State of the United States, if they do not want it torn down by force, if they do not desire the success of the public enemy, what disqualifies them? This is but a provision for the ascertainment of that fact. And it is no more dishonorable for a man to take the oath, than to be searched when a pocket book has been stolen and a suspected thief is to be found. We make no discrimination. We call upon everybody to take this oath. We purge the whole community. We take it ourselves. We ask everybody to take it. I say that it does not injure anybody's feelings. I do not know where it applies, nor do I care; but I say that the man who refuses to take that oath, either refuses to take it because he is at heart a traitor, or because from a misapprehension of his own rights he does not understand the position in which he is placed.

I want to say one word with regard to the soldiers' vote. I do not see how any proper objection can be urged against it, because it does not, as my colleague who has addressed the convention (Mr. Stockbridge) has shown, either admit any new class of persons to vote or exclude any old class of persons from voting. These people are qualified to vote. It is a mere question of fact whether there shall be authority of law to enable them to vote, to provide a place where they can cast their votes. This convention has authority to take the sense of the people of this State upon the adoption of this constitution. That is a broad power, a power to be exercised not technically but liberally; in such a manner as to ascertain the true sense of the people of the State. In point of fact and in point of law a large part of the voters of this State are in the service of the United States and out of the State. Any submission of the question to a vote, which does not take their sense of it, does not take the sense of the people of the State. It was upon that ground that I argued last winter that the legislature possessed this power. I held that even if the legislature could not give the soldier the right to vote out of the State at our State elections, that under the power given to the legislature to take the sense of the people in regard to calling a convention, which was not a strict technical power, but a power to be exercised upon broad constitutional principles, and which the legislature could not fairly exercise unless they did take the sense of the soldiers. They could authorize the soldiers to vote on that question. I never claimed that it was clear as a mere question of law to allow soldiers to vote at all elections, but I confined my bill expressly to allowing them to vote upon the call of the convention.

It has been a very grave question of doubt whether the legislature has not a right to provide for the vote of the soldiers at any election. I admit that the decision of most of the courts is against it; but no court has decided that the soldiers may not vote for or against a constitution. That is always to be taken liberally; and I hold therefore that under the constitution as it now exists we have the right in taking the sense of the people to provide for taking the sense of the soldier. I think there cannot be any misunderstanding about it. It is not a question of attempting to enfranchise unqualified persons. They are all qualified under the constitution. The only difficulty is that from their situation they cannot get their votes into the ballot-box; and this is simply a provision for the purpose of enabling qualified citizens of Maryland to vote.

Mr. SMITH, of Carroll. The objection to this report upon the part of the minority appears to be two-fold; first, to allowing the soldiers in the field to vote, and the other, to imposing an oath upon voters. In the discussion of the question before the convention a great latitude has been indulged in. We seem to have resolved ourselves into a committee for stump-speaking; and I suppose I shall not be violating precedent if I take part in that discussion. My friend from Calvert (Mr. Briscoe,) last night or this morning has cited Henry Clay as an evidence against the party now in power. He has cited his testimony against the terrible effects of the accession of that party to power, and claims that the prophecy which he uttered has been faithfully filfilled. I am not here as an advocate of the republican party. I do not belong to it. I have been a whig all my life; and whenever I have departed from the straight path of whiggery, it was only because I thought I could do more to aid in breaking up the worst party in the world, the democratic party. But I say the democratic party have no right to take on their tongues the words of that glorious patriot, Henry Clay. He was their victim from his first entry into public life down to the day of his death, hunted down by the whole party, and especially by that unfortunate, feeble old man in Lancaster, who is now shunned as a leprous man by every one who feels that he has a moral principle in him. I say that whatever Henry Clay may have said with regard to the abolition party who would have abolished slavery without reference to forms of law, Henry Clay has never put on record any testimony in favor of the old party called the democratic party, but he has again and again denounced it, and his whole life was one witness against it. And he said something better than the gentleman has quoted, and he sustained it by the whole course of his glorious and beautiful political life, that if the time should ever come when there should be two parties in this country, one for the Union and the other against the Union, he had no hesitation on which side he would array himself, for under the dear old flag of his country he would stand forever. [Applause, promptly suppressed by the President.] I trust there will be no demonstrations of this kind during my remarks.

If he were living to-day, he would stand just where the gallant Douglas stood when he found there were two parties, one for the Union and the other against the Union, one loyal and the other traitor.

What has this democratic party done? They say that the abolition party of this country has brought on the war. I deny it. I say now, as I said before, that it arose from the acts of the democratic party, when they arrayed themselves against this Union. I believe it as firmly as I believe in the existence of an all-wise God, that on the democratic party of this country, as it is now organized, rests the terrible and eternal responsibility of all the blood that has been spilled in this war. It is referred to an arbitrament to which I am willing to leave it. It is referred to history; and history will do them justice. What are the democratic party now doing? Clamoring for peace. At Chicago they have presented a platform and a candidate; a peace candidate with shoulder-straps and a sword by his side; a peace candidate opposed to arbitrary arrests, who arrested and imprisoned our noble legislature at Frederick; a peace candidate, unwilling to interfere with our erring sisters, anxious to bring them back, driving them to the walls of Richmond on paper, and retreating down and clinging to his gunboat on James river all the while. He is indeed the peace candidate in one sense; it has been suggested with a great deal of force and propriety, that he never did the rebels much harm, and therefore ought to be regarded as a peace man.

As the gentleman from Baltimore city, who has just taken his seat, has said, this is a general and comprehensive proposition. It applies with equal force to us and to the gentleman upon the other side. It makes no discrimination. It does not allow men to do as has been done in previous elections, select out some individual against whom they have some enmity, and for the purpose of exciting him and perhaps preventing his voting, challenge that man. But it makes every man take the oath. What oath? An oath of allegiance to the government of the United States. An oath to protect this government which protects them. If I entertained in my heart the sentiments which I know are rankling in the bosoms of men in my county and throughout this whole State, the blush of shame would mantle on my cheek, and I should feel like a felon if I should dare to offer to vote in the State of Maryland. They have no sympathies here. Their prayers rise to high heaven for success to the rebel army. They look with delight on conflagration, to see the fiery figures of flame dart up in the air, destroying the homes of our own citizens, and kindled by rebel hands. They look upon it, in the shades of night, while it makes thousands homeless, and they feel that there is music in it. The constitution can be violated in every letter and in all its spirit by Jeff. Davis and his minions, and they are satisfied. Yet if Abraham Lincoln departs one scintilla from its provisions for the purpose of protecting the government and preserving it from destruction, he is to be arrayed before the world for all time as a tyrant and a usurper.

After all, how much better is General McClellan. If the gentleman who represents the first district of Maryland in Congress is to be believed—and will any man tell me that he is not—he says, and he says truly, that he cannot go home to Maryland and ask his constituents to vote for the man who drove the Maryland legislature out of their seats. But says the gentleman from Prince George's (Mr. Marbury) he acted then as a subordinate. Where is the evidence? He acted on his own authority. His whole life shows that his heart was at first engaged in this contest; and if he had listened to the speech of gentlemen to-day he might well say in the language of Henry Clay, "God save me from my friends;" for he is put in the same category with that most execrable Don Carlos Buell, who said, while he wore the shoulder stars of a major-general, that he had no heart in this contest. I believe George B. McClellan is made of better stuff than that. I believe he has fallen into the hands of men who are using him for their own base purposes. I believe that let alone he has a high, generous, honorable nature; but I do not think he has the material in him to crush out this rebellion; and I would rather trust it to the powers that be. I believe that those who nominated him desire his election. I believe his election will be promoted by federal defeat. I believe as a necessary consequence therefore that those who desire his election desire a federal defeat.

Ought any man in this loyal State of Maryland to be permitted to vote who does not support the Union? I find no fault with gentlemen for entertaining sympathies with the south if they choose to do so. I find no fault with gentlemen for disagreeing with me on that subject; but if a man has them he must keep them within his own bosom. He has no right to contaminate the purity of the ballot-box by testifying practically to his treason to this government.

Now as to the vote of the soldiers. Last winter, when this discussion was going on in the senate, I looked on, and considered the subject, and took a great deal of interest in it. I heard the gentleman representing Baltimore city in the senate, nobly and patriotically impress upon the minds of the senate his views upon that subject. Who is more entitled to vote than the brave soldier in the field? Why do we retain our privilege of voting? Why are we not driven away from our homes? It is because they have bared their breasts against the bullets of the foe.—Leaving all the endearments of life, they have perilled their lives on the altar of their country for our advantage; to sustain the Union and all that makes life beautiful and holy.—Why should not Bradley Johnson, general commanding in the forces invading our State, be permitted, pistol in hand, to vote according to law? He is only temporarily absent, discharging a high public function in the south. A renegade Marylander, leading a tatterdemalion host of renegade Marylanders, he appears before Cumberland, and demands the surrender of our American flag on the penalty of utter annihilation. Yet that man, unless we restrict the vote, is just as much entitled to vote as I am. It is a proposition upon its face and its terms utterly absurd, that we should permit it. No man has a right to vote, and no man should be permitted to vote who does not believe in the supremacy of this government, and whose heart is not in the maintenance of its integrity and in the suppression and crushing out utterly and forever of this foul and accursed rebellion.

Mr. Briscoe. I should like to know upon what authority it is said that a man who comes within the provisions of our present constitution, unless he takes the oath of allegiance, is not entitled to vote in this State.—Has any court so decided? But if they do not pay any more attention to the oath of allegiance down in the army than up here, it will not do any harm. I have said about all I desire to say. I shall vote for the amendment with great pleasure.

Mr. CHAMBERS. One word, Mr. President; although I do not intend to take any part in this electioneering debate which has been carried on here, not being in the category of gentlemen one side or the other. As long as they choose to occupy the stump I shall listen to them certainly with pleasure. The last remark of the gentleman from Carroll (Mr. Smith) amused me exceedingly. The gentleman said what, if he had been on the stump, would have been a most appropriate thing, but which could hardly be called a constitutional argument, with which alone we have anything to do. McClellan is before the people, and Lincoln is before the people—no doubt about that—and one of them is to be elected. Give them a fair field; that is all I want. Let them be who they may, and let their politics be what they may, give them a fair chance.

In the mean time I have something to say about the State of Maryland, upon a subject that seems to have been lost sight of for some time. The argument which I had the honor to submit, has not, in my humble judgment, been met. I stated the language of this oath to be such that it would embarrass men whose conduct was as free from reproach as that of any man on this floor or any man elsewhere. The only sort of an answer that I have heard is that of the gentleman from Howard (Mr. Sands,) that that is a matter of interpretation. It is not denied that the language does include such individuals; but it is answered that individuals must judge for themselves; that it is a matter of interpretation. Now I wish to submit this question to the majority of this house. I wish to submit it to any gentleman who wishes to deal fairly with the people of the State; to deal fairly, not with traitors, rebels, prisoners in the armies, and all that sort of thing, but with honest men, with an honest purpose; with loyal men who have always been loyal. If there are doubts in the phraseology of this oath, calculated to embarrass men. who do not wish to see how near they can come to an obligation which the words might embrace, or how near to a violation of their conscience they can come by an oath, if that is the case, why not put into the oath language which does not leave room for interpretation? Gentlemen know how to frame these matters. They have here stated that no man shall be permitted to vote unless he swears that he has never given aid, comfort or countenance to any one who has been in the rebel army.

Mr. STIRLING. No, sir; it does not say that. It is no one in armed rebellion.

Mr. CHAMBERS. That is the interpretation. Why not put it in the language?

Mr. STIRLING. I have; just as well as I can express it.

Mr. CHAMBERS. Here it is; to be administered to any person offering to vote:

"I do swear or affirm that I am a citizen of the United States, that I have never given any aid, countenance or support to those in armed hostility to the United States," &c.

Mr. STIRLING. Now I will ask the gentleman to explain whether a man lying wounded and sick in a hospital is in armed rebellion, or in armed hostility to the United States?

Mr. CHAMBERS. A man who has been in armed rebellion is as much in this category, in my judgment, as if he were to-day unwounded and unimprisoned. I want to know what sort of "aid, countenance or support" is contemplated. A man to-day in prison receives from me one hundred dollars in money to add to his comfort. He is exchanged to-morrow, and the next day is in arms against the government of the United States. Gentlemen may raise their hands and stare their eyes as much as they please; that is the very language: "I have never given any aid, countenance or support to those in armed hostility to the United States." I understand that to mean to any one in armed hostility to the United States. Did I not give aid and comfort in the case supposed? Is not he in armed opposition to the government? Is not that the language of the oath? You know how to put it in terms that lead to no difficulty. Why not do it?

But I rose now to say that I heard with the most infinite amazement, the assertion made upon this floor that the elections had been conducted in the last election without military interference. That any man with eyes in his head and ears to hear should rise and take the responsibility of making that assertion is to me a matter of amazement. I do not profess to know in many districts in the State what occurred at the election; but so far as I do know there was inspection at every district. I make this assertion, and it can be proved by as respectable testimony as can be furnished to prove any fact on oath, that in my county not only did military interference prevent men from voting, but the military made the proposition to individuals. If you will vote for the gentleman who is now in power and has control, you may vote the balance of the ticket as you like. Yes, sir; by military men such an offer was made; you may vote provided you will vote a given ticket. Does any man pretend to say he does not know that the member of congress in our district would not have received, if a fair vote had been allowed, one vote—I was about to say in ten—scarcely more than that? And yet here we are told that there was no military interference.

But even that perhaps would not have induced me to leave my seat if the gentleman from Baltimore city (Mr. Stockbridge) had not thought proper to introduce an illustration in terms very offensive, without the least shadow of fact upon which to base it. The gentleman must be aware that the terms of an illustration should always be consistent with the character and deportment of gentlemen, and not offensive. After noticing my illustration of the language of this oath, asking if it would exclude me from voting, and stating the peculiar facts of my case, the gentleman replied, by saying, that if I had furnished money, if I had advised my grandson to unite with the Southern army, and all that sort of thing, producing a case very contrary to any shadow of foundation in truth, then I was to be excluded. All I have to say is that no gentleman has a right to put such a supposititious case involving facts offensive to the moral conduct of an individual. It is a liberty which no gentleman has a right to take; and of which I only rose upon the present occasion to say that it was without the slightest foundation in point of fact I do not mean to argue this question. I have said what I thought about it.

We have heard from the gentleman from Baltimore city last up (Mr. Stirling) some authority upon another subject. These conventions of other States are held, as ours is, by virtue of acts of assembly. They are held by virtue of provisions of which I know nothing, and the effect of which I cannot argue. It is the opinion of a large majority here, it is intimated but I hope it is not so, that the legislature in passing the convention bill and the people in confirming it, imposed obligations to the full extent of its provisions. If that be the doctrine—it is not mine; I only argued it last evening as obligatory upon those who had advanced it here—we must first know what the acts of assembly of Virginia and other States authorized to be done. If the Virginia legislature in providing for the action of the convention authorized them to extend the right of voting—a very probable fact, which I have not had an opportunity of investigating—if that was done, there is no parallel about it; because our legislature have expressly said that before this constitution shall have effect it shall be submitted to the people; whereas, after taking an oath to support the present constitution, and after the people have indorsed the declaration of the legislature that this is not the constitution and does not supersede the other until it is submitted, we are here making it obligatory as part of the organic law of the State.

That is the difficulty, and I do not see how the gentlemen can possibly escape it. They say the law is obligatory; that the people have imposed obligations upon us through that law. The law says that the constitution shall not go into force until it shall be submitted to and passed upon and approved by the people. If so, it is, as I remarked, a dead letter until then. If it be a dead letter until then, how can you give it vitality in these two most important particulars, one of which lessens the number of those who constitutionally now have the right of voting, and the other of which gives authority to vote to those who never had it before? This is not the constitution before it is confirmed. According to your own account you have taken a solemn oath to regard the existing constitution until this has superseded it, and it cannot supersede it until it is submitted. I have heard no answer to this argument.

With regard to the argument made last night by the gentleman from Baltimore county (Mr. Ridgely) as to the proper interpretation of the act of assembly which called us together, the gentleman certainly made the very best of his case. But as shown by my friend from Anne Arundel (Mr. Miller) it was only a specious case made by arguing a part of the law. The law is that the qualified voters, the persons entitled to vote, shall vote at the time, those persons entitled to vote shall vote at the place, those persons entitled to vote shall vote under the regulations which this body may adopt. Will any philologist, any lawyer, any logician, stand up here and say that to regulate a thing is to put it aside, create it anew, and change it altogether? That is not regulation. To regulate a thing is to control a certain particular object. That particular object must remain to be controlled, to be managed, to be arranged, or it is not regulated at all. It does not propose to decide who are the voters. The constitution decides who have the right to vote. Those people are to vote; and the convention are to regulate other matters with regard to those people. I do not object to that. I do not deny your power to do that.

That is my view of the case; and I do not see how the argument can be avoided. I have not heard any attempt to refute it. If the argument of the gentleman from Baltimore county could have been sustained, and if this could have been brought within the power of this body by the convention bill, those who take that theory would have been justified. Will any man on the face of the earth stand up here and say that the authority to appoint time and place and regulate the manner of voting, is authority to make a rule to decide who are the constituency to vote? I will only say that I will not believe that there is a man in this house unprejudiced and unaffected by party sympathy, undisturbed by the peculiar condition of our affairs, who would take that view of the question. I cannot believe that there is a man who in a calm moment would entertain a doubt upon the subject. Certainly I do not.

Mr. Dellinger moved that the convention take a recess.

Mr. Ridgely asked and obtained leave of absence for to-morrow morning.

Mr. THOMAS asked and obtained leave of absence.

The convention then took a recess until half-past three o'clock, P. M.

AFTERNOON SESSION.

The convention reassembled at half-past 3 o'clock, P. M.

The roll was called, and the following members answered to their names:

Messrs. Goldsborough, President; Annan, Audoun, Baker, Barron, Belt, Billingsley, Blackiston, Brooks, Chambers, Clarke, Crawford, Cunningham, Cushing, Dail, Davis, of Charles, Davis, of Washington, Dellinger, Dent, Earle, Ecker, Edelen, Galloway, Greene, Hatch, Hebb, Henkle, Hollyday, Horsey, Johnson, Jones, of Cecil, Kennard, King, Lansdale, Lee, Marbury, Markey, McComas, Mitchell, Morgan, Mullikin, Murray, Nyman, Parker, Parran, Pugh, Purnell, Russell, Scott, Smith, of Carroll, Smith, of Dorchester, Smith, of Worcester, Sneary, Stirling, Stockbridge, Swope, Thomas, Todd, Turner, Valliant, Wickard, Wilmer, Wooden—63.

LEAVE OF ABSENCE.

Mr. WICKARD. On yesterday I asked leave of this convention to be absent until this morning, but the vote was rather equivocal, and I declined going last evening. I now ask leave to be absent until to-morrow morning.

Leave was accordingly granted.

SCHEDULE.

The convention then resumed the consideration of the report of the committee on the schedule, which was on its second reading.

VOTE ON THE CONSTITUTION.

The section under consideration was the following:

"At the said election, the vote shall be by ballot, and each ballot shall describe thereon the words 'for the constitution,' or 'against the constitution,' as the voter may elect, and it shall be conducted in all respects as the general elections of this State are now conducted. The judges of election shall administer to every person offering to vote, the oath or affirmation prescribed by this constitution, and should any person offering to vote refuse or decline to take said oath, he shall not be permitted to vote at such election, but the taking of such oath or affirmation shall not be deemed conclusive evidence of the right of such person to vote; and it shall be the duty of the return judges of said city and of the several counties of the State, having counted the votes given for or against the adoption of this constitution, to certify the result thereof in the manner now prescribed by law, accompanied with a special statement that every person, who has voted, has taken the oath or affirmation prescribed by the constitution; and the governor upon receiving such result and ascertaining the aggregate vote throughout the State, shall by his proclamation make known the same, and if a majority of the votes cast shall be for the adoption of the constitution, it shall go into effect on the first day of November, eighteen hundred and sixty-four."

The pending question was on the motion of Mr. DENT to amend the section, by striking out the following words:

"The judges of election shall administer to every person offering to vote, the oath or affirmation prescribed by this constitution, and should any person offering to vote refuse or decline to take said oath, he shall not be permitted to vote at such election, but the taking of such oath or affirmation shall not be deemed conclusive evidence of the right of such person to vote."

Mr. BILLINGSLEY. When this test oath, as reported by the committee on the elective franchise, was under consideration, and was amended on motion of the gentleman from Baltimore city (Mr. Stirling,) it was my intention to have addressed the convention upon that subject. But after the honorable gentleman from Baltimore city (Mr. Stirling) had concluded his argument, the previous question as usual, was called and sustained by this house, and I was denied the privilege of speaking.

I regret that the honorable gentleman from Baltimore city has thought it his duty to introduce that amendment, which has now become part and parcel of the constitution, as passed under the article of elective franchise. I regret it the more, because having served with that honorable gentleman in the Senate of Maryland, and having realized through his aid and liberality the success of some very important local measures before that body, I entered this house with the most kindly feelings toward him. And although I felt that at that period he entertained very mistaken, and as I thought dangerous, views in regard to the powers of the federal government, yet I had hoped that time, with the horrors of this sanguinary struggle, and the present condition of our bleeding country, had made some changes or modifications in his opinions. And exercising, as he does here, all his talents and his abilities, and a most important influence upon the deliberations of this body, I did hope that it would have been his pleasure as also his duty to have introduced some measure or measures looking to a compromise of our difficulties, and the bridging of this unfortunate chasm, and the healing of the divisions by which we are surrounded. In this hope, and in this expectation I have been doomed to disappointment.

I find that that amendment, which went much farther than the report of the committee on elective franchise, has been made the ground-work upon which has been based another provision contained in this report of the committee on the schedule, and which is more objectionable than the oath which was incorporated in the article on the elective franchise. That was but the beginning of the end.

Now, so far as I am concerned, I am free to confess here that I did not enter this convention with any political prejudices. I did not come into this convention for any other purpose than to make such an organic law as would be acceptable to the people at large. It was the remark of a heathen philosopher, and it is applicable to the present day, "*Sci se tuum.*" I know that of all the problems presented to the human mind, that is the most difficult of solution. The scriptures tell us that "the heart of man is deceitful above all things, and desperately wicked." So far as regards my own individual feelings and wishes, I came here under the impression I have always entertained in regard to these political exacerbations, political excitement, political vituperation and political prosecution. And were I to-day in the same position with the honorable gentleman from Baltimore city (Mr. Stirling,) in this convention, I assure you that I would be guilty of no act which would be calculated to oppress my fellow citizens.

In all governments, from the very foundation of society to the present period, changes and mutations have taken place. And there never has existed a government even anterior to the light of revelation, but what it was the duty of the ruler as well as of the citizen to adhere to the principles of that government. And whenever there has been a departure from the established laws of the land, from the established organization of any government, you will find that is has always sooner or later eventuated in revolution. If we take for instance the history of Rome. It was founded by Romulus. It was a legal government, and under five successive reigns it flourished and advanced in power and conquest, and everything connected with the peculiar organization of that government. But upon the accession of Tarquin, when contrary to every principle of justice and every principle of morals, there was an outrage offered to a Roman matron, in the conduct of Sextus towards Lucretia, what was the consequence? It eventuated in the dowfall of Rome, and the expulsion of the Tarquin family from the kingdom. It was an immaterial point, it is true, in the history of Rome, as compared with the peculiar organization under which it has succeeded and flourished. But when we take into consideration that it was an outrage to an individual, to a female, we will recollect that Brutus took the dagger all reeking with blood, and swore that it should never be returned to its scabbard until the liberties of Rome were achieved. And then it followed that the kingly government of Rome was abolished. And so it will be with any free government.

Here we have lived under a government of equal laws, and equal justice, and equal rights. Here we have been taught to believe that eternal vigilance is the price of liberty, and that public men and public measures were the legitimate subjects of criticism. Does it follow, of course, because we do not believe in the policy of this government, because we do not believe that that policy is calculated to advance the interest and prosperity of the country in which we live—does it follow that we are rebels? Does it follow, as a necessary consequence, because we do not sustain the government in all its acts, do not sustain this convention in all its outrages, that we must necessarily be rebellious? Does it follow that because we believe you have done us injustice, that you have deprived us of that which did not belong to you, but which was ours by all the guarantees of the laws and the constitution of the country; because we cannot sustain you in all these acts of outrage, does it follow that you are to pass test oaths here, by which you are to perpetuate your power, representing as you do but one-third of the population of this State; perpetuating your power by putting oaths to us which are offensive, which are contrary to the constitution and laws of the land, and which are contrary to the very principle of the very law under which this convention is assembled.

Why do you propose to embody this test oath in your constitution, and to make it a part of your constitution? Why do you require the citizens of Maryland to take that oath before the constitution has been submitted to the people for their ratification or rejection? What does the constitution of the State of Maryland, under which we are living, say in regard to this oath? It says that we shall true allegiance bear to the State of Maryland, and support the constitution and laws of the United States. What was the oath embodied in the article on the elective franchise? That you shall bear true allegiance to the State of Maryland, and that you shall support the laws and constitution of the United States. Was not that enough? Was it necessary that the law should be retrospective, that it should look back? What says Mr. Lincoln's amnesty proclamation? And yet under this provision, if any man comes back to Maryland who has been in the Southern army and takes the oath of allegiance to this government he is not entitled to vote. If any gentleman in the city of Baltimore was found on the 19th of April, 1861, under the excitement of the moment, with a musket upon his shoulder for the purpose of driving back, as he believed, the invaders of the soil of Maryland, can he consistently take this oath? And any man who has ever professed any sympathy with the government across the Potomac, who at any period of his life has expressed any sympathy or feeling in their behalf, no matter what may be his feelings and opinions now, he is precluded by this oath. Can any man who had done this, whatever may be his position now, no matter what may be his situation now, no matter however desirous he may be for the restoration of the government, can he under this test oath, under the oath of this schedule, be allowed to vote?

And do you intend, do you desire to impose such restrictions upon your fellow-citizens as that? It is contrary to the principles of the Christian religion. [Laughter.] You may laugh, but it is nevertheless so. When our Saviour came upon earth, for what did he come? He came for the purpose of proclaiming peace, and repentance and confession of your sins. And if you will come and confess your sins, God is faithful and just and will forgive you your sins, and cleanse you from all unrighteousness. But according to the theory of this test oath you cannot purge yourself. How are you going to purge yourself? You impose this oath to be taken before you submit the question of this constitution to the people of Maryland. It does seem to me to be the strangest thing that ever happened.

The gentleman from Baltimore city (Mr. Cushing) said that he gloried in having voted for the act of emancipation. And having gloried in voting for the act of emancipation, as I presume you all do who voted for that act, you deny to those whom you have robbed of their property by that act of emancipation the right of passing upon that act——

Mr. BARRON. I call the gentleman to order.

The PRESIDENT. The gentleman will state his point of order.

Mr. BARRON. He has called us robbers, and I won't stand that.

The PRESIDENT. I do not suppose the gentleman meant anything personal.

Mr. BILLINGSLEY. Certainly not.

Mr. BARRON. He says we have robbed him. I do not think he has lost a cent—not a copper.

Mr. DAVIS, of Charles. I hope my friend from St. Mary's will take his seat if he cannot speak without interruptions.

Mr. BARRON. I will interrupt him when he calls us such names as that.

The PRESIDENT. The gentleman from Baltimore city (Mr. Barron) will not interrupt the gentleman from St. Mary's.

Mr. DAVIS, of Charles. Then I ——

The PRESIDENT. The gentleman is out of order. The chair will protect the gentleman from St. Mary's (Mr. Billingsley) in his rights, without the interposition of the gentleman from Charles (Mr. Davis.) The chair does not suppose the gentleman meant anything personal. He will proceed with his remarks.

Mr. BILLINGSLEY. What I say here I say politically. The gentleman from Baltimore city said that he gloried in his vote upon the act of emancipation.

Permit me to say that, so far as it regards the abstract question of slavery, I can see that any man may be honest in whatever opinions he may entertain upon that subject. I deny to no man the right honestly and conscientiously to entertain his opinions in regard to the abstract question of slavery. He may look upon it as a sin. He may look upon it as a foul stain upon the statute book of Maryland. He may look upon it as a cancer upon the body politic. He may look upon it as the cause of perpetuating the war, and he may even think that the destruction of slavery may be the means of bringing to us peace and tranquillity, and restoring the government. But how any gentlemen entertaining these views can deny to me the right to compensation is to me a very different question. You take away from me my vested rights—my rights under the constitution—the rights which you have heretofore protected—rights which I had every reason to believe would be perpetual. And after having taken them away then you deny to me, believing, as you say you do, that those rights were an injury to the government and to the State, you deny to me the right to compensation. I do think that this is a most singular and extraordinary proposition—that you can take away my property and yet not compensate me for it. Yet this you have done.

And now by this test oath you deny to me the privilege of testing this question before the people. I do not say that you have deprived me particularly, but you have deprived those men who are conscientious in regard to the oath itself, and who perhaps, under the operation of this oath, it being retrospective, might feel some conscientious scruples in regard to taking it, although they are as desirous as any man in this convention of having this government restored, with all the rights of the States as they were before the separation, and the constitution as it now is.

When we passed the bill submitting the question of a convention to the people, it was distinctly and emphatically expressed in that bill that the whole constitution should be submitted to the people.

The PRESIDENT informed the member that his time had expired under the rule.

Mr. AUDOUN. I had not intended to say anything at all upon this question. Nor should I feel it my duty to do so now, but for the fact that I have seen from the first day of the session until now a determination on the part of the minority of this convention to vote against every measure calculated to assist the government. But for that I should still be silent.

They protest against this and that clause of this and that report. They protest most particularly against allowing the soldiers to vote. I ask, why not allow those to vote who have been fighting for their homes and our homes, for their country and our country—men who have been baring their breasts to the bayonet to preserve our rights—men to whom we owe the fact that our State has so far been protected from the horrors of war? Yet we are told that they are not entitled to vote. Have they lost all their rights and privileges by doing as they have done? Or is this objection raised because it is believed that the soldiers will cast their ballots for this constitution and thereby indorse the work of this convention and assist in burying this damning institution of slavery so deep that it will never be heard from again in our State?

I call upon the majority of this body to exercise the power given them by the people. Let every one of their votes be cast for this and every other section in this report. Let it go forth and thereby gladden the hearts of those men to whom the whole people of this State owe a deep debt of gratitude. The whole effort of the opponents of this report is against the men who have been bearing aloft the old starry banner. The cry of "law," "law," is raised to arouse hatred to those men because they are soldiers in the armies of the United States. So far as I am concerned, I tell gentlemen that I intend he shall be allowed to vote who has been willing to lay down his life for his country, and that he who is not willing to take the oath prescribed in this constitution, and thereby give some evidence of his attachment to this Union, shall not be allowed to vote.

I desire to say further, that if the friends of the Chicago convention want bullets instead of ballots, as was said upon this floor this morning, so far as the people whom I have the honour in part to represent are concerned, they are perfectly willing to give them as many as they want. I heard here this morning, as I have heard nearly every day since this convention met, language, which if used down South against the rebel government, would, to say the least of it, cause to be sent beyond their lines those using it. And I thought to myself, this morning, of the oath we all took up in the chamber of the governor. I made up my mind that no matter what oath we might put in the constitution these men would gulp it down. And so we have been told upon this floor. I know, gentlemen, that the test about to be administered to you is a bitter one. I would that it were more so, and that it might purge you of every disloyal sentiment and idea that you now possess.

Mr. Daniel. I have a few remarks which I wish to submit upon this question. I shall not travel into the political view of the question. But I have an opinion or two upon the legal question, which so far as I now recollect, has not yet been presented by any gentleman, precisely in the form in which it has struck my own mind.

What are the theories advanced here as to the powers of this convention? One is that we are confined by the restrictions which are contained in the bill calling this convention, and which was submitted to the people, and whose provisions it has been contended have been adopted by the people. The other theory is that we are not restrained by anything in that bill, except so far as it is our pleasure to observe its provisions. That, as a sovereign convention, we have of ourselves all power, and that we are under no restrictions. Now I do not see how gentleman can sustain themselves upon any other theory than the one which has been adopted by the gentleman from Kent (Mr. Chambers) and by every other gentleman, except the gentleman from Anne Arundel (Mr. Miller) who addressed the convention last night.

The gentleman from Anne Arundel, consistent with himself, for he has heretofore advocated that theory upon this floor, held that we were bound by the provisions of the act which called us into being, that this convention was the mere creature of that act. And the gentleman argued that view very ably, when the question was presented about the right of certain members to their seats in this convention.

Now, I adopt that theory. I think that so far as the provisions of the act which called us into being are applicable to us, they do govern us. And this convention has practically so said, by its observing the restrictions contained in the provisions of that act. This convention has acted upon the provision giving us our per diem and upon other provisions, thereby showing that it considered itself bound by the provisions of that act.

Now, taking that act as my standard, and looking to the provisions of that act, starting from the very point from whence the gentleman from Anne Arundel (Mr. Miller) started, I come to a very different conclusion in my construction of that act. I come to the conclusion that the provision we are now about to adopt, requiring an oath to be taken by voters at the polls, is the very provision, in substance at least, if not in so many words, which is sanctioned and authorized by that act. The gentleman from Baltimore county (Mr. Ridgely) based his argument in favor of the section now under consideration, upon that portion of the sixth section of the convention bill which authorized this convention to submit the new constitution to the people "subject to such rules and regulations as said convention may prescribe." My friend from Anne Arundel (Mr. Miller) in reviewing that argument said that the gentleman (Mr. Ridgely) had carefully excluded from consideration the latter part of that sixth section, which reads as follows:

"And the provisions hereinbefore contained for the qualifications of voters, and the holding of the elections provided in the previous sections of this act, shall be applicable to the election to be held under this section."

Now, it is upon that part of the section that I intend to base the view which I shall take of this subject; that part which my friend from Anne Arundel said my friend from Baltimore county had carefully avoided.

"Provisions hereinbefore contained for the qualification of voters." What are the provisions for the qualifications of voters contained in this convention bill, and which are to be applicable when they vote for the constitution, or against the constitution, as they were applicable when they voted for a convention or against a convention? The gentleman from Anne Arundel admits that the people ratified the provisions of this act when they voted for it. And he has argued that the provisions of this act apply to this convention, although every other gentleman of his party has been forced to flee from that conclusion, in order to avoid the necessary implication that this oath was legal, and to plant themselves upon the sovereign powers of this convention, and to hold that there is no legal qualifications except those contained in the constitution.

The gentleman from Montgomery (Mr. Peter) was very careful this morning to note certain qualifications laid down in the first section of the convention bill; that is, those prescribed for voters in electing delegates to the general assembly. And then he read a certain oath which the members were required to take. But there was another part of the first section which he did not read, but which I will now read:

"And the judges of election shall at said election (for the convention) administer the oath or affirmation to every person offering to vote, whose vote shall be challenged on the ground that such person has served in the rebel army, or has either directly or indirectly, given aid, comfort or encouragement to those in armed rebellion against the government of the United States, or is for any other reason not a legal voter in the manner and form provided by section twenty-one of article thirty-five of the Code of public general laws, relating to elections."

Now the article of the Code referred to simply allows the judges of election in ordinary cases to administer the oath to the party touching his right to vote, as regards his residence. But it gave them the power to ask such questions as they might deem it necessary to put to the voter. That, therefore, in connection with the first section of this convention bill, gave the judges complete power to ask as many questions as they pleased, and in any manner they pleased in order to purge the conscience of the voter, and to bring out from him any of these facts, viz: whether he had ever served in the rebel army, or had either directly or indirectly given aid, comfort or encouragement to those in armed rebellion against the government of the United States.

Now here is the point I make upon that. I say that the sixth section of the convention bill says that the same provisions in regard to the qualifications of voters shall be applicable when this constitution is submitted to the people, as were required by the first section of that act when the question of a convention was submitted to the people. And among those provisions is this, that the judges of election were authorized to put every man on his oath as to whether he had ever served in the rebel army, or had ever directly or indirectly given aid, comfort, or encouragement to those engaged in armed rebellion against the government of the United States. Now I ask, in what respect does this oath which we propose to prescribe in this schedule, differ from the one which the judges of election were empowered to administer to every man who voted upon the calling a convention? The judges might have gone on, under the very bill which called this convention together, and ask all the questions now proposed by the committee on the schedule. The only difference, if it be a difference, that this report, instead of allowing the judges to put their questions in their own way, has included in the form of an oath to be taken by the voter, what the judges under the convention bill could have accomplished by questions put to the voter. What is the oath prescribed by this report of the committee on the schedule, being the oath contained in the article on elective franchise?

"I do swear or affirm that I am a citizen of the United States, that I have never given any aid, countenance or support to those in armed hostility to the United States, that I have never expressed a desire for the triumph of said enemies over the arms of the United States, and that I will bear true faith and allegiance to the United States and support the constitution and laws thereof as the supreme law of the land, any law or ordinance of any State to the contrary notwithstanding, and will in all respects demean myself as a loyal citizen of the United States, and I swear this without any reservation or evasion."

Mr. Edelen. Do I understand the gentleman from Baltimore city (Mr. Daniel) to give his opinion here as a lawyer, that the oath he has just read, is substantially the same oath which is prescribed by the first section of the convention bill?

Mr. Daniel. Yes, sir. I say this, that

section one of the convention bill implies everything that is contained in this oath. The only difference is this: that in the one case it is drawn out in the form of an oath, while in the other case it was left to the judgment of the judges of election to draw out the very same thing by as many questions as they pleased. And it is well known that a great many of the judges had question upon question printed, which they put to the voters. And if those questions were answered under oath, they would amount to more than this oath. One of the questions which I am told some of the judges asked of the voters, was, if the two armies came to fight, which army would they prefer to see succeed? Now I ask whether that is not the precise point reached by this oath, whether they have expressed a desire for the triumph of the enemy? Therefore I say this is no broader than the other. On the contrary, you gave the judges more power under the convention bill, which did not define what questions they might ask a voter, than you do under this oath, which does define what is to be asked. I make that as an argument, in addition to what has already been urged by the gentleman from Baltimore county (Mr. Ridgely.)

I wish now to reply to one argument urged here again and again by the gentleman from Prince George's (Mr. Clarke.) He made the same argument when he made his first speech, and he made it again to-day. In reference to the status of a man who had been in the rebel army, he took the ground that because the supreme court of the United States, in their decisions in reference to the prize cases, had said that the southern confederacy, or those in armed rebellion against the government were belligerents, therefore they occupied the position of foreigners, and could not vote by virtue of that very position. I say that the supreme court of the United States have made no such decision, because that point was never before them. The court was called upon to decide whether the laws of war applied to a civil war so far as vessels endeavoring to run the blockade were concerned. The court did decide that the laws of war did apply to the property, but not to the persons, except so far as to acknowledge that they were belligerents for the time being, in order to enable the government to enforce the right of blockade. My point is this, that while they have decided that those in armed rebellion were belligerents for the time being, in order to enforce the right of blockade, they also decided that these belligerents still owed allegiance to the government of the United States, and could be punished as traitors. Now, if the position is true, and I will show that that is the construction upon that decision by Hon. Reverdy Johnson, one of the most eminent lawyers of the United States, that they are only belligerents for the time being, then I ask how can you deprive them of the right to vote, until you have by due course of law, convicted them as traitors? If they are still held to be subjects, and to owe allegiance to the government of the United States, then they can return and claim and exercise all their rights under that government until they have been properly prosecuted, and judgment of condemnation entered against them.

I beg leave to read a few extracts from that decision. It will be found in Black's Reports, vol. 2, page 667, &c. In that decision Justice Grier says:

"They claim to be in arms to establish their liberty and independence, in order to become a sovereign State, while the sovereign party treats them as insurgents and rebels, who owe allegiance, and who should be punished with death for their treason."

That he states to be their status. Then he goes on to quote Vattel:

"'A civil war,' says Vattel, 'breaks the bands of society and government, or at least suspends their force and effect; it produces in the nation two independent parties, who consider each other as enemies, and acknowledge no common judge. These two parties therefore, must necessarily be considered as constituting, at least for a time, two separate bodies, two distinct societies. Having no common superior to judge between them, they stand in precisely the same predicament as two nations who engage in a contest and have recourse to arms.'"

On page 669 he says:

"It is not the less a civil war, with belligerent parties in hostile array, because it may be called an 'insurrection' by one side, and the insurgents be considered as rebels or traitors."

Not the less a civil war because they are rebels or traitors, showing that the government has always held them as rebels or traitors, and not as public enemies except for the purposes of that decision.

"It is not necessary that the independence of the revolted province or State be acknowledged, in order to constitute it a party belligerent in a war, according to the law of nations."

But I will not take up further time with that.

Now I wish to read the opinion of Hon. Reverdy Johnson, on the point of the status of these people after this war is over, to show how utterly inconsistent it is with the position of the gentleman from Prince George's (Mr. Clarke.) Mr. Johnson, in a speech delivered in the senate of the United States, April 5, 1864, says:

"He (Mr. Sherman, of Ohio,) tells us, and in this he was, as I think, partly correct, but for his object substantially incorrect, that the supreme court of the United States, at the last term, in what are called the prize cases, decided that there existed between the rebellious States and the United States a condition of war which places the two in the relation of belligerents, and gives to each all the rights which belong to belligerents in an international war.

"I believe I speak advisedly when I say that, whatever may be their language, the court designed and affirmed no such general proposition. They held what, indeed, cannot be denied, because your legislation recognizes its existence, and because, independent of that recognition, the fact is apparent that a state of war exists. That the insurrection, however at the first it might have been arrested by the mere civil power, had culminated to a point which places it beyond that power, or any other but the power of war. In saying this, however, the court referred only to the particular cases which were before them, and cases of like character, and to the particular questions presented by such cases. They relied upon belligerent rights growing out of the actual war, merely with the view to show that the goods captured upon the high seas, coming from the territorial limits of the rebellious States were to be considered, under the prize law, as prize of war; and that the question whether legal prize or not was to be determined by the principles of the prize law as a part of the law of nations. But in so ruling, in answer to the objection, that although in one sense a war, it was a rebellion in which each citizen in the rebellious States was guilty of treason against the United States, they said that that was true, but that such parties were not the less to be esteemed enemies because they were traitors.

"The court never intimated, as I read their opinion, that the existence of a belligerent relation between the two forces terminated the civil obligations which the citizens of the rebellious States are under to the government of the United States; but, on the contrary, announced, as before stated, that their being traitors did not, in the view of the prize law, show that they were not also enemies. The court, I understand, decided that each of the citizens or inhabitants of the rebellious States still owes, as before, unqualified allegiance to the government of the United States, and to be under an obligation to fulfil it; and consequently, that when the authority of the United States shall be restored, such of them may be proceeded against as traitors who may have voluntary aided the rebellion."

There is the construction of what this court has said. Then I ask, if you do not have some such restriction as this, what is to hinder such men as Bradley T. Johnson, and others engaged in this rebellion, from coming back here and claiming the right to vote, and thus overturning our free institutions by bringing treason to corrupt the very purity of the ballot-box? We need just such an oath as this in order to purge men. And as has been so well said here to-day by my colleagues, why should men claim the right to vote, or want to vote under the government protecting them, when their avowed purpose is to destroy and break up the government under which they claim their rights and privileges?

I say that if gentlemen are right on this question, if they do not sympathize with the rebellion, they have only to say so to be allowed the same rights that others have. But as I had occasion to say on this floor once before, if I were under Jeff. Davis' government, and wanted to overthrow that government, as an honest man I never would hold office under it, or take an oath to support it. I would do neither of those things unless in my heart I wanted that government to prevail. And I do not believe any other honest man in heart will offer to vote under a government which he is trying to destroy.

Mr. Barron moved the previous question, which was seconded.

Mr. Davis, of Charles. I rise for the purpose of making a personal explanation.

The President. That is not now in order. The previous question has been moved and seconded. And the question now is upon ordering the main question to be put.

Upon this question Mr. Marbury called for the yeas and nays, which were ordered.

The question was then taken, by yeas and nays, and resulted—yeas 35, nays 23—as follows:

Yeas—Messrs. Goldsborough, President; Abbott, Annan, Audoun, Baker, Barron, Cunningham, Cushing, Daniel, Davis, of Washington, Dellinger, Ecker, Galloway, Greene, Hebb, Jones, of Cecil, Kennard, King, Markey, McComas, Mullikin, Murray, Parker, Pugh, Purnell, Russell, Schlosser, Scott, Smith, of Worcester, Sneary, Stirling, Stockbridge, Swope, Todd, Wooden—35.

Nays—Messrs. Belt, Billingsley, Blackiston, Brown, Chambers, Crawford, Davis, of Charles, Dent, Duvall, Edelen, Hollyday, Horsey, Johnson, Lansdale, Lee, Marbury, Mitchell, Miller, Morgan, Parran, Peter, Smith, of Dorchester, Turner—23.

The main question was accordingly ordered.

The following explanations, pending the call of the yeas and nays, were made by members as their names were called:

Mr. Belt. One or two other gentlemen, myself among the number, desire to be heard a few minutes upon this question. If every one had been heard who desired to speak, of course I should have no objection to the previous question being called. But as that is not the case I vote "no."

Mr. Davis, of Charles. I shall be compelled to vote in the negative on this question. We have adopted a rule here restricting each member to twenty minutes in the expression of his views upon any question that may be under consideration. Some two or three gentlemen obtain the floor and make their speeches, and then the previous question is sprung upon us. Now I submit it to the justice of the convention to say whether that is fair. If all the gentlemen who desire to speak had spoken, I should vote to sustain the previous question. But I shall vote against it now, because I think that each gentleman who wishes to avail himself of the brief time allowed under the rule, should have that privilege. And injustice is done to every gentleman who is cut off by the previous question. I vote "no."

Mr. EDELEN. I shall vote against sustaining the call for the previous question, although I am not influenced at all by any desire to prolong this discussion to any considerable length. I tried to get the floor to make a remark or two in reply to the gentleman who last spoke (Mr. Daniel.) I shall vote "no" on this question, in order that I may have the opportunity of correcting one or two errors into which I think he has fallen.

Mr. MILLER. I will say that having been one of those who have participated in the privileges of debate upon this question, under the twenty minute rule I cannot vote to cut off any gentleman who desires to debate this question, from the privilege of doing so. And I cannot see how common courtesy and common honesty can allow any gentleman who has spoken upon this question, to vote for sustaining the previous question.

The PRESIDENT. The gentleman from Anne Arundel (Mr. Miller) is out of order.

Mr. BARRON. That is twice we have had such language applied to us this afternoon. Once we were called robbers, and now we are told that we have not got common honesty.

Mr. MILLER. I said nothing about common honesty.

Mr. BARRON. Yes, you did; you said those very words.

The PRESIDENT. The president will not permit any member to impugn the motives of this convention.

Mr. MILLER. I did no such thing.

The PRESIDENT. The gentleman used the expressions "common courtesy" and "common honesty." No gentleman can be allowed to occupy the floor for the purpose of imputing improper motives to members of this convention, as if gentlemen were voting here with a view to deprive members of their constitutional rights.

Mr. MILLER. If I used the words "common honesty," I did so unintentionally. I meant common courtesy.

The PRESIDENT. It was the manner of the gentleman more than anything else, which attracted the notice of the chair.

Mr. MILLER. I disclaim any intention of using such language. I vote "no."

Mr. PETER. I do not desire to exercise any right upon this floor which I am not willing to extend to others. And as I have had an opportunity to speak upon this question, and other gentlemen desire to do the same, I shall vote "no."

Mr. PUGH. Being one of those who have not spoken upon this question, I feel much less hesitation in voting than some of the gentlemen who have spoken. I might possibly, if the opportunity were afforded me, have somewhat to say upon this question. But I would long since have voted "aye" on a call for the previous question, had it been made, for the reason that I think everything has already been said upon this question that can be said. Further debate is only going over the same old ground, and I am tired of it. I vote "aye."

The question was upon the amendment of Mr. DENT, to strike out the following words:

"The judges of election shall administer to every person offering to vote, the oath or affirmation prescribed by this constitution, and should any person offering to vote refuse or decline to take said oath, he shall not be permitted to vote at such election, but the taking of such oath or affirmation shall not be deemed conclusive evidence of the right of such person to vote."

Mr. DAVIS, of Charles. I now rise to a personal explanation.

The PRESIDENT. It is not in order at this time. The ordering the previous question compels the house to proceed and take a vote upon the pending amendment and upon the section. After that is done the gentleman will have ample opportunity for explanation.

Mr. DENT called for the yeas and nays upon his amendment, and they were ordered.

The question was then taken by yeas and nays, and resulted—yeas 25, nays 35—as follows:

Yeas—Messrs. Belt, Billingsley, Blackiston, Brown, Chambers, Crawford, Dail, Davis, of Charles, Dent, Duvall, Edelen, Henkle, Hollyday, Horsey, Johnson, Lansdale, Lee, Marbury, Mitchell, Miller, Morgan, Parran, Peter, Smith, of Dorchester, Turner—25.

Nays—Messrs. Goldsborough, President; Abbott, Annan, Audoun, Baker, Barron, Cunningham, Cushing, Daniel, Davis, of Washington, Dellinger, Ecker, Galloway, Greene, Hebb, Jones, of Cecil, Kennard, King, Markey, McComas, Mullikin, Murray, Parker, Pugh, Purnell, Russell, Schlosser, Scott, Smith, of Worcester, Sneary, Stirling, Stockbridge, Swope, Todd, Wooden—35.

The amendment was accordingly rejected.

The question then recurred upon the section as reported by the committee.

Upon this question Mr. DUVALL called for the yeas and nays, and they were ordered.

The question was then taken, by yeas and nays, and resulted—yeas 35, nays 25—as follows:

Yeas—Messrs. Goldsborough, President

Abbott, Annan, Audoun, Baker, Barron, Cunningham, Cushing, Daniel, Davis, of Washington, Dellinger, Ecker, Galloway, Greene, Hebb, Jones, of Cecil, Kennard, King, Markey, McComas, Mullikin, Murray, Parker, Pugh, Purnell, Russell, Schlosser, Scott, Smith, of Worcester, Sneary, Stirling, Stockbridge, Swope, Todd, Wooden—35.

Nays—Messrs. Belt, Billingsley, Blackiston, Brown, Chambers, Crawford, Dail, Davis, of Charles, Dent, Duvall, Edelen, Henkle, Hollyday, Horsey, Johnson, Lansdale, Lee, Marbury, Mitchell, Miller, Morgan, Parran, Peter, Smith, of Dorchester, Turner—25.

The section was accordingly adopted.

Mr. Davis, of Charles, when his name was called, said: I was cut off by the previous question from explaining my views upon this question, and I will therefore avail myself of this opportunity to explain my vote. I have heard it said over and over again that gentlemen could not understand why members could not vote for this oath, unless it was because they were traitors. Now I think I have a reason for not voting for this oath, one certainly satisfactory to myself, and I think it will be satisfactory to this convention; at least every member who will divest himself of passion, and let reason have sway. I do not think I am the material of which to make a traitor. That I might be driven to rebellion is possible; but that, thank God, I have never as yet felt the necessity of doing. I hold that this convention has no power to pass one single section, paragraph, line or word in this constitution, and adopt it and make it binding upon the people of this State at the election when this constitution shall be submitted to them for their ratification or rejection, and I shall vote against this oath, because I believe there is no such power in this convention. This oath to me would be just as easily taken, and as easily kept, as the one I took when I took my seat in this body. I can conscientiously take it, and I am sure I would keep it. But I shall refuse to take it, and I expect to vote without taking it, for that is my determination, as I advertise here beforehand. My reason for not taking it is not because it is so very objectionable in its feature or form, but because you have no right to require me to take it. If you will, put it in the constitution, and let it go forth to the people for their ratification. If they ratify the constitution, and the oath with it, then I shall not have the slightest objection, at any subsequent election, to take it; and if I violate it I will abide by the consequences. I vote "no.'

After the result of the vote had been announced,

Mr. Davis, of Charles, said: I now rise to a personal explanation. When the gentleman from St. Mary's (Mr. Billingsley) was making his speech, the gentleman from Baltimore city (Mr. Barron) interrupted him for a considerable length of time. I arose and said that I hoped the gentleman from St. Mary's would take his seat if he was not allowed to proceed without interruption. The chair made some remark in reference to the gentleman from Charles, myself, which I did not distinctly understand. I understood the chair to say that the gentleman from St. Mary's would be allowed to proceed without the interposition of the gentleman from Charles.

The President. The president said that the gentleman from Charles (Mr. Davis) need not interpose, because the chair would see that the gentleman from St. Mary's (Mr. Billingsley) was protected in all his rights.

Mr. Davis, of Charles. When one member interrupts another, particularly for any considerable length of time, I do not think it is at all out of place for any friend of the member who is interrupted to request him to take his seat until he can proceed in order. I thought the remark of the chair was entirely uncalled for, and intended to be very unkind.

The President. The chair had no unkind feelings towards the gentleman; not the slightest. The chair only desired to assure the gentleman from Charles (Mr. Davis) that he need not interpose, because the chair would see that the gentleman from St. Mary's was fully protected in all his rights.

Mr. Davis, of Charles. The gentleman from Baltimore city (Mr. Barron) continued to interrupt the gentleman from St. Mary's.

The President. The chair does not deny that fact, because the chair interposed at once upon the suggestion of the gentleman from Charles.

Mr. Davis, of Charles. I accept very willingly and gladly the explanation of the president.

The President. The president does not know that he has any explanation to make, because there is no difference in point of fact between the gentleman from Charles (Mr. Davis) and the chair. The only point is that the chair assured the gentleman from Charles that he need not interpose as the chair would see that the gentleman from St. Mary's was fully protected.

Mr. Davis, of Charles. I think I had the right.

The President. The gentleman has the right, no doubt. But the chair did not interpose from any unkind feeling.

Mr. Davis, of Charles. I am glad to hear that. I did not understand the remarks of the chair, and I wished to do so; for the reason that gentlemen on this floor called my attention particularly to the fact, that the chair had been unkind to me in his remarks; and I myself had thought so. I never wish to be captious, and I never object to anything said to me until I am sure it is intended to be objectionable, or unkind to me.

The President. I assure the gentleman that I do not entertain the slightest unkind feeling towards him or any other gentleman upon this floor. The chair is indebted to the gentleman for giving him the opportunity of saying so.

Mr. BILLINGSLEY. I assure the president that, so far as I am concerned, I conceive that he discharged his duties as the presiding officer of this body, and protected me in every right that belongs to me as a member of this convention.

Mr. BARRON. I suppose an explanation is due from me. I find that the dignity of the chivalry is very much touched if a man objects to being called a robber by them. I do not know that they pay their honest debts any better than I do. When the gentleman from St. Mary's (Mr. Billingsley) said we had robbed him of his property, to whom was he talking? To this convention; to you, and to me. "You have robbed us of our property." I rose to a point of order, not out of any disrespect towards him. In the few humble remarks I made here some time ago, I used no such language towards him. I did not say to him, "You give a negro four pounds of meat and a peck of corn meal to live on for a week, and then you pocket the proceeds of their labor, the sweat of their brow." No, sir; I kept that to myself. I did not charge them with standing up here as if they were gods with whips in their hands to lash humanity as they pleased.

But to-day it is necessary I should throw down the gauntlet, and talk the matter over plainly, and not handle it with gloved hands. Think how great they are! Are they any more than men? The blood in my veins is just as good as the blood in theirs. And no man on this floor, independent of you, Mr. President, shall ever charge me with being a robber without my noticing it.

And what occurred in less than thirty minutes afterwards? Because I called the previous question, without desiring to be heard upon this question myself, I was accused by the gentleman from Anne Arundel (Mr. Miller) with not having common honesty. That was modest in that gentleman certainly. I thank him for it.

Mr. MILLER. I disavow any intention to use that expression. If it escaped from me, it did so inadvertently.

Mr. BARRON. I do not care how high-born the chivalry are; as long as I stand in this convention I am the peer of the best of them here. I am to-day a man just as God made me, and that man is not in this convention, and does not tread the face of this earth, to whom I am afraid to speak my mind. With this explanation I am willing to let this matter drop.

The PRESIDENT. The chair is fully satisfied that the gentleman from St. Mary's (Mr. Billingsley) from his manner and mode of expression, and from his generally gentlemanly deportment in this convention, did not entertain the slightest intention to reflect upon the motives of any gentleman in this convention. The chair does not believe that the gentleman from St. Mary's entertained any such sentiment. The chair has to judge by the manner in which gentlemen express themselves. What harm is it to any individual to use the word "robber" in a political sense? There is no gentleman in this convention but what has used equally as strong expressions. The attention of the gentleman from St. Mary's being called to it, he instantly disclaimed any intention to offend any gentleman in this convention. It is utterly impossible for the chair to restrain gentlemen on account of their particular modes of expression. Men have different ways of expressing themselves. I could have checked every gentleman in this convention, if I had chosen to put a literal, strict interpretation upon their words. There is not a man in this convention but what, from a strict interpretation of his language, has committed an insult to this body. It is a peculiarity attending all political debates. It is a part of the freedom of speech allowed to gentlemen for the purpose of enabling them to exercise freely and fully a right guaranteed to them under the constitution and laws of this State. If gentlemen here say that they have been robbed of their property, it does not mean that each one here who voted for that measure has participated in any such thing as is commonly understood by the term "robbery." It is spoken in a political sense. That is the only sense in which the word is used.

I checked the gentleman from Anne Arundel (Mr. Miller,) and I believe it is the second instance only in which I have been compelled to check gentlemen, on the ground that the use by him of the words "common honesty," the manner in which he used them, the apparent warmth with which he used them, indicated that he imputed improper motives to the members of this convention. It is the duty of the president of the convention to protect the rights and honor of every member here. The gentleman from Baltimore city (Mr. Barron) is the peer of every other man in this body. The gentleman from Kent (Mr. Chambers,) the gentleman from St. Mary's (Mr. Billingsley,) and the gentleman from Charles (Mr. Davis,) are equally the peers of every other man in this body. We all stand upon the same common platform, subject to those frailties that are incident to human nature. We can none of us claim any superiority over the others. It is the duty of the presiding officer to see that equal justice is meted out to every one of you, and that he will do under all circumstances and upon all occasions. And he will further say, that if any gentleman violates intentionally or knowingly the rules of this body, he will put him in such a situation as will render it very unpleasant to him, he cares not what may be his threats in regard to the matter. The chair is something like other individuals, not to be intimidated by anything at all.

Mr. MARBURY. I ask leave of the convention to offer the following additional section:

"Sec. —. It shall be the duty of the general assembly, at its first session after the adoption of this constitution, to provide by law that all taxes paid by individuals on slaves emancipated by this constitution, since the ——— day of ——— shall be returned to the persons so paying them."

The PRESIDENT. The chair does not consider that that matter pertains to this report. It is not germain in any way.

Mr. DENT. I would submit that a proposition of this character might be entertained under the head of "miscellaneous." A new article might be inserted in the constitution. I only make the suggestion that the gentleman could reach his object in that way, without opening any other article.

The PRESIDENT. It cannot be entertained at this time.

Mr. BELT. The proposition of my colleague (Mr. Marbury) does not look to the incorporation of any permanent policy into the constitution. It does not propose that there shall be a remission of certain taxes year after year. It is but a temporary affair, and therefore I thought it would properly fall within this report upon the schedule, because I understood the schedule was designed to cover these temporary affairs.

Mr. HEBB. It is not customary to introduce any new section to a report, until the report has been read through.

The PRESIDENT. The chair rules the amendment of the gentleman from Prince George's (Mr. Marbury) to be out of order.

Mr. EDELEN. I was cut off, by the operation of the previous question, from introducing an amendment to this section. It is in these words——

The PRESIDENT. The section has been adopted.

Mr. EDELEN. Then I will read it for the information of the convention.

Mr. PUGH. I object to that.

Mr. EDELEN. Then I will offer it as an additional section as follows:

"Sec. —. The obligation of the judges of election to administer the oath required in section two, shall only exist in those cases whenever the vote of the person offering to vote may be challenged."

My reason for introducing it is to meet the view of my friend from Baltimore city (Mr. Daniel.) The whole of his argument was founded upon the sixth section of the convention bill, from which he sought to derive the authority to give us the perfect right to put in here the oath prescribed.

Mr. HEBB. I rise to a point of order. There was no section before the convention when this proposition was offered. The gentleman from Charles (Mr. Edelen) proposes to amend the whole report. Now, in conformity with the uniform decision of the chair, no new section can be introduced until we get through the report.

Mr. MILLER. Several reports have been subdivided into different parts; the judiciary report was so divided. This schedule is divided into several parts—"general provisions," "vote on the constitution," and "soldiers' vote." We are now about concluding that portion of this report which relates to the vote upon the constitution, before we come to the subdivision entitled "soldiers' vote." In the case of the judiciary report, new sections were received at the conclusion of each subdivision. If the new section now proposed is germain to the particular subdivision of the report under consideration, it seems to me proper that it should be allowed to come in here.

Mr. HEBB. The gentleman from Charles (Mr. Edelen) proposes to offer an amendment to the whole report, to introduce a new section. My point of order is that there is nothing before the convention until some section is read. We have adopted section two, and that is not any longer before the house.

Mr. PUGH. It has been the custom heretofore to admit new sections under the different subdivisions of a report, but that was because no objection was raised. The idea is that the new section shall be offered after the report is read through, and then it can be put in its proper place, if it is adopted.

The PRESIDENT. The usual course is to admit new sections only after the report has been read through.

Mr. EDELEN. Then I will give notice that at the proper time I will offer this as an additional section.

SOLDIERS' VOTE.

The following section was then read:

"Section 1. Any of the qualified voters of this State, who shall be absent from the county or city of his residence, by reason of being in the military service of the United States, so as not to be able to vote at home, on the adoption or rejection of this constitution, or for all State officers elected on general ticket, and for presidential electors, and for members of congress, at the election to be held on the Tuesday next after the first Monday in November, eighteen hundred and sixty-four, shall be entitled to vote at such elections as follows: A poll shall be opened in each company of every Maryland regiment in the service of the United States, or of this State, on the day appointed by this convention, for taking the vote on the new constitution or on some day not more than five days thereafter, at the quar ters of the commanding officer thereof, and voters of this State belonging to such company who shall be within ten miles of such quarters on the day of election, may vote at such poll; the polls shall be opened at eight o'clock, A. M., and close at six o'clock, P. M.; the commissioned officers of such company or such of them as are present at the opening of the polls, shall act as judges, and any one officer shall be competent so to act, and if no officer be present, then the voters in such company present, shall elect two of the voters present to act as judges of the election; before any votes are received, each of the judges shall take an oath or affirmation, that he will perform the duties of judge according to law, will prevent fraud and observe and make proper return thereof, and such oath the judges may administer to each other; the election shall be by ballot, and any voter may vote in writing either 'for the new constitution,' or 'against the new constitution.'"

Mr. BELT. I move to strike out this section. And not having had an opportunity to be heard upon the general subject to-day, I beg leave to remark, upon this matter of soldiers' voting, that, so far as I am concerned, it is an entire misapprehension to suppose that the general principles I have ever held, or hold now, or expect to hold, would induce me upon any occasion to deprive any one of his just and fair right to the elective franchise. I am not only in favor of soldiers voting, but of everybody voting. I am not only opposed to depriving soldiers of their right to vote, but I am opposed to depriving civilians of their right to vote after they have been years and years in this State, without having been out of it at all.

But the real objection that has obtained in this State, and in all other States on this side of the military line, to soldiers voting in camp, is not that anybody wants to deprive them of a fair right to vote under the same conditions under which civilians vote. If they can procure furloughs, or be detached and come home and vote as they have done heretofore, under the same conditions that civilians vote, there would be no objection on earth to it. But the objection arises from the circumstance that it is proposed that these people shall vote nobody knows where, no matter how many hundreds of miles away from the place where the election is conducted. It is the total abnegation of all protection against fraud. Nobody can guarantee a fair election under these circumstances.

And another objection, and a strong and conclusive one to my mind, against the policy proposed to be inaugurated, not from any indisposition that the right of suffrage shall be exercised, is that it is to be conducted by persons who are not officers of the law, and therefore a discrimination is made between one part of our people who are in the State, and those who happen to be in the military service, in favor of those who are in that service. I am opposed to a policy which gives to men, because they happen to be in the army and out of the State, who are in a service which they have chosen with all the known disabilities of it, an immense advantage of this sort over our whole civil population. It is upon this ground and this only that I am opposed to this system.

The question was then taken upon striking out the section, and it was not agreed to.

No amendment was offered to the section.

The next section was then read as follows:

"Section 2. The judges may swear any one offering to vote, as to his being a legal voter of this State. The judges shall take down on a poll book or list the names of all the voters as their votes are taken, and the tickets shall be placed in a box as taken; after the polls are closed, the tickets shall be counted and strung on a thread, and the judges shall make out a certificate, which they shall sign, addressed to the governor, in which they shall state that they have taken the oath hereby prescribed, and shall certify the number of votes taken, and the number of votes for and against the constitution; the said certificates shall be accompanied with the names of the voters, and shall be plainly expressed, but no particular words shall be required."

Mr. DAVIS, of Charles. I move to strike out the word "may," in the first line, and insert the word "shall." I can see no reason for swearing voters in the State and not swearing those out of the State.

Mr. PUGH. My understanding of this section is this; that these judges are to exercise their discretion just as other judges do; but they shall not be required by this constitution to swear a man whom they know to be a citizen, though they may do so if they choose.

Mr. DAVIS, of Charles. The gentleman has voted for a provision requiring judges of elections to swear all civilians offering to vote.

Mr. PUGH. These judges are taking the votes of soldiers in the field, and they are supposed to know all the men who compose their companies.

Mr. DAVIS, of Charles. I think there is a much greater necessity for swearing voters who are out of the State than those who are in it.

Mr. MARBURY. I think it is clearly established upon the authority of the best legal minds of the country that the word "may" here means "shall," and leaves no discretion whatever.

Mr. CUSHING. The officers are convinced of the loyalty of their men.

Mr. DAVIS, of Charles. They must be citizens of the State; not only loyal, but citizens of the State.

Mr. HEBB. The requirements of the oath in regard to civilians are not in relation to their residence, but their loyalty. The judges of election in the army know that a soldier is loyal because he has a gun in his hand.

The question was upon the motion of Mr. DAVIS, of Charles, to strike out the word "may" in the first line, and insert the word "shall."

Upon that question Mr. DAVIS, of Charles, called the yeas and nays, and they were ordered.

The question was then taken by yeas and nays, and resulted—yeas 24, nays 35—as follows:

Yeas—Messrs. Belt, Billingsley, Blackiston, Brown, Chambers, Crawford, Davis, of Charles, Dent, Duvall, Edelen, Henkle, Hollyday, Horsey, Johnson, Lansdale, Lee, Marbury, Mitchell, Miller, Morgan, Parker, Parran, Smith, of Dorchester, Turner—24.

Nays—Messrs. Goldsborough, President; Abbott, Annan, Audoun, Baker, Barron, Carter, Cunningham, Cushing, Daniel, Davis, of Washington, Dellinger, Ecker, Galloway, Greene, Hebb, Jones, of Cecil, Kennard, Markey, McComas, Mullikin, Nyman, Peter, Pugh, Purnell, Russell, Schlosser, Scott, Smith, of Worcester, Sneary, Stirling, Stockbridge, Swope, Todd, Wooden—35.

The amendment was accordingly rejected.

The following explanations were made, pending the call of the yeas and nays, by members when their names were called:

Mr. BELT. I am, as a general proposition, opposed to having any one sworn. But as the convention has decided that civilians shall be forced to take the oath, I shall vote to put all on an equality. I vote "aye."

Mr. CHAMBERS. I believe of all persons who should swear when they come to vote, these soldiers should do so. An officer from Massachusetts commands a company, a dozen men of which may claim to be citizens of Maryland. The officer knows nothing about it; he knows no more where they come from than he does what is going on in the farthest end of the world. I suppose the result will be that if a man professed to be of his politics he would take his vote, without swearing. If he professed to be of different politics the officer, who is the judge, would swear him. That is not right. It strikes me that the only way to have common justice is to swear all. It is bad enough under any circumstances. But it seems to me that if the citizens are made to take the oath, all should be made to do so. I vote "aye."

Mr. DAVIS, of Charles. I did not mean in offering this amendment to sanction the propriety of administering this oath. I merely offer it to remove the distinction made between the two classes of voters. In the first place the judges of election are required to administer the oath to all civilians. But in the case of soldiers voting it is provided that they *may*, not that they *shall*, administer the oath. I want to remove that restriction.

Mr. PETER. It strikes me that we have no authority to pass any such provision as this, and therefore I vote "no."

Mr. BELT moved to amend the section by adding thereto the following:

"Provided, however, that no votes of soldiers cast at any one polling place or camp shall be valid or taken into account in any case where the total number returned shall exceed the numbers of record in the office of the adjutant general.

Pending the consideration of which,

On motion of Mr. DAVIS, of Washington,

The convention took a recess until eight o'clock, P. M.

EVENING SESSION.

The convention reassembled at eight o'clock, P. M.

The roll was called, and the following members answered to their names:

Messrs. Goldsborough, President; Abbott, Annan, Audoun, Baker, Barron, Billingsley, Blackiston, Carter, Crawford, Cunningham, Cushing, Dail, Daniel, Davis, of Charles, Davis, of Washington, Dellinger, Dent, Duvall, Earle, Ecker, Edelen, Galloway, Greene, Hebb, Hodson, Hollyday, Hopper, Horsey, Johnson, Jones, of Cecil, Keefer, Kennard, King, Lansdale, Lee, Marbury, Markey, McComas, Mitchell, Morgan, Mullikin, Murray, Nyman, Parker, Parran, Pugh, Purnell, Russell, Schley, Schlosser, Scott, Smith, of Carroll, Smith, of Dorchester, Smith, of Worcester, Sneary, Stirling, Stockbridge, Swope, Sykes, Todd, Wooden—62.

SCHEDULE.

The convention then resumed the consideration of the report of the committee on the schedule, which was on its second reading.

SOLDIERS' VOTE.

The section under consideration was the following in relation to soldiers voting:

"Sec. 2. The judges may swear any one offering to vote as to his being a legal voter of this State. The judges shall take down on a poll book or list the names of all the voters as their votes are taken, and the tickets shall be placed in a box as taken. After the polls are closed the tickets shall be counted and strung on a thread; and the judges shall make out a certificate which they shall sign, addressed to the governor, in which they shall state that they have taken the oath hereby prescribed, and shall certify the number of votes taken, and the number of votes for and against the constitution; the said certificates shall be accompanied with the names of the voters, and shall be plainly expressed, but no particular words shall be required."

The pending question was upon the motion of Mr. BELT to amend the section by adding thereto the following:

"Provided, however, that no votes of soldiers cast at any one polling place or camp shall be valid or taken into account in any case where the total number returned shall exceed the numbers of record in the office of the adjutant general."

Mr. MARBURY. My colleague (Mr. Belt,) who offered this amendment, is not here now. I therefore move to postpone the further consideration of this section until to-morrow.

Mr. AUDOUN. I hope this convention will not postpone the consideration of this section until to-morrow. There is no reason why we should not go on and close up the work of the convention. We have been here long enough, rather too long, I think; at any rate longer than I have been willing to remain here. If gentlemen have absented themselves from the convention to-night it is their own fault and not the fault of the majority, who are here ready to transact business. I hope, therefore, the convention will refuse to postpone the consideration of this section.

Mr. MARBURY. My colleague (Mr. Belt,) who offered this amendment is detained from the convention by very important business, or I would not ask to have this section postponed.

The question was then taken upon the motion to postpone, and it was not agreed to.

The question was then taken upon the amendment of Mr. BELT, and it was rejected.

No further amendment was offered to the section.

The next section was then read, as follows:

"Section 3 The judges shall, as soon as possible, transmit said returns, with the tickets so strung, to the governor, who shall receive the returns of the soldiers' vote, and shall cast up the same, and judge of the genuineness and correctness of the returns, and may recount the threaded tickets, so as to satisfy himself, and the governor shall count said vote with the aggregate vote of the State on the adoption or rejection of this constitution, and shall wait for fifteen days after the day on which the State vote is taken, so as to allow the returns of the soldiers' vote to be made, before the result of the whole vote is announced. The governor shall receive the returns of the soldiers' vote on said election for State officers, presidential electors, and members of congress, and shall count the same with the aggregate home vote on State officers, and the aggregate home vote in each district respectively for members of congress."

Mr. DUVALL. I move to amend this section by striking out the words "may recount the threaded tickets," and insert "shall recount or have recounted the threaded tickets."

The question being taken upon the amendment of Mr. DUVALL, it was rejected.

Mr. TODD. I move to amend by inserting the words "and county" after the word "State" in the following sentence of this section: "The governor shall receive the returns of the soldiers' vote on said election for State officers," &c. It would seem from the wording of the section that there was some doubt as to whether the soldiers would be authorized to vote for county officers.—My object in offering this amendment is to place that matter beyond doubt, and give them the right to vote for county as well as State officers.

Mr. CUSHING. That would necessitate that every man's residence should be registered in the district in which he lives; a thing almost impossible to be done in the army. It would be almost impossible for soldiers to vote for county officers.

Mr. STIRLING. The chairman of this committee (Mr. Ridgely) is absent. The committee on the schedule I know had this matter under consideration. The chairman of the committee had a conversation with me about it. The provision as here reported was determined upon advisedly, because it was impossible to make any provision by which soldiers could cast their votes for county officers, without going into an extensive series of provisions, which would encumber the constitution to an extent which would be manifestly improper. We have proposed to let them vote for State officers, because all that would be required of them would be to show that they are residents of the county, and there will be but one return to be sent to the governor. But if they are allowed to vote for county officers, then the judges of election in the camp would have to make out a return of the votes for every single officer voted for in the county. We have certainly gone as far as we can, in providing for the vote to be taken on the day of the presidential election. And we must trust to the legislature to make provision for the future. Besides, the only officers to be elected in 1864 are State officers and members of the general assembly; there are no county officers to be elected in 1864.—The committee were unable to provide, consistently with the length of a provision in the constitution, for soldiers to vote upon county officers.

Mr. TODD. The remarks of the gentleman from Baltimore city (Mr. Stirling) have satisfied me of the difficulty of any attempt to make provision for soldiers voting for county officers. And as the legislature can provide for that, I will withdraw my amendment.

The amendment was accordingly withdrawn.

No further amendment was offered to this section.

The next section was then read as follows:

"Section 4. The governor shall make

known to the officers of the State regiments the provisions of this article of the schedule, and request them to exercise the right hereby conferred upon them, and shall take all means proper to secure the soldiers' vote; and the general assembly at its first session after the adoption of this constitution, shall make proper appropriation to pay any expense that may arise herein."

Mr. DUVALL moved to amend the section by inserting the following after the words "means proper to secure the soldiers' vote:"

"And if any officer or person shall give or offer to give directly or indirectly, any bribe, present, or reward, or any promise, or any security for the payment or delivery of money or any other thing to induce any voter in the military service of the United States to refrain from casting his vote, or forcibly to prevent him in any way from voting, or to procure a vote for any candidate or person proposed or voted for as elector of president and vice-president of the United States, or representative in congress, or for any office of profit or trust created by the constitution or laws of this State, or by the ordinances or authority of the mayor and city council of Baltimore, the officer or person giving or offering to give, and the voter receiving the same, and the officer or person who gives or causes to be given an illegal vote, knowing it to be such, at any election to be hereafter held in this State, or under the provisions of sections 1, 2, 3, 4 and 5 of schedule, relating to the 'vote' of those persons in the military service of the United States, &c."

Mr. SCOTT. I see no use in cumbering this section of the report with this amendment. We have the same provision in the article on elective franchise.

Mr. DUVALL. I desire to make the provision applicable to officers in the army as well as to citizens.

Mr. SCOTT. It applies to every case now. Any attempt to make it more definite would be like saying "the whole world and the rest of mankind."

The question was upon agreeing to the amendment of Mr. DUVALL.

Upon this question Mr. MARBURY called for the yeas and nays, which were ordered.

The question was then taken by yeas and nays, and resulted—yeas 19, nays 41—as follows:

Yeas—Messrs. Billingsley, Blackiston, Crawford, Dail, Davis, of Charles, Dent, Duvall, Edelen, Hodson, Hollyday, Horsey, Johnson, Lansdale, Lee, Marbury, Mitchell, Morgan, Parran, Smith, of Dorchester—19.

Nays—Messrs. Goldsborough, President; Abbott, Annan, Audoun, Baker, Barron, Carter, Cunningham, Cushing, Daniel, Davis, of Washington, Dellinger, Ecker, Galloway, Greene, Hebb, Hopper, Jones, of Cecil, Keefer, Kennard, King, Markey, McComas, Mullikin, Nyman, Parker, Pugh, Purnell, Russell, Schley, Schlosser, Scott, Smith, of Carroll, Smith, of Worcester, Sneary, Stirling, Stockbridge, Swope, Sykes, Todd, Wooden—41.

The amendment was accordingly rejected.

Pending the call of the yeas and nays, the following explanations were made by members as their names were called:

Mr. ABBOTT. Believing that that difficulty is already sufficiently covered, I vote "no."

Mr. AUDOUN. Believing that this amendment is only offered for the purpose of retarding the progress of the convention, I vote "no."

Mr. DUVALL. I disclaim the imputation made by the gentleman from Baltimore city (Mr. Audoun.) I am as truly anxious that this convention shall close its labors as any man upon this floor. I vote "aye."

Mr. SMITH, of Carroll. For the simple and only reason that full provision is made for the punishment of the crime indicated in this proposition, I vote "no."

No further amendment was offered to this section.

The next section was then read as follows:

"Section 5. If this constitution shall be adopted by the people, the provisions contained herein for taking the soldiers' vote on the adoption of the constitution, shall apply to all elections to be held in this State, until the general assembly shall otherwise provide."

Mr. STOCKBRIDGE. I desire to offer an amendment to this section, in order to make it what the committee evidently designed it should be. As it now stands it seems to me that the committee have left a loose joint in one place. It now reads that the provisions "for taking the soldiers' vote on the adoption of the constitution shall apply to all elections held in this State, until the general assembly shall otherwise provide." Now that "otherwise provide" might be held to mean that the legislature could provide that the soldiers' vote should not be taken at all. I therefore move to amend by striking out the words "otherwise provide," and inserting "provide some other mode of taking the same."

The question being taken, the amendment was adopted.

No other amendment was offered to this section.

On motion of Mr. STIRLING,

The vote by which the following section was adopted was reconsidered:

"Sec. 3. The judges shall, as soon as possible, transmit said returns, with the tickets so strung, to the governor, who shall receive the returns of the soldiers' vote, and shall cast up the same, and judge of the genuineness and correctness of the returns, and may recount the threaded tickets, so as to satisfy himself, and the governor shall count said vote with the aggregate vote of the State on the adoption or rejection of this constitution, and shall wait for fifteen days after the day on which the State vote is taken, so as to allow the returns of the soldiers' vote to be made, before the result of the whole vote is announced. The governor shall receive the returns of the soldiers' vote on said election for State officers, presidential electors, and members of congress, and shall count the same with the aggregate home vote on State officers, and the aggregate home vote in each district respectively for members of Congress."

Mr. STIRLING moved to amend the section by adding thereto the following:

"And the governor shall exclude from count the votes of any county or city, the return judges of which shall fail to certify in the returns as provided by this schedule, that all persons who have voted have taken the oath prescribed to be taken, unless the governor shall be satisfied that such oath was actually administered, and that the failure to make the certificate has been from inadvertence or mistake."

The question being then taken, the amendment was adopted.

The section as amended was then adopted

Mr. DUVALL. I move to add the following as an additional section:

"The style of this State on the adoption of this constitution shall be "South Massachusetts; and the committee on revision are hereby authorized to erase —— "

The PRESIDENT. That is out of order.

Mr. EDELEN. According to notice already given, I offer the following as an additional section:

"Sec. —. The obligation of the judges of election to administer the oath required in section 2, shall only exist in those cases where the vote of the person offering to vote may be challenged."

Had not the previous question been called when we were considering section two, I should have offered this as an amendment to that section. I do not know what ground was taken by the chairman of the committee on the schedule (Mr. Ridgely) in the discussion last evening. But so far as I observed the course of the discussion this morning, the great bulk, I might say almost the whole of it, was of a political character, and with the exception of the argument of the gentleman from Baltimore city (Mr. Daniel,) in my humble judgment very little of that discussion was applicable to the question before the house for consideration.

I understood that gentleman to base the right of this convention to incorporate this oath in this constitution, and make it operative upon the people when they came to vote upon the adoption or rejection of this constitution, he based it upon the sixth section of the convention bill; the latter clause of it, which reads: "and the provisions hereinbefore contained for the qualification of voters, and the holding of the elections provided in the previous sections of this act, shall be applicable to the election to be held under this section"—that is, when this constitution is submitted to the people.

Now, while I do not concede the ground taken by him to be true, valid, and tenable ground, I make this point. And I insist that the gentleman from Baltimore city (Mr. Daniel) and those who hold the opinions that he entertains upon this question, shall be compelled, by logical consistency at least, to vote for the provision, I now propose to incorporate in this report as an independent section. My friend from Baltimore city (Mr. Daniel) then proceeded to read the concluding portion of section one of the convention bill, which is in these words:

——"and the judges of election shall at said election administer the oath or affirmation to every person offering to vote, whose vote shall be challenged on the ground," etc.

Now the sum and substance of the proposition I have offered is, that it shall be the duty of the judges to administer this oath to a voter only in case where his vote is challenged. I plant myself upon the doctrine that gentlemen upon the majority side of this convention have assumed upon this question; that they derive their whole power and authority to incorporate this provision in the constitution solely from the concluding portion of the first section of this convention bill.

Now I need not tell my friend from Baltimore city (Mr. Daniel) that it is a plain and incontrovertible proposition of law that in the construing of all penal enactments you are to be held to a strict construction. And I submit to him, as a lawyer, whether he can take one part of this section and plant himself upon it, and in the very same breath reject another and a very important part of the same section. And I submit here that all these outside oaths, which the judges in the several election districts propounded to voters on the 6th day of April last, were directly in the teeth of, and in contravention of the language of this first section. For this section makes it their clear and imperative duty to administer this oath, and exclude votes upon the grounds set forth, only when the vote is challenged.

And I will remark here that in our county cavalry came there with the written instructions, and they acted upon that ground in two precincts, that they would not require the judges to put the oath to any man except where he was challenged. And a refusal to take the oath after challenge in two precincts was made the ground for arrest. In another precinct it merely deprived the man of his vote, without causing his arrest.

My friend from Baltimore city (Mr. Daniel) in answer to a question which I put to him, whether the oath which is required to be taken by this schedule, differed from that prescribed by the first section of this convention bill, said that they were the same. Now let us see how consistent gentlemen are with themselves. They plant themselves here upon a theory, and when we ask them to carry that theory out to its logical consequences and conclusion, they fly from it; they take a part and reject the rest. Here are the words of this convention bill. Admit, for the sake of the argument, that we are bound and concluded by it, and that gentlemen have a perfect right to put this into the constitution, because this convention bill was indorsed by the people at the polls in April last. Here are the words of the convention bill:

"And the judges of election shall at said election administer the oath or affirmation to every person offering to vote, whose vote shall be challenged on the ground that such person has served in the rebel army, or has either directly or indirectly given aid, comfort or encouragement to those in armed rebellion against the government of the United States."

That is all; these were the disqualifications pointed out by the convention bill. A man who had been in open war against the government, serving in the rebel army, or who had directly or indirectly given aid, comfort, or encouragement to those in armed rebellion against the United States. All the time looking to overt acts and demonstrations; not seeking to go down into and probe the secret recesses of a man's heart and mind, and parade them upon the hustings as a reason for disqualifying a man from voting who was otherwise entitled to vote.

Now what is the oath prescribed by this convention? After going on and putting in here a list of disqualifications that covers absolutely nearly the whole of a page of the journal, then comes the oath:

"I do swear or affirm that I am a citizen of the United States, that I have never given any aid, countenance or support to those in armed hostility to the United States."

So far you are in substantial keeping and accord with the provisions of the convention bill. If this oath had gone no farther than that, then my friend from Baltimore city (Mr. Daniel) could have well answered me that there was no substantial difference between the two. But the oath goes on to say:

—— "that I have never expressed a desire for the triumph of said enemies over the arms of the United States," etc.

Now is there no difference between overt acts, and the mere expression of opinion, perchance in a man's private chamber, library, office, or anywhere else? Does not the gentleman from Baltimore city (Mr. Daniel) know full well, as a lawyer, that the acts covered by this convention bill, and spoken of in the first part of this oath, are what the law would call treason, coming within the definition of the word "treason" as defined in the constitution of the United States? Section three, article three, of that constitution says:

"Treason against the United States shall consist only in levying war against them, or in adhering to their enemies, giving them aid and comfort. No person shall be convicted of treason, unless on the testimony of two witnesses to the same overt act, or confession in open court."

Must you not in all cases have the overt act, in order to make the party amenable for the crime of treason? And yet the gentleman from Baltimore city, and others who take the same ground, with a show of consistency which will not bear the test for one moment of a close and careful scrutiny, plant themselves upon this convention bill, and insist here that the oath they have incorporated in this new constitution, and which they have put in this schedule for voters upon this constitution to take, is one and the same thing as that spoken of and contemplated by the convention bill. The purpose of my proposition is to carry us back to the true intent and meaning of the language of this latter clause of the first section of the convention bill; that it shall not be the duty of the judges of election to administer this oath to any voter, except he be challenged, just as the convention bill requires.

I will make one reference to a quotation which my other friend from Baltimore city (Mr. Stirling) made from the constitution of Virginia. If he is not in error about it, it certainly has created doubt in my mind. The quotation he made was from section three of the schedule of the constitution of Virginia:

"And such officers (judges of election) keeping said polls open for the space of three days, shall then and there receive, and record in said poll-book, the votes for and against this constitution and schedule, of all persons qualified, under the existing or amended constitution to exercise the right of suffrage."

To what does that term "amended constitution" refer? In the preamble of this constitution of Virginia, we learn that in 1776 the people of Virginia framed their first constitution; and in 1829 they framed what they speak of in all their proceedings as their "amended constitution." And I doubt not that when, in this very section of the schedule, they speak of "the existing or amended constitution" reference was had exclusively to that which was known as the "amended constitution" of Virginia, the constitution of 1829.

Mr. Stirling. The gentleman is mistaken. The constitution of Virginia, from which I read, and from which the gentleman is reading, is the constitution which enacted universal suffrage. And that convention submitted that constitution to those to whom they were about to extend that right of suffrage. And it is an acknowledged and well-known fact that they did so, and that was the reason they put that provision in their schedule.

Mr. EDELEN. It would have been more appropriate, if they had used the term "this constitution."

Mr. STIRLING. The gentlemen from Kent (Mr. Chambers) admitted that they had extended the right to persons not previously qualified to vote, but said they had not excluded those who were previously qualified.

Mr. EDELEN. I do not know that the gentlemen can claim that interpretation for the ordinance submitting the co stitution of Tennessee to the people. The first section of that ordinance contains this:

"*Provided*, That no person shall be deemed a qualified voter in said election, except such as are included within the provisions of the first section of the fourth article of this amended constitution."

Unless the gentleman can follow that up and show that the antecedent constitution of the State of Tennessee was different in that respect from their "amended constitution," he cannot claim that they meant to put in any new qualifications for voting and make it apply before their new constitution went into operation. It is only a way, I doubt not, a very succinct, clear and concise way, they had of describing those qualified to vote on the constitution. It does not appear on the face of the constitution, or from anything which the gentleman from Baltimore city (Mr. Stirling) has brought to the notice of the convention, but that this very identical section referred to in the new constitution of Tennessee was a copy of the section in the old constitution.

But I do not wish to occupy the time of the convention longer. I really think that the question amounts to nothing more nor less than this; that this convention says in so many words that one part of this constitution shall go into operation on the second Wednesday of October next, when it is to be submitted to the people for their ratification or rejection; and the rest of it shall go into operation when the people shall so signify by their votes in its favor. While they submit a part of the constitution, they make the other part, by the omnipotent fiat of this convention, go into operation *eo instanti*.

Since I have taken my seat in this convention, I have heard it conceded by every gentleman who has spoken upon this question, that even apart from that provision in the convention bill, no man upon this floor has ever dreamed of making any portion of this constitution operate as the organic law of this State, until the people by their votes have so declared. This constitution is nothing more in effect than a blank piece of paper, until the people so pronounce.

Now I really hope that this house will be consistent, and as they say they are bound by this convention bill, they will not take a part of it and reject the rest. My amendment is a very important part of that section one of the convention bill, making it the imperative duty of the judges of election to have the voter challenged before they propose this oath.

Mr. CUSHING. I had supposed that the whole debate upon this subject was concluded this morning. I had thought that everything had been said that could be said, about the outrages committed upon the people of Maryland by the government of the United States; the outrages committed upon the people of Maryland by this convention. I had supposed that the whole political and moral question of slavery, and the right and want of right to compensation, had been thoroughly gone over; and that this house had decided definitely that they would not change the provisions for submitting this constitution to the people for their action. With that view I had not intended myself to trouble this house with any more remarks.

But when I find to-night that this whole question is opened again, that this old charge of inconsistency is again thrown back upon us; with no further argument; not one single point touched which was made this morning by the members of the majority of this house; not one single fact which they adduced disproved; but the mere repetition of assertions which, in my humble judgment, are entirely destitute of foundation in law or in fact—under these circumstances I think it incumbent upon me simply to express that opinion to the house, and to give some few reasons why I entertain that opinion.

The gentleman from Charles (Mr. Edelen) has again brought in here the constitution of the United States as it has again and again been brought in here, to be used to defeat measures designed to strengthen the operation of that very constitution. He thought, possibly, that the members of the majority of this house had never read that document, or that they had come here with deliberate intention to destroy it; and that we must go to the delegation from Charles county to be instructed as to what does or does not constitute treason.

Now I will take the definition of treason as the gentleman from Charles has read it to us from the constitution of the United States, and every single thing which a man in this oath in the article on elective franchise, is required to swear he has not done. I contend that the open expression of opinion in this State, in the length and breadth of this land, or of any portion of it, the expression of one single desire that the enemies of this nation may triumph, is treason for which, as one of a jury of twelve men, on the testimony of two witnesses, I would hang any citizen of the United States or any resident of the State of

Maryland. Treason is made a little thing throughout this State; nothing has been deemed treason unless you deliberately go out in open arms against your country to destroy its defenders. Now I want to express my opinion upon the floor of this house, that there are many minor grades of acts which constitute treason.

And I comparatively honor and esteem the men who believing that this constitution had been violated by the northern States, honestly believing that the right of revolution was there and that the time to revolt had come, have openly and honestly taken their lives in their hands, and gone gladly off to risk anything for what they believe to be right, rather than those men who have remained at home and attempted to undermine and stab secretly their government, who, not going out into the field, not even going out into the community with clear voice and uplifted hand, speaking or acting against the government, but have, in their own secluded localities, or in the coteries of their own friends, uttered treason against the United States and have incited others, bolder, braver, better men than they are to do the deeds of arms which they shrank from doing. That is not only treason, but it is treason complicated with cowardice.

If I could have got a more stringent oath than this, I would have had one that would go where this does not go, to the thoughts and wishes of men. There is no one political right under the constitution of the United States or under the constitution and laws of the State of Maryland, which inheres to any single individual who desires the success of the so-called southern confederacy. He has by his own wish, by the operation of his own heart, put himself beyond the pale of the protection of those laws or those constitutions. I hold him to be an outcast in the world, without any country whatever. The southern confederacy spews him out of her mouth, because he has not gone and helped her in her hour of trial. The State of Maryland will have nought of him, except that fervent prayer and wish that he may go beyond her borders. No land under the broad rule of almighty God calls him its child. The southern confederacy cannot be called his country, for it does not exist. Every time its flag has been seen beyond the confines of its own domain, it has been in reality the black flag, the death's head and cross bones of the pirate, although the red and the white of "the stars and the bars" were painted over it as a thin disguise.

Into this question, and on the floor of this house, has been dragged by the gentleman from Prince George's (Mr. Marbury) a matter which I had hoped would never have been spoken of in this house, without all the indignation, all the deprecation, all the sorrow that the English tongue could give, or the energies of any man here could prompt him to pour out before this body. He has dragged before this body the emaciated limbs, the idiotic intellect of the starved and the dying, aye, the dead, of our brave heroes in the prisons of Richmond. He has dragged them forth and mocked and jeered at their sufferings, by saying that the government of the United States have traded for political capital upon the photographs taken of these men in the hospitals in our State. He has thrown the blame of these barbarities, the like of which were never before heard of except in the Black Hole of Calcutta, and even there only dimly shadowed forth—he has thrown the blame of these atrocities upon the government of the United States. He had not one word of indignant protest in the sight of God and man; he made not one single assertion that any man with a heart for freedom, or any love of humanity in his bosom, would be expected to make, or who could ever be supposed under any circumstances, or contingencies, or conditions, to sympathize with, desire the success of, do otherwise than hate and contemn and scorn those who would commit such atrocities.

Why, sir, it would be better to go forth into the wild forests of Germany and lie down with the unfed hungry bear, than to fall into the hands of these civilized, christian southern chivalry. It would be better to make one's bed in hell, for there the almighty God could be with a man and sustain him, than to fall into the hands of these high-toned gentleman of the nineteenth century.

The gentleman from Charles (Mr. Edelen) complains that we do not act consistently on this question of the soldiers' vote. I trow we could act consistently; we could do as Mr. Jefferson Davis has done—refuse the votes of these forty thousand men of Maryland, spoken of here to-day, on the ground that we believe them to be unsympathetic with the cause of the government. That would be consistent; that would be carrying out the strict line of justice to its full extent. But we have tempered our justice with mercy. We have put into this constitution an oath of such a character that if any man refuse to take it, he ought never to vote in Maryland or even to live. There is not one single provision in that oath, given as it is to every voter in the State of Maryland, which ought in the slightest degree to stir up the remotest particle of repugnance in the breast of any loyal man. I shall find no difficulty in taking that oath. It does not make me at all feel as if the iron heel of the oppressor was on my neck, or as if any instinct of freedom in my heart was being crushed out. I would be willing to swear that oath every time I voted, from now until my lips grow cold in death, without feeling that any single privilege of mine had been curtailed.

It is to me a thing strange, and a thing incredible, that constituencies announced upon this floor to be as loyal as any man upon the floor of this house, into whose minds their inmost and secretest minds, the thought of disloyalty has ever come—whole constituencies, forty thousand men in number, should be found to which this oath would be disfranchisement. The estimate of loyalty must differ vastly between the gentlemen who represent these constituencies and myself. I do not esteem a man at all loyal to the government who could hesitate to take this oath; I do not hold that there is an element of loyalty in him.

I can understand that a man might be simply obedient, so far as not to risk his life in treason, and yet decline to take this oath. I can understand that a man might not have been found raising the banner of revolt, or inciting insurrection in his district, and yet refuse to take this oath. But loyalty and obedience are different things. A man, who through fear has all his lifetime been kept in bondage, is not a loyal man. Loyalty takes hold of the heart, and the soul, and the life; it impregnates a man with devotion to the country he calls his own. It bids him give, according to the best of his judgment, his every power to the service of his country. And I go farther; I much question the loyalty of any man, in any portion of this country who, through three years of civil war, has never made his voice heard, to any person, or assemblage of persons, strongly, openly, clearly and unequivocally in favor of the government which protects him. Loyalty is something which does, and not a thing which merely leaves treason undone.

We are told that we extend the right of suffrage. I deny that as a fact. That question was argued before you so ably this morning that it seems almost trifling at this hour to bring it again before the house. I had not supposed there was an individual who would for one single instant maintain that under our present laws soldiers are not entitled to vote. This is solely and simply a question in relation to the place of voting. It is astonishing that, after hearing fifteen or sixteen speeches upon this subject, law essays, appeals to your judgments, your hearts, your passions, denunciations of your course, there should still be found some gentlemen in this convention who cannot understand the perfectly clear words of a portion of that bill under which we are assembled here. It does seem as if much words had confused their counsel; and that the more they heard, and the longer they read that bill and the constitution, and the longer they talked about treason, and against treason, and what treason was, they finally got so they could not make the distinction between what law was and what was not law; what constitutes treason and what was not treason; what made a man loyal, and what did not.

I was much astonished at one argument of the gentleman from Prince George's (Mr. Marbury,) which struck me as strange from an ardent lover of freedom; from a man who desired this constitution to be preserved; from a man who, morning, noon, and night prayed the Almighty to grant us this one thing of constitutional liberty, and that freedom might be preserved upon this continent. He complained of the government of the United States that it had used any means that came into its hands to preserve itself. He actually upon the floor of this house did complain of and denounce this government, and did justify the cruelties practiced upon our suffering prisoners in Richmond, because the government of the United States had taken men with black skins and put them in the front to be shot. The gentleman phrased it differently: he called it "putting slaves into the army." But I ask what is the difference? I simply put it in the other form, that they took men of color and put them in the front to be shot, that the gentleman from Prince George's, myself, and others might not be shot. That is only a different way of stating just the same fact. And I cannot understand on what ground he does, on the floor, to some extent excuse the atrocities of these fiends at Richmond upon our unarmed prisoners in their hands, because of the use by the government of the United States of negro soldiers; when we have had members of this convention from his own county urging upon the majority of this body to take measures for having the slaves enlisted in the armies of the United States from Prince George's county, credited to their quota. It is strange, to say the least of it.

The gentleman from Calvert (Mr. Briscoe) has alluded in remarks here to a foreigner named Haynau. I suppose that, in his own judgment, he found a counterpart to that Austrian different from the one I found. I doubt me if the gentleman would have gone as far south as Richmond to have found him. But I know of no other place upon the civilized earth that produces such men in such boundless profusion as does the city of Richmond. Every man there, from the so-called president of the so-called confederate States, down to the meanest and pettiest underling whom he controls, who has in the slightest degree countenanced that treatment of prisoners, is in comparison with Haynau a very fiend of darkness; and at the judgment bar that Austrian butcher will have a luminous radiance around his head in comparison with the blackness of despair which will settle upon the hearts of those men at Richmond.

This whole discussion upon the subject of this oath reminds me of those trite lines:

"Let the galled jade wince; my withers are unwrung."

Now, if gentlemen will read this oath and apply it to the hearts of the loyal constituencies they represent, they may find the reason why this oath is so unpleasant to them.

And summing up briefly what we have heard here to-day, we are acting clearly and indisputably within our powers as a convention. We have but extended the oath to be taken upon the vote for and against this constitution. We have not extended the right of suffrage. We have clearly, and carefully, and conscientiously kept within the limits of our power. We have, as we believe, done no wrong to any man, or set of men, in Maryland. But we have given them all an opportunity to purge themselves, and to put Maryland in her proper position before the other States of this Union; and to disprove the assertion that has often been made, that the majority of her citizens are secessionists. And these gentlemen, I know, convinced of this on reflection, will go home to their loyal constituencies, and will represent to them that this oath is one which they ought to take, not only one which they ought to take, but one which they ought to delight to take. They will also represent to them that under this provision of the constitution the elective franchise is not extended to any human being who did not have it before; but all that is done is to provide means whereby those brave men who are fighting in the field for those loyal constituencies, or are lying in suffering hospitals or in prison—those of them who at the time of the taking of this vote may be left alive and are under our care, will have a chance to vote. And if in the hearts of those 40,000 loyal constituents there is one generous impulse, they will hail with joy the opportunity of allowing those brave men in the field the privilege of exercising this right.

What more is needed? Having had it proved to them that the law is on our side, that justice is on our side, that the right remains with us in our action, I certainly hope that when these gentlemen come to canvass their communities upon this constitution, though there be nothing else found in it which they can support, this at least will commend itself to them; that they will not be led away by the gentleman from Kent (Mr. Chambers,) that ministering to a prisoner is aiding the rebellion, that carrying clothes and comforts to a prisoner, by permission of the lawful authorities, is rebellion. But they will tell the people that this one thing alone in the constitution is so great a boon to them, and to all loyal men, to all generous, freedom loving men, that they should swallow the whole constitution with all its objectionable features, for the sake of doing this single act of justice; to many of those 40,000 loyal constituents perhaps the first act of loyalty they have ever done in their lives.

Mr. Mullikin moved the previous question, which was seconded, and the main question ordered.

The question was upon the additional section offered by Mr. Edelen, as follows:

"Sec. —. The obligation of the judges of election to administer the oath required in section two, shall only exist in those cases whenever the vote of the person offering to vote may be challenged."

Upon this question Mr. Edelen called for the yeas and nays, and they were ordered.

The question was then taken by yeas and nays, and resulted—yeas 14, nays 40—as follows:

Yeas—Messrs. Billingsley, Dail, Davis, of Charles, Dent, Duvall, Edelen, Hollyday, Horsey, Johnson, Lansdale, Lee, Marbury, Mitchell, Morgan—14.

Nays—Messrs. Goldsborough, President; Abbott, Annan, Audoun, Baker, Barron, Carter, Cunningham, Cushing, Daniel, Davis, of Washington, Ecker, Galloway, Greene, Hebb, Hopper, Jones, of Cecil, Keefer, Kennard, King, Markey, McComas, Mullikin, Murray, Parker, Pugh, Purnell, Russell, Schley, Schlosser, Scott, Smith, of Carroll, Smith, of Worcester, Sneary, Stirling, Stockbridge, Swope, Sykes, Todd, Wooden—40.

The section was accordingly rejected.

Mr. Marbury. The gentleman from Baltimore city (Mr. Cushing) who last addressed the house, has hitherto conducted the debate, at least so far as I am concerned, with a great deal of courtesy. And I am sure he did not intend to misrepresent me on this occasion. He said that I had dragged in here the emaciated forms of the prisoners from Richmond; that I had not had one word of sympathy to express for them, but that on the contrary I had justified the whole course of the South in this respect. Now, I wish it to be understood once for all, that I have the deepest and most profound sympathy for the sufferings of all these prisoners, and for the sufferings of humanity everywhere. What I said was this: that it was the opinion of some of the best judging men of this country, both in civil and in military life, that it was most impolitic to put negro slaves into the army of the federal government; that it would be the means of raising the black flag; that it would produce all these evil effects.

The President. The chair must check the gentleman; these remarks are altogether out of order.

Mr. Marbury. I want to explain what I said. I do not want these statements to go out to the world as mine, when I did not make them. I want to put myself in a correct position.

The President. If the gentleman's motives had been assailed in any way, it would be proper for him to explain.

Mr. Marbury. The gentleman said I had no sympathy for these prisoners; that I considered them properly treated. Is not that a reflection upon any man, to say that he has no spark of human sympathy about him? I must appeal from the decision of the chair.

The PRESIDENT. The gentleman will state the ground of his appeal.

Mr. MARBURY. It is this: I was explaining my position, which the gentleman from Baltimore city (Mr. Cushing) has misrepresented.

The PRESIDENT. The chair does not understand the gentleman from Baltimore city, (Mr. Cushing) to reflect upon the motives of the gentleman from Prince George's (Mr. Marbury,) in the slightest degree.

Mr. DAVIS, of Charles. The gentleman from Baltimore city stated that the gentleman from Prince George's used certain language, which he (Mr. Marbury) says he did not use. He (Mr. Marbury) claims now the right to state what he did say.

The PRESIDENT. The chair permitted the gentleman from Prince George's to deny the facts stated by the gentleman from Baltimore city. But the gentleman from Prince George's was proceeding to make an argument which the chair did not think was proper.

Mr. DAVIS, of Charles. The gentleman is only repeating what he had said. I would advise the gentleman from Prince George's to call upon the reporter to read what he did say.

The PRESIDENT. If the gentleman from Prince George's did so, the gentleman from Baltimore city would have the right to reply to him. If that is allowed the convention would soon become involved in interminable discussions of this character. If the gentleman from Prince George's thinks his character has been assailed, or his motives improperly impugned, the chair will allow him ample opportunity to correct that. But the gentleman from Prince George's can very readily perceive that if the chair were to permit the discussion to continue, whenever the facts stated by one gentleman, were repeated by another, and his interpretation placed upon them, there would be no end to the discussion. The chair is not aware of any case where it has ever been done or permitted. If the gentleman from Prince George's conceives that his motives have been assailed in any manner by the gentleman from Baltimore city, he will be permitted to make his explanation. But the chair does not understand the gentleman so to say.

Mr. MARBURY. I do consider that my motives have been improperly construed; that the gentleman has represented me as being influenced by motives of inhumanity, motives that would reflect upon me as a christian man, as a good citizen of any State, and under any government. I consider this a reflection upon me.

I was going on to state simply the reasons upon which I based my judgment, to show the gentleman that he could not consistently impute any such motives to me. I was going on to say that at the time the exchange of prisoners was refused, it was a notorious fact, known all through the country, heralded in every newspaper, you heard it at every turn and corner, that the southern country was in a starving condition, that they had neither bread, meat, sugar, tea nor coffee; that flour was $200, $300 and $400 a barrel; that such was the condition of the southern people. At that crisis, at that very time, there was a proposal for the exchange of prisoners. I say this government ought not to have stood upon a punctilio, but should have delivered these men from their position.

The PRESIDENT. The chair must say that that is a mere matter of difference of opinion, between the gentleman from Prince George's (Mr. Marbury) and the gentleman from Baltimore city (Mr. Cushing.) The gentleman from Baltimore city has as perfect a right to entertain his opinion in regard to the course of the government of the United States as has the gentleman from Prince George's. How the gentleman from Prince George's can draw the conclusion that that is an imputation upon his motives, the chair cannot perceive. The chair does not regard this as a matter of personal imputation at all.

Mr. MARBURY. Very well; I will waive my appeal.

Mr. LANSDALE. I move to substitute the report of the minority of the committee on the schedule, for that part of the report of the majority which relates to soldiers voting.

The report of the minority was as follows:

"The undersigned, a minority of the members of the committee on provisions and ordinances as may be desirable to carry into effect amendments to the constitution, report that they dissent from the report submitted by the majority of the committee.

"First. Because they believe the authority given to soldiers in camp to vote at all elections, will utterly fail to have the effect proposed by those who advocate the measure; on the contrary, as the undersigned believe, it will enable the officers who command the soldiers, to control the votes of those who feel and know the power of their officers, to make them suffer in various ways the penalty of disobedience to their wishes. To a soldier on duty, the first great lesson taught, is obedience to his commanding officer. Military necessity requires a rigid exaction of this duty; it allows of no discussion or discretion. To fail in the smallest respect insures harsh treatment, even in cases where martial law prescribes no specific penalty. It will not be doubted that the only safe approach to the favor of an officer is to gratify his wishes by voting his ticket.

"Second. But whatever may be the propriety of taking the votes of soldiers or their officers, the undersigned cannot permit themselves to doubt of the concurrence of the convention in their determined opposition to so much of the report of the majority as provides for the immediate operation of portions of the constitution before its adoption by the people. Surely if any one proposition, in regard to our proceedings was universally accepted by all who voted, whether for or against a convention, it was this, that its work was to be submitted to and accepted by the people of the State before it should have any effect. Yet the majority propose that now at the very moment when the question of adoption is being taken, in the very act of taking that question, the people shall be bound and governed by it, so far as it relates to some of its most important and vital changes of the existing system of government. What a strange spectacle would be exhibited if the provisions now proposed should be enforced as part of the new constitution, in direct opposition to the existing constitution, and yet the result show that the people will not accept the new constitution? The present constitution exists until the new one is adopted. How then can the provisions of the present constitution be violated, or interfered with, until the new one has an existence by the adoption of the people? The great purpose of the majority seems to be, to deprive those who form the constituency of this convention of the privilege secured to them by the present constitution of passing upon the work of this body, and to this end, by newly contrived oaths and by the aid of the military, to confirm their proceedings. For these, amongst other reasons, the undersigned protest against the report in the particulars mentioned. All which is respectfully submitted."

Mr. STOCKBRIDGE. There is nothing presented in that report in the form of a section or an article. It is simply a protest against the report of the majority; assigning reasons why that report should not be adopted.

The PRESIDENT. The gentleman from Montgomery (Mr. Lansdale) cannot move this as a substitute for the article reported by the majority of the committee on the schedule. It is in the character of a mere protest. The convention have already determined to take up the majority report, and have acted upon it, and have gone through it.

Mr. ECKER. I move the following as an additional section:

"Sec. —. Any of the qualified voters of this State, who may be absent from the city or county of his residence on the day for taking the vote on the adoption or rejection of this constitution by reason of his being in the military service of the United States, but shall be at some hospital or military post, or on duty within this State, and not with his company, may vote at the nearest polls to such place on satisfying the judges that he is a legal and qualified voter of this State."

My reason for offering this section is this; there are a great many soldiers in the hospitals in this State, a great many in the hospitals in this city, for instance. Now if only a hundred, or fifty, or even five of them are Maryland soldiers, they certainly are entitled to vote. I spoke to the chairman of the committee on the schedule (Mr. Ridgely) upon this subject, and he approved of it.

The question was then taken upon the additional section, and it was adopted.

Mr. KENNARD. I desire the assent of the convention to return to the first section under the caption of "vote on the constitution." I desire to offer an amendment to it, which relates merely to the details of it, to make it conform to the act of assembly now in force in relation to the hours for holding elections. As the section now stands, it rather conflicts with the provisions of that act in relation to the hours for holding the election in Baltimore city.

No objection being made, the section was taken up for consideration.

The section was as follows:

"Section 1. For the purpose of ascertaining the sense of the people of this State, in regard to the adoption or rejection of this constitution, the governor shall issue his proclamation within five days after the adjournment of this convention directed to the sheriff of the city of Baltimore, and to the sheriffs of the several counties of this State, commanding them to give notice in the manner now prescribed by law, that an election will be held in the city of Baltimore and in the several counties of the State, at the usual places of holding elections in said city and counties, for the adoption or rejection of this constitution, on the twelfth day of October, in the year eighteen hundred and sixty-four, which election shall be held between the hours of eight o'clock, A. M., and six o'clock, P. M." &c.

Mr. KENNARD. I move to insert after the words "between the hours of eight o'clock, A. M. and six o'clock P. M." the words "in the several counties of the State, and between the hours of eight o'clock, A. M., and five o'clock, P. M., in the city of Baltimore."

The act of assembly has fixed the hours of eight o'clock, A. M., and six o'clock, P. M., for the counties, and the hours of eight o'clock, A. M., and five o'clock, P. M., for the city of Baltimore. As the section now stands, the polls would be kept open in Baltimore city one hour later than the act of assembly now provides.

Mr. STIRLING. This was an inadvertence, I suppose. I hope the convention will adopt the amendment. It so happens that the day on which this vote is to be taken, is the day for the municipal election in Baltimore city. The act of the assembly requires the polls to be closed at five o'clock for the municipal election. And as the vote upon the constitution is to be taken upon the same ticket with the vote for municipal officers, there may be some question as to whether the judges of election can keep the polls open after five o'clock.

The question being taken, the amendment was adopted.

The section as amended was then adopted.

Mr. DAVIS, of Charles. I move to reconsider the first section of this report, in relation to general provisions. By that section all officers are required to pay into the treasury of the State all excess of fees over $3,000. Now, it seems to me they should be allowed something for collecting those fees, keeping the books, etc. An officer whose fees amount to exactly $3,000, would be paid for all the work done in his office, while another officer, whose fees amount to $5,000, is required to pay over the excess, of $2,000, and is allowed nothing by this section for keeping the books, etc. I wish to allow him some compensation for his extra work.

The PRESIDENT. The chair is of opinion that that question was acted upon the other day.

The motion to reconsider was not insisted upon.

The report of the committee on the schedule, as amended, was ordered to be engrossed for its third reading.

On motion of Mr. GALLOWAY,

The convention then adjourned.

EIGHTY-EIGHTH DAY.

FRIDAY, September 2, 1864.

The convention met at 9½ o'clock, A. M.

Prayer by the Rev. Mr. Patterson.

The roll was called, and the following members answered to their names:

Messrs. Goldsborough, President; Abbott, Annan, Audoun, Baker, Barron, Belt, Billingsley, Bond, Brooks, Brown, Carter, Chambers, Crawford, Cunningham, Cushing, Dail, Daniel, Davis, of Charles, Davis, of Washington, Dellinger, Dent, Earle, Ecker, Farrow, Galloway, Greene, Hatch, Hebb, Henkle, Hodson, Hoffman, Hollyday, Hopper, Horsey, Johnson, Jones, of Cecil, Keefer, Kennard, King, Lansdale, Larsh, Lee, Marbury, Markey, McComas, Mitchell, Miller, Morgan, Mullikin, Murray, Negley, Nyman, Parker, Parran, Peter, Pugh, Purnell, Ridgely, Russell, Schley, Schlosser, Scott, Smith, of Dorchester, Sneary, Stirling, Stockbridge, Swope, Sykes, Thomas, Todd, Turner, Valliant, Wickard, Wilmer, Wooden—76.

The journal of yesterday was read and approved.

On motion of Mr. WOODEN,

It was ordered to be entered on the journal that Mr. Smith, of Carroll, is detained from his seat in consequence of urgent business engagements.

FORWARDING DEBATES AFTER ADJOURNMENT.

On motion of Mr. TODD,

The convention proceeded to the consideration of the following order submitted by Mr. HEBB, on Wednesday last:

"*Ordered*, That the secretary and Collins Tatman, folder, be directed to forward to the several members of the convention after its adjournment, their copies of the journal of debates until it shall have been completed—and the president is requested to issue his certificate for the usual per diem so long as they shall be so employed."

The pending question was upon the motion of Mr. DAVIS, of Washington, to strike out the words "the secretary and."

Mr. GREENE. I move the following as a substitute for the whole proposition:

"*Ordered*, That the secretary be directed to provide for the folding, and addressing and mailing of that portion of the journal of the debates of this convention, which shall not have been delivered to the members at its adjournment *sine die*; and, as in full compensation for such service, the president is hereby requested to issue his certificates to the said secretary, at the rate of six dollars for each thousand copies of said journal thus folded, addressed and mailed."

Mr. TODD. This convention appointed Mr. Tatman to the office of folder.

Mr. HEBB. They appointed two folders.

Mr. TODD. And I suppose when that appointment was made, it was not the intention of the convention to oust that gentleman from his office until he had finished his labors. I do not know of any act of his, in his official relation to this body, that is deserving of any such treatment at our hands. I have not been advised that he has in any instance failed in the performance of his duty. I have on the contrary understood that he has been exceedingly diligent and faithful in the performance of his duties, and been accommodating, and polite, and gentlemanly to all who have been associated with him. He has remained here when this convention adjourned, and has prosecuted his work, and kept that work up, and that, too, when he has been under the necessity of prosecuting that work alone, without the aid of the gentleman whom this convention appointed to assist him. That gentleman has been called away by providential circumstances, and the whole work for the last three weeks has devolved upon Mr. Tatman.

It seems to me that if this convention adopt the substitute offered by the gentleman from Allegany (Mr. Greene,) it will be, to say the least of it, offering an insult to a gentleman whom they have deliberately appointed to do this work. It will be very undeserved treatment, treatment that has not been merited by him. And I think this convention will compromise its dignity by thus offending him. We have made this contract; let us stick to it like men, and let Mr. Tatman be continued in his office until he shall have accomplished the work to which we have appointed him. I have no disrespect for any other gentleman connected with this body as an officer. So far as I know they have performed their duties faithfully. And if it be necessary that the clerk of this body, or any other officer, should be associated with Mr. Tatman, in the performance of this, as it appears to me, his legitimate duty, and that fact can be shown, I have no objection to it. But I do protest against ousting a man from his office, whom we have placed there.

Mr. PURNELL. I indorse with great pleasure everything that has been said by my friend from Caroline (Mr. Todd) in relation to Mr. Tatman. I think he has performed the duties which have devolved upon him with singular fidelity. It is true that for the last two weeks he has performed the entire labor himself. Mr. Collins, his associate, as has been stated, has been called home by serious indisposition in his family, scarlet fever in a very malignant form prevailing among them, and he has necessarily been detained by their bedsides. That has devolved the whole duty upon Mr. Tatman; and I think that should entitle him to some little consideration in disposing of the patronage which this convention may have in its power.

I shall with great pleasure vote for the order introduced by the gentleman from Allegany county (Mr. Hebb) dividing this duty between Mr. Tatman and the secretary. It seems to me that their spheres are different. It was not contemplated that the folder should direct and distribute the matter to the various members; that more properly belongs to the secretary of this body. I am in favor of retaining both of them. And with that conviction of justice and right on my mind, I shall vote for the first order.

Mr. NEGLEY. Would it be in order to move to amend this substitute?

The PRESIDENT. Not now.

Mr. NEGLEY. Then I indorse everything that has been said by the gentleman from Caroline (Mr. Todd.) And I cannot agree with the gentleman from Worcester (Mr. Purnell,) that it is proper to divide this labor with the secretary. If there are two persons at all needed, the labor should be divided between those employees to whom the duty legitimately and properly belongs. The secretary has no connection whatever with the distribution of the documents of this convention. The folder and the postmaster are the proper parties for the distribution of these papers. And if there is to be any division of labor which will have to be performed by the employees of this convention, those two officers are the only two employees who have any legitimate connection with this matter. The folder to fold them, and the postmaster to direct and frank them to the different members. I submit to gentlemen whether that duty does not legitimately belong to the postmaster. It is no part of the duties of the folder to direct and frank these documents. And at the proper time I will move to connect the postmaster with the folder. I am certainly opposed to ousting the folder. I think the duty should not be taken away from him, because it naturally and properly belongs to him.

Mr. GREENE. If any wrong has been done to anybody, it seems to me it has been done to the folder appointed by this convention, whose name was omitted by the gentleman from Caroline (Mr. Todd.) The convention at the commencement of its session appointed two folders; one of whom has been left entirely out of the question.

Mr. TODD. The folder from Worcester county, Mr. Collins, was under the necessity of returning home in consequence of the serious indisposition of his family. When he left he said he would not be able to be back, and gave over to Mr. Tatman all claim whatever to any position after the convention adjourned. That was the understanding between them.

Mr. GREENE. Every member desires to have sent to him the remaining sheets of the debates. We have probably not yet received the half of them, and it will be months before their distribution is completed. Some person should be kept here to direct these debates, and perhaps a folder to fold them. The receiving and folding these documents will involve the much larger portion of the expenses. I do not know the folder; I do not know how far he is competent to the duty of addressing a thousand copies per day.

Mr. TODD. He is an excellent penman, and very rapid.

Mr. GREENE. I am glad to hear it. But the labor of addressing a thousand copies a day is very arduous. I contemplate in my order that the secretary be furnished with the names of the parties to whom members desire to have these debates sent. And he can fold them and address them in Baltimore, where they are printed, and mail them in the Baltimore city post office And it strikes me that the amount of compensation fixed, six dollars per thousand copies, is a limited one, and vastly cheaper than the other plan. And I think that we would be vastly more likely to receive the remaining copies of the debates in the way I propose, than we would be to receive them from Annapolis. That is all the object I have in offering this. I would be very glad to do anything for Mr. Tatman that I could do properly.

Mr. STOCKBRIDGE. This is perhaps rather a small matter, this squabbling over a residuary legacy. But after all it amounts to something as far as the members and the State are concerned. I believe that it is conceded on all hands that the remainder of the journal of debates should be forwarded to members after they leave this place. The only question with me is, how it can be the most surely done, with the least expense to the State. I wish that was the question with everybody.

Mr. GREENE. That is my object.

Mr. STOCKBRIDGE. I have no doubt of it. I have no desire to confer favors upon anybody, or to oust anybody from his place. If we can save the State one dollar it is our duty to do so. It is certain that this matter must continue from two to four months. The debates are almost two full months behind. And if this work is to be done by the folder remaining here and receiving his per diem precisely as he has done since we have been in session here, we can form no idea in reference to the expense. I think it is better to place it in the hands of some officer in whom we can have confidence, and not parcel it out to two or three or half a dozen men. I do not think they should continue on *ad infinitum*, I had almost said for years, to do so very small a work, and to receive so large a pay as this.

Mr. TODD. Does the gentleman mean to insinuate that the gentleman named in my order cannot be trusted?

Mr. STOCKBRIDGE. I do not know anything about him. I would not know him if he were to come in here now. I suppose he is competent to do the work for which he was appointed.

Mr. TODD. He is competent to do anything this convention may desire to have done.

Mr. HEBB. I do not know that this office of folder was intended to last forever. Nor do I know that it is necessary for any one to rise in his place here and deliver a eulogy upon any officer of this convention for the faithful manner in which he has discharged his duties. I do not rise now to deliver any eulogy upon the secretary of this convention. But the secretary certainly has as much right to expect that he will be continued in office to discharge this duty, as one of the folders has. The former convention and our legislature have universally continued the secretary in office after adjournment for as many days as was necessary. And the secretary of this convention, supposing that he would be required to perform this duty in conformity with precedent and custom heretofore, has had prepared a list as far as he could, and expects to have the list made complete, of all those to whom members desire to have these debates forwarded. The last convention gave the secretary a compensation of one dollar a day for six months, to discharge this duty. The price fixed by the substitute of my colleague (Mr. Greene,) is six dollars for one thousand copies, which is six cents for every ten copies folded, addressed and mailed, which I think is as small a compensation as could be asked As the gentleman from Baltimore city (Mr. Stockbridge) has said, if the folder is required to stay here until this is done, he will be here over two months.

Mr. STIRLING. It seems to me that the decision of this question depends very much upon matters of fact. I do not think that anybody is specially entitled to anything from this convention. The question is how far the public business and convenience can be subserved. These debates are printed in Baltimore city; and I can see no use in having them sent to Annapolis, and somebody kept here for the purpose of mailing them somewhere else. It has been very often said, that the road to "no place" lies through Annapolis. And the idea of having the debates sent here for the purpose of sending them somewhere else, is absurd. I understand that the printer is willing to deliver these debates in Baltimore city, already folded, at three dollars per thousand sheets. And we want somebody to supervise the work, and to attend to what other labor there may be connected with it. If these matters are printed in Baltimore, and the secretary goes to Baltimore, and the revising clerk goes to Baltimere when the convention adjourns, what is the use of keeping anybody here in Annapolis to receive these debates and send them off?

The question was upon the motion of Mr. DAVIS, of Washington, to amend the original order submitted by Mr. HEBB, by striking out the words "the secretary and," leaving the folder to perform the work contemplated by the order.

Mr. NEGLEY. I move to amend the amendment of my colleague (Mr. Davis, of Washington,) so that the words "the postmaster and" be inserted in place of the words he proposes to have stricken out.

Mr. DAVIS, of Washington. I will accept that amendment.

The PRESIDENT. If any objection is made the gentleman cannot modify his amendment.

Mr. HEBB. I object.

The question was then taken upon the amendment of Mr. DAVIS, of Washington, and it was rejected.

The question was then upon the substitute offered by Mr. GREENE.

Mr. DAVIS, of Charles. I understand that the offer has been made to do this work for three dollars a thousand sheets. I move to amend the substitute by striking out the word "six" and inserting the word "three" before the words "dollars for each thousand copies."

Mr. GREENE. That offer was in regard to the folding alone. There still remains the addressing and mailing. The addressing is certainly a much more laborious part of the work than the mere folding.

Mr. DANIEL. Six dollars a thousand is little enough for doing this work; that is only three-fifths of a cent for folding, directing and mailing each copy.

Mr. DAVIS, of Washington. It will cost three hundred and sixty dollars besides the postage.

Mr. NEGLEY. I understand that there will be about two thousand copies delivered daily. At that rate it would be infinitely cheaper for the convention to retain its present folder, and have them sent to members from this point. The contract with the printer is that he must deliver these debates here in Annapolis; the convention is not bound to pay for their transmission from Baltimore city to this place; that is the duty of the printer. It was contemplated originally, I presume, that the printing should be done here; at least the contract was made with the printer in this place, and of course this is the point where these documents must be delivered. The convention is not charged with any expense that is consequent upon their transmission to this place, and if two thousand copies daily are to be printed, folded and distributed, it would be cheaper for the convention to continue the folder, who says he can do all that. That would be only four dollars a day, instead of twelve dollars. The present folder says he can fold and send to members two thousand copies a day.

Mr. PUGH. I understand we have only about a thousand a day now.

Mr. TODD. There will be two forms a day struck off after the convention adjourns.

Mr. DAVIS, of Charles. I will modify my amendment, so as to strike out the words "six dollars" and insert the words "four dollars."

Mr. MILLER. I think if the debates are kept up hereafter as they have been heretofore, we shall want about three hundred dollars to pay the secretary. I notice that the second volume of the debates has been commenced. There were some forty-nine or fifty signatures in the first volume, and there will probably be as many in the second volume. Then at the rate of six dollars a signature of a thousand copies, there would be paid to the secretary about three hundred dollars. If we keep the folder for seventy-five days, and pay him four dollars a day, as we are now paying him, that will take three hundred dollars. I do not suppose the debates will all be printed short of seventy-five days. Therefore, as a matter of economy, it will make very little difference whether we employ the secretary to do this work at six dollars a thousand copies, or the folder at four dollars a day.

Mr. CUSHING. If this amendment prevails, and the printer requires three dollars a thousand for folding, that will leave only a dollar a thousand for directing and affixing the stamps. No man would do that work for that.

Mr. DAVIS, of Washington. I suppose the gentleman who offered to do the folding for three dollars a thousand, expected to make considerable profit. If the secretary undertakes to do this work himself, he will have the dollar a thousand, and a portion of that three dollars as profit besides.

Mr. DAVIS, of Charles. The gentleman from Baltimore city (Mr. Cushing) thinks that a dollar a thousand is not remuneration enough for directing these debates.—Now the printers have a system of printing the directions, as we all know from the newspapers we receive, and can furnish them to the secretary for a mere trifle, and he can get off from eight to ten thousand copies a day. He will not have to write the name of every person on the wrapper, merely to paste on the printed name. The cost of directing will be a mere trifle.

The question was upon the motion of Mr. DAVIS, of Charles, to strike out the words "six dollars," and insert the words "four dollars" in the substitute of Mr. GREENE.

The question being then taken, upon a division—ayes 42, noes not counted—the motion was agreed to.

Mr. NEGLEY moved to amend the substitute by striking out the word "secretary," and inserting the word "folder."

The question being taken, the amendment was rejected.

The question was then upon agreeing to the substitute, as amended, which was as follows:

"*Ordered*, That the secretary be directed to provide for the folding, and addressing and mailing of that portion of the journal of the debates of this convention, which shall not have been delivered to the members at its adjournment *sine die;* and, as in full compensation for such service, the president is hereby requested to issue his certificates to the said secretary, at the rate of four dollars for each thousand copies of said journal thus folded, addressed and mailed."

Upon this question Mr. TODD called for the yeas and nays, and they were ordered.

The question was then taken, by yeas and nays, and resulted—yeas 50, nays 21—as follows:

Yeas—Messrs. Goldsborough, President; Audoun, Baker, Barron, Belt, Billingsley, Bond, Brooks, Chambers, Cunningham, Cushing, Dail, Daniel, Davis, of Charles, Dent, Duvall, Earle, Ecker, Farrow, Greene, Hatch, Hebb, Hodson, Johnson, Jones, of Cecil, Keefer, Kennard, King, Lansdale, Larsh, Marbury, Markey, McComas, Mitchell, Miller, Morgan, Negley, Parker, Pugh, Ridgely, Russul, Schley, Schlosser, Scott, Smith, of Dorchester, Sneary, Stirling, Stockbridge, Sykes, Thomas—50.

Nays—Messrs. Abbott, Annan, Brown, Carter, Davis, of Washington, Dellinger, Galloway, Henkle, Hoffman, Hollyday, Hopper, Horsey, Lee, Mullikin, Murray, Nyman, Peter, Purnell, Todd, Turner, Wilmer—21

The substitute was accordingly adopted.

Pending the call of the yeas and nays, the following explanations were made by members as their names were called:

Mr. ABBOTT. I sha'l vote "no" on this proposition, as I have an amendment which I desire to offer, and which I very much prefer to this.

Mr. BELT. I think the secretary is the proper officer to represent this convention after it adjourns; and the proper officer to have charge of this matter, whoever else may be under him. I would like to pay him a more liberal compensation: but as I believe that this is the best that can be done, I shall vote for it. I vote "aye."

Mr. GALLOWAY. I am in favor of having Mr. Tatman with the secretary to perform this work; and therefore upon this proposition I vote "no."

Mr. NEGLEY. As the house has refused to insert the name of the folder, who I believe should be the one to have this work, and have manifested a determination to give it on these terms to the secretary, I vote "aye."

Mr. PETER. I believe the folder is the proper person to do this work. He was selected for this purpose; and believing that this is throwing him out of what properly belongs to him, I shall vote "no."

Mr. TODD. I have no personal feeling against any officer of this body. But simply upon the ground of economy I shall be compelled to vote in the negative upon this proposition. I have been informed by the chairman of the committee on printing (Mr. Valliant) that two forms a day will be struck off—that is, two thousand copies a day. I have been informed by Mr. Tatman that he could fold and send off those two thousand copies a day, which will be at a cost of five dollars; whereas, by the adoption of this order the convention will pay eight dollars a day. I therefore vote "no."

Mr. MILLER. I move to reconsider the vote by which the amendment of the gentleman from Charles (Mr. Davis) was adopted, striking out "six dollars" and inserting "four dollars." I voted for that amendment without properly reflecting upon the extent of the labor to be imposed upon the secretary in folding, directing and mailing this large number of debates. A few days ago a book was passed around to members of this body, requesting them to write in it the names and addresses of those persons to whom they were in the habit of sending copies of the journal of debates. Now, if the secretary, under this order, takes a book of that kind, and addresses these debates to each individual named in that book, it will certainly be no easy task for him to perform the merely clerical labor of directing a thousand copies in that way. You could not go into a counting house in Baltimore city and get a clerk to do it for one dollar. The folding will be three dollars a thousand according to the estimate made here. The only compensation, therefore, for doing this large amount of work will be but one dollar a thousand copies, which is certainly a very small compensation. The printer, I understand, is to furnish the wrapping paper and fold these documents.

The PRESIDENT. That paper will be furnished by the State.

Mr. MILLER. The gentleman from Caroline (Mr. Todd) spoke of the number to be sent off each day. We are entitled to but ten copies each of each signature of these debates, and if two signatures a day are printed then the sooner the debates will be completed. It is only four or six dollars a signature, and the printing of two signatures a day will only be getting through the matter sooner. I make this motion to reconsider for the reason that the merely clerical work of directing a thousand copies of these debates in the way in which we direct them here at our desks every day, to be sent to our friends, will not be properly compensated by one dollar. I would not ask any person in the world to do it for that.

Mr. DAVIS, of Charles. I will explain to the gentleman how the thing is to be done, and he will then see that there will be no clerical labor. The directions on these wrappers will be printed before these sheets are folded, and when the folding is done all the directing is done, just as the directions on newspapers which one sees every day, and one dollar a thousand is, I think, an ample compensation.

Mr. DAVIS, of Washington. I will state another thing about this folding. I am satisfied the secretary can employ a boy to fold them for seventy-five cents a thousand, and any boy can fold two thousand a day. If the State furnishes the paper, and he can employ a boy for seventy-five cents a thousand, I think the balance of the four dollars a thousand will pay him very handsomely, even if he should use a pen for directing every one of them.

Mr. PETER. I will second the motion of the gentleman from Anne Arundel (Mr. Miller) to reconsider this matter, with a view to retain the folder as well as the secretary; to let each one of them finish up his respective labors here. We have selected them for that purpose. They have been with us all the time. They understand all their duties. And even if it should cost a little more, let it be done right. Let us be enabled to look with certainty to receiving these sheets of debates, which are important to us, and also that the files we have attempted to keep here shall be made complete. Therefore, if the matter is reconsidered, I shall move to keep the secretary and folder both.

Mr. NEGLEY. I do not think we ought to

expect all this labor of directing to be done by the secretary. Would it not be infinitely better to have him fold each copy by itself, put a stamp upon it, and then wrap up the ten copies for each member in a bundle and direct that bundle to the member, who can direct each single copy as he pleases? It would save a great deal of trouble to the secretary, and I think would be infinitely better.

Mr. ECKER. That would require double postage; the postage upon each single copy, and then the postage upon each bundle of ten copies.

The question was then taken upon the motion of Mr. MILLER to reconsider, which was not agreed to.

ONE HUNDRED DOLLARS EXTRA MILEAGE.

Mr. DELLINGER submitted the following:

"*Ordered*, That the committee on accounts, in auditing the per diem and mileage accounts of members of the convention, be and they are hereby instructed to make such audit, in conformity to the convention bill, by allowing to each member five dollars per day, and the mileage allowed to the members of the last general assembly of this State."

The PRESIDENT. Does that include the hundred dollars extra mileage?

Mr. DELLINGER. That is the object.

The PRESIDENT. The object is to appropriate one hundred dollars to each member, according to the practice of the last legislature, unsanctioned by any law or authority.

Mr. BAKER. I hope that order will not be adopted. It is not sustained by any precedent.

Mr. DANIEL. I would like to hear this order explained.

Mr. DELLINGER. I do not think, for my part, that it requires any explanation. The law is perfectly clear to my mind, although I am no lawyer. I will state that I have no doubt upon the subject myself. The committee on claims of the last legislature made this report:

"The committee on claims, to which was referred an order of the house of the second day of March, 1864, instructing them to readjust the mileage of the members of the general assembly, respectfully report:

"That the constitution of Maryland provides that the members of the general assembly shall receive a per diem of four dollars, and such mileage as may be allowed by law. This constitutional provision seems to justify the conclusion, that while the per diem of members is fixed unchangeably, their mileage is left to be adjusted according to the varying circumstances which might arise.

"The committee, having in view the peculiar and unprecedented condition of the currency of the country at this time, and the greatly enhanced cost of travel and living in consequence thereof, have deemed it just and right to provide as near as may be for equalizing the compensation of members with that of the previous legislatures, and therefore would respectfully recommend the adoption of the following joint resolution:

"*Resolved by the General Assembly of Maryland*, That the sum of one hundred dollars, in addition to their usual mileage, be paid to each of the senators and delegates of the general assembly."

Mr. STOCKBRIDGE. Will the gentleman read the names appended to that report?

Mr. DELLINGER. There are no names to the report. I now read from section three of the bill calling this convention together:

"And the compensation of the delegates to said convention shall be five dollars per day, and the mileage allowed to members of the general assembly of this State."

The PRESIDENT. That does not say members of the last general assembly.

Mr. DELLINGER. But the last legislature fixed the mileage under the resolution I have read. And the act calling this convention together clearly says that members of this convention shall receive the same mileage as members of the legislature. The only question is: Did the legislature intend that the convention should have the mileage they received, or did they intend that they should only receive the mileage of previous legislatures? which to my county is forty-one dollars.

Mr. SCHLEY. Can the gentleman inform me whether the convention bill was passed prior to the adoption of the joint resolution fixing the mileage of members of the general assembly?

Mr. DELLINGER. I cannot give that information; I presume it was, however. Nevertheless, that does not make any difference at all, according to my judgment. I am one of those who believe that the last legislature of the State of Maryland had no right or power, under the constitution of this State, to fix even the per diem of members of this convention, let alone their mileage; that is a subject which exclusively belongs to this body. And I say that, looking at the constitution in relation to calling this convention together, that legislature clearly transcended its powers when it attempted to say to the sovereign convention of the State of Maryland, brought here by the voice of the sovereign people, that their per diem should be but five dollars a day, and their mileage the same as received by former general assemblies of this State. In addition to that I will say that I am informed that a proposition was before the last legislature of Maryland, to fix the per diem of members of this body at seven dollars. And I am told—and the gentleman from Worcester (Mr. Purnell) who was a member of that body will remember—that in the senate a motion was made to insert the sum of ten dollars as the per diem of members of this body.

Now so far as living and other expenses are concerned, they have increased fifty per cent. over what they were at the meeting of the last general assembly of this State. I think that in view of everything that is stated here in the report of the committee of the last general assembly, and in view of the law, this convention ought to be liberal enough to allow the poor members of this convention the amount asked for in this order.

Mr. STIRLING. I wish to say a word upon this subject, because I am not in the habit of refusing to acknowledge anything I have done. It has been said or insinuated here, that those who reported that resolution in the last general assembly were not to be respected, so far as their judgments were concerned, and were not quite to be respected so far as their motives were concerned. That resolution passed both houses of the general assembly, by a large majority. And so far as I have heard, with the exception of one gentleman, whom I have heard of since, every member of both houses took the money. And I think that anybody who took that money has no right to say anything against the legislature for voting it. I voted for that resolution, and I stand here responsible for having voted for it. And the reason why I shall not vote for the order of the gentleman from Washington (Mr. Dellinger) is that the per diem of the members of the last general assembly was only four dollars, and more than a hundred dollars in addition to that has already been received by members of this convention whose per diem is five dollars.

Mr. RIDGELY. Consistently with my own views of law, I reach a very different conclusion from that just communicated by the gentleman from Baltimore city (Mr. Stirling.) I do not think this convention has any right to decide this question at all. If this convention bill is susceptible of the construction which has been put upon it; if it will admit of the interpretation which the gentleman from Washington county (Mr. Dellinger) has put upon it, and I think it will, that appears to me to be an end of the question. This convention bill is no longer an act of assembly. It ceased to be an act of assembly the moment the people passed upon it and indorsed it. When the people passed upon it and indorsed it, it became the law, and imperative in all its parts. We have no discretion to relax it or to extend it. If the convention bill be susceptible of the interpretation and construction put upon it by the gentleman from Washington county, then I say you are bound to pay the mileage received by the members of the last legislature, because the people have said so.

I care nothing about the proposition itself. I rise simply to express an opinion upon the law of the case. And I go further; and I do it with great deference and respect. I believe that each member of this convention has a legal right to this amount, and that that legal right could be enforced by a mandamus. I think, therefore, it is no longer a question of discretion, but imperatively a question of right which we cannot resist.

Mr. STOCKBRIDGE. I do not see either the right or the justice of it. The phraseology of the convention bill is: "and the compensation of the delegates to said convention shall be five dollars per day, and the mileage allowed to members of the general assembly of this State." Now what does that mean? Does it refer to one single exceptional case in all the State's history, or does it refer to the customary and usual mileage? That is the question. At the time of the passage of this convention bill, there had never been in the State of Maryland, so far as I know, but one rate of mileage established by law; certainly not more than one rate for many years at least.

The PRESIDENT. It had been so from the days of the revolution.

Mr. STOCKBRIDGE. There had been but one rate of mileage, and that is what it was at the time this convention bill was passed. I submit to the convention, with great deference, that a single, wrongful, exceptional case, transpiring after the passage of this convention act, should not in this case have any influence upon the minds of members of this convention. What is mileage? A certain fixed rate allowed as travelling expenses; nothing else. There are members sitting here whose homes can be hit with a stone thrown from the steps of this State-house. A hundred dollars mileage to them for travelling expenses to those homes? The proposition is absurd upon its face. It is a wrong upon the State which we have no right to perpetrate. I hope this order will not be adopted.

Mr. DELLINGER. The gentleman from Baltimore city (Mr. Stockbridge) cannot throw a stone to my house, at any rate. I would inquire of the honorable gentleman from Baltimore city (Mr. Stockbridge) whether he took the mileage that was allowed by the last general assembly to every one of its members? I know one thing; it has cost me a great deal more than the mileage I receive, to travel to my home and back. It is well known to members of this convention that we had to leave the city of Annapolis upon a certain occasion, and I could only reach my home then by going around by the way of Philadelphia and Harrisburg. I have gone to my home and come from my home, but once since I have been a member of this convention, directly by the Baltimore and Ohio Railroad. I have been subjected to extra expense every time I have gone home from here, which has been but three times. And I would ask whether the cost of everything has not increased at least fifty per cent. beyond what it was when the last general assembly of Maryland passed this resolution?

Mr. STOCKBRIDGE. The expense of travelling by railroad has not.

Mr. DELLINGER. What was the price of gold then, and what is it now?

Mr. PURNELL. I see it stated in the papers that the railroad fare from Philadelphia south has been increased thirty-three per cent.

Mr. DELLINGER. I know very well—at least I am so informed by members of the last general assembly—that board in this city is higher now than it was then. And certainly all the expenses to which members of the convention are subjected, have been greatly increased over those of the members of the last general assembly. If the committee on accounts do not chose to allow the one hundred dollars, let them readjust the mileage, and say what the members from Anne Arundel shall receive, and what the members from Washington and Allegany, who live farthest away from the seat of government, shall receive. Let us have it fair and equitable. I think I am entitled to something more than I am getting, and therefore I must insist upon this order.

Mr. MILLER. Without stating whether I am or not in favor of this proposition as it has been advanced, I merely rise now for the purpose of replying to a remark made by the gentleman from Baltimore city (Mr. Stockbridge) in reference to members of the last general assembly, whose homes were within a stone's throw of the State house, on receiving one hundred dollars for their mileage.

Mr. STOCKBRIDGE. I made no such statement. I said that there were members sitting in this hall now, whose homes might be reached by a stone thrown from the steps of this State house.

Mr. MILLER. It may be applied to members of the last general assembly.

Mr. STOCKBRIDGE. The gentleman may apply it to any one he pleases.

Mr. MILLER. The only gentleman of the last legislature who refused to take the money, but returned the hundred dollars to the treasury, was a senator from Anne Arundel, who lives some twelve or fourteen miles from Annapolis. I am informed, without knowing the fact, that the gentleman from Baltimore city (Mr. Stockbridge) received his hundred dollars extra, although it cost him but a dollar to go from Annapolis to Baltimore.

Mr. STOCKBRIDGE. I propose to reply to this *argumentum ad hominem*. It is known to everybody here, that the moment that infamous proposition was presented in this hall last winter I arose and denounced it. I did my utmost to prevent its passage, uniformly, persistently. The president of this convention knows that I called his attention to it, when it was originally but a mere order, as being without any authority of law that would justify him, as the comptroller of the State, in paying it. And that gave rise to the joint resolution which was subsequently introduced and put through here.

As to any compensation which I received then, I received not one cent until after the general assembly had adjourned, when a certain amount of money was brought and placed in my hand. Whether it included the hundred dollars or not, I did not know then, and do not now, but presume it did. At that time I was in somewhat of a bad humor. The house of delegates had passed an appropriation for the care of our sick and wounded soldiers. That went to the senate, and the senate cut it down to one-sixth of what we had voted. They sent it back here, and the house refused to accede to their amendment, but returned it to the senate, and asked them to recede. We said that it was due to the soldiers that they should receive from the State that amount of money. We did our utmost to get it through; but we failed, and were obliged at the last moment, late in the session, to accept what we could get—one-sixth of what we had passed. In no very amiable mood when I received the money, presuming that it contained the hundred dollars, I said, "This hundred dollars belongs to the State; I will pass it over to the State where it should be put." And I passed it over to the benefit of the sick and wounded soldiers. That is the history of that hundred dollars. If that is wrong, let it be so.

Mr. ECKER. As I am somewhat interested in this matter myself, I rise to corroborate what has been said by the gentleman from Baltimore city. When that proposition was introduced last winter, that gentleman arose with some show of indignation, as he frequently does, and made a very excellent speech on the subject. The proposition came up before the house of delegates, and was voted down—I think the vote stood 40 to 22. We supposed that that matter was at an end, and turned our attention to other matters. But a very particular friend from Harford county, watched his opportunity, counted noses, and when he found my worthy friend (Mr. Stockbridge,) and those who voted the other way, out of the house, he slipped around to another member from a neighboring county, whose name I will not mention ——

Mr. CHAMBERS. Give the name.

Mr. ECKER. No, it is too near home. He slipped around to him and said, "Let us reconsider this matter." And it was reconsidered and carried. When I called for my money, I counted it over, but made no calculation at all, and put it into my pocket. I had a neighbor from Frederick county who sat near me. He took his money and put it into his pocket, intending to keep it, not supposing that Frederick county would notice it. But when he got home he found his neighbors and friends down on him like a thousand of brick for taking the money. So he brought it back and paid it in to the credit of the State. Whether he is entitled to any particular credit for that, I do not say.

Now, so far as I was myself concerned, I was in the same fix. My people came down on me, too, like a thousand of brick. So I came down to Baltimore and paid the hundred dollars into the sanitary fair. I acknowledge the corn that I took it, though at the time I took it I did not know it. The legislature had refused to give a certain amount to the poor soldiers; had cut the appropriation down to one-sixth, which I considered an outrage. Therefore when gentlemen come to look at this matter right and properly, I am inclined to think that matters stand about as they ought.

Now in regard to the price of board about which the gentleman from Washington county (Mr. Dellinger) has spoken. I know I paid ten dollars a week last winter, and when I came back here last spring the same man offered to board me for eight dollars. And I do not know of a single gentleman now who pays as much board as last winter. I know one gentleman who paid seventeen or eighteen dollars a week last winter, and I know no gentleman who pays over fourteen or fifteen now.

Mr. Scott. I hope the members of this convention will take warning from the dilemma in which the members of the general assembly got themselves, requiring so much explanation before the people, and compelling those who took the money to disgorge, in order to put themselves right on the record. I hope members here will avoid getting into the same trouble.

Mr. Stockbridge. I wish to disclaim having disgorged anything. I never asked the question how it would affect my popularity, and what is more, I do not care.

Mr. Scott. My remark applied more properly to the gentleman from Carroll (Mr. Ecker.)

Mr. Stockbridge. No complaints were ever made until made here. I do not care whether my constituents were in favor of it or not.

Mr. Ecker. The gentleman from Cecil (Mr. Scott) is the member who, upon the first day of the session, proposed that each member of the convention be furnished with a gold pen. I disclaim any disgorging.

Mr. Scott. I have always been accustomed to using a good pen myself. I do abominate a pen that will not write; it invariably puts me in a bad humor. And as the legislature had set the example, I thought we might as well have good pens as they. In regard to disgorging, the gentleman said he spent the money at the sanitary fair, because his neighbors were down on him like a thousand of brick. If that is not disgorging, I do not know what is.

Mr. Purnell. I should not say a word on this subject but for the reference made by the gentleman from Washington county (Mr. Dellinger) to the action upon the proposition before the senate. The resolution originated in the house of delegates, a co-ordinate branch of the government; it passed that body, I do not recollect by what majority; I have never had occasion to refer to the journal to satisfy myself in regard to the vote. It went to the senate, at all events, with the high indorsement of the house of delegates, and the senate with that sort of courtesy that distinguishes that body, passed it very quickly. There was a proposition made there to increase the compensation of members of the convention from five to ten dollars a day. My recollection does not bear me out in that fact fully. I do not think anything was said upon that subject. The question was put and decided very quietly. So far as receiving the hundred was concerned, I received it, and had no compunctions of conscience in doing so. I received it under what I supposed to be the action of the general assembly, and considered myself entitled to it. I have seen no cause to regret it since. Without indicating what my action on this proposition will be, I will say that I did not then have, nor have I since had occasion to feel under the necessity of disgorging it, in order to purge myself of any iniquity. My constituents have never called me to account. I am ready at any time to vindicate my vote.

Mr. Dent. I merely desire to express the opinion that it is perfectly competent for the committee on accounts, without any action of this body, to allow the members of this convention the same amount of mileage which was allowed the members of the last general assembly. The last legislature passed the convention bill and fixed the mileage of members of this convention at the same as they received themselves; and they authorized the payment of a certain per diem. With that view I believe that the committee on accounts are competent to make the allowance without any action by this body.

Mr. Dellinger. I can assure every member of this convention that I have been influenced by no improper motives in bringing this subject before this house. Having consulted with some legal gentleman upon the subject, and having been assured by them that the law of the last legislature calling this convention together gives us this one hundred dollars additional mileage; I then consulted with several other members of this body, and they agreed to support the proposition if it was introduced here. I then concluded I would introduce it. And if it be a duty, I have discharged that duty here.—Whether this convention shall adopt this order or not, I am free to confess is a matter of perfect indifference to me. If they shall adopt it, I shall take the mileage, most unquestionably. If they do not adopt it, as a matter of course, I cannot receive it.

I attach a great deal of weight to the opinion which has been expressed by the gentleman from Baltimore county (Mr. Ridgely.) If I had not him upon my side, if he did not support my proposition, I should feel very much inclined to withdraw it. But I believe he is right. I am satisfied I have done nothing wrong in submitting this proposition to the convention. It is for the convention to decide upon it. I do feel, I must confess, some inclination to withdraw it. But as that perhaps would not meet with the approbation of those who have advocated it, I will not do so. If the yeas and nays are called I shall vote in favor of the proposition, because I believe it to be just and right and proper. If I did not so think I should record my vote against it.

Mr. BELT. I desire to add one sentence to the strong view my friend from Baltimore county (Mr. Ridgely) has taken upon this question. I would state my impression that the mileage allowed to members of the general assembly of this State from time immemorial was not regulated by any constitutional provision. It was regulated either by the custom of the general assembly, or by statute.

Mr. STIRLING. It was regulated by statute law; one of the old laws.

Mr. BELT. My impression was that it was regulated by statute; and I have been trying to find the statute, but have not done so.—Being regulated by statute, of course it was competent to be changed by statute. Here then a certain statute existed allowing a certain mileage to members of the general assembly. The last general assembly repealed that statute. And I hold as a matter of law that that repeal operates until another general assembly shall restore the old provision. I do not know any authority which any officer of the State has to refuse to comply with the new statute, for it supersedes the old one.

As regards the suggestion made by the gentleman from Baltimore city (Mr. Stockbridge) that the act calling this convention was passed before the appropriation bill changing the mileage of members of the general assembly. That has no force in it, for the reason that the general appropriation bills are about the last acts passed at any session. Therefore that appropriation bill, like all others, operates *nunc pro tunc;* it takes action back. I shall therefore cheerfully vote for this proposition.

The question was upon the order submitted by Mr. DELLINGER.

Upon this question Mr. BAKER called for the yeas and nays, which were ordered.

The question was then taken by yeas and nays, pending the call of which, the following explanations were made by members, as their names were called:

Mr. ABBOTT. When this proposition was first presented, after hearing the explanation of the gentleman from Baltimore county (Mr. Ridgely,) I intended to vote for it. But when I came to hear the explanations of members of the last general assembly, and found out what effect it had upon them, that they did not know they had a hundred dollars too much or too little, fearing it might have the same effect upon me, I shall vote "no."

Mr. CHAMBERS. I have no doubt about the authority of this convention to pass this order, and to prescribe their own pay, their mileage, their emoluments, or anything else. But seeing from the indications here that the gentlemen of the majority do not choose to take the responsibility of this upon themselves, I have no idea of putting money in their pockets against their will. I therefore vote "no."

Mr. NEGLEY. I believe with the gentleman from Baltimore county (Mr. Ridgely) that it is perfectly right and proper that this proposition should carry. But I see clearly that it is lost, and therefore there is no use for me to vote in the affirmative. I therefore vote "no."

Mr. RIDGELY. For the reasons I have already given, I cannot consistently vote in any other way than in the affirmative. I therefore vote "aye."

Mr. STIRLING. My vote upon this question will be given upon this ground: I believe that the joint resolution of the last general assembly is the law. And I believe that by the force of that law the members of this convention are entitled to this additional mileage.—But as the question is presented to me here whether I think it expedient, and according to my wishes and preferences at the present time to receive this money, I vote "no."

Mr. WOODEN. Being a member of the committee on accounts, I ask to be excused from voting.

The question being taken, the convention refused to excuse the member from voting.

Mr. WOODEN. Then I vote "no."

After the call of the roll had been completed, but before the result of the vote was announced, several members changed their votes as follows:

Mr. HODSON changed his vote to "no."
Mr. DUVALL changed his vote to "no."
Mr. TURNER changed his vote to "no."
Mr. PARRAN changed his vote to "no."
Mr. LEE changed his vote to "no."
Mr. JOHNSON changed his vote to "no."
Mr. HENKLE changed his vote to "no."
Mr. DAIL changed his vote to "no."
Mr. GALE changed his vote to "no."
Mr. CRAWFORD changed his vote to "no."

Mr. BELT. I am still inflexibly in favor of the opinion I have expressed, and which my friend from Baltimore county (Mr. Ridgely) has indorsed. And I have no doubt that those who have voted with me in favor of this proposition have been thrown in a false position by the gentlemen of the majority, who have cast their votes against this proposition when more of them are in favor of it than there are of the minority of this house. Having no desire to occupy that position, I am compelled, against my judgment, to change my vote to "no."

Mr. DELLINGER. I wish to change my vote to "no," and I ask the unanimous consent of the house, if it can be done, to withdraw this order.

Mr. STOCKBRIDGE. O! no! let it stand.

Mr. DELLINGER. I am induced to take this course by the remarks made by the gentleman from Baltimore city (Mr. Stirling.)

Mr. MARBURY. For the reasons stated by my colleague (Mr. Belt,) I change my vote to "no."

Mr. RIDGELY. I ask leave to change my vote to "no." But I desire to say that I am decidedly of the opinion that the proposition of the gentleman from Washington (Mr. Dellinger) is right and sustained by the law. But as the direction which this matter has taken has been contrary to my expectations, I ask permission to put myself right by changing my vote to "no."

Mr. KING changed his vote to "no."

Mr. DAVIS, of Charles, who was not present when his name was called, now voted "no."

Mr. THOMAS, who was not present when his name was called, also voted "no."

The PRESIDENT then announced that the order was rejected by the following vote:

Yeas—Messrs. Billingsley, Bond, Dent, Lansdale, Morgan—5.

Nays—Messrs. Goldsborough, President; Abbott, Annan, Baker, Belt, Brooks, Brown, Carter, Chambers, Crawford, Cunningham, Cushing, Dail, Daniel, Davis, of Charles, Davis, of Washington, Dellinger, Duvall, Earle, Ecker, Farrow, Gale, Galloway, Greene, Hatch, Hebb, Henkle, Hodson, Hoffman, Hollyday, Hopper, Horsey, Johnson, Jones, of Cecil, Keefer, Kennard, King, Larsh, Lee, Marbury, Markey, McComas, Mitchell, Miller, Mullikin Murray, Negley, Nyman, Parker, Parran, Pugh, Purnell, Ridgely, Russell, Schley, Schlosser, Scott, Smith, of Dorchester, Sneary, Stirling, Stockbridge, Swope, Sykes, Thomas, Todd, Turner, Wickard, Wilmer, Wooden—69.

Mr. SCHLEY. I move that the gentleman from Washington county (Mr. Dellinger) be allowed to withdraw the order he introduced in relation to the milage of members.

Mr. STOCKBRIDGE. I object to that.

Mr. SCHLEY. I hope the objection to my motion will be withdrawn. The course the house has taken in regard to this matter shows the propriety of the course I have suggested.

Mr. STOCKBRIDGE. What will be the effect of allowing this order to be withdrawn? Can it be renewed to-morrow or next day?

The PRESIDENT. Certainly.

Mr. STOCKBRIDGE. Then I think it better be left as it now stands.

Mr. DELLINGER. It will not be renewed again.

The PRESIDENT. Objection having been made to the withdrawal of the order, the question must be submitted to the convention.

The question being taken, permission was granted, and the order was accordingly withdrawn.

Mr. VALLIANT. I desire to ask the consent of the convention to allow the committee on reporting and printing to retire. We desire to have a meeting, and it will be perhaps somewhat protracted. We have been trying to get a meeting during the present week, and sometimes have succeeded in getting on during the intervals between the sessions. But those intervals have been so brief, and being obliged to get meals during the intervals, or not get them at all, we have not been able to accomplish our business. I therefore ask leave of the convention for that committee to retire in order that it may do what it has heretofore been unable to do.

Leave was accordingly granted.

EXTRA COMPENSATION TO COLLINS TATMAN.

Mr. RIDGELY. I offer the following order, in regard to which I will add one word of explanation:

Ordered, That the sum of one hundred dollars be paid Collins Tatman as extra compensation."

When the proposition was before the house touching the duties devolving upon the secretary in relation to transmitting documents to members after the adjournment of the convention, I voted for the proposition to devolve those duties upon the secretary for the reason assigned by the gentlemen from Prince George's (Mr. Belt) that it was eminently proper that the secretary, being the proper and responsible officer of this body, should have the superintendence of the duties to be performed after its adjournment. Many members of the convention thought it was unkind and unfair towards the folder, whose special duty it was to have charge of that department. I now offer this order, at the suggestion of some of those gentlemen for the reason that this folder has been employed for the last two or three weeks in the exclusive performance of that duty, in consequence of the unavoidable absence of the one associated with him. I offer this proposition with a view to harmonize upon that subject.

The question was upon agreeing to the order.

Upon this question, Mr. DAVIS, of Washington, called for the yeas and nays, and they were ordered.

The question was then taken, by yeas and nays, and resulted:

Yeas—Messrs. Goldsborough, President; Abbott, Barron, Billingsley, Brooks, Carter,

Chambers, Cushing, Dellinger, Dent, Earle, Gale, Galloway, Greene, Hodson, Hollyday, Hopper, Johnson, King, Lansdale, Larsh, Marbury, Markey, McComas, Morgan, Mullikin, Murray, Negley, Nyman, Peter, Pugh, Purnell, Ridgely, Schley, Scott, Smith, of Dorchester, Sneary, Swope, Sykes, Thomas, Todd, Turner, Wooden—42.

Nays—Messrs. Annan, Baker, Bond, Brown, Crawford, Cunningham, Dail, Daniel, Davis, of Charles, Davis, of Washington, Duvall, Hatch, Hebb, Henkle, Hoffman, Horsey, Jones, of Cecil, Keefer, Kennard, Lee, Mitchell, Miller, Parker, Russell, Schlosser, Stirling, Stockbridge, Wilmer—28.

The order was accordingly adopted.

Pending the call of the yeas and nays, the following explanations were made by members, as their names were called:

Mr. CUSHING. I shall vote for this order, both from a sense of justice, and a desire to be right. I voted for an order to pay the secretary extra compensation for doing in addition to his own work, the work of the assistant secretary while the latter was absent. And I voted for extra compensation to the assistant secretary under similar circumstances. I shall therefore vote to increase the pay of the folder for doing the work of two folders. I vote "aye."

Mr. DAVIS, of Washington. In order to be consistent, as the gentleman from Baltimore city (Mr. Cushing) is, as I am opposed to all this matter of extra compensation, I vote "no."

Mr. HEBB. I am compelled with some reluctance to vote against this proposition, as I consider it a bad precedent to pay the folder for twenty-five days extra work, inasmuch as some other proposition may be introduced to pay the postmaster and the pages who assisted him in that work. I therefore vote "no."

Mr. STIRLING. I regret very much to vote against any order of this sort. I am always in favor of paying everybody who has done work for us. I am not very well acquainted with the facts in this case. But I understand that while some additional labor has been thrown upon this folder, still he has been assisted by the pages and other officers of this house. I do not gather that he has done the whole of the work himself. I vote "no."

BOUND COPIES OF THE CONSTITUTION.

Mr. GREENE submitted the following order:

"*Ordered*, That the State librarian be and he is hereby directed to purchase of James Wingate two hundred and fifty copies of the constitution passed by this convention, when adopted by the voters of this State, said constitution shall contain an elaborate index, prepared with references to articles and sections, and also to the page, said constitution shall be printed in the best style, (with side notes,) on fair white paper with large fair type and well bound, and shall contain the names of the members of this convention, said constitution shall contain the certificate of the clerk of the court of appeals, that it is a true copy of the constitution passed by this convention; and the indexing and publication of said constitution shall be approved by the president of this convention.

"And the State librarian shall distribute said copies of the constitution, as follows:

"One copy to each member of the convention; to the governor, lieutenant governor, comptroller, treasurer, attorney general, adjutant general, superintendent of public education, and commissioner of the land office, each one copy; to the judges and clerks of the circuit courts, and the courts of Baltimore city, each one copy; to the judges and the clerk of the court of appeals, each one copy; to the orphans' courts of the State, each one copy; to the State's attorneys, each one copy; to the register of wills, each one copy; to the boards of county commissioners, each one copy; to the mayor of Baltimore city, one copy.

"And the remaining eleven copies shall be retained in the State library, subject to the disposition of the general assembly.

"And the president of this convention is hereby authorized and directed to pay James Wingate one hundred dollars, for preparing said carefully elaborated index and side notes to said constitution, and also two dollars per copy for said constitution when published by James Wingate."

Mr. THOMAS. I move that this order be laid over, so that it may be printed upon the journal, and an opportunity given members to examine it.

Mr. GREENE. I hope the convention will pass upon this order at once. It is merely following the precedent of the convention of 1850. There is nothing so very extraordinary about the order as to require twenty-four hours consideration.

The question was then taken upon the motion of Mr. THOMAS, that the order be laid over, and it was not agreed to.

The question was upon agreeing to the order.

Mr. BARRON. Did this order come from the committee on printing?

The PRESIDENT. No, sir; it was offered by the gentleman from Allegany (Mr. Greene.)

Mr. BARRON. I think it should come from that committee.

Mr. THOMAS. I understand that the committee is in session now, considering among other subjects the very one to which this order relates.

Mr. GREENE. I think my friend from Baltimore city (Mr. Thomas) is misinformed. Different members of that committee have been consulted with in regard to this order, and I think all of them have agreed to it.

Mr. THOMAS. I think the committee on printing should consider this matter. I therefore move that this order be referred to the committee on printing.

Mr. STIRLING. What has the committee on printing and reporting got to do with the printing of the certified copies of the constitution after the convention adjourns? They are to have charge of the current printing of this convention. They have nothing to do with a proposition of this sort. Whether it be expedient or inexpedient is a matter for the convention to determine.

Mr. SCHLEY. I understand the proposition is to have the constitution printed and bound in the style of the edition printed by Murphy & Co. in 1855. I am very sure if the party, who it is proposed shall furnish these books, shall get them up in that style for two dollars a copy his margin of profit will be exceedingly small. I think it is a very economical plan for such an edition, and I shall support the proposition.

The question was then taken upon the motion to refer the order to the committee on reporting and printing; and, upon a division—ayes 29, noes 22—the motion was agreed to.

ENGROSSED COPY OF THE CONSTITUTION.

Mr. STIRLING. I move to reconsider the order adopted on Wednesday last, on motion of my friend from Baltimore county (Mr. Ridgely,) providing for four manuscript copies of the constitution as finally passed upon by this convention. I voted for that order, but upon reflection since then I am apprehensive that if it is carried out we will get ourselves into difficulty. In the first place it will take more time than we can afford. And then there may be some difficulty in having four originals. They may not all be exactly alike, and if they are not there is no authority to decide which original shall control. I think it much safer to have but one original of the constitution. The order as passed reads as follows:

"*Ordered*, That four copies of the constitution when finally adopted by the convention, be copied on parchment or detached sheets of bill paper, that the same be subscribed by the president and members of the convention, attested by the secretary, and that one copy thereof be deposited with the executive, one copy with the clerk of the court of appeals, one copy with the comptroller, and one copy with the librarian."

The question was then taken upon the motion to reconsider, and it was agreed to.

The question then recurred upon adopting the order.

Mr. STIRLING. I offer the following as a substitute for the order:

"*Ordered*, That the constitution when finally adopted by the convention, be written on parchment or detached sheets of bill paper, that the same be subscribed by the president and attested by the secretary of the convention, and be deposited with the clerk of the court of appeals."

I think there may be some question as to what the subscription by the members, as mentioned in the original order, may mean; whether it means that all who choose may sign it, or the majority of the members, or all the members. And it may be contended that the proper subscription is necessary to the legal efficacy of the paper. There may be some questions raised about it which I think better not be encountered.

Mr. RIDGELY. I do not know what is the object of the gentleman from Baltimore city, (Mr. Stirling.) I will only state that my purpose in offering the original was that one copy of course should be the original, and as the original should be deposited with the clerk of the court of appeals, who, I suppose, would be the proper depository. The other copies would be considered as duplicates, and would be deposited in the other offices named, with a view of preserving an authenticated copy of the constitution in the contingency of the original being lost or destroyed. That was the sole purpose I had in view; it was from abundance of caution to have duplicates of the original preserved. I do not know the object my friend has in view in the change he proposes.

Mr. STIRLING. The gentleman was out when I made my former statement. He interprets the order as I suppose he meant it to be interpreted. But it provides that there shall be four "copies." Copies of what? As I understand the meaning of the order, it is that there shall be one original and three copies, and so the gentleman explains it. That relieves it from some of the objections which I urged against it a few moments since. "Three copies and one original" is very different from "four copies." I think there need be only the one original.

Mr. RIDGELY. I do not object to that.

The question being then taken upon the substitute offered by Mr. STIRLING, it was adopted.

JOURNAL OF DEBATES.

Mr. STOCKBRIDGE. I submit the following:

"*Ordered*, That the revising clerk be requested to have appended to the report of debates a copy of the official vote upon the question of calling this convention, and also of the vote upon the question of the ratification of the constitution which we shall submit to the people."

Any gentleman who will look at the journal of the last convention will find in a little appendix at the close, the vote by counties for and against that convention. But it has not the vote upon the adoption of the constitution framed by that convention. It would be very little to do, would make but a page or two, and may be very useful in time to come.

The question being taken, the order was adopted.

Mr. GALLOWAY called up the following report, which was read and adopted:

"The committee on accounts in compliance with the order passed the 30th instant, respectfully report that, after a careful examination of said order, they recommend that the president of the convention pay all bills for reporting and printing of the journal of debates remaining unpaid after the adjournment of the said convention, when the same are duly certified as correct by Mr. Joseph H. Audoun, or some other member of the committee on reporting and printing."

ELECTIVE FRANCHISE.

Mr. EARLE, from the committee of revision, reported back to the convention the article on the elective franchise, with amendments; and recommended that said amendments be concurred in by the convention.

The first section of this article as adopted by the convention reads:

"All elections shall be by ballot, and every white male citizen of the United States of the age of twenty-one years or upwards, who shall have resided in the State one year next preceding the election and six months in the city of Baltimore or in any county, shall be entitled to be registered as a legal voter; and such registration made in accordance with such provisions as the general assembly may prescribe, together with the muster rolls of all such soldiers as may be entitled to be registered in the State, and who may be serving in the army of the United States, shall be held and taken as the only evidence of qualification to vote at any election hereafter, and the general assembly shall by law provide for taking the votes of soldiers serving in the army of the United States, in the field; and in case any county or city shall be so divided as to form portions of different electoral districts for the election of congressman, senator, delegate, or other officer or officers, then to entitle a person to vote for such officer, he must have been a resident of that part of the county or city which shall form a part of the electoral district in which he offers to vote, for six months next preceding the election; but a person who shall *not* have acquired a residence in such county, or city, entitling him to vote at any such election, shall be entitled to vote in the election district from which he removed, until he shall have acquired a residence in the part of the county or city to which he has removed."

This section as remodeled by the committee of revision reads in the following manner:

Section 1. All elections shall be by ballot, and every white male citizen of the United States of the age of twenty-one years or upwards, who shall have resided in the State one year next preceding the election, and six months in any county, or in any legislative district of Baltimore city, and who shall comply with the provisions of this article of the constitution, shall be entitled to vote at all elections hereafter held in this State. And in case any county or city shall be so divided as to form portions of different electoral districts for the election of congressman, senator, delegate, or other officer or officers, then to entitle a person to vote for such officer, he must have been a resident of that part of the county or city which shall form a part of the electoral district in which he offers to vote, for six months next preceding the election; but a person who shall have acquired a residence in such county or city, entitling him to vote at any such election, shall be entitled to vote in the election district from which he removed, until he shall have acquired a residence in the part of the county or city to which he has removed.

The proposed changes in the section will be seen by comparing the above forms, one with the other.

The second section of this article recommended by the committee, is a new one, though it contains no new matter.

It embraces the seventh section as adopted by the convention, and such parts of the first section, as the committee rejected in *their* first section. It relates to the registration of voters, and to the vote of the soldiers in the United States service, and reads thus:

Section 2. The general assembly shall provide by law for a uniform registration of the names of voters in this State, which registration shall be evidence of the qualification of said voters to vote at any election thereafter held. But no person shall be excluded from voting at any election on account of not being registered until the general assembly shall have passed an act of registration, and the same shall have been carried into effect, after which no person shall vote unless his name appears on the register. The general assembly shall also provide by law for taking the votes of soldiers in the army of the United States serving in the field.

The committee recommend that the sixth section of this article be made the third section. It specifies a class of persons who shall not be entitled to vote, and this is evidently its most appropriate place.

The section has been slightly modified by the committee, and as changed will read thus:

Section 3. No person above the age of twenty-one years convicted of larceny or other infamous crime, unless pardoned by the governor, shall ever thereafter be entitled to vote at any election in this State; and no lunatic or person non compos mentis shall be entitled to vote.

The next section relates to the test oath for

voters. The committee propose to number it as the fourth instead of the second section.

The oath as referred by the convention to the committee reads thus:

"I do swear or affirm that I am a citizen of the United States, that I have never given any aid, countenance or support to those in armed hostility to the United States, that I have never expressed a desire for the triumph of said enemies over the arms of the United States, and that I will bear true faith and allegiance to the United States and support the constitution and laws thereof as the supreme law of the land, any law or ordinance of any State to the contrary notwithstanding, and will in all respects demean myself as a loyal citizen of the United States, and I swear this without any reservation or evasion."

The committee recommend alterations in this oath; as altered, it will read:

"I do swear or affirm that I am a citizen of the United States, that I have never given any aid, countenance or support to those in armed hostility to the United States, that I have never expressed a desire for the triumph of said enemies over the arms of the United States, and that I will bear true faith and allegiance to the United States, and support the constitution and laws thereof as the supreme law of the land, any law or ordinance of any State to the contrary notwithstanding; that I will in all respects demean myself as a loyal citizen of the United States. And I make this oath or affirmation without any reservation or evasion, and believe it to be binding on me."

The committee propose to make the third section of this article as adopted by the convention, the fifth section. It relates to bribery, and provides, "that any person who shall give or offer to give directly or indirectly any bribe, present, or reward, or any promise or any security for the payment or delivery of money or any other thing to induce any voter to refrain from casting his vote, or forcibly to prevent him in any way from voting, shall on conviction in a court of law, in addition to the penalties now or hereafter to be imposed by law, be forever disqualified to hold any office of profit or trust or to vote at any election thereafter." The same provision is made in the present constitution, and the members of the committee are of the opinion, that this section should be so modified as to embrace all cases which may have arisen under that provision; they therefore recommend that the first part of this section be amended to read thus:

"Section 5. If any person shall give or offer to give directly or indirectly, or since the fourth day of July, eighteen hundred and fifty one, hath given or offered to give, any bribe, present, or reward," &c.

In the last line of this section, the committee recommend that the words "*an election*" be changed to read "any election."

The committee have no material change to recommend in the sixth and seventh sections of this article, and which were the fourth and fifth sections of said article as adopted in convention.

In the sixth section, they propose that the words "*in the first article of the constitution*" be stricken out, and the words "*in this article*" inserted. In the second line of the seventh section, they recommend that the words "*this constitution*" be substituted for "*the constitution.*"

The eighth and last section of this article reads as follows:

"Section 8. Every person holding any office of trust or profit under the late constitution, or under any law of this State, and who shall be continued in office under this constitution, or under any law of the State, shall within thirty days after this constitution shall have gone into effect, take the oath or affirmation set forth in the fifth section of this article, and if any such person shall fail to take said oath his office shall be *ipso facto void.*"

"The fifth section" above referred to having become the seventh section, the appropriate change should be made.

And the committee recommend as an addition to the end of the eighth section, the following:

"And every person hereafter elected or appointed to office in this State, who shall refuse or neglect to take the oath or affirmation of office provided for in the said seventh section of this article, shall be considered as having refused to accept the said office, and a new election or appointment shall be made as in case of refusal to accept or resignation of an office. And any person swearing or affirming falsely in the premises, shall, on conviction thereof in a court of law, incur the penalties of wilful and corrupt perjury, and thereafter shall be incapable of holding any office of profit or trust in this State."

This closes the report of the committee on the elective franchise.

They respectfully recommend that the proposed changes be concurred in by the convention.

GEORGE EARLE, Chairman.

When the second section reported by the committee was read,

Mr. STIRLING said: That section embraces an amendment which was submitted by myself when the report was under consideration in the convention. The committee on revision has united it with another section of the report, and put it together in a much better form than it was originally.

Mr. EARLE. The second section is composed, in part, of the first section as originally adopted by the convention, and of the seventh section which was proposed by the gentleman from Baltimore city (Mr. Stirling.) That part which was compiled from the first section sets forth, that the general assembly shall provide by law for the registration of voters; the seventh section declares that until such provision shall be made by the general assembly no person shall be excluded from voting because of not being registered. The two sections relate to the same subject-matter, hence the committee concluded to unite them in one section.

The recommendations of the committee as to changes and alterations in the article on the elective franchise were then severally read and concurred in.

EXECUTIVE DEPARTMENT.

Mr. Earle, from the same committee, reported back to the convention the article on the executive department, and recommended the following changes.

The first clause of the second section reads thus:

"Section 2. The first election for governor under this constitution shall be held on the Tuesday next after the first Monday of November, in the year eighteen hundred and sixty four, and on the same day and month in every fourth year thereafter."

This identical phraseology is used in the present constitution, but it is clearly incorrect, and the committee recommend that the words "the first election" be stricken out, and the words "an election" be substituted in their place. That part of the section will then read:

Section 2. An election for governor, under this constitution, shall be held on the Tuesday next after the first Monday of November, in the year eighteen hundred and sixty-four, and on the same day and month in every fourth year thereafter.

The sixth section of this article now reads:

"Section 6. A lieutenant governor shall be chosen at every regular election for governor in the same manner, to continue in office for the same time, and possess the same qualifications as the governor."

The committee recommend that this section be modified to read thus:

Section 6. A lieutenant governor shall be chosen at every regular election for governor. He shall continue in office for the same time, shall be elected in the same manner, and shall possess the same qualifications as the governor.

In the first line of the eighth section the committee have inserted "the" before the word "death," and in the fourth line have stricken out the word "or" before the word "removal," and after the word "removal," have inserted the words, "or other disqualification."

In the first line of the ninth section the word "the," before governor, has been stricken out. And in the last line but one, the word "senate" has been substituted for "senators," "its" for "their," and "members" for "number."

In the first line of the fourteenth section the word "any" has been stricken out, and "of" substituted. And in the last line of the twenty-first section the word "influenced" has been substituted for "influence."

The committee have no further amendments to make to this article, but respectfully recommend the adoption of those reported.

George Earle, Chairman.

On motion of Mr. Hebb, the amendments of the committee were concurred in by the convention.

EDUCATION.

Mr. Earle, from the committee of revision, also reported back to the convention the article on education, and recommended the following amendments:

After the word "qualified" in the sixth line of the first section, commence a new sentence with the words "He shall." In the eighth line of the same section insert "shall" before "report." In the tenth and eleventh lines for the expression "free public school education" substitute "free public schools," and in the eleventh line insert "shall" before the word "perform."

The section as amended will then read as follows:

Section 1. The governor shall, within thirty days after the ratification by the people of this constitution, appoint, subject to the confirmation of the senate at its first session thereafter, a State superintendent of public instruction, who shall hold his office for four years, and until his successor shall have been appointed and shall have qualified. *He shall* receive an annual salary of twenty-five hundred dollars, and such additional sum for travelling and incidental expenses as the general assembly may by law allow; *shall* report to the general assembly within thirty days after the commencement of its first session under this constitution, a uniform system of *free public schools*, and *shall* perform such other duties pertaining to his office, as may from time to time be prescribed by law.

In the second line of the second section insert the word "State" before "superintendent."

In the seventh line insert "shall" before "be appointed," and in the ninth line strike out "made" after "time," and insert the same word after "be."

In the second line of the third section after the word "governor" strike out "of the State." Also strike out "the president of the senate." And instead of "State's superintendent" in the fourth line, insert "State superintendent."

The committee also recommend that these sections (second and third) be transposed. The third section creates the board of education, and the second section makes it the duty of that board to appoint "school commissioners."

Having regard to symmetry, the board of education should be created before performing duties; for this reason the committee recommend the transposition.

In the fourth section it is proposed to insert the word "free" before "public schools" in the eighth line. And in the last line but one of the fifth section, the word "by" is inserted before the words "the mayor," and the word "and" after the word "mayor."

In the sixth section where the expression "free common schools" is used, the committee propose to strike out the word "common" and insert "public." The object is to make the expression referring to the public schools uniform throughout this article.

This closes the report of the committee of revision on the article styled education.

They recommend that the changes proposed be concurred in by the convention.

George Earle, Chairman.

Pending the consideration of that part of the above report which recommends striking out from the third section, the words "the president of the senate,"

Mr. Davis, of Washington, said: I understood it was the determination of the house not to strike out the words "the president of the senate" in this section.

Mr. Chambers. I understand it to be the business of the committee on revision to revise what has been done by the convention; and not to do as they seem to have done here, propose changes and alterations just as if they were a committee to prepare articles for the constitution.

The Chairman (Mr. Daniel.) I believe it has always been held that the committee on revision have power to suggest alterations for the consideration of the house.

Mr. Chambers. I suppose amendments cannot be made to these reports after their third reading, except in a certain manner. All that the committee on revision has to do is to see that the language is correct.

Mr. Stirling. I understand that the reason why the committee recommend the striking out of the words "the president of the senate," is that they are in this section by mistake. The committee propose no alterations except in the phraseology.

Mr. Miller. I would ask if the committee have not reported additional words to the election oath?

The Chairman (Mr. Daniel.) The chair is of opinion that the committee have proposed no substantial alterations.

Mr. Stirling. The committee on revision examine the articles after they have been passed by the convention, and then bring them in here with such suggestions in the way of alterations as they deem proper. It s for the convention to adopt them or reject hem.

Mr. Brown. I would like to inquire if these reports of the committee on revision are to be printed. It seems to me that very material alterations are proposed here, which we are passing upon without understanding them properly. I understand that an additional section has been reported to the article on elective franchise. Will that be printed without an order of the house?

The Chairman (Mr. Daniel.) The next printing will probably be in the form of the entire constitution.

The question was then taken upon the recommendation of the committee on revision to leave out the words "the president of the senate," in the third section, and it was agreed to.

The other amendments as proposed by the committee on revision were then severally read and adopted.

MILITIA.

Mr. Earle, from the committee of revision, recommended a modification of the third section of the article on militia.

The said section as adopted by the convention reads:

"Section 3. The adjutant general shall be appointed by the governor, by and with the advice and consent of the senate. He shall hold his office during the pleasure of the governor, and receive for his services such compensation as is now or may be hereafter fixed by law."

The same section as modified by the committee reads:

Section 3. There shall be an adjutant general, who shall be appointed by the governor, by and with the advice and consent of the senate. He shall hold his office at the pleasure of the governor; shall perform such duties, and shall receive such compensation or emoluments as are now or may be hereafter fixed by law.

George Earle, Chairman.

The recommendation of the committee, on being read, was concurred in by the convention.

ATTORNEY GENERAL AND STATE'S ATTORNEYS.

Mr. Earle, from the committee of revision, next reported back to the convention the article on attorney general and State's attorneys.

The changes proposed in this article are as follows:

In the first section insert the word "the" before the word "Tuesday" in the second line, and the words "the month of" before "November," in the third line. This change makes the time for electing an attorney general read, "on the Tuesday next after the first Monday in the month of November." The same phraseology is found in other parts of this constitution, and the object of the change here is to preserve uniformity. The same change is made in the ninth section of this article, when referring to the election of State's attorneys.

In the eighth line of the first section the committee recommend that the word "therefrom" after the word "removal," be stricken out. After the word "them" in the ninth line of the third section, that the words "or either of them," be inserted.

And in that part of the third section which says the attorney general "shall commence and prosecute or defend any suit or action, in any of said courts, on the part of the State *as* the general assembly shall direct," the committee propose to strike out the word "as" and insert "which."

The fourth section of the article now reads:

"Section 4. No person shall be eligible to the office of attorney general who has not been admitted to practice the law in the State, and who has not practiced the law therein for seven years, and who has not resided in the State for at least seven years next preceding his election."

The committee recommend that this section be modified to read as follows:

Section 4. No person shall be eligible to the office of attorney general who has not resided and practiced law in this State for at least seven years next preceding his election.

The first clause of the ninth section now reads, "The State's attorney shall perform such duties and receive such fees and commissions as are now prescribed by law, and such other duties, fees and commissions as may hereafter be prescribed by law." The committee recommend that this clause be made to read as follows: "The State's attorney shall perform such duties and receive such fees and commissions as are now, or may be hereafter prescribed by law."

This ends the committee's report on this article.

George Earle, Chairman.

Pending the consideration of this report, Mr. Chambers said: How can you amend an article after it has passed its third reading? And yet you are now passing upon amendments, without even calling the yeas and nays to show that they are made part of the constitution.

The Chairman (Mr. Daniel.) The chair understands the committee on revision to say that they have recommended no material amendments. They have merely suggested certain changes in the phraseology.

Mr. Earle. The chair is correct so far as relates to amendments, recommended by the committee of revision, to the article now under consideration; but there are other articles of the constitution in which the committee propose material and substantial changes. I had supposed that the reports from this committee would be printed. They certainly should be. Otherwise they cannot be properly understood, and acted upon by the convention.—This committee, composed, as it is, of but five members—only four of whom so far have been in attendance—is pressed for time. There is an evident disposition to terminate the sessions of the convention at an early day. To review the constitution is a work of no small magnitude. It would be wonderful if the committee of revision, in the hurry and excitement which always attends the closing sessions of a convention, should not overlook many amendments which ought to be recommended; and equally wonderful should they not propose amendments which, on mature deliberation, should be rejected. The review of the committee may and probably will need revision. But we can have no such revision unless the reports of the committee are printed, and presented to the members of the convention in that form for their consideration. I hope the reports will be printed.

Mr. Cushing. I object very decidedly to the idea of printing all the reports of the committee of revision, which are merely verbal alterations, not affecting the sense of the propositions. To print them would simply be a waste of time. As I understand it we are working now in the hope of finishing up our whole work to-morrow, and if we wait for these reports to be printed, that will take till next Thursday, and then we shall not get through our labors until the end of next week. Any gentleman by taking the printed report which he has before him, can follow the reading and ascertain the changes which the committee on revision propose. If he considers any proposed change a material one, he can call the yeas and nays, and go through all the formalities he may desire. But all the amendments which I have heard are merely verbal amendments, and do not alter the sense of any proposition which the convention has already passed. There is no reason at all why we should delay the action of this body for the time it would take to have these reports printed.

Mr. Chambers. Reports are brought in here, laid upon the secretary's table and adopted, and made part of the constitution without the formalities which your rules require. I do not speak of mere verbal alterations and amendments, for that is the appropriate business of the revising committee. But that committee has no more business to make amendments, substantially changing the character of any provision referred to them, than they have to do anything else; not a bit. It is their business to revise what we have been doing, what has been done by the convention, to see if any alteration is necessary in the verbiage, to see that the grammar is all right. But to introduce totally new provisions and pass them, as has just been done, I say is in violation of the rules.

Mr. Cushing. What rules?

Mr. CHAMBERS. The rules of this body.

Mr. STOCKBRIDGE. I rise to a point of order. The report of the committee on revision upon the article on State's attorneys is now being read; and all this discussion and vituperation of the past action of the house has no connection with the report under consideration. So far as we have gone in relation to the report now before the convention, there is nothing but verbal changes; no material alteration of the report, and that report and nothing else is now before the house.

Mr. CHAMBERS. Matters have been presented here and declared a part of the constitution which this body has never adopted.

Mr. STIRLING. I understand perfectly well what use can be made and will be made of this matter, and I will move to reconsider the vote by which the convention has just adopted the report of the committee on revision on the article on elective franchise, and if it is found that any material change has been made in that article, I will call the yeas and nays on it.

Mr. STOCKBRIDGE. I raise the point of order that that motion is not in order, until the report now under consideration is disposed of.

The CHAIRMAN (Mr. Daniel.) The point of order is well taken. The motion to reconsider is not now in order.

The various amendments suggested by the committtee on revision to the article on State's attorneys were severally agreed to.

ELECTIVE FRANCHISE.

Mr. STIRLING. I now move to reconsider the vote by which the report of the committee on revision on the article on elective franchise was adopted. My object in making this motion is this: objection has been raised that words have been put in that article which materially affect its substance, and some objections have been made that the forms required by our rules have not been strictly observed. Now I do not intend that any such objections shall be made. I therefore move to reconsider that report, in order that the several amendments proposed may be spread upon the journal, and the yeas and nays be taken upon concurring in the report of the committee, so that no objection can be made to our action here.

Mr. CHAMBERS. I would ask the gentleman if he does not consider that objection well taken?

Mr. STIRLING. I say that when the convention concurs in the report of the committee on revision, then the changes they recommend become a part of the constitution. If the committee, under the authority of the rules of this house, make a recommendation to the convention, and it is concurred in, that is all that is required.

Mr. BROWN. Has not a section been introduced in this article by the committee on revision, which was submitted to the convention and rejected?

Mr. STIRLING. No, sir; only a sentence added to a section already adopted.

Mr. EARLE. I hope the report will be reconsidered, and that the changes proposed will be printed, or stated fully to the convention, so that every member can act understandingly upon them.

The question being then taken upon the motion to reconsider, it was agreed to.

The question was upon concurring in the report of the committee on revision.

The amendments proposed by the committee were again read.

Mr. NEGLEY. I would ask whether, according to the rules of this convention, it would not be necessary to move to reopen the article so as to permit these amendments to be made? Upon the third reading of any article no amendment can be made to it except upon the vote of a majority of the members elected to this convention, or on a motion to suspend the rules, requiring a vote of three-fifths of the members present.

The CHAIRMAN (Mr. Daniel.) This article having passed its third reading, now comes up as a matter not strictly provided for by the rules. In the opinion of the chair it is competent for the convention to take any action upon it they may think proper.

Mr. CUSHING. I move that the convention concur in the report of the committee on revision, and on that question I call for the yeas and nays.

The yeas and nays were ordered accordingly.

Mr. BELT. I would ask if the committee on revision can make any substantial addition or amendment to any report referred to them? Take the earliest instance we have of the action of a committee on revision, in the convention of 1787, which framed the constitution of the United States. The distinguished committee of revision of that body, in determining on their duties, determined that they were authorized merely to make verbal changes, changes of words, not to add anything which was substantial.

The CHAIRMAN (Mr. Daniel.) In the opinion of the chair, any substantial change or alteration would have to be reported to this convention, and the vote taken upon it by yeas and nays. The chair thinks it is competent for the convention to make such changes and alterations at this stage; otherwise after the convention has passed any article, if any mistake was discovered in it, the work of the body could never be perfected. The committee on revision certainly can report what changes and alterations they deem necessary to be made, and it is in the power of the convention to take such action upon their report as they may think proper. The chair thinks any substantial change should be passed upon by yeas and nays.

Mr. DAVIS, of Charles. Would it be competent for any member to offer an amendment to this article at this time?

The CHAIRMAN. The chair thinks not.

Mr. DAVIS, of Charles. How then is it competent for a committee to do what a member of this body cannot?

Mr. PUGH. I understand that the question before the house is upon concurring in the report of the committee on revision. I do not know that that committee has had any special instructions from this house, as to what they shall do, or what they may report. There seems to be some doubt as to whether these proposed changes come strictly within the purview of the powers of the committee on revision.—They are a committee organized by and acting under the authority of this body. This convention certainly has the right to accept or reject the report of the committee. The committee may report as they see fit, in regard to changes to be made in the articles referred to them. That is my understanding of the matter. If the house shall determine differently, then I shall pursue a different course, and move to suspend the rules, so that these amendments can be received and acted upon. But I think the committee have a right to report to this convention, and we can then adopt or reject their report as we see fit.

The CHAIRMAN (Mr. Daniel.) The chair is of the opinion that it would be out of order for any member of the convention to offer any amendment to any article after it has been read the third time and passed. But the committee on revision having been appointed for this purpose, more especially to make corrections so far as verbal alterations are concerned, if they choose to report material alterations, it is competent for the convention to take them into consideration and act upon them, and as they may materially affect the provisions of the constitution it is proper that they should be passed upon by yeas and nays.

Mr. EARLE. As the reports from the committee of revision are not to be printed before being acted upon by the convention, I wish to call attention to an amendment recommended by the committee in the first section of the article on the elective franchise. I read that part of the section which is to be affected by the change:

"And in case any county or city shall be so divided as to form portions of different electoral districts for the election of congressman, senator, delegate, or other officer or officers, then to entitle a person to vote for such officer, he must have been a resident of that part of the county or city which shall form a part of the electoral district in which he offers to vote, for six months next preceding the election, but a person who shall *not* have acquired a residence in such county or city, entitling him to vote at any such election, shall be entitled to vote in the election district from which he removed, until he shall have acquired a residence in the part of the county or city to which he has removed."

The committee recommend that the word "not" in this section be stricken out.

With the exception of this word, the language of the section is identical with that used in the first section of the first article of the present constitution.

In general terms, the section provides, that in case any county shall be so divided as to form portions of different electoral districts for the election of congressman, or other officer, to entitle a person to vote, he must have been a resident of that part of the county which shall form part of the electoral district in which he offers to vote, for six months next preceding the election Baltimore county, for example, is thus divided. Part of it is in the second, and the remaining part in the fifth congressional district. Without a residence of six months in the county previous to an election, no person is entitled to vote there; neither in that part of the county which is embraced in the second, nor in that part which is embraced in the fifth congressional district; neither in an electoral district to which he has removed, nor in one from which he has removed. The county residence of six months is an indispensable prerequisite. Having acquired that residence, a person may remove from one part of the county to another—from one election district in the county to another election district in the same county, without forfeiting his right of suffrage.

The committee having examined the subject with care, are unanimous in recommending, that the word "not" be stricken out.

Mr. CHAMBERS. The convention determined that it ought to be there.

Mr. STIRLING. The convention can now determine otherwise.

Mr. HEBB. I understand the chair to say that the yeas and nays will have to be called on all these amendments.

The CHAIRMAN. On all material amendments.

Mr. HEBB. The yeas and nays are to be called on all articles. The last convention did not take the yeas and nays on these reports of the committee on revision. Some propositions were introduced from the revisory committee by the gentleman from Kent himself (Mr. Chambers,) and no yeas and nays were called on them. If the convention see proper, they have the right to reconsider everything they have done, and make a new constitution. The majority of the convention have the right to do what they please in this matter.

Mr. CHAMBERS. I beg leave to read the fifteenth rule, as follows:

"Every report from a committee containing articles or sections proposed to be made a part of the constitution, shall be read on three different days of the session, previous to its adoption, unless two-thirds of the members present otherwise determine; the first of which readings shall be by the title only, unless a majority of the convention shall otherwise order."

Mr. CUSHING. I would suggest to the house that that rule does not apply to this case.—The revising committee report neither new sections nor new articles, but simply some slight changes in the phraseology.

Mr. STIRLING. This rule says that reports of committees proposing articles to be incorporated into the constitution shall be read on three several days, etc. That is a rule applicable to the manufacture of the constitution, while in progress of framing. But those committees have now reported; the articles have now been adopted, and have become parts of the constitution, and the rule has ceased to have any further application to them.

Another rule provides for a committee on revision, whose duty it is to take the articles that have been adopted by the convention, that have been made parts of the constitution, that have been read three times, and finally passed by yeas and nays, and examine them carefully and revise them. What does that mean? It means that the committee shall take the articles which you have adopted, according to your rules, examine them and bring them back here with such alterations, amendments, and modifications as may be necessary to carry out the intentions of the convention in passing them. The convention votes either to concur in the alterations proposed by the committee on revision, or not to concur. If they concur, then those alterations are incorporated in the constitution; if they do not concur, then the alterations are left out.

The committee do not here propose any new section or article. What is the meaning of a rule which says the committee shall revise, if they can make no changes? It is not an ordinary committee of this body, whose reports must be read three times on three several days and then passed by yeas and nays. That rule relates solely to the committees whose duty it is to frame the several articles to be incorporated into the constitution. This committee is engaged in the mere matter of recasting the phraseology. And even if they do report a matter of substantial change, it is a matter within the power of the revisory committee. No member can propose amendments now, after these articles have been passed. It is the business of the committee on revision to report such changes and alterations as they may deem necessary to be made. They have reported these changes, and it is now for the house to determine whether they will concur in the report of the committee.

I want the yeas and nays called upon concurring in this report, for I want it distinctly to go upon the journal that this change was made. Are we to stand here and have all our work paralyzed by the misapplication of a rule requiring these reports to be read on three several days, and passed by the yeas and nays? I stand here ready to defend the work which we have been doing, and do not intend it shall be interrupted by any such sophistical objections.

The CHAIRMAN (Mr. Daniel.) The chair decides, that the fifteenth rule has no application to the report of the committee on revision.

Mr. CHAMBERS. I protest against this process of doing business.

Mr. BROWN. Is there no matter incorporated in this report by the committee of revision, which was before the convention and rejected?

Mr. EARLE. In answer to the gentleman from Queen Anne, I reply that the convention adopted the last clause of the first section of the article on elective franchise in the following form:

"But a person who shall NOT have acquired a residence in such county or city entitling him to vote at any such election, shall be entitled to vote in the election district from which he removed, until he shall have acquired a residence in the part of the county or city to which he has removed."

A proposition to strike the word "not" from this clause was rejected in convention. The whole subject was then referred to the committee of revision, and the members of that committee having arrived at the plain, but, as they thought, logical conclusion, that a person who had not acquired a residence in a county or city, should not be entitled to vote in any part of that county or city, respectfully recommended that the word "not" in the aforesaid section be stricken out; this, I presume, is the matter alluded to by the gentleman from Queen Anne.

Mr. STIRLING. As to the word "not," that certainly is a matter for the committee of revision to examine and report upon.

Mr. MILLER. As I understand the report of the committee of revision, they have added an entirely new section to the article on elective franchise.

Mr. EARLE. The gentleman from Anne Arundel is mistaken. No entirely new section has been added by the committee of revision to the article on the elective franchise. Several of the sections have been remodeled. Parts of two or more sections, in some instances, have been consolidated into one section. Some sections have been divided, others transposed, but no entirely new section has been introduced.

Mr. STOCKBRIDGE. For symmetry's sake the section has been divided into two sections. There is no new matter recommended by the committee on revision.

The PRESIDENT having resumed the chair, announced that the question was upon concurring in the report of the committee on revision in relation to the article on the elective franchise.

Mr. Chambers. I will state in a few words what has occasioned all the difficulty. I objected to the course being pursued as being contrary to what the rules of the body required. A committee on revision has been appointed. An article adopted by this body has been referred to that committee for revision. They have made various changes in the language of that article, and, except in one instance, without the slightest objection on the part of any individual, so far as I know. But in one instance they have undertaken to erase a word which by a positive vote this house refused to have erased. I voted with those of this house who voted that the word should be erased, in order to carry out the sense which was intended to be given to the section. The committee, under the name of revising, have undertaken to go contrary to that vote of the house, and to strike out what the house voted to retain, which, I think, is wrong. I have no material objection, however, to that verbal alteration.

The committee, however, have gone further. They have made a specific amendment, a substantial amendment to one of the sections. Now I say that the fifteenth rule directs how to dispose of the report of a committee, if this is to be regarded as a valid report. I say this committee on revision have no business to suggest new matter. But if this house adopt the idea that the committee have acted within the range of their authority, and this is a report of a committee of this house, then upon that subject the fifteenth rule is just as precise as language can make it. That is my idea; that there is no mode consistently with our rules by which any provision can be inserted in the constitution in the manner now suggested.

The President. The chair has no difficulty in regard to this question. The work of this convention has in effect been accomplished, and all the provisions of the standing rules have been complied with, by the reports of the committees having been made in regular form, read the first, second and third times, and finally passed by yeas and nays. The work contemplated by the standing rules of the house has, therefore, been completed.

For the purpose of ascertaining that the constitution is complete in all its parts, the convention has appointed an additional committee, called the committee on revision, for the purpose not only of revising any verbal or other errors which may have occurred, but also for the purpose of suggesting for the consideration of this house any matter which the committee may deem important and necessary to perfect any article or section in that constitution. That the chair regards as coming strictly within the purview of the committee. If the suggestions made by this committee meet with the sanction of this house, they will stand; if not, they will be of no avail. This whole subject depends upon the will of the majority. The convention has the right to reject or adopt any suggestion of the committee, whether the particular subject has been acted upon by this convention or not. In other words, the work of this convention resolves itself into the will of the majority.

Mr. Belt. Allow me to state a point to the chair, in order that I may understand this matter more clearly. I suppose nothing has given more trouble or anxiety to this convention than our judicial system. We have decided in favor of an elective judiciary. Suppose that the committee on revision should undertake to strike out all that establishes the elective principle, and to insert the appointive principle. Would that come within the proper scope of the committee on revision?

The President. The chair has no doubt upon this question. The committee on revision has the entire control of the constitution, and can make any suggestions it pleases in regard to it. It can suggest to this convention to strike out this or that paragraph or section; but that does not strike it out. It is still left to the judgment of this body whether it shall be stricken out or retained. The whole matter resolves itself into the judgment of the house. If the house determine to make any change, they can do so They can do so in concurrence with the action of the committee, or contrary to the action of the committee. Of course there is a limit to the proper prudence to be exercised by a committee of this character. It is not to be supposed that the committee, in direct violation of the judgment of the house, would strike out any important provision or principle. But in the hurry of business the convention may overlook some important provision, which may be brought to the attention of the committee on revision, who may bring it to the consideration of the convention in the shape of a report. When they do that their work is complete. They can suggest the striking out of a provision, or the insertion of an additional provision; but no provision is stricken out or inserted except by the deliberate judgment and action of the house. In other words, this is a short mode of enabling the convention to perfect its labors, relieving them of the necessity of going through all the formalities required by the standing rules.

Mr. Chambers. Can you by this process avoid or evade a rule which requires that no section or paragraph shall be incorporated into the constitution except in accordance with a certain course of action?

The PRESIDENT. The gentleman from Kent (Mr. Chambers) can very easily understand that the convention is not required to do its work over twice. If all that is contained in the standing rules have been fully complied with, then the rule is exhausted.

Mr. CHAMBERS. Not in regard to new matter.

The PRESIDENT. The work has passed over into the hands of the committee on revision for the purpose of suggesting any alteration, or recommending anything which they in their judgment deem proper for the perfecting of the instrument. Of course their recommendation does not of itself change the instrument. It is still left to the determination of the convention whether the change shall be made or not. That question is to be determined by the vote of the house upon concurring in the report of the committee.

The question was upon concurring in the report of the committee in relation to the article upon the elective franchise.

Upon this question the yeas and nays had been ordered.

The question being then taken by yeas and nays, it resulted—yeas 44, nays 19—as follows:

Yeas—Messrs. Goldsborough, President; Abbott, Annan, Audoun, Baker, Barron, Cunningham, Cushing, Daniel, Davis, of Washington, Dellinger, Earle, Ecker, Farrow, Galloway, Greene, Hebb, Hoffman, Hopper, Jones, of Cecil, Keefer, Kennard, King, Larsh, Markey, McComas, Mullikin, Murray, Negley, Nyman, Parker, Pugh Purnell, Ridgely, Russell, Schley, Schlosser, Stirling, Stockbridge, Swope, Sykes, Thomas, Todd, Wooden—44.

Nays—Messrs. Belt, Bond, Brown, Chambers, Crawford, Davis, of Charles, Dent, Duvall, Hollyday, Horsey, Lansdale, Lee, Marbury, Mitchell, Miller, Parran, Peter, Smith, of Dorchester, Wilmer—19.

The report of the committee on revision was accordingly concurred in.

Mr. KING. I would ask if we of the committee on revision have not a right to make verbal changes and other suggestions to be brought before this house? Because if we are merely to take these articles into the committee room and bring them back again, without making any alterations, you might as well dispense with the committee of revision altogether. My idea was that we had a right to make these verbal changes, and at the same time make suggestions to be submitted to the house.

The PRESIDENT. The gentleman is correct. This committee is a very different thing from a committee appointed after the session of the legislature. In that case the committee has no power to revise the work of the legislature; they are confined strictly to the correction of any verbal errors. But this committee is under the control of this house, and all the powers of the house are confided to it over any article before it.

Mr. KING. That is the way I understood it. But according to some of the arguments here we were authorized merely to take the document into the committee room and bring it back again entirely unchanged.

TREASURY DEPARTMENT.

Mr. EARLE, from the committee of revision, reported back to the convention the article on the treasury department, and recommended that the first section of that article be remodeled. This section as adopted by the convention reads thus:

"Section 1. There shall be a treasury department, consisting of a comptroller, chosen by the qualified electors of the State at each general election of members of the general assembly, who shall receive an annual salary of twenty-five hundred dollars, and of a treasurer, to be appointed by the two houses of the general assembly at each regular session thereof, on joint ballot, who shall also receive an annual salary of twenty-five hundred dollars, and neither of the said officers shall be allowed or receive any fees, commissions, or perquisites of any kind, in addition to his salary, for the performance of any duty or service whatever. In case of a vacancy in either of the offices by death, or otherwise, the governor, by and with the advice and consent of the senate, shall fill such vacancy by appointment, to continue until another election by the people, or a choice by the legislature as the case may be, and the qualification of the successor. But the comptroller chosen at the first election under this constitution, and the treasurer appointed at the first session of the general assembly held under this constitution, shall not enter upon the discharge of the duties of their respective offices until the expiration of the terms of the present incumbents, unless the said offices, or either of them shall become vacant by death, resignation, removal from the State, or other disqualification of the said incumbents, or either of them. The comptroller and treasurer shall keep their offices at the seat of government, and shall take such oath and enter into such bonds for the faithful discharge of their duties as are now or may hereafter be prescribed by law."

From the reading of this section it will be seen that the comptroller is elected by the qualified voters of the State, and the treasurer by the general assembly.

The offices are distinct and should not be embraced in one section. The members of the committee are of the opinion that this section could be divided with advantage into at least three. They therefore recommend the following sections:

"Section. 1 The treasury department of

this State shall consist of a comptroller and a treasurer."

"Sec. 2. The comptroller shall be chosen by the qualified electors of the State at each regular election for members of the general assembly. He shall hold his office for two years, commencing on the second Wednesday in January next ensuing his election, and shall receive an annual salary of twenty-five hundred dollars, but shall not be allowed, nor shall he receive any fees, commissions, or perquisites of any kind, in addition thereto, for the performance of any official duty or service. He shall keep his office at the seat of government, and shall take such oath and enter into such bond for the faithful performance of his duty as are now or may hereafter be prescribed by law. A vacancy in the office of comptroller shall be filled by the governor for the residue of the term. The first election for comptroller under this constitution shall be held on the Tuesday next after the first Monday in the month of November, in the year eighteen hundred and sixty-four, but the comptroller then elected shall not enter upon the discharge of the duties of his office until the expiration of the term of the present incumbent, unless the said office shall sooner become vacant."

Under the recommendation of the committee of revision to divide the first section of this article, the second section will become the third. It relates exclusively to the duties of the comptroller, and no change in it is proposed.

The fourth section is a new one, though in substance it is the same as that part of the original first section, which relates to the treasurer It reads thus:

"Section 4. The treasurer shall be elected, on joint ballot, by the two houses of the general assembly, at each regular session thereof. He shall hold his office for two years, and shall receive an annual salary of twenty-five hundred dollars, but shall not be allowed, nor shall he receive any fees, commissions or perquisites of any kind in addition thereto, for the performance of any official duty or service. He shall keep his office at the seat of governments and shall take such oath, and enter into such bond for the faithful discharge of his duty as are now or may hereafter be prescribed by law. A vacancy in the office of the treasurer shall be filled by the governor for the residue of the term. The general assembly, at its first session after the adoption of this constitution, shall elect a treasurer, but the treasurer then elected, shall not enter upon the discharge of the duties of his office, until the expiration of the term of the present incumbent, unless the said office shall sooner become vacant."

The third section of this article, as it stood when referred to the committee of revision will, under the new arrangement of sections, become the fifth section, and the fourth will become the sixth.

The committee having no further recommendations to make, close their report on the treasury department.

GEORGE EARLE, Chairman.

All the recommendations of the committee set forth in the above report, on being read, were considered and adopted by the convention.

PUBLICATION OF THE CONSTITUTION.

The PRESIDENT, in accordance with an order of the convention adopted on Tuesday last, announced the following members as the committee to contract for the printing of the constitution for general distribution:

Messrs. STOCKBRIDGE, RIDGELY, and STIRLING.

Mr. STOCKBRIDGE. I desire to make one request of the members of the convention. The convention has ordered the printing of 50,000 copies of the constitution in the English language, and 10,000 copies in the German. On behalf of the committee just announced by the president, I would request members to notify the committee what number of copies in the German language they will desire, and what number in the English language.

SENATOR BATES, OF DELAWARE.

Mr. CHAMBERS. I have had my attention called to some remarks made by the gentleman from Worcester (Mr. Purnell) and which will be found on page 794 of the journal of debates. That gentleman during the course of his remarks asserted that Mr. Cabell, of Georgia, Mr. Hilliard, of Alabama, and Mr. Bates, of Delaware, were ministers. I stated at the time that Mr. Bates was a lawyer. I knew his history far enough to know that he was a school-master, had studied medicine and become a doctor, and afterwards had studied law and become a lawyer. I notice by the printed debates that in answer to my suggestion that Mr. Bates was a lawyer, the gentleman from Worcester (Mr. Purnell) replied—"and a minister, too, for I have heard him preach often." I understand from a gentleman who is a friend of Mr. Bates, that this is a mistake; that Mr. Bates never was a minister of any church. At the request of that gentleman I suggest to the gentleman from Worcester the propriety of correcting this statement of fact. He may have heard Mr. Bates declaim in a sort of meeting.

Mr. PURNELL. Perhaps I may have been unfortunate in my discrimination between a minister and a lawyer. I am not a member of the church to which Mr. Bates belonged. He, I believe, was a very worthy member of the Methodist church. It is very true I have often heard him exhort. Now I cannot discriminate between preaching and exhorting; it may have been a lecture. Nevertheless, it was that sort of harangue that I have frequently listened to from persons who have been denominated ministers. Mr. Bates, as has been very properly remarked by the gentleman from Kent (Mr. Chambers,) was a very good lawyer. It may have been a very high compliment to have connected him with the ministry. In making the remark I did, in debate, I did not intend to say that Mr. Bates was a regular licentiate, or that he had charge of any particular church or congregation. I merely meant to say, what I now say, that he was a good man, I believe, and a very worthy and acceptable member of the Methodist church, and was in the habit of lecturing, or exhorting, or preaching, or whatever you may call it; I cannot discriminate. I said he was a good "preacher-lawyer." If that term does not suit, then I will say "exhorter;" if not that, then I will say he was a good "lecturer." And if that does not suit, I do not know what to call him.

SCHEDULE.

On motion of Mr. HEBB,

The convention proceeded to consider the report of the committee on the schedule, which was on its third reading.

The report was then read the third time, and passed, by yeas and nays, (under rule forty-three,)—yeas 43, nays 18,—as follows:

Yeas—Messrs. Goldsborough, President; Abbott, Audoun, Baker, Barron, Brooks, Cunningham, Cushing, Daniel, Davis, of Washington, Dellinger, Ecker, Farrow, Galloway, Greene, Hebb, Hoffman, Hopper, Jones, of Cecil, Keefer, Kennard, King, Larsh, Markey, McComas, Mullikin, Negley, Nyman, Parker, Pugh, Purnell, Ridgely, Russell, Schley, Schlosser, Stirling, Stockbridge, Swope, Sykes, Thomas, Todd, Wickard, Wooden—43.

Nays—Messrs. Belt, Bond, Brown, Chambers, Crawford, Davis, of Charles, Dent, Duvall, Hollyday, Horsey, Lansdale, Lee, Marbury, Mitchell, Miller, Parran, Peter, Wilmer—18.

JUDICIARY DEPARTMENT.

On motion of Mr. CUSHING, the convention then resumed the consideration of the report of the committee on the judiciary department, which was on its second reading.

NEGRO APPRENTICESHIP.

Mr. BARRON moved to reconsider the vote by which section twenty-nine of the report as amended had been adopted.

The section was as follows:

"It shall be the duty of the orphans' court of the several counties and the city of Baltimore to bind out, until they arrive at the age of twenty-one years for males, and eighteen years for females, all negroes emancipated by the adoption of this constitution, who are minors, incapable of supporting themselves, and whose parents are unable to maintain them, subject to such regulations as are now or may hereafter be prescribed by law; and in all cases the preference shall be given to their former masters, when in the judgment of the said courts they are suitable persons to have charge of them."

The motion to reconsider was seconded by Messrs. FARROW and HEBB.

Mr. TODD moved a call of the house, which was ordered.

Pending the call of the roll,

Mr. CUSHING moved that further proceedings under the call be dispensed with—which was not agreed to.

The call of the roll was then completed, and the following members answered to their names:

Messrs. Goldsborough, President; Abbott, Annan Audoun, Baker, Barron, Belt, Bond, Brooks, Brown, Carter, Chambers, Crawford, Cunningham, Cushing, Daniel, Davis, of Charles, Davis, of Washington, Dellinger, Dent, Duvall, Ecker, Farrow, Galloway, Greene, Hatch, Hebb, Hoffman, Hollyday, Hopper, Horsey, Jones, of Cecil, Keefer, Kennard, Lansdale, Larsh, Lee, Marbury, Markey, McComas, Mitchell, Miller, Mullikin, Negley, Parker, Parran, Peter, Pugh, Purnell, Ridgely, Russell, Schley, Schlosser, Smith, of Dorchester, Stirling, Stockbridge, Swope, Sykes, Thomas, Wickard, Wilmer, Wooden—63.

On motion of Mr. KENNARD,

Further procedings under the call were dispensed with.

The question was upon the motion to reconsider.

Mr. BARRON. I find upon referring to the journal, that I was not present when this twenty-ninth section was adopted. I suppose, therefore, that it is not competent for me to move a reconsideration of that section.

Mr. FARROW renewed the motion to reconsider, which was seconded by Messrs. HEBB and GREENE.

Mr. MARKEY moved that the convention now take a recess; not agreed to.

ADJOURNMENT TILL MONDAY.

Mr. DELLINGER moved that when the convention adjourn, it stand adjourned till Monday next at twelve o'clock, M.

Mr. ECKER. I have been among the number of those who have been as steady in their attendance here, as any member of this convention, with the exception perhaps of the president. But for the last hour I really have not been able to comprehend or understand one particle of what has been going on here. And if that manner of proceeding is to be carried on until we adjourn, I am inclined to think we shall be in the predicament which my honorable friend from Kent (Mr. Chambers) says they got into in the last convention; that we will have something in the constitution that ought not to be in there, or leave something out that ought to be put in. I am as anxious to get our business done, so that it is done properly, and go home, as any member can be. But I see no necessity for this crowding matters through in such a way that we common folks cannot understand what is being done. As we have already spent so much time here over this business, I think we better stay here two or three days longer, and do it carefully so that we can all understand it. I see no reason for crowding this thing through, so as to adjourn to-morrow night. Let us do things decently and in order. If we cannot find anything to do now, let us adjourn over until Monday, and give the committee on revision time to do their work. And then on Monday, or Tuesday, when they bring in their work, let us take it up and go through with it carefully, decently and in good order.

Mr. DANIEL. We have plenty to do yet.

Mr. ECKER. I see no necessity at all for crowding matters in this way. I am astonished that members who have stayed away from the convention and retarded its business, should now be so very fierce to crowd everything through at once. If they had remained here and attended to the work of the convention, we could have got through by the fourth of July. I do not refer to the minority of the convention, because we do not expect anything of them.

Mr. CHAMBERS. I have no responsibility for the work done here; God forbid that I should have. But I was here at the close of the last convention, and I have no desire to see such another exhibition; of a piece of paper purporting to be, but not in fact, the constitution, and signed by the president and the secretary, and then be obliged to appoint a committee to examine after we went away and see what the constitution really was. There was altogether such a scene of confusion that, to say the least of it, was certainly not at all respectable.

I have as much desire to get away from here, and go home, as any member can have. I think I have been here about as regularly as any member has. I thought the doings of this convention required watching about as much as anything could. I have tried, by staying here, to avert as much mischief as I could. I have suffered as much pecuniary loss in this matter as anybody has. But I do not desire to hurry matters through unreasonably. Let the articles which have been acted upon here be carefully revised; let your clerks arrange them and put them in proper order. And then when they have done that, let us know what the constitution is. I have already mentioned in this convention one item which was left out of the last constitution. And just as sure as we leave here, in the hurry the last convention left in, there may be half a dozen important matters left out of this one. Not that I would object to leaving out a great deal of it, if I had the power. But although I am one of the minority, differing very greatly with the majority in regard to political sentiments, I certainly desire as much as anybody else to see everything that is done, done properly, done decently and in good order, as the gentleman from Carroll (Mr. Ecker) says.

Mr. STOCKBRIDGE. Before the vote is taken on the motion of the gentleman from Washington county (Mr. Dellinger,) I wish the convention would revert to the position in which the work of this convention now stands. We have passed through their second and third readings all the reports made to the convention but two. There is the very short report of the committee on usury, and the very long report—no; that is not a report at all, but the long judiciary article; the report of the committee on the judiciary was abolished long ago. It is important that those two matters should be acted upon, before we adjourn, in accordance with the proposition of the gentleman from Washington. Otherwise, when we come here on Monday, we would have to take up those reports, act upon them, go through their third reading, and pass them over to the committee on revision, who would have to take at least a day to dispose of them. I trust there will be no adjournment over until we have gone through the third reading of those reports. Then if it is necessary to adjourn over, in order to enable the committee on revision and the clerks to bring up their work, I will not object.

Mr. DELLINGER. I will withdraw the motion to adjourn until Monday, and renew the motion to take a recess.

The question being taken, the motion was agreed to;

And the convention accordingly took a recess until half past three o'clock, P. M.

AFTERNOON SESSION.

The convention met at half-past 3 o'clock, P. M.

The roll was called, and the following members answered to their names:

Messrs. Goldsborough, President; Abbott, Audoun, Baker, Belt, Brooks, Brown, Carter, Crawford, Cunningham, Cushing, Daniel, Davis, of Charles, Davis, of Washington, Dellinger, Dent, Duvall, Earle, Ecker, Farrow, Galloway, Greene, Hatch, Hebb, Hoffman, Hollyday, Hopper, Horsey, Jones, of Cecil, Keefer, Kennard, King, Larsh, Lee, Marbury, Markey, McComas, Mitchell, Miller, Morgan, Mullikin, Murray, Negley, Nyman, Parker, Parran, Pugh, Purnell, Ridgely, Russell, Schley, Schlosser, Scott, Smith, of Dorchester, Stirling, Stockbridge, Swope, Sykes, Todd, Wickard, Wilmer, Wooden—62.

NEGRO APPRENTICESHIP.

The convention resumed the consideration

of the report of the committee on the judiciary department.

Mr. FARROW, (seconded by Messrs. HEBB and GREENE,) moved to reconsider the vote by which the twenty-ninth section of the report was adopted.

The section was the following:

"SEC. 29. It shall be the duty of the orphans' court of the several counties and the city of Baltimore to bind out, until they arrive at the age of twenty-one years for males, and eighteen years for females, all negroes emancipated by the adoption of this constitution, who are minors, incapable of supporting themselves, and whose parents are unable to maintain them, subject to such regulations as are now or may hereafter be prescribed by law; and in all cases the preference shall be given to their former masters, when in the judgment of the said courts they are suitable persons to have charge of them."

Mr. MILLER. I rise to a point of order, whether the gentleman from Worcester (Mr. Farrow) is entitled to make that motion. My friend from Baltimore county (Mr. Ridgely) who has looked at the authorities can make the question clearer than I can, but I will simply suggest that the point of order is this: The motion is, after the convention has passed upon this section as an entirety, to open it for consideration as a whole section. The gentleman from Worcester, who makes the motion, only voted in favor of incorporating one branch of that section into the constitution. He voted against the incorporation of the second branch of the proposition. In order to get the whole section open for consideration, I say that the motion to reconsider must come from some member of the convention who voted in favor of both branches of that proposition.

Mr. RIDGELY. When that section was under consideration, and the house was called to pass upon it, a division of the question was asked for. It is on page 545 of the journal, [August 26.] On the first branch of the proposition the gentleman who moved the reconsideration voted in the affirmative. On the second branch of the proposition they voted in the negative. The point is this: that on taking the vote on the second branch of the proposition, the proposition became an entirety. The vote being taken on the first branch of the proposition, but half the vote was taken. It became necessary to take the other half of the vote to perfect the vote upon the proposition. The vote being taken on the second branch of the proposition, the proposition became an entirety; and now it exists as an entirety. It is in your constitution; and the motion to reconsider that as an entire proposition must come from a member who voted for it as an entire proposition, and not from a member who voted for but one-half.

The only authority I have upon the subject, which is a very remote one, because I have not found that this question has ever been raised, although I have made a very diligent search through all the manuals that have been in my reach, is one supporting the last view that the proposition only becomes an entire proposition after the question has been taken upon all its branches. It is Jefferson's Manual, page 184, sec. 36.

"When a question is divided, after the question on the first member, the second is open to debate and amendment; because it is a known rule that a person may rise and speak at any time before the question has been completely decided, by putting the negative as well as affirmative side. But the question is not completely put when the vote has been taken on the first member only. One-half of the question, both affirmative and negative, remains to be put."

And until the other half is put, the house does not determine the question. That being put, the question then becomes an entire question. It is not susceptible of reconsideration by branches. No motion could be entertained to reconsider one branch of an entire proposition. The only motion that could be entertained would be a motion to reconsider the whole proposition. The question is who is entitled under the general rule to move a reconsideration under circumstances of this kind, as having voted in the majority. I hold that according to all reasonable views of the subject, the party must show that he was friendly to the measure, that he voted for the whole proposition as an entire proposition. If the question had come before the house as a whole proposition he would have been found with the majority. It is very clear that the parties here who propose to reconsider were unfriendly to the second branch of the proposition, and could not have voted for the proposition as a whole. Therefore the point is raised that they are not competent as friends of the proposition that was adopted, being with the majority, to move to reconsider.

Mr. STIRLING. There is nothing in the rules upon this subject except the proposition in the 44th rule, which says:

"*Rule* 44. When a question has once been decided in the affirmative or negative, a motion of reconsideration shall be in order, if made by one member and seconded by two others who voted in the majority; and no motion for reconsideration shall be postponed or laid on the table."

Then the rule in regard to the division of the question is this:

"*Rule* 40. Any member may call for the division of a question, which shall be divided, if it comprehend propositions in substauce so distinct that, one being taken away, a substantive proposition shall remain for the decision of the convention."

The principle of the right of division originates from the fact that nobody has a right to say, when two propositions are put in such a form as to make one question, that a member who is in favor of one of them shall not vote for it unless he will vote for the whole. You have no right to say to a member, you must vote for the whole or against the whole. The very reason for the rule allowing the division of a question is to enable members to vote for one portion of it who are unwilling to vote for the whole. The idea that a man must be friendly to a whole proposition in order to have a right to divide it, would destroy the whole right of division. So far as friendliness is concerned, it is often the case that a member votes for a proposition with a distinct statement that he intends to move a reconsideration, and votes for it for that reason.

After the proposition was divided, the question was first on the first branch, and the yeas and nays were taken on that, and then the question was taken on the second branch, and the yeas and nays were taken on that. Now the rule is that any vote taken in the convention may be reconsidered on motion of any person who voted in the majority in that vote. In this case, it is the more evident that a member voting for the first branch can move to reconsider, because the first branch of the proposition is really the substantive portion of it. The latter branch is only a provision that the thing required to be done by the first branch, shall be done in a particular way. The first branch was the real substantive thing. Strike out the first branch, and the second falls as a matter of course.

Mr. Miller. If that were so, under the rule you would have no power to divide it.

Mr. Stirling. I think it could be divided, because the first branch was a substantive proposition in itself. At any rate it was decided that it could be divided, and that decision cannot now be reversed. That decision must stand. A division presupposes that members will vote for one part and against another. The power to vote under the rule for reconsideration, is connected with the power to change the vote, if it should be effective But if you adopt the rule contended for, you say that a member voting for a proposition that may prevail, upon a division of a question, shall not move to reconsider; which is a restriction of the right of reconsideration. The gentleman says that somebody must move the reconsideration of the section as a whole who voted for it as a whole. There is not a member of the convention who voted for it as a whole. The vote was taken by divisions. There were two questions, two calls of the yeas and nays, and I hold that a member who voted in the majority upon either of those two questions may move to reconsider the vote upon that question.

Mr. Pugh. I was the party who called for a division of the question. I had no idea at that time that in exercising my right to call for a division of the question, I was putting myself in such a position as to cut myself off from the right that every member has here, when he votes for a proposition that is carried to call for its reconsideration if he wishes it to be reconsidered. I did not intend, when I called for a division of the question to vote for either branch of it; but there were several members here who were perfectly willing to vote for the first part of it. But if I had decided at that time to vote for it, I should not have been under the impression which the gentleman from Baltimore county (Mr. Ridgely) seems to wish to prevail here, that in voting for that proposition which, as the gentlemsn from Baltimore city (Mr. Stirling) says was the substantive proposition, the question for the consideration of the house, I had cut myself off from being in a position to move a reconsideration of the question.

The gentleman from Baltimore county has referred to Jefferson's Manual, and probably he has some other authorities to refer to. I refer to our course in this convention from its commencement until now.

Mr. Stirling. It has been suggested to me that the journal will show that upon the precise point of a divided question the motion to reconsider has been entertained.

Mr. Pugh. Yes, sir; that is the practice of this convention. No man who ever voted for any proposition has been denied the right. No man here has ever questioned the right of the member who votes in favor of any question to move a reconsideration. The rules show that the motion may be introduced by any member who voted for the proposition. It would be more particularly unjust now since it has heretofore been the practice of the convention to concede that rule for all who voted in the majority in any instance.

Mr. Hebb. With regard to this question, I will say that those who voted for the first branch of this proposition have the right either to move the reconsideration of that branch of the proposition, or to move the reconsideration of the whole proposition. After the first branch of the proposition was adopted, and the second branch was adopted, the chair passed over the proposition. In other words, by the consent of the whole house the proposition was passed on its second reading. Therefore every member, in that light, can be considered as entitled to move a reconsideration of the whole proposition. Those who voted in the majority on the first branch of the proposition, could move a reconsideration of that branch. Certainly these members could move a reconsideration in one case or the other; and it is immaterial which.

The President. As the president understands this subject, it arises on a section of the report introduced by a member. Another member, under the rules of the convention, called for a division of the question—a division of the section, under the impression that the section contained two questions about which members could differ in opinion, adopting the one and rejecting the other. The adoption of one, and rejection of the other branch, would of course have incorporated the branch adopted to the exclusion of the other branch.

In this state of the case, the question arises, and the chair is of opinion that it has never yet been formally decided by the convention, whether it is competent for a member to move to reconsider that action, who voted for one branch of the section and did not vote for the other.

The object of reconsideration is to enable the convention to retrace their steps, if an error has been committed by surprise or inadvertence, or if there should be a change in the judgment or determination of the convention. There is a very broad latitude allowed by our rules, for the motion to reconsider may be made at any time. This privilege however is conceded only to those who voted in the majority upon a question. It is from them only that this motion can emanate.

The subject then resolves itself into this simple question: Is this section susceptible of division under our rules? Does it embrace distinct subjects? If so, in the judgment of the chair any gentleman voting for either of the branches of this section can move a reconsideration. You cannot divide the section now. If a gentleman that voted for the first branch of the section moves a reconsideration, it opens the entire section. Or if a gentleman who voted in the affirmative upon the second branch, and who may have voted against the first branch, moves a reconsideration, the whole question is open. The effect of it is to give those who voted in the majority upon either of these questions an additional privilege that is not conceded upon a simple isolated question. That is the only effect of the parliamentary law, to give a member a double advantage, in dividing a question; because if a member who voted in the majority upon either branch moves a reconsideration, the necessary consequence of opening that branch is to open the other. It is therefore the judgment of the chair that the motion to reconsider is in order.

Mr. RIDGELY demanded the yeas and nays, and they were ordered.

The question being taken upon reconsidering the adoption of the section of the judiciary report providing for the apprenticeship of colored minors, the result was—yeas 38, nays 23—as follows:

Yeas—Messrs. Abbott, Annan, Audoun, Baker, Brooks, Cunningham, Cushing, Daniel, Dellinger, Dent, Duvall, Ecker, Farrow, Greene, Hatch, Hebb, Henkle, Hopper, Keefer, Kennard, Lansdale, Marbury, McComas, Mitchell, Negley, Parker, Pugh, Purnell, Russell, Schley, Schlosser, Scott, Sneary, Stirling, Stockbridge, Thomas, Wickard, Wooden—38.

Nays—Messrs. Goldsborough, President; Belt, Brown, Carter, Crawford, Davis, of Washington, Galloway, Hoffman, Hollyday, Horsey, Jones, of Cecil, Larsh, Lee, Markey, Miller, Morgan, Mullikin, Parran, Ridgely, Swope, Sykes, Todd, Valliant—23.

When their names were called,

Mr. MILLER said: I conceive the article adopted to be but a recognition of the existing laws of the State in reference to apprenticeship. All negro minors under the emancipation clause after the constitution is adopted, will become free and subject to the operation of these apprentice laws; and it is a matter of perfect indifference to me whether the convention adopt this section or not. Having voted however originally for the proposition to incorporate this provision into the constitution, and supposing that the object of the reconsideration is to strike it out, for the sake of consistency I vote "no."

Mr. SCOTT said: I was not here when this question was up before, and I deem it due to myself to say that as we have abolished slavery by the action of this convention with a considerable flourish of trumpets, I shall with a great deal of pleasure vote to reconsider the matter in order to put an end to an institution which we first declared was abolished, and the existence of which we then covertly attempted to prolong. I vote "aye."

Mr. NEGLEY at first voted "no," but afterwards said: As the gentleman from Worcester moves the reconsideration, and as the section can only affect the Eastern Shore, I will change my vote and vote "aye."

The motion to reconsider accordingly prevailed.

The question recurred upon the adoption of the twenty-ninth section.

Mr. SYKES demanded the yeas and nays, and they were ordered.

The question being taken, the result was—yeas 18, nays 43—as follows:

Yeas—Messrs. Goldsborough, President; Belt, Carter, Farrow, Hoffman, Jones, of Cecil, Larsh, Markey, Mitchell, Miller, Morgan, Mullikin, Parran, Purnell, Ridgely, Swope, Todd, Valliant—18.

Nays—Messrs. Abbott, Annan, Audoun, Baker, Brooks, Brown, Chambers, Crawford, Cunningham, Cushing, Daniel, Davis, of Washington, Dellinger, Dent, Duvall, Ecker, Galloway, Greene, Hatch, Hebb, Henkle, Hollyday, Hopper, Horsey, Keefer, Kennard, Lansdale, Lee, Marbury, McComas, Negley, Parker, Pugh, Russell, Schley, Schlosser, Scott, Sneary, Stirling, Stockbridge, Sykes, Thomas, Wickard, Wooden—43.

When their names were called,

Mr. FARROW said: I moved the reconsideration of this section expecting an amendment to be offered. Believing that the present law would be much more likely to be abused than this, I vote "aye."

Mr. HEBB said: I desire to state why I shall now vote against this proposition, when before I voted for it. An amendment I offered was accepted by the gentleman from Caroline (Mr. Todd) limiting the operation of the apprenticeship system so as to apply only to those minors incapable of supporting themselves and whose parents are unable to maintain them. Having told the gentleman from Caroline that if he would incorporate that amendment I would vote for the section, I did so at that time. Believing that the law is sufficient and will be much better carried out as it is than with this section together with the other section adopted on the motion of the gentleman from Baltimore city (Mr. Audoun,) I vote "no."

Mr. McCOMAS said: I voted for this proposition before; but after more mature deliberation I think it is improper matter to incorporate into the constitution. It is impossible to attach to it here those barriers which should exist against abuse. I therefore now vote "no."

Mr. NEGLEY said: Our friends who are much more interested in this than we are, having deserted it, I feel no hesitation in doing so likewise, and I therefore vote "no."

Mr. PURNELL said: When this section was before the convention I supported it in a feeble way. I have maturely considered it since, and I see nothing whatever objectionable in it. I voted a few moments since for a reconsideration of the proposition for the purpose of giving those who are opposed to it an opportunity of modifying it, improving it, or amending it in any form to make it acceptable to them, preserving the substance and tenor of the section. They have not done so. Seeing no cause whatever to change my tactics in this matter, I shall adhere to my original vote. I vote "aye."

Mr. RIDGELY said: As I understand the laws of the State as they now exist, the orphans' courts have power to bind out such a class of people in their own discretion as vagrants and those that are incapable of supporting themselves. The difference between the existing law and the provision under consideration is this, that this provision restrains that discretion, and limits its exercise only to those who are loyal. The house have voted to strike that out. I think it ought to remain there. I vote "aye."

Mr. TODD said: In offering this proposition I acted from conscientious motives of right and justice. I see no reason whatever for changing my position; and I therefore vote "aye."

Mr. CHAMBERS said: I understand that this is the question whether to accept the proposition originally introduced by the gentleman from Caroline (Mr. Todd) as it stands, encumbered with loyalty oaths, &c., or to leave the matter as it was before. Is that the character of it?

The PRESIDENT. Yes, sir; that is the character of it.

Mr. CHAMBERS. I vote "no," not to accept this.

The twenty-ninth section was accordingly rejected.

Mr. CHAMBERS. I understand that that is not the section that imposed the restriction.

The PRESIDENT. I suppose that to be consistent the convention will strike out the other section.

Mr. AUDOUN. When the twenty-ninth section was adopted a few days ago, for the purpose of meeting it, I offered the 30th. The 29th has been stricken out, and I see no use in retaining the 30th section. I therefore move to reconsider the vote by which that was adopted.

The motion to reconsider was seconded by Messrs. CUSHING and HEBB.

The section was the following:

"Sec. 30. It shall be the duty of the judges of the several orphans' courts of this State, before they shall proceed to bind any negroes as apprentices, to administer to the party to whom he or she is to be bound, the same oath as prescribed for voters by this constitution, in the article on the elective franchise, and upon the refusal of the said party to take and subscribe to said oath, the said courts shall hold the person so refusing to be an unsuitable person to have charge of such negro; and the fact of such oath having been taken by the party to whom such negro has been bound, shall be expressed in the indenture."

The motion to reconsider was agreed to.

The question recurred upon the adoption of the section, and it was rejected.

Mr. CHAMBERS. Will it now be in order to offer the original proposition of the gentleman from Caroline as a new section, and let the house vote nakedly upon it?

The PRESIDENT. That amendment has been virtually voted upon by the house already.

JUDICIARY REPORT.

Mr. HEBB. I move to strike out the word "associate" in section two, line one, being an error. It reads:

"The judges of the several courts, except the associate judges of the orphans' courts," &c.

The amendment was agreed to.

On motion of Mr. THOMAS,

Sec. 42, line 9, was amended by striking out "thirty-third" and inserting "forty-first," a change rendered necessary by the renumbering of the sections.

The report was then ordered to be engrossed for a third reading.

BIENNIAL SESSIONS.

Mr. MILLER. I ask for information whether the legislative article as a whole is before the house?

The PRESIDENT. No, sir; it is divided into three reports.

Mr. MILLER. Is any part of it before the house?

The PRESIDENT. The report of the committee on usury is still unacted upon.

Mr. MILLER. If that report is before the house, or if it is in order, I should like the sense of the house to be taken, in order to put myself right upon the record, upon the proposition for which I voted at the time for the purpose of moving a reconsideration; the question whether the sessions of the legislature shall be annual or biennial. I hope, having voted for it for the purpose of reconsideration, that there will be no objection to a vote of the convention upon it.

The PRESIDENT. The gentleman can offer an order to go upon the journal.

JUDICIARY REPORT.

On motion of Mr. PUGH,

The rules were suspended in order to place the judiciary report upon its third reading.

The title having been read,

Mr. CUSHING moved that so much be considered the third reading of the report.

Mr. STOCKBRIDGE. I hope that motion will not prevail. This report is a long one. It is known to all sides of the house that this is not at all the system which was reported, but was made up, on successive days, from an endless amount of amendments, more amendments than improvements I fear. That however is with the convention, and I do not impeach their judgment in the matter. But these amendments have been put together, and I greatly fear there may be incongruities in the report. I think that in order that it be perfected as a system, it is essential that we shall go over it, reading it in detail. I certainly do not propose to offer any amendment to it in substance; only what may seem absolutely necessary to harmonize one section with another, if any amendment should be found necessary. I think it is important that for that purpose it should be read over.

Mr. MILLER. I would be in favor of that, but that the committee of revision will have that very thing under their charge; and they have power to make a report making such alterations and dovetailing it together in any way they please. I think if this long report is read over here in convention, there will not be more than two or three that will pay much attention to it.

The motion was rejected.

The secretary proceeded to read the report section by section.

The 8th section having been read as follows:

"Sec. 8. The general assembly shall provide for the trial of causes in case of the disqualification of all the judges of the circuit, to hear and determine the same, but in case of such disqualification, the parties thereto may, by consent, appoint a person to try the same; and the parties to any cause may submit the same to the court for determination without the aid of a jury."

Mr. STOCKBRIDGE (by unanimous consent) submitted the following amendment:

Strike out the words "all the judges of the circuit" and insert "the judge of the circuit, or of the superior court, court of common pleas, circuit court or criminal court in Baltimore city."

The amendment was agreed to.

The 16th section having been read as follows:

"Sec. 16. The salary of the justices of the court of appeals shall be $3,000 per annum, payable quarterly."

Mr. MILLER said: There is a slight verbal inaccuracy in this section, and I ask the unanimous consent of the convention to move to strike out the word "three" and insert the word "five." [Laughter.]

Objection was offered.

Mr. STOCKBRIDGE. In this same section, in which the gentleman discovers that inaccuracy, the judges of the court of appeals are called justices, while in other places they are called judges.

Mr. CHAMBERS. It is an error in section 15. It was intended that the designation should be justices of the court of appeals; and I move that it be corrected.

There being no objection, the word "justices" was substituted for "judges" in sections 12, 13, 15 and 17.

Mr. STOCKBRIDGE. In the 18th line of section 12, is the expression "the first Monday of November." The law of congress reads, "the first Monday in the month of November."

There being no objection the amendment was made; and a similar amendment in section 22.

The 25th section having been read as follows:

"Sec. 25. In case of the death, resignation, removal or other disqualification of a judge by the courts of this State, the governor, by and with the advice and consent of the senate, shall thereupon appoint a person duly qualified, to fill said office until the next general election for members to the general assembly thereafter, at which time an election shall be held as herein prescribed, for a judge, who shall hold said office for the term of fifteen years, and until the election and qualification of his successor."

Mr. STIRLING said: The judges of the court of appeals are elected for fifteen years. They could hardly be elected always on the general election day.

Mr. HEBB. It will be necessary either to change the term to fourteen or sixteen years, or to have elections in the year when the county officers are elected.

Mr. STOCKBRIDGE. This section is among the provisions relating to circuit courts. The whole difficulty will be obviated if the word "circuit" is inserted before the word "courts."

The PRESIDENT. Is the case of the death, resignation, &c., of justices of the court of appeals provided for elsewhere?

Mr. CHAMBERS. Why not wait until the general election, and let the governor's appointee remain in office until then?

On motion of Mr. STIRLING, and by unanimous consent,

The second line was so amended as to read "of a judge of any court;" and the fifth line so as to read, "the next general election thereafter, whether for members of the general assembly or county officers."

On motion of Mr. STOCKBRIDGE, and by unanimous consent,

The section was transferred to part I, to come in after the 11th section.

CIRCUIT COURTS.

Mr. STOCKBRIDGE. I observe in the 19th section a slight inaccuracy, like that of my friend from Anne Arundel (Mr. Miller.) Since this matter was brought before the convention my attention has been called to it, and I am assured that the first three circuits might without any injury to the business be consolidated into two: St. Mary's, Charles and Prince George's, the first; and Anne Arundel, Calvert and Montgomery, the second. I am not sufficiently familiar with the business of those counties to speak of my own knowledge, and do not profess to do so. But if that statement be correct, gentlemen here may know it; and if they can be consolidated it will save one judge. I therefore call attention to it.

The 19th section as adopted on the second reading, was as follows:

"Sec. 19. The State shall be divided into thirteen judicial circuits, in manner following: The counties of St. Mary's and Charles, shall constitute the first circuit; the counties of Anne Arundel and Calvert, the second; the counties of Prince George's and Montgomery the third; the county of Frederick, the fourth; &c.

Mr. MILLER. I hope the gentleman will move to open the section for the purpose of making that amendment. I know that our friends from Prince George's are anxious that it should be done. We desired a judge for each county; but failing in that I am satisfied that the judge of the lower district, St. Mary's and Charles, would have very little to do; and the judge for Anne Arundel and Calvert may very well have attached to his circuit, I think, the county of Montgomery.

Mr. STOCKBRIDGE. Distinguished citizens of those counties have assured me so; and that is the reason I called attention to it, thinking that if we could save the expense of a judge, it was an item worth considering. I will now move that these three circuits be so consolidated that St. Mary's, Charles and Prince George's shall constitute the first, and Anne Arundel, Calvert and Montgomery, the second.

Mr. ABBOTT. What do they expect to do when they get a population of forty, fifty, or sixty thousand inhabitants? These circuits must remain until the constitution is altered.

Mr. MILLER. When we get that large number I hope we shall throw this constitution aside.

Mr. CUSHING. The gentleman from Prince George's said when the subject was before us on the second reading, that it was almost impossible for the business to be done; that he had known in the winter season of men lying in jail six months at a time; and that justice could not be rendered in that circuit on account of its extent. Now it is proposed to put the circuit back, when we have diminished it on account of the representation of gentlemen from Prince George's, that justice could not be done, and that men were lying in jail six months at a time, and again to make it what the gentleman from Prince George's considered monstrous and unjust.

Mr. PARRAN. I hope the report will not be opened. As a member from Calvert county, I am very well satisfied with the present arrangement. If to gratify the gentlemen from Prince George's, they are to go back to the old circuit, what becomes of Montgomery? As a necessary consequence, it must go back to Anne Arundel and Calvert, or else make a separate circuit. I do not presume it is intended to make that a separate circuit, the object being to reduce the number of circuits. Montgomery therefore is to be put in the circuit with Calvert and Anne Arundel. I think the present arrangement is better; and I hope the convention will not open the report.

The motion was not agreed to.

ORPHANS' COURT.

By unanimous consent the 26th and 27th sections were transposed.

The 27th section having been read,

Mr. PUGH moved to amend by striking out the words, "at the time of his election," in the 16th line, and transposing the last two clauses of the section, so that the words "to be paid by the said counties and city respectively," should be inserted next after the word "compensation."

The latter portion of the section, as adopted upon the second reading was:

"No person shall be elected judge of the

orphans' court unless he be a citizen of the United States, and resident for twelve months in the city or county for which he may be elected at the time of his election; each of said judges shall receive such compensation as is now or may hereafter be fixed by the general assembly, to be paid by the said counties and city respectively."

The amendment was agreed to, by unanimous consent.

On motion of Mr. STIRLING, and by unanimous consent,

The words "at the time of his election" were inserted next after the words "unless he be" in the fourteenth line.

DETENTION IN SLAVERY.

The thirty-first section having been read, as follows:

"Section 31. Any person who shall, after this constitution shall have gone into effect, detain in slavery any person so emancipated by the provisions of this constitution shall, on conviction, be fined not less than five hundred dollars, nor more than five thousand dollars, or be imprisoned not more than five years; and any of the judges of this State shall discharge, on *habeas corpus*, any person so detained in slavery;"

On motion of Mr. STIRLING, and by unanimous consent,

The word "so" was stricken out in the second line.

Mr. MILLER. I was not here at the time this provision was adopted, and I move that the report be opened for the purpose of enabling me to move to strike out this section. It must be acknowledged that after we have declared that slavery or involuntary servitude shall no longer exist in the State, there can be no such thing as detaining any emancipated slave in slavery. It seems to me a contradiction in terms, and rather mars the symmetry of this great work in the estimation of gentlemen, to say that a man can be detained in slavery after you have said that slavery shall not exist.

Mr. STIRLING. A man is detained in slavery who is taken by a slave ship, and he might escape punishment, although it is piracy by the laws of the country.

Mr. MILLER. The laws of the United States provide for that.

Mr. BELT. I trust that my friend from Anne Arundel (Mr. Miller) will withdraw his motion. I desire to vote for that section, taking it as a recognition of slavery.

Mr. PUGH. I have no objection whatever to all the comfort there is in it being administered to the gentleman.

The motion was rejected.

SUPERIOR COURT OF BALTIMORE CITY.

The thirty-fourth section having been read as follows:

"Section 34. The superior court of Baltimore city shall have jurisdiction over all suits where the debt or damage claimed, exclusive of interest, shall exceed the sum of one thousand dollars, and in case any plaintiff or plaintiffs shall recover less than the sum or value of one thousand dollars, he or they shall be allowed or adjudged to pay costs in the discretion of the court. The said court shall also have jurisdiction as a court of equity within the limits of the said city, and in all other civil cases which are not hereinafter assigned to the court of common pleas, and shall also have jurisdiction in all cases of appeals from the commissioner for opening streets; provided all cases now pending on the law side of said court, where the debt or damage claimed is less than one thousand dollars, shall be prosecuted to final judgment in said court, as though its jurisdiction had not been changed;"

Mr. CHAMBERS said: I would ask why the provision is made that the principal, rather than the principal and interest, shall exceed the sum of one thousand dollars. By this provision a verdict of one thousand dollars and interest could not be entered; and I do not see why the interest, every dollar of it, is not as important to the plaintiff as the principal. If the debt amounts to more than one thousand dollars, I do not see why it may not as well be interest as anything else. The value consists in the sum of money due. I would suggest that the words "exclusive of interest" be stricken out.

Mr. STOCKBRIDGE. These words were put in for the reason that in many cases where the time was a little uncertain, the mere matter of interest would change the jurisdiction; and there have been cases where persons have been thrown in costs because the jury took a certain view as to the point of time from which interest could be properly claimed. It was thought more safe for suitors that the matter of interest should not be included in the sum determining the jurisdiction; and these words were inserted to avoid that practical difficulty.

Mr. CHAMBERS. In an action the party plaintiff claims that his principal amounts to one thousand dollars, and the case is tried before a jury, and they bring in a verdict of eleven hundred dollars. You cannot tell how much is principal and how much is interest. They consolidate it. The law requires them to bring in the aggregate amount. Then the question must be opened before the court to decide that. It strikes me that where a party can recover more than one thousand dollars, he should be heard in the superior court, no matter whether it is principal or principal and interest. So before a justice of the peace, a man may claim ninety-nine dollars principal and ninety-nine dollars interest. The law does not allow the justice of the peace to decide upon a claim amounting in the aggregate to more than one hundred dollars.

Mr. STOCKBRIDGE. There have been all sorts

of difficulties growing out of the same thing my friend refers to. Men have brought suits in which they did not claim any interest; and at other times they have claimed so much money with interest from such a date; and the entire question of jurisdiction has grown out of the question whether they were entitled to claim interest from the time specified or from a subsequent time. For instance, a man has a claim for one thousand dollars, and interest for two years and a half, amounting to one hundred and fifty dollars. He thinks he is entitled to interest for that period of time. He brings his suit. The jury, when they come to take the matter in hand, decide that he is entitled to the principal; but for some reason he is not entitled to interest. He is then in the position of being entirely at the court's mercy whether he shall not be compelled to pay costs for bringing his suit there instead of in the other court. I think it is preferable as it stands; and I wish it was the same in the case of justices of the peace.

Mr. MILLER. I will suggest that the jurisdiction prescribed for the superior court is "over all suits where the debt or damage claimed, exclusive of interest, shall exceed the sum of one thousand." When a suit is brought, whether upon a promissory note, or for other debt or damage, exceeding that amount, it comes within the jurisdiction of that court. A suit may not be tried for two or three years, and interest running all the while. When the jury make up their verdict at the trial of the cause they bring in, including interest, a sum exceeding one thousand dollars, as the sum total of their verdict; and as the sum rendered exceeds or is less than one thousand dollars, it will come within the jurisdiction of one court or the other. I think it is very clear that these words should be left out.

Mr. STOCKBRIDGE. I do not think so; but I am ready to vote on the gentleman's motion if he makes one.

No amendment was offered.

On motion, and by unanimous consent,

Section thirty-seven was amended by striking out the word "city," in the designation of the criminal court of Baltimore.

Section thirty-nine having been read, as follows:

"Section 39. All causes pending in the several courts of Baltimore city, at the adoption of this constitution, shall be prosecuted to final judgment, as though the jurisdiction of the several courts in which they may be pending had not been changed;"

Mr. STOCKBRIDGE said: I move to open section thirty-four for amendment, in order to strike out from line ten to the end of the section, as follows: "provided all cases now pending on the law side of said court, where the debt or damage claimed is less than one thousand dollars, shall be prosecuted to final judgment in said court, as though its jurisdiction had not been changed." The thirty-ninth section provides precisely the same thing for all the courts, of course including the superior court.

The motion was agreed to.

The amendment was adopted.

CLERKS OF BALTIMORE COURTS.

The 41st section having been read, as follows:

"Sec. 41. There shall be a clerk of the superior court of Baltimore city, and a clerk of the circuit court of Baltimore city, and a clerk of the court of common pleas in Baltimore city, and a clerk of the criminal court of Baltimore city, and each of the said clerks shall be elected by the legal and qualified voters of said city, and shall hold his office for six years from the first day of January succeeding his election, and until his successor is elected and qualified, and be re-eligible thereto, subject to be removed for wilful neglect of duty or other misdemeanor in office, on conviction in a court of law. In case of a vacancy in the office of a clerk of any of the said courts, the judge of the court of which he was clerk, shall have the power to appoint a clerk until the general election for county officers held next thereafter."

On motion of Mr. STIRLING, and by unanimous consent,

The words "in Baltimore city" were stricken out from the designation of the court of common pleas, and the word "city" from the designation of the criminal court of Baltimore.

Mr. MILLER. I see that in case of a vacancy, the judge is to have power to fill the vacancy until the general election for county officers held next thereafter. There is no provision to show whether that election shall be for the full term of six years, or for the remainder of the term thus vacated. I think there ought to be some provision to explain that.

Mr. STIRLING. Why are they to hold office "from the first day of January?" The present constitution says the clerks shall hold office from the time of their election. I move to open the section to amend it.

Mr. HEBB. I think the change ought to be made. The clerks of the circuit courts hold from the time of their election.

The motion was agreed to.

On motion of Mr. STIRLING,

The section was amended by striking out "first day of January succeeding," and inserting "time of."

Mr. STOCKBRIDGE. A vacancy is to be filled "until the general election for county officers held next thereafter." We do not happen to have "county officers" in the city.

Mr. STIRLING. Yes, sir; the sheriff and orphans' court judges are county officers.

Section 42d having been read,

On motion of Mr. STIRLING,

The section was opened for amendment, in

order to insert the words in the fifth line, "and until their successors are elected and qualified;" and the amendment was adopted.

By unanimous consent,

The word "41st" was stricken out in line nine, and "39th" inserted, to correspond with the renumbering of the sections.

Section 43d having been read,

On motion of Mr. RIDGELY, and by unanimous consent,

The word "legislature" was stricken out, and the words "general assembly" were inserted in the first line.

The 44th section was read as follows:

"Sec. 44. The clerk of the court of common pleas shall have authority to issue within said city, all marriage and other licences required by law, subject to such provisions as the legislature have now or may hereafter prescribe, and the clerk of the superior court of said city shall have the custody of all deeds, conveyances and other papers now remaining in the office of said court, and shall hereafter receive and record all deeds, conveyances and other papers which are required by law to be recorded in said city. He shall also have custody of all other papers connected with the proceedings on the law or equity side of Baltimore county court, and of the dockets thereof so far as the same have relation to the city of Baltimore."

On motion of Mr. MILLER, and by unanimous consent,

The word "other" was stricken out in the ninth line, so as to read, "he shall also have custody of all papers" &c.

Mr. HEBB, by unanimous consent, submitted the following amendment:

Insert as section 26, the following:

"The judges of the respective circuit courts of this State, or of the courts of the city of Baltimore, shall render their decision in all cases argued before them, or submitted for their judgment, within two months after the same shall have been so argued or submitted."

Mr. HEBB said: I have known cases retained in courts of law over two years.

The amendment was agreed to.

Section 45th having been read,

On motion of Mr. STOCKBRIDGE, and by unanimous consent,

The expression "the mayor and city council of Baltimore" was substituted for "the mayor and council of the city of Baltimore."

SHERIFFS, &C.

The 47th section having been read,

Mr. STOCKBRIDGE said: There is an inaccuracy in that, arising from the change in the courts of Baltimore city. It provides that in case of vacancy the circuit court shall appoint a person to be sheriff. I hope that will be modified.

Mr. STIRLING. I move to open the section and strike out "circuit court" and insert "governor." That will apply to the whole State, and give the governor the power to fill a vacancy in the office of sheriff.

Mr. CHAMBERS. What is the difficulty as it stands?

Mr. STIRLING. We have four judges in the city of Baltimore, and the question is who shall make the appointment.

The motion to open the section was agreed to, and the amendment was adopted.

Mr. MILLER. I have another suggestion to make. The time of the election of sheriffs is not fixed.

Mr. STIRLING. I have an amendment to offer; and I do not know whether it is germain here or in the schedule. I will move to add this section to the report; and if the committee of revision think it belongs anywhere else they can change it.

"Sec.— There shall be an election held in the several counties and in the city of Baltimore, on the Tuesday next after the first Monday in the month of November in every second year. The first election to be held in the year eighteen hundred and sixty-five, at which elections all clerks of courts and registers of wills, judges of the orphans' court, sheriffs, county commissioners, and all other county officers elected by the people shall be chosen whenever an election for any such officer is required to be held, but this shall not apply to the municipal officers of any incorporated town or city."

The motion to open the report to admit the amendment was agreed to.

Mr. NEGLEY. It seems to me that this ought to go into the schedule.

Mr. STIRLING. The schedule is already passed upon.

Mr. HEBB. There is a provision now that all officers now in office shall hold their offices until their present terms expire.

Mr. MILLER. This provides for an election in 1865. Do the terms of the judges of the orphans' court expire in 1865?

Mr. MULLIKIN. I have an objection to this section, that we must have an election in the county every year.

Mr. STIRLING. That is already provided for in the constitution. It is very important that this should be perfectly clear; and as there seems to be some doubt about it, I will withdraw the amendment.

Mr. HEBB. Will it be in order to refer the amendment to the committee of revision?

The PRESIDENT. The amendment can be sent to the committee on revision to accompany the report.

Mr. HEBB. Then I make that motion.

The motion was agreed to.

Mr. MARBURY moved to open the nineteenth section of the report, in order to restore the old circuit system.

The motion was not agreed to.

The report on the judiciary department

having been read the third time, was passed by yeas and nays, as follows:

Yeas—Messrs. Goldsborough, President; Abbott, Annan, Audoun, Baker, Carter, Cunningham, Cushing, Daniel, Davis, of Washington, Dellinger, Earle, Ecker, Farrow, Galloway, Greene, Hatch, Hebb, Hoffman, Hopper, Jones, of Cecil, Keefer, Kennard, King, Larsh, McComas, Mullikin, Negley, Nyman, Parker, Pugh, Purnell, Ridgely, Russell, Schley, Schlosser, Scott, Sneary, Stirling, Stockbridge, Swope, Sykes, Thomas, Todd, Valliant, Wickard, Wooden—47.

Nays—Messrs. Belt, Brown, Chambers, Crawford, Dent, Hollyday, Horsey, Lee, Marbury, Mitchell, Miller, Parran—12.

When their names were called,

Mr. CHAMBERS said: So far as I am concerned, I have voted thus far against every bill; and I shall vote against this, not upon the ground of opposition to everything that is done here; but I cannot vote for a judicial system with a tenure for a term of years. My opinion is that it ought to be during good behaviour. Upon that ground I shall vote "no," although I am glad to see an approach towards the correct tenure in this report.

Mr. MILLER said: The subject of the judiciary has been one in which I have felt more interest than almost any other question before this convention. I voted against the call of the convention of 1850, and against the adoption of the present constitution of 1850, because it changed the judiciary system of the State from an appointive system with a life tenure to an elective system for a term of years. I have had all my life a great and strong feeling upon that subject, and I never will vote for an election, or a term of years. I vote "no."

Mr. STOCKBRIDGE said: I must be allowed, contrary to my usual custom, to say one word in explanation of my vote upon the question before the convention. It is very well known to members that this judiciary article, as now prepared, is a very different one from what I had hoped to see adopted by this convention. I think it defective and wrong in many respects. But the question is not what I would like to see it. If that were the question; if it were a question between adopting this and something better, I should most readily vote "no." But the question is between this and the existing article upon that subject. I consider the article as now completed a decided improvement upon the existing article in many features. I am not aware that it is worse in any respect. The features that are most objectionable to me are similar to those in the present constitution. On other points I consider it a decided advance; and I shall therefore vote for the article as it stands. I vote "yes."

Mr. VALLIANT said: My explanations have been frequent here; but I have not troubled the convention very much with speech making. This system is not as I would have it. It does not meet with my entire approbation; but as has been remarked by the gentleman from Baltimore, I believe it is an improvement upon the old system. I prefer the life tenure; and I prefer the appointive system; but as this is a nearer approach to my views than the old system, I vote for it. I vote "aye."

Mr. BELT said: One single remark. Inasmuch as I misunderstood the effect of the proposition of my friend from Baltimore city (Mr. Stockbridge) at the time he offered it a little while ago, and did not say what I would like to have said then, I will do it now in explanation of my vote. There are many objections to the report on general principles, and one feature of it is so objectionable to my people and those of the surrounding counties that it is impossible for me to vote for the article with that provision in it. I refer to the provision in the nineteenth section which redistricts the lower counties. The proposition that we have made to the convention several times, and which I do not think and am sorry that it has never yet been understood, is to put Prince George's, Charles and St. Mary's into one circuit, as they are now, and Calvert, Anne Arundel and Montgomery into one, relieving them of Howard county which goes into another circuit.

The immediate effect of it is to save the expense of one judge, saving one circuit. There is not one feature of this constitution so productive of feelings of regret and sorrow in those counties, as this arrangement which has been made for them. We would ten-fold rather have the three counties in one circuit than any two of them. As represented upon this floor, I believe the arrangement is without a single voice in any of five of the counties. Five out of the six counties are earnestly in favor of the old system being re-established.

The PRESIDENT. The gentleman from Calvert (Mr. Parran) objected to the amendment.

Mr. BELT. I speak of the other five counties. The sixth, Calvert, which here opposes the re-establishment, is the smallest county of the whole six. As to the practical question, the reason for my vote, it is this. We made a proposition with almost the universal assent of the people of six counties, to be re-established in our old relations, and to save the State one judge and one circuit; and we are refused so reasonable a proposition as that. I am therefore compelled to vote "no."

The report on the judiciary department, as amended, was accordingly passed.

USURY.

Mr. STOCKBRIDGE. I now move to take up the usury report, our last report. I have no objection to taking a recess when that is taken up; but I want gentlemen to understand that it is to come up this evening.

The motion was agreed to.

On motion of Mr. STIRLING,

The convention took a recess until 8 o'clock.

EVENING SESSION.

The convention met at 8 o'clock, P. M.

The roll was called, and the following members answered to their names:

Messrs. Goldsborough, President; Abbott, Annan, Audoun, Baker, Belt, Brooks, Brown, Carter, Chambers, Crawford, Cunningham, Cushing, Daniel, Davis, of Washington, Dellinger, Dent, Duvall, Earle, Ecker, Farrow, Galloway, Greene, Hatch, Hebb, Hoffman, Hollyday, Hopper, Horsey, Jones, of Cecil, Keefer, Kennard, King, Larsh, Lee, Marbury, Markey, McComas, Mitchell, Miller, Morgan, Mullikin, Murray, Negley, Parran, Pugh, Purnell, Ridgely, Russell, Sands, Schley, Schlosser, Scott, Sneary, Stirling, Stockbridge, Sykes, Thomas, Todd, Valliant, Wickard, Wooden—62.

THE SOLDIERS' VOTE.

Mr. DANIEL. I ask the consent of the house to make a statement with reference to some remarks that were made in the debate yesterday. It will be recollected by the house that one of the gentlemen from Prince George's (Mr. Marbury) yesterday, in a speech, made reference to a certain vote that had been taken among the soldiers encamped here, at which vote, I think he stated that all had voted for McClellan except seven, and these would have voted for him if they had not been afraid. There were at that time some officers present who were surprised at the announcement, and believing that injustice would be done them, or a large proportion of them, if such a report were to go out uncontradicted, they felt it their duty to call a meeting and take a vote; and they desire me to present the result to the convention. I ask therefore that this paper, showing the result of the vote, be entered upon the record of the debates of this convention.

Mr. MILLER. Is that in order?

Mr. CUSHING. Quite as much so as the personal character of Mr. Williams.

Mr. BELT. That was not so much the character of Mr. Williams as the character of Mr. Valliant.

The paper was read as follows:

OFFICERS' HOSPITAL,
Annapolis, Md., Sept. 2, 1864.

The wounded officers at this hospital, representing some two hundred and fifty different regiments, met to-day to give expression to their choice of candidates for the presidency.

The meeting was called to order by Dr. Comstock. On motion, he was called on to preside over the meeting.

Lieutenant Ball, of the second Maryland volunteers, was appointed secretary, and the following officers tellers: Captain Little, 187th Pennsylvania volunteers, Captain Wells, 1st New York dragoons, and Lieutenant Davis, second infantry, United States army.

Lieutenant Colonel Adney, of the 36th Ohio, was called upon to address the meeting, when he proceeded to make a few appropriate remarks, which were received with great applause. He was followed by Colonel De-Forrest, of the 11th Massachusetts volunteers, and Colonel Massey, 2nd Maryland volunteers, and others.

The following named officers were appointed a committee to wait upon the Maryland State Convention, now in session here, with the result of the ballot:

Lieutenant Colonel Adney, 36th Ohio volunteers, D. H. Armstrong, Surgeon, United States volunteers, and Captain DeKay, 14th infantry, United States army.

The ballot was then taken with the following result:

Lincoln and Johnson	237
McClellan and Pendleton	32
Fremont and Cochrane	1
Total	270

Lincoln majority, 204.

WM. B. BALL,
2nd Md. Vols., Secretary.

[Applause.]

Mr. BELT. As my colleague who made the statement is not here, I will say I have no doubt that the explanation of it is this: We know very well that night by night those who constitute the soldiers here, are coming and going between two suns. The vote he referred to was taken I believe some days ago, at least. I understood yesterday that on the night before there had been a very large arrival of troops from Maine; and I do not suppose anybody expects Maine men will vote for McClellan, soldiers or not. No doubt it was the Maine vote that carried the result against us.

Mr. CUSHING. I should like to have the gentleman from Prince George's explain to us the process by which broken limbs can be cured between sun and sun, in order that these men who come here with a wounded leg or arm, or a hole in the breast or stomach, may be cured and sent away. The information might be valuable to surgeons.

Mr. BELT. I have been here four months, and I have never seen any arrival of wounded men, and I have never seen any departure of them in the day time; and hence I conclude they are moved at night. I suppose the reason the government moves the men at night is that it is more salubrious, on account of the coolness of the atmosphere.

Mr. DANIEL. These officers say that they represent "some two hundred and fifty different regiments. So many could not have come from Maine. [Laughter and applause.]

Mr. SANDS. I would like to say a word.—

I have only to say in reply to my friend that if there were soldiers here from anywhere else who voted for McClellan, I am very glad they are gone. And if those who are here came from Maine, voting as they have voted on this occasion, I am very glad they are here; and I hope they will stay here long enough to make good Union people out of some other people that are here. As to the merits of these two gentlemen—the candidates for the presidency of the United States—they are before the world. As to General McClellan, all I have to say of him is this, that I feel toward him as a simple lad felt about a sheep on a certain occasion. The father died, leaving two sons. In his estate, to be divided, was a flock of sheep. One of the brothers was sharp-witted and the other was dull; and the latter was particularly attached to Billy, his pet lamb.

Mr. MILLER (in his seat.) We have heard that story before.

Mr. SANDS. It may do you good to hear it again, and if it is not a new story, it is a new application of an old story.

The sharp brother went to work and divided the sheep into two lots, putting all the best into one lot, and all the good-for-nothing and scabby ones into the other, and then put Billy, the pet lamb among the scabby sheep, confident that his silly brother would choose the flock to which Billy belonged. The half-witted young man came to the pen and looked at his favorite. "Billy, I love you. I have always liked you, Billy. I like you still, Billy. I would like to keep you, Billy, but I can't do it; you are in bad company, and I must quit you."

That is exactly the way I feel toward General McClellan. He has got into company I cannot possibly keep, and if I quit him it is his fault and not mine. He is now the candidate of the peace democracy, who illustrated their peace principles out at Chicago the other day by a fight upon the floor of their convention. He is the gentleman of whom my friend from St. Mary's (Mr. Harris,) following Mr. Long, said: "For Heaven's sake, don't put such a weight as this upon a weak platform. The platform is bad enough, but put this man on it and he will crush you."

I would not have said anything that I sympathize with the class of men who voted, more than I do with the peace advocates upon this floor. They are men who have risked their lives in the cause of the country. They have left home and all that is dear to them, and spent their time for years and their blood in oceans for the land of my birth, and I love them. I am sure that the vote placed upon our record here to-night is only a faint indication of that which is going to be placed in the ballot-box in November next; for I am sure that the brother soldiers of those who voted for McClellan have since expressed themselves ashamed of the act. I trust that whatever may be the result of these little indications, in hospitals, railway cars, and steamers, the people mean to press onward to the great end to be accomplished in the next four years—the preservation of their country from disruption and destruction, which is the object every true patriot has at heart. It is not the question of any little party power, which may result in placing McClellan, or anybody else, in high position, but of such action as is going to result in the re-establishment of this Union in all its integrity and power. The people have made up their minds to this, and even if they have to war four years longer, and wade through a deeper sea of blood, they are going to that end. God speed them to it. It is your salvation and mine to war on this side of the Potomac with those who are now striving to divide the country in order to get you and me by the throat to become their victims. I trust in God first to preserve my country, and then I trust in the brave men who are battling for it this day.

Mr. BELT. I desire simply to say that the magnificent and characteristic reply of the gentleman from Baltimore city (Mr. Daniel) did not come upon us more like a thunderbolt than the appearance of the gentleman from Howard (Mr. Sands.) If anybody had known he was in the house there would not have been a word said. If he had been here the remarks of my colleague would unquestionably never have been uttered. The gentleman left here with an open, public declaration, that he had gone home to attend court, and did not intend to come back any more.

Mr. SANDS. The gentleman is as wide from the facts there as with regard to the soldiers voting. I expected to be back last night but was kept away by important business.

Mr. BELT. With reference to any hopes that the remarks of any person here will now change any one's politics, I am astonished that after four months of tri-weekly war-speeches, harangues in support of the administration, and demonstrations against the peace party, the gentleman should ever have supposed that those who had proved refractory under that infliction, or that administration of physic, I may say, would ever be capable of being cured by the application of anything of a sterner sort.

There is only one remark more I have to make to close this matter up, so far as I am concerned, and that is that I do not want my coming to the support of this cause to be taken in the widest sense, as an entire indorsement of the action of the democratic party. That may require some consideration. Although being very practical in my political course, I think it quite probable that I may agree to the present arrangements.

ADJOURNMENT OVER.

Mr. RIDGELY. I do not rise to say anything upon the subject before the house, but to bring the house to the consideration of business. I move that when the convention adjourns to-night, it stand adjourned until Monday next, at 12 o'clock, M.

Mr. NEGLEY. I move to amend by striking out "Monday" and inserting "Tuesday." I do not think we ought to adjourn at all, unless we adjourn to that time.

Mr. CUSHING. I should like to hear some reason for the adjournment while in the full tide of successful work.

Mr. RIDGELY. The reason lies in a very narrow compass. It is known to the whole convention that we have but one more subject to consider, and that is the usury report The committee of revision are engaged industriously in the revision of the work that has been done, and I am informed that that committee do not expect to be able to complete their labors until late in the day to-morrow; and it will therefore be impossible for us to go through with our business until the committee on revision are prepared to make a final report. Besides which, the entire constitution by the order of the house, is to be engrossed for the signature of the presiding officer. Under these circumstances the house will be without any kind of employment to-morrow, supposing the usury report, which is very short, to be passed tonight. If the house determines to adjourn to-night, such members as desire it may leave in the morning train and return on Monday, when the committee on revision will be able to submit their final report, and the house will be able to act deliberately, doing things, as the gentleman from Carroll observed this morning, decently and in order, instead of having the business all crowded upon us during the day to-morrow.

Mr. NEGLEY. In addition to what the gentleman from Baltimore county has said, we know that there are now before the committee on revision seven or eight reports—about half of all the reports. We know by the experience of this convention that it took the whole afternoon to go over the judiciary report. And I do not see how it is possible for any committee to go over that report carefully and deliberately, comparing the different sections with each other, and correcting the verbal mistakes, if there are any, in the manner they should go over it, in less than half a day. What is the use of one day at the heel of a session of four months? What are two days, or half a week, at the heel of the session? Would we not a great deal better spend two days more, and give this committee time to go over its revision carefully, systematically, and in such a manner that we can depend upon their work, when they report to this body. It is not to be expected that we will give it much more attention, when we adjourn to-night to meet again on Monday or Tuesday. We shall be in no frame of mind to go into a critical examination of the report of the committee on revision. Therefore, I say, let us give them ample time. Let them complete their work. I know the chairman of that committee (Mr. Earle) is competent to do it, and I believe the other members will assist him, and we may rely upon their work. The State, I am satisfied, would much rather see this thing done up neatly and effectually, and with propriety. There is no necessity for hurrying over this matter.

Again, I think our friends from Baltimore county and city ought to have a little compassion on the members who live a little further away from the seat of government. It is very easy for them to come here to-morrow morning, to be there on the Sabbath, and return here on Monday morning. We of the western counties cannot do that. We can go home and spend the Sabbath with our families and be here on Tuesday at 12 o'clock. I think if you adjourn to that time you will have a quorum and a full house; but I very much doubt whether you will have a full house on Monday; and at the final adoption of this constitution I would like to see a full house. I would like to impress upon members of the convention the necessity and the propriety of being here in force on Tuesday. If you adjourn to Monday, you will not have a full house that day. If I go home, and I shall be sorely tempted to do so, I am certain I cannot be here before Tuesday morning. Adjourning until Tuesday, you will give the committee an additional twenty-four hours. They need it—they want it. Let them have that ample time. I do hope that we shall adjourn over to that time.

Mr. CUSHING. I have listened with attention to the reasons urged by the gentleman from Washington (Mr. Negley;) but I must say that I remain as yet unconvinced that we cannot finish the whole work before the convention by to-morrow, if necessary at midnight. The committee on revision presented to us this morning their report on a number of articles, some of them of a great deal of importance. We acted on these in a few minutes; and I think the majority of the convention thought we acted decently and in order, and acted knowingly. The judiciary report, which the gentleman says took all the afternoon, I would remind him was complicated with several other things besides merely correcting it. Besides, the house having corrected the judiciary report mainly, the work the committee on revision will have to do upon it will be very slight. If the house adjourns until Monday or Tuesday, it will probably, on the day fixed, be without a quorum; for many of the members will go home to-morrow morning, and they will not be back on Monday or Tuesday morning. This house will find itself in the condition of staying here a whole day with no quorum to do business, sending despatches and writing to members asking them for God's sake to come down that the convention may do its work. We passed an order to adjourn on the 31st of August. That time is already now passed two days. Going over to Monday morning, that will be the 5th of September; and the convention will not adjourn until Tuesday morning, the 6th; and possibly it will then be without a quorum, and the end of next week may find the convention still in session.

The committee on revision sits throughout the whole session of this house. Admitting that the judiciary report would take them half a day, that will take more time than all the rest of the work they have to do. There is not the slightest objection to their calling in extra aid. If they request of this house that their committee be enlarged to twice its numbers, I have no doubt that request would be acceded to. We have provided in our schedule that after the adoption of this constitution by the convention the governor shall have five days before he shall be required to issue his proclamation; and if we remain here five days more, we shall hardly have the customary twenty days notice before the election of State officers; and we desire, in addition, as much time as we can possibly have for the dissemination of the printed copies of the constitution throughout the State, and in the army, that the soldiers and the people at home may knowingly vote upon its provisions. Every day of time that we allow ourselves here, is diminishing our time for the accomplishment of these objects just one day. We propose to lose the whole of to-morrow. In reference to the engrossment of the reports, I have been informed that the clerks of this house have been and are now engaged in engrossing as many of the reports as the committee on revision have acted upon; and, in all probability, if the committee on revision should conclude its labor to-night, by the expenditure of a small sum for additional clerical force, the whole constitution could be presented to this body to-morrow morning. Or, admitting that the committee on revision do not get through, or we do not get through acting upon their reports, all their reports which may have been acted upon will be engrossed by the clerks; and during the morning, as fast as they are passed upon, they will be engrossed by the clerks; and at the afternoon session to-morrow, or at the furthest by the night session, we can act upon the whole constitution, engrossed by the clerks. And when we adjourn to-morrow, we may adjourn having finished our work.

But if we break the continuity of exertion, by which the convention has for the last week kept up three sessions a day, and if the members go to their respective homes, they will find claiming their attention so many private interests, that it is very doubtful whether they will be able to return from Washington and other distant counties in season to proceed on Monday or Tuesday. The gentleman from Washington (Mr. Negley) asks what does it matter, after a session of four months, if we take a week or two weeks. I have no personal objection to adjourning. I should much desire it for my own sake. But I think it is for the interest of the constitution to allow as much time as possible after its passage; and for that reason I think the convention should finish its work before it adjourns.

I have presented my views as they have suggested themselves to me; and if they have made the impression upon our friends that the work can be completed by extra exertion by to-morrow night, I hope they will vote against the adjournment. I would rather sit here the whole of the night than go away and have to come back again to finish our work.

Mr. Pugh. I am satisfied that the members of the convention have made up their minds with regard to the matter that it is only the question whether the committee on revision will be prepared to furnish the convention with work to-morrow, or whether we shall stay here all day to-morrow and make speeches. I am well satisfied that the committee cannot get through to-night.

Mr. Cushing. Not if the committee is enlarged to three times its present number?

Mr. Pugh. That is not the proposition before the house. I have been informed by the chairman of the committee on revision that they cannot get through to night unless they work all night. They worked a large portion of last night, and have worked all day, and are at work to-night. For one, I am not disposed, if the committee cannot furnish us work to do, to stay here to-morrow and listen to speeches.

Mr. King (a member of the committee) said: I am pretty certain that we will not be able to get through our work to-morrow. We have worked all day yesterday and to-day, and, as we are going on, to do it correctly, if the house want it brought in as it ought to be, it will be impossible for us to finish it to-morrow.

Mr. Negley. To show the necessity for care in this, I will state that I have been informed that it has been discovered that no provision has been made for contested elections in the judiciary. This shows the necessity for care and deliberation on the part of the committee on revision. We know further that a whole new section has been referred to that committee in regard to the judiciary report. I hope the convention will not hurry through things at the last moment.

Mr. AUDOUN. The gentleman from Baltimore county (Mr. King,) a member of the committee, has stated to the house that it is utterly impossible for them to get through their work. We have that information from the committee, and I think we ought now to be ready to act on the question.

Mr. GREENE. What shall we gain by adjourning over to-morrow and Monday? Is it the intention to have the committee sit during the recess? If not, what shall we gain by this adjournment?

The PRESIDENT. The chairman of the committee (Mr. Earle,) who has been sent for by the chair, is now present, and will please to inform the convention how far the committee have progressed in the revision of these reports.

Mr. ABBOTT. Will the gentleman also please to inform us whether another committee could aid them in this work?

Mr. EARLE (chairman of the committee on revision) said: We have several of the articles yet to act upon. The judiciary article only came into our hands this afternoon. We have not commenced that. The schedule also came to us to-day.

The PRESIDENT. Is there any probability that the committee will be able to get through by to-morrow?

Mr. EARLE. It would require very hard work to get through by to-morrow night; and I do not believe it would be possible for the work to be entirely finished and the constitution copied off and read here to-morrow.

The PRESIDENT. Would extra clerical force be of assistance?

Mr EARLE. I do not think that extra clerical force would accomplish it. Appointing one or two more committees to take up different articles might accomplish it.

Mr. HEBB. Is there any work for the committee clerks to-morrow, unless the convention remain here to act upon the reports?

Mr. EARLE. They have now the articles passed upon to-day. I think most of them have been copied. Unless other articles are acted upon, or unless the clerks go on and copy it just as we give it to them, without waiting for the action of the convention, they would not be employed.

The PRESIDENT. All the reports have been sent to the committee, excepting the report of the committee on usury, a very short report not yet acted upon by the convention.

Mr. MILLER called for the previous question; and it was sustained.

Mr. PURNELL (addressing Mr. Earle.) Mr. Chairman, could you have the report ready by 12 o'clock on Monday?

Mr. EARLE. Yes, sir; I think we can have all the reports ready by 12 o'clock on Monday. We could review the different articles and have them copied I think. But if the convention is going to adjourn over, I would greatly prefer their adjourning until Tuesday. I think the committee could do their work more satisfactorily if they could have that time.

The question being stated upon the amendment submitted by Mr. NEGLEY, to substitute "Tuesday" for "Monday."

Mr. HEBB demanded the yeas and nays, and they were ordered.

The question being taken the result was—yeas 31, nays 33—as follows:

Yeas—Messrs. Audoun, Brooks, Brown, Carter, Chambers, Dellinger, Dent, Duvall, Earle, Ecker, Galloway, Hatch, Hoffman, Hollyday, Hopper, Horsey, Jones, of Cecil, Kennard, King, Larsh, Lee, McComas, Mitchell, Miller, Negley, Parker, Parran, Ridgely, Sneary, Sykes, Thomas—31.

Nays—Messrs. Goldsborough, President; Abbott, Annan, Baker, Belt, Crawford, Cunningham, Cushing, Daniel, Davis, of Washington, Farrow, Greene, Hebb, Keefer, Marbury, Markey, Mullikin, Murray, Nyman, Pugh, Purnell, Russell, Sands, Schley, Schlosser, Scott, Stirling, Stockbridge, Swope, Todd, Valliant, Wickard, Wooden—33.

When his name was called,

Mr. HEBB said: I vote against this proposition because I cannot get home. The gentlemen from Baltimore city can go home. On Tuesday morning we shall be here, and then it will take us two days to get through the work. I vote "no."

The amendment was accordingly rejected.

The question recurred upon the original motion submitted by Mr. RIDGELY to adjourn over to Monday at 12 o'clock, M.

Mr. CUSHING demanded the yeas and nays, and they were ordered.

The question being taken, the result was—yeas 35, nays 29—as follows:

Yeas—Messrs. Goldsborough, President; Audoun, Brooks, Brown, Chambers, Cunningham, Davis, of Washington, Dellinger, Dent, Duvall, Earle, Ecker, Galloway, Hatch, Hollyday, Horsey, King, Larsh, Lee, Markey, Mitchell, Miller, Murray, Negley, Parker, Parran, Purnell, Ridgely, Schlosser, Scott, Sneary, Stockbridge, Sykes, Thomas, Todd—35.

Nays—Messrs. Abbott, Annan, Baker, Belt, Carter, Crawford, Cushing, Daniel, Farrow, Greene, Hebb, Hoffman, Hopper, Jones, of Cecil, Keefer, Kennard, Marbury, McComas, Mullikin, Nyman, Pugh, Russell, Sands, Schley, Stirling, Swope, Valliant, Wickard, Wooden—29.

The motion was accordingly agreed to.

USURY.

The convention proceeded to the consideration of the report of the committee on interest and the usury laws, which was read the third time, as follows:

"That the rate of interest in this State shall not exceed six per cent. per annum, and no higher rate shall be taken or demanded, and the legislature shall provide, by law, all necessary forfeitures and penalties against usury."

Mr. Belt. I had the misfortune to be absent from the house when the original report for which I was in a measure responsible, as chairman of the committee, was taken up; and I regretted on my return to find that the section we unanimously reported as embodying the views of the entire committee was stricken out and superseded by the action of the convention by a very decided vote, by the adoption of the section in the present constitution. The report of that committee was on my part the result of a very earnest conviction entertained all my life that there is no more false system on the face of the earth than that which continues in force those laws which are known as usury laws. It is not my intention in any manner to debate this question as fully as I would like to have done in the early part of the session.

The original clause in the constitution was that now before us. The committee appointed to consider the subject soon found that there was not the slightest difference of opinion among them as to the principle on which their report should be based; and by general consent the consideration of the subject was postponed until after the greater reports had been made to the convention. When we did meet I had prepared a report. It is no violation of the confidence of the committee for me now to state, since it has been rejected, that it was drawn up almost in the words of the British statute upon the subject. It is within the knowledge of most gentlemen present that what are known as usury laws were abolished in England in 1854, ten years ago. For the information of the house, and to show the foundation of the original report submitted by the committee I will read the act which passed the British Parliament on August 10th, 1854, and which will be found in the public general statutes, 17 and 18 Victoria:

"Cap. XC.—An act to repeal the laws relating to usury and to the enrolment of annuities:

Whereas, It is expedient to repeal the laws at present in force relating to usury: Be it enacted by the Queen's most excellent Majesty, by and with the consent and advice of the Lords spiritual and temporal, and Commons, in this present Parliament assembled, and by the authority of the same, as follows:

I. The several acts and parts of acts made in the parliaments of England and Scotland, Great Britain and Ireland, mentioned in the schedule hereto, and all existing laws against usury, shall be repealed.

II. Provided always, that nothing herein contained shall prejudice or affect the rights or remedies of any person, or diminish or alter the liabilities of any person, in respect of any act done previously to the passing of this act.

III. When interest is now payable upon any contract expressed or implied, for payment of the legal or current rate of interest, or whereupon any debt or sum of money interest is now payable by any rule of law, the same rate of interest shall be recoverable as if this act had not been passed.

IV. Provided always, that nothing herein contained shall extend, or be construed to repeal or affect any statute relating to pawnbrokers; but that all laws touching and concerning pawnbrokers shall remain in full force and effect to all intents and purposes whatsoever as if this act had not been passed."

The first report we considered in committee established the principle of the abolition of the usury laws with these several qualifications contained in the British statute, except that in relation to pawnbrokers—the last. I suggested that we should include insurance brokers as well as pawnbrokers. On considering the subject, we came to the conclusion that as these provisions of the British statute more particularly pertained to the legislative functions of the government than to the framing of our organic law, we would embody in our report merely the principle we had agreed upon; and so our report was made in these words:

Section —. The legal rate of interest in this State shall be six per centum per annum, except in cases where a different rate may be agreed upon between contracting parties; and in all cases of private contract, the rate of interest agreed on, or contracted for, shall be recoverable; and the general assembly shall pass all laws that may be necessary to carry this section into effect.

I have the honor now to propose, the house having very decidedly passed their censure upon the report as submitted, a section in lieu of that reported by the committee. Finding that we cannot probably carry the principle of leaving interest absolutely free, which is my own preference, which is the doctrine I have ever held and believed to be the enlightened doctrine of modern times, of political economists, and of commercial men, I am willing to take the best we can get, advancing towards that principle.

In explanation of the substitute I propose to offer, I will say that the highest rate of interest that is allowed in any of the States anywhere in the Union, is ten per cent. In Maryland it is six per cent and in New York it is seven. The result is that several of the surrounding States and more particularly New York, the commercial and monetary centre, having a rate of interest a little higher than ours, capital is carried out of Maryland on the least financial pressure, for investment in New York, or in other States. Comparatively few of the States have a rate as low as six per cent. The substitute is intended to preserve the legal rate of interest at six per cent., so that where there is no contract no higher rate shall be recoverable, so that in all proceedings in law or equity where no rate is proved to have been agreed upon between the parties six per cent. may be recoverable, restricting the rate to six per cent. in that respect, but leaving the parties free to contract for a higher rate up to ten per cent.; which puts our people upon precisely the same footing with other States, in making special contracts up to the highest rate of interest that prevails. My substitute is in these words:

"That the legal rate of interest in this State shall be six per centum per annum, except in cases of agreements between contracting parties; and in all such cases parties contracting shall have power to contract, and to recover any rate of interest not exceeding ten per centum per annum."

Mr. ECKER. I would suggest that it is necessary to move to open the report.

Mr. ABBOTT. I have an amendment which I desire to offer to the article as it stands.

Mr. STIRLING. I am very desirous that the gentleman from Prince George's (Mr. Belt,) who is the chairman of the committee, should have an opportunity to express his views; and I think if the house should after consideration conclude to make some modification in the report it would do no harm. I move to reconsider the vote by which the report was ordered to a third reading, so that it may again be open to amendment. It cannot take long to consider the matter, and if the house is disposed to recede from its judgment, they will have the opportunity.

I said before that I was not prepared to go as far as the committee went upon the abstract principle; but I do think that some modification should be made so that reasonable contracts may be made at a higher rate than six per cent. I have had information coming to me from good authority, from my own constituents, that the commercial class in the city of Baltimore have a vast interest in this matter. I had the honor to present the other day a petition which did not come from pawnbrokers, stockbrokers, money-lenders, Shylocks, or anything of the sort, but the paper was signed by men engaged in legitimate and honest commercial business, as respectable as the merchants of any city in the Union, the Baltimore Flour Exchange; men who are agents for the distribution of agricultural products, who are so using capital as to develop as far as possible the agricultural resources of the State. They have sent here a memorial asking for some relief; asking that they shall not be tied down and fettered by the absurd and useless prejudices of the last five hundred years, but may be put upon some sort of equality with the great commercial centre of the Union. I am not disposed to go for an absolutely unrestricted rate of interest; but something should be done to enable contracting parties to exceed the usual rate to some extent when they find it necessary. I hope the convention will reconsider the vote ordering this report to a third reading; that we may take up the subject for consideration whether or not we will amend it; and at least give some opportunity for the chairman of the committee (Mr. Belt) to express his views upon the subject.

The motion to reconsider was seconded by Messrs. PURNELL and KENNARD.

Mr. CHAMBERS. One would suppose that this question had been passed upon, and the vote had been taken without debate, without giving even the chairman of the committee an opportunity to say a word upon it, or to make any argument.

Mr. STIRLING. The chairman of the committee was not here.

Mr. CHAMBERS. The subject was debated; fully debated. The gentleman talks about the wants of Baltimore. The wants of Baltimore were ascertained before. We were informed before that persons engaged in business in Baltimore differed widely upon the matter; but I have heard no one deny that six per cent. is as much as a farmer can afford to pay for money. There is no question that there is a wish very generally entertained among certain classes that the restriction may be removed in order that they may be able to make ten per cent., taking advantage of the necessities of borrowers. Whatever the limit is, that is the amount that will be charged and received. I rise to protest against any departure from the ordinary practice of the house I am perfectly willing that the gentleman from Prince George's (Mr. Belt) should be heard; but I should desire that the field should be open for all sides, and not for one gentleman exclusively.

Mr. BELT. I wish to say by way of explanation, while thanking my friend from Baltimore city (Mr. Stirling) for his intended courtesy, that I have said all I propose to say upon the question, unless a debate should arise and cause me to say something in answer to gentlemen. That I do not anticipate. It is too late in the day to make an argument, particularly after a judgment has been given. I only desire to submit this new proposition and have it decided in some way or other. It occurred to me that perhaps, if the house is not prepared to go to the extent they have gone in England, the total abolition of usury, which I regard as of no use and of no practical effect, they would at least be willing to put the people of this State, and the commercial interests of the whole people upon the same basis as in other States. But I am perfectly content, and so I am sure will the whole committee be, to have it fairly decided in any way the convention think proper.

Mr. ABBOTT. Before the vote is taken, I desire simply to give notice of my amendment for the information of the convention.

It is to insert after the words "per annum" in the second line, the following:

"But such rates may be contracted for as Congress have or may hereafter allow on any loans of the United States."

Mr. KENNARD. Before action is had upon the motion to reconsider, I wish to say that I hope the convention will reconsider. My views have undergone some change with reference to the subject. My opinions have always been in favor of six per cent., and my action has adhered to that; but I am somewhat unsettled in my views in reference to it. I desire to conform to that which is right and just, as far as I can; and I should be glad to review this question. There may be other gentlemen similar to myself in that particular. I hope the motion to reconsider will prevail.

Mr. NEGLEY. I hope that this report will be opened. I am very glad to find that the gentleman from Prince George's (Mr. Belt) has supplied a bit of testimony which the other day, on the argument of the case, was not at hand. I am very happy to find that he has entirely overthrown the positions, as to the law, of the gentleman from Anne Arundel (Mr. Miller,) who assumed the other day that the legal rate of interest in England was five per cent., and read some decisions then where parties, I believe, were arraigned and convicted of usury. I suppose the decisions are all right I replied to the gentleman at that time, taking the ground, not having the statute by which the usury laws were abolished in England, that the position assumed by the gentleman from Anne Arundel was false, because the Bank of England changed its rate of interest just as the pressure was upon the money market. If money was abundant its rate of interest went down perhaps to three and-a-half per cent., and if it was scarce it went up as high as eight or nine per cent I argued from that fact that it was not possible that the theory of the law assumed by the gentleman from Anne Arundel was correct. I am glad to find that I was correct in the argument I then made. I hope the convention will review this matter. Maryland is behind the age. The gentlemen from Anne Arundel (Mr. Miller) and Kent (Mr. Chambers) are eminent lawyers; but I do not think they are eminent authorities upon matters of finance. I would pay every respect to their legal opinions, but I have not a single particle of confidence in them as financiers.

Mr. MILLER. When the question is opened for debate I wish to be heard upon it. I must confess that I was not aware of this statute repealing the usury laws at the time I made my argument the other day. The date of the law is 1854. The gentleman brings to-day a manuscript copy. I suppose he saw the original statute and has accurately copied it. It certainly has not got into our recent law books on the subject, and I was not aware that England had gone so far as to repeal all her usury laws.

Mr. BELT. I trust the gentleman does not mean to cast any doubt upon the fact.

Mr. MILLER. Not at all. I see the gentleman has obtained it. I had no access to it myself. Of course I accept his version of it, as the law of England at the present day. All the remaining portions of the argument which I had the honor to submit on that occasion are just as forcible now as they were at the time they were uttered. I stated that the laws of England were like the old statutes of Maryland. My information was from the statute books, so far as I had seen them, at the time my remarks were made. But whatever England may have done, it is perfectly clear that the commercial States of this country have not undertaken to go to the extent of the original report about which we were then arguing. And the usury laws of the neighboring State of Pennsylvania are precisely the same as the usury laws of Maryland under our present constitution. So in New York, with simply the exception that New York allows seven per cent. as the legal rate of interest.

Mr. CUSHING. Is the gentleman any more sure that he now has the latest law of Pennsylvania and New York than he was the other day that he then had the latest law of England?

Mr. MILLER. Yes, sir. I have the latest volume of reports made in the State of Pennsylvania; a volume published very recently, containing a case in which an action was brought by one man against another to recover excessive interest paid under a contract, and the law was sustained, and the judges confirmed the policy of the usury law. It was the law of the State of Pennsylvania and the decision was made by the supreme court of the State of Pennsylvania.

As I am up now, I may as well say about this question that I have strongly settled opinions upon the subject, and have always had them, and I do not intend by any vote I give here to do anything to aid usury. If you adopt the amendment proposed by my friend from Prince George's (Mr. Belt) allowing parties to contract up to ten per cent., you might as well say at once to-day that the legal rate of interest shall be ten per cent.; because if you give parties power to do it, they will always contract up to that point. Contracts will be made. If they are allowed to go up to ten per cent., they will not lend their money for six per cent. I have no sympathy for, and no good feelings towards, men who are in the proper sense of the term called usurers. I am not going to do anything which will help them to get usury, or what I believe to be excessive rates of interest. There is a great deal of good sense in the old laws upon that subject; no matter what the later statutes of England may have been about it. The statutes were against it in early times in very broad terms. One of their statutes after premising that usury is by the word of God utterly prohibited as a vice most odious and detestable, practiced only by uncharitable and covetous persons, who thereby exposed themselves to the terrors of God's eternal wrath and vengeance, justly hanging over them, goes on to provide temporal punishment to restrain men from that crime.

To a certain extent modern commerce, civilization and advancement have taken away the odium which originally attached to the system of usury. I have much respect for merchants and traders in their lawful traffic, and in all legitimate gains and profits from the use of his capital, I wish him success. But I have no sympathy with the men who do nothing but sit down in their counting houses and make their contracts for gold and silver.

Mr. RIDGELY. I rise to a question of order; whether it is in order to discuss the merits of the question upon a motion to suspend the rules for the purpose of amendment.

The CHAIRMAN (Mr. Dent.) It is not strictly in order. The chair has not restrained the discussion, because it has been allowed to on heretofore. The question is upon the motion to reconsider.

Mr. CHAMBERS. Can you reconsider the vote ordering the report to its third reading? Is there any way to amend it except by the motion to open the section to amendment? I understand the motion to reconsider not now to be in order. I understand the decision of the president to have been that when an article had passed to the third reading, the only mode by which it could be altered, except by the revising committee, was by moving to open the subject for the purpose of offering an amendment, and we have acted upon that plan.

The CHAIRMAN (Mr. Dent.) The present incumbent of the chair understands the practice to have been different.

Mr. DANIEL. The forty-fourth rule provides for reconsideration at any time. That is another question, and a different mode of amending from that we have adopted in some other cases.

The CHAIRMAN. It has been the practice of the chair to allow a motion to open the section for special amendments; but the motion now made is to reconsider the vote ordering the section to a third reading, which would bring it back to the condition of the second reading.

Mr. CHAMBERS demanded the yeas and nays, and they were ordered.

The question being taken, the result was—yeas 32, nays 24—as follows:

Yeas—Messrs. Abbott, Annan, Audoun, Baker, Belt, Brooks, Brown, Cunningham, Cushing, Daniel, Dellinger, Farrow, Greene, Hatch, Hebb, Hoffman, Hopper, Kennard, Larsh, Marbury, Negley, Parker, Purnell, Ridgely, Schley, Scott, Sneary, Stirling, Stockbridge, Todd, Valliant, Wickard—32.

Nays—Messrs Carter, Chambers, Crawford, Davis, of Washington, Dent, Duvall, Ecker, Galloway, Hollyday, Horsey, Jones, of Cecil, Keefer, Lee, McComas, Mitchell, Miller, Mullikin, Parran, Pugh, Russell, Sands, Schlosser, Swope, Wooden—24.

The motion was accordingly reconsidered; and the question recurred upon ordering the section to a third reading.

Mr. ABBOTT submitted the following amendment:

Amend by inserting after the word "per annum," in the second line, "but such rates may be contracted for as congress have or may hereafter allow on any loans of the United States."

Mr. BELT submitted the following amendment:

Amend the report by substituting in lieu thereof the following:

"That the legal rate of interest in this State shall be six per centum per annum, except in cases of agreements between contracting parties; and in all such cases parties contracting shall have power to contract, and to recover any rate of interest not exceeding ten per centum per annum."

The question was first upon the amendment submitted by Mr. ABBOTT to perfect the section before a decision upon striking it out.

Mr. NEGLEY submitted the following amendment to the amendment:

Strike out all after the words "contracted for," and insert the words "as shall be agreed upon between the parties, not exceeding eight per centum per annum."

Mr. ABBOTT. If the government goes higher, does the gentleman wish to confine it to eight per cent.?

Mr. NEGLEY. This was so indefinite that nothing would be constitutional but the amount allowed by the government. If that were ten per cent. that would be the constitutional rate. If it were five per cent. that would be the constitutional rate I think it would be better to fix upon some limit as the one to which the contract may go. I think it would be better to make the legal rate six per cent., with the privilege of contracting to a higher amount, not exceeding eight per cent.

Mr. MARBURY. I am opposed to all these amendments. I was favorable to the reconsideration of this subject in order that I might get further light upon it; but as at present advised I am opposed to the whole thing. It seems to me that it is a blow at the agricultural interests of this country. It may be that it is politic for the government of England to repeal their usury laws. England is in a prosperous condition, at perfect peace with the whole world. They have opportunities to develop their resources At present the agricultural interest of this State is prostrated. Labor of every sort, so far as one portion of our State is concerned, is all gone. If you raise the rate of interest now, you paralyze the great agricultural interest of the country. A large majority of the land-holders of this State, in consequence of the oppressive taxation, and the losses and burdens that have fallen upon them for the last few years, are borrowers of money. If you raise the rate of interest, or open the door to its being raised to a certain height, to that extent you put a burden upon the agricultural interests of the State. I am satisfied it is the view of a large majority of the agriculturalists of this State that there should be no change whatever made in this law, as a matter of general policy. Under certain circumstances, and at certain times, it may be a very wise provision; but certainly at this time, in my humble opinion it is very odious to a large majority of the people of the State, and I shall therefore vote against any change whatever in the law upon this subject.

Mr. SANDS. I trust this amendment will not prevail. When it was up before I thought it had received its quietus. No such large vote has been given against any proposition urged upon this floor, as was given against the proposition to increase the legal rate of interest. The proposed amendment renders utterly nugatory the action which the convention by a vote of 63 to 8, took when the subject was before it on a former day.

What does the proposed amendment do? It utterly contradicts the section. The legal rate shall be 6 per cent., says the section; and then it is proposed to go on and say that it shall be lawful to bargain for, and claim for, and sue for and recover a larger amount. How do gentlemen reconcile this? First, the section provides that the legal rate which alone is recoverable at law, shall be fixed at 6 per cent.; and then it is proposed to say that it shall be lawful, although that is the legal rate of interest, to demand, and sue for and recover a greater amount. Not content with allowing the rate of interest to run to seven and three-tenths per cent., which is the meaning of the amendment, other gentlemen urge even larger rates. I am utterly and entirely opposed to this matter for the reasons I have stated here upon this floor once before.

Money does not need protection. It is the great lever of society. The man who has it is always safe, always secure; while he that is to pay the percentage on it is often in circumstances that leave him utterly at the mercy of the usurer. I remember that one gentleman upon the floor here, when he argued the matter, put the case thus: Suppose the furniture of a man was under execution or distraint. He could go out into the street, and he could pay a high rate of interest to get the money to meet the case and relieve him from his difficulty. Does not this illustrate the whole of this matter, that its purpose and working is to put that unfortunate man utterly at the mercy of any one who chooses to play Shylock and demand his pound of flesh? I am not aware what new light has dawned upon the minds of members since we argued this matter before. If I had heard any new views on the matter, anything which was not then urged, and which could be considered a fair argument for abandoning a position taken by an overwhelming vote, I should know how to meet that new view.

You are legislating between two very different classes of interests in this matter; the rich who hold the money, and the necessitous who often require it. If they can show us that there has been any good reason why money is worth more than they decided it to be worth a few days ago, let us have it. It was decided here the other day, on evidence that everybody seemed to think conclusive, that money was not worth more than six per cent. because it was to be had in quantities large and small, for six per cent., and even lower;—it was offered in the advertising columns of the "American" for five per cent.

Another consideration I have to offer, which I think ought to appeal to certain members upon this floor if not to all. Just so much as you raise the rate of interest, do you take advantage of the circumstances in which the government is placed—the great power in the land. The people have got to pay six per cent. for the government. I am paying my share of it. Every man in the State of Maryland has got to pay his share of this interest. Why are we paying six per cent. on the national debt? If you had been about the purlieus of that New York legislature when it struck out six and put in a higher rate ——

Mr. CUSHING. Do you know what rate that was?

Mr. SANDS. I do not. It makes no difference whether it was ten or twenty. I say it is a matter notorious to the country at large, that the monetary classes of New York manage their legislative bodies where their interests are concerned. And as I was saying, if the government has to-day accumulated an enormous debt upon which she pays an enormous interest, it was because that change was made in New York; because capitalists, moneyed men, were seeking how to add to their stores; and the government being forced to go to the great moneyed centre of the country to borrow what it required to meet its pressing necessities, is of course obliged to pay seven and three-tenths per cent. I ask gentlemen whether they believe that the secretary of the treasury is advertising for loans at seven and three-tenths per cent. because he thinks money is fairly worth it, or simply because the legislative body of the great State of New York, the moneyed centre, fixed the rate of interest at that rate.

Mr. ABBOTT. Will the gentleman allow me a question?

Mr. SANDS. Yes, sir.

Mr. ABBOTT. If the government is paying seven and three-tenths per cent., can I borrow money at six per cent. while the government is in the market?

Mr. SANDS. I can get as much money as I want to-morrow at six per cent.; and so can you, I have no doubt. Take up your paper to-day, and you can have the money to-morrow.

Mr. NEGLEY. Does the gentleman mean to say or to insinuate that the credit of the government is not as good as his?

Mr. SANDS. Did the gentleman say or insinuate so?

Mr. NEGLEY. That is the result of it.

Mr. SANDS. The gentleman says and means to say, that the reason why the government is paying this is because the local legislation of New York fixed the rate of interest at that; and the government in its necessities was forced into the market, and had to pay their price. I ask gentlemen this question. Suppose the legislature had fixed the rate of interest at six per cent. and no more, would the government be asking loans at seven and three-tenths per cent.?

Mr. NEGLEY. Has not New York paid seven per cent. for twenty years? And did not the government borrow money at five per cent.? Did the seven per cent. of New York then compel the government to give seven per cent. or five?

Mr. SANDS. The government has borrowed money, I believe, as low as four and a half per cent., borrowed it from New York capitalists. But what is the result? Gold is at two fifty to-day. Do you, as a loyal man, say there is just ground for this? It is not true. Look how it operates. The government borrows five hundred millions in New York. The legal price upon that, suppose it to be six per cent. or five per cent.—I will assume it to be five per cent., taking the gentleman's figures—and the interest upon five hundred millions will be twenty-five millions of dollars. These money people, who always take care of their own interest, get this interest paid in gold. What do they do with the twenty-five millions paid them by the government of the United States in gold? They control the money market of the country, forcing gold up to its present prices. They get their twenty-five millions of dollars of interest, and go right down into Wall street, and for that gold they ask and receive sixty-two and a half millions of dollars. How much per cent. is that on five hundred millions. It is twelve and a half per cent. That is what they receive according to the present rates of gold. Out of a legitimate interest of five per cent. upon five hundred millions of dollars which they hold, these men every year manage to make sixty-two and a half millions, or twelve and a half per cent. on their capital. That is in plain figures. They get their interest of twelve and a half per cent., and they go out into the market and buy up government bonds at par; and the bonds thus purchased pay them now seven and three-tenths per cent. That is the secret of the price of gold this day; that and nothing else.

I am opposed to the amendments from these considerations, leaving all other considerations entirely out of the case, because we are all borrowers, all debtors paying interest so long as this government stands. I am paying my tax, and every man paying his tax is paying the money lenders, the usurers, the government interest. I am therefore interested for myself and for the people, in fixing the rate of interest so that it shall not grind the people of the country further into the dust. Heaven knows we are burdened enough as it is. Heaven knows that at six or five per cent. you have got enough to carry. The people have enough to pay annually in the way of interest. Your taxes are only taxes in name; they are interest in fact; and at the present rates of gold they are interest at twelve and a half per cent. You propose to raise it still higher. You propose, lest the people of the United States should not be sufficiently burdened with taxes, to raise the rate of interest still higher.

Take the rate of seven and three-tenths per cent., and make the calculation. I think we have now a debt of about $2,000,000,000. At this rate of interest the country will be forced hereafter for all time to pay $146,000,000 annually; and she must double the sum if she has any hope of the time coming when the people shall escape from the burden of the present rate of taxation.

It has been argued here that by not raising the rate of interest equal to that in New York, you will keep capital out of the State. There are also facts to answer this. One gentleman upon this floor told me he knew of $10,000,000 looking for investment now in Maryland, at the present rate of six per cent. in Maryland lands and Maryland mines, looking for investment here, in the faith that Maryland with her resources will become the little empire she ought to be. In my own county, for instance, look at the large amounts of Northern capital, New York city capital. If my colleague is here he will assure you that in our county large and magnificent estates have been bought recently at half price, and paid for by New York capital, where they pay seven per cent., brought here to pay for Maryland lands. Why? Because they know these lands are going to enhance in value. The seven per cent. does not tie capital to New York, and it will not keep capital out of Maryland; because any shrewd New Yorker knows well the fact that $100 laid out in Maryland lands to-day, will be in a few years $200; and he is not going to wait for seven per cent. And that is the whole of the argument, I understand, that has been urged upon this floor, with the least semblance of fairness, that if Maryland kept her interest at six per cent., New York seven per cent. capital would be kept out of the State. Yet this is a fact notorious to every gentleman upon this floor. Can any gentleman tell me how old the New York interest is?

Mr. Cushing. It is older than the gentleman.

Mr. Hopper. I know that it is over thirty years old.

Mr. Sands. In the face of the fact then that the rate of seven per cent. in New York is older than I am, New York capital is coming in a constant stream into Maryland to-day. Is it because they believe you will raise the rate of interest to seven or seven and three-tenths per cent.? Not a whit of it; but it is because they see the wealth that is in your fields, in your mines, along your streams.—Look down here just at the edge of the bay—a thing untold of in Annapolis—and you will see a large factory springing up there. Is it because they expected the rate of interest to be seven and three-tenths per cent.? No, sir; it is because they know that your State was growing and going to grow. The argument is not worth a straw that the difference of one per cent. in the rate of interest between New York and Maryland is keeping capital out of the State. In my humble judgment—I have never had the benefit of an education in August Belmont's office—

Mr. Cushing (in his seat.) That is very evident.

Mr. Sands. And what is just as certain, I do not desire to be impregnated with the principles upon which he operates. I want to keep out of his office, and I want to keep out of the society and influences of all mere money-gamblers and usurers. I don't want to go there and learn; still less do I want to practice his teachings. But I know this, as a plain common sense business man, that capital is coming to your State; and you know it too, in streams such as never flowed hither heretofore. And now you propose to help it onward by raising the rate of interest three-tenths per cent. higher than it is in New York. I do not think you will do more, in taking this view, than to bring upon us as a body the just condemnation of the great body of the people, who are the borrowers and not the lenders. The lenders are few compared with the borrowers of money; and I think we ought not to advance the rate. Six per cent. n my opinion is as much as money is worth.

Mr. Chambers. I have as much anxiety perhaps upon this subject as any gentleman upon this floor. I feel deeply for the interest of the agricultural portion of the State particularly. I feel deeply for the interest of the young in every department of human life. I feel that this is to be a departure from the long established custom, and from the long established system of law which has worked well and has never failed to do good, has never done mischief, and which ought to be persevered in. I regret that the condition of my health does not permit me to remain here. I can scarcely hope in the present temper of the house that they will defer the further consideration of this question; but if not I shall be obliged to leave, and to omit to vote upon a question in which, as I said before, I take the deepest interest. I feel bound before I go to move that the house do now adjourn.

Mr. Cushing. I ask the decision of the chair whether I am privileged to ask a question?

Mr. Chambers. I will withdraw my motion to enable the gentleman to ask a question.

Mr. Cushing. For fear the house should come to the conclusion from the remarks of the gentleman from Howard (Mr. Sands) that it was contemplated to institute an insurrection against every man owning over one hundred dollars, I ask what is the subject before the house?

The question was stated, upon the amendment submitted by Mr. Negley, to the amendment submitted by Mr. Abbott.

Mr. Chambers renewed his motion to adjourn.

The motion was not agreed to.

Mr. Ridgely. I propose to say a very few words. The remarks which the gentleman from Howard (Mr. Sands) has made seem to require at least some reply. I may be in error, but I think I have taken the common sense view. If I had any doubts upon the subject before—and I confess I had doubts before—I am very free to confess that those doubts have been entirely removed by the speech of the gentleman from Howard, if I have correctly understood that speech, and the train of argument in which he has indulged.

This is a question of finance. It concerns the money capital of the country. The great object is to protect and advance the great commercial interests of the country. It is a question which almost exclusively addresses itself to that interest, and all other interests are here collateral and incidental to that great interest.

Mr. Sands. Will the gentleman allow me to ask one question? How do the commercial and producing—I mean the agricultural interests of the State—compare?

Mr. Ridgely. I am going on to show that there are certain paramount interests, and others incidental and auxiliary to them; and that the protection or encouragement of the one, is necessarily that of the other; that they are all inseparably blended, and that the prosperity of one necessarily implies the prosperity of the others. They are like members of the body. I regard this as a great question of capital and of finance. As I said before, it addresses itself more especially to the great commercial interests of the country. And it is that sort of capital which is actively and constantly and continuously employed, which is seeking active motion daily. It is that sort of capital which transfers itself promptly and immediately and is convertible immediately. It is not that sort of money capital which seeks permanent investment; not that which is put away; but it is the sort of capital which is the life of trade, easily convertible, and constantly subject to transition.

I have one plain fact to state in connection with that sort of capital. It is like water.—It seeks and will find its level. It seeks and will find its profitable employment, and where that level is, where that profitable employment is, it is bound to go. The gentleman from Howard (Mr. Sands) tells you that he has heard no argument upon this question. I have heard an argument which has been irresistible to my mind—I do not remember now by whom it was employed—but the argument is that wherever active money, active capital, the life-blood of trade, can demand a higher rate there that capital will go. There is no answer to that argument. It is an irresistible argument. It has not been answered by the case which he supposes. It has not been answered by the illustration which the honorable gentleman gave, by the fact that thousands and tens of thousands of dollars are seeking permanent investments in our lands here. If it has, it has been answered negatively to his theory; because his theory was that money was not worth more than six per cent.; and yet in the same breath he tells us that that money was seeking investment at two and three hundred per cent.

Mr. Sands. I said that in the counties money loaned on interest was not worth more than six per cent. I did not say that money invested in reality would not bring more than six per cent.

Mr. Ridgely. So I understood you; that money employed for loans was not worth more than six per cent.; and he gave us a practical illustration of his theory of the value of money generally by stating that New York capital was coming to Maryland for investment, because the price of lands would be so enhanced that money could be more profitably employed here than at seven per cent. in New York. It leaves New York at seven per cent. and obtains three hundred per cent. here, according to his own illustration, that lands may be bought for one hundred dollars per acre which are worth three hundred dollars.—Hence the fallacy of the argument. I am no financier. I know nothing of financiering. But there are some plain matters of hard fact that come home to the understanding of plain men that are not familiar with peculiar subjects. I regard this as one of those questions. I have not heard an argument that overthrows the position that money, like water, will seek its level. If the State of New York allows seven per cent. for money, the banking men, the financial men, the men of capital whose particular interest it is to convert it easily, will send it to New York for ordinary investment, ordinary business transactions, and ordinary purposes of trade. What will be the effect of such a transfer of capital from your main city, Baltimore, to the city of NewY ork? It will be, to the extent that the money is withdrawn from the money market of Baltimore, that just to that extent will the money facilities of Baltimore be contracted, and to that extent will the commercial interests of Baltimore suffer.

These appear to me to be plain views of this question. They strike me as unanswerable. They are not my own. I have been convinced by the force of these arguments—I am but repeating them—and they have not, it seems to me, been met either by the honorable gentleman from Kent (Mr. Chambers,) or by the honorable gentleman from Howard. For these considerations I am induced to change my vote. I voted for the proposition which was ordered to be engrossed for a third reading. I shall now vote, under this light, for the proposition of the gentleman from Prince George's (Mr. Belt.)

Mr. Negley. I think the strangest and most unheard of argument I have ever heard adduced, has fallen from the lips of the gentleman from Howard (Mr. Sands.) He absolutely charges our national debt on paying interest on money.

Mr. Sands (interposing.) The gentleman is entirely mistaken.

Mr. Negley. He absolutely charges the national debt upon paying interest on money, when men have been paying interest on money ever since money has been invested.

Mr. Sands (interposing.) When the gentleman states as a fact that which is not a fact, all I can do is to contradict it.

Mr. Negley. That is the legitimate inference from his argument; that this national debt has been heaped upon us because men pay interest on money. That is not all. There has been a suspension of specie payment throughout the entire land, because interest has been paid on money. Is not that the sublimest argument that ever fell from the lips of mortal man—the idea that specie payment has been suspended in this land because New York charges seven per cent. interest? Who ever heard of such an argument? That is not all. It is not all that we have accumulated this immense debt by reason of the payment of interest; it is not all that specie payment has been suspended by reason of the payment of interest; but even our taxes, the taxes under which we groan, both State and federal, are attributable to this horrible system of paying interest on money. If this is not the most extraordinary argument I ever heard! I paid careful attention to the gentleman's argument, and it seemed to be that all the accumulated woes under which the world labors are attributable to the horrible practice of paying interest on money! I would advise the gentleman to abandon the profession of the law for the writing of treatises on political economy, and especially on the subject of interest. All the treatises on political economy on that subject are entirely thrown in the shade. The world is travelling backwards instead of forwards if the theory which he advances is true. It is a great and monstrous sin! I suppose it is the cause of original sin perhaps! I should not wonder if it should turn out in the end that this horrible practice was the cause of our unfortunate mother Eve eating the apple! I should not be surprised if the gentleman should conjure it up as the cause of the epidemics that traverse the entire world, causing the yellow fever in the south, and perhaps the Asiatic cholera, and the plague that ran over the east in olden times! We have now got new light upon the subject of finance, certainly. It is a very plain thing; but the system of the gentleman is to befog the minds of this convention and to becloud them. He is like the cuttle fish in the sea, that to avoid detection beclouds the water around him. If anybody can listen to such an argument as that, and not be beclouded, he has got more than mortal faculties.

Mr. SANDS. The gentleman is evidently in a cloud.

Mr. NEGLEY. I do not know, if the gentleman had continued, where I would have got to. I could not for the soul of me keep up with the gentleman, and got pretty nearly as wild as he was in trying to keep up with him.

This is a very plain thing. Why can you not let money alone, as you let anything else alone? Why can you not let money be a subject of bargain and sale, just as you leave anything else to be a subject of bargain and sale? Money has two characters. It has the character of being the instrument of effecting exchanges between man and man. In that character there is no interest accruing from it. While a man has money in his pocket, while it is passing day by day from one man to another, it pays no interest. It is used as an instrumentality to effect the exchanges of the world. That is one character. But money has another character; that of property. A great many men have their property in lands. A great many men have their property in ships on the sea. A great many have their property in houses, or in factories. A great many have their property in the merchandise of the world; and a great many have their property—their all—in money. What is the difference? If a man has ten thousand dollars and does not use that for the purpose of exchanging commodities, it is to him property. What does he do? He goes into the market, and he loans it to his neighbor or hires it to his neighbor as he hires his horse, as he hires his house, as he hires his land, as he hires anything that he can use and that another man can use, for a consideration. Now, in the name of common sense, why can you not let a man, when he has money, go into the market and make a disposition of it?

The commercial world to-day is getting out of that age in which the gentleman's mind seems to live, out of that beclouded state of intellect that was prevalent five hundred years ago. I think a lawyer is the poorest and most unsafe of all financial advisers. He is very good authority in law; very good authority in cases that have been tried in the courts; but send him down to the exchange in Baltimore, and he would be like a fish out of water. We have here a petition of some of the most respectable men and the best informed men in Maryland as to the effect of this restriction—the gentlemen of the Maryland Corn Exchange. Is their opinion entitled to no respect? Must we follow the gentleman from Howard in his lucid arguments, and transcendently convincing, reasoning and abandon the experience of the commercial world, and especially the unanimous voice of the people of Baltimore city, who absolutely pay one-half the taxes into the treasury of the State of Maryland? Are you to turn a deaf ear to them, and pay no attention to them? If they were ignorant, if they were actuated by any political considerations or improper motives, we might have some reason to doubt it. But here are men of all shades of politics, of all kinds of business, who come before you and make a statement and reiterate the very argument that we heard here on a former occasion; and it is the experience of the world.

We merely ask you to keep your hands away from money; not to protect it, not to legislate for it, but to quit protecting it, to quit legislating for it. Money will take care of itself; and the people who have it will take care of it, just as they take care of any other species of property. That is what usury means, legislating about a thing that ought not to be legislated about. That is all we ask. Can we not come up to the enlightened view of our sister States. The States in the west have done this—the new States—and even the old governments of England and France have done it. It is so in all the commercial centres in the world; and perhaps Baltimore is the only city practically cut off from it. It may be that Philadelphia is subjected to the same restrictions. But do these restrictions keep money from going up and down? Do not we all know, by looking at the papers day by day, under the head of "finance," that paper is worth sometimes even to nine, and again is down to six per cent., according to the character of the paper and the rate in other places? Can you fix the value of money? You may legislate until you grow as old as Methusaleh, and you can never possibly fix and maintain in a fixed condition the value of money. It will break away from all your restraints. There is no species of legislation by which you can tie it down. No human power can tie it down. The legislation of the world on this subject never has done any good and never will do any good. The old constitution, as it was, did not prevent the taking of seven per cent., eight, nine, ten, and even twenty-four per cent., as I am informed. The constitution never did prevent it; but it made men go into their closets, to do secretly and clandestinely that which they were afraid to do in the open daylight; not because it was a *malum in se*, not because there was moral turpitude in the act, but because the folly of the age had made that illegal which never ought to have been made so, for it had no moral turpitude about it. I have seen it in my own county, and the gentlemen from Baltimore city assure you that it is there the daily practice to pay even eight and nine per cent. One of the members of this house, who has been in business there for a great number of years, told me the other day that he believed he had never borrowed money there at six per cent.; but that was about the average, ranging from seven and eight down to five.

This legislation never does any good and never will. Let us make one step forward; and let us not be stationary in this old beaten track. The whole world is moving on. It will do no harm to leave men to make their own bargains; and that is all we ask. We do not ask you to put the poor men into the hands of the rich. You cannot legislate money out of the pockets of the rich man. You cannot force him to lend his money at six per cent. You can say that shall be the legal rate, but you never can force him to lend money at that rate. It is absurd. He will send it where he can get higher rates of interest. As the gentleman from Baltimore county (Mr. Ridgely) has just said, it is like water, seeking its own level. Wherever the rate of interest is higher there it will tend, just as certainly as water tends to run down hill. That is all we ask. I will withdraw my amendment. I have no objections to the amendment of the gentleman from Baltimore city (Mr. Abbott) or to that of the gentleman from Prince George's (Mr. Belt.) They are simply one a little more advanced than the other. But let us at least have some progress in this matter.

Mr. Daniel. I will try not to occupy the time of the convention long. As has well been said, money will command its price, like any other commodity in the market. If our fixing the rate of interest here would confine money to that rate, if it would prevent it from ever asking a higher rate, if it prevented men from being defrauded, there would be great justice in the plea that money ought to be fixed as urged by gentlemen here. But what is the experience of every man who knows anything of financial arrangements and business habits, especially in the large commercial cities? As I stated the other day, I know of my own knowledge that money is loaned every day in Baltimore on mortgage at from twelve to fifteen per cent. without any sort of scruple. A man advertises in the paper that he has got $100,000, and men go to him and ask what he charges for it; and he will have no more scruple in telling you twelve or fifteen per cent. than any other man would have in telling you six per cent. Gentlemen ask how he will recover that; how the arrangement is made. I will tell you how it is done; and I know what I say to be the fact; and it is known to the experience of other gentlemen here. The gentleman says, "money is worth twelve per cent., and I will lend you money for twelve per cent." He deducts six per cent. as the premium, or $60 from $1,000, and then takes a note for $1,000 and takes a mortgage for security, at six per cent. interest, for the $940 which he pays. That is done every day.

Then it is asked whether he can recover the amount. What is the law upon that subject? If the man goes into court, it has been decided to be the law of Maryland that, unless he pleads usury and tenders the amount, the plaintiff can recover whatever he has contracted for. As I stated the other day, that has been decided in a case in Baltimore since the passage of our last constitution. Unless the defendant values his character so little, having gone into market and contracted fairly to give a certain rate, as to come into court and plead usury to meanly evade his obligation—and no man with any respect for his business character would ever do it—the plaintiff can recover even fifteen per cent. under his contract. Indeed I recovered eight per cent. the other day from a man who tried in every way to evade it, but although he was a great sharper and skinflint, he had too much respect for his character in the public market to plead usury.

There are other ways of doing it. The court of appeals have decided that you can buy up paper at any amount you please. A goes to B, and wants to borrow money of C. A makes a note to B, payable to B's order. B is merely a man of straw, a third man. B indorses it, and offers it to C. If it is a note of $500, C says "I will give you $400 for that note." B puts his name on it and passes it over, and the money passes directly to A. It is all understood between A and C from the beginning. The court of appeals say that is not illegal; that you can buy up paper at any price you please. So the law can be evaded that way; and it is done every day. You cannot stop it. But you do this by fixing a certain rate of interest. You drive honest men to invest their money in stocks, which are more profitable, rather than put that amount of money into the market where the poor men can get it, and where the rate of interest would range lower than it does when you have it at a certain fixed rate. As I said to my friend from Howard (Mr. Sands) the other day, you put the poor men into the hands of the sharpers, because honest men will invest their money otherwise where they can get more for it; and the sharpers are the men who lend to the poor. You throw the poor men into their hands entirely, and they charge all the more for being obliged to evade the law, and for taking that risk. They have to pay men for taking the risks of the law and evading it; and they always have to pay more on that account.

I have stated what I know, that in the city of Baltimore some of the first banks, notwithstanding what the gentleman from Howard (Mr. Sands) may state about money not going out of the State of Maryland at this rate of six per cent. to go to New York for seven, some of the strongest banks in Baltimore have as much New York paper as they care about discounting at seven per cent. Some leading bank men tell me that they do not care about doing any business in Baltimore, and do not do anything except for their own immediate friends, for their accommodation, because they find at their counters in the morning as much New York paper at seven per cent., and as good paper as they can ask, as they can discount. And they are sending money every day to New York, because the rate is seven per cent. there and six per cent. here.

The argument of the gentleman from Howard that because men invest money in Maryland lands, and mines, &c., therefore money is plenty here at six per cent., is no answer to the fact that money is actually going to New York at seven per cent. For suppose that money is invested here; how long is it going to remain here? It goes into the hands of capitalists after it is brought here, and finds its way right back to New York and other places where the rate of interest is higher. Although it may come here, it will not stay here.

I will not detain the house longer. I shall vote with great pleasure for the amendment of the gentleman from Prince George's, because it does not raise the rate of interest, but simply allows contracts to be made up to ten per cent., saying they shall not go beyond that. It seems to me that that is as much as we could ask upon this subject.

Mr. Belt. As I said a short time ago, this has always been a favorite subject of study with me; and I had proposed to myself, in case there should be a debate upon it, to deliver some remarks to the convention. I had prepared some minutes upon the subject, with a view to discuss it in its historical and financial aspects. But I did not expect the subject to come up to-night, and not having my notes here, and the subject having rather gone out of my mind, and not having at hand the authorities I intended to quote to the house in opposition to the views that I supposed would be advanced; and I have abandoned the idea of addressing the convention at any length; and will only make one or two observations in reply to gentlemen who have spoken.

The first impulse which I had to doubt the scientific accuracy of the policy embraced in the usury laws, was in considering the policy embraced in what are known as free-trade laws. It was in opposition to interference by the State with the natural laws of trade, no matter what the subject-matter of interference might be. We all know that in the early history of the country, not only in other nations but in our own, down to a period comparatively modern, the State interfered with all subjects, not only moral subjects like religion, but actually fixed the prices of articles; and the most ridiculous laws formerly existed in the colonies, until the light of political economy, which appears never to have entered the minds of some gentlemen, broke in and dispelled the cloud, and the sumptuary laws were repealed. It was my detestation of that policy of unnecessary interference by the State with matters of trade, that led me to object to interference with money as much as with anything else; with a bargain between you and me as to what we may choose to do with our money on the one side or to pay for it on the other; with a trade in money, as well as with the sale of cattle, a horse and carriage, or a house.

Arriving at an interest in this subject from these general views, I may say that I found them supported by every single modern authority of any weight, I believe, without a single exception, from the time of Jeremy Bentham to the present hour. Every one of any weight, who has written either in the interest of the strictly financial circles, or who has written in the interest of what may be called the commercial class, or who has written, as many of them have, in the interest of the agricultural part of the community, in England and elsewhere, no matter in what interest they have written upon political economy, yet in relation to trade and finance every single one of any weight has indorsed the principle of the absolute freedom of trade in money just as trade ought to be absolutely free in reference to its exercise on other subjects. I have never had any doubt on the subject in my mind since I first became acquainted with the celebrated work of Jeremy Bentham to which he gave the quaint title of "Defence of Usury." I do not believe any one else ever rose up to answer his arguments. Macleod and others whose names are household words in the modern science of finance, took the same view; and the result has been that in England, in our own day, after a warfare in parliament and government circles for thirty or forty years, a contest including the whole British population, for the parliament is not controlled by the commercial interests, but as much as any body on the face of the earth by the agricultural interests, and a contest conducted there in an enlightened and scientific spirit, there was passed the act of Parliament passed in 18th and 19th Victoria, which I have read to the convention.

My friend from Anne Arundel (Mr. Miller) in the course of his observations made one remark on which I will make a single comment. He quoted Lord Coke, among other antiquated authorities, who spoke of this especially in its spiritual relations. I do not know whether my friend indorses that antiquated view when he follows it up with the common opinion then entertained, and which a great many people I believe still entertain that the Bible in some sort condemns the loaning of money at any other than a fixed rate. As I remarked before I am not in a position to make exact citations; but if I recollect aright, the matter of usury among the Jews was simply the direction under the theocracy, that no Jew should take usury from another, either for money, cattle, horses, or any other property. I believe those are nearly the exact words of the Old Testament. But while by this municipal arrangement among the Jews, the Jew was forbidden to take usury for money, cattle, or anything else, from a Jew, he might take as much usury as he pleased from an outsider. Everybody who knows these facts, and who knows what political economists have said upon the subject, knows that every writer upon the subject accepts the investigation which Bentham first made upon the subject as conclusive evidence that there cannot be said to be any moral wrong in what is known as usury, —if anybody can define what is usury, which I will come to it in a moment. There cannot be any moral wrong in it, because the commandment came to the Jews in the first place merely as a municipal arrangement among them, for their profit in some way which we know nothing about, for some purpose in the divine wisdom which we cannot penetrate; and in the second place, because while forbidden to take usury of one another they were at perfect liberty to take it of strangers. It would not have been permitted to take it of strangers if there was any moral wrong in it.

But if it is wrong to take usury, who shall fix what usury is? Here it is above six per cent. In New York it is above seven per cent. Somewhere else, in other States, it is above ten per cent. Who shall say that it is usury to take seven per cent. in Maryland, but that in New York eight per cent. is usury? If there is any moral wrong in it, anything essentially ruinous in it, it ought to be condemned, and it ought to be stopped; but why should we not be able to determine and point out the amount necessary to constitute usury? That cannot be immoral here which is moral in New York. If you cannot fix the rate up to which it shall be called interest and is perfectly right and proper, and beyond which it is to be called usury, and is fraudulent and extortionate, how can you claim that any rate is in itself wrong? The rate of interest at the bank of England goes up and down day by day according to the pressure of the demand by the whole population in the cities and the country.

That brings me to an observation made by my colleague, who bases his opposition to any change here upon the agricultural interest, the interest the people have in it. Of course, as my colleague is aware, and I think I have given pretty strong evidence of it during our sessions here, that there is no interest I am more ready to protect. It is for the very reason that I want to advance and to protect the agricultural interest, and to aid in all that will help to support the agricultural interest ultimately, that I am in favor of this change. I do not favor it because it is going to benefit usurers, or benefit rich men at the expense of poor men—the cry raised here upon every question—but because it tends to the advancement of the whole community by the adoption of what is regarded in modern times by those who think upon the subject, as a great scientific advance.

I will not argue these points, because they have already been so elaborately covered.—My friend from Baltimore county (Mr. Ridgely) has exhausted pretty much what I should have said upon the question if I had spoken at length. It is not the raising of the rate of interest, but leaving money free here which will bring money into the State. I do not ask the convention to consent to the permanent raising of the rate of interest to say ten per cent. instead of six. I only say, set money free; and the effect of it will be that capital will flow into the State instead of daily and hourly flowing out of it; it will be that interest will eventually and permanently fall; it will be that money will be more plenty, and there will be more seeking for investment; and in the course of a few years the rate of interest will be more likely to sink to four per cent. than to rise to eight per cent.

In reference to the question of the rich and the poor, which has been alluded to—the gentleman from Howard (Mr. Sands) had a drive at that—that it puts the poor into the hands of the rich, and oppresses the poor men, I would like to have anybody tell me, in the position of things to-day, the rich men having money, and the poor men wanting to borrow it and obliged to have it, whether it is not in the power of the rich man now to extort his usury. He has nothing to do but to take his discount in advance. What is to prevent it. On the other hand, if the poor man's necessities are such that they must have the money is it for his interest that the State should prohibit him from paying for it what it is worth, and thus restrain him from getting it upon any terms? That single illustration shows us the philosophy of this question; that the value of money as of anything else varies with every man according to his necessities. The whole difficulty arises from attempting to fix the value, which is regulated by the great principles of exchange and finance that control all matters relating to money and its operations, and which cannot be predetermined or controlled by legislative enactment.

The gentleman from Howard made one other observation, if I heard him distinctly, that I ought not to pass by, because I did not think it was even in that gentleman's capacity not to perceive so plain a matter. He asked why it was necessary, if a clause like this was to be adopted allowing private contracts up to ten per cent., to mention six per cent. at all. I will give him a simple answer in passing. If he will read the clause he will be sufficiently answered. The object is to make six per cent. the legal standard of interest in the absence of contracts, so that if parties neglect or do not choose to contract, the rate of interest recoverable in a suit at law shall be six per cent. That is the plain object of it. If interest were left entirely free, it might be supposed that if no interest were agreed upon none could be recovered

This is no longer a question of government, but simply of dealings between one man and another. It is not a question of the Jew in the olden time under a theocracy, under the old dispensation, trading with another Jew and lending him money, and prohibited by the fulminations against usury from making such a demand. It is a question of finance, subject to the laws of trade, regulating all commercial transactions between man and man, laws applicable to the whole world and ruling money as they rule every other article.

Gentlemen have repeated here the old maxim of Aristotle, that usury is not to be allowed because money produces nothing and is a fixed standard. What has produced more than money? What is more flexible, more fluctuating in its value, than money? I need not refer to any other illustration than our daily commercial intercourse. Those that are engaged in that business see the effect of it.—We know how prices rise and fall as specie rises and falls. We know how prices rise and fall as current funds generally rise and fall. We also know that the effect of that rise and fall is that it comes to every man's door. We pay for the necessities of life one price to-day, and another price to-morrow. What is that payment? It is paying exchange. Though he may not know it, in the price of the bread that a man and his children eat for the morning or evening meal, is a practical recognition of the very doctrine we claim here, of freedom for money; for at every meal he is paying a higher or a less rate of interest.—That is the practical operation of it. It all comes from exchange and the scientific principles of trade which control everything bought and sold, even the most common articles of domestic consumption.

As I said before, this is a mere remnant, and about the last remnant, of the old theory and doctrine of sumptuary laws which so long controlled men's minds; and we have before us the brilliant example of England, in abandoning, after scientific inquiry, the laws restricting interest on money within a certain fixed rate. If we shall be wise enough and scientific enough, in constructing our organic law, I hope we may follow in her wake.

Mr. Negley renewed his amendment, to strike out all after the words "contracted for," and to insert the words "as shall be agreed upon between the parties, not exceeding eight per centum per annum."

Mr. King called the previous question, and it was sustained.

Mr. Sands demanded the yeas and nays on the amendment of Mr. Negley, and they were ordered.

The question being taken, the result was —yeas 22, nays 38—as follows:

Yeas—Messrs. Audoun, Baker, Brooks, Brown, Cushing, Daniel, Dellinger, Greene, Hebb, Hoffman, Hopper, Kennard, Lansdale, Markey, Negley, Parker, Schley, Scott, Sneary, Stirling, Sykes, Todd—22.

Nays—Messrs. Abbott, Annan, Belt, Carter, Crawford, Davis, of Washington, Dent, Duvall, Ecker, Farrow, Galloway, Hatch, Henkle, Horsey, Jones, of Cecil, Keefer, King, Larsh, Lee, Marbury, McComas, Mitchell, Miller, Morgan, Mullikin, Murray, Myman, Parran, Pugh, Purnell, Ridgely, Russell, Sands, Stockbridge, Swope, Valliant, Wickard, Wooden—38.

When their names were called,

Mr. Ecker said: I had promised some gentlemen that I would vote for a modification of the provision as it now stands, but the argument has changed my mind. We might as well say that capital punishment for murder should be done away with because an occasional murder is committed. The argument of the gentleman from Washington county (Mr. Negley) has entirely changed my mind; and therefore I vote "no."

Mr. McComas said: Considering this a matter in which the people are very deeply interested, and not knowing fully the wishes of my constituents on this subject, I shall vote against any proposition to change the rate of interest, on the ground that the constitution can be easily changed by submitting the question to the people.

Mr. PUGH said: I had intended to submit a few remarks on this question if the previous question had not been called. I am influenced in my vote upon this question by my own view of it, which is altogether different from any which I have heard presented here. I shall not pretend to take up the time to present my peculiar view. I do not think any serious injury will be done to business men in any community in the State by obliging them, at least for the present, to pay as much interest as the government thinks proper to pay. While the United States government pays that amount, I am willing that all who are borrowers should pay the same. For that reason I vote against the amendment of the gentleman from Washington county (Mr. Negley,) and shall vote in favor of the amendment of the gentleman from Baltimore city (Mr. Abbott.) I vote "no."

Mr. RIDGELY said: I vote against this amendment in the hope that I shall have an opportunity to vote for the proposition of the gentleman from Prince George's (Mr. Belt.) I vote "no."

Mr. BELT said: My object is, so far as I can, to set trade free—money and everything else. If I cannot free them entirely I want to free them as far as possible. But this proposition not coming up to the point I hope we can attain, I shall vote in the negative.

The amendment was accordingly rejected.

The question recurred upon the amendment submitted by Mr. ABBOTT, to insert after the words "per annum" in the second line, the words "but such rates may be contracted for as Congress have or may hereafter allow on any loans of the United States.

Mr. SANDS demanded the yeas and nays, and they were ordered.

The question being taken, the result was —yeas 19, nays 40—as follows:

Yeas—Messrs. Abbott, Annan, Brown, Cushing, Daniel, Dellinger, Greene, Hebb, Hoffman, Hopper, Lansdale, Markey, Negley, Parker, Pugh, Scott, Sneary, Stirling, Todd—19.

Nays—Messrs. Audoun, Baker, Brooks, Belt, Carter, Crawford, Davis, of Washington, Dent, Duvall, Ecker, Farrow, Galloway, Hatch, Henkle, Horsey, Jones, of Cecil, Keefer, Kennard, King, Larsh, Lee, Marbury, McComas, Mitchell, Miller, Morgan, Mullikin, Murray, Nyman, Parran, Purnell, Ridgely, Russell, Sands, Stockbridge, Swope, Sykes, Valliant, Wickard, Wooden—40.

When their names were called,

Mr. ABBOTT said: Every member here will see that the proposition which I have offered does not alter the section in the least. My object in offering it and in voting for it, is simply to make it in conformity with the wishes, as I think, of most of our people, that they may be allowed to make such contracts and subscribe for such amounts of government bonds as they may desire to do, without running counter to the fundamental law of our State, and to put our people on a par with the offers that the government may make, that our citizens may not be debarred from lending their money to one another by the higher rates of interest that the government may offer. I vote "aye."

Mr. MILLER said: Notwithstanding what has been so ably and eloquently urged by my friend from Prince George's (Mr. Belt) about the laws of trade, I believe the effect of allowing the rate of interest to rise above six per cent. to seven and three-tenths or eight per cent., will be immediately to cause all the banking institutions of the State to raise their rate of discount to the maximum rate for which they are allowed to contract; and the people whom I represent and those in other agricultural portions of the State, who have been in the habit of obtaining discounts upon their crops at the rate of six per cent., will immediately have to pay ten per cent. instead of six, notwithstanding all that is urged here.

The amendment was accordingly rejected.

The question recurred on the substitute submitted by Mr. BELT, as follows:

"That the legal rate of interest in this State shall be six per cent. per annum, except in cases of agreements between contracting parties; and in all such cases parties contracting shall have power to contract and to recover any rate of interest not exceeding ten per centum per annum."

Mr. KING demanded the yeas and nays, and they were ordered.

The question being taken, the result was —yeas 22, nays 37—as follows:

Yeas— Messrs. Belt, Brooks, Brown, Cushing, Daniel, Dellinger, Hatch, Hebb, Hoffman, Lansdale, Larsh, Markey, Negley, Parker, Pugh, Ridgely, Schley, Scott, Sneary, Stirling, Stockbridge, Sykes—22.

Nays—Messrs. Abbott, Annan, Audoun, Baker, Carter, Crawford, Davis, of Washington, Dent, Duvall, Ecker, Farrow, Galloway, Greene, Henkle, Hopper, Horsey, Jones, of Cecil, Keefer, Kennard, King, Lee, Marbury, McComas, Mitchell, Miller, Morgan, Mullikin, Murray, Nyman, Parran, Purnell, Russell, Sands, Swope, Todd, Valliant, Wooden—37.

When their names were called,

Mr. KENNARD said: I was in favor of and supported the reconsideration of this question because I was open to conviction, and was willing to modify my views respecting it; and I have done so to some extent, but still my views have not been modified so far as to authorize me to vote for the proposition before the convention; and I therefore vote "no."

Mr. PUGH said: Seeing that it is impossible to get any nearer approach to my view of this subject, I shall be obliged to vote for this. My idea was that parties contracting should certainly be allowed to contract to pay as much interest as the government of the United States allows to its creditors. For this reason I vote "aye."

The amendment was accordingly rejected.

The question recurred upon ordering the report to be read a third time, which was agreed to.

On motion of Mr. STOCKBRIDGE,

The rules were suspended to permit the third reading to take place immediately.

The report was then read a third time, and the question was stated upon its passage.

Mr. STIRLING. This provision is the same as the law now stands upon the statute books and has stood since 1845, to allow six per cent. interest and no more. As I think it is the safest plan to let the whole matter stand as it is in the code, I shall vote against introducing this provision into the constitution.

Mr. SANDS. I hope that this convention, having expressed so decidedly its conviction that that ought to be the rate of interest, we shall not leave it to the legislature to bandy up and down under the influence of capital.

The question being taken upon the passage of the report, by yeas and nays, under the rule, the result was—yeas 32, nays 27—as follows:

Yeas—Messrs. Annan, Audoun, Carter, Crawford, Davis, of Washington, Dent, Duvall, Ecker, Farrow, Galloway, Henkle, Horsey, Jones, of Cecil, Keefer, Kennard, King, Marbury, McComas, Mitchell, Mullikin, Murray, Nyman, Parran, Purnell, Russell, Sands, Swope, Thomas, Todd, Valliant, Wooden—32.

Nays—Messrs. Abbott, Baker, Belt, Brooks, Brown, Cushing, Daniel, Dellinger, Greene, Hatch, Hebb, Hoffman, Hopper, Larsh, Lee, Markey, Negley, Parker, Pugh, Ridgely, Schley, Scott, Sneary, Stirling, Stockbridge, Sykes, Wickard—27.

The report was accordingly passed.

SHERMAN IN ATLANTA.

Mr. STOCKBRIDGE read the following telegram:

"*Office Annapolis Telegraph Company.*

The following message was received at this office at — o'clock, Sept. 2nd, 1864, dated Baltimore, Sept. 2nd, 1864:

JOHN MCGARIGLE, *of Baltimore American:*

Official announcement just recieved, that Sherman's advance entered Atlanta, Georgia, to-day. ALEXANDER FULTON."

[Enthusiastic applause.]

On motion of Mr. MULLIKIN,

The convention adjourned.

EIGHTY-NINTH DAY.

MONDAY, September 5, 1864.

The convention met at 12 o'clock, M.

Prayer by the Rev. Mr. Owen.

The roll was called, and the following members answered to their names:

Messrs. Goldsborough, President; Abbott, Annan, Audoun, Baker, Belt, Berry, of Baltimore county, Bond, Brooks, Brown, Carter, Chambers, Clarke, Crawford, Cunningham, Cushing, Dail, Daniel, Davis, of Charles, Davis, of Washington, Dellinger, Dent, Duvall, Earle, Ecker, Farrow, Galloway, Greene, Hatch, Hebb, Hoffman, Hollyday, Horsey, Jones, of Cecil, Jones, of Somerset, Keefer, Kennard, King, Lansdale, Larsh, Lee, Markey, Mayhugh, Mitchell, Miller, Morgan, Mullikin, Murray, Negley, Nyman, Parker, Parran, Purnell, Ridgely, Russell, Schley, Schlosser, Scott, Smith, of Dorchester, Sneary, Stirling, Stockbridge, Swope, Thomas, Todd, Turner, Valliant, Wickard Wilmer, Wooden—70.

The journal of Friday was read and approved.

PUBLISHING THE CONSTITUTION.

Mr. WICKARD submitted the following order:

"*Ordered*, That the special committee on publishing the new constitution, be instructed to authorize the publication of the same in two newspapers in each county of the State, (in which there are two printed,) and in three in the city of Baltimore, at least three times before the day on which it shall be submitted to the people for their ratification or rejection; provided it can be done at a cost of one dollar per square."

Mr. NEGLEY. Would it not be better to leave the amount to be paid open for negotiation? I have heard some gentlemen suggest fifty cents per square.

Mr. RIDGELY. I do not think that that order ought to pass. The whole object of the order adopted by the convention authorizing the publication of 60,000 copies of the constitution in the English and German languages, was to supersede the necessity of this sort of publication. The idea was that a single paper should publish a supplemental edition of the constitution, and distribute to the newspapers throughout the State as many copies as they might require to supply their subscribers. In that manner the constitution would be distributed over the State in every direction, and abundant information conveyed to the people, and this mode of publication will be rendered unnecessary.

Mr. NEGLEY. I understand from my colleague (Mr. Sneary) who was a printer at the time the last constitution was adopted, that a similar provision was made to that adopted here; that the newspapers of the county were not engaged to publish the constitution. My colleague gives it as his experience that not one-quarter of the copies of the constitution prepared for distribution were ever distributed, for it was really no favor to the county papers to supply them to their subscribers. The Union papers have taken a great interest in this constitution, and in the Union cause generally; and they think that it is not more than right that the publication should be given to them. And besides, there are hundreds and hundreds of families in the country that never see any paper but the one published in the county where they live. And I think it is advisable that this constitution should be brought fully before as large a number of the people in this way as can be done.

Mr. STOCKBRIDGE. The purpose of the order adopted by the convention the other day, as I understood it, was to furnish gratuitously to the publishers of those papers throughout the State, as many copies of this constitution headed "Extra," as they might require to send one to each subscriber, and send it as an extra of their own paper. The difference between the two plans is this; as the order now stands adopted, the type are set in one place for the whole State; while according to the plan now proposed they must be set twice in every county in the State. Gentlemen will of course see at once the very great difference as regards the matter of expense to the State.

I am not sufficiently acquainted with these things to know what would be the expense of publishing this constitution as an advertisement in the county newspapers; but it seems to me it would be enormous. I suppose there are gentlemen here in the convention who can form some reasonable conjecture as to the number of squares this would occupy. My own impression is that it would cost the State for that operation a great many thousand dollars. And unless it be necessary I shall be opposed to incurring that expense. Before voting on this proposition I would like to know whether it is the design to have this constitution published in the newspapers in addition to what has already been ordered; or whether this order is intended to be a substitute for the other.

Mr. DAVIS. I desire to move to amend this order by inserting after the words "three times," the words "at least two weeks before the election." Otherwise this constitution might be published three times within three days of the election.

Mr. NEGLEY. My colleague (Mr. Sneary,) who is a practical printer, and thoroughly conversant with the business, states that it would not cost over fifteen hundred dollars.

Mr. STOCKBRIDGE. In forty-four papers?

Mr. SNEARY. I meant to say this: I am not now connected with any newspaper, but I was in 1851. At that time the convention authorized the publication of the constitution in bill form. A large number of copies were sent to our county, but not one of them was ever distributed. I do not think that one person in five in the county ever saw the constitution before he was called upon to vote upon it. And under the post office law, editors are not permitted to enclose any matter in their papers other than that which belongs to the papers themselves; and if they do they violate the law of Congress. They are permitted to send only their papers free of postage, through the counties, but not permitted to enclose any circular or anything of that sort in them.

I presume it might cost from fifteen hundred to two thousand dollars, perhaps more, to print this constitution in the newspapers. Some limit should be placed upon it of course. But the newspaper press is the medium through which the people of the counties look for information in regard to such matters as these. I have no interest in the newspaper press now. I know very well that what is everybody's business is nobody's business. The copies of the constitution sent to my county some thirteen years ago, were not generally distributed among the people. The result was that comparatively few people saw the constitution. To print the constitution in the papers might lead to an expense something over and above the printing of the 60,000 copies as proposed. I do not know what they would cost; I am not able to say as to that. But I know this, that by inserting it in the newspapers it would have a much more general circulation, and be much more gratifying to the people, for they look to the papers as the channel through which such information is to be communicated. And the press of the State expect it. I would suggest that this order be substituted for the other.

The PRESIDENT. Does the gentleman from Allegany (Mr. Wickard) offer this as an additional order to the one already adopted by the convention?

Mr. WICKARD. I offer it as an additional order.

The question was then taken upon the amendment of Mr. DAVIS, of Charles, to insert after the words "three times," the words "at least two weeks before the election," and it was rejected.

The question then recurred upon adopting the order submitted by Mr. WICKARD.

Upon this question Mr. WICKARD called for the yeas and nays, and they were ordered.

The question was then taken, by yeas and nays, and resulted—yeas 28, nays 40—as follows:

Yeas—Messrs. Abbott, Annan, Audoun, Baker, Belt, Brooks, Chambers, Clarke, Davis, of Washington, Dellinger, Dent, Duvall, Greene, Hebb, Jones, of Somerset, Kennard, Lansdale, Miller, Morgan, Negley, Nyman,

Schley, Sneary, Swope, Thomas, Valliant, Wickard, Wooden—28.

Nays—Messrs. Goldsborough, President; Berry, of Baltimore county, Bond, Brown, Carter, Crawford, Cunningham, Cushing, Dail, Daniel, Davis, of Charles, Earle, Ecker, Farrow, Galloway, Hatch, Hoffman, Horsey, Jones, of Cecil, Keefer, King, Larsh, Lee, Markey, Mayhugh, Mitchell, Mullikin, Murray, Parker, Purnell, Ridgely, Russell, Schlosser, Scott, Smith, of Dorchester Stirling, Stockbridge, Todd, Turner, Wilmer—40.

The order was accordingly rejected.

Mr. Cushing, when his name was called, said: I think this would be an extremely expensive business. I think the newspapers of the counties would publish this constitution at once, for the sake of furnishing the news to their readers. We have provided for the printing of 60,000 copies, to be sent to the newspapers, to be distributed to their respective subscribers. This would be putting the State to an additional expense of six or eight thousand dollars for no purpose whatever, and I therefore vote "no."

Mr. Schley, when his name was called, said: The experience of this State has shown that the reason assigned by the gentleman from Baltimore city (Mr. Cushing) for voting against this order, is not well founded; that is, that the newspapers would publish this constitution as an item of news. That was not our experience at the time of the last convention. This order provides that this constitution shall be published in two newspapers in each county, where two newspapers are published. I am not prepared at this time to say how many counties have each two newspapers. But I think there are not more than five counties in which two newspapers are published at this time.

The President. There are five on the eastern shore. I do not know about the western shore.

Mr. Schley. I am sure not half of them. But even if all the counties had two newspapers each, I do not believe that the cost of its publication would be twenty-five hundred dollars for the State. But the sum is unimportant compared with the necessity and advantage of bringing this constitution in a familiar newspaper form home to every man's door. That I consider wholly outside of the question here. I shall therefore cheerfully vote "aye."

MISCELLANEOUS.

Mr. Abbott submitted the following:

"*Ordered*, That this convention recommend the governor, immediately after the adoption of the new constitution, to issue pardons to all persons now held in confinement for any violation of the laws made for the protection of slavery in this State."

Mr. Mayhugh moved to lay the order on the table.

Upon this question Mr. Cushing called for the yeas and nays, but they were not ordered.

The question was then taken upon the motion to lay the order on the table, and it was agreed to.

Mr. Greene submitted the following order:

"*Ordered*, That the committee on accounts be directed to adjust the per diem and mileage, according to law, of the several members of the convention up to and inclusive of Tuesday, the sixth day of September, 1864, and to issue certificates for the same to members on and after that day."

Mr. Greene said: The object of that order is to enable the committee on accounts to make up the several accounts of members, and have their certificates prepared in anticipation of the time of adjournment. I think the convention has already decided that it will not adjourn *sine die*, but adjourn subject to the call of the President. In the absence of any such order as this it strikes me that the committee on accounts will be unable to finish up its accounts by to-morrow.

Mr. Daniel. I suppose it is pretty certain that we will adjourn to-morrow.

Mr. Cushing. O! yes.

The question was then taken upon the order, and it was adopted.

Mr. Valliant. I submit the following, in regard to which I propose to make a word or two of explanation:

"*Ordered*, That the committee on accounts pay John McGarigle, one hundred dollars for extra services rendered, as superintendent of the printing of the debates of this convention."

This order has been prepared by the committee on printing and reporting. In so doing they have been actuated by this consideration: when the contract was made with Mr. McGarigle to superintend the printing for the sum of three hundred dollars, it was expected that the deliberations of this convention would not continue longer than from two to three months. The convention has not yet adjourned, although more than four months have elapsed since the organization of the convention. We therefore think Mr. McGarigle ought to receive more money than the amount contracted for. In addition to this reason, the printing of the debates of this convention will not be completed for perhaps two months to come, and during all that time the printing of the convention is to receive the attention of Mr. McGarigle. His services will therefore continue from six to seven months, whereas the committee, and Mr. McGarigle, and the people of the State, thought at the time the contract was made that the deliberations of this body would not continue longer than from two to three months, and he thought his services would not be required more than that time. But since his services have been much more arduous than the committee at first apprehended, the committee think that he ought to receive one hundred dollars more. He thinks he ought to get more than that.

The question being then taken, the order was adopted, upon a division—ayes 45, noes not counted.

Mr. VALLIANT. I have another order of a similar character. I confess that I submit it with a great deal of reluctance, not because I do not think that the party is justly entitled to receive what is proposed in this order, but because it somewhat resembles some proceedings of this convention which have not met my entire approbation. But I think that the explanation I can give will fully satisfy every member of this convention that the order should be adopted. The order is as follows:

"*Ordered*, That the committee on accounts be, and they are hereby instructed to pay to Mr. Daniel M. Moore, the sum of two hundred dollars, for extra services rendered, for indexing the works of this convention."

About the time this convention was organized, Mr. Moore proposed to index the constitution, the journal of debates, and the journal of proceedings for the sum of five hundred dollars. Or rather, he wanted a much larger sum than that, but finally consented to take the sum of five hundred dollars. There was some little difficulty about the employment of Mr. Moore; the only difficulty was that another person had offered to do the same, and some other work for the same sum. We did not give it to the other person because we did not think he could do all the work. We finally contracted with Mr. Moore to do the indexing for three hundred dollars, with the understanding on the part of every member of the committee I believe, that we would recommend to this convention that he be paid a larger sum, if we deemed his services to be worth more.

The indexing the work of the last convention was done for the sum of eight hundred dollars, at a time when gold was at par. The work of this convention is much larger than that of the last convention; that is, the work of indexing. The debates of the last convention amounted to about nine hundred or one thousand pages; the number of pages of our journal of debates will not be less than sixteen hundred or seventeen hundred, and if eight hundred dollars was a fair compensation for indexing the debates of the last convention, twelve or fourteen hundred dollars would not be more than a fair compensation for our indexing. Yet the committee have determined not to pay Mr. Moore so much as that, but to pay him in all five hundred dollars, which is three hundred dollars less than was paid for indexing the work of the convention of 1851.

It is my honest conviction, from a careful investigation, that five hundred dollars is not a fair compensation to Mr. Moore, and he is not willing to do it for that, only he has contracted to do it. It is my judgment that he is entitled to more than that. The majority of the committee, however, would not consent to give him more. Perhaps I ought not to mention that. The committee are unanimous in their recommendation to give Mr. Moore this additional two hundred dollars.

Mr. THOMAS. I move to strike out "two hundred," and insert "three hundred."

Mr. MILLER. Does that include the indexing of the journal of proceedings as well as the journal of debates?

Mr. VALLIANT. Yes, sir.

Mr. MILLER. I understand that the indexing of the journal of debates of 1850 cost eight hundred dollars.

Mr. VALLIANT. The indexing of all the work of the convention of 1850: by that I mean the journal of debates, the journal of proceedings, and the constitution. The indexer then received eight hundred dollars in gold, or what was tantamount to gold. We propose to give Mr. Moore five hundred dollars; that is, we have already contracted to give him three hundred dollars, and we propose now to give him two hundred more.

Mr. MILLER. If the indexer of the convention received eight hundred dollars, he received more than he ought. There were but a few pages of index, which I think could have been made out by a competent person in a week's time.

Mr. VALLIANT. From 1850 to the present time, the smallest amount paid for indexing the journals of the generally assembly has been four hundred and fifty dollars, and from that amount up to seven hundred and fifty dollars.

The question was then taken upon the motion of Mr. THOMAS to strike out "two hundred," and insert "three hundred," which was not agreed to.

The question recurred upon the original order.

Mr. MAYHUGH called for the yeas and nays upon this question, but they were not ordered.

The question was then taken, and upon a division—ayes 41, noes not counted—the order was adopted.

BOUND COPIES OF THE CONSTITUTION.

Mr. VALLIANT, from the committee on reporting and printing, made the following report:

The committee on reporting and printing, to whom was referred the order offered September 2, 1864, by Mr. GREENE, of Allegany, very respectfully beg leave to report, that after mature deliberation they have concluded that said order ought not to be adopted, and herewith offer the following instead thereof:

Ordered, That the comptroller of the treasury be authorized, and is hereby directed to contract with Mr. Richard P. Bayly, of Annapolis, printer to the convention, for the printing and binding of five hundred copies of the constitution when adopted by the people of Maryland; said copies to be printed in the same style, on such quality of paper, and bound in like manner to the edition of the present constitution, published by Murphy & Co., of Baltimore.

Mr. GREENE. I offer as a substitute for the order reported by the committee on reporting and printing, the following, which is a copy of the original order offered by me on Friday last:

Ordered, That the State librarian be and he is hereby directed to purchase of James Wingate two hundred and fifty copies of the constitution passed by this convention, when adopted by the voters of this State; said constitution shall contain an elaborate index, prepared with references to articles and sections, and also to the page, said constitution shall be printed in the best style, (with side notes,) on fair white paper with large fair type and well bound, and shall contain the names of the members of this convention; said constitution shall contain the certificate of the clerk of the court of appeals, that it is a true copy of the constitution passed by this convention; and the indexing and publication of said constitution shall be approved by the president of this convention.

And the State librarian shall distribute said copies of the constitution, as follows:

One copy to each member of convention; to the governor, lieutenant governor, comptroller, treasurer, attorney general, adjutant general, superintendent of public education, and commissioner of the land office, each one copy; to the judges and clerks of the circuit courts, and the courts of Baltimore city, each one copy; to the judges and the clerk of the court of appeals, each one copy; to the orphans' courts of the State, each one copy; to the State's attorneys, each one copy; to the register of wills, each one copy; to the boards of county commissioners, each one copy; to the mayor of Baltimore city, one copy.

And the remaining eleven copies shall be retained in the State library, subject to the disposition of the general assembly.

And the president of this convention is hereby authorized and directed to pay James Wingate one hundred dollars, for preparing said carefully elaborated index and side notes to said constitution, and also two dollars per copy for said constitution, when published by James Wingate.

Mr. BERRY, of Baltimore county. I would suggest to the gentleman from Allegany (Mr. Greene,) to include in his order a sufficient number of copies to be placed at the disposal of the governor to enable him to send one to the governor of each State. That, I believe, has been the uniform practice of all the States.

Mr. GREENE. I think that is a very proper suggestion, and with the consent of the convention, I will modify accordingly the order I submitted.

No objection being made, the substitute of Mr. GREENE was modified by increasing the number of copies to three hundred, and inserting before the words "and the remaining eleven copies," &c., the words "and fifty copies to the governor for distribution to the governors of the several States."

The question was upon adopting the substitute as modified.

Mr. VALLIANT. The committee considered the question of economy, and it was their judgment that the order which I have submitted would be a saving to the State of about one hundred dollars, besides providing at the same time for more copies for the use of the State than is provided for by the order of the gentleman from Allegany (Mr. Greene.) Then another thing; I presume that the whole work to be done in accordance with the provisions of the order submitted by the gentleman from Allegany will be done by strictly loyal men. I presume so, because I have no special reason to believe otherwise. But I can say with certainty, in relation to the order I have submitted, that if it is adopted, the work will be performed by those who are strictly loyal. How far that consideration should govern this convention I do not pretend to say. I did not know but it was well enough to mention these little matters.

The PRESIDENT. One issue of Murphy & Co. is of large full type, the other is smaller.

Mr. VALLIANT. The edition to which the committee have reference is the one of large type; the one of 1855. That is the edition, a copy of which I now hold in my hand, which was before the committee on reporting and printing at the time they framed this order. I will ask permission, in order to make that certain, to add to the order, the words "in 1855."

The order was modified accordingly.

Mr. GREENE. According to my recollection of the order as I heard it read, it does not appear certain that it will be an edition like this of 1855. It says similar to that published by Murphy & Co., of Baltimore. They published an edition in 1862, which is the common edition of the constitution, and smaller than the one of 1855. The copy which I hold in my hand, and which is a copy of the edition of 1855, and which is intended to be the model on which the constitution is to printed according to my order, is very considerably different from the other edition. I do not know that the edition of 1855, was ever published and offered for sale.

The PRESIDENT. Yes, sir; it has been published and sold. And the order of the gentleman from Talbot (Mr. Valliant) has been modified so as to make it designate that edition.

Mr. GREENE. Then there is another thing in the order offered by the chairman of the committee on reporting and printing. There is no provision requiring proper marginal notes and references. That is a matter of very considerable importance. The order offered by me prescribes the quality of paper, the character of the printing, and full marginal notes and references.

Mr. VALLIANT. I will state an additional fact of which the gentleman has reminded me. Our regular printer, named in my order, has offered to do all the annotating free of charge. If he does the printing, it will be done as nearly as possible according to the contract which he has made with the comptroller of the State, and the marginal references will be made without any additional charge whatever. He has been in the habit of making the marginal references for a number of years, in printing the journals of the two houses of the legislature, and has never made any charge of it.

Mr. HEBB. The committee on revision, I understand, are ready to make several reports. I therefore move a suspension of the rules, in order that they may make their reports, and let the convention act on them, so that the committee clerks may have something to do.

The PRESIDENT. The subject before the convention must be disposed of in some way.

Mr. JONES, of Somerset, moved that it be informally passed over.

The question was then taken, and upon a division—ayes 38, noes 30—the motion was agreed to.

On motion of Mr. HEBB,

The rules were then suspended, in order to allow the committee on revision an opportunity to make their reports.

AMENDMENTS OF THE CONSTITUTION.

Mr. EARLE, from the committee of revision, reported back to the convention the article on the amendments of the constitution.

He stated that no change had been made by the committee in the second and third sections of that article, but that the first section had been materially modified.

That section, as referred to the committee, reads thus:

"Section 1. Either branch of the general assembly may propose amendments to this constitution; and if the same shall be agreed to by three-fifths of the members elected to each house, such proposed amendments shall be entered on the journals, with the yeas and nays taken thereon, and shall be published in two newspapers in each county in the State where two are published, and in three newspapers in the city of Baltimore, one of which shall be German, for three months preceding the next election for senators and representatives, at which time the same shall be submitted to the electors for their approval or rejection; and if a majority of the electors voting at such election shall adopt such amendments the same shall become a part of the constitution. When more than one amendment shall be submitted at the same time, they shall be so submitted as to enable the electors to vote on each amendment separately."

This section remodeled by the committee reads as follows:

"Section 1. The general assembly may propose any amendment or amendments to this constitution which shall be agreed to by three-fifths of all the members elected to both houses. Such proposed amendment or amendments, with the yeas and nays thereon, shall be entered on the journal of each house, shall be printed with the laws passed at the same session, and shall be published by order of the governor in all the newspapers printed in the different counties of this State, and in three newspapers printed in the city of Baltimore, one of which shall be printed in the German language, for at least three months preceding the next election for members of the general assembly, at which election the said proposed amendment or amendments shall be submitted to the qualified electors of the State for their confirmation or rejection; and if it shall appear to the satisfaction of the governor, from the returns of said election made to him by the proper authorities, that a majority of the qualified votes cast at said election were in favor of the said proposed amendment or amendments, he shall, by proclamation, declare said amendment or amendments to be part of the constitution of this State. When two or more amendments shall be submitted by the general assembly to the qualified electors of the State at the same election, they shall be so submitted that the electors may vote for or against each amendment separately."

Recommending the adoption of this section as modified, the committee close their report on the article styled "amendments of the constitution."

GEORGE EARLE, Chairman.

Mr. CHAMBERS. I will take the opportunity to recur to a remark made by me yesterday, as to the power of a revisory committee. I understand that some gentlemen have supposed that the action of the last convention, the revisory committee of which I was a member, should have been recollected by me. It was not, though I knew there was a committee of revision in that body. I find by reference to the journals that that committee acted under the express orders of the body to make amendments which were published. I have turned to the order appointing that committee, and find that it was appointed on the order of Judge Tuck, who moved "that the chairman of the several standing committees should constitute a committee of revision to which should be referred all articles of the constitution after they shall have been passed upon by the convention, to be examined and printed for the use of the convention prior to their final adoption." All those articles were printed, and every member had an opportunity to examine them. It was made a part of the duty of that committee to make those suggestions.

Now I submit that we cannot fairly comprehend the details of the amendments reported by the committee of revision of this body without having them printed. If the convention is to remain in session until tomorrow, I see no reason why, when the committee proposes any material changes, they should not be printed and acted on to-morrow. If it is the determination of members to close the session to-night, of course it would be impracticable to have these amendments printed. I can only express my regret at being called upon to act upon very important articles without having an opportunity to know the exact import of them.

From the reading of the first section of the article on amendments to the constitution as proposed to be changed by the committee on revision, I presume that it means that to adopt an amendment by the people after it has received a three-fifths vote of the legislature, it must receive a majority of the votes cast at that election. If I am correct, I would ask whether that should be so? If there are more votes for than against the amendment, is not that all that should be required? I would ask for information, whether this section requires a majority of the whole number of votes given at that election, or merely a majority of the votes cast for and against the proposed amendment to the constitution?

Mr. Earle. The section says expressly "a majority of the qualified votes cast at said election." There is another change proposed in the language of this section. The article as passed by the convention says that "either branch of the general assembly may propose amendments to this constitution." The committee recommend that the phraseology be changed, by saying, that the general assembly may propose any amendment or amendments to this constitution which shall be agreed to by three-fifths of all the members elected to both houses.

Mr. Chambers. That is the same in substance. There can be no objection to that.

Mr. Earle. The committee next recommend that all amendments to the constitution proposed by the general assembly shall be printed with the laws passed at the same session and submitted to the qualified electors of the State for their confirmation or rejection. If confirmed by a majority of the qualified votes cast at the election, the governor shall, by proclamation, declare the same to be part of the constitution of the State.

Mr. Chambers. I would suggest the propriety of having this report recommitted to the committee on revision, with the view of having inserted here what I suppose was designed by the convention—that the majority of the votes for and against should decide the question. That is not the case with the section as it now stands. Suppose that there are ten thousand votes given for and against some candidate on the day of election, and only three thousand votes are cast for the proposed amendment to the constitution. Seven thousand of the voters say nothing about it, and care nothing about it, or they fail to attend to it properly. There is not a vote cast against the proposed amendment. There is no evidence that there is a voter in the county who is opposed to it. Yet the votes affirmatively given do not operate to adopt the amendment, because they do not amount to a majority of all the votes cast at that election. I presume that was not the intention of the convention, and if not, then there should be some change in this phraseology.

Mr. Stirling. The section as reported by the committee provides that the vote upon any proposed amendment to the constitution shall be taken upon the day of the election of members to the general assembly, and it goes on to say that if a majority of the votes cast at said election are in favor of the proposed amendment, then it shall be adopted. Now the argument of the gentleman from Kent (Mr. Chambers) is perfectly correct. If two thousand people in the county vote for State officers, and only five hundred vote in favor of the proposed change in the constitution, although no one votes against it, because a majority of the votes cast at that election were not cast in favor of the proposed amendment.

Mr. Stockbridge. I have no objection whatever to having the phraseology of this section modified by the insertion of the necessary words. But I do not think it necessary as a question of law, disagreeing in that respect with both the gentleman from Kent, (Mr. Chambers) and my colleague (Mr Stirling.) A majority of the votes cast is required to carry any measure or candidate at an election. In the case supposed by the gentleman from Kent, there are three thousand votes for the proposed amendment to the constitution, and seven thousand blanks. In that case the blanks are not counted at all. So far as the amendment is concerned there are but three thousand votes cast at that election. An amendment to the constitution stands precisely upon the same ground as a candidate for governor. The candidate for governor to be elected must have a majority of the votes cast. Suppose there are 100,000 votes cast at an election in the State for members of the house of delegates. And suppose a candidate for governor receives 35,000 votes, and no other candidate receives any, would there be a doubt that the candidate receiving the 35,000 votes would be elected governor, he receiving a majority of the votes cast for that office? And if so in the case of governor, would it not be precisely so in the case of an amendment to the constitution? The law of the State provides that blanks shall not be counted. It would be precisely the same, I apprehend, in reference to an amendment to the constitution, as in reference to an election to any office. Still I have no objection to the change in this section, if any person has any doubt upon the subject.

Mr. CHAMBERS. Respectable persons do doubt; I doubt, and the gentleman from Baltimore city (Mr. Stirling) doubts.

Mr. EARLE. Will these words remove the difficulty? After the expression "a majority of the qualified votes cast at said election," insert "on the proposed amendment or amendments."

Mr. CHAMBERS. That is right.

Mr. EARLE. That part of the section will then read, "And if it shall appear to the satisfaction of the governor, from the returns of said election made to him by the proper authorities, that a majority of the qualified votes cast at said election, on the proposed amendment or amendments, were in favor of the said proposed amendment or amendments, he shall, by proclamation, declare said amendment or amendments to be part of the constitution of the State."

The report of the committee of revision, in relation to the article on "amendments to the constitution," was then concurred in.

VOTE ON THE CONSTITUTION.

Mr. RIDGELY. In connection with the subject of the committee on revision, I have an order which I wish to submit to the house. It is as follows:

Ordered, That the committee on revision be instructed so to modify that part of the schedule which provides for the taking of the vote on the constitution on the 12th day of October, 1864, so as to extend the said time for two days, including the 13th day of October, 1864."

I offer that for this reason: the provision in the schedule requires that the oath shall be administered to every voter. It has been thought by a great many persons that it would be impossible to take the vote in one day in some of the counties, where the districts are large, and there are many voters.

Mr. HEBB. I am not prepared to vote upon that question just now. I move that it be passed over until the committee on revision get through making their reports.

The PRESIDENT. As the committee on revision are now engaged in making their reports, this order cannot now be received except by unanimous consent.

Mr. RIDGELY. I have no objection to having it laid over until the committee get through their reports.

SUNDRY OFFICERS.

Mr. EARLE, from the committee on revision, made the following report on the article on "sundry officers."

The first section of this article, as referred to the committee by the convention, reads as follows:

"The governor, the comptroller of the treasury and the treasurer shall constitute the board of public works, who shall exercise a diligent and faithful supervision of all public works in which the State may be interested as stockholder or creditor, and shall appoint the directors in every railroad or canal company in which the State has the legal power to appoint directors, which said directors shall represent the State in all meetings of the stockholders of every railroad or canal company in which the State is a stockholder; said board of public works shall require the directors of all said public works, from time to time, and as often as there shall be any change in the rates of toll on any of said works, to furnish said board a schedule of such modified rates of toll, and shall use all legal powers which they may possess to obtain the establishment of rates of tolls, which may prevent an injurious competition with each other, to the detriment of the interests of the State, and so to adjust them as to promote the agriculture of the State; the said board of public works shall keep a journal of their proceedings, they shall hold regular sessions in the city of Annapolis, on the first Wednesday in January, the first Wednesday in April, the first Wednesday in July, and the first Wednesday in October in each year, and oftener if necessary, at which sessions they shall hear and determine such matters as affect the public works of the State, and the general assembly may confer upon them the power to decide; they shall at each regular session of the general assembly make a report to the general assembly and recommend such legislation as they shall deem necessary and requisite to promote or protect the interests of the State in the public works, and perform such other duties as may be hereafter prescribed by law; and a majority of them shall be competent to act. The governor, the comptroller of the treasury and the treasurer shall receive no additional salary for the services rendered as members of the board of public works."

This section is very long, and somewhat confused in expression. The committee recommend that it be modified, though not changed in substance, and that it be divided into two sections, which shall read as follows:

Sec. 1. The governor, the comptroller of the treasury, and the treasurer, shall constitute the board of public works in this State;

they shall keep a journal of their proceedings, and shall hold regular sessions in the city of Annapolis, on the first Wednesday of January, April, July and October in each year, and oftener if necessary, at which sessions they shall hear and determine such matters as affect the public works of the State, and as the general assembly may confer upon them the power to decide.

Sec. 2. They shall exercise a diligent and faithful supervision of all public works in which the State may be interested as stockholder or creditor, and shall appoint the directors in every railroad or canal company in which the State has the legal power to appoint directors, which said directors shall represent the State in all meetings of the stockholders of every railroad or canal company in which the State is a stockholder; they shall require the directors of all said public works, from time to time, and as often as there shall be any change in the rates of toll on any of said works to furnish said board of public works a schedule of such modified rates of toll, and shall use all legal powers which they may possess to obtain the establishment of rates of toll, which may prevent an injurious competition with each other, to the detriment of the interests of the State, and so to adjust them as to promote the agricultural interest of the State; they shall report to the general assembly at each regular session, and recommend such legislation as they shall deem necessary and requisite to promote or protect the interests of the State in the said public works; they shall perform such other duties as may be hereafter prescribed by law, and a majority of them shall be competent to act. The governor, comptroller and treasurer shall receive no additional salary for services rendered by them as members of the board of public works.

The next section relates to the commissioner of the land office. The committee recommend that the word "the" in the second line be inserted before the word "Tuesday." In the sixth line strike out the words "the first day of January next after his election," and insert "the first Monday in January ensuing his election." In the eighth line strike out the word "any" before the word "two." In the eighth, ninth and tenth lines, after the expression "shall direct a new election to be held by writs to the sheriffs of the several counties," add "and of the city of Baltimore." In the event of a tie between two or more candidates, the governor in ordering a new election will then issue writs not only to the sheriffs of the several counties, but also to the sheriff of Baltimore city, which is an important matter, as the election for a commissioner of the land office is by general ticket throughout the State. In the thirteenth and fourteenth lines after striking out the words "and shall be keeper of the chancery records," insert "and shall also be the keeper of the chancery records." In the seventeenth line strike out the words "the said commissioner of the land office," and insert the word "he" in place of them. At the end of the section add the following clause:

"In case of vacancy in land office by death, resignation, or other cause, the governor shall fill such vacancy until the next general election for members of the general assembly thereafter, when a commissioner of the land office shall be elected for the full term of six years ensuing."

The fourth section relates to the State librarian. The committee recommend that the words "the legislature" in the fourth line be stricken out, and in their place be inserted the words "and the general assembly." In the fifth line strike out the word "an" and substitute the word "any." Add the following clause at the end of the section: "In case of a vacancy in the office of State librarian from death, resignation or other cause, the governor shall fill such vacancy until the next meeting of the general assembly thereafter, and until a successor be elected and qualified."

The next section provides for the election of county commissioners; their compensation; their powers and their duties. As it stood after its adoption in convention it was enumerated as section four, instead of section five, and reads thus:

"The county commissioners shall be elected by general ticket by the voters of the several counties. An election for county commissioners shall be held on Tuesday next after the first Monday of November, 1865; as nearly one half as may be of said commissioners shall hold their office for two years, and the other half for four years, and at the first meeting after their election and qualification, or as soon thereafter as practicable, they shall determine by lot which of their number shall hold his office for two and four years respectively, and thereafter there shall be elected as aforesaid, at each general election for county officers, county commissioners for four years to fill the places of those whose term has expired; said commissioners shall exercise such powers and perform such duties only as the legislature may from time to time prescribe; but such powers and duties shall be similar, and the tenure of office uniform throughout the State, and the legislature shall have power to pass such laws as may be necessary for determining the number for each county, fixing the salary, and ascertaining and defining the powers, duties, and tenure of office of said commissioners, and the commissioners elected under this constitution shall have and exercise all the powers and duties in their respective counties, now exercised by the county commissioners under the laws of the State, and they shall receive the same salary, and their present number in the several counties shall remain the same until changed by law.

The committee recommend that this section be modified to read as follows:

Sec. 5. The county commissioners shall be elected, on general ticket, by the qualified voters of the several counties in this State; an election for county commissioners shall be held on the Tuesday next after the first Monday in the month of November, 1865, and as nearly one half as may be of said commissioners shall hold their office for two years, and the other half for four years; at the first meeting after their election and qualification or as soon thereafter as practicable the said commissioners shall determine by lot, which of their number shall hold office for two and four years respectively; and thereafter there shall be elected as aforesaid, at each general election for county officers, county commissioners for four years to fill the places of those whose term has expired. The said commissioners shall exercise such powers and perform such duties, which shall be similar throughout the State, as are now or may hereafter be prescribed by law. Their number in each county, and their compensation, their powers and duties, may at any time hereafter be changed and regulated by the general assembly.

The committee recommend that the seventh section of this article, which was the sixth as adopted in convention, be remodeled as hereinafter proposed. This section at the time of its being referred to the committee read thus:

"Sec. 7. The qualified voters of each county and the city of Baltimore shall, on Tuesday next after the first Monday of November, in the year eighteen hundred and sixty-five, and every two years thereafter, elect a surveyor for the counties and city of Baltimore respectively, whose duties and compensation shall be the same as are now prescribed by law for the county and city surveyors respectively, or as may hereafter be prescribed by law. The term of office of said county and city surveyors respectively shall commence on the first Monday of January next succeeding their election. And vacancies in said office of surveyors by death, resignation or removal from their respective counties or city shall be filled by the commissioners of the counties, or by the mayor and city council of Baltimore respectively, for the residue of the term thus made vacant."

This section, according to the proposed amendments of the committee, will read thus:

Sec. 7. The qualified voters of each county and of the city of Baltimore shall, on the Tuesday next after the first Monday in the month of November, in the year eighteen hundred and sixty-five, and every two years thereafter, elect a surveyor for the counties and the city of Baltimore respectively, whose term of office shall commence on the first Monday of January next ensuing their election, and whose duties and compensation shall be the same as are now or may hereafter be prescribed by law. Any vacancy in the office of surveyor shall be filled by the commissioners of the counties, or by the mayor and city council of Baltimore respectively, for the residue of the term.

In the eighth section of this article the committee recommend the following amendments:

Insert the word "the" before the word "Tuesday" in the first line. Strike out the word "prescribed" after the word "now" in the fifth line. Also the words "by death, resignation or removal from the county," in the eighth line, and the words "thus made vacant" in the tenth line.

This closes the report of the committee on the article "sundry officers."

GEORGE EARLE, Chairman.

All the recommendations of the committee of revision relating to the article on "sundry officers" were concurred in by the convention.

On motion of Mr. CHAMBERS,

The convention took a recess until half past 3 o'clock, P. M.

AFTERNOON SESSION.

The convention reassembled at half past 3 o'clock, P. M.

The roll was called, and the following members answered to their names:

Messrs. Goldsborough, President; Abbott, Annan, Audoun, Baker, Berry, of Baltimore county, Bond, Brooks, Brown, Carter, Crawford, Cunningham, Cushing, Dail, Daniel, Davis, of Charles, Dellinger, Dent, Duvall, Earle, Ecker, Farrow, Galloway, Greene, Hatch, Hebb, Hoffman, Hollyday, Horsey, Jones, of Cecil, Jones, of Somerset, Keefer, Kennard, Lansdale, Larsh, Lee, Markey, Mayhugh, Mitchell, Morgan, Mullikin, Murray, Negley, Parker, Parran, Purnell, Ridgely, Russell, Schley, Schlosser, Scott, Smith, of Dorchester, Sneary, Stirling, Stockbridge, Swope, Todd, Turner, Valliant, Wickard, Wilmer, Wooden—62.

ABSENT MEMBERS.

On motion of Mr. WICKARD,

It was ordered to be noted upon the journal that Dr. Hopkins left his seat in the hall on Wednesday afternoon on account of his wife's illness, and has been detained since on account of his own.

VOTE ON THE CONSTITUTION.

Mr. DAVIS, of Charles, submitted the following resolution:

Resolved, That it is the sense of this convention, that all constitutions framed by conventions, called by the voters of any State for that purpose subject to their ratification, ought to be submitted to the legal voters of such State for their ratification or rejection before such constitution or any part thereof should go into operation, and any attempt by a convention to adopt and put in force a constitution or any part thereof in violation of promises to the people, that the constitution to be framed should be submitted to them, would be a breach of faith, and any convention acting in such manner as above described ought to forfeit the confidence of the people

Which was read the first time.

PUBLICATION OF THE CONSTITUTION.

Mr. NEGLEY. I submit the following order:

Ordered, That the committee on publication be directed to have the constitution published in one or more newspapers in each county, and the city of Baltimore once a week for three successive weeks before the day of its ratification or rejection.

I really think that it is of the utmost importance that this convention should make provision for the publication of this constitution in the newspapers of the counties. I know from experience that it is utterly useless to have a large quantity of constitutions printed and sent to the counties for distribution. They will, just as certainly as anything in the world, never reach the destination designed for them, but will be allowed to lie around, and be used as wrapping paper by those in whose hands' they are left. The newspapers will not distribute them; there is no doubt about that. The proprietors of the county papers will not put them in their own papers, and distribute them in that way. If they are distributed at all, it must be in some other way; and if it is done in some other way it will not be done as it was before. Would it not be infinitely better to decrease the number to be printed in the way proposed by the order already adopted; say twenty thousand in the English language and five thousand in the German, and then have it published in the different papers in the counties? It would be gratifying to the editors of those papers, and would enlist them in behalf of the constitution. And I am certain this constitution will not reach the eyes and come to the observation of numbers of the people who get no papers at all except their country papers. You cannot reach them in any other way. I think this convention will be very remiss in bringing this constitution before the people, if they do not adopt this joint system of publication and distribution.

Perhaps I better withdraw this order for the present, and I will do so.

The order was accordingly withdrawn.

Mr. NEGLEY. I move to reconsider the order directing the printing of sixty thousand copies of the constitution. I do so for the purpose of submitting a motion to decrease the number.

The question being then taken upon the motion to reconsider, it was agreed to.

The question recurred upon agreeing to the order, which was as follows:

"*Ordered*, That the chair appoint a committee of three to contract with the Baltimore American or some other newspaper or newspapers, for the publication of the constitution entire in extra newspaper form, ten thousand copies in the German language and fifty thousand in the English, to be distributed as follows: two hundred copies to be furnished to each member of the convention, and the remainder to be equally distributed by said committee among the various county newspapers and postmasters who will promptly distribute the same among the people, the copies to be furnished by the contractor for printing the same within one week after the final adjournment of this convention."

Mr. NEGLEY. I move to amend the order by striking out the words "ten thousand" and inserting "five thousand;" also by striking out the words "fifty thousand" and inserting "twenty thousand."

Mr. STIRLING. I should like to have time to consider this matter. I think it will be a very good thing to make some provision for publishing the constitution in the newspapers. But even if we do that, I think we would do well to carry out the order we once adopted. For I think we can distribute the copies published in that way. There are some counties in which the county newspapers are hardly read at all. The gentleman from Worcester, over the way, remarked to me just now that so far as his county was concerned, the county newspapers have no circulation at all, and all the distribution the constitution will get in his county, would be in the way provided by this order. There are some counties in which there are no newspapers at all. I should like to hear first what is to be the expense of publishing these sixty thousand copies.

The PRESIDENT. The president thinks it would cost a great deal.

Mr. JONES, of Somerset. I think that perhaps two hundred dollars a paper would cover all the expense in the counties.

Mr. STIRLING. I was asking what would be the expense of publishing these sixty thousand copies under the order as we adopted it; not in regard to the newspapers.

Mr. STOCKBRIDGE. I had hoped that this matter would not be called up until to-morrow, by which time I hope to be able to give some definite statement as to the cost of this publication. I made repeated efforts on last Saturday to obtain an estimate, but was unsuccessful. I wrote this morning about it, and I presume the return mail of to-night will bring some reply. At this time I am entirely in the dark in regard to the matter.

On motion of Mr. NEGLEY,

The further consideration of this subject was postponed until to-morrow.

BOUND COPIES OF THE CONSTITUTION.

The convention then resumed the consideration of the following order from the committee on reporting and printing:

"*Ordered*, That the comptroller of the treasury be authorized, and is hereby directed to contract with Mr. Richard P. Bayly, of Annapolis, printer to the convention, for the printing and binding of five hundred copies of the constitution when adopted by the people of Maryland; said copies to be printed in the same style, on such quality of paper, and bound in like manner to the edition of the present constitution, published by Murphy & Co., of Baltimore, in 1855."

The pending question was upon the amendment of Mr. GREENE, to strike out all after the word "ordered," and insert the following:

"That the State librarian be and he is hereby directed to purchase of James Wingate three hundred copies of the constitution passed by this convention, when adopted by the voters of this State; said constitution shall contain an elaborate index, prepared with references to articles and sections, and also to the page; said constitution shall be printed in the best style, (with side notes,) on fair white paper with large fair type and well bound, and shall contain the names of the members of this convention; said constitution shall contain the certificate of the clerk of the court of appeals, that it is a true copy of the constitution passed by this convention; and the indexing and publication of said constitution shall be approved by the president of this convention; and the State librarian shall distribute said copies of the constitution, as follows: One copy to each member of convention; to the governor, lieutenant governor, comptroller, treasurer, attorney general, adjutant general, superintendent of public education, and commissioner of the land office, each one copy; to the judges and clerks of the circuit courts, and the courts of Baltimore city, each one copy; to the judges and the clerk of the court of appeals, each one copy; to the orphans' courts of the State, each one copy; to the State's attorneys, each one copy; to the register of wills, each one copy; to the boards of county commissioners, each one copy; to the mayor of Baltimore city, one copy; and fifty copies to the governor for distribution to the governors of the several States; and the remaining eleven copies shall be retained in the State library, subject to the disposition of the general assembly; and the president of this convention is hereby authorized and directed to pay James Wingate one hundred dollars, for preparing said carefully elaborated index and side notes to said constitution, and also two dollars per copy for said constitution, when published by James Wingate."

Mr. AUDOUN. I desire to state for the information of the house that the committee on printing have already made provision for the indexing of the constitution by Mr. Moore, who has contracted to prepare an index for the debates, proceeding, and constitution. I therefore can see no necessity for paying one hundred dollars to some one else for doing the same work. Mr. Moore is compelled under his contract to do the indexing of the constitution. We have already voted an extra sum to Mr. Moore for doing this work, and I see no necessity of paying one hundred dollars, as proposed by the gentleman from Allegany (Mr. Greene) to some one else to do the same work.

Mr. GREENE. My proposition is not merely to make an index. It contemplates a careful and elaborate index prepared with reference to articles and sections, and also complete and carefully prepared marginal notes and references. That certainly is not embraced in the contract with Mr. Moore.

Mr. AUDOUN. The very same thing precisely. The committee would not make a contract with the party unless he contracted to do the entire work. They do not propose to have it half done, or that the convention shall pay an extra sum to some one else to do the very work they have already contracted to have done. We have already agreed to pay for that work, and expect it will be done in good style, and will see that it is done. There is no necessity to pay any one else to do that work.

Mr. VALLIANT. There is one thing perhaps which the convention ought to know; and that is, that the regular printer of the convention proposes to print an edition precisely similar to the edition published by Murphy & Co., of Baltimore city, in 1855. A specimen copy was before the convention this morning. The proposition is to have it printed on precisely the same kind of paper, and if in the judgment of the comptroller and the convention it is desired, he proposes to use the same kind of type, and have it bound in the same manner. We stated to Mr. Bayly, it may be well enough to say, that it had been proposed to the convention that these copies should not cost more than two dollars each. And we asked him if he could make it less expensive to the State by getting up this work at less cost. He made an estimate and then said he would guarantee that they should not cost over one dollar and ninety cents each, how much less I do not know. I felt it my duty to state this fact to the convention, to assist them in making up their judgment. I have the kindest feelings in the world towards the reporter of the Baltimore Sun (Mr. Wingate,) but think this proposition of the committee is better for the State.

Mr. WICKARD. I would like to know how

it is that Mr. Wingate can come into this convention and propose work for himself, and afterwards get propositions offered as substitutes for the action of a committee of this body?

Mr. GREENE. So far as the remarks of my colleague (Mr. Wickard) refer to me, all I have to say is that I do not recognize his right to catechise me in any shape whatever as to my action.

The question was upon agreeing to the substitute proposed by Mr. GREENE.

Upon this question Mr. THOMAS called for the yeas and nays, which were ordered.

The question was then taken by yeas and nays, and resulted—yeas 24, nays 32—as follows:

Yeas—Messrs. Berry, of Baltimore county, Bond, Brown, Chambers, Crawford, Dail, Daniel, Dent, Duvall, Greene, Hebb, Hoffman, Hollyday, Jones, of Somerset, Lansdale, Lee, Mitchell, Morgan, Parran, Ridgely, Schley, Scott, Stirling, Turner—24.

Nays—Messrs. Abbott, Annon, Audoun, Baker, Carter, Cunningham, Cushing, Dellinger, Farrow, Galloway, Hatch, Horsey, Jones, of Cecil, Keefer, Kennard, King, Larsh, Mayhugh, Mullikin, Murray, Negley, Parker, Purnell, Russell, Schlosser, Sneary, Swope, Thomas, Todd, Valliant, Wickard, Wooden—32.

The substitute was accordingly rejected.

Mr. STOCKBRIDGE, when his name was called, said: If I understand this matter aright the proposition of the gentleman from Allegany (Mr. Greene) was before the convention, and was referred to the committee on printing.—That committee have reported a substitute for that proposition, and we are now voting upon the order of the gentleman from Allegany (Mr. Greene.)

Mr. AUDOUN. I can explain this matter so that the gentleman can understand it exactly.

Mr. STOCKBRIDGE. Well, I will not vote.

The CHAIRMAN (Mr. Purnell.) Does the gentleman ask to be excused from voting?

Mr. STOCKBRIDGE. I asked information from the chair, and did not get it.

The CHAIRMAN. The gentleman from Baltimore city (Mr. Audoun) being a member of the committee, proposed to give the information.

Mr. AUDOUN. I am perfectly willing the chair should give it, if my colleague (Mr. Stockbridge) refuses to receive it from the committee on printing.

The CHAIRMAN. Does the gentleman ask to be excused from voting?

Mr. STOCKBRIDGE. Yes, sir; I do not understand the question.

The question was then taken upon excusing Mr. STOCKBRIDGE from voting, and the convention refused to excuse him.

Mr. STOCKBRIDGE. I will not vote in this convention upon any measure in regard to which I do not know how to vote. I decline voting, and it may be so entered upon the journal, if any gentleman wishes.

It was accordingly ordered to be entered upon the journal that Mr. STOCKBRIDGE refused to vote upon the question under consideration.

The question recurred upon agreeing to the order reported by the committee on reporting and printing.

Mr. THOMAS. I desire to offer as an amendment that portion of the order of the gentleman from Allegany (Mr. Greene,) which is in relation to the distribution of these constitutions.

Mr. GREENE. I have an amendment to offer to define the character of the publications, and I shall take it from the description in the order which I offered. My only object is to secure a handsome and well printed edition of the constitution.

Mr. THOMAS. My amendment can come in after that proposed by the gentleman from Allegany (Mr. Greene) has been acted upon.

Mr. GREENE. I move to strike out all after the words "when adopted by the people of Maryland," and insert the following:

"The said constitution shall contain an elaborate index, prepared with reference to articles and sections, and also to the page.—The said constitution shall be printed in the best style, (with side notes,) on fair, white paper, with large, fair type, and well bound, and shall contain the names of the members of this convention, and a certificate of the clerk of the court of appeals that it is a true copy of the constitution passed by this convention; and the cost shall not exceed two dollars per copy."

Mr. VALLIANT. I have no objection to that.

Mr. THOMAS. I move to amend the amendment by adding to it the following:

"And the State librarian shall distribute said copies of the constitution as follows:

"One copy to each member of the convention; to the governor, lieutenant governor, comptroller, treasurer, attorney general, adjutant general, superintendent of public education, and commissioner of the land office, each one copy; to the judges and clerks of the circuit courts and the courts of Baltimore city, each one copy; to the judges and the clerk of the court of appeals, each one copy; to the orphans' courts of the State, each one copy; to the State's attorneys, each one copy; to the register of wills, each one copy; to the boards of county commissioners, each one copy; to the mayor of Baltimore city, one copy, and fifty copies to the governor for distribution among the governors of the several States.

"And the remaining copies shall be retained in the State library, subject to the disposition of the general assembly."

Mr. GREENE. I will accept the amendment.

The question was then taken upon the amendment as modified, and it was adopted.

The order reported by the committee, as amended by the convention, was then adopted.

PER DIEM OF THE PRESIDENT.

Mr. RIDGELY. I offer the following:

"*Ordered*, That the president of this convention be allowed a per diem of seven dollars, and that the committee on accounts audit his account accordingly."

I have only to say that it is customary with every deliberative body to make an additional allowance to its presiding officer, in view of the extraordinary labors which that officer has to perform. It was done in the last convention, and I believe has been the custom of every deliberative body.

Mr. HEBB. I would state in regard to this order that I would vote for it very cheerfully, but there was a motion made in the house of delegates when the convention bill was pending, to make the *per diem* of the president of the convention six dollars a day, and it was voted down.

Mr. JONES, of Somerset. There is nothing in the convention bill that fixes the *per diem* of the president; that matter was left to the convention. I second the proposition of the gentleman from Baltimore county (Mr. Ridgely.)

Mr. DELLINGER. If it be in order, I move to postpone this order until to-morrow. I will perhaps then offer an amendment to it, if the committee on accounts refuse to allow the amount which the convention this morning ordered it to allow.

The CHAIRMAN (Mr. Purnell) stated the question to be upon the motion to postpone until to-morrow.

Mr. RIDGELY. I will state that it is uniformly the rule in every deliberative body to make an extra allowance to its presiding officer; and it does not depend upon any other contingency. This house surely will not undertake to connect with this proposition any independent matter that has no relation to it whatever. I trust the house will act upon this proposition as it stands, and decide it upon its own merits. When the other proposition comes up the gentleman will find that I will be a friend to it, and will advocate it, believing as I do that it is founded in justice, in equity, and in right. But I desire this proposition to be considered independently, and so acted upon by the house.

Mr. DELLINGER. I will withdraw the motion to postpone. I am one of those who believe that the legislature have no power under the constitution to fix the per diem of members of this convention. I believe it is perfectly competent for this convention to fix the per diem of its own members, and to say what their services are worth, and what they shall receive. Being under that impression, I shall vote for this as an independent proposition, to allow the president this additional compensation. But I think it more proper that this matter should be referred to the committee on accounts, and I therefore make that motion. Let this proposition, as well as the claim which members of this body make for their services here, go together to the committee on accounts.

Mr. JONES, of Somerset. The committee on accounts can do nothing in the world with this matter. They have no power to fix the compensation of the presiding officer.

Mr. RIDGELY. This is a proposition to instruct the committee on accounts, in auditing the accounts of the president of this convention, to conform to the suggestion of allowing him seven dollars a day. Now what purpose is to be served by referring this to the committee on accounts? If the house do not desire to give those instructions they can vote it down. Its reference to the committee on accounts will accomplish no purpose whatever, because it will go to them without any instructions from the house. It will therefore be idle legislation to refer this proposition to the committee on accounts. If the house is disinclined to vote that amount, it would be infinitely better to vote down the proposition But I trust they will not do so.

Mr. DANIEL. I should have less difficulty in voting for this proposition, if this question, as has been stated, had not come directly before the legislature, which voted down a proposition to give the president an increase of per diem.

Mr. RIDGELY. What has the legislature to do with it?

Mr. DANIEL. Upon the theory that the gentleman and I adopt—for I have agreed with him on that theory in regard to the powers of this convention—we have adopted the theory that this convention is bound by the provisions of the act of the legislature which called us into being, so far as those provisions are applicable, and the legislature having fixed the compensation at five dollars a day, I cannot vote for more. Now if I assumed the theory that this convention was not bound by that act, that we had a right to make our own rules and regulations, and to determine upon all these questions, I should vote for this proposition with great pleasure, because then I should believe this convention had the power to do it. But having adopted the other theory, that so far as the convention act is applicable it does bind the convention, and that act having received a construction by the legislature, they having voted down a proposition to increase the per diem of the president, I cannot vote for it.—I will say at the same time that there is no gentleman here who has a higher regard and respect for the able manner in which the chair has discharged his duties, and for him personally, and in every other way, than I have.

Mr. DELLINGER withdrew the motion to refer to the committee on accounts.

The question was upon adopting the order.

Mr. RIDGELY. I ask leave to amend this order. I have been mistaken in the amount of per diem named. I had supposed that the present constitution provided an extra compensation of two dollars per day for the speaker of the house of delegates; but upon examination I find it allows but one dollar a day additional. I therefore ask leave to strike out "seven dollars" and insert "six dollars."

No objection was made, and the order was modified accordingly.

Mr. STIRLING. The act of assembly says: "and the said convention shall have power to appoint such clerks and other officers as they may deem necessary to facilitate the transaction of the business of the convention, and to fix their compensation." Now I submit that the president of this convention is an officer of this convention. I find that the same interpretation was put upon the act of 1849 by the convention of 1850, and a precisely similar order adopted. The bill under which that convention was called fixed the per diem at four dollars. That convention, acting under precisely the same authority that we are acting under, under a bill of precisely the same language in this respect, passed an order granting the president of that convention two dollars additional per diem, as an officer of the convention distinct from a member.

ONE HUNDRED DOLLARS EXTRA MILEAGE.

Mr. LEE moved to amend the order by adding the following:

"And that the committee on accounts be hereby instructed to audit the mileage account of each member of this convention according to the joint resolution of the general assembly of this State at its last session, adjusting the mileage of the members of that body."

Mr. ABBOTT. I move to lay that amendment on the table.

The CHAIRMAN (Mr. Purnell.) That carries the whole subject with it.

Mr. ABBOTT. Then I withdraw the motion.

Mr. DANIEL. I hope this matter will be acted upon now. We voted upon this matter the other day, and voted it down by a very large majority, so large that a motion was made and adopted to withdraw the proposition and have no mention made of it on the journal. I understand now that it is proposed by the committee on accounts to allow this extra mileage. I do think that before they allow it, it ought to be determined by the house. The committee on accounts I know are in difficulty and trouble about this matter, and I think it is a proper thing for the house to determine. For one I do not think any member is entitled to it any more than I think the members of the last legislature were. Therefore I shall vote against it. But I think the house ought to pass upon it now, and relieve the committee on accounts from all further trouble in regard to the matter.

Mr. NEGLEY. I move that the whole subject be referred to the committee on accounts, with instructions to inquire into the law and report accordingly.

Mr. MILLER. The amendment that has been offered, and is now before the house, is simply carrying out, as I conceive, the provisions of the law as it now stands. With the propriety or impropriety of the action of the last legislature this body has nothing in the world to do. The convention bill under which we are assembled, and which declares that the per diem of members of this body shall be five dollars, and the mileage shall be the same that is fixed by law, is the law to guide us in this matter. Our per diem is fixed absolutely at five dollars. To what law are we to go to ascertain what is our mileage? What has been done in reference to mileage? Mileage has been a matter of legislative determination from the time the legislature was first established in this State, and has been changed from time to time from then till the present. In early times, when railroad facilities for travel and communication were wanting, mileage was allowed at a certain rate. It has been modified from time to time, by acts of the legislature, down to 1864, when the legislature by joint resolution raised the mileage for considerations set forth in the preamble. That joint resolution is just as much a law as if it had been passed under the words "Be it enacted by the general assembly of Maryland." That joint resolution was passed in just the same way as every other law was passed. And then comes in the convention bill, which says that we shall receive the mileage allowed by law.

Mr. JONES, of Somerset. It says "the mileage allowed to members of the general assembly of this State."

Mr. MILLER. Exactly; and the law, in the shape of a joint resolution, says that there shall be allowed as mileage to members of the general assembly so much. Therefore it is the law which allows mileage to the general assembly, and we are covered by that law. If we are going to do as they did in the long parliament, pass a self-denying ordinance, and make ourselves out to be great patriots by not taking what the law allows us, then let us take that ground at once. But will we say that the legislature has not fixed the mileage that we are to receive? or shall we say, under that law, that we are not worthy to receive it, and we will deny ourselves and will not take it? It seems to me that standing upon the matter of law, this is the true construction, and no other construction can be put upon it. As I understand, the amendment offered by the gentleman from Queen Anne (Mr. Lee) has been offered for the purpose of relieving the committee on accounts from all doubt. That doubt it seems to me is removed by the act of assembly. As some gentlemen have requested it, I will read the reasons for passing that joint resolution:

"The committee on accounts, to which was referred an order of the house of the second day of March, 1864, instructing them to readjust the mileage of the members of the general assembly."

They were instructed to readjust it, to fix it as a readjustment of the mileage, which it was perfectly within the power of the legislature to do.

"——respectfully report, that the constitution of Maryland provides that the members of the general assembly, shall receive a per diem of four dollars, and such mileage as may be allowed by law. This constitutional provision seems to justify the conclusion that, while the per diem of members is fixed unchangeably, their mileage is left to be adjusted according to the varying circumstances which might arise. The committee having in view the unprecedented condition of the currency of the country, and the greatly enhanced cost of travel and living in consequence thereof, have deemed it just and right to provide as near as may be for equalizing the compensation of members with that of previous legislatures."——

That is the ground upon which they put it. It is an equalizing of the compensation of members with that of previous legislatures.—And nobody can doubt that four dollars a day ten years ago is infinitely superior to five dollars a day now.

"——and therefore, respectfully recommend the adoption of the following joint resolution:

"*Resolved by the general assembly of Maryland,* That the sum of one hundred dollars, in addition to their usual mileage, be paid to each of the senators and delegates of the general assembly."

Then our convention bill comes in and says, we shall receive the same mileage as members of the general assembly. Is not this joint resolution the law for our guidance? I ask lawyers of this convention to say whether that is so or not. Personally, I do not care whether the hundred dollars comes to me or not; I do not care a straw about it. But I say that the law is clear upon that subject.

Mr. STOCKBRIDGE. From the determined assurance with which the gentleman who has just taken his seat (Mr. Miller) has spoken, one would suppose that this whole matter of mileage had been arranged by law upon some fixed principle in this State, time out of mind. He said it was regulated by act of assembly, which had been modified from time to time.—Now I suppose, as a lawyer, that statement would have been entitled to much more weight if he had referred to the acts of assembly by which mileage has been regulated and modified from time to time. But I say it would have been no easy task for him, or any other gentleman, to have produced any such authority.

The earliest reference to mileage which I find upon the statute books of Maryland, is in 1796, chapter 41, which fixes the per diem of members at four dollars, and then at the close simply says "besides the accustomed itinerant charges and ferriage" That is the earliest act of assembly upon the subject which I have been able to find. In 1811 there was an increase of fifty cents a day made to the per diem. It was so construed, although the words "per day" were left out, simply providing that members of the general assembly, should have an additional fifty cents. The same phraseology is used there in reference to mileage, "the accustomed itinerant charges and ferriage." I find no other modifications or changes. So far as I have been able to discover, it stood so until the adoption of the constitution of 1850. What does that constitution say upon the subject?

"The senators and delegates shall receive a per diem of four dollars, and such mileage as may be allowed by law."

That is all with reference to their pay. "A per diem of four dollars, and such mileage as may be allowed by law." What the per diem is everybody understands; it is a rate of four dollars a day. Now what is mileage? Worcester says—and Webster uses precisely the same language—"*Mileage:* Fees paid for travel by the mile." That is mileage. It is competent for the members of the general assembly to receive four dollars a day, and a certain allowance, fixed by law, as "fees for travel by the mile." There has been no modification of the law on the subject of mileage since the constitution of 1850 was adopted. It is not in the power of the general assembly to vary their per diem, for that is fixed by the constitution. But a desire having been felt to receive some compensation, or some money out of the State treasury, beyond "the four dollars per diem, and the amount of fees for travel by the mile which was fixed by law," a very innocent looking order was introduced:

"*Ordered,* That the committee on accounts readjust the mileage of members."

A readjustment of the mileage could be but one of two things: a re-regulation of the number of miles travelled, to conform to the change of roads, or the mode of communication; or an increase or decrease of the amount allowed for travel. Did the general assembly attempt to do either? I say, and I ask the attention of the convention to this one thing—they did neither the one nor the other. They did not touch, or attempt to touch, the mileage of members; they did not assume to do it. But they wanted to appropriate a certain amount. They could not appropriate a hundred dollars under the head of per diem, because the constitution fixed how much per diem they were to receive. They could not appropriate a hundred dollars under the head of mileage, because travelling such unequal distances, it would have led to so great confusion that it would have amounted to an impossibility to arrange it.

What then did they do? They say they make an effort to equalize the compensation of members with that of previous legislatures. They do not propose to affect in the slightest the amount allowed for travel by the mile; but they propose to equalize the compensation of members with that of previous legislatures. And how do they propose to do that?

"*Resolved by the general assembly of Maryland*, That the sum of one hundred dollars, in addition to their usual mileage, be paid to each of the senators and delegates of the general assembly."

Paid as what? As additional compensation? As additional mileage? As arbitrary mileage? They do not say any such thing as that. Why do they not say—"paid as an addition to their per diem?" Because it might have seemed to some of them that that would look too much like running in the face of the constitution. Nor do they say, "allowed as additional mileage." They do not bring it under either head. But they say "in addition to their usual mileage." It is not mileage; not a rate of compensation for travel by the mile, which is the definition of mileage. It is an arbitrary matter, as gentlemen will see at once upon reflection.

Is this hundred dollars mileage? Suppose, for example, that there is a case of contested election before the house of delegates, and witnesses are brought here to testify. So far as I know, witnesses are allowed mileage the same as members of the general assembly. That is to say, the same compensation for travel rated by the mile. If this hundred dollars bonus is mileage, then witnesses, on the same principle, would be allowed this hundred dollars as well as members of the general assembly. But the hundred dollars was not allowed to the witnesses before the last general assembly, and their name was legion.

But this hundred dollars was a bonus granted to members, and by nearly the same vote to all the officers of that general assembly, whether they resided in Annapolis, Baltimore city, Allegany county, or upon the eastern shore, this hundred dollars was allowed to each one as a bonus, not as mileage. It is upon that point that this whole thing may turn. For if that hundred dollars be not mileage, then it is not allowed to the members of this convention, under this convention bill, which allows only two things, per diem and mileage. If it be mileage, then I will thank any gentleman on the floor of this convention to tell me what is the rate of "fees for travel by the mile" fixed by law for members of the general assembly and of this convention. Is there any rate that can be specified? It is possible to find out these things somehow. And what is the rate per mile, if this hundred dollars bonus is mileage?

Heretofore mileage has always been adjusted by a fixed rule. The rate per mile is ten times as much for one hundred miles as it is for ten miles, and cannot be anything else. If it is mileage it must be that. And a member of this convention, or a member of the general assembly who lives in Allegany county is entitled to very different mileage from that allowed to the man who lives in Anne Arundel county or Baltimore city.

I say, then, that this is not mileage. And if the convention chooses to vote to themselves such compensation as that, let them vote it straight out, just what the thing is. Let us not try to deceive ourselves or others by calling that mileage, which is not mileage; let us call it what it really is. I am not here to argue the question of the justice or injustice, propriety or impropriety of the matter. But let us call things by their right names. If it is mileage, let us know how much we are to have per mile. If it is not mileage, then let us call it a bonus, or anything else that men may choose to call it. But I insist it is not mileage, as contemplated by this act. How can it be? All money paid out of the treasury of the State must be under appropriations by law. The general assembly in calling this convention made their appropriation, and told at what rate it should be allowed. But I will not trespass further upon the convention.

Mr. DANIEL. I have a remark or two to make in addition to what my colleague (Mr. Stockbridge) has said. In the first place, it was not carrying out the principle embraced in the order of the general assembly to their committee on accounts, which was to readjust the mileage. It ought to have been upon some principle, and if upon any principle, then surely the gentleman living in Anne Arundel county, or in Annapolis, or in the city of Baltimore, is not entitled to the same mileage as the gentleman from Allegany county. And yet under the pretence of mileage every member, those living in Annapolis and Baltimore city as well as those in Allegany and Worcester, received the same amount of additional compensation; each received the hundred dollars.

Now if the mileage is to be readjusted, let it be adjusted according to principle. And if you do that, then the members from Worcester and Allegany ought to receive more than the members from Anne Arundel county or Baltimore city, according to the difference in the distance they live from this place. But it is contrary to any principle to call this hundred dollars mileage, or to take it as mileage.

And in reply to the gentleman from Anne Arundel (Mr. Miller) who says that if we do not take it we adjudge ourselves to be not as worthy as members of the legislature, I say that if the convention adopts this order, it will adjudge itself very unworthy. I hope we are not so unworthy as to take it.

Another point which I wish to state is just this: It is a rule of construction that where there is a doubt as to what a law means, you must arrive, if you can, at the intention of the law-makers; and that intention, if it can be clearly arrived at, will aid you in construing the law. Now when the bill was passed calling this convention together, the joint resolution in relation to mileage had not been passed by the general assembly. The convention bill was passed on the 3d of February, 1864. That bill says that the members of the convention should receive the same per diem as members of the general assembly. Up to that time no member of the legislature had ever received " one hundred dollars, in addition to his usual mileage." The joint resolution in relation to mileage was passed on the 9th of March, 1864, more than a month after the convention bill had been passed. Now, will it be said that the legislature intended the members of this convention to receive this additional hundred dollars, when that thing had never been heard of when the convention bill was passed? How could they have contemplated any such thing? They said that the members of the convention should receive the same mileage that had always been allowed and received up to that time. It is clear to my mind, that they did not intend, when they passed the convention bill, for us to have this hundred dollars; and that if we take it, we take it without any real principle to justify us in doing so. As my colleague (Mr. Stockbridge) says, if we are going to take it, let us take it as a bonus, or extra compensation, or something of that kind; let us call it by its right name, and take it upon the theory adopted by same members of this convention, that we are not bound by the convention bill at all. Do not let us do in a roundabout way that which we would not do directly.

Mr. Ridgely. This subject has taken a most extraordinary turn. The gentleman from Baltimore city (Mr. Daniel) has referred to the proceedings which took place in the general assembly at the time of the passage of those two propositions—the convention bill and joint resolution number four. As I understand him, he has invoked those proceedings as furnishing a key for unlocking the meaning of this law. If I have understood him correctly, then this is the first time that I have ever in my life heard that the transactions which took place in a legislative body could be invoked as a means of interpreting the meaning of a statute. You might as well call the members of the legislature into a court of justice, and ask them to testify upon the witness stand as to their intention and their purpose when they voted for any particular law, as to invoke them under circumstances of this kind. When we are called upon to expound a statute, we are to take its contents and to arrive at the meaning of the law from the statute itself, and not go behind the statute into the proceedings of the legislature for lights by which we are to be guided in reaching the true meaning of the contents of the statute.

We cannot go behind the law. That law I hold in my hand, and in my judgment it is clear of all ambiguity in its context. What are its words?

" And said convention shall have full power and authority to determine on the validity of the election and qualification of its members; and the compensation of the delegates to said convention shall be five dollars per day, and the mileage allowed to the members of the general assembly of this State."

They do not call it "bonus." They do not call it by any other name than its proper name—"and the mileage allowed to the members of the general assembly of this State." What general assembly? Any particular general assembly? The general assembly of last year, or year before last, or four or five years before?

Mr. Miller. Not "as is now allowed," but as "is allowed to members of the general assembly."

Mr. Ridgely. Yes, sir. Can there be any ambiguity about the phraseology of that law? True, I concede to the gentleman from Baltimore city (Mr. Daniel) that you are to look to the intention of the legislature. But you are to look to the text of the law from which to gather that intention of the legislature. Did the legislature mean to convey the idea that this was to be received as a bonus—as a compensation in the form of extra per diem? On the contrary, the phraseology used shows that it was to be received as mileage. As mileage in what connection? As mileage in connection with the mileage which was to be received by members of the general assembly, and the legislature received the mileage prescribed in resolution number four. What is that resolution?

"*Resolved by the general assembly of Maryland*, That the sum of one hundred dollars, in addition to their usual mileage, be paid to each of the senators and delegates of the general assembly."

Not in addition to their per diem—not in addition to any other compensation which shall be received by that body. But it was in connection with the word " mileage." It was to be received "in addition to their usual mileage." It will be in vain for honorable gentlemen to seek to bring in here lexicographers and dictionaries with which to determine the meaning of the word "mileage." It has a very wide and comprehensive meaning. If we take the meaning adopted by the general government heretofore, we will find "mileage" to be a very different thing from what gentlemen would confine it to here.

I hold, upon theories which I advanced here the other day, and which I regard as still stronger than the theories derived from the law itself, that this law is the fundamental law. It is fixed by the people who have prescribed what your compensation is to be, and you cannot go behind their verdict. They have said that you shall receive the mileage allowed to members of the general assembly of this State. It is a right which belongs to members of this body, and I trust there will be no extraordinary fastidiousness of conscience upon the subject. If there are gentlemen here who do not feel that they can conscientiously take this money, then I hope they will not take it; and I trust they will make no mistakes when they come to settle up their mileage accounts. It is perfectly easy for them to adjust those accounts without mistakes. For my part, I feel that I am asking no favor—that I am receiving no gratuity—that I am receiving nothing at the hands of this body but what my constituents and the great body of the people voted to me, and if it is withheld by a vote of this house, it is withheld under a mistaken sense of duty.

Mr. Ecker. It is rather presumption in me, I know, to get up here and say one word after the very able argument of the gentleman from Baltimore county (Mr. Ridgely.) That gentleman says this hundred dollars was received in addition to their mileage.

Mr. Miller. In addition to their usual mileage.

Mr. Ecker. Every man got a hundred dollars besides his mileage. I got one hundred and twenty-four dollars. But according to the construction of the gentleman, I should have taken the twenty-four from the hundred dollars and received seventy-six dollars. If they had adjusted the mileage in that kind of style, taken the usual mileage from the hundred dollars, how would it have worked? We had a very worthy friend from Anne Arundel county, who resided in the city of Annapolis. He would have got his hundred dollars straight out, because he had no mileage to deduct from it, while the members from Allegany and Worcester and Washington and Somerset, would have got their one hundred dollars, with their mileage off.

Now this whole thing is nothing more nor less than a raid upon the State treasury. When I reached home last Saturday morning, my friends asked me, when we were going to adjourn? I said, "We have got all through, except stitching the pieces together, and making a book of it"—and then I added in a joking way—"No, there is forty thousand dollars of the appropriation left yet, and we are going back to distribute that on Monday and Tuesday next." Now, from indications here, I am beginning to be afraid that what I said as a joke will turn out to be the fact. I should be very sorry to have my words prove true. I therefore move that we adjourn.

The motion to adjourn was not seconded.

Mr. Bond. The mileage now claimed under the amendment of the gentleman from Queen Anne (Mr. Lee,) is claimed as a matter of law, as an absolute right of members of this convention, under the existing law of this State. It seems to me that there are one or two lawyers here who differ from that opinion. Yet the other lawyers are of the opinion that this claim is right according to the law. Now, if it be that there is a doubt as to whether this be the law or not, then I say there are circumstances now existing which ought to give that doubt in favor of those claiming this mileage.

What is the state of the case now as compared with the state of the case when this resolution number four was passed? On that day—and I have looked at the record for the purpose of ascertaining that fact—gold was at a premium of 67½—now it is 1.50 per cent. premium. And if the reason then given for increasing the mileage was a good one, how much stronger is the argument now? In point of fact five dollars a day now is very little more than two dollars a day in coin; and yet that is the rate at which we are now being paid. It is for this reason that I say that if there be any doubt about the matter at all—though I do not think there is any—if there be any doubt at all upon the question of the law, it should be given in favor of the claimants.

But this question, according to my judgment, has been settled; and I confess I have had but little experience in the construction of statutes. The legislature undertook to adjust—what? To adjust the mileage to which members were entitled. Was it necessary that, according to my friend from Baltimore city (Mr. Stockbridge,) they should have descended to count the number of miles that each member lived away from here, and say that he was entitled to so much mileage? No, sir. They had the right to give the gross sum if they chose. They did give it—whether rightfully or wrongfully as regards the different members it is not for us to inquire. The matter of adjusting the mileage was referred to the committee on accounts. They did adjust the mileage, and under that adjustment they awarded one hundred dollars to each member of the legislature. Then came the law calling this convention together, which says, that in addition to the five dollars per diem, the members of the convention should be entitled to the mileage allowed to members of the general assembly. Nothing to my mind can be clearer than that is, in regard to the law of this matter.

But suppose we take another view of this matter. Suppose we say (and that is my doctrine) that this body represents the sovereign power of the State—that it is bound by no legislative act whatever. Then what is the condition of things? If we are left to fix our own compensation, is it too much to say that one hundred dollars, in addition to the five dollars a day should be allowed?—making it, perhaps, not more than three dollars a day in gold.

I contend, therefore, that in every view of the case, both as a matter of law, and as a matter of justice, this amendment should be adopted. There is nothing in it that I can see except a squeamishness of the conscience of a few gentlemen here to prevent the adoption of this amendment. If there are any such, then let them refuse to take the money. I shall not refuse to take it.

Mr. STOCKBRIDGE. When this matter was before the convention last Friday ——

Mr. LANSDALE. The gentleman is out of order; he has already spoken twice.

Mr. ABBOTT. The gentleman (Mr. Stockbridge) was a member of the last legislature, which passed this mileage resolution, as it is called. I understood him the other day to say that he received the hundred dollars. Now I would like to ask him this question; suppose this constitution is not adopted by the people, and he comes back here to the next legislature; would he not receive this hundred dollars again without another act of the legislature?

Mr. STOCKBRIDGE. I will remark, in answer to that question, that these personal arguments which we have so much of in cases like these, amount to nothing in my opinion. They are very good to turn a laugh sometimes, but really they are not arguments at all. In answer, however, to the question whether this resolution of the last general assembly creates a mileage of eight or ten cents a mile, or whatever rate it may be, and the one hundred dollars in addition for the members of all succeeding legislatures; I will say that no proposition can be clearer to my mind that the hundred dollars under that resolution cannot be allowed to the members of any subsequent legislature, if the constitution we are now framing be not adopted. I do not believe it is a law of the State, in default of our making a constitution which the people accepts. Upon its face it does not pretend to call it mileage. It does not say "the sum of one hundred dollars additional mileage," or "mileage in addition to that which has heretofore been allowed." As they say in their report, it was an effort to equalize the compensation of members with that of previous legislatures.

Now there were two or three ways of doing that. One was to raise the per diem; but the constitution stood in the way of that. Then they could increase the mileage, giving to each member in the State an additional amount of "fees for travel by the mile." But that would not do, for the simple reason that all the increase would go to the members who came from the greatest distance, and there would be no increase of compensation to those who lived near by. Therefore, it would not do to call it "mileage." They accordingly ordered that the round sum of one hundred dollars be paid to each member. That is what it reads. It does not say "one hundred dollars more mileage than usual," because they cannot deceive themselves into the idea that they are receiving more mileage.

The thing is just here; if this be the law of the State regulating the matter of mileage, then there is no necessity for this convention to do anything. Because if it be the law then the committee on accounts of this convention are bound by it; the comptroller is bound by it; the law officers and the disbursing officers of the State are bound by it. If it be the law of the State, then they will obey it, and there is no necessity for us to do anything; they are under a sworn obligation to obey the law. And therefore if it be the law, I say it is unnecessary for us to act in the matter. If it be not the law, then the question arises whether we will make it so. On that point, I will say that I am not ready at this time to make it the law. I think this proposition is unjust. Just look at it. How will it apply to the legislature? The legislature cannot increase the compensation of any officer; the constitution prohibits it. It says:

"No extra compensation shall be granted or allowed by the general assembly to any public officer, agent, servant, or contractor, after the services shall have been rendered or the contract entered into; nor shall the salary or compensation of any public officer be increased or diminished during his term of office."

Now, will any gentleman, lawyer or not lawyer, tell me that the general assembly could say that the judges of the circuit courts should receive an additional thousand dollars as compensation for riding through their circuits?

Mr. JONES, of Somerset. The constitution does not provide that they should have mileage.

Mr. STOCKBRIDGE. It does not say they shall or shall not; it fixes their salaries. Can you give them a thousand dollars additional mileage?

Mr. BELT. I believe it is provided in the constitution in the case of the general assembly, but not in the case of the judges, that they shall be entitled to such per diem as the constitution fixes, and such mileage as is allowed by law.

Mr. STOCKBRIDGE. It is.

Mr. Belt. If the law in reference to judges was that they should be entitled to twenty-five hundred dollars a year, and such mileage as should be fixed by law, would not the legislature have the right to fix that mileage at such sum as they pleased?

Mr. Stockbridge. Unquestionably. But if it went on to state that the salary or compensation of any officer should not be increased or diminished during his term of office, I greatly question whether you could affect the amount of the compensation of a judge during his term. If it can be done in regard to the members of the general assembly what is there to limit them? Because if they can vote into their own pockets, under any name or any pretence, any sum that they please from the State treasury, then there is nothing upon earth to check them. Imagine for a moment a general assembly so corrupt that they should see fit to put into their own pockets a thousand dollars in addition to their usual mileage. If they can put in ten dollars or a hundred dollars lawfully, they can put in a thousand dollars just as lawfully and legally. There is no reason why they should not do the one as well as the other.

And if this amendment be passed, I take it for granted that, as in the last legislature, an order will be offered to-morrow morning that all the officers of the convention shall receive one hundred dollars in addition to their usual mileage; the secretaries, the sergeant-at-arms, the door-keepers and pages. That will be the necessary consequence. And though it be a little matter to each individual, it will take, unwarrantably I believe, about twelve thousand dollars at once out of the State treasury.

The other day when this same proposition was up, and members changed their votes so as not to be on record in favor of this proposition, and it was proposed to withdraw it so that it should not appear on the journal, I then inquired whether it was withdrawn for the purpose of having it offered again. I was answered on all sides that it would not come up again. I had supposed that that was the end of it.

Now I do believe that we have no warrant of law for it. If we have the warrant of law for it, then there is no necessity for any action on our part; the officers of the State will act on the law. But if there is no warrant of law for this thing, then I am not disposed to make a law which shall take from the treasury of the State, over and above what the convention bill authorizes, twelve thousand dollars and put it into the pockets of the members and officers of this convention.

And I am equally clear upon the main proposition. The question was asked here, I remember it distinctly, whether the president of the convention was to be allowed any pay in addition to that of the members. There was but one response in the house of delegates; that the duties of the president were not more arduous than those of some of the members, and that he should stand upon the same footing with them. It was a matter of discussion in the legislature at the time the convention bill passed; and the compensation was fixed at five dollars a day, with the distinct understanding that that included the president as well as all the other members. Highly as I esteem our president, there are other reasons why I should not be disposed, why I should think it would be highly inappropriate, to increase the amount of his compensation. As the convention bill was originally presented, it contained an increased allowance for the president. That was subsequently cut down in the legislature, and it was done intentionally. And standing here as he does, an officer of the State, subjected to no additional expense for his attendance here, I think it would be singularly inappropriate for us to make any addition to his compensation. And I am confident—although I say so without any conversation with him upon the subject—that it would not be acceptable to him.

Mr. Chambers. This it seems has become strictly a legal question; I do not wish to say, in advance, from what I consider a misconstruction of the law. I am free to say, though I voted against this hundred dollar proposition the other day, that I consider the question, upon the proceedings of the legislature, as clear a question as could well be presented to the legal mind. I do not agree to the obligation of this body to obey any mandate of the legislature. I say, as I have said all along, the legislature have the right to call us together, to appoint the time, place and manner of our meeting. But when we get here we are omnipotent in regard to these matters. But to those gentlemen who adopt the theory that the act of assembly is obligatory upon us, I am bold to say that they have not only the right, but they are bound by that law to require the payment of this sum.

I mean simply to argue the legal question. The theory, remember, is that the law passed last February, having been submitted to the people, and by the people having been confirmed, is now constitutional law; and obligatory upon this body, Now let us look at the language of that law. The language of that law is this:

"and the compensation of the delegates to said convention shall be five dollars per day, and the mileage allowed to the members of the general assembly of this State."

Now, then, let us take up the objections. First, it is said that this is not strictly mileage. Agreed; be it so. What did the legislature call mileage? We are to understand the meaning of the legislature. Where are we to go to get it? To the act of the legislature, recorded as their proceedings, their laws and resolutions. What do we find there? We find that the legislature expressly stated that this hundred dollars was to be allowed as mileage. "Resolved that the sum of one hundred dollars, in addition to their usual mileage," etc. And that resolution is accompanied by a report which begins:

"The committee on claims, to which was referred an order of the house, of the second day of March, 1864, instructing them to re-adjust the mileage of the members of the general assembly, respectfully report," &c.

I do not say it is mileage; that is another affair. I say the legislature called it mileage. However, more of that presently.

Now I want this question answered. Suppose the convention bill, instead of saying we shall be allowed "the mileage allowed to the members of the general assembly of this State," had said—"shall be allowed the hundred dollars allowed to the members of the present general assembly." Would there then be any difficulty about it? Would any man here doubt? Could he doubt, if the bill said expressly "the hundred dollars allowed as mileage to the members of the present general assembly?" There would be no doubt then, would there? And yet the same objection would apply to the term "mileage." That objection therefore is not sufficient; it is not available. It is not for us to determine whether this is properly termed "mileage;" the legislature have determined that.

Suppose another case; suppose the legislature had violated the law, for that makes no difference in the argument. Suppose that instead of four dollars a day they had taken eight dollars a day, and that in this convention bill that had said in so many words—"the members of the convention shall receive the per diem which the present lagislature have received." That bill goes before the people, and the people confirm it. It is no longer the work of the legislature, gentlemen say, but it is the work of the people. The people therefore have said, not at all giving an opinion as to whether it was right or wrong, as regards the legislature, the people have said that that bill should be the law of the convention. What then would have been the per diem of members of this body? Four dollars? or eight dollars? Would gentlemen have gone back of the act of assembly? There is the law. You say it is obligatory. And that law says you shall have eight dollars a day, says it just as much as if it had been in these words, instead of "the per diem which the members of the present legislature have received." You would not have gone back of that for any law about the matter. The first canon of interpretation is that when a matter is referred to, it is just the same thing as if it had been introduced without a reference. When you refer to what the legislature received, it is just exactly the same as if you stated in so many words what the legislature did receive.

Now, having relieved this matter from these difficulties, as to whether it be right or wrong, or whether it be mileage or not, I admit that it is not mileage according to the dictionary. But the legislature called it mileage, and received it as mileage. Nobody can doubt that we are to receive for mileage what was allowed to the general assembly. The only difficulty is, what did the legislature receive as mileage. This business of increasing the mileage was no new thing in 1864. Here is a joint resolution passed on the 4th of May, 1861.

"*Resolved by the general assembly of Maryland*, That the sum of eighteen dollars, in addition to their usual mileage, be paid to each of the senators and delegates, and the officers of each house, from the following counties and Baltimore city, to wit: Cecil, Kent, Talbot, Queen Anne's, Caroline, Dorchester, Somerset, Worcester, St. Mary's, Charles, Calvert, Anne Arundel, Prince George's, Montgomery, Harford, Carroll, Baltimore county, Baltimore city, and Howard."

Here is another resolution passed on the 19th of June, 1861.

"*Resolved by the general assembly of Maryland*, That the members and officers of the senate and house of delegates be allowed for this adjourned session, commencing on the fourth day of June last, the per diem for the time they have been in actual session, and the sum of twenty dollars, as an increase to the mileage of each member and officer, except the mileage due to officers appointed from Frederick city, and the same be received as full compensation for all demands for per diem and mileage at this adjourned session."

Then comes the resolution of 1864. The mileage we are to have is the mileage allowed to the general assembly. What general assembly? The Frederick general assembly, that passed the resolution of May, 1861? Or the assembly of 1864, that passed the convention bill? The gentleman from Baltimore city (Mr. Stockbridge) goes back to the law regulating the mileage. The convention bill does not say a word about the law. It is not "the mileage allowed by law." That is a very different sort of thing. If it was "the mileage allowed by law," then the question of what was the mileage allowed by law would come up. But that is not the thing here. It is "the mileage allowed to the general assembly." Which general assembly? That is the whole question involved. Which general assembly did they mean? If you do not go to the general assembly that made this law, which general assembly shall you go to? One of the two whose resolutions I have read, or some other?

I say, therefore, that this law is to have just exactly the same force as if it had given the number of dollars, and had expressly stated the general assembly referred to to be the general assembly that passed this law. I feel bound to say this, because I have been in the habit of trying to have the law distinctly understood by those concerned in it, and I could not agree with gentlemen here. I do say, therefore, never mind whether the law was right or wrong, whether lawful or unlawful, whether constitutional or unconstitutional, that, according to the theory which gentlemen have supported here, when that bill was submitted to the people and was adopted and sanctioned by them, that bill is a rule of conduct for us. We need not go back and ask what the law was before. That is the law from that hour.

These are the views I entertain, and they lead me to believe that any matter involving a simpler and plainer question of law, cannot well be contemplated.

Mr. DELLINGER moved the previous question.

Mr. JONES, of Somerset. This is a question of legal construction, and I think it is hardly proper to call the previous question on such a question until it is fully discussed.

Mr. SCOTT. I would ask the gentleman from Washington (Mr. Dellinger) to withdraw his motion for the previous question.

Mr. DELLINGER. I withdraw it.

Mr. BELT. I would like, in reply to some observations that fell from the gentleman from Baltimore city (Mr. Stockbridge,) to add one single remark to what has been said by my distinguished friend from Kent (Mr. Chambers,) and my learned friend from Baltimore county (Mr. Ridgely.) I understood the train of the argument of the gentleman from Baltimore city to be to the effect that the last general assembly, in voting this hundred dollars additional, had practically perpetrated some fraud, or exercised some corruption. Now I put it to that gentleman, and to every lawyer here, whether it is not a received principle of law in any body, especially one like this founded upon a law, and especially in a convention like this sitting at the very root of all law, that the first and primary rule of construction in reference to the act of a body like the general assembly of this State, is that it is to be interpreted in accordance to the best intent that can be put upon it? Every intendment of the law, every construction, every presumption is to be made in favor of the proper action of the legislature; not only upon the common maxim of law, that all things that are done, are presumed to be rightly done until the contrary appears, but as was most ably and splendidly set forth, I remember, in Judge Martin's decision, and afterwards in the decision of the court of appeals confirming it; I refer to the police law. He said that he first felt bound to say that the law was to be presumed to be constitutional, because everything done by the general assembly was presumed to be constitutional.

And so in this case. Here the general assembly pass a joint resolution, nominally and expressly for the very purpose, as they say, for revising the law of mileage. And the resolution does so far revise it as to affix to it a certain sum, as had been done by previous legislatures. It comes before us as the act of the regularly organized legislative branch of the State government. And are we to stand here and say that it was the result of fraud and corruption? Is it proper legal construction for us to take the ground that that act of the legislature was done in any except the most honorable and proper mode in which they can exercise their legislative functions? Not only are we bound to presume that, but if there are different constructions which can be placed upon the law, are we bound, as lawyers and legislators, to search about among the different constructions that can be found, so as to put upon it precisely that construction which would tally with the constitutional power of the legislature. And if we can possibly find such a construction, we are bound to take it and none other.

Now the construction which has received the assent of nearly all the lawyers of this body, is that this act of the legislature was a change, a readjustment of the question of mileage, and was entirely proper and constitutional. And it seems to me that, upon every just principle of law, it is our duty, until the contrary shall be made manifest by evidence, to take that as the proper rule of action for this body. These are all the observations I desire to make.

Mr. ECKER moved the previous question.

Mr. JONES, of Somerset. I trust that will not be sustained.

The motion for the previous question was not seconded.

Mr JONES, of Somerset. This question is entirely new to me, not having been present when it was agitated on a former occasion. But on listening to the debate, and looking at the law, I entirely concur in the opinion expressed by the gentleman from Anne Arundel (Mr. Miller) and the gentleman from Kent (Mr. Chambers.) It is a question of statutory construction, and I was surprised to hear gentlemen so well versed in the rules of law which govern such a question as the gentlemen from Baltimore city, (Messrs. Stockbridge and Daniel,) referring to what took place in the house of delegates of the last general assembly, and to the injustice and inequality of the resolution about mileage adopted by that assembly, as reasons for their construction. We must look at the law as it stands upon the statute book, and interpret its meaning by the well known rules of construction of statutes. Now what is the case? The constitution provides that "no money shall be drawn from the treasury of the State, except in accordance with an appropriation made by law." The existing constitution is in full force, and will so continue until a new one is substituted, in proper manner, by the vote of the voters of the State. Hence the idea which some gentlemen seem to entertain that this, being a sovereign convention, has unlimited control of the treasury and everything else in the State, is a very great mistake. The purpose and powers of this convention are expressed in the act of assembly, and said to be indorsed by the people, in calling and constituting this convention.—The general assembly made an appropriation by law of a sum of money to defray the expenses of the convention; otherwise not a dollar could have been drawn from the treasury. The expenditure of so much of the sum thus appropriated, as may be necessary, was intrusted to the discretion of this convention. The compensation of the delegates was fixed by the law at "five dollars per day *and the mileage allowed to the members of the general assembly of this State;*" and in my judgment, the convention have no authority to alter or change that provision.

Then it is said, the president being a delegate can receive no additional compensation, especially and mainly because, as the gentleman from Baltimore city (Mr. Stockbridge) alleges, the house of delegates expressly refused to allow the president six dollars per day. Now whatever votes the house of delegates may have given upon separate propositions, the *law* passed by the general assembly provides for paying "to the officers of the convention, upon the order of the president, such compensation as the convention shall allow." There is no exception in the law. If the president is an "officer of the convention," in the meaning of the law, can there be any doubt that the convention may allow him, as such officer, the additional dollar per day for his constant and faithful services as its presiding officer? Whatever may have been the intention and meaning of the house of delegates, is there any pretence that the senate had any other intention than the language of the law plainly implies? And who ever heard of the proceedings of one or even both houses of a legislature being brought into court to enable a judge to decide on the meaning of a law?

And then as to the question of "mileage allowed to the members of the general assembly of this State," to which the delegates are entitled under the law. It is known that previous to the last general assembly, the mileage of the members had been fixed, I believe, by immemorial usage, with reference to the distance of the counties from the seat of government. But the last assembly passed the following resolution:

"*Resolved by the general assembly of Maryland,* That the sum of one hundred dollars, *in addition to their usual mileage,* be paid to each of the senators and delegates of the general assembly."

Can any one doubt that the plain import and meaning of that resolution is "one hundred dollars *as additional mileage?*" It is plain there was, in the contemplation of the legislature, "usual mileage" to which the members were entitled. In "addition" to *that,* they allowed one hundred dollars; yet gentlemen argue, with many hard sayings and insinuations against that assembly, that they *meant* one hundred dollars additional per *diem.* I can hardly think if the gentleman near me (Mr. Stockbridge) were sitting as judge, (a position he may hereafter fill with dignity and ability,) he could give the resolution such a construction, even with the aid of the report of the committee, which precedes the resolution, which like the preamble to a law, may be considered as *aiding* in its construction, but not as controlling or contradicting the plain import of the language used in the law. That report is in these words:

"The committee on claims, to which was referred the order of the house of the second day of March, 1864, instructing them to readjust the mileage of the members of the general assembly, respectfully report:

"That the constitution of Maryland provides that the members of the general assembly shall receive a per diem of four dollars, and such mileage as may be allowed by law. This constitutional provision seems to justify the conclusion that while the per diem of members is fixed and unchangeable, their mileage is left to be adjusted according to the varying circumstances which might arise.—The committee, having in view the peculiar and unprecedented condition of the currency of the country at this time, and the greatly enhanced cost of travel and living in consequence thereof, have deemed it just and right to provide as near as may be for equalizing the compensation of members with that of previous legislatures; and therefore recommend the adoption of the following joint resolution," etc.

The committee were instructed "to readjust the *mileage.*" They notice that while the constitution fixes the *per diem* at four dollars, which cannot be increased, the mileage is left to be adjusted by the general assembly "according to the varying circumstances which might arise," and the committee mention the "condition of the country at this time, and the greatly enhanced cost of travel and living," as reasons "for equalizing the compensation of members with that of previous legislatures," which they propose to do by paying the members of the general assembly "one hundred dollars in *addition* to their usual *mileage.*"

Considering the question as one of statutory construction, it does seem to me impossible to say they meant the hundred dollars as additional per diem, in the face of their declaration that by the *constitution* "the per diem of members as fixed and unchangeable." It was doubtless their purpose "to equalize the compensation of members with that of previous legislatures," and having the constitutional right to increase their mileage, they did so—very inequitably and unfairly, I admit, as to the distant members from Allegany, Worcester and Somerset; but I have got to learn that the unfair or even iniquitous *effect* and *operation* of a law, in particular instances, can control a judge in pronouncing upon the true legal construction of a statute.

The only remaining question is, did the resolution apply to members of that general assembly only, or does it fix the mileage "allowed by law," for future general assemblies until changed by law? I see nothing in the case, which limits the allowance to members of that particular general assembly. If such were their purpose, the language should have been "the senators and delegates of *this* general assembly." In the absence of any such restrictive words, whatever may possibly or even probably have been the selfish motives of those who voted for the resolution, as charged here, and under all the circumstances, in terms harsh and perhaps unjust, I am of opinion that the resolution is equivalent to a public general law, fixing the mileage until duly changed. The delegates to this convention being entitled under the law of their creation, to "the mileage allowed to members of the general assembly of this State," I am clearly of the opinion that they are entitled to the mileage fixed by the resolution aforesaid. I admit that it operates most unfairly to the distant members, but that we cannot now help or avoid. A future legislature will doubtless correct this inequality. As to the indelicacy of deciding the question in our own favor, we cannot avoid a decision, as there is no other tribunal to decide. Gentlemen who doubt, or differ from us in our construction, ought to vote against the amendment. If our construction of the law is correct, there is no altered "condition of the currency or the cost of travel and living," except for the worse, which ought to be considered as rendering it improper for the delegates to accept the mileage allowed by the law.

Mr. Dellinger moved the previous question, which was seconded, and the main question ordered.

The question was upon the amendment of Mr. Lee, to add to the order offered by Mr. Ridgely the following:

"And that the committee on accounts be hereby instructed to audit the mileage account of each member of this convention according to the joint resolution of the general assembly of this State at its last session, adjusting the mileage of the members of that body."

Upon the question Mr. Daniel called for the yeas and nays, and they were ordered.

Mr. Stockbridge moved a call of the house, which was ordered.

Pending the call of the roll—

On motion of Mr. Negley,

Further proceedings under the call were dispensed with.

Mr. Scott moved to adjourn.

The Chairman. That motion is not now in order. The rule requires the vote to be taken, after the yeas and nays have been ordered, before any adjournment can take place.

The question was then taken upon the amendment by yeas and nays.

After the call of the roll had been commenced,

Mr. Daniel said: I want to ask a question for information.

Cries of "Order," "Order," from various parts of the house.

Mr. Daniel. I want to ask ——

Mr. Jones, of Somerset. I call the gentleman to order. The secretary having commenced to call the roll, it is not in order for the gentleman to say anything until his name is called.

The Chairman. (Mr. Purnell.) The point of order is well taken. The gentleman from Baltimore city (Mr. Daniel) must take his seat.

Pending the calling of the yeas and nays, the following explanations were made by members, as their names were called:

Mr. Cushing. I have not the slightest doubt as to the legality of paying this hundred dollars to every member; that does not trouble me the slightest. I think it was the duty of the committee on accounts, if they had any doubt as to the law, to have sought advice and decided the matter for themselves. In a case affecting myself, I prefer to be on the safe side, and to vote against taking this money, rather than assume a duty which I think the committee on accounts ought to have taken upon themselves. I therefore vote "no."

Mr. Daniel. I shall vote "no" on this proposition, because I am opposed to the amendment, and shall be opposed to the original proposition as amended, if this be adopted. The question I want to ask is, whether, if this order is amended, it can be divided. I could vote for the first part of it, but I must vote against the whole if this is put in, and it cannot be divided.

Mr. Dent. I rise merely to say that I have no difficulty, either in law or in morals, in voting for this proposition; none whatever. I vote "aye."

Mr. Ecker. I do not rise to make any explanation. But I want the clerk and the reporter to put down to my name "NO" in the largest kind of capitals they can use.

Mr. Galloway. Being the chairman of the committee on accounts, to which this question was referred this morning, I ask to be excused from voting.

The gentleman was accordingly excused.

Mr. HARWOOD. I have no objection to voting additional compensation to any employee of this house who has faithfully discharged his duties. But I am not willing to pay any member of this house an additional hundred dollars. I vote "no."

Mr. HOLLYDAY. Being perfectly satisfied, from the arguments I have heard here, that we are justly entitled to this money, and being of the opinion that the convention has the right to fix their own per diem, I vote "aye."

Mr. JONES, of Somerset. I shall vote for this amendment solely upon the ground that it is in accordance with what I believe to be the standing law of the State. And I shall vote for the original order, if it is amended in this way, to give the president six dollars a day, because I consider that the compensation of the president, he being an officer of this house, is within the control of the house by the act under which we are called together.

Mr. DANIEL. I call the gentleman to order. We are not voting upon the compensation of the president.

Mr. JONES, of Somerset. When my name is called, I have a right to assign my reasons for the vote I give. I should have done so in fewer words, if the gentleman from Baltimore city (Mr. Daniel) had not interrupted me. I am in favor of the original proposition. The president being an officer of the house, appointed by the house, and compelled to be here at the exact time for the meeting of the house, to a minute, I think it but fair to give him the additional compensation which it is customary for every deliberative body to give its presiding officer. I shall vote for this hundred dollars, because I think it is the law of the land. I vote "aye."

Mr. KENNARD. I am of the opinion that this matter is wrong in law, equity and morals. As the question was tied up in such a legal net-work, I think it was the province of this body to cut the gordian knot, and determine not to take this money. I shall therefore vote "no."

Mr. MULLIKIN. I believe that the naked letter of the law would give us this money. But I do not believe the legislature ever intended it for us. I therefore vote "no."

Mr. NEGLEY. Under the unanswerable exposition of the law which we have had here to-day, I believe this to be entirely legal. I further believe that it is entirely right, and that it is not against morals, or law, or virtue, or anything else that is proper and good. I therefore vote "aye."

Mr. RIDGELY. I regret that the original proposition which I offered has been somewhat embarrassed by this amendment. Nevertheless, as I am in favor of both propositions, I shall vote for the amendment. I would have done so with much greater pleasure, after voting for the original proposition, as an independent proposition. I vote "aye."

Mr. SCOTT. I have views somewhat different from any I have heard yet expressed upon this subject. I believe that if the president were in his place, he would reject the offer to give him this hundred dollars additional compensation. And as I claim to be his particular personal friend, in his name I protest against it. Nevertheless, I believe that he has just the same right, and no more, to this extra compensation than any other member of this house. I shall vote "aye" on this proposition, and then when the question comes up on the amended order, I shall vote against the whole proposition.

Mr. STIRLING. As I said before, I have no doubt as to the legality of this matter, as a question of law. But I know that I did not expect to receive this money when I came down here. I know it can do no harm not to take it. I am satisfied it may do some public harm if the convention does take it. And as the question is submitted to me whether I will take it or not, I shall vote "no."

Mr. WOODEN. Being a member of the committee on accounts, I ask to be excused from voting.

The gentleman was not excused; upon a division—ayes 25, noes 30—and voted "no."

After the call of the roll had been completed, but before the result of the vote was announced, several members changed their votes, as follows:

Mr. CHAMBERS changed his vote to "aye."

Mr. SCOTT. I have come to the conclusion to change my vote to "no."

Mr. PARRAN, who had not voted, now voted "aye."

Mr. NYMAN, who had not voted, now voted "no."

Mr. BELT. I think the course pursued by my learned friend from Baltimore city (Mr. Stirling) is a very safe one, to advocate a proposition and then vote against it.

Mr. STIRLING. I call the gentleman to order. If he wants any explanation of my vote I will give it to him here or elsewhere. I am not afraid of taking the consequences of any vote I may give.

Mr. BELT. I will change my vote to "no."

Mr. JONES, of Somerset. Although I am perfectly clear that the mileage is fixed by law, yet I will follow the good example set by gentleman on the other side. I will change my vote to "no."

Mr. BROWN changed his vote to "no."

Mr. MAYHUGH changed his vote to "no."

Mr. NEGLEY changed his vote to "no."

Mr. STOCKBRIDGE. Is it in order to examine the vote before it is announced, and then change your vote, if you see it is sure to go against you?

Mr. HEBB. Is it in order to move that the polls be closed?

The CHAIRMAN (Mr. Purnell) then announced that the amendment of Mr. LEE had been rejected by—yeas 25, nays 38—as follows:

Yeas—Messrs. Abbott, Audoun, Berry, of Baltimore county, Bond, Carter, Chambers, Crawford, Dail, Dellinger, Dent, Duvall, Hatch, Hollyday, Jones, of Cecil, King, Lansdale, Larsh, Miller, Morgan, Murray, Parran, Ridgely, Swope, Turner, Wickard—25.

Nays—Messrs. Annan, Baker, Belt, Brown, Cunningham, Cushing, Daniel, Davis, of Washington, Ecker, Farrow, Greene, Harwood, Hebb, Hoffman, Horsey, Jones, of Somerset, Keefer, Kennard, Lee, Markey, Mayhugh, Mitchell, Mullikin, Negley, Nyman, Parker, Purnell, Russell, Schley, Schlosser, Scott, Sneary, Stirling, Stockbridge, Thomas, Todd, Valiant, Wooden—38.

The question then recurred upon the original order offered by Mr. RIDGELY, as follows:

"*Ordered*, That the president of this convention be allowed a per diém of six dollars, and that the committee on accounts audit his account accordingly."

Upon this question Mr. CUSHING called for the yeas and nays, which were ordered.

The question was then taken, by yeas and nays, and resulted—yeas 20, nays 44—as follows:

Yeas—Messrs. Brown, Cunningham, Cushing, Dellinger, Dent, Farrow, Greene, Harwood, Hollyday, Jones, of Somerset, Lansdale, Morgan, Murray, Negley, Parker, Purnell, Ridgely, Schley, Thomas, Valiant—20.

Nays—Messrs. Abbott, Annan, Audoun, Baker, Belt, Berry, of Baltimore county, Bond, Carter, Chambers, Crawford, Dail, Daniel, Davis, of Washington, Duvall, Ecker, Galloway, Hatch, Hebb, Hoffman, Horsey, Jones, of Cecil, Keefer, Kennard, King, Larsh, Lee, Markey, Mayhugh, Mitchell, Miller, Mullikin, Nyman, Parran, Russell, Schlosser, Scott, Sneary, Stirling, Stockbridge, Swope, Todd, Turner, Wickard, Wooden—44.

The order was accordingly rejected.

Mr. CUSHING, when his name was called, said: I have great pleasure in voting in the affirmative for this order, as it is for an officer of the convention, who has well performed his duties. I hope this vote will be conclusive, and that gentlemen will not detain the house with long speeches in favor of this proposition and then vote against it.

Mr. STIRLING, when his name was called, said: I shall be governed in my vote on this proposition by precisely the same considerations which governed my vote on the other. I do not doubt the power of the convention to do this thing. Yet, not because I am afraid to assume personally the responsibility of voting for it, but because I do not think it can have any bad effect not to give it, and as I think the action of this convention is likely more or less to influence the fate of our work, I shall vote to have our work as cheap as we can. I therefore vote "no."

THANKS TO THE PRESIDENT.

Mr. CHAMBERS. I am about to perform a duty which I trust will be accepted as one due from every member of this body. I believe that so far as I can speak the sentiments of those with whom I have the most personal intercourse, it does speak the general sentiments of them all, expressing the entire satisfaction which the conduct of the presiding officer of this body has given to those members. Believing it to be the unanimous opinion of this house, I shall ask to have the resolution which I am about to read adopted, and shall ask the secretary to enter it on the journal as the unanimous opinion of this house. I offer the following resolution:

"*Resolved*, That the thanks of the convention are due and are hereby tendered to the Hon. Henry H. Goldsborough, the presiding officer of the convention, for his dignified, efficient and impartial discharge of the duties of the chair."

These motions are very often made as matters of form. I desire to have it distinctly understood that so far as I am concerned, and so far as I know the sentiments of this house, this is offered from a deliberate judgment that this tribute has been fairly and honorably won by our presiding officer.

Mr. JONES, of Somerset. I take great pleasure in indorsing every word which the gentleman from Kent (Mr. Chambers) has said, in reference to the dignity, ability and impartiality of our presiding officer.

Mr. DENT. I desire to say that I support this proposition most cordially. So far as I have been able to judge, I can bear testimony to the great promptness, strict impartiality, and general efficiency of the presiding officer of this house. And it gives me much pleasure to bear this testimony in his favor.

Mr. MILLER. I wish to add my testimony to that which has been so well given by the gentleman from Somerset (Mr. Jones,) the gentleman from St. Mary's (Mr. Dent) and the gentleman from Kent (Mr. Chambers.) As one of the minority, I can say that the president has discharged his duties with the utmost impartiality.

Mr. BOND. I also take pleasure in indorsing the sentiments of this resolution.

On motion of Mr. CHAMBERS,

The rules were suspended, the resolution read the second time, and unanimously adopted.

On motion of Mr. BROWN,

The convention took a recess until 8 o'clock.

EVENING SESSION.

The convention reassembled at 8 o'clock, P. M.

The roll was called, and the following members answered to their names :

Messrs. Goldsborough, President; Abbott, Annan, Audoun, Baker, Berry, of Prince George's, Bond, Brown, Carter, Crawford, Cunningham, Cushing, Dail, Daniel, Davis, of Washington, Dent, Duvall, Earle, Ecker, Edelen, Farrow, Galloway, Greene, Harwood, Hatch, Hebb, Hoffman, Hollyday, Hopper, Horsey, Jones, of Cecil, Jones, of Somerset, Keefer, Kennard, King, Larsh, Lee, Markey, McComas, Mitchell, Mullikin, Murray, Negley, Nyman, Parran, Pugh, Purnell, Ridgely, Russell, Schley, Schlosser, Scott, Sneary, Stockbridge, Swope, Sykes, Thomas, Todd, Valliant, Wickard, Wooden—61.

DISTRIBUTION OF THE DEBATES.

Mr. PURNELL. I ask leave to submit the following order:

Ordered, That the State librarian, in distributing the debates under the order adopted on the 26th of July, 1864, deliver one copy of the same to each of the chaplains of this convention.

I offer this order at the wish of the chaplains of this convention, who have manifested a great deal of interest in the various propositions discussed before the convention, and who have expressed a desire to receive a copy of these debates.

Mr. STOCKBRIDGE. This is perhaps as good a time as any, while the matter is before the convention, to provide for the distribution in full. The order adopted on the 26th of July, is as follows :

"*Ordered*, That the State librarian shall have bound 1,000 copies of the journal of proceedings, and 1,000 copies of the debates of this convention, at a cost not to exceed the rates per volume of binding the laws and journals of the last general assembly, and shall distribute the same as the laws and journals are now distributed, and the same amount allowed by law, to pay the expenses of distributing the laws and journals, is hereby directed to be paid for distributing the journal and debates of this convention. The remaining copies to remain in the library."

I concur fully in the order offered by the gentleman from Worcester (Mr. Purnell.) But I would be very glad to have him modify it, so as to include some other officers of this convention. I wish he would include six copies for the official reporter of the convention.

Mr. VALLIANT. I was about to submit an order to that effect.

Mr. PURNELL. I will accept the amendment.

Mr. HEBB. Under the order passed on the 26th of July, none of the members of the convention would get any bound copies of the debates. I had drawn up an order to meet that case.

Mr. VALLIANT. I have an order prepared, making provision for the entire distribution, which will perhaps meet the purpose of gentlemen here. I will read it, and if anybody has any better order than this, let him present it, and I will vote for it.

Mr. STOCKBRIDGE. This order of the 26th of July does not say to whom these debates shall be distributed.

Mr. VALLIANT. I offer this as a substitute for the order of the gentleman from Worcester (Mr. Purnell.)

Ordered, That the librarian be and is hereby directed to distribute the journal of debates as early as practicable, after the same shall have been printed and bound, as follows :

"One copy to each loyal State and territorial governor within the limits of the United States; six copies to the official reporter of the convention; two copies to each member of the convention; one copy to each officer of the convention; one copy each to the judges and clerks of the circuit courts, the several courts of the city of Baltimore, and of the court of appeals; one copy to each register of wills in the State, and one copy each to the governor, lieutenant governor, and the superintendent of public instruction."

Mr. HEBB. I will read the order I had prepared :

"*Ordered*, That the bound copies of the journal of proceedings and of the debates be placed in the State library, and that the librarian distribute such number of the same as may be necessary, in the same manner and to the same persons, and the same officers as the laws of the general assembly are distributed; also to each member of the convention two copies of the debates, and one copy of the journal of proceedings; to the official reporter three copies of the debates; to the assistant reporter three copies of the debates; to each chaplain, officer and appointee of the convention one copy of the journal of proceedings and one copy of the debates; and the remaining copies of the journal of proceedings and of the debates shall be retained in the library, subject to the future order of the general assembly; and the president of the convention is hereby authorized to issue to the librarian his certificate for such sum as may be necessary to defray the expenses of such distribution."

Mr. PURNELL. I withdraw my order in favor of the one offered by the gentleman from Allegany (Mr. Hebb.)

Mr. VALLIANT. I withdraw the substitute I offered.

The question was upon the order of Mr. HEBB.

Mr. ABBOTT. I move to amend by striking out "three" and inserting "six" as the number of copies for the chief reporter. It is well known that the chief reporter has occasion to use these specimens of his work when applying for other work. He brought here a copy of the debates of another constitutional convention of which he was the official reporter, and presented it to the authority having the appointing of the reporter to this convention, as an evidence of his ability as a reporter.

The question being taken, the amendment was adopted.

The order as amended was then adopted.

THANKS TO THE SECRETARIES, &C.

On motion of Mr. DUVALL, it was

"*Ordered*, That the thanks of this convention are due to and are hereby tendered Wm. R. Cole and John H. Shaw, secretary and assistant secretary, and all other officers connected with the convention, for the faithful and efficient manner in which they have discharged their respective duties."

LEGISLATIVE DEPARTMENT.

Mr. EARLE, from the committee of revision, reported back to the convention the article on the legislative department; and preparatory to offering amendments, proposed a rearrangement of the sections according to the following table. The first column represents the number of each section as arranged in committee; the second column the corresponding number as adopted in convention:

1		1
2	Basis of representation	1
3	Basis of representation	2
4	Basis of representation	3
5		2
6		3
7		4
8		7
9		8
10		9
11		31
12		26
13		5
14		6
15		27
16		22
17		24
18		10
19		11
20		12
21		13
22		23
23		25
24		14
25		37
26		16
27		17
28		15
29		30
30		28
31		18
32		19
33		20
34		21
35		33
36		40
37		42
38		43
39		44
40		32
41		29
42		34
43		35
44		36
45		41
46		46
47		47
48		48
49		49
50	Usury	1
51		45
52		38
53		39
54	Schedule	8
55	Schedule	4

The above rearrangement of sections having been adopted by the convention,

Mr. EARLE, on behalf of the committee, recommended the following verbal amendments:

In the first line of the third section after the word "each," strike out "district of the city of Baltimore" and insert "of the legislative districts of Baltimore city." In the fourth line of the same section strike out the word "who;" and in the fifth line, before the word "election," strike out "their" and insert "his." At the end of the section add these words: "Subject to the classification of senators hereinafter provided for."

In the third, sixth and tenth lines of the fourth section insert the word "legislative" before the word "districts." And in the same section strike out these words: "Upon this principle and until the next national census or State enumeration of inhabitants, the house of delegates shall consist of seventy-nine members distributed as follows," and insert the following: "Upon this principle, and as soon as practicable after each national census or State enumeration of inhabitants, the general assembly shall apportion the members of the house of delegates among the several counties, and the several legislative districts of Baltimore city, according to the white population of each. But until such apportionment is made, the house of delegates shall consist of eighty members, distributed as follows."

In the fifth line of the fifth section, strike out "city of Baltimore," and insert "the legislative districts of Baltimore city."

In the fifth line of the eighth section after the word "or" and before the word "city," insert "in the legislative district of Baltimore," and in the sixth line of the same section, strike out the word "city," and insert "legislative district of said city."

In the seventeenth section insert "spoken" for "spoke."

In the second line of the eighteenth section insert "shall" before "appoint." And in the fifth line of the same section after "number" insert "of members elected."

In the first line of the nineteenth section after the word "of" insert "members elected to."

And in the second line of the twenty-fifth section insert the word "elected" after the word "members," and the same word after the word "senators" in the seventh line.

Insert "nor" for "or" in the fourth line of the twenty-sixth section, and in the fifth line of the twenty-eighth section make the same change.

In the first line of the thirty-first section insert "general assembly" for "legislature."

In the second line of the thirty-eighth section insert "nor" for "or." And in the tenth line strike out the word "article" and insert the word "section."

In the third line of the forty-fourth section insert "registers" for "register." And in the second line of the forty-seventh section insert "presidents" for "president."

Recommending the adoption of these verbal changes, the committee of revision close their report on the legislative department.

GEORGE EARLE, Chairman.

On being read, all the amendments proposed above were concurred in by the convention.

JUDICIARY DEPARTMENT.

Mr. EARLE, from the committee of revision, reported back to the convention the article on the judiciary department.

The committee recommend that the fourth part of this article, which relates to the orphans' courts, and the fifth part, which relates to the courts of Baltimore city, be transposed. This arrangement will cause the courts of Baltimore city, which are included in the thirteenth judicial circuit of the State, to follow the third part of this article, which relates exclusively to circuit courts.

The committee further recommend that the different sections of this article be rearranged according to the following table. The first column gives the number of each section as arranged by the committee; the second column refers to the corresponding number of each section as the sections now stand:

1	1
2	2
3	3
4	4
5	25
6	5
7	6
8	8
9	9
10	11
11	10
12	31
13	7
14	New sections.
15	
16	
17	12
18	13
19	14
20	15
21	16
22	17
23	18
24	19
25	20
26	21
27	22
28	23
29	24
30	29
31	33
32	40
33	34
34	35
35	36
36	37
37	38
38	39
39	41
40	42
41	43
42	44
43	27
44	26
45	28
46	32
47	45
48	46
49	47
50	48

The rearrangement of the different parts and sections of this article, as recommended by the committee, having been adopted by the convention,

Mr. EARLE, on behalf of the committee, proposed the following amendments:

In the fourth and fifth lines of the first section, strike out the words "all said courts shall be courts of record, and have a seal," and insert "all said courts shall be courts of record, and each shall have a seal."

In the first line of the second section strike out the word "associate." In the third line of the same section insert the word "residents" after the word "and." In the fifth line of the same section strike out the words "by death, resignation or otherwise." In the sixth line of the same section add the words "or appointment" after the word "election," and in the line below, the words "or appointed," after the word "elected."

In the fourth section before the words "on impeachment" insert the word "or."

In the fifth section, after the words "judge of any court of this State," insert "except of the orphans' court."

At the end of the tenth section add the following words: "In all the courts of this State."

In the second line of the twelfth section strike out the word "so" before the word "emancipated."

The committee recommend the adoption of the following sections:

"Section 14. All elections of judges and other officers provided for by this constitution, State's attorneys excepted, shall be certified, and the returns made by the clerks of the respective counties to the governor, who shall issue commissions to the different persons for the offices to which they shall have been respectively elected; and in all such elections, the person having the greatest number of votes, shall be declared to be elected.

"Section 15. If in any case of election for judges, clerks of the courts of law, and registers of wills, the opposing candidates shall have an equal number of votes, it shall be the duty of the governor to order a new election; and in case of any contested election, the governor shall send the returns to the house of delegates, who shall judge of the election and qualification of the candidates at such election.

"Section 16. All public commissions and grants shall run thus: 'The State of Maryland, &c.," and shall be signed by the governor, with the seal of the State annexed; all writs and process shall run in the same style, and be tested, sealed and signed as usual; and all indictments shall conclude 'against the peace, government and dignity of the State.' "

In the first line of the twenty-second section strike out the word "provisions" and insert "provision."

In the twenty-third section insert the words "in office" after the word "misdemeanor."

In the thirty-first section strike out the words "their offices," and insert the words "his office." The sentence will then read as follows:

"Each court shall consist of one judge, who shall be elected by the legal and qualified voters of said city, and shall hold his office for the term of fifteen years."

In the thirty-third section insert the word "commissioners" for "commissioner," and strike out all the section from and after the word "streets."

In the thirty-sixth section, for "the criminal court of Baltimore city" insert "the criminal court of Baltimore."

In the thirty-ninth section strike out the following words: "There shall be a clerk of the superior court of Baltimore city; and a clerk of the circuit court of Baltimore city, and a clerk of the court of common pleas in Baltimore city, and a clerk of the criminal court of Baltimore city. And each of the said clerks shall be elected by the legal and qualified voters of said city," and insert therefor these words:

"There shall be a clerk of each of the said courts of Baltimore city, who shall be elected by the legal and qualified voters of said city." At the end of this section add the following: "When a clerk of said court shall be elected to serve for six years thereafter."

In the forty-second section, strike out the word "legislature" and insert "general assembly." Also strike out the words "shall have the custody of all deeds, conveyances and other papers now remaining in the office of said court, and hereafter." Also strike out the word "other" before the word "papers" in the same section.

Strike out the first sentence of the forty-third section, and insert therefor the following:

"Section 43. There shall be an orphans' court in the city of Baltimore, and in each of the counties of this State."

In the forty-fifth section, instead of "the said orphans' court" read "the orphans' court."

And in the forty-seventh section, after the words "subject to such right of appeal in all cases," insert "from the judgment of justices of the peace."

The committee now close their report on the judiciary.

GEORGE EARLE, Chairman.

The amendments above recommended by the committee were adopted by the convention.

COUNTIES AND TOWNSHIPS.

Mr. EARLE, from the committee of revision, reported back to the convention the article on counties and townships, without amendment.

SCHEDULE.

Mr. EARLE. I am instructed by the committee of revision to report back to the convention the article "schedule," with the following proposed amendments:

First, strike out the second section. This section reads as follows: "The common law and statute law now in force, and not repugnant to this constitution, shall remain in force until they expire by their own limitation, or are altered by the general assembly."

The substance of this section is embraced in the fourth article of the declaration of rights; the section therefore is unnecessary.

The committee next recommend that the fourth section of this article be transferred to the article on the legislative department.—This section reads as follows:

"Section 4. The general assembly shall have power to pass all such laws as may be necessary and proper for carrying into execution the powers vested by this constitution in any department or office of the government, and the duties imposed upon them thereby."

The committee recommend that the eighth section of this article be also transferred to the article on the legislative department. This section is in the words following:

"The general assembly shall have power to regulate by law, not inconsistent with this constitution, all matters which relate to the judges of election, time, place and manner of holding elections in this State, and of making returns thereof."

In the third section of this article strike out the word "on" and insert the word "at." In the second line of the same section insert the word "an" before the word "equal," and in the fourth line insert the word "for" after the word "provided." In the same line strike out the word "otherwise" after the word "specially."

In the second line of the fifth section insert the words "of law" after the word "courts," and in the third line the words "*in controversy*" after the word "amount."

The committee further report that they have considered the section which was specially referred to them by the convention. That section reads thus:

"Section —. There shall be an election held in the several counties and in the city of Baltimore on the Tuesday next after the first Monday in the month of November, in every second year. The first election to be held in the year eighteen hundred and sixty-five, at which election all clerks of courts and registers of wills, judges of the orphans' courts, sheriffs, county commissioners and all other county officers elected by the people, shall be chosen whenever an election for any such officer is required to be held, but this shall not apply to the municipal officers of any incorporated town or city."

The committee recommend the adoption of this section in the following modified form.

Section 7. General elections shall be held throughout the State, on the Tuesday next after the first Monday in the month of November of each and every year. At the election held in the year eighteen hundred and sixty-four, all State officers required to be elected under this constitution during that year shall be elected, and in like manner in every second year thereafter an election shall be held for those State officers whose terms are about to expire. At the election held in the year eighteen hundred and sixty-five, all county officers required to be elected under this constitution, in that year, shall be elected, and in like manner, in every second year thereafter, an election shall be held for those county officers whose terms are about to expire; provided, however, the judges of the several courts of this State (except the judges of the orphans' courts,) shall be elected at the regular election, whether for State or county officers as the case may be, immediately preceding the expiration of the term of the incumbent whose place is to be filled.

Mr. DENT. I would inquire how that section affects the provisions of section six, which has been adopted. That section reads:

"All officers, civil and military, now holding office, whether by election, or appointment, under the State, shall continue to hold and exercise their offices according to their present tenure, unless otherwise provided in this constitution, &c."

It was supposed that under that provision the clerks of the several courts throughout the State would continue in office, until the terms for which they had been elected would expire. It occurs to me that the section just read might affect this section, and create a necessity for the election of clerks before the period contemplated by this ninth section.

Mr. PUGH. I would suggest that the words in the proposed section—"whose terms are about to expire"—meets that ground.

Mr. STIRLING. It strikes me that it would be better, instead of saying "county officers," to name the officers intended to be embraced by that term. I do not know what effect it may have in the city of Baltimore, where we make a distinction between county and city officers.

Mr. HEBB. It is stated in the body of the constitution itself in what years all officers shall be elected. All that this section does, is to say that there shall be a new election in the year when their terms expire.

Mr. STIRLING. I am not speaking in regard to the expiration of the terms of office, but in regard to what is meant by "county officers." There are certain officers elected in the city of Baltimore, by general ticket, who are municipal officers; yet they occupy the same ground as county officers. The original resolution I offered, and which was referred to the committee on revision, contained a proviso which I will move to have inserted here, as follows:

"Provided that this shall not be taken to include the municipal officers of any incorporated town or city."

I do that for fear the words "county officers" might lead to some misconstruction.

Mr. HEBB. The section proposed by the committee on revision speaks of those county officers required to be elected under this constitution. I am not aware that this constitution provides for the election of any municipal officers of any incorporated town or city.

Mr. STIRLING. Very well; my amendment may not be necessary, and I will withdraw it.

The section, as proposed by the committee on revision, was then adopted.

VOTE ON THE CONSTITUTION.

Mr. EARLE. The next amendment proposed by the committee, is to the first section of that part of the schedule which relates to the "vote on the constitution." It is in accordance with the suggestion made this morning by the gentleman from Baltimore county (Mr. Ridgely.) It proposes to strike out so much of said section as extends from the word "law" in the seventh line down to the word "and" in the thirteenth line as printed in bill form, and in place of the part thus stricken out to insert the following words, to wit:

"That an election will be held in the city of Baltimore on the twelfth day of October, in the year eighteen hundred and sixty-four, and in the several counties of this State, on the twelfth and thirteenth days of October in the same year, at the usual places of holding elections in said city and counties, for the adoption or rejection of this constitution, which election shall be held in the said city of Baltimore, on the twelfth day of October, eighteen hundred and sixty-four, between the hours of eight o'clock, A. M., and five o'clock, P. M., and in the said several counties of this State, on the said twelfth and thirteenth days of October, eighteen hundred and sixty-four, between the hours of eight o'clock, A. M., and six o'clock, P. M."

Mr. CHAMBERS. This experiment of two days election is perhaps a little unsafe in itself. I have a very distinct recollection of a three days election at one time, and I have also a very distinct recollection—as my venerable friend with the white head in front of me (Mr. Ridgely) will no doubt testify—that after the first day there was a sort of battle royal at the hustings. It was a very confused, and perhaps without misapplying the term, I may say a very riotous proceeding.

I do not object to the two days election in this case particularly. But the two days will afford sufficient time certainly if the hours of voting be limited to between the hours of 8 o'clock, A. M., and 5 o'clock P. M., instead of 8 o'clock, A. M., and six o'clock, P. M., as proposed here. The lateness of the hour will probably increase the excitement of the day, and of those who may be at the polls. I would therefore suggest that 5 o'clock, P. M., at that season of the year is quite late enough. It is sundown in the month of October, before 6 o'clock. I would suggest 5 o'clock instead of six as likely to lead to more quiet at the polls.

Mr. EARLE. Many members of the convention expressed a preference for seven o'clock, P. M., as the hour for closing the polls, and solicted the committee of revision to recommend that change. But, if we are to have a two days election, the vote of the State can certainly be taken between the hours of eight o'clock, A. M., and five o'clock, P. M. Without the slightest violation of confidence, or the privacy of the committee room, I may be permitted to state, that the amendment now under consideration was reported to the convention according to instructions from the committee of revision. Personally, I have no preference for the two days election. On the contrary, as at present advised, I am of the opinion, that the entire vote of the State can be taken in one day. Others, I know, entertain very different views, and I hope we shall have a full expression of opinion on the subject from gentlemen representing the different divisions of the State. My own vote may be influenced to some extent by the opinions expressed.

Mr. STOCKBRIDGE. I am greatly afraid of this experiment of two days election, and nothing would reconcile me to it, but the probability that it would be absolutely impossible to poll the whole vote within the hours allowed in one day. I do not know how it may be in the various election districts in the counties; and before voting upon this proposition I would like very much to hear from members representing the various counties whether it would be impossible for them to poll their full vote in one day. Unless that would probably be impossible, I would very much prefer to have but one day's election. I believe that more than one day's election has operated badly in other States, and nothing but the impossibility of polling the entire vote would reconcile me to the experiment in this case.

Mr. GREENE. In answer to the inquiry of the gentleman from Baltimore city (Mr. Stockbridge,) I would say that the district in which I reside is one of large territorial extent, and polls upwards of seven hundred votes, when the whole vote of the district is out. And it has appeared to me from the beginning that the usual hours of election would hardly be sufficient to secure the administration of the oath to all the voters. I have been desirous of obtaining all the time I could in order to take the whole vote of the district. It has been the habit of the voters of that district to come in to the polls at a late hour of the day; especially those engaged in the mines. They finish their day's work, and come up to the polls somewhat late in the afternoon.

Mr. ECKER. My colleague (Mr. Smith, of Carroll,) who is now absent, I know thinks it would be utterly impossible to get all the votes in in one day. So far as my district is concerned, we poll between three and four hundred votes, and could probably get through in one day. But Taneytown polls five hundred votes, and Manchester about six hundred. And I would therefore prefer to have two days for the election.

Mr. RIDGELY. I would say, in answer to the inquiry of the gentleman from Baltimore city (Mr. Stockbridge,) that so far as Baltimore county is concerned, in the four districts lying immediately on the city line, the first, third, ninth and twelfth districts, in all contested elections the vote ranges from eight to nine hundred votes. If there is to be a full vote cast, it would be utterly impossible to take the vote of those districts in one day if every voter is to be sworn.

Mr. PUGH. So far as I am concerned, I am perfectly willing to vote for whichever plan the majority of the convention may deem most advisable. But at the same time I wish to state that unless it is as stated by the gentleman from Allegany (Mr. Greene,) and the gentleman from Baltimore county (Mr. Ridgely,) that they have a very large vote to poll, I should be opposed to extending the time over one day, for several reasons. One of them is to a certain extent based upon my experience in this respect. I have seen elections extended over one day. In the progress of elections, as gentlemen are very well aware, there is always considerable excitement. And if the election is carried over to the second day, the excitement is sure to be increased during the intervening night. In the district represented by my colleague (Mr. Scott,) the ballot-box and all in it might disappear during the night. And except for the very serious objections stated by the gentleman from Allegany and the gentleman from Baltimore county, I should object to extending the election over one day; extending the excitement over that much more time, and increasing by that extension the chances of disturbances at the polls, and the chances of not getting a correct expression of the sentiments of the people throughout the State.

I would ask gentlemen if the business could not be expedited by swearing a dozen, or fifteen, or twenty voters at one time? In my district we do not poll so large a vote as in the district represented by the gentleman from Allegany (Mr. Greene,) and the gentleman from Baltimore county (Mr. Ridgely.) Therefore we are not in a position to state properly what would be our opinion in regard to this matter, provided we had a large vote to poll. I am perfectly satisfied that in the district I represent we can poll our entire vote in one day. And I am also satisfied that if it be possible to poll the entire vote of the State in one day, it would certainly be wise to do so.

Mr. SCHLEY. In answer to the inquiry of the gentleman from Baltimore city (Mr. Stockbridge,) I would state that on my visit home on Saturday last, this very subject was a matter of conversation and discussion among many gentlemen of my acquaintance there. The general impression was that the entire vote could not be taken in one day, unless the convention made some provision for administering the oath in a different manner than at the polls. I am convinced that in the election district in which I reside, where there are some eighteen hundred votes, and only two voting places—at one of which there is a much larger number of voters than at the other—the vote cannot be taken in one day. I am glad that the subject has been brought to the consideration of the convention, and trust that some remedy may be provided.

It has occurred to me—I merely throw out the suggestion for what it is worth—that the judges of election might be directed, by some provision in this schedule, to administer the oath in advance of the day of election, on the day before, or some other day. If that cannot be conveniently done, there is an evident necessity for holding the election on two days, for I do not believe the full vote of the State can be polled in one day.

Mr. PUGH. The judges of election have a discretion in the matter. They know how many votes they have to poll in each district, and they can arrange matters accordingly. They can provide beforehand for administering the oath to a dozen or twenty-five, or as many as they can get together at a time. There would be no difficulty about it if the judges would make that arrangement.

Mr. PURNELL. When this proposition was first introduced, I felt very much inclined to favor it, because I thought I saw some necessity for it. But upon reflection, I am disposed to think that in the county I have the honor in part to represent, although it is a very large county, and polls a very large vote, it can all be polled in one day. We have sometimes polled as high as six hundred votes in the district in which I reside. But I think that with a little diligence, and swearing a number together in the manner proposed by the gentleman from Cecil (Mr. Pugh,) the vote can all be polled within the hours precribed by law.

However, I am inclined to yield to whatever the majority of the convention may deem necessary in the matter. But it is my impression that not only in the county I represent (Worcester county,) but also in the adjoining counties, where they do not poll so many votes as in the county of Worcester, the vote can all be taken in one day. I think there is some danger, in protracting the time, that the results might ensue which have been apprehended by some gentlemen who have taken part in this discussion.

Mr. CHAMBERS. I move to change the time from six o'clock P. M., to five o'clock P. M., for closing the polls in the counties where two days will be occupied in the election.

Mr. HEBB. Inasmuch as the committee have reported in favor of keeping the polls open for two days, I think it would be far preferable to close the polls at five o'clock in the afternoon, for if there is any disposition to riot it will be very apt to be manifested from five to six o'clock. I am therefore in favor of the amendment of the gentleman from Kent (Mr. Chambers.)

Mr. NEGLEY. The district in which our town (Hagerstown) is situated, polls nearly eleven hundred votes, and I doubt if we shall be able to swear all the voters and get in all the votes in one day. And there are some other districts in the county of Washington which poll larger votes. They are spread over considerable territory, and I think a fuller vote would be obtained if two days were allowed. And I think further, that it would accommodate the voters in the country districts, because it might not be convenient for them to come in on one day, and they could come in on the other. In Virginia they have kept the polls open for three days; it is true the vote there was *viva voce*. I do not suppose there will be any danger of anybody running away with the ballot-boxes, for I suppose the judges would exercise proper precaution in putting them away and guarding them.

The question was upon the amendment proposed by Mr. CHAMBERS, to change the time of closing the polls from six o'clock to five o'clock.

Mr. STIRLING. I think it would be better to take the vote first upon the amendment reported by the committee on revision. If we are to have two days for the election, I think every one will agree that the polls better be closed at five o'clock.

The PRESIDENT. If no objection is made, the question will be first taken upon the amendment reported by the committee on revision, to assign two days for taking the vote in the counties upon the constitution.

The question was then taken upon the amendment recommended by the committee, and upon a division—ayes 34, noes 23—it was concurred in.

The amendment moved by Mr. CHAMBERS, to close the polls at five o'clock, instead of six o'clock, was then adopted.

Mr. EARLE. The committee next recommend a verbal change in the eighth section of the article schedule. It is simply to insert the word "for" after the word "provided," in the eighteenth line.

In the sixteenth line of the ninth section, insert "this constitution" for "the constitution." And in the eighteenth line of the same section after the word "State," insert the following words, "including the soldiers' vote hereinafter provided for." And in the twentieth line of the same section insert "this constitution," for "the constitution."

At the end of section nine of this article, add the following, as

Section 10. And the governor shall exclude from count the votes of any county or city, the return judges of which shall fail to certify in the returns as provided by this schedule, that all persons who have voted have taken the oath prescribed to be taken, unless the governor shall be satisfied that such oath was actually administered, and that the failure to make the certificate has been from inadvertence or mistake.

SOLDIERS' VOTE.

In the first line of the eleventh section of this article, which is the first section of the subdivision "soldiers' vote," strike out the words "any of the qualified voters," and insert "any qualified voter." In the twentieth line of the same section insert the word "no" before the word "officer," and in the same line of the same section insert "voters" for "votes."

In the twenty-sixth line of the same section strike out the words "in writing." And in the twenty-seventh line of the same section, strike out the word "new" in two places, before the word "constitution."

At the end of the eleventh section insert the following as

"Section 12. Any qualified voter of this State, who shall be absent from the city or county of his residence on the day for taking the vote on the adoption or rejection of this constitution by reason of his being in the military service of the United States, but shall be at some hospital or military post, or on duty within this State, and not with his company, may vote at the nearest polls to such place, on satisfying the judges that he is a legal and qualified voter of this State."

In the first line of the thirteenth section strike out the word "or," and insert therefor the word "as." And in the seventh line of the same section after the word "governor" insert the words "at Annapolis."

In the ninth line of the same section, after the word "for" insert the words "the constitution."

The committee further report that they have rearranged the different sections of this article. This became necessary, inasmuch as one section was stricken out, two were transferred to the legislative department, and several new ones added.

And now the committee have the honor of reporting to the convention, that they have completed their revision of the different articles of the constitution. The work has been performed with too much speed to be thorough, but it will be remembered that most important articles of the constitution have been referred to the committee within the last few days, and the convention is evidently determined to close its sessions forthwith. Under the circumstances a more thorough revision was impossible.

To-morrow the committee will be prepared to present to the convention, for its final action, an engrossed copy of the declaration of rights and constitution.

All of which is respectfully submitted.

GEORGE EARLE, Chairman.

On motion of Mr. HEBB, all the above amendments recommended by the committee of revision, were concurred in by the convention.

FINAL READING OF THE CONSTITUTION.

Mr. ABBOTT. I move that the final reading of the constitution be made the special order for to-morrow at 12 o'clock, M.

Mr. CUSHING. I would suggest 10 o'clock to commence the reading. It will take some time.

Mr. ABBOTT. I accept the amendment.

The motion as modified was then agreed to.

DESCRIPTIVE AND HUMOROUS.

Mr. SCOTT. Our session is about to close. As we are in a pretty good humor at present, I have a little bit of pleasantry which I wish to perpetrate, at my own expense, and the expense of some others. I will say in advance, that as we will probably never all see each other's faces again, it will be a pleasant recollection to me all my life, to have met with the gentlemen who compose this body, and to have spent our time here so agreeably, and as I believe to our mutual satisfaction.

The *Sands* of this body are finally run out—not played out. [Laughter.] Our cherished *Chambers* will shortly know us no more as a Convention; and the pleasant *Hollyday* which we have enjoyed will soon be passed away. Though a democratic body, this Convention presents the anomaly of having in its midst a *Lord*, a *Noble*, a *Barron* and an *Abbott*, an *Earle*, and a *King*, with a *Mace*. In addition to gentlemen of learned professions, we have a *Turner* and a *Carter*, a *Miller* and a *Baker*, and a number of *Smiths*. Where there are streams there should be bridges; hence Baltimore city sends *Stockbridge*, with her *Brooks;* her *Stirling* men repose confidently on her *Cushing;* [laughter] her *Hatch* never breeds mischief; her *Daniel* is no false prophet, and her *Thomas* is neither doubting nor doubtful. St. Mary's county put her *Dent* in the Convention, but did not dinge the Constitution; Talbot glories in having sent her most *Valliant* man; Prince George's rejoices in her *Clarke* (clerk,) who sounds the key note of her choir, while, with her elegant *Belt*, she adorns this body. Queen Anne's, from windward to *Lee* is done *Brown;* Frederick, through her *Schley*-man, has made her *Markey* in the Constitution, and her *Cunning-ham* will appear anon (*Annan.*) Worcester is no *Farrow* kine when she can raise such men as she sends to this House. The *Hopper* of Harford is well filled. [Laughter.] Allegany not being afflicted with *Hebb*-itude, *Thrust-on* the Convention one wicked (*Wickard*) man; her delegation, though fully ripe, contains one eminent *Greene*. Of the Washington county delegates I have only to say that the nigh man (*Nyman*) is worthy of his associates, and I hope they all *Mayhugh* their way to fortune and to fame. I have no fears that Anne Arundel will repudiate the work of the Convention, since she gives us her duly executed *Bond*. Baltimore county and Prince George's county of their first fruits gave us their choice *Berries*. Somerset, though a quiet county, blew up a heavy *Gale;* [laughter] while Dorchester permits us to look upon her chosen *Dail* (dale.) Caroline's best *Todd*-y sparkles in our debates. Carroll, having furnished one of the *Smiths* whose sturdy blows helped to forge the Constitution, thought she might be allowed to fill out her delegation with a *Wooden* man. [Laughter.] Cecil is never in the wrong *Pugh* (pew,) and I hope from imputations of offensive personalities to escape *Scott* free. I will conclude with the remark that the Secretary is a live *Cole*, to which his assistant may properly say pshaw! (*Shaw.*) Mr. President, I am a modest man, and shrink from notoriety; and I am admonished by the presence of the *ever-ready little Mac* of the *American*, that

"A chiel's amang ye takin' notes,
And faith he'll print 'em."

On motion of Mr. THOMAS,

The Convention adjourned.

NINETIETH DAY.

TUESDAY, September 6, 1864.

The convention met at 9½ o'clock, A. M.

Prayer by Rev. Mr. Patterson.

The roll was called, and the following members answered to their names:

Messrs. Goldsborough, President; Abbott, Annan, Audoun, Baker, Barron, Belt, Berry, of Prince George's, Bond, Brooks, Brown, Carter, Chambers, Crawford, Cunningham, Cushing, Dail, Daniel, Davis, of Charles, Davis, of Washington, Dellinger, Dent, Duvall, Ecker, Farrow, Gale, Galloway, Greene, Hatch, Hebb, Henkle, Hodson, Hoffman, Hollyday, Hopper, Horsey, Jones, of Cecil, Jones, of Somerset, Keefer, Kennard, King, Lansdale, Larsh, Lee, Marbury, Markey, Mayhugh, McComas, Mitchell, Miller, Morgan, Mullikin, Murray, Negley, Nyman, Parker, Parran, Peter, Pugh, Purnell, Ridgely, Russell, Schley, Schlosser, Scott, Smith, of Dorchester, Sneary, Stirling, Stockbridge, Swope, Sykes, Thomas, Todd, Turner, Valliant, Wickard, Wilmer, Wooden—78.

The journal of yesterday was read and approved.

OFFENCES UNDER THE SLAVE CODE.

Mr. ABBOTT moved to take from the table for consideration the following order submitted by him on yesterday:

"*Ordered*, That this convention recommend the governor, immediately after the adoption of the new constitution, to issue pardons to all persons now held in confinement for any violation of the laws made for the protection of slavery in this State."

Upon this motion Mr. PUGH called for the yeas and nays, and they were ordered.

The question being then taken by yeas and nays, the motion was agreed to—yeas 41, nays 33—as follows:

Yeas—Messrs. Goldsborough, President; Abbott, Annan, Audoun, Baker, Barron, Berry, of Baltimore county, Brooks, Carter, Cushing, Daniel, Davis, of Washington, Dellinger, Ecker, Farrow, Galloway, Greene, Hatch, Hoffman, Hopper, Keefer, Kennard, King, McComas, Murray, Negley, Nyman, Parker, Pugh, Purnell, Ridgely, Russell, Schley, Schlosser, Scott, Sneary, Stirling, Stockbridge, Swope, Sykes, Valliant—41.

Nays—Messrs. Belt, Bond, Brown, Chambers, Crawford, Cunningham, Dail, Davis, of Charles, Dent, Duvall, Gale, Henkle, Hollyday, Horsey, Jones, of Cecil, Jones, of Somerset, Lansdale, Larsh, Lee, Marbury, Markey, Mayhugh, Mitchell, Miller, Morgan, Mullikin, Parran, Peter, Smith, of Dorchester, Todd, Turner, Wilmer, Wooden—33.

The question was upon the adoption of the order.

Mr. Miller. It is perfectly well known that under the present constitution the executive has the power to pardon all offences which have been committed against the laws of the State. The order which is now under consideration is a recommendation that the governor should exercise the executive clemency in behalf of a certain class of offenders. If the governor should take this order as an imperative direction, or look upon it as imposing a sort of imperative obligation upon him, the duty thereby imposed would go to this extent. It is perfectly well known that a great many offences of this class have been perpetrated by a portion of the colored people of the State. Under existing laws those negroes, instead of being confined in the penitentiary or jail, have been ordered to be sold for a term of years, and purchasers have made their purchases of those negroes, and have paid their money for them. Do you wish that this convention should recommend to the governor the pardon of such cases as those? If the convention desires to go that far they can do so. I merely desire to call the attention of the convention to the extent to which the order goes.

Mr. Pugh. I look upon this order as meaning simply what it states in words. It is simply a recommendation to the governor. And I cannot for the life of me see how this convention could do less than simply recommend to the governor that these people, in the opinion of this convention, are no longer criminals, as this convention has decided that slavery shall no longer exist in this State.

Mr. Jones, of Somerset. Except for crime.

Mr. Pugh. Certainly. This is simply a recommendation to the governor. He is not bound by it. It is simply an expression of opinion upon the subject. It may not be noticed. An expression of opinion made by this convention, upon a former occasion, to the President of the United States and military commanders, was not noticed much. This is merely an expression of opinion on the part of this convention in regard to this class of offences. The governor will act as he deems best. This is not binding upon him. It is simply a recommendation to him, calling his attention to the fact. The governor, in spite of anything we might do here, has the right to pardon all criminals. We neither add to nor take from that right by the adoption of this order. If circumstances appear to him such as to justify the exercise of executive clemency, he can exercise it. For my part I think it is perfectly proper for the convention to pass this order.

The President announced that the hour had arrived for proceeding to the order of the day, being the final reading of the constitution as a whole.

On motion of Mr. Abbott,

The order of the day was postponed until eleven o'clock.

Mr. Jones, of Somerset. The circumstances under which the executive is to exercise this prerogative of pardoning criminals are regulated by law. Application for the pardon must be made. The application must be published in the newspapers, objections are to be filed by a particular day, and then the governor acts upon the application according to his discretion, and what is due to public justice and the good order of society. This order conflicts with the law, by recommending to the governor to violate these provisions of the law, and to order a wholesale delivery of a certain class of offenders. I think we better leave the matter where it is. Cases will come before the governor upon their merits; and in view of all that has been done the governor, no doubt, will discharge his duty faithfully. I am opposed to this interference with the law which regulates the mode in which the governor shall exercise the prerogative of pardon.

Mr. Stirling. It strikes me that my friend from Somerset (Mr. Jones) is a little inaccurate in regard to the operation of that part of the constitution which affects the pardoning power. The constitution does say that the executive, before granting any pardon, shall give notice that he is about to take the case up, and in regard to any applications for pardon, shall keep them on file so that they may be inspected by the general assembly. But the constitution never meant to say that the governor should never pardon any one, except when he was requested to do so. It never meant to take away from the governor the power to initiate the proceeding upon his own motion. If one person petitions for a pardon the governor may set the case down for a hearing. But if nobody petitions for it, the governor, knowing that public opinion is in favor of it, can still exercise his authority in that respect. The extent of the law is that the governor must give notice that he is going to take the case up for consideration.

This order does not conflict with that in the least. If the governor acts upon this recommendation, he has the power to give all the notice that the law requires to be given.

Now, in regard to what the gentleman from Anne Arundel (Mr. Miller) says about certain persons having been sold, and those who have bought them having an interest in their labor—I do not think those cases could come within the purview of this order. I should have been better satisfied with the order if it had been confined to persons in the penitentiary. So far as I have heard, or believe, I do not think there is a single negro who has been convicted for these offences who has not been sold out of the State.

Mr. JONES, of Somerset. They are all sold in the State.

Mr. MILLER. I suppose that within the last year ten or a dozen have been sold in this county.

Mr. STIRLING. The governor has a discretion in regard to them. I do not think any harm can result from the adoption of this order. So far as my experience goes, the amount paid for these persons is not much, and probably full value has been returned long ago.

Mr. MILLER. I know persons who have paid as high as two hundred dollars.

Mr. STIRLING. However, that does not at all touch the question of power. The governor, under the constitution, is not bound to observe any such obligation as that. No matter if the criminal in the penitentiary is bound by a contract to work for those who contract with the penitentiary, he can be pardoned, and when he goes out, the contract, so far as he is concerned, it is at an end. I have never had my attention called to the people of which the gentleman speaks. I know there are a great many cases in the penitentiary involving great hardship—of persons who have been sent there because the judges of the courts had no discretion in the matter.

I know of a case in Allegany county, where a man was accused of running off a number of servants, they being his own children. It was proved before the court that he wanted to keep them from being taken by the rebels. Yet he was sentenced to the penitentiary for five or ten years. I call upon the members from Allegany to say whether that is not the fact, or very near the facts? I may have misstated them somewhat, but I am satisfied I have stated them very nearly right.

Mr. GREENE. The case arose in this way: at a time when it was supposed the town of Cumberland was in danger of being taken by the rebels, this old negro man gathered up his children, who were slaves, and took them off to Pennsylvania. He made no concealment of what he was doing; the fact was observed by everybody. Yet he was convicted and sentenced. The judge, the jury, and nearly all the leading citizens of Cumberland, including the owner of the slaves that had been run off, signed a petition to the governor requesting a pardon.

Mr. JONES, of Somerset. And the governor has granted it?

Mr. GREENE Not yet.

Mr. STIRLING. There is one man now in the penitentiary under a sentence for forty years, for an offence of this kind; a man against whose private character no one entertains a doubt, but who under mistaken notions undertook to carry out his own convictions in regard to the law. It is one of that class of offences which no one regards as *malum in se*, but an offence against those laws which were necessary to keep up the institution of slavery. He was sent from Prince George's county for forty years. When there is no longer any necessity for such laws, why keep him there?

Mr. BELT. What was the case? One of insurrection?

Mr. STIRLING. No; being engaged in the underground railroad. He was convicted on five or six indictments, probably more, at the same term of the court.

Mr. BELT. The most remarkable feature about this discussion, is this extraordinary sympathy for the negro. Not satisfied with devoting nearly the whole of the session of the convention to the consideration of the negro in his various interests and relations, here at the very heel of the session, on the very brink of adjournment, we are called upon to stop our legitimate business, and pass an order recommending the governor to open the door of the penitentiary to the negro and the negro stealer; for nine-tenths of the people tried for these offences against the policy of slavery are negroes. Why not extend your clemency and leniency and mercy to white men? Many a white man is in the penitentiary for other offences, and there unjustly. I have vainly tried, during the session of the convention, to have some action taken here that would release from the penitentiary men who have been sent there, and who have since become lunatics. You can get nothing done for innocent white people who are confined for minor offences upon slender evidence.—Nothing can be done except for Mr. Negro; he is to be relieved. It is preposterous, ridiculous, disgusting.

Mr. STIRLING. The gentleman can entertain himself what opinions he pleases about what is preposterous and disgusting. I choose to entertain my own. I would like to know what this convention has to do with particular cases of wrongful imprisonment? This order, whether right or wrong, is based upon the ground that there is a certain class of offences, action upon which is rendered no longer necessary by the action of this body.

If the gentleman can discover anything disgusting in that he is welcome to do so.

Now as regards innocent persons being sent to the penitentiary. I know they have been sent to the penitentiary, although known to be innocent, as the proper place to confine them, the object being to get rid of their support. And it is the fact that almost all those cases come from a particular section of the State. The judges have the discretion to send them to a proper place of confinement, and they have designated the penitentiary as the proper place.

Mr. Dent. I am not aware of any such instances from the county which I represent.

Mr. Belt. Never any from my own official circuit.

Mr. Stirling. I know the fact from the statements of the officers of the penitentiary; and they are in the penitentiary now.

Mr. Jones, of Somerset. None from my district.

Mr. Stirling. I am willing to take the testimony of those connected with the penitentiary, if such is not the fact.

Mr. Miller. I know of no such cases from our county.

Mr. Abbott. My object in offering this order was simply to call the attention of the governor to this subject, and to back up his disposition to relieve certain parties now in confinement for offences against laws which we are about to abolish. If this constitution is adopted, slavery will no longer exist in this State, and consequently with slavery go all the laws made to protect it. There are a large number of persons in our State who are now suffering punishment for a breach of those laws. If the law is repealed, there can no longer be any breach of it. It only reaches that class of persons who are confined for any violation of the laws made for the protection of slavery. I carefully worded it so as not to include kidnappers, and such persons. That class of persons would not properly come within the limits of this order. I intended it to reach only those persons who have offended against the laws for the protection of slavery, which laws we are about to abolish.

Mr. Pugh. In answer to the statement of the gentleman from Prince George's (Mr. Belt,) that there is a great disposition on the part of this convention to take care of the negro, I would suggest that we are peculiarly situated in that respect, having been sent here, as was pretty generally understood—and I suppose the gentleman from Prince George's had such an idea—mainly for the purpose of abolishing slavery in this State. It so happens that all the slaves are called negroes; consequently we could not very well avoid dealing with negroes, they being the persons held in slavery. The gentleman himself has, I believe, avoided all sympathy for the negro.

Mr. Belt. I have more true sympathy for the negro than the gentleman himself has.

Mr. Pugh. Very many of the party with whom the gentleman acts, were very anxious to have the negro represented in the legislature. I for one was opposed to that, and am still opposed to it. The gentleman's colleague (Mr. Clarke)—I do not hold the gentleman responsible for that at all—introduced an order here to relieve the negro from military duty. I was opposed to it. I do not think the gentleman, if he will examine the record, will find that the party with whom he has acted here, are any more wanting in their sympathy for the negro than we are.

Mr. Belt. In reply to the remarks of my friend from Cecil (Mr. Pugh,) I would say that it is not any particular philanthropy for the negro at all that that was asked. It was because it has been done from the very foundation of the government. The negro has always been represented and counted in the population, upon the theory that all classes of people, whether they were voters or not, whether they were endowed with political privileges or not, who ministered to the production and wealth of the State, ought to be included within the basis of representation. Here is one single fact, which being stated, nothing further need be said upon the subject. The very instant you free the negro slaves in Maryland, that very instant, by the very operation of law, they become represented man for man, poll for poll, in the national congress. Now if negroes are to be represented in the national congress, why not here? Under the law of federal numbers, negroes are represented in the national congress only to the extent of three-fifths. But the moment they are set free, they are represented there as fully as we are.

Mr Berry, of Baltimore county. I would like to make one statement in reply to the gentleman from Baltimore city (Mr. Stirling) and the gentleman from Allegany (Mr. Greene.) I understood the gentleman from Allegany to say that at the time it was supposed Cumberland was about to be invaded, this man, Harris, gathered his own children together and carried them into Pennsylvania, and that the judge, and the prosecuting attorney, and the jury had signed a petition stating these facts. If I am wrong in my statement of what the gentleman from Allegany said, I would be glad to be corrected.

The President. The gentleman from Allegany is not now in his seat.

Mr. Berry, of Baltimore county. However, the facts of the case are simply these: a petition was drawn up and sent to the governor, with this simple statement, that these children were seen to be carried from the town of Cumberland some ten miles and put into a stage; and were then carried on to the next stopping place, where they were crowded out of the stage by an overplus of passengers. The petition makes no particular statement in regard to any danger of invasion; but simply states that these children were the children and grandchildren of Harris. The judge did not sign the petition; the prosecuting attorney did not sign it. The jurors, and the members of the last legislature from that county, signed it, and it is now on file in the executive department.

The question was upon adopting the order of Mr. ABBOTT.

Upon this question Mr. PUGH called for the yeas and nays, and they were ordered.

The question was then taken, by yeas and nays, and resulted—yeas 34, nays 34—as follows:

Yeas—Messrs. Goldsborough, President; Abbott, Annan, Audoun, Baker, Barron, Brooks, Carter, Cunningham, Cushing, Daniel, Dellinger, Ecker, Farrow, Galloway, Harwood, Hatch, Hebb, Hopper, Keefer, Kennard, Markey, Mayhugh, McComas, Negley, Pugh, Purnell, Russell, Schley, Schlosser, Stirling, Stockbridge, Swope, Valliant—34.

Nays—Messrs. Belt, Berry, of Baltimore county, Bond, Chambers, Crawford, Dail, Davis, of Charles, Dent, Duvall, Gale, Henkle, Hodson, Hoffman, Hollyday, Horsey, Jones, of Cecil, Jones, of Somerset, King, Lansdale, Larsh, Lee, Marbury, Mitchell, Miller, Morgan, Mullikin, Parker, Peter, Ridgely, Smith, of Dorchester, Sykes, Turner, Wilmer, Wooden—34.

The order was accordingly rejected, it being a tie vote.

COMPENSATION FOR SLAVES.

On motion of Mr. BERRY, of Baltimore county,

The convention took from the table the following resolution offered by Mr. CLARKE, and laid on the table on the 2d of June:

"*Resolved*, That a select committee to consist of nine members, of which committee the president of the convention shall be chairman, be appointed by the chair, whose duty it shall be to confer with the President of the United States, our senators and representatives in congress, and the appropriate committees of congress, to ascertain and report to this convention, what appropriation if any, will be made by congress, in pursuance of the recommendations contained in the messages of the President of the United States, of December, 1862, and December, 1863, and the joint resolutions of congress No. 26, approved April 10th, 1862, to aid the State of Maryland in the adoption of a system of emancipation, and "to be used by said State in its discretion to compensate for the inconveniences, public and private, produced by such change of system."

Mr. BERRY, of Baltimore county, had given notice that when the resolution was again taken up for consideration, he would offer the following substitute:

"*Resolved*, That a special committee, to consist of seven members be appointed by the president of the convention, of which the president shall act as chairman, whose duty it shall be to confer with the President of the United States, our senators and representatives in congress, and the appropriate committees of congress, to ascertain what appropriation, if any, will be made by the federal government in compliance with the recommendations contained in the messages of the President of the United States of March 6th, 1862, and December 1st, 1862, and the joint resolution of congress, approved April 10th, 1862, in the following words, to wit:

"That the United States ought to co-operate with any State which may adopt gradual abolishment of slavery, giving to such State pecuniary aid, to be used by the State in its discretion, to compensate for inconveniences, public and private, produced by such a change of system."

Mr. BERRY, of Baltimore county. As congress has adjourned, the substitute of which I gave notice is no longer appropriate. I therefore withdraw it, and offer the following as a substitute for the original order of the gentleman of Prince George's (Mr. Clarke):

"*Resolved*, That a special committee to consist of seven members, be appointed by the president of the convention, of which he shall act as chairman, whose duty it shall be to visit and confer with the President of the United States, respecting an appropriation on the part of the federal government to the State of Maryland, in conformity to the recommendations of the messages of the President of the United States of March 6th, 1862, and December 1st, 1862, and the joint resolution of congress, approved April 10th, 1862, declaring "that the United States ought to co-operate with any State which may adopt gradual abolishment of slavery, giving to such State pecuniary aid, to be used by the State in its discretion, to compensate for inconveniences, public and private, produced by such a change of system.

"The committee will submit to the President of the United States article 24th of the declaration of rights, as adopted by this convention, and respectfully ask in behalf of this body, that, upon the ratification of said 24th article by the people of this State, he will recommend to congress at its next session to make such appropriation as will compensate loyal owners for the inconveniences and losses sustained in the premises."

Mr. AUDOUN moved to lay the subject on the table.

On this motion, Mr. BERRY, of Baltimore county, called for the yeas and nays, which were ordered.

The question being then taken, by yeas and nays, it resulted—yeas 18, nays 55—as follows:

Yeas—Messrs. Abbott, Annan, Audoun, Barron, Brooks, Cushing, Ecker, Greene, Harwood, Hatch, Hebb, Keefer, Kennard,

Pugh, Schley, Schlosser, Stirling, Wooden—18.

Nays—Messrs. Goldsborough, President; Baker, Belt, Berry, of Baltimore county, Bond, Brown, Carter, Chambers, Crawford, Cunningham, Dail, Daniel, Davis, of Charles, Dent, Duvall, Farrow, Gale, Galloway, Henkle, Hodson, Hoffman, Hollyday, Hopper, Horsey, Jones, of Cecil, Jones, of Somerset, King, Lansdale, Larsh, Lee, Marbury, Markey, Mayhugh, McComas, Mitchell, Miller, Morgan, Mullikin, Murray, Negley, Nyman, Parker, Peter, Purnell, Ridgely, Russell, Smith, of Dorchester, Stockbridge, Swope, Sykes, Todd, Turner, Valliant, Wickard, Wilmer—55.

Accordingly the motion to lay on the table was not agreed to.

Mr. Berry, of Baltimore county, moved the previous question, which was seconded, and the main question ordered.

The first question was upon the substitute offered by Mr. Berry, of Baltimore county.

Upon this question Mr. Stirling called for the yeas and nays, which were ordered.

The question was then taken, by yeas and nays, and resulted—yeas 49, nays 24—as follows:

Yeas—Messrs. Goldsborough, President; Baker, Belt, Berry, of Baltimore county, Bond, Brown, Carter, Chambers, Crawford, Dail, Daniel, Davis, of Charles, Dellinger, Duvall, Farrow, Gale, Galloway, Henkle, Hodson, Hoffman, Hollyday, Hopper, Horsey, Jones, of Cecil, Jones, of Somerset, King, Lansdale, Larsh, Lee, Markey, Mayhugh, McComas, Mitchell, Miller, Morgan, Mullikin, Murray, Parker, Peter, Purnell, Ridgely, Russell, Smith, of Dorchester, Swope, Sykes, Todd, Turner, Valliant, Wilmer—49.

Nays—Abbott, Annan, Audoun, Barron, Brooks, Cunningham, Cushing, Dent, Ecker, Greene, Harwood, Hatch, Hebb, Keefer, Kennard, Marbury, Negley, Pugh, Schley, Schlosser, Stirling, Stockbridge, Thomas, Wickard, Wooden—24.

The substitute was accordingly adopted.

Pending the calling of the yeas and nays, the following explanations were made by members as their names were called:

Mr. Brooks. I shall vote against this proposition for this reason: when the offer was tendered by the general government, some of our representatives in congress, said that they looked upon it as an insult to the State, and that they spit upon it. That is one reason. Another reason is this: I never will by any vote of mine acknowledge the right of property in man. I therefore vote "no."

Mr. Negley. If this resolution had been made broad enough to cover the losses which our people in western Maryland have sustained by reason of rebel invasions, I would have voted for it. But I never will vote for any resolution which looks to only one species of property, that has reference to but one kind of loss, and that kind of loss being very questionable, namely, that of the negro. I never will vote for any resolution that looks to nothing else but property in the negro, and that does not cover losses we have sustained in property, about the right to which there is no question. I vote "no."

Mr. Pugh. There are one or two reasons, probably more, why I cannot vote for this proposition. In the first place, under the operation of the previous question—there has been some trouble heretofore about the previous question; but this is the most remarkable instance of the application of the previous question that has come under my observation. Under the operation of the previous question, I had no opportunity, nor had any other member, to offer an amendment to this proposition, when it is well known to everybody in this convention that there is nothing so liable to be misunderstood as the word "loyal" in this State, unless properly explained. It has never been used at any time by this convention without a full explanation accompanying it. We little know, from the terms of this resolution, who will receive this compensation if any is granted. There are people in this State who will apply for it, whom I know and you know very well to be not loyal. I wanted some definition of the term. As the resolution does not contain that, I vote "no."

Mr. Stirling. I desire to say that while it is very well known that I was very anxious, when this question was first discussed before congress, that this relief should be granted in anticipation of emancipation, yet I cannot vote for this resolution, because I know it is keeping before the people of the State a mere delusion; and holding out expectations which cannot and will not be realized. And as I regard it as extremely unfortunate that any such course should now be pursued, which will result in no practical good, and can only tend to deceive the people, I shall vote "no."

Mr. Stockbridge. I am always opposed to this sending of committees on errands like this. For that reason, if there were no other, I should vote against this proposition. So far as my observation extends, such conferences always result in misunderstandings.—We have reports of the recollections of various parties; not written statements of what passed, reduced to writing beforehand in the form of address and reply. I shall therefore vote against this and all such propositions to send committees on any such errands. If it had been a proposition to communicate in writing the sense of this convention, it would have been a very different thing. I vote "no."

Mr. Valliant. I dislike very much to trouble the convention with any explanation of my vote. But justice to myself, I think, demands it on this occasion. I do not desire that my vote in favor of this proposition should be construed as anything like a recognition of the natural right of property in man. I deny that any one man has a natural right to hold another as a slave. My principle reason, and I think I may safely say my only reason, for voting in favor of this proposition is, that I stand pledged to my constituents to do it. I am indifferent as to whether this resolution is adopted or not. If I have any feeling one way more than the other, I believe it is against it. I think it would be gratifying to my feelings to have it rejected. But standing pledged to my constituents to vote for a proposition of this character in case it came up, I feel bound to comply with that promise; and therefore I vote "aye."

The PRESIDENT subsequently announced the following committee in accordance with the above order:

Messrs. Goldsborough, (chairman,) Berry, of Baltimore county, Purnell, Negley, Todd, Smith, of Carroll, and Hopper.

ONE HUNDRED DOLLARS EXTRA MILEAGE.

Mr. BELT. Last night there was an order under consideration providing for the compensation of the president of this convention, as one of the officers of this house, to which an amendment was offered looking to the instruction of the committee on accounts in relation to the mileage of members. They were defeated by a small vote. I now move to reconsider the vote by which they were rejected.

Mr. STOCKBRIDGE. That matter has been pretty thoroughly canvassed a dozen times in this convention. I therefore move that this whole matter be indefinitely postponed.

The PRESIDENT. The question before the house is the motion to reconsider. Rule forty-four says: "No motion for reconsideration shall be postponed or laid on the table."

Mr. STOCKBRIDGE. Then I call for the yeas and nays on the motion to reconsider.

The yeas and nays were accordingly ordered.

The question was then taken by yeas and nays, and resulted—yeas 39, nays 29—as follows:

Yeas—Messrs. Abbott, Audoun, Barron, Belt, Berry, of Baltimore county, Bond, Brooks, Carter, Chambers, Crawford, Dail, Dellinger, Dent, Duvall, Gale, Hatch, Henkle, Hodson, Hollyday, Jones, of Cecil, Jones, of Somerset, King, Lansdale, Larsh, Lee, Marbury, Mayhugh, Miller, Morgan, Negley, Peter, Ridgely, Smith, of Dorchester, Swope, Sykes, Turner, Wickard, Wilmer, Wooden—39.

Nays—Messrs. Annan, Baker, Cunningham, Cushing, Daniel, Davis, of Charles, Ecker, Farrow, Greene, Harwood, Hebb, Hoffman, Horsey, Keefer, Kennard, Markey, McComas, Mitchell, Mullikin, Parker, Pugh, Purnell, Russell, Schley, Schlosser, Scott, Stirling, Stockbridge, Thomas—29.

The motion to reconsider was accordingly agreed to.

Pending the calling of the yeas and nays, the following explanations were made by members as their names were called:

Mr. ECKER. As I understand it, this is a motion to reconsider the vote by which the convention refused to allow each of its members to steal a hundred dollars. Now I have nothing to say more than I have already said on this subject. This question has been already decided by the convention two or three times. I have the floor now, and if the chair decides that I can hold it until eleven o'clock (the hour for the special order, the reading of of the constitution,) I shall most certainly do it.

The CHAIRMAN (Mr. Purnell.) The gentleman cannot do that. He must vote.

Mr. ECKER Then I vote "no."

Mr. JONES, of Somerset. I changed my vote to the negative last night, because there was a very thin house, and there seemed to be a very great indisposition upon the part of some gentlemen to vote in the affirmative, although many of them avowed that, after the exposition of the law as it stood, they had no sort of question but the law fixed the mileage at one hundred dollars in addition to the usual mileage. That, I admit, is a very unequal distribution of the mileage. But it is the law. And those who think they ought not to take the money can leave it in the treasury, where it ought to be left. I trust they will not withdraw it from the treasury, and then bolster up a character for charity by giving it to somebody else. The committee on accounts, as I understand, are embarrassed to know what the law is in reference to mileage, and they want the instruction of the house upon the question. The house must either say that the committee shall disregard this part of the law fixing the mileage, and act as if it did not exist; or else they must affirm this to be a part of the law regulating mileage, and instruct the committee on accounts accordingly. The committee certainly ought to have some expression of the opinion of the house upon this subject. I shall therefore vote for the reconsideration, in order that we may have an opportunity of fixing what the committee on accounts shall regard as the mileage of members. I vote "aye."

Mr. SCHLEY. This appeal to the cupidity of members, for I regard this proposition in no other light, has been solemnly decided adversely three times by this convention. I had hoped that there was an end to it. I had hoped that we had arrived at something like a definite decision of this matter. I had hoped that the temptation to appropriate this money would be finally resisted. I was very much surprised last night to hear it laid down as law, by gentlemen learned in the law, that we had a clear right to this appropriation.—With all deference to their arguments, and I do defer to gentlemen of the law, I must insist that it is at least not just to take this money. I know that the sentiment of the people everywhere was against the action of the last general assembly in this respect. I do not care what decision this convention comes to, I as one of its members, entertaining the opinion I do, shall positively decline to take this money out of the State treasury. I therefore vote "no."

Mr. STOCKBRIDGE. The gentleman from Baltimore county (Mr. Ridgely) submitted an order to the convention, to which the gentleman from Queen Anne (Mr. Lee) proposed an amendment. Upon which of those propositions is the motion to reconsider?

The CHAIRMAN (Mr. Purnell.) Upon both.

Mr. STOCKBRIDGE. There were two distinct motions.

Mr. BELT. I never heard of anybody who doubted on a question of this sort.

Mr. STOCKBRIDGE. I made an inquiry of the chair.

The CHAIRMAN. The chair understood the motion to be to reconsider the whole subject; the order of the gentleman from Baltimore county (Mr. Ridgely) as amended, on motion of the gentleman from Queen Anne (Mr. Lee.)

Mr. STOCKBRIDGE. It was not amended; the amendment was rejected.

The CHAIRMAN. Both the order and the amendment were lost.

Mr. STOCKBRIDGE. Then I vote "no."

The order submitted by Mr. RIDGELY was as follows:

"*Ordered*, That the president of this convention be allowed a per diem of six dollars, and that the committee on accounts audit his account accordingly."

To which Mr. LEE proposed to add the following:

"And that the committee on accounts be hereby instructed to audit the mileage account of each member of this convention according to the joint resolution of the general assembly of this State at its last session, adjusting the mileage of the members of that body."

The question was upon the amendment proposed by Mr. LEE.

Mr. SCHLEY. I call for the order of the day, the hour of eleven having arrived.

Mr. MILLER moved that the order of the day be postponed until half past eleven o'clock.

Upon this question Mr. STOCKBRIDGE called for the yeas and nays, which were ordered.

The question was then taken by yeas and nays, and resulted—yeas 41, nays 21—as follows:

Yeas—Messrs. Abbott, Audoun, Barron, Belt, Berry, of Baltimore county, Bond, Brooks, Carter, Crawford, Cunningham, Dail, Davis, of Charles, Dellinger, Dent, Duvall, Gale, Hatch, Henkle, Hodson, Hollyday, Horsey, Jones, of Cecil, Jones, of Somerset, Lansdale, Larsh, Lee, Marbury, Markey, Mayhugh, Miller, Morgan, Negley, Ridgely, Schlosser, Smith, of Dorchester, Swope, Sykes, Turner, Wickard, Wilmer, Wooden—41.

Nays—Messrs. Annan, Baker, Daniel, Ecker, Farrow, Greene, Harwood, Hebb, Hoffman, Keefer, Kennard, McComas, Mullikin, Parker, Pugh, Purnell, Russell, Schley, Scott, Stirling, Stockbridge—21.

The order of the day was postponed accordingly.

Mr. GALE moved the previous question, which was seconded, and the main question ordered.

The question was upon the amendment offered by Mr. LEE.

Upon this question Mr. STOCKBRIDGE called for the yeas and nays, which were ordered.

The question was then taken by yeas and nays, and resulted—yeas 38, nays 33—as follows:

Yeas—Messrs. Abbott, Audoun, Barron, Belt, Berry, of Baltimore county, Bond, Brooks, Carter, Crawford, Dail, Dellinger, Dent, Duvall, Gale, Hatch, Henkle, Hodson, Hollyday, Jones, of Cecil, Jones, of Somerset, King, Lansdale, Larsh, Lee, Marbury, Mayhugh, Miller, Morgan, Negley, Peter, Ridgely, Smith, of Dorchester, Swope, Sykes, Turner, Wickard, Wilmer, Wooden—38.

Nays—Messrs. Annan, Baker, Cunningham, Cushing, Daniel, Davis, of Charles, Davis, of Washington, Ecker, Farrow, Galloway, Greene, Harwood, Hebb, Hoffman, Horsey, Keefer, Kennard, Markey, McComas, Mitchell, Mullikin, Nyman, Parker, Pugh, Purnell, Russell, Schley, Schlosser, Scott, Sneary, Stirling, Stockbridge, Thomas—33.

The amendment was accordingly adopted.

Pending the call of the yeas and nays, the following explanations were made by members as their names were called:

Mr. DANIEL. Believing, as I have already stated, that this proposition is contrary both to law and principle, and calculated, if it prevails, merely to despoil the treasury of so much money, I shall vote against it. And if it is adopted, I shall feel it to be my duty to return to the treasury of the State the amount I may receive under this proposition. I am very sorry to see that a great many members who have been here least are the most anxious in advocating this amendment. I vote "no."

Mr. DAVIS, of Charles. Some of my friends around me seem to think that this is a mere question of law. Now I do not differ with them at all in regard to the construction of the law. I believe the law is on the side of those who contend that they have a right to this extra compensation. But I do not believe the people of the State so understood it. I know I did not so understand it at the time of the election. Believing that the people did not understand the law in that way, I am compelled to vote "no."

Mr. MITCHELL. I shall vote against this order in the first place, because, notwithstanding the elaborate arguments by which it is supported, I am not convinced of our right or power to take this money. And I am opposed to it in the next place for the reasons set forth by my colleague (Mr. Davis, of Charles.) I vote "no"

Mr. PUGH. I have not the least doubt that the gentlemen who support this proposition, do so in good faith. I have not a particle of doubt that they so interpret the law. I have examined the matter in every possible way, but I cannot so understand it. At the time I was elected to come to this convention, I never expected to get this extra compensation. I shall vote conscientiously upon this matter; I am not actuated by any buncombe feeling. I shall act just according to my convictions. I do not think I am entitled to this money, and I do not want it. I vote "no."

Mr. RUSSELL. This matter has been decided several times in the convention, and in the committee on accounts. I am very sorry to see it introduced here again. I believe most conscientiously that neither legally nor morally are we entitled to it. And if this proposition is adopted, I shall decline to receive the money. I vote "no."

Mr. SCHLEY. I merely wish to say that by the operation of the previous question, I have been prevented from offering an amendment to the pending proposition, which I think would have been received by the convention. It is unnecessary for me to repeat my views upon the question now pending. I shall most assuredly decline to receive the money, if this shall be adopted, which I hope will not be the case. I vote "no."

Mr. STOCKBRIDGE. I regret extremely that our record should be marred with this subject. I shall vote against this proposition because I do not think it right. There is no temptation, were the sum much larger than it is to induce me to do otherwise. At the same time I desire to say with reference, not to myself, but to others, that I hold the decision of this convention to make this matter equally applicable to all members, notwithstanding any sneer about being charitable at the expense of others. If the decision of this convention makes this legal for one, it is legal for all. If any one chooses to decline to receive it on moral grounds, it is right to do as he pleases. But no one has a right to point any sneer at another who has persistently objected to this proposition, but considers himself overruled by the better judgment of the convention. I vote "no."

The question recurred upon adopting the order as amended, as follows:

"*Ordered*, That the president of this convention be allowed a per diem of six dollars; and that the committee on accounts audit his accounts accordingly; and that the committee on accounts be hereby instructed to audit the mileage account of each member of this convention according to the joint resolution of the general assembly of this State at its last session, adjusting the mileage of the members of that body."

Upon this question Mr. SCHLEY called for the yeas and nays, which were ordered.

The question was then taken by yeas and nays, and resulted—yeas 39, nays 34—as follows:

Yeas—Messrs. Abbott, Audoun, Barron, Belt, Berry, of Baltimore county, Bond, Brooks, Brown, Carter, Crawford, Dail, Dellinger, Dent, Duvall, Gale, Hatch, Henkle, Hodson, Hollyday, Jones, of Cecil, Jones, of Somerset, King, Lansdale, Larsh, Lee, Marbury, Mayhugh, Miller, Morgan, Negley, Peter, Ridgely, Smith, of Dorchester, Swope, Sykes, Turner, Wickard, Wilmer, Wooden—39.

Nays—Messrs. Annan, Baker, Cunningham, Cushing, Daniel, Davis, of Charles, Davis, of Washington, Earle, Ecker, Galloway, Greene, Harwood, Hebb, Hoffman, Horsey, Keefer, Kennard, Markey, McComas, Mitchell, Mullikin, Murray, Nyman, Parker, Pugh, Purnell, Russell, Schley, Schlosser, Scott, Sneary, Stirling, Stockbridge, Thomas—34.

The order as amended was accordingly adopted.

Mr. MCCOMAS, when his name was called, said: Though in favor of the former part of this proposition, yet considering the latter part of it one of the worst acts of selfish and iniquitous legislation that ever characterized the general assembly of Maryland, I shall have to vote against the whole proposition, especially after having recorded my vote, with others, in favor of allowing future general assemblies of this State five dollars a day and no mileage. There was not one of us who was elected to this convention who expected to receive this mileage. I vote "no."

Mr. PUGH. I should like very much to have had an opportunity to vote for the first part of this proposition, because I believe it is justified by precedent and is nothing more than right. But as the matter now stands, it is impossible for me to vote for the first part without indorsing the rider. I am altogether opposed to that portion of it, and am therefore obliged to vote "no."

Mr. SCHLEY. I ask the unanimous consent of the convention to have the following entered on the journal.

"*Ordered*, That it be entered on the journal that Frederick Schley, one of the delegates from Frederick county, dissenting from the decision just come to by the convention, respectfully protests against its action in appropriating one hundred dollars to each member for extra itineracy, and declines to take from the treasury of the State, the amount of additional compensation so awarded to him."

Mr. DENT. The gentleman from Frederick (Mr. Schley) has already fully stated his objections to the adoption of this order, and those objections have gone upon the journal of debates. It appears to me, therefore, that it is unnecessary for the purpose of our understanding his position, that any such protest as this should be entered upon the journal of proceedings. He has stated his objections very clearly, and they are already on the journal of debates. And it appears to me that it is rather out of place to attempt to put such a protest upon the journal of proceedings. I shall therefore object to it going upon the journal. If his objections had not already been properly put upon the journal of debates, I would not make any such objection to it.

Mr. JONES, of Somerset. I desire to ask the gentleman from Frederick (Mr. Schley) whether he voted in the affirmative to enter upon the journal the protest of thirty-five members of this house. If he did not, will he ask a courtesy for himself, which he refused to extend to thirty-five gentlemen here?

The PRESIDENT. The gentleman from Frederick (Mr. Schley) asks the consent of the house to have this protest entered upon the journal. Objection being made, the chair will put the question to the house.

The question was then taken, and the request of Mr. SCHLEY was refused.

Mr. BARRON. I shall offer no protest. But if I get this hundred dollars, I shall lay it out in a proper channel. I was here last winter.

Mr. DENT (in his seat.) You are not in order.

Mr. BARRON. The gentleman from St. Mary's (Mr. Dent) tells me I am not in order; so I will not go on.

COMPENSATION FOR SLAVES.

Mr. AUDOUN submitted the following:

"*Ordered*, That before any person shall receive the benefits to be derived from the resolution offered by the gentleman from Baltimore county (Mr. Berry,) they shall take and subscribe to the oath as prescribed in this constitution, in the article on elective franchise."

Mr. BERRY, of Baltimore county. Will the gentleman from Baltimore city (Mr. Audoun) so amend his order as to state what the resolution was, that it was in regard to compensation from the general government for losses sustained in consequence of the abolition of slavery?

Mr. AUDOUN. I have no objection to that.

The order was modified accordingly.

The PRESIDENT announced that the hour had arrived for taking up the order of the day.

On motion of Mr. GALLOWAY,

The order of the day, (being the reading of the constitution,) was postponed until twelve o'clock.

The order of Mr. AUDOUN was passed over informally.

THE PUBLCATION OF THE CONSTITUTION.

On motion of Mr. NEGLEY,

The convention then proceeded to consider the following resolution, which was reconsidered yesterday, and then postponed until to-day:

"*Ordered*, That the chair appoint a committee of three to contract with the Baltimore American, or some other newspaper or newspapers, for the publication of the constitution entire in extra newspaper form, ten thousand copies in the German language, and fifty thousand in the English, to be distributed as follows: two hundred copies to be furnished to each member of the convention, and the remainder to be equally distributed by said committee among the various county newspapers and postmasters, who will promptly distribute the same among the people, the copies to be furnished by the contractor for printing the same within one week after the final adjournment of this convention."

The pending question was upon the motion of Mr. NEGLEY to amend by striking out "ten thousand," and inserting "five thousand," and striking out "fifty thousand," and inserting "twenty thousand."

Mr. NEGLEY. If this amendment is adopted, I will then move an additional amendment, providing for giving the publication of this constitution to the newspapers in the several counties, in addition to this. I think this constitution should be brought generally before the people; and I feel certain that will not be done, unless it is published in at least one newspaper in each county. This proposition to distribute did not work well in regard to the last constitution. A great number of copies were sent to our county, and long after the adoption of the constitution they were lying about and being used as waste paper by the parties to whom they were sent; they were really not distributed at all. I think you cannot better bring this constitution before the people, than by publishing it in the newspapers. My colleague (Mr. Sneary) says he does not think the expense of publishing it in the county newspapers, will be any greater than publishing it in the other way.

Mr. STIRLING. I hope this amendment will not be adopted. I think the gentleman from Frederick (Mr. Schley) has an order, which he has shown me, which he desires to introduce, and which I shall be very happy to support. I would be very willing to vote for some provision to publish the constitution in the county newspapers. But I am opposed to cutting down the number provided by this resolution. These copies can all be distributed. The reasons assigned by my friend from Washington (Mr. Negley) are not applicable to this constitution, because the condition of things now is very different from what it was in 1850. It is perfectly well known that the last constitution was submitted to the people without any canvass either for or against it. There was no political party, no organization that took any interest in it. There was no organization for the purpose of distributing copies of the constitution. The whole thing was left to take its course.

We are now about to submit this constitution on the eve of a presidential election. We are about to submit it with party influences and organizations, on the one side and the other, in every county in the State, besides our central organization. We have meetings organized all over the State in reference to this constitution and the presidential election. These copies can all be distributed at these public meetings, and by the action of independent special committees who feel an interest in this matter. There are none too many. A certain amount will be wasted, of course; we cannot help that, and you need not try. In order to guard against that, you must have a certain number in excess. I am satisfied, from what I have heard, that those who are interested in the adoption of this constitution, have already taken measures by which these copies will all be distributed.

Mr. MILLER. I will merely say that I voted for the order for publishing and distributing these sixty thousand copies of the constitution. I am also in favor of the proposition of the gentleman from Washington county (Mr. Negley) or some similar proposition, by which this constitution can be published in our county papers, and in the papers in the city of Baltimore. There are a great many people in the State who are deeply interested in this subject, who would like, before they vote upon this constitution, to have its provisions before them so that they can read them. I know farmers who would like to take their county paper, with this constitution in it, and read it over by their firesides at night in the presence of their families, and discuss its provisions. Many of those people will be reached by the county papers. A fair and impartial judgment ought to be expressed upon this constitution by those who are entitled to vote upon it. It is but right and just that it should be made as public as possible. The time allowed before we are to vote upon it is limited. I do not think we should consider the additional expense of a few hundred dollars for publishing it in the papers.

Mr. STOCKBRIDGE. I had but one purpose in offering the order which was adopted; and that was to secure the circulation and distribution of this constitution as widely as possible throughout the State. I suppose that many of the county papers, being small, if they were to publish this constitution, would contain nothing else; it would fill up their papers entirely. And I thought the publishers of those papers would be very glad to be able to furnish it, without additional expense to themselves, to their subscribers in addition to their usual matter. If the contract with the Baltimore American should be made by the committee, this constitution will certainly appear in that paper within the next two or three days. By that arrangement alone, without any expense whatever, there will be struck off about fifty thousand copies to be circulated far and wide throughout the State. There will then be published the sixty thousand copies called for by this order, the expense of which will be far less than publishing it in forty or even twenty papers throughout the State. I therefore do not see the utility of having it so published, and am satisfied it will be attended with great expense.

I am satisfied also, that these "extras" can without any difficulty be distributed everywhere through the means of public meetings. For instance, the members from Washington county will have twelve hundred copies for them to distribute in that county. And then by distributing other copies at the public meetings which are already announced for that county, it seems to me this constitution will reach every household in that county. If it can be done in that way, and this very considerable item of expense saved, I would be glad of it. I would be glad to see it published in every county newspaper, if it could be done without too great expense to the State. I would be glad to save any unnecessary expense, and not have it added to the $10,000 or $12,000 we have already this morning unnecessarily imposed upon the State.

Mr. NEGLEY. The sole object I have in going for this publication at all is to bring this constitution to the notice of the people. The plan proposed by the gentleman from Baltimore city (Mr. Stockbridge) is a good one, I admit, if it will work; if the object it proposes can be attained, it is a good one. I know that twelve hundred copies will be sent to my county; I will have two hundred of them; I know we can distribute them among our people. But there is a large number of our people who do not come out to our political gatherings; they only come out to vote. They are a reflecting and reading and thinking people. How will you reach them? If you trust to these copies, you will have to get a colporteur in each county, put him on horseback, and send him out to distribute them. We have six thousand vot rs in our county. I know that the only means by which you can reach our people is by publishing this constitution in the papers.

Now, let us have a reasonable number of these "extra" copies. But if the object be to bring this constitution before the people, there is no mode so effectual as to publish it in the county newspapers. There is a large class of agriculturists in our county, and this year especially, as work is crowded upon them by the scarcity of labor, they will pay but little attention to your political meetings. But they get their county paper every week, and at night they sit down and read it. It is a habit with that kind of people in our county, and in every county in this State and in every State; they regard it as a sort of duty and privilege to read their county newspapers. They will absolutely wade through things there that might as well not be read. And from that very habit, they will read the constitution if printed in their paper, when they would not, if sent to them in the form of an "extra."

I am not anxious either one way or the other. My only object is to get this constitution before the people, as thoroughly and completely as we can. If it takes a few hundred or a few thousand dollars more, be it so. If gentlemen think we better hold on to this fifty thousand copies in English, and ten thousand in German, let that be done. But there ought to be some provision made for the publication of this constitution in the county newspapers. The editors of those papers take a deep interest in this movement. And I think it is no more than right that they should have this opportunity of spreading this matter before the people, and that they should be remunerated properly for it, when the public good is to be benefitted by it. You will necessarily enlist them in behalf of the constitution. And in counties where there are opposition papers, it infinitely better be published in those papers, and go out with all the animadversions of the editors. Let the document itself go before the people, so that they can correct the misrepresentations of its opponents. I shall therefore move an amendment that it be published in the papers.

The question was upon the motion of Mr. NEGLEY, to decrease the number of copies of the constitution to be published from fifty thousand to twenty thousand in the English language, and from ten thousand to five thousand in the German.

The question being taken, the motion was not agreed to.

Mr. NEGLEY. I move to amend the order by adding the following:

"And that the committee on publishing be directed to have the constitution published in one or more newspapers in each county and the city of Baltimore, once a week for three successive weeks before the day of its ratification or rejection."

Mr. DAVIS, of Washington. I would ask my colleague (Mr. Negley) to add the following to his amendment:

"Provided, it can be done at a cost of not more than $75 to each paper in which it is published."

Mr. NEGLEY. I accept the amendment.

Mr. PUGH. Is it possible to get this constitution published for that sum? If not it might lead to trouble to adopt this proposition.

Mr. NEGLEY. My colleague (Mr. Sneary,) who is a practical printer, says that it can be done for that.

Mr. DAVIS, of Washington. I think our papers will publish it for that sum.

The time for the special order having arrived,

Mr. NEGLEY moved to postpone the special order until the pending subject was disposed of.

Mr. ABBOTT moved a call of the house, which was ordered.

The roll was then called, and the following members answered to their names:

Messrs. Goldsborough, President; Abbott, Annan, Baker, Barron, Berry, of Baltimore county, Bond, Brown, Carter, Cunningham, Dail, Daniel, Davis, of Charles, Duvall, Earle, Ecker, Farrow, Galloway, Greene, Hatch, Hebb, Hodson, Hoffman, Hopper, Horsey, Jones, of Cecil, Keefer, Kennard, King, Lansdale, Larsh, Lee, Marbury, Markey, Mayhugh, McComas, Mitchell, Miller, Morgan, Mullikin, Murray, Negley, Parker, Pugh, Purnell, Russell, Schlosser, Scott, Smith, of Dorchester, Sneary, Stirling, Stockbridge, Swope, Sykes, Thomas, Valliant, Wickard, Wilmer, Wooden—58.

On motion of Mr. PUGH,

Further procedings under the call were dispensed with.

The question was then taken upon the motion of Mr. NEGLEY, to postpone the special order, until the pending subject was disposed of—and the motion was agreed to.

The question was then taken upon the amendment of Mr. NEGLEY, providing for the publication of the constitution in the newspapers, and it was adopted.

The order as amended was adopted.

THE CONSTITUTION.

Mr. EARLE said: On behalf of the committee on revision, I now present to this convention for its final action, a revised copy of the constitution of Maryland. After careful examination we are prepared to report, that this constitution as revised and engrossed, corresponds in all respects with the different articles and sections heretofore adopted in detail by the convention. I therefore move that this constitution, in its present form, as one entire instrument, be now read and adopted.

The entire constitution was then read through. [See close of volume 2, of debates.]

Mr. HEBB moved a call of the house, which was ordered.

The roll was then called, and the following members answered to their names:

Messrs. Goldsborough, President; Abbott, Annan, Audoun, Baker, Barron, Belt, Berry, of Baltimore county, Bond, Brooks, Brown,

Carter, Crawford, Cunningham, Cushing, Dail, Daniel, Davis, of Charles, Davis, of Washington, Dellinger, Dent, Earle, Farrow, Gale, Galloway, Greene, Hatch, Hebb, Hollyday, Hopper, Horsey, Jones, of Cecil, Jones, of Somerset, Keefer, Kennard, King, Lansdale, Larsh, Lee, Marbury, Markey, Mayhugh, McComas, Mitchell, Miller, Morgan, Mullikin, Murray, Negley, Nyman, Parker, Parran, Peter, Pugh, Purnell, Ridgely, Russell, Schley, Schlosser, Scott, Smith, of Dorchester, Sneary, Stirling, Stockbridge, Swope, Sykes, Thomas, Todd, Turner, Valliant, Wickard, Wilmer, Wooden—73.

On motion of Mr. Audoun,

Further proceedings under the call were dispensed with.

The President. The constitution having now been read through, the question is upon its adoption, which will be taken by yeas and nays.

The question was then taken by yeas and nays, and resulted—yeas 53, nays 26—as follows:

Yeas—Messrs. Goldsborough, President; Abbott, Annan, Audoun, Baker, Barron, Berry, of Baltimore county, Brooks, Carter, Cunningham, Cushing, Daniel, Davis, of Washington, Dellinger, Earle, Ecker, Farrow, Galloway, Greene, Hatch, Hebb, Hoffman, Hopper, Jones, of Cecil, Keefer, Kennard, King, Larsh, Markey, Mayhugh, McComas, Mullikin, Murray, Negley, Nyman, Parker, Pugh, Purnell, Ridgely, Russell, Schley, Schlosser, Scott, Sneary, Stirling, Stockbridge Swope, Sykes, Thomas, Todd, Valliant, Wickard, Wooden—53.

Nays—Messrs. Belt, Bond, Brown, Chambers, Crawford, Dail, Davis, of Charles, Dent, Duvall, Gale, Henkle, Hodson, Hollyday, Horsey, Jones, of Somerset, Lansdale, Lee, Marbury, Mitchell, Miller, Morgan, Parran, Peter, Smith, of Dorchester, Turner, Wilmer—26.

Absent and not voting—Messrs. Berry, of Prince George's, Billingsley, Blackiston, Briscoe, Clarke, Dennis, Edelen, Harwood, Hopkins, Johnson, Mace, Noble, Robinette, Sands, Smith, of Carroll, Smith, of Worcester, and Thruston—17.

The constitution as engrossed and read, was accordingly adopted.

Pending the call of the yeas and nays, the following explanations were made by members as their names were called:

Mr. Dent. I shall vote against this constitution for the following reasons:

First. Because I believe that the election by which this convention was called, and its members elected, was not free for the legal voters of the State, but was held and conducted in clear violation of the legal rights of voters, in consequence of which a majority of the legal voters of the State was excluded from the polls.

Second. Because by this constitution the cardinal principles of the rights of the State have been repudiated, and a rapid stride is taken towards centralization of power in the Federal government.

Third. Because by this constitution citizens of the State have been unjustly deprived of millions of dollars worth of property by the abolition of slavery, and no compensation to the owners has been provided; and not only so, but the legislature is expressly prohibited from providing compensation hereafter.

My fourth objection is because the right of suffrage is so impaired, or attempted to be impaired, by the provisions for submitting this constitution to the voters of the State, that there cannot be a free exercise of the invaluable right of suffrage on its adoption or rejection.

Besides these cardinal objections, I have many comparatively minor objections to this constitution, and believe that, taken as a whole, it is an instrument of wrong and oppression, unparalleled in the history of American constitutions, and ought not to be adopted. I vote "no."

Mr. Jones, of Somerset. I have urged my objections to various parts of this constitution, from time to time, as they have successively come before the convention, as will appear by the debates. I desire now to urge an additional reason why I cannot vote to adopt it. This convention was called "to frame a new constitution and form of government." The sixth section of the law authorizing this convention provides "that the constitution and form of government adopted by the said convention, shall be submitted to the legal and qualified voters of the State for their adoption or rejection." The existing constitution declares that "every free white male person of twenty-one years of age or upwards, who shall have been one year next preceding the election a resident of the State, and for six months a resident of the city of Baltimore, or of any county in which he may offer to vote, being a citizen of the United States, shall be entitled to vote in the ward or election district in which he resides, in all elections hereafter to be held." These are "the legal and qualified voters of the State" to whom your proposed constitution must be submitted. I understand that during my absence the convention have decreed that their work shall be submitted to those only of said voters who shall submit to take a detestable oath, purging themselves of a long catalogue of supposed political offences against the United States government, and even then they are not to be allowed to vote unless the judges of election shall choose to permit them. I protest against such an attempt to subvert the present government of Maryland, as a revolution by usurpation.

In addition to the objections I urged against the oath, on a former occasion, one of the offences proposed to be tried before judges of election and punished by disfranchisement, amounts to treason against the United States, for the trial and punishment of which the law of congress provides. I submit that the constitutional jurisdiction of the United States courts over this and other criminal offences against the United States, is exclusive of State jurisdiction to try and punish the same offences in any way whatever. I vote "no."

Mr. MITCHELL. I am here from a county whose people almost unanimously voted against the calling this convention together. But I came here prepared to unite with gentlemen in framing such a constitution that if adopted would be for the interest of the people of this State. In that I have been disappointed. I have found that no proposition coming from the minority upon this floor, has been acceptable, unless indorsed by certain gentlemen of the majority. Upon the only two or three occasions when I could have wished to express my opinions, or join in the debate, I have been cut off by the operation of the previous question, and the operation of the most stringent rules ever adopted by any legislative body.

I shall vote against this constitution, and therefore I have taken no active part in the proceedings of this body, but have contented myself with simply voting. I shall vote against this constitution, first, because it affects my own county by the abolition of slavery in perhaps a greater degree than any other county in the State. I coincide with and represent the opinions of my constituents upon that subject. And even had I agreed to the necessity of a provision of that sort, I never could have voted for it, when it refused compensation to the holders of that property, who have been ruined by this measure. You have not only refused that compensation, but you have put into your organic law a provision prohibiting the legislature from hereafter making any such compensation.

And I do not see that the people of this State will be benefited by the changes made in the constitution in other respects. But I do see that a large portion of them have been disfranchised by the test oaths you have incorporated here.

And more than that; if I approved this constitution in all other respects, I could not, with my views, vote for any proposition which seeks to go against the law which called this convention into being, and regulated its proceedings so far as the legislature had the right to do it. I could not go for a provision which puts a portion of this constitution into force before its adoption by the people, and which if rejected would present the anomalous spectacle of a body whose acts have been rejected, having legislated in such a manner as to affect the rights of the people. I vote "no."

Mr. PUGH. I have only this to say: I tried hard to be elected to come to this convention. And I am free to say that there has never been afforded to me in my life so far, any opportunity in which I have more reason to rejoice, than I have in voting for this constitution. I vote "aye."

Mr. CHAMBERS. I regard this constitution as a most unwarrantable seizure of property, and a wanton attack upon the rights of those in regard to whom we were sent here to afford protection for their persons, liberty, property, and every other political right. So regarding it, I vote against its adoption. I vote "no."

The PRESIDENT and SECRETARY then proceeded to sign the constitution in due form.

On motion of Mr. HEBB, it was

Ordered, That the secretary of the convention proceed forthwith to deposit the constitution as adopted, passed, signed and attested, in the office of the clerk of the court of appeals.

THANKS TO THE OFFICIAL REPORTERS.

On motion of Mr. THOMAS, it was

Ordered, That the thanks of this convention are due and are hereby tendered to Wm. Blair Lord, Esq., the reporter, and to Henry M. Parkhurst, Esq., assistant reporter, for the impartial, faithful and efficient manner they have reported the debates of this convention.

COMPENSATION FOR SLAVES.

On motion of Mr. AUDOUN,

The convention resumed the consideration of the order submitted by Mr. AUDOUN this morning, and informally passed over, which order was as follows:

"*Ordered*, That before any person shall receive the benefits to be derived from the resolutions offered by the gentleman from Baltimore county (Mr. Berry,) [namely, providing for the general assembly to receive such moneys as the government may think proper to appropriate to loyal owners of slaves in this State,] the persons so claiming shall take and subscribe to the oath as prescribed in this constitution, in the article on the elective franchise."

The question was upon the adoption of the order.

Upon this question Mr. AUDOUN called for the yeas and nays, which were ordered.

The question was then taken, by yeas and nays, and resulted—yeas 50, nays 25—as follows:

Yeas—Messrs. Goldsborough, President; Abbott, Annan, Audoun, Baker, Barron, Berry, of Baltimore county, Brooks, Carter, Cunningham, Cushing, Daniel, Davis, of Washington, Dellinger, Ecker, Farrow, Galloway, Greene, Hatch, Hebb, Hoffman, Hopper, Jones, of Cecil, Keefer, Kennard, King, Larsh, Markey, Mayhugh, McComas, Mullikin, Murray, Negley, Nyman, Parker, Pugh, Purnell, Ridgely, Russell, Schley, Schlosser, Scott, Sneary, Stirling, Swope, Sykes, Todd, Valliant, Wickard, Wooden—50.

Nays—Messrs. Belt, Bond, Brown, Chambers, Crawford, Dail, Davis, of Charles, Dent, Duvall, Gale, Henkle, Hodson, Hollyday, Horsey, Jones, of Somerset, Lansdale, Lee, Marbury, Mitchell, Miller, Morgan, Peter, Smith, of Dorchester, Turner, Wilmer—25.

The order was accordingly adopted.

Mr. Ridgely, when his name was called, said: I do not understand what effect this order can have. It certainly is not intended to form a part of the constitution. It can have no force or effect as law or anything else. According to my understanding it is not a part of the constitution, and can in no way at all have any effect of law. I vote for it nevertheless, because I believe it to be harmless. I vote "aye."

OPERATION OF THE CONSTITUTION.

Mr. Davis, of Charles, moved to suspend the rules, in order to proceed to the consideration of the following order submitted by him on yesterday:

"*Resolved*, That it is the sense of this convention, that all constitutions framed by conventions, called by the voters of any State for that purpose subject to their ratification, ought to be submitted to the legal voters of such State for their ratification or rejection before such constitution or any part thereof should go into operation, and any attempt by a convention to adopt and put in force a constitution or any part thereof in violation of promises to the people, that the constitution to be framed should be submitted to them, would be a breach of faith, and any convention acting in such manner as above described ought to forfeit the confidence of the people."

The question being taken on the motion to suspend the rules, it was not agreed to.

ADJOURNMENT SINE DIE.

Mr. Belt. I move that this convention now adjourn *sine die*.

Mr. Audoun. There was an order adopted on the 21st of last month in relation to the adjournment of this convention.

Mr. Belt. I will explain my motives for making this motion. I was not present at the time of the adoption of the order referred to. My view of our duty to the people is that when we finish our business here, we ought to adjourn *sine die*, and submit our work to the people who sent us here. We were not sent here to constitute ourselves into a sort of long parliament, with a committee of safety at the head of it, to regulate the affairs of the State. Nobody can tell the effect of continuing the session of this convention. Suppose among other things that this constitution should be rejected by the people. Is this convention to be reassembled for the purpose of framing another?

Mr. Stirling. The resolution states expressly that if there is no interruption in the State between now and the time the people are called upon to vote on the constitution, and the vote is fairly taken upon it, then the president shall declare this convention adjourned *sine die*.

Mr. Belt. Can a parliamentary body delegate to any one the right to adjourn it? I am opposed to the constitution of any long parliament in this State. I demand a vote on my motion to adjourn *sine die*.

The President. The motion is in order. It is competent for the convention to repeal any order heretofore made.

Mr. Audoun. If I understand the object of my colleague (Mr. Abbott) in offering the order to which I have referred, it was for the purpose of providing against any emergency that might occur. Under that resolution I believe three or four members of this convention are designated to act as president, in case of the death of the now president of the convention, for the purpose of calling this convention together, in the event of an invasion of this State, to prevent the vote being taken upon the adoption of this constitution. Such a thing might occur, and I have no doubt that there are some upon this floor who desire it, and feel anxious that it should take place. But I say openly here, that the majority of this house have provided against any such emergency, and we are determined to prevent any such thing occurring.

Mr. Belt. Does the gentleman from Baltimore city (Mr. Audoun) allude to me in the remarks he has just made?

The President. The difficulty in which the chair is placed is this: The convention being a deliberative body can, like all other deliberative bodies, change or alter any of its rules, or any action which it may have taken. It is utterly impossible for the chair to restrict gentlemen in any motion they may choose to make, provided they catch the eye of the president. The gentleman from Prince George's (Mr. Belt) was recognized by the chair as being entitled to the floor. He submits a motion for this body to adjourn *sine die*. If the convention determines to do so, the chair knows of no parliamentary rule to forbid it. The chair conceives the motion of the gentleman from Prince George's to be in order, upon the supposition that the convention may desire to retrace its steps, and rescind the resolution it has adopted. The question is not debatable.

The question was upon the motion of Mr. Belt to adjourn *sine die*.

Upon this question Mr. Belt called for the yeas and nays, and they were ordered.

The question was then taken by yeas and nays, and resulted—yeas 25, nays 49—as follows:

Yeas—Messrs. Belt, Bond, Brown, Chambers, Crawford, Dail, Davis, of Charles, Dent, Duvall, Gale, Henkle, Hodson, Hollyday, Horsey, Jones, of Somerset, Lansdale, Lee, Marbury, Mitchell, Miller, Morgan, Peter, Smith, of Dorchester, Turner, Wilmer—25.

Nays—Messrs. Goldsborough, President; Abbott, Annan, Audoun, Baker, Barron, Berry, of Baltimore county, Brooks, Carter, Cunningham, Cushing, Davis, of Washington, Dellinger, Earle, Ecker, Farrow, Galloway, Greene, Hatch, Hebb, Hoffman, Hopper, Jones, of Cecil, Keefer, Kennard, King, Markey, Mayhugh, McComas, Mullikin, Murray, Negley, Nyman, Parker, Pugh, Purnell, Ridgely, Russell, Schley, Schlosser, Scott, Stirling, Stockbridge, Swope, Sykes, Thomas, Todd, Valliant, Wickard, Wooden—49.

The convention accordingly refused to adjourn *sine die.*

ADJOURNMENT.

Mr. Hebb submitted the following order:

"*Ordered*, That when this convention adjourns to-day, it stands adjourned in pursuance of a resolution of the convention passed upon the 21st day of August, 1864."

The resolution referred to, of the 21st of August, is as follows:

"*Resolved*, That in view of the uncertain condition of affairs in this State, owing to the possibility of an invasion by the public enemy, which may interfere with the expression of the popular will on the day to be fixed for voting on this constitution, that this convention, when it adjourns, for the purpose of taking the sense of the people on this constitution, it stand adjourned subject to the call of the president, and in case of the death or disqualification of the president (H. H. Goldsborough,) Frederick Schley, of Frederick county; Joseph B. Pugh, of Cecil county; Henry Stockbridge, of Baltimore city; Wm. T. Purnell, of Worcester county, be and they are hereby authorized, in the order in which they are named, to act as president, and call the convention together; but should the day appointed for the adoption or rejection of this constitution pass without interruption, then the president shall declare, through the public press, the final adjournment without day of this convention, and no per diem shall be allowed for the recess."

The question being taken upon the order of Mr. Hebb, it was adopted.

Mr. Hebb moved that the convention do now adjourn, which was agreed to.

ADDRESS OF THE PRESIDENT.

The President, before announcing the vote, addressed the convention as follows:

Gentlemen of the Convention:—The time has now arrived when, as your presiding officer, it becomes my duty to declare the termination of the labors of this body. In so doing it would not be proper to omit the observance of the time-honored custom of giving utterance to some brief and friendly words of parting.

We have been engaged for the past four months in the work of framing anew the organic law of this State. However easy the task may appear to many, and especially to those who have never participated in such a work, yet I am sure you will concur with me that its difficulties, not a few even in times of profound peace, have been greatly increased by the condition of things by which we were surrounded.

Amid a civil war of the most gigantic proportions, our minds have been constantly disturbed by the ever recurring consideration whether the institutions, under which we have prospered so long as a nation, were to stand or fall amid the conflicts of the day. While the nation has been thus agitated throughout its entire limits, our own State has been the theatre of the most bitter contests between social and political classes ever experienced, and which it could have been wished should not have existed while we were engaged in a work of so much importance and magnitude. Our labors, though thus interrupted by scenes calculated to create the most embittered feeling, and to provoke discussions of the most exciting character, have not been marred by any of those personal animosities or collisions which might have been anticipated, and which have so often characterized the proceedings of other deliberative bodies. This is a matter of sincere congratulation, and if your president has succeeded in the accomplishment of this object, he has been encouraged and sustained by a conviction of your belief in his conscientious discharge of duty, and in his faithful endeavor at all times to award to each individual member, irrespective of party designations or particular localities, that impartial justice which should always control the action of a presiding officer of a deliberative body.

We are now about to separate for our respective homes. In all human probability the most of us may never meet again. As actors in the past and present eventful scenes, can we *not all*—dismissing the memory of every embittered feeling, before parting—unite in the prayer so often repeated at this desk, that the same *ever living God*, who has heretofore protected and defended us as one people, may, notwithstanding our civil broils, our many sins and misgivings, still "preserve us under the shadow of his wing" as one undivided nation; that whatever changes may be occasioned by the rapidly transpiring events of the day—whatever modifications may be produced in the character of our social institutions, the *Union*, as the great ark of our national safety, with the constitution, may be vouchsafed to us and our children; and that *ere many years shall roll around*, we may all look again with fond delight upon the same gorgeous emblem of our nationality still floating over us, affording equal protection to the rights of all, at home and abroad, not a star erased, nor a stripe obscured.

Representatives of Maryland—Freemen of a central State of a once proud galaxy of States—citizens of a national government, unequalled in its fostering protection by any other upon earth, your hearts and mine I know beat responsive to a wish for the restoration of our federal government, and a return of that period when we shall all, irrespective of geographical lines or sectional parties, recognize "the constitution and the laws and treaties made in pursuance thereof, as the supreme law of the land." Is there a man so indifferent to the blessings of republican liberty, as not to cherish a hope of a speedy realization of such a result? Who does not desire a peace—permanent, substantial peace—a peace commanding the obedience of all men, in all parts of our common country, to those who have been or may be chosen to administer the government? Who will not hail with pleasure the end of scenes of blood and desolation, if it can be obtained by an unconditional submission of those proud domestic foes, wherever located, who have been and are now engaged in plotting our destruction, and whose treasonable schemes, I hope, in the providence of God, may be defeated, whether sought to be accomplished by the sword or by a surreptitious use of the ballot? "The union of the States, the majority must govern, it is treason to secede," is as truthful now as in the earlier days of the republic, or even in the Madisonian era of unsuspected State rights republicanism. The will of the people must be respected. It must be enforced, and although we may cry "peace, peace," there will be no peace until every armed foe shall be made to acknowledge the paramount authority of our federal government.

In the momentous struggle which has for the past three years agitated this State, your president has not been an inactive participant. He has witnessed the rapid change of public sentiment in relation to a domestic institution heretofore protected by law to such an extent as almost to suppress all freedom of speech and freedom of action. In an evil hour, initiated by the loss of place, and in the full-blown pride of power, its supporters sought to extend and perpetuate its rule, even though it involved the destruction of the best government on earth. Scarcely awaiting the announcement of the result of the presidential canvass, they openly proclaimed their fixed determination to disregard the popular will as expressed in the choice of a chief magistrate, and mocking all the ordinary restraints of law, proceeded in their work of disintegration and dismemberment, regardless of all consequences. Such traitorous proceedings culminated, as might have been expected and foreseen, in all the horrors of civil war. In such acts are to be discovered the true cause of all our trials and sufferings, as well as the history of that determined popular clamor for this convention, as the most effectual means to check such movements within our State. The draft of a constitution now about to be submitted, is but one of the legitimate fruits of rebellion, to be followed by other similar enactments, until the popular will shall be reflected in an absolute extinguishment of this institution. Slavery interwoven with our social and domestic relations, and accustomed to control our national policy, could not brook the antagonism of free speech and free labor. In its mad appeal to the dread arbitrament of the sword, there has been disclosed the secret history and ambitious designs of many party leaders who have long sought to divide our country by sectional lines for the gratification of their own personal ends. That God, in the providence of His ways, will effectually thwart the machinations of such schemers and plotters of disunion, I have not a doubt. Believing that He has permitted this state of things for the accomplishment of some great national good, I have an abiding faith that the great mass of the American people, whose generous patriotism, unflinching courage and unselfish devotion to their country's cause is without a parallel in the history of the world, will emerge from this terrible ordeal, much better prepared to appreciate the blessings of free institutions, and to provide in a constitutional mode for the removal of every obstacle to the perpetuation of a united government, constituting us one people, so dear to every true American heart. This problem of *universal freedom* is being fast wrought out by the current events of the day, to the satisfaction of every loyal man, while in the blood of patriotic sons and sires will be found the surest guarantees against all future enemies, foreign or domestic, of that liberty and union which should be one and inseparable, now and forever.

In this State the institution of slavery is dead. Those who have tears therefor, prepare to shed them now. It is not *now* in your power, or mine, or that of any living mortal to revive or resuscitate it. I congratulate you upon the accomplishment of this work, which I doubt not the people will seal with their approbation. Even those of your constituents who do not now coincide with your views, after the asperities of the day shall have ceased, will, I doubt not, hail with pleasure this great social revolution, opening as it does, the fair fields of Maryland to the hand of honest industry, in all its diversified forms, and enabling each and every man, *irrespective of color*, to enjoy, as God intended, the fruits of his own personal labor. The sons of honest toil, the farmer, the mechanic and the manufacturer will be elevated in the scale of humanity. Free and untrammelled—with the avenues of wealth, power, and distinction open to all classes of the white race, every one, whether native or naturalized, becomes the peer of every other man—nay, even of the proudest aristocrat, who will have either to content himself with the daily contact of the things he loathes or seek other more congenial climes for the enjoyment of the peculiar blessings of an institution which, in its mad efforts to discredit free labor and free institutions, has destroyed itself.

This change alone, of itself, will more than compensate the people of Maryland for all their trials and sufferings. As a central State her future is most auspicious, bringing with it wealth, prosperity and population, the sure concomitants of free labor. She will henceforth begin to experience the truth of her motto "*Crescite et multiplicamini,*" and, with the increase of her people, I hope the love she has ever manifested for the Union and Constitution will be strengthened, purified and intensified.

Permit me, gentlemen, in conclusion to express my thanks for your emphatic approval of my official course, for your courteous and kind deportment at all times, and in bidding you *farewell*, to renew my wishes for the prosperity and happiness of each individual member of this convention.

I do now proclaim this convention adjourned, in accordance with a resolution heretofore adopted.

CONSTITUTION OF MARYLAND,

ADOPTED IN CONVENTION,

Which Assembled at the City of Annapolis, on the Twenty-seventh Day of April, Eighteen Hundred and Sixty-four, and Adjourned on the Sixth Day of September, Eighteen Hundred and Sixty-four.

DECLARATION OF RIGHTS.

WE, the people of the State of Maryland, grateful to Almighty God for our civil and religious liberty, and taking into our serious consideration the best means of establishing a good constitution in this State, for the sure foundation and more permanent security thereof, declare:

Article 1. That we hold it to be self-evident that all men are created equally free; that they are endowed by their Creator with certain unalienable rights, among which are life, liberty, the enjoyment of the proceeds of their own labor, and the pursuit of happiness.

Art. 2. That all government of right originates from the people, is founded in compact only, and instituted solely for the good of the whole; and they have at all times, the unalienable right to alter, reform, or abolish their form of government, in such manner as they may deem expedient.

Art. 3. That the people of this State ought to have the sole and exclusive right of regulating the internal government and police thereof.

Art. 4. That the inhabitants of Maryland are entitled to the common law of England, and the trial by jury according to the course of that law, and to the benefit of such of the English statutes as existed on the fourth day of July, seventeen hundred and seventy-six, and which, by experience have been found applicable to their local and other circumstances, and have been introduced, used and practiced by the courts of law or equity, and also of all acts of assembly in force on the first day of June, eighteen hundred and sixty-four, except such as may have since expired, or may be inconsistent with the provisions of this constitution, subject, nevertheless, to the revision of, and amendment or repeal by the legislature of this State; and the inhabitants of Maryland are also entitled to all property derived to them from or under the charter granted by his majesty Charles the First, to Cæcilius Calvert, Baron of Baltimore.

Art. 5. The constitution of the United States, and the laws made in pursuance thereof, being the supreme law of the land, every citizen of this State owes paramount allegiance to the constitution and government of the United States, and is not bound by any law or ordinance of this State in contravention or subversion thereof.

Art. 6. That all persons invested with the legislative or executive powers of government, are the trustees of the public, and as such accountable for their conduct; *wherefore*, whenever the ends of government are perverted, and public liberty manifestly endangered, and all other means of redress are ineffectual, the people may, and of right ought to reform the old or establish a new government. The doctrine of non-resistance against arbitrary power and oppression is absurd, slavish and destructive of the good and happiness of mankind.

Art. 7. That the right of the people to participate in the legislature is the best security of liberty, and the foundation of all free government; for this purpose elections ought to be free and frequent, and every free white male citizen having the qualifications prescribed by the constitution, ought to have the right of suffrage.

Art. 8. That the legislative, executive and judicial powers of government ought to be forever separate and distinct from each other; and no person exercising the functions of one of said departments, shall assume or discharge the duties of any other.

Art. 9. That no power of suspending laws, or the execution of laws, unless by or derived from the legislature, ought to be exercised or allowed.

Art. 10. That freedom of speech and debate or proceedings in the legislature, ought not to be impeached in any court of judicature.

Art. 11. That Annapolis be the place for the meeting of the legislature; and the legislature ought not to be convened or held at any other place but from evident necessity.

Art. 12. That for the redress of grievances, and for amending, strengthening and preserving the laws, the legislature ought to be frequently convened.

Art. 13. That every man hath a right to petition the legislature for the redress of grievances in a peaceable and orderly manner.

Art. 14. That no aid, charge, tax, burthen, or fees, ought to be rated or levied, under any pretence, without the consent of the legislature.

Art. 15. That the levying of taxes by the poll is grievous and oppressive, and ought to be prohibited; that paupers ought not to be assessed for the support of the government, but every other person in the State, or person holding property therein, ought to contribute his proportion of public taxes, for the support of government, according to his actual worth in real or personal property; yet fines, duties, or taxes may properly and justly be imposed or laid, with a political view, for the good government and benefit of the community.

Art. 16. That sanguinary laws ought to be avoided as far as it is consistent with the safety of the State; and no law to inflict cruel and unusual pains and penalties ought to be made in any case, or at any time hereafter.

Art. 17. That retrospective laws, punishing acts committed before the existence of such laws, and by them only declared criminal, are oppressive, unjust and incompatible with liberty; wherefore, no *ex post facto* law ought to be made.

Art. 18. That no law to attaint particular persons of treason or felony, ought to be made in any case, or at any time hereafter.

Art. 19. That every man, for any injury done to him in his person or property, ought to have remedy by the course of the law of the land, and ought to have justice and right, freely without sale, fully without any denial, and speedily without delay, according to the law of the land.

Art. 20. That the trial of facts where they arise, is one of the greatest securities of the lives, liberties, and estate of the people.

Art. 21. That in all criminal prosecutions, every man hath a right to be informed of the accusation against him; to have a copy of the indictment or charge, in due time (if required) to prepare for his defence; to be allowed counsel; to be confronted with the witnesses against him; to have process for his witnesses; to examine the witnesses for and against him on oath; and to a speedy trial by an impartial jury, without whose unanimous consent he ought not to be found guilty.

Art. 22. That no man ought to be compelled to give evidence against himself in a criminal case.

Art. 23. That no man ought to be taken or imprisoned, or disseized of his freehold, liberties or privileges, or outlawed, or exiled, or in any manner destroyed, or deprived of his life, liberty or property, but by the judgment of his peers, or by the law of the land.

Art. 24. That hereafter, in this State, there shall be neither slavery nor involuntary servitude, except in punishment of crime, whereof the party shall have been duly convicted; and all persons held to service or labor as slaves, are hereby declared free.

Art. 25. That excessive bail ought not to be required, nor excessive fines imposed, nor cruel or unusual punishment inflicted by the courts of law.

Art. 26. That all warrants, without oath, or affirmation, to search suspected places, or to seize any person or property, are grievous and oppressive; and all general warrants to search suspected places, or to apprehend suspected persons, without naming or describing the place, or the person in special, are illegal, and ought not to be granted.

Art. 27. That no conviction shall work corruption of blood, nor shall there be any forfeiture of the estate of any person for any crime, except treason, and then only on conviction.

Art. 28. That a well regulated militia is the proper and natural defence of a free government.

Art. 29. That standing armies are dangerous to liberty, and ought not to be raised or kept up without the consent of the legislature.

Art 30. That in all cases and at all times the military ought to be under strict subordination to, and control of the civil power.

Art. 31. That no soldier shall in time of peace be quartered in any house without the consent of the owner, nor in time of war, except in the manner prescribed by law.

Art. 32. That no person, except regular soldiers, mariners, and marines in the service of this State, or militia when in actual service, ought in any case to be subject to, or punishable by martial law.

Art. 33. That the independency and uprightness of judges are essential to the impartial administration of justice, and a great security to the rights and liberties of the people; wherefore the judges shall not be removed, except for misbehavior, on conviction in a court of law, or by the governor, upon the address of the general assembly; *provided*, that two-thirds of all the members of each house concur in such address. No judge shall hold any other office, civil or military, or political trust or employment of any kind whatsoever, under the constitution or laws of this State, or of the United States, or any of them, or receive fees or perquisites of any kind for the discharge of his official duties.

Art. 34. That a long continuance in the executive departments of power or trust is dangerous to liberty; a rotation, therefore, in those departments is one of the best securities of permanent freedom.

Art. 35. That no person ought to hold at the same time more than one office of profit created by the constitution or laws of this State; nor ought any person in public trust to receive any present from any foreign prince, or State, or from the United States, or any of them, without the approbation of this State.

Art. 36. That as it is the duty of every man to worship God in such manner as he thinks most acceptable to Him, all persons are equally entitled to protection in their religious liberty, wherefore, no person ought, by any law, to be molested in his person or estate on account of his religious persuasion or profession, or for his religious practice, unless under the color of religion any man shall disturb the good order, peace, or safety of the State, or shall infringe the laws of morality, or injure others in their natural, civil, or religious rights; nor ought any person to be compelled to frequent or maintain, or contribute, unless on contract, to maintain any place of worship or any ministry; nor shall any person be deemed incompetent as a witness or juror who believes in the existence of God, and that under His dispensation such person will be held morally accountable for his acts, and be rewarded or punished therefor, either in this world or the world to come.

Art. 37. That no other test or qualification ought to be required on admission to any office of trust or profit, than such oath of allegiance and fidelity to this State and the United States, as may be prescribed by this constitution, and such oath of office and qualification as may be prescribed by this constitution, or by the laws of the State, and a declaration of belief in the Christian religion, or in the existence of God, and in a future state of rewards and punishments.

Art. 38. That every gift, sale, or devise of land, to any minister, public teacher or preacher of the gospel, as such, or to any religious sect, order or denomination, or to or for the support, use or benefit of, or in trust for any minister, public teacher or preacher of the gospel as such, or any religious sect, order or denomination, and every gift or sale of goods or chattels to go in succession, or to take place after the death of the seller or donor, to or for such support, use or benefit; and, also, every devise of goods or chattels, to or for the support, use or benefit of any minister, public teacher or preacher of the gospel, as such; or any religious sect, order or denomination, without the prior or subsequent sanction of the legislature, shall be void; except always, any sale, gift, lease, or devise of any quantity of land, not exceeding five acres, for a church, meeting house, or other house of worship, or parsonage, or for a burying ground, which shall be improved, enjoyed, or used only for such purpose, or such sale, gift, lease, or devise, shall be void.

Art. 39. That the manner of administering an oath or affirmation, to any person, ought to be such as those of the religious persuasion, profession, or denomination, of which he is a member, generally esteem the most effectual confirmation by the attestation of the Divine Being.

Art. 40. That the liberty of the press ought to be inviolably preserved; that every citizen of the State ought to be allowed to speak, write and publish his sentiments on all subjects, being responsible for the abuse of that liberty.

Art. 41. That monopolies are odious, contrary to the spirit of a free government and the principles of commerce, and ought not to be suffered.

Art. 42. That no title of nobility or hereditary honors ought to be granted in this State.

Art. 43. That the legislature ought to encourage the diffusion of knowledge and virtue, the extension of a judicious system of general education, the promotion of literature, the arts, sciences, agriculture, commerce and manufactures, and the general melioration of the condition of the people.

Art. 44. This enumeration of rights shall not be construed to impair or deny others retained by the people.

Art. 45. That the legislature shall pass no law providing for an alteration, change, or abolishment of this constitution, except in the manner therein prescribed and directed.

CONSTITUTION.

ARTICLE I.

ELECTIVE FRANCHISE.

Section 1. All elections shall be by ballot, and every white male citizen of the United States, of the age of twenty-one years or upwards, who shall have resided in the State one year next preceding the election, and six months in any county, or in any legislative district of Baltimore city, and who shall comply with the provisions of this article of the constitution, shall be entitled to vote at all elections hereafter held in this State; and in case any county or city shall be so divided as to form portions of different electoral districts for the election of congressmen, senator, delegate, or other officer or officers, then to entitle a person to vote for such officer he must have been a resident of that part of the county or city which shall form a part of the electoral district in which he offers to vote for six months next preceding the election; but a person who shall have acquired a residence in such county or city entitling him to vote at any such election shall be entitled to vote in the election district from which he removed, until he shall have acquired a residence in the part of the county or city to which he has removed.

Sec. 2. The general assembly shall provide by law for a uniform registration of the names of voters in this State, which registration shall be evidence of the qualification of said voters to vote at any election thereafter held, but no person shall be excluded from voting at any election on account of not being registered until the general assembly shall have passed an act of registration, and the same shall have been carried into effect, after which no person shall vote unless his name appears on the register. The general assembly shall also provide by law for taking the votes of soldiers in the army of the United States serving in the field.

Sec. 3. No person above the age of twenty-one years, convicted of larceny or other infamous crime, unless pardoned by the governor, shall ever thereafter be entitled to vote at any election in this State, and no lunatic, or person *non compos mentis*, shall be entitled to vote.

Sec. 4. No person who has at any time been in armed hostility to the United States, or the lawful authorities thereof, or who has been in any manner in the service of the so-called "Confederate States of America," and no person who has voluntarily left this State and gone within the military lines of the so-called "Confederate States or armies" with the purpose of adhering to said States or armies, and no person who has given any aid, comfort, countenance or support to those engaged in armed hostility to the United States, or in any manner adhered to the enemies of the United States, either by contributing to the enemies of the United States, or unlawfully sending within the lines of such enemies money or goods, or letters, or information, or who has disloyally held communication with the enemies of the United States, or who has advised any person to enter the service of the said enemies, or aided any person so to enter, or who has by any open deed or word declared his adhesion to the cause of the enemies of the United States, or his desire for the triumph of said enemies over the arms of the United States, shall ever be entitled to vote at any election to be held in this State, or to hold any office of honor, profit or trust under the laws of this State, unless since such unlawful acts he shall have voluntarily entered into the military service of the United States, and been honorably discharged therefrom, or shall be on the day of election, actually and voluntarily in such service, or unless he shall be restored to his full rights of citizenship by an act of the general assembly passed by a vote of two-thirds of all the members elected to each house; and it shall be the duty of all officers of registration and judges of election carefully to exclude from voting, or being registered, all persons so as above disqualified; and the judges of election at the first election held under this constitution shall, and at any subsequent election may, administer to any person offering to vote the following oath or affirmation: I do swear or affirm that I am a citizen of the United States, that I have never given any aid, countenance or support to those in armed hostility to the United States, that I have never expressed a desire for the triumph of said enemies over the arms of the United States, and that I will bear true faith and allegiance to the United States and support the constitution and laws thereof as the supreme law of the land, any law or ordinance of any State to the contrary notwithstanding; that I will in all respects demean myself as a loyal citizen of the United States, and I make this oath or affirmation without any reservation or evasion, and believe it to be binding on me; and any person declining to take such oath shall not be allowed to vote, but the taking of such oath shall not be deemed conclusive evidence of the right of such person to vote; and any person swearing or affirming falsely shall be liable to penalties of perjury, and it shall be the duty of the proper officers of registration to allow no person to be registered until he shall have taken the oath or affirmation above set out, and it shall be the duty of the judges of election in all their returns of the first election held under this constitution to state in their said returns that every person who has voted has taken such oath or affirmation. But the provisions of this section in relation to acts against the United States shall not apply to any person not a citizen of the United States who shall have committed such acts while in the service of some foreign country at war against the United States, and who has, since such acts, been naturalized, or may be naturalized, under the laws of the United States, and the oath above set forth shall be taken in the case of such persons in such sense.

Sec. 5. If any person shall give, or offer to give, directly or indirectly, or hath given or offered to give, since the fourth day of July, eighteen hundred and fifty-one, any bribe, present, or reward, or any promise, or any security for the payment or delivery of money or any other thing, to induce any voter to refrain from casting his vote, or forcibly to prevent him in any way from voting, or to procure a vote for any candidate or person, proposed or voted for as elector of President and Vice-President of the United States, or representative in congress, or for any office of profit or trust created by the constitution or laws of this State, or by the ordinances or authority of the mayor and city council of Baltimore, the person giving or offering to give, and the person receiving the same, and any person who gives or causes to be given an illegal vote, knowing it to be such, at any election to be hereafter held in this State, or who shall be guilty of or accessory to any fraud, force, surprise, or bribery to procure himself or any other person to be nominated to any office, National, State or municipal, shall on conviction in a court of law, in addition to the penalties now or hereafter to be imposed by law, be forever disqualified to hold any office of profit or trust, or to vote at any election thereafter.

Sec. 6. It shall be the duty of the general assembly to pass laws to punish with fine and imprisonment any person who shall remove into any election district or precinct of any ward of the city of Baltimore, not for the purpose of acquiring a *bona fide* residence therein, but for the purpose of voting at an approaching election, or who shall vote in any election district or ward in which he does not reside, (except in the case provided for in this article,) or shall at the same election vote in more than one election district or precinct, or shall vote or offer to vote in any name but his own, or in place of any other person of the same name, or shall vote in any county in which he does not reside.

Sec. 7. Every person elected or appointed to any office of trust or profit under this constitution, or under the laws made pursuant thereto, before he shall enter upon the duties of such office, shall take and subscribe the following oath or affirmation: I, ———, do swear, (or affirm, as the case may be) that I will, to the best of my skill and judgment, diligently and faithfully, without partiality or prejudice, execute the office of ———, according to the constitution and laws of this State, and that since the fourth day of July, in the year eighteen hundred and fifty-one, I have not in any manner violated the provisions of the present, or of the late constitution, in relation to the bribery of voters, or preventing legal votes or procuring illegal votes to be given, (and if a governor, senator, member of the house of delegates, or judge,) that I will not, directly or indirectly, receive the profits or any part of the profits of any other office during the term of my acting as ———. I do further swear or affirm, that I will bear true allegiance to the State of Maryland, and support the constitution and laws thereof, and that I will bear true allegiance to the United States, and support, protect and defend the constitution, laws and government thereof, as the supreme law of the land, any law or ordinance of this or any State to the contrary notwithstanding; that I have never directly or indirectly, by word, act or deed, given any aid, comfort, or encouragement to those in rebellion against the United States, or the lawful authorities thereof; but that I have been truly and loyally on the side of the United States against those in armed rebellion against the United States; and I do further swear or affirm that I will to the best of my abilities protect and defend the Union of the United States, and not allow the same to be broken up and dissolved, or the government thereof to be destroyed, under any circumstances, if in my power to prevent it; and that I will at all times discountenance and oppose all political combinations having for their object such dissolution or destruction.

Sec. 8. Every person holding any office of trust or profit under the late constitution, or under any law of this State and who shall be continued in office under this constitution, or under any law of the State, shall within thirty days after this constitution shall have gone into effect take and subscribe the oath or affirmation set forth in the seventh section of this article, and if any such person shall fail to take said oath his office shall be *ipso facto* vacant. And every person hereafter elected or appointed to office in this State, who shall refuse or neglect to take the oath or affirmation of office provided for in the said seventh section of this article shall be considered as having refused to accept the said office, and a new election or appointment shall be made as in case of refusal to accept or resignation of an office. And any person swearing or affirming falsely in the premises shall, on conviction thereof in a court of law, incur the penalties for wilful and corrupt perjury, and thereafter shall be incapable of holding any office of profit or trust in this State.

ARTICLE II.

EXECUTIVE DEPARTMENT.

Section 1. The executive power of the State shall be vested in a governor, whose term of office shall commence on the second Wednesday of January next ensuing his election, and continue for four years, and until his successor shall have qualified, but the governor chosen at the first election under this constitution shall not enter upon the discharge of the duties of the office until the expiration of the term for which the present incumbent was elected, unless the said office shall become vacant by death, resignation, removal from the State, or other disqualification of said incumbent.

Sec. 2. An election for governor under this constitution shall be held on the Tuesday next after the first Monday of November, in the year eighteen hundred and sixty four, and on the same day and month in every fourth year thereafter, at the places for voting for delegates to the general assembly, and every person qualified to vote for delegates shall be qualified and entitled to vote for governor ; the election to be held in the same manner as the election of delegates, and the returns thereof, under seal, to be addressed to the speaker of the house of delegates, and enclosed and transmitted to the secretary of State, and delivered to the said speaker at the commencement of the session of the general assembly next ensuing said election.

Sec. 3. The speaker of the house of delegates shall then open the said returns in the presence of both houses, and the person having the highest number of votes, and being constitutionally eligible, shall be the governor, and shall qualify in the manner herein prescribed, on the second Wednesday of January next ensuing his election, or as soon thereafter as may be practicable.

Sec. 4. If two or more persons shall have the highest and an equal number of votes, one of them shall be chosen governor by the senate and house of delegates; and all questions in relation to the eligibility of governor, and to the returns of said election, and to the number and legality of votes therein given, shall be determined by the house of delegates; and if the person or persons having the highest number of votes be ineligible, the governor shall be chosen by the senate and house of delegates. Every election of governor by the general assembly shall be determined by a joint majority of the senate and house of delegates, and the vote shall be taken *viva voce*. But if two or more persons shall have the highest and an equal number of votes, then a second vote shall be taken, which shall be confined to the persons having an equal number; and if the votes should be again equal, then the election of governor shall be determined by lot between those who shall have the highest and an equal number on the first vote.

Sec. 5. A person to be eligible to the office of governor must have attained the age of thirty years, and must have been for five years a citizen of the United States, and for five years next preceding his election a resident of the State.

Sec. 6. A lieutenant governor shall be chosen at every regular election for governor. He shall continue in office for the same time, shall be elected in the same manner, and shall possess the same qualifications as the governor. In voting for governor and lieutenant governor, the electors shall state for whom they vote as governor, and for whom as lieutenant governor.

Sec. 7. The lieutenant governor shall, by virtue of his office, be president of the senate, and whenever the senate are equally divided, shall have the right to give the casting vote.

Sec. 8. In case of the death, resignation, removal from the State, or other disqualification of the governor, the powers, duties and emoluments of the office shall devolve upon the lieutenant governor; and in case of his death, resignation, removal, or other disqualification, then upon the president of the senate for the time being, until the disqualification or inability shall cease, or until a new governor shall be elected and qualified; and for any vacancy in said office, not herein provided for, provision may be made by law, and if such vacancy should occur without such provision being made, the general assembly shall be convened by the secretary of State for the purpose of filling said vacancy.

Sec. 9. Whenever the office of governor shall be administered by the lieutenant governor, or he shall be unable to attend as president of the senate, the senate shall elect one of its own members as president, *pro tempore.*

Sec. 10. The lieutenant governor, while he acts as president of the senate, shall receive for his services the same compensation which shall for the same period be allowed to the speaker of the house of delegates, and no more.

Sec. 11. The governor shall be commander-in-chief of the land and naval forces of the State, and may call out the militia to repel invasions, suppress insurrections, and enforce the execution of the laws; but shall not take the command in person without the consent of the general assembly.

Sec. 12. He shall take care that the laws be faithfully executed.

Sec. 13. He shall nominate, and by and with the advice and consent of the senate, appoint all civil and military officers of the State, whose appointment or election is not otherwise herein provided for, unless a different mode of appointment be prescribed by the law creating the office.

Sec. 14. In case of vacancy, during the recess of the senate, in any office which the governor has power to fill, he shall appoint some suitable person to said office, whose commission shall continue in force till the end of the next session of the general assembly, or till some other person is appointed to the same office, whichever shall first occur, and the nomination of the person thus appointed during the recess, or of some other person in his place, shall be made to the senate within thirty days after the next meeting of the general assembly.

Sec. 15. No person after being rejected by the senate, shall be again nominated for the same office at the same session, unless at the request of the senate; or be appointed to the same office during the recess of the general assembly.

Sec. 16. All civil officers appointed by the governor and senate, shall be nominated to the senate within fifty days from the commencement of each regular session of the general assembly; and their term of office, except in cases otherwise provided for in this constitution, shall commence on the first Monday of May next ensuing their appointment, and continue for two years (unless sooner removed from office,) and until their successors respectively qualify according to law.

Sec. 17. The governor may suspend or arrest any military officer of the State for disobedience of orders, or other military offence, and may remove him in pursuance of the sentence of a court-martial; and may remove, for incompetency or misconduct, all civil officers who received appointments from the executive for a term not exceeding two years.

Sec. 18. The governor may convene the general assembly, or the senate alone, on extraordinary occasions; and whenever, from the presence of an enemy, or from any other cause, the seat of government shall become an unsafe place for the meeting of the general assembly, he may direct their sessions to be held at some other convenient place.

Sec. 19. It shall be the duty of the governor semi-annually, and oftener if he deem it expedient, to examine the bank book, account books, and official proceedings of the treasurer and comptroller of the State.

Sec. 20. He shall from time to time inform the general assembly of the condition of the State, and recommend to their consideration such measures as he may judge necessary and expedient.

Sec. 21. He shall have power to grant reprieves and pardons, except in cases of impeachment, and in cases in which he is prohibited by other articles of this constitution, and to remit fines and forfeitures for offences against the State; but shall not remit the principal or interest of any debt due to the State, except in cases of fines and forfeitures; and before granting a *nolle prosequi*, or pardon, he shall give notice in one or more newspapers of the application made for it, and of the day on or after which his decision will be given; and in every case in which he exercises this power, he shall report to either branch of the general assembly, whenever required, the petitions, recommendations and reasons which influenced his decision.

Sec. 22. The governor shall reside at the seat of government, and shall receive for his services an annual salary of four thousand dollars.

Sec. 23. A secretary of State shall be appointed by the governor, by and with the advice and consent of the senate, who shall continue in office, unless sooner removed by the governor, till the end of the official term of the governor from whom he received his appointment, and shall receive an annual salary of one thousand dollars.

Sec. 24. The secretary of State shall carefully keep and preserve a record of all official acts and proceedings, which may at all times be inspected by a committee of either branch of the general assembly, and shall perform such other duties as are now or may hereafter be prescribed by law, or as may properly belong to his office.

ARTICLE III.

LEGISLATIVE DEPARTMENT.

Section 1. The legislature shall consist of two distinct branches, a senate and a house of delegates, which shall be styled "the general assembly of Maryland."

Sec. 2. Immediately after the adoption of this constitution, and before there shall have been held any general election under it, the mayor and city council of Baltimore shall proceed to lay off and divide the said city into three several districts, of equal population and contiguous territory, as near as may be, which said districts shall be called the first, second, and third legislative districts of Baltimore city.

Sec. 3. Every county in the State, and each legislative district of Baltimore city, as hereinbefore provided for, shall be entitled to one senator, who shall be elected by the qualified voters of the counties, and of the legislative districts of Baltimore city, respectively, and shall serve for four years from the date of his election, subject to the classification of senators hereinafter provided for.

Sec. 4. The white population of the State shall constitute the basis of representation in the house of delegates, and the apportionment of the delegates among the several counties and legislative districts of the city of Baltimore, shall be as follows: For every five thousand persons, or a fractional part thereof above one-half, one delegate shall be chosen, until the number of delegates in each county and legislative district of the city of Baltimore, shall reach five; above that number, one delegate shall be chosen for the next twenty thousand persons, or a fractional portion over one-half thereof, in each county and legislative district of the city of Baltimore; above that number, each county and legislative district of the said city, shall elect one delegate for every eighty thousand persons, or fractional portion thereof, above one-half. Upon this principle, and as soon as practicable after each national census, or State enumeration of inhabitants, the general assembly shall apportion the members of the house of delegates among the several counties, and the several legislative districts of Baltimore city, according to the white population of each.—But until such apportionment is made, the house of delegates shall consist of eighty members, distributed as follows: Allegany, five members; Anne Arundel, two; each of the three legislative districts in Baltimore city, six; Baltimore county, six; Calvert, one; Caroline, two; Carroll, five; Cecil, four; Charles, one; Dorchester, two; Frederick, six; Harford, four; Howard, two; Kent, two; Montgomery, two; Prince George's, two; Queen Anne's, two; St. Mary's, one; Somerset, three; Talbot, two; Washington, five; Worcester, three.

Sec. 5. The members of the house of delegates shall be elected by the qualified voters of the counties and the legislative districts of Baltimore city respectively, to serve for two years from the day of their election.

Sec. 6. The first election for senators and delegates shall take place on the Tuesday next after the first Monday in the month of November, eighteen hundred and sixty-four; and the elections for delegates, and as nearly as practicable for one-half of the senators, shall be held on the same day in every second year thereafter.

Sec. 7. Immediately after the senate shall have convened after the first election under this constitution, the senators shall be divided by lot into two classes, as nearly equal in number as may be—senators of the first class shall go out of office at the expiration of two years, and senators shall be elected on the Tuesday next after the first Monday in the month of November, eighteen hundred and sixty-six, for the term of four years, to supply their places; so that after the first election, one half of the senators may be chosen every second year. In case the number of senators be hereinafter increased, such classification of the additional senators shall be made as to preserve, as nearly as may be, an equal number in each class.

Sec. 8. No person shall be eligible as a senator or delegate who, at the time of his election, is not a citizen of the United States, and who has not resided at least three years next preceding the day of his election in this State, and the last year thereof in the county or in the legislative district of Baltimore city which he may be chosen to represent, if such county or legislative district of said city shall have been so long established, and if not, then in the county or city from which, in whole or in part, the same may have been formed; nor shall any person be eligible as a senator unless he shall have attained the age of twenty-five years, nor as delegate unless he shall have attained the age of twenty-one years at the time of his election.

Sec. 9. No member of congress, or person holding any civil or military office under the United States, shall be eligible as a senator or delegate; and if any person shall, after his election as a senator or delegate, be elected to congress, or be appointed to any office, civil or military, under the government of the United States, his acceptance thereof shall vacate his seat.

Sec. 10. No person holding any civil office of profit or trust under this State, except justices of the peace, shall be eligible to the office of senator or delegate.

Sec. 11. No collector, receiver or holder of public moneys, shall be eligible as senator or delegate, or to any office of profit or trust under this State, until he shall have accounted for and paid into the treasury all sums on the books thereof charged to and due by him.

Sec. 12. In case of death, disqualification, resignation, refusal to act, expulsion, or removal from the county or legislative district of Baltimore city for which he shall have been elected, of any person who shall have been chosen as a delegate or senator, or in case of a tie between two or more such qualified persons, a warrant of election shall be issued by the speaker of the house of delegates or president of the senate, as the case may be, for the election of another person in his place, of which election not less than ten days' notice shall be given, exclusive of the day of the publication of the notice and of the day of election; and in case of such resignation or refusal to act, being communicated in writing to the governor, by the person so resigning or refusing to act, or if such death occur during the legislative recess, and more than ten days before its termination, it shall be the duty of the governor to issue a warrant of election to supply the vacancy thus created, in the same manner the said speaker or president might have done during the session of the general assembly; *provided*, *however*, that unless a meeting of the general assembly may intervene, the election thus ordered to fill such vacancy shall be held on the day of the ensuing election for delegates and senators.

Sec. 13. The general assembly shall meet on the first Wednesday of January, eighteen hundred and sixty-five, and on the same day in every second year thereafter, and at no other time, unless convened by the proclamation of the governor.

Sec. 14. The general assembly shall continue its session so long as in its judgment the public interest may require, and each member thereof shall receive a compensation of five dollars per diem, for every day he shall attend the sessions unless absent on account of sickness; *provided*, however that no member shall receive any other or larger sum than four hundred dollars. When the general assembly shall be convened by proclamation of the governor, the session shall not continue longer than thirty days, and in such case, the compensation shall be at the rate of five dollars per diem.

Sec. 15. No book or other printed matter not appertaining to the business of the session shall be purchased or subscribed for for the use of the members of the general assembly, or be distributed among them at the public expense.

Sec. 16. No senator or delegate, after qualifying as such, notwithstanding he may thereafter resign, shall during the whole period of time for which he was elected, be eligible to any office which shall have been created, or the salary or profits of which shall have been increased during such term, or shall, during said whole period of time, be appointed to any civil office by the executive or general assembly.

Sec. 17. No senator or delegate shall be liable in any civil action or criminal prosecution whatever for words spoken in debate.

Sec. 18. Each house shall be judge of the qualifications and elections of its members, subject to the laws of the State; shall appoint its own officers, determine the rules of its own proceedings, punish a member for disorderly or disrespectful behavior, and with the consent of two-thirds of its whole number of members elected, expel a member; but no member shall be expelled a second time for the same offence.

Sec. 19. A majority of the whole number of members elected to each house shall constitute a quorum for the transaction of business; but a smaller number may adjourn from day to day, and compel the attendance of absent members in such manner and under such penalties as each house may prescribe.

Sec. 20. The doors of each house and of the committees of the whole shall be open, except when the business is such as ought to be kept secret.

Sec. 21. Each house shall keep a journal of its proceedings, and cause the same to be published. The yeas and nays of members on any question shall, at the call of any five of them in the house of delegates, or one in the senate, be entered on the journal.

Sec. 22. Each house may punish by imprisonment, during the session of the general assembly, any person not a member for disrespectful or disorderly behavior in its presence, or for obstructing any of its proceedings, or any of its officers in the execution of their duties; provided such imprisonment shall not, at any one time, exceed ten days.

Sec. 23. The house of delegates may inquire, on the oath of witnesses, into all complaints, grievance and offences, as the Grand Inquest of the State, and may commit any person for any crime to the public jail, there to remain until discharged by due course of law; they may examine and pass all accounts of the State, relating either to the collection or expenditure of the revenue, and appoint auditors to state and adjust the same; they may call for all public or official papers and records, and send for persons whom they may judge necessary in the course of their inquiries concerning affairs relating to the public interest, and may direct all office bonds which shall be made payable to the State, to be sued for any breach thereof.

Sec. 24. Neither house shall, without the consent of the other, adjourn for more than three days at any one time, nor to any other place than that in which the house shall be sitting, without the concurrent vote of two-thirds of the members present.

Sec. 25. The house of delegates shall have the sole power of impeachment in all cases, but a majority of all the members elected must concur in an impeachment; all impeachments shall be tried by the senate, and when sitting for that purpose, the senators shall be on oath or affirmation to do justice according to the law and evidence, but no person shall be convicted without the concurrence of two-thirds of all the senators elected.

Sec. 26. Any bill may originate in either house of the general assembly, and be altered, amended, or rejected by the other; but no bill shall originate in either house during the last ten days of the session, nor become a law until it be read on three different days of the session in each house, unless three-fourths of the members of the house where such bill is pending shall so determine.

Sec. 27. No bill shall become a law unless it be passed in each house by a majority of the whole number of members elected, and on its final passage the ayes and noes be recorded.

Sec. 28. The style of all laws of this State shall be, "*Be it enacted by the general assembly of Maryland*," and all laws shall be passed by original bill, and every law enacted by the general assembly shall embrace but one subject, and that shall be described in the title; and no law nor section of a law shall be revised or amended by reference to its title or section only; and it shall be the duty of the general assembly, in amending any article or section of the code of laws of this State, to enact the same as the said article or section would read when amended. And whenever the general assembly shall enact any public general law, not amendatory of any section or article in the said code, it shall be the duty of the general assembly to enact the same in articles and sections, in the same manner as the said code is arranged; and to provide for the publication of all additions and alterations which may be made to the said code.

Sec. 29. Every bill, when passed by the general assembly and sealed with the great seal, shall be presented to the governor, who shall sign the same in the presence of the presiding officers and chief clerks of the senate and house of delegates. Every law shall be recorded in the office of the court of appeals, and in due time be printed, published, and certified under the great seal to the several courts, in the same manner as has been heretofore usual in this State.

Sec. 30. No law passed by the general assembly shall take effect until the first day of June next after the session at which it may be passed, unless it be otherwise expressly declared therein; and in case any public law is made to take effect before the said first day of June, the general assembly shall provide for the immediate publication of the same.

Sec. 31. No money shall be drawn from the treasury of the State, except in accordance with an appropriation by law, and every such law shall distinctly specify the sum appropriated and the object to which it shall be applied; provided that nothing herein contained shall prevent the general assembly from placing a contingent fund at the disposal of the executive, who shall report to the general assembly at each session the amount expended, and the purposes to which it was applied; an accurate statement of the receipts and expenditures of the public money shall be attached to and published with the laws, after each regular session of the general assembly.

Sec. 32. The general assembly shall not pass local or special laws in any of the following enumerated cases, viz:

For the assessment and collection of taxes for State or county purposes, or extending the time for the collection of taxes;

Providing for the support of the public schools;

The preservation of school funds;

The location or the regulation of school-houses;

Granting divorces;

Relating to fees or salaries;

Relating to the interest on money;

Providing for regulating the election or compensation of State or county officers;

Or designating the places of voting;

Or the boundaries of election districts;

Providing for the sale of real estate belonging to minors or other persons laboring under legal disabilities, by executors, administrators, guardians or trustees;

Giving effect to informal or invalid deeds or wills;

Refunding money paid into the State treasury; or releasing persons from their debts or obligations to the State, unless recommended by the governor or officers of the treasury department;

Or establishing, locating or affecting the construction of roads, and the repairing or building of bridges.

And the general assembly shall pass no special law for any case for which provision has been made by an existing general law. The general assembly at its first session after the adoption of this constitution, shall pass general laws providing for the cases enumerated in this section, and for all other cases where a general law can be made applicable.

Sec. 33. No debt shall be hereafter contracted by the general assembly, unless such debt shall be authorized by a law providing for the collection of an annual tax or taxes sufficient to pay the interest on such debt as it falls due, and also to discharge the principal thereof within fifteen years from the time of contracting the same, and the taxes laid for this purpose shall not be repealed or applied to any other object until the said debt and interest thereon shall be fully discharged. The credit of the State shall not, in any manner, be given or loaned to, or in aid of any individual, association or corporation, nor shall the general assembly have the power in any mode to involve the State in the construction of works of internal improvement, nor in any enterprise which shall involve the faith or credit of the State, nor make any appropriations therefor. And they shall not use or appropriate the proceeds of the internal improvement companies, or of the State tax now levied, or which may hereafter be levied, to pay off the public debt, to any other purpose until the interest and debt are fully paid, or the sinking fund shall be equal to the amount of the outstanding debt; but the general assembly may, without laying a tax, borrow an amount never to exceed fifty thousand dollars, to meet temporary deficiencies in the treasury, and may contract debts to any amount that may be necessary for the defence of the State.

Sec. 34. No extra compensation shall be granted or allowed by the general assembly to any public officer, agent, servant or contractor, after the services shall have been rendered or the contract entered into; nor shall the salary or compensation of any public officer be increased or diminished during his term of office.

Sec. 35. No lottery grant shall ever hereafter be authorized by the general assembly.

Sec. 36. The general assembly shall pass no law, nor make any appropriation to compensate the masters or claimants of slaves emancipated from servitude by the adoption of this constitution.

Sec. 37. No person shall be imprisoned for debt.

Sec. 38. The general assembly shall grant no charter for banking purposes, nor renew any banking corporation now in existence, except upon the condition that the stockholders shall be liable to the amount of their respective share or shares of stock in such banking institution for all its debts and liabilities upon note, bill or otherwise; and upon the further condition that no director or other officer of said corporation shall borrow any money from said corporation; and if any director or other officer shall be convicted upon indictment of directly or indirectly violating this section, he shall be punished by fine or imprisonment at the discretion of the court. The books, papers, and accounts of all banks shall be open to inspection, under such regulations as may be prescribed by law.

Sec. 39. The general assembly shall enact no law authorizing private property to be taken for public use without just compensation as agreed upon between the parties or awarded by a jury, being first paid or tendered to the party entitled to such compensation.

Sec. 40. Any citizen of this State who shall, after the adoption of this constitution, either in or out of this State, fight a duel with deadly weapons, or send or accept a challenge so to do, or who shall act as a second, or knowingly aid or assist in any manner those thus offending, and any citizen who has thus offended, or who has so aided or assisted those thus offending, since the first Wednesday of June, eighteen hundred and fifty-one, shall ever thereafter be incapable of holding any office of trust or profit under this State.

Sec. 41. The general assembly shall pass laws for the preservation of the purity of elections by the registration of voters, and by such other means as may be deemed expedient; and to make effective the provisions of the constitution disfranchising certain persons, or disqualifying them from holding office.

Sec. 42. The general assembly shall pass laws necessary to protect the property of the wife from the debts of the husband during her life, and for securing the same to her issue after her death.

Sec. 43. Laws shall be passed by the general assembly to protect from execution a reasonable amount of property of a debtor, not exceeding in value the sum of five hundred dollars.

Sec. 44. The general assembly shall provide a simple and uniform system of charges in the offices of clerks of courts and registers of wills, in the counties of this State and the city of Baltimore, and for the collection thereof; provided the amount of compensation to any of said officers shall not exceed the sum of twenty-five hundred dollars a year over and above office expenses, and compensation to assistants; and provided further, that such compensation of clerks, registers, assistants and office expenses, shall always be paid out of the fees or receipts of the offices respectively.

Sec. 45. The general assembly shall have power to receive from the United States any grant or donation of land, money or securities, for any purpose designated by the United States, and shall administer or distribute the same according to the conditions of the said grant.

Sec. 46. The general assembly shall make provision for all cases of contested elections of any of the officers not herein provided for.

Sec. 47. The general assembly shall pass laws requiring the president, directors, trustees, or agents of corporations created or authorized by the laws of this State, teachers or superintendents of the public schools, colleges, or other institutions of learning; attorneys-at-law, jurors, and such other persons as the general assembly shall from time to time prescribe, to take the oath of allegiance to the United States, set forth in the first article of this constitution.

Sec. 48. The general assembly shall have power to accept the session of any territory contiguous to this State, from the States of Virginia and West Virginia, or from the United States, with the consent of congress, and of the inhabitants of such ceded territory, and in case of such cessions the general assembly may divide such territory into counties, and shall provide for the representation of the same in the general assembly, on the basis fixed by this constitution, and may for that purpose increase the number of senators and delegates, and the general assembly shall enact such laws as may be required to extend the constitution and laws of this State over such territory, and may create courts conformably to the constitution for such territory, and may for that purpose increase the number of judges of the court of appeals.

Sec. 49. The general assembly shall provide by law for the registration of births, marriages and deaths, and shall pass laws providing for the celebration of marriage between any persons legally competent to contract marriage, and shall provide that any persons prevented by conscientious scruples from being married by any of the existing provisions of law, may be married by any judge or clerk of any court of record, or any mayor of any incorporated city in this State.

Sec. 50. The rate of interest in this State shall not exceed six per centum per annum, and no higher rate shall be taken or demanded, and the general assembly shall provide by law, all necessary forfeitures and penalties against usury.

Sec. 51. Corporations may be formed under general laws, but shall not be created by special act, except for municipal purposes and in cases where, in the judgment of the general assembly, the object of the corporation cannot be attained under general laws. All laws and special acts, pursuant to this section may be altered from time to time, or repealed: *Provided*, nothing herein contained shall be construed to alter, change or amend, in any manner, the section in relation to banks.

Sec. 52. The governor, comptroller and treasurer of the State are hereby authorized, conjointly, or any two of them, to exchange the State's interest as stockholder and creditor in the Baltimore and Ohio railroad company for an equal amount of the bonds or registered debt now owing by the State; and subject to such regulations and conditions as the general assembly may from time to time prescribe, to sell the State's interest in the other works of internal improvement, whether as a stockholder or a creditor; also, the State's interest in any banking corporation, and receive in payment the bonds and registered debt now owing by the State, equal in amount to the price obtained for the State's said interest; *Provided*, that the interest of the State in the Washington branch of the Baltimore and Ohio railroad be reserved and excepted from sale; and, *provided further*, that no sale or contract of sale of the State's interest in the Chesapeake and Ohio canal, the Chesapeake and Delaware canal, and the Susquehanna and Tide-Water canal companies shall go into effect until the same shall be ratified by the ensuing general assembly.

Sec. 53. The general assembly before authorizing the sale of the State's interest in the Chesapeake and Ohio canal, and before prescribing regulations and conditions for said sale, shall pass all laws that may be necessary to authorize the counties of Allegany, Washington, Frederick and Montgomery, or any one of them, to create a debt by the issue of bonds or otherwise, so as to enable them, or any of them to become the purchasers of said interest.

Sec. 54. The general assembly shall have power to regulate by law, not inconsistent with this constitution, all matters which relate to the judges of election, time, place and manner of holding elections in this State, and of making returns thereof.

Sec. 55. The general assembly shall have power to pass all such laws as may be necessary and proper for carrying into execution the powers vested by this constitution, in any department or office of the government, and the duties imposed upon them thereby.

ARTICLE IV.

JUDICIARY DEPARTMENT.

Part I.—General Provisions.

Section 1. The judicial power of this State shall be vested in a court of appeals, circuit courts, orphans' courts, such courts for the city of Baltimore as may be hereinafter prescribed or provided for, and justices of the peace; all said courts shall be courts of record, and each shall have a seal, to be used in the authentication of all process issuing from them. The process and official character of justices of the peace shall be authenticated as hath heretofore been practiced in this State, or may hereafter be prescribed by law.

Sec. 2. The judges of the several courts, except the judges of the orphans' courts, shall be citizens of the United States, and residents of this State, not less than five years next preceding their election, or appointment by the executive in case of a vacancy; and not less than one year next preceding their election or appointment, residents in the judicial district or circuit, as the case may be, for which they may be elected or appointed; they shall be not less than thirty years of age at the time of their election, and selected from those who have been admitted to practice law in this State, and who are most distinguished for integrity, wisdom and sound legal knowledge.

Sec. 3. The judges of the court of appeals shall be elected by the qualified voters of the State; and the governor, by and with the advice and consent of the senate, shall designate the chief justice; and the judges of the judicial circuits shall be elected by the qualified voters of their respective circuits; each judge of the court of appeals and of each judicial circuit shall hold his office for the term of fifteen years, from the time of his election, or until he shall have attained the age of seventy years, whichever may first happen, and be re-eligible thereto until he shall have attained the age of seventy years, and not after.

Sec. 4. Any judge shall be removed from office by the governor on conviction in a court of law, of incompetency, of wilful neglect of duty, misbehavior in office, or any other crime; or on impeachment according to this constitution, or the laws of the State; or on the address of the general assembly, two-thirds of each house concurring in such address, and the accused having been notified of the charges against him, and had opportunity of making his defence.

Sec. 5 In case of the death, resignation, removal, or other disqualification of a judge of any court of this State, except of the orphans' courts, the governor, by and with the advice and consent of the senate, shall thereupon appoint a person duly qualified to fill said office until the next general election thereafter, whether for members of the general assembly or county officers, whichever shall first occur, at which time an election shall be held as herein prescribed, for a judge who shall hold said office for the term of fifteen years, and until the election and qualification of his successor.

Sec. 6. All judges shall, by virtue of their offices, be conservators of the peace throughout the State, and no fees or perquisites, commission or reward of any kind, shall be allowed to any judge in this State, besides his annual salary or fixed per diem for the discharge of any judicial duty.

Sec. 7. No judge shall sit in any case wherein he may be interested, or where either of the parties may be connected with him by affinity or consanguinity, within such degrees as now are or may hereafter be prescribed by law, or where he shall have been of counsel in the case.

Sec. 8. The general assembly shall provide for the trial of causes in case of the disqualification of the judge of the superior court of Baltimore city, the court of common pleas, the circuit court of Baltimore city, and the criminal court of Baltimore, and also in case of the disqualification of any judge of other circuit courts of this State, to hear and determine the same, but in case of such disqualification, the parties thereto may, by consent, appoint a person to try the same; and the parties to any cause may submit the same to the court for determination without the aid of a jury.

Sec. 9. The judge or judges of any court of this State, except the court of appeals, shall order and direct the record of proceedings in any suit or action, issue or petition, presentment or indictment pending in such court, to be transmitted to some other court in the same or any adjoining circuit having jurisdiction in such cases, whenever any party to such cause, or the counsel of any party shall make it satisfactorily appear to the court that such party cannot have a fair and impartial trial in the court in which such suit or action, issue or petition, presentment or indictment is pending; and the general assembly shall make such modifications of existing law as may be necessary to regulate and give force to this provision.

Sec. 10. The judge or judges of any court may appoint such officers for their respective courts, as may be found necessary, and it shall be the duty of the general assembly to prescribe by law a fixed compensation for all such officers.

Sec. 11. Every person being a citizen of the United States shall be permitted to appear to and try his own case in all the courts of this State.

Sec. 12. Any person who shall, after this constitution shall have gone into effect, detain in slavery any person emancipated by the provisions of this constitution, shall on conviction, be fined not less than five hundred dollars nor more than five thousand dollars, or be imprisoned not more than five years; and any of the judges of this State shall discharge, on *habeas corpus*, any person so detained in slavery.

Sec. 13. The clerks of the several courts created or continued by this constitution, shall have charge and custody of the records and other papers, shall perform all the duties and be allowed the fees which appertain to their several offices as the same now are or may hereafter be regulated by law.

Sec. 14. All elections of judges, and other officers, provided for by this constitution, State's attorneys excepted, shall be certified and the returns made by the clerks of the respective counties to the governor, who shall issue commissions to the different persons for the offices to which they shall have been respectively elected; and in all such elections, the person having the greatest number of votes shall be declared to be elected.

Sec. 15. If in any case of election for judges, clerks of the courts of law, and registers of wills, the opposing candidates shall have an equal number of votes, it shall be the duty of the governor to order a new election; and in case of any contested election, the governor shall send the returns to the house of delegates, who shall judge of the election and qualification of the candidates at such election.

Sec. 16. All public commissions and grants shall run thus: "The State of Maryland," &c., and shall be signed by the governor, with the seal of the State annexed; all writs and process shall run in the same style, and be tested, sealed and signed as usual; and all indictments shall conclude "against the peace, government and dignity of the State."

Part II.—Court of Appeals.

Sec. 17. The court of appeals shall consist of a chief justice and four associate justices, and for their selection the State shall be divided into five judicial districts, as follows, viz: Worcester, Somerset, Dorchester, Talbot, Caroline, Queen Anne, Kent and Cecil counties shall compose the first district; Harford and Baltimore counties, and the first seven wards of Baltimore city, shall compose the second district; Baltimore city, except the first seven wards, shall compose the third district; Allegany, Washington, Frederick, Howard and Carroll counties, shall compose the fourth district; St. Mary's, Charles, Anne Arundel, Calvert, Prince George's and Montgomery counties, shall compose the fifth district, and one of the justices of the court of appeals shall be elected from each of said districts, by the qualified voters of the whole State. The present chief justice and associate justices of the court of appeals shall continue to act as such until the expiration of the term for which they were respectively elected, and until their successors are elected and qualified; and an election for a justice of the court of appeals, to be taken from the fourth judicial district, shall be held on the Tuesday next after the first Monday in the month of November, eighteen hundred and sixty-four.

Sec. 18. The court of appeals shall hold its sessions in the city of Annapolis, on the first Monday in April and the first Monday of October, of each and every year, or at such other times as the general assembly may by law direct, and it shall be competent for the justices of said court, sufficient cause appearing to them, temporarily to transfer their sittings elsewhere.

Sec. 19. The jurisdiction of the court of appeals shall be co-extensive with the limits of the State, and such as now is or may hereafter be prescribed for it by law, and its sessions shall continue for not less than ten months in the year, if the business before it shall so require.

Sec. 20. Any three of the justices of the court of appeals may constitute a quorum, but no cause shall be decided without the concurrence of at least three justices in the decision; and in every case decided an opinion in writing shall be filed within three months after the argument or submission of the cause, and the judgment of the court shall be final and conclusive.

Sec. 21. The salary of the justices of the court of appeals shall be three thousand dollars each per annum, payable quarterly.

Sec. 22. Provision shall be made by law for publishing reports of all causes argued and determined in the court of appeals, which the justices shall designate as proper for publication.

Sec. 23. The court of appeals shall appoint its own clerk, who shall hold his office for six years, and may be re-appointed at the end thereof; he shall be subject to removal by the said court for incompetency, neglect of duty, misdemeanor in office, or such other cause or causes as may be prescribed by law.

Part III.—Circuit Courts.

Sec. 24. The State shall be divided into thirteen judicial circuits, in manner following: The counties of St. Mary's and Charles shall constitute the first circuit; the counties of Anne Arundel and Calvert, the second; the counties of Prince George's and Montgomery, the third; the county of Frederick, the fourth; the county of Washington, the fifth; the county of Allegany, the sixth; the counties of Carroll and Howard, the seventh; the county of Baltimore, the eighth; the counties of Harford and Cecil, the ninth; the counties of Kent and Queen Anne's, the tenth; the counties of Talbot and Caroline, the eleventh; the counties of Dorchester, Somerset and Worcester, the twelfth; and the city of Baltimore, the thirteenth.

Sec. 25. One court shall be held in each county of the State; the said courts shall be called circuit courts for the county in which they may be held, and shall have and exercise all the power, authority and jurisdiction, original and appellate, which the present circuit courts of this State now have and exercise, or which may hereafter be prescribed by law.

Sec. 26. For each circuit (the thirteenth excepted) there shall be one judge, who shall be styled circuit judge, who, during his term of office, shall reside in one of the counties composing the circuit for which he may be elected; the said judges shall hold a term of their courts in each of the counties composing their respective circuits at such times as now are or may hereafter be fixed by law, such terms to be never less than two in each year in each county; special terms may be held by said judges in their discretion, whenever the business of their several counties renders such terms necessary.

Sec. 27. The present judges of the circuit courts shall continue to act as judges of the respective circuit courts within the judicial circuits in which they respectively reside, until the expiration of the term for which they were respectively elected, and until their successors are elected and qualified, viz: the present judges of the first, second, third, fourth, sixth and eighth judicial circuits, as organized at the time of the adoption of this constitution, shall continue to act as judges respectively of the first, second, fourth, fifth, ninth and twelfth judicial circuits, as organized under this constitution; and an election for judges of the third, sixth, seventh, eighth, tenth and eleventh judicial circuits shall be held on the Tuesday next after the first Monday in the month of November, in the year eighteen hundred and sixty-four.

Sec. 28. The salary of each judge of the circuit court shall be twenty-five hundred dollars per annum, payable quarterly, and shall not be increased or diminished during his continuance in office.

Sec. 29. There shall be a clerk of the circuit court for each county, who shall be elected by a plurality of the qualified voters of said county; he shall hold his office for the term of six years from the time of his election, and until a new election is held and his successor duly qualified; he shall be re-eligible at the end of his term, and shall at any time be subject to removal for wilful neglect of duty, or other misdemeanor in office, on conviction in a court of law. In the event of any vacancy in the office of the clerk of any of the circuit courts, said vacancy shall be filled by the judge of said circuit in which said vacancy occurs, until the next general election for county officers, when a clerk of said circuit court shall be elected to serve for six years thereafter.

Sec. 30. The judges of the respective circuit courts of this State, and of the courts of Baltimore city, shall render their decisions in all cases argued before them, or submitted for their judgment, within two months after the same shall have been so argued or submitted.

Part IV.—Courts of Baltimore City.

Sec. 31. There shall be in the thirteenth judicial circuit four courts, to be styled the superior court of Baltimore city; the court of common pleas; the circuit court of Baltimore city; and the criminal court of Baltimore; each court shall consist of one judge, who shall be elected by the legal and qualified voters of said city, and shall hold his office for the term of fifteen years, subject to the provisions of this constitution with regard to the election and qualification of judges, and their removal from office, and shall exercise the jurisdiction hereinafter specified.

Sec. 32. Each of said judges shall receive an annual salary of three thousand dollars, payable quarterly.

Sec. 33. The superior court of Baltimore city shall have jurisdiction over all suits where the debt or damage claimed, exclusive of interest, shall exceed the sum of one thousand dollars, and in case any plaintiff or plaintiffs shall recover less than the sum or value of one thousand dollars, he or they shall be allowed or adjudged to pay costs in the discretion of the court. The said court shall also have jurisdiction as a court of equity within the limits of the said city, and in all other civil cases which are not hereinafter assigned to the court of common pleas, and also have jurisdiction in all cases of appeals from the commissioners for opening streets.

Sec. 34. The court of common pleas shall have civil jurisdiction in all suits where the debt or damage claimed, exclusive of interest, shall be over one hundred dollars, and shall not exceed one thousand dollars; and shall also have jurisdiction in all cases of appeal in civil cases from the judgment of justices of the peace in the said city, and shall have jurisdiction in all applications for the benefit of the insolvent laws of this State, and the supervision and control of the trustees thereof.

Sec. 35. The circuit court of Baltimore city shall have jurisdiction concurrent with the superior court of Baltimore city, in all cases in equity, in cases arising under the act to direct descents, and its supplements, and shall exercise all the power that is now conferred by law, provided said court shall not have jurisdiction in applications for the writ of *habeas corpus*, in cases of persons charged with criminal offences.

Sec. 36. The criminal court of Baltimore shall have and exercise all the jurisdiction now held and exercised by the criminal court of Baltimore, except in cases of appeals from commissioners for opening streets, and shall have jurisdiction in all cases of appeals from justices of the peace in said city, for the recovery of fines, penalties and forfeitures.

Sec. 37. The present judges of the several courts of Baltimore city, shall continue to act as such until the expiration of the terms for which they were respectively elected, and until their successors are elected and qualified.

Sec. 38. All causes pending in the several courts of Baltimore city at the adoption of this constitution shall be prosecuted to final judgment, as though the jurisdiction of the several courts in which they may be pending had not been changed.

Sec. 39. There shall be a clerk of each of the said courts of Baltimore city, who shall be elected by the legal and qualified voters of said city, and shall hold his office for six years from the time of his election, and until his successor is elected and qualified, and be re-eligible thereto, subject to be removed for wilful neglect of duty, or other misdemeanor in office on conviction in a court of law. In case of a vacancy in the office of a clerk of any of the said courts, the judge of the court of which he was clerk, shall have the power to appoint a clerk until the general election for county officers held next thereafter, when a clerk of said court shall be elected to serve for six years thereafter.

Sec. 40. The present clerk of the superior court of Baltimore city and of the court of common pleas, and of the criminal court of Baltimore, shall continue to act as clerks of said courts respectively during the time for which they were severally elected, and until their successors are elected and qualified, and in case of the death, resignation or disqualification of either of said clerks before the expiration of the time for which they were elected, the judge of the court where such death, resignation or other disqualification may occur, shall have the power to appoint a clerk as provided by the thirty-ninth section of this article. The present clerk of the circuit court of Baltimore city shall continue to act as clerk of said court until the first election for county officers next after the adoption of this constitution, when a clerk of said court shall be elected in the same manner, and hold his office for the same time, and be subject to the same provisions of this constitution, as the clerks of the courts in said city.

Sec. 41. The general assembly shall, whenever it may think the same proper and expedient, provide by law another court for the city of Baltimore, to consist of one judge, to be elected by the legal and qualified voters of said city, who shall be subject to the same constitutional provisions, hold his office for the same term of years, and receive the same compensation as the judge of the superior court of said city, and said court shall have such jurisdiction and powers as may be prescribed by law; and the general assembly may re-apportion the civil jurisdiction among the several courts in Baltimore city from time to time, as in their judgments the public interest and convenience may require.

Sec. 42. The clerk of the court of common pleas shall have authority to issue within said city, all marriage and other licenses required by law, subject to such provisions as the general assembly have now or may hereafter prescribe, and the clerk of the superior court of said city shall receive and record all deeds, conveyances, and other papers which are required by law to be recorded in said city. He shall also have custody of all papers connected with the proceedings on the law or equity side of Baltimore county court, and of the dockets thereof, so far as the same have relation to the city of Baltimore.

Part V.—Orphans' Courts.

Sec. 43. There shall be an orphans' court in the city of Baltimore, and in each of the counties of this State. The qualified voters of the city of Baltimore and of the several counties of the State shall, on the Tuesday next after the first Monday in the month of November, eighteen hundred and sixty-seven, elect three men to be judges of the orphans' court of said city and counties respectively; one of the said judges first elected shall hold his office for two years, one for four years and the other for six years; and at the first meeting after their election and qualification, or as soon thereafter as practicable, they shall determine by lot which one of their number shall hold his office for two, four and six years, respectively, and thereafter there shall be elected as aforesaid, at each general election for county officers, one judge to serve for the term of six years. No person shall be elected judge of the orphans' court unless he be at the time of his election a citizen of the United States and a resident for twelve months in the city or county for which he may be elected; each of said judges shall receive such compensation, to be paid by the said counties and city respectively, as is now or may hereafter be prescribed by the general assembly.

Sec. 44. In case of the death, resignation, removal or other disqualification of a judge of an orphans' court, the governor by and with the advice and consent of the senate, shall appoint a person duly qualified to fill said office for the residue of the term thus made vacant.

Sec. 45. The orphans' courts shall have all the powers now vested by law in the orphans' courts of this State, subject to such changes as the general assembly may prescribe, and shall have such other jurisdiction as may from time to time be provided by law.

Sec. 46. There shall be a register of wills in each county of the State and in the city of Baltimore, to be elected by the legal and qualified voters of said counties and city respectively, who shall hold his office for six years from the time of his election, and until his successor is elected and qualified; he shall be re-eligible and subject at all times to removal for wilful neglect of duty or misdemeanor in office in the same manner that the clerks of courts are removable. In the event of any vacancy in the office of register of wills, said vacancy shall be filled by the judges of the orphans' court in which such vacancy occurs, until the next general election for county officers, when a register shall be elected to serve for six years thereafter.

Part VI.—Justices of the Peace.

Sec. 47. The governor, by and with the advice and consent of the senate, shall appoint such number of justices of the peace, and the county commissioners of the several counties, and the mayor and city council of Baltimore, shall appoint such number of constables for the several election districts of the counties and wards of the city of Baltimore, as are now or may hereafter be prescribed by law; and justices of the peace and constables so appointed, shall be subject to removal by the judge having criminal jurisdiction in the county or city for incompetency, wilful neglect of duty, or misdemeanor in office, on conviction in a court of law. The justices of the peace and constables so appointed and commissioned shall be conservators of the peace, shall hold their office for two years, and shall have such jurisdiction, duties and compensation, subject to such right of appeal in all cases from the judgment of justices of the peace, as hath been heretofore exercised, or shall be hereafter prescribed by law.

Sec. 48. In the event of a vacancy in the office of a justice of the peace, the governor shall appoint a person to serve as justice of the peace for the residue of the term, and in case of a vacancy in the office of constable, the county commissioners of the county in which the vacancy occurs, or the mayor and city council of Baltimore, as the case may be, shall appoint a person to serve as constable for the residue of the term.

Part VII.—Sheriffs.

Sec. 49. There shall be elected in each county, and in the city of Baltimore, in every second year, one person, resident in said county or city, above the age of twenty-five years, and at least five years preceding his election, a citizen of this State, to the office of sheriff. He shall hold his office for two years and until his successor is duly elected and qualified; shall be ineligible for two years thereafter, shall give such bond, exercise such powers, and perform such duties as now are or may hereafter be fixed by law.—In case of a vacancy by death, refusal to serve, or neglect to qualify or give bond, by disqualification or removal from the county or city, the governor shall appoint a person to be sheriff for the remainder of the official term.

Sec. 50. Coroners, elisors, and notaries public may be appointed for each county and the city of Baltimore, in the manner, for the purposes, and with the powers now fixed or which may hereafter be prescribed by law.

ARTICLE V.

ATTORNEY GENERAL.

Section 1. There shall be an attorney general elected by the qualified voters of the State, on general ticket, on the Tuesday next after the first Monday in the month of November, in the year eighteen hundred and sixty-four, and on the same day in every fourth year thereafter, who shall hold his office for four years from the first Monday of January next ensuing his election, and until his successor shall be elected and qualified, and shall be re-eligible thereto, and shall be subject to removal for incompetency, wilful neglect of duty, or misdemeanor in office, on conviction in a court of law.

Sec. 2. All elections for attorney general shall be certified to, and returns made thereof by the clerks of the circuit courts for the several counties, and the clerk of the superior court of Baltimore city, to the governor of the State, whose duty it shall be to decide upon the election and qualifications of the person returned, and in case of a tie between two or more persons to designate which of said persons shall qualify as attorney general, and to administer the oath of office to the person elected.

Sec. 3. It shall be the duty of the attorney general to prosecute and defend, on the part of the State, all cases which at the time of his election and qualification, and which thereafter may be depending in the court of appeals, or in the supreme court of the United States, by or against the State, or wherein the State may be interested; and he shall give his opinion in writing, whenever required by the general assembly, or either branch thereof, the governor, the comptroller, the treasurer, or any State's attorney on any matter or subject depending before them, or either of them, and when required by the governor or the general assembly, he shall aid any State's attorney in prosecuting any suit or action brought by the State, in any court of this State; and he shall commence and prosecute or defend any suit or action in any of said courts, on the part of the State, which the general assembly or the governor acting, according to law, shall direct to be commenced, prosecuted or defended, and he shall receive for his services an annual salary of twenty-five hundred dollars; but he shall not be entitled to receive any fees, perquisites or rewards whatever, in addition to the salary aforesaid, for the performance of any official duty, nor have power to appoint any agent, representative or deputy, under any circumstances whatever.

Sec. 4. No person shall be eligible to the office of attorney general who has not resided and practiced law in this State, for at least seven years next preceding his election.

Sec. 5. In case of vacancy in the office of attorney general, occasioned by death, resignation, or his removal from the State, or his conviction, as hereinbefore specified, the said vacancy shall be filled by the governor for the residue of the term thus made vacant.

Sec. 6. It shall be the duty of the clerk of the court of appeals, and the commissioner of the land office, respectively, whenever a case shall be brought into said court or office, in which the State is a party, or has interest, immediately to notify the attorney general thereof.

THE STATE'S ATTORNEYS.

Sec. 7. There shall be an attorney for the State in each county and the city of Baltimore, to be styled "the State's attorney," who shall be elected by the voters thereof, respectively, on the Tuesday next after the first Monday in the month of November, eighteen hundred and sixty-seven, and on the same day every fourth year thereafter, and shall hold his office for four years from the first Monday in January next ensuing his election, and until his successor shall be elected and qualified, and shall be re-eligible thereto, and be subject to removal therefrom for incompetency, wilful neglect of duty or misdemeanor in office, on conviction in a court of law.

Sec. 8. All elections for the State's attorney shall be certified to, and returns made thereof, by the clerks of the said counties and city to the judges thereof having criminal jurisdiction, respectively, whose duty it shall be to decide upon the elections and qualifications of the persons returned, and in case of a tie between two or more persons, to designate which of said persons shall qualify as State's attorney, and to administer the oaths of office to the persons elected.

Sec. 9. The State's attorney shall perform such duties and receive such fees and commissions as are now or may hereafter be prescribed by law, and if any State's attorney shall receive any other fee or reward than such as is, or may be allowed by law, he shall, on conviction thereof, be removed from office; provided, that the State's attorney for Baltimore city shall have power to appoint one deputy, at a salary of not more than fifteen hundred dollars per annum, to be paid by the State's attorney out of the fees of his office, as has heretofore been practiced.

Sec. 10. No person shall be eligible to the office of State's attorney who has not been admitted to practice law in this State, and who has not resided for at least one year in the county or city in which he may be elected.

Sec. 11. In case of vacancy in the office of State's attorney, or of his removal from the county or city in which he shall have been elected, or on his conviction as herein specified, the said vacancy shall be filled by the judge of the county or city, respectively, having criminal jurisdiction in which said vacancy shall occur, for the residue of the term thus made vacant.

ARTICLE VI.

TREASURY DEPARTMENT.

Section 1. The treasury department of this State shall consist of a comptroller and a treasurer.

Sec. 2. The comptroller shall be chosen by the qualified electors of the State, at each regular election for members of the general assembly. He shall hold his office for two years, commencing on the second Wednesday in January next ensuing his election, and shall receive an annual salary of twenty-five hundred dollars; but shall not be allowed, nor shall he receive any fees, commissions or perquisites of any kind, in addition thereto, for the performance of any official duty or service. He shall keep his office at the seat of government, and shall take such oath, and enter into such bond, for the faithful performance of his duty, as are now or may hereafter be prescribed by law. A vacancy in the office of comptroller, shall be filled by the governor for the residue of the term. The first election for comptroller under this constitution, shall be held on the Tuesday next after the first Monday in the month of November, in the year eighteen hundred and sixty-four, but the comptroller then elected shall not enter upon the discharge of the duties of his office, until the expiration of the term of the present incumbent, unless the said office shall sooner become vacant.

Sec. 3. The comptroller shall have the general superintendence of the fiscal affairs of the State; he shall digest and prepare plans for the improvement and management of the revenue, and for the support of the public credit; prepare and report estimates of the revenue and expenditure of the State; superintend and enforce the collection of all taxes and revenue; adjust, settle and preserve all public accounts; decide on the forms of keeping and stating accounts; grant, under regulations prescribed by law, all warrants for moneys to be paid out of the treasury, in pursuance of appropriations by law; prescribe the formalities of the transfer of stock or other evidences of the State debt, and countersign the same, without which such evidences shall not be valid; he shall make full reports of all his proceedings, and of the state of the treasury department within ten days after the commencement of each session of the general assembly, and perform such other duties as are now or may hereafter be prescribed by law.

Sec. 4. The treasurer shall be elected on joint ballot by the two houses of the general assembly at each regular session thereof.—He shall hold his office for two years, and shall receive an annual salary of twenty-five hundred dollars, but shall not be allowed, nor shall he receive any fees, commissions, or perquisites of any kind in addition thereto, for the performance of any official duty or service. He shall keep his office at the seat of government, and shall take such oath and enter into such bond for the faithful discharge of his duty as are now or may hereafter be prescribed by law. A vacancy in the office of treasurer shall be filled by the governor for the residue of the term. The general assembly at its first session after the adoption of this constitution shall elect a treasurer, but the treasurer then elected, shall not enter upon the discharge of the duties of his office until the expiration of the term of the present incumbent, unless the said office shall sooner become vacant.

Sec. 5. The treasurer shall receive and keep the moneys of the State, and disburse the same upon warrants drawn by the comptroller and not otherwise; he shall take receipts for all moneys paid by him, and all receipts for moneys received by him shall be indorsed upon warrants signed by the comptroller, without which warrant, so signed, no acknowledgment of money received into the treasury shall be valid; and upon warrants issued by the comptroller, he shall make arrangements for the payment of the interest of the public debt, and for the purchase thereof, on account of the sinking fund. Every bond, certificate or other evidence of the debt of the State shall be signed by the treasurer and countersigned by the comptroller, and no new certificate or other evidence intended to replace another shall be issued until the old one shall be delivered to the treasurer, and authority executed in due form for the transfer of the same shall be filed in his office, and the transfer accordingly made on the books thereof, and the certificate or other evidence cancelled; but the general assembly may make provision for the loss of certificates or other evidence of the debt.

Sec. 6. The treasurer shall render his accounts quarterly to the comptroller, and on the third day of each regular session of the general assembly he shall submit to the senate and house of delegates fair and accurate copies of all accounts by him from time to time rendered and settled with the comptroller. He shall at all times submit to the comptroller the inspection of the moneys in his hands, and perform all other duties that are now or may hereafter be prescribed by law.

ARTICLE VII.

SUNDRY OFFICERS.

Section 1. The governor, the comptroller of the treasury and the treasurer shall constitute the board of public works in this State; they shall keep a journal of their proceedings, and shall hold regular sessions in the city of Annapolis, on the first Wednesday in January, April, July and October in each year, and oftener if necessary, at which sessions they shall hear and determine such matters as affect the public works of the State, and as the general assembly may confer upon them the power to decide.

Sec. 2. They shall exercise a diligent and faithful s pervision of all public works in which the State may be interested as stockholder or creditor, and shall appoint the directors in every railroad or canal company in which the State has the legal power to appoint directors, which said directors shall represent the State in all meetings of the stockholders of every railroad or canal company in which the State is a stockholder; they shall require the directors of all said public works from time to time, and as often as there shall be any change in the rates of toll on any of said works, to furnish said board of public works a schedule of such modified rates of toll, and shall use all legal powers which they may possess to obtain the establishment of rates of toll which may prevent an injurious competition with each other to the detriment of the interests of the State, and so to adjust them as to promote the agricultural interests of the State; they shall report to the general assembly at each regular session, and recommend such legislation as they shall deem necessary and requisite to promote or protect the interests of the State in the said public works; they shall perform such other duties as may be hereafter prescribed by law; and a majority of them shall be competent to act.

The governor, comptroller and treasurer, shall receive no additional salary for services rendered by them as members of the board of public works.

Sec. 3. There shall be a commissioner of the land office, elected by the qualified voters of the State, on the Tuesday next after the first Monday in the month of November, in the year eighteen hundred and seventy, and on the same day in every sixth year thereafter, who shall hold his office for the term of six years from the first Monday in January ensuing his election. The returns of said election shall be made to the governor, and in the event of a tie between two or more candidates, the governor shall direct a new election to be held by writs to the sheriffs of the several counties, and of the city of Baltimore; who shall hold said election after at least twenty days' notice, exclusive of the day of election. He shall perform such duties as are now required of the commissioner of the land office, or such as may hereafter be prescribed by law, and shall also be the keeper of the chancery records. He shall receive a salary of two thousand dollars per annum, to be paid out of the treasury, and shall charge such fees as are now or may be hereafter fixed by law. He shall make a semi-annual report of all the fees of his office, both as commissioner of the land office and as keeper of the chancery records, to the comptroller of the treasury, and shall pay the same semi-annually into the treasury. In case of vacancy in said office by death, resignation or other cause, the governor shall fill such vacancy until the next general election for members of the general assembly thereafter, when a commissioner of the land office shall be elected for the full term of six years ensuing.

Sec. 4. The State librarian shall be elected by a joint vote of the two branches of the general assembly for four years, and until his successor shall be elected and qualified. His salary shall be fifteen hundred dollars per annum, and the general assembly shall pass no law whereby he shall receive any additional compensation. He shall perform such duties as are now or may hereafter be prescribed by law. In case of a vacancy in the office of State librarian from death, resignation and other cause, the governor shall fill such vacancy until the next meeting of the general assembly thereafter, and until a successor be elected and qualified.

Sec. 5. The county commissioners shall be elected, on general ticket, by the qualified voters of the several counties in this State; an election for county commissioners shall be held on the Tuesday next after the first Monday in the month of November, eighteen hundred and sixty-five, and as nearly one-half as may be of said commissioners shall hold their office for two years, and the other half for four years. At the first meeting after their election and qualification, or as soon thereafter as practicable, the said commissioners shall determine by lot which of their number shall hold office for two and four years respectively; and thereafter there shall be elected as aforesaid, at each general election for county officers, county commissioners for four years to fill the places of those whose term has expired. The said commissioners shall exercise such powers and perform such duties (which shall be similar throughout the State) as are now or may hereafter be prescribed by law. Their number in each county, and their compensation, their powers and duties, may at any time hereafter be changed and regulated by the general assembly.

Sec. 6. The general assembly shall provide by law for the appointment of road supervisors in the several counties by the county commissioners, and the number of said supervisors as well as their powers and duties in the several election districts in the several counties, shall be determined by the said county commissioners.

Sec. 7. The qualified voters of each county and of the city of Baltimore shall on the Tuesday next after the first Monday in the month of November, in the year eighteen hundred and sixty-five, and every two years thereafter, elect a surveyor for the counties and city of Baltimore respectively, whose term of office shall commence on the first Monday of January next ensuing their election, and whose duties and compensation shall be the same as are now or may hereafter be prescribed by law. Any vacancy in the office of surveyor shall be filled by the commissioners of the counties or by the mayor and city council of Baltimore respectively, for the residue of the term.

Sec. 8. The qualified voters of Worcester

county shall on the Tuesday next after the first Monday in the month of November, in the year eighteen hundred and sixty-five, and every two years thereafter, elect a wreck master for said county, whose duties and compensation shall be the same as are now or may be hereafter prescribed by law; the term of office of said wreck master shall commence on the first Monday of January next succeeding his election, and a vacancy in said office shall be filled by the county commissioners of said county for the residue of the term.

Sec. 9. The general assembly may provide by law for the election or appointment of such other officers as may be required, and are not herein provided for and prescribe their tenure of office, powers and duties.

ARTICLE VIII.

EDUCATION.

Section 1. The governor shall, within thirty days after the ratification by the people of this constitution, appoint, subject to the confirmation of the senate, at its first session thereafter, a State superintendent of public instruction, who shall hold his office for four years and until his successor shall have been appointed and shall have qualified. He shall receive an annual salary of twenty-five hundred dollars, and such additional sum for travelling and incidental expenses as the general assembly may by law allow; shall report to the general assembly within thirty days after the commencement of its first session under this constitution, a uniform system of free public schools, and shall perform such other duties pertaining to his office as may from time to time be prescribed by law.

Sec. 2. There shall be a State board of education, consisting of the governor, the lieutenant governor, the speaker of the house of delegates, and the State superintendent of puplic instruction, which board shall perform such duties as the general assembly may direct.

Sec. 3. There shall be in each county such number of school commissioners as the State superintendent of public instruction shall deem necessary, who shall be appointed by the State board of education; shall hold office for four years, and shall perform such duties and receive such compensation as the general assembly or State superintendent may direct; the school commissioners of Baltimore city shall remain as at present constituted, and shall be appointed, as at present, by the mayor and city council, subject to such alterations and amendments as may be made from time to time by the general assembly, or the said mayor and city council.

Sec. 4. The general assembly, at its first session after the adoption of this constitution, shall provide a uniform system of free public schools, by which a school shall be kept open and supported free of expense for tuition in each school district, for at least six months in each year; and in case of a failure on the part of the general assembly so to provide, the system reported to it by the State superintendent of public instruction, shall become the system of free public schools of the State; *Provided*, That the report of the State superintendent shall be in conformity with the provisions of this constitution, and such system shall be subject to such alterations, conformable to this article, as the general assembly may from time to time enact.

Sec. 5. The general assembly shall levy at each regular session, after the adoption of this constitution, an annual tax of not less than ten cents on each hundred dollars of taxable property throughout the State, for the support of the free public schools, which tax shall be collected at the same time and by the same agents as the general State levy; and shall be paid into the treasury of the State, and shall be distributed under such regulations as may be prescribed by law, among the counties and the city of Baltimore, in proportion to their respective population between the ages of five and twenty years: *Provided*, That the general assembly shall not levy any additional school tax upon particular counties, unless such county express by popular vote its desire for such tax; the city of Baltimore shall provide for its additional school tax as at present, or as may hereafter be provided by the general assembly, or by the mayor and city council of Baltimore.

Sec. 6. The general assembly shall further provide by law, at its first session after the adoption of this constitution, a fund for the support of the free public schools of the State, by the imposition of an annual tax of not less than five cents on each one hundred dollars of taxable property throughout the State, the proceeds of which tax shall be known as the public school fund, and shall be invested by the treasurer, together with its annual interest until such time as said fund shall, by its own increase and any additions which may be made to it from time to time, together with the present school fund, amount to six millions of dollars, when the tax of ten cents in the hundred dollars, authorized by the preceding section, may be discontinued in whole or in part, as the general assembly may direct; the principal fund of six millions hereby provided, shall remain forever inviolate as the free public school fund of the State, and the annual interest of said school fund shall be disbursed for educational purposes only, as may be prescribed by law.

ARTICLE IX.

MILITIA AND MILITARY AFFAIRS.

Section 1. The militia shall be composed of all able-bodied male citizens, residents of this State, being eighteen years of age, and under the age of forty-five years, who shall be enrolled in the militia, and perform mili tary duty in such manner, not incompatible with the constitution and laws of the United States, as may be prescribed by the general assembly of Maryland, but persons whose religious opinions and conscientious scruples forbid them to bear arms, shall be relieved from doing so on producing to the proper authorities satisfactory proof that they are thus conscientious.

Sec. 2. The general assembly shall provide at its first session after the adoption of this constitution, and from time to time thereafter, as the exigency may require, for organizing, equipping and disciplining the militia in such manner, not incompatible with the laws of the United States, as shall be most effective to repel invasion and suppress insurrection, and shall pass such laws as shall promote the formation of volunteer militia associations in the city of Baltimore and in every county, and to secure them such privileges or assistance as may afford them effectual encouragement.

Sec. 3. There shall be an adjutant general, who shall be appointed by the governor, by and with the advice and consent of the senate. He shall hold his office at the pleasure of the governor; shall perform such duties, and shall receive such compensation or emoluments as are now or may be hereafter fixed by law.

ARTICLE X.

COUNTIES AND TOWNSHIPS.

Section 1. The general assembly may provide for organizing new counties, locating and removing county seats and changing county lines, but no new county shall be organized without the consent of a majority of the legal voters residing within the limits about to form said county, nor shall the lines of any county be changed without the consent of a majority of the legal voters residing within the limits of the lines proposed to be changed, nor shall any new county contain less than four hundred square miles nor less than ten thousand white inhabitants, nor shall any county be reduced below that amount of square miles, nor below that number of white inhabitants.

Sec. 2. The general assembly shall provide by general law for dividing the counties into townships or permanent municipal corporations, in place of the existing election districts, prescribing their limits and confiding to them all powers necessary for the management of their public local concerns; and whenever the organization of these township corporations shall be perfected, all officers provided for in this constitution, but whose official functions shall have been superseded by such organizations shall be dispensed with, and the affairs of such townships and of the counties as affected by the action of such townships shall be transacted in such manner as the general assembly shall direct.

ARTICLE XI.

AMENDMENTS OF THE CONSTITUTION.

Section 1. The general assembly may propose any amendment or amendments to this constitution which shall be agreed to by three-fifths of all the members elected to both houses. Such proposed amendment or amendments with the yeas and nays thereon, shall be entered on the journal of each house; shall be printed with the laws passed at the same session, and shall be published by order of the governor, in all the newspapers printed in the different counties of this State, and in three newspapers printed in the city of Baltimore (one of which shall be printed in the German language,) for at least three months preceding the next election for members of the general assembly, at which election the said proposed amendment or amendments shall be submitted to the qualified electors of the State for their confirmation or rejection; and if it shall appear to the satisfaction of the governor, from the returns of the said election made to him by the proper authorities, that a majority of the qualified votes cast at said election on the proposed amendment or amendments, were in favor of the said proposed amendment or amendments, he shall, by proclamation, declare said amendment or amendments to be part of the constitution of this State. When two or more amendments shall be submitted by the general assembly to the qualified electors of the State at the same election, they shall be submitted so that the electors may vote for or against each amendment separately.

Sec. 2. Whenever two-thirds of the members elected to each branch of the general assembly shall think it necessary to call a convention to revise, amend or change this constitution, they shall recommend to the electors to vote at the next election for members of the general assembly for or against a convention; and if a majority of all the electors voting at said election shall have voted for a convention, the general assembly shall, at their next session, provide by law for calling the same.

The convention shall consist of as many members as both houses of the general assembly, who shall be chosen in the same manner, and shall meet within three months after their election for the purpose aforesaid.

Sec. 3. At the general election to be held in the year one thousand eight hundred and eighty-two, and in each twentieth year thereafter, the question "Shall there be a convention to revise, alter or amend the constitution," shall be submitted to the electors of the State; and in case a majority of all the electors voting at such election shall decide in favor of a convention, the general assembly at its next session shall provide by law for the election of delegates and the assembling of such convention, as is provided in the preceding section; but no amendment of this constitution agreed upon by any convention assembled in pursuance of this article shall take effect until the same shall have been submitted to the electors of the State, and adopted by a majority of those voting thereon.

ARTICLE XII.

SCHEDULE.

Section. 1. Every person holding any office created by or existing under the constitution or laws of the State, the entire amount of whose pay or compensation received for the discharge of his official duties shall exceed the yearly sum of three thousand dollars, except wherein otherwise provided by this constitution, shall keep a book in which shall be entered any sum or sums of money received by him or on his account as a payment or compensation for his performance of official duties, a copy of which entries in said book, verified by the oath of the officer by whom it is directed to be kept, shall be returned yearly to the comptroller of the State for his inspection, and that of the general assembly of the State, and each of the said officers, when the amount received by him for the year shall exceed three thousand dollars, shall yearly pay over to the treasurer of the State, the amount of such excess by him received, subject to such disposition thereof, as the general assembly may direct; any such officer failing to comply with this requisition, shall be deemed to have vacated his office and be subject to suit by the State for the amount that ought to be paid into the treasury.

Sec. 2. The several courts, except as herein otherwise provided shall continue with like powers and jurisdiction, both at law and in equity, as if this constitution had not been adopted, and until the organization of the judicial department provided by this constitution.

Sec. 3. If at any election directed by this constitution, any two or more candidates shall have the highest and an equal number of votes, a new election shall be ordered, except in cases specially provided for by this constitution.

Sec. 4. In the trial of all criminal cases, the jury shall be the judges of law as well as fact.

Sec. 5. The trial by jury of all issues of fact in civil proceedings in the several courts of law in this State, where the amount in controversy exceeds the sum of five dollars, shall be inviolably preserved.

Sec. 6. All officers, civil and military, now holding office, whether by election or appointment under the State, shall continue to hold and exercise their offices, according to their present tenure, unless otherwise provided in this constitution, until they shall be superseded pursuant to its provisions, and until their successors be duly qualified, and the compensation of such officers which has been increased by this constitution, shall take effect from the first day of January, eighteen hundred and sixty-five.

Sec. 7. General elections shall be held throughout the State on the Tuesday next after the first Monday in the month of November of each and every year; at the election held in the year eighteen hundred and sixty-four, all State officers required to be elected under this constitution during that year shall be elected, and in like manner in every second year thereafter, an election shall be held for those State officers whose terms are about to expire; at the election held in the year eighteen hundred and sixty-five, all county officers required to be elected under this constitution in that year shall be elected, and in like manner in every second year thereafter, an election shall be held for those county officers, whose terms are about to expire; *Provided*, however, the judges of the several courts of this State, except the judges of the orphans' courts, shall be elected at the regular election, whether for State or county officers, as the case may be, immediately preceding the expiration of the term of the incumbent whose place is to be filled.

VOTE ON THE CONSTITUTION.

Sec. 8. For the purpose of ascertaining the sense of the people of this State in regard to the adoption or rejection of this constitution, the governor shall issue his proclamation within five days after the adjournment of this convention, directed to the sheriff of the city of Baltimore, and to the sheriffs of the several counties of this State, commanding them to give notice, in the manner now prescribed by law, that an election will be held in the city of Baltimore on the twelfth day of October, in the year eighteen hundred and sixty-four, and in the several counties of this State on the twelfth and thirteenth days of October, in the same year, at the usual places of holding elections in said city and counties, for the adoption or rejection of this constitution, which election shall be held in the said city of Baltimore on the twelfth day of October, eighteen hundred and sixty-four, between the hours of 8 o'clock A. M. and five o'clock P. M., and in the said several counties of this State on the said twelfth and thirteenth days of October, eighteen hundred and sixty-four, between the hours of eight o'clock A. M. and five o'clock P. M., and the judges of election of said city and of the several counties of the State, shall receive at said election the votes only of such electors as are qualified according to the provisions of this constitution, who may offer to vote at such election, and the said sheriffs shall also give notice on or after the twelfth day of October, eighteen hundred and sixty-four, for all elections provided for by this constitution, to be held during that year.

Sec. 9. At the said election the vote shall be by ballot, and each ballot shall describe thereon the words "For the Constitution" or "Against the Constitution," as the voter may elect, and it shall be conducted in all respects as the general elections in this State are now conducted. The judges of election shall administer to every person offering to vote the oath or affirmation prescribed by this constitution, and should any person offering to vote refuse or decline to take said oath, he shall not be permitted to vote at such election, but the taking of such oath or affirmation shall not be deemed conclusive evidence of the right of such person to vote, and it shall be the duty of the return judges of said city, and of the several counties of the State, having counted the votes given for or against the adoption of this constitution, to certify the result thereof in the manner now prescribed by law, accompanied with a special statement, that every person, who has voted has taken the oath or affirmation prescribed by this constitution; and the governor upon receiving such result, and ascertaining the aggregate vote throughout the State, including the soldiers' vote, hereinafter provided for, shall, by his proclamation make known the same, and if a majority of the votes cast shall be for the adoption of this constitution, it shall go into effect on the first day of November, eighteen hundred and sixty-four.

Sec. 10. And the governor shall exclude from count the votes of any county or city the return judges of which shall fail to certify in the returns, as provided by this schedule, that all persons who have voted have taken the oath prescribed to be taken, unless the governor shall be satisfied that such oath was actually administered, and that the failure to make the certificate has been from inadvertence or mistake.

SOLDIERS' VOTE.

Sec. 11. Any qualified voter of this State who shall be absent from the county or city of his residence by reason of being in the military service of the United States, so as not to be able to vote at home, on the adoption or rejection of this constitution, or for all State officers elected on general ticket, and for presidential electors and for members of congress, at the election to be held on the Tuesday next after the first Monday in the month of November, eighteen hundred and sixty-four, shall be entitled to vote at such elections as follows: A poll shall be opened in each company of every Maryland regiment in the service of the United States or of this State on the day appointed by this convention for taking the vote on the new constitution, or some other day not more than five days thereafter, at the quarters of the commanding officer thereof, and voters of this State belonging to such company who shall be within ten miles of such quarters on the day of election may vote at such poll; the polls shall be opened at eight o'clock A. M. and close at six o'clock P. M; the commissioned officers of such company, or such of them as are present at the opening of the polls, shall act as judges, and any one officer shall be competent so to act, and if no officer be present then the voters in such company present shall elect two of the voters present to act as judges of the election; before any votes are received each of the judges shall take an oath or affirmation that he will perform the duties of judge according to law; will prevent fraud and observe and make proper return thereof, and such oath the judges may administer to each other; the election shall be by ballot, and any voter may vote either "For the Constitution" or "Against the Constitution."

Sec. 12. Any qualified voter of this State who shall be absent from the city or county of his residence on the day for taking the vote on the adoption or rejection of this constitution by reason of his being in the military service of the United States, but shall be at some hospital or military post, or on duty within this State, and not with his company, may vote at the nearest polls to such place on satisfying the judges that he is a legal and qualified voter of this State.

Sec. 13. The judges may swear any one offering to vote as to his being a legal voter of this State. The judges shall take down on a poll-book or list the names of all the voters as their votes are taken, and the tickets shall be placed in a box as taken; after the polls are closed the tickets shall be counted and strung on a thread, and the judges shall make out a certificate which they shall sign, addressed to the governor at Annapolis, in which they shall state they have taken the oath hereby prescribed, and shall certify the number of votes taken, and the number of votes for the constitution and against the constitution; the said certificates shall be accompanied with the names of the voters, and shall be plainly expressed, but no particular words shall be required.

Sec. 14. The judges shall, as soon as possible, transmit said returns, with the tickets so strung, to the governor, who shall receive the return of the soldiers' vote, and shall cast up the same, and judge of the genuineness and correctness of the returns, and may recount the threaded tickets so as to satisfy himself, and the governor shall count said vote with the aggregate vote of the State on the adoption or rejection of this constitution, and shall wait for fifteen days after the day on which the State vote is taken, so as to allow the returns of the soldiers' vote to be made, before the result of the whole vote is announced. The governor shall receive the returns of the soldiers' vote on said election for State officers, presidential electors and members of Congress, and shall count the same with the aggregate home vote, on State officers, and the aggregate home vote in each district respectively for members of Congress.

Sec. 15. The governor shall make known to the officers of the State regiments the provisions of this article of the schedule, and request them to exercise the rights hereby conferred upon them, and shall take all means proper to secure the soldiers' vote; and the general assembly at its first session after the adoption of this constitution shall make proper appropriation to pay any expense that may arise herein.

Sec. 16. If this constitution shall be adopted by the people, the provisions contained herein for taking the soldiers' vote on the adoption of the constitution shall apply to all elections to be held in this State until the general assembly shall provide some other mode of taking the same.

Done in convention, the sixth day of September, in the year of our Lord one thousand eight hundred and sixty-four, and of the independence of the United States the eighty-ninth.

HENRY H. GOLDSBOROUGH,
President of the Convention.

Attest—W. R. COLE,
Secretary.

STATE OF MARYLAND, *Sct.:*

I, George Earle, clerk of the court of appeals of Maryland, do hereby certify that this constitution was, on this sixth day of September, in the year of our Lord one thousand eight hundred and sixty-four, filed in this office.

Witness my hand:

GEORGE EARLE,
Clerk of the Court of Appeals.

ADJOURNMENT OF THE CONVENTION.

NOVEMBER 1, 1864.

The balloting upon the question of the adoption of the Constitution having been peaceful and uninterrupted, the President this day announced as follows:

IN CONVENTION,
ANNAPOLIS, November 1, 1864.

In pursuance of instructions contained in a resolution passed by the Maryland State Constitutional Convention, as President of said body I do hereby proclaim the said convention adjourned *sine die.*

HENRY H. GOLDSBOROUGH,
President.

APPENDIX.

CONSTITUTION SUBMITTED TO THE PEOPLE.

In obedience to the requirements of the sixth section of the 12th article of the constitution, and for the purpose of ascertaining the sense of the people of the State in regard to the adoption or rejection of the constitution the governor on the 9th day of September issued the following proclamation:

STATE OF MARYLAND,
EXECUTIVE DEPARTMENT.

To the Sheriffs of the Several Counties of the State and of the City of Baltimore:

Whereas, by an act of the general assembly of Maryland, passed at January session, in the year eighteen hundred and sixty-four, entitled "An act to provide for the taking of the sense of the people upon the call of a convention to frame a new constitution and form of government for this State, to provide for the election of delegates to said convention, and the assembling thereof, it was among other things enacted that the constitution which might be framed by said convention should be submitted to the legal and "qualified voters of the State for their adoption or rejection, at such time, in such manner and subject to such rules and regulations" as said convention should prescribe; and—

Whereas, the said convention assembled in conformity to said act, and did adopt a new constitution, in which they provided that for the purpose of ascertaining the sense of the people of this State in regard to the adoption or rejection of said constitution an election should be held in the city of Baltimore on the twelfth day of October, in the year 1864, and in the several counties of this State on the twelfth and thirteenth days of the same month, and did direct that the governor should issue his proclamation to the sheriffs of the said city and counties, directing them to give the usual notice of said election.

Therefore, you are hereby commanded to give notice in the manner now prescribed by law, that an election will be held in the city of Baltimore on the twelfth day of October next, and in the several counties of the State on the twelfth and thirteenth days of October next, at the usual places of holding elections in said city and counties, for the adoption or rejection of said constitution by ballot, in the manner by said constitution provided, which election shall be held as aforesaid between the hours of eight o'clock A. M. and five o'clock P. M., on the day or days so respectively appointed for said city and counties, and the judges of election "shall receive at said election the votes only of such electors as are qualified according to the provisions of said constitution"

Given under my hand and the great seal of the State at the city of Annapolis [L. S.] this ninth day of September in the year eighteen hundred and sixty-four.

By the Governor,
A. W. BRADFORD.

WM. B. HILL, Secretary of State.

CORRESPONDENCE.

After the issuing of this proclamation, doubts were expressed as to the legality of the provisions of the constitution, by which its adoption was to be submitted to a vote of the people. While these doubts were agitating the public mind the following correspondence took place and about the fifth of October was made public, viz:

FIRST LETTER OF MR. VICKERS.

CHESTERTOWN, September 14, 1864.

His Excellency, A. W. Bradford, Governor of Maryland:

My Dear Sir—I beg leave, most respectfully, to call your attention to the proceedings of the late convention, which assembled at the city of Annapolis to remodel the constitution or propose a plan of a constitution for the State. I am now living under the only constitution of the State in existence, framed and adopted in the year 1851. That constitution secures to the male inhabitants of the State, over twenty-one years of age, and resident twelve months in the State and six in the county (or city) in which they may reside, by its first section, the right to vote in the ward or election district in which they reside, *in "all elections hereafter to be held."*

The act of the general assembly passed on

*The following pages—detailing events occurring after the adjournment of the convention—are here published as a portion of the history of the constitution.—*J. McGarigle, Sup't Printing Debates of Convention.*

the 3d February, 1864, directed a vote to be taken upon the call of a convention; if a majority should decide in favor of the call, an election of delegates was to be held in the manner directed by the act, which also prescribed an oath to be taken by the challenged voter (of very doubtful legality.) The sixth section provides that the form of government prepared by the convention shall be submitted to the legal and qualified voters of the State for their adoption or rejection; that the provisions of said act *for the qualification of voters*, and the holding of the elections provided for in the previous sections, shall be applicable to the election to be held under that section. The eighth section provides, that if a majority of the legal voters shall adopt the said form of government as a constitution, the governor shall issue his proclamation declaring the fact.

In the form of government fabricated by the convention and submitted to the people, a provision exists, requiring as an essential qualification for the legal voters of the State, before casting their ballots for or against the said paper, that they shall take an oath not provided for in the constitution under which we live, or any law to be found upon the statute books, and in express violation of the requirements of the act of 1864, under which a legal existence was derived to the convention. This attempted innovation upon the constitution and statutes of the State must be designated for some sinister object, no less, we presume, than a disfranchisement of a large portion of the qualified voters, whose residence, property and interests identify them with the State. If a majority of the voters shall reject the said plan of government it will be inoperative and as a piece of blank paper. It is *now* of no more force or validity than any act reported to either branch of the legislature and not acted upon. It is a mere proposition which is to be accepted or repudiated. It is but a skeleton, a form or plan, without vitality or energy. It requires the people to breathe into it life and power; till then it is as a feather floating upon the breeze of popular opinion. If this be the true character of the instrument, how can it now, inert, inactive, without any symptoms of legal existence, contain power to disfranchise a voter, and subject him to a trial and ordeal unknown to the constitution and laws under which we are living? We hold our property, our rights and privileges under the constitution of 1851, and the laws of the State made in pursuance thereof. Could the proposed constitution, before its adoption, deprive a man of his property or liberty if it contained such provisions? No one would assert it. How then can it affect a voter's constitutional right to vote at "*every election*" to be held? The same reason would apply to both, because of its inherent want of life and energy. It follows that the provision is unconstitutional. The convention exceeded its authority, and as far as that excess extends its pretended enactment is inoperative and void. But as judges of elections, who are not supposed to be very conversant with law, and may deem themselves under an obligation to conform to its provisions in the respect mentioned, and as the legal and qualified voters must look to another and higher source of power and authority for anticipated redress and a vindication of their constitutional and legal rights, they naturally turn to *you*, the chief executive of the State, and ask your prompt and efficient interposition by a proclamation or letter of instruction to the judges of election to disregard the unjust and illegal requirements attempted to be put upon the loyal voters of the State. The fourth article of the bill of rights declares that the executive is the trustee of the public. The fifth article says that "every free white male citizen, having the qualifications prescibed by the constitution, ought to have the right of suffrage." The ninth section of the first article of the constitution declares that the governor shall be commander-in-chief of the land and naval forces of the State, and may call out the militia, repel invasions, suppress insurrections, and *enforce the execution* of the laws. The next section, ten, declares that the "governor *shall take care that the laws be faithfully executed*." A law is a rule of action prescribed by the supreme power of the State. The legislature is the law-making power. If it should be convened by your excellency, it would now be the supreme and only law-making department of the government within constitutional limits. As there cannot be two law-making powers in existence at the same time, it is evident that the action of the convention in the matter referred to is nugatory and should be held to be of no avail. If the law as it now exists is suffered to be overcome or overridden by the unlawful assumptions of the convention, then are the laws not executed in the State in a matter vital to the best interests of the citizen? The manner of preventing such an outrage upon the rights of the citizen is left to the executive. It was never intended to be a barren power that was not to be wielded in a crisis like the present. There is no authority to redress the wrong after it is perpetrated. The mischief once done is irreparable. There is no tribunal to which the people can appeal but to you. You hold their rights and privileges in your keeping. You are a "trustee" for them, and you have all the discretion and latitude of power to prevent the wrong as the nature of the case demands. The rejected voters may sue the judges of election, but that will not prevent the consummation of the outrage. Whatever the case requires, you have the power commensurate with the necessity. You are to "take care that the laws be faithfully executed;" to take care looks to the past, the present and the future. It implies to search, look after, guard, protect, defend. I am loyal and can take the oath required, but the convention seeks to destroy a great constitutional principle which lies at the very foundation of the government There is no enemy to be dreaded more than he who cloaks his ulterior and hidden designs under tests and oaths unknown to the laws and violative of great political rights. The true conservative patriot is he who tolerates differences of opinion, and sets up the constitution and the laws as his constant rule and guide.

The attempt to pass an election law to be executed in Virginia or elsewhere than where is found the voters' legal residence, and to appoint officers or soldiers in the ranks within confederates lines judges of election, and to receive and count such votes, contrary to the express law in the code, article thirty-five, section one, which enacts that "the county commissioners in each county shall appoint three persons for each election district of the *county, residents in such districts*, judges of the election; of the fourth section, which directs the sheriff to serve the notices on the judges, and the fifth section, which directs the judge to attend in his district, is so palpably repugnant to every principle of law, of duty and of justice, that the broadest mantle of charity cannot cover the motives and sinfulness of the act. Your name and history are linked with this proffered constitution—if it can be disguised by that name. You are to proclaim it if adopted.

These times of excitement, passion and prejudice must pass away. A reaction must come when the impartial mind must record the true character of the men and the events passing before us. Party success is ephemeral, and its measures can never be permanently fastened on a free people. They can never remain manacled by the shackles forged by interested politicians. An enlightened, chastened, and true public sentiment must succeed the agitations and injustice of those days. "Truth is mighty and must prevail," was a motto of the lamented Clay. Justice, integrity and right, will be elements in that public opinion which will consign many of the dominant and prominent actors of these days to an obloquy which will scarcely find a parallel in the annals of history.

You have an honored name. I wish you to present a fair record when the truth of history shall be vindicated by the pen of the faithful historian. The history of this tendered constitution, the actions, speeches and motives of its principal and inferior authors and abettors will be written in living letters to be read of all men. We desire that the recorder shall disconnect your name from those of its makers and assistants, and place it in a niche in the temple of fame, on the side of the just, the true, the honored of our day.

With great regard, and as ever, yours,

[Signed] GEORGE VICKERS.

GOVERNOR BRADFORD'S REPLY.

STATE OF MARYLAND,
EXECUTIVE DEPARTMENT, ANNAPOLIS,
September 19, 1864.

George Vickers, Esq.:

My Dear Sir:—I have received your letter of the 14th inst., and given to it the attentive consideration due alike to the importance of the subject to which it relates, and to the sincere respect I always entertain for your opinions. You therein call my attention to the proceedings of the late convention, and more especially that provision found in the constitution which they framed which prescribes an oath to be taken by the voter when offering to vote at the election at which that constitution is submitted for the adoption or rejection of the voters of the State. You refer also to another part of it wherein provision is made for taking the vote of the soldiers of Maryland regiments, who are absent from the State at the time of said election, and designating these clauses of the new constitution, as palpably in conflict with the constitution of 1851, which must subsist until the new one is adopted by a vote of the people; you appeal to me to interpose and prevent the execution of these provisions, and to instruct the judges of election to disregard the clause requiring the oath aforesaid.

It is not my purpose, nor is it necessary, in the view which I take of my duty in the premises, to undertake to show that the convention possessed the power to make the provisions in question; still there are some considerations which it may not be amiss to notice, calculated to show that in so doing, they have not so manifestly exceeded their authority as your argument assumes. You, for instance, say that the oath prescribed by the convention is not only an innovation upon the existing constitution, but is in express violation of the act of 1864, from which the convention derived its existence. That act, however, in providing for the submission of the constitution to the vote of the people, declares that it shall be submitted "at such time, in such manner, and *subject to such rules and regulations* as said convention may prescribe."

I am aware that to this may be replied that the legislature which passed this act could have prescribed no such additional qualification for those who should vote upon the adoption of this constitution, and that possessing itself no such power, it could therefore confer none such upon the convention. But was it in fact necessary for the legislature to have required the submission of the constitution for the ratification of the people at all? It was, doubtless, a very just requirement, but our first constitution was, I think, never ratified by a vote of the people, and, if I mistake not, other State constitutions, since adopted, have been made to operate immediately and without such ratification. From this it would seem to follow that if it was not essentially necessary to submit the constitution to the ultimate vote of the people in order to give it vitality, the legislature in so directing it to be submitted, was not so manifestly exceeding its authority in qualifying the manner of voting upon it or empowering the convention to do so.

But apart from any authority which the general assembly has or might have delegated to the convention on the subject, we can all remember that the powers claimed for the people in the institution of their organic law, and for a convention duly elected by them for such a purpose, have been of such a character as to permit, in previous instances, of the apparent disregard of existing constitutional requirements. The constitution of 1776, for instance, declared in one of its articles, "that this form of government and declaration of rights, and no part thereof, shall be altered, changed or abolished, unless a bill so to alter, change or abolish the same shall pass the general assembly, and be published at least three months before a new election, and shall be confirmed by the general assembly after a new election of delegates, in the first session after such new election." Yet the constitution of 1851, under which we at present live, was not ordained in the manner thus limited and prescribed, but was the work of a convention, and its validity was chiefly maintained upon the ground of the paramount authority of the people on the subject, and the plenary powers possessed by such a convention. I would not be understood as concurring in all these conclusions, but I advert to such cases to show that the proceedings of this convention of which you complain, may not be so unquestionably unconstitutional as to warrant upon that ground, as you suppose, the executive action you invoke. I think it would have been wiser for the convention to have avoided the exercise of all doubtful powers, but having, after due deliberation and discussion, adopted the changes in question, had they, in so doing, as clearly exceeded their authority, in my opinion, as they have in yours, I should still consider myself as obnoxious to the same objection, were I to interfere in the manner you request, for the purpose of nullifying their action. This convention was elected by a majority of the voters of the State, and charged with the most important duty that they could delegate to representatives—the formation of a new constitution. These delegates have discharged that duty, and in the constitution which they have adopted, they have by a very decided majority, introduced the provisions to which you object; for the executive of the State to interpose in such a case, instruct the officers of the State to disregard these provisions, and to disregard them himself upon the ground that he considers them unconstitutional, would not only be a precedent fraught with the most dangerous consequences, but would be the assumption of a judicial function which he is not at liberty to exercise, and a denial of the ordinary respect due to the proceedings of a deliberative body, and to the constituency they represent. Nor can I agree with you that "there is no authority to redress the wrong after it is perpetrated," and that "there is no tribunal to which the people can appeal but to you" (me). If any wrong has been perpetrated by the convention, or any one should suffer in person or property by its wrongful action, surely the judicial tribunals of the State are the proper ones to redress the injury, and possess the power to do so.

You refer to "these times of exciting passion and prejudice," and to the period when "an enlightened, chastened and true public sentiment must succeed the agitation and injustice of these days." No one, I assure you, regrets such a state of things more than I do, or would go farther to promote such a chastened public sentiment, but I cannot but think that were I to interfere in the manner you propose, and undertake to annul the action of such a convention, the agitation and excitement you so justly deprecate would fearfully exceed any we have yet witnessed, and more especially so as the most obvious and only effect of such interference would be to allow those to vote who could not conscientiously swear that they had never given aid, countenance or support to the rebellion, and to deny that franchise to others who are daily shedding their blood that the rebellion may be subdued.

Regretting, as I sincerely do, that I have not the support of your judgment in the convictions I entertain of my duty in the premises,

I am very truly, yours, &c.,

[Signed] A. W. Bradford.

SECOND LETTER OF MR. VICKERS.

Chestertown, September 27, 1864.

His Excellency A. W. Bradford, Governor of Maryland:

My Dear Sir—Your favor of the 19th was received last week. My business engagements have prevented me from acknowledging its receipt sooner. I regret very much that you have come to the conclusion not to interfere in preventing the unconstitutional measures of the convention from being imposed upon the people of the State. It is unpleasant to differ in opinion from you, especially on a subject of so much importance, and when my own conviction of the wrongful and illegal requisition is without a shadow of doubt. I have received from you so many proofs of your regard and confidence, communicated in a manner so very flattering and agreeable, that it enhances my regrets at the different views I have to take of constitutional law and executive duty. In what may be further said, I beg to assure you that I shall do so with perfect respect to you and your views, and yet with the freedom which a friend and citizen may take, when in his own mind he is vindicating the cause of truth and of law.

It is scarcely necessary to say that the objectional provisions of the proposed constitution would not prevent the enjoyment of my suffrage, and that I have no other interest in the matter than as a citizen of the State, who desires the constitution to be observed and the law respected.

In regard to the unconstitutionality of the provision which requires an oath of voters unknown to the constitution and in repugnance to it and to the law, I did not suppose that any lawyer in the State (outside of the convention) could entertain a doubt, nor do I understand you to express any, and I am sure if you entertained one, no one could find language more expressive and cogent than yourself to declare it. But you are too good a lawyer to entertain such an opinion, and your unwillingness to interfere must be predicated on other grounds. You refer to the first constitution as not having been submitted to the people, and express the opinion that such reference was not essential to its validity. I have not the data and the facilities to examine into the history of that constitution, and cannot therefore venture an opinion upon the fact of its submission to a popular vote, but I may safely lay down as a postulate, that if the law which called the convention required its submission, it was done; if it did not require it, it gave plenary power to the convention to form a constitution by its own acts. Another postulate I may safely advance is, that if an act of the assembly, authorizing a vote of the people upon the question of convention or no convention, directs the manner of electing delegates, and requires their work, when done, to be submitted to the voters of the State, the convention cannot make a constitution that would be binding without its submission to and ratification by the people. You refer to an irregularity in calling the convention of 1851, and the provisions of the old constitution upon the subject of its amendment. I believe that some did think the manner of the call irregular, but not that the people could be restrained from making another constitution. However, if it proves anything, it is only as to the manner of calling it, not to any abridgment of the people's rights under it. The call, if irregular, was made by the people, for their benefit, to enable them to form such a constitution as they wished, embracing their views and opinions which the changed circumstances and progress of the age made expedient, but there was no complaint that the sovereign people were affected or prejudiced in their rights by any innovation. If the opinion was well founded, it only shew that the people were sovereign, and did not feel bound by forms and regulations which affected only the time and manner of doing what they thought should be done in a briefer period and a different mode. It was the *people* who did and sanctioned it. If then these irregularities existed, of which you write, they were those of the people, the *masters*, to carry out and effectuate their own will, and not those of their own agents or deputies appointed by them, and whose acts are now attempted to be set up to defeat the will and purposes of their principals and sovereigns. It would be an anomaly to allow an agent to prescribe terms to his principal to restrict him and deprive him of his primary and essential rights; or where there were a number of principals, that the agent should select such as he pleased to adjust their accounts, or make conditions precedent that would exclude some from any participation in the settlement. But the reason applies with greater force where a constitution is to be made for all time, when the prohibition is to be perpetual, binding not only the present but future generations.

If the late convention had authority to insert the oath as a prerequisite to the right to vote, they had equal authority to insert other provisions upon that subject. The constitution declares that voting shall be by ballot. Had the convention power to change that requirement and say it should be *viva voce?* The constitution enacts "that every free white male person of twenty-one years of age, who shall have been one year next preceding the election a resident of the State, and for six months a resident of the city of Baltimore, or of any county, in which he may offer to vote, and being at the time a citizen of the United States, *shall be entitled to vote* in the ward or election district in which he resides, *in all elections hereafter to be held*, and at all such elections the vote shall be by ballot." (Article 1, section 1.) Would it not, therefore, have been as competent for the convention to abrogate the ballot as the elective franchise of those who, in the same article, are declared to be entitled to exercise it? Suppose the convention had required of every one offering to vote, to swear that he was worth five hundred acres of land and a stated amount of personal estate? Suppose it had asserted that every free male person, without distinction of color, over twenty-one years of age, &c., should be entitled to vote, would these attempts be more palpably unconstitutional than the other in regard to the oath? To be sure, they strike the moral sense with more force and shock the judgment; but analyzed, are they greater violations than the other? They all violate the letter and spirit of the constitution and the genius of our government, and undermine its foundation.

You refer to the language of the act of 1864, which, in providing for the submission of the constitution to the people, declares that it shall be submitted "at such time and in such manner and subject to such *rules and regulations* as said convention may prescribe."—You do not, however, contend that these expressions, quoted and italicised, give to the convention the power they have assumed. The fixing of the time for holding the election should of course be given to the convention, because it was uncertain when they would adjourn, and also of the manner, &c.; these minor or inferior powers were intended to subserve the great object of calling the convention; that is, to form a constitution and obtain in a manner most convenient and agreeable to the people their true sentiments upon it.

The same act required it to be submitted to the people, by its sixth section, in these words: "That the constitution and form of government adopted by the said convention *shall be submitted to the legal and qualified voters* of the *State*, for their adoption or rejection," &c. Who were the legal and qualified voters of the State? Were they not such as elected the legislature? "White male persons of twenty-one years of age?" &c. The constitution being the supreme law, the "legal and qualified voters of the State" are such as have the constitutional qualifications. Can there be any other? But when we read the whole section from which you quote, I find immediately following the words "rules and regulations as said convention may prescribe," these words, "and the provisions hereinbefore contained for the *qualification of the voters* and the holding of the elections provided in the previous sections of this act, *shall be applicable to the election to be held under this section.*" The convention has not only overstepped the constitution, but the very charter under which they received their legal existence from the people. The rules and regulations must be in accordance and not in conflict with the words that follow them, which confine and restrict them to such form, &c., as may be necessary and proper to execute the purposes of the law by which they are commanded not to go beyond them, and yet they have transcended them.

You decline to interfere to protect the elective franchise, for the reasons indicated in your letter, that it is a judicial question and that it might produce agitation and excitement, and the "effect would be to allow those to vote who could not conscientiously swear, &c., and to deny that franchisè to those who are daily shedding their blood that the rebellion may be subdued." I do not understand you to say that the "*effect*" of a measure is to determine its legality, and that the consequences of the exercise of a constitutional power by the executive to protect a portion of the people of the State in their rights are to be weighed in the scales of expediency, and made to cast a shadow of doubt upon the power itself. If the convention has violated the constitution and the act of 1864, and the executive has the power to correct the abuse, the effects that may follow such correction should not I think weigh a feather against the exercise of it, although I think they would redound to your advantage. The last legislature refused to pass a law to allow soldiers distant from home and beyond the limits of their county and State, to vote abroad; that body was largely and eminently Union, and no suspicion was ever entertained of the character of its loyalty. They must have believed the measure repugnant to the constitution; they *refused* to clothe the convention with that power, and the clause embracing the "rules and regulations" will not aid the argument for it.

The first section of the act of 1864 provides that "on the first Wednesday of April next, at the *same places* where the *polls* are by *law* held in the *several counties* and city of Baltimore for the election of delegates to the general assembly, shall vote, &c.;" and in the sixth section it is said "that the provisions hereinbefore contained for the qualification of voters and the *holding* of the elections provided in the previous sections of this act, *shall be applicable* to the election to be held under this *section*." The election law provides (1 Code, 258,) that the judges of election shall be residents of the election districts; that if they remove out of the district others are to be appointed—warrants to be delivered to them in five days by the sheriff. If a judge shall not attend at the time appointed, *in his district*, he shall forfeit fifty dollars. If they fail to attend, the justices of the peace, present at the *place of election*, to open polls, &c.; all pointing to the locality of election districts as the place for holding the election; and the constitution, in its first article, declares that a person shall be "entitled to vote *in the ward or election district* in which he resides."

If it be lawful to take votes in the army, why not in the navy? Are the marines not as gallant as the soldiers? If votes may be taken in Virginia, South Carolina, &c., why not on board the national ships under Farragut, Porter, &c.? and why not in foreign as in domestic waters? Is not every illegal and improper vote given a fraud upon the legal voters? Are not the election laws framed to protect the ballot-box, and throw around it all possible safeguards? Would army elections promote these ends? I would have every soldier and sailor to vote if he could do so legally and constitutionally, and I would do anything reasonable to procure for them furloughs to return to their homes to vote as they may please; but I would not, and I do not believe you would, advocate an unconstitutional measure, or vindicate it when done, although done for the brave and patriotic men in the armies of the Union.

But you say, "If any wrong has been perpetrated by the convention, or any one should suffer in person or property by its wrongful actions, surely the judicial tribunals of the State are the proper ones to redress the injury, and possess the power to do so." It is a maxim of law, I know, that there is no right without a remedy; this, of course, refers to rights of persons and property under existing laws; but I am not satisfied that there is a remedy always in the law for the infraction of political rights. Will you point out the mode or manner of redress to one-third of the legal voters of the State after they may be wrongfully excluded from the polls, and by that act of exclusion a new government is instituted and officers are sworn to support it? The right of suffrage is a political right guaranteed by the constitution. If it be obstructed, and the party be injured, he may sue the judges of election, but that only awards him a pecuniary compensation and does not restore his right nor prevent the public wrong done by the rejection of his vote. How could suits be maintained by one-third of the voters of the State against the judges of election? Could any judge be supposed capable of liquidating, in money, the enormous amount of costs and damages that might be awarded? In a single case it might be so, but in such a multiplicity how could it be? The very jurors and judges who would be called to support the new constitution would have to decide upon his case. Could that be a "relief" of the injury? How few would be able to engage in such litigation? But how can the injury be prevented? Is it by *mandamus?* How can it be obtained and prosecuted by the masses? Judges of elections are being constantly changed—their appointments are frequently on the eve of an election. If absent, others are to be elected, and sometimes on the morning of the election, at which time they qualify.

Would it be practicable for every voter to apply for and obtain such a writ, and have it served and the case argued before election day, or on that day? The writ is not one of right, but rests in the judge's discretion, and we might have the anomalous spectacle of one judge granting the writ and another refusing it, and thus the election be conducted on different principles in different judicial districts. The theory of judicial redress may do for individual cases in matters of property and the rights which appertain to it, but how can it be applied or executed in a great political question which strikes at the fundamentals of the government? If the courts could, by possibility, pronounce the proceedings of the convention unconstitutional in a case where an individual was a party, that decision would not affect the government, nor its administration; it would not destroy the government *de facto*, and it would continue its functions; the maxim of nought without a remedy, is only applicable where the remedy is co-extensive with the right and the injury, and its exercise fully adequate to the exigencies of the case. Do you not agree with me in these principles? But if it were a judicial question, it does not follow that it is not a political one. Is it not essentially political? If it is, to whom are the people to look for a preventive remedy? Can it be to any one but yourself, who are clothed with the powers of the government, civil and military, to enforce the laws. I respectfully lay down the following positions:

First—That the acts of the convention in respect to a test oath and soldiers voting out of the State, are clearly unconstitutional.

Second—That the execution or enforcement of those acts may inflict a permanent and flagrant wrong upon the people of the State by putting into operation an unconstitutional instrument.

Third—That the consummation of a wrong so great and enormous ought to be avoided.

Fourth—That the power to prevent it is somewhere.

Fifth—That the courts cannot effectually exercise the power; for their redress would succeed and not precede the perpetration of the wrong.

Sixth—That the executive has the appropriate and full power to prevent the wrong, and should exercise it.

On the 27th October, 1863, Gen. Schenck, then in military command of the middle department (Maryland,) issued an order to influence the then approaching elections. It recited "that there are many evil disposed persons now at large in the State of Maryland who have been engaged in rebellion against the government, or have given aid and comfort or encouragement to others so engaged, and who may avail themselves of the indulgence of the authority which tolerates their presence, to embarrass the approaching election," and he therefore commanded "all provost marshals and other military officers to arrest all such persons found at or hanging about or approaching any poll or place of election on the 4th November, 1863," &c. This order ostensibly professed to prevent disloyal persons who had been in rebellion or engaged in giving aid and comfort to the confederates, from embarrassing the election, and to protect and develop the Union sentiment of the State. On the 2d November, immediately on receiving notice of the order, you very properly issued a proclamation in which you denounced the military order, and called upon the constituted authorities to disregard it. I quote an extract: "I avail myself of the occasion to call to the particular attention of the judges of election the fact that they are on the day of election clothed with all the authority of conservators of the peace, and may summon to their aid any of the executive officers of the county, and the whole power of the county itself, to preserve order at the polls, and *secure the constitutional rights of the voters.*" The true conservative, patriotic sentiment of the State sustained you, and would have rallied to your support in any mode you might have designated. You further stated, that "whatever power the State possesses shall be exerted to protect them (the judges of election) for anything done in the proper execution of its laws." That was nobly and patriotically said. But, my dear sir, what drew forth your laudable and fervent indignation? The order of General Schenck *professed* to be to assist loyal voting and prevent traitors, rebels and disloyal persons from interfering with the elections. You took the liberty of scanning the notices and purposes of this major general, and determined to protect the "constitutional rights of the voters." You took a correct view of the subject, and resolved as far as practicable to carry out and execute the constitution. You declared in that paper, pointedly and emphatically, in reference to the judges of election: "I need not, I am sure, remind them of the terms of the oath they are required to take before entering upon their duties, and according to which they swear to 'permit all persons to vote who shall offer to poll at the election,' &c., who, *in their judgment*, shall, according to the directions contained in the *constitution and laws*, be entitled to poll at the said election," &c.

I cordially approved your course and sentiments in the issuing and composing of that paper, and with fresh remembrance of it, was it unreasonable to suppose that you would again address the judges of election to prevent a greater and more flagitious wrong than was attempted by the military order of General Schenck? Then the election was but an ordinary one, except that certain officers were to be chosen. Now it is for a constitution—a fundamental law—that is designed to be continued for many years, and which may disfranchise many persons, as well as inflict the grossest injustice upon other large classes of the community. If the act of General Schenck was unconstitutional, so is that of the convention. If the order of Gen. Schenck was covertly designed to favor a certain political party, so is that of the convention If General Schenck's order was to prevent legal voters from voting, so is that of the convention. If the rejected voters are now to be referred to the judiciary, should they not then have been thus referred? Was not the question as much of a judicial one then as now? Could not a voter sue the judge if he rejected his vote in 1863, or any one who arrested or molested him when attempting to approach the polls? It was the unconstitutionality of the act that prompted your just and timely interference; an equally unconstitutional effort is now making to obstruct what you then called "the constitutional rights of the voters." The attempt to commit a grievous wrong upon the legal voters of the State, differs only in form. If General Schenck had said that the judges should administer an oath to every voter that he would at the next presidential election support the re-election of the present incumbent of the executive chair as a test of loyalty, it would have been no more unconstitutional than what he did, and it would have equally aroused your indignation. If the convention had inserted a similar clause, would you not deem it alike contrary to the constitution, and issue a proclamation to the judges of election to counteract it?

It is not the nature of the requirement only, but the usurpation of power, which characterizes the act and makes it unconstitutional. If there be usurpation, why not act upon it? In your message to the legislature in January, 1864, while referring to the outrages committed at the previous election, and the course you had taken, you used this language: "If, with these facts before me, and seeing the judges of election, sworn to conduct it according to the laws of the State, openly menaced with arrest unless they recognized the military authority and conducted it by the rules which that authority prescribed, I had stood silently by and failed to assure them of the protection of the State to the extent of its ability, I should have felt myself utterly unworthy of the place of its chief magistrate."

Now, governor, did not these precedents justify an expectation that you would interpose in a similar manner to prevent a greater wrong? a wrong not only to those whose votes may be rejected, but grievous injustice to others by reason of that rejection, who are and have been as loyal as any in the State?

Should not a constitution fraught with such momentous interests, having no parallel in our State, nor in any other State of the Union, be fairly and honestly submitted to all the constitutional and legal voters of the State? The occasion and the crisis are extraordinary, and of intense and vital interest to the people of the State—*the whole people.* If the vote be fairly, freely, fully taken, and the constitution be adopted, all good citizens will submit; but if the vote be partial, limited, unfair; if party spirit is to be subserved, and not the public interest; if wrong and injustice prevail; if an unconstitutional oath is forced upon the people, and votes taken without the territorial limits of the State, then what respect can be paid to a constitution thus adopted, and what excitement and bitterness of feeling will not be engendered?

I desire no office, and try to look exclusively at this subject through the medium of right, justice and patriotism. I cast aside all parties and party affinities, when an appeal is made to my sense of justice, to my integrity and honor. I do hope, for the reasons stated in my last, and for those now respectfully offered, that you will reconsider this subject, and if you should even have a shadow of doubt about the exercise of the power you are called upon to exert, let the consideration that it is best to be on the side of the constitution, the laws, the people, of justice and of right, determine the preponderance, and lead you to prompt and efficient action. I have written hastily and cursorily, because of want of time, but I hope considerately and after due reflection. I must beg you to excuse my imperfections of language, as well as my prolixity, and believe that in anything I may have written, nothing has been intended inconsistent with the high regard I entertain for one who has shown me so many signal manifestations of his partiality and favor.

With my best wishes for your health and prosperity, I am as ever, yours,

GEORGE VICKERS.

P. S. Since writing, a gentleman, (a judge of the election by appointment in our county,) called upon me and said, substantially: "What are we to do about administering the oath laid down in the proposed constitution? I consider it unconstitutional and improper; I shall be sworn to discharge my duty according to law—how can I administer an oath I deem contrary to law, and not found in any law? It is a subject that causes unpleasant reflections." He then asked what would be the consequences if he refused to administer it. I told him you had the power in that paper to reject votes, unless certified that the oath had been administered. He inquired if you would reject legal votes on that ground? I replied that I would write to know whether you would count votes not certified to be voted by those who took the new oath. He exacted a promise of me to advise him of your determination. Yours, G. V.

RESPONSE OF GOVERNOR BRADFORD.

STATE OF MARYLAND,
EXECUTIVE DEPARTMENT, ANNAPOLIS,
October 3, 1864.

George Vickers, Esq., Chestertown, Md.;

Sir—Your letter of the 27th ultimo, received on Saturday, is before me, and whilst I have certainly no inclination whatever for controversy, and but little time for argument, such as the subject of these letters requires, I cannot forbear from again briefly adverting to it, and some of the considerations by which I feel constrained to take the course I have already indicated.

I am fully aware that in coming to a different conclusion you are influenced by no personal motives, and that you can take the oath prescribed by the convention as conscientiously as myself; such a conviction, however, only the more inclines me to make manifest, if I can, the reasons that compel me to differ with you.

In adverting to that clause of the act of assembly which authorizes the convention to submit the constitution to the people, *subject to such rules and regulations* as it might prescribe, and to which I had previously called your attention, you seem to think that the legislature in the use of these terms only meant to confer upon the convention "minor and inferior powers," such as "the fixing of the time for holding the election," and also "of the manner, &c.," and that it was never thereby intended to give to the convention the power it has assumed; but the more I reflect upon the purport of these terms the more I am inclined to think that in the use of them the general assembly meant to confer some such power. If this was not their meaning, and they really intended, as you assume, only to allow the convention to provide for the *time* and *manner* of the election, why was not the clause concluded with the "minor powers" thus conferred? Already, in express terms, the convention had been authorized to submit their work to the people, "at such time and in such manner," &c. What, then, was meant by the further provision, that they should submit it, "*subject to such rules and regulations*" as they might prescribe? A well known rule of construction requires us to give effect to every member of a sentence if it be possible, and if it was not intended that these rules and regulations to be prescribed by the convention were to embrace the subject of the voter's qualification, to what other subject could the legislature have possibly meant them to apply.

But again, you argue that this construction is inconsistent with the terms used in the latter clause of the same section, requiring the constitution to be submitted "to the legal and qualified voters of the State," and from which you infer that no other qualification could have been contemplated but that provided in the existing constitution. But with great deference I submit that this is by no means a logical inference.

If the legislature referred at all to the *persons* by whom the constitution was to be ratified, it could only have referred to them as *voters*—of course, as *legal and qualified voters;* to have said that it should be submitted to the *people*, or the *citizens*, or the *inhabitants*, would have been to make it subject to the ratification of people of all ages and both sexes. In designating, therefore, the class of persons who were to ratify the constitution, the act of assembly necessarily uses the phrase *legal and qualified voters;* but whether qualified according to the rules and regulations ordained by the old constitution, or those which the convention were authorized to prescribe, is the very question in issue.

In reply to my suggestion that this is a legal question, more properly belonging to the judicial than to the executive department of the State, you argue against the correctness of such a view, and claim the right to ask for executive interference upon the ground of there being no adequate and practicable remedy which a court of law could conveniently apply, and you apparently assume that the substantial injury inflicted is upon the individual voter who is precluded from the exercise of his rightful franchise, and you advert to the practical inconvenience of attempting to remedy that wrong by suits or writs of *mandamus*, brought by every voter thus disfranchised, against the judges of election. To all that I agree—but have not numerous questions of the same kind constantly arisen out of every election we have ever had? Is not the rejection of legal and the taking of illegal votes a subject of complaint always occurring at elections, and has there been yet found no remedy for such abuses but suits by the individual voters against the judge?

The chief wrong inflicted in such cases has been generally supposed to consist in the election of one officer and the defeat of another, resulting from such abuse of the elective franchise, and when an account is kept, as it always may be, of the votes wrongfully admitted or excluded, the tribunals invested with the power of canvassing the matter, when they have purged the polls and counted or excluded the legal or illegal votes, have afforded what has been generally regarded as an adequate remedy, and sufficiently vindicated the disfranchised voter by thus ultimately making his vote effectual.

And so, in the case under consideration, does not the wrong supposed to be occasioned by the action of the convention consist really and substantially more in the other provisions which its constitution has introduced than in qualifying the elective franchise of those to whom it is submitted; and, is not the subject of most absorbing interest connected with the approaching election the question whether that constitution is to supplant the old one, rather than whether this man or that is deprived of the right of voting on it. If this be so, why may not the injuries apprehended from the new constitution be still obviated as in cases of other elections, if it be adopted by what can hereafter be shown to be the unlawful exclusion of those who, if permitted, would have voted against it?

But whatever may be the inconveniences which you recapitulate of seeking a remedy through the courts of law, and however such a consideration might operate in determining me to execute an *admitted* power, it cannot have, and I think you will agree with me, ought not to have any weight in inducing me to employ one of most questionable authority.

Again, you say that if this "were a judicial question it does not follow that it is not a political one," and you intimate the opinion that for the infraction of *political* rights, such as the right of franchise, the law does not always profess to furnish a remedy, and that the executive is clothed with authority to apply one. Doubtless this is in some respect a *political* question, and I may admit, too, that such question may at times arise that can be solved only by the political power of the State; but where is the authority for the assumption that such power is embodied in its executive?

The people of the State are the source of that power, and, according to the acknowledged theory and practice of our form of government we are to search for its representatives among those whom they have duly delegated to ordain or alter their organic law, rather than any where else. I felt, if you will allow me to say so, some surprise that one of your discriminating mind should have referred, at such length, to the proceedings, in the case of General Schenck's order at the election of 1863, and to my action in connection therewith, for the purpose of showing that in the oath which the convention has prescribed there is an interference with the constitutional rights of the voters as unwarrantable as that which General Schenck undertook to exercise, and the same necessity for my interference. I deem it proper to say that my sentiments in regard to that military movement have undergone no change whatever, but I confess myself unable to perceive any analogy between the cases. In the one a military commander arranges the form of an oath which he requires the judges of election in certain cases to administer, menaces them with arrest if they refuse, and sends a squad of soldiers to the polls to see that this order is enforced. I did in that case issue a proclamation, and called to the attention of the judges of election the law they were sworn to administer. No one pretended that any other law existed, and the quotation you make from my message correctly shows my object, and the feeling which prompted my action.

The judges were menaced with arrest for refusing to obey an unauthorized military order instead of the undisputed laws of the State, and I said to them that for thus doing their duty they should be protected to the extent of any power that I possessed.

How does the case stand that we are now considering? The constitution is of course the same to-day that it was a year ago. But the people of the State have declared, in the manner provided by law, their intention to change it. They have elected delegates for that purpose—their delegates assembled in pursuance of that authority—they frame a constitution—a large majority of its members, after months of deliberation and discussion, adopt it—they are to submit the work of their hands to their constituents—they require, however, that all who offer to vote upon it shall swear that they have never given aid, countenance or support to the rebellion which is seeking to overthrow the government of which they are part—they claim to do this not merely as the representatives of the people intrusted by them in such cases with powers adequate to such a proceeding, but they rely upon the grant of express authority to that effect by the legislature which provided for their meeting, and upon the authority of similar proceedings by other conventions.

You and I may look at these transactions from different points of view, but I think it must be admitted I have correctly recited the leading facts in the two cases, and, assuming this to be so, can it be contended that there is any similitude between them, and that because in the one I promised that the power of the State should be exerted to defend the judges in the execution of its unquestioned laws, I should now interfere, not as then, to protect them for obeying these laws, but to become the exponent of what these laws are in a case where the people of the State differ widely in opinion, whether the law of the next election is to be found in the old constitution or the new?

You, I know, consider the action of the convention a usurpation. I have briefly stated some of the reasons why, to my mind, that is not so palpable. Not because in the plenitude of the powers with which such conventions are supposed to be invested, and to which I have occasionally referred, they can do no wrong—for we can imagine that such a body, as well as an individual, might assume an authority that would be a flagrant usurpation.

If the people, for instance, at the election at which the members of this convention were chosen had voted that we should have no convention, and these members had still insisted on assembling; or if some small number of those elected, confessedly less than a quorum had undertaken to form a new constitution—these would have been such unquestionable usurpations, revolutionary almost in their character, that no officer in the State would be bound to regard them; but to my mind the difference between such cases and the one we are discussing is very obvious.

I referred in my previous letter, in illustration of the powers claimed for a convention of this character, to the present constitution of the State, inaugurated as it was in a manner forbidden by the constitution which it superseded. You object to that precedent as not applicable to the present case, because the part of the old constitution disregarded, related only to the *manner* of amending it, and did not affect the rights of the people under it.

Let me cite another authority, the applicability of which I think you will not deny, and which supports the course of the late convention in the proceeding in question as far as precedent possibly can.

In 1829 a constitutional convention assembled in Virginia. A recurrence to a list of its members will show a roll of illustrious names, surpassed in character and talent by none that ever formed a similar assembly.

They adopted a new constitution, which, like ours, was only to become operative when ratified by the people. The concluding lines of its preamble declared that "We, therefore, the delegates and representatives of the good people of Virginia, elected and in convention assembled, &c., *do submit and propose to the people* the following constitution."

Now, who were the people to whom they thus submitted it? The qualification required of a Virginia voter, like our own, was precisely defined by their constitution. None but freeholders were qualified to vote. They alone had enjoyed the right of suffrage for fifty years, and they alone had elected that convention.

The constitution which secured to them this exclusive privilege was still in force, and must so continue until they adopted another, and, as you say in reference to ours, the new constitution proposed to them, until so adopted, was a mere proposition without vitality or energy. To apply to it your comments in this case, until then it was "but a skeleton," "a feather floating upon the breeze of popular opinion," and "required the people to breathe into it life and power." Using your argument in the present case, the rights and property of the people of the State were held under the old constitution, the qualifications by it prescribed for the voter must continue as the only qualification until another ratified by these qualified voters took its place. Hence your conclusion that to allow a new qualification to be required before that time was an infraction of constitutional rights, and to provide for the taking the vote of soldiers out of the State, when that was not permitted by the existing constitution, was a flagrant usurpation of authority. This, undoubtedly, is your argument, briefly stated. Now, under the constitution of Virginia, all who were not freeholders were as effectually excluded from the elective franchise as their negro population, and yet the convention, in submitting the new constitution to the people, allowed large classes to vote, such as owners of leasehold, householders who paid a tax, and many others who had never before exercised the right of suffrage.

The convention allowed them to vote. They did vote, and undoubtedly by their vote the constitution was carried. The only possible difference between the authority o that convention and ours was in the fact that there was no ambiguity in the terms of the act of assembly providing for its exercise. The act directed that they should submit the constitution either to those whom the convention might authorize to vote for members of the legislature, or upon the ratification of the constitution. But this clause of the act of assembly cannot, from the whole tenor of your argument, make any distinction between the cases; for, certainly, I do not understand you as in any respect admitting that had our act of assembly, in terms ever so unequivocal, prescribed a new oath for the voters, and made provision for the soldier's vote, or had explicitly authorized the convention to do so, that the constitutional provisions could be put aside by such legislation. Nor was any peculiar power claimed by the Virginia convention on such ground; on the contrary, Mr. Thompson, one of the most prominent debaters in behalf of the power claimed, in effect repudiated such a derivative authority.

Referring to that clause of the act, he said, "the whole object of this provision was to declare *what it was supererogatory to affirm*, that if it should be the pleasure of this body to designate the persons to whom our work should be submitted *we had the power to do so*, and in the event of our silence on this subject, the sheriffs should on question of ratification or rejection take the votes of all qualified under the new constitution." Nor were those who opposed the exercise of the power less confident in their denunciation of the measure as a usurpation than yourself.

They pursued the same line of argument. Mr. Nicholas, who was one of these opponents, after declaring that as a general principle there were two ways by which a government could be changed—the one by revolution, and the other by those from whom the powers of government are derived, agreeing to modify its existing institutions, says: "If it be admitted that the change in the government can only be made with the assent of those who possess the power, the reference of the question to those not now entitled to vote would present a curious political anomaly. In the first place, on a question whether the constitution is to be adopted, we are to anticipate that it will be so adopted, and give the decision to those who possess no political power until after the event takes place, instead of obtaining the assent of those in whose hands the power of government is, we are to unite in the decision numerous classes who constitute no part of the actual government."

He then puts the case of the majority of the freeholders voting one way, and of the new voters the other, and in which case the form of government, instead of being altered with the assent of the existing authorities, would be so altered in defiance of them.

Mr. Randolph, another opponent of the proposed submission of the constitution to those who were not allowed to vote under the existing one, denounces the proposition still more emphatically. He says:

"I consider this as the greatest question which has been presented to this body since it assembled. Is it not obvious that if the commonwealth consists of freeholders and non-freeholders, and the non-freeholders are—as we are told they are—the most numerous of the two, that the worst of constitutions might have been imposed upon the commonwealth by those who, in the language of a gentleman on this floor, are out of the constitution, against the voice of every freeholder in the county? Sir, what sort of a tribunal do you elect when you admit those who have no part or lot in our acts to pass judgment upon them? Sir, you might as well refer the constitution to the people of Ohio, or the people of Kentucky, or, I will go further, to the people of Japan. Yes, sir, they have just as good a right to decide upon it."

Mr. Randolph then moved the following resolution:

"*Resolved*, That the amended constitution adopted by this convention be submitted on the respective election days in the month of April next *to the persons qualified to vote under the existing constitution for members of the general assembly*."

The ayes and nays were taken upon the adoption of the resolution, and it was defeated by a vote of more than two to one. The new constitution was submitted to voters who were not qualified under the existing one, and among those voting with the majority were Ex-President Madison, Chief Justice Marshall, Chapman Johnson, Philip P. Barbour, and others of scarcely inferior celebrity.

Now, my dear sir, whatever opinion you may still entertain of the proceeding of our convention, I hope and think that with such a precedent before us you will no longer press me to interpose the executive arm to arrest it upon the ground of its being a palpable violation of constitutional rights, "having no parallel in our State or any other."

In regard to the query propounded by one of your judges of election, and mentioned in your postscript, as to whether I would refuse to count the votes of a district where the judges did not certify that the oath required by the convention had been administered, I would say, what you are, of course, aware of, that by another clause in the constitution proposed I am expressly enjoined not to count such votes. That for the reasons already given I hold myself bound by that requirement, and were I to disregard it, it would be as effectually to annul the action of the convention as if I had acceded to your request, and directed the judges of election not to administer the oath required.

With sincere respect, I am, yours, &c.,

A. W. BRADFORD.

DUTIES OF JUDGES OF ELECTION.

Further to guard against any informalities in the returns of the election, the governor deemed it his duty to address the following circular to the judges of election, and it was published and circulated throughout the State on the tenth and eleventh days of October:

EXECUTIVE DEPARTMENT,
ANNAPOLIS, October 8, 1864.

To the judges of the election throughout the State on the question of the adoption or rejection of the constitution.

You have been apprised by my letter, recently published, of the necessity of accompanying your returns of the election about to be held on the question of adopting the new constitution with a certificate that the oath prescribed in the said constitution has been administered to all voters at the election; and I deem it also proper to call your attention to another certificate required in connection with said returns, which not being a customary one, may be otherwise overlooked.

The act of 1864, authorizing the convention, contains the following provision, which, by another clause of the act is made applicable as well to said election now about to be held, as to the last one at which members of said convention were elected:

"The said judges in said return shall certify that no organized military or other armed force had appeared at the place where the polls had been held and interfered with said election, unless such military force shall be called for by the said judges of election, or by other civil authority charged with the preservation of the peace."

Your returns, therefore, to the executive should distinctly state that the oath, required by the convention to be taken by all voting on the question of adopting or rejecting the constitution, had been administered by you, and you should also therein further certify that no military or other armed force had appeared at the place of voting and interfered with said election, unless under the call of the civil authorities as therein provided; and should such force appear without said call, you should certify that fact under oath.

A. W. BRADFORD,
Governor of Maryland.

JUDICIAL PROCEEDINGS.

The election was held as provided for in the twelfth article of the constitution, on the twelfth and thirteenth days of October, eighteen hundred and sixty-four. On the twenty-fourth of October an application was made to the superior court of Baltimore city, Hon. Robert N. Martin, judge, on behalf of Samuel G. Miles, for a *mandamus* to be directed to A. W. Bradford, governor of the State, commanding him to exclude all votes cast at any place outside of the State of Maryland from the count upon the question of the adoption of the constitution. The petition for the mandamus recited the fact of the convention, that it had adopted what is termed the "New Constitution," section eight of article twelve thereof providing that an election should be held in the city of Baltimore on the twelfth day of October, and on the twelfth and thirteenth of the month in the several counties of the State, &c: that all persons duly qualified to vote for delegates to the general assembly should vote at said election, excepting nevertheless that in sections eight and nine of the same article it is provided that no person should be permitted to vote unless he should first take the oath prescribed by article first, section four, of said constitution, and that the taking of said oath should not be conclusive evidence of his right to vote as aforesaid, whereby in addition to the qualifications prescribed by article first of the present constitution, (which the petitioner is advised, is under the constitution of the United States, the supreme law of the State of Maryland,) and as the condition on the performance of which, only the citizens of the State of Maryland should be entitled to vote, he is required to take the following oath, which will be found in the constitution.

The petitioner further shows that he is a free white person, upwards of twenty-one years of age, and that on the said twelfth day of the present month of October, was a citizen of the State of Maryland and of the United States, and on said day and month aforesaid, and for many years next preceding said day continuously, had been a resident of the city of Baltimore, and of the fourteenth ward of said city, and of the first precinct of said ward, in which he tendered his ballot, and had not been at any time convicted of bribery, false swearing, larceny or other infamous crime, or otherwise, according to the form and effect of the existing constitution, or any law made pursuant thereto, rendered incapable of exercising his elective franchise as aforesaid; and being so qualified to vote at all elections to be held in the said precinct and ward and city aforesaid, he did, on the said twelfth day of the present month of October, attend at the place appointed for the holding the aforesaid election in said precinct, at the hour of 12.30 or thereabouts in the afternoon of the day aforesaid, and did then and there tender to the duly qualified judges of the said election, then and there acting as such judges, a ballot, whereon was written "Against the Constitution," and did there and then require the said judges to receive said ballot, and to deposit the same in the ballot-box provided by the said judges for the deposit of ballots tendered by persons qualified to vote at the said election; that the said judges, although they well knew that your petitioner was duly qualified, as aforesaid, to vote at all elections held in said ward, and especially at the election then holding as aforesaid, did then and there refuse to receive said ballot, so as aforesaid tendered by your petitioner, and did then and there require your petitioner to answer whether he would take oath so as aforesaid prescribed to be taken by the said new constitution, and *because* and *only because*, of the refusal of your petitioner to take said oath, the said judges refused to deposit the said ballot in the ballot-box aforesaid; but, on the contrary, took the said ballot from him and deposited it in one other box, which they, the said judges, had then and there provided for the deposit and safe-keeping of ballots received by them but rejected as having been tendered by persons not qualified to vote.

The petitioner, after stating that the governor has declared and insisted that he will count the votes of persons in the military service, returned to him, and will not exclude them from the count in ascertaining the aggregate vote cast at said election, avers that even if the provisions of the constitution allowing the taking of soldiers' votes, away from their residences, are in themselves liable to no constitutional objections, yet the governor is bound to exclude all the soldiers' votes which have been returned to him, from count in estimating the votes "for" or "against" the said new constitution, because, as your petitioner avers, the new constitution itself requires that the soldiers who shall vote on its adoption shall, as well as those who are not soldiers, take the aforesaid oath as a necessary preliminary to the exercise of the right to vote on said constitution, whereas, as your petitioner avers, the returns as made to the governor of said soldiers' votes, do not show that said soldiers took, or were asked to take, the said oaths; and your petitioner avers that the fact is, that none of those whose votes are returned to the governor did take, nor were they required to take, the said oath, and he also avers that if said soldiers' votes should be excluded from count by the governor, the said new constitution has failed to receive, by at least eighteen hundred votes, a majority of the votes cast on the twelfth and thirteenth of the present month of October, at the said election on the adoption or rejection of the said instrument, and that, too, even if the ballots tendered by persons qualified to vote, and were not received by said judges as the votes of persons qualified to vote, are excluded from the count.

The petitioner avers that an inspection will show that many of said returns of soldiers' votes, as made to said governor, are invalid, because of the neglect on the part of those making them to observe the requirements of the said instrument called the new constitution; and that, on each and all of the aforegoing grounds, the said governor is bound to exclude the said soldiers' votes, so as aforesaid returned to him, in casting up the votes for and against the said new constitution; but to exclude which, as above averred, the said governor refuses; and the said governor also refuses to ascertain and count the votes of those persons qualified to vote under the existing constitution of the State whose votes were rejected because of their refusal to take the oath as heretofore recited; and refuses also to count the votes so aforesaid placed in the ballots, described "rejected ballot" boxes, which, your petitioner avers, are by law required to be safely kept sealed up by the police commissioners until called for, and which are therefore readily accessible to the said governor.

The petitioner further states that he is advised that the course which the governor intends to pursue and is now pursuing, by which he proposes to execute and carry into effect all the provisions of the said proposed "new constitution," in reference to said election or voting, although on the day on which said vote was taken the said instrument had not been adopted, but was then for the first time submitted for adoption or rejection by the people, and although some of said provisions conflict with the existing and only constitution of the State of Maryland, is in violation of the rights of your petitioner and others of his fellow-citizens of the State of Maryland. The petitioner further states that he is the owner of slaves of large value, held and owned by him in this State under the constitution and laws thereof, and that by the 24th article of the declaration of rights prefixed to the said new constitution, slavery is abolished in this State, and all slaves are declared to be free, so that your petitioner will be deprived of his said slave property without any compensation therefor, if the said "new constitution" should go into effect, because the 36th section of the 3d article of the said proposed new constitution declares that the general assembly shall make no law, nor make any appropriation to compensate the masters or claimants of slaves emancipated from servitude by the adoption of this constitution.

And your petitioner is advised that, as a qualified voter of this State, as hereinbefore stated, and as the owner of slaves in this State, he is entitled to demand of your honor a *mandamus* directed to the governor of the State, commanding him to do certain acts required by the constitution of the State and the laws passed in pursuance thereof, and without the doing of which your petitioner will be remediless in the premises.

After reciting that since said election a vacancy in the office of the judge of the circuit court of Anne Arundel county had occurred, and that Governor Bradford passes much of his time in the city of Baltimore, where he transacts much of his official business, &c., the petitioner prays that the governor may be ruled by some early day to show cause, if any he has, why a writ of *mandamus* ought not to be issued, commanding him in ascertaining the number of votes cast at the said late election held as aforesaid "for or in favor of" the said new constitution, and the number of votes cast at the said late election against the said new constitution, to count such votes as shall appear by the returns made to him as aforesaid to have been cast or given by persons duly qualified to vote at elections according to the form and effect of the first article of the existing constitution relating to the elective franchise, and at the election districts, precincts and places respectively where the said persons so casting or giving their votes as aforesaid are, or were authorized, severally and respectively, as aforesaid, to cast or give their said votes and also all other votes or ballots as shall appear by evidence satisfactory to his judgment, to have been tendered at the said election by persons duly qualified under the existing constitution, and at the several and respective precincts or districts or places where such persons were qualified to vote as aforesaid, and which ballots shall appear to him to have been rejected or excluded from the returns made him as aforesaid by reason or because of the refusal of the persons so tendering said ballots respectively to take the oath required to be taken by article 1st, section 4, of the said "new constitution," and *to exclude* from his said count any and every vote which from the returns made him as aforesaid, shall appear to have been cast at any place, other than the election district, precinct or place at which the person so casting said vote was qualified to vote, according to the form and effect of the aforesaid article one of the existing constitution, and to exclude all votes cast at any place outside of the State of Maryland. And if the said A. W. Bradford, Governor of Maryland, as aforesaid, shall shew for cause that the said ballots so as aforesaid supposed to have been rejected by reason or because of the refusal of the persons tendering the same to take the oath required by the 4th section of article 1st of the new constitution, were rightfully rejected as aforesaid; and that the votes cast by persons in the military service of the United States were not unlawfully cast because or by reason of the holding of the polls at which said votes were cast, at places different from and out of the election district, precinct or place, at which the persons so voting as aforesaid severally and respectively were qualified to vote by the existing constitution, and the laws passed in pursuance thereto, then and in such event that the said A. W. Bradford, Governor of Maryland, and as aforesaid, do further show cause as aforesaid, wherefore he should not be commanded to exclude from his said count as aforesaid, any and every ballot which shall appear to have been cast by a person in the military service of the United States, unless it shall appear affirmatively from the returns made of said vote that the person casting said ballot did before casting said vote take the oath prescribed to be taken by the said 4th section of the 1st article of the new constitution, and unless the said returns shall also show affirmatively a compliance with all the other requirements relating to taking and returning the votes of persons in the military service of the United States, which are contained in the said new constitution.

This petition was dismissed by the court in the following order:

"In the superior court of Baltimore city, this 24th day of October, 1864, on consideration of the aforegoing petition, the court being of opinion that no sufficient ground is stated therein for the interposition of this court, in the matter thereof, it is ordered that the said petition be and the same is hereby dismissed."

From this order an appeal was at once taken to the court of appeals. Prior to its being taken up in that court, the same petition precisely, was presented in the circuit court of Anne Arundel county (Judge Wm. H. Tuck,) and by that court in like manner dismissed. From that order dismissing the petition, an appeal was also taken.

Pending these proceedings a petition was presented to the circuit court of Baltimore county (Judge John H. Price,) on behalf of E. F. Chambers and others, for an injunction to restrain the governor from counting the votes cast on the question of the adoption of the constitution outside of the State of Maryland, and from issuing his proclamation declaring the adoption of the constitution. This petition was dismissed by the court, and an appeal at once taken to the court of appeals. The same petition in behalf of the same complainants was then presented to the circuit court of Anne Arundel county, and dismissed in like manner by Judge Tuck. From his decision and order dismissing the petition, there was also an appeal.

These four appeals standing for hearing in the court of appeals, the application for an injunction was taken up by that court on the 27th of October. After argument had commenced Judges Bowie and Goldsborough announced that being themselves slaveholders, they had the same interest in the decision of the cause before them which the parties complainant in the cause had, and were therefore, under the fifth section of the fourth article of the existing constitution, disqualified from sitting in the case; and the court ordered its clerk to certify the fact to the governor, that he might commission the requisite number of persons for the trial and determination of the case.

The court then proposed, with the consent of counsel who were present as *amici curiæ*—the governor having declined to appear by counsel—to take up and dispose of the application for a *mandamus*. To this, that the question might be adjudicated, the counsel agreed. The argument proceeded upon the appeal from the superior court of Baltimore city, and the principles involved were discussed at length by I. N. Steele, Wm. Schley and T. S. Alexander, Esqs., on behalf of the appellants, and by Hon. Henry Stockbridge—who was chairman of the judiciary committee in the convention—and Hon. H. Winter Davis, of Baltimore, on the other side. On the 29th of October the court, through Hon. Richard J. Bowie, chief justice, gave its decision, and unanimously affirmed the order of Judge Martin. The chief justice said:

The peculiar circumstances surrounding this case requiring it should be promptly decided, we have only time to announce the conclusions arrived at, and refer to a few of the leading authorities on which these are based.

The case has been argued with an admirable spirit of courtesy and moderation, and much eloquence and learning.

The brief of the relator's counsel states: "The object of the proceedings is to obtain an exposition of the rule of law which ought to guide the *discretion* of the governor in his ascertainment of the result of the late election had for the adoption or rejection of the new constitution."

The relator's prayer substantially is, that the governor of Maryland show cause "why a writ of mandamus ought not to be issued, *commanding* him in ascertaining the number of votes cast at the said late election held as aforesaid," to count certain votes which were tendered and rejected, and to exclude certain votes which shall appear to have been cast at any other place than the election precinct at which the person voting was qualified to vote.

From this brief analysis it appears the proceeding is one of the most momentous consequence, and should be treated with the greatest deliberation. Our first duty is to inquire whether it is a proper subject for judicial interpretation and interposition.

By our organic law, the powers of government are distributed into legislative, executive and judicial. We are admonished by the declaration of rights that these powers "ought to be forever separate and distinct from each other; and no person exercising the functions of one of said departments shall assume or discharge the duties of any other."

The second article of the constitution is, "The executive power of the State shall be vested in a governor."

"He shall take care that the laws be faithfully executed."

The sixth section of the convention law required the constitution and form of government adopted by the convention to be submitted to the legal and qualified voters of the State for their adoption or rejection, at such time, in such manner, and subject to such rules and regulations as said convention may prescribe; and the provisions thereinbefore contained, for the qualification of voters and the holding of elections, provided in the previous sections of the act, were made applicable to the election to be held under that section.

The eighth section further enacts that when the governor shall receive the returns of the number of ballots cast in this State for the adoption or rejection of the constitution submitted by the convention to the people, if, upon counting and casting up the returns as made to him, as hereinbefore prescribed, it shall appear that a majority of the legal votes cast at said election are in favor of the adoption of the said constitution, he shall issue his proclamation to the people of the State, declaring the fact, and he shall take such steps as shall be required by the said constitution to carry the same into full operation and to supersede the old constitution of this State.

Is the power and authority conferred on the governor by this act, a political or judicial power?

A late eminent jurist, whose recent death has been lamented as a national calamity, in the case of Luther *vs.* Borders, *et. al.*, 7 Howard, 39, expressed himself thus strongly: "Certainly the question which the plaintiff proposed to raise by the testimony he offered, has not heretofore been recognized as a judicial one in any of the State courts. In forming the constitution of the different States, after the declaration of independence and in the various changes and alterations which have since been made, the *political department has always* determined whether the proposed constitution or amendment was ratified or not by the people of the State, and the judicial power has followed its decision."

Courts of law will not interfere with the exercise of high *discretionary* powers vested in the chief magistrate of the State, for obvious political reasons:

Among others, "Because, as Governor of the State, deriving his powers from the constitution thereof, he has been made a co-ordinate, separate, distinct and independent department of the government."

In the case of Low *vs.* Towns, governor of Georgia, the supreme court of that State said: "The ultimate effect of this remedy, (mandamus,) in case of refusal by the governor to obey the laws of the land, would be to deprive the people of the State of the head of one of the departments of the government." (8 Geo., 372.)

Chief Justice Marshall, in the case of Marbury & Madison, (1 Cranch,) says "that the President is invested with certain important political powers, in the exercise of which he is to use his own discretion, and is accountable only to his country, in his political character, and to his own conscience."

The chief magistrate or governor of the State bears the same relation to the State that the President does to the United States, and in the discharge of his political duties is entitled to the same immunities, privileges and exemptions—*vide* Hawkins *vs.* the Governor, 1 Ark. Rep. 586.

Independently of all political considerations, if the question was a purely judicial one, this court could not consistently with decisions in other States and in our own, grant the prayer of the relator.

The general principle laid down in all these, almost without exception, is, that where the act to be done requires the exercise of judgment and discretion in the officer against whom the mandamus is prayed, it will be refused. *Vide* cases collected 12 Md., Purnell *vs.* Green, 336; 17 Howard, 230. The result of these decisions is, that the duty and power to decide the questions which we are asked to determine are devolved upon the officer, or governor, without appeal, over whom, in that respect, the judiciary have no control or revisory power.

We have thus succinctly announced the general principles which lead us to the adoption of the conclusion that the order of the superior court in this case should be affirmed.

The court has been invoked to enter into the constitutional powers of the convention and express opinions upon the validity of their acts even if they should hold that the right to issue a mandamus did not exist, and they have been referred to the eminent examples of the supreme court, through their chief justices in some cases, where they declared the law although they could not enforce it. Without dwelling on the immense moral, political and legal influence of that tribunal, to which we cannot pretend, we respectfully suggest there is no parallel between the cases. Those cases in which the supreme court adopted that course, with one notable exception, were not cases in which society was shaken to its foundations by civil discord, and parties arrayed against each other with intense bitterness. If we cannot subdue the strife, we will not add fuel to the flame. All that we can do is to show such reverence for constitutional government, by confining ourselves to the strict limits of our authority, as may induce others, who love "liberty regulated by law," to cherish all its muniments and observe all their obligations.

Test: GEORGE EARLE,
Clerk Court of Appeals of Maryland.

Justice Bartol delivered the following separate opinion:

I assent to that part of the opinion of a majority of the court which denies the mandamus asked for, on the ground that the duties devolved upon the governor, by the act of 1864, chapter 5, in ascertaining and announcing the legal votes upon the adoption or rejection of the proposed new constitution are not purely ministerial in their character, but that they require the exercise of judgment and discretion on his part, necessarily devolving upon him the duty of passing upon and deciding the various questions argued before us, and upon which we have been called upon to pass. In such case the law is well established that a writ of mandamus will not be granted.

Green *vs.* Purnell, 12th Maryland, 329, and the cases there referred to and many other cases might be cited.

I do not agree, however, with my brothers in thinking the power devolved upon the governor, now under consideration, is in any sense a political-executive power belonging to him *virtute officii*, and not a proper subject for judicial investigation. That subject, however, having been submitted by law to the decision of the governor, I forbear the expression of any opinion upon it.

Test: GEORGE EARLE,
Clerk Court of Appeals of Maryland.

While these proceedings were in progress an application was made to the governor for permission to canvass the returns made to him of the soldiers' votes, and to show cause why certain of these votes should be rejected in the count. This privilege was accorded by the governor; the votes and returns were canvassed in detail, and the questions raised upon such canvass were argued at length by William Schley, Esq., against the admissibility of the votes, and by Hons. Alexander Randall and Archibald Stirling, Jr., on behalf of their admissibility. The points thus presented to the governor were disposed of by him in the subjoined

OPINION OF THE GOVERNOR.

STATE OF MARYLAND, EXECUTIVE DEP'T.,
ANNAPOLIS, October 28, 1864.

In the matter of objections made to the sufficiency and correctness of returns of soldiers' vote:

A request was made of me recently by a committee of gentlemen representing, as I understood, those opposed to the adoption of the new constitution, that before issuing any proclamation, as required by its terms, I would allow counsel to inspect the returns of the soldiers' vote, provided for by that instrument, and submit to me such objections thereto as they thought could be made. Although the proposition was a novel one, and I believe no other instance exists in which election returns, filed as they are annually or biennially in this department, have ever been subjected to a legal scrutiny as a preliminary to executive action, I did not feel at liberty to refuse the request, and at once agreed that counsel should have full access to these returns, stipulating only that, as according to the view I took of the case, there were no facts about which I could inquire except such as were suggested on the face of the returns; that all objections or discussion should be limited accordingly, and that the friends of the constitution should be advised of the proceeding and allowed the opportunity of answering these objections, as well as making any other to the home vote that might occur to them.

The past two or three days have been devoted to this examination, and a great number of exceptions have been taken to these returns, and argued with the ability that distinguishes the learned counsel who conducted the examination. He had been already apprised that my previous examination of that subject had brought my mind to the conclusion, several times expressed, that so far as my action was concerned I was bound by the provisions of the constitution which the convention had adopted, and whilst we differed widely as to its authority, he very courteously waived all discussion upon that subject, and confined his argument to exceptions taken to the sufficiency or correctness of the military returns, and those I now propose to consider.

The first point raised in the argument is that the oath required by the constitution to be taken by voters was required of the soldiers voting under its special provision as well as of the citizen voting at the county polls, and as the returns of the soldiers' vote, except in two or three cases, fail to show that such oath was administered, that their vote must be rejected. The requirements of the constitution in this respect seem to me very plain. In directing the manner of voting on the constitution, provision is first made for the vote in the counties of the State, and afterwards, and under a distinct heading entitled "Soldiers' Vote" special provision is made for the vote of those in the military service. In the former, and the former only, is anything said about the oath. After directing on what days in the counties and city of Baltimore the election is to take place, the section proceeds to require that the judges *of the said city and the several counties of the State* "shall receive at said election the votes only of such electors as are qualified according to the provisions of this constitution,"—thus expressly showing that the limitation upon the elective franchise thus imposed was confined to those voting before the ordinary judges of election appointed by the county and city authorities. And when in a subsequent clause—still however on the subject of the home vote, and before reaching the article relating to the soldiers—it is said that "the judges of election shall administer to every person offering to vote the oath," &c., the same judges of election previously indicated are manifestly referred to, a conclusion confirmed by the tenor of the succeeding section on the same subject, wherein the governor is required to exclude from count the votes *of "any county or city"* where the judges fail to certify that the oath has been taken.

When in the subsequent part of the same article the special provision is made for the vote of the soldiers, although it is minute in its directions as to the course they are to pursue, not a word is said on the subject of any oath to be taken by them. Indeed, I understand the learned counsel in making this objection to admit that, looking only to the language of the constitution, the oath is not required of the soldiers, but he thinks they come within the spirit and purview of that instrument and should take the oath required of all others. It seems to me that the very contrary is the unavoidable inference, and that the whole scope and spirit of the constitution show that it was not intended that the soldiers should take the oath. In providing as it does in the fourth article that no person who has ever been in armed hostility to the United States, or has given aid or comfort to those who have, &c., &c., shall exercise the right of suffrage, it expressly excepts from the operation of that disqualifying provision those who have "since such unlawful acts voluntarily entered into the military service of the United States," &c., or "*shall be on the day of election* actually and voluntarily in such service." So far, therefore, from the soldiers being required either by the words or spirit of the constitution to take the oath in question, although a man may have committed all the acts denied by the terms of the oath, his employment in the military service at the time he offers his vote completely condones his past offence and entitles him to vote. And an examination of the returns of the soldiers' vote will show that in every instance they certify affirmatively that the persons voting were in the military service of the United States.

The next of the objections, reviewing them according to what I consider the order of their importance, is that founded on the assumption that no soldier belonging to any company of Maryland volunteers can vote unless such company is attached to a Maryland *regiment;* and therefore that the members of the different batteries of artillery, of the four companies of the late third regiment of infantry, now reduced to a battalion, the four independent cavalry companies (not a part of any regiment,) and the independent company of infantry known as the Patapsco Guards, are, by the terms of the constitution, all excluded from the right of suffrage, and the counsel accordingly insists that their votes should not be counted. To suppose that the convention meant to establish a discrimination among the soldiers of the State so manifestly unjust, would require either the suggestion of some most obvious reason therefor, or a purpose to that effect so unequivocally expressed in the constitution as to make that construction of it unavoidable. No attempt has been made, I believe, to assign any reason for so arbitrary a distinction, and, indeed, looking at it from every possible point of view, any such discrimination would seem as unreasonable as it is unjust. Is there, in the next place, any such positive restriction of the right to vote to those who are a part of some regiment as to oblige us to exclude all others? That will depend on the terms, spirit and intent of the instrument. Let us examine it to that end.

The very first line of the first clause of the article relative to the soldiers' vote rebuts the idea that the convention meant to restrict the right of suffrage to any particular class or organization of Maryland soldiers. It declares that "*Any* qualified voter of this State who shall be absent from the county or city of his residence by reason of his being in the military service of the United States, so as not to be able to vote at home on the adoption or rejection of this constitution, or for all State officers, &c., &c., shall be entitled to vote," &c. Not only in the commencement of the article is the purpose manifest to secure the right to vote to any soldier, but in all other parts of it where it refers to the subject, a similar determination is manifested. In the succeeding section, for instance, where provision is made for a soldier who may be in some hospital or military post within the State, on the day of the election, "and not with his company," and who is authorized to vote at the nearest election polls, such authority is not limited to those who belong to a regiment; and again in the fifteenth section the same anxious purpose is displayed to secure—not the votes of soldiers attached to some regiment merely—but the soldiers' vote generally, and the governor is enjoined to "take all means proper to secure *the soldiers' vote*."

Whence, then, the idea that no company can vote unless incorporated with a regiment? The sentence relied upon for that construction is found at the end of the first clause in the article already quoted, whereby, after declaring in the words I have cited, that any one absent from the county or city where he resides, by reason of being in the military service, may vote, the clause proceeds to point out *how* he may vote, and in giving direction on that subject it is stated that a "poll shall be opened in each company of every *Maryland regiment*," &c., and because in thus directing how the votes are to be given the convention has used these terms, it is argued that none but those so attached to a regiment can vote at all. This inference, in the face of the injustice and unreasonableness of such a restriction, and of the express purpose to the contrary so clearly exhibited throughout the article, is not warranted, I think, by any fair construction. Did the convention really mean thereby that none should vote except at the polls of a company belonging to a regiment, and where that was impossible by reason of there being no regiment, that the companies should not vote at all? or were the terms "of any Maryland regiment," used as they were by civilians unfamiliar with military technicalities, meant merely in the same sense as though they had said a poll shall be opened in each company of Maryland volunteers? A regard to the primary object of the constitution, and to the effectuation of its substantial purpose, force me to adopt the latter conclusion. The principal object of the convention doubtless was to secure the right of voting to every Maryland soldier who was a qualified voter at home. That essential purpose is, if possible, to be gratified, and if that object cannot be accomplished consistently with all the mere directory parts of the same provision, the latter should be sacrificed rather than the former. The convention had no right; and, as I have endeavored to show, they have made no attempt to discriminate between these soldiers; they were all alike voters at home; they had all alike left their home that they might the better protect it against invasion. If they voted at the company quarters of their commanding officer, they have, I think, sufficiently complied with the directions of the constitution.

The next general objection embraces the cases of several company commands acting at the time of election on detached duty. These detachments were sometimes composed of parts of several companies, and sometimes consisted of a part of one company only. They were stationed in some cases within, and in others without the State, and it is objected that they had no right to vote, because they were not *companies* in the sense of that term as used in this part of the constitution. By the terms of the constitution a poll is to be opened in every *company*, the commissioned officers of the *company*, or any one of them, may act as the judge of the election, and voters of this State belonging to such *company* may vote thereat, &c., and it is contended that by the word company, as thus used, is meant only the organized military command forming one of the ten subordinate divisions which compose a regiment. I can see nothing in the language or spirit of this article in the constitution that should restrict us to this limited and technical application of the term. It is in the first place opposed to the manifest object of the convention to which I have already called attention, which was to authorize every qualified voter in the military service of the United States to exercise the right of suffrage, which he could not do in the ordinary way by reason of his absence from home. A company used in the technical sense here insisted on as an integral part of a regiment is required to consist of a prescribed number of men, not less than sixty-four, nor more than eighty-two privates, with a specified number of commissioned and non-commissioned officers. It is hardly to be presumed that the convention, in framing this section, had in view any such precise or professional idea of the word *company;* on the contrary, I think they certainly used it in its ordinary acceptation, as any civilian would be most likely to do, and as signifying any organized military association less than a battalion or regiment; and if a detachment, whether made up of a part of one or more companies, technically so called, was, on the day of election, in an organized condition, acting under the command of a company officer, as was the case of all the detachments whose votes have been received, I think it came within the meaning of the term company, as used in said section, and the voters belonging to it were authorized to vote at the quarters of its commanding officer.

Another objection is made to the vote of these detachments, where they are stationed within the State, upon the ground that by the 12th section of the same article in the constitution provision is made for their votes by allowing them to vote at the nearest election polls. My construction of that section is that it was designed only for *individual* cases, in hospitals or elsewhere on duty in the State, and did not apply to organized companies stationed within the State whose members were absent from their usual place of residence. The terms of the section expressly limit the privilege therein given of voting at the nearest polls (which I understand to mean the nearest district polls) to those qualified voters in the service and absent from home, who are "not with their company;" and, if I am right in the views previously presented, that a detachment under command of an officer is a company within the meaning of that term as used in the constitution, then the proper place of voting for that detachment is the quarters of its commanding officer, and not the nearest district polls.

Objections are made to the returns in some three or four cases upon the ground of irregularity in showing, as in one case they do, that three non-commissioned officers acted as judges, when only two could properly be elected for that purpose, and again in another case that only one acted; that in one case a commissioned officer was united with a non-commissioned officer as the judges, and in another case with a private, and that these were improper conjunctions and vitiated the election. These may have been irregularities, but according to the authorities on the subject, they were not, I think, of such a character as to require a rejection of the vote; at all events, in the absence of anything going to show that any one has lost his vote thereby, or voted when he was not entitled. If in any of these cases complaints existed of frauds or unfairness practiced at the polls where these judges presided, the imputed irregularities of the kind noted might be entitled to some weight, but the leading principle in such cases is, says Mr. Cushing, in his work on Legislative Assemblies, "sanctioned both by law and common sense, that where the provisions of law, whatever they may be, are imperative and peremptory, any neglect of the returning officers to observe them will render their proceedings void; but that where the law is *merely directory*, no neglect or mistake, or even improper conduct or irregularity on their part will be fatal, if in other respects *there has been a substantial or good election.*"

And again, he says, "that whether a neglect of the requisitions of a directory statute will be fatal or not to the proceedings, does not depend so much upon the nature of the neglect as *upon its influence in producing the result of the election.*"

It would certainly be very difficult to suggest any reason for believing that the irregularities herein referred to could have exerted any influence upon the vote of the particular companies in which they occurred. The same author cites a variety of cases of irregularity upon the part of the returning judges of election, apparently far more important than those here suggested, which, however, were held not to invalidate the election. In one case the clerks of the election "were not sworn till after the election" or "not sworn at all;" in another, "the poll was not kept open each day the number of hours required by law;" in another, the ballot-box, which was required by law to be locked, "was only tied with a tape, and was also placed in the custody of a person not authorized to have charge of it."

In all these cases (says the author) there being a substantial and good election, notwithstanding the irregularities complained of, the proceedings were not invalidated.—(*Cushing on Legislative Assemblies*, 74-5.)

Other objections have been taken to the sufficiency of these returns upon the ground that where the commissioned officers do not act as judges, it should appear affirmatively upon the face of the returns that they were not present, and that the voters present elected others in their places, who must also be certified to be qualified voters, and therefore various returns are said to be defective, because in different cases without making these averments the returns commence by saying, "We, the sergeants of company A;" or, "we, the judges of company E;" or, "we, the lawfully appointed judges of company F;" or, "we, being two voters of company G;" or, "we, enlisted members of company B," &c., &c.; but in every one of these cases the certificate thus commencing proceeds to declare that "we did then act as judges of election at an election then held at the quarters of the commanding officer," and the necessary presumption and intendment coming in aid of all these general averments, if any aid is necessary, supply all that is necessary to show that, so acting as judges, they acted by competent authority. Were it not so it would be difficult to find any returns from any county in the State at this or any other election on file in this office that would not be obnoxious to the same or much graver objections. Indeed, the learned counsel who has presented these objections has been himself obliged to rely upon presumptions to supply defects in returns from several counties casting large majorities against the constitution, which have been made subjects of exception by the opposing counsel, and which I think furnish examples of irregularities quite as important, to say the least of them, as most of those suggested against the sufficiency of the military returns. Several of these make no statement of the time during which the polls were opened; in two cases they fail to show that the vote was by ballot—in one, instead of positively certifying, as they are required so explicitly to do, that every voter has taken the oath prescribed by the constitution, they only certify in the way of preamble that it so appears from the certificates made out at the district polls; and in another county the returns, instead of being made and directed to the governor, are made and directed to the clerk of the circuit court, and a certified copy enclosed by that officer. But I am of opinion that these returns being substantially correct, are entitled to the benefit of all reasonable presumptions to cure their defects; and surely, returns made in the field, and by officers who, as well as the county judges, are sworn to observe the law, ought not to be subject to any more rigid scrutiny.

The circumstances under which they were prepared entitle them to the most liberal construction, and the convention very justly looked to these circumstances in providing, as they did against all unimportant irregularities, by declaring "that no particular words shall be required."

I proceed to a brief notice of some particular objections applied to different returns of several companies, which, whilst they are generally, I think, within the reasons suggested against other objections taken, it may be proper to advert to, as they were of a more special description. The vote of company B, of 2d regiment of infantry, is objected to on the ground that the caption to the list of voters accompanying the return represents that the polls were opened at the quarters of "the judges." Adverting to the certificate of return itself, it will be found to recite that the election was "held at the quarters of the commanding officer of said company"—and whilst the list of votes accompanying that certificate might be admitted to explain any ambiguity on its face, it cannot, without the signature of any official, be allowed to contradict the regular certificate of the judges made out under their hand and seal.

Objection is taken to the returns of company C, of 12th regiment infantry, upon the ground that it appears by a letter accompanying the return, that the polls were not opened until after the appointed hour, eight o'clock, A. M. The captain, however, distinctly states that though not opened at the hour required, "abundant time and opportunity were given to secure the entire vote of the company"—a fact that can scarcely be doubted when we perceive that the company polled twenty-three votes, and no other in the regiment, though apparently with the poll opened during the whole time required, voted more than twenty-eight. Under such circumstances, and with no complaint made that any member of the company lost his vote by reason of the delay, it would seem to be a most harsh and unreasonable proceeding to refuse to count the votes that were given. This view of the case is sustained too by the authority of the writer already quoted, who enumerates, among the irregularities insufficient to invalidate the proceedings, a case "where the opening of the meeting was delayed for two hours beyond the time fixed." The vote of company K, 1st regiment, P. H. B., is objected to on the ground that others not members of that company voted with it. The certificate of the judges show no such fact, but states the election to have been by the members of company K, but a letter accompanying it states that "the accompanying list of voters consist of members of company K, and a detachment of companies A, C and F, of same regiment, *serving under the command of the officers of company K, the officers of companies A, C and F, having been mustered out of service.*" These men, therefore, were incorporated into company K. Companies A, C and F cast no vote, and these members of said companies, consolidated apparently with company K, had a right to vote at the quarters of that company, and even if they had not it would be as unreasonable to reject the whole vote of the company on such account as it would be to reject the vote of an entire election district because its poll-books showed that sundry illegal voters had participated in the election.

Objection is made to company H, 1st Potomac Home Brigade, upon the ground that twenty-three "blue tickets" are returned with the ballots, which I am asked to reject.

The objection is founded on the 9th section of the act of 1864, providing for the call of the convention, which directs that the ballots "shall be written or printed on white paper." The paper on which these twenty-three ballots were written is what is commonly known as "blue-laid" letter paper, quite as commonly used as the "white-laid," and I can scarcely think it comes within the proscription of the act of assembly. The object of that prohibition was to prevent the judge or any one else from knowing, by the different color of the ballots, for what party or on which side of a question a voter voted—an object that was wholly unnecessary in the case in question, as all the ballots of the company, of every hue, were on the same side. But even if these ballots were on a prohibited kind of paper, the law puts upon the *judge* the duty of rejecting them, declaring that ballots so printed "shall not be received by said judges," and I have no greater power to reject them than I would have to reject any other illegal ballot which they had received.

The vote of a company of recruits at Camp Bradford is objected to on the ground, as I understand it, that they are not yet assigned to any regiment. I have already noticed the objection taken to the votes of companies unconnected with a regiment, and I perceive nothing in the condition of this company that particularly distinguishes it from other unattached companies. If it is a company—so far organized as to be under a company commander, it would seem to have the same right to vote at his quarters as any other company not connected with a regiment. The return sets forth that it is "a company of recruits"—that they are "in the military service of the United States," and a company officer of one of the Maryland regiments appears as its commanding officer, makes the return, and certifies that the election was held at his quarters. This, I think, embraces every necessary averment to entitle the company to vote.

Companies D and K, of the 1st regiment of cavalry, it is objected, voted together. It appears that there were only four votes in the two companies, and the commissioned officer who took them describes himself in the return as the commanding officer of the said two companies, and the strong presumption is that the two had been consolidated. I think it but reasonable so to consider them, and accept their four votes.

I proceed now to notice briefly some objections to the sufficiency of other returns that I think better founded. The vote of the whole 1st regiment of infantry is objected to on the ground that the entire regiment, instead of voting by companies at the headquarters of each company commander, voted together at one regimental polls.

The learned counsel appearing in support of these returns have endeavored to sustain this one upon the ground that a separate list of the voters of each company accompanies the certificate of the judges, from the caption of which lists it would seem that the voters therein named had deposited their ballots "at the quarters of the commanding officer" of said companies. However, these captions might help a return otherwise insufficient, they cannot control or contradict the express certificate of the judges, which not only declares that they were the judges of the 1*st regiment*, but that they opened the polls for said *regiment* at the quarters of the commanding officer of said *regiment*, and in two places erase the printed word *company* and insert *regiment*.

Under such circumstances it is difficult to presume that each company voted at its company quarters as required, and I feel compelled to reject their vote.

Another well founded objection is made to the votes taken at a second election in two companies (F and I,) of first Eastern Shore regiment. These companies having opened a poll at a proper time and place, and taken the votes of a portion of each company, several days afterwards re-opened the polls and received in one company twenty-one and in the other fifteen votes of men who were either absent or declined to vote at the first election. This fact appears by a note annexed by the judge- to the foot of the return, and as there was no authority for a second day's voting, these votes must be rejected.

Objection is also well taken to the votes of fourteen persons who voted at the quarters of company I, 1st Eastern Shore regiment. This appears by a memorandum indorsed upon the list of voters and certified by the captain, who stated that these fourteen soldiers, "absent from their proper command," voted at the polls of this company, and, as the whole number of votes polled by the company, 133, were given "for the constitution," there is no difficulty in making the deduction.

The vote of thirteen field and staff officers, voting in the 5th and 8th regiments, at special polls opened for such officers, must also be rejected. It is unnecessary to determine whether their vote could have been taken at either of the company polls of their respective regiments, or whether the convention has neglected altogether to provide for their vote; but it is certain, I think, that they could not vote as they have done at a special poll, and their votes will be deducted. In three other cases, embracing in all, I think, eight votes of persons voting at company quarters with which they had no connection, and where the facts are so noticed and reported by the returning judges, the objection is sustained. The sum of the votes so deducted, for reasons apparent on the face of the return, amounts to 285 votes for and 5 against the constitution; and leaves the number counted on the soldiers' vote 2,633 for and 263 against the constitution. The aggregate of the home and soldiers' vote then being 30,174 for and 29,799 against the adoption of the constitution.

I regret that the multiplicity of the objections suggested, and the short time allowed since the conclusion of the discussion to-day, have not allowed me to review them as thoroughly or satisfactorily as I could desire. I am gratified, however, that these returns of the soldiers' vote have passed under the searching scrutiny of the able counsel who has inspected them. They will satisfy him, I think, of a purpose everywhere manifested on their face to state frankly and without reserve the facts as they really occurred. Indeed, in several of his objections, and in nearly all of those that have been sustained, the very foundation of the objection has been furnished by letters filed with, or special statements annexed, to the regular returns, which but for these special annexations would have presented no cause of objection, and I rejoice to see, as I think these circumstances obviously show, a purpose on the part of the soldiers to abide strictly by the law, and avail themselves of no privileges except what the law allows. A month before the election, as I fully explained to the committee to whom I have herein referred, I caused to be printed and sent to all our organized commands a circular of instruction, calculated not only to insure an observance of the law, but to guard against any one's being permitted to vote who would not be entitled to do so if he had been at home.

The entire vote authorized by the constitution having been thus accurately ascertained, it becomes my duty in obedience to its mandate to proclaim the result and its adoption. I propose to do this simultaneously with the publication of this opinion. The very near approach of the day appointed for the constitution to take effect, and an important election so soon afterwards depending on this announcement, will not permit of longer delay.

The duty thus imposed upon me is a plain proceeding of a purely ministerial and executive character, which leaves me no discretion, and which I dare not disobey.

A. W. BRADFORD.

THE CONSTITUTION ADOPTED.

In obedience to the conclusions to which the governor had thus arrived, and to the requirements of section nine of article XII of the constitution, the governor at the same time published the following proclamation:

STATE OF MARYLAND.
EXECUTIVE DEPARTMENT.

Whereas, by an act of the general assembly of Maryland, passed at January session, eighteen hundred and sixty-four, entitled "an act to provide for the taking of the sense of the people upon the call of a convention to frame a new constitution and form of government for this State, to provide for an election of delegates to said convention, and the assembling thereof," it is provided that the constitution and form of government adopted by the said convention, as aforesaid, "shall be submitted to the legal and qualified voters of the State, for their adoption or rejection, at such time, in such manner, and subject to such rules and regulations as said convention may prescribe."

And whereas, it is further provided by said act "that when the governor shall receive the returns of the number of ballots cast in this State for the adoption or rejection of the constitution submitted by the convention to the people, if upon counting and casting up the returns as made to him, as hereinbefore prescribed, it shall appear that a majority of the legal votes cast at said election are in favor of the adoption of the said constitution, he shall issue his proclamation to the people of the State, declaring the fact, and he shall take such steps as shall be required by the said constitution to carry the same into full operation, and to supersede the old constitution of this State."

And whereas, in pursuance of the said act and of a vote of a majority of the people of the State, taken in conformity to its provisions, and in favor of the assembling of said convention, that body did convene at the city of Annapolis, on the day appointed by said act, and did on the sixth day of September last adopt a new constitution and form of government; and did therein direct that the same should be submitted for the adoption or rejection of the people of the State at an election to be held in the several counties of the State and the city of Baltimore for that purpose, at a certain time therein specified; and did also therein provide that an election should be held likewise for a similar purpose "in each company of every Maryland regiment in the service of the United States or of this State."

And whereas, by said constitution it was further provided that the governor, upon receiving the result of said elections, and ascertaining the aggregate vote throughout the State, including the soldiers' vote aforesaid, should by his proclamation make known the same, and if a majority of the votes cast should be for the adoption of said constitution, it should go into effect on the first day of November, eighteen hundred and sixty-four.

And whereas, the elections as provided for were held in the said counties of the State and the city of Baltimore, and in the said military companies in the service of the United States.

And whereas, the results of said elections have been duly certified to me by the proper judges of the said several elections, and upon accurately counting and casting up the votes so returned to me for and against the said constitution, including the soldiers' vote aforesaid, it doth appear that there were thirty thousand one hundred and seventy-four (30,174) ballots for the constitution, and twenty-nine thousand seven hundred and ninety-nine (29,799) ballots against the constitution, and that there were sixty-one (61) blank ballots, and that there were thirty-three (33) ballots reported as given against the constitution, but not counted, the persons offering them refusing to take the oath required by said constitution; and there being, therefore, of the aggregate vote so cast a majority in favor of the adoption of said constitution—

Now, therefore, I, AUGUSTUS W. BRADFORD, Governor of the State of Maryland, in pursuance of the authority so vested in me by the said act of assembly, and the constitution aforesaid, do by this my proclamation, declare and make known that the said constitution and form of government so framed and adopted by the convention aforesaid has been adopted by a majority of the voters of the State, and that in pursuance of the provision therein contained the same will go into effect as the proper constitution and form of government of this State, superseding the one now existing, on the first day of November next.

Given under my hand and the great seal of the State of Maryland, at the city of Annapolis on the twenty-ninth day of October, in the year of our Lord, eighteen hundred and sixty-four. [L. S.]

A. W. BRADFORD.

By the Governor:

WM. B. HILL, Secretary of State.

THE OFFICIAL VOTE ON THE CONSTITUTION.

The following are the official returns of the vote for and against the constitution, as on file among the records of the Executive Department at Annapolis:

Counties.	*For.*	*Against.*
Allegany county	1,839	964
Anne Arundle	281	1,360
Baltimore city*	9,779	2,053
Baltimore county	2,001	1,869
Carroll	1,587	1,690
Caroline	471	423
Calvert	57	634
Cecil	1,611	1,611
Charles	13	978
Dorchester†	449	1,486
Frederick‡	2,908	1,916
Harford‖	1,083	1,671
Howard§	462	583
Kent	289	1,246
Montgomery¶	422	1,367
Prince George's	149	1,293
Queen Anne's**	220	1,577
Somerset	464	2,066
St. Mary's	99	1,078
Talbot	430	1,020
Washington	2,441	985
Worcester††	486	1,666
	27,541	29,536
Soldiers' vote	2,633	263
	30,174	29,799
	29,799	
	375	

* 8 votes (against) not counted, voters refusing oath. † 2 blanks. ‡ 23 blanks. ‖ 19 blanks. § 15 votes not included in these, (given against the constitution by voters who did not take the oath.) ¶ 14 blanks, and 10 against the constitution not included in those counted—voters refusing to take the oath. ** 2 blanks. †† 1 blank.

INDEX.

www.ingramcontent.com/pod-product-compliance
Lightning Source LLC
LaVergne TN
LVHW021107110826
845150LV00001B/191

* 9 7 8 1 4 2 5 5 6 4 7 2 8 *